AN ANNOTATED SECONDARY BIBLIOGRAPHY SERIES ON ENGLISH LITERATURE IN TRANSITION 1880–1920

1880–1920

HELMUT E. GERBER

GENERAL EDITOR

W. SOMERSET MAUGHAM

JOSEPH CONRAD

THOMAS HARDY

E. M. FORSTER

JOHN GALSWORTHY

GEORGE GISSING

D. H. LAWRENCE

H. G. WELLS

WALTER PATER

G. B. SHAW

THE CONTRIBUTORS

With the exception of the translators mentioned in the acknowledgments, Frederick P. W. McDowell abstracted all items in this volume.

ERRATA

Page 7, line 12. Period after THE ABINGER PAGEANT; delete colon

Page 10, 4 lines from bottom. Should read, "as one of the master works of the century."

Page 12, line 13. Should read, Hugh Maclean

Page 14, 9 lines from bottom. Should read, (see entries, respectively, for 1966, 1971, 1972, 1974, and 1975)

Page 16, line 27. Should read, "E. M. Forster at Ninety" (1968)

Page 18, line 20. Delete Gokulāstami

Page 63, entry 134, line 1 of entry. Should read, interpretation

Page 93, entry 227, line 1 of title. Should read, "Casual Criticisms,"

Page 95, entry 234, next to last line of entry. Should read, does not figure in this part of the discussion

Page 115, entry 281, line 4 of entry. Should read, "so alive and so consistently inconsistent."

Page 163, entry 411, line 8 of entry. Should read, "Co-ordination."

Page 213, entry 523, line 3 of title. Should read, Münster

Page 235, entry 569, 5 lines from bottom. Should read, EMF feels that his type of liberal thought

Page 238, entry 577, line 8 of entry. Should read, in Freedom, Democracy, Humanity, and Culture

Page 251, entry 613, line 5 of entry. Should read, life is made to seem more casual and more arbitrary than it really is

Page 256, entry 628, last line. Should read, *A Passage to India*

Page 273, entry 662, line 2 of entry. Should read, see Lawrence (1948)

Page 321, entry 785, line 1 of title. Should read, "Mr. E. M. Forster as a Symbolist,"

Page 350, entry 839, first word of entry. Should read, Nietzschean

Page 353, entry 841, next to last line of entry. Should read, because He *is* and they *are*

Page 371, entry 883, line 12 of entry. Should read, A separation or death aspect

Page 375, entry 890, line 5 of entry. Should read, virtuosity

Page 386, entry 912, line 5. Should read, it is only one among many possible passages

Page 387, entry 916, line 3. Should read, disputations

Page 389, entry 922, line 6 of entry. Should read, also resembled

Page 405, entry 940, 10 lines from bottom. Should read, to admit this prosaic world into his fiction

Page 417, entry 954, 17 lines from bottom. Should read, the Hindu view

Page 434, entry 994, line 13. Should read, L'EDUCATION SENTIMENTALE

Page 441, entry 1008, line 6 of entry. Should read, somehow kept going anti-materialist values

Page 444, entry 1013, line 2 of entry. Should read, THE OLD WIVES' TALE

Page 474, entry 1082, line 3 of entry. Should read, agnostic and anti-clerical; politically, he is liberal

Page 482, entry 1094, 8 lines from bottom. Should read, the discords between people are erased

Page 489, entry 1111, line 19 of entry. Should read, the informative into the sensational mode

Page 492, entry 1119, line 1 of title. Should read, Husain, Syed Hamid

Page 493, entry 1124, last line of entry. Should read, identification

Page 530, entry 1196, 14 lines from bottom. Should read, inspired in EMF a love of the classics

Page 538, entry 1198, 3 lines from bottom. Should read, SCRUTINY (1938; rpt date, 1952)

Page 553, entry 1226, 10 lines from bottom. Should read, the Wilcox children are excluded from him

Page 562, entry 1248, line 17. Should read, "the normal elements of action and characters,"

Page 585, entry 1282, line 6 of entry. Should read, as EMF sees them

Page 596, entry 1307, line 3 of title. Should read, Siddharth

Page 610, entry 1332, at end of entry. Should add, [In French.]

Page 620, entry 1356, line 13. Should read, his sexual lapse in the past

Page 623, entry 1359, line 1 of title. Should read, PAN, THE GOAT-GOD, HIS MYTH IN MODERN TIMES. Line 5 of entry. Should read, the ineffable 'beyond the veil' "

Page 649, entry 1427, line 1 of entry. Should read, prejudice

Page 684, entry 1514, line 1 of entry. Should read, stressing influence of G. E. Moore

Page 695, entry 1545, line 1 of title. Should read, Gransden, K. W. Line 2 of title. Should read, ENCOUNTER

Page 730, entry 1629, line 2 of entry. Should read, His nonexistence. Line 21 of entry. Should read, *because* Mrs. Moore is a

Page 740, entry 1644, line 9 of entry. Should read, "Arthur Snatchfold"

Page 751, entry 1668, line 3 from bottom. Should read, "The Machine Stops" rptd. "Notes on the Authors"

Page 804, entry 1791, line 1 of title. Should read, D. H. LAWRENCE: THE WORLD OF THE MAJOR NOVELS

Page 816, entry 1819, last line of entry. Should read, reduced circumstances

Page 841, entry 1879, line 11. Should read, divisiveness and exclusiveness is the thematic motif

Page 853, entry 1897, line 4 from bottom. Should read, J. M. E. McTaggart's idealism

Page 854, entry 1898, line 1 of title. Should read, THE RAZOR EDGE OF BALANCE: A STUDY OF VIRGINIA WOOLF

Page 858, entry 1903, line 2 from bottom. Should read, represents *saguna* (personal, with attributes) Brahmin

E. M. Forster

AN
ANNOTATED
BIBLIOGRAPHY
OF WRITINGS
ABOUT HIM

COMPILED AND EDITED BY
FREDERICK P. W. MCDOWELL

NORTHERN ILLINOIS UNIVERSITY PRESS
DE KALB, ILLINOIS

Frederick P. W. McDowell is a professor of English at the University of Iowa.

Library of Congress Cataloging in Publication Data

McDowell, Frederick P. W.
    E. M. Forster, an annotated bibliography of writings
about him.

    (An Annotated secondary bibliography series on English
literature in transition, 1880-1920)
    Includes indexes.
    1. Forster, Edward Morgan, 1879-1970—Bibliography.
I. Title. II. Series.
Z8309.3.M33   [PR6011.058]   016.823'9'12   73-18797
ISBN 0-87580-046-7

Preface

My aim in compiling this bibliography has been for completeness. The entries begin in 1905, when E. M. Forster made his arresting debut with *Where Angels Fear to Tread,* and end in 1975. As other compilers have done in the previous volumes in this series, I have noted publications of all sorts. I have included reviews, general appreciations, bibliographies, biographies, critical books, documented articles, chapters in books, scattered references in books and articles, Ph. D. dissertations, letters to the editors of major newspapers and journals, introductions to editions of Forster's works, and explications in anthologies and case books. I have also noticed author entries in encyclopedias and literary dictionaries. For Forster there are the contents of three *Festschrift* volumes and many reviews of these, obituary comment, and discussions of his controversial posthumously published works.

The extent to which I have fallen short of completeness I shall learn with time. There must be other works in German and Italian besides those that I have been able to trace, and there must be other significant reviews of Forster's books. I have been able to include a cross section of the review comments on Forster's fiction as they appeared in newspapers and magazines of many previous years, and these should be of particular interest. Subsequent to my compiling this bibliography and abstracting these reviews, many of them were made available in Philip Gardner's E. M. FORSTER: THE CRITICAL HERITAGE (1973). My entries for 1974 and 1975 are incomplete because the bibliographical publications upon which I depend to check my own listings have been slow to appear for these years.

For all the more significant items abstracted, I have appended critical comments in brackets. Forster is a writer for whom the secondary materials existing are sufficiently limited to make it possible for one person to do all the abstracting. I have abstracted everything myself except for about half the German items and items in other foreign languages (except for those in French, which I abstracted). I have been able, therefore, to perceive more of the connections and cross references among all these accounts than would have been possible otherwise. I have not been able to make all the judgments that I would have liked, since it is difficult to keep all these materials firmly in mind when one has been able to read through the completed manuscript only once. Yet the reader can be assured of a consistency in judgment not always present in a collaborative effort. Some of my own admiration for Forster, his fiction, and his humanism will, I hope, be discernible in what I have written.

For the most part I have placed entries under the date of their first publication and there noted the reprintings. But I have also noted certain items at a later date when there have been significant revisions. Whenever a book appeared in England and America during the same year, I have placed first in the title caption the edition that I consulted, since I was not able usually to consult both the British and the American editions of the same book. When the book appeared in different years in England or America, I placed it under the earliest year and indicated that I used the later of the two editions when in fact I had to do so. As a result I have checked the page numbers for either the British or the American edition, sometimes for both.

Generally I have not included reviews of secondary works, though for some of the major books on Forster I indicate them at the end of the abstract. I did include these reviews whenever the critic made general observations of significance apart from a mere appraisal of the book itself. Thus most of the reviews for Rose Macaulay's THE WRITINGS OF E. M. FORSTER (1938) are important as witness to Forster's reputation at that time. The same cannot be said for all of the reviews of Wilfred Stone's THE CAVE AND THE MOUNTAIN (1966). Most of the reviews or review-articles on K. Natwar-Singh's E. M. FORSTER: A TRIBUTE (1964) and Oliver Stallybrass's ASPECTS OF E. M. FORSTER (1969) go beyond mere description of the contents of the books or perfunctory judgments upon them. As Teets and Gerber do in the Conrad volume, I list Ph. D. dissertations involving Forster, and abstracts for most of these can be found in DISSERTATION ABSTRACTS or DISSERTATION ABSTRACTS INTERNATIONAL.

The interest in Forster continues unabated. If there is to be the same flow of articles and books within the next few years as has characterized the 1960s, a supplement to this bibliography will be inevitable.

ACKNOWLEDGMENTS

The University of Iowa has been generous to me in my teaching schedule and its allocation to me of research assistants and funds for the preparation of this book. These graduate students, as my research assistants over the years, have contributed much to the compilation of this book: Mary Jo Small, Michael W. Sewell, Richard T. Cecil, Patrick White, John Hazlett, Jenny Spencer, Martha Petry, Bartley Garvey, and James Degan. The University of Iowa paid for the typing of this outsize manuscript and allocated money for the abstracting of articles from Italian and Japanese. Dean Duane Spriestersbach and Associate Dean Charles M. Mason of the University of Iowa Graduate College have been sympathetic to my various requests for funds. Professor John C. Gerber, the Head of the University of Iowa's English Department and the Director of the School of Letters at the University, has helped by freeing me from an undue amount of committee and administrative work and by his personal encouragement. For the typing of the manuscript I am principally indebted to Catherine Hahn and Christine M. Heuer. Christine Heuer was not only expert in her typing of a difficult manuscript but helped in many other ways in compiling it. In arranging for the typing, John B. Harper, the administrative assistant of the English Department, was helpful.

For assistance in translating or abstracting writings from foreign languages I am indebted to the following: Margaret Seigel for items in Italian, Takako Lento for items in Japanese, Louis M. Bell of the University of Iowa for an article in Hungarian, Richard Martin of the Aachen Institut für Anglistik for about half the items in German, Matti Rissanen of the University of Helsinki for an article in Finnish, Lee Croft of Arizona State University for an article in Serbo-Croatian, and Thomas E. Sheahan of the University of Nebraska Press for articles in Danish.

Without the help of the University of Iowa Library's Reference Department, this book could not have appeared in its present form. Julia Bartling, Ada M. Stoflet, Keith A. Rageth, and Lois L. Horstman have always been cheerful in responding to the demands that I have made upon them. The Interlibrary Loan Service under Keith Rageth solved many difficult problems for me and procured almost every obscure item for me that the library did not have in its own collection.

Numerous Forster scholars have assisted me. Among those to whom I am most indebted are Helmut E. Gerber, George H. Thomson, Richard Martin, and Alan Wilde. All of them called my attention to articles and books that I would otherwise have overlooked. I owe a great debt to P. N. Furbank and Oliver Stallybrass for helping me locate reviews of Forster's early books. This last endeavor would not have been successful without the help of the King's College Library, Cambridge, and its staff, past and present. Thanks in particular must go to A. L. N. Munby, Elizabeth Ellem, and Penelope Bulloch. As this volume goes to press, I have been assisted by Philip Gardner's Critical Heritage volume on Forster in locating some more obscure items.

My wife Margaret has helped me principally by seeing that my time was not devoured by other activities and projects which seemed always at the moment more pressing than the completion of this book.

FREDERICK P. W. McDOWELL

Contents

NOTE ON ENTRY STYLE

Titles of Forster's books appear in italic type; titles of his stories, in roman capitals and lower case with quotation marks. Titles of books by other authors, collections of stories and letters edited by other writers, and names of periodicals and newspapers appear in capitals and small capitals. The translations appearing in parentheses are confined to meanings of the phrases; however, it should be noted that the titles of translations are seldom literal ones.

E. M. Forster

AN ANNOTATED BIBLIOGRAPHY
OF WRITINGS ABOUT HIM

A Checklist

NOTE: In this listing I have included important American and later editions and reprintings of some of the major works, especially the fiction, when it has seemed helpful to do so. I am greatly indebted to B. J. Kirkpatrick's A BIBLIOGRAPHY OF E. M. FORSTER (Lond: Rupert Hart-Davis, 1965; 2nd rvd ed, 1968).

I. FICTION
A. SEPARATE WORKS

Where Angels Fear to Tread. 1st ed, Edinburgh & Lond: William Black-wood, 1905; 1st American ed, NY: Alfred A. Knopf, 1920; 2nd English ed (Uniform Edition), Lond: Edward Arnold, 1924; American ed rptd, NY: Alfred A. Knopf, 1943; 3rd English ed (Pocket Edition), Lond: Edward Arnold, 1947; 2nd American ed, NY: Vintage Books, 1958; 4th English ed, Harmondsworth: Penguin Books, 1959.

The Longest Journey. 1st ed, Edinburgh & Lond: William Blackwood, 1907; 1st American ed, NY: Alfred A. Knopf, 1922; 2nd English ed (Uniform Edition), Lond: Edward Arnold, 1924; American ed rptd, Norfolk, Conn: New Directions, 1943; 3rd English ed (Pocket Edition), Lond: Edward Arnold, 1947; 4th English ed, Harmondsworth: Penguin Books, 1960; 5th English ed (World's Classics) with Introduction by Forster, Lond: Oxford UP, 1960; 2nd American ed, NY: Vintage Books, 1962.

A Room with a View. 1st ed, Lond: Edward Arnold, 1908; 1st American ed, NY & Lond: G. P. Putnam's Sons, 1911; 2nd American ed, NY: Alfred A. Knopf, 1923; 2nd English ed (Uniform Edition), Lond: Edward Arnold, 1924; rpt, 2nd American ed, Norfolk, Conn: New Directions, 1943; 5th English ed (Pocket Edition), Lond: Edward Arnold,

1947; 6th English ed, Harmondsworth: Penguin Books, 1955; 3rd American ed, NY: Vintage Books, 1960.

Howards End. Lond: Edward Arnold, 1910; 1st American ed, NY: G. P. Putnam's Sons, 1910 (actually publd, Jan 1911); 2nd American ed, NY: Alfred A. Knopf, 1921; 1st ed rptd (Uniform Edition), Lond: Edward Arnold, 1924; 2nd English ed, Harmondsworth: Penguin Books, 1941; 3rd English ed, Harmondsworth: Penguin Books, 1943; 2nd American ed rptd, NY: Alfred A. Knopf, 1943; 4th English ed (Pocket Edition), Lond: Edward Arnold, 1947; 5th English ed, Harmondsworth: Penguin Books, 1955; 3rd American ed, NY: Vintage Books, 1954; rptd, with rvd text, as Volume 4, *The Abinger Edition of E. M. Forster*, ed by Oliver Stallybrass, Lond: Edward Arnold, 1973; see also Volume 4A, *The Abinger Edition*, *The Manuscripts of Howards End*, Lond: Edward Arnold, 1973.

The Celestial Omnibus and Other Stories. 1st ed, Lond: Sidgwick & Jackson, 1911; 1st ed (3rd printing), American issue, NY: Alfred A. Knopf, 1923; stories republd with those in *The Eternal Moment* (1928, see below), in *The Collected Tales of E. M. Forster* (1947, see below). Contents: "The Story of a Panic," "The Other Side of the Hedge," "The Celestial Omnibus," "Other Kingdom," "The Curate's Friend," "The Road from Colonus."

The Story of the Siren. 1st ed, Richmond: Hogarth P, 1920; rptd in *The Eternal Moment* (1928, see below) and *The Collected Tales of E. M. Forster* (1947, see below).

A Passage to India. 1st ed, Lond: Edward Arnold, 1924; 1st American ed, NY: Harcourt, Brace, 1924; 1st English ed rptd (Uniform Edition), Lond: Edward Arnold, 1926; 2nd English ed, Harmondsworth: Penguin Books, 1936; 1st American ed rptd, NY: Modern Library, 1940; 1st American ed rptd, NY: Harcourt, Brace, 1944, 1958 and later imprint dates as Harbrace Modern Classics; 3rd English ed (Everyman's Library) with Foreword and Notes by E. M. Forster, Lond: J. M. Dent & Sons, the notes rvd for 1957 printing; 4th English ed (Pocket Edition), Lond: Edward Arnold, 1947; 5th English ed, Harmondsworth: Penguin Books, 1950.

The Eternal Moment and Other Stories. 1st ed, Lond: Sidgwick & Jackson, 1928; 1st American ed, NY: Harcourt, Brace, 1928; stories republd with those in *The Celestial Omnibus* (1911, see above) in *The Collected Tales of E. M. Forster* (1947, see below). Contents: "The Machine Stops," "The Point of It," "Mr. Andrews," "Co-ordination," "The Story of the Siren," "The Eternal Moment."

The Collected Tales of E. M. Forster. 1st ed, NY: Alfred A. Knopf, 1947; 1st English ed, as *Collected Short Stories of E. M. Forster*, Lond: Sidgwick & Jackson, 1948; 2nd English ed, Harmondsworth: Penguin Books, 1954. Contents: "The Story of a Panic," "The Other Side of the

Hedge," "The Celestial Omnibus," "Other Kingdom," "The Curate's Friend," "The Road from Colonus," "The Machine Stops," "The Point of It," "Mr. Andrews," "Co-ordination," "The Story of the Siren," "The Eternal Moment."

Albergo Empedocle and Other Writings by E. M. Forster, ed by George H. Thomson. Contains "Albergo Empedocle," hitherto uncollected short story, rptd from *Temple Bar,* CXXVIII (Dec 1903), 663–84. For remaining contents of volume see II. "Nonfiction," below.

The Life to Come and Other Stories. Lond: Edward Arnold, 1972; *The Abinger Edition of E. M. Forster,* ed by Oliver Stallybrass, Volume 8; as *The Life to Come and Other Short Stories* (NY: Norton, 1972). Contents: "Introduction," "Ansell," "Albergo Empedocle," "The Purple Envelope," "The Helping Hand," "The Rock," "The Life to Come," "Dr. Woolacott," "Arthur Snatchfold," "The Obelisk," "What Does It Matter? A Morality," "The Classical Annex," "The Torque," "The Other Boat," "Three Courses and a Dessert" ("The Second Course" by E. M. Forster).

B. DRAMATIZATIONS

Tait, Stephen, and Kenneth Allott. *A Room with a View: A Play, Adapted from the Novel by E. M. Forster.* Lond: Edward Arnold, 1951.

Rama Rau, Santha. *A Passage to India: A Play in Three Acts. From the Novel by E. M. Forster.* Lond: Samuel French, 1960; 2nd ed, Lond: Edward Arnold, 1960; 1st American ed, NY: Harcourt, Brace & World, 1961. London run: 20 April–3 December 1960; New York run, 31 January–10 May 1962.

Hart, Elizabeth. *Where Angels Fear to Tread: A Play in Two Acts.* Lond: Samuel French, 1963. London run, 9 July 1963–25 January 1964.

Sieveking, Lance, and Richard Cotrell. Dramatization of *Howards End.* London run, 28 February 1967–1 April 1967.

II. NONFICTION
A. BOOKS AND PRINCIPAL PAMPHLETS

Egypt. Lond: Labour Research Department, 1920.

Alexandria: A History and a Guide. 1st ed, Alexandria: Whitehead Morris, 1922; 2nd English ed, Alexandria: Whitehead Morris, 1938; 1st American ed, Garden City, NY: Doubleday, Anchor Books, 1961 (text is that of 1st ed; new introduction by E. M. Forster).

Pharos and Pharillon. 1st ed, Richmond: Hogarth P, 1923; 1st American ed, NY: Alfred A. Knopf, 1923; 3rd English ed, Lond: Hogarth P, and

American issue, NY: Alfred A. Knopf, 1961. Contents: *Pharos:* "Pharos," "The Return from Siwa," "Epiphany," "Philo's Little Trip," "Clement of Alexandria," "St. Athanasius," "Timothy the Cat and Timothy Whitebonnet," "The God Abandons Antony, by C. P. Cavafy"; *Pharillon:* "Eliza in Egypt," "Cotton from the Outside," "The Den," "The Solitary Place," "Between the Sun and the Moon," "The Poetry of C. P. Cavafy," "Conclusion."

Anonymity: An Enquiry. Lond: Hogarth P, 1925; rptd in *Two Cheers for Democracy.*

Aspects of the Novel. 1st ed, Lond: Edward Arnold, 1927; 1st American ed, NY: Harcourt, Brace, 1927 (further printings, 1928, 1929, 1937, 1940, 1947, 1948, 1949, 1950 and as Harbrace Modern Classics, 1954, 1958, 1961, 1962); 2nd English ed (Pocket Edition), Lond: Edward Arnold, 1949; 2nd American ed, NY: Harvest Books, 1956; 3rd English ed, Harmondsworth: Penguin Books, 1962.

A Letter to Madan Blanchard. Lond: Hogarth P, 1931; 1st American ed, NY: Harcourt, Brace, 1932; rptd in *Two Cheers for Democracy.*

Goldsworthy Lowes Dickinson. 1st ed, Lond: Edward Arnold, 1934, rptd in Pocket Edition, 1962; 1st ed, American photo-offset rpt, NY: Harcourt, Brace, 1934; rptd in Volume 13, *The Abinger Edition of E. M. Forster, Goldsworthy Lowes Dickinson and Related Writings,* ed by Oliver Stallybrass, Lond: Edward Arnold, 1973; the related writings comprise "G. L. Dickinson: A Tribute," "A Great Humanist: E. M. Forster on Goldsworthy Lowes Dickinson," "Preface" to *The Greek View of Life,* "Introduction" to *Letters from John Chinaman and Other Essays,* "Pilgrim's Progress" (review of *The Magic Flute*), and "A Broadcast Debate" (review of *Points of View*).

Pageant of Abinger. Lond: Athenaeum P, 1934; rptd as "The Abinger Pageant," *Abinger Harvest.*

Abinger Harvest. 1st ed, Lond: Edward Arnold, 1936; 1st American ed, NY: Harcourt Brace, 1936, rptd, NY: Noonday P, 1955 in Meridian Books; 2nd English ed (Pocket Edition), Lond: Edward Arnold, 1953. Contents: 1, THE PRESENT: "Notes on the English Character," "Mrs. Grundy at the Parkers'," " 'It Is Different for Me,' " "My Wood," "Me, Them and You," "A Voter's Dilemma," "Our Graves in Gallipoli," "Happiness!" "Roger Fry: An Obituary Note," "Our Diversions: 1, The Scallies; 2, The Birth of an Empire; 3, The Doll Souse; 4, Mickey and Minnie; 5, Chess at Cracow; 6, The Game of Life; 7, My Own Centenary," "Liberty in England"; 2, BOOKS: "A Note on the Way," "Forrest Reid," "Ibsen the Romantic," "T. S. Eliot," "Proust," "Wordmaking and Sound-taking," "The Early Novels of Virginia Woolf," "Ronald Firbank," "Howard Overing Sturgis," "Sinclair Lewis," "Joseph Conrad: A Note," "T. E. Lawrence," "Jane Austen: 1, The Six Novels; 2, Sanditon; 3, The Letters"; 3, THE PAST: "The Consolations of

History," "Malcolnia Shops," "Cnidus," "Gemistus Pletho," "Cardan," "Voltaire's Labratory: 1, How they Weighed Fire; 2, Troublesome Molluscs," "Captain Edward Gibbon," "Trooper Silas Tomkyn Comberbacke," "Mr. and Mrs. Abbey's Difficulties," "Mrs. Hannah More," "Battersea Rise"; 4, THE EAST: "Salute to the Orient!" "The Mosque," "Wilfrid Blunt: 1, The Earlier Diaries (1888–1900); 2, The Later Diaries (1900–1914)," "A Flood in the Office," "For the Museum's Sake," "Marco Polo," "The Emperor Babur," "Adrift in India: 1, The Nine Gems of Ujjain; 2, Advance, India!; 3, Jodhpur; 4, The Suppliant; 5, Pan," "Hickey's Last Party," "Two Books by Tagore: 1, Chitra; 2, The Home and the World," "The Mind of the Indian Native State," "Hymn before Action"; 5, THE ABINGER PAGEANT: "A Flood in the Office" was omitted after the first printing of 1st ed.

What I Believe. Lond: Hogarth P, 1939; rptd in *Two Cheers for Democracy.*

England's Pleasant Land: A Pageant Play. Lond: Hogarth P, 1940.

Nordic Twilight. Lond: Macmillan, Macmillan War Pamphlets, 1940.

Virginia Woolf. 1st ed, Cambridge: Cambridge UP, The Rede Lecture, 1942; 1st American ed, NY: Harcourt, Brace, 1942; rptd in *Two Cheers for Democracy.*

The Development of English Prose between 1918 and 1939. Glasgow: Jackson, Son & Co., The Fifth W. P. Ker Memorial Lecture, Glasgow University Publications, Vol 63, 1945; rptd as "English Prose between 1918 and 1939" in *Two Cheers for Democracy.*

Two Cheers for Democracy. 1st ed, Lond: Edward Arnold, 1951; 1st American ed, NY: Harcourt, Brace, 1951; rptd, NY: Harvest Books, 1962; rptd as Volume Eleven, *The Abinger Edition of E. M. Forster,* ed by Oliver Stallybrass, Lond: Edward Arnold, 1972. Contents: Part I, THE SECOND DARKNESS: "The Last Parade," "The Menace to Freedom," "Jew-Consciousness," "Our Deputation," "Racial Exercise," "Post-Munich," "Gerald Heard," "They Hold Their Tongues," "Three Anti-Nazi Broadcasts: 1, Culture and Freedom; 2, What Has Germany Done to the Germans?; 3, What Would Germany Do to Us?" "Tolerance," "Ronald Kidd," "The Tercentenary of the 'Areopagitica,' " "The Challenge of Our Time," "George Orwell"; Part II, WHAT I BELIEVE: "What I Believe"; ART IN GENERAL: "Anonymity: An Enquiry," "Art for Art's Sake," "The Duty of Society to the Artist," "Does Culture Matter?" "The *Raison d'Être* of Criticism in the Arts," "The C Minor of That Life," "Not Listening to Music," "Not Looking at Pictures"; THE ARTS IN ACTION: "John Skelton," "*Julius Caesar,*" "The Stratford Jubilee of 1769," "Gibbon and His Autobigraphy," "Voltaire and Frederick the Great," "George Crabbe and Peter Grimes," "Bishop Jebb's Book," "Henry Thornton," "William Arnold," " 'Snow' Wedgwood," "William Barnes," "Three Stories by Tolstoy," "Edward Carpenter," "Webb and Webb," "A Book That Influenced Me," "Our Second

Greatest Novel?" "Gide and George," "Gide's Death," "Romain Rolland and the Hero," "A Whiff of D'Annunzio," "The Complete Poems of C. P. Cavafy," "Virginia Woolf," "Two Books by T. S. Eliot," *The Ascent of F6*," "*The Enchafèd Flood*," "Forrest Reid," "English Prose between 1918 and 1939," "An Outsider on Poetry," "Mohammed Iqbal," "Syed Ross Masood," "A Duke Remembers," "*Mrs. Miniver*," "In My Library," "The London Library"; PLACES: "A Letter to Madan Blanchard," "India Again," "Luncheon at Pretoria," "The United States," "Mount Lebanon," "Ferney," "Clouds Hill," "Cambridge," "London Is a Muddle," "The Last of Abinger."

Billy Budd, Opera in Four Acts, Music by Benjamin Britten; Libretto by E. M. Forster and Eric Crozier, Adapted from the Story by Herman Melville. Lond, NY, Toronto, Sydney, Capetown, Buenos Aires, Paris, Bonn: Boosey & Hawkes, 1951.

The Hill of Devi Being Letters from Dewas State Senior. 1st ed, Lond: Edward Arnold, 1953; 1st American ed as *The Hill of Devi*, NY: Harcourt, Brace, 1953.

Marianne Thornton, 1797–1887, A Domestic Biography. 1st ed, Lond: Edward Arnold, 1956; 1st American ed as *Marianne Thornton. A Domestic Biography 1797–1887*, NY: Harcourt, Brace, 1956.

Albergo Empedocle and Others Writings by E. M. Forster, ed by George H. Thomson. NY: Liveright, 1971. Contents: "Introduction"; AN EARLY SHORT STORY: "Albergo Empedocle"; CAMBRIDGE HUMOR: "On Grinds," "A Brisk Walk," "On Bicycling," "A Long Day," "The Pack of Anchises," "The Cambridge Theophrastus" (two sketches), "A Tragic Interior" (two dramatic sketches), "Strivings After Historical Style," "A Day Off," "An Allegory"; BOURGEOIS VALUES VERSUS INSPIRATION: "Rostock and Wismar," "Literary Eccentrics: A Review," "Mr. Walsh's Secret History of the Victorian Movement," "Inspiration"; FOR THE WORKING MEN'S COLLEGE: "Pessimism in Literature," "Dante," "The Beauty of Life," "The Functions of Literature in War-Time"; INDIA: "Iron Horses in India," "The Age of Misery," "The Indian Boom," "The Indian Mind," "A Great Anglo-Indian," "The Elder Tagore," "The Gods of India," "The Mission of Hinduism"; THE ARTS AND WAR: "The Wedding," "The Rose Show," "To Simply Feel," "A New Novelist," "Short Stories from Russia," "Tate versus Chantrey," "Reconstruction in the Marne and the Meuse."

For contributions to books and for uncollected writings in periodicals, see B. J. Kirkpatrick's A BIBLIOGRAPHY OF E. M. FORSTER (Lond: Rupert Hart-Davis, 1965; 2nd rvd ed, 1968).

Introduction

The writings on E. M. Forster divide into three periods: from 1905 to 1938, from 1938 to about 1957, and from 1958 to the present. In the period 1905 to 1938 Forster produced his chief volumes of fiction and nonfiction, except for *Two Cheers for Democracy* (1951). During this time review comment prevails. The creative efflorescence in the years 1905–1910 generally brought favorable reactions. Most of the critics recognized a new and significant talent, but some were puzzled by Forster's tough irony, his latent pessimism, his mordant tone, and his fondness for violence. Forster was a bit too abrasive for some of these critics, though accounts such as those by C. F. G. Masterman, R. A. Scott-James, Edward Garnett, Virginia Woolf, and the anonymous reviewers of *The Longest Journey* and *Howards End* deserve to be better known. Most of these reviews have now been collected in E. M. FORSTER: THE CRITICAL HERITAGE (1973), edited by Philip Gardner.

With the publication of *Pharos and Pharillon* (1923), *A Passage to India* (1924), the American editions or reissues of his novels, and *Aspects of the Novel* (1927), Forster could be seen in perspective and judged for the important writer that he is. *Pharos and Pharillon* resulted in at least one review of weight, John Middleton Murry's "The Magic of E. M. Forster" (1923). Reviews of *A Passage to India* by Herbert Gorman, L. P. Hartley, Robert Morss Lovett, H. W. Massingham, Kenneth Muir, Rose Macaulay, Henry W. Nevinson, Leonard Woolf, Ralph Wright, and Elinor Wylie are important for suggesting not only the greatness of the novel but the stature of Forster as a writer. Readers greeted *Aspects of the Novel* enthusiastically, and this book added considerably to Forster's reputation as a man of letters. Some of the general accounts of Forster which appeared in the 1920s have become standard and indicate that his reputation was beginning to solidify. I refer to the essays of such writers as Gerald Bullett (1926), I. A. Richards (1927), Edward Shanks (1927), Bonamy Dobrée (1929), and Virginia Woolf (1927).

The 1930s saw a number of other such comprehensive surveys of Forster's work—those by Howard M. Doughty, Jr. (1932), Peter Burra (1934), Montgomery Belgion (1934), E. B. C. Jones (1936), Derek A. Traversi (1937), and Austin Warren (1937). These are serious, well-informed, sensitive critiques, still of value to the contemporary student. The critics recognize Forster as a writer of merit but do not often assert the same degree of significance which he has achieved for most readers in the 1970s. Forster kept before the public, not with the fiction which everyone hoped to see coming from him but with many essays, reviews, and broadcasts, with a biography of one of his mentors (*Goldsworthy Lowes Dickinson*, 1934), and with a collection of miscellaneous writings, *Abinger Harvest* (1936). The last-named book led to other reasoned estimates of Forster's achievement by such critics as Elizabeth Bowen, George Dangerfield, Basil de Sélincourt, David Garnett, Christopher Isherwood, Louis Kronenberger, Peter Monro Jack, Q. D. Leavis, Phillip Littell, V. S. Pritchett, John Crowe Ransom, R. A. Scott-James, and Orlo Williams. Clearly the time was ready for Rose Macaulay's full-length study, THE WRITINGS OF E. M. FORSTER (1938). Miss Macaulay was appreciative and enthusiastic; she attempted a full survey of Forster's work and career; and she formulated a number of insights which make her book still profitable to consult, though she was too relaxed in her approach and too concerned with Forster's characters for her study to be definitive. Almost as important as the book were the reasoned estimates of Forster that it prompted, those by Elizabeth Bowen, Séan O'Faoláin, Desmond MacCarthy, Forrest Reid, Lionel Trilling, Morton Dauwen Zabel, and, above all, F. R. Leavis. Miss Macaulay's book and the reviews of it suggested that the time was soon to come for a more authoritative and systematic appraisal of Forster's work and for a consolidation of existing opinion.

This expectation was to be met a few years later with Lionel Trilling's E. M. FORSTER (1943), which at the time seemed the definitive statement on Forster. At least this book caused Forster to be viewed as a major writer. The 1940s proved to be an auspicious time for the inauguration of a Forster revival. Forster's humanism and liberalism spoke directly to those who were fighting to preserve the traditions of Western civilization; his offhand, ironic, understated manner appealed to a generation of intellectuals alienated by the pretentious and by the irrational appeals to the mass psyche prevalent in the 1930s and the 1940s. His sardonic, somber, intermittently cyncial, and sometimes tragic world view (with its recognition of the evil forces in man's nature and the disparity between his aspirations and his limited capabilities), and, above all, his projection of an imaginative world in his fiction notable for its aesthetic beauty, consistency, and lucidity appealed to a world beleagured by war and the problems engendered by its aftermath. Suddenly Forster seemed to stand clear from Edwardian contemporaries, such as Galsworthy, Bennett, and George Moore, as the incomparably superior novelist; and *A Passage to India* was increasingly seen as the master work of the century. The full significance of *A Passage to India*, however, was to depend upon critics of a later generation, more sensitive than Trilling or Leavis had been to its subtleties and complexities. Its aesthetic, philosophical, and metaphysical dimensions were only to become fully apparent with the critical resurgence of interest in Forster beginning about 1957. Trilling's book seemed more definitive to contemporary readers and scholars than it in fact was, and so did F. R. Leavis's influential essay, occasioned by Rose Macaulay's book and reprinted in THE COMMON PURSUIT (1952). The authoritative, not to say dogmatic, pronouncements of these critics discouraged widespread writing on Forster during the early 1950s, though some worthwhile essays did appear. Some of the best accounts written during these years were inspired by Trilling's book and by the American reissue of the first four novels: reviews and review-essays by Newton Arvin, Carlos Baker, Clifton Fadiman, Eleanor Godfrey, Howard Mumford Jones, Alan Pryce-Jones, John Crowe Ransom, Cuthbert Wright, and Morton Dauwen Zabel in 1943, by Noel Annan, F. R. Leavis, and Rose Macaulay in 1944. The most important essays to appear in the 1940s were those by E. K. Brown (especially the sections on Forster in RHYTHM IN THE NOVEL, 1950), Hyatt Howe Waggoner (1945), Peter Ault (1946), Lee Holt (1946), and Lord David Cecil (1949).

Though he did not publish any fiction, Forster kept before the public in the 1940s and the 1950s. He became a Cambridge institution after he was appointed fellow of King's College in 1946; he did much reviewing in the LISTENER and elsewhere, and he frequently wrote occasional essays or letters to the editor in which he gave his views on a wide variety of subjects. He gathered together his short stories in 1947 and some of his miscellaneous essays in 1951 in *Two Cheers for Democracy;* he collected his own letters and impressions of his Indian experiences in *The Hill of Devi* (1953); and he celebrated his Clapham ancestors in the biography of his great-aunt, *Marianne Thornton* (1956). Each of his books occasioned notable commentary: Carlos Baker, George Painter, Philip Toynbee, Hyatt Howe Waggoner, and Richard Watts on the short stories; Jacques Barzun, Robert Gorham Davis, Irving Howe, Joseph Wood Krutch, Michael Oakeshott, Gouverneur Paulding, Katherine Anne Porter, and V. S. Pritchett on *Two Cheers;* Newton Arvin, L. P. Hartley, Richard Hughes, Steven Marcus, Raymond Mortimer, William Plomer, V. S. Pritchett, and Santha Rama Rau on *Devi;* and Noel Annan, Ronald Bryden, Lord David Cecil, Louis Crompton, Naomi Lewis, Harold Nicolson, Lionel Trilling, Rex Warner, and Eudora Welty on *Marianne Thornton.* J. K. Johnstone's THE BLOOMSBURY GROUP (1954) emphasizes Forster's work in relation to its Bloomsbury affiliations but fails to be a definitive book on the subject. The excellent essay-reviews occasioned by this book give us more insight into Bloomsbury than Johnstone had himself given—the critiques of Maurice Bowra, Maurice Cranston, Richard Hughes, Vivian Mercier, Geoffrey Moore, Edwin Muir, and Benedict Nicolson. All of these essays ought to be better known, as should William Van O'Connor's authoritative "Toward a History of Bloomsbury" (1955).

Journal essays on Forster before 1957 were few in number, although some, especially those on *A Passage to India* that tried to lift the book from the depressed status accorded it by Trilling, are important in the unfolding of Forster's reputation. Reuben Brower's critique in his THE SHORES OF LIGHT (1951), despite his recognition of the complexity and paradoxical nature of the novel, was ultimately unsympathetic because he denigrated the "Temple" sequence. Gertrude White (1953) and Glen O. Allen (1955) wrote standard essays on *Passage*, though White does not steer clear of Trilling's begrudging estimate of novel, and Allen, despite the subtlety of his Hindu reading of the novel, rather surprisingly maintains that the philosophy of proportion inculcated in *Howards End* is more important to Forster than the mystical wholeness propounded in *Passage*. W. A. S. Keir (1952), Hugh N. Maclean (1953), and D. J. Enright (1957) all recognized the stature of *Passage* in their essays and did something to raise it in general esteem. No survey of these years should omit Rex Warner's still informative and discerning pamphlet in the Writers and Their Work series (1950), Stephen Spender's provocative "Personal Relations and Public Powers" (THE CREATIVE ELEMENT, 1953), Alwyn Berland's strong "James and Forster: The Morality of Class" (1953), Richard Voorhees's scrutiny of Forster's complexities in "The Novels of E. M. Forster" (1954), and William York Tindall's shrewd analysis of Forster's symbols (THE LITERARY SYMBOL, 1955).

An important 1953 doctoral dissertation became the book that inaugurated the third phase of recent Forster criticism, James McConkey's THE NOVELS OF E. M. FORSTER (1957). Its impact on Forster studies was somewhat delayed, as it was not widely noticed on publication. The importance of McConkey's book lay in his subtle reading of the novels. McConkey demonstrated especially the richness of Forster's symbolism, the finished artistry of the novels despite their flaws, and the greatness of *A Passage to India*. Critics, readers, and students now began to see that Trilling and Leavis had not said the last word and that much more remained to be said. How much more is apparent in the bulk and the excellence of the criticism written after 1957.

Upwards of fifteen books solely on Forster have appeared since 1960. Not all of them are important, but the best ones represent a high standard of critical discourse and have been instrumental in consolidating the view that Forster is an important writer and, at least intermittently, a great one. H. J. Oliver's THE ART OF E. M. FORSTER does not reach the depths of McConkey's study, but at least four volumes published from 1962 to 1964 have become standard for the study of Forster. J. B. Beer's THE ACHIEVEMENT OF E. M. FORSTER (1962) focuses upon the debts which Forster owes to nineteenth-century romanticism and elucidates, convincingly, many of the symbolic patterns in the fiction. K. W. Gransden's E. M. FORSTER (1962) is a model overall study of Forster, for the edification of both the general reader and the specialist. It is a shrewder, more flexible, and more sophisticated study than Trilling's. Frederick C. Crews has written a challenging book, E. M. FORSTER: THE PERILS OF HUMANISM (1962). Its premise that *A Passage to India* represents a culmination of Forster's pessimism is debatable or overstated, but the readings of the individual works reveal tact, originality, insight, and imagination. If one can discount to some degree the thesis, Crews's critique remains the best single book yet written on Forster. Alan Wilde, in ART AND ORDER: A STUDY OF E. M. FORSTER (1964), maintains that Forster finds in art the order that eludes him when he interprets life; and he has written a book, like Crews's, that is remarkable for the depths and subtlety of his readings of the novels. The books by V. A. Shahane (1962), David Shusterman (1965), Norman Kelvin (1967), Laurence Brander (1968), Denis Godfrey (1968), Martial Rose (1970), and Richard Martin (1974) are more perfunctory or idiosyncratic and are not up to the general standard of the books I just mentioned.

Forster studies have been redirected by the appearance of two more or less controversial books, Wilfred Stone's THE CAVE AND THE MOUNTAIN: A STUDY OF E. M. FORSTER (1966) and George Thomson's THE FICTION OF E. M. FORSTER (1967). Whatever the final opinion on these books may be, they represent fresh attempts to interpret Forster, and they reveal minds operating critically at enviable depths. By its length and inclusiveness, Stone's would seem to be the definitive book on Forster. But Stone is ultimately too specialized in his approach, too limited in his sympathies toward the earlier fiction and Forster himself, to justify our regarding it, uncritically, as the final word on Forster. He is overly disposed toward a Jungean interpretation of the fiction and overly concerned with questions of Forster's biography as it relates to the novels to achieve a balanced interpretation. On the other hand, his critique of *A Passage to India* is superb, since that book is capacious enough to absorb a Jungean interpretation (and, in fact, almost any other approach used by a critic). Stone's work was widely reviewed, and its originality and vigor were applauded, although a number of critics also expressed some of the same reservations that I have just elaborated. The book also inspired at least three essays of first importance: Stuart Hampshire's "Two Cheers for Mr. Forster" (1966), Robert Langbaum's "A New Look at E. M. Forster" (1968), and Martin Price's "E. M. F. and D. H. L." (1966).

Thomson's book conclusively demonstrates that Forster belongs, at least in part, to the romance tradition in Western fiction rather than to the tradition of realism. Despite his tendency at times to elevate his partial truth into the whole truth, Thomson has been salutary in exposing the fallaciousness of influential estimates of Forster's position such as Leavis's and Trilling's. Thomson's book shares honors with Crews's in providing the maximum number of insights per page in the reading of Forster's fiction.

Other books on Forster I shall have to pass under briefer review. In my

Twayne English Authors Series book, E. M. FORSTER (1969), I attempt to summarize Forster studies until 1968, building on the findings of others rather than ignoring them. June Perry Levine's CREATION AND CRITICISM (1971) is the first book devoted entirely to one Forster novel, *A Passage to India*. Levine is good on the background and the texts of *Passage* but inadequate on the scholarship completed on the book or the critical problems posed by it. Forster has also been the subject for three collections of original essays. E. M. FORSTER: A TRIBUTE, edited by K. Natwar-Singh (1964), illustrates the high regard which Indian intellectuals have for Forster, as well as his own tenderness toward things Indian. A GARLAND FOR E. M. FORSTER, edited by H. H. Anniah Gowda (1969) contains some criticism of value, but the essays are not up to the standard set by Oliver Stallybrass in 1969 with his ASPECTS OF E. M. FORSTER. From ASPECTS, the essays by Wilfred Stone, Elizabeth Bowen, Malcolm Bradbury, Edward Garnett, Oliver Stallybrass, and George H. Thomson merit the attention of Forster scholars. The review-essays occasioned by Stallybrass's collection are, many of them, important as valuations of Forster, especially those by P. N. Furbank and Raymond Mortimer in 1968 and by J. B. Beer in 1969. Bonnie Blumenthal Finkelstein's FORSTER'S WOMEN: ETERNAL DIFFERENCES (1975) is a competent and often cogent analysis of a timely subject, and she demonstrates conclusively that Forster was much concerned with the cause of liberating women from constricting sexual, social, and political conventions.

Other articles that have appeared as chapters in books since 1957 are less crucial than the journal contributions written during these years. Nevertheless, one must single out G. D. Klingopulos's "Mr. Forster's Good Influence" (1961), which celebrates Forster's influence during the critical years of World War II and his maturing sensibility from 1905 to 1924; C. B. Cox's essay in THE FREE SPIRIT (1963), which looks critically on Forster's liberalism and his lack of direct participation in politics; and H. A. Smith's "Forster's Humanism and the Nineteenth Century" (1966), which sorts the rationalistic and romantic elements in Forster.

The interest that Forster generated after 1960 is attested to in other ways. More than twenty theses which treat his work in whole or in part have been completed. Those by Alan Friedman, June Perry Levine, Calvin Bedient, Richard Martin, and Bonnie Blumenthal Finkelstein have been published as books, probably in revised form (see entries, respectively, for 1966, 1971, 1972, and 1975). Robert Ligon Harrison's "The Manuscripts of *A Passage to India*" (1965), though it remains unpublished, has become a standard reference for Forster scholars. Numerous interviews date from the late 1950s and early 1960s when Forster was still in good health; and *A Passage to India, Where Angels Fear to Tread*, and *Howards End* were dramatized respectively in 1960, 1963, and 1967 and held the stage for varying periods in London (*Passage* also ran in New York in 1962; and *A Room with a View* had been dramatized earlier, in 1951). B. J. Kirkpatrick's

Soho Bibliography of primary writings appeared in 1965 (revised edition, 1968), a special E. M. Forster number of MODERN FICTION STUDIES came out in 1961, and interpretative bibliographies of secondary materials on Forster have been running in ENGLISH LITERATURE IN TRANSITION since 1957. One must also mention the perceptive work of foreign scholars, among whom Anna Maria Fadda and Agostino Lombardo (in Italian), Gerhard Stebner and Heinz-Joachim Müllenbroch (in German), and Ineko Kondo (in Japanese) are the most outstanding. The Abinger Edition of E. M. Forster, under the skillful editorship of Oliver Stallybrass, is currently (early 1975) bringing together previously collected writings and hitherto uncollected and unpublished works. This edition will round out the canon of Forster's work, make all his writings readily available, and supply an interim definitive text for them. The introductions to the Abinger Edition often provide excerpts from unpublished journals, notebooks, and letters, materials indispensable for the appraisal of Forster's work and significance. Stallybrass himself describes this edition, his aims in editing it, and the problems that he has encountered in "The Abinger Edition of E. M. Forster" (1973).

Forster's Bloomsbury connections, at once strong and tenuous, have been amplified by the publication of numerous background studies and materials. Among the most important are Virginia Woolf's A WRITER'S DIARY (1953) and her COLLECTED ESSAYS (4 volumes, 1966–1967), Clive Bell's OLD FRIENDS (1956), Leonard Woolf's series of autobiographies in the 1960s, Michael Holroyd's LYTTON STRACHEY (1967, 1968), Quentin Bell's BLOOMSBURY (1968) and VIRGINIA WOOLF (1972), CARRINGTON: LETTERS AND EXTRACTS FROM HER DIARIES (1970), LETTERS OF ROGER FRY (1972), and THE AUTOBIOGRAPHY OF G. LOWES DICKINSON (1973). Central to an understanding of Forster's personality and values are the reminiscences, occasioned by his death, of those who knew him casually or closely (as the case might be), and certain of the interim obituary accounts: articles by Patrick Anderson, Noel Annan, Evert Barger, Denis Brogan, R. C. Churchill, P. N. Furbank, Frank Kermode, James Kirkup, K. Natwar-Singh, V. S. Pritchett, Alec R. Vidler, and Stephen Spender, all from 1970, and articles by J. R. Ackerley, K. W. Gransden, and Glenway Wescott from 1971. These essays are not all of a piece, for some of the writers stress Forster's kindliness, his generosity, and his saintly and self-abnegating qualities, while others see as central his hedonism, his astringency, his strong sexuality, and his consistent egotism. Nor are these commentators unanimous in their judgments of his work. Some emphasize the passion which they see in it and its inclusiveness and relevance; some others feel that sexual passion is attenuated in it, that his writing is bloodless, and that, in point of view, he is solipsistic, parochial, and self-enclosed. Virtually all of his critics regard the style as refracting the man's temper; most are favorable in discussing it, though some have expressed reservations about an allegedly mannered aspect. Most critics find that Forster's humanism and liberalism, as he formulated it, possesses vitality and significance for the present-day reader. Clearly Forster was not an easy writer to sum up. Clearly, opposing strains formed the complicated and fascinating personality and writer that made of Forster an institution and legend in his years at Cambridge after 1945. THE LETTERS OF J. R. ACKERLEY (1975) also do much to illuminate Forster's personality and psyche.

Since 1957 the bulk of the scholarly and critical writing on Forster has appeared in journals and magazines; and any attempt to survey it has to be at best selective. The most rewarding inquiries of a more general sort have emphasized specific subjects or thematic content rather than technique or artistry. The essays which touch Forster's social concerns are perhaps the most interesting. Donald Hannah in "The Limitations of Liberalism in E. M. Forster's Work" (1962) feels that only in *A Passage to India* does Forster transcend the limitations of his liberalism, whereas Willis H. Truitt in "Thematic and Symbolic Ideology in the Works of E. M. Forster" (1971) finds strong evidence that Forster depicts shrewdly and sympathetically the Marxist class struggle in *The Longest Journey* and *Howards End*. Thus with an open-ended, elusive, indeterminate, paradoxical fiction such as Forster's, contrary approaches often have almost equal validity. This, actually, is the point that Dan Jacobson makes in one of the best short essays on Forster, "Forster's Cave" (NEW STATESMAN, ns LXXII [14 Oct 1966], 560) in which he concludes that *A Passage to India* contains both the pessimism and the optimism which Crews and Stone respectively see in the novel. Herbert Howarth in "E. M. Forster and the Contrite Establishment" (1965) demonstrates persuasively that the origins of Forster's acute social awareness are to be found in the INDEPENDENT REVIEW and its contributors. V. S. Pritchett in "E. M. Forster at Ninety" asserts the paradoxical view that Forster's ideas have made his books seem dated, precisely because we have assimilated so completely their manner and their valuations of experience. Other notable essays of a general kind are Edwin Nierenberg's "The Prophecy of E. M. Forster" (1964), which analyzes perspicuously the classical, romantic, Christian, and Hindu elements in Forster's religious philosophy, and Samuel Hynes's "E. M. Forster at Ninety" (1969), which emphasizes how Forster values the non-heroic virtues at the expense of the heroic and how he exists more fully in his books as wholes than in his characters. Among the recent first-class essays on Forster is A. Woodward's "The Humanism of E. M. Forster" (1963), which effectively relates the humanistic, realistic, religious, and symbolist aspects of the fiction to each other.

On more literary matters, Mark Goldman's "Virginia Woolf and E. M. Forster: A Critical Dialogue" (1966) and Frederick P. W. McDowell's "E. M. Forster's Theory of Literature" (1966) attempt a synthesis of Forster's aesthetic ideas. Alan Wilde in "Depths and Surfaces: Dimensions of Forsterian Irony" (1973) traces the inferiority (as he sees it) of the posthumous works to a disappearance of Forster's irony, and Elizabeth Heine in "The

Significance of Structure in the Works of E. M. Forster and Virginia Woolf"
(1973) finds that Forster's novels follow far more consciously imposed
external patterns than do the more internally centered, organically conceived novels of Virginia Woolf.

Other essays have focussed on the implications of Forster's homosexuality or on his relationships with his contemporaries. Forster's homosexuality, to the fore in discussion about him since his death, figures as a principal
subject in Norman Pittenger's "E. M. Forster, Homosexuality and Christian
Morality" (1971), Cynthia Ozick's "Forster's Homosexuality" (1971), Molly Haskell's "A Refuge among Contemporary Novels" (1972), Jeffrey Meyers's "Fizzling Sexual Time Bombs" (1973), and David Jago's "School and
Theater: Polarities of Homosexual Writing in England" (1974). Jago sees
Forster not as an exponent of revolution in matters of sexual morality but
as an advocate for the integration of the homosexual into modern society.
Donald Salter has made the most searching inquiry into Forster's homosexual writings in "That Is My Ticket: The Homosexual Writings of E. M.
Forster" (1975) and finds them to be aesthetically and ideologically inferior
to the works published during Forster's lifetime. Martin Price in "E. M. F.
and D. H. L." (1966) and Jeffrey Meyers in "E. M. Forster and T. E.
Lawrence" (1970) say the first, and perhaps the last, word on Forster's
relationships to the two Lawrences. Recent essays by Quentin Bell, Frederick P. W. McDowell, and Robert Nye, all from 1973 and inspired by the
simultaneous appearance of the Abinger Edition of *Goldsworthy Lowes
Dickinson* and THE AUTOBIOGRAPHY OF G. LOWES DICKINSON, have helped
to clarify Forster's relationship with Dickinson, one of his most important
mentors.

Next to MOBY DICK, LORD JIM, WUTHERING HEIGHTS, and ULYSSES, *A
Passage to India* must be the most thoroughly explicated novel in English.
The critics in the 1960s, at least by implication, rejected Trilling's misleading view of the novel as primarily a social and political testament and his
denigration of its characters as inadequate for Forster's purposes. The consensus now is that *A Passage to India*, not *Howards End*, is Forster's
masterpiece. The mythical, philosophical, religious, symbolical, and metaphysical dimensions of the novel have most intrigued recent commentators.
Louise Dauner's "What Happened in the Cave?" (1961) seems to anticipate
much of the succeeding commentary when she presents the Marabar Caves
as highly complex, archetypal, paradoxical images which are simultaneously negative and positive in meaning. Keith Hollingsworth in "*A Passage to
India:* The Echoes in the Marabar Caves" (1962) has followed too closely
the schematic formulations of Glen O. Allen in aligning the Caves with
Western rationalism, though Hollingsworth's explanation of the cause, in
the aridity of Western positivistic science, for the disillusionment of Mrs.
Moore and Adela Quested is provocative. In "Thematic Symbol in *A Passage to India*" (1961), George H. Thomson has been concerned with the

symbolical, archetypal dimensions of the novel, an approach which he develops still further in THE FICTION OF E. M. FORSTER (1967). Other critics have followed the lead of Thomson, notably Ellin Horowitz, Edgar A. Austin, and John S. Martin. Horowitz, in "The Communal Ritual and the Dying God in E. M. Forster's *A Passage to India*" (1964), demonstrates how Frazerian concepts of the savior who must die to bring fertility again to his native land were formative in Forster's conception of Mrs. Moore and how they are illustrated in her death and apotheosis. Austin, in "Rites of Passage in *A Passage to India*" (1964), focuses upon the relationship of the rituals in *Passage* to the findings of the Cambridge anthropologists of the early century. Martin, in "Mrs. Moore and the Marabar Caves: A Mythological Reading" (1965), finds convincing resemblances between Mrs. Moore and the Roman Cumaean Sibyl. Again, Wilfred Stone's masterful "*A Passage to India:* The Great Round" (THE CAVE AND THE MOUNTAIN [1966]) must be mentioned, as he relates the novel most subtly to Jungian theories of the unconscious and to Indian religion and philosophy.

The abundance, variety, and excellence of recent commentaries on *A Passage to India* are remarkable. The more formal aspects of Forster's thematic content and the presentation and resolution of dichotomies to attain some kind of unity are explored in such thoughtful Gokulāstami essays as Guttikonda Nageswara Rao's "Gokulāstami: The Resolution of the Antithesis in Forster's Art" (1965) and H. M. Daleski's "Rhythmic and Symbolic Patterns in *A Passage to India*" (1966). The best discussion of Hinduism in *Passage* is Michael Spencer's little-known essay of 1968, "Hinduism in E. M. Forster's *A Passage to India.*" Benita Parry also appreciates the role of Hindu inclusiveness as tending to heal the divisions among the characters ("Passage to More than India," 1966), and J. A. Ramsaran asserts that India, especially through the agency of Hinduism, allows for connections and fulfillments not found elsewhere ("An Indian Reading of E. M. Forster's Classic," 1969). A recent attempt to define more precisely the Hindu content of the novel is S. V. Pradhan's "A 'Song' of Love; Forster's *A Passage to India*" (1973), though his denial of all Hindu relevance to Mrs. Moore is debatable. Other excellent essays comprise Svetozar Koljević's "E. M. Forster: Sceptic as Novelist" (1965), wherein Forster's skepticism is seen as mitigated to a degree by his honest confrontation of it, and Roy Thomas's and Howard Erskine-Hill's "*A Passage to India:* Two Points of View" (1965), wherein Thomas sees the novel as an exercise in irony and detachment with an emphasis on separation, while Erskine-Hill views it primarily in terms of the multiplicity, diversity, inclusiveness, and final possible unity of our experience. Malcolm Bradbury's "Two Passages to India: Forster as Victorian and Modern" (1969) is one of the best critiques yet written on the novel. He sees the realistic and the symbolic levels of the novel reinforcing each other as varying aspects of Forster's temperament and his views of experience—the realistic subsuming his roots in aesthetic and philosophic tradition deriving from the eighteenth century, the symbolic indicating his modern open-ended tendencies in technique and philosophy, deriving from nineteenth-century romanticism and its later manifestations. Hélène Webner's "E. M. Forster's Divine Comedy" (1971) is interesting for its analysis of the Christian elements in *Passage*, which tend to be obscured in discussion of the novel because the Moslem and Hindu cultures are so prominent in it.

In spite of Andrew Shonfield's derogation of Forster's presentation of the Indian scene ("The Politics of Forster's India," 1968), the consensus is that Forster did have brilliant insight into the real India and into the British in India. Most critics feel that Forster's arrogant and unimaginative Anglo-Indians were all too typical of the colonial administrators. Jeffrey Meyers in "The Politics of *A Passage to India*" (1971) refutes Shonfield implicitly by demonstrating the truth of Forster's depiction of the Anglo-Indians and the definite references in the novel to contemporary Indian events and nationalistic aspirations. M. M. Mahood in "Amritsar to Chandrapore: E. M. Forster and the Massacre" (1973) supports Meyers's contention that Forster is conscious of postwar Indian history and politics. Benita Parry in her monumnetal DELUSIONS AND DISCOVERIES (1972) also demonstrates, by considering in detail other Anglo-Indian novelists, how Forster condemns the typical formulations of race superiority voiced, sometimes unconsciously, by earlier writers of Anglo-Indian fiction. Her critique of *Passage* conclusively reveals its reflections of the various strands in Indian culture—the Moslem, Jain, and Hindu. Kenneth Burke has written a difficult and involuted, yet strikingly perceptive essay ("Social and Cosmic Mystery: *A Passage to India*," 1966). Burke stresses the role of the novel as evoking in the reader a mood of "ironically sympathetic contemplation" and analyzes its linguistic and ideological content, concluding that caste and class differences that result in muddle can be tentatively but not completely resolved when they are seen in full perspective. Paul Scott in "India: A Post-Forsterian View" (1970) suggests that Forster in *Passage* epitomized the alienation felt not only by Anglo-Indians early in the century but still felt by present-day resident technicians in the former British dependencies, and Andrew Deacon in "*A Passage to India:* Forster's Confidence" (1971), with a modicum of success, argues that the novel fails, in some aspects, to be as intellectually and emotionally rigorous as it ought to have been. Excellent short monographs on *Passage* have appeared, especially in England, by W. H. Mason (1965), J. A. Boulton (1966), John Colmer (1967), and Phillipa Moody (1968).

Though most commentators feel that Hinduism is essential to a knowledge of Forster's full meaning in *A Passage to India*, V. J. Emmett, Jr. ("Verbal Truth and Truth of Mood in E. M. Forster's *A Passage to India*," 1972), with some plausibility, argues that Fielding and his humanism stand at the center of the novel, rather than Godbole and his Hinduism and Mrs.

Moore and her mysticism. Contrasting views to Emmett's had been asserted by Glenn Pederson ("Forster's Symbolic Form," 1959) who has argued convincingly for the centrality of Mrs. Moore and her affinities with Hinduism to the structure and meaning of the novel and by Edwin M. Moseley in "Christ as One Avatar: Forster's *Passage to India*" (1962) who argued for an identification of Mrs. Moore with Christ, Shri Krishna, and Kali, the Earth Mother. Edwin Nierenberg in "The Withered Priestess: Mrs. Moore's Incomplete Passage to India" (1964) attempted, without much success, to overturn this view of Mrs. Moore as a positive, mythic figure. Somewhat analogous was David Shusterman's attempt ("The Curious Case of Professor Godbole: *A Passage to India* Re-examined," 1961) to undermine the spiritual authority which most critics have attributed to Professor Godbole.

Howards End has also led to considerable commentary. One of the best essays, James Hall's "Forster's Family Reunions" (1958) indicates how Forster's dialectic in the novel runs in several directions and how the connection established finally between the Schlegel sisters outweighs in importance Margaret's rapprochement with Henry Wilcox. Frederick P. W. McDowell, George H. Thomson, Cyrus Hoy, and Frederick Hoffman have explained the symbolic and thematic aspects of the novel in essays written in 1959, 1960, and 1961. Easily the best separate treatments of *Howards End* are Malcolm Bradbury's "E. M. Forster's *Howards End*" (1962) and John Edward Hardy's "*Howards End:* The Sacred Center" (in MAN IN THE MODERN NOVEL, 1964). Bradbury finds that the novel has much general, social, and philosophical significance and notes how the symbolic and realistic levels of the novel reinforce each other as expressions respectively of the poetic and the comic elements in Forster's temperament; Hardy also finds many universal intonations of meaning in the novel, especially in his ritualistic interpretation of the finale which, he says, disappoints only when it is judged by realistic canons. These critics, therefore, are at variance with Walter Allen, F. R. Leavis, and Virginia Woolf, who hold that the poetry in *Howards End* does not "work." Other critics have taken the novel in directions of their own without causing undue distortion: Edwin M. Moseley ("A New Correlative for *Howards End:* Demeter and Persephone," 1961) perceptively traces mythological analogues in the novel; Thomas Churchill ("Place and Personality in *Howards End*," 1962) finds Ruth Wilcox and Howards End to be at the center of the novel rather than the Schlegel sisters; Barry R. Westburg ("Forster's Fifth Symphony: Another Aspect of *Howards End*," 1964) emphasizes Helen Schlegel's positive role in the novel, in her imaginativeness and creativity; and Paul B. Armstrong in "E. M. Forster's *Howards End:* The Existential Crisis of the Liberal Imagination" (1973) adroitly suggests how Forster would have needed the resources provided by the existential imagination to resolve the "liberal" problem he had developed of the need for his characters to achieve purposeful connection.

Other Forster works have had less extensive analysis. As for *The Longest Journey*, John Harvey in "Imagination and Moral Theme in E. M. Forster's *The Longest Journey*" (1956) emphasized the alleged symbolic weaknesses in the novel, though he may have overstated matters by adopting the realistic criteria of F. R. Leavis and Lionel Trilling for his method and appraisal (the limitations of this approach George H. Thomson was to expose in THE FICTION OF E. M. FORSTER, 1967). Frederick P. W. McDowell in "Forster's Many-Faceted Universe: Idea and Theme in *The Longest Journey*" (1960) vindicates Rickie Elliot to the extent possible and sees him as a more positive character than do most critics, though he may overstate his case. John Magnus's masterly "Ritual Aspects of E. M. Forster's *The Longest Journey*" (MODERN FICTION STUDIES, XIII (Summer 1967), 195–210) supports Thomson and Stone in their view that *Journey* is ultimately romance, and no critic has more persuasively explored the connections between the intellectual issues in the novel (their background in contemporary philosophy and Forster's own progress from the mysticism of McTaggart and Dickinson to the rationality of G. E. Moore and Bertrand Russell), the characters, and the symbols than has Elizabeth Heine in "Rickie Elliot and the Cow: The Cambridge Apostles and *The Longest Journey*" (1972).

Where Angels Fear to Tread, despite the high regard in which critics hold it, has generated little independent inquiry. The most striking brief treatment is Carolyn Heilburn's "Speaking of Books: A Modern among Contemporaries" (1966) in which she demonstrates that the tensions enclosed in this novel are distinctly modern in their implications. *A Room with a View* has fared better with serious critics and has occasioned distinguished essays such as those by John Lucas ("Wagner and Forster: PARSIFAL and *A Room with a View*," 1966, on the relations of *Room* to Wagner, especially to PARSIFAL), Jeffrey Meyers ("'Vacant Heart and Hand and Eye': The Homosexual Theme in *A Room with a View*," 1970), and Elizabeth Ellem ("E. M. Forster: The Lucy and New Lucy Novels: Fragments of Early Versions of *A Room with a View*," 1971).

The reviews and articles on the posthumously published *Maurice* (1971) comprise an important accession to the critical writing on E. M. Forster. Opinion concerning the book is sharply divided. Brigid Brophy, Oswell Blakeston, Samuel Hynes, Julian Mitchell, and Philip Toynbee come down heavily on the negative side; John Colmer, Nigel Dennis, and Bernard Levin come down just as heavily on the positive; most other critics come down somewhere between the extremes. In this latter group are a number of thoughtful critics who have written stimulating commentary on Forster and his career as a whole: A. Alvarez, Noel Annan, Douglass Bolling, Cyril Connolly, Joseph Epstein, Frank Kermode, Arnold Kettle, David Lodge, Frederick P. W. McDowell, Vivian Mercier, Jeffrey Meyers, V. S. Pritchett, Michael Ratcliffe, C. Rising, C. P. Snow, Stephen Spender, George Steiner, Paul Theroux, Richard Wasson, and Colin Wilson. The critiques of *Maurice* are important in shaping our sense of Forster and his total contemporary significance. *The Life to Come and Other Stories*, a second posthumous volume published in 1972, has not caused much positive commentary, though Eudora Welty's review in the NEW YORK TIMES BOOK REVIEW (1973) is appreciative and discriminating. Melvin Bragg, David Craig, Samuel Hynes, Jeffrey Meyers, Karl Miller, Roger Scruton, and Donald Salter have also written with discernment on *The Life to Come*, perhaps the most difficult to appraise of all Forster's works.

The fact that *Maurice* was so widely noticed indicates how important Forster had become not only as writer but as cultural arbiter. The extent of the writing on *Maurice* and the volume of the journal articles on Forster in the last decade signify that he is now a writer with whom all literary historians must reckon. That few people now question his eminence is best conveyed by the way in which he now, almost automatically, figures in chapters of recent critical books. For James Gindin in HARVEST OF A QUIET EYE: THE NOVEL OF COMPASSION (1971) Forster is one of the chief novelists of sensibility and compassion who protested against the emotional aridity of realistic fiction; for Calvin Bedient in ARCHITECTS OF THE SELF (1972) he is the writer who best achieved a middle course between George Eliot's intellectuality and D. H. Lawrence's primitivism; for Naomi Leibowitz in HUMANISM AND THE ABSURD IN THE MODERN NOVEL (1971) he is a voice of sanity who recognizes the paradoxical (and absurd) nature of contemporary existence, without losing his humanistic balance; and for Jonah Raskin in THE MYTHOLOGY OF IMPERIALISM (1971) he is an imperfectly emancipated, timorous liberal who failed to achieve a genuine inclusiveness in his philosophy such as D. H. Lawrence attained. William Barrett in TIME OF NEED (1972) regards Forster's sensitivity to the abyss and his formulation of the message of the Caves as his contribution to an understanding of contemporary chaos and the devastating tensions present in the modern age; Jeffrey Meyers in FICTION AND THE COLONIAL EXPERIENCE (1973) alleges that Forster has written the pivotal book in the literature of imperialism, appropriating Kipling's imaginative apprehension of India yet connecting with other more recent writers on the colonial theme, such as Joyce Cary and Graham Greene who are aware of the native population as comprised of individuals; and Benita Parry in DELUSIONS AND DISCOVERIES (1972) finds that Forster is the source of light at the end of the tunnel that includes all other less sensitive and gifted writers of Anglo-Indian fiction. Stephen Spender in LOVE-HATE RELATIONS (1974) conceives of Forster as a "poet-novelist" who wrote elegies in his fiction for a bygone England, while he projected characters in whom the essential spirit of that England might still survive. The testimony of these important books, all appearing between 1971 and 1974, is that Forster is a writer representative and significant enough to be considered in any discussion of contemporary literature.

In the bibliography which follows I have sought to evaluate entries according to principles which underlie my understanding of Forster's work, mind, and art. For the early novels, I believe that Philip Herriton and Caroline Abbott in *Where Angels Fear to Tread* are changed as a result of their Italian experiences. I also think that Gino Carella is not altogether successful as a character, though the violence in the novel is on the whole aesthetically justified. With respect to *The Longest Journey* I regard Rickie Elliot as an interesting and significant character, philosophically and morally, despite his eventual failure as a person and moral agent. I feel that he has more strength and resources than some critics admit and that it is a fatal conjunction of circumstance with temperament which undoes him. Like most other critics, I do not regard Stephen Wonham as fully formed in his double capacity as natural man and symbolic entity. He is relatively convincing when he is viewed in either aspect, but he does not fuse the two sides of his nature adequately. Primarily, as George H. Thomson thinks, he is to be regarded as an archetypal presence. Stewart Ansell has limitations as a person, I think, in addition to being a source of light in the novel. The book is more fully articulated and aesthetically compelling than some critics have been willing to admit; and I would say that, on the whole, it forcefully unites realism and symbolism. The style and technique both betray some weakness which is, however, not overpowering. With respect to *A Room with a View*, the Emersons are not fully persuasive as imaginative creations; in particular, Mr. Emerson as a sententious man with myth-like authority is inadequately envisioned. Lucy Honeychurch and George Emerson are appealing though they are only moderately perceptive. I do not greatly believe in Charlotte Bartlett's change of heart that enables her to assist the lovers, nor is Mr. Beebe's contrary change quite fully adumbrated. Mr. Beebe, Mr. Eager, Miss Lavish, Cecil Vyse, and Charlotte Bartlett are great comic creations, the last two being extensively developed.

Howards End is the most controversial of Forster's novels. Some critics like John Edward Hardy and Lionel Trilling have found it to be Forster's best novel, whereas F. R. Leavis has thought it an outright failure. The great majority regard it as an important and weighty work but flawed, yet in importance and stature second only to *A Passage to India*. The novel is more completely planned and patterned than some commentators have granted, and I think that the realistic and symbolic levels, on the whole, merge without undue aesthetic fracture. While the design is schematic, the characters in general are sufficiently rounded to flesh out the skeletal plan. Leonard Bast I consider an original and vital character, although Forster's treatment of him betrays some uncertainty, as he wavers between sympathy for him and ridicule of him. Henry Wilcox is very much alive and a forceful if often misguided individual. But Forster's emotional antipathy for him outruns his intellectual valuation of him. The marriage between Margaret Schlegel and Henry is probable rather than incredible, as Alan Wilde in Art and Order (1964) has so well demonstrated, although it is difficult always to credit Margaret's continuing blindness to Henry's major defects. I would say that Helen Schlegel did not forget that she was a "lady" with Leonard, but was so blindly smarting with passion at the social injustice done to the Basts by Henry Wilcox that she gave herself to Leonard out of pity for him and as a vehement gesture against the Wilcoxes. The ending of the novel has often been slated. Whereas there are improbabilities in the sequence considered as an exercise in realism, this last sequence in the main convinces philosophically as part of Forster's unfolding pattern for the novel, as John Edward Hardy has asserted. Helen and Margaret are essentially admirable if fallible characters (the position of James Hall, for example, in "Forster's Family Reunions," 1958) and are not the consciously superior or even malignant figures that Wilfred Stone and Walter Allen have them as being.

As for *A Passage to India*, I believe that Aziz is a creditable protagonist and that Forster was justified in using a Moslem rather than a Hindu, as it suited his purpose and inspiration to do so. Aziz is, in any case, balanced by Godbole, whom I regard as a central spiritual presence in the novel and not as the malign force that David Shusterman has seen him as. And Mrs. Moore has been similarly discredited by Edwin Nierenberg. She is, rather, a regenerative agent in the novel, as Ellin Horowitz views her; her true significance is evident only when she is translated into a popular Hindu deity after her death, and Godbole inexplicably recalls her presence to mind. Forster was intrigued by Hinduism, and the novel is to be explained philosophically (as James McConkey, Wilfred Stone, and Michael Spencer, among others, have contended) in terms of the inclusiveness of Hinduism and its stress upon cosmic love. I hold the Temple sequence to be a dynamic and aesthetically successful rendition of Forster's positive views, with his major dependence on Oriental religion and his rejection of Western rationalism as insufficient to account for life's mysteries and discords. The total drift of the novel is not negative or pessimistic as Reuben Brower and Frederick C. Crews have held; there is, as Stone and Jacobson have asserted, a dimension in which the novel lies beyond optimism and pessimism and includes both. The Marabar Caves comprise another inclusive entity that lies beyond good and evil while it includes them. Good implies evil; evil, good. The absence of God implies His eventual presence; the presence of God, His soon-to-be-encountered absence. As for Fielding there is much to be said for his humanism as it balances the barbarism of the Anglo-Indians, the emotionalism of Aziz, and the mysticism and social indifference of Godbole. The comprehensiveness of Hinduism is all in its favor; its passivity in the face of social disaster is its limitation.

I am of the opinion that the short stories should be interpreted "straight" and that characters like Mr. Lucas ("The Road from Colonus") and Miss Raby ("The Eternal Moment") are not "ironically" conceived and meant by Forster to be regarded satirically. The volumes of nonfictional prose are important, though I would not challenge the view that Forster's chief fame will derive from his novels. I think that critics like Lionel Trilling and C. B. Cox have overemphasized Forster's alleged passivity and non-involvement. Forster has shown always an interest in social and political issues, and this interest became more pronounced in the 1930s and later. Indeed, Forster did much to form the intellectual temper of the age after World War I and the age after World War II; and he has been, for a writer, rather more than less widely influential upon the general reading public.

More than in the case of most authors, the commentary written on E. M. Forster has resulted in his being accepted as an outstanding writer. Without the support of the discerning critics and scholars who have written on him, especially since World War II, it is doubtful whether he would stand in such high repute as he now does. The criticism on E. M. Forster illustrates, among other things, the recovery of a literary reputation after a time of obscurity and the reestablishment of it on a firmer, less arbitrarily defined basis.

The Bibliography

1905

---

1 "Books in Brief: Fiction," PALL MALL GAZETTE, 7 Oct 1905, p. 9; rptd in E. M. FORSTER: THE CRITICAL HERITAGE, ed by Philip Gardner (Lond & Boston: Routledge & Kegan Paul, 1973), p. 46.
Where Angels Fear to Tread is not a particularly interesting story of Lilia and of her widower, a picturesque but disreputable Italian.

2 "Fiction," SPEAKER (Lond), 21 Oct 1905, p. 90; rptd in E. M. FORSTER: THE CRITICAL HERITAGE, ed by Philip Gardner (Lond & Boston: Routledge & Kegan Paul, 1973), p. 49–51.
In *Where Angels Fear to Tread* EMF has exposed with refreshing and original touch Sawston's ideals and ways of life in the warm Italian sun. The five Herritons and Caroline Abbott represent middle-class England and are opposed to "the subtle, graceful, materialistic, and full-natured" Gino Carella. EMF is in full control of his materials in this clash of national types. Caroline's confession of passion for Gino is not quite credible since EMF does not view her romantic fervor at all critically. The temperamental affinities are really stronger between her and Philip Herriton. EMF gives their relationship, which seems so colorless, much interest.

3 "Fiction," TIMES LITERARY SUPPLEMENT (Lond), 29 Sept 1905, p. 319; rptd in E. M. FORSTER: THE CRITICAL HERITAGE, ed by Philip Gardner (Lond & Boston: Routledge & Kegan Paul, 1973), p. 43.
Some of the incidents in *Where Angels Fear to Tread* are so original as to be farcical. It has an "odd" individuality, as do its characters. The writing is good and witty.

4 Masterman, C. F. G. "A Book of the Day: A Remarkable Novel," DAILY NEWS (Lond), 8 Nov 1905, p. 4; rptd in E. M. FORSTER:

THE CRITICAL HERITAGE, ed by Philip Gardner (Lond & Boston: Routledge & Kegan Paul, 1973), pp. 52–55.

Where Angels Fear to Tread conveys impression of power and thorough mastery of its materials. Its qualities of style and thought are a satisfaction and a delight: EMF's stylistic taste, his keen relish of the humor of life, his challenge to normal concerns. EMF weaves a vision that is at once an approval and a criticism of life. He explores the clash of diverse racial traits and lets erupt what is ordinarily hidden in polite, civilized existence. The story manifests the triumph of the ordered conventional world "over the revolt of incongruous, queer, and passionate desires." EMF conveys the reality of this conflict and presents an all too seldom challenge to ultimate things, in charting the effects of Gino's primitive energies and those of his Italy upon the English visitors. EMF is dispassionate in his treatment of opposed cultures which have little direct connection with each other. EMF's direction in *Angels* seems to be this: "The conquering Briton has gained the whole world; perhaps the Italian, amongst the ruins of populous cities, has preserved his own soul." The two cultures will afterwards retain their separate identities, but in their momentary clash, "something unaccountable, almost elfish and fantastic, has been revealed of the queer, irrational material of the soul of woman and of man." The deftness, lightness, grace of touch, and the radiant atmosphere of the humor in *Angels* are remarkable. [The most important of the first reviews of EMF's work.]

5 "More Novels," DAILY MAIL (Lond), 5 Oct 1904, p. 4.

Where Angels Fear to Tread breaks in two with the death of Lilia Herriton. The relationship between Lilia and her husband, Gino Carella, is convincing; but events after her death are less so, especially the attraction finally felt by Caroline Abbott for Gino.

6 "New Novels," MANCHESTER COURIER, 13 Oct 1905, p. 3; rptd in E. M. FORSTER: THE CRITICAL HERITAGE, ed by Philip Gardner (Lond & Boston: Routledge & Kegan Paul, 1973), p. 48.

Where Angels Fear to Tread is an accomplished apprentice novel, though EMF treats his somewhat unpleasant characters too savagely. He reveals "originality of conception and attitude" and reality of character and incident. He lets comedy give way to ironical tragedy, turning upon trivial causes.

7 "Novel Notes," BOOKMAN (Lond), XXIX (Oct 1905), 40–41; rptd in E. M. FORSTER: THE CRITICAL HERITAGE, ed by Philip Gardner (Lond & Boston: Routledge & Kegan Paul, 1973), pp. 43–44.

Where Angels Fear to Tread modulates from triviality to profundity; it is a mixture of jocularity and truthfulness. It is unusual and convincing, "its uniqueness and its persuasion accomplished in an unexpectedly fresh manner."

8 "Novels," SPECTATOR (Lond), XCV (23 Dec 1905), 1089–90; rptd in E. M. FORSTER: THE CRITICAL HERITAGE, ed by Philip Gardner (Lond & Boston: Routledge & Kegan Paul, 1973), pp. 56–58.

Where Angels Fear to Tread is a clever and painful story. EMF reveals tact and reticence in handling a difficult theme; he is not cruel nor anarchical, although he is concerned with those elements in modern society that make for disintegration. His tale is steeped in disillusionment. He reveals how the love felt by a good woman may be a retrogression to primitive instinct, "a mark of degradation rather than elevation." None of the characters are heroic. EMF's real concern is with the emergence of primitive instincts in educated and repressed natures. There is cruelty and callousness in Mrs. Herriton. EMF reveals the tragic possibilities which occur when unimportant people seek to emancipate themselves from convention or to control others who have been conditioned by a different set of traditions. He does not give offense, but his book is painful and disquieting. "Let us hope that so original and searching a talent may yet give us a story in which the fallibility of goodness and the callousness of respectability are less uncompromisingly insisted upon." [Review is both perceptive and imperceptive, and typical of the reaction that EMF's early novels may have provoked among cultivated but conventional readers.]

9 "Novels and Short Stories," BIRMINGHAM DAILY POST, 13 Oct 1905, p. 4; rptd in E. M. FORSTER: THE CRITICAL HERITAGE, ed by Philip Gardner (Lond & Boston: Routledge & Kegan Paul, 1973), p. 47.

There is much to commend in *Where Angels Fear to Tread*, but the character of Gino Carella taxes credulity. After his misconduct helps bring about his wife's death, how could her best friend come so readily under his spell?

10 "Novels and Stories," GLASGOW HERALD, 5 Oct 1905, p. 61; rptd in E. M. FORSTER: THE CRITICAL HERITAGE, ed by Philip Gardner (Lond & Boston: Routledge & Kegan Paul, 1973), p. 45.

Where Angels Fear to Tread is fresh and convincing; its characters seem as if copied from life. The method used to contrast the English and Italian natures is ingenious and effective. Lilia Herriton prefers the decisive masculinity of the Italian Gino Carella to the passivity of Englishmen like Philip Herriton, her brother-in-law. The absurdity of the events adds to the enjoyment gained from *Angels*.

11 "Recent Fiction," YORKSHIRE POST (Leeds), 6 Dec 1905, p. 5; rptd in E. M. FORSTER: THE CRITICAL HERITAGE, ed by Philip Gardner (Lond & Boston: Routledge & Kegan Paul, 1973), p. 55.

Where Angels Fear to Tread reveals some skill but is pervaded "by an atmosphere of snobbishness and vulgarity." Only the despised Gino Carella apparently merits sympathy.

12 V. "New Novels," MANCHESTER GUARDIAN, 4 Oct 1905, p. 5; rptd in E. M. FORSTER: THE CRITICAL HERITAGE, ed by Philip Gardner (Lond & Boston: Routledge & Kegan Paul, 1973), pp. 44–45.
Where Angels Fear to Tread "is not mawkish or sentimental or commonplace." The setting and treatment are original. EMF's cynicism is persistent, perhaps repellent, but it is not deep-seated. He protests the conventionalities of "refinement" and "respectability." Mrs. Herriton and Harriet Herriton are too repellent to be real, but the other four main characters are true-to-life. In the mismatching of Lilia Herriton and Gino Carella there is Meredithian comedy. EMF could be more charitable without loss of force and originality.

1906

[No entries for this year.]

1907

---

13 "Books in Brief: Fiction," PALL MALL GAZETTE, 11 May 1907, p. 4; rptd in E. M. FORSTER: THE CRITICAL HERITAGE, ed by Philip Gardner (Lond & Boston: Routledge & Kegan Paul, 1973), p. 81.
EMF is a sensitive and well-endowed writer, but he lacks dramatic feeling; the result is that Rickie Elliot in *The Longest Journey* comes through as a "case" rather than as a human being. Rickie's experiences are developed with much consistency, but human interest is lacking.

14 "A Clever Book," OBSERVER, 26 May 1907, p. 7.
The Longest Journey is a clever book but not a satisfactory novel. The characterization of the book is expert; EMF has an insider's knowledge of Rickie Elliot as he disintegrates. The moral passion of the author is diminished by the crudenesses in the book.

15 de Wyzewa, T. "Le Roman Anglais en 1907: II, Les Nouveaux Venus" (The English Novel in 1907: The Newcomers), REVUE DES

DEUX MONDES, XLII (15 Dec 1907), 896–920, espec pp. 916–17; discussion of EMF, rptd and trans as "A Newcomer," in E. M. FORSTER: THE CRITICAL HERITAGE, ed by Philip Gardner (Lond & Boston: Routledge & Kegan Paul, 1973), pp. 95–96.

The Longest Journey is unskillful in the telling, and EMF is ignorant of the usual narrative techniques. He fails to highlight his scenes and gives too much detail in Rickie Elliot's Cambridge and Sawston careers. Still, the book is full of observation and poetry. Rickie is sensitive and resigned, and appealing as hero. In contrast to EMF, John Galsworthy is the most skillful new English novelist. [In French.]

16 "Fiction," CAMBRIDGE REVIEW, XXVIII (16 May 1907), 408; rptd in E. M. FORSTER: THE CRITICAL HERITAGE, ed by Philip Gardner (Lond & Boston: Routledge & Kegan Paul, 1973), pp. 85–86.

With *Where Angels Fear to Tread* and *The Longest Journey* to his credit, the public will soon realize that EMF is a genius. In *Journey* EMF has caught the mental atmosphere of undergraduate life. Rickie Elliot alters his views, but Stewart Ansell is inflexible. Stephen Wonham is a "glorious pagan" and complementary to Rickie. The design falls short of the workmanship, but *Journey* is a remarkable novel.

17 "Fiction," TIMES LITERARY SUPPLEMENT (Lond), 26 April 1907, p. 134; rptd in E. M. FORSTER: THE CRITICAL HERITAGE, ed by Philip Gardner (Lond & Boston: Routledge & Kegan Paul, 1973), pp. 67–68.

By its cleverness and adroitness *The Longest Journey* seems to be a young book; EMF again exposes the suburbs and the values of their denizens. EMF manifests skillful and subtle conduct of the story as it is concentrated in Rickie Elliot, yet it does not afford so much satisfaction as the dexterity of the writer might warrant. The comedy is a little too shrill. EMF's faculty of manipulating his facts, theories, and people is remarkable. Agnes Pembroke is a success; Mrs. Failing is not. EMF conveys a sense of a larger background; the Greeks are there, if only to contradict the power of the Sawstonians, just as Rickie's vision is always alloyed by a "pellet of suburban mud." [Perceptive review.]

18 L., R. W. "Some Books Worth Reading," BLACK AND WHITE (Lond), XXXIII (11 May 1907), 658; rptd in E. M. FORSTER: THE CRITICAL HERITAGE, ed by Philip Gardner (Lond & Boston: Routledge & Kegan Paul, 1973), pp. 81–83.

EMF reveals much talent. *The Longest Journey* is not well-constructed, though the opening and closing chapters are excellent. Stephen Wonham is a blurred conception, and so is the plot-line which concerns him. The real interest in the novel is the gradual degradation of Rickie Elliot. Rickie is an excellent character study, except that he ought not to have given in so easily.

19 *"The Longest Journey,"* MORNING POST (Lond), 6 May 1907, p. 2; rptd in E. M. FORSTER: THE CRITICAL HERITAGE, ed by Philip Gardner (Lond & Boston: Routledge & Kegan Paul, 1973), pp. 78–80.

EMF's people in *The Longest Journey* are unpleasant but absorbing. He subjects many of them to a diabolic humor: Agnes Pembroke, Mrs. Failing, Mr. Elliot, Herbert Pembroke, even Rickie Elliot himself. Stephen Wonham escapes EMF's criticism, but as a blend of pagan god and young hooligan he is not convincing. EMF can be "tenderly imaginative" as well as mordant, but *Journey* is more provocative than satisfying. It does not hang together formally; the death rate among the main characters is 44 percent. Still, EMF is a writer of performance and promise.

20 "The Man Who Failed," TRIBUNE (Lond), 22 April 1907, p. 2; rptd in E. M. FORSTER: THE CRITICAL HERITAGE, ed by Philip Gardner (Lond & Boston: Routledge & Kegan Paul, 1973), pp. 65–66.

The Longest Journey is a striking novel about failure. Rickie Elliot is a fool of the nobler type who is surrounded by less admirable people. There is an overabundance of such characters from whom sympathy is withheld for the book to be great. Agnes Pembroke is a memorable character, and the contrast between Rickie and Stephen Wonham is well-done. Rickie's character is too carefully drawn or too different from the ordinary man to be fully convincing. [Excellent review.]

21 Masterman, C. F. G. "A Book of the Day: The Soul in Suburbia," DAILY NEWS (Lond), 3 May 1907, p. 4; rptd in E. M. FORSTER: THE CRITICAL HERITAGE, ed by Philip Gardner (Lond & Boston: Routledge & Kegan Paul, 1973), pp. 73–76.

The promise of *Where Angels Fear to Tread* is more than fulfilled in *The Longest Journey:* "It is difficult, elusive, exasperating: with something of the cleverness of the young in it, and something of the cruelty." *Journey* is a bitter satire on respectability and a visionary novel, with the roots of the visionary often latent in everyday experience. It is not a great book but has elements of greatness. Rickie Elliot is born to the city and suburbia; and after a few years at Cambridge, the dead values of urban life again enmesh him at Sawston. *Journey* is full of suggestion, insight, and cleverness and reveals a writer determined to face the real world. [Sympathetic discussion.]

22 "Mr. E. M. Forster," BOOKMAN (Lond), XXXII (June 1907), 81–82; rptd in E. M. FORSTER: THE CRITICAL HERITAGE, ed by Philip

Gardner (Lond & Boston: Routledge & Kegan Paul, 1973), pp. 61–64.

EMF is an authentic "new novelist" on the strength of *Where Angels Fear to Tread* and *The Longest Journey*. He has had courage to use tentative or unhappy endings when it is fitting to do so. His wit and humor, irony, and living and human characters are noteworthy. "He writes imaginatively, with spiritual insight, and an underlying sense of the beauty, and sordidness, and pathos of mortal life." *Journey* is an even stronger book than *Angels*. Both books herald even more interesting work to be done in the future. [Important early article.]

23 "New Books," Scotsman (Edinburgh), 25 April 1907, p. 2.
Philosophical gravity and academic seriousness give to *The Longest Journey* a monotonous, somber tone. The novel is a commentary on the vanity of intellectual pride. EMF's treatment, revealing refinement and literary ability, mitigates the sadness.

24 "New Novels," Athenaeum, No. 4151 (18 May 1907), 600–601; rptd in E. M. Forster: The Critical Heritage, ed by Philip Gardner (Lond & Boston: Routledge & Kegan Paul, 1973), pp. 86–87.
The Longest Journey dramatizes the situation of an impassioned idealist who is forced to shed his ideals or witness their disintegration and partial reconstruction. The Pembrokes have much vitality and force. Rickie Elliot is anemic; his falling away, his precipitate regeneration, and final immolation are not convincing nor is Stephen Wonham. The cynical aunt is well-done, as are the minor characters. The construction is lax, and death is used in too catastrophic a way for the purposes of art.

25 "Novel Note," Evening Standard and St. James's Gazette (Lond), 30 April 1907, p. 5; rptd in E. M. Forster: The Critical Heritage, ed by Philip Gardner (Lond & Boston: Routledge & Kegan Paul, 1973), p. 72.
The Longest Journey has a touch of genius. The outlook, the style, the dialogue, and the development are original; the flashes of wit are impressive. There is too much contrivance. The commonplace people are too much disparaged by the author; Agnes Pembroke is not "allowed the qualities of her defects." Stephen Wonham is too contradictory, alternately too degraded and too exalted in spirit, but his letter to the unwholesome schoolboy is delightful.

26 "Novel Notes," Bookman (Lond), XXXII (June 1907), 109.
The Longest Journey has some of the same cleverness and glamor as *Where Angels Fear to Tread* and is arresting in its own right. The characters are uncommon; unfortunately, too many of them are abnormal, with the result

that EMF has fallen into crudities and violences in depicting them. The book is not a progression from *Angels*, which revealed unusual power; there is more of the unusual than of power in *Journey*, though EMF does portray a glowing inner life and reveals much insight in so doing. He needs to look at life sanely and steadily as well as sympathetically to distinguish more clearly the fine line between the effective and the ludicrous.

27 "The Novel of the Week," Nation (Lond), I (27 April 1907), 357–58; rptd in E. M. Forster: The Critical Heritage, ed by Philip Gardner (Lond & Boston: Routledge & Kegan Paul, 1973), pp. 68–71.

The Longest Journey is elusive, actual, and ordinary but discloses "the finest shades of spiritual meaning." Style and method are as original as the point of view, as unusual as the subject matter is common and everyday. In the last third of the book, the reader will be struck by the complexity and strangeness of life, by the alternation of meaninglessness with profundity. The novel contains a criticism of ordinary life that is philosophical and witty, spiritual and full of humorous by-play. The novel contrasts those who think for themselves with those who are molded by convention. The rendition of the Pembrokes with their "banal insincerity of spirit" and "cultured Philistinism" is masterly. The Pembrokes are the children of this world, not the children of light. Mrs. Failing and Stephen Wonham are well drawn. The vigor of the country life at Cadover owes something to Meredith. Sudden death is used too often, especially in Rickie's case; but the squabble between Herbert Pembroke and Stephen over Rickie's literary remains is consummately done. EMF's vision is that of a poet fused with that of a humorist; the book as a result has freshness and depth. [Perceptive discussion.]

28 "Novels," Outlook (Lond), XX (13 July 1907), 55; rptd in E. M. Forster: The Critical Heritage, ed by Philip Gardner (Lond & Boston: Routledge & Kegan Paul, 1973), p. 94.

The Longest Journey is the most impossible book in many years; there is no "gleam of Nature" in it. It is difficult to find plain meaning in such "deliberately obscure verbiage."

29 "Novels," Spectator (Lond), XCIX (6 July 1907), 24–25; rptd in E. M. Forster: The Critical Heritage, ed by Philip Gardner (Lond & Boston: Routledge & Kegan Paul, 1973), pp. 91–94.

EMF's characters in *The Longest Journey* are disagreeable and abnormal; they lack geniality. EMF has the power to invent memorable phrases. His humor is excellent, though it is often at the service of an "almost brutal cynicism." The portrayal of the teachers at Sawston School is first-rate. The philosophical undergraduates are not so special as they think they are; "culture" itself is suspect when it causes so many crises. The novel is worth considering for what EMF may yet do, "unless . . . the 'abnormality' of his invention is constitutional and ineradicable." [Reaches toward some truths about *Journey*.]

30 "Novels of the Day," STANDARD (Lond), 14 May 1907, p. 5; rptd in E. M. FORSTER: THE CRITICAL HERITAGE, ed by Philip Gardner (Lond & Boston: Routledge & Kegan Paul, 1973), p. 83.

There is a repulsive note in EMF's realism. He generates disgust rather than wonder or awe in *The Longest Journey;* at times, the atmosphere becomes "hot, acrid, and oppressive."

31 "Pages in Waiting: New Novels," WORLD (Lond), LXVI (21 May 1907), 924; rptd in E. M. FORSTER: THE CRITICAL HERITAGE, ed by Philip Gardner (Lond & Boston: Routledge & Kegan Paul, 1973), pp. 87–88.

The Longest Journey is puzzling and elusive "in its short sentences, in its scrappy indications of who's who, in its abruptness." There are no shades or perspective provided in it; the narrative lacks consecutiveness. The Cambridge undergraduates are not so much unconventional as impossible. The book's purpose is difficult to discover.

32 "Recent Fiction," BIRMINGHAM DAILY POST, 24 May 1907, p. 4; rptd in E. M. FORSTER: THE CRITICAL HERITAGE, ed by Philip Gardner (Lond & Boston: Routledge & Kegan Paul, 1973), pp. 90–91.

In *The Longest Journey* the haphazard method interposes difficulties for the reader. The limitations of Rickie Elliot and Stephen Wonham are mitigated when EMF's symbolical purposes are recognized. The Sawston School sequences and Agnes Pembroke's genuine appeal, but ghastly personal relations, are strengths in the novel.

33 "Recent Fiction," LIVERPOOL DAILY POST AND MERCURY, 22 May 1907, p. 8; rptd in E. M. FORSTER: THE CRITICAL HERITAGE, ed by Philip Gardner (Lond & Boston: Routledge & Kegan Paul, 1973), pp. 88–89.

The subtlety of *The Longest Journey* is so great that it is difficult to grasp its intent. It is not a novel so much as "a bundle of wonderful studies in human psychology." EMF studies "the abnormalities in the normal," the "eccentricities in the commonplace." Its tragic close is a blemish since Rickie Elliot had the ability to organize himself and Agnes the capacity to reform her marriage; yet the characters also have qualities that inevitably result in tragedy. The novel provides, with all its subtleties, its speculative aspects, and its demands on our rational faculties, an experience of life. By the end we know more of the characters than the writer has told us. He demonstrates for us "the hardest of life's ironies with . . . intense conviction." [Excellent review.]

34 St. Barbe. "Books and Their Writers," QUEEN, THE LADY'S NEWSPAPER (Lond), 11 May 1907, p. 880; rptd in E. M. FORSTER: THE CRITICAL HERITAGE, ed by Philip Gardner (Lond & Boston: Routledge & Kegan Paul, 1973), p. 80.

The Longest Journey does not fulfill the promise revealed in *Where Angels Fear to Tread.* EMF loses himself in "a labyrinth of characterisation." The plot is devoid of climaxes; the lack of straightforwardness makes *Journey*'s interest meager.

35 "Two New Novelists," DAILY MAIL (Lond), 4 May 1907, p. 4. The section of *The Longest Journey* dealing with Rickie Elliot's marriage and the characterizations are strong; the deaths are contrived. *Journey* is a subtle and clever novel.

36 V. "New Novels," MANCHESTER GUARDIAN, 15 May 1907, p. 5; rptd in E. M. FORSTER: THE CRITICAL HERITAGE, ed by Philip Gardner (Lond & Boston: Routledge & Kegan Paul, 1973), pp. 84–85.

The Longest Journey is as brilliant, incoherent, original, and pessimistic as *Where Angels Fear to Tread.* It reveals strong and vivid writing. It is full of eccentricities and abruptnesses which subject the reader to a succession of shocks. EMF writes in a spirit of revolt, but he identifies the real too greatly with the grotesque and the eccentric. His studies of the unreal person, especially Herbert Pembroke, are excellent.

1908

37 "A Clever Novel," MORNING POST (Lond), 23 Nov 1908, p. 4; rptd in E. M. FORSTER: THE CRITICAL HERITAGE, ed by Philip Gardner (Lond & Boston: Routledge & Kegan Paul, 1973), p. 110.

A Room with a View is a strong and admirable novel, and with it EMF consolidates his reputation. His satire is pointed but good-natured. Life triumphing makes Lucy Honeychurch fresh, natural, and adorable; art, in Charlotte Bartlett and Cecil Vyse, influences Lucy to become conventional. George Emerson is well presented. His love for Lucy is spontaneous and sure, not vulgar and uncontrolled; he has within him "the genius of love" that allows him to break all bonds, discern the truth, and become the means by which others can recognize it.

38 F. "A Notable Novel," MANCHESTER GUARDIAN, 4 Nov 1908, p. 5; rptd in E. M. FORSTER: THE CRITICAL HERITAGE, ed by Philip Gardner (Lond & Boston: Routledge & Kegan Paul, 1973), pp. 107–8.

George Emerson plays a decisive role in Lucy Honeychurch's development in *A Room with a View* when he leaves his note with a question mark on it over her washstand in Florence. He incarnates his father's philosophy. Belief in joy is a primary value: "in the joy of the sun and the free air, in sincerity of soul, and in passion." In Cecil Vyse there are echoes from Bernard Shaw, and an indebtedness to Meredith is present throughout. But EMF has his own humor, philosophy, and style.

39 "Fiction," SCOTSMAN (Edinburgh), 2 Oct 1908, p. 3.

Individuality of style and method are again pronounced in *A Room with a View*. Narrative and characterization are achieved with light strokes, but every stroke tells. The theme is "the everlasting struggle" between convention and passion.

40 "Fiction under Three Heads: Humorous," PALL MALL GAZETTE, 6 Nov 1908, p. 4; rptd in E. M. FORSTER: THE CRITICAL HERITAGE, ed by Philip Gardner (Lond & Boston: Routledge & Kegan Paul, 1973), p. 108.

A Room with a View is original and delightful; it has quiet humor and penetrating observation. The characters are admirably drawn and true to life; the Emersons are new creations in the novel. The book might have as its text Dr. Johnson's "Clear your minds of cant." It is characterized by "delightful 'unexpectedness.'"

41 "For Booklovers," DAILY MAIL (Lond), 31 Oct 1908, p. 8; rptd in E. M. FORSTER: THE CRITICAL HERITAGE, ed by Philip Gardner (Lond & Boston: Routledge & Kegan Paul, 1973), pp. 106–7.

A Room with a View is a clever and entertaining novel. The characters are clear and salient, as in Sargent portraits. The story is interesting and real, though the character of Mr. Beebe is baffling in its development. EMF is an important novelist.

42 "Limitations," MORNING LEADER (Lond), 30 Oct 1908, p. 3; rptd in E. M. FORSTER: THE CRITICAL HERITAGE, ed by Philip Gardner (Lond & Boston: Routledge & Kegan Paul, 1973), p. 106.

In *A Room with a View* EMF makes clear the limitations of the cultured middle class. EMF's characters reveal themselves with "complete naturalness and complete self-condemnation."

43 [Masterman, C. F. G.] "The Half-hidden Life," NATION (Lond), IV (28 Nov 1908), 352, 354; rptd in E. M. FORSTER: THE CRITICAL

HERITAGE, ed by Philip Gardner (Lond & Boston: Routledge & Kegan Paul, 1973), pp. 111–15.

All EMF's novels reveal individuality, distinction, and power of suggestion. All his characters are content with their "room," but they also have some element in them which wishes for a "view." The two main places in *A Room with a View*, Italy and Surrey, are outposts of man's civilization and places of danger. In Florence the life of passion erupts in the scene of violence in the square and the threatening power of death; also primitive nature is a force in Italy. In Surrey the primitive gods survive beneath the surface of the ordinary world and engender a hidden life that EMF seeks to evoke. In their struggle to attain a valid life Lucy Honeychurch and George Emerson have the advantage of there being weak spots in the conventions which enfold them. Mr. Emerson's revolt is in large part superficial, but he does instruct his son in the worth of instinct; and Lucy has a passion for music and a receptivity to spiritual restlessness. The fusion of a satiric scrutiny of convention with the hidden life of nature and of the spirit forms a novel humorous and arresting and gives it "compelling strength and emotion." [Thoughtful comment.]

44 "New Novels," ATHENAEUM, No. 4234 (19 Dec 1908), 784; rptd in E. M. FORSTER: THE CRITICAL HERITAGE, ed by Philip Gardner (Lond & Boston: Routledge & Kegan Paul, 1973), p. 116.
A Room with a View has characters that are too commonplace and flat for sustained enjoyment. The dialogue is amateurish, and EMF's satire against convention is not always consistent.

45 "Novel Notes," EVENING STANDARD AND ST. JAMES'S GAZETTE (Lond), 30 Dec 1908, p. 5; rptd in E. M. FORSTER: THE CRITICAL HERITAGE, ed by Philip Gardner (Lond & Boston: Routledge & Kegan Paul, 1973), p. 117.
A Room with a View is less arresting than *The Longest Journey* but confirms EMF's stature as a writer. It is full of "wonderful impressions and radiant sayings." Its point of view is new in the sense of EMF's seeing experience in a new way. The character of George, the scene in the Italian square, and the bathing scene in Surrey are "probably faultless in psychology" and are most delicately rendered.

46 "Novels," OUTLOOK (Lond), XXII (26 Dec 1908), 906; rptd in E. M. FORSTER: THE CRITICAL HERITAGE, ed by Philip Gardner (Lond & Boston: Routledge & Kegan Paul, 1973), p. 116.
A Room with a View is an irresponsible work about people who never act or talk sanely. EMF overindulges his gift for "quaint dialogue." He needs more common sense in his approach to life. His experience of modern life seems "exceptionally curious," or else his focus is wrong.

47 O'Brien, Desmond B. "Letters on Books," TRUTH (Lond), LXIV (9 Dec 1908), 1403–4.

A Room with a View is a charming novel in its presentation of a woman who does not understand herself. The characters are well drawn and the scenes natural and interesting.

48 "Recent Fiction," EAST ANGLIAN TIMES (Ipswich), 26 Oct 1908, p. 5.

Characterization, plot, satirical humor, and keenness of wit make the exposé of bourgeois banality in Room with a View worthy of the reputation which EMF has already established.

49 "A Room with a View: Conversational Banalities Satirized," WESTERN MAIL (Cardiff), 21 Nov 1908, p. 7.

EMF has written a clever book but not one that will satisfy public taste, despite its humor, "quaint dialogue," and its satire upon "conversational banalities."

50 Scott-James, R. A. "A Book of the Day: A Novel of Character," DAILY NEWS (Lond), 20 Oct 1908, p. 4; rptd in E. M. FORSTER: THE CRITICAL HERITAGE, ed by Philip Gardner (Lond & Boston: Routledge & Kegan Paul, 1973), pp. 101–4.

What is wrong with A Room with a View (too many articulated views, overplayed subtlety) disappears before its brilliance. It changes from a "brilliantly dull" novel to a "humanly absorbing" one. The sequences at Windy Corner in Surrey reveal a more searching irony and a more genuine effect of passion than do the early sequences. The book becomes more genuine as EMF celebrates the force of the primitive and forgets "his horrible artificialities." [Interesting review.]

51 [Woolf, Virginia.] "A Room with a View," TIMES LITERARY SUPPLEMENT (Lond), 22 Oct 1908, p. 362; rptd in Virginia Woolf, CONTEMPORARY WRITERS, ed by Jean Guiguet (Lond: Hogarth P, 1965; NY: Harcourt, Brace & World, 1966), pp. 49–50 (NY); and in E. M. FORSTER: THE CRITICAL HERITAGE, ed by Philip Gardner (Lond & Boston: Routledge & Kegan Paul, 1973), pp. 104–5.

A Room with a View has "that odd sense of freedom which books give us when they seem to represent the world as we see it." EMF makes us partisans for his characters, but if we are honest we must recognize that the view we finally get is smaller than we had anticipated. Some belittlement cramps the souls of the characters. Lucy Honeychurch's conversion is trifling, and the views of the Emersons seem less striking than we had thought they would be. But the book has cleverness, much fun, occasional beauty, originality, and observation. [Important early appreciation.]

52 "A Young Woman in a Muddle," OBSERVER (Lond), 8 Nov 1908, p. 4; rptd in E. M. FORSTER: THE CRITICAL HERITAGE, ed by Philip Gardner (Lond & Boston: Routledge & Kegan Paul, 1973), p. 109.

A Room with a View might have been called "A Young Woman in a Muddle." As an average young woman, Lucy Honeychurch learns slowly to find what she wants from life. *Room* is full of humor and "delightful, commonplace people." EMF's "gift for sighting the comedy of ordinary social intercourse amounts to genius."

1909

---

53 "Novels," SPECTATOR (Lond), CII (2 Jan 1909), 23–24; rptd in E. M. FORSTER: THE CRITICAL HERITAGE, ed by Philip Gardner (Lond & Boston: Routledge & Kegan Paul, 1973), pp. 118–20.

A Room with a View is superior to *Where Angels Fear to Tread* and *The Longest Journey*. EMF stands apart in excellence from most contemporary novelists. *Room* reveals a greater interest in the characters than does *Journey*. The humor is more genial and kind than in the earlier work. While he keeps his freshness and unconventionality of approach, he has come "to regard the human comedy with greater respect and sanity." Lucy Honeychurch habitually misinterprets her genuine instincts. EMF engages sympathy for Lucy in her emancipation from convention, but he also does justice to those who thwart her in her progress: Charlotte Bartlett and Cecil Vyse. Mr. Beebe's inhumanity at the close of the novel is inadequately motivated. The writing is epigrammatic and witty. There are no remarkable or heroic characters in *Room*, but EMF is able to make "stupid people interesting and tiresome people amusing." [Perceptive review.]

1910

---

54 "Connect!" MORNING POST (Lond), 24 Nov 1910, p. 3; rptd in part in E. M. FORSTER: THE CRITICAL HERITAGE, ed by Philip Gardner (Lond & Boston: Routledge & Kegan Paul, 1973), pp. 149–50.

In *Howards End* "connect" not only means the merging of sensual instincts and ascetic revulsions of the individual, but also implies that philanthropy cannot become a system nor can business be divorced from morals. EMF would insist that "the harmony so lacking in our modern life is to be found in it somehow or other." The design is not altogether achieved, but *Howards End* is impressive. EMF is moving towards a comprehensive view that he has not yet achieved despite his "highly sensitized imagination and real intellectual ability." Thus some crucial incidents—Helen Schlegel's affair with Leonard Bast and Leonard's death—are unreal. Later EMF may more truly connect "objective" and "subjective." The characters are alive, the conversation is adroit, the style is subtle, the descriptions are vivid, and the contrasts in point of view are dramatic. The sequences featuring the Basts are "Hogarthian" in their satiric thrust. [Excellent review.]

55 "Current Literature," DAILY TELEGRAPH (Lond), 2 Nov 1910, p. 14; rptd in E. M. FORSTER: THE CRITICAL HERITAGE, ed by Philip Gardner (Lond & Boston: Routledge & Kegan Paul, 1973), pp. 130–31.

EMF is one of the great novelists. As exemplified in *Howards End* his stories are life, and his characters are real; he has the intelligence that probes the actions of his characters and the spirit that connects. The intellectual atmosphere of the Schlegel household is well suggested. Howards End house furnishes a dominating leitmotif; the variations are subtle and excellent. Leonard Bast reveals EMF's genius, but, also, he does not quite ring true. All blemishes aside, *Howards End* reveals art and power.

56 "Fiction," SCOTSMAN (Edinburgh), 31 Oct 1910, p. 2.

EMF is distinctive in his psychic insight into character and in his appreciation of the *genius loci* (which is used as a touchstone for evaluating character). In *Howards End* the interest lies not only in the clash of the Schlegels and the Wilcoxes but in the incidents that arise from the impressionableness of the Schlegels. His skill at differentiating shades of thought and feeling is remarkable.

57 "Fiction," TIMES LITERARY SUPPLEMENT (Lond), 21 Oct 1910, p. 412; rptd in E. M. FORSTER: THE CRITICAL HERITAGE, ed by Philip Gardner (Lond & Boston: Routledge & Kegan Paul, 1973), pp. 125–26.

EMF's talent has found full and ripe expression in *Howards End*. More than its predecessors this is a novel at unity with itself. EMF's power of generalization holds the complex plot together. He works from the center outwards; the graces and humors of the novel's surface have a firm structure beneath. His principal generalization is that there are two types of people: those who feel the primacy of personal relationships and those who do not. EMF's character portrayal reveals both shrewdness and clarity. In *Howards End* there is "the odd charming vein of poetry" revealing itself at unpredictable times. The poetic suggestiveness belongs to a subtle realism rather than to romance. The novel reveals deftness of manner and "a sensitive reflection of life." [Extensive plot summary.]

58 "A Fine Novel," DAILY GRAPHIC (Lond), 19 Nov 1910, p. 4; rptd in E. M. FORSTER: THE CRITICAL HERITAGE, ed by Philip Gardner (Lond & Boston: Routledge & Kegan Paul, 1973), p. 146.

In spite of his unevenness EMF reveals the highest kind of talent in *Howards End.* There is some crudity or formlessness in the incidents that bring about or accompany the finale, but the book has great "descriptive and reflective power."

59 [Garnett, Edward]. "Villadom," NATION (Lond), VIII (12 Nov 1910), 282, 284; rptd in E. M. FORSTER: THE CRITICAL HERITAGE, ed by Philip Gardner (Lond & Boston: Routledge & Kegan Paul, 1973), pp. 139–42.

Howards End is noteworthy for its farsighted criticism of middle-class ideas; it says those things which the intelligent minority feel but seldom arrive at formulating. Howards End house provides the spiritual background against whose unobtrusive charm and settled standards the aggressive Wilcoxes are measured. In depicting the destinies of the two families EMF reveals "his rare gift of philosophic criticism." His characters are real as people but also exist as contemporary signposts: "the ideas behind them, the code of manners and morals, and the web of forces, material and mental, that are woven before our eyes in the life of London" are all-important. EMF reveals much ingenuity in working out his design but sacrifices artistic truth to the requirements of his philosophical moral. His purposes strain character and incident and thereby rob the work of artistic inevitability. The value of the novel consists in its acute analysis of British bourgeois values in the Wilcoxes and their "villadom." [Important early article.]

60 *"Howards End,"* EAST ANGLIAN DAILY TIMES (Ipswich), 29 Oct 1910, p. 6.

Howards End reveals the same imaginative abundance and skill in plot invention as the early novels. The chief characters register as individuals, but their actions are uninteresting. The book is most notable for its reflective passages.

61 *"Howards End:* A Story of Remarkably Queer People," WESTERN MAIL (Cardiff), 10 Dec 1910, p. 9; rptd in E. M. FORSTER: THE CRITICAL HERITAGE, ed by Philip Gardner (Lond & Boston: Routledge & Kegan Paul, 1973), pp. 153–54.

All the characters in *Howards End*—Schlegels, Wilcoxes, Basts—are strange and atypical, except for Charles Wilcox and his wife, who "shine like a green oasis in this wilderness of eccentrics." All the characters become a bit more normal by the conclusion of the novel.

62 M[arshall], [Archibald]. "The Season's Great Novel," DAILY MAIL (Lond), 17 Nov 1910, p. 6; rptd in E. M. FORSTER: THE CRITICAL HERITAGE, ed by Philip Gardner (Lond & Boston: Routledge & Kegan Paul, 1973), pp. 143–45.

Howards End is a riper work than *A Room with a View* and establishes EMF as a foremost contemporary novelist. The house [Howards End] plays an important part throughout. The confrontation between Margaret Schlegel and her husband Henry Wilcox concerning the pregnant but unmarried Helen Schlegel is realized masterfully. The happiness imputed for those at Howards End at the close of the novel is not completely convincing. The merits of the book outshine its faults: its characters live; they are seen in memorable action; they are revealed through vivid incident; and EMF has much inventiveness as a novelist. [Important review.]

63 M[onkhouse], A. N. "A Novel of Quality," MANCHESTER GUARDIAN, 26 Oct 1910, p. 5; rptd in E. M. FORSTER: THE CRITICAL HERITAGE, ed by Philip Gardner (Lond & Boston: Routledge & Kegan Paul, 1973), pp. 123–24.

Howards End is written with brilliant perception. Henry Wilcox is not "in the front of civilization," but at its base. The marriage between him and Margaret Schlegel is difficult for readers to take: though life is a compromise, the spirit needs more than mere "solidities" of the Wilcox sort. The Schlegel sisters are vivid and true. There is "an immense liberality" and notable sympathy in the book, a humanity in the presentation even of those with whom we find it difficult to sympathize. [Perceptive review.]

64 "New Novels," ATHENAEUM, No. 4336 (3 Dec 1910), 696; rptd in E. M. FORSTER: THE CRITICAL HERITAGE, ed by Philip Gardner (Lond & Boston: Routledge & Kegan Paul, 1973), p. 151.

EMF is one of the handful of notable writers. There are three major defects in *Howards End:* its protagonists are points of view rather than characters; Margaret's marriage and Helen's seduction are unconvincing; and the moral direction is wrong, as the finer feelings ought not to be sacrificed for enlarged sympathies. The great thing in the novel is the personal relationship between the Schlegel sisters. The brilliant and delicate strokes in the novel reveal subtle states of mind and elusive traits of character.

65 "New Novels," MANCHESTER COURIER, 2 Nov 1910, p. 9.

Howards End is distinctive for its "independent style." The Schlegels are erratic and conventional, blending unsatisfyingly a "glossy culture and plebeian predilection." Nor do the Wilcoxes appeal, because EMF's touch is uncertain. The novel is unsuccessful as a satire.

66 "New Novels," OBSERVER (Lond), 6 Nov 1910, p. 8; rptd in E.
   M. FORSTER: THE CRITICAL HERITAGE, ed by Philip Gardner (Lond
   & Boston: Routledge & Kegan Paul, 1973), pp. 134–35.
EMF is a clever writer. If in *Howards End* he is acquiring greater range and
subtlety, it is at the expense of the humor revealed in his earlier books. A
similarity exists between his approach to society and John Galsworthy's in
A MAN OF PROPERTY. Margaret Schlegel's affection bridges the gap between the modes of life represented by the Wilcoxes and the Schlegels. The
confrontation at Howards End between Margaret and Henry Wilcox is
masterful, but Helen's fall is "disagreeable." EMF's observation and sense
of character are remarkable; his art is "undeniable."

67 "New Novels," WESTMINSTER GAZETTE, 19 Nov 1910, p. 16;
   rptd in E. M. FORSTER: THE CRITICAL HERITAGE, ed by Philip Gardner (Lond & Boston: Routledge & Kegan Paul, 1973), pp. 147–48.
Howards End is a remarkable book but not quite satisfactory as a novel.
EMF is good at depicting personal relations, especially in the Schlegel
sisters, and at presenting the symbols through which their minds operate.
He has envisioned the Schlegels vividly, especially Margaret; he gets into
her innermost self. He also imagines well the more conventional types like
the Wilcoxes. He has little sense of form, of "constructive harmony" in this
work. He is something of a seer and mystic. He suggests much concerning
Howards End and Miss Avery but fails to convey Mrs. Wilcox's imputed
extraordinary nature. [Perceptive review.]

68 "Novels," SATURDAY REVIEW, CX (26 Nov 1910), 688.
Where Angels Fear to Tread announced a new writer with gifts of characterization; *The Longest Journey* revealed "Meredithian powers of suggestion
and psychology"; *A Room with a View* revealed a fine gift for high comedy.
In all of EMF's narratives (including the stories) there is "a delicate sensibility to the beauty and divinity in things animate and inanimate." *Howards
End* is too intricate to be epitomized; its characters are complex in their
gentleness; the great theme is "personal relations." EMF has the ability to
convey the living essence of places and things and has a true comic sense
that makes use of colloquial speech to convey nuances of personality in his
speakers. *Howards End* is too large a work to be immediately apprehended.
[Important review.]

69 "Novels," SPECTATOR (Lond), CV (5 Nov 1910), 757; rptd in E.
   M. FORSTER: THE CRITICAL HERITAGE, ed by Philip Gardner (Lond
   & Boston: Routledge & Kegan Paul, 1973), pp. 132–34.
In EMF's work, surprise is essential to his method; his novels are unpredict-
able. *Howards End* is a set of variations upon the misfortunes of those who
love. Helen's lapse with Leonard Bast and Leonard's death are not probable.
EMF's handling of incident is often arbitrary, the progress of his narrative

disjointed. He lacks self-effacement and reveals himself too frequently. But his merits balance his defects: "vivid characterisation, a happy command of dialogue, and a freakish humour." He conveys memorably the clash of modern culture and modern materialism. [Extended plot analysis.]

70 "Novels of the Week," STANDARD (Lond), 28 Oct 1910, p. 5; rptd in E. M. FORSTER: THE CRITICAL HERITAGE, ed by Philip Gardner (Lond & Boston: Routledge & Kegan Paul, 1973), pp. 128–30.
Howards End reveals the all-pervading influence of place. Everyone is tested by Howards End house, but the house itself is established by the power of suggestion. The characters are incisive, some of the scenes are unforgettable, and the humor is engaging.

71 P. and Q. "New Novels," WORLD (Lond), LXXIII (20 Dec 1910), 943; rptd in E. M. FORSTER: THE CRITICAL HERITAGE, ed by Philip Gardner (Lond & Boston: Routledge & Kegan Paul, 1973), pp. 154–55.
Howards End is less great than Arnold Bennett's CLAYHANGER, but EMF has made great strides since *A Room with a View.* EMF reveals ingenuity in plot and truth in character portrayal, but there are too many surprises, as in the Helen Schlegel–Leonard Bast sexual affair. He has a sense of humor alive to the incongruities in things usually accepted, a power of description, and a wide sympathy. But his views of the Wilcoxes are prejudiced, as are those of Wells, Galsworthy, and Bennett on such people.

72 "The Part and the Whole," MORNING LEADER (Lond), 28 Oct 1910, p. 3; rptd in E. M. FORSTER: THE CRITICAL HERITAGE, ed by Philip Gardner (Lond & Boston: Routledge & Kegan Paul, 1973), pp. 127–28.
EMF's characters in *Howards End* are representative as well as individual, but the events are not always representative, as at the end where artifice takes over. EMF does not treat strong passions powerfully, but he is inimitable in depicting class distinctions, manners, and conventions. He is an author of distinction and ability.

73 "Recent Fiction," YORKSHIRE POST (Leeds), 21 Dec 1910, p. 5.
In *Howards End* EMF stresses the need for trusting "differences" in people. The Schlegel sisters are remarkable characters. The novel is full of insight, strong characterization, humor, and arresting quality.

74 Scott-James, R. A. "A Book of the Day: The Year's Best Novel," DAILY NEWS (Lond), 7 Nov 1910, p. 4; rptd in E. M. FORSTER: THE CRITICAL HERITAGE, ed by Philip Gardner (Lond & Boston: Routledge & Kegan Paul, 1973), pp. 135–39.

With *Howards End* EMF has written a connected novel in which real characters have a more general meaning. Howards End house is always a presence, "a symbol of everything in England, old and new, changeless, yet amid flux." For Mrs. Wilcox Howards End was a home; for her family it is only a house. Helen Schlegel and Charles Wilcox are polar characters, all passion and all prose respectively. *Howards End* is a philosophical novel but rooted thoroughly in the realities of life.

75 "Some Novels of the Season," Outlook (Lond), XXVI (5 Nov 1910), 663.

Howards End is a symbolic novel in the succession of Henry James and Meredith. The acts of the characters are less important than their morals and states of mind; they approach the allegorical. But EMF individualizes his characters; their human aspect saves the novel from pedantry. It is good that a Germany of intellect and culture rather than a militant and materialistic Germany is presented through the Schlegels.

76 "The Week's Best Novel," Daily Mail (Lond), 29 Oct 1910, p. 8.

Howards End places EMF in the front rank of contemporary novelists. It is a finer and riper book than his others. It reveals his humor, his powers of observation, his skill at character drawing, his inventive powers, and his stylistic gifts. He has used these qualities to dramatize a weighty theme: the contrast between the Schlegels, who value personal relations, and the Wilcoxes, who live by telegrams and anger. He has much talent in the art of storytelling. His qualities are epitomized in his charting the effects of Ruth Wilcox's death. There is much wit and wisdom in the book. [Frank Swinnerton in The Georgian Scene (1934, p. 344) asserts that this notice or the one by Marshall (or perhaps both) gave EMF "a colossal boost" in both reputation and sales. Excellent review.]

77 "A Work that Should Count," Pall Mall Gazette Illustrated Literary Supplement, 28 Oct 1910, p. 8.

The opening of *Howards End* is tame and somewhat absurd, but the book becomes a searching analysis of motive. The characters are amply developed. The contrast between the Wilcoxes and Helen Schlegel is dramatic, as is also the chapter in which Margaret Schlegel fails to get Henry to connect his past trespass against Ruth Wilcox with Helen's.

1911

78 "A Book of Phantasies," DAILY MAIL (Lond), 19 May 1911, p. 10; rptd in E. M. FORSTER: THE CRITICAL HERITAGE, ed by Philip Gardner (Lond & Boston: Routledge & Kegan Paul, 1973), p. 170.
EMF's tales in *The Celestial Omnibus and Other Stories* are individual in confronting sympathetic (and unsympathetic) moderns with "the old gods of the woods and the fields" to make his points about good and evil. They reveal a feeling for nature and a refreshing paganism.

79 "Current Literature," DAILY TELEGRAPH (Lond), 17 May 1911, p. 4.
EMF is sometimes vague and elusive as in "Other Kingdom." "The Story of a Panic" is poetic and delightful, full of charm and power (so is "The Curate's Friend"). "The Celestial Omnibus" pits imagination against common sense. His mode of writing is a bit private; it is to be hoped that he will escape the precious. [Review of *The Celestial Omnibus and Other Stories*.]

80 E., E. F. "*Howards End:* A Variable Discussion of Human Eccentricities," BOSTON EVENING TRANSCRIPT, 18 Jan 1911, p. 22.
Howards End is not a novel so much as "a disconnected series of impressions of humanity." It is a scrapbook that EMF has gathered, without form or coherence. He has profound ideas about human actions and the human mind but little structural sense; his book is as chaotic as life itself. He has little sense of the passage of time. His obvious purpose is to contrast the ideal with the real, the fantastic with the commonplace; and this he has done by opposing the Schlegels to the Wilcoxes. The novel does display a calm, incisive wit, and it presents objectively many kinds of eccentricity. EMF seems to apprehend life in sections rather than as a whole. He regards eccentricity as originality and as admirable—in Helen Schlegel, for instance, whose smartness is "impudence" and whose brilliance moves toward "lunacy." Howards End house is featured too little. A novel should be a comment on life and contain a story that makes comment possible: *Howards End* has much comment, little life, and a negligible story. EMF's wit is his undoing. He has talent, and if he restrains himself, he may write a first-class novel. [Interesting but quirky discussion.]

81 "Fiction," SCOTSMAN (Edinburgh), 11 May 1911, p. 2.
The interest of the stories in *The Celestial Omnibus and Other Stories* resides in their interweaving of the real world with an ideal one, with a consequent confusion of the boundaries between them. The ideal world depends on an organic, fresh, and natural use of classical mythology for its definition.

82 "Fiction," TIMES LITERARY SUPPLEMENT (Lond), 22 June 1911, p. 238; rptd in E. M. FORSTER: THE CRITICAL HERITAGE, ed by Philip Gardner (Lond & Boston: Routledge & Kegan Paul, 1973), pp. 175–76.
The stories in *The Celestial Omnibus and Other Stories* have originality and grace. They are so insubstantial as to elude criticism; there is nothing solemn or heavy about them. They contrast those who are in rapport with nature and poetry with those who are not. The style is not always "equable," but such a style may be partly intended, since EMF characteristically uses a stupid person as narrator.

83 "*Howards End* by E. M. Forster," NEW YORK TIMES, 19 Feb 1911, p. 94; rptd in E. M. FORSTER: THE CRITICAL HERITAGE, ed by Philip Gardner (Lond & Boston: Routledge & Kegan Paul, 1973), pp. 157–58.
EMF's forte is conventional comedy, for which his gifts are adequate. Unlike John Galsworthy and May Sinclair, he has neither the power nor the inclination to confront any vital human problems. [Mostly plot summary, focusing on the role of the three main families.]

84 "Like Father, Like Son," NEW YORK TIMES, 30 July 1911, p. 472; rptd in E. M. FORSTER: THE CRITICAL HERITAGE, ed by Philip Gardner (Lond & Boston: Routledge & Kegan Paul, 1973), pp. 121–22.
The pretentious philosophizing present in *Howards End* is absent from *A Room with a View*. The only leading idea is the need to reckon honestly with nature. EMF satirizes those people who stifle their natural impulses. Mr. Emerson and his son George cause havoc among the middle class at a Florentine pension and later in English suburbia because they take themselves and their feelings "with a candid and innocent seriousness." There is unusual freshness and originality in *Room*. In his use of an irony characterized by lightness of touch EMF reveals the influence of Meredith, but not in his style.

85 "Literature," INDEPENDENT, LXX (27 April 1911), 903–4.
A house is central in *Howards End*. Here two families are brought together: the Wilcoxes—hard, cold, and clear like their diamonds—and the Schlegels,

whose "opal" qualities continually shift and change. The conflict between the materialism of business (in the Wilcoxes) and "the unbalanced idealism of modern culture" (in the Schlegels) is disastrous for all. EMF reveals mastery of dialogue, character depiction, and interaction between character and circumstances.

86 "The New Books," OUTLOOK (NY), XCVIII (10 June 1911), 310.

There is a subtle suggestion in *A Room with a View*. The novel is true to life in depicting the foibles and hypocrisies of the upper middle class, and witty writing in the novel is attractive.

87 "New Fiction," SUNDAY TIMES (Lond), 4 June 1911, p. 7.

The stories in *The Celestial Omnibus and Other Stories* may err on the side of displaying too much skill and literary correctness. "The Story of a Panic" reveals much delicacy in emotion; so does "Other Kingdom," which also has a delicate satire.

88 "Our Library Table," ATHENAEUM, No. 4366 (1 July 1911), 12; rptd in E. M. FORSTER: THE CRITICAL HERITAGE, ed by Philip Gardner (Lond & Boston: Routledge & Kegan Paul, 1973), p. 177.

The stories in *The Celestial Omnibus and Other Stories* are united by "the fantastically supernatural." They are not completely successful or original in their design. EMF's methods are original, though the tales are too often whimsical. It is difficult to find a meaning in "Other Kingdom." The stories are monotonous and facetious; they have the atmosphere of a young writer's spirited "lark."

89 Peattie, Elia. "Rare Power Displayed in *Howards End*," CHICAGO DAILY TRIBUNE, 28 Jan 1911, p. 9.

The sensibility revealed in *Howards End* is so keen that the novelist must have been a woman. This kind of writer is not interested in plot so much as in character and psychology, and he (or she) transcends mere science by his art, imagination, and subtlety. A work like *Howards End* is not a finished tale but closes with a question. One of the themes dramatized in the fate of the Schlegel sisters is the missed expectation, "the frustration of brave effort." EMF is also concerned with the implied waste of feminine power. He shows, moveover, how the vulgar, the aggressive, and the active individual tends to triumph over the aspiring, mentally fine, and delicate individual; theory is at the mercy of materialism. These two kinds of individuals are often envious of each other, as EMF demonstrates in this novel. Those with aspiration are often defeated by those with efficiency, but EMF in *Howards End* tries to reconcile the two groups. The Schlegels are not really successful in their attempts to connect with people from other

segments of the middle class; they are, in a way, besmirched by "the triumphant vulgarity" of the Wilcoxes and by "the timorous vulgarity" of the
Basts. The novel also demonstrates how an act of careless selfishness has
many unforeseen consequences. EMF is an impressive moralist. [Penetrat-
ing, imaginative discussion.]

90 "Recent Fiction and the Critics," CURRENT LITERATURE (NY),
L (April 1911), 451–54, espec p. 454; rptd as "An American Sum-
ming-up," in E. M. FORSTER: THE CRITICAL HERITAGE, ed by Philip
Gardner (Lond & Boston: Routledge & Kegan Paul, 1973), pp.
159–60.
[Survey for recent criticism of *Howards End*. The author of this article is
puzzled and bored by the acclaim given *Howards End*.]

91 "Reviews," CAMBRIDGE REVIEW, XXXIII (19 Oct 1911), 40;
rptd in E. M. FORSTER: THE CRITICAL HERITAGE, ed by Philip Gardner (Lond & Boston: Routledge & Kegan Paul, 1973), p. 178.
The best short stories of today are in EMF's *The Celestial Omnibus and
Other Stories*. "The Story of a Panic" is superior to *Where Angels Fear to
Tread*, "The Celestial Omnibus" to *The Longest Journey*. "Other Kingdom" and "Panic" almost reach the poetry of the "Florentine meadow"
scene in *A Room with a View*.

92 Scott, Dixon. "The Pipes of Puck," MANCHESTER GUARDIAN, 24
May 1911, p. 5; rptd in E. M. FORSTER: THE CRITICAL HERITAGE, ed
by Philip Gardner (Lond & Boston: Routledge & Kegan Paul,
1973), pp. 171–73.
The accolade extended to EMF for his stories has been excessive. "The
Story of a Panic" and "The Curate's Friend" are too pointed in their
classical references. The tales are incompletely fantastic, charming instead
of terror-inspiring. We need another symbol for the primitive, since Pan has
become so domesticated. In "The Celestial Omnibus" Puck rather than Pan
dominates, and the story is all the better for it, full of perfume and caprice.
The stories in *The Celestial Omnibus and Other Stories* bewitch us in spite
of ourselves, as EMF prepares his own concoction of myth, modernity, and
original sin. No other writer has his gift for capturing the otherworldly, and
we should not urge him to drop this bent (he seems to have done so to some
degree, as *Howards End* focuses on the real world). [Fresh discussion.]

93 "Stories of the Supernatural," NATION (Lond), IX (10 June
1911), 408, 410; rptd in E. M. FORSTER: THE CRITICAL HERITAGE, ed
by Philip Gardner (Lond & Boston: Routledge & Kegan Paul,
1973), pp. 174–75.
In *The Celestial Omnibus and Other Stories* EMF divides villadom against

itself: its sensitive and superior individuals struggle with their Philistine brethren. In "The Story of a Panic" EMF reveals how cultivated people regard incredible events as beautiful to read about in the classics but are hostile to them when these events are seen to apply, spiritually, to themselves. In "The Road from Colonus" modern insincerity is burlesqued. As in "Other Kingdom" things of the spirit are in league with the supernatural powers, and at war with prosaic, inorganic, modern-day existence. An uncanny quality in the tales makes them successful, the insight that the unexpected prevails in the everyday life of men: the appeal is constantly from man-made law to the free workings of nature. [Good discussion.]

94 Tonson, Jacob [pseud of Arnold Bennett]. "Books and Persons in London and Paris," NEW AGE, nsVIII (12 Jan 1911), 257; rptd in "Books of the Year," BOOKS AND PERSONS (NY: Doran; Lond: Chatto & Windus, 1917), pp. 292–93; and in E. M. FORSTER: THE CRITICAL HERITAGE, ed by Philip Gardner (Lond & Boston: Routledge & Kegan Paul, 1973), p. 156.

Howards End has been discussed by the elite as no other novel has for many years, though it is not EMF's best book. It is popular with the elite in spite (or because) of its criticism of them. EMF can become the most fashionable novelist in England if he turns out one book a year according to formula. But if he writes solely to please himself, he may produce some first-class literature. [EMF did choose to please himself, and instead of turning out a novel each year, he published no novel between 1910 and 1924. *A Passage to India* is "first-class!"]

1912

[No entries for this year.]

1913

[No entries for this year.]

1914

[No entries for this year.]

1915

[No entries for this year.]

1916

[No entries for this year.]

1917

95 Walpole, Hugh. JOSEPH CONRAD (Lond: Nisbet & Co, 1917), pp. 116–17.
Conrad's romantic-realism was formative on younger novelists at the time, including EMF. EMF is "a romantic-realist of most curious originality" whose novels *The Longest Journey* and *Howards End* may provide a historian of English literature with dates as important as 1895, the date of Conrad's ALMAYER'S FOLLY.

1918

96 George, W. L. "Who Is the Man?" A NOVELIST ON NOVELS (Lond: Collins, 1918), pp. 62–89, espec 65, 86–87; rptd (Port Washington, N.Y.: Kennikat P, 1970); and as LITERARY CHAPTERS (Bost: Little, Brown, 1918), pp. 44–73; espec 47, 70–71.
Who will take the positions now occupied by Bennett, Conrad, Galsworthy, Hardy, and Wells as premier novelists? There are seven main candidates: J. D. Beresford, Gilbert Cannan, EMF, D. H. Lawrence, Compton Mackenzie, Oliver Onions, and Frank Swinnerton. [This grouping is also discussed

by Frank Swinnerton, SWINNERTON: AN AUTOBIOGRAPHY (1936) and by Alec Waugh, "E. M. Forster's World" (1972).] EMF might even be "the" young man, although he has not published since 1910. An autobiographical element is apparent in *A Room with a View* and *The Longest Journey; Howards End* was both popular and of high merit. In the last there is a fusion of the particular and the general, the local and the cosmic; EMF has caught the qualities of the cultured, the untaught, and the rulers. His own self colors all he writes and gives it an individual stamp. He urges tolerance and a synthesis of mind and body; in a word, "mystic athleticism." EMF is a man of both perceptions and ideas.

97 Williams, Harold. MODERN ENGLISH WRITERS, BEING A STUDY OF IMAGINATIVE LITERATURE, 1890–1914 (Lond: Sidgwick & Jackson, 1918; NY: Knopf, 1919), pp. 384–85; 3rd rvd ed, 1925 [materials on EMF unchanged].

The stories in *The Celestial Omnibus* may be nearer to EMF's thought and art than the novels; the stories reveal poetic imagination, thought, and satiric bent. In the novels the satire is more pronounced, revealing Meredith's influence. In *Where Angels Fear to Tread* the characters live; EMF is successful in epigram, and he thinks for himself; but the comedy is farcical and approaches the ridiculous. In *The Longest Journey*, there is an advance in concentration, a sustained effect, and notable characters who pursue truth; with the stories, this novel comprises the best of EMF's writing. *A Room with a View* is more commonplace. *Howards End* is difficult and not wholly consistent. It reveals originality of insight and independence of thought but the development of the characters is unconvincing—their emotions are too strong for the situation. [Interesting early account.]

1919

[No entries for this year.]

1920

98 Boynton, H. W. "Good Novels of Several Kinds," BOOKMAN (NY), LI (May 1920), 339–45, espec 342.

Where Angels Fear to Tread reveals "an unfamiliar touch or flavor"; it is a comedy with "tragic shadows." Gino Carella is "irresistible" as the embodiment of Italian character and tradition, and Philip Herriton is "irrefutable" as the Briton. [Notice of 1st American ed of *Angels.*]

99 "Briefer Mention," DIAL, LXVIII (May 1920), 665.
Meredith would call *Where Angels Fear to Tread* a comedy; the gallery would call it tragedy. The contrast between "childlike sinfulness and the sunshine of medieval towns" is refreshing after the unimaginativeness of the English family. [Notice of 1st American ed of *Angels.*]

100 M[ansfield], K[atherine]. "Throw Them Overboard!" ATHENAEUM, No. 4711 (13 Aug 1920), 209–10; rptd in NOVELS AND NOVELISTS, ed by John Middleton Murry (NY: Knopf; Lond: Constable, 1930), pp. 246–48; and in E. M. FORSTER: THE CRITICAL HERITAGE, ed by Philip Gardner (Lond & Boston: Routledge & Kegan Paul, 1973), pp. 184–86.
EMF compels our curiosity and admiration as few writers do. His novels have delicate atmosphere and precision of expression, and his appreciation of the uniqueness of his characters gives him his special humor, "half whimsical, half sympathetic." In *Howards End* he conveys the impression that vision reigns within, but the impression, too, that he has not used his imaginative powers fully. In his style there is a leisurely quality that charms, but might not such a leisurely approach encourage him to drift? He fails to commit himself wholly and seems altogether too detached. His sensitiveness and sense of humor perhaps make him a spectator in his own country. The officious aunt and the garrulous chaplain (in "The Story of the Siren") are too familiar props in his work and suggest a too ready resort to contrivance. Their background presence dissipates, in part, the enchantment to be found in this story. [Interesting, subtle remarks.]

101 "Some Tabloid Reviews," BOOKMAN (NY), LII (Oct 1920), 175.
Where Angels Fear to Tread is notable for its fusion of laughter and tears and for EMF's ability to both scoff at life and enjoy it. One word describes the book: "human." [Review of 1st American ed of *Angels.*]

102 "Tears and Laughter," NEW YORK TIMES BOOK REVIEW, 11 April 1920, p. 168.
In *Where Angels Fear to Tread* there is a skillful blending of comedy and tragedy. The married life of Lilia Herriton and Gino Carella is strikingly portrayed. EMF knows provincial Italy and the Italian character. The rendition of the performance of LUCIA DI LAMMERMOOR is diverting. [Detailed summary of plot. Review of 1st American ed of *Angels.*]

103 West, Rebecca. "Notes on Novels," NEW STATESMAN, XV (28 Aug 1920), 576; rptd in E. M. FORSTER: THE CRITICAL HERITAGE, ed by Philip Gardner (Lond & Boston: Routledge & Kegan Paul, 1973), pp. 186–89.

There is softness and strength, humanity and inhumanity, twilight beauty and desolation in EMF's work. He is aware of the state of man's mind in the present and in antiquity (and its manifestations in beauty), but about his work there is also a "grey magic of inhumanity." The opening sequence of the narrator's notebook falling through the water is arresting. EMF's story is a real myth, "the adequate symbol of a spiritual adventure." EMF reveals a fascination with the cruelty, primitive and uncivilized, of his characters. EMF as a classicist distrusts the emotions we have imported into our relationships; he writes books, therefore, that are "cold variations of human relationships" that play down emotional warmth, and he tries to bring back into his books an authentic paganism. Since paganism is a dead religion and cannot be recreated, EMF's attempt gives his work a ghostly quality that is "faintly terrifying." [Incisive and imaginative criticism. Review of *The Story of the Siren* and narratives by other writers.]

104 *"Where Angels Fear to Tread,"* SPRINGFIELD SUNDAY REPUBLI- CAN, 21 March 1920, p. 11A; rptd in E. M. FORSTER: THE CRITICAL HERITAGE, ed by Philip Gardner (Lond & Boston: Routledge & Kegan Paul, 1973), pp. 59–60.

The "subtle comprehension, the subdued irony, the charm of temperament, and the delicacy of style" found in *Where Angels Fear to Tread*, as in EMF's other books, are praiseworthy. In *Angels* as in *Howards End* there is a merging of comedy and tragedy. The plot is built by contrasts but is not simplistic, since EMF's irony plays over all the characters. "The brightness, the suppleness, the alacrity of the style" makes for a mastery in the compo- nent parts, though construction may be faulty. [Review of 1st American ed of *Angels.*]

1921

---

105 B., L. "Shorter Notices," FREEMAN (NY), III (13 July 1921), 431.

A lucid and logical mind is in control in *Howards End.* EMF touches his narrative with irony and illuminates it with his grasp of motive and char- acter. [Notice of American reissue of *Howards End.*]

106 "Briefer Mention," DIAL, LXXI (Oct 1921), 483; rptd in E. M. FORSTER: THE CRITICAL HERITAGE, ed by Philip Gardner (Lond & Boston: Routledge & Kegan Paul, 1973), p. 165.

In *Howards End* EMF has the true novelist's sensitivity to casual encounters. His people are real, but his symbolism is blurred. [Notice of American reissue of *Howards End.*]

107 Chevalley, Abel. LE ROMAN ANGLAIS DE NOTRE TEMPS (The Modern English Novel) (Lond: Milford, 1921), pp. 128, 202; rptd as THE MODERN ENGLISH NOVEL, trans by Ben Ray Redman (NY: Knopf, 1925), p. 132.

The Longest Journey and *Howards End* have confirmed EMF's reputation. The first part of *Howards End* is full of intellectual and sentimental pith, having a quality of "learned freshness." The second half verges on melodrama and does not fulfill the formal promise of the first part. [In French.]

108 H., R. "*Howards End,*" NEW REPUBLIC, XXVI (20 April 1921), 246; rptd in E. M. FORSTER: THE CRITICAL HERITAGE, ed by Philip Gardner (Lond & Boston: Routledge & Kegan Paul, 1973), pp. 163–64.

Howards End reveals a remarkable sense of the elusive and the intangible, which EMF connects, however, with the other aspects of human life. The need for connection is perennial, but it is essayed in *Howards End* with ironic insight and originality. EMF expertly realizes the dramatic values in his subject. [Review of American reissue of *Howards End.*]

109 Mais, S. P. B. "E. M. Forster," WHY WE SHOULD READ (NY: Dodd, Mead; Lond: Grant Richards, 1921), pp. 152–56.

EMF is more interested in classical mythology than in his readers; he is satiric when he treats the modern. We read *Howards End* for its unexpectedness, its elliptical talk (which characterizes his people), its manifestation of the Comic Spirit, the skill with which EMF exposes the soul of Leonard Bast, and the merciless sketch of Henry Wilcox. Characters in his books, however, go to prison or die too arbitrarily. Helen Schlegel's gift of herself to Leonard Bast "is absolutely true to life." EMF has the two main requisites of a modern writer—the ability to reveal life as it is and an articulated philosophy.

110 Manly, John Matthews, and Edith Rickert. CONTEMPORARY BRITISH LITERATURE: BIBLIOGRAPHIES AND STUDY OUTLINES (NY: Harcourt, Brace, 1921), pp. 61–62.

[Short biographical account and bibliography.]

111 "Recent Books in Brief Review," BOOKMAN (NY), LIV (Oct 1921), 172–73.

EMF's diction in *Howards End* has charm, and the book reveals inimitable humor and generous humanity. To contrast with many other modern books, in this one there are "graciousness, untypified human beings, and faith in personality whether of houses or people." Howards End house dominates the book and finally assimilates into itself both the idealists and the materialists. [Review of American reissue of *Howards End.*]

1922

112 "Books of the Day—Birthright: *The Longest Journey*," Boston Evening Transcript, Part III, 19 April 1922, p. 5; rptd in E. M. Forster: The Critical Heritage, ed by Philip Gardner (Lond & Boston: Routledge & Kegan Paul, 1973), p. 98.

The theme of *The Longest Journey* is the need to return to "the Greek ideal of beauty as a panacea for the ills of modern life." This novel is one of "dreary pessimism" and has a "harsh and obscure style." [Review of 1st American ed of *Journey.*]

113 Dutton, George B. "*Howards End* Shows Up Disjointed Living," Springfield Sunday Republican, 1 Jan 1922, p. 11A; rptd in E. M. Forster: The Critical Heritage, ed by Philip Gardner (Lond & Boston: Routledge & Kegan Paul, 1973), pp. 165–67.

EMF in *Howards End* plays variations upon the theme of "only connect"; the novel represents an "adventure among generalizations." The generalizations are not economic or sociological but philosophical, involving "ultimate questions about personality, its development, and its value"; and these generalizations are embodied in substantial men and women. The novel is not perfect; it is a bit didactic and the characters are not always credible, but it has space, amplitude, and sanity. [Excellent review of 2nd American ed of *Howards End.*]

114 "Medallions IV.—Mr. E. M. Forster: The Spirit of Beethoven," Times (Lond), 17 June 1922, p. 14.

EMF believes that man has a soul; he has some of the artistic vision most masterfully expressed in Beethoven's music. EMF has written (in *Howards End*) the only literarily endurable description of Beethoven's Fifth Symphony. EMF's awareness of man's spiritual dimension may account for his having stopped writing, for it takes much time to trace the implications of this kind of awareness. EMF's stories are fumbling and their solutions to problems are too easily won. The spiritual life makes great demands on the artist who would express it, whether he be Beethoven, Dostoevski or, in a more minor category, EMF. [Important appreciation at its date.]

115 "A Tragic Hero," SPRINGFIELD SUNDAY REPUBLICAN, 29 Oct 1922, p. 7A; rptd in E. M. FORSTER: THE CRITICAL HERITAGE, ed by Philip Gardner (Lond & Boston: Routledge & Kegan Paul, 1973), pp. 99–100.

There is a similarity in theme and treatment in *The Longest Journey* and in Willa Cather's ONE OF OURS, "the same tragedy of sensibility, imaginativeness and a delicate sense of honor thwarted by the world." *Journey* subtly contrasts "the spiritual heritage of man" (and its background in nature) with Rickie Elliot's small realization of it. EMF shows the possibilities for the modern novel, especially in his combination of irony and poetry. The novel has charm and attains beauty, though in its elucidation of spiritual values it is somewhat attenuated. [Excellent review of 1st American ed of *Journey*.]

1923

116 "Books in Brief," NATION (NY), CXVII (5 Sept 1923), 247.

In *The Celestial Omnibus* EMF is interested in literature for "its quickening values"; his work has gaiety and philosophical charm. The stories in the book are not in a conventional mode but are fantasies which are, however, still concerned with truth.

117 "Celestial Omnibus," NEW YORK TIMES BOOK REVIEW, 5 Aug 1923, p. 17.

In the six stories of *The Celestial Omnibus* there is a sure and delicate touch, a striking union of fantasy with realism. A clean and wholesome paganism characterizes the stories, also a keen but gentle humor ("Pan laughing at mortals for their stupidity") deriving from the contrast between stolid respectable people and "the Ariel-like quality of the beings or the influence that disconcerts them." In these stories EMF is searching for some poetic and elemental reality. [Perceptive review.]

118 Dickinson, G[oldsworthy] Lowes. "Mr. Forster's New Book," NATION AND ATHENAEUM, XXXIII (26 May 1923), 273; NEW YORK EVENING POST LITERARY REVIEW, 30 June 1923, p. 800.

EMF's *Pharos and Pharillon* is modest and demure in contrast to many nineteenth-century edifices which celebrate Alexandria and its past. His best talent is his ability to present people from the past as if they were living now. EMF has the tenderness, humor, and insight characteristic of the present age; he resembles Anatole France, but he is humorous rather than witty, and he implies that a faith may lurk behind his skepticism. EMF's "courage of skepticism" provides a foundation upon which mankind may yet build. [Perceptive review.]

119 Forman, Henry James. "Tardy Recognition of an English Novelist's Qualities," NEW YORK TIMES BOOK REVIEW, 4 Feb 1923, p. 3.

EMF's coolness derives from sheer mastery of his material; he never loses his emotional balance. He is detached and aloof, but sympathetic. Everything that happens in his novels is fresh, unhackneyed, and original. He is not indecent or obscene like Joyce but is modern at heart despite his classicism. In *A Room with a View* he masterfully renders Lucy's revolt against the artificial, the unnatural, and the unreal; she eventually attains the right view. EMF hates the muddle deriving from suburban values. The tragedy of the baby's death in *Where Angels Fear to Tread* derives from this muddle, the hold of rigid convention, and the suppression of the natural. There is a pagan quality in his books, especially to the fore in *The Longest Journey*. EMF manages coincidences well. "He is brilliant, humorous, subtle, original, but never unconvincing." [Review of 2nd American ed of *Room*.]

120 "Forster's Alexandria," NEW YORK TIMES BOOK REVIEW, 2 Sept 1923, p. 15.

One reason for the success of *Pharos and Pharillon* is EMF's finely poised intellect from which romantic preconceptions are absent. He seems to have been aware of two civilizations striving for supremacy, Greek (paganism) and Asian (Christianity). The result was that "civilized existence spun on its axis here and faced in a new direction." "Pharos" (the first section) reveals unforced and leavening humor, EMF's sensitivity to the passing of time, and his sympathetic approach to personalities from the Alexandrian past, especially to Alexander. In "Pharillon" (the second section) the city becomes an atmosphere, not a backdrop for great figures. The modern city is different from the ancient; it is no longer a city of the soul but of modern industry. *Pharos* is not history but "a series of spiritual attitudes brooding over a fragment of fact until he has evolved from it a recreated atmosphere." It is as much a revelation of the many-sided EMF as a presentation of Alexandria. He writes often with "a sense of poetic values," and his humor is kind and gentle. In *Pharos* we have a compelling sense of a spiritual unity between EMF and Alexandria. [Penetrating review.]

121 "In This Month's Fiction Library," LITERARY DIGEST INTERNATIONAL BOOK REVIEW, I (Oct 1923), 68–69.

Lucy Honeychurch in *A Room with a View* is obtuse and uninteresting, Cecil Vyse is a prig and a snob, and George Emerson is a prig and a boor. EMF's triumph of passion over convention is not sympathetic because of the limitations of his characters. [Review of 2nd American ed of *Room.*]

122 L., I. W. "Books of the Day: *The Celestial Omnibus,*" BOSTON
EVENING TRANSCRIPT, Section VI, 11 Aug 1923, p. 6.
The central figures in *The Celestial Omnibus and Other Stories* know Pan
well. Eustace in "The Story of a Panic" is the most memorable example.
"The Other Side of the Hedge" is subversive of a strenuous, earnest morality. "The Celestial Omnibus" is a beautiful but strange story. The most
brilliant character who embraces the spontaneous life is Evelyn in "Other
Kingdom." "The Road from Colonus" is the tale with the most intellectual
substance. The book emphasizes the importance of spontaneous perceptions
in our inner lives.

123 L., I. W. "*Pharos and Pharillon,*" BOSTON EVENING TRAN-
SCRIPT, Section VI, 22 Sept 1923, p. 5.
Pharos and Pharillon is not a solemn undertaking but a book which sparkles
and delights. *Pharos* is authentic; having spent some time in Alexandria,
EMF is equipped to write about it. [Extended summary of book.]

124 M., R. "Things That Have Interested Mr. Forster," NEW
STATESMAN, XXI (16 June 1923), 302, 304.
EMF should write a novel with an Oriental setting now that he has so well
encapsulated Alexandria and its history in *Pharos and Pharillon.* More
extended treatment of Alexandrian science and poetry would have been
appropriate, as found in EMF's *Alexandria: A History and a Guide.* EMF
treats historical individuals as real people. He writes of those people and
those facets of Alexandria and its history that interest him. His irony is
unobtrusive; his skepticism covers a mystical quality of mind. In his description of C. P. Cavafy as a writer not interested in "facile beauty" and as one
who remains "at a slight angle to the universe," EMF is describing himself.
As in Cavafy's work, in EMF's there is a union of appreciation and detachment. In *Pharos* EMF's sympathy, humor, intellect, and individuality are
abundantly present. [Perceptive commentary.]

125 Murry, John Middleton. "The Magic of E. M. Forster," NEW
REPUBLIC, XXXV (8 Aug 1923), 293–94.
In *Pharos and Pharillon,* EMF captures the essence of Alexandria's "debatable ground." EMF is in this book at the center of his subject and himself.
Like the poet C. P. Cavafy EMF has made Alexandria his own; and like him,
he stands "at a slight angle to the universe." All of his observations about
the city and its history have become personalized; and to some people this
will seem an impertinence and an arrogance. In Alexandria EMF found "a
lucid confusion of the categories" that he enjoyed and on occasion tried to
reconcile. *Pharos* is all of it good: "in Alexandria Mr. Forster found his

spiritual home." EMF seems to have gained there the courage of his own vision and ventured into a "field rightly his own." [Implicit in these remarks is a realization that only at "a slight angle" to an alien civilization could EMF realize his own creative potential and actualize his vision, as in *A Passage to India;* a most penetrating discussion of *Pharos.*]

126 Pure, Simon [pseud of Frank Swinnerton]. "The Londoner," BOOKMAN (NY), LVI (Feb 1923), 735–40, espec p. 738.
An EMF work-in-progress (*A Passage to India*) will be welcome when it is published. "Forster is one of the very best brains of his generation, refined, scrupulous, educated."

127 "A Room with a View," LITERARY DIGEST INTERNATIONAL BOOK REVIEW, I (Oct 1923), 68–69.
Cecil Vyse in *A Room with a View* is a snob and a prig; George Emerson is a prig and a boor. The triumph is not a sympathetic one, since "the limitations of all his characters are too disagreeably obvious." [Review of American reissue of *Room.*]

128 Stallings, Laurence. "A Reviewer's Excursion among the Short Stories," NEW YORK WORLD. 29 Sept 1923, p. 9.
EMF's stories in *The Celestial Omnibus* are marked by "pagan symbolism and flair for fine prose effects." In EMF's emphasis on the Great God Pan, he is similar to Arthur Machen but lacks his demonic and sexual preoccupations. "The Story of a Panic" resembles Machen's fantasies but is more shadowy and delicate; "The Celestial Omnibus" is an excellent tale.

129 Stone, Percy N. "Novels à la Carte," BOOKMAN (NY), LVII (April 1923), 210–12.
The love affair in *A Room with a View* is a bit too contrived. But there is much to enjoy, especially the general quality of the comedy: "He touches and runs. He doesn't attempt to smash." [Review comment on 2nd American ed of *Room.*]

130 "Unusual Short Stories," NEW YORK EVENING POST LITERARY REVIEW, 29 Sept 1923, p. 83; rptd in E. M. FORSTER: THE CRITICAL HERITAGE, ed by Philip Gardner (Lond & Boston: Routledge & Kegan Paul, 1973), pp. 179–80.
EMF is good at conveying the elusive and supernatural. He can create atmosphere and tell a good story with completeness and with the ability to satisfy our sense of structural unity. "The Celestial Omnibus" is the gem of the volume. "Philosophical subtlety, humor, and fantasy" combine in the typical EMF story. [Singles out in *The Celestial Omnibus and Other Short Stories*, "Other Kingdom" and "The Road from Colonus" for praise.]

131 "A Vision of Alexandria," TIMES LITERARY SUPPLEMENT (Lond), 31 May 1923, p. 369.

In *Pharos and Pharillon* EMF reveals that Alexandria is a land where Greece and Asia strove for harmony and where the human sought the infinite; as such the city belongs as much to imagination as to history. In *Pharos* EMF is both at the center of his subject and at the center of himself. Alexandria becomes a manifestation of EMF especially as he stands (like C. P. Cavafy) "at a slight angle to the universe." Where the two worlds of Greece and Asia, of the finite and the infinite, come together EMF puts his ear to the crack which resulted. *Pharos* is better than his preceding books because in Alexandria EMF found a spiritual home. He has never been so convincing as in this book and so different from his fellow writers. [Interesting account, as it defines some of the substrata from which *A Passage to India* was to develop.]

1924

132 A., S. "Mr. Forster's India," SPRINGFIELD SUNDAY REPUBLICAN, 19 Oct 1924, p. 5A.

A Passage to India is characterized by absolute objectivity of presentation, lucidity and "graceful ease" of writing, mastery in dialogue, and delicate irony.

133 Butler, W. W. "*A Passage to India,*" NEW STATESMAN, XXIII (23 Aug 1924), 568.

Neither Horne nor EMF in *Passage to India* ever mentions the devotion shown by conscientious British officials in India to the Indians in their charge. [See E. A. Horne, "Mr. Foster's *A Passage to India,*" no. 142.]

134 Douglas, A. Donald. "Plumbing the Depths of India's Mystery," LITERARY DIGEST INTERNATIONAL BOOK REVIEW, II (24 Sept 1924), 719, 759.

Any writer's intepretation of India is bound to be both partial and personal. EMF is the first to admit that *A Passage to India* is only one passage to India. He displays "the wisdom and the sadness of the historian rather than the antic and frenzy of the poet deluded by the splendor of his own fantasies." In *Passage* EMF presents "life in all its confusion and diversity." He has intellectual control and firm grasp of the realities of the situation he presents. His story is long "in that it is complicated and difficult like life." He resists the temptation to melodrama and sensationalism.

135 Fassett, I. P. "Books of the Quarter," CRITERION, III (Oct 1924), 137–39; rptd in E. M. FORSTER: THE CRITICAL HERITAGE, ed by Philip Gardner (Lond & Boston: Routledge & Kegan Paul, 1973), pp. 273–75.

EMF has found no answer to his question concerning India in *A Passage to India:* she remains elusive. *Passage* is logically thought out and completely wrought but lacks an arresting aspect that would raise it above the level of "Sound Contemporary Fiction." Mrs. Moore is a "sinister, obscure, horrible" woman. EMF does convince us that he is correct in regarding India not as a promise but as an appeal. [Interesting ambivalent review.]

136 G., C. W. [Review of *A Passage to India*], ENGLISHMAN (Calcutta), 25 September 1924, p. II; rptd in E. M. FORSTER: THE CRITICAL HERITAGE, ed by Philip Gardner (Lond & Boston: Routledge & Kegan Paul, 1973), pp. 270–72.

The writer who treats Indian station life and cultural and racial conflict has the responsibilities to be fair and truthful. EMF does not assume these responsibilities in *A Passage to India* because he lacks knowledge and understanding of Indian station life and of India in general. [Typical reaction of the Anglo-Indians hostile to *Passage*. Benita Parry in DELUSIONS AND DISCOVERIES (1973) traces in detail the racial antipathies between the British and the Indians and demonstrates that EMF gave, in general, a true picture of relationships between the races.]

137 Gaines, Clarence H. "Some Philosophers in Fiction," NORTH AMERICAN REVIEW, CCXX (Dec 1924), 375–78, 384; rptd in E. M. FORSTER: THE CRITICAL HERITAGE, ed by Philip Gardner (Lond & Boston: Routledge & Kegan Paul, 1973), pp. 285–87.

EMF is a distinctive talent because his philosophy, while profound and pessimistic, expresses itself through the comic mode. He is "at once a philosopher, a humanist, and a wit"—and a civilized novelist. He is not a romantic like Kipling but a realist like Chekhov, discerning not only people's motives "but the very wrinkles in their consciousness." Unlike Chekhov EMF is always the artist and never the diagnostician. [Review of *A Passage to India;* the other "philosophers" are May Sinclair, Arthur Train, A. C. Benson, and Thomas Nelson Page.]

138 Gorman, Herbert S. "Challenge and Indictment in E. M. Forster's Novel," NEW YORK TIMES BOOK REVIEW, 17 Aug 1924, p. 6.

A Passage to India justifies the enthusiasm of EMF's admirers; it is "one of the saddest, keenest, most beautifully written ironic novels of the time." It is a challenge, an indictment, and a revelation. The characterization is outstanding. Ronny Heaslop is conscientious but obtuse, as his success depends on his being obtuse. The fine irony and the control that EMF displays in the club scene after Aziz's arrest are noteworthy. There is an Olympian quality in such irony and control: to the Englishmen their troubles are real, but seen from EMF's perspective these problems hardly exist. EMF, in this novel, is at the height of his powers, by virtue of "the crystal-clear portraiture, the delicate conveying of nuances of thought and life, and the astonishing command of his medium." [Penetrating comment.]

139 Gould, Gerald. "New Fiction," SATURDAY REVIEW (Lond), CXXXVII (21 June 1924), 642; rptd, with a few additions, in THE ENGLISH NOVEL OF TO-DAY (Lond: John Castle, 1924), pp. 183–89;

and in original form in E. M. FORSTER: THE CRITICAL HERITAGE, ed by Philip Gardner (Lond & Boston: Routledge & Kegan Paul, 1973), pp. 218–20.

The fairy-tale quality of *A Passage to India* accounts for the unreality and thinness of the characters: "His wealth of wit and poetry is marked, or at any rate limited, by something between pity and contempt for that witless and unpoetic race, the human." EMF's great theme is the failure of communication among human beings. The details of the novel are more important than its center. The characters do not have separate lives, but their circumstances and their thoughts are exquisitely rendered. There is much dramatic power, but the novel fails to be great because of EMF's lack of creative force in envisioning his characters. [Extensive plot summary. Interesting if unusual reaction to *Passage*. In THE ENGLISH NOVEL OF TO-DAY Gould acknowledges the sympathy, wit, knowledge, and charm to be found in *Howards End*, but the novel is at one remove from life. EMF's imperfect realism and his excessive fantasy are present even in *Passage*.]

140 Hartley, L. P. "Mr. E. M. Forster's New Novel," SPECTATOR (Lond), CXXXII (28 June 1924), 1048, 1050; rptd in E. M. FORSTER: "A PASSAGE TO INDIA": A CASEBOOK, ed by Malcolm Bradbury (Lond: Macmillan, Casebook Series, 1970), pp. 47–50; and in E. M. FORSTER: THE CRITICAL HERITAGE, ed by Philip Gardner (Lond & Boston: Routledge & Kegan Paul, 1973), pp. 225–27.

Some constriction or idiosyncrasy in outlook marred EMF's earlier books. Now in *A Passage to India* his artistry is more mature and considered. He finds fault with both Indians and Anglo-Indians, though his sympathies lie with the Indians. The book is more than political; it is intensely personal, intensely comic. The characters, except for Fielding, are at the mercy of mood and nerves and have little hold over themselves; they are infinitely receptive and suggestible. They desire intimacy, but their personalities or circumstances interfere with their achieving it. EMF gives the affair of the Marabar a peculiar horror; he dissociates it from our ordinary experiences. There is no emotional repose or security in the book: "it is for ever puncturing our complacence, it is a bed of thorns." EMF's humor and irony leave a sting; all emphasis in the book is on the present moment, with all its discontent and pain. "The action of the book is not fused by a continuous impulse; it is a series of intense isolated moments." [Interesting, deep-reaching discussion.]

141 Harwood, H. C. "New Books," OUTLOOK (Lond), LIII (14 June 1924), 412; rptd in E. M. FORSTER: THE CRITICAL HERITAGE, ed by Philip Gardner (Lond & Boston: Routledge & Kegan Paul, 1973), pp. 202–3.

EMF's irony is superior to the ordinary expression of irony in adding interest to amusement. In *A Passage to India* the irony reveals intelligence, not facility. *Passage* corrects the extravagances of Indian partisans of all sorts. Aziz is the central figure: pathetic in his fate, presumptuous in his success, a poet and religious individual. His ruin emerges out of nothing and is an accident. At the end he becomes a passionate Mohammedan caught between the "chilly English" and the "flabby Hindus."

142 Horne, E. A. "Mr. Forster's *A Passage to India*," NEW STATESMAN, XXIII (16 Aug 1924), 543–44; rptd as "An Anglo-Indian View," in E. M. FORSTER: THE CRITICAL HERITAGE, ed by Philip Gardner (Lond & Boston: Routledge & Kegan Paul, 1973), pp. 246–51.

EMF's capacity to identify himself with the world he is describing accounts at once for the virtues and the limitations of *A Passage to India*. This novel is not about India but about Indians, especially Indian Mohammedans. Aziz is a fine portrait, but we know nothing of his social and political antecedents. The hallucination in the Caves was Aziz's. His is a sexual vanity, the physical obsession with the opposite sex, and he transfers his obsessive feeling to Adela Quested. The Anglo-Indians are unreal, and so are some aspects of their background in India. EMF knew India but not the Anglo-Indians at firsthand, nor did he have enough affection for them to render them truly. [See W. W. Butler, "*A Passage to India*," no. 133.]

143 Kendon, Frank. "Belles-Lettres," LONDON MERCURY, IX (March 1924), 549–50.

In *Pharos and Pharillon*, EMF writes with amusing irony about the ancient theological squabbles in Alexandria. His sketches are enlivened with a "tart" humor. *Pharos* suggests that EMF could himself compose an impressive and entertaining history of Alexandria.

144 Lovett, Robert Morss. "*A Passage to India*," NEW REPUBLIC, XL (27 Aug 1924), 393–94; rptd in THE CRITIC AS ARTIST: ESSAYS ON BOOKS 1920–1970, ed by Gilbert H. Harrison (NY: Liveright, 1972), pp. 243–46.

A Passage to India has the same quality as *Howards End:* "the delicate perception of character as it expresses itself in tones of feeling and shades of manner." There is a grim struggle for survival in the British ruling class in India. The novel is marked by "the humor of infinitely incongruous relations." EMF has developed a novel of manners against a background of conquest, "a human comedy within the frame of the huge imperial joke. He has raised the racial question from the murky region of politics to the lighter air of social life." EMF treats both sides with sympathy and satire. [Genuine feeling for *Passage* is revealed.]

145 Lynd, Sylvia. "A Great Novel at Last," TIME AND TIDE, V (20 June 1924), 592–93; rptd in E. M. FORSTER: THE CRITICAL HERITAGE, ed by Philip Gardner (Lond & Boston: Routledge & Kegan Paul, 1973), pp. 215–18.

A Passage to India is a great book. Like Jane Austen, EMF makes things happen naturally; he applies her qualities to a consideration of relationships between East and West: impartiality, humor, irreverence, candor. *Passage* is both comical and agonizing. His Indians are not all of one sort. He conveys the exquisite discomfort involved in trying to bridge the racial gulf. At a crisis each character reveals himself clearly. The book's contribution is as an enlargement of knowledge, not just about India but about human motives.

146 M., C. "New Novels," MANCHESTER GUARDIAN, 20 June 1924, p. 7; rptd in abrgd form in E. M. FORSTER: THE CRITICAL HERITAGE, ed by Philip Gardner (Lond & Boston: Routledge & Kegan Paul, 1973), pp. 212–13.

EMF's *A Passage to India* has "the involuntary fairness of the man who sees." *Passage* is a personal impression complete with the prejudices and limitations of the writer. He is examined by India in the novel; it is his confession. Its principal qualities are imagination (giving him the power to see and hear internally) and humor (EMF enjoys his people instead of satirizing them). The friendship between Fielding and Aziz is founded on affection, but it is also at the mercy of feelings rising from the depths of racial consciousness. We are left with a realization that the blending of the races is a four-dimensional problem. If anything, EMF leans towards his own race in their difficulties, but presents all his people as they really are. [Thoughtful remarks.]

147 M., D. L. "Books of the Day: *A Passage to India*," BOSTON EVENING TRANSCRIPT, Section II, 3 Sept 1924, p. 6; rptd in E. M. FORSTER: THE CRITICAL HERITAGE, ed by Philip Gardner (Lond & Boston: Routledge & Kegan Paul, 1973), pp. 261–64.

EMF has a sharp sense for words, so that his command of language may obscure the technical accomplishment present in *A Passage to India*. He is always master of his medium. *Passage* penetrates more deeply into its subject of Anglo-Indian relationships than any other novel. EMF has done full justice to India itself, not dismissing it or Indians as other novelists have tended to do (who seem to have aped the dismissive Ronny Heaslop in *Passage*). EMF is aware of the weaknesses of the Indian: his unreliability, his tendency to fit the facts to the occasion rather than to serve disinterested truth. On both sides, a sense of fatalism precludes meaningful communication: see the exaggerated reactions after Adela Quested announces the presumed assault upon her in the Caves. She is the only English woman at

Chandrapore brave enough to have withdrawn a charge like hers. The part of *Passage* after the trial is anticlimax, and the novel would have ended more effectively with the trial [as, in fact, Santha Rama Rau's dramatization (1960) was to do]. *Passage* evinces both subtlety and power in EMF's depicting the minds of the Hindu, the Moslem, and the Anglo-Indian. [Excellent comment.]

148 Macaulay, Rose. "Mr. Forster's New Novel," DAILY NEWS (Lond), 4 June 1924, p. 8; rptd in E. M. FORSTER: THE CRITICAL HERITAGE, ed by Philip Gardner (Lond & Boston: Routledge & Kegan Paul, 1973), pp. 196–98.

EMF is the most attractive, exquisite, and truthful of practicing novelists. His delicacy of character portrayal, his pervading humor, his conveying of the beauty and absurdity of life, his sensitivity to nuances of behavior, his forthright thought, his poetry, and his ironic wit are his excellences. He also appreciates the interaction between fantasy and ordinary life. In *A Passage to India* his picture of the ruling race is convincing, pathetic, amusing, and sympathetic. He is excellent with the sensitive, elderly Mrs. Moore and with the slightly gauche, imperceptive, stolid, and honest Adela Quested. *Passage* is a story about the Anglo-Indian wall and the futile attempts on either side to surmount it. The novel is an ironic tragedy and a brilliant comedy of manners. EMF's range here is wider and deeper than in his other novels, and *Passage* lacks their occasional preciousness. It is EMF's best and most interesting book. [Sensitive review.]

149 Massingham, H. W. "The Price of India's Friendship: Mr. Forster's Great Novel," NEW LEADER, VII (27 June 1924), 10; rptd, slightly rvd, with note by H. J. Massingham as "E. M. Forster and India," H. W. M.: A SELECTION FROM THE WRITINGS OF H. W. MASSINGHAM, EDITED WITH A PREFACE AND NOTES BY H. J. MASSINGHAM (NY: Harcourt, Brace; Lond: Jonathan Cape [1925]), pp. 195–200 (see 1925 entry for H. J. Massingham); rptd in original form, slightly abrgd, in E. M. FORSTER: THE CRITICAL HERITAGE, ed by Philip Gardner (Lond & Boston: Routledge & Kegan Paul, 1973), pp. 207–10.

A Passage to India has to be read not only in aesthetic terms, if only because of EMF's gifts as writer—his analytic ability, his discernment of the hidden sides to human nature and of the ironies of existence, his ability to present the thoughts of men against the scenes in which they occur, his use of rich detail, and his power to suggest the color and movement of the life toward which he is both disdainful and sympathetic. EMF has something important to say about India. He emphasizes the honesty, the arrogance, the intellectual shallowness, the physical courage, and "the moral tremors" of the ruling race, and the "super-sensitiveness," impulsiveness, charm, and weakness of Mohammedan and Hindu India. His sympathies are with the Indians and not with the governing caste: see his liking for Aziz and his disdain for Major Callendar. Knowing the weakness of a non-English India (the antagonism between Hindu and Moslem), EMF would hope that the Fieldings and Mrs. Moores might retrieve some of the lost English credit. But the picture of India presented by EMF is also something that cannot last; the present situation cannot be saved and will disappear. Still, Aziz represents something that can and ought to be won in India. Yet there are immense difficulties in the way—too little character and clear purpose on one side, too little understanding on the other. The political and actual subject must not be ignored, though the charm of the novel lies in the precision of the detail and the way in which the whole panorama retreats into the mystical background where half-revealed forces have sway. The Anglo-Indian scene is thus a tangle of "obscure and warring spiritualities" and absurdities (Aziz himself is mercurial and absurd). EMF's conclusion: to counter the undermining effects of fear and suspicion, love and understanding might bring reconciliation. But how can the disparate races understand one another? The Englishman must realize both the difficulty and the importance of understanding India. [Judicious, perceptive account.]

> **150** Miles, Hamish. "E. M. Forster," DIAL, LXXVI (May 1924), 452–56; rptd in E. M. FORSTER: THE CRITICAL HERITAGE, ed by Philip Gardner (Lond & Boston: Routledge & Kegan Paul, 1973), pp. 191–95.

EMF invokes the vision of a modest country manor; he is eminently civilized. His work is distinguished by its origins in the richness of human experience, its "delicate sensibility to humane values." The need to "connect" develops in him a consistency of temper and sensibility. His short stories reveal EMF's "touch of Pan" upon our modern civilization, and they have enlarged our imagination and understanding. *Pharos* is "a distillation of a tenderly ironic spirit" that sees things in its own individual way. [Important in the history of EMF's reputation. Review-essay on American eds of *Howards End* (1921), *Pharos and Pharillon* (1923), and *The Celestial Omnibus and Other Stories* (1923).]

> **151** "Mr. E. M. Forster's New Novel," OBSERVER (Lond), 15 June 1924, p. 5; rptd in abrgd form in E. M. FORSTER: THE CRITICAL HERITAGE, ed by Philip Gardner (Lond & Boston: Routledge & Kegan Paul, 1973), pp. 211–12.

A Passage to India reveals less the ingenuity and hopelessness of *Howards End* than the spiritual, "less insolently bored tone" of *A Room with a View*. *Passage* reveals a wise and sensitive writer, alert to the nuances of human feeling and tolerant in his point of view, critical only of spiritual arrogance. He portrays well Anglo-India and Mohammedan India, but Hindu India does not come through forcefully in the fanciful figure of Godbole. EMF is a fine storyteller and a fine painter of scenes; but the story exists primarily for us to get to know the characters.

152 "Mr. Forster's Novel of India," BIRMINGHAM POST, 20 June 1924, p. 3; rptd in E. M. FORSTER: THE CRITICAL HERITAGE, ed by Philip Gardner (Lond & Boston: Routledge & Kegan Paul, 1973), pp. 214–15.

EMF in *A Passage to India* has a distinctive style recalling that of Henry James, yet his manner is very much his own. His novel reveals distinction of style, keen analysis of character, creation of a rich atmosphere, and profundity of emotion. It captures well the undercurrents of feeling between East and West. Philosophy and atmosphere build up to a crisis that strips away the superficial aspects of civilization and penetrates to "naked passions of loyalty and hate"; the personal conflict then ceases, but India remains. "The passions have broken themselves, and those who felt them: we are left with only East and West—as before; together, and yet apart."

153 Muir, Edwin. "Mr. Forster Looks at India," NATION (NY), CXIX (8 Oct 1924), 379–80; rptd in E. M. FORSTER: THE CRITICAL HERITAGE, ed by Philip Gardner (Lond & Boston: Routledge & Kegan Paul, 1973), pp. 278–80.

EMF's work shows the influence of the Lytton Strachey "ironical" school, but his work is more deft and indirect than that of many writers influenced by Strachey. His work is "a work of inclinations"; he has much control and can go halfway at will in any direction because he knows where the halfway point is. Assurance is present, but is profundity? The intellect is not pushed to its extreme by going only halfway in all directions. EMF lacks wisdom and the passion for truth which inspires great art; but "he has an intelligence of greater force and purity than that of any other imaginative writer today." *A Passage to India* shows EMF's cultivation more than his intuition; he convinces us that he understands the misunderstandings of his characters but not that he understands his characters. The party at Fielding's, the trial, and the riot are praiseworthy. EMF's art is impressionistic but at the same time detached and objective. The festival is feeble and unconvincing. "The novel is a triumph of the humanistic spirit over material difficult to humanize." *Passage* is an exquisite rather than a profound work of art, and it is a graphic picture of India "seen through a very unembarrassed and courageous intelligence." [Important and perceptive review of *Passage*.]

154 Murry, John Middleton. "Bou-oum or Ou-boum?" ADELPHI, II (July 1924), 150–53; rptd in E. M. FORSTER: THE CRITICAL HERITAGE, ed by Philip Gardner (Lond & Boston: Routledge & Kegan Paul, 1973), pp. 236–38.

In *A Passage to India* EMF has reached the end of what he can say. EMF's stance is so intellectual and impersonal and so skeptical of the heart's affirmations that he ends on a negative and pessimistic note. [Interesting review of *Passage*.]

155 Nevinson, Henry W. " 'India's Coral Strand,' " SATURDAY REVIEW OF LITERATURE (NY), I (16 Aug 1924), 43; rptd in E. M. FORSTER: THE CRITICAL HERITAGE, ed by Philip Gardner (Lond & Boston: Routledge & Kegan Paul, 1973), pp. 256–60.

There are three stages in our recognition of India: (1) the age of the nabobs, when India was seen as a fabulous land of great wealth, ripe for plunder; (2) the age of India as "the coral strand," when it was seen as the land of exotic and extreme behavior on the part of the Indians; and (3) the time of Kipling, when natives and jungle beasts were dominated and ruled over for their own good by the English. The falseness of the preconceptions determining these formulations led to a lack of interest in India and reliance upon activities of the India Civil Service, in lieu of more personal contact with, and fuller understanding of, the subcontinent. World War I, the growing independence of Indians, and, above all, the Amritsar massacre were crucial in changing our views of both India and England; the result is that *A Passage to India* is the right novel appearing at the right time. It is not the story but the picture of Anglo-Indian life and character on the one side and of the Indian life and character on the other that is significant. "I have never known so accurate, so penetrating, and so sympathetic an account of these divergent characters and lives as this." [Nevinson quotes his own writings to support EMF's negative views of the Anglo-Indians. This review of *Passage* is essential to correct disparaging judgment of EMF's treatment of Indians voiced by Nirad Chaudhuri, "Passage to and from India" (1954) and Andrew Shonfield, "The Politics of Forster's India" (1968).]

156 "New Novels," DAILY TELEGRAPH (Lond), 24 June 1924, p. 15.

In *A Passage to India*, EMF presents the Anglo-Indians in a hard, dry light, unmodified by kinship of race with them. The Hindus are minor characters. The English are neither interesting nor ridiculous. EMF accepts the Indian as he is but realizes the importance of what the English can give him. Aziz is an original character, representative of national India, neither idealized nor ridiculed. The Anglo-Indians make Aziz embittered and cynical because he is as he is and they are as they are.

157 "New Novels," GLASGOW HERALD, 26 June 1924, p. 4.

There are few incidents in *A Passage to India;* and its interest lies in its convincing portraiture. Aziz is the cleverest and most realistic study in the novel. His high ambitions are modified by poverty and by association with a contemptuous, superior race; his flexible standards of honesty and truthfulness are too elastic to be understood by the European mentality. It is a novel marked by life and reality.

158 "New Novels," TIMES LITERARY SUPPLEMENT (Lond), 12 June 1924, 370; rptd in E. M. FORSTER: THE CRITICAL HERITAGE, ed by Philip Gardner (Lond & Boston: Routledge & Kegan Paul, 1973), pp. 199–200.

A Passage to India reveals EMF's fairness; he blends observation and insight. Its appeal is more precise than that of his earlier novels; it is "a definite picture rather than a creative imagining." Adela Quested sees India as a frieze, not as a spirit; she can't understand the aloofness and the apathy of the Anglo-Indians, including her fiance, Ronny Heaslop. If he is arrogant, Adela is inexperienced. By their warmth and social imagination, Mrs. Moore and Fielding overcome Aziz's suspicion and compel his friendship. Aziz's resentment contributes to his disaster. In Adela's case, her repentance is worthless to Aziz because justice and honesty mean little in India without some show of passion. The book is noteworthy for its subtle portraits, its insight into the Moslem and Hindu mind, its irony and poetry. All these aspects contribute to its "imaginative breadth and generosity."

159 Niles, E. A. "Oriental Mystery," INDEPENDENT, CXIII (30 Aug 1924), 134.

A Passage to India is a novel of problems, though nothing is solved; EMF broaches important questions for the reader himself to decide. EMF works "at a slight angle to the universe," that which penetrates into the minds of individuals. He has penetrated into the Indian mind, and he also has a genius for place. *Passage* reveals "fine and thoughtful writing, original, compressed; and compact of observation."

160 Paterson, Isabel. "Drawing Room Fiction," BOOKMAN (NY), LX (24 Dec 1924), 494–98, espec 495.

A Passage to India is the best novel of the year. The theme is "stupendous," the plot simple. EMF has weighed "the imponderables." *Passage* is remarkable for "the subtlety of [EMF's] shading, his hair's breadth accuracy in catching mental moods and inflections." Speech, action, and thought are organic expressions of individual personality, racial culture, or national ethos. EMF is also adept at exposing stupidity. His keenness and clairvoyance may work against his popularity with general readers.

161 Priestley, J. B. "Fiction," LONDON MERCURY, X (July 1924), 319–20; rptd as "A Review" in E. M. FORSTER: "A PASSAGE TO INDIA": A CASEBOOK, ed by Malcolm Bradbury (Lond: Macmillan, Casebook Series, 1970), pp. 55–58; and in E. M. FORSTER: THE

CRITICAL HERITAGE, ed by Philip Gardner (Lond & Boston: Routledge & Kegan Paul, 1973), pp. 228-30.

EMF brings back into the English novel his own exquisite sanity and curious sensitivity. An English subject would have been preferable. The figures are all treated with the detached sympathy that is "the very height of human justice." The evocative and pregnant style of *Howards End* is not quite attained in *A Passage to India*, but there are no major improbabilities, such as the marriage of Margaret and the seduction of Helen. EMF has opened in contemporary fiction a window to the outside air. [Review of *Passage* followed by comments on novels by other writers.]

162 Pure, Simon [pseud of Frank Swinnerton]. "The Londoner," BOOKMAN (NY), LIX (Aug 1924), 701-7, espec 705-6.

EMF is a scholar; he is witty and has the ability to write well. He has an attractive if elusive personality. He has knowledge and also an insight that transcends mere knowledge. His books reveal brilliance and disdain (by virtue of his wit) of the common mind. The books prior to *Howards End* are preferable because they are more open, especially *A Room with a View*. In *Howards End*, the texture is heavy, probability is lacking, and the tone is disagreeable. Perhaps his promise as a writer will be fulfilled in his new novel. [Discussions of EMF, the man and his work, immediately prior to publication of *A Passage to India.*]

163 "Race Conflict in a New Novel: E. M. Forster Suggests a Passage to 'More than India,'" CURRENT OPINION (NY), LXXVII (Oct 1924), 445-46.

In *A Passage to India* EMF's point of view is that of a disillusioned observer; he has an intellectual detachment equal to Galsworthy's. His inspiration is partly from Whitman's "Passage to India." Ironic agnosticism is the chief note, and EMF does not flatter either the English or the Indians. The deterioration of relationships between the races is tragic because good intentions are subverted by untoward circumstances.

164 Ratcliffe, S. K. "*A Passage to India*," NEW STATESMAN, XXIII (23 Aug 1924), 567-68; rptd as "Another Anglo-Indian View," in E. M. FORSTER: THE CRITICAL HERITAGE, ed by Philip Gardner (Lond & Boston: Routledge & Kegan Paul, 1973), pp. 251-53.

A Passage to India is the only recent book that has imperial significance. E. A. Horne in his letter on *Passage* (see entry no. 142) incorrectly asserts that EMF's Anglo-Indians are false to reality. Rather, the details in EMF's presentation are often wrong, but the Anglo-Indians are truly depicted in essentials of character and attitude. The message of *Passage* is that the society, relation, and system presented in the novel are in the long run impossible. The Indian characters are the ones discredited.

165 "Recent Fiction," TIMES OF INDIA (Bombay), 23 July 1924, p. 13; rptd in E. M. FORSTER: THE CRITICAL HERITAGE, ed by Philip Gardner (Lond & Boston: Routledge & Kegan Paul, 1973), pp. 239–40.

In *A Passage to India* EMF sees Anglo-India as it is, not as a violent partisan or a vehement satirist. As a picture of educated India (in Aziz and others), the novel is outstanding. It also provides insight into relations between the races and creeds in India.

166 Redman, Ben Ray. "The Anglo-Indian Problem," BOOK REVIEW (Sept 1924), 18.

A Passage to India has been worth the long wait, but EMF has not given fully of his talent in it. The situation in the novel rather than any of its characters is to blame for what happens. EMF reveals excellent writing, humor, and keen observation in *Passage;* but he fails to use his materials dramatically. The result: a pictorial rather than a narrative success.

167 Roberts, R. Ellis. "E. M. Forster's New Novel," BOOKMAN (Lond), LXVI (July 1924), 220–21; rptd in E. M. FORSTER: THE CRITICAL HERITAGE, ed by Philip Gardner (Lond & Boston: Routledge & Kegan Paul, 1973), pp. 231–33.

As novelist of manners and society, EMF creates flesh and blood characters. In *A Passage to India* he has also written a novel "rich in colour . . . lively in sensation . . . varied in aspect." He controls his "freakishness" in this book in the interest of creating believable characters. In Aziz, EMF has created a character of much psychological depth. The analysis of Fielding and the other Anglo-Indians is excellent. With Godbole, EMF gives us externals without understanding his inner aspects. The descriptive scenes in *Passage* are unexcelled; the book gains in power after the incident in the Marabar Caves.

168 Singh, St. Nihal. "Indians and Anglo-Indians: As Portrayed to Britons by British Novelists," MODERN REVIEW (Calcutta), XXXVI (Sept 1924), 251–56; rptd in E. M. FORSTER: THE CRITICAL HERITAGE, ed by Philip Gardner (Lond & Boston: Routledge & Kegan Paul, 1973), pp. 264–69.

EMF presents his characters faithfully in *A Passage to India*, although Indians are not all so full of religious prejudice or so muddled as EMF conceives them to be. The Anglo-Indians demonstrate, by their arrogance and lack of sympathy, that Indians must separate from England in order to solve their political problems.

169 "The Spirit of Modern India," DAILY GRAPHIC (Lond), 6 June 1924, p. 13.

A Passage to India is less interesting than *Howards End* because England's problems are more relevant to us than India's. But EMF captures the spirit of modern India as no other writer has.

170 Stallings, Laurence. "When Rudyards Cease Their Kiplings and Haggards Ride No More," NEW YORK WORLD, 13 Aug 1924, p. 9; rptd in E. M. FORSTER: THE CRITICAL HERITAGE, ed by Philip Gardner (Lond & Boston: Routledge & Kegan Paul, 1973), pp. 240–42.

A Passage to India is the most sensitive work of fiction in years. It is concerned with the transmission of ideas (or with the misunderstandings) between the races. The Western mind and the Eastern mind have been defined and revealed in *Passage*. The style has clarity and smooth penetration and lacks diffuseness. EMF is impartial and unprejudiced as he pits second-rate government officials against medium-grade Indians. Any element of propaganda is absent. His prose does not easily come apart, a train of ideas giving rise to a thousand following grains of thought. EMF has a subtlety and complexity lacking in Kipling.

171 "A Striking Novel," STATESMAN (Calcutta), 15 Aug 1924, p. 6; rptd in E. M. FORSTER: THE CRITICAL HERITAGE, ed by Philip Gardner (Lond & Boston: Routledge & Kegan Paul, 1973), pp. 244–46.

As a portrayer of character EMF is outstanding in *A Passage to India*. His Anglo-Indians are especially well drawn. The trial is not a well-done sequence; it is full of technical errors and is a travesty of the reality. EMF is well informed and insightful about some aspects of India but ignorant about some others.

172 Walker, Charles R. "The Atlantic's Bookshelf," ATLANTIC MONTHLY, CXXXIV (Dec 1924), 14, 16.

EMF's craftsmanship in *A Passage to India* gives him unusual power; he is able to convey the sounds, the smells, the psychology of India. Officialism envelops the scene, while kindness, Western science, and Oriental tradition try to break the web but only pierce it at points. It is Adela Quested's tale because she never conforms to British India or to Indian India. Out of the picnic to the Marabar Caves, EMF distills Indian landscape and character and suggests the complexity of Anglo-India in the events that follow. The friendship of Fielding for Aziz and the difficulties involved in the relationship provide a unifying force for the novel.

173 Watson, Blanche. "*A Passage to India*," WORLD TOMORROW (NY), VII (Dec 1924), 382.

A Passage to India is aesthetically good, structurally a masterpiece, but spiritually lacking in insight [incomprehensible judgment]. EMF lacks sympathy for the inarticulate millions of Indians for whose misery England is responsible. He depicts with insight the antagonism between the races but has chosen to formulate his spiritual and moral aversions rather than his love. He shows India as it is, not as it could be. [Reviewer seems blind to implications of "Temple."]

174 West, Rebecca. "Interpreters of Their Age," SATURDAY REVIEW OF LITERATURE (NY), I (16 Aug 1924), 41–42; rptd in E. M. FORSTER: THE CRITICAL HERITAGE, ed by Philip Gardner (Lond & Boston: Routledge & Kegan Paul, 1973), pp. 253–56.

Bernard Shaw and Thomas Hardy are the two great literary men of the early twentieth century, and Hardy is the greater of the two. EMF is a candidate for like literary greatness as a result of *A Passage to India*. He may well inherit their position as interpreter to an age and become, like them, the literary figure in his age. Although *Passage* is a political novel, it has much universal interest. EMF has the equipment of a poet, especially a sensitivity of perception. Being in possession of his facts, he can synthesize them compellingly. The mute commentary of the punkah wallah at the trial where the races contend with each other is exactly right. EMF's passion for understanding a complex situation renders the book authentic and modern. [The prophecy of EMF's greatness was to be fulfilled but twenty years later and with no more novels to his credit than at the time of this excellent and perceptive article.]

175 Woolf, Leonard. "Arch Beyond Arch," NATION AND ATHENAEUM, XXXV (14 June 1924), 354; rptd in E. M. FORSTER: THE CRITICAL HERITAGE, ed by Philip Gardner (Lond & Boston: Routledge & Kegan Paul, 1973), pp. 204–6.

Hopes concerning *A Passage to India* have been realized: the novel is superbly written; EMF finds the exact words to convey his thoughts. Like his preceding novels this one reveals a subtle and individual humor, lifelike characters, ability to write dialogue, and "the power of opening windows upon what is both queer and beautiful." There are none of the lapses into silliness that had been present in the preceding books. *Passage* is remarkable for the large number of "themes" that account for its strange and beautiful texture. The book reverberates in the mind; there is arch beyond arch of meaning, and beyond the remotest silence in the book there is an echo. "The themes are woven and interwoven into a most intricate pattern, against which, or in which, the men and women are shown to us pathetically, rather ridiculously, entangled." [Discerning review.]

176 Woolf, Virginia. MR. BENNETT AND MRS. BROWN (Lond: Hogarth P, 1924); appeared as "Character in Fiction," CRITERION, II

(July 1924), 409–30; rptd in NEW YORK HERALD TRIBUNE BOOKS, 23 Aug 1925, pp. 1–3, and 30 Aug 1925, pp. 1–4; in HOGARTH ESSAYS (NY: Doubleday, Doran, 1928), pp. 1–29; in CRITICISM: THE FOUNDATIONS OF MODERN LITERARY JUDGMENT, ed by Mark Schorer, Josephine Miles, and Gordon McKenzie (NY: Harcourt, Brace, 1948), pp. 66–75; in THE CAPTAIN'S DEATH BED AND OTHER ESSAYS (NY: Harcourt, Brace; Lond: Hogarth P, 1950), pp. 94–119; and in COLLECTED ESSAYS (Lond: Hogarth P, 1966; NY: Harcourt, Brace & World, 1967), I, 319–37.

EMF and Lawrence are only imperfect Georgians in their early work; they compromised and tried to combine their sense of the unique reality of Mrs. Brown with the Edwardians' subservience to external facts. In the end they rejected the practice of the Edwardian realists and tried to rescue Mrs. Brown from them. [In this manifesto, Mrs. Woolf divides current writers into Edwardians (realists enslaved to fact, such as Wells, Bennett, and Galsworthy) and Georgians (those emancipated from tyranny to fact and dedicated to capturing the essence of Mrs. Brown), writers with whom Mrs. Woolf aligns herself—EMF, D. H. Lawrence, Strachey, Joyce, and T. S. Eliot.]

177 Wright, Ralph. "New Novels," NEW STATESMAN, XXIII (21 June 1924), 317–18; rptd as "A Review" in E. M. FORSTER: "A PASSAGE TO INDIA": A CASEBOOK, ed by Malcolm Bradbury (Lond: Macmillan, Casebook Series, 1970), pp. 50–55; and in E. M. FORSTER: THE CRITICAL HERITAGE, ed by Philip Gardner (Lond & Boston: Routledge & Kegan Paul, 1973), pp. 221–25.

EMF reflects the desire of the people in his age to know the truth; and he has tried to give us the truth about a complex situation in *A Passage to India*. After the arrest of Aziz, Indians and English alike cease to be individuals and become part of one of the herds. EMF is fair although he delivers no ostensible judgments; he refuses to generalize. His aim is "sight and insight —the distinguishing of the individual problem from the obscuring mass." The mystery of the Caves is overdone, and none of the characters is sympathetic; but *Passage* is full of knowledge and perceptiveness and is beautifully written. It is better proportioned and more mature than *Howards End*. [Important review.]

178 Wylie, Elinor. "Passage to More Than India," NEW YORK HERALD TRIBUNE BOOKS, 5 Oct 1924, 1, 2; rptd in E. M. FORSTER: THE CRITICAL HERITAGE, ed by Philip Gardner (Lond & Boston: Routledge & Kegan Paul, 1973), pp. 276–77.

EMF is a master of the art of prose. *Howards End* now no longer seems surprising but true. It was doubtful if EMF could surpass his achievement in this book and in *A Room with a View*, but he has not disappointed with

A Passage to India. The passage in the novel is no voyage of discovery but one through confusion and ignorance. However, the frustration presented in it is more illuminating than the successes of stupidity. The brilliant portraits of individuals are less important than the spirit of the book; its humanity, insight, and disturbing justice. *Passage* is beautiful, ironic, clear, exquisite, profound. *Passage* is poetry, melodrama, philosophy, and realism all in one. [Discerning review.]

179 Yust, Walter. "A Fascinating Journey," NEW YORK EVENING POST LITERARY REVIEW, 10 Aug 1924, p. 963.

In *A Passage to India* substance and form and style aptly fit each other. Penetration, subtlety, and insight in *Passage* are praiseworthy. Its skillful rendition of the nuances of mental states and its presentation of the "scarcely conscious combats of personality" are notable.

1925

180 "Anonymity," TIMES LITERARY SUPPLEMENT (Lond), 17 Dec 1925, p. 879.

EMF's essay "Anonymity" gives us basis for understanding EMF's own reticences and detachment toward experience and his view that art can be enjoyed apart from our knowledge of the artist.

181 Massingham, H. J. "Note," to "E. M. Forster and India," by H. W. Massingham [rpt of "The Price of India's Friendship"; see 1924 entry], H. W. M.: A SELECTION FROM THE WRITINGS OF H. W. MASSINGHAM, EDITED WITH A PREFACE AND NOTES BY H. J. MASSINGHAM (NY: Harcourt, Brace; Lond: Jonathan Cape [1925]), pp, 199–200.

H. W. Massingham may have been too "tender" toward Aziz, more so than EMF, who tends to regard Aziz more as a ruin than an ennobled victim. In either case, Aziz well represents "the nemesis of the imposition of an alien civilization upon his race."

182 Pure, Simon [pseud of Frank Swinnerton]. "The Londoner," BOOKMAN (NY), LXI (April 1925), 187.

A Passage to India is popular, but whether the book will outlast this popularity is problematical. EMF has a subtle mind, is an accomplished writer, and holds attention in the early chapters. Later he has recourse to "morbid hallucinations" when he needs emotion. EMF may not properly be a novelist and might use his gifts of mind and style to more advantage in writing history or biography.

183 Shanks, Edward. "Fiction," LONDON MERCURY, XVIII (May 1925), 96–98.

In *The Eternal Moment and Other Stories*, "The Story of the Siren" is "mysteriously lovely"; the other stories are only moderately successful. "The Machine Stops," for example, fails to satirize significant tendencies because EMF failed to observe closely the social scenes. "Co-ordination" is the second best story [this judgment is unique, I think, with Shanks].

184 Weygandt, Cornelius. A CENTURY OF THE ENGLISH NOVEL (NY: Century, 1925), pp. 379, 382, 433–34, 437, 441, 479.

EMF's attack on conventions is original. He writes of cultivated people, as Henry Handel Richardson does. Both novelists reveal the influence of the later, psychologically oriented George Gissing. EMF can bestow personality with a touch; his people are often painfully real. His characters make fateful mistakes—sometimes accidentally, sometimes predictably. The intimacy of his knowledge of people is at times "appalling." An absence of richness may tell against his permanent reputation. D. H. Lawrence, James Stephens, EMF, and Francis Brett Young are the best of the novelists who have emerged in the period 1910–1925.

1926

185 Bullett, Gerald. "E. M. Forster," MODERN ENGLISH FICTION: A PERSONAL VIEW (Lond: Herbert Jenkins, 1926), pp. 70–85.

EMF's work elicits contrary reactions—admiration and dislike—because of his unexpectedness, elusiveness, and embodiment of contradictory qualities. "He is at once tolerant and fastidious, sensitive and sensible, passionate and cool." In *Howards End* his constant theme is the conflict between the commercial civilization of the Wilcoxes and the culture of the Schlegel sisters that stresses an inner rather than a material reality. Helen Schlegel's sudden intoxication with Paul Wilcox is believable, but Margaret's attraction to Henry Wilcox remains inexplicable, given the individual that she is. Henry reveals obtuseness, narrow-mindedness, and complacency; and his charm is stated rather than conveyed. After the marriage the collision between Margaret and Henry becomes inevitable. The Wilcoxes lack the "coordinating imagination" that would save them from hypocrisy; they lack a sense of complexity, ultimately of charity. The catastrophe and the reconciliation in the last chapter are difficult to credit, but the affection that binds the sisters is firmly realized.

EMF again shows a lack of probability in the postponement of the engaged lovers' kiss in *A Room with a View* and in Adela Quested's retraction of her charge against Aziz in *A Passage to India*. In the early books, theme sometimes obtrudes at the expense of story: old Mr. Emerson in *Room* is too directly an embodiment of EMF's point of view and reveals also a failure in EMF's tact and humor. His work remains "exquisite, penetrating, and urbane." His style has charm, his total work a pervasive wisdom; his work is as truthful as it is subtle. The element of commentary is a quality of the fiction rather than a blemish. Like many other contemporary writers, EMF combines the qualities of fiction and essay in his books. EMF has also, with notable success, arrived close to innermost reality in his fiction. [Important earlier account.]

186 Drew, Elizabeth A. THE MODERN NOVEL: SOME ASPECTS OF CONTEMPORARY FICTION (NY: Harcourt, Brace, 1926), pp. 35–36; rptd Port Washington, NY: Kennikat P, 1967.
Like Conrad in his fiction, EMF in *A Passage to India* refuses to make absolute statements, since life is unpredictable, complicated, impenetrable, formidable, and provisional. The futilities and frustrations in the lives of Indians and English alike are emphasized, as an indifferent cosmos surrounds and impinges on them.

187 "E. M. Forster," SIXTEEN AUTHORS: BRIEF HISTORIES, TOGETHER WITH LISTS OF THEIR RESPECTIVE WORKS (NY: Harcourt, Brace, 1926), pp. 7–8.
EMF lives a retired existence in the country and writes carefully and slowly. He is not the active man of the world his education may have trained him to be; he has been a man of leisure and a dedicated artist. His sympathies lie with the past and the East rather than with the present and the West, despite his short residence in India (his long-time sojourn in Alexandria during World War I may have encouraged his Eastern sympathies). His best friend is Syed Ross Masood, an Indian Mohammedan. [Interesting if brief contemporary account.]

188 Kent, Muriel. "A New Study of an Old Problem," HINDUSTAN REVIEW (Allahabad), XLIX (April 1926), 348–49.
EMF's study of the race-consciousness of the British in India is cool and sane in *A Passage to India;* his presentation of the conflict between British and Indians is marked by detachment. EMF's artistic instinct was sound when he made Adela Quested a plain woman, without charm but possessing honesty. The word-pictures in *Passage* are impressive.

189 Moody, William Vaughn, and Robert Morss Lovett. A HISTORY OF ENGLISH LITERATURE (NY: Scribner's, 3rd ed, 1926), pp.

474–75; substantially the same as 1930 and 1935 eds; see also Millett (1943).

In his fiction, EMF illustrates the modern tendency of precision in developing character and in the projection of human relationships. *A Passage to India* is a masterpiece that will survive because of its relevance and art. [Survey of the novels.]

190 Murry, John Middleton. "Lemonade?" ADELPHI, IV (Sept 1926), 139–49; rptd in part as "Proust, Joyce, Forster, and Lawrence," in POETS, CRITICS, MYSTICS: A SELECTION OF CRITICISMS WRITTEN BETWEEN 1919 AND 1955 BY JOHN MIDDLETON MURRY, ed by Richard Rees (Carbondale & Edwardsville: Southern Illinois UP; Lond & Amsterdam: Feffer & Simons, Crosscurrents/Modern Critiques, 1970), pp. 55–58.

Oswald Spengler's THE DECLINE OF THE WEST should be considered in conjunction with four other remarkable books of imagination that could only have been produced in this era: Proust's REMEMBRANCE OF THINGS PAST, Joyce's ULYSSES, D. H. Lawrence's novels from AARON'S ROD to THE PLUMED SERPENT, and EMF's *A Passage to India*. Religiousness shapes a culture, or a period of creativity, which is then succeeded by a civilization. A primary sense of purpose or "religiousness" is present in all symbolisms of literature, and it is necessary for full human reality or greatness. Proust and Joyce lack this sense; Lawrence and EMF possess it. EMF has it more intellectually and tentatively; he has a sense of the otherness of an exotic culture, also of the futility involved when this sense of purpose is lacking (as it is for Mrs. Moore in the Marabar Caves). Thus EMF could visit India, savor its otherness, experience with Mrs. Moore the futility engendered by the Marabar Caves, and comprehend how the echo is symbolic of the lack of purpose in our whole modern life. Proust unconsciously reveals our absence of religiousness; Joyce exhibits it with "blinkered awareness"; EMF is genuinely aware of it, intellectually; and Lawrence realizes it dynamically and reveals religiousness in his fiction, rebelling against a society and an age that do not have it. [Review article on THE DECLINE OF THE WEST. Suggestive account.]

191 Overton, Grant. "An Author You Should Know and Why," MENTOR, XIV (April 1926), 49.

[Note, mostly descriptive, concerning *A Passage to India*.]

192 Watts, Harvey M. "The Real India and the Brahminic Propaganda," LITERARY DIGEST INTERNATIONAL BOOK REVIEW, IV (March 1926), 228–30.

A Passage to India would appear to be a balanced presentation of complex issues if certain Hindu propagandists had not called it a revelation. EMF portrays well the prejudiced British mugwump intellectual and meddler [McBryde, the District Superintendent of Police?]. [Review-essay of recent books on India, including *Passage.*]

1927

193 "Speaking of Books: The Inevitable Leeway," OUTLOOK (NY), CXLVIII (9 Nov 1927), 314–15.

Aspects of the Novel has authority and wide appeal. Though EMF shows that plot and characters are often in conflict, the best books, like EMF's own *A Passage to India* and *A Room with a View*, reveal these elements in "triumphant amity."

194 Benson, E. F. "A Literary Mystification," SPECTATOR (Lond), CXXXIX (29 Oct 1927), 732; rptd in E. M. FORSTER: THE CRITICAL HERITAGE, ed by Philip Gardner (Lond & Boston: Routledge & Kegan Paul, 1973), pp. 329–31.

EMF, in *Aspects of the Novel*, opens many matters but does not pursue them. In describing a novelist's concerns EMF excludes too much: all but the experience of love, for example, from the psychic life. EMF's unfavorable judgments of Meredith and Scott are questionable. *Aspects* is stimulating but lacks sustained thought.

195 Boyd, Ernest. "Readers and Writers," INDEPENDENT, CXIX (3 Dec 1927), 555.

EMF in *Aspects of the Novel* rightly holds that the English novel is not so adult nor so distinguished as the continental novels of Dostoevski, Tolstoy, Flaubert, and Balzac.

196 D., C. [pseud of T. E. Lawrence]. "D. H. Lawrence's Novels," SPECTATOR (Lond), CXXXIX (6 Aug 1927), 223; rptd as "A Review of Novels by D. H. Lawrence," in MEN IN PRINT: ESSAYS IN LITERARY CRITICISM BY T. E. LAWRENCE, ed by A. W. Lawrence (Lond: Golden Cockerel P, 1940), pp. 23–29; and in abrgd form as "T. E. Lawrence on Forster and D. H. Lawrence," in E. M. FORSTER: THE CRITICAL HERITAGE, ed by Philip Gardner (Lond & Boston: Routledge & Kegan Paul, 1973), pp. 317–18.

D. H. Lawrence and EMF were the leading novelists at the beginning of World War I, which profoundly disturbed both of them. They turned from politics and action to character to escape external chaos. They are similar yet contrasting figures. EMF is a comic writer drawing typical characters;

Lawrence seeks always the individual. EMF is clever and subtle; at his best, Lawrence has a shattering simplicity and marked poetic intensity. [Review of Lawrence's THE PLUMED SERPENT.]

197 Deutsch, Babette. "How to Tell a Plot from a Story," NEW YORK EVENING POST, 19 Nov 1927, p. 6.
EMF tells us nothing new but illuminates the art of the novel for us. [Summary account of *Aspects of the Novel.*]

198 "East and West," NEW STATESMAN, XXIV (4 June 1927), 253.
EMF's *A Passage to India* is better written than Edward Thompson's AN INDIAN DAY. Thompson's book reveals a greater and more precise knowledge of Indian life, however. Thompson's rendition of India under the English is more concrete than EMF's. Both Thompson and EMF have the same purpose: to show how complex the problem of the English in India really is. Thompson has therefore no reason to be defensive about *Passage.* [Review of Thompson's AN INDIAN DAY.]

199 [Editorial comment], NEW STATESMAN, Literary Supplement, IX (5 Nov 1927), ix.
[Stresses the expertise of EMF's colloquial method revealed in *Aspects of the Novel.*]

200 Ford, Ford Madox. "Cambridge on the Caboodle," SATURDAY REVIEW OF LITERATURE (NY), IV (17 Dec 1927), 449–50.
Early in the century EMF was the leading influence on the Hampstead intelligentsia; Ford was thus put off from reading him, but he did read *A Room with a View* and became EMF's warm admirer though aware of "his aspect of aloofness, awfulness, chaste reason, tenuity, sobriety." EMF's attitude toward the art of the novel is lacking in seriousness. EMF reveals, unfortunately, the attitude of the Cambridge don toward serious subjects in *Aspects of the Novel* in his remark that Gide was a little too "solemn . . . at the whole caboodle." An element of dedication, of *saeva indignatio,* is lacking in EMF's view of the novelist and his craft. EMF gives us too little of his own problems and experiences as an artist. His ahistorical approach denigrates the seriousness of the novel since the novel does have a history; this approach also slights the difficulties involved in technique and the fact that technique evolves. [Review article on *Aspects.* Ford failed to see that EMF's relaxed attitude is consonant with seriousness and that the informal approach does not dominate the book: see EMF's well-reasoned and provocative remarks on plot, prophecy, pattern rhythm, etc. Ford left us no book as a technician in the novel comparable to EMF's.]

201 H[artley], L. P. "The Novel," SATURDAY REVIEW (Lond), CXLIV (17 Dec 1927), 858–59; rptd in E. M. FORSTER: THE CRITI-

CAL HERITAGE, ed by Philip Gardner (Lond & Boston: Routledge & Kegan Paul, 1973), pp. 336–38.

EMF's charm of style and his elegant, controversial manners predispose us in favor of the ideas set forth in *Aspects of the Novel*. He is sometimes too exclusive in his range, not mentioning Balzac, Stendhal, and Turgenev, for instance. He is excellent in seeing resemblances between novelists and has succeeded in "cutting several royal roads through his subject."

202 Heurgon, Jacques. "Les Romans de E. M. Forster" (The Novels of E. M. Forster), REVUE DE PARIS, CXCIX (April 1927), 701–9; rptd and trans as "The Novels of E. M. Forster," in E. M. FORSTER: THE CRITICAL HERITAGE, ed by Philip Gardner (Lond & Boston: Routledge & Kegan Paul, 1973), pp. 297–305.

EMF's greatest gifts are his inventing strong and vivid detail, his power of discrimination, and his firm intelligence. He has held to the rights of the individual against institutions. His characters must decide whether a given situation or value is real. In *Howards End* EMF finds reality in uniting the man of the world with a woman of sensibility, in uniting action and thought. The same theme of the nature of reality is explored with greater objectivity, immediacy, and fullness in *A Passage to India*. EMF is in the symbolist tradition in his search for a reality that transcends the immediate and the physical. [In French.]

203 Hutchison, Percy. "E. M. Forster Discusses The Art of the Novel," NEW YORK TIMES BOOK REVIEW, 27 Nov 1927, p. 2.

EMF may be unduly harsh in *Aspects of the Novel* upon English literature in comparison with Russian. He is an original mind approaching "a fairly threadbare subject" in an original way.

204 L., R. "What Author, Please?" NEW REPUBLIC, XLIX (19 Jan 1927), 248–49.

[Commentary on *Anonymity: An Enquiry*. Agrees with EMF's ideas as presented in his essay.]

205 Mirsky, D. S. "Literary History and Criticism," LONDON MERCURY, XVII (Dec 1927), 208–10.

Aspects of the Novel has informality, freshness, and wisdom. EMF is fundamentally a moralist, and his approach to fiction is ethical. He is interested in character and in prophecy and has an antifeminist bent. EMF has little interest in the style of novelists, and this is a chief limitation of his criticism.

206 "Mr. Forster on the Novel," TIMES LITERARY SUPPLEMENT (Lond), 3 Nov 1927, p. 784.

The final impression conveyed in *Aspects of the Novel* is not merely a sense of the continuity of the English novel but its peculiar and intrinsic reality, which is different from the reality of everyday life. The wit and vigor of EMF's writing is noteworthy, revealing as it does "the apparent mischief of Mr. Forster's businesslike manner." [Informed, lucid summary of contents.]

207 "New Books in Brief Review," INDEPENDENT, CXIX (24 Dec 1927), 637.

Aspects of the Novel lacks the defects but also some of the virtues of scholarly writing: precision and definiteness. The book is worth reading, although EMF does not elucidate fully "the principles which he practices so deftly."

208 Priestley, J. B. THE ENGLISH NOVEL (Lond: Ernest Benn, Benn's Essex Library, 1927), pp. 144–45.

EMF forms a complete contrast with Galsworthy; he cares little for breadth and is subtle, and he does not provide a realistic transcription of life. With EMF characters are often vague and incidents absurd; there is something freakish and attenuated about his world in which will and passion scarcely exist. His style is evocative rather than descriptive; he goes after an essential reality. He stays on the surface, then suddenly plunges to the depths of a character's mind.

209 Richards, I. A. "A Passage to Forster: Reflections on a Novelist," FORUM, LXXVIII (Dec 1927), 914–20; rptd in FORSTER: A COLLECTION OF CRITICAL ESSAYS, ed by Malcolm Bradbury (Englewood Cliffs, NJ: Prentice-Hall, Spectrum Books, 1966), pp. 15–20.

EMF's odd or special quality is not very usual; it impregnates his whole writing and is difficult to isolate. In his early books his characters are less social studies than embodiments of moral forces. *Where Angels Fear to Tread* is nearer to being a mystery play than a comedy of manners. Part of his difficulty for the reader is his adherence always to the concrete facts, to the actuality rather than to abstractions. His real audience is youth at the point when it is trying to cast off conventions without seeing how difficult it is to do so. His readers, as they grow older, feel less sympathy with his directness than they did when young. He offers his discomfiting vision in an urbane manner, yet his work is more pessimistic than that of any other writer one can readily cite. The rawness, crudeness, and violence of *The Longest Journey* reveal the intensity of EMF's dissatisfaction with things as they are. His fiercely critical sense of values revealed in *Journey* resulted in revolt but has since led to "an almost weary pessimism." In *Pharos and Pharillon* and *A Passage to India* he consoled himself by the cultivation of a less militant and more humorous irony. He has become the observer of whom he had disapproved in *Angels* (Philip Herriton). But he is still dissatisfied with the artificial, the spurious, the institutional. He embraces the spontaneous as his final standard; to his hatred of the nonspontaneous we owe much in the books that may seem unconnected and accidental. His great theme is a preoccupation with the continuance of life that is almost mystical in intensity. When automatisms and social pressures threaten continuity, he is most concerned. Rickie's dream in *Journey* in which his mother's spirit says, "Let them die out," is one of the most dreadful dreams in fiction. *Howards End* is the book that best represents, despite its defects, the several sides of EMF's value. The conflict, not completely resolved, between the theme of survival and the theme of class conflict disqualifies it from being one of the world's great novels. When Margaret Schlegel tells her sister Helen of her engagement, the subsequent description of the Purbeck Hills scenery is excessive. The relations of the Wilcoxes with the Schlegels is best defined through their contacts with Leonard Bast; he is crude as compared with the Schlegels, feeble as compared with the Wilcoxes, but a victim and "horribly alive." Leonard is best presented in his life with Jacky; and this part of the book is masterful. Leonard is less alive when the theme is survival. Charles Wilcox and Mrs. Wilcox are free from this subtle inner disharmony because they represent respectively the outer and the inner in its purity and are not used for a double purpose. Leonard's being given a child is arbitrary, though we understand why EMF wants him to live on. [An interesting essay, still of value, especially in its discussion of Leonard Bast.]

210 Shanks, Edward. "Mr. E. M. Forster," LONDON MERCURY, XVI (July 1927), 265–74; rptd in E. M. FORSTER: THE CRITICAL HERITAGE, ed by Philip Gardner (Lond & Boston: Routledge & Kegan Paul, 1973), pp. 306–16.

Howards End is the culminating book of the early novels. EMF's books are subjective; their note is "considerate impartiality, verging at times on vacillation." His novels reveal their own inconclusiveness, his disabling sense (as with Rickie Elliot in *The Longest Journey*) that good and evil are forever locked in combat with each other. This personal or moral difficulty, dramatized in his fiction, becomes "the active principle of his genius." His novels treat of dichotomies and polarities, and his mind actively balances the claims of each contrasting entity. EMF is on the side of the dynamic and vital but also recognizes the claims of the material and the traditional. The first four novels mirror the intellectual life of 1890–1914 with its heavy emphasis on the need for culture, even at a remove from the life of the world. EMF tends to balance his judgments, and the result is "an action of low tones, of suppressed crises." Though the crises are mental and subtly conveyed, they are often punctured by violence, especially sudden death. The violence is sometimes aesthetically unfortunate and does not consort well with an art that is mainly "dispassionately evocative" or "compassionately ironical." He is more successful in establishing a compassionate irony

in his interior scenes than in the world outside. He does evoke this outside
world consummately in *Where Angels Fear to Tread.* He loses some of his
spontaneous vision when he seeks for deeper expression as in *Journey.* In
Howards End the conflicts are fuller, and the characters convince by "a
transcending artistic necessity" rather than by EMF's conscious efforts. His
vision of life is now so certain that he does not need to draw explicit
conclusions from his materials. In "The Story of the Siren," there exists a
wonder that is "meaningless" yet "full of unattainable meanings." There is
"demurely bloodless gaiety" in *Pharos and Pharillon. A Passage to India*
is EMF's masterpiece. He has overweighted the political, presenting his
imagined events as if they must have happened. Fielding is too consciously
a mediator between the races and comments too explicitly on a local political situation. EMF's impartiality prevents him from arriving at any conclusions when discussing politics. *Passage* is not so much a political novel as
"an agonized and delighted contemplation of the contrasts of different
kinds of life." A balance is maintained in *Passage* between effort expended
by EMF and his attained purpose. EMF convincingly reveals life in all its
diversity in *Passage,* and he has laid aside all schemes and formulas. The
comedy surrounding Aziz and his friends in his illness, the slow and inevitable death of Mrs. Moore, and the brilliant impressionism in "Temple" are
noteworthy. In *Passage* EMF achieves a state of transcendent understanding, "the poetic state of mere wonder," and he also convinces his readers.
[A brilliant essay of permanent value.]

211 "Speaking of Books: 'The Inevitable Leeway,'" OUTLOOK
(NY), CXLVII (9 Nov 1927), 314–15.
Aspects of the Novel will appeal to everyone interested in the reading or
writing of fiction. EMF's conception of the omnipresent conflict between
plot and character is resolved in *A Passage to India* and *A Room with a View*
where "people and plot have achieved triumphant amity." [Summary of
Aspects.]

212 Woolf, Virginia. "Is Fiction an Art?" NEW YORK HERALD TRIB-
UNE BOOKS, 16 Oct 1927, pp. 1, 5–6; rvd and rptd as "The Art of
Fiction," NATION AND ATHENAEUM, Literary Supplement, 12 Nov
1927, pp. 247–48; rvd essay rptd in THE MOMENT AND OTHER ES-
SAYS (Lond: Hogarth P, 1947; NY: Harcourt, Brace, 1948), pp.
106–12; in COLLECTED ESSAYS (Lond: Hogarth P, 1966; NY: Harcourt, Brace & World, 1967), II, 51–55; and E. M. FORSTER: THE
CRITICAL HERITAGE, ed by Philip Gardner (Lond & Boston: Routledge & Kegan Paul, 1973), pp. 332–36.
In *Aspects of the Novel* EMF organizes his discussion formally, but his
method is relaxed, as befits a discussion of his charming and multiform
subject. In his remarks on Scott he dismisses perhaps too readily Scott's

great creativity by saying that Scott knows only how to tell a story. The criticism of fiction needs to work from firmer principles and to be practiced more rigorously than EMF apparently wishes. His judgments on Meredith, Hardy, and James imply that he is more involved with the life that goes into fiction than with the fiction itself. [EMF's unaesthetic attitude leads Mrs. Woolf to the conclusion that critics are not enough concerned with the art of fiction. But EMF's book and his sensitivity lead her to hope that eventually the idea of fiction may be enlarged. Essay is much condensed (though the argument remains the same) as "The Art of Fiction."]

213 Woolf, Virginia. "The Novels of E. M. Forster," ATLANTIC MONTHLY, CXL (Nov 1927), 642–48; rptd in THE DEATH OF THE MOTH AND OTHER ESSAYS (NY: Harcourt, Brace; Lond: Hogarth P, 1942), pp. 104–12; in COLLECTED ESSAYS (Lond: Hogarth P, 1966; NY: Harcourt, Brace & World, 1967), I, 342–51; in part in A LIBRARY OF LITERARY CRITICISM: MODERN BRITISH LITERATURE, ed by Ruth Z. Temple and Martin Tucker (NY: Frederick Ungar, 1966), I, 308–10; in part in E. M. FORSTER: "A PASSAGE TO INDIA": A CASEBOOK, ed by Malcolm Bradbury (Lond: Macmillan, 1970), pp. 73–76; and in E. M. FORSTER: THE CRITICAL HERITAGE, ed by Philip Gardner (Lond & Boston: Routledge & Kegan Paul, 1973), pp. 319–28.

There is something perplexing in the nature of EMF's talent. He is a keen social observer, but this kind of observation is not an end in itself; it leads to a desire to escape the mundane and to that balance of forces which emerges as a structural principle in his novels: "Sawston implies Italy; timidity, wildness; convention, freedom; unreality, reality." Beneath the objects of reality, its people, and its conventions lies the soul, reality, truth, poetry, love. EMF achieves this further reality when he is least intent on doing so, for example, in the great scene at the opera in *Where Angels Fear to Tread.* In *The Longest Journey* he accentuates the opposition of "truth and untruth; Cambridge and Sawston; sincerity and sophistication"; he sees beauty and the prison from which she must be extricated. "A mocking spirit of fantasy" is at odds with his seriousness; there is a central tension between an Austenesque gift of social comedy and the impulses of a poet. He tries to weld "satire and sympathy; fantasy and fact; poetry and a prim moral sense." *Journey* does not produce the unified impression that EMF hoped for; he has not mastered his perspective. He is both a prose artist and a prophetic, didactic writer. His artistic merits are "an exquisite prose style, an acute sense of comedy, a power of creating characters in a few strokes which live in an atmosphere of their own"; but he is also the bearer of a message. He strives for an Ibsenian combination of realism and mysticism; he attempts to unite the reality of the suburb with that of the soul. In his attempts to connect the actual with its inward and universal meaning, he is not always successful. He is unable to make the solid object "luminously transparent" at the same time. He is too much the observer; his objects have too much solid reality for them to take on an ineffable, symbolical dimension. The gap between the real and the symbolical is fatal—it makes us doubt both realms of experience; his ambiguities are not always adequately formulated. He did not attain an adequate subject until *Howards End*, which if it fails is still impressive. *Howards End* has "elaboration, skill, wisdom, penetration, beauty"; but these elements do not fuse and cohere. The novel lacks force. The characters impress, but the complete effect is less satisfying than in *Angels*. His perspective continually changes from the poetic back to the factual, so that the lyrical passages in the novel are blurred. The characters are real, the ordering of the story is skilled, intelligence is in the atmosphere, reality and the sham engage in significant conflict, the comedy is shrewd, and the observation excellent; then EMF's presence obtrudes and his effects are dissipated; we are shoved from the world of imagination to that of theory. (This stricture is not true of the comic scenes.) EMF is less an obtruding presence in *A Passage to India;* his characters are more free, his world is larger, the double vision is in the process of becoming single, and he has almost succeeded in charging the observed facts with spiritual light. [A well-reasoned, judicious, if severe essay that represents the line taken by F. R. Leavis, "E. M. Forster" (1938) and Walter Allen, THE ENGLISH NOVEL (1954); most present critics attribute to EMF a more organic fusion of fact and symbol than Woolf finds.]

214 Zabel, Morton Dauwen. "Competitive Criticisms," COMMONWEAL, VII (26 Dec 1927), 880.

Howards End represents a culmination of EMF's early works. There is in all of them a balance between thought and art, as EMF defines the conflicts between sense and spirit, scourges cant and hypocrisy, and penetrates to "life's soundest truth and saving beauty." In *A Passage to India* EMF enlarges his art and thought. In *Aspects of the Novel* he evinces the same creative vigor. *Aspects* is notable for its wit, incisiveness, and flexible style. EMF rejects the easy or expeditious in his critical discourse as in his fiction. EMF's central premise would be: "Not by technical mastery alone were the great novels written, neither by an ogling omniscience about life." [Important and incisive review of *Aspects*, with much general commentary.]

1928

---

215 Asper. "Reading and Writing: Other Books," NEW YORKER, IV (19 May 1928), 97.

The Eternal Moment and Other Stories suggests that EMF is better at short story writing than at writing novels. "The Machine Stops" is a satire on our mechanical civilization; "The Eternal Moment" is the best in the volume. The stories herald *A Passage to India.*

216 B., A. S. "Hommage à Monsieur Forster (By an Indian)," NATION AND ATHENAEUM, XLIII (4 Aug 1928), 589–91; rptd in E. M. FORSTER: THE CRITICAL HERITAGE, ed by Philip Gardner (Lond & Boston: Routledge & Kegan Paul, 1973), pp. 289–92.

EMF's sympathy for India is that of the artist, a sympathy conjoined with detachment. We respond to it by submitting to a new orientation. EMF humanized the Easterner in English literature; "he is the first to raise grotesque legendary creatures and terracotta figures to the dignity of human beings." The position of the Indian visitor in England has much improved as a result of *A Passage to India.*

217 Beer, Thomas. "In Six Fantasies, E. M. Forster Freshens Stale Conceptions and Credits His Readers with Sense," NEW YORK EVENING POST, 12 May 1928, p. 8.

EMF is elusive rather than didactic; he gets new meaning from worn materials as in "The Machine Stops." In this story (and elsewhere in *The Eternal Moment and Other Stories*) he contracts rather than dilates "his scales." He also knows what not to do in the way of suggestion. His powers of establishing scene and incident are extraordinary, and he conveys consummately "the awkwardness of living."

218 Beresford, J. D. "E. M. Forster and the Anarchist," NEW ADELPHI, I (June 1928), 366–67.

In *Aspects of the Novel* EMF is impatient with the canons of literary criticism and with the need to formulate principles by which to consider the novel.

219 "Books in Brief," NATION (NY), CXXVI (8 Feb 1928), 169.

In *Aspects of the Novel* EMF has presented truths that are so fundamental and simple that they often escape formulation.

220 "Briefer Mention," DIAL, LXXXIV (March 1928), 255.

Despite EMF's candor and informality, *Aspects of the Novel* contains many profound truths about the writing of fiction. His undogmatic mind and his humor make him persuasive.

221 Chevalley, Abel. "Temps—Histoire—Roman" (Time—History—The Novel), REVUE DE LITTÉRATURE COMPARÉE (Paris), VII (April 1928), 205–41.

In *Aspects of the Novel* EMF is an "enemy of Time," considered as a factor in understanding novels and their history. As an enemy of time and of categories, he is inconsistent, for he introduces many such categories of his own, including "seven" aspects of the novel. Modernity tends to ignore historic and specific time as an important element in the novel and the artist's vision and disregards the fact that the artist's unique vision is rooted in a definite time (he expresses something never before expressed and that something has actual basis in fact, and by implication, in time). If art is immutable to a degree, it is also the function of criticism to understand the work of art in relation to its own milieu and time. EMF would make an absolute of the novel and eliminate from it the element of time (in its aspects of succession and duration), the expression of which may, in fact, reach its ultimate in the novel. He is uninformed on historical fact, attributing to a writer like Defoe an originality that he did not possess, as the female rogue had been a staple in narrative before Defoe's age. EMF does better with contemporary writers, when so great an historical transplantation is not necessary. EMF does not see that in order to get beyond time in our judgments we must pass through time and assimilate it, not reject it out of hand. These considerations account for EMF's impatience with the story as a temporal element in the novel. His best chapters in *Aspects* are those which depend least upon an active sense of history working in the critic, those on "Fantasy," "Prophecy," and "Pattern and Rhythm." In life, as in viewing the novel, people are either the enemies or the friends of time. Certain modern historians (as enemies of time) tend to deny the validity of the historical fact as such, and they regard the past as inhering in the present, and both as reaching their apogee in the future. The novel is by nature realistic, dealing with an objective reality in an apprehensible time, with historical elements concretely there. As we view social and psychological reality, we should discern a temporal succession as well as unbroken duration, discontinuity as well as continuity. The novelist and the historian have the same problem: to recover the past. But the novelist does so in a more imaginative, personal way. Time, history, and the novel can help an individual define his identity through the concretions that ultimately compose each. Time, history, and the novel do not exist just to dissolve such an identity. [Long and closely argued essay, relating EMF to some of the philosophic currents of the age and viewing these critically.] [In French.]

222 Connolly, Cyril. "New Novels," NEW STATESMAN, XXX (31 March 1928), 796–97; rptd in E. M. FORSTER: THE CRITICAL HERITAGE, ed by Philip Gardner (Lond & Boston: Routledge & Kegan Paul, 1973), p. 340.

The stories in *The Eternal Moment and Other Stories* are, except for the title story, visions of judgment or of the machine age, revealing EMF's characteristic "demure malice." They are all excellent, if slight—pagan, supernatural, youthful in the best sense. "The Eternal Moment" is weaker, although within it there is present all of EMF's world. He is unable to describe a woman to make her appear attractive or a crisis so that it is real.

223 Cross, Wilbur L. THE MODERN ENGLISH NOVEL: AN ADDRESS BEFORE THE AMERICAN ACADEMY OF ARTS AND LETTERS (New Haven: Yale UP; Lond: Humphrey Milford, Oxford UP, 1928), pp. 17, 19.

EMF in *A Passage to India* captures the soul of India as Kipling did not. Kipling was a romancer; EMF is a psychologist. In *Passage* he presents the native as he appears to himself, as he appears to the British official, and as he is when his mind is laid bare, away from the influence of the West.

224 Cross, Wilbur. "Novelists at a Round Table," YALE REVIEW, nsXVII (July 1928), 792–94.

EMF in *Aspects of the Novel* stresses similarities in temperament as uniting novelists of different eras rather than influences operating historically from early novelists to later ones. Contrary to EMF's views, English and continental novelists differ not so much in art and aesthetic quality as in the traditions from which they spring; it is misleading thus to elevate continental novelists over the English. EMF rightly says that the novelist presents us with characters that we know more fully in his art than we could in life.

225 Dandieu, Arnaud. "*Les Aspects du Roman:* E. M. Forster contre le Temps" (*Aspects of the Novel:* E. M. Forster Against the Times), BULLETIN DE L'ASSOCIATION FRANCE–GRANDE BRETAGNE, N. 75 (April 1928), 1–7.

EMF's theorizing in *Aspects of the Novel* is more amusing and penetrating than that of any other critic. There are two objections to EMF's book: (1) the English novel is not necessarily inferior to the Russian or French; (2) EMF's attack on historicism is not justified (the institutions of an age do cause modifications in human nature that is not, in fact, unchanging, as EMF asserts). [In French.]

226 "E. M. Forster's Stories," SPRINGFIELD SUNDAY UNION AND REPUBLICAN, 20 May 1928, p. 7F.

In EMF's vein of fantasy the best story is "The Machine Stops"; "The Eternal Moment" is a brilliant and skillful character study. The stories in *The Eternal Moment and Other Stories* are more substantial than are most such exercises in fantasy.

227 Frierson, William C. "Casual Criticism," SEWANEE REVIEW, XXXVI (July 1928), 376–77.

Aspects of the Novel is "the only adequate analysis of fiction in the language." EMF is at his best when he "rambles."

228 Hartley, L. P. "New Fiction," SATURDAY REVIEW (Lond), CXLV (28 April 1928), 530–32; rptd in E. M. FORSTER: THE CRITICAL HERITAGE, ed by Philip Gardner (Lond & Boston: Routledge & Kegan Paul, 1973), pp. 348–49.

Criticism of EMF is difficult because he so well attains his purpose and because he writes with such polish. But when one considers subject, the ironic fantastic tales in *The Eternal Moment and Other Stories* do not seem entirely satisfying. They are expressions of dissatisfaction that avoid moral indignation but sometimes descend into querulousness. EMF starts from the premise that the letter killeth and the spirit giveth life; but the spirit is too often identified with a fanciful race of Panlike and faunlike figures. "The Story of the Siren" and "The Eternal Moment," in particular, are enjoyable and impressive.

229 Kronenberger, Louis. "E. M. Forster in the Vein of Fantasy," NEW YORK TIMES BOOK REVIEW, 6 May 1928, p. 9.

For those who like fantasy, EMF's stories in *The Eternal Moment and Other Stories* will appeal, especially "The Machine Stops," which is original in showing the breakdown of the machine age. "The Point of It" is EMF's one failure in fantasy. "The Eternal Moment," not a fantasy, is the best story of all, showing in Miss Raby "the impotence of both fine intelligence and fine emotion" when there is no one to appreciate them.

230 M., C. "The Human Scale," MANCHESTER GUARDIAN (20 April 1928), p. 7; rptd in E. M. FORSTER: THE CRITICAL HERITAGE, ed by Philip Gardner (Lond & Boston: Routledge & Kegan Paul, 1973), pp. 344–45.

By the standard expressed in "The Machine stops," man is the measure. By this criterion, "The Eternal Moment" is the best story in *The Eternal Moment and Other Stories*, and "Mr. Andrews" next. The other stories, such as "The Machine Stops," are not quite successful in contrasting a human reality with a mechanical dream or nightmare. These stories represent the inventive stage of a writer who has since come to the stage of creation.

231 Manly, John Matthews, and Edith Rickert. CONTEMPORARY BRITISH LITERATURE: OUTLINES FOR STUDY, INDEXES, BIBLIOGRAPHIES (NY: Harcourt, Brace, 1928), pp. 143–44.

[Secondary bibliography enlarged from 1921 ed.]

232 Marble, Annie Russell. "Novelists of Anglo-India," A STUDY OF THE MODERN NOVEL, BRITISH AND AMERICAN SINCE 1900 (NY & Lond: D. Appleton, 1928), pp. 43, 97, 110–15, 228, espec 113–14.

EMF's *A Passage to India* reflects his sharp observation and a bias toward the philosophy of Nietzsche. He has analyzed well the Hindu mind and the Anglo-Indian. The tendency of the work is toward pessimism, though the will to live survives.

233 Muir, Edwin. "The Eternal Moment," NATION AND ATHENAEUM, XLIII (12 May 1928), 184; rptd in E. M. FORSTER: THE CRITICAL HERITAGE, ed by Philip Gardner (Lond & Boston: Routledge & Kegan Paul, 1973), pp. 351–52.

In fantasy, the justice and originality of EMF's imagination are best displayed. The quality of genius—doing what no one else can—is better displayed in *The Eternal Moment and Other Stories* than in *A Passage to India*. The best stories are deliberately symbolical: "The Point of It" and "The Story of the Siren." In "The Point of It" the evocation of Hell is psychologically profound. "The Story of the Siren" impresses by its suggestive and sheer imaginative power. The other stories are less convincing. In "The Machine Stops" EMF does not write as well about the future as when he writes about Heaven and Hell.

234 Muir, Edwin. THE STRUCTURE OF THE NOVEL (Lond: Hogarth P, Hogarth Lectures on Literature, No. 6, 1928), pp. 8, 10, 13–15, 25–26, 49–50, 135–46; later imprints apparently unrvd.

EMF reveals an impatience with "form" in *Aspects of the Novel:* his instincts are correct, since "structure" is a more flexible and inclusive concept for the organization of fiction. EMF rightly states, with respect to James's excessive patterning, "All that is prearranged is false." Discussions of form in *Aspects* depend upon question-begging terms originating in James; some of these terms have been popularized by EMF, e.g., "pattern" and "rhythm." EMF is critical of Hardy's insufficiency of psychic causality, but he overlooks Hardy's powers of invention. There is a distinction between the novel of character (inhabited by individuals who do not change but who are progressively revealed and are therefore examples of EMF's "flat" characters) and dramatic novels (inhabited by individuals who change and develop and are examples of EMF's "round" characters). EMF has a begrudging attitude toward "flat" characters, although his discussion of them is sound, particularly his view that they must surprise us. EMF does not realize that such characters, if not fully developed, have a richer and fuller life than the idiosyncrasy that defines each one of them. [Muir is concerned with the novel considered organically, with structure rather than form. He also defines "romance" (emphasis on action), chronicle (panoramic novel of universal import), and period novel (emphasis on the recording of social fact at a given time), but EMF does not figure into this part of the discussion. Numerous incidental references to *Aspects.*]

235 "The New Books," SATURDAY REVIEW OF LITERATURE (NY), V (13 Oct 1928), 250.

In the stories of *The Eternal Moment and Other Stories* fantasy has "gravity and intention," the underlying motif being that the heightened moments of experience, whether ecstatic or painful, must be accepted for the insight they give and the salvation that they afford ("Mr. Andrews," "The Story of the Siren"). Passivity is the first stage on the road to Hell (see "The Machine Stops" and "The Point of It"). Story and allegory are perfectly fused in "The Point of It."

236 "New Fiction," SCOTSMAN (Edinburgh), 20 April 1928, p. 2.
The stories in *The Eternal Moment and Other Stories* suggest a preoccupation with what lies beyond life or the incomplete present; into this realm man feels compelled to project his imagination. In "The Eternal Moment" there is more a note of irony than of mystery.

237 "New Novels," TIMES LITERARY SUPPLEMENT (Lond), 5 April 1928, p. 256; rptd in E. M. FORSTER: THE CRITICAL HERITAGE, ed by Philip Gardner (Lond & Boston: Routledge & Kegan Paul, 1973), pp. 341–42.
In the stories of *The Eternal Moment and Other Stories* mood and substance are more important than method. EMF's emphasis is on the theme "only connect." He is searching for "the true essence of life," perhaps impatiently, as if seeking too easy an explanation for the fatuity of existence.

238 "New Novels," TIMES (Lond), 30 March 1928, p. 22.
EMF's intention to cease writing fantasy is regrettable. No one has better expressed the fear of the machine and man's enslavement to it than EMF has done in "The Machine Stops." [Review of *The Eternal Moment and Other Stories.*]

239 "Novel Notes," BOOKMAN (Lond), LXXIV (May 1928), 138; rptd in E. M. FORSTER: THE CRITICAL HERITAGE, ed by Philip Gardner (Lond & Boston: Routledge & Kegan Paul, 1973), pp. 349–50.
EMF's gift is his sense of the idiosyncrasies in human character and his sense of a spiritual power that sustains his people. These pre-1914 stories do not date. "The Machine Stops" is still pertinent in demonstrating the need for personal relationships and the disasters which follow when they are denied. "The Eternal Moment" shows the triumph of modern mechanism and conveniences over "the exquisite verities" of village life in Italia Irredenta. "The Story of the Siren" reveals the tragedy resulting from the denial of the vision of beauty in our lives. The stories are low-toned but posit a belief "in the validity, if not in the temporal triumph, of splendid and eternal things." [Excellent discussion of *The Eternal Moment and Other Stories.*]

240 "Readers' Reports," LIFE AND LETTERS, I (June 1928), 70–71.
In *The Eternal Moment and Other Stories* EMF reworks his old themes: stripping middle age of its "warm and decent clothing" and "tracking the prig" even into the next world (see the dreary hell in "The Point of It" and the dreary heaven in "Mr. Andrews"). Passivity, as in "The Point of It," is the sin against the Holy Ghost. The tone of the stories is spinsterish: weary, distinguished, witty, and irritable (the irritability of the sensitive). "The Machine Stops" lacks the gusto it requires. EMF is a master of foreground detail, though some aspects of his larger scenes elude him.

241 Riding, Laura. "Jocasta," ANARCHISM IS NOT ENOUGH (Garden City, NY; Doubleday, Doran; Cape, 1928), pp. 41–132, espec 48–51.
A Room with a View has charm but is too charming. [It affects Riding as would the sight of a ripe pimple that needs to be squeezed. Protests against the solipsistic and excessively symbolical method of the individual-real in the writing of fiction, wherein everything is strained through the writer's sensibility, represented in the novels of Virginia Woolf and also in EMF's *Room*. The collective-real, to be found in the work of Oswald Spengler is no more adequate as a version of truth; man is only to be defined as he aligns himself with the "unreal."]

242 Ross, Mary. "Forster's Early Tales," NEW YORK HERALD TRIBUNE BOOKS, 22 April 1928, pp. 3–4; rptd in E. M. FORSTER: THE CRITICAL HERITAGE, ed by Philip Gardner (Lond & Boston: Routledge & Kegan Paul, 1973), pp. 346–47.
"The Machine Stops" has much contemporary relevance; all the stories in *The Eternal Moment and Other Stories* reveal a rich vein of fantasy in them. "The Eternal Moment" reveals the clashes between cultures, races, and individualities that were to be developed more fully in *A Passage to India*. The stories are still fresh and provocative, though they represent a mode to which EMF should probably not return (as he himself realizes).

243 S., J. F. "The Eternal Moment," BOSTON EVENING TRANSCRIPT, 12 May 1928, p. 4; rptd in E. M. FORSTER: THE CRITICAL HERITAGE, ed by Philip Gardner (Lond & Boston: Routledge & Kegan Paul, 1973), pp. 353–54.
Fantasy has not really retreated since the war (as EMF maintains in the foreword to *The Eternal Moment and Other Stories*), nor have these stories of his lost their life and significance. They are unusual since they combine irony with fantasy. The irony is especially prevalent and effective in "The Machine Stops." "The Point of It" reveals EMF's implied regret at the passing of Greek ideals of bodily and mental vigor. The otherworldly orientation of "Mr. Andrews" and "Co-ordination" is persuasive. "The Story of

the Siren" is inferior [a minority judgment]. "The Eternal Moment" is not a fantasy but a firm and impressive psychological work, revealing, like all other tales, EMF's obsessive reaction against "progress."

244 Scott-James, R. A. THE MAKING OF LITERATURE: SOME PRINCIPLES OF CRITICISM EXAMINED IN THE LIGHT OF ANCIENT AND MODERN THEORY (NY: Henry Holt; Lond: Martin Secker [1928]), pp. 254, 343–46, 363, 365, 369, 372.

EMF gives too much support to the view that it is art that gives some characters their reality, although elsewhere he says that the novelist, by virtue of his actual experience, knows more about his characters than we can know of actual people. EMF states that the novel, because we know its people perfectly, gives us a truer view of social reality than does history. Even Virginia Woolf and EMF are reluctant to regard art as amenable to judgments based on critical principles, though both also imply at times that the novel is a work of art. But Percy Lubbock in THE CRAFT OF FICTION is too absolute in insisting that the critic of the novel ought to be limited to matters of form and technique. Transcending such considerations is the author's ability to "bounce" us [EMF's expression] into accepting his view of reality. Fiction is more closely related to life than are the other forms of literary art because of the "grossness of its material" [EMF's phrase]. [In working out his Arnoldian view that literature and life are closely related, Scott-James refers to some of EMF's ideas elaborated in *Aspects of the Novel*. Reveals rapid assimilation of the ideas developed in *Aspects*.]

245 Taylor, Rachel Annand. "Hardy's Little Ironies," SPECTATOR (Lond), CXL (7 April 1928), 543–44; rptd in E. M. FORSTER: THE CRITICAL HERITAGE, ed by Philip Gardner (Lond & Boston: Routledge & Kegan Paul, 1973), pp. 343–44.

In *The Eternal Moment and Other Stories*, "The Machine Stops" hardly convinces one that the revolt against the machine has begun; but the genius for rebellion is stronger in most people than in EMF's "conscious and uncertain characters." The fantasies are not so good as those in *The Celestial Omnibus and Other Stories* because EMF has invested existence after death with a nebulous imagery. "The Eternal Moment" is not psychologically true. "The Story of the Siren" is excellent with its "Latin brutality, sharp scepticism, and wild sea-magic." His style has astringent beauty; his comments on humanity are profound. [Review also of THE SHORT STORIES OF THOMAS HARDY.]

246 Taylor, Rachel Annand. "The Post-War English Novel," SOCIOLOGICAL REVIEW (Manchester, England), XX (July 1928), 177–96, espec 192.

EMF's cool disinterestedness toward his characters makes them hard to understand. "The Celestial Omnibus" has more beauty and tenderness than any of the novels, including *A Passage to India*, though this book has an admirable felicity in style. The controlled style is not in tune with the age. EMF has a distaste for inquiring into the hearts of women.

247 Vines, Sherard. MOVEMENTS IN MODERN ENGLISH POETRY AND PROSE (Lond: Oxford UP, 1928), pp. 185, 198, 199, 229, 232–37, 238, 321–26, 327, 347.

EMF's essay "Anonymity" is an instance of the modern tendency to avoid the personal in art. EMF's essay on Virginia Woolf implies that her art is very personal; EMF thus goes contrary to the views expressed in "Anonymity" that great art ranges beyond reflection of the artist's personality. EMF's attempt in "Anonymity" to separate surface personality from the deeper is questionable. *A Passage to India* is a good example of the new didactic writing. It is marked by a sense of ironical justice and by a passionate descriptive faculty; it conveys the lack of atmosphere in India. It is not so well written as Kipling's KIM but comes from a finer spirit. EMF is not as good as Kipling or Tolstoy, but his intelligence is powerful and he has a bardic quality. EMF portrays the elusiveness of India and the difficulty involved in the Anglo-Indians and the natives understanding each other. The white well-wisher is misunderstood by both groups. Unreason is more powerful with the Anglo-Indians than with the Indians. EMF's novel reveals that the didactic is more effective when the work goes beyond the didactic. [Idiosyncratic.]

248 Ward, A. C. TWENTIETH-CENTURY LITERATURE: THE AGE OF INTERROGATION 1901–1925 (Lond: Methuen, 1928), pp. 52, 207; rptd with additions in Ward, A. C. TWENTIETH-CENTURY LITERATURE 1901–1940 (Lond: Methuen, 1940 [7th rvd ed]), and with further additions in TWENTIETH-CENTURY LITERATURE 1901–1950 (Lond: Methuen, 1956 [12th rvd ed]).

The atmosphere of EMF's books is "bracing," but also too "rarefied" for the characters to live full lives; they are overstrung and tend toward hysteria. His style is "luminous" and "sensitive"; his books have beautiful passages; his satire is incisive; and his irony relentlessly relates the trivial cause to the massive effect. His characters, however, seem "caged in the author's mind, unable to escape into actuality."

249 Warren, Dale. "Forster on the Novel," FORUM, LXXIX (March 1928), xii, xv.

The essence of *Aspects of the Novel* is in the chapters "Fantasy" and "Prophecy." Herein EMF strikes out in a new direction. His book is wise, intelligent, and provocative, though the subject still eludes its critic.

250 Williams, Orlo. "Recent Books," CRITERION. VII (Feb 1928), 176–79.

In *Aspects of the Novel* EMF does not give us criticism so much as "reflections upon the problems of novel-writing that occur to an experienced novelist" as he considers those who have written before him. EMF's emphasis is practical and psychological rather than critical. He is best in discussing such questions as the place of the story in a work of fictional art and the difference between characters and living people. EMF seems distressed by the presence of love in fiction. He says nothing decisive about beauty (and pattern), but he is perceptive in writing about fantasy and prophecy. His criticisms are only partial, but his ideas are stimulating. [Perceptive review.]

251 Wilson, Edmund. "Three English Critics," NEW REPUBLIC. LIV (22 Feb 1928), 21–22.

EMF's *Aspects of the Novel* comes out of reading the literature of the novel. The tone is a bit kittenish at times; but, contrary to Ford Madox Ford's view ["Cambridge on the Caboodle," SATURDAY REVIEW OF LITERATURE (1927)], EMF appreciates all kinds of "form" and is actually less parochial than a formalist like Ford, who appreciates only one kind of novel, the Jamesean-Flaubertian. EMF's best discussion is on prophecy, but he reveals a constriction of sympathy when he discusses Henry James and Joyce. [Review of *Aspects*, Edmund Gosse's LEAVES AND FRUIT, and Gilbert Murray's THE CLASSICAL TRADITION IN POETRY.]

252 Woolsey, Dorothy Bacon. "Bards of Passion and of Mirth," NEW REPUBLIC, LVI (29 Aug 1928), 54; rptd in E. M. FORSTER: THE CRITICAL HERITAGE, ed by Philip Gardner (Lond & Boston: Routledge & Kegan Paul, 1973), p. 355.

The tales in *The Eternal Moment and Other Stories* deal with the preternatural and are all tinged with a grim or rueful irony. EMF's prophetic stance is genuine if less intense than D. H. Lawrence's. His accents are those of "unearthly comedy"; ironic pity is the "bardic quality" most apparent in his stories. [Review also of D. H. Lawrence's THE WOMAN WHO RODE AWAY.]

253 Zabel, Morton Dauwen. "Border-Line Fiction," COMMONWEAL, VIII (20 June 1928), 190–91.

The short stories in *The Eternal Moment and Other Stories* date from before World War I and reveal that EMF from the first found a style and viewpoint essentially his own to which he had adhered. The supernatural, indigenous to the novels, is even more patently embodied in the short stories. The conflicts are less realistically oriented than in the novels, and some of the figures in the stories are actual supernatural beings. These tales are characterized by understatement and salient poetic insight. [Penetrating early discussion.]

1929

254 Arns, Karl. "Besprechungen" (Reviews), ENGLISCHE STUDIEN (Leipzig), LXIV (1929), 145–46.

Aspects of the Novel is noteworthy for its cosmopolitan and non-insular quality. EMF is not bound by theory and has intuitive insight into the makeup of a novel. With him technique is less important than morality and atmosphere. He speaks with authority because of his own achievement as novelist. [In German.]

255 Dobrée, Bonamy. "E. M. Forster," THE LAMP AND THE LUTE: STUDIES IN SIX MODERN AUTHORS (Oxford: Clarendon P, 1929), pp. 66–85; 2nd ed as THE LAMP AND THE LUTE: STUDIES IN SEVEN AUTHORS (Lond: Frank Cass; NY: Barnes & Noble, 1964), pp. 65–81; rptd in part in A LIBRARY OF LITERARY CRITICISM: MODERN BRITISH LITERATURE, ed by Ruth Z. Temple and Martin Tucker (NY: Frederick Ungar, 1966), I, 306–7.

EMF is a "newer" novelist who says "this is what people are like" instead of "this is how things happen." With the collapse of religious values, the mind becomes more important as it recognizes and expresses the importance of the personal relation. *Where Angels Fear to Tread* reveals EMF's preoccupation with this subject. He contrasts the respectable (the stronger) and the vital (the brighter), and he values highly the interior life and the various forms of love. He is preoccupied with the nature of reality in *The Longest Journey*. *Howards End* stresses the need to connect the unseen with the seen. Ruth Wilcox hovers over all the characters; she "connects" by affection and by doing nothing. There is danger in EMF's stress upon the personal relation; it makes reality overly mental. In spite of his concern with ideas, EMF's novels are aesthetic entities, and his people are real people, given perspective by his "elfin irony." A "demure seriousness" underlies his satire. His authorial comments do not put us off but allow us to share the intimate lives of his characters and lend excitement to his work. EMF is scrupulous yet is not quite fair, since he makes the people that he dislikes "flat" and lets them attain the social, but not the personal, emotions. His sense of a life-force strengthens the personal relation, as does his stress on emotion, kindness, and "the mother passions." For real greatness his work is not quite "anonymous" enough, and the stress on the personal relation is perhaps too prescriptive. [Essay important in history of EMF's reputation and still of value.]

256 Harwood, H. C. "Recent Tendencies in English Fiction," QUARTERLY REVIEW, CCLII (April 1929), 321–38, espec 326–27 on *A Passage to India*.

A Passage to India is the greatest novel of the century. EMF has advanced "from personal relations to the wide and generally impersonal play of human intercourse." *Howards End* was subtly good and mentally satisfying—almost readable—and this is more than subtle novels usually are. EMF's shyness with respect to the passions may militate against his being accepted by posterity. [Other novels discussed: Aldous Huxley's POINT COUNTER POINT, D. H. Lawrence's THE PLUMED SERPENT, F. Brett Young's PORTRAIT OF CLAIRE, Ford Madox Ford's THE LAST POST, and Virginia Woolf's ORLANDO.]

257 Herrick, Robert. "Hermaphrodites," BOOKMAN (NY), LXIX (July 1929), 485–89, espec 488.

Some qualities such as subtlety are not sexual attributes. *A Passage to India* is subtle but far-reaching in implication. EMF presents with insight the unconscious arrogance and hypocrisy inherent in displays of racial superiority. Though *Passage* is subtle, it has compelling form and meaning and is "male" from beginning to end. [Herrick deplores the tendency of writers of one sex to assume, for negligible reasons, the qualities of the other.]

258 Seldes, Gilbert. "Form and the Novel," BOOKMAN (NY), LXX (Oct 1929), 128–31.

Howards End succeeds by its form despite EMF's contention that the writer's ability to "bounce" his reader is more important than form. [Considers works on the novel by Edwin Muir, Edith Wharton, John Carruthers, Virginia Woolf, Storm Jameson, Ford Madox Ford, Percy Lubbock, and EMF (*Aspects of the Novel*).]

259 Sp[arrow], J[ohn]. "Edward Morgan Forster," ENCYCLOPAEDIA BRITANNICA (NY & Lond: Encyclopaedia Britannica, 14th ed, 1929), IX, 520; in succeeding eds until 1961 ed inclusive.

EMF has two types of characters who live on two different planes: those who live by instinct versus those who live by convention, those who value property and propriety versus those who value personal relationships. He is at home in presenting both worlds. [Short sketch of career.]

1930

260 Thompson, Edward. RECONSTRUCTING INDIA (NY: Dial P, 1930), pp. 39, 41; THE RECONSTRUCTION OF INDIA (Lond: Faber, 1930).

EMF's *A Passage to India* mirrors the division between the races in pre-World War I India. [Thompson resented EMF's book at first but then admired its truthfulness in depicting provincial life in an upcountry station before World War I.]

1931

261 Charteris, Evan. THE LIFE AND LETTERS OF SIR EDMUND GOSSE (Lond: Heinemann; NY: Harper, 1931), 323–24.
Letter to Edward Marsh (27 Dec 1910): Gosse is severely critical of *Howards End;* it does not fulfill the promise of *Where Angels Fear to Tread* or *A Room with a View.* EMF has listened to people who have told him "that he should give more 'story,' and that he should be coarse in morals, and that he should coruscate in style." The book is "sensational and dirty and affected"; it is disgusting for a highbred maiden (Helen Schlegel) to have an illegitimate baby. The closing chapters reveal "lurid sentimentality, preposterous morals, turgid and sickly style." "The real talent of the author is for delicate, ironic painting of straightforward natures." The portrait of Aunt Juley Munt is persuasive: "The quiet lives of people of that type, to whom nothing happens, . . . that is what your author was born to depict." [EMF could shock a genteel critic.]

262 Dilly Tante [pseud of Stanley Kunitz]. "E. M. Forster," LIVING AUTHORS: A BOOK OF BIOGRAPHIES (NY: H. W. Wilson, 1931), pp. 130–31.
EMF's first four novels are an attempt to pronounce upon the eternal conflict between good and evil. In this series, *Howards End* is the final statement. These novels reflect the life of the upper middle classes from about 1890 to 1914. [Description of EMF, evidently from personal observation. Summary of his career, his Indian sojourns, and his books until 1928.]

1932

263 Doughty, Howard N., Jr. "The Novels of E. M. Forster," BOOKMAN (NY), LXXV (Oct 1932), 542–49; rptd in E. M. FORSTER: THE CRITICAL HERITAGE, ed by Philip Gardner (Lond & Boston: Routledge & Kegan Paul, 1973), pp. 356–67.
EMF was caught between the prewar and the postwar world. As Virginia Woolf asserts ["The Novels of E. M. Forster" (1927)], the strains of fantasy, realism, and sociology do not coalesce satisfactorily in his novels. Such lack

of integration is a failure in technique. Like the Fielding of *A Passage to India*, EMF has sacrificed passion to clarity. He has elected to be truthful rather than impressive; D. H. Lawrence at his best could be both truthful and impressive. Like Lawrence, EMF is devoted to anarchic individualism and suspects industrialism and the regimentation it has brought. For EMF the life of the body is fundamental; as it manifests itself in sex and mating, it leads to concepts of generation and continuity so predominant in EMF. For the inner spiritual life to be worthwhile, it must recognize the body, social realities, and the world of action. In *Where Angels Fear to Tread* EMF condemns in Philip Herriton the aestheticism and the indifference that interfere with the life of the spirit. In Rickie Elliot in *The Longest Journey* EMF deals with one of Philip's qualities of mind as a fixed state of character: the tendency to idealize. Though Rickie is likeable and the best of the Elliots, his mother (in Rickie's dream) prefers Stephen Wonham as her true issue and would have the Elliots, including Rickie, die out. Mrs. Elliot is one of the mystic mothers in EMF's fiction who embody racial continuity. Stephen is unreal because he is placed in a social vacuum so that his mythic significance will register clearly. But as Mrs. Elliot's partly mythic son, he has literary verisimilitude. In *A Room with a View* EMF handles the emancipation of women with more insight than H. G. Wells in ANN VERONICA. In *Howards End* EMF is concerned with whether a healthy individual life is possible in modern society. The path of withdrawal and escape is not to be condoned, but the possibilities of nourishment are not great. In *Howards End* EMF impressively presents the truth about a whole society. The Schlegel sisters already exhibit futility in spite of their vitality and responsiveness. With respect to Margaret's marriage to Henry Wilcox, with its portrayal "of a hopeful member of the intelligentsia taking up with a representative of Capital and trying to make it over," we are given the thrust of prewar reform movements. Leonard Bast illustrates what democracy and machinery have done to yeomanry; he is what Stephen might have become if society could have claimed him. It is over Bast that shipwreck occurs: even the Schlegel efforts drive him from bad to worse, and finally to his death. Helen does act, does get her child, does go to the future, does redeem Leonard's past, all with the apparent concurrence of the dead but pervasive Earth Mother, Mrs. Wilcox. The conflict between heart and head is not forcible enough, and the redemptive value of the pastoral life is questionable. Fielding represents what the Schlegel culture leads to: a thorough disillusion. In Fielding's and Mrs. Moore's disillusion EMF has written "finis" to all that Mrs. Wilcox and the Schlegels stood for in *Howards End*. The beneficent Earth Mother had disappeared in the years between *Howards End* and *Passage*. Pessimism characterizes the work of both EMF and Lawrence because a creative balance between the self and society is no longer possible. [Many insights of value in this early discussion.]

264 Lawrence, D. H. THE LETTERS OF D. H. LAWRENCE, ed by Aldous Huxley (Lond: Heinemann; NY: Viking P, 1932), pp. 224, 552, 605, 613, 615, 728, 783–85; rptd except for Postcard to EMF, Summer 1924, in THE COLLECTED LETTERS OF D. H. LAWRENCE, ed by Harry T. Moore (NY: Viking P; Lond: Heinemann, 1962), I, 315, II, 716, 799, 811–12, 1122–25.

Letter to EMF (April 1915) [dated (? Feb 1915) in Harry T. Moore's ed, (1962)]: Glad EMF is not Buddhist in point of view and glad that he can enlist EMF's help in the war "against the fussy Mammon." Letter to EMF (20 Sept 1922): Comments that "glorifying those *business* people in *Howards End*" was a great mistake, because business is no good. Letter to Martin Secker (23 July 1924): Praises *A Passage to India*, but it makes him "wish a bomb would fall and end everything." EMF is too preoccupied with people rather than with the undercurrents of life. Postcard (Summer 1924): Urges EMF to send him *Passage* despite John Middleton Murry's comments about it; his "*Bou-oum* crit.—but even that is better than his *miaow*" [reference is to Murry's "Bou-oum or Ou-boum?" ADELPHI (1924)]. Letter to J. M. Murry (3 Oct 1924): Agrees with Murry that EMF does not understand his Hindu in *Passage* and that India for EMF is negative, but Lawrence feels that EMF does repudiate thoroughly "our white bunk" in India. Letter to Lady Ottoline Morrell (5 Feb 1929): Mentions "a silly, funny little letter from E. M. Forster, telling me à propos of nothing that he admires me but doesn't read me."

265 Leavis, Q. D. FICTION AND THE READING PUBLIC (Lond: Chatto & Windus, 1932), pp. 38, 62, 76–77, 232, 264–65.

The subtlety of EMF's exposure of the inner life in *A Passage to India* contrasts with the lack of subtlety in bestsellers, but *Passage* is one of the few novels since George Eliot's to have reached all levels of the reading public. The terms (*Aspects of the Novel*) to which EMF gave popularity are not useful in the evaluation of literature.

266 Linati, Carlo. "*A Passage to India,*" SCRITTORI ANGLO AMERICANI D'OGGI (Anglo-American Writers of Today) (Milano: Corticelli Editore, [1932]), pp. 117–21.

Considering the prevalence of every type of writing about India, the uniqueness and success of *A Passage to India* is all the more significant. EMF undertakes a study of the complex social and psychological relationships between the English colonial rulers and the native Indians whose traditions are threatened by English domination. EMF first studied this problem in Egypt; and today, it is an even more delicate and dangerous problem because of the emergence of nationalistic sentiment. A multitude of characters and situations are interwoven in the novel as in a chronicle. Scenes, episodes, conversations, glimpses of British functionaries, and glimpses of sensitive and bizarre Indians follow one another against a background of a "vast, brimming, feverish, innocent" India, ruled over by the bright and implacable sun. EMF's style is severe, unadorned, marked by dry dialogue, the narrative often achieving the quality of cutting commentary. His earliest novels established him as not only a writer of sensitivity but as a cunning and biting humorist. *The Longest Journey, Where Angels Fear to Tread, A Room with a View,* and *The Celestial Omnibus* are distinguished by a crystalline style, precise and disillusioned views on the qualities of life and society, and a richness of experience. *Howards End* demonstrates EMF's great evocative power and his unique, magical, pulsating style. After fourteen years EMF again impressed the critics with *Passage,* many of whom had remained loyal to him. [In Italian.]

267 Lovett, Robert Morss, and Helen Sard Hughes. "The Georgians: Edward Morgan Forster," THE HISTORY OF THE NOVEL IN ENGLAND (Boston: Houghton Mifflin, 1932), pp. 416–21.

Viewing EMF as traditionalist we may miss the originality of his work; susceptible to its charm, we may miss its solidity. Three of his five novels have foreign scenes, but his cosmopolitanism is more intellectual and spiritual than geographical. He reveals the effects of mental provincialism and the efforts of ordinary people to transcend it. Provincialism persisted in results in misunderstanding; tolerance is both the reward and the symptom of growth. *Howards End* explores the interaction of rival viewpoints: "smug conservative, prosperous progressive, and aspiring underprivileged." *A Passage to India* is a tragicomedy of misunderstandings between individuals magnified into that between races. His characters again represent groups (English, Hindu, Moslem) with their mingled virtues and defects. His characters are "round" and are capable of development. EMF is aware of the complexity of life; he achieves a balance between "large issues and minor circumstances," the individual and his environment. His preoccupation is with the inner life; he combines a sense of beauty and mystery of life with an objective humor. The element of fantasy in his short stories is translated into eccentricity of character and manipulation of incident in the novels. Character development is all-important for his dramatization of theme. His handling of incident is arbitrary; he is willing to sacrifice suspense by telling us the outcome of a situation in advance. He foregoes sympathy for individual characters by assuming-an attitude of charity for all of them. His sympathy is matched by his detachment; he understands his characters through perspective rather than through participation. EMF recognizes that morals, manners, and men are closely united; this realization makes of him our "most civilized writer." [Important early appreciation that associates EMF with Huxley, Lawrence, Joyce, and Woolf rather than with Edwardian writers.]

268 Sheean, Vincent. "Lytton Strachey: Cambridge and Bloomsbury," NEW REPUBLIC, LXX (17 Feb 1932), 19–20.

Bloomsbury was really conceived in Cambridge. A group consciousness and underlying similarities characterize the members of the group: (1) exact definition of a problem is stressed, (2) certainty is impossible, (3) good is to be measured by results, and (4) the highest good consists in personal relationships and aesthetic enjoyment. Strachey was at the center of Bloomsbury with his amazing critical intelligence; with his death Bloomsbury would lose some of its coherence. [Incidental mention of EMF.]

1933

269 Bennett, Arnold. THE JOURNALS OF ARNOLD BENNETT, Vol. III, 1921–1928, ed by Newman Flower (Lond: Cassell, 1933), pp. 67, 69–70, 177; entry for 27 Jan 1927 rptd in E. M. FORSTER: THE CRITICAL HERITAGE, ed by Philip Gardner (Lond & Boston: Routledge & Kegan Paul, 1973), pp. 287–88.

Entry for 27 Jan 1925: The central part of *A Passage to India*—the trial scene, etc.—is superb, as is EMF's depiction of the herd instinct among the British at Chandrapore. But one finds it difficult to know quite what the book is about. The religious life in Mau is well presented, but it is not related to the earlier part of the novel. The details are all good in this last section, but they do not produce a definite impression. Entry for 31 Dec 1926: EMF says that he has no ideas for a new novel. EMF should be cursed into getting on with one, but "curses" will probably do no good.

270 Charques, R. D. "The Bourgeois Novel," CONTEMPORARY LITERATURE AND SOCIAL REVOLUTION (Lond: Martin Secker, [1933]), pp. 83–129, espec 90, 122–24; also 159.

EMF's books belong, in their enduring qualities (fineness of sympathy, humor, feeling for character, restraint and reasonableness, and a sense of proportion) to the period before the war. *Howards End* brought to a close a period in the English novel. *A Passage to India* is luminous, sensible, ironical, and eloquent yet somewhat old-fashioned in the mode of *Howards End;* however, a little more skepticism, dryness, and irony are present. On the one side, there is exploitative imperialism in action (it is significant that EMF returned to fiction with analysis of a social problem); on the other side, there is the echo in the Marabar Cave. Modern life is not favorable to "the exercise of his sensitive and balanced genius of sympathy." "Anonymity" (1921; rptd in *Two Cheers for Democracy*) lends support to the view that artists are often driven by the need for publicity and by material gain when they insist upon signing their work; they are not content to remain anonymous, as devoted artists once were.

271 Mackenzie, Compton. Literature in My Time (Lond: Rich & Cowan, 1933), pp. 189, 191.

Before World War I, EMF and D. H. Lawrence sounded a note of defiance. *Howards End* preserved traditional form but revealed that a new kind of mind could be appreciatively feminine as well as masculine. EMF is an admirable writer, but his values make it impossible to enjoy his work.

1934

---

272 Auden, W. H. "Lowes Dickinson," Scrutiny, III (Dec 1934), 303–6.

It requires love to write so successfully a biography of a teacher, as EMF does in *Goldsworthy Lowes Dickinson*. The sense of the mystery of life, the hatred of prescriptive systems, and the love of individuality that both Dickinson and EMF shared may account for EMF's success. Dickinson is revealed as a man of destiny, and he illustrates the fact that intellectual curiosity and isolation go together. He remained true to his commitment to a life of understanding, but he also worked outward from the self to others. Dickinson and EMF would counsel those who are dedicated to a life of "mental fight" not to lose patience.

273 Belgion, Montgomery. "The Diabolism of Mr. E. M. Forster," Criterion, XIV (Oct 1934), 54–73.

EMF is a novelist of distinction though not a perfect one. His women, except for Margaret Schlegel, are not real; Leonard Bast is too "different" as a clerk to be quite credible. But EMF's subtlety of style and of narration has appeal. He has something to say, but there is a sameness of invention in his work—the bantering of certain characters by the author, the use of rooms and buildings for decor, the "beefy male" as sadist and the assertive female as sadist, the big scene in which one character instructs another. Such scenes, incidents, and characters EMF finds to be particularly symbolical. His works exist, in his view, to connect prose with passion. But what is the background of "value" in his work? No one has yet expounded it. G. E. Moore's "personal affections" and "aesthetic enjoyments" partly define EMF's world view. In a number of his works EMF implies that it is wrong to control people against their will. In *The Longest Journey* Stewart Ansell's remark that he cannot "coach people" betrays an unconscious patronage in his very fear of patronizing others, just as the Schlegels are perhaps too self-congratulating in their conscious need to be kind to servants. The question of whether EMF is a "sound thinker" is difficult to decide. *Goldsworthy Lowes Dickinson* does not allay this discomfort. The intellectual enthusiasms of Dickinson—Shelly, Plato, and Goethe—are incongruous and indicate his confusion, a confusion that EMF's explanations do not clarify. EMF himself is confused when he prefers Dickinson to Socrates, betraying at least a lack of proportion. For EMF the capital sin is to miss opportunities to be oneself (to muff the symbolical moment), as Rickie Elliot does in *Journey* when he refuses to recognize Stephen Wonham as his half-brother. The "response" one makes is the crucial element in behavior because one is then oneself; one must respond to poetry, which is one's link with the unseen (poetry is equivalent to instinct that gives us entrance to the world of spirit). The spirit world is not the world of organized religion (or religion at all), but it may be the world of mystical and aesthetic experiences. Romantic beauty, poetry, passion (and the moment of passion) are all-important to EMF. Those who cannot thus respond (or connect the prose with passion by being responsive) are outsiders whom EMF condemns; they are the goats (often being clergyman, businessman, and laymen). The goats follow their instincts too; and the only way to distinguish among these instincts is through instinct itself. EMF would have us rely on instinct alone in ethical matters and in determining value, and that reliance is insufficient. The combination of rich talent in EMF with this emphasis on the importance of instinct is pernicious, even diabolical. [Reasoning here is elliptical and circuitous; and the essay does not seem to quite define a difficult subject, i.e., the validity of EMF's romanticism.]

274 "A Beloved Don," DAILY TELEGRAPH (Lond), 24 April 1934, p. 8.
Dickinson's chief desire was to serve humanity. His elusive, magnetic personality is revealed in EMF's *Goldsworthy Lowes Dickinson;* he was a disciple of Socrates and was himself like Socrates.

275 Brickell, Herschell. "The Literary Landscape," NORTH AMERICAN REVIEW, CCXXXVIII (Aug 1934), 190.
Goldsworthy Lowes Dickinson is full of sympathy and understanding as well as being "an admirable piece of writing." EMF's task was difficult: to write a moving book about a superior individual who was not great in any usual sense.

276 Brown, E. K. "E. M. Forster and the Contemplative Novel," UNIVERSITY OF TORONTO QUARTERLY, III (April 1934), 349–61; rptd in E. M. FORSTER: THE CRITICAL HERITAGE, ed by Philip Gardner (Lond & Boston: Routledge & Kegan Paul, 1973), pp. 369–78.
EMF's novels illustrate "the chasm between the world of actions and the

world of being." His most common situation is for an inhabitant of the world of being to try to conduct himself in the world of actions according to his inner light, his contemplative values. Those who dwell in the world of actions are obtuse, complacent, trivial, or ludicrous. In *Howards End* Margaret Schlegel, though a devotée of the inner life, is unable to perceive at first that the Wilcox extravert life is an illusion. She experiences the same muddle as Rickie Elliot (*The Longest Journey*) and Adela Quested (*A Passage to India*). Old Mr. Emerson (*A Room with a View*) and Stewart Ansell (*Journey*) are the most elaborate but not the most successful portraits of the true contemplative. More successful are Mr. Failing, Mrs. Wilcox, and Mrs. Moore because they are contemplatives who are removed from the world of actions. Mr. Failing's wisdom derives from the life within; it is superior to both Rickie's and Ansell's and is akin to Edward Carpenter's. Ruth Wilcox in *Howards End* differs in quality from those who surround her and has a wisdom that goes far beyond theirs. She solves problems rather than talking about them; her dimension of wisdom is apparent only to Margaret. With Mrs. Moore (*Passage*) we enter the world of prophecy. In Mrs. Wilcox and Mrs. Moore the real and the visionary worlds are blended, and these characters cause the world of actions to be absorbed into a larger reality that they themselves represent. [Essay has some insights but is diffuse and excessively relaxed.]

277 Burra, Peter. "The Novels of E. M. Forster," NINETEENTH CENTURY AND AFTER, CXVI (Nov 1934), 581–94; rptd as "Introduction," *A Passage to India* (Lond: Dent, Everyman's Library, 1942), pp. xi–xxviii, with EMF's notes, pp. xxxi–xxxii [in 1957 and later imprints, pp. xi–xxviii, with EMF's revised notes, pp. xxix–xxx]; rptd in FORSTER: A COLLECTION OF CRITICAL ESSAYS, ed by Malcolm Bradbury (Englewood Cliffs, NJ: Prentice-Hall, Spectrum Books, 1966), pp. 21–33; and in part in E. M. FORSTER: "A PASSAGE TO INDIA": A CASEBOOK, ed by Malcolm Bradbury (Lond: Macmillan, Casebook Series, 1970), pp. 61–72.

In EMF's work a disparity exists between his tendency toward the abstract (to get at the essence of things) and the novel form, which is the least abstract of aesthetic forms. As artist he is on the fringe of social reform; he is interested in causes. Despite this philosophical bent and his impatience with story as such, expressed in *Aspects of the Novel*, he often stresses incident at the expense of the experiencing sensibility. The short stories, for example, are full of exaggerated events and shocks of violence, although this violence alternates with gentler moods. In the first four novels the story element is not credible; EMF wishes to "bounce" us into accepting what he says, something he usually succeeds in doing. An operatic quality about these incidents allows them to function in their context but does not conduce to a realistic appraisal of them. Thus in *The Longest Journey* Stewart

Ansell's denunciation at Sawston School of Rickie Elliot for the rejection of his half-brother Stephen Wonham has this sort of operatic truth, though it is not convincing on a realistic level. EMF's plots represent distinguished craftsmanship. He contrives plot only for developing his characters, at least in the first four novels; however, in *A Passage to India* the realistic and the extraordinary are more completely part of one another. In his plotting he uses hints to foreshadow succeeding events, and for incremental emphasis he uses the repeated image or leitmotif, such as the level-crossing in *Journey* and the wasp in *Passage*. These images readily become symbolic in intonation if not explicitly so, as they would be likely to do in Virginia Woolf's fiction. EMF often uses buildings, places, and names of places as symbols and parts of the framework for his books. The three-part divisions of *Journey* and *Passage* are like the movements of symphonies, especially in their intercalations with each other. In *Passage* all leads up to the Caves, and all reflects back to them. The leitmotifs, the modulating irony, and the resulting symbolic intonations of the materials in his books form the modern equivalent of the classical unities, with none of their disadvantages. He is passionately interested in human beings; his observation is precise, yet his people are elusive, a quality which makes them more real. He describes men against their social setting, and this tendency accounts for his use of social comedy rather than a purer, more musical kind of fiction. His work revolves around the clashes, often violent, of opposites. The conflict in *Passage* is personal rather than racial, the difference of race only heightening the personal divisions. In each book there are elemental characters whose vision is clear and who see to the realities beneath appearances. Gino Carella (*Where Angels Fear to Tread*), Stephen Wonham (*Journey*), George Emerson and his father (*A Room with a View*), Mrs. Wilcox (*Howards End*), and Mrs. Moore (*Passage*) are such characters. With the men EMF stresses the athletic element; with the women, the intuitive. Mrs. Moore and Mrs. Wilcox withdraw from a stupid world. They belong to the enemy's camp (though they are not the enemy) and so prepare the way for the merging of opposites. The elemental men dispense with the disguises which the rest of the characters wear. Stephen is life in its essence, a simplicity transformed by EMF's vision; he is a great creation. George and Gino represent the same athletic honesty. As for Gino, George, and Stephen, each realizes his importance in the continuance of the race. EMF presents the clash as well as the merge of opposites: types for him are never absolutely distinct. Though EMF exalts the return to nature, he also demonstrates that tragedy arises in *Journey* from Rickie's faith in the earth. Heroically, Rickie refuses to heed the warning of his aunt (Mrs. Failing) concerning the malignancy of earth. People like Mrs. Failing, whom imagination never visits, are always apparently right. The two sides are presented in *Howards End* with as exact a balance of sympathy as possible. Margaret Schlegel sees that love is greater than opinions and that one should not ruin one's chance for sexual intimacy by adhering inflexibly to abstract principles. Concerning her views that the empire builder is superior to the empire and that war is horrible but soldiers are not, such inconsistency is at the heart of EMF's philosophy: for him a man is always greater than his opinions. The Anonymous Prophecy, the great beauty of Mosque and Temple, and the athletic body of Stephen comprise the essence of the novels. [An early essay in appreciation, with many striking insights. An essay of lasting value. EMF's notes in the Everyman ed of *Passage* are invaluable in locating the originals of places, objects, persons, allusions, and incidents. The notes for both 1942 and 1957 imprints should be consulted; dedication is omitted in 1957 imprint.]

278 "Check List of New Books," AMERICAN MERCURY, XXXIII (Nov 1934), x, xi.
Goldsworthy Lowes Dickinson fails to bring the man to life. The man's portrait is pallid, and his intellectual influence and distinction are not created.

279 Dobrée, Bonamy. "Description of Action," MODERN PROSE STYLE (Oxford: Clarendon P, 1934), pp. 15–38, espec 36–38; 2d ed (1964).
In the opening three paragraphs from Chapter XVII of *Howards End* it is difficult to separate the philosophic meaning from the narrative. EMF hints that his ideas have something to do with us; he is at the right distance. Nearer he would seem obtrusive; further away, too abstract. There is no flatness but variety and careful balance in the writing. His mind is at work in his prose, appealing to his reader's mind. His epigrammatic mode and his constant humor prevent the intrusion of sentimentality.

280 Dobrée, Bonamy. "The Novel: Has It a Function To-Day?" ESSAYS BY DIVERS HANDS, ed by W. B. Maxwell (Lond: Oxford UP, nsXIII, 1934), pp. 57–76, espec 62–64, 73.
The novel from Defoe to George Eliot took society as its chief theme. A change began with Meredith, who emphasized the importance of the individual. This interest was refined by EMF into a concern with the personal relation. In EMF's fiction society exists as a background for presenting personal relationships; he would have the novel change people by making them look at themselves in a new way. With D. H. Lawrence, Virginia Woolf, and Joyce the novel became less concerned with the individual in his relation to others (as in EMF's novels) and more interested in his relationship to himself. The novelist always presents what is to him the most important reality; this reality is now the individual, whereas it was once society. The stable social fabric disappeared after the war; the prewar EMF was the last novelist who could rely upon it. But the novel at present needs to do more than to present personal issues; it needs genuine social orienta-

tion, theme, underlying idea, concern with a problem, and contemporary consciousness, such as EMF had in dramatizing the conflicts between those who in *Howards End* embrace the outer life and those who embody the internal.

281 Forster, E. M. *Goldsworthy Lowes Dickinson* (NY: Harcourt, Brace; Lond: Edward Arnold, 1934), pp. 215–17; rptd, Pocket edition (Lond: Edward Arnold, 1962), pp. 215–17; and *The Abinger Edition of E. M. Forster*, vol. 13, *Goldsworthy Lowes Dickinson and Related Writings*, ed by Oliver Stallybrass (Lond: Edward Arnold, 1973), pp. 179–81.

Letter to EMF (2 June 1926): In *A Passage to India* EMF analyzes well the subject of the incompatibility of the Indians and the English. He has lifted a corner of the veil and seen something beyond that is disquieting. Aziz is a triumph, "so alive and consistently inconsistent." What happens in the Caves is puzzling; and the sequence ought possibly to have been more explicit. The double vision in this novel—combining this world with a world or worlds beyond—does not "squint," as it does in some of EMF's other works. *Passage* should become a classic "on the strange and tragic fact of history and life called India." Letter to EMF (19 April 1928): EMF's stories are not entirely satisfactory; he does not bring realistic life into persuasive contact "with the background of values," though admittedly this contact is difficult to achieve. "The Eternal Moment" and "The Machine Stops" are the best stories. "The Machine Stops" turns inside out "the Wells-Shaw prophecies."

282 Garnett, David. "Current Literature: Books in General," NEW STATESMAN AND NATION, nsVII (21 April 1934), 600.

EMF's *Goldsworthy Lowes Dickinson* is a living portrait of a distinguished man. It is excellent by virtue of what he and Dickinson have in common: personal qualities and sense of humor. (Their tastes were often different, EMF not finding Shelley, Plato, and Goethe congenial writers, and Dickinson preferring China to India.) EMF's book could have been more authoritative if additional material on Dickinson's friendships and conversations had been included.

283 Gillett, Eric. "Literary History and Criticism," LONDON MERCURY, XXX (July 1934), 271–73.

Dickinson had a genius for friendship but a dislike for actual contact with public life. Aside from his work for the League of Nations, he existed as a "personality"; and it is fitting that EMF should thus commemorate him. In *Goldsworthy Lowes Dickinson* EMF presents Dickinson with a casual air, which shows us the man as he was.

284 "G. Lowes Dickinson," SPRINGFIELD DAILY REPUBLICAN, 7 June 1934, p. 10.

EMF's book is a convincing interpretative portrait of his friend and mentor, though some of EMF's own comments on education and society seem "capricious and trivial." [Informed summary of *Goldsworthy Lowes Dickinson* and some of Dickinson's main concerns.]

285 "G. Lowes Dickinson," TIMES (Lond), 24 April 1934, p. 19.

EMF, with tact and sympathy, makes Goldsworthy Lowes Dickinson a Socrates and sees Cambridge as Platonic in atmosphere. EMF both admits the reader to and excludes him from this milieu. This exclusion is a limitation in *Goldsworthy Lowes Dickinson* but also a virtue in suggesting depths in Dickinson that cannot be conveyed in a written account. EMF makes an unadventurous life adventurous.

286 H., L. "Mr. E. M. Forster on Lowes Dickinson," MANCHESTER GUARDIAN, 30 May 1934, p. 7.

In *Goldsworthy Lowes Dickinson* EMF has interpreted the facts with patience and imagination and has written with courage as well as perspicacity, alive both to the limitations and the greatnesses of Dickinson. Dickinson as a man motivated by love of truth and by humanity is well summarized in EMF's portrait.

287 Hobson, J. A. "New Books," PHILOSOPHY, IX (July 1934), 377–78.

Dickinson was a seeker who never found an absolute or ultimate. He displayed clear thought in the fields of personal and social conduct, and he had a deep concern for civilization which drew him out of his donnish seclusion. He retained a faith in progress despite the challenges made to it in his lifetime. [Review of *Goldsworthy Lowes Dickinson*.]

288 Hutchison, Percy. "E. M. Forster on Lowes Dickinson," NEW YORK TIMES BOOK REVIEW, 10 June 1934, p. 6.

EMF's *Goldsworthy Lowes Dickinson* is an affectionate and intimate portrait of a great man. Dickinson was no doctrinaire pacifist but wanted people to live amicably so that war would not be necessary. EMF presents convincingly Dickinson's change at Cambridge from interest in poetry and philosophy to interest in international polity.

289 Kingsmill, Hugh. "Lowes Dickinson," ENGLISH REVIEW, LVIII (June 1934), 746–49.

In *Goldsworthy Lowes Dickinson* there is presented a pleasant portrait of a sincere and thoughtful man and an academic millenarian. He emerges as excessively unnerved by the war; he seems always, even in his efforts on behalf of the League of Nations, to have been retreating from the horrors of existence.

290 Lovett, Robert Morss. "Portrait of a Gentleman," NEW REPUBLIC, LXXX (26 Sept 1934), 192.
EMF as a novelist has a major capacity for "scenting the rare, strange, elusive traits of personality." He reveals the same gift in *Goldsworthy Lowes Dickinson.* EMF has tried for a biography that would be a personal portrayal, and he has caught Dickinson's likeness. EMF's manner, "his very self-consciousness, deprecation, evasion, his tentative approach and uncertain strokes," fit his subject. He has also set Dickinson against the Cambridge of the late Victorian Age. EMF reveals a sensitive man, a man whose career had its tragic aspect in the failure of the League of Nations he had helped bring into being.

291 "Lowes Dickinson," TIMES LITERARY SUPPLEMENT (Lond), 19 April 1934, p. 279.
Goldsworthy Lowes Dickinson is excellent because of EMF's thoroughness of research, a process which EMF at one point decries. EMF reproduces sympathetically the tension in Dickinson between the Socratic intellectual and the public servant. The book is especially good in its treatment of Dickinson's public career. [Informative review by a writer familiar with Dickinson as a person. Valuable for its appraisal of EMF's treatment of Dickinson.]

292 Lucas, F. L. "Goldsworthy Lowes Dickinson: The Laughing Philosopher," OBSERVER (Lond), 6 May 1934, p. 4.
Goldsworthy Lowes Dickinson led an uneventful life, but in EMF's *Goldsworthy Lowes Dickinson* it does not seem so. The sadder Dickinson, not the laughing philosopher, predominates too much in EMF's book. EMF rightly divines that Dickinson is not important for what he did or wrote but for what he was—a saint and a sage. He lived his wisdom and seemed always young in essence.

293 MacCarthy, Desmond. "Culture and Kultur: The Life of G. Lowes Dickinson," SUNDAY TIMES (Lond), 22 April 1934, p. 8.
EMF is successful in his labor of love, *Goldsworthy Lowes Dickinson.* Dickinson was important, not so much for his rare personality (as EMF emphasizes), as for being a Representative Man, an advocate of Liberal Culture. Dickinson was more interested in ends than in means; he wished to bring into controversy the spirit of liberal culture, "its impartiality without its aloofness, its superiority without its superciliousness." EMF's biography is of special use in emphasizing Dickinson's impulse to be of service to his fellow men. Dickinson's faith in Liberal Culture received a great shock

in World War I, though he still addressed men as if they could be rational. EMF's book brings us into full contact with the mind behind Dickinson's many activities, private and public. In his life and work he was the exponent of culture against Kultur with its compulsory uniformity. [Stimulating discussion by a member of the Bloomsbury inner circle.]

294 Martin, Kingsley. "Book Reviews," POLITICAL QUARTERLY, V (July 1934), 447–52.

EMF in *Goldsworthy Lowes Dickinson* does not emphasize enough Dickinson's political and philosophical tendencies. On the personal side EMF's book is outstanding. Dickinson developed away from religion and authority to a concern with the individual and so reversed the course of the development of his mentor Plato. [Informed summary of Dickinson's philosophical and political development.]

295 Peel, Robert. "Latter-Day Platonist," CHRISTIAN SCIENCE MONITOR, 9 June 1934, p. 14.

The informality of EMF's procedure in *Goldsworthy Lowes Dickinson* recreates the essence of Dickinson.

296 P[ippett], R[oger]. "When a Guardian Angel Writes," DAILY HERALD (Lond), 19 April 1934, p. 8.

Dickinson deserves the biography that EMF, a kind of guardian angel, writes in *Goldsworthy Lowes Dickinson.* Dickinson's rare personality comes through; he was "a humanist with intense social hopes and enthusiasms."

297 "Plato's Britannia," LIFE AND LETTERS, X (June 1934), 374–76.

Goldsworthy Lowes Dickinson escaped, by his sense of the ridiculous and by the extraversion of his impulses, into such causes as the League of Nations, the absurdity sometimes connected with academic life. The biographer and his subject are well suited to each other in EMF's *Goldsworthy Lowes Dickinson.* Dickinson had the Platonic mind, not quite at its best. Such a "second-best" Platonist reaches synthesis too readily. Although he lacks rigor, he is a "Good Siren" rather than a "Bad Siren."

298 Ponsonby. "The Modern Platonist," LISTENER, XIX, Supplement (2 May 1934), viii,xi.

EMF has done almost the impossible in *Goldsworthy Lowes Dickinson;* he has been able to recreate a personality of an intangible distinction. He has given us the dimensions of a contemplative mind, Dickinson's inner development, and the course of the ideas that led to action. EMF shows a capacity for both accurate and brilliant portraiture. EMF's memorial is worthy of Dickinson and may extend his mentor's influence.

299 R., G. R. B. "An Eminent English Scholar in His Placid Environment," BOSTON EVENING TRANSCRIPT, "Book Section," 16 June 1934, pp. 1, 3.

Dickinson's life was uneventful, but the man did count. As an affectionate, intelligent, witty, charming, inspiring individual he merits the treatment accorded him in EMF's *Goldsworthy Lowes Dickinson*. EMF does not romanticize Dickinson but makes him an individual of continuing interest. The charm of the man's life and EMF's re-creation of him result in a lasting contribution to the understanding of recent civilization and international reform. The book reveals wisdom, graciousness, tolerance, and fine artistry in the subject and in its interpreter.

300 S., A. "Philosopher Prophet," SATURDAY REVIEW (Lond), CLVIII (8 Sept 1934), 88.

EMF reveals both the strengths and the weaknesses of the man in his monumental *Goldsworthy Lowes Dickinson*. Dickinson had much influence over the young, though the modern age paid little attention to him as prophet.

301 Sheppard, J. T. "Lowes Dickinson," SPECTATOR (Lond), CLII (27 April 1934), 664.

Dickinson was a greater influence at Cambridge than EMF allows in *Goldsworthy Lowes Dickinson*. Dickinson worked for university reforms. He also had a more robust kind of humor than is evident in EMF's biography. Still the book provides an excellent portrait of Dickinson, enriching the subject. This book is the chronicle of a man who devoted his life to a quest for spiritual satisfaction and to the service of others.

302 Singh, Bhupal. "E. M. Forster and Edward Thompson," A SURVEY OF ANGLO-INDIAN FICTION (Lond: Oxford UP, 1934), pp. 1, 221–232, 233; rptd in abrgd form as "Forster's Picture of India," in E. M. FORSTER: THE CRITICAL HERITAGE, ed by Philip Gardner (Lond & Boston: Routledge & Kegan Paul, 1973), 293–94.

EMF's analysis of characters in *A Passage to India* is impartial. Critics who condemn his treatment of the Anglo-Indians forget that he is portraying individuals as well as types (he combines both admirably). He is a psychologist rather than a portrait painter, giving us in his Anglo-Indians individuals as they would act under specific circumstances. Ronny Heaslop is being transformed into the Anglo-Indian bureaucrat in danger of degeneration. EMF's portrait of the Moslem, Aziz, is compelling; despite his fine qualities, he has many repellent ones and is not superior to Adela Quested, Mrs. Moore, or Fielding. EMF did not know Hindus well and did Godbole from the "outside." The Gokul Ashtami sequence is, however, impressive, "a beautiful picture of Hindu superstitions, faith and fervour, vulgarity and mysticism." Aziz may represent EMF's mature thought when he muses, "The song of the future must transcend creed." [Analysis of *Passage*, stressing relationships between English and Indians. Excellent account.]

303 Stawell, F. M. "Book Reviews," OXFORD MAGAZINE, LII (7 June 1934), 807–8.

As EMF says in *Goldsworthy Lowes Dickinson*, Dickinson knew more about flight than many who went higher than he did, but he had to forgo much in his service to humanity. He was committed both to the work of making the world better (the Religion of Time) and the contemplation of the world as perfect (the Religion of Eternity). He knew that often a choice had to be made among goods but deplored the fact that this choice must be made.

304 Sunne, Richard. "Men and Books," TIME AND TIDE, XV (28 April 1934), 542.

Before 1914 Goldsworthy Lowes Dickinson was not an impressive figure, and even EMF in *Goldsworthy Lowes Dickinson* cannot make him seem so. He was an amiable don, a belated romantic as interpreter of the Greeks, a scholar of less importance than Walter Headlam or W. A. Verrall or Gilbert Murray, an essentially unoriginal humanist, and an undistinguished writer of dialogues. EMF overrates Dickinson's beneficent influence and that of King's College. The important Dickinson is the writer of THE INTERNATIONAL ANARCHY, the opponent during World War I of both savage nationalism and militant pacifism, and the man who helped bring into being the League of Nations. [Excellent review.]

305 Swinnerton, Frank. "Post-Freud: E. M. Forster," THE GEORGIAN SCENE: A LITERARY PANORAMA (NY: Farrar & Rinehart, 1934), pp. 390–401; also 52, 298, 344, 347, 374, 384, 409, 487; rptd as THE GEORGIAN LITERARY SCENE (Lond: Hutchinson, 1934; rvd ed, 1938); sixth rvd ed as THE GEORGIAN LITERARY SCENE: 1910–1935: A PANORAMA (NY: Farrar & Straus; Lond: Hutchinson, 1950), discussion "Post-Freud," pp. 406–18; references to EMF passim; discussion of EMF in rvd eds unchanged except for slight changes in comments on Leonard Bast (*Howards End*).

EMF is above all a moralist. His books reveal an active intelligence that plays with a theme; they have little warmth. His chief concern is with "Nature, Honesty, the need for mutual comprehension, the Good Life." At Cambridge Goldsworthy Lowes Dickinson helped him attain increased clarity. *Where Angels Fear to Tread* and *A Room with a View* are brilliant exercises in comedy. *The Longest Journey* and *Howards End* are not altogether intelligible presentations of middle-class dilemmas; *A Passage to*

India is a subtle analysis of the Anglo-Indian situation. The first two novels and *Passage* are brilliant with "radiant intelligence"; all five embody a style formal, cool, witty, and original in phrasing; all are fantastic. The fantasy works to advantage in *Angels* and *Room*, to disadvantage in *Journey* and *Howards End*, and becomes a bewilderment in *Passage*. *Angels* is his most successful book; it has vivid characters, lively talk, zestful invention; obscurity and contradiction do not mar the effect. In *Journey*, though Agnes Pembroke is cruel to Rickie Elliot, EMF persecutes her unduly. Stephen Wonham is not convincing to the reader though he represents something symbolically valuable to EMF. EMF is so full of animosity toward convention that he cannot present it scrupulously. As for *Room*, its composition will not bear looking into; its message is trite, and the book is sentimental in its appeal to faunishness and eccentricity. *Howards End* is a mature and diversified book, but it is puzzling because EMF's invention is arbitrary. The Basts are incredible as clerk and wife; they are fantastic people offered as realities [note that Leonard Woolf in his GROWING (1961, pp. 63ff.) attests to the reality of the Bast-type in Dutton, an Anglo-Indian magistrate in Ceylon.] The inconsecutiveness of the story is not the inconsecutiveness of life. *Passage* is coherent; it is a vehicle for EMF's ideas and is more interesting for its crystallization of EMF's thoughts and emotions about India than as a novel. EMF's reservations about the story element in fiction (*Aspects of the Novel*) illuminate his talents and gifts. Despite his faults, he has intelligence, deftness and perceptiveness, originality, a flair for comedy, a feeling for milieu, and exceptional understanding when his sympathies are engaged, as in his portrait of Margaret Schlegel. As moralist he protests against inhibiting social forces, hypocrisies, sham, and tyranny. He has an individual integrity that is heartening and that seldom interferes with the workings of his imagination. [Extended summary of *Howards End*. Several mentions, passim. Interesting remarks by a literary contemporary.]

306 T., R. "Two Literary Lives," CURRENT HISTORY (NY), XL (Sept 1934), vii, xii.
Edith Wharton and Goldsworthy Lowes Dickinson led secluded lives. EMF's biography is a candid appraisal of Dickinson and a model biography. [Review of Wharton's A BACKWARD GLANCE and *Goldsworthy Lowes Dickinson*.]

307 Tigner, Hugh Stevenson. "An Urbane Critic of Society," CHRISTIAN CENTURY, LI (12 Sept 1934), 1150–51.
EMF in *Goldsworthy Lowes Dickinson* gives us the view that Dickinson was more important as a person to those who knew him than as an intellectual force. EMF's biography does not "get off" as a biography; the drama— mostly intellectual—of Dickinson's life escapes EMF.

308 Tilby, A. Wyatt. "Riddle of Lowes Dickinson: Poet, Politician, Mystic—and Relative Failure," YORKSHIRE POST (Leeds), 19 April 1934, p. 6.

Goldsworthy Lowes Dickinson was a force rather than an influence in the Cambridge of his time. He was too much the poet to be a philosopher, in the opinion of his friends; too much the philosopher to be a poet, in the opinion of his enemies. He could not accept religious orthodoxy but was mystic in temperament; he was an idealist but could not explain away pain and evil. In politics he tended to be too removed from the sphere of critical action; during the war he was pacifist in sympathy but not entirely without militarist leanings. His failure, as EMF makes clear in *Goldsworthy Lowes Dickinson*, was the result of his extreme fastidiousness, his lack of driving power, and his high expectations.

309 Tomlinson, H. M. "Mr. E. M. Forster on Lowes Dickinson," DAILY TELEGRAPH (Lond), 19 April 1934, p. 4.

Goldsworthy Lowes Dickinson is EMF's best book. The spirits of subject and of biographer are so in accord that one seems to be overhearing confidences between them as he reads. Dickinson's regard for truth and his directness in going after it were remarkable. During World War I he became an inspiration; he represented the existence of mind, wisdom, and good will.

310 Trilling, Lionel. "Politics and the Liberal," NATION (NY), CXXXIX (4 July 1934), 24–25.

The charm of Dickinson's personality is conveyed in *Goldsworthy Lowes Dickinson*, and the charm is important because of the tradition Dickinson represents. This tradition is impotent because, in spite of Dickinson's sensitivity and idealism, he could not relate its ideals to the passions and interests of men. (He confessed to this failure.) His was the failing of a whole generation of liberal-humanist intellectuals. The League of Nations was another of Dickinson's ideals that the passions and interests of the nations defeated; he did not consider enough the realities of class and economics. EMF does well with this analysis of Dickinson's mind because it was so much his own. As a novelist EMF rises above the politicians of his class; the future will not be interested in his novels because they are too narrowly based on individualistic values and on the need for tolerance. In politics these values mean little, though they still do dictate the provenance of our personal lives. [Interesting, as these comments bear upon Trilling's politically oriented study of EMF which inaugurated the EMF revival in 1943. He seems to have found the novels more important in 1943 than in 1934.]

311 Van Doren, Carl. "'A Gentler Socrates in a Safer Athens,'" NEW YORK HERALD TRIBUNE BOOKS, 10 June 1934, p. 5.

"If Dickinson had been more energetic and more fertile, and if he had had less of the monotony of excellence," he might have been a great influence. Instead he was a casualty of his times, believing too hopefully in reason. He was greater than the liberal intellectuals he represents, and he deserves this biography (which is at times too reticent). It is excellent as a biography of the mind. [Review of *Goldsworthy Lowes Dickinson.*]

312 Van Gelder, Robert. "Books of the Times," NEW YORK TIMES, 9 June 1934, p. 13.

Goldsworthy Lowes Dickinson is more interesting for its author than for its subject. EMF writes with an easy style and a "mature surety." The book is unsparing yet sympathetic; it makes its subject come alive. [Summary of Dickinson's opinions derived from EMF's biography.]

313 Williamson, Hugh Ross. "Notes at Random," BOOKMAN (Lond), LXXXVI (May 1934), 87–90, espec 87–88.

In *Goldsworthy Lowes Dickinson* EMF has at once presented Dickinson to a wider circle and perpetuated his charm for posterity; but he has also shown, unconsciously perhaps, the escapism of dons and their "dupes." Dickinson's one great accomplishment was the League of Nations. His books will probably not endure; THE GREEK VIEW OF LIFE, for example, is not appreciative enough of the violence which partly formed Greek culture.

314 Wingfield-Stratford, Esmé. "The Last Victorian," SATURDAY REVIEW OF LITERATURE, X (9 June 1934), 739.

Goldsworthy Lowes Dickinson is bowdlerized, and Dickinson was a more human, earthy, and fallible man than EMF presents him as being. He will be remembered as a character and an influence.

1935

315 M., M. C. "New Books," CATHOLIC WORLD, CXL (Feb 1935), 630–31.

In *Goldsworthy Lowes Dickinson* EMF conveys the charm of his subject in a "lucid and plastic style." He also establishes close rapport between a theme (the strength of Dickinson's idealism and its being undermined by the war) and its expression. Dickinson's ideal of the good life was pagan and aesthetic, and probably did not go far enough.

316 Millet, Fred S. CONTEMPORARY BRITISH LITERATURE: A CRITICAL SURVEY AND 232 AUTHOR BIBLIOGRAPHIES BY FRED S. MILLETT: THIRD REVISED AND ENLARGED EDITION, BASED ON THE SECOND REVISED AND ENLARGED EDITION BY JOHN M. MANLY AND EDITH RICKERT (NY: Harcourt, Brace, 1935), pp. 33, 230–31.

EMF is a minor Edwardian, along with Samuel Butler, Maurice Hewlett, Arthur Machen, Frank Swinnerton, J. D. Beresford, and Gilbert Cannan, in contrast to "major" figures such as Wells, Galsworthy, Bennett, Moore, and Conrad. EMF's art is one of implication rather than of explication; important are "the refinement of his psychological observation and notation," his individuality in choice of themes and milieus, his technical expertise, and his sympathy for the fate of the sensitive individual. EMF is "a distinguished but imperfectly satisfying novelist of a rather uncreative variety." [Valuable for reflecting the negative critical opinion of EMF in the 1930s.]

317 Oda, Masanobu. "Aspects of E. M. Forster," STUDIES IN ENGLISH LITERATURE (Tokyo), XV (1935), 91–109.

EMF's desire, in the early novels, to attain a harmony between prose and passion is stressed, together with his inability to achieve any kind of solution to the human dilemma in *A Passage to India.* His desire to achieve harmony was his basic impulse as a writer; he may have stopped writing fiction when he was no longer able to achieve this harmony. [Overview of EMF's career as novelist and writer.] [In Japanese.]

318 Owen, David. "Two Liberals," YALE REVIEW, nsXXIV (March 1935), 628–30.

EMF reveals in *Goldsworthy Lowes Dickinson* a person rather than a career. In focusing on a personality EMF tends to discount Dickinson's wider influence. Works like "A Modern Symposium" and "Letters from a Chinese Official" did contribute to the new liberalism of the early Twenties. [The other liberal discussed is C. P. Scott of the MANCHESTER GUARDIAN.]

1936

319 Bowen, Elizabeth. "*Abinger Harvest*," SPECTATOR (Lond), CLVI (20 March 1936), 521; rptd as "E. M. Forster, I," in COLLECTED IMPRESSIONS (Lond: Longmans, Green; NY: Knopf, 1950), pp. 119–22; rptd in E. M. FORSTER: THE CRITICAL HERITAGE, ed by Philip Gardner (Lond & Boston: Routledge & Kegan Paul, 1973), pp, 380–82.

EMF's books are inscrutable, though they are few in number. There is nothing factitious in these occasional essays in *Abinger Harvest*. They are arranged in sections that give the book unity. They reveal EMF's maturity from the beginning of his writing career. The continuity characteristic of his book results from the fact that his personality has not altered significantly. Intellect does not so much control susceptibility as balance it. EMF's prose makes his subjects appear brighter than they are; the prose is at the call of his subject and is full of vitality. The passion in these essays ultimately obtrudes from beneath the irony. [Stimulating commentary.]

320 Dangerfield, George. "Scenario of a Civilized Mind," SATURDAY REVIEW OF LITERATURE, XIV (30 May 1936), 7.

EMF is a man, an artist, and a thinker of the liberalizing and individualistic type. Such men are contemplatives and support the "lost cause." Today we approve of men who act directly, but the future will turn to truth-seekers such as EMF. EMF in his literary and artistic criticism pierces through the work to the man behind it; and his essays in *Abinger Harvest* represent a triumph of personality. [Important discussion.]

321 de Sélincourt, Basil. "Mr. E. M. Forster's Essays," MANCHESTER GUARDIAN, 20 March 1936, p. 7; rptd in abrgd form in E. M. FORSTER: THE CRITICAL HERITAGE, ed by Philip Gardner (Lond & Boston: Routledge & Kegan Paul, 1973), p. 379.

The impression produced by the essays in *Abinger Harvest* is that of a conservative, sweet temper reluctantly admitting the presence of other and alien influences in the world about him. As a novelist EMF is more interested in people as they are than in ascertaining how or why they are that way. His observations, revealing his taste and perceptiveness, may lead us to overestimate his power. His view that the English are "unformed" may be a merit as well as a defect in the English. On ultimate issues his remarks are tentative and fumbling; see his failure to define the nature of English tradition in his essay on Eliot. His book is notable for its sympathies, its stylistic felicity, and its illumination rather than for its philosophic grasp. [Suggestive remarks in a brief review.]

322 Garnett, David. "Current Literature: Books in General," NEW STATESMAN AND NATION, nsXI (21 March 1936), 459; rptd in E. M. FORSTER: THE CRITICAL HERITAGE, ed by Philip Gardner (Lond & Boston: Routledge & Kegan Paul, 1973), pp. 383–86.

In time of stress someone like EMF speaking of old values and of sanity is especially welcome. EMF is allied with three men, recently deceased, in outlook and philosophy—Goldsworthy Lowes Dickinson, Lytton Strachey, and Roger Fry. Their minds did not need propping; they believed in reason and they mistrusted intuition. In EMF's novels his emotionalism makes for obscurity; in his essays we see his mind in its great clarity. In his politics he protests against the encroachments by government or other forces upon individual liberty. EMF's humor is truly individual; he uses it to define a new truth and to reveal the thing itself. [Interesting contemporary account by a Bloomsbury associate. Review of *Abinger Harvest.*]

323 Henderson, Philip. "Bloomsbury: Virginia Woolf, E. M. Forster," THE NOVEL TODAY: STUDIES IN CONTEMPORARY ATTITUDES (Lond: John Lane, 1936), pp. 87–96; also 19–23, 28, 43, 248, 251.

EMF's assumption, expressed in *Aspects of the Novel*, that history changes while literature stands still, is questionable. Ideally, literary art does not stand still but ought to affect positively and dynamically the culture that it reflects. EMF in *A Passage to India* would encourage "tact, delicacy and patient understanding" on the part of the British toward the Indians. The book is courageous and admirable but exposes too little and does it too politely. EMF criticizes the instruments of British colonial policy rather than the policy itself. For him the remedy for existing abuses lies in the employment of decent people in the Civil Service rather than relinquishing colonial rule. He says nothing of the exploited millions from the lower classes in India.

324 Hillhouse, James T. THE WAVERLEY NOVELS AND THEIR CRITICS (Minneapolis: University of Minnesota P; Lond: Oxford UP, 1936), p. 256.

In *Aspects of the Novel* EMF oversimplifies Scott's novels by emphasizing only the simple plot line and its melodramatic qualities. Edie Ochiltree in

THE ANTIQUARY is a great character, and the Mucklebackits have much human depth.

325 Isherwood, Christopher. "Mr. Forster Tidies Up," LISTENER, XV (25 March 1936), 603.
Abinger Harvest is more than the usual collection of miscellaneous writings by an established author. It becomes EMF's "own involuntary autobiography." EMF's characteristics as a novelist are present: the capacity for self-orientation, the faculty of seeing other people objectively in the round, and the touches of irony. EMF is both the uncommitted artist and the committed political intelligence who has come to feel that "the slighter gestures of dissent" are not enough. [Important review.]

326 Jack, Peter Monro. "E. M. Forster's Delightful Essays," NEW YORK TIMES BOOK REVIEW, 24 May 1936, p. 2.
The five sections of *Abinger Harvest* are a dramatization of EMF's self in five scenes. "The Abinger Pageant" is the most revealing section and includes, in essence, all the other sections. Despite EMF's cultivated and literary qualities, it is his "unforced eloquence" on Abinger and its woods that forms the secret of his power. "Notes on the English Character" is an exercise in intellectual perspective. EMF has been too much praised for the quality of his intelligence at the expense of the powerful feeling in his work, in these essays as in his novels. The biographical interest in these essays is strong ("My Wood," "Liberty in England," etc.). He reveals himself as a liberal with stoic endurance. The book is uneven, the essays in "The Present" being inadequate to the subject. His critiques of writers reveal charm and critical knowledge. He writes in "The Past" with authority; the essays in "The East" could only have been written by him. EMF writes for the older generation but speaks to the new. His book is noteworthy as an exposition of reason, tolerance, and tradition. [Excellent review.]

327 Jenckes, Edward N. "A Novelist's Essays," SPRINGFIELD REPUBLICAN, 4 July 1936, p. 6.
An occasional incoherence in the subject matter rather than monotony of material and form prevents the essays collected in *Abinger Harvest* from being a unified collection. EMF's strictures against the middle class are unsupported by cogency on his part as the critic. In the literary essays he reveals insight but no marked power of generalization.

328 Jones, E. B. C. "E. M. Forster and Virginia Woolf," THE ENGLISH NOVELISTS: A SURVEY OF THE NOVEL BY TWENTY CONTEMPORARY NOVELISTS, ed by Derek Verschoyle (Lond: Chatto & Windus; NY: Harcourt, Brace, 1936), pp. 261–76 (NY ed, pp. 281–97).
EMF's novels are traditional; the relation between writer and reader is that

between guide and traveler, with EMF appearing in passages of reflection, analysis, or philosophy. With EMF, comradeship is exalted at the expense of sex. Other loves than the sexual are actualized with complete success in his work; see Gino Carella's passion for his child (*Where Angels Fear to Tread*), the sisters' affection in *Howards End*, Mrs. Wilcox's love for Howards End, the accord between George Emerson and his father (*A Room with a View*), Lucy Honeychurch and her brother (*Room*), Rickie Elliot and Stewart Ansell (*The Longest Journey*). The speech of EMF's characters is life-like without diffuseness, except in crises when they talk too much like EMF. In his style there is an elegant colloquialism; the thoughts of the characters and the authorial asides are necessary for the unfolding of the story. EMF is much concerned with the conflict between first-hand and second-hand reactions to life. In *Howards End* Margaret Schlegel is poised between outer and inner worlds; at the end Henry Wilcox's compromise with the personal view is superficial because there is no real change of heart. Ruth Wilcox, the Emersons, Stephen Wonham, and Mrs. Moore are "first-hand" people who stand outside the battle but who have an unconscious force that influences others. Mrs. Moore "lives through her possession of the deeply moral quality of taste," which the intellect alone cannot reach. The two chief themes of *A Passage to India* are the difficulties of communication among human beings and the dependence of salvation upon personal integrity and truth to the self. Such salvation Mrs. Moore attains as if to illustrate T. S. Eliot's "Teach us to care and not to care." In *Passage* EMF implies that the antithesis between spirit and matter is false; these are two sides of an ultimate reality, though imagination is the most real quality in his world. [Some insights of lasting value.]

329 Kelly, Blanche Mary. THE WELL OF ENGLISH (NY & Lond: Harper, 1936), p. 320.
A Room with a View represents insouciance in love. In *Howards End* the conventional standpoint is represented by the Wilcoxes, the adventurous spirit of youth by the Schlegels. Helen Schlegel's willed sacrifice of her "virtue" to Leonard Bast because life had been unfair to him and EMF's portrayal of the ineptitude of Bast's life (reminiscent of Jude Fawley's in Hardy's JUDE THE OBSCURE) anticipate in spirit the postwar novel.

330 Kronenberger, Louis. "Mr. Forster's Harvest," NATION (NY), CXLII (17 June 1936), 780–81.
EMF is less mannered, less self-indulgent, and less self-conscious than other members of his group. All his essays reveal "the same gusto tempered by caution, the same sensibility disciplined by toughness, the same humor and grace and generosity." He is the best type of modern liberal; his lapses result from a deficiency of intensity, not of integrity. [Important commentary on *Abinger Harvest.*]

331 Leavis, Q. D. "Mr. E. M. Forster," Scrutiny, V (June 1936), 100–105; rptd in A Selection from Scrutiny, ed by F. R. Leavis (Cambridge: Cambridge UP, 1968), I, 134–37.

Abinger Harvest is a disappointing book, but it furnishes a key to EMF's poise, which comprises the originality of his novels and from which his irony springs. There is a split in EMF's mind or personality; he cannot decide whether to be critical or charming, and this conflict between the serious and the playful often leads him into whimsy. His literary criticism is often notable for its insights, but he does not know how to consolidate. In his literary criticism he reveals a lack of discipline and of sustained effort, and he is unable to take advantage of his best discriminations. When EMF writes of the past, his treatments of it are picturesque and overly personal. Some social feeling is present in some essays, but EMF unfortunately tends to identify with group values. His best essays are on the East, wherein he is witty in a serious cause and is responsible; best is "The Mind of the Native Indian State." "Liberty in England" has this same note of responsibility, and EMF says things in it for which all civilized people should be grateful. "A Note on the Way" is personal in the best sense; EMF's courage is less to be associated here with his irony than with "his delicate emotional machinery." EMF lacks rigor and the intellectual strength that the major novelists of the century reveal. [A probing if severe essay.]

332 Littell, Philip. "E. M. Forster," New Republic, LXXXVII (8 July 1936), 273–74.

"A Flood in the Office" is a fresh, discerning essay. [This essay was dropped from later eds because of libel action against its being reprinted.] The most amusing essays in *Abinger Harvest* are the "loveliest." EMF is a good guide to the past and to "distant presents." The essays possess variety of subject and mood; beauty and humor in them are one; there are no set pieces. In some ways the War and the Peace may have made EMF harder, but they have also made him more sensitive. Despair has sharpened his compassion and generosity, and he is now emphatic about social and political issues concerning which he feels deeply. His work is spontaneous, as the work of Galsworthy and Beerbohm is not. He "improvises his distance" when he writes. For a man with a generalizing mind, EMF lives close to sense data: "Mr. Forster rings little bells of change not from word to word, but from perception to perception." The vision in these essays is not always single, but this fact mostly indicates the richness of the vision. EMF invites us not to change our opinions but "to use our senses afresh"—thereby will our minds be opened, our beliefs seen anew, our first principles doubted. EMF is above all "a disturber of values, a changer of perspectives." [Subtle, meaningful appreciation of EMF's qualities.]

333 "Mr. E. M. Forster Past and Present," Times Literary Supplement (Lond), 21 March 1936, 239.

The contents of *Abinger Harvest* are rich and diverse. The divisions of the volume—"The Present," "Books," "The Past," "The East," and "The Abinger Pageant"—are convenient. Another order, the chronological, suggests itself. Such an arrangement would allow us to trace EMF's spiritual history and that of an age through him. The groups would then appear in this order: "The Past," "The East," "Books," "The Past" (for the essays written after 1918), and "The Present." The present as EMF treats it is all too insistent and disturbing. EMF feels called upon to defend our traditional liberties in view of the threats to our existence. There is no weariness in these essays; there is the presence of "the imaginative realism which sees and accepts life, naked and whole"; EMF seeks no escape from this world out of disgust with it.

334 "Mr. E. M. Forster's Essays: A Varied Harvest," TIMES (Lond), 20 March 1936, p. 19.
In *Abinger Harvest* EMF reveals the "luxury" of his mind, presenting aspects of many realms of experience that figure in his novels. The book exhibits diversity of subject and of the author's mind: EMF is "at once wit, poet, scholar, impressionist, propagandist." He has integrated all his gifts into essays that are works of art, delightful and disturbing at the same time.

335 Orwell, George [pseud of Eric Blair]. "Some Recent Novels," NEW ENGLISH WEEKLY, IX (24 Sept 1936), 397–97; rptd as "Review," in THE COLLECTED ESSAYS, JOURNALISM AND LETTERS OF GEORGE ORWELL, ed by Sonia Orwell and Ian Angus (NY: Harcourt, Brace & World; Lond: Secker & Warburg, 1968), I, 230–32.
A Passage to India is not the perfect novel about India, but it is as good as we are likely to get, since no one capable of writing a good novel can be made to stay in India long enough to assimilate the atmosphere completely.

336 Paterson, Isabel. "Mr. Forster, Cultured, Tolerant, Urbane," NEW YORK HERALD TRIBUNE BOOK REVIEW, 31 May 1936, p. 6.
The essays in *Abinger Harvest* contain notes and hints of EMF's antecedents and their bearing upon the formation of the liberal mind. The contents are rich and diverse if personal and idiosyncratic. "Liberty in England" is an honest defense of the liberal mind. *Abinger* acquaints us with "a cultured, tolerant, and urbane mind."

337 Pritchett, V. S. "Mr. Forster Speaks for the English Middle Class," CHRISTIAN SCIENCE MONITOR, "Weekly Magazine," 29 April 1936, p. 11.
Sanity and good sense account in part for EMF's influence, but more to the point is his integrity. He may have detached his reason from passion, and

he may have accepted freedom as a result of the sacrifice of others; but he has heart, unlike certain other intellectuals. His examination of the English character is perceptive; the Englishman is impervious perhaps, but he is not unsubtle, as EMF's own criticism proves. "The middle class whom Mr. Forster represents have reached their aristocratic period, and their charm and lucidity are all the more delightful and dangerous." [Review of *Abinger Harvest*. Incisive commentary.]

338 Ransom, John Crowe. "Gestures of Dissent," YALE REVIEW, nsXXVI (Sept 1936), 181–83.

Abinger Harvest is a notable miscellany; EMF reveals sensibility, wit, and a narrative gift. He was not born in the right age. His fame rests on his novels, especially *A Passage to India*, but the comic attitude is untenable in this age. His novels are comedies; he has stopped writing fiction as if to acknowledge that comedy runs counter to the time-spirit. The essays on literary criticism are praiseworthy. EMF is a casualty, intellectually and artistically, of the war. [Stimulating commentary.]

339 Reilly, Joseph J. "Made by Time," COMMONWEAL, XXV (25 Dec 1936), 255.

Abinger Harvest reveals an essayist of charm and humor who declines to take himself too seriously. "The Abinger Pageant" has much pathos: it asks if nature can stand up to industrial progress. EMF is uneven as a critic; he is best on Sinclair Lewis, unsatisfying on Proust, inadequate on T. S. Eliot. He is at his best in picturing personalities (in his biographical sketches). He is a sane, sensitive, and delightful writer.

340 Schnell, Jonathan. "Books: A Causerie," FORUM, XCVI (July 1936), iv–vii.

Abinger Harvest reveals English culture at its best, although EMF is also interested in exposing the imitation English gentleman. EMF manifests "a profound humanity" and has "a sense of solidarity with all human beings." He has also absorbed, to his advantage, some of the culture of the East. The book reveals a writer of "enlightenment, humor, and knowledge."

341 Scott-James, R. A. "E. M. Forster," LONDON MERCURY, XXXIII (April 1936), 635–36.

EMF's books show the continuity of his intellectual interests. He is leisured in his responses but can react precipitously. He sees experience clearly and unconventionally; his language corresponds, being "direct, easy, free from affectation, and choice." His humor, ironic sense, and intellect save him from the occasional sentimentality of Charles Lamb. He has a wide range and an impressive balance of thought and feeling, "where all that is expressed has passed through the fine mechanism of sensibility, having the self-consistency of what is consistent with himself." [Perceptive review of *Abinger Harvest.*]

342 Simonds, Katharine. "Sketches by a Novelist," ATLANTIC MONTHLY, CLVIII (Aug 1936), front pages.
Abinger Harvest reveals EMF's quasi-novelistic, quasi-essayistic talents as they capture the essence of personality, the motivations of those he writes about, and their values.

343 Swinnerton, Frank. SWINNERTON: AN AUTOBIOGRAPHY (Garden City, NY: Doubleday, Doran, 1936; Lond: Hutchinson, 1937), pp. 112, 186, 280–81, 290, 292–94.
In W. L. George's list of the promising novelists at the time of World War I (NOTES ON NOVELISTS [1918]), EMF was the one regarded as the intellectual of the hour. EMF feels no compulsion to write for a living; his work has, therefore, the grace and ease of a dedicated amateur and an imposing clarity. EMF's clarity, thoughtfulness, insistence in conversation, intelligence, and constraint tend to make his associates self-conscious. EMF detests insincerity; he does not feel or provoke resentment; his mind is luminous. He is "spinsterish" in his sedateness, his occasional malice, and his determination to stand by reason; but he also has a totally admirable integrity, purity, and beauty. EMF, however, lacks "reciprocative vivacity."

344 Van Gelder, Robert. "Books of the Times," NEW YORK TIMES, 28 May 1936, p. 21.
EMF voices a despair in *Abinger Harvest*, modulated by his perfect prose. There are a few escapes for him—the past, music, the imaginative world of literature—but these are not infallible. He responded, in World War I, to the feeble protest of T. S. Eliot against the twentieth century, and because it was feeble (rather than self-confident) EMF found it congenial. Sometimes as in "Howard Overing Sturgis" he reveals himself as overcivilized. "Sinclair Lewis" and "Joseph Conrad: A Note" are excellent.

345 Williams, Orlo. "Books of the Quarter," CRITERION, XV (July 1936), 694–97.
EMF is not always at his best as occasional writer, but his work in this form is still thought-provoking even when it is at its most amusing. In almost all he does there is a hint either of the elemental and sinister under the pleasant surfaces or of the extraordinary underlying the ordinary. EMF is a fine literary critic. His essays on the East are also excellent. "The Consolations of History" illustrates all of EMF's merits. In addition to aesthetic distinction, this essay reveals a profound discontent at its base, a hint of the demonic (not the diabolic). "Liberty, humanity, humility and mutual comprehension between all men are the things he loves; tyranny, violence, pride

and prejudice are what he loathes." The misery on which civilization is based provides the basis of EMF's horror, which was accentuated by the war. EMF's liberalism is not quite extinguished, but it seems "a rather pathetic flame." [A profound and stimulating critique of *Abinger Harvest* and EMF.]

1937

346 Bayliss, Stanley A. "E. M. Forster and Music," CHESTERIAN, XVIII (Jan–Feb 1937), 61–65.

In *Aspects of the Novel* EMF's discussion of Tolstoy (whose WAR AND PEACE, he says, resounds with chords) and his discussion of rhythm in fiction; the famous Fifth Symphony description in *Howards End* and his use of the Beethoven "Eroica" Symphony in "Co-ordination" (*Collected Tales*); Lucy Honeychurch's playing of Beethoven's Opus 111 (*A Room with a View*) are all indicative of his knowledge of music. EMF uses music in his fiction with superb dramatic effect, despite the fact that the music he alludes to in *Room* (Opus 111, "Parsifal," Gluck's "Armide") may not be commonly known and available to all of his reading public. [Pedestrian and rather obvious article, less valuable than Benjamin Britten's "Some Notes on Forster and Music" (1969).]

347 Caudwell, Christopher [pseud of Christopher St. John Sprigg]. "Liberty: A Study in Bourgeois Illusion," STUDIES IN A DYING CULTURE (Lond: Macmillan, 1937; NY: Dodd, Mead, 1938), pp. 193–228, espec 204, 210–11 (NY ed).

EMF, along with Bertrand Russell and Wells, is an exemplar of bourgeois freedom, a man who wishes a liberation from conventions only. True freedom is less absolute and individualistic; it involves a consciousness of "causality" and can only be attained in a society wherein men cooperate in the process of economic production.

348 Routh, H. V. TOWARDS THE TWENTIETH CENTURY: ESSAYS IN THE SPIRITUAL HISTORY OF THE NINETEENTH (NY: Macmillan; Cambridge: Cambridge UP, 1937), pp. 161, 181, 365.

Ruskin in his compulsion to ground abstractions on individual sense impressions anticipates the inductions of Bergson, who was to influence writers like D. H. Lawrence, Virginia Woolf, EMF, and Proust. D. H. Lawrence and EMF have continued Matthew Arnold's quest for spiritual self-possession begun in the nineteenth century. In EMF the spirit springs to life only when it meets a kindred spirit and establishes affinities with him. [Notes the psychological basis of the important twentieth century novelists of whom EMF is one.]

349 Traversi, D[erek] A. "The Novels of E. M. Forster," Arena (Lond), I (April 1937), 28–40; rptd in E. M. Forster: The Critical Heritage, ed by Philip Gardner (Lond & Boston: Routledge & Kegan Paul, 1973), pp. 387–99.

How far does EMF criticize the one-sidedness of modern literature and how far does he transcend it? In *Howards End* the kind of sensitivity and sincerity present in Margaret Schlegel is the note most often struck in EMF's novels. He wishes to bring the Schlegel middle-class idealism and integrity into contact with actuality. He does so in all his books by a shock or a crisis that interrupts the even tenor of social life and confronts the middle class with its insufficiency. In *A Room with a View* Mr. Emerson upsets the conventional attitudes of the English by guiding them about Santa Croce; in *Howards End* Mrs. Wilcox introduces the Schlegel sisters to a profounder actuality at Howards End; in *A Passage to India* Adela Quested's hysterical experiences in the Marabar Caves affect her marriage to Ronny Heaslop, Aziz's surface attachment to Islam, and the depth of Mrs. Moore's despair. Mrs. Wilcox, Mrs. Moore, Mr. Emerson, and George Emerson are free within their conventional limitations. They are aware of the crisis which confronts them but do not fathom its meaning. They reveal the chief discrepancy in EMF's work, that between an insistence on awareness or intensity of experience and the corresponding sense of vacancy and futility that unexpectedly meets it [a most perceptive formulation]. EMF places his hope in the weakness of logic ("logic" for him is an awareness of devaluing contemporary tendencies). His drift is toward pessimism but one honest enough to interpret the contemporary situation with passion and integrity. His hope centers too much on the past (an organic community with roots in rural life) and is too little directed to the present and the future. The heritage from the past wears thin: hence the somewhat sentimental nostalgia in his works. He suggests that the life found in Howards End is only temporarily eclipsed and will later triumph, but his assurance lacks "verification from experience." Mrs. Wilcox does not have noticeable connections with England and with actual life, and so fails to come alive. EMF is a social novelist, aware of the sterility of his society but unable to find a mode of living for his people that would assimilate them to a wider, less personal context, and so relieve them of their self-importance and triviality. Intelligence in Margaret needs to be fused with something more comprehensive than big business and insensitivity as Henry Wilcox embodies them; and Henry is too sentimentally justified in terms of work and honesty. EMF is sensitive to his own experience, expresses it in "clear, supple and passionate prose," and thus remarkably recreates the intense moment. Yet he is unable to bring these separate moments of feeling into a continuous, personal unity.

In *Howards End* he does not believe deeply enough in the value of strong personal relations; the connections he wishes for are, therefore, emotionally unrealized. But in *Passage* his critical pessimism is not sentimentality; his values in India are set off by something frightening and unmanageable. There is in India a unity between man and nature, but one that stresses an impersonal identity and the unimportance of the spirit. This unimportance robs us of the drama—the crisis of despair—and leaves only a void and uncertainty. India becomes the "solvent" by which EMF analyzes the faith that he derived from European culture, "in causality, in the spirit, in the significance of events." His sense for values is contrasted in India with the spiritual vacancy inherent in the Caves. What gives his pessimism a unique quality is an intense concern for values and the keenness with which he apprehends them. Mrs. Moore senses "the infinite possibilities of experience," and yet realizes their lack of importance. The unfathomable arch of the sky suggests in structure a small regular cave; just so, "an unending echo" is the end result of any decisive human act. Love attempts to break down barriers, but its inability to do so is emphasized by Adela's experiences in the Caves. The gradually extinguished flames in the Cave walls after a match is lit connote the inability of two people to merge in love. The flames also suggest, in EMF, a clash between an ideal that "breathes air" (a self-transcending union through love) and the incapacity of his self-awareness that "breathes stone," to actually accept that ideal. [A searching commentary and still one of the best essays on EMF, though it is relatively unknown.]

350 Warren, Austin. "The Novels of E. M. Forster," AMERICAN REVIEW, IX (Summer 1937), 226–51; rvd and rptd in RAGE FOR ORDER: ESSAYS IN CRITICISM (Chicago: University of Chicago P, 1948), pp. 119–41; in CRITIQUES AND ESSAYS ON MODERN FICTION: 1920–1951, ed by John W. Aldridge (NY: Ronald P, 1952), pp. 447–87; in part in FORSTER: A COLLECTION OF CRITICAL ESSAYS, ed by Malcolm Bradbury (Englewood Cliffs, NJ: Prentice-Hall, Spectrum Books, 1966), pp. 48–55.

EMF's masters are Austen, Butler, and Dostoevski. For EMF the novel has as its function "a persuasive equilibrium: it must balance the claims of the existence and the essence, of personalities and ideas." Values are more important than facts to him, values such as friendship, intellectual exploration, insight and imagination, the pursuit of the inner life. EMF has ideas but no "idea" (or dogma). In *Howards End* he expresses this view: though it is possible either to see life steadily or to see it whole, he prefers to see it whole. His cardinal virtues are "courage, candor, insight, disinterestedness"; he can, in fact, find worth in everything except humbug and muddledom. In EMF's view human beings have, different as they are, a common obligation to attain self-knowledge. He concentrates on the upper middle class and the academic intelligentsia and excludes from his purview aristo-crats, sadistic peasants, cruelty, and lust. The vice of the bourgeois is "self-complacent, unimaginative respectability"; the vice of the intelligentsia is "the snobbery of 'culture.' " "Culture" is often exposed as thin, bloodless, and lifeless, as in Rev. Cuthbert Eager (*A Room with a View*), Cecil Vyse (*A Room With a View*), and Leonard Bast (*Howards End*). EMF would urge that culture and conduct connect (Mr. Bons fails to connect them in "The Celestial Omnibus"). A truer culture is presented in another aspect of Cecil Vyse, in Tibby Schlegel (*Howards End*), Philip Herriton (*Angels*), Rickie Elliot (*The Longest Journey*), Stewart Ansell (*Journey*), and the Rev. Mr. Beebe (*Room*). These men are ascetics, scholars, aesthetes, detached ob-servers, and contemplatives, not capable of passion for women or people in general. Cecil Vyse is a genuine if restricted person and is only absurd when he pretends to ranges of feeling (sexual love) which lie beyond him. Philip Herriton develops from a culture snob into a man of insight and goodwill. At times the life of culture becomes bloodless; then EMF turns to primiti-vism (as with Gino Carella [*Angels*] and Stephen Wonham [*Journey*]) or to healthy extraverts like the Wilcoxes (*Howards End*). Throughout, EMF has felt the attraction of his opposites, the child, the animal, the Philistine, Italy and the Italians. But his main impulse is to let reason rule and to harmonize opposites. As with Santayana, so with EMF, everything ideal has a natural basis, and there is nothing in nature "incapable of ideal fulfill-ment." The individual can never become, in all respects, the universal person; but the large-minded individual, like Margaret Schlegel (*Howards End*), will try to become as univeral as possible by virtue of his or her ranging sympathies. Such a person attempts to reconcile the disparities of existence. The golden mean is not tepidity, mechanical compromise, or apathetic good humor. True moderation is thus an achievement, not an endowment; the attainment of proportion is the work of a lifetime. EMF agrees with Goldsworthy Lowes Dickinson that reason as such is both important and unimportant. It is to be balanced by a sense of a world or worlds beyond this one. This kind of double vision EMF projects in his tales and preeminently in his clairvoyant women, Mrs. Wilcox (*Howards End*) and Mrs. Moore (*A Passage to India*). There are three kinds of human contact: the insensitive and impersonal, the personal, and the transcenden-tally impersonal (EMF cherishes the last two, exposes the first). Without any practical political sense, Mrs. Moore affirms the oneness of all humani-ty, and she influences all with whom she comes in contact. The center of *Passage*, structurally and psychologically, is the excursion to the Marabar Caves. The echo is that of eternity, infinity, the absolute but is also an appalling, frightening vision. Mrs. Moore's pessimism is only possible for one reared in the Christian tradition that posits a personal relationship with a beneficent God. The Caves insinuate, instead, that human values have no basis in the nature of things, that moral distinctions are irrelevant, that the cosmos does not distinguish between sinner and saint, and that cosmic forces are indifferent, even malignant. The echo levels all religion to the same substratum of disillusion. Fielding, in his pleasure with the measurable harmonies of Venetian culture on his way back to England, speaks in part for EMF. Yet *Passage* does offer "a chastened hopefulness," since Mrs. Moore and her younger children do reach, in part, the alien world of India even if they don't understand it completely; their dedication to the personal still has value in an impersonal world. It is from the standpoint of an ideal, spiritual wholeness that EMF criticizes racial shortcomings. He himself has tried to reach wholeness and steadiness of vision; he knows that no one race has ever achieved perfection. As a novelist he lacks conscious eccentricities; he is, however, sometimes lacking in power. But his sensitivity and his stylistic distinction will insure his survival. [An essay of permanent value and many striking insights; especially good on the role of Mrs. Moore in *Passage.* The 1948 revision has many stylistic changes and some excisions, including the final judgment that EMF's novels will take their place with those of Hawthorne, Turgenev, and Austen.]

1938

351 Batho, Edith, and Bonamy Dobrée. THE VICTORIANS AND AFTER: 1830–1914 (NY: Robert M. McBride; Lond: Cresset P, Introductions English and American Literature, IV, 1938), pp. 18, 78, 79, 100–101, 211, 274, 275, 321, 334; 2nd rvd ed (Lond: Cresset P, 1950), pp. 18, 76, 77, 97–98, 205, 267, 268, 314, 327 (EMF discussions unchanged).

EMF takes the novel in the direction of the personal relation away from conflict in society. EMF reacted strongly to all that Kipling stood for; his world, for EMF, was the outer world of "telegrams and anger, of futile efficiency, of misdirected effort." For EMF the important values are inner ones; his is a world of introspection rather than an extraverted one. The delicacy of his prose matches the delicacy of his characters' sentiments; his people value an inner integrity. His reputation, especially with novelists, has gradually grown; the earlier novels were a bit clumsy and uncertain. Most of his work has an undeniably moving quality. [Bibliographical listing and brief discussion of EMF's nonfiction, p. 321, updated in 2nd ed, p. 314.]

352 Bell, Quentin (ed). "Preface, by Charles Mauron," "War and Peace: A Letter to E. M. Forster" [by Julian Bell], "Notes for a Reply, by E. M. Forster," JULIAN BELL: ESSAYS, POEMS AND LETTERS WITH CONTRIBUTIONS BY J. M. KEYNES, DAVID GARNETT, CHARLES

MAURON, C. DAY LEWIS, E. M. FORSTER (Lond: Hogarth P, 1938), pp. 233–56, 335–89, 391–92; also 304, 320, 324.

[In "Preface, by Charles Mauron," Mauron indicates a will to power in Julian Bell that led him to reject the "democratic epicureanism" of EMF and other twentieth-century liberals. In "War and Peace: A Letter to E. M. Forster," Bell praises many of EMF's qualities: "tolerance, reasonableness, charity; a clear and deep conviction of the value of certain states of mind; a readiness to listen to opponents and a sympathy for the young." While Bell appreciates these qualities, he feels that they are inadequate to cope with the international power struggle and with the force of fascism. The military virtues must be cultivated in order to fight fire with fire. In "Notes for a Reply," EMF defends his liberalism and notes the contradictory elements in Bell's letter: a conviction that men are evil or at least indifferent to evil and a need to save them through Marxism. In "Letter to A," Bell sees his relationship to Roger Fry in the same terms as those EMF used to describe his relationship to Goldsworthy Lowes Dickinson, that of disciple to a Socrates figure. In "The Proletariat and Poetry: An Open Letter to C. Day Lewis," Bell maintains that the work of Keynes, EMF, and Wells may represent "a higher, more mature, and dignified and assured culture than the 'left.'" Many individual references to EMF and his Bloomsbury connections. See also Frederick Grubb, A VISION OF REALITY: A STUDY OF LIBERALISM IN TWENTIETH-CENTURY VERSE (1965), and Peter Stansky and William Abrahams, JOURNEY TO THE FRONTIER: TWO ROADS TO THE SPANISH CIVIL WAR (1966).]

353 Bowen, Elizabeth. "Mr. Forster," NEW STATESMAN AND NATION, nsXV (2 April 1938), 572, 574; rptd as "E. M. Forster, II," in COLLECTED IMPRESSIONS (Lond: Longmans Green; NY: Knopf, 1950), pp. 122–26.

Like Chekhov, EMF is a civilized man who has had to witness a decline. His point of view has been mature from the first and has remained the same since his twenties. Intellect gives his novels their structure, and it edits feeling. His novels show control; they all smile, even the grim *The Longest Journey;* they engross us with their stories. He writes a personal fiction; his irony is deadly and seldom gentle. In the moral war he depicts, there is no private justice; individual fates are insignificant. His bad characters fail to change and are the enemy; they do not generate evil but store it. His good characters have imagination and expose themselves; they are anti-heroic (Margaret Schlegel, Fielding). He also has neutral characters like Philip Herriton in *Where Angels Fear to Tread* and Rickie Elliot in *Journey.* A fourth kind of character is the non-moral, naturalistic individual, Gino Carella in *Angels,* Helen Schlegel in *Howards End,* Aziz in *A Passage to India.* His admirable characters may dread the forces let loose against them but are not intimidated by these forces. Rose Macaulay in THE WRITINGS

OF E. M. FORSTER (1938) writes for both the amateur and the professional. [Incisive essay. In part a review of Macaulay's book.]

354 Church, Richard. "A Study in Sympathies," CHRISTIAN SCIENCE MONITOR, Magazine, 11 May 1938, p. 10.
Rose Macaulay is the ideal critic to write about EMF: they both love individuality, delight in characters, detest uniformity, and value freedom. She also pursues EMF's indebtedness to many cultures and can define his essence as a mind and sensibility. Her analysis of his fiction is firm. His chief concern, she realizes, is the contrast between the permanent and the transient. She uses language in the same precise and vivid way as EMF does. [Review of Rose Macaulay's THE WRITINGS OF E. M. FORSTER, 1938.]

355 Collier, John. "Beside Tourgeniev?" LISTENER, XXIX (16 March 1938), supplement, p. xv.
Rose Macaulay's THE WRITINGS OF E. M. FORSTER (1938) is unsatisfactory because it neglects EMF's craft and artistry. Like Turgenev, EMF can indulge with absolute security in "a certain amateurishness of design" because his form is perfect enough to allow such a departure. The crystal technique expands to the proportions revealed in *A Passage to India* and remains essentially unchanged. EMF's genius recalls Turgenev's. EMF's characters are less simple and magnificent though more subtle than Turgenev's. EMF is "our only novelist of European importance."

356 Connolly, Cyril. ENEMIES OF PROMISE (Lond: Routledge & Kegan Paul, 1938; Boston: Little, Brown, 1939); rvd ed (NY: Macmillan, 1948; Lond: Routledge & Kegan Paul, 1949); (pages are for NY eds): 1939, pp. 7, 31–32, 62, 107, 122, 158; 1949, pp. 6, 26–27, 49, 81, 92, 119; materials on EMF only slightly rvd in 1948–1949 ed; rptd in part in A LIBRARY OF LITERARY CRITICISM: MODERN BRITISH LITERATURE, ed by Ruth Z. Temple and Martin Tucker (NY: Frederick Ungar, 1966), I, 307.
The best literary work explodes with delayed impact, as EMF's parables, written twenty to thirty years ago, now have done. His vision was firm enough, his characters representative enough, his social consciousness strong enough for his works to appeal to present-day intellectuals; his style also remains fresh. His style, in its simplicity, its absence of subordinating clauses, and its everyday language, represents a revolt against the mandarin style. EMF is a true innovator because *The Longest Journey* and *Howards End* adumbrated a point of view, a technique, and an attitude to the reader to be followed by psychological novelists in the next thirty years, notably Virginia Woolf, Katherine Mansfield, David Garnett, and Elizabeth Bowen. The new writer can gain much from "the cursive style, the agreeable manners, the precise and poetical impact of EMF's diction" and the individual

qualities to be found in Maugham, Hemingway, Isherwood, Lawrence, and Orwell. Virginia Woolf developed away from EMF "with his artlessness and simple, poetic, colloquial style" into a more lyrical kind of writing.

357 Dangerfield, George. "E. M. Forster: A Man with a View," SATURDAY REVIEW OF LITERATURE (NY), XVIII (27 Aug 1938), 3–4, 14–16.

It is sometimes difficult to discover EMF's direction; the difficulty is one of understanding the liberal temperament, which offers a Protest, not a Plan, in the interests of freedom. This temperament protests against tyranny, but its answers are vague when a means to prevent oppression is sought. EMF's four prewar novels center on the necessity for personal relationship as opposed to stupidity, snobbery, and muddle. In *A Room with a View*, as in the other novels, EMF's keen observation, marvellous ear, and sly and demure wit are omnipresent. He is uneasy with sexuality in women (even with the Schlegel sisters the interest in sex is offhand). When he denies the life of the senses in sex, this life gets back through shock, sometimes even through death, which is sometimes made clumsy and irrelevant. These faults are not disastrous: love, for example, is seen as companionship and understanding even when sex is denied. In *Howards End* EMF is infused with his characters; through this means EMF gives us both glory and comment. The characters are so full of EMF that they sometimes reflect adversely on him: the condescension expressed by the Schlegels toward Leonard Bast is really EMF's, not theirs. The liberalism, in its attempts at fairness to the Wilcoxes, is at times too close to the sentiments of John Bright and Adam Smith. The Protest is sometimes murky. *A Passage to India* has for its theme the muddle that is life. The English are drawn with a cruelty intensified over that present in the depiction of some characters in the early novels; it has become impersonal, the English are victims of an abstraction—the White Man's Burden. But the Indians reveal limitations, especially the rivalry between Muslim and Hindu, though EMF presents them with subtlety and tenderness. This novel also registers only a Protest, not a Plan. The inconclusiveness, the Protest that is necessary if sometimes inconvenient and obtrusive, is expressed so well that EMF's work will survive as an embodiment of it. [Authoritative and too little known essay; incidentally a review of Rose Macaulay's THE WRITINGS OF E. M. FORSTER (1938).]

358 Elting, M. L. "The Book Forum," FORUM, C (Sept 1938), iv–v.

EMF has taken, somewhat reluctantly, to the defense of democratic liberty against fascism. His stature increases because of his vigorous endeavors to keep his "quiet excellence" loved in a raucous world. [Remarks are from review of Rose Macaulay's THE WRITINGS OF E. M. FORSTER (1938).]

359 Endicott, N. J. "Most of Us," CANADIAN FORUM (Toronto), XVIII (June 1938), 88–89.
Rose Macaulay's comment on EMF the individual has more distinction, in THE WRITINGS OF E. M. FORSTER (1938), than her critiques of his novels. EMF does have the qualities which she claims for him: a feeling for idiom and a sensitivity to "minor registrations and differentiations." His liberalism has been insistent, a liberalism that emphasizes "ruthless analysis and cultured tradition" [EMF's phrase].

360 Fausset, H. I'A. "E. M. Forster," MANCHESTER GUARDIAN, 18 March 1938, p. 7.
Rose Macaulay in THE WRITINGS OF E. M. FORSTER (1938) magnifies the creative force of EMF's fastidious sensitivity. Her appraisal of him as a writer "who invites us not to pass judgment on life but to understand and cherish it" is clear-sighted.

361 Fremantle, Anne. LOYAL ENEMY (Lond: Hutchinson, 1938), pp. 53, 54, 56, 68, 112, 129, 344, 441.
By many of his admirers, Marmaduke Pickthall was thought to have been the prototype of Fielding in *A Passage to India.* [Numerous references are made to EMF's remarks on Pickthall, contained in "Salute to the Orient" (*Abinger Harvest*), and to some of EMF's other writings on the East, supportive of Pickthall's views.]

362 Hoare, Dorothy M. "E. M. Forster," SOME STUDIES IN THE MODERN NOVEL (Lond: Chatto & Windus, 1938; NY: Prospect P, 1940; Chester Springs, Pa: Dufour, 1953), pp. 68–96.
EMF reveals Meredith's influence: see EMF's embracing of the comic, his conviction that women are men's equals, his neo-paganism (this last is memorably expressed in "The Story of the Siren"). He is better with groups than with individuals, and as comic artist is then on surer ground. *The Longest Journey* presents a contrast between the forces of free instinct and restrictive convention, with Rickie Elliot caught between them. EMF's tendency is to check enthusiasm or vision by acid comment or intrusive incident (i.e., Rickie breaks his aunt's teacup as he meditates on his new freedom. In the upshot he retreats to convention yet ultimately dies to insure Stephen Wonham's salvation.) In *Where Angels Fear to Tread* EMF further reveals his method of ironic juxtaposition of incident and opposing values; the significance of Lilia's situation for Mrs. Herriton is on a par with her troubles over the cook and the garden. In Italy the situation is not that simple—it involves the inner transformation of Philip Herriton and Caroline Abbott and the death of Gino Carella's child. In *Journey* EMF valued the symbolic moment as having inescapable importance for the individual; in *Angels* the value of trivial incidents is stressed, when Caroline asserts that

any one of our actions may have consequences "hanging on it forever." In his novels the emphasis on free, vital, and total response and involvement leads to a valuing of the extraordinary aspects of experience: accidents, passion, sudden death. EMF criticizes the passivity toward life exemplified by Philip Herriton. EMF does not build his emotional universe on false foundations; the antagonistic force always breaks in to balance the scene, as it would in life (note that Philip's and Caroline's differing sexual exaltations in the last scene of *Angels* are deflected by the cinder in Harriet Herriton's eye). EMF thus allows for the materialism, the convention, and the pettiness that he despises, instead of suppressing it. In *Howards End* the Schlegels realize the sacredness of personality, while the Wilcoxes do not. Personal relations acquire a religious sanction, whereas in the early novels the free life of impulse had substituted for religion. The regeneration of the Wilcoxes is asserted almost at the expense of "pure" feeling, represented in the relationship between Helen Schlegel and Leonard Bast. The dichotomy between convention and instinct has become less simple and stark. The "free" characters in the late novels, Mrs. Wilcox and Mrs. Moore, are also more elusive and complex. *A Passage to India* denies both free impulse and personal relationship as ultimate sanctions and gives us Mrs. Moore and what she stands for. She embodies a visionary intuition of reality, a mode of communication based on sympathy. Mrs. Moore bridges two ranges of experience: the romantic, the impulsive, an integral mode of feeling versus the ironic, the mood of disillusion, a negation of value. She unites these opposing attitudes and embodies mystery as well as muddle; in so doing she helps create an atmosphere of ironic detachment and intellectual aloofness to balance sympathy and an interest in the ineffable. [Perceptive remarks by an early critic, especially good on Mrs. Moore's function in *Passage*.]

363 Isherwood, Christopher. LIONS AND SHADOWS: AN EDUCATION IN THE TWENTIES (Lond: Hogarth P, 1938; Norfolk, Conn: New Directions, 1947), pp. 167–68, 173–75, 258.
[Chalmers (Edward Upward) and Isherwood read Gide's LES FAUX-MONNAYEURS (THE COUNTERFEITERS), as a result of reading about it in EMF's *Aspects of the Novel.* Isherwood was more intrigued by EMF's conception of the book than by the book itself, although Gide's idea of the novelist as enduring protagonist was similar to the situation in one of Isherwood's own works. Chalmers was enthusiastic about EMF's modernity in *Howards End.* EMF is modern because he is comic rather than tragic and because his technique is based (in a now famous phrase) "on the tea-table": important incidents are minimized, downplayed, and presented in an offhand manner. Chalmers and Isherwood attempt to apply this conception in a book that Isherwood is writing, in which a violent accident is thus to be "tea-tabled." The ending of this book becomes "an apotheosis of the Tea-Table, a decrescendo of anti-climaxes."]

364 Jameson, Storm. THE NOVEL IN CONTEMPORARY LIFE (Boston: The Writer, Inc., 1938), pp. 7–8.

The writer in 1937 finds it difficult to write because he cannot find, in the chaos outside him, meaningful experience for his art. EMF does know what is going on (witness the speech he made at the First International Congress of Writers in Paris in 1935; see "Liberty in England," *Abinger Harvest*). In this time of crisis EMF regards the role of the novelist as temporary; the task of civilization will fall to others than to the present generation of novelists. But EMF's courage and personal integrity do not provide the mood in which it is worthwhile to write a meaningful novel. Significant novels do not result from "pottering about with old tools, waiting stoically for the roof to fall in." There is "a gap in the continuity of consciousness" [D. H. Lawrence's phrase] in contemporary culture, and it is difficult now for the writer to form a conception of life that will be basic to the novels that he writes. To arrive at a new consciousness of reality, the novelist must make a willing and passionate surrender to experience, and he must practice an absolute truthfulness in turning emotion into words.

365 Lawrence, T. E. THE LETTERS OF T. E. LAWRENCE, ed by David Garnett (Lond: Jonathan Cape, 1938; NY: Doubleday, Doran, 1939), pp. 374, 435–36, 455–58, 460–62, 466–67, 473, 486–87, 496–97, 531–32, 536–38, 553–55, 593–95, 622–26, 641, 646, 737–38, 759–60, 804–5, 864–65, 871.

Letter to EMF (20 Feb 1924): *Howards End*, "The Story of the Siren," and *Pharos and Pharillon* put EMF among the elect. EMF's distinction between active and passive books is valid; SEVEN PILLARS OF WISDOM is passive or static rather than active like EMF's books. Letter to EMF (24 July 1924): [Detailed criticism of *A Passage to India.*] EMF gets continent of India on canvas complete; then the characters become so lively that the continent fades. *Passage* has a multiplicity of effects and cross-lights and bearings. The roof conversation between Aziz and Fielding, the orgiastic festival, and the club and Cave sequences are excellent. "One feels all the while the weight of the climate, the shape of the land, the immovable immensity of the crowd behind . . . all that is felt, with the ordinary fine human senses." Letter to Edward Garnett (16 Sept 1924): EMF's greatness is doubtful, though he is an excellent writer. Letter to EMF (29 Sept 1924): One critic's judgment of EMF—that he plays the flute exquisitely but cannot command an entire orchestra—is beside the point; all great works are essentially solo performances [the critic is probably Edward Garnett]. Letter to Edward Garnett (9 April 1925): [Lawrence is "Struck all of a heap" by *The Longest Journey*, "though it is as faulty as Verga."] Letter to E. Palmer (10 Dec 1925): [Lawrence saw EMF at King's College, "large as life, but sad-looking, wasted almost."] Letter to EMF (26 April 1926): EMF will yet do something bigger than *Passage*, though he may feel empty for the moment and may have to wait ten years to do it. Letter to EMF (14 July 1927): Many passages when excerpted from the novels do not seem like EMF. Hopefully, EMF's critical lectures [*Aspects of the Novel*] will be published, "a flag as guide to your course." Letter to EMF (8 Sept 1927): *Aspects* is superb, like hearing Adam discourse on gardens. The difference in tone between EMF and Percy Lubbock is marked; Lubbock treats the novel "like the glazed unapproachable pictures in a public gallery," while EMF regards novels "as though they were things one writes." As for an unpublishable short story of EMF's ["Dr. Woolacott," in *The Life to Come*], there is nothing wrong with it. [As for an unpublished novel *Maurice* that EMF invited him to read, Lawrence did not want to risk altering his present conception of EMF by commenting on it.] *Howards End* and *Passage* are popular with airmen in Karachi; *Journey* is not. They feel that EMF does not "clear things up much" without realizing that he has "cleared a mist of reality from their eyes." The sudden, off-stage deaths in *Journey* bother him. Letter to Dick Knowles (7 Dec 1927): [Robert Graves said that Lawrence is like a unicorn because he is different from his fellow beasts.] Possibly EMF is a unicorn, when he writes from Edinburgh: "so I'm at peace and quite happy. But I do not know why every year it becomes more difficult to write down those last two words." Letter to EMF (16 April 1928): EMF's works are all rewarding even when he may not be at his best and at his highest standard. The less good work is still valuable for the intentions visible behind the performance. [Would like EMF to read his manuscript concerning life in the service (THE MINT) if EMF could bring himself to do it.] Letter to EMF (20 Aug 1928): EMF's good words on THE MINT are gratifying, since EMF is "one of the shining ones of the English language." Letter to James Hanley (28 Dec 1931): [EMF was struck with Hanley's work when he read it while visiting Lawrence in Plymouth. Lawrence found EMF "a very subtle and helpful critic" when he was writing SEVEN PILLARS OF WISDOM. All of EMF's notes on books or writing are workmanlike since he writes himself, "a very witty, pointed, shy, emancipated person."] Letter to EMF (24 May 1934): *Goldsworthy Lowes Dickinson* is notable for its restraint, tidiness, subtlety, commonsense, glorification of quiet, care for the average man, wit, and assimilated quotations. Letter to D. J. Greenwood (5 April 1935): EMF is a possibility to render help for the defense in the prosecution of James Hanley's BOY. EMF's mind is most subtle. [Rpts letter to Robert Graves (24 Jan 1933), pp. 759–60; see T. E. Lawrence, T. E. LAWRENCE TO HIS BIOGRAPHERS, entry no. 366.]

366 Lawrence, T. E. T. E. LAWRENCE TO HIS BIOGRAPHER, ROBERT GRAVES: INFORMATION ABOUT HIMSELF IN THE FORM OF LETTERS, NOTES AND ANSWERS TO QUESTIONS, EDITED WITH A CRITICAL COMMENTARY. (Garden City, NY: Doubleday, Doran, 1938; Lond: Fa-

ber & Faber, 1939); reissued in T. E. LAWRENCE TO HIS BIOGRA-
PHERS, ROBERT GRAVES AND LIDDELL HART (Garden City, NY:
Doubleday; Lond: Cassell, 1963), pp. 35, 58, 116, 144, 157, 170
[1938 ed unobtainable].
Letter (21 Oct 1925): EMF's *Alexandria* is great literature and should be
boosted. Letter (24 Dec 1927): Bennett, Wells, Galsworthy, EMF, Tomlinson, and Kipling are preferable to Wyndham Lewis, Joyce, and Stein. Letter
(6 Nov 1928): Those writers who try to better their everyday speech are the
most admirable and enjoyable: Wells, Bennett, Sir Thomas Browne, Rosset-
ti, Morris, and EMF. Letter (24 January 1933): EMF is one of the three
people Lawrence cares for most now that D. C. Hogarth is dead; the others
are the writer Frederick Manning and an Irish-Armenian physician, Dr.
Altounyan.

367 Leavis, F. R. "E. M. Forster," SCRUTINY, VII (Sept 1938),
185–202; rptd in THE IMPORTANCE OF SCRUTINY, ed by Eric Bentley
(NY: G. W. Stewart, 1948), pp. 295–310; rptd in rvd form in F. R.
Leavis, THE COMMON PURSUIT (Lond: Chatto & Windus; NY: G. W.
Stewart, 1952; NY: New York UP, 1964), pp. 261–67; and FORSTER:
A COLLECTION OF CRITICAL ESSAYS, ed by Malcolm Bradbury (En-
glewood Cliffs, NJ: Prentice-Hall, Spectrum Books, 1966), pp. 34–
37; and in part in A LIBRARY OF LITERARY CRITICISM: MODERN BRIT-
ISH LITERATURE, ed by Ruth Z. Temple and Martin Tucker (NY:
Frederick Ungar, 1966), I, 311–12.
It is difficult to define EMF's peculiar but real distinction. EMF is, in his
comedy, "the born novelist," but in his attempts to convey "a poetic communication about life" he is unsuccessful. The paradox is this: as a novelist
of personal relations, wherein his distinction lies, he is dissatisfied with the
quality of the civilization he writes about. His preoccupation with emotional
vitality takes him beyond the comic toward the poetic and the cosmic (away
from Jane Austen and toward D. H. Lawrence), where his touch is unsure.
Where Angels Fear to Tread is the most successful of the early novels; there
is no clash of modes or tones in it; the life in the book emanates from a
center. *A Room with a View* is readable and enjoyable, but there is a
"spinsterish inadequacy" in his presentation of love; also old Mr. Emerson
is not so wise as EMF takes him to be. The poetic intention is disciplined
in these two novels, but in *The Longest Journey* and *Howards End* the
element of distancing and control is in abeyance, to the detriment of these
works. The assuredness of EMF's comedy emphasizes the immaturity, the
unsureness, and the crudity of the poetic elements. The action surrounding
Stephen Wonham is especially unconvincing. *Howards End* is more mature
and less autobiographical than *Journey;* EMF's intentions in it or the means
he takes to realize them are dubious. Margaret Schlegel's marriage to Henry
Wilcox is not believable. EMF wishes to show the inadequacies of Marga-

ret's culture; but in bringing in Henry, he makes her situation desperate in a way that undercuts what she stands for. He conceives the Wilcoxes incorrectly; they aren't what he takes them to be. The symbology connected with Howards End house is not realized, with the result that the end of the book is sentimental. *A Passage to India* is a classic of liberal culture and escapes most of the foregoing strictures. Fielding is a far more mature figure of enlightenment than the Schlegels. Some weakness is present in the imputing of supernatural power to Mrs. Moore and her children, Ralph and Stella; it is too easily done. Even in *Passage* there are lapses in style, and the personal quality sometimes becomes more of a tonal liability than an asset. EMF's intelligence lacks force and authority for one who is so perceptive and sensitive; a general lack of vitality is perhaps too prevalent. This same weakness in tone and grasp is present in his essays; their "incompleteness" undoubtedly reflects the Bloomsbury milieu from which he developed. With all reservations made, EMF represents the free play of critical intelligence; he embodies the liberal point of view, "the humane, decent and rational— the 'civilized'—habit, of that tradition." [A germinal if somewhat rigid treatment of EMF's work, setting the stage for the later Forster "revival" of the 1940s. Essay is incidentally a review of Rose Macaulay's THE WRITINGS OF E. M. FORSTER (1938): for later revisions see Leavis, THE COMMON PURSUIT (1952).]

368 Macaulay, Rose. THE WRITINGS OF E. M. FORSTER (Lond: Hogarth P; NY: Harcourt, Brace, 1938); reissued (Lond: Hogarth P; NY: Barnes & Noble, 1970), with rvd bibliography; excerpts rptd in A LIBRARY OF LITERARY CRITICISM: MODERN BRITISH LITERATURE, ed by Ruth Z. Temple and Martin Tucker (NY: Frederick Ungar, 1966), I, 308.

Chapter I, "Setting": EMF derives from the Edwardian upper middle class. Rebelling against the unimaginative aspects of his tradition, he formulated the basic antithesis in his work: between the real and unreal, the true and false, being and not being. Chapter II, "Beginnings": EMF began writing with fantastic sketches and stories that stress the necessity for getting in touch with nature. "The Eternal Moment," contrasting the forces of sham and reality, is excellent; "The Machine Stops" is the least Forsterian tale; "The Story of the Siren" reveals the temporary victory of convention; "The Other Side of the Hedge" balances the forces, and neither side wins. Chapter III, *"Where Angels Fear to Tread"*: EMF traces the conquest of suburban English respectability by Italian charm and paganism. He reveals a mastery of plot despite his protests against the story element in fiction. He does not know his people well, especially the Italians; nevertheless they emerge solid and round. Chapter IV, *"The Longest Journey"*: Sawston is like a dark wood, a hell of lost souls in which Rickie Elliot is caught; his deterioration rather than his misery gives the Sawston scenes a nightmare quality. Agnes

Pembroke is a memorable portrait; she is at once better and worse than Herbert Pembroke, more subtle and sinister. We identify with the weak and sensitive Rickie, though his disgust with his father for supposedly engendering an illegitimate son is excessive. Gerald Dawes is a distorted figure; EMF's sure touch with the brainless athlete is missing here. Stewart Ansell is convincing as a denunciatory angel, a damning and bitter-tongued friend, and an undergraduate philosopher. Stephen Wonham is a magnificent conception, a reality that thrusts into perspective the artifices and conventions of Ansell, Mrs. Failing, Agnes, and Rickie. [Unlike most later critics, Macaulay has no reservations about Stephen's characterization.] Mrs. Failing is both a "sheep" and a "goat," ambiguous in her qualities and the effects she produces. Cambridge represents truth and life; Sawston, lies and darkness; and Wiltshire, recovery into truth and life. Cambridge is seen in too golden a light; Mr. Failing's essays are platitudinous; EMF's mysticism obtrudes too greatly. [This chapter is Macaulay's best.] Chapter V, "Modern Literature and Dante": [Discusses EMF's lectures to the Working Men's College, "Pessimism in Literature" and "Dante."] EMF distrusts Dante's rigor, though he and Dante share many traits: interest in people, history, and human character; respect for grandeur; a mystic belief in the greatness of life or the reality of salvation and damnation. Chapter VI, "*A Room with a View*": Old Mr. Emerson is EMF's spokesman, maintaining that until we find Italy in the spirit we remain in muddle. In EMF's comedies the symbolical mounting of the forces making for good and evil is like that in morality plays. *Room* is less arresting for its philosophy than for the conversations, relationships, and mutual reactions of its characters. EMF's triumph is his expressing through the means of a witty comedy the fact that life is struggle. [Extensive discussion of the characters.] Chapter VII, "*Howard's End*" [Full discussion.] Chapter VIII, "Interval": [EMF went to India for the first time and wrote articles about it.] Chapter IX, "Guidebook": In *Alexandria: A History and a Guide* EMF champions Greek and Ptolemaic culture and is critical of Christian orthodoxy. Chapter X, "Alexandrian Essays": [Contains descriptive summary of *Pharos and Pharillon.*] Chapter XI, "Other Essays": EMF in his essays after the war reveals disgust with the present and nostalgia for the past. His portraits in them reveal the insight and skill of the novelist. Chapter XII, "*A Passage to India*": [Extensive thematic summary.] The spoken idiom of the British in India is wonderfully recorded, though their behavior at the time of the trial is overdone. Adela Quested seems to derive more from life than from fiction. Mrs. Moore's characterization is excellent; she is intelligent where Mrs. Wilcox was stupid, and her behavior has the unexpectedness of actuality. Though kindness should be practiced and the personal relationship is important, they are irrelevant to the solution of the differences between the races, sometimes to those between individuals. The beauty of *Passage* is its most impressive aspect, though it is important also as a socio-political tract, a psychological novel, a character study, and an absorbing story. Chapter XIII, "Ironies and Appreciations": EMF's later essays are anti-imperialist, anti-capitalist, and pro-rebel in tendency. They reveal also EMF's controlled subjectivity. Chapter XIV, *"Aspects of the Novel"*: [Descriptive summary of EMF's treatise.] Chapter XV, "The Sinister Corridor": [Discussion of EMF's literary criticism and the troubled political writings of the early 1930s.] Chapter XVI, "Biography": [Discussion of *Goldsworthy Lowes Dickinson,* to the writing of which EMF brought his novelistic gifts.] Chapter XVII, "Some Conclusions": EMF is noteworthy for the charged effect of his prose. He reveals a movement from a faith in the individual and in personal relationships as an axis for a troubled world to active speculation about more general human concerns. [The first critical book on EMF, it is somewhat lacking in method and solidity but appreciative of EMF's mind and art, still engaging if lacking in profundity. For reviews see Bowen, Church, Collier, Dangerfield, Elting, Endicott, Faussett, and Leavis, above; MacCarthy, Merton, O'Faolain, Reid, Strauss, Trilling, and Zabel, below; see also below, "The Work of E. M. Forster: Miss Macaulay's Appreciation." See also B. M., "New Books," DALHOUSIE REVIEW, XVIII (July 1938), 271; "Briefly Noted," NEW YORKER, XIV (20 Aug 1938), 50; E. H. W., "The Season's Books," QUEEN'S QUARTERLY, XLV (Autumn 1938), 416–19; and "Recent Books," TIME, XXXII (22 Aug 1938), 56.]

369 MacCarthy, Desmond. "E. M. Forster," SUNDAY TIMES (Lond), 15 May 1938, p. 6; rptd in E. M. FORSTER: THE CRITICAL HERITAGE, ed by Philip Gardner (Lond & Boston: Routledge & Kegan Paul, 1973), pp. 400–404.

The absence of concepts in EMF's mind clamoring to be embodied in fiction is regrettable. EMF's difficulty in writing fiction stems from the fact that private life is so important to him. He is also indifferent to success and reputation, and he has concentrated upon a few aspects of experience, which he treated by 1924. In his conflicts of good with evil, the real with the sham, there are gradations. His point of view is feminine rather than masculine. The masculine impulse is to compartmentalize; the feminine, to see life as a continuum. His message is "Connect!" The style is personal, subtle, and precise. His chief weakness is that crucial events take place offstage. [Important essay by a Bloomsbury intimate. Incidentally a review of Rose Macaulay's THE WRITINGS OF E. M. FORSTER (1938).]

370 MacNeice, Louis. MODERN POETRY: A PERSONAL ESSAY (Lond & NY: Oxford UP, 1938), pp. 12–13.

T. S. Eliot's poetry in EMF's "T. S. Eliot" (*Abinger Harvest,* reflecting his view of Eliot in World War I) is seen as escapist and as thereby preserving humane tradition. Ten years later the humane tradition was to be preserved by poets using more direct means and committed attitudes than the one EMF imputed to Eliot.

371 Merton, John Kenneth. "Criticism," COMMONWEAL. XXVIII (23 Sept 1938), 562.

All of EMF's novels reveal a dramatic quality, especially notable in *A Passage to India*, which is a great tour de force. The details are not all correct, but the dexterity is great, and the character drawing and dialogue are flawless. EMF has a bloodless quality that prevents him from achieving first rank: he is an impeccable, not a great writer, remaining "donnish" in spite of his hatred of dons. [Review of Rose Macaulay's THE WRITINGS OF E. M. FORSTER (1938).]

372 O'Faoláin, Seán. "E. M. Forster," LONDON MERCURY. XXXVII (April 1938), 643–44.

Macaulay in THE WRITINGS OF E. M. FORSTER (1938) is solemn, but she lacks irony and detachment. She takes all EMF's work too seriously; she is overly concerned with theme, idea, and message without seeing that the message is organically embedded in most of EMF's fictional works. The message is too explicit in *A Passage to India*, however; *Howards End* is his best work, a book where the themes do not obtrude. EMF has been led into ephemeral utterances in the essay form which are partly dishonest; his Epicurean philosophy, in its pure form, is exclusive and faintly precious. But the essential EMF, at least by implication, repudiates these attitudes and activities. He leaves them behind in his novels. [Excellent critique.]

373 Reid, Forrest, "E. M. Forster," SPECTATOR (Lond), CLX (25 March 1938), 532, 534.

Rose Macaulay in THE WRITINGS OF E. M. FORSTER (1938) correctly demonstrates that EMF's development was in enlarging his artist's vision rather than in terms of style, which was excellent in EMF's first works. No finer prose is written today: "It is individual, yet in its freedom from mannerism, in its purity and restraint and natural grace, it has something that to me has always suggested the freshness and charm of Greek poetry." But there is a personal note to the prose also. EMF's tales, with their fauns and dryads and his feeling for nature, are genuine and unique. [Interesting commentary by a fellow novelist and friend of EMF.]

374 Strauss, Harold. "Rose Macaulay's Study of E. M. Forster," NEW YORK TIMES BOOK REVIEW, 4 Sept 1938, p. 8.

Rose Macaulay's treatment of EMF, the man and his world view, is inadequate in THE WRITINGS OF E. M. FORSTER (1938). She does not appreciate fully his subtleties and indirections; she also does not discuss the reasons for his failure to write more novels. She slights the central problem: his belief in moral patterns but his inability to project them upon a world that he judges to be amoral.

375 Trilling, Lionel. " 'The Primal Curse,' " NEW REPUBLIC, XCVI (5 Oct 1938), 247.

EMF's work appears to be soft, but it is hard inside (and below the surface) when he treats such apparently trite themes as "the need for tolerance, for sympathy, for freedom." He has "an absolutely ruthless moral realism." Rose Macaulay in THE WRITINGS OF E. M. FORSTER (1938) brings out EMF's softness and obscures his toughness. He leads us into ambiguity, in distinction to most other novelists. He is a follower of the true Montaigne of creative skepticism and critical intellect. At this time an awakening of interest in liberal humanism is occurring; a liberal humanism like EMF's may correct the flatness of recent radical literature. EMF may be a more valuable, because less portentous, guide to liberal politics and their literary and cultural ramifications than Thomas Mann. [Interesting as early expression of Trilling's view on EMF, and different in emphasis from his 1934 review of *Goldsworthy Lowes Dickinson*.]

376 "The Work of E. M. Forster: Miss Macaulay's Appreciation," TIMES LITERARY SUPPLEMENT (Lond), 19 March 1938, p. 185.

Rose Macaulay gives a positive and sound appreciation of EMF in THE WRITINGS OF E. M. FORSTER (1938), but she has not related his work to those inner depths from which it has arisen.

377 Zabel, Morton Dauwen. "E. M. Forster," NATION (NY), CXLVII (22 Oct 1938), 412–413, 416.

EMF has written little but has made it count for much. EMF is the only novelist emerging between 1895 and 1914, besides Conrad and Lawrence, who still counts as a force in the literary public. He would rank above James, Lawrence, or Eliot if one were to establish the intellectual provenance of Auden's generation. His sensitive treatment and his tough critical mind in combination were formative. Rose Macaulay's THE WRITINGS OF E. M. FORSTER (1938) is appreciative and might have been written by an EMF heroine, a Margaret Schlegel. EMF deserves a more thorough book, but Macaulay's will gain readers for EMF. He follows Arnold in an attempt to see life steadily and see it whole. His origins are in Cambridge; later formative forces upon him were the humanism of Greece, the civilization of Italy, Dante ("whom he evaded intellectually only to find him the modern man's severest spiritual guide"), Egypt and Asia Minor ("with their lessons in decadence"), and India ("with its image of man's supreme division between matter and essence, mortality and spirit"). These forces were brought to bear upon the narrow, intolerant, complacent middle-class culture that he had inherited and upon a tendency toward the mystic and the identification with the impenetrable forces of human nature. Out of this conflict were bred his liberal skepticism ("morally uncompromising and ruthless, with its dialectic of refusing to simplify opposites by dogma or mandate, whether studied in men, nations, or events") and the basic theme of his books, the need to connect. There is "fundamental realism" in his concept of human nature. He avoids being one of Dante's "trimmers" by virtue of "a remorseless passion for human nature, as well as the art to express it." In EMF's books, those who espouse the prose in life are opposed by those who espouse the passion in life, and there are disillusioned intelligences like Ansell and Fielding or mystics like Mrs. Wilcox and Mrs. Moore to act as mediating influences. Occasionally love will triumph, or positive forces will be in the ascendant at the end of the novels; but mostly the characters and plot are left as complex and unresolved as EMF found them. The struggle between the forces of light and darkness goes on forever, "the blight of skepticism must be fought and fought again, the futility of human desolation must be routed, and life must be affirmed." Today the problems of personal morality may seem irrelevant because of the magnitude of our social and political problems, and these problems may be beyond EMF as a creative intelligence to use in his art. Our age would profit by a novel from him, as it has already profited by the hard intelligence in his writing and his articulation of relevant moral problems. He has become an instructor of a new generation of English writers; he himself has gone beyond his original detachment to the formulation of positive values. [Zabel's first essay on EMF, a most important essay in its own right and in the history of EMF's reputation; most of its salient points were repeated in Zabel's "E. M. Forster: The Trophies of the Mind," CRAFT AND CHARACTER: TEXTS, METHODS, AND VOCATION IN MODERN FICTION (1957).]

1939

378 Auden, W. H. "To E. M. Forster," JOURNEY TO A WAR, with Christopher Isherwood (Lond: Faber; NY: Random House, 1939), p. 11; rptd in THE COLLECTED POETRY OF W. H. AUDEN (NY: Random House, 1945), p. 53; in COLLECTED SHORTER POEMS 1930–1944 (Lond: Faber & Faber, 1950), p. 72; and in rvd form as sonnet xxi, "Sonnets from China," COLLECTED SHORTER POEMS 1927–1957 (Lond: Faber & Faber, 1966; NY: Random House, 1967), p. 138.

EMF reminds us that the inner life will pay [*Howards End*] and deflects us from Hate and Madness. Like Lucy Honeychurch [*A Room with a View*], Turton, an Anglo-Indian [*A Passage to India*], and Philip Herriton [*Where Angels Fear to Tread*], we are anxious to join "the jolly ranks" of the benighted, denying Reason and Love. Miss Avery [*Howards End*], carrying her sword (belonging to the deceased Ernst Schlegel), interrupts us as we try to do so.

379 Ellis, G. U. TWILIGHT ON PARNASSUS: A SURVEY OF POST-WAR FICTION AND PRE-WAR CRITICISM (Lond: Michael Joseph, 1939), pp. 87, 128, 176, 236, 343, 344, 354, 405.

David Garnett's technique of authorial effacement in NO LOVE contrasts with EMF's intrusiveness as author. Garnett does not efface himself fully. His inclusiveness mitigates against his book's effectiveness as art. A successful social novel confines itself to a segment of society that the writer defines precisely, as EMF does in *A Room with a View*. EMF wishes to balance nuances of sensibility in his characters and to present a cross-section of a society in which people can develop such sensibility. He utilizes as a standard by which to measure his characters one drawn from a point outside this world. EMF's standard is this: "The delicate presentation of the minor maladjustments of life ... to illustrate the conflict between the human individual and the world around him." There are similarities between Rose Macaulay's satiric novels and EMF's use of the unspectacular in human experience. She admired his dramas of sensibility but saw that they were less significant than he sometimes thought them to be. She also perceived that his coolness of temper might cause him to fail in his rendering of physical passion. [Several mentions of *Aspects of the Novel.*]

380 Galinsky, Hans. "Englische und Angloirische Dichtung" (English and Anglo-Irish Literature), DIE GEGENWARTSDICHTUNG DER EUROPÄISCHEN VÖLKER (Present-Day Literature of the European Nations), ed by Kurt Wais (Berlin: Junker & Dunnhaupt, 1939), pp. 76–160, espec 79, 102, 129–30, 134.

In *A Passage to India* there is an epic-like presentation of the problem of India, political in its implications but stretching beyond them to the metaphysical and religious. In *Passage* EMF reveals a mastery of the novel form, a clear analysis of the soul, and a critical, ironical, fantastic, and bizarre tone. The first four novels also reveal this characteristic tone. In *Passage* the significance inheres in the conflict between the Mohammedan doctor, Aziz, and a young English woman, Adela Quested. The tendency of *Passage* is an acceptance of the hedonism of the moment, since all other facets of experience seem irrelevant in India. A Christian charity is supplanted by a mysticism based on a double vision. No rationale is presented for continued British suzerainty; political matters are to be measured in terms of the relationships among people. Honesty is a great value. EMF's final position: a liberalism with some basis in mysticism. [In German.]

381 Maugham, W. Somerset. "Introduction," TELLERS OF TALES, 100 SHORT STORIES FROM THE UNITED STATES, ENGLAND, FRANCE, RUSSIA AND GERMANY, ed by W. Somerset Maugham (NY: Doubleday, Doran, 1939), pp. xiii–xxxix, espec xviii, xxx; rptd in SELECTED PREFACES AND INTRODUCTIONS OF W. SOMERSET MAUGHAM (NY: Doubleday, 1963; Lond: Heinemann, 1965), pp. 90–122, espec 96, 110.

EMF in *Aspects of the Novel* tends to derogate the story element because he himself has never been able to devise a plausible story [whether story need be plausible Maugham does not consider. Maugham's definition of the short story is broad enough to include anything approaching fiction not of excessive length; he was therefore able to include some atypical things like EMF's "Mr. and Mrs. Abbey's Difficulties" (rptd in TELLERS OF TALES, pp. 904–10), which is a bit of literary history disguised as fiction.]

382 Trilling, Lionel. MATTHEW ARNOLD (NY: Norton; Lond: Allen & Unwin, 1939), pp. x, xii, 120, 154, 346; EMF materials unchanged in later eds.

EMF wrongly asserts that Arnold was preoccupied with personal problems, and he dismisses Arnold, the prose writer, without seeing that the poet's vision gave the prose writer and man of the world his goal. His prose writings extend the poetry, and Arnold in his poetry and prose wished to apprehend the object as it really is. The sustaining quality of literature is present in the writings that Arnold repudiated, i.e., literature expressing the dialogue of the mind with the self as in "Empedocles on Etna." Arnold was concerned with morality not just in a prescriptive sense but in its ramifications into a realm beyond conscious motivation, the realm of such novelists as Dostoevski and Tolstoy, Henry James, Lawrence and EMF, Santayana and Aldous Huxley—all concerned "with the quality of *style* in morality." [EMF is quoted on the sustaining quality of literature (his remarks on Huysmans in "T. S. Eliot," *Abinger Harvest*).]

1940

383 Dataller, Roger (pseud of Arthur A. Eaglestone). "The Social Novel," The Plain Man and the Novel (Lond & NY: Nelson, 1940), pp. 149–69, espec 165–69; also xi.
With respect to the Indian problem, EMF would seek a *modus vivendi* between two parties: (1) the valuable administrators and solidly established British mercantile interests, and (2) the self-conscious and well-educated Indians. "With Forster it is a contest of equals at a time when the galling priorities still obtain." Although EMF is sympathetic to the oppressed Indians, he is also sympathetic with enlightened British aims and policies in India. Is the tendency of *A Passage to India* to urge home rule or continued British domination? The problem is not answered in the novel, but the two sides are presented in a masterly way. "The book is a satire of contrasts, through which perhaps the irreconcilable may be reconciled by such an attitude as that displayed by Fielding and Mrs. Moore."

384 Evans, B. Ifor. A Short History of English Literature (Harmondsworth, Middlesex & Baltimore: Penguin Books, 1940), pp. 183–84; rvd eds, (Lond: Staples P, 1949), discussion of EMF unchanged; and (Lond: Macgibbon & Kee, 1964), discussion rvd to include the early novels.
The spread of EMF's reputation has been slow, though discerning critics recognized the merits of *Howards End. A Passage to India* enlarged his reputation. It is based on personal knowledge; its governing mood is satirical. It serves as a corrective to Kipling, revealing not the romance of the East but the Indians as they actually are. [For expanded version, see entry for 1964.]

385 H., H. W. "Murder of the Mind," Spectator (Lond), CLXV (20 Sept 1940), 296.
For EMF in *Nordic Twilight* the Nazis represent "the murder of the mind." He also stresses physical and political freedom as basic to intellectual

creativity. The Nazis are enemies to an intellectual culture and to the communication of ideas that makes such a culture possible.

386 Orwell, George [pseud of Eric Blair]. "Inside the Whale," INSIDE THE WHALE AND OTHER ESSAYS (Lond: Victor Gollancz, 1940), pp. 131–88, espec 182–84; rptd in NEW DIRECTIONS IN PROSE AND POETRY 1940, ed by James Laughlin (Norfolk, Conn: New Directions, 1940), pp. 205–46, espec 242–43; in ENGLAND YOUR ENGLAND AND OTHER ESSAYS (Lond: Secker & Warburg, 1953), pp. 94–142, espec 137–39; in SUCH, SUCH WERE THE JOYS (NY: Harcourt, Brace, 1953), pp. 154–99, espec 194–96; in A COLLECTION OF ESSAYS BY GEORGE ORWELL (NY: Doubleday Anchor, 1954), pp. 215–56, espec 252–53; in SELECTED ESSAYS (Harmondsworth, Middlesex: Penguin Books, 1957 and 1960 [as INSIDE THE WHALE AND OTHER ESSAYS, 1962 and later rpts]), pp. 9–50, espec 46–47; in COLLECTED ESSAYS (Lond: Secker & Warburg, 1961), pp. 118–59, espec 155–56; and in THE COLLECTED ESSAYS, JOURNALISM AND LETTERS OF GEORGE ORWELL, ed by Sonia Orwell and Ian Angus (NY: Harcourt, Brace & World; Lond: Secker & Warburg, 1968), I, 493–527, espec 523–25.

EMF had a sure feeling concerning the spiritual influence of World War I. His reading of T. S. Eliot was deliberately escapist because Eliot was not concerned with moral and political issues at that point in his career. EMF wished to stay human amid dehumanizing pressures, even if to do so he had to be an escapist. Louis MacNeice in the committed generation of the 1930s condemned this Olympian attitude of EMF's in MODERN POETRY: A PERSONAL ESSAY (Lond & NY: Oxford UP, 1932). But EMF was justified in his actions because he was in the War and knew it for what it was, whereas MacNeice was not.

387 Pellow, J. D. C. "The Beliefs of E. M. Forster," THEOLOGY, XL (April 1940), 278–85.

Like EMF (who does not realize it) the Christian is skeptical of many of the "faiths" that surround him which encourage a belief in wrong objects. The very act of publishing "What I Believe" (1939, in *Two Cheers for Democracy*) demonstrates that EMF is not altogether a skeptic and that he believes in some things: an appeal to a common mind, the worth of individualism, and "Love the Beloved Republic." He also believes in personal relations, but what happens when the other individual is unreliable? EMF is uneasy in moving about in the larger world of society and politics. He does believe provisionally in a democracy, which for him is government "by reason, discussion, and agreement." Force, he says, is the ultimate reality; if so, how have creativeness, sympathy, and loyalty come into being and been kept alive? And is not force required to contain violence? EMF feels that men act better in the individual sphere than in social and political spheres. A strong opposition prevails between the pure and free spirit of man and the corrupt organization of human beings in society. He places blame on political institutions, not on the nature of man himself. He will not recognize that the will of man is corrupt, not just his institutions. But EMF as an opponent to Christianity cannot admit that truth. EMF wrongly holds that a creative aristocracy can save the world because its members may have lapses and those who wield power selfishly may be capable of goodness in some relationships. Rather, if an enlightened regime in society materializes, it will derive from the efforts of sinners who themselves need redemption. Violence is internal, not external; this EMF will not allow. He denies that we need a change of heart; rather, all that is necessary is to make more effective the goodness now available and to shut up force within its box. Liberals like EMF cannot now deny the facts which make them so uncomfortable. They will not reject the dogma of the goodness of man or accept the idea of original sin. They will not admit that dictatorships arise from a cult of "the free and unchecked expansive impulses of human nature." EMF places emphasis on individuality but concedes also (and creditably) the resemblance of one individual to another: the individual's commonness, his likeness to others, alone can provide the only possible basis for a valid assessment of human nature and a defense against the forces which threaten it. "The individualist atomization of society" causes the individual to be submerged, robbing him of initiative and responsibility. The dictator is, therefore, a symptom of this process rather than a cause of it. [Keen analysis of EMF's values by a Christian thinker.]

388 Reid, Forrest. PRIVATE ROAD (Lond: Faber, 1940), pp. 58, 77, 85, 115–16, 239–41.
[Glimpses of EMF by an old friend; EMF wrote appreciatively of Reid (see *Abinger Harvest*). Disagrees with EMF's praise of Ronald Firbank in *Abinger*. EMF agreed with Reid's publisher that additional chapters would improve THE BRACKNELS. The book brought Reid the friendship of Walter de la Mare and EMF. EMF took Reid to a London graveyard frequented by cats and provided him with a scene for THE RETREAT.]

389 Ward, A. C. TWENTIETH-CENTURY LITERATURE 1901–1940 (Lond: Methuen, 1940 [7th rvd ed]), pp. 17, 64, 75, 77.
[Repeats material in first edition (1928). Quotes from EMF's 1938 essay "The Ivory Tower," in commenting upon the socially oriented literature of the 1930s (the individual *and* the society are important). Mentions the austerity of EMF's work, which is less to the fore in his *Abinger Harvest* essays. Notes affinity between Virginia Woolf's delicacy and sensitivity in THE VOYAGE OUT and EMF's similar qualities.]

390 Woolf, Virginia. ROGER FRY: A BIOGRAPHY (NY: Harcourt, Brace; Lond: Hogarth P, 1940), pp. 240, 253, 292.

Fry praises texture and writing in *A Passage to India* but feels that EMF's mysticism is too obtrusive, also that he tries to explain too insistently his ideas and emotions and so "misses the great thing." Fry at one point was to collaborate with Charles Mauron on a translation into French of *Passage*. EMF's obituary essay on Fry is briefly quoted. [See also LETTERS OF ROGER FRY, ed by Denys Sutton, Vol II, 1913–1934 (Lond: Chatto & Windus, 1972; NY: Random House, 1973), pp. 554–55.]

1941

391 A[dams], J. D[onald]. "Speaking of Books," NEW YORK TIMES BOOK REVIEW, 9 Feb 1941, p. 2.

EMF in *Aspects of the Novel* is concerned with form, though he feels pattern can be slighted in pursuit of human values. [Commends the chapter on rhythm and notes the symphonic structure in Elizabeth Madox Roberts's novels where, at the end, chords strike and convey the "expansion" which EMF describes as the result of the novelist's having achieved difficult rhythm (in contrast to the easy rhythm of repetition with variation).]

392 Sampson, George. THE CONCISE CAMBRIDGE HISTORY OF ENGLISH LITERATURE (Cambridge: Cambridge UP, 1941), p. 969.

EMF's work has a "shy, unworldly quality" and is diffidently presented. *Aspects of the Novel* contains a definite but narrow view of the novel, revealing a lack of sympathy with larger, more exuberant works. At heart he is a scholar, and he lacks inventiveness. [Judgments seem mostly off the mark.]

1942

393 Bowen, Elizabeth. ENGLISH NOVELISTS (Lond: Collins, Britain in Pictures, 1942), pp. 47–48.

EMF's novels are more straightforward and more in the familiar manner than Virginia Woolf's; they have developed plots, fully fleshed characters, ironic comedy, and incisive dialogue. Their mental climate is the new feature in them, also the nature of other people's predicaments. Contrast is not only a structural principle but a mode of psychological organization; the central character is kept at "the high tension of a continuous decision." The character makes an inner journey, often a lonely one. The controlled style is often beautiful.

394 Burnham, David. "The Invalid Lady of Bloomsbury," COM-MONWEAL, XXXVI (2 Oct 1942), 567–68.
In *Virginia Woolf* EMF mentions Woolf's snobbery (which is really her candid evaluation of her situation) and her aesthete's stance. But her writing, he says, "was not about something. It was something." [Mostly discussion of Woolf's THE DEATH OF THE MOTH and David Daiches's VIRGINIA WOOLF.]

395 Colum, Mary M. "Heir to Tradition and Free to Experiment," NEW YORK HERALD TRIBUNE BOOKS, 4 Oct 1942, p. 3.
Virginia's Woolf's judgments of EMF (in THE DEATH OF THE MOTH) are just. EMF's *Virginia Woolf* represents "an ingenious, ... perhaps partly unconscious, denigration of a dead author by a living one." His appreciation of her is minimal; he stresses unduly her aestheticism and artiness, and he lacks the intelligent, full, fair-minded qualities of David Daiches, found in his VIRGINIA WOOLF. [Extended discussion of Woolf's THE DEATH OF THE MOTH.]

396 Dunbar, Olivia Howard. "Virginia Woolf," NEW REPUBLIC, CVII (12 Oct 1942), 471–72.
In *Virginia Woolf* EMF writes of Woolf as a human being and stresses her love of writing. [Discussion of Woolf's THE DEATH OF THE MOTH and David Daiches's VIRGINIA WOOLF.]

397 Endicott, N. J. "The Novel in England Between the Wars," UNIVERSITY OF TORONTO QUARTERLY, XII (Oct 1942), 18–31.
The criticisms leveled against the realistic novel by Virginia Woolf were too sweeping, since they included EMF and the early Lawrence as well as the Edwardian realists such as Bennett, Wells, and Galsworthy. Lawrence thought that EMF was too realistic and too indulgent toward the Wilcoxes in *Howards End.* Such criticisms fail to appreciate EMF's subtlety and discrimination. [Essay mostly concerned with Woolf, Joyce, Lawrence, and Huxley, but EMF discussed on p. 19.]

398 Frierson, William C. THE ENGLISH NOVEL IN TRANSITION 1885–1946 (Norman: University of Oklahoma P, 1942), pp. 142, 148, 168–72, 243
The traditional element in EMF's work is a reliance on plot that "depends upon an irrational mistake, an accident, or a fortuitous event"; his technique is sometimes dramatic in the worst sense. EMF was influenced by ideas of his day and has in turn influenced current ideas. Like H. G. Wells, EMF

feels civilization is out of joint and wishes for a new understanding, new values, a new man. EMF's influence on D. H. Lawrence is especially evident in the similarity of the basic situation in *Where Angels Fear to Tread* and THE LOST GIRL. Both writers present characters in conflict, in actions that are symbolic. There is a similarity between Stephen Wonham (*The Longest Journey*) and Mellors (LADY CHATTERLEY'S LOVER). Stephen is not likeable but real. In *Howards End* the rural simplicities will not restore the Wilcoxes. *Angels* exposes aestheticism and indifference; *A Room with a View* is in part concerned with emancipation of women; *A Passage to India* exposes British imperialism and is sympathetic with the Indians. EMF works in the vein of Bennett and Galsworthy as a novelist of ideas. Gilbert Cannan, May Sinclair, W. L. George, W. Somerset Maugham, and EMF all "adapted naturalistic techniques and Wellsian or other ethical concepts to private designs for individual utterance." [Valuable for relating EMF to some of his less obvious (to us) contemporaries; some interesting suggestions, considering date of essay, but facile, and overstresses EMF's "realism."]

399 Gerould, Gordon Hall. THE PATTERNS OF ENGLISH AND AMERICAN FICTION: A HISTORY (Boston: Little, Brown, 1942), pp. 456–57. EMF was one of the few novelists in the period 1900–1914 who was influenced by Henry James, in that he was concerned with individuals reacting against something in their environment. As a novelist he has "modest but genuine gifts."

400 Gregory, Horace. "Virginia Woolf's THE DEATH OF THE MOTH," NEW YORK TIMES BOOK REVIEW, 27 Sept 1942, p. 2. In *Virginia Woolf* EMF stresses authoritatively the charm, the unpredictability, and the responsiveness of Woolf's personality, its freedom within the limits she set for herself, and her knowledge of her own social position. [Primarily a discussion of Woolf's THE DEATH OF THE MOTH.]

401 Karr, Dorothy. "Along the Bookshelves," CHURCHMAN (Lond), CLVI (1 Dec 1942), 156. EMF in *Virginia Woolf* discerns Mrs. Woolf's delight in writing and words, but she also had stature as critic and feminist. Her THE DEATH OF THE MOTH illustrates all these aspects of her work.

402 Kronenberger, Louis. "Virginia Woolf as Critic," NATION (NY), CLV (17 Oct 1942), 382, 384–85. EMF's *Virginia Woolf* is "full of sharp comments and animating touches" but too brief for what it might say. [Mainly comment on Woolf as a literary sensibility and critic; discussion of David Daiches's VIRGINIA WOOLF and Woolf's THE DEATH OF THE MOTH.]

403 Kunitz, Stanley J., and Howard Haycraft. "E. M. Forster,"
TWENTIETH CENTURY AUTHORS: A BIOGRAPHICAL DICTIONARY OF
MODERN LITERATURE (NY: H. W. Wilson, 1942), pp. 477–78.
Aspects of the Novel is a well-reasoned discussion of the novel, which sees
its pretensions as an art form in perspective. *Abinger Harvest* reveals EMF
as "a critic of agile mind and nice appreciation." He is "the complete man
of letters," and has enlisted in liberal causes, protesting against Nazi censorship and oppression abroad and unenlightenment at home. He is likely to
have a permanent place in literature by virtue of his "power of characterization, subtlety in plot, wit, irony, and resilient style." [Biographical account
using standard facts; relatively complete.]

404 Mortimer, Raymond. "Books in General," NEW STATESMAN
AND NATION, nsXXIII (13 June 1942), 390.
EMF's *Virginia Woolf* is "a summing up exemplary in its shrewdness and
delicacy." EMF's main points: Virginia Woolf had many interests and much
curiosity; she was "sensitive but tough"; she respected knowledge and believed in wisdom; and she was a poet writing novels. [Also discusses Woolf's
THE DEATH OF THE MOTH.]

405 Orwell, George [pseud of Eric Blair]. "Rudyard Kipling,"
HORIZON, V (Feb 1942), 111–25, espec 115; rptd in CRITICAL ESSAYS
(Lond: Secker & Warburg, 1946), pp. 100–14, espec 104; in DICK-
ENS, DALI AND OTHERS (NY: Reynal & Hitchcock, 1946), pp. 140–
60, espec 146 (this pagination from 1963 rpt, Harcourt, Brace &
World); in A COLLECTION OF ESSAYS BY GEORGE ORWELL (NY:
Doubleday Anchor, 1954), pp. 134–28, espec 127–28; in THE OR-
WELL READER, ed by Richard Rovere (NY: Harcourt, Brace, 1956),
pp. 271–83, espec 274; in COLLECTED ESSAYS(Lond: Secker & War-
burg, 1961), pp. 179–94, espec 183; and in THE COLLECTED ESSAYS,
JOURNALISM AND LETTERS OF GEORGE ORWELL, ed by Sonia Orwell
and Ian Angus (NY: Harcourt, Brace & World; Lond: Secker &
Warburg, 1968), II, 184–97, espec. 187.
The Anglo-Indians of the nineteenth century, with whom Kipling partly
identifies himself, were people who did things and could not have maintained themselves in power at all if their outlook had been that of EMF.

406 Roberts, R. Ellis. "A Biographer Manquée," SATURDAY
REVIEW OF LITERATURE (NY), XXV (3 Oct 1942), 9.
EMF's *Virginia Woolf* is a tribute to a friend and artist. In ROGER FRY,
Woolf suppresses herself, according to EMF, but the great biographer does
not do so. The essays in THE DEATH OF THE MOTH and in THE COMMON
READER series are biography at its best, for the reason that Woolf does not
suppress her personality. EMF is wrong to think of her as a "snob"; she

knew her own social position for what it was, and she did not condescend to women whose backgrounds were different from her own. [Extended discussion of THE DEATH OF THE MOTH.]

407 Roscoe, Theodora. "Literary Supplement," CONTEMPORARY REVIEW, CLXII (Sept 1942), 192.

EMF in *Virginia Woolf* sees Woolf not as a legendary figure but as a human personality. EMF celebrates her for her honesty and love of truth; these traits would make her welcome this tribute.

408 Sato, Ineko. "The Novels of E. M. Forster," STUDIES IN ENGLISH LITERATURE (Tokyo), XXII: 4 (1942), 456–69.

In *A Passage to India* EMF has developed further in his characterizations; Mrs. Moore is a firmer character than Mrs. Wilcox in *Howards End;* his appreciation of Italian character in the early novels has helped him interpret the Indian. Fielding's function parallels Margaret Schlegel's in *Howards End.* An otherworldly quality characterizes the relationship between Aziz and Mrs. Moore; this supernatural aspect acts as a redeeming force at the end of the novel. In "A Note on Forster and Dostoevsky" Mrs. Moore is seen to be an advance on Mrs. Wilcox because she is speculative. EMF admitted [in note to Sato] that Dostoevsky may have influenced him in imagining Mrs. Moore's speculations during and after the visit to the Marabar Caves. EMF regards Dostoevsky's characters as real through what they imply and through their capacity of extending themselves throughout a novel. In such ways Mrs. Moore is like a character out of Dostoevsky. [For its date a sympathetic and full discussion but relies too greatly on plot summary; by modern standards most of the points made are obvious. Discussion is centered on the need of EMF's central characters to achieve "salvation" and on the importance of the symbolic moment.]

409 "Shorter Notices," SPECTATOR (Lond), CLXVIII (5 June 1942), 540.

In *Virginia Woolf* EMF attempts "not judgement, but justification." He presents Woolf as she was—"a poet-novelist, a critic, a biographer, a short story writer, an experimentalist, an essayist, a scholar, a feminist, a gourmet, a practical-joker, a woman, a lady, a snob: a civilised being, respecting knowledge and believing in wisdom."

410 Stonier, G. W. "Books in General," NEW STATESMAN AND NATION, nsXXIV (21 Nov 1942), 341.

EMF is an elusive writer. He seems a "half-hog" writer rather than one who goes whole-hog; his characters seem half-hearted because he dominates them so greatly and refuses to let them go. He recalls Jane Austen by virtue of his ironic stance and subtle dialogue, but there is also a spiritual "large-ness" about his work. His presence, and the enlightenment it conveys, means that his characters change, sometimes almost imperceptibly, even if they do not develop radically. There is psychic movement, for example, in his prigs. Though his characters are individual and lifelike, they are all minor. They are, however, "quietly remarkable," writing and talking more pointedly than most characters in fiction. His style is the most individual and pleasing of any living novelist and exactly suited to its functions and circumstances. It is the style of "the pure novel," combining art with spon-taneity. EMF never overstates. If he is elusive, he is, like Chekhov, settled, operating from a fixed set of values. This is true for all his novels except *The Longest Journey*, which is a failure. All his novels are equally mature; all seem equally good; there is little progress but rather an enlargement of scale. Physical magnitude is beside the point when we consider such finished works as his novels. *A Passage to India* is more topical than ever. Mood and fact are wonderfully mingled. His conclusion is that there is no secret in India. The book tails off a bit: Mrs. Moore is a dummy, and the lukewarm lovers (Adela Quested and Ronny Heaslop) are unimpressive. Small touches create EMF's inimitable spell; he is "the master of the half-heard and enchanting strain in prose." [Review of Everyman ed of *Passage*. Excellent commentary.]

411 Tillotson, Geoffrey. "Things in Heaven," ESSAYS IN CRITICISM AND RESEARCH (Cambridge: Cambridge UP, 1942; Hamden, Conn: Archon Books, 2nd ed, 1967), pp. 193–203, espec 201–3.

In Western literary tradition Heaven was first conceived as an otherworldly place, following St. John; then as an extension of existence in this world (Charles Lamb, Leigh Hunt); and, in the modern age, as an emptiness for writers to fill as they see fit. EMF is such a writer, giving us a heaven of his own imagining. In "Mr. Andrews" both Andrews and the Turk find no satisfaction in a traditionally conceived heaven; they reject it to merge into the world soul. The heaven presented is concrete if idiosyncratic; so is the heaven presented in "Coordination." In this story Beethoven and Napoleon give apparently absurd orders to the members of a girl's school. These two great men insist that their triumphs be experienced by these girls and teachers of a later century, but the triumphs are transmuted for them. The girls hear a wonderful cavalry band and the teacher and principal a fine tune from a shell cocked to their ears (instead of a perfect performance of the A minor quartet); and Miss Haddon achieves victory through a legacy which enables her to retire from her hated post at school (instead of her experiencing, with her pupils, Napoleon's triumph at Austerlitz). EMF's rendition of heaven is still definite. This definiteness is lacking in A. E. Coppard's depiction of heaven in "Clorinda Walks in Heaven" (to the detriment of the story).

412 Trilling, Lionel. "E. M. Forster," KENYON REVIEW, IV (Spring 1942), 161–73; rptd, slightly rvd, as "Introduction: Forster and the Liberal Imagination," E. M. FORSTER (Norfolk, Conn: New Directions, The Makers of Modern Literature, 1943; Lond: Hogarth P, 1944), pp. 7–24.

EMF has less of a reputation in America than he deserves. His comic manner puts off some readers who feel that literature ought to be serious and solemn. Also EMF's "refusal to be great" alienates some readers. But his manner also has validity, since exaggeration and improbability are often keys to the truth about life. EMF like Hawthorne is a "moral realist," concerned not so much with morality as with "the contradictions, paradoxes and dangers of living the moral life." EMF is much concerned with the interplay of Good and Evil as they are projected in the dualities "of Life and Death, Light and Darkness, Fertility and Sterility, Courage and Respectability, Intelligence and Stupidity." His plots suggest "eternal division," but his manner implies reconciliation. EMF is at war with the liberal tradition that emphasizes such entities as "progress, collectivism and humanitarianism." [Trilling here is guilty of what he accuses liberals, being reductive in his thinking. Questionable also are Trilling's premises that the liberal characteristically espouses absolutes, that he is at a loss when those absolutes are threatened, and that he is offended by subtlety and complexity.] EMF has also a respect for tradition, something especially absent from American writers [simplified statement]. Believing in the past, he is also able to believe in the present; he is worldly in a constructive sense, in his acceptance of man's present condition "without the sentimentality of cynicism and without the sentimentality of rationalism." [In my view Trilling's quarrel with the naive, socially orientated literary critics of the 1930's adds little to his discussion of EMF.]

413 "Virginia Woolf: Mr. Forster's Impressions," TIMES LITERARY SUPPLEMENT (Lond), 23 May 1942, p. 260.

EMF's essay is illuminating and derives from much knowledge of his subject. [Mostly summary of EMF's *Virginia Woolf.*]

1943

414 Adams, J. Donald. "Speaking of Books," NEW YORK TIMES BOOK REVIEW, 10 Oct 1943, p. 2.

EMF, in *Aspects of the Novel*, rightly holds that the appeal of fiction is perennial, especially to our sense of curiosity about other people and their motives and to our own desire to achieve "the illusion of perspicacity and power" [EMF's phrase].

415 Adams, J. Donald. "Speaking of Books," NEW YORK TIMES BOOK REVIEW, 31 Oct 1943, p. 2.

Sinclair Lewis in GIDEON PLANISH does better than in his other recent books because his qualities, so admirably defined in EMF's "Sinclair Lewis" (*Abinger Harvest*)—his materialistic realism and his photographic inclusiveness —are more in evidence.

416 Anand, Mulk Raj. "English Novels of the Twentieth Century on India," ASIATIC REVIEW (Lond), nsXXXIX (July 1943), 244–51; discussion of article, pp. 251–57.

The Anglo-Indian writers have concentrated on the English in India and their London orientation, and they reflect the attitudes toward empire prevailing in the period in which they wrote. Flora Annie Steel and EMF had much more sympathy with and understanding of the Indians than did Kipling. EMF's earlier work is personally rather than politically oriented, in the English tradition of Austen and Meredith supplemented by Flaubert. In *A Passage to India* he did not depart from his theme of personal relations and the failure of the British middle class to embody such relations. The Indians do not fare well; they are infected with the neurosis that, to EMF, attacks a subject people. *Passage* is the first English novel about India to suggest the scope and nuances of India. Edward Thompson and Dennis Kincaid continued the liberal tradition of EMF and wrote of India realistically and sympathetically. [Discussion follows. In a letter, EMF contends that Anand views Kipling's KIM too much as a political and social statement. Anand maintains that *Passage* is outstanding because of its accuracy or truth. George Orwell's comments testify to the annoyance caused to British colonial servants by *Passage*, with its theme that real intimacy between British and Indian is impossible while the first rules the second. Illuminating article.]

417 Arvin, Newton. "Two Cheers for Forster," PARTISAN REVIEW, X (Sept–Oct 1943), 450–52.

EMF's work is a protest against pedantry and priggishness; Lionel Trilling in E. M. FORSTER (1943) has also written without either. Trilling is in sympathy with EMF's comic insight, his distrust of absolutism, his hatred of smugness, his rejection of moral dualisms for a more flexible and relativistic morality. EMF's fiction asserts the claims of imagination, irony, taste, and "hilarity" in our troubled age. Trilling does not quite account for EMF's less than great stature. EMF's limitation is that his connections are not firm and difficult enough; the connections need to be between a harsher prose and a fiercer passion. His irony is not so searching nor his "double vision" so double as they ought to be; he has achieved a silver rather than a golden mean. His prose essays contain too many false alternatives and humorous simplifications; they reveal a "soft" humanist like Michael of "The Point of It." [Review-essay on Trilling's E. M. FORSTER and the American reissue of the first four novels. An incisive and stimulating essay.]

418 Baker, Carlos. "New Biography of E. M. Forster," NEW YORK TIMES BOOK REVIEW, 15 Aug 1943, p. 4.

EMF is a social critic, a humanist, an ironist, and a genuine stylist. His characters are alive, the atmosphere of his books is authentic, his resolutions are genuine. He has a "roughness of surface" that "scratches" the intellect and sensibilities. His books are not dated but possess "unwavering contemporaneousness"; he is able to depict with insight the significance of unimportant relationships. EMF's style, "firm without being dense," is inadequately analyzed in Lionel Trilling's book. EMF's comic manner is a greater asset for the public than Trilling believes, but in E. M. FORSTER (1943) Trilling rightly holds that EMF has serious moral intentions. EMF appreciates humble people whose flaws enable them to escape their mediocrity; his books are impressive though they lack magnificence. [Review of Trilling's E. M. FORSTER and the American reissue of the first four novels. Perceptive critique.]

419 Cowley, Malcolm. "E. M. Forster's Answer," NEW REPUBLIC, CIX (29 Nov 1943), 749–50.

Christine Weston's INDIGO reproduces EMF's characters. Her style, however, is inferior to EMF's. Her sense that the people of India are not grotesques (as some of the Anglo-Indians tended to be in *A Passage to India*) is her one advantage over him. She feels that Indians and Europeans cannot now be friends and so supports EMF's conclusion at the end of *Passage;* but she also shows that they might have been close allies before World War I.

420 "Current Revival of Interest in E. M. Forster's Novels," PUBLISHERS' WEEKLY, CXLIV (25 Sept 1943), 1161–62.

[Details of reissue of EMF's books in United States in 1943. Valuable for bibliographical information and for history of EMF's reputation. Also see "First American Publication of E. M. Forster," below.]

421 Fadiman, Clifton. "E. M. Forster," NEW YORKER, XIX (14 Aug 1943), 68, 70.

EMF's books are alive by virtue of their stylistic distinction and their seriousness and subtlety of subject matter. His focus is inward rather than outward; his influence has been pervasive rather than decisive. The novels are so "relaxed" that it is difficult to use the terms "genius" or "great" with respect to them or their author. EMF's chief theme is that of "the undeveloped heart," but his condemnations or commendations are never absolute. Lionel Trilling's study is a model of informed academic criticism. [Excellent review-essay on Trilling's E. M. FORSTER (1943) and the reissue of the first four novels in America.]

422 "First American Publication of E. M. Forster," PUBLISHERS' WEEKLY, CXLIV (16 Oct 1943), 1518.
[Adds details to account given in "Current Revival of Interest in E. M. Forster's Novels" (see above). EMF's first publisher in America was Putnam (*Howards End* and *A Room with a View*, 1911).]

423 "Forster and the Human Fact," TIME, XLII (9 Aug 1943), 98, 100, 102, 104.
The reissuing of the earlier EMF books and the publication of Lionel Trilling's E. M. FORSTER (1943) resulted in the widespread realization that EMF is the most distinguished living novelist. [Review-essay on Trilling's E. M. FORSTER. Article important for documenting the EMF "revival."]

424 Gillett, Eric, and William J. Entwistle. THE LITERATURE OF ENGLAND A.D. 500–1942 (Lond, NY, & Toronto: Longmans, Green, 1943), pp. 219–20, 250; 2nd ed as THE LITERATURE OF ENGLAND A.D. 500–1946 (1948), pp. 223–24, 232, 259; 3rd ed as THE LITERATURE OF ENGLAND A.D. 500–1950 (1952), pp. 226–27, 235, 268; 4th ed as THE LITERATURE OF ENGLAND A.D. 500–1960 (1962), pp. 209, 215, 246.
EMF is fastidious, but his creative impulse is not very strong. He is more interested in life and letters than in writing fiction and perhaps writes best in the essay form. He has great qualities as a creator of character, within narrow limits. He is better as a commentator in his fiction; when he attempts action he often attains only melodrama. [In 2nd and later eds, *A Room with a View*, *Howards End*, and *A Passage to India* are judged to be his best books.]

425 Godfrey, Eleanor. "The Unbuttoned Manner," CANADIAN FORUM (Toronto), XXIII (Oct 1943), 154–55.
EMF was in revolt against nineteenth-century tendencies to deprive man of his natural dignities and irreverences and to curb "adventurers" in their revolt against repressive moral conventions. Like Bernard Shaw he protested against this "self-conscious, power-ridden, proprietorial society," but he did not crusade or project his protest into great themes and persons. His characters are almost too human and are sometimes trivial; at his best "the relaxed will" allows them to be persuasive. EMF demonstrates how high motives are corrupted by concern for class, pride, money, race, and egotism;

he urges us not toward reform but toward awareness. The elemental characters are more vital, not necessarily more moral, than the others; they are complex individuals. EMF is too easygoing in constructing his novels, too often disregarding the need for artistic proportion. [Thoughtful review-essay on Trilling's E. M. FORSTER (1943).]

426 Jones, Howard Mumford. "E. M. Forster and the Liberal Imagination," SATURDAY REVIEW OF LITERATURE (NY), XXVI (28 Aug 1943), 6–7.

EMF achieves a union of thoughtfulness and sensibility, verging into sensuality. EMF's "otherworldliness" is neither completely pagan nor mystic "but a product of a heightened and educated sensibility." EMF recognizes the splendor and strength of the liberal tradition and bypasses the economic divisions of mankind to achieve "a deep and tender spirituality." [Review of Lionel Trilling's E. M. FORSTER (1943) and the American reissue of the first four novels.]

427 Mayberry, George. "The Forster Revival," NEW REPUBLIC, CIX (6 Sept 1943), 341.

EMF's short fiction and essays suffer from lack of rigor. His style, while magnificent at times, has been overpraised; it is often platitudinous, his metaphors are often strained, and his manner is frequently "overblown." Lionel Trilling wrongly judges *Howards End* to be EMF's best novel. *A Passage to India* is greater and *The Longest Journey* more representative— Forsterian in essence, even if a failure. Lionel Trilling takes EMF too seriously, as have reviewers. [Essay-review on Trilling's E. M. FORSTER (1943) and the American reissue of the first four novels.]

428 Millett, Fred B. "Twentieth Century Literature: Prose Fiction," A HISTORY OF ENGLISH LITERATURE, by William Vaughn Moody and Robert Morss Lovett (NY: Charles Scribner's Sons, 6th ed, 1943), pp. 423–44, espec 427–28; identical account in 1956 and 1964 eds; see also Moody (1926).

EMF takes part in the attack on realism in the early twentieth century. His surface manner is realistic, but his use of violence and accident and his juxtapositions of a romantic figure with a realistic environment (*The Longest Journey*) or of a realistic figure in a romantic environment (*A Room with a View*) reveal his impatience with realism. His chief theme, the conflict between a sensitive individual and convention, allows range for delicate perceptions and tough irony. His early novels are experiments that are not altogether successful, but with his masterpiece, *A Passage to India*, his experimental stage is left behind. *Passage* is an "infinitely perceptive study of inter-racial psychology and attitudes."

429 Nicholson, Norman. "The Satirists," MAN AND LITERATURE (Lond: S. C. M. Press; Toronto: Macmillan, 1943; 2nd ed, Lond: S. C. M. Press, 1944), pp. 157–61.

EMF is supreme among the modern satirists, with his subtle debunking of "natural man" [certainly an overstatement]. He is different from Bennett and Wells in his concern with the surface of thought rather than the external world and with the interplay of motive and response in conversation and action. He is disdainful of plot but provides one in every novel; his condescension in doing so is enjoyable, the plots often being outrageous, fantastic, arbitrary. The opening of *Howards End* is masterful; the ingenious situation, once set up, is then thrown aside casually. All the contrasting characters are treated with quiet irony. *The Longest Journey* is a satire against the cult of the primitive (though it was not EMF's intention to make it so). Rickie Elliot is forced to realize that Stephen Wonham, drunk on the railway tracks, is "neither a monster nor a paragon, but only a human being."

430 Pryce-Jones, Alan. "Books in General," NEW STATESMAN AND NATION, nsXXVI (6 Nov 1943), 303.

The margin by which EMF's art avoids the "commonplace" is narrow; he does so by his use of nuance and shading. Like others in his generation, EMF, in his art, suggests "abstinence, devotion, exactitude"; but these qualities are balanced by his humanity. His genius is an attitude of mind, and he expresses it "in the most limpid, unforced prose." The ultimate EMF is "a tone of voice, solitary, passionate, politely ironical, paradoxically fluent considering how seldom it speaks." The battle between Sawston and Italy is an eternal one, with EMF on the side of Italy, passion, and truth rather than on the side of Sawston and "the undeveloped heart." "Sawston, stupidity, the unvarying clock: all are faces of the same enemy." [An appreciative essay, occasioned by the appearance of Lionel Trilling's E. M. FORSTER (1943).]

431 Rahv, Philip. "Mrs. Woolf and Mrs. Brown," KENYON REVIEW, V (Winter 1943), 147–51.

EMF's *Virginia Woolf* is a tribute rather than an analysis, and "it shines with the grace of the occasion." EMF rightly says that she can give us "life on the page" but not "life eternal"; yet this judgment does not go far enough. Actually, Mrs. Woolf does not penetrate to the mystery of Mrs. Brown; she merely spiritualizes the novel instead of materializing it. [Also discusses David Daiches's VIRGINIA WOOLF and Woolf's THE DEATH OF THE MOTH.]

432 R[ansom], J[ohn] C[rowe]. "Editorial Notes: E. M. Forster," KENYON REVIEW, V (Autumn 1943), 618–23.

EMF has five times studied, with merciless intelligence, a group of characters whose fortunes are closely related to the reader's. Intellectually, EMF finds his contemporaries wanting in imagination, perceptiveness, and sense of beauty; emotionally, in tolerance, fair play, and gentleness. He has no faith in social establishments as such. The novels are exposures, and they "bear destructively upon our habits and institutions." Wit is EMF's chief weapon. He writes in the liberal tradition of Butler and Shaw, but he falls short of it by being relatively unconcerned with the positive—with formulating a constructive "Plan"—and rises above it aesthetically. EMF's skepticism of social and political formulas is profound. The only possible program for EMF is a "Benevolent Anarchism": "The community of good persons, of whom none would be capable of taking advantage of his superior strength, even in order to impose his superior illumination upon the others." Under the institution lurks for EMF a natural goodness, and his society would be founded on this residual goodness, not on the evil of men (as in Christianity). EMF would urge us to live and let live and to try to love. The rich, stable society in Henry James's fiction had been disestablished, but it is still partly alive in EMF's world. EMF dissociates himself from the grimness of worldly pursuits and has imagination enough to see that the mansions of beauty are still intact, despite the eclipse of an opulent regime. Aesthetically, he transcends others in the liberal tradition by the beauty and purity of his style and by his ability to ascribe aesthetic vision to his positive characters and to absorb it into his own consciousness when the occasion arises (which is often). EMF owes much to Meredith: (1) the collocation of wit and poetry, (2) the exuberance of his wit, which he carries sometimes to the point of farce, (3) an innocence and lack of venom in his view of life, and (4) the daring use of a ubiquitous poetry and a conscious mythologizing (drawing especially from Greek sources). EMF is essentially "a purified Meredithian, like the second and improved generation of a stock." EMF's cardinal dogma is agrarian; he stresses "the primacy of scene in developing our sensibility, as in gentling our hearts." Society is to be rooted in its sense of soil; his best characters appreciate nature as well as their social relations. EMF loves nature; his landscapes are the best in English fiction, and even the subtle ones are conveyed. He reveals a kind of claustrophobia that seeks relief in the out-of-doors, and he champions, therefore, an "untidiness" in both interior and exterior scene. He embraces abundance and fecundity and is suspicious of Positive modes of thought and action that would eliminate the untidy. One may either embrace the untidy for the life it embodies or reject it as ugly and hateful. To embrace untidiness in art, as EMF does, is an ontological act. [General essay inspired by Lionel Trilling's E. M. FORSTER (1943) and the American reissue of the first four novels. A valuable and virtually unknown account by one of America's finest critics.]

433 "Re-Discovering E. M. Forster," CHRISTIAN SCIENCE MONITOR, "Weekly Magazine Section," 25 Sept 1943, p. 13.

Lionel Trilling's E. M. FORSTER and the American reissue of EMF's first four novels will allow Americans to know EMF's work. EMF is an accomplished stylist, an acute delineator of character, and a master of flexible dialogue. He knows how to use suspense, which often ends in violence. His principal themes are the conflict between the intellectual life and the material world and the conflict between the individual and conventional society.

434 Schorer, Mark. "Virginia Woolf," YALE REVIEW, nsXXXII (Winter 1943), 377–81.
EMF is right in *Virginia Woolf* in saying that Woolf will be judged as a novelist rather than as an essayist. Her essays reveal the novelist's temperament rather than the critic's. EMF's distinction about Woolf having "life on the page" but not "life eternal" is only partly true; but he does well to emphasize her love of writing. [Also discusses Woolf's THE DEATH OF THE MOTH.]

435 Spectorsky, A. G. "E. M. Forster—A Critical Biography, Four Novels," CHICAGO SUN, "Book Week," 22 Aug 1943, p. 10.
The reprinting of the novels and the publication of Lionel Trilling's study will enable Americans to know an outstanding English writer. EMF's books are fresh, alive, contemporary. They are vibrant, the characters and plots are vital, and his unobtrusive style can be savored for its fine qualities. [Review of American reissue of first four novels and Trilling's E. M. FORSTER (1943).]

436 Trilling, Lionel. E. M. FORSTER (Norfolk, Conn: New Directions, The Makers of Modern Literature, 1943; Lond: Hogarth P, 1944; 2nd ed, with Preface and rvd bibliography, NY: New Directions, New Directions Paperback, 1964); rpts, slightly rvd, as "Introduction: Forster and the Liberal Imagination," "E. M. Forster," KENYON REVIEW, IV (Spring 1942), 161–73; Chapter 1, "Introduction: Forster and the Liberal Imagination," rptd in FORSTER: A COLLECTION OF CRITICAL ESSAYS, ed by Malcolm Bradbury (Englewood Cliffs, NJ: Prentice-Hall, Spectrum Books, 1966), pp. 71–80; Chapter 7, "*Howards End*," rptd in MODERN BRITISH FICTION: ESSAYS IN CRITICISM, ed by Mark Schorer (NY: Oxford UP, Galaxy Books, 1961), pp. 195–209; Chapter 8, "*A Passage to India*," rptd in E. M. FORSTER: "A PASSAGE TO INDIA": A CASEBOOK, ed by Malcolm Bradbury (Lond: Macmillan, Casebook Series, 1970), pp. 77–92; in part in PROSE AND CRITICISM, ed by John Hamilton McCallum (NY: Harcourt, Brace & World, 1966), pp. 730–39; in TWENTIETH CENTURY INTERPRETATIONS OF "A PASSAGE TO INDIA," ed by Andrew Rutherford (Englewood Cliffs, NJ: Prentice-Hall, Spectrum Books, 1970), pp. 17–32; and extracts from the entire book

E. M. FORSTER

rptd in CONTEMPORARY LITERARY CRITICISM, ed by Carolyn Riley (Detroit: Gale Research Co., 1973), I, 104–5.
Chapter 1, "Introduction: Forster and the Liberal Imagination" [see Trilling, "E. M. Forster" (1942)]. Chapter 2, "Sawston and Cambridge": EMF's work is to be explained in terms of his emphasis upon the disastrous effects of "the undeveloped heart." Sawston represses the natural impulses of the heart, whereas Cambridge encourages them. EMF is aware of the complex relationships between the public and the private life; he feels that private acts and emotions have social and political implications. EMF's style best reveals his nature; the style is plain but replete with wit, eloquence, and intensity. Chapter 3, "The Short Stories: A Statement of Themes": "The Road from Colonus" and "The Eternal Moment," which are the least fantastic of the stories, endure the best. "The Story of the Siren" has power; "The Point of It" contrasts a pointless life and a glorious death. Among the themes present in the stories which are developed in the novels: the idea of the inadequate heart, the insufficient imagination, the nature and significance of death, the role of money, snobbery, the conditions for salvation, the Pan theme (the role of vital nature), racial survival, the meaningful appreciation of art versus an artificial reverence for it. [Discussion is a bit obvious.] Chapter 4, *"Where Angels Fear to Tread"*: This novel reveals the Forsterian intelligence in control of its materials. *Angels* is a novel of learning and growth; a novel of broken ties; a novel of questioning, disillusionment, and conversion; and a novel of sexuality. It begins as a comedy of manners, goes on to violence and melodrama, and ends in "enlightened despair." The sudden deaths imply that life is capricious and uncertain. The aesthetic impressiveness is largely the result of the meaning that EMF derives from his plot. Gino Carella's demonic behavior and cruelty when he hears of the death of his child is more excusable than the malignant cruelty of the respectable Harriet Herriton. Italy has been educative for Philip Herriton and Caroline Abbott; things will never again be the same in Sawston for them. Chapter 5, *"The Longest Journey"*: *Journey* is "the most brilliant, the most dramatic, and the most passionate of his works"; it does not so much fall apart as "fly apart." The theme is the tragic consequences of mistaking the unreal for the real (the real is the inner life, which Rickie Elliot loses through a wrong sort of devotion to it). He mistakenly idealizes Agnes Pembroke as reality, whereas she does not even exist for Stewart Ansell. Rickie should have identified himself with Mrs. Elliot, Robert (her lover), Mr. Failing, Ansell, and Stephen Wonham, who choose the equable human way, but instead he aligns himself, through a distorted view of reality, with the Pembrokes and becomes vulnerable to Mrs. Failing [this formulation of Trilling's is valid but somewhat simplistic]. Rickie joins the multitude and deteriorates; he is saved by Ansell and Stephen, but he is later destroyed since he still demands from life what is unreal. He suffers from the knowledge of good-and-evil in his intellect, but spiritually he

demands absolutes from life. After his death, his generosity and spiritual dignity survive in Stephen and Stephen's farm, wife, and child. Chapter 6, *"A Room with a View": Room* is slighter than *Angels* or *Journey* but embodies a sense of melodramatic evil more frightening than anything in the other two novels. The most memorable effects are of impalpability, brightness, and nature in motion; of darkness and lurking evil at the end of the novel. The Rev. Mr. Eager mistakenly turns life into art; George Emerson is imprisoned by his neurotic *fin de siècle* pessimism; Lucy Honeychurch, by respectability; and Cecil Vyse, by egotism and a false conception of culture. Cecil tries to shape Lucy as Sir Willoughby Patterne in Meredith's THE EGOIST had tried to shape Clara Middleton. Sexuality and right political feeling converge when Lucy criticizes Cecil for his "democratic" intention in bringing the Emersons to the neighborhood villa. The final irony of the novel is in the reversal of roles: Charlotte Bartlett now works to bring the lovers together, whereas the Rev. Mr. Beebe resents Lucy's happiness since it is sexual in kind. Chapter 7, *"Howards End": Howards End* is EMF's masterpiece; the earlier novels represented a simplistic confrontation of good and evil, in contrast to the complexities dramatized in *Howards End.* It is a novel of the class war, kept within the sections of the middle class. Henry Wilcox is one of Plato's Artisans, whereas Ernst Schlegel is one of Plato's Watchdogs, the military elite from whom the Philosophical Guardians were chosen. Mrs. Wilcox has strength as a presence but is more successful as a real woman than as a symbol. She comes from the yeoman class rather than from the middle class, and her wisdom is traditional and ancestral. As intellectuals, the Schlegel sisters touch the extremes of their class, Margaret reaching up to the Wilcoxes, Helen down to the Basts. The novel is also about the war between men and women. The Wilcoxes represent the masculine principle but suffer from sexual deficiency and arrested personal development. Class feeling and his obsession with culture prevent Leonard Bast from seeing the Schlegels as they are; class feeling prevents the Schlegels and the Wilcoxes from seeing Leonard as he is. Helen is vengeful rather than humane in bringing the Basts to Shropshire. The outer life betrays Margaret; it is the inner life with Helen, Margaret finds, that "pays." In furnishing Howards End house with the Schlegel books, EMF adds, through the agency of Miss Avery, the stuff of the intellect to traditional England. Margaret and Helen have the names of the two chief women in Goethe's FAUST and are heroines, respectively, of the outer life and the inner. At the end sexual deprivations mar the idyllic note: Henry is too completely feminized; Helen is neurotic in her recoil from a lover; and Margaret is too limited in her deficient maternal feeling. Helen's child is a Euphorion figure (the child of Faust and Helen) and a classless heir of all classes and a symbol of the epigraph in the novel, "Only Connect!" To him Howards End, the symbol of England, will eventually belong. [This is the best chapter in the book.] Chapter 8, *"A Passage to India": Passage* is restrained, objective in approach, and written in a chastened and more public style than the earlier novels. The manner is less arbitrary, but EMF is also less in control of the truth than he was in the earlier books. The English officials and the Indians are presented with great honesty, though the Indians, if charming, have little dignity. The characters lack sufficient dimensions for the underlying story and are effective only at the level of plot. England has lost India because of an undeveloped heart and a public-school attitude transferred to the administration of empire. The theme of separation (race from race, sex from sex, culture from culture, man from himself) is paramount. The plot is concerned with the Moslem characters, the story with Mrs. Moore and the Hindu theme (she moves nearer to Indian ways of feeling when she finds that Christianity is inadequate). Her recognition of the wasp and Godbole's acknowledgment of it and of Mrs. Moore carry the story line. Though Mrs. Moore is immobilized by her experiences in the Caves, her influence later augments and she comes to dominate the action. The Shri Krishna festivities in "Temple" lead to the abolition of barriers but to no firm solution of the problems raised in the novel. EMF's novel is not about India but about all of human life. [This last, central insight Trilling fails to develop. The discussion of *Passage* is superficial, condescending, and misleading, the weakest part of this book.] Chapter 9, "Mind and Will: Forster's Literary Criticism": EMF is a greater essayist than a literary critic. [This is not the consensus view.] The response to *Aspects of the Novel* is likely to be genial and admiring, but not strong or creative. [Trilling downgrades the book.] EMF's literary criticism is vitiated by his lack of a set philosophy or formal principles: his liberalism verges on anarchy and "is an affront to the Western mind." [A pompous and arbitrary judgment, overlooking the fact that not all critics can work from, or toward, the abstract.] EMF undercuts the intellect and the whole structure of order and law so that he can thereby reassert them more forcefully. [Trilling's book is of immense significance in the present-day acknowledgment of EMF as a major figure. Trilling focused attention on EMF in intellectual circles and was greatly instrumental in the EMF revival. The book is not as good as later books by McConkey, Crews, Beer, Stone, and Thomson. Its Olympian quality and its attitude of superiority to its subject detract from its present effectiveness, though many scholars rate the book more highly than I do. For review comment, see items above by Arvin, Baker, Fadiman, Godfrey, Jones, Mayberry, Pryce-Jones, Spectorsky, Whicher, Wright, and Zabel. See also "Forster and the Human Fact," "Re-discovering Mr. Forster," and "Notes on Current Books," VIRGINIA QUARTERLY REVIEW, XIX (Autumn 1943), xxxvii, xc. See also Annan, Leavis, Macaulay, and O'Brien (1944); " 'Undeveloped Hearts': Mr. E. M. Forster and the Modern World" (1944). See Daiches (1945), Putt (1951), Thomson (1962), and Barbara Hardy, "The Personality of Criticism," SOUTHERN REVIEW, nsIII (Autumn 1967), 1001–9.]

437 Wagenknecht, Edward. CAVALCADE OF THE ENGLISH NOVEL (NY: Henry Holt, 1943, 2nd ed, with supplementary bibliography, 1954), p. 555.

EMF is the voice of English liberalism—"anti-imperialist, anti-capitalist, anti-regimentarian, pro-mystical, anti-ecclesiastical." His reputation rests on *Howards End* and *A Passage to India*. He is the champion of the individual; his villains prefer things to people; his "skeptical urbanity" is conjoined to a preoccupation with the struggle between good and evil. [Of interest to demonstrate that by 1943 the revolution in taste that elevated EMF and Ford Madox Ford to major status had not occurred; in this sensible and perceptive book they are included only in an appendix, "Some Nineteenth and Twentieth Century Novelists not Considered in the Text."]

438 Whicher, George F. "A Modern Rational Mind," NEW YORK HERALD TRIBUNE WEEKLY BOOK REVIEW, 5 Sept 1943, p. 7.

Lionel Trilling's praise of EMF in E. M. FORSTER (1943) is deserved but unexpected, since EMF is no strict contemporary but an Edwardian novelist who represents "the uncertainties of pure intellectualism and the decline of liberal culture in the modern world." Free intelligence characterizes both EMF and Trilling. Trilling makes the case for EMF in terms of the importance of the modern rational mind. If this mind, as represented by EMF, is sometimes oversubtle and tolerant, it has lucidity, quiet life, and relevance as a viable force in the modern world.

439 Wright, Cuthbert. "The Damned and the Saved," COMMONWEAL, XXXVIII (24 Sept 1943), 557–61.

The categories of sheep and goats do not apply fully to judgments made about EMF's characters; we might substitute "fauns" for "goats." EMF is distrustful of absolutes and regards human nature as unpredictable and mixed. EMF does not descend from Meredith or James but from the simpler tradition of Jane Austen and Samuel Butler. EMF writes in a vernacular tradition, but his effects are often suffused with poetry. Rickie Elliot (*The Longest Journey*) is a "faun" who gets involved with bad sheep. EMF attacks vices of the heart more than he does those of the body; as in Dante spiritual pride and envy are greater evils than lust and anger. EMF advocates neither asceticism nor self-indulgence. He is Christian in preferring the Publican to the Pharisee, the children of this world to the Children of Light (who are often the monsters of EMF's novels). [Review-essay on Lionel Trilling's E. M. FORSTER (1943) and the American reissue of the first four novels. Important essay in history of EMF's reputation.]

440 Zabel, Morton Dauwen. "A Forster Revival," NATION (NY), CLVII (7 Aug 1943), 158–59.

The reissue of the first four novels by Knopf and New Directions and the appearance of Lionel Trilling's E. M. FORSTER (1943) are welcome. Not only is Trilling's the best study of its subject yet written, but also the writing of it is a public service. EMF's books are among the wittiest, most original, and most stimulating of the modern age. EMF deserves attention at a time when the novel is so uninspired, when human and moral values seem to be in a state of atrophy or abdication, or when in some quarters they have been oversimplified. EMF "is the historian of the fatal estrangements that underlie the defeats and humiliations of his age." His chief limitation is his apparent abandonment of his creative temperament and action. His chief distinction: "A restless disquiet of moral sensibility, an uncompromising empiricism of sympathy and sincerity, the impulse, *ondoyant et divers*, of the skepticism of Socrates and Montaigne which takes as its duty the quickening to consciousness of human values and necessities that are eternally betrayed to the intolerance and brutality of social prejudice and force." EMF has applied this sensibility to many problems and has thereby illuminated them. He has placed his gifts at the disposal of statesmen, moralists, and educators; it is their tragedy and ours that they have not been utilized. Trilling's book is an examination of the conscience of contemporary literature and thinking. It has this ramification, but it will also stand as the classical treatment of EMF's fiction. [Review-essay on Trilling's E. M. FORSTER. Zabel's second essay on EMF is intelligent and shrewd in its own right, and important in the EMF "revival." Most of its salient points are repeated in Zabel's "E. M. Forster: The Trophies of the Mind," CRAFT AND CHARACTER: TEXTS, METHODS, AND VOCATIONS (1957).]

1944

441 Annan, Noel. "Books in General," New Statesman and Nation, nsXXVIII (7 Oct 1944), 239–40.

Lionel Trilling is right (in E. M. Forster [1943]) to feel that EMF is as concerned with public as private life. Trilling fails to note influence of G. E. Moore on EMF and his contemporaries. Moore's "concern for clarity, his insistence on the importance of *states of mind*, and that one must analyze *meaning*" were formative for EMF. Under Moore's aegis, EMF no longer was able to accept ready-made virtues and vices. His comic manner owed as much to Bloomsbury as it did to Fielding, Dickens, Meredith, and James, especially in the conjoining of high-mindedness and ruthless honesty with a sense of comicality. His style and method are modern; but his plots have a Victorian caprice, his settings and characters a Victorian vitality. EMF is a moralist, though sometimes he is too moralizing or else excludes too much—the will, for example—in favor of the heart. EMF's "artistic and creative conviction with which he states his vision of life" will assure him survival. In the final judgment, "we are held by his subtle, evocative imagination, his exquisite counterpoint and ... by his rattling stories." The supreme quality in his fiction is the passionate honesty characterizing G. E. Moore's circle of forty years ago. [Important article.]

442 Babcock, V. A. "East is West?" Time, XLIV (11 Sept 1944), 6.

No book gives a more incorrect impression of India and Indians than *A Passage to India*. Indians are businessmen, intelligentsia, government officials, and politicians, "like the people we know at home." [A letter protesting Time review, "The Only One of Its Kind," below.]

443 Brown, E. K. "The Revival of E. M. Forster," Yale Review, nsXXXIII (Summer 1944), 668–81; rptd in Forms of Modern Fiction: Essays Collected in Honor of Joseph Warren Beach, ed by William Van O'Connor (Minneapolis: University of Minnesota P, 1948), pp. 161–74.

In our age the best attempt to write the novel of ideas has been EMF's; he has been aware of the dangers in the form, so he tries to circumvent them. In *The Longest Journey*, for example, his redemptive and radical spokesman, Anthony Failing, is dead, and Failing's spiteful widow is penning a scornful memoir. The absurdities of another such spokesman, Mr. Emerson in *A Room with a View*, make him credible, though not entirely so. *Howards End* is a redoing of *Journey*, with a more incisive redemptive figure and a larger canvas (the business world is substituted for the academic); *A Passage to India* is a redoing of *Room*. In *Where Angels Fear to Tread*, the "Panic" figure, Gino Carella, who is not quite redemptive, emerges and later receives fuller embodiment in the Stephen Wonham of *Journey*. Stephen is a pure expression of the novel of ideas (he is nature, similar to Robinson Jeffers's male nature figures), but he is not fully successful as a character. Ruth Wilcox is a far more convincing redemptive figure; when she ceases to be "dreary," she takes us with her as she "soars." Mrs. Moore in *Passage* is even more commanding. [Brown traces in detail her personal decline in India.] She is a most convincing character in a novel of ideas. EMF's figures of convention are excellent, especially the men. However, he is sometimes unable to focus his materials. The deaths of major characters (Gerald Dawes, Mrs. Wilcox, Mrs. Moore) are too quietly and coldly done, for example. The novels often don't come off at the realistic level; writing novels of ideas, EMF sometimes fails to find appropriate embodiments for his themes. [Superficial essay; the judgment by standards of realism seems irrelevant; not up to Brown's other work on EMF.]

444 Churchill, R. C. ENGLISH LITERATURE AND THE AGNOSTIC (Lond: Watts, The Thinker's Forum, No. 32, 1944), pp. 19–20, 23. In EMF's books, as in those of Woolf, Conrad, Galsworthy, Bennett, Douglas, Stella Benson, Huxley, and Joyce, a keen sense of liberal religious values informs them, but these novelists do not try to justify their agnosticism as do D. H. Lawrence, T. F. Powys, and L. H. Myers. [Pamphlet is an apologia for agnosticism, seen as a middle way between the supernatural mysticism of the religious temperament and the materialism of certain followers of Darwin.]

445 Connolly, Cyril. "E. M. Forster," BRITAIN TO-DAY, No. 104 (Dec 1944), 20–24; rptd as "The Art of Being Good: A Note on Maugham and Forster: II, The Undeveloped Heart," THE CONDEMNED PLAYGROUND, ESSAYS: 1927–1944 (NY: Macmillan, 1945; Lond: Routledge & Kegan Paul, 1946), pp. 254–59. EMF is a moralist with a clear-cut system in a skeptical age. His writing is rapid, vivid, and impressionistic, characterized by exactness of observation and felicity of imagery. An ascetic delight determines the quality of his sensibility. His "religion" is "a primitive pantheistic paganism" overlaid by an Oriental preoccupation with nonattachment and abnegation, modulated by his inherited moralism. In "The Eternal Moment," EMF reveals his typical moral insight, lyricism, and ascetic vitality; and he attacks modern destructiveness and money values. He is "a political writer who prefers unpolitical themes," though he is on the side of the oppressed in *Howards End* and *A Passage to India*, which are in part "tales of the barricades and the class war." He is not only liberal but libertarian in his opposition to imposed authority. Though he believes in original sin, he also stresses human dignity, courage, and freedom. His philosophy is best expressed in "What I Believe" (1939; rptd in *Two Cheers for Democracy*). [Incisive discussion.]

446 Leavis, F. R. "Meet Mr. Forster," SCRUTINY, XII (Autumn 1944), 308–9.

The emancipative aspect of the Cambridge presented in *The Longest Journey* is questionable. The Hellenism and liberalism of those days have not had the best consequences, and the university did not equip EMF to deal with Bloomsbury: "How can so sensitive, decent and generous a mind have allowed itself to be so much *of* a milieu so inferior?—so provincially complacent and petty?" The inequalities in the work should have prevented Trilling from taking intention for achievement, as in his judgment of *Howards End.* [Review of Lionel Trilling's E. M. FORSTER (1943).]

447 Macaulay, Rose. "Selected Notices," HORIZON, X (Nov 1944), 432–34.

In E. M. FORSTER (1943), Lionel Trilling is able to formulate principles and to refer EMF's books to them, but he lacks the quick, intuitive, empirical, flickering quality of EMF's mind. He misses some of the humor and the idiom. He is more discerning about ideas, attitudes, and themes than about the characters. Miss Raby ("The Eternal Moment") is hardly the ancestor of Mrs. Wilcox, Mrs. Moore, Mrs. Elliot, and Margaret Schlegel: Evelyn Beaumont ("Other Kingdom") is hardly the progenitor of Lucy Honeychurch and Helen Schlegel. The clergymen, Rev. Mr. Eager and Rev. Mr. Beebe, of *A Room with a View*, are different from each other. Trilling's analyses of the novels are excellent.

448 McLuhan, Herbert Marshall. "Kipling and Forster," SEWANEE REVIEW, LII (Spring 1944), 332–43.

In *A Passage to India*, India scrutinizes the reigning Wilcoxes far more pitilessly than the Schlegels scrutinized them in *Howards End. Passage* is unique as an expression of EMF's artistry and understanding. For the most part he never overcame the dichotomies of his world by understanding them. In this respect he is similar to Kipling. Both EMF and Kipling were unable to resolve the contradictions and cleavages existing between art and action. Kipling exemplifies the public school code; EMF deplores it but is unduly obsessed with it. *Passage* is superior to *Howards End* because the Indians are more convincing incarnations of personal values than the Schlegels; and Ronny Heaslop and the other government officials are more dramatically engaged in their milieu than are the Wilcoxes. The Wilcoxes are too ineffectual as persons to be credible as characters. The Schlegels are vacuous and dull, and they lack insight into art and life; the Wilcoxes do not believe in themselves or exert real power over their lives. There is obtuseness rather than subtlety behind EMF's dichotomizing; he makes absolutes in turn out of each pole in a contrast, but he also hopes that the poles will merge to contribute to a larger whole. His observations and his analyses of characters are often not profound, nor are all his characters passionately engaged in or by life. His novels are too purposive and end by seeming like "tracts for the times." In *Passage*, Mrs. Moore's vision is really "nostalgic agnosticism," in her conclusion that values are "wishful fictions." With Mrs. Moore the double vision depends on glandular and somatic decline; action is now impossible for her, with the result that she is bemused "by the pseudo-horrors of Heaven, Hell, and Annihilation." EMF seems unable to say that action, if an illusion, is preferable to the life of reflection, detachment, and art. Mrs. Moore's repudiation of relationships in favor of people is given no firm basis. The lyricism of the novels is not always under control, or it is artificial and willed. EMF is interested not in the normal emotions of humanity but in the unexpected emotions deriving from unexpected quarters. Melodrama mars his work, separating a given sequence or character from the rest of the book by overemphasis, and emotion in his characters is overcerebralized. [The negative criticisms of EMF and his work are mostly asserted rather than demonstrated.]

449 O'Brien, Kate. "Refusal of Greatness," SPECTATOR (Lond), CLXXIII (1 Dec 1944), 508, 510.

Lionel Trilling in E. M. FORSTER (1943) is thorough and intelligent, but he does not document why a writer as confident and talented as EMF can sometimes be so feeble, and why his passion and irony fail to be sustained. In EMF's refusal to be great may lie his true quality, though he may have actually achieved greatness in one book, *A Passage to India*. We do not admire the novels so unreservedly as Trilling indicates. At moments of descending grace in his fiction, EMF lacks the ability to be completely and perfectly simple. His irony may be less great a gift than seriousness and simplicity would be.

450 "The Only One of Its Kind," TIME, XLIV (24 July 1944), 90, 92, 94.

From India EMF derived the materials which, by some visit of inspiration, "lifted his sardonic talent to genius" in the writing of *A Passage to India*, a novel that is "beautiful, ironic, crystal-clear, intense." No other British novel on India has attained its delicacy, toughness, and clarity. EMF's great gift is keeping his characters, their mental lives and their expectations, in a continual state of suspension. The pathos and irony of *Passage* reside in the people of good intentions on both sides in the racial situation doing nothing more than complicating the problem. As Mrs. Moore and Aziz proceed toward intimacy, the forces of misunderstanding and suspicion intensify, with the result that the city is finally in revolt. Mrs. Moore set a large portion of the empire on edge simply by being herself in a totally different world. The contradictions in Aziz make of him an impressive imaginative creation. The surface action seems less impressive than it once did, but "the brilliant characterizations, the religious and political insights, the atmosphere" more so. In particular, the portrait of Aziz has gained depth. [Review of 1944 American rpt of *Passage*.]

451 Orwell, George [pseud of Eric Blair]. "As I Please," TRIBUNE (Lond), 13 Oct 1944, p. 11; rptd in THE COLLECTED ESSAYS, JOURNALS AND LETTERS OF GEORGE ORWELL, ed by Sonia Orwell and Ian Angus (NY: Harcourt Brace & World; Lond: Secker & Warburg, 1968), III, 252–55.

What kind of "patron" must an artist have if he is to be free to devote his energies to his art? The problem is not easy to solve; but government subsidy is hardly a perfect answer. Can one envision the British government commissioning EMF to write *A Passage to India?* It was possible for him to write it because he was not dependent on state aid.

452 Plomer, William. "An Introduction to E. M. Forster," PENGUIN NEW WRITING (Harmondsworth, Middlesex: Penguin Books, 1944), XX, 138–41.

EMF had great influence among his thoughtful contemporaries. His two most oustanding books are *Howards End* and *A Passage to India*, which are notable for their range of human interest and for their intricacy of construction. They are concerned with the contrast between sensitive, spiritually oriented, imaginative human beings and those who are insensitive, exclusively materialistic, and unimaginative. *Howards End* deals with English life in the materialistic Edwardian Age. EMF had the happy inspiration to dramatize how necessary to each other a woman of feeling and a man of action are. The types are complementary and the world needs both. In *Passage* EMF looks toward a world in which the races and continents will understand each other and work in harmony. He not only dramatizes the divisions in human nature but notes those subtle and elusive signs which indicate that communication is taking place. EMF is unobtrusive in appearance, original of mind, has a modest manner, a capacity for friendship, and a love of French culture. [Analyzes at some length "What I Believe," (1939; rptd in *Two Cheers for Democracy*).]

453 S., G. "Mystic Realist," ROCKY MOUNTAIN REVIEW, VIII (Winter 1944), 62–63.

EMF is a "metaphysical" novelist who combines the mystical and realistic in a way acceptable to the modern temper. The "unseen" is the superior category for EMF, and those who are alive to it have the author's approval most. A catalyst in each novel connects the opposing camps and brings about the denouement. *A Passage to India* is greatest since the roles of "cognizance" are passed back and forth, owing to EMF's combination of his own metaphysics with Hinduism. There is structural unity, order, and balance in the novels; they are almost "classical." EMF unembarrassedly resorts to coincidence in working out his plots. His interest is in pattern, and he suggests the universal by a deft symbolism. [Important notice for spread of EMF's reputation in America in World War II and after.]

> **454** Savage, D. S. "E. M. Forster and the Dilemma of Liberalism," Now (Lond), III (ca. 1944), 4–13; IV (ca. 1944), 21–29; rptd in abrgd form as "Examination of Modern Authors: 4—E. M. Forster," Rocky Mountain Review (Salt Lake City), X (Summer 1946), 190–204; rptd in abrgd form as "E. M. Forster," Writers of Today, ed by Denys Val Baker (Lond: Sidgwick & Jackson, 1946; NY: Vanguard, 1947), pp. 154–69; rptd in Savage, The Withered Branch: Six Studies in the Modern Novel (Lond: Eyre & Spottiswoode, 1950; NY: Pellegrini & Cudahy, 1952), pp. 48–69; rptd, slightly abrgd, in Forster: A Collection of Critical Essays, ed by Malcolm Bradbury (Englewood Cliffs, NJ: Prentice-Hall, Spectrum Books, 1966), pp. 56–70.

EMF has no central core of political belief. In his early novels he too readily equates erotic emotion and the natural with spirituality, and he oversimplifies convention. The division between good and bad types is not consistent; in a bourgeois civilization, no consistent system of moral symbolism is possible. EMF's concept of the inner life, as dramatized in *Howards End*, is weakened by its dependence for validity upon nature and money instead of the supernatural. Accordingly, his portraits of the Schlegels and Leonard Bast are falsified. The pessimism of *A Passage to India* further indicates the powerlessness of a cultured liberalism to become effective in the political and social world. [An adverse critique on EMF which maintains that the tendency of liberalism toward compromise, represented in EMF's work, results not so much in reconciliation as confusion. Attack is too absolute and lacks the reasoned quality of the best essay in this vein, C. B. Cox's "E. M. Forster's Island," The Free Spirit (1963).]

> **455** Thompson, Edward. Robert Bridges 1844–1930 (Lond: Oxford UP, 1944), p. 89.

[Bridges had remarked to Thompson that EMF had the most brilliantly photographic mind he had ever encountered. Thompson agrees, remembering that in *A Passage to India* EMF had utilized details that Thompson had overlooked in India, or else not remembered, but that he recognized as being unmistakably accurate when EMF thus called attention to them (e.g., the hot-weather squirrel hanging downward in the sun, glued to where it clings).]

456 " 'Undeveloped Hearts,' " TIMES LITERARY SUPPLEMENT (Lond), 7 Oct 1944, p. 1.
Lionel Trilling in E. M. FORSTER (1943) traces the theme of the "undeveloped heart" in EMF's works. EMF is interested in character and reveals a fastidious care for style (the colloquialism tends to conceal the art); the ramifications of his style are mainly political (and liberal). The uniqueness of EMF is the quality of his intentions, "its effective execution, its individualism." Trilling is on surer ground when he analyzes EMF's literary criticism than when he attempts to deduce EMF's presuppositions from the complicated novels.

457 Ward, A. C. "Epilogue," ENGLISH LITERATURE: MODERN 1450–1939, by G. H. Mair (Lond & NY: Oxford UP, 1944 [2nd ed; Home University of Modern Knowledge, No. 27]), pp. 223–24; as "The Twentieth Century (II)," MODERN ENGLISH LITERATURE 1450–1959 (3rd ed, 1960), pp. 224–26.
EMF appeals to other writers (as he did to Virginia Woolf), rather than to the average reader. His appeal lies in his distinction of manner, not in his stories. His subjects—the tension between the inner and outer lives, social snobbery, and domestic neuroses—are less important than his sanity and balance of mind and his assured style. Virginia Woolf and EMF reveal that the "new novel" is inadequate "as a medium for reflective prose of the modern philosophical-critical-poetic kind." The new novel needs to be delivered from bondage to plot and incident and the use of usual character types. *Howards End* reveals mature intelligence as it treats significant themes but falls below its own high standard in a resort to coincidence and in the character of Leonard Bast ("a piece of mere mental slumming").

1945

458 Adams, J. Donald. "Speaking of Books," NEW YORK TIMES BOOK REVIEW, (11 Nov 1945), p. 2.
The essence of EMF's *Aspects of the Novel* is in the chapter "People." The difference between people in the novel and actual people is a matter of the author's temperament. EMF rightly holds that great fiction goes beyond the "evidence."

459 Belgion, Montgomery. "Second Lecture: Novels," READING FOR PROFIT: LECTURES ON ENGLISH LITERATURE DELIVERED IN 1941, 1942 AND 1943 TO BRITISH OFFICERS PRISONERS OF WAR IN GERMANY (Harmondsworth, Middlesex & NY: Penguin Books, Pelican, 1945), pp. 40–62, espec 48–53, 58–60.

Fielding and Aziz are the only real characters in *A Passage to India*, but Aziz is a bit shadowy; his true self is never quite made clear. Fielding is the hero; his private philosophy of the good life is somewhat inadequate and vague, since it is the result of his personal effort alone and does not have secure social foundations. In light of it he tries to understand the Indians and their institutions (no other white man does so), but he does not make corresponding efforts to understand the English. He is also aware that he does not live up to his own philosophy and that his philosophy does not go far enough. How does Fielding and his situation affect us? Is there in *Passage* seriousness of theme and seriousness of treatment? Not altogether so, probably. That the English are swept by waves of irrationality in their view of Aziz and his guilt is graphically demonstrated and is a convincing picture of "lynch-law" mentality. The total picture, however, is unfair and lacking in full verisimilitude; at least some conscientious readers have thought so. Is the characterization adequate? Not quite. The women are "dummies." Mrs. Moore's portrait is "theoretical and frigid"; as for Adela Quested, EMF does not care about her. The Anglo-Indian officials are seen only from the outside; there is no sympathy shown for them. In view of these considerations, *Passage* may be judged as on the way to being literature rather than being at this point literature. The lack of understanding among men is the reason for the existence of this novel; it is set in India because there misunderstandings are highlighted by the tension between the races. The novel has significance as a result, yet the form and characterization are unsatisfactory. Dickens's BLEAK HOUSE has a poetry and an imaginative grasp exceeding that found in *Passage*, just as *Passage* in turn is superior in this respect to James Hilton's RANDOM HARVEST. [Belgion recommends *Aspects of the Novel*.]

460 Connolly, Cyril. "The Defects of English Novels," "The Novel-Addict's Cupboard," THE CONDEMNED PLAYGROUND, ESSAYS: 1927–1944 (NY: Macmillan, 1945; Lond: Routledge & Kegan Paul, 1946), pp. 101–3; 112–17; rpts "E. M. Forster" (1941) as "The Art of Being Good: A Note on Maugham and Forster: II, The Undeveloped Heart," pp. 254–59.

"The Defects of English Novels": The defects are thinness of material, poverty of style (there are two principal styles, the academic, mandarin style, and the style avoiding the intellectual by an extreme simplicity; EMF, David Garnett, and Dorothy Edwards are examples of the latter), and lack of power. Regretfully, in the years ahead EMF will be neglected because his excellence is inconvenient. "The Novel-Addict's Cupboard": EMF is "anti high-brow," in that he dislikes intellectual presumption and spiritual pride. He is a revolutionary writer, attacking the arrogant individualism of the nineties and writing of "plain men and plainer women." Having written only one novel since 1910, he is waiting for English fiction to catch up to him.

461 Daiches, David. "Reviews," ACCENT, IV (Autumn 1945), 61–62.

EMF is transitional between the militant revolt of nineteenth-century liberals and the cynical revolt of the disillusioned generation of the 1920s. First, EMF's hero stands between Butler's Ernest (THE WAY OF ALL FLESH) and Huxley's Dennis (CHROME YELLOW). Second, like other moderns, EMF confuses myth (an external pattern to which all else relates) and symbol (the part that characters and incident play in the plot), sometimes to the aesthetic detriment of his work. This second aspect of his work is perhaps related to the transitional aspect. Lionel Trilling in E. M. FORSTER (1943) enlightens us on EMF's historical place and helps explain EMF's confusion, but he shirks the final responsibility of the critic, which is evaluation rather than description.

462 Guidi, Augusto. "Prefazione" (Preface), *Passagio all'India* (A Passage to India) (Roma: Perrella, 1945), pp. 7–9.

A Passage to India is perhaps EMF's central work. EMF is an impressionistic and intimate writer, convinced that human life is an individual phenomenon, whose dominating motives remain unexpressed or can only be expressed with difficulty. A searching psychology interests EMF more than abstract truth. At the novel's center is the enormous problem of the relations between the governing English and the governed Indians, a problem treated impartially and a more important theme than those problems dramatized in the earlier novels. The novel's focus is on the friendship between Fielding, who alone among the British views the Indian people without prejudice, and the young Indian doctor, Aziz. EMF's dedication of the novel to his friend, Syed Ross Masood, and Fielding's interior speculation and unswerving honesty leave no doubt that the novel is autobiographical. Mrs. Moore embodies the best qualities of a British woman, but she also offers an ideological contrast with Fielding's atheism. EMF's language is nervous, rich, full of rapid impressions and suggestions, at times even reticent and impatient. *Passage* reveals a writer of notable humanity who lived for some time in India and who assimilated the country and its inhabitants into his vision. The most genuine aspect of his humanity is the dominating theme of friendship. EMF values the type of friendship that Bacon said leads humanity toward perfection. [In Italian.]

463 Lunan, N. M. "The Novels of E. M. Forster," DURHAM UNIVERSITY JOURNAL, nsVI (March 1945), 52–57.

Lionel Trilling, in E. M. FORSTER (1943), wrongly emphasizes the casual anarchism of the novels. EMF either defines the good society directly (as in his presentation of Italy in *Where Angels Fear to Tread* and *A Room with a View*) or else he presents a deficient society (Sawston in *Angels* and *The Longest Journey*, Anglo-India in *A Passage to India*, the Wilcox world of "telegrams and anger," "panic and emptiness" in *Howards End*). He is looking for a society in which he can feel at home, and he wishes to define the true meaning of culture. [EMF is regarded as a constructive social thinker who tries to establish through his fiction the values of a good society. Essay is perfunctory. EMF is better presented as a "social thinker" in C. B. Cox's THE FREE SPIRIT (1963) and in Willis H. Truitt's, "Thematic and Symbolic Ideology in the Works of E. M. Forster: In Memoriam" (1971).]

464 Morton, A. L. "E. M. Forster and the Classless Society," THE LANGUAGE OF MEN (Lond: Cobbett P, 1945), pp. 78–88.

EMF writes for the classless society that will grow up "on the far side of the Revolution," because he realizes how important personal relations will be in such a society. In his novels the new is at work "within the substance of the old." EMF is on the side of Victory, as is Beethoven in *Howards End*. Though the Schlegels are honest, sensitive, and generous, they injure Leonard Bast irreparably. He only glimpses the kind of life of which he is capable. In *The Longest Journey* Rickie Elliot dies after failing in everything that he undertook, betraying his deepest instincts for expedient approximations. Because EMF has made a leap into the future, he is serene about the present. In spite of presenting failure, suffering, and death, EMF is on the side of Victory (the classless society) in the future, of Revolution in the present. Almost alone among contemporary writers, he has the ability to deal with important issues and the courage to write about them. His Cambridge manner with its gentleness and diffidence conceals passionate conviction of which he is not completely confident. He understates, and he writes of inconclusive people or else of elemental people who seem more prophecies than people (old Mr. Emerson in *A Room with a View*, Stephen Wonham in *Journey*), by virtue of his poetic wistfulness. His plots are preposterous; his novels are really built around themes which are developed as they would be in music. Though his works are thematic, they do not explicitly convey a "moral"; the abstraction is not there just to illustrate the story but is organic to it. Beethoven is EMF's most authentic spiritual ancestor. EMF is finally a poet, and as poet he is most clearly the harbinger in his work of the classless society. [Essay is dated 1932.]

465 Orwell, George [pseud of Eric Blair]. "Introduction," Talking to India, ed by George Orwell (Lond: Allen & Unwin, 1945), pp. 7–9.

[Recounts circumstances of EMF's broadcast talks to India at time of World War II. Prints early versions of "Gibbon and His Autobiography" and "Three Stories by Tolstoy" (*Two Cheers for Democracy*) as "Edward Gibbon" and "Tolstoy's Birthday."]

466 Orwell, George [pseud of Eric Blair]. "Through a Glass, Rosily," Tribune (Lond), (23 Nov 1945), p. 8; rptd in The Collected Essays, Journalism and Letters of George Orwell, ed by Sonia Orwell and Ian Angus (NY: Harcourt, Brace & World; Lond: Secker & Warburg, 1968), IV, 34–37.

During World War II, the Germans broadcast works or excerpts damaging to British prestige. Among them was *A Passage to India*. The Germans did not have to resort to dishonest quotation to reveal that the English had been deficient in some aspects of colonial administration. Thus, essentially truthful books can also serve the cause of enemy propaganda when they are quoted out of context.

467 Waggoner, Hyatt Howe. "Exercises in Perspective: Notes on the Uses of Coincidence in the Novels of E. M. Forster," Chimera, III (Summer 1945), 3–14; rptd in Forster: A Collection of Critical Essays, ed by Malcolm Bradbury (Englewood Cliffs, NJ: Prentice-Hall, Spectrum Books, 1966), pp. 84–89.

In EMF there is a religious view of life, a need to carry us "beyond convention, beyond personal and individual instincts, desires, and ideas, beyond worldliness and subjectivity." He arranges views and perspectives; his views are more inclusive than those of James—his sense of oppositions in tension, his sense of the known as opposed to the vast unknown. He is aware of the universal backdrop behind his stories: he is a keen novelist of manners but also sees what lies deeper than manners. He is able to carry us from the human to the natural and the eternal. Thus, coincidence is significant both formally and philosophically; he enlarges our perspectives by its use, just as his authorial asides do. Sudden deaths are part of an aesthetic, philosophical, and ethical pattern. In *A Passage to India* what ought to have been the dramatic peak, Mrs. Moore's death, is as offhand in EMF's treatment of it as the whisper in the Cave itself. The casualness is deliberate, but so is life deliberately casual. These deaths pinpoint "the intrusion of the unknown, the unpredictable, into our ordered and secure existence"; they destroy the most carefully cherished illusion of our culture, the illusion of security. Those who pin their hopes on political or social reform or on applied science do not yet realize that men cannot control nature enough to eliminate natural evil, let alone moral evil. EMF's novels are disillusioning; they open up "fissures in the structure of our secular faith," fissures through which we may see the darkness surrounding our easy, well-lighted, secure existences. They imply that our illusion of salvation by works is as dubious as is the possibility of salvation by faith. The coincidences of the novels show the endless web of connections (as the meeting of Henry Wilcox and Jacky at Evie Wilcox's wedding) in which we are involved. Coincidences help us to connect, to realize the interdependence of "matter" and "spirit," to relate the behavior of barnyard creatures, for example, to that of Henry Wilcox and Margaret Schlegel. EMF's novels never suggest that the individual must not choose and must not try to retain his integrity, but they reveal the limitations within which an individual must work. They suggest the conditions to which the will is subject; the coincidences illustrate the reality of freedom within necessity. His novels are tissues of "interwoven contradictory, mutually modifying perspectives." His coincidences seem more accidental to those who lack vision (Lucy Honeychurch in *A Room with a View*) than to those who possess it (Mr. Emerson in *Room*). If ideals depend on fact, they do not do so overwhelmingly; coincidence itself is seen in perspective. EMF's novels are open and dynamic in accordance with the findings of modern physics, and he rejects the static materialism of early post-Darwinian thought; his world illustrates a "Whiteheadian" conception of *process* in which there are "neither gaps in the tissue of connections nor easy mechanistic answers to complex questions." The coincidences, if they accentuate the strange, also dilate the natural to include all possibilities. His novels are naturalistic but not dogmatically so, idealistic without sanctioning untenable illusions. He arranges his synthetic patterns of experience to show that he is aware of fact, of paradox, and of mystery; and the use to which he puts coincidence is part of this larger awareness. [A stimulating essay, definitive on its subject, an essay which answers critics who regard the sudden deaths and the melodramatic incidents in the novels only as implausible and as artistic blemishes.]

468 Wingfield-Stratford, Esmé. BEFORE THE LAMPS WENT OUT (Lond: Hodder & Stoughton, 1945), pp. 176–79.
In *Goldsworthy Lowes Dickinson* EMF idealized Dickinson too greatly; as a man Dickinson had his quirks and crotchets of character that earned him the name of "Dirty Dick." EMF does not capture in his book "the dapper, fussy, sensitive, slightly absurd, but wholly lovable little man" the author once knew.

1946

469 Ault, Peter. "Aspects of E. M. Forster," DUBLIN REVIEW, CCIX (Oct 1946), 109–34.

EMF's intent was expressed by Lowes Dickinson (in *Goldsworthy Lowes Dickinson*): "to bring realistic life into contact with the background of value." Where such an attempt has been made, we should examine the psychological traits, the prejudices, and the metaphysical beliefs that form the writer's temperament and point of view; we should examine the scope and limits of the experience presented; and we should determine whether we can assimilate seeming abnormalities in his vision to his general world view. Mr. Emerson in *A Room with a View* is an agnostic of the first generation, with his tranquil unbelief. George (his son) and EMF are agnostics of the second generation, visited by doubt, despair, acedia (Mrs. Moore in *A Passage to India* is also an example). EMF, through G. E. Moore, is a kind of Cambridge Utilitarian in ethics, deprecating fanaticism, cherishing civilization, and stressing the importance of aesthetic and personal satisfactions. The defect of this view is the lack of any object absolutely pleasurable that would inspire us to live in the failure of our natural appetites. But John Stuart Mill and EMF would still hope that one is immortal and that civilization is eternal, though rationally these men know that such propositions are false. This tendency of EMF to hope despite "inconceivable disaster" is the special mark of the supernatural faith he has rejected. The memory of religious hope still plagues EMF and people like him. He is not quite satisfied with things as they are; but when he seems on the point of revelation, the revelation eludes him and us in the end. The inability to formulate or understand the ineffable—as in the Beethoven Fifth Symphony episode in *Howards End*, in the Caves sequence in *Passage*, or in Lucy's playing piano music in *Room*—is often the result of EMF's use of music and musical sounds. Music alone can express for him "fundamental notions on the nature and significance of life" when language becomes inadequate. The result is that conceptions of the greatest depth and significance are sundered most from the control and understanding of the reason, and it becomes impossible to express in a single vision the actuality of life and its significance. EMF exemplifies in his work T. S. Eliot's concept of the dissociation of sensibility in the modern age—the inability of men to integrate the knowledge of sense and the knowledge of value. Such dissociation in the modern agnostic writer like EMF leads also to a failure in sensibility. The supernatural order thereby has become extruded from our representations of experience, whereas the actualization of the supernatural is necessary to give a proper form to moral value and a precise rendition of the phenomena of the senses. With the supernatural eliminated, the goods of life are reduced to animal comfort, mental refinement, and personal affection. These are changing objects; what we need is a changeless object as the goal of our ambition. Our sense of the miraculous in the modern world is often kept in abeyance except in the experiences of love and death, when a realm of value beyond the empirical seems to assert itself. Romantic love had been sponsored by Western religion; with the decline in religious authority, romantic love has been attenuated. Three types of personal contact are possible: friendship, passion or romance, and marriage. EMF values passion highly, but he is unable to conceive impassioned human beings in a sustained association with more ordinary moments. He thus has a notional, but not a real, belief in passion, and his renditions of love and marriage are weakened. EMF reveals a lack of imaginative power also in presenting types who represent values higher than utility, in conceiving heroic individuals who are willing to die for something as well as live for it, "be it region or religion, honour or love": the soldier, sailor, murderer, or saint. This inability to imagine people responsive to such motivation demonstrates his failure "to realize the fullness of natural life." In his work there is no place for death, no rationale for inflicting or accepting it. An ambiguity about belief is typical of EMF's fiction and of the Western mind: a mixture of intellectual detachment and pragmatic attachment, an intellectual rejection of it and a spiritual hankering for its comforts and promised rewards. There are three possible attitudes concerning death: We must attempt to understand it, determine to endure it, or agree to disregard or forget it. EMF's views are a mixture of the first (the explanation of religion which removes the fear of death and accepts it even with joy) and the second (the stance of Stoicism). The third is the Chinese way and has been little practiced in the West. EMF's beliefs make of him a stoic, while his temper craves the comforts of religion. Musing over Ruth Wilcox's death and Leonard Bast's death to the effect that some hope may emanate from these occurrences, EMF is revealed as unable to explain death but unwilling to accept his inability. Throughout his work he fails to establish a coherent attitude about death. Death comes as a shock. If death is regarded as only a natural process, it will seem most normal when most sudden. We have little knowledge of just how Lilia Herriton (*Where Angels Fear to Tread*) or Leonard Bast die. Because EMF lacks a coherent attitude toward death, it will seem outside nature, as Leonard's is described as being. EMF, if nothing else, reveals the effects of loss of belief upon men's sensibilities in the modern age. The modern mind cannot connect the catastrophic moment with the ordinary moment, cannot see life and death as parts of one integrated pattern. EMF's work points to this unfortunate truth: "For without belief in death our life at best can be little better than a joyless, frivolous, passionless existence." [A cogent, closely reasoned essay; starting from its Christian premises, one finds the logic and the conclusions reached unassailable. But as even Ault admits, EMF is important for revealing the spiritual consequences of agnosticism; and, aesthetically considered, these consequences are more of a characteristic than a defect in his works. There are elements also of visionary enthusiasm and mystical transcendence in EMF's work that may have greater authority than Ault as a Christian apologist may be willing to grant. Helen Schlegel in *Howards End* also criticizes the Wilcoxes for their evasion of "the idea of Death," and she apparently speaks for EMF.]

470 Brower, Reuben A. "Beyond E. M. Forster: Part I—The Earth," FOREGROUND (Cambridge, Mass.), I (Spring–Summer 1946), 164–74.

The obscurity in EMF's novels may be the result of his confusion as well as of profundity. There is a need, therefore, to define with clarity EMF's symbols. Of these, "the earth" is one of the most important. In *The Longest Journey* there is a profusion of Demeter images; her picture in the attic is a kind of totem for Stephen Wonham. In both *Journey* and *Howards End*, the earth represents an antithesis of modern civilization. In *Journey* Rickie is made aware of the squalor of the modern city through the beauty of the earth; for Margaret Schlegel in *Howards End*, earth points up the evils she had recognized instinctively in London. *Howards End* is about the opposition of two modes of living: the rural, in which personal relations are the prime value, and the urban, in which they are ignored. Helen's child at the end is a weak symbol because he represents neither the country stock of his father nor the business class: he fits in badly with contemporary social and economic fact. This sequence relies too much on the possibility of an occult harmony between the child and Mother Earth. There are too many symbols like the wych elm and the pig's teeth that are mysterious rather than precise. Still, *Howards End* is a more mature book than *Journey* because there is less talk in it about confirmation by the earth. There is a contradiction [questionable] between Mrs. Failing's advice to Rickie to beware of the earth and EMF's glorification of the earth at the novel's end. There is a conflict [questionable] between the EMF who accepts a Wordsworthian rhetoric of Nature with its mysticism and the EMF who is skeptical of all rhetorics except those that have become assimilated to a particular social experience. EMF was part of the Cambridge represented by Goldsworthy Lowes Dickinson, not of that part represented by the analysts of language: G. E. Moore, Ogden, and Richards. [Brower does take the novels seriously, in spite of some questionable interpretations.]

471 Gilomen, W. "Fantasy and Prophecy in E. M. Forster's Work," ENGLISH STUDIES (Amsterdam), XXVII (Aug 1946), 97–112.

EMF's prophetic gifts were first used to explore differences in national cultures. Sawstonians in England thrive on the distinction between rigid principles of right and wrong. In *Where Angels Fear to Tread* and *A Room with a View*, the good is opposed to the respectable, the beautiful to the petty, the true to the adequate, the reality to the sham. In *The Longest Journey* Rickie Elliot goes to Wiltshire from Cambridge through inhibiting Sawston, which is a static, unimaginative milieu. [A convincing parallel between Rickie and Alastor (in Shelly's "Alastor") is developed; in both figures a fixated imagination operates disastrously.] EMF's moral dichotomies are less sharply drawn in *Howards End;* in Henry Wilcox, for example, some complexities of temper make of him an imperfect example of some-times reprehensible extravert values. In *A Passage to India*, the English-man's difficulty in his rapprochement with the Indians is elaborated, even in Fielding, who becomes an Anglo-Indian by the end of the novel. [Gilo-men overemphasizes this change.] EMF often presents characters who are too weak to live up to the vitality suggested by their instincts, such as Mr. Lucas in "The Road from Colonus" and Lilia Herriton in *Angels*. [Surveys, in EMF's fiction, the elements of "fantasy" (induced when a god, ghost, mythic being, monster, etc., is used to express the supernatural; when an ordinary man is introduced into the future, the past, or other remote or unusual region; or when personality is divided or dived into) and of "prophecy" (induced when ranges of experience are seen to have a universal or unitary significance and when characters and events stand for more themselves, reaching out toward the infinite). The survey in "Fantasy" is perfunctory; there are a few insights of value under "Prophecy." Commen-tary is diffuse and overextended.]

472 Hamill, Elizabeth. "E. M. Forster," THESE MODERN WRITERS: AN INTRODUCTION FOR MODERN READERS (Melbourne: Georgian House, 1946), pp. 137–44; also 122–23, 145, 147.

EMF's work is a link between the liberal thought of the generation of Shaw, Wells, and Chesterton and contemporary socialist thought in English litera-ture. EMF is no ivory-tower figure; he stresses the need for the artist to participate "in the vulgar political conflicts which are shaping the world and the role of artists for the future." In so doing he rejects the supreme artistic detachment found in Joyce. Among contemporary writers EMF has been almost alone in combining the artist with the good citizen. In his work he stresses the fact that there is "a Truth, a Way, and a Life which we constant-ly miss or falsify by hypocrisy, conventional humbug and dreary muddle." In his early work he uses pagan myths to symbolize this state; in his later work he uses, for the same purpose, a more organic supernatural symbolism. In *A Passage to India* EMF depicts mass misunderstanding between two races, fostered mostly by British arrogance. [Extensive plot summary of *Passage*.] EMF concludes in this novel, reluctantly, that kindness, good will, and personal relations are not enough to solve the problems of empire. Still, for EMF himself, his individualism of the liberal humanist cast forms the basis for his own philosophy and political views. He has, therefore, a hatred of fascism and only a modified enthusiasm for communism. [By 1946 EMF's reputation had been revived; he merits a separate chapter in com-mon with T. S. Eliot, D. H. Lawrence, Huxley, Katherine Mansfield and Virginia Woolf, and Joyce.]

473 Holt, Lee Elbert. "E. M. Forster and Samuel Butler," PUBLICA-TIONS OF THE MODERN LANGUAGE ASSOCIATION, LXI (Sept 1946), 804–19.

In EMF's *Where Angels Fear to Tread* occurs the same contrast as in Butler's works (especially ALPS AND SANCTUARIES) between English hypocrisy and restraint, and Italian genuineness and spontaneity. Neither writer feels that the Italian devotion to instinct and spontaneity are completely admirable. Lilia Herriton's initial flight is symbolically right, though it results in disaster. She is unable to complete what she had begun: Gino Carella's animal stupidity is too much for her. As in THE WAY OF ALL FLESH, the bigoted religionist (Harriet Herriton) produces disastrous results. In *The Longest Journey* the theme is Butlerian, the bitter effects resulting from self-serving egotism (see Mrs. Failing and Agnes Pembroke, who make Rickie Elliot their victim). Stephen Wonham and Mr. Failing represent the natural and genuine life to which Rickie aspired but did not attain, a life of which Butler was also an exponent. Alethea Pontifex in THE WAY OF ALL FLESH is a savior, as is Stephen Wonham in *Journey*. He has been thwarted in his development by Mrs. Failing; otherwise, he might have been as great as Mr. Failing. Mr. Emerson in *A Room with a View* is the most forthright Butlerian in EMF's novels. He alone among EMF's guardian figures is successful in imparting his knowledge to others. Especially Butlerian is his emphasis upon the need for sincerity and truthfulness as the requisites for a happy life. In *Howards End* the emphasis upon money and its positive effects is Butlerian. Margaret Schlegel's ability to compromise is Butlerian; she saves both Helen Schlegel and Henry Wilcox from different kinds of excess. In *A Passage to India* Mrs. Moore has the wisdom of the East though she comes from the West. She becomes a positive influence only after sickness and death claim her, though the Western mind (see her son Ronny Heaslop) tends to connect her ability to see the truth and to bring about effective action with her sickness and death. Fielding is Butlerian in his pragmatism, enlightenment, liberalism, and unconventionality. [A sound essay demonstrating Butler's unmistakable influence over EMF, though some aspects of that influence seem slighted.]

474 Macaulay, Rose. "E. M. Forster: An Appreciation," LISTENER, XXXVII (12 Dec 1946), 845–47; rptd, slightly rvd, as "E. M. Forster," LIVING WRITERS, ed by Gilbert Phelps (Lond: Sylvan P, c. 1947), pp. 94–105.

EMF is our greatest living novelist. It is absurd to condemn him (as D. S. Savage [1944] does) for depicting the upper middle class. He is a good story teller, despite his impatience with story expressed in *Aspects of the Novel:* events do more than form a plot and are symbolic. His presentation of people is most delicate and exact; he captures the essence and the quirks of personality, and he has much skill with speech and dialogue. For EMF the real tragedies are not sudden deaths but "the failures in human relationships, the betrayals, the hates, the inability to understand." Prophecy in his novels involves the moral or mystical element that differentiates the saved from the damned. In *A Passage to India* "personal friendship is an irrelevant affirmation in a huge negation." The earlier novels in which there is incessant conflict between the vivid and the dull, the living and the dead, are preferable; they have also acquired a wonderful period flavor. EMF's novels have a Dantesque quality in their concern with "hell," which is the present. [Appreciative and discerning essay.]

475 McCullough, Bruce. REPRESENTATIVE ENGLISH NOVELISTS: DEFOE TO CONRAD (NY: Harper & Row, 1946), pp. 164, 283, 352. Becky Sharp in VANITY FAIR does not develop as EMF says a "round" character should, though EMF classifies her as being "round." EMF disparages Henry James unduly in contending that life has been drained from his fiction in the interest of form. [EMF's cited opinions are from *Aspects of the Novel.*]

476 Reed, Henry. THE NOVEL SINCE 1939 (Lond & NY: Longmans Green, Arts in Britain: No. 4, 1946), p. 12.
EMF has been influential upon Christopher Isherwood, Elizabeth Bowen, and William Plomer. His comic manner heightens the tragedy in his books; his urbane and clear style, his sensitiveness, and his comic genius have caused him to survive the presence of Joyce, with whom he shares a hatred of clichés. EMF was inspiriting during World War II because he was bold, honest, and incapable of being deceived.

477 Routh, H. V. "The Pioneers of the Twentieth Century: Edward Morgan Forster," ENGLISH LITERATURE AND IDEAS IN THE TWENTIETH CENTURY: AN INQUIRY INTO PRESENT DIFFICULTIES AND FUTURE PROSPECTS (Lond: Methuen, 1946; NY: Longmans Green, 1948), pp. 58–62, 69 (NY ed).
Cambridge was formative for EMF. The classics taught him to examine human nature in its essentials and to realize the value of words (and by implication the value of precision in the statement of ideas). He learned there the value of intellectual conversation, the cooperative search for truth; in this quest, Goldsworthy Lowes Dickinson aided him. One chief theme of his fiction Cambridge helped him define: the need to distinguish true culture from pseudo-culture. His admired novelists were Defoe, Richardson, Sterne, Austen, White Melville, Emily Bronte, Tolstoy, Henry James, Proust, and Lawrence. All were concerned, as was EMF, with the deeper workings of the mind and with the conflict between class thinking and individual self-expression. He was interested in combining nineteenth-century thought and style with the most arresting aspects of twentieth-century mentality. In *Where Angels Fear to Tread* the theme of continuity is obscured by the conflict between cultures; the book lacks intimacy. Thus, *The Longest Journey* became a human document, with EMF's manifest involvement with Rickie Elliot. We understand Rickie's character but not his

destiny. *A Room with a View* is a concentrated and comic book, but the values are not entirely clear. In this early fiction, individuals feel their way amid kindred sensibilities, but they find no answers to their perplexities. EMF gives human nature another chance in *Howards End*. This novel reveals his sense of humor, and the minor characters are impressive. The conflicts are well dramatized; but the story line sometimes wavers, the characters are sometimes undeveloped, and the texture is occasionally loose so that we cannot be sure of the validity of our interpretations. *A Passage to India* is a remarkable experiment; the novel is in tune with the time-spirit, since it is cosmopolitan and since the characters are placed against an alien civilization. EMF has greater mastery of his material; the descriptions are more impressive and the characters more incisive, especially Fielding and Aziz. He is expert in dialogue and in creating personalities, and his plots are meaningful with respect to increasing our knowledge of the characters. Moral earnestness combines with wit, satire, poetry, humor, and a classic prose style. EMF is a traditionalist in fabricating organic and consequential plots and in organizing his narratives about central individuals who possess definite motives; his treatment is dramatic. But he outruns his methods because he believes in accident rather than in character or destiny (a modern predisposition). The characters are in search of a more satisfying way of life, so action needs to be inner as well as outer. EMF is, in essence, a master of nineteenth-century technique who is unable to do justice to his twentieth-century materials.

478 Shahani, Ranjee G. "Some British I Admire: V.—Mr. E. M. Forster," ASIATIC REVIEW (Lond), nsXLII (July 1946), 270–73.
EMF is difficult to write about; his great charm, one's fear of offending him, and his reticence are obstructions. His place in literature is not clear. He is a gifted stylist; but his work finally disappoints, since it does not create a single impression. He is not at his best in works of large design; he was cut out to be a short story writer. [Finds (rather questionably) EMF's best work to be in *The Celestial Omnibus*.] EMF has an astonishing power of observation, but also uses trivial, irrelevant details. He lacks the artist's vision of shaping masses of material into creative wholes. His social comedy is superb in *Where Angels Fear to Tread;* his seriousness in *The Longest Journey* is less impressive. The feminine element in his temper is too obtrusive. He is a splendid satirist but is overly conscious of his victories. His poetry is genuine but too erratic; he seems to want to extinguish it. The quality of his morality is not arresting. In *A Passage to India* he has not penetrated to the essentials of the Indian mind and character. He is bigger as a person than as a writer. [Praises *Aspects of the Novel.* Tone of article is condescending.]

1947

479 Bailey, J. O. PILGRIMS THROUGH SPACE AND TIME: TRENDS AND PATTERNS IN SCIENTIFIC AND UTOPIAN FICTION (NY: Argus Books, 1947), pp. 133–34, 197, 199, 249, 262, 278, 308–10.
"The Machine Stops" is a satire upon impersonal aspects of our present machine age. [Numerous other mentions of this story in a book analyzing many other examples of scientific and Utopian fiction.]

480 Baker, Carlos, "E. M. Forster's Quality of Insight," NEW YORK TIMES BOOK REVIEW, 13 July 1947, pp. 5, 27.
In *The Collected Tales of E. M. Forster* EMF writes of the Wordsworthian theme that, by following false influences, we lay waste our powers of imagination. EMF's heroes and heroines have the purest insight and are the characters in his works most capable of being educated by life. In EMF's world, fantasy serves (1) "as messenger from the gods to men," (2) "as breaker of dictatorial machines and false images," and (3) as conductor of souls to the hereafter. EMF is memorable as the breaker of images and repressive machines in "The Machine Stops." "The Story of a Panic" and "The Road from Colonus" are better stories than "The Machine Stops" and "The Celestial Omnibus," the most anthologized pieces. EMF's irony is muted but "rings clear and true." [A discussion of more than ordinary insight.]

481 Bookwright. "Reprints, New Editions," NEW YORK HERALD TRIBUNE WEEKLY BOOK REVIEW, 6 April 1947, p. 25.
[Favorable notice of American reissue of *Aspects of the Novel*, stating that the book is both intelligent and intelligible.]

482 Bookwright. "Reprints, New Editions," NEW YORK HERALD TRIBUNE WEEKLY BOOK REVIEW, 27 July 1947, p. 14.
The tales in *The Collected Tales of E. M. Forster* are "delicately conceived and intelligently executed." The best of them (e.g., "The Celestial Omnibus") are substantial as fantasies.

483 [Breit, Harvey?] "People Who Read and Write: At Last, Mr. Forster," NEW YORK TIMES BOOK REVIEW, 29 June 1947, p. 8.

In appearance, EMF seems "a little bit like a spare, intelligent, ruffled heron"; he is youthful, disarming, modest, quietly witty. He has come, he says, on this first visit to the United States because Lionel Trilling wrote a book about him and made him a celebrity. He had expected Americans to be kind and gentle but had not expected their great charm. He likes Eudora Welty's short stories and finds F. Scott Fitzgerald "puzzling and fascinating, and possessing a fine sense of mystery."

484 Burger, Nash K. "Books of the Times," New York Times Book Review, 10 July 1947, p. 19.
EMF's work is noteworthy for its polished style, its ironic and compassionate point of view, and its mastery of emotional and psychological nuances. He has been compared to Meredith, Henry James, and Lawrence, although he has not been read enough in his own right. He is not strident but accomplishes his destructive purpose by ironic wisdom. He uses Greek myths vitally, as in "The Road from Colonus." "The Story of a Panic" and "Other Kingdom" combine the value of feeling and the truth of myth with incisive satire upon modern society. "The Machine Stops" is terrifying. The symbolism is puzzling or elusive in "The Story of the Siren" and "The Point of It." "The Eternal Moment" effectively dramatizes moral complications. [Excellent review of *The Collected Tales of E. M. Forster.*]

485 "Fables in Fantasy," Time, L (11 Aug 1947), 101–2, 104.
The Collected Tales of E. M. Forster reveal a "disembodied timelessness." They exploit comic improbabilities in their fantasy, and predominantly contrast the presence of Pan with staid respectability. Simple instinct is shown to be superior to "the taboos and sophistries of social custom" ("The Machine Stops"). EMF emphasizes that man's salvation lies in his return to nature's nakedness, as in "The Road from Colonus." Here, as in his other tales, it is the seeking of beauty, not the finding of it, that matters. One cannot isolate one's paradise ("Other Kingdom"), nor overtly publicize it ("The Eternal Moment").

486 Farrelly, John. "Distinguished Visitor," New Republic, CXVII (28 July 1947), 28–29.
EMF prefers the decentralized organization of English universities, prevalent at least before the war, to the centralized arrangements at American universities. Conversation in America concerns the Russian menace; in England it is about food shortages. EMF liked the Menotti operas, The Medium and The Telephone and saw them twice. [Interview. Stresses EMF's deprecatory and tentative manner and opinions.]

487 Hardwick, Elizabeth. "Fiction Chronicle," Partisan Review, XIV (Sept–Oct 1947), 533–38.

Whether the fantasy element is successful in EMF's tales is questionable. There is a monotonous quality about EMF's heaven. Lionel Trilling, in E. M. FORSTER (1943), rightly holds that the stories are interesting mostly as they prefigure characters and themes developed in the novels. Two of the most prominent themes present in the tales are (1) the meaning of art and the false use of it, and (2) the dangers and challenges inherent in a vital life. EMF's stories lack the strength that passion, though submerged, would have provided. His tone is restrained and controlled, but something also creeps in that is akin to haughtiness; "an excessive and morbid pride," rather than lack of energy, may ultimately inhibit him. There is imagination, wit, and irony in these tales, but there is also a faintly apologetic tone. [Review of *The Collected Tales of E. M. Forster* and works by John Paul Sartre and J. P. Powers. Perceptive cricitism.]

488 Jackson, Joseph Henry. "A Bookman's Notebook," SAN FRANCISCO CHRONICLE, 25 July 1947, p. 12.
The Collected Tales of E. M. Forster reveal EMF in the mode of fantasy, and his intelligence and irony reveal the possibilities inherent in the mode. In "The Story of a Panic" (as in "The Celestial Omnibus") youth and simplicity are more open to the truth than are age and reason. In "The Other Side of the Hedge" and "The Machine Stops," there is the perspective given by a leap into another dimension. "The Machine Stops" answers H. G. Wells in his own terms and seems contemporary in its relevance.

489 Lazarus, H. P. "The 'Slighter Gestures' of E. M. Forster," NATION (NY), CLXV (29 Nov 1947), 598–600.
The essay form, as EMF uses it in *Abinger Harvest*, suits him because he grasps the relaxed relationship necessary between writer and reader. Sometimes EMF's essays deal with the trivial and the merely personal; sometimes the manner obtrudes and becomes arch. In some essays, especially those based on persons from history, EMF subordinates his materials too thoroughly to his sensibility; and he sometimes fails to generalize or to form judgments upon general and impersonal questions. These limitations are usually absent in the literary criticism; the essays on Howard Overing Sturgis and Proust, for example, reveal EMF in perfect sympathy with his subjects. This rapport is also found in the accounts of his Clapham ancestors and in "Notes on the English Character," perhaps his masterpiece in the essay; also in the component essays of "Adrift in India." His wit is a distinctive literary quality. EMF is too preoccupied with "the slighter gestures of dissent" to reach the larger issues. The presence and the relevance of these slighter gestures do comprise the greatness of the novels, which chronicle the alienation, the isolation, and the futile lives of his middle-class characters; the importance and inadequacies of human relationships; the difficulties involved in leading the individual life; and the process of con-

fronting negations in experience. But there are whole expanses of life that the characters do not traverse, confined as they are to "their self-constricted, untranscendable small worlds." [Review of 1947 rpt of *Abinger*. Perceptive commentary.]

490 Liddell, Robert. "A Novelist May Use His Range to Its Limits: Forster, Isherwood, Maugham," and "The Foregoing Principles Applied: A Brief Examen of Mr. E. M. Forster's Novels," A TREATISE ON THE NOVEL (Lond: Cape, 1947), pp. 44–46, 64–70; also pp. 14, 19, 21, 56, 84, 91, 93, 154, 156, 159; rptd in ROBERT LIDDELL ON THE NOVEL WITH AN INTRODUCTION BY WAYNE C. BOOTH (Chicago: University of Chicago P, 1969).

EMF has deliberately and tactfully narrowed his range to the "tea-table" perspective, as Christopher Isherwood had described it in LIONS AND SHADOWS (1938). When EMF tries to extend this range to scenes of violence and passion, he is not successful, and when he stops short of such scenes, we see his limitations. There is a defense of culture and civilization in all EMF's works. He proclaims two false doctrines: (1) the "great refusal," as in Rickie Elliot's denial of his brother at a symbolic moment in *The Longest Journey* [in Liddell's view, EMF puts too much stress on such a moment]; (2) the noble savage, the overvaluing of passion and instinct in figures like Stephen Wonham (*Journey*) and George Emerson (*A Room with a View*). [Other incidental references, mostly to *Aspects of the Novel.*]

491 Marshall, Margaret. "Notes by the Way," NATION (NY), CLXV (16 Aug 1947), 166.

Lionel Trilling rightly asserts, in E. M. FORSTER (1943), that "The Road from Colonus" and "The Eternal Moment" endure best from *The Collected Tales of E. M. Forster*. "The Other Side of the Hedge" is uneven in conception and execution; "The Machine Stops" is heavy-handed. "Other Kingdom," "The Curate's Friend," and "The Celestial Omnibus" are pleasing exposés of bourgeois values and represent, in relation to the novels, informal experimental exercises.

492 Mulgan, John, and D. M. Davin. AN INTRODUCTION TO ENGLISH LITERATURE (Oxford: Clarendon P, 1947), pp. 153–56.

EMF's urbanity traces back to Addison, his concern with unpretentious people to Jane Austen and Trollope. He awards praise or blame to his characters according to whether they use convention to reinforce and enhance their living or fail to break from it when it imposes inhibitions upon a free life. His first four novels reveal the conflict between vitality and defunct convention; but his irony is directed as much against the conventional rebel as against convention. He is an artist before he is a satirist and so creates living people; a skepticism of his own authority allows him to imply accusation but not to condemn. He prefers, notably in *A Passage to India*, to portray emotion sympathetically but not emotionally. His Indians are drawn more fully and sympathetically than the Italians in the earlier novels. His theme is misunderstanding and the larger consequences of misunderstanding. With EMF human relationships are paramount; life and truth are his two ultimate standards. EMF and Virginia Woolf are both a bit thin-blooded. Both show perceptiveness, intelligence, and refined sensibilities and analyze people whose lives are undistracted by struggle for a livelihood.

493 Prescott, Orville. "Outstanding Novels," YALE REVIEW, nsXXXVII (Autumn 1947), 189–92, espec. 190.

The stories in *The Collected Tales of E. M. Forster* are not of the same excellence as *A Passage to India*, which "seems timeless in its profound preoccupation with the painful issues of psychology and race." The stories are dated, reflecting the mannered world of Henry James and Max Beerbohm. They are fantasies, many concerned with classical myths and the contrast between a freer pagan past and the restricted bourgeois world of the present.

494 R., W. K. "Fantasy Without Apology," CHRISTIAN SCIENCE MONITOR, 4 Aug 1947, p. 18.

In *The Collected Tales of E. M. Forster*, EMF's fantasy recaptures a sense of the ancient myths underlying Italian and English nature or else it creates a vision of the future. He has a sympathy with children of nature. Some tales are especially contemporary in their relevance: "The Machine Stops" reveals the horrors of the machine age, and "Co-ordination" is an attack on progressive education.

495 Rago, Henry. "Books of the Week," COMMONWEAL, XLVI (2 May 1947), 73–74.

EMF's opinions in *Aspects of the Novel* are still fresh because of his personal style. Some memorable discriminations are made, but the tone of his work is coy; the statements are indirect and prolix; and his critical work becomes doctrinaire because he insists on not being doctrinaire. No work of art can be saved from the critical rigor that EMF seems so anxious to evade.

496 Redman, Ben Ray. "New Editions," SATURDAY REVIEW OF LITERATURE (NY), XXX (12 July 1947), 32.

The Collected Tales of E. Forster are fantasies, "little stories of revolt and escape"—revolt against the bourgeois conventions of Edwardian England. Since that age is gone, they now have a nostalgic quality. None are great, although all reveal EMF's craftsmanship.

497 Spencer, Theodore. "A Novelist's Advice, Reissued," NEW YORK TIMES BOOK REVIEW, 11 May 1947, p. 4.

Charm, unpretentious wisdom, and lack of pedantry are present in *Aspects of the Novel*. EMF is not enough concerned with the development of the novel or with historical and environmental differences (human nature is not so unchanging as EMF would say; for example, novelists now lack the moral security present in former ages). EMF is not concerned enough with causes, though he is wise in his discussion of results. The generalizations as well as the individual judgments are perceptive (a few of the latter are now dated). [Review of 1947 rpt of *Aspects*.]

498 "The Talk of the Town: Tourist," NEW YORKER, XXIII (3 May 1947), 27–29.

EMF says that he is something of a "bore" and would prefer, if he could, to be "bright" in conversation. EMF is glad that those who invited him to come to Harvard University to deliver "The *Raison d'Etre* of Criticism in the Arts" (*Two Cheers for Democracy*) divined that he was interested in music. He is detached now from his novels; sometimes they don't even seem to be his. His individualism comes out when he says that he does not like to be "shepherded" in air travel. He is fond of scenery and has climbed a lot of low mountains in Massachusetts and plans to visit the Grand Canyon. He will visit the Empire State Building but will forego Niagara Falls, since he has seen Victoria Falls. He finds it unsettling to have "deep" readers "turning up hidden meanings" in his works. He maintains that he still looks at things from a novelist's point of view, although he now primarily writes essays.

499 Tindall, William York. "Right," "Disenchantment and Fantasy," and "Myth and the Natural Man," FORCES IN MODERN BRITISH LITERATURE, 1885–1946 (NY: Knopf, 1947), pp. 63–111, espec 75–76; 112–44, espec 114–16; 360–86, espec 365–66, 380–81; also 30, 59, 140, 300, 320; materials somewhat abrgd in FORCES IN MODERN BRITISH LITERATURE, 1885–1956 (NY: Vintage Books, 1956), pp. 62, 95–96, 107n, 199n, 200, 213n, 287, 290–91, 300, 309, 312n.

In *A Passage to India* EMF exposes the injustice of the officials, the shoddiness of the educated natives, and the Anglo-Indian dilemma. All else, however, is dwarfed by the echo in the Caves which affects directly the lives of Aziz, Adela Quested, and Mrs. Moore. Compared to Mrs. Moore's disillusionment and apathy, the white man's burden seems irrelevant. EMF suggests, by his use of the echo, that the Empire may be "bottomless." EMF's aim is more impressive than his achievement; the apparatus of exposure is more elaborate than the results require. *Howards End* is more complex and of greater value than Galsworthy's THE MAN OF PROPERTY. [The characters are analyzed as social symbols.] EMF sees his people as mixed and as dubious as "gryphons." The dull Ruth Wilcox alone gains full approbation. Henry Wilcox is real, but Leonard Bast is not. In *Passage*, EMF is more effective in depicting victims, since he knows the Indians better than the people of the lower middle class. In *The Longest Journey* EMF is concerned with the nature of reality (for him, Stephen Wonham symbolizes the truest reality) and with Cambridge, which represents intellect, imagination, and humanism (Stewart Ansell is its main representative). In *A Room with a View* the Emersons are outsiders of low degree who represent Life, Passion, and Beauty in conflict with middle-class insensitivity. Passion and Beauty are not present in the Florentine honeymoon; they are only in EMF's mind. *Where Angels Fear to Tread* and *Passage* are his best novels. *Angels* is the most perfect and Jamesean novel. Gino Carella has a vitality lacking in Stephen Wonham and in the Emersons, and he is the agent whereby the Sawstonians are exposed or improved. *Angels* has much impact since even melodrama serves its purposes. The commenting author is often too obtrusive; the urbanity, irony, and restraint provide comment not only on his characters but adversely upon himself. And melodrama is sometimes abused in the fiction. EMF's primitive men (oafs and lower-class men) are not ideal personages (contrary to similar figures in D. H. Lawrence). They uncover the defects of society, but they are not better than their society. Stephen Wonham is not so much natural man as what society has made of natural man. This ambiguity is also present in "The Story of a Panic," in the case of Gennaro, the primitive who sells his friend in exchange for gold. EMF uses myth as a structuring device in "The Road from Colonus"; he also uses Orion in other stories as a symbol of desired vitality. [Perceptive judgments for their date, and many of them still pertinent.]

500 Warshow, Robert. "The Legacy of the 30's," COMMENTARY, IV (Dec 1947), 538–45; rptd in THE IMMEDIATE EXPERIENCE: MOVIES, COMICS, THEATRE, AND OTHER ASPECTS OF POPULAR CULTURE (Garden City, NY: Doubleday, 1962), pp. 33–48.

The oversimplifications involved in the communist-dominated intellectual scene of the 1930s account for the superficiality of Lionel Trilling's THE MIDDLE OF THE JOURNEY. The novel is very similar to *Howards End*, but Trilling lacks EMF's specific literary gifts: a complex sense of character and a richness of wit. Trilling makes melodrama of his deeper content instead of investing the deeper content, as did EMF, with a melodramatic tone. Trilling lacks EMF's detachment and his ability to embody, organically, an idea within the character himself.

501 Watts, Richard, Jr. "Ironic Speculation," NEW REPUBLIC, CXVII (14 July 1947), 27–28.

The tales in *The Collected Tales of E. M. Forster* "have imagination without extravagance, charm without preciousness and delicacy without bloodlessness. They are neither coy nor whimsical, and there is always a hard core of unsentimental intelligence beneath their romantic paganism." Like the novels, they give the sense of a yawning abyss underneath the surfaces of life. They are nondidactic, but it is almost impossible not to speculate on their moral implications. EMF satirizes racial bigotry ("The Eternal Moment"), cultural snobs ("The Celestial Omnibus" and "Other Kingdom"), mechanized civilization ("The Machine Stops"), and tepid intellectualism ("The Point of It"). [Appreciative account.]

1948

502 Acton, Harold. MEMOIRS OF AN AESTHETE (Lond: Methuen, 1948), pp. 160, 330, 382.
Mussolini extinguished the gracious ease of Florentine life for the English visitor and expatriate, the life given a classic literary representation in EMF's *A Room with a View*. [MEMOIRS OF AN AESTHETE 1939–1969 (NY: Viking P, 1971) is same as MORE MEMOIRS OF AN AESTHETE (Lond: Methuen, 1970) and has no important references to EMF.]

503 Allen, Walter. ARNOLD BENNETT (Lond: Home & Van Thal, The English Novelists, 1948; Denver: Alan Swallow, The English Novelists, 1949), pp. 64, 66, 102, 103 (American ed).
EMF is correct in his judgment, in *Aspects of the Novel*, that the distinction of THE OLD WIVE'S TALE lies in Bennett's handling of time. Bennett's novel misses absolute greatness because of its failure sufficiently to transcend time. EMF did not share Virginia Woolf's distaste for Bennett evinced in "Mr. Bennett and Mrs. Brown" (1924). Bennett's novels, to quote EMF, are "strong, sad, sincere" but lack some other elements of imaginative greatness.

504 Bentley, Phyllis. "The Novels of E. M. Forster," ENGLISH JOURNAL, XXXVII (April 1948), 163–70; COLLEGE ENGLISH, IX (April 1948), 349–56.
Where Angels Fear to Tread reveals in essence all of the distinctly Forsterian qualities. The plot is but the integument for the inner drama; love for Italy and the Italian landscape give warmth and color; the characters are handled with EMF's "deft, light, sure touch." The style and writing are lucid; the dialogue is convincing. The narrative passages are light, resilient, and tough as a spider's web, capable of bearing the weight of violent emotions and large themes. *The Longest Journey* explores the same dichotomy as *Angels:*

"Truth and life against lies and spiritual death." The same theme predominates in *A Room with a View*—as Freddy Honeychurch says of Lucy's
singing a song that urges renunciation: "The tune's right enough but the
words are rotten. Why throw up the sponge?" [Thematic summary of *Howards End* is given.] *A Passage to India* is noteworthy for the powerfully
evoked landscapes, the "enthralling" story and "terrific" court scene, and
the wide range of Indian life presented. The character drawing is uneven;
there is a greater mixture of flat and round characters than usual. The
English, except for Mrs. Moore and Adela Quested, are flat; but the Indians,
especially Aziz and Godbole, are seen in the round. The theme is that
conquerors and the conquered cannot be friends; even Mrs. Moore brings
disaster to Aziz, and Aziz and Fielding must part. EMF's qualities include:
the ease and economy of his narrative; his essentially modern and economic
style; his pungent and fitting dialogue; his beautiful or squalid landscapes,
always organic to the novel; his ironical, playful, urbane wit; his lifelike and
clear characters, especially the multifarious women and the middle-aged
and elderly men; and his exploring the life by values, through the intelligence leavened by affection, understanding, and tolerance. He realizes, like
Magistrate Das in *Passage*, that "life is not easy as we know it on the earth."
[Appreciative, genial, though scarcely profound essay.]

505 Brocklehurst, A. G. "The Short Stories of E. M. Forster,"
MANCHESTER LITERARY CLUB PAPERS, LXVII (1948–1949), 86–104.
There are four categories of story in *The Collected Short Stories of E. M.
Forster*: pure fantasies ("The Other Side of the Hedge," "The Celestial
Omnibus," "The Point of It," "Mr. Andrews," and "Co-ordination"); fanta-
sies bordering on the occult ("The Story of a Panic," "Other Kingdom,"
"The Curate's Friend," and "The Story of the Siren"); comparatively realis-
tic—and artistically more successful—stories ("The Road from Colonus"
and "The Eternal Moment"); and a futurist Utopia or anti-Utopia ("The
Machine Stops"). "The Story of a Panic," "Other Kingdom," and "The
Celestial Omnibus" have for theme the belief that certain truths are re-
vealed to the young, the small, the weak, the deficient, and the abnormal.
[Extended analyses, mostly descriptive, of "Panic," "The Point of It,"
"Colonus," "The Eternal Moment," and "Omnibus."]

506 Brower, Reuben A. "Beyond E. M. Forster: The Unseen,"
CHICAGO REVIEW, II (Fall–Winter 1948), 102–12.
EMF's two chief metaphors are "the earth" and "the unseen," which sometimes connect, although "the unseen" is often referred to independently.
The references to the unseen in *Howards End* are through crude metaphors;
in *A Passage to India* through a series of symbols. The experience of the
invisible does not have to be religious in any traditional sense; it can be the
result of discipline of the self. In *Passage* the Mosque symbolizes fine

relationships between human beings (Aziz and Mrs. Moore, Aziz and Fielding); the Caves provide an ironic negation of the Mosque symbol and connote the failure of the inner life (see Adela's unimaginative approach to Aziz); the Temple symbolizes (together with the sky) mystical and visionary experience. The vision can also be disconcerting and unpleasant (see the goblins in *Howards End* and Mrs. Moore's trauma after being in the Marabar Caves in *Passage*). Mrs. Moore's experience in the Caves does not represent evil in the Christian sense; it is, rather, the collapse of all order and myth; it is muddle and chaos. The sequence is well prepared for. It is unconvincing to make Mrs. Moore both an agent of redemption and a woman who loses all sense of values [she is, however, able to be a savior, precisely because she is sensitive enough to feel horror as well as ecstasy]. The conclusion is unsatisfying because the experiences of Mrs. Moore at the cave had been too compelling. In "Temple" EMF fails to maintain his ironic detachment, and unproductive ambiguities ensue. EMF's wistful desire for unity undermines the strength of the novel. [The literal interpretation of Mrs. Moore reveals a misunderstanding of EMF's purpose, as does the denigration of "Temple." Discusses myth of the unseen in *Howards End* and *Passage* (some of the discussion in greatly revised form appears in THE FIELDS OF LIGHT, 1951).]

507 Chapman, R. W. JANE AUSTEN: FACTS AND PROBLEMS (Oxford: Clarendon P; NY: Oxford UP, 1948), pp. 43, 106–8, 110, 170–71, 193, 208.

EMF's strictures on Jane Austen's letters should be modified. EMF's fiction resembles Miss Austen's in its concern for domestic interiors; his criticism of it in this aspect is subtle and sympathetic. [EMF's criticism of Jane Austen ("Jane Austen," *Abinger Harvest*) is discussed, and there are many incidental references to it.]

508 Chew, Samuel C. "The Nineteenth Century and After (1787–1939)," A LITERARY HISTORY OF ENGLAND, ed by Albert C. Baugh. (NY: Appleton-Century-Crofts, 1948; Lond: Routledge & Kegan Paul, 1950 [2nd ed, NY, 1967; Lond, 1968]), p. 1569 (and p. S1569 in 2nd ed, containing bibliography).

A Passage to India owes its fame partly to considerations other than its high merits in style, pattern, and characterization. There are "veins of quietism and symbolism" in EMF, with persistent contrast between inner life and outer. EMF suddenly interrupts psychological analysis with episodes of melodramatic violence. EMF is indebted to Henry James and Gissing, and probably influenced D. H. Lawrence. EMF's subtle but limited opinions on the art of fiction are found in *Aspects of the Novel*.

509 Curtis, Anthony. "E. M. Forster: The Man and His Work," WORLD REVIEW (Lond), (May 1948), 44–47.

In *Where Angels Fear to Tread* EMF achieves a perfect matching of story and plot, of the life in time and the life by values (see EMF's *Aspects of the Novel* for discussion of these terms). In *A Room With a View* and *The Longest Journey* the realism is more acceptable than the symbolism, and Stephen Wonham and George Emerson are only convincing as symbols, not as real men. EMF's work presents the pagan view that conflict can be resolved by mutual participation in athletic experiences (see the polo match in *A Passage to India* between the racist British subaltern and Aziz). In *Journey* the relentlessly marshalled events and the choric comments by the narrator are reminiscent of the structural patterns found in Greek drama. A mystical element intrudes with Mrs. Wilcox and Miss Avery in *Howards End* and Mrs. Moore in *Passage*. *Howards End* is a work of social criticism as well as of symbolical mysticism. EMF centers *Passage* about an inexplicable and fantastic moment (in the Marabar Caves), and the repercussions which follow it. The incident connects the opposing sides. The Council of War scene in the club after the alleged rape of Adela Quested is effective. [Discusses "What I Believe."] EMF's fiction also has its strength in his championing of individual liberty. [Accounts for EMF's silence in the novel by the restrictions imposed on the individual's liberty since World War I. An illuminating pioneer essay.]

510 Evans, B. Ifor. "E. M. Forster," ENGLISH LITERATURE BETWEEN THE WARS (Lond: Methuen, 1948; 3rd ed, Chester Springs, Pa: Dufour, 1949), pp. 27–39; also 3, 21.

EMF is an example "of the very aristocracy of liberal intellectualism." As long as his values seemed secure he did not intrude into politics, but when they were challenged he adjusted his tenets and his attitude toward politics. Even in his early work he knew that life was complex, strange, and mystical on the one side, cruel and disconcerting on the other. In his novels there is always the conflict between good and evil, the good associated with perception and sensitivity, the evil with their absence. His travels to the East erased the Faustian elements in his concept of personality and replaced them with an emphasis upon gentleness and quiescence; he recognized, however, that gentleness was not possible in the cruel world of the 1930s. His work has lightness of touch and sensibility, but he is always aware of the presence of death and of man's capacity for cruelty. He has a great power of storytelling, an ability to draw characters, a capacity to write rhythmic and natural prose, and a flair for comedy, Meredithean but lighter in touch, coming from his full confidence in his materials. *Where Angels Fear to Tread* is a mixture of comedy with violence and tragedy. So is *The Longest Journey*, except that the portrait of Agnes Pembroke has an emphatic bitterness in it. In *A Room with a View* he reached full maturity and artistic command. *Howards End* is his highest achievement because of its variety of character and complexity of motive. *A Passage to India* contains nothing technically to give it precedence over *Howards End.* In *Passage* he again reveals his ability to move from the colloquial to the sublime within a sentence; thought and comment are organically mingled with the language and lives of his characters. EMF's embracing of individual values will still be attractive even when this kind of life may be less possible to realize. [Sound presentation but somewhat ordinary.]

511 Lawrence, D. H. D. H. LAWRENCE'S LETTERS TO BERTRAND RUSSELL, ed by Harry T. Moore (NY: Gotham Book Mart, 1948), pp. 29–35; rptd in THE COLLECTED LETTERS OF D. H. LAWRENCE, ed by Harry T. Moore (NY: Viking P; Lond: Heinemann, 1962), I, 316–21.

D. H. Lawrence to Bertrand Russell (12 Feb 1915), EMF is inhibited by nature, and he lacks positive enthusiasm (*"he does not believe that any beauty or any divine utterance is any good any more"*). He is unable to act decisively. He settles for love of humanity instead of passion for a woman.

512 Lehmann, John. "E. M. Forster," GATE (Lond), II (March–May 1948), 23–27.

EMF qualifies today as "an oracle of sanity and guidance." He has a light touch but is also deadly earnest on many things. A clear idea of his unique personality and his ideas (and the reasons for his intellectual influence) are well conveyed in "The Challenge of Our Time" (*Two Cheers for Democracy*). His "message" has become increasingly important. His reputation has also grown because of his style. *A Passage to India* reveals his insight into both the political and the metaphysical realms. *Passage* also had much direct influence.

513 Painter, George D. "New Novels," LISTENER, XXXIX (22 April 1948), 674.

The greatness of *The Collected Short Stories of E. M. Forster* does not lie in their number, variety of subject, or variety of treatment but in their exploration of the Good Life conceived as a combination of passion and discipline. Our hope for salvation, EMF maintains, lies in grace rather than in goodness. He is the patriot, the sociologist, and the comedian, but above all the moralist.

514 Stewart, Douglas Alexander. "Irreconcilable India," THE FLESH AND THE SPIRIT: AN OUTLOOK ON LITERATURE (Sydney: Angus & Roberton, 1948), pp. 17–24.

EMF's subject in *A Passage to India* is man's ultimate loneliness; he struggles for communion with his fellows but fails to attain it. EMF has a detached irony, but is acid when dealing with the English, sympathetic when dealing with Aziz. The trial and the circumstances surrounding it are absurd, but the consequences are lamentable. EMF means to say that if the Turtons and the Burtons had known Aziz as they should have (with their hearts), they could never have suspected him of the crime. The friendship fails between Aziz and Fielding because Aziz wants more than justice. The Hindu and Moslem are both inefficient when away from the English. Fielding and Aziz part because both revert to their respective types; the races are incompatible. Aziz's prevarications and evasions cause some of the trouble. The empire, in short, is difficult for everyone.

515 Stringer, Arthur. RED WINE OF YOUTH: A LIFE OF RUPERT BROOKE (Indianapolis & NY: Bobbs-Merrill, 1948), p. 116.
In a letter to Edward Marsh c. 1911, Brooke in Florence relates how he is living in a *pension* frequented by EMF characters, "English clergymen and ladies." To live among them is perplexing: "The quaint remarks fall all round one during meal-times, with little soft plups like pats of butter."

516 Toynbee, Philip. "Short Stories," NEW STATESMAN AND NATION, nsXXXV (17 April 1948), 317.
The Collected Short Stories of E. M. Forster reveal that EMF's ideas (the love of pagan energy, and his pleas for love, freedom, and connection) require a more capacious form than that provided by the short story. At times his stories become simplistic, false, and whimsical.

517 Trilling, Lionel. "Manners, Morals, and the Novel," KENYON REVIEW, X (Winter 1948), 11–27, espec 24–25; rptd in THE LIBERAL IMAGINATION: ESSAYS ON LITERATURE AND SOCIETY (NY: Viking P, 1950; Lond: Secker & Warburg, 1951), pp. 205–22, espec 218–19.
Manners are "a culture's hum and buzz of implication." The novel finds its way into reality by a concern with manners that reflect appearances. (American fiction is deficient in embodying social reality, partly because of the lack of rich traditions and manners to express them.) In our modern culture we tend to regard reality as something hard and abstract, not as something to be modulated by the individual's relation to it or as something that must be personally felt. Stephen Wonham in *The Longest Journey* illustrates EMF's view that reality must be personally felt; he would shock intelligent, liberal, democratic people by his violent reactions toward a friend who has reneged on a bargain. The Princess in Henry James's THE PRINCESS CASAMASSIMA pursues too relentlessly a "strong" reality and so lacks flexibility. Both novels descend from DON QUIXOTE: the heroes (Hyacinth Robinson and Rickie Elliot) pursue to their personal detriment perconceived ideas; both are concerned with appearance versus reality; *Journey* explicitly so, THE PRINCESS CASAMASSIMA by indirection. Both novels get at reality through the conflict of classes and the manners that they

embody. The leading characters in both protest against social injustice and are right in doing so. Yet both authors realize that the achievement of social justice provides no full solution to moral problems and generates problems of its own.

518 Waggoner, Hyatt Howe. "Symbol and Substance in Recent Fiction," WESTERN REVIEW, XII (Winter 1948), 120–22.

In *The Collected Tales of E. M. Forster* only "The Road From Colonus" and "The Eternal Moment" approach the power and richness of EMF's novels. His distinctive irony is present in the rest of the tales in only a rudimentary way; multiple perspectives are absent. The abstract nature of substance and idea tends to make them mechanical allegories. Like Hawthorne, EMF has never quite found and mastered his medium; he is not satisfied with the essay nor at home with fiction.

1949

519 Breit, Harvey. "Talk with E. M. Forster," NEW YORK TIMES BOOK REVIEW, 19 June 1949, p. 35; rptd as "E. M. Forster," THE WRITER OBSERVED, ed by Harvey Breit (Cleveland: World, 1956), pp. 53–56; 2nd ed (NY: Collier Books, 1961), pp. 40–42.

EMF is in America for his second visit [his first was in 1947; see Breit, "People Who Read and Write: At Last, Mr. Forster," NEW YORK TIMES BOOK REVIEW, 29 June 1947, p. 8, and "The Talk of the Town: Tourist," NEW YORKER, XXIII (3 May 1947), pp. 27–28.] He has had a less strenuous time than before; his major activity has been to deliver "Art for Art's Sake" (*Two Cheers for Democracy*) for the American Academy and National Institute of Arts and Letters. His publishers are preparing another of EMF's miscellanies [*Two Cheers*]; he is bewildered by New York. He has revised his opinion on Joyce, recognizing Joyce's greatness though still not appreciating him adequately. His estimation of George Eliot has risen: he recognizes her civilized quality, whereas he had previously stressed her pedestrianism [revisions of judgments in *Aspects of the Novel*]. Matthew Arnold has also influenced EMF. He was civilized, especially in his prose. Arnold foresaw our troubles with the detachment of one from another time (EMF did not get this kind of help from the Greeks, though Goldsworthy Lowes Dickinson did). Among American writers, EMF admires Katherine Anne Porter, Eudora Welty, and Willard Motley (for KNOCK ON ANY DOOR).

520 Cecil, David. "Two Twentieth-Century Novelists: Virginia Woolf and E. M. Forster," and "E. M. Forster," POETS AND STORY-

TELLERS: A BOOK OF CRITICAL ESSAYS (NY: Macmillan; Lond: Constable, 1949), pp. 155–59, 181–201; "E. M. Forster" is rptd, with slight revisions, from "E. M. Forster," ATLANTIC MONTHLY, CLXXXIII (Jan 1949), 60–65.

"E. M. Forster": EMF is a didactic writer like George Eliot. His originality lies in his fresh, private, independent, firm vision. He reveals himself as tender-hearted yet unattached. He is not responsive to the forces that unite men into a group ("national feeling, class feeling, family feeling, comradely feeling") or to those private emotions they may share; he centers on the individual and on personal relationships. His first desire is for human beings to be united in love; the first fact that he sees is that they are not so united. He is a moralist to the extent that he judges adversely the forces that prevent this union. In his early books he finds a remedy in nature, which is the enemy of artificial divisions like those of class, convention, and nation. In *Howards End* it is nature as Ceres rather than as Pan that effects the reconciliation. In *A Passage to India* nature is malignant except for its transient beneficence at the Mau Festival. In order to communicate this moral purpose EMF has had to unite the real world with the symbolic; his thesis, not character or probability, determines plot. His talents are these: mastery of form and the art of story-telling, economy in the use of detail, ability to recreate the actual movements of the human mind, ability to convey the nuances of motive and emotion, and a mastery of humor, irony, and comedy (in the tradition of Jane Austen, but adding "an airy whimsicality" of his own). His comic art implies the presence of the author. He does best with those people who naturally arouse a smile: maiden ladies like Miss Bartlett or Miss Lavish (*A Room with a View*), contradictory personalities like Aziz, unself-conscious children of nature (Gino Carella in *Where Angels Fear to Tread*). EMF does not do so well with dignified characters. His lyric sensibility is also intense. His lyricism modifies his comedy; he satirizes not from the standpoint of common sense but of "uncommon sensibility." His effects are complex, with the poet, satirist, and moralist all contributing to them. His work has much suggestion, emphasized by his distinctive style, "infinitely sensitive, infinitely dexterous, infinitely graceful." He does not always succeed, however, in harmonizing realism and symbolism. The element of probability is violated too sharply in Helen Schlegel's seduction of Leonard Bast (*Howards End*) and in Rickie Elliot's fainting at the Cadbury Rings when Mrs. Failing tells him about his half-brother (*Journey*). EMF's symbolism takes him too far out of his range (neither Stephen Wonham's primitive virility [*Journey*] nor George Emerson's philosophical talk [*Room*] is convincing.) He believes in the elemental quality of love but can't convey it. His heroines are sexless; they are too preoccupied with intellectual problems. His professed beliefs do not always correspond to his instinctive moral feelings; he professes tolerance and sympathy but is not actually tolerant and sympathetic in his fiction. He dislikes their vices so much that he can't be fair to the Wilcoxes; nor does he have the courage of his dislikes.

A gap between his intention and performance makes suspect his renditions of ecstasy. His moral relations to his subject matter are confused enough to make his moral world an unstable one. "Two Twentieth Century Novelists: Virginia Woolf and E. M. Forster": Judging contemporary writers is difficult; but the achievements of Virginia Woolf and E. M. Forster as artists justify the attempt. They have enough in common to be considered together: intelligence and exquisite sensibility and a common social and cultural tradition, combining material security and intellectual freedom. They were mentally sheltered yet were vigorous in their defenses of individualism against authority, tradition, and convention. [Stimulating remarks, though some of the judgments are now more obvious or more questionable than they once appeared to be.]

521 Grebanier, Bernard D., Samuel Middlebrook, Stith Thompson, and William Watt (eds). "Edward Morgan Forster," ENGLISH LITERATURE AND ITS BACKGROUNDS, VOL II: FROM THE FORERUNNERS OF ROMANTICISM TO THE PRESENT (NY: Dryden P, rvd ed, 1949), pp. 980–81; EMF materials not in 1st ed (1941).

EMF is a brilliant ironist aware of delicacy in relationships among human beings and of the elusive influence of environment. The first four novels are ironic pictures of the British middle class. Human perception characterizes EMF's depiction of Indians and Anglo-Indians in *A Passage to India.* In his essays and fiction EMF emphasizes that for a genuinely civilized human being "souls are more important than systems." In the atomic age EMF's tragi-comic "The Machine Stops," with its underworld civilization, takes on a grim new significance. [Summary of career. "The Machine Stops" rptd pp. 981–95.]

522 Howe, Susanne. NOVELS OF EMPIRE (NY: Columbia UP, 1949), pp. 6, 11, 22, 33–35, 38, 54–56, 71, 78, 79, 80, 164.

The Oakfield of William D. Arnold's OAKFIELD (1853) is similar to EMF's Fielding in *A Passage to India:* both men question the values of imperialism, both are unable to reach a stand on this issue, and both are very much alive by virtue of their perplexities. Many writers on India (Flora Annie Steel, E. J. Thompson, EMF) seem appalled by the size of the subcontinent and the magnitude of the misunderstandings possible between the races. The typical Indian novel with English participants emphasizes their homesickness, especially for the pastoral beauty of England as opposed to the formidable "simmering vagueness" of India and its landscape. OAKFIELD and *Passage* both indicate that Englishmen have left their manners, and sometimes their morals, behind at the Cape of Good Hope. EMF presents a woman in *Passage* who is against missionaries and in favor of chaplains because the latter do not work to get Indians into heaven where they would be out of place. EMF mentions in *Goldsworthy Lowes Dickinson* the positivist cast of mind evinced by the Indian princes who wished to have definite answers to questions about God. In W. W. Hunter's THE OLD MISSIONARY, the Reverend James Williamson becomes a legend in his district after his saintlike death, just as Mrs. Moore does after people learn of her death at sea. Both Arnold and EMF deplore the trivial leisure-time activities of the English in India, though other novelists have exploited these materials with relish. Only a great writer can treat of the incomprehensible, elusive Indian scene without presenting too much for the requirements of art or oversim-plyfying and so destroying the truth. In novels about India the need for British endurance within the Indian scene or against it is somewhere stressed and is seen to be doomed from the start. Modern novelists of empire such as Winifred Holtby, Joyce Cary, William Plomer, and EMF know that the Juggernaut of Empire cannot be stopped; but they satirically expose, with inclusiveness, indignation, and ruefulness, the damage that it has caused. [For another discussion of Arnold's OAKFIELD in relation to *Passage*, see Irene A. Gilbert's "Public and Private Virtue in British India," SOUTH ASIAN REVIEW, VIII (April 1974), 209–22.]

> **523** Junker, Rochus. Studien zur Romanwelt von E. M. Forster"
> (Studies in the World of E. M. Forster's Novels). Unpublished
> dissertation, University of Munster (1949). [Listed in Lawrence F.
> McNamee, DISSERTATIONS IN ENGLISH AND AMERICAN LITERATURE
> (NY & Lond: Bowker, 1968).]

EMF has a message for the postwar years: for the young he fights against conventions and authority and for the older generation he inspires with his humanism and philosophy of life. [In German.]

> **524** Keynes, John Maynard. "My Early Beliefs," TWO MEMOIRS:
> DR. MELCHIOR, A DEFEATED ENEMY, AND MY EARLY BELIEFS, with
> "Introductory Note," by David Garnett (Lond: Hart-Davis; NY:
> A. M. Kelley, 1949), pp. 75–103, espec 81; rptd in ESSAYS AND
> SKETCHES IN BIOGRAPHY (NY: Meridian Books, 1956), pp. 239–56,
> espec 241; and in THE COLLECTED WRITINGS OF JOHN MAYNARD
> KEYNES, Vol. X: ESSSAYS IN BIOGRAPHY (Lond: Macmillan, 1972),
> pp. 433–50, espec 435.

[In "Introductory Note" by David Garnett, the reactions of D. H. Lawrence to Keynes and his Cambridge-Bloomsbury circle are recounted (see F. R. Leavis, "Keynes, Lawrence and Cambridge" [1949]). In "My Early Beliefs" Keynes recalls the inability of prewar Cambridge and Lawrence to under-stand each other and feels that Lawrence's criticism of the men in Keynes's circle may have had some point.] These men adhered to "The Ideal," as G. E. Moore defined it; they were swayed by Moore's passion for clear think-ing (his "What *exactly* do you mean?"); and they embraced an improvised rationalism with its implication that all men could be virtuous. They disregarded the irrational aspects of human nature, the value of the spontaneous emotions as such, the existence of original sin, and the significance of order and pattern in the communal aspects of human existence. This philosophy was inadequate to the culture that followed World War I and led to a superficiality of judgment and feeling. EMF was on the fringes of this group of intellectuals, "the elusive colt of a dark horse." [EMF, being more of a "romantic" by disposition than others affiliated with Bloomsbury, intuitively arrived earlier at much the same conclusions as Keynes. This fact may explain why he was not at the center of this group.]

525 Leavis, F. R. "Keynes, Lawrence and Cambridge," SCRUTINY. XVI (Sept 1949), 242–46; rptd in THE COMMON PURSUIT (Lond: Chatto & Windus; NY: G. W. Stewart, 1952 and New York UP, 1964), pp. 255–60.

John Maynard Keynes in "My Early Beliefs" (TWO MEMOIRS [1949]) sees some of the inadequacies of the Cambridge ethos and culture, deriving from G. E. Moore, which was formative for Bloomsbury (and for EMF as an associate of Bloomsbury). Keynes treats these inadequacies with a friendly irony and reveals thereby his essential endorsement of these views and attitudes. He goes along with some of Lawrence's strictures on the Cambridge-Bloomsbury circle, in particular its disregard of irrational forces and its naive reliance on reason, though he attributes [wrongly, to Leavis] some of Lawrence's hostility to jealousy. Lawrence was the intellectual superior of this Cambridge-Bloomsbury circle and would not have been jealous of it. Keynes, according to Leavis, does not realize the essential drift of Lawrence's criticism, the triviality of intellectual Cambridge in the early twentieth century, exemplified most forcibly in its exaltation of Lytton Strachey as writer and intellect. Strachey's popularity reveals how Cambridge culture had declined from the day of Sidgwick, Maitland, and Leslie Stephen. [An interesting footnote on Bloomsbury, predisposed to Lawrence's hostile view of it.]

526 Lynes, Russell. "Highbrow, Lowbrow, Middlebrow," HARPER'S MAGAZINE, CXCVIII (Feb 1949), 19–28, espec 22–23; rptd in THE TASTE-MAKERS (NY: Harper & Brothers, 1949), pp. 210–33, espec 316–17, and in CONFESSIONS OF A DILETTANTE (NY: Harper & Row, 1966), pp. 119–38, espec 128–29.

The highbrow artist (such as T. S. Eliot, EMF, Picasso, and Stravinsky) does not consciously set out to create art. Rather, he wishes to communicate ideas within a formal framework; and if his work does become art, he regards it as a by-product of creation. The highbrow artist is then taken up by the highbrow consumer who purveys his works to the public.

527 Mortimer, Raymond. "Mr. E. M. Forster: A 70th Birthday Appreciation," SUNDAY TIMES (Lond), 2 Jan 1949, p. 3.

EMF has now become a popular writer as well as a writer's writer. His style is "more distinguished than distinctive"; he is subtle and evasive because he finds it so difficult to define the truth, which he has to approach obliquely. He has a message that he implies but does not preach: "Pursue truth, respond to beauty, cherish friendship, cultivate good will." EMF deplores narrowness of heart; he is a humanist whose standards of benignity and brotherhood are almost saintly. He values spontaneity, has humor, shows disgust for quantity as opposed to quality, and champions liberty. He is "aloof, persuasive, and intensely individual," and now a world-wide influence. [A perceptive notice.]

528 "Mr. E. M. Forster," TIMES LITERARY SUPPLEMENT (Lond), 1 Jan 1949, p. 9.
[Convincing birthday tribute, stressing EMF's "lonely eminence" and noting that he stopped writing because "the general deterioration of civilized life made it no longer possible for him to give pleasure."]

529 Sale, William M., James Hall, and Martin Steinmann. "The Road from Colonus," CRITICAL DISCUSSIONS FOR TEACHERS USING "SHORT STORIES: TRADITION AND DIRECTION" (Norfolk, Conn: New Directions, 1949), pp. 30–33.
On a literal level, Mr. Lucas, with the help of the Greek natives, is prevented in "The Road from Colonus" from doing as he likes by his daughter and two friends. On a thematic level, the meaningfulness of primitive vital life close to nature is in conflict with the meaninglessness of conventional, civilized life. The conflict is resolved with the triumph of folly over wisdom, of the forces of spiritual death over those of spiritual life, of death-in-life over life-in-death.

1950

530 Blöcker, Günter. "Das unzerstörbare Herz: E. M. Forster's Roman *Howards End*" (The Indestructible Heart: E. M. Forster's Novel *Howards End*), DER TAGESSPIEGEL (Berlin), 10 Sept 1950. For EMF the novelist and for EMF the theoretician of *Aspects of the Novel*, the same lively dislike of being forced into an aesthetic straightjacket prevails. *Howards End* embodies the world of property and conventions; whenever the book threatens to become dull, EMF makes use of the sword of fate. EMF is comparable to Fontane as a revolutionary, even an anarchist, in the cause of individualism. In *Howards End* EMF strives for a synthesis between extreme individualists and acquisitive conformists. After the disaster, personal relationships are still sought in an exclusively upper middle-class world. Such restricted scope, together with EMF's preference for a "salon atmosphere," accounts for the lessening of his effectiveness after 1945. [Review of German translation of *Aspects*.] [In German.]

531 Boyle, Alexander. "The Novels of E. M. Forster," IRISH MONTHLY (Dublin), LXXVIII (Sept 1950), 405–15.
EMF is an important writer, despite the slenderness of his canon and the remoteness in time of the publication of his novels. He is a representative figure. He can be read for the story element, but his view of life is also important, tentative, and exploratory in an age often characterized by strident dogmatism. His mood is critical; his technique is suggestive because it is symbolic. The antitheses in *Howards End* are less stark; it is the work of an adult intelligence. The child of nature is repudiated; as such a child, Helen Schlegel comes to disaster by following her impulses. Margaret Schlegel, who represents the spirit of compromise, survives and saves Helen and Henry Wilcox from despair. Margaret has a foot in the camps of both Law and Nature and synthesizes the antitheses present in the earlier novels. *Howards End* is complicated by the introduction of the working-class man Leonard Bast; both the Wilcox and Schlegel ways of life retreat before his challenge. The ghost of Leonard refused to be exorcized; EMF's conscience was troubled, and he projected into Aziz the problem of the dispossessed that had troubled him in Leonard. *A Passage to India* is a fascinating and technically accomplished book. Superb descriptions and minutely observed scenes abound; the characters are interesting and absorbing. In *Passage*

EMF develops the same problems as in *Howards End* but does not solve them: Aziz is another Bast, Fielding has a foot in both camps like Margaret Schlegel (but is less effective), and Adela Quested suffers from violence, as does Helen Schlegel. Aziz grows in stature. EMF detests the Anglo-Indian officials and is sympathetic to the Indians but patronizing toward them. His irony is absent only in presenting Aziz. Personal relationships are not effective in India; EMF's point of view seems pessimistic. The festival seems as if added to the book and represents an intense mood that did not last long. EMF's true feelings are those of Fielding when the latter appreciates the seemliness of Mediterranean civilization [questionable]. EMF was unable to write further novels because he lacked a system of belief. If he did not achieve religious certainty, he had artistic integrity and stopped writing when he had nothing more to say. [Routine discussion of *The Longest Journey* and *A Room with a View*. Essay tends to be superficial in spite of some shrewd comments.]

> **532** Brown, E. K. "Phrase, Character, Incident," "Expanding Symbols," "Interweaving Themes," "Rhythm in E. M. Forster's *A Passage to India,"* RHYTHM IN THE NOVEL (Toronto: University of Toronto P; Lond: Oxford UP, 1950), pp 3–30, espec 4, 5, 6, 7, 25, 28; 33–59; 63–86; 89–115; "Rhythm in E. M. Forster's *A Passage to India,"* rptd in FORSTER: A COLLECTION OF CRITICAL ESSAYS, ed by Malcolm Bradbury (Englewood Cliffs, NJ: Prentice-Hall, Spectrum Books, 1966), pp. 134–59; and in E. M. FORSTER: "A PASSAGE TO INDIA": A CASEBOOK, ed by Bradbury (Lond: Macmillan, Casebook Series, 1970), pp. 93–113.

["Phrase, Character, Incident" reveals Brown's great indebtedness to EMF's *Aspects of the Novel* for conception, plan, and methods used in the book. "Expanding Symbols" analyzes certain novels for images (or incidents, characters, etc.) that accrete meaning as a result of their being repeated with variations, like Vinteuil's sonata phrase from Proust's REMEMBRANCE OF THINGS PAST (cited in *Aspects*).] In *Howards End* "hay" is a symbol comparable to Vinteuil's musical phrase. Hay appears in a variety of forms (wisps of hay, bunches of weeds, trickling grass, hay fever, the grass on the Six Hills burial mounds, the bumper crop of hay at the end) and represents the natural, subjective values that oppose the materialistic, extravert values of the Wilcoxes. In its final ramifications hay is associated with all that stands opposed to Wilcoxism (with the countryside and the past, Helen's revolt, Margaret's cult of personal relations, with the poor as it refers to the child who will inherit Howards End and England, etc.). Symbols of comparable intent are the vine and the wych-elm at Howards End. The symbols in *A Room with a View* are recurrent (or fixed) rather than expanding, except for water. Such symbols tend to have a fixed and precise meaning rather than to develop incrementally. [In "Interweaving

Themes," a third type of rhythm (or symbology) is defined, the sort that depends on the intricate relationship between the larger units of a novel, analogous to the relationship between movements in a sonata or a symphony (in essence, this is the "difficult" rhythm that EMF discusses in *Aspects*).] This rhythm is largely the result of thematic interweavings. *A Passage to India* is an excellent example of a novel with this kind of rhythm. So is *The Longest Journey*, in which the interweaving of themes is so complex that it defeats attempts to analyze it briefly. [EMF is alluded to in discussions of Virginia Woolf's To THE LIGHTHOUSE and Tolstoy's WAR AND PEACE.] [In "Rhythm in E. M. Forster's *A Passage to India*," *Passage* is analyzed as exemplifying all three kinds of rhythm.] Aziz repeats a phrase instinctively to Ralph Moore at the end of the novel, "You are an Oriental," that he had uttered instinctively to Mrs. Moore at the beginning. Ralph and Stella Moore repeat their mother and exert her influence, though Ralph may lack some of his mother's complexity. The wasp is an expanding symbol rather than a repeated motif. The wasp is unable to discriminate a house from a tree; the wasp thus symbolizes the lack of clear distinctions prevalent in India generally and comments on the Western mind that operates according to fixed ideas and sharp categories. It is fitting that Godbole think of Mrs. Moore, in "Temple," when he is attempting to evoke the strongest attachments he has known, and then of a wasp. The reality of the wasp indicates how mysteriously alike Godbole and Mrs. Moore are. The bees are a related symbol; they are, however, a divisive rather than a unitary agent. Their rage against the intruder (Ralph Moore) recalls Aziz's rage against the intruder into the Mosque (Mrs. Moore); their rage is like Aziz's rage with Fielding at the time of the friends' last ride. Yet bees are not totally divisive since they bring Aziz and Ralph Moore together. The echo is the foremost expanding symbol. Before the Caves episode, Adela Quested has been frustrated by the Indians, by the "echoing walls of their civility." An increase in the use of sound (Godbole's song, and the wheels of the train) occurs as events lead to the Marabar. These sounds, like the echo, have a quality of indistinctness with which the Westerner must come to terms; he must learn to discriminate among such indistinctions if India is not to overwhelm him. Fielding has difficulty with the echo since he can make little of indistinct meanings. For Fielding the echo is evil; he functions best in the realm of personal relationships in which there are definite obligations. The echo at the time of the trial disappears from Adela's consciousness when Mrs. Moore's name is invoked by the crowd outside; the chanting of the crowd has its parallel in the Radhakrishna chanting in "Temple." The opening chapters of each part of *Passage* interweave themes: in "Temple" the first chapter opens with a reference to the Caves, and "Mosque" is recalled in this first chapter by the presence of Aziz in Mau. The parts of the novel are structural blocks with many intercalated connections; the whole book opens out to achieve the total suggestiveness supplied by the presence of interweaving themes. The final structure of the book is a kind of "rhythmic rise-fall-rise." Evil has been contained but not cancelled; order is restored but an order that can only be glimpsed, never completely seized. Godbole and Mrs. Moore achieve a mystery that has more of order than of muddle. EMF's imaginative sympathies outrun his intellectual convictions as he aligns himself with Mrs. Moore rather than with Fielding. Mrs. Moore and Adela did not understand that the lack of form (illustrated in the Caves) is not negation, that the presence of evil means only the receding of good, not its vanquishment. The minds of the two women, Western, modern, complex, are unable to operate at the level of primitivism which the Hills and the Caves signify; EMF takes the women purposely beyond their depth. Both characters do come to terms with the Caves in the course of the novel, Mrs. Moore after her death. The echo in the Caves (analogous to the goblins of evil in *Howards End*) is routed in the Mau festivities, and the characters are reconciled in the boat collision in the tank. [A pioneering work, classic for its discussion of the wasp and bee motifs and the importance of "Temple"; otherwise, despite valuable insights, the discourse is a bit relaxed and diffuse.]

533 Einsiedel, Wolfgang von. "Einbildungskraft des Herzens: Der Erzähler E. M. Forster" (The Strength of the Heart's Imagination: The Novelist E. M. Forster), MERKUR (Stuttgart), IV (June 1950), 629–39.

Why should EMF be so influential when he has not been a revolutionary figure in fiction like Joyce, Lawrence, Huxley, or Woolf? He has been popular in Germany since the last war, despite his not being a prolific writer. His moral authority has been recognized here as elsewhere. Although the middle class was formative for him and supplied his milieu and even some of his values, he is in fundamental rebellion against the rigidity of its conventions and its penchant for "unreality." EMF has no dogmatic system of his own; he prizes the individual and is against collectivism of any sort. For him the natural, primitive man is the paramount reality. EMF measures the worth of the individual not by class canons but by his ability to attain harmony. The unspoiled child of nature whom he prizes is anti-puritan in attitude. In this type lies EMF's hope for reform and salvation. He is a writer of comedy in the succession of Meredith, not a satirist: the comedy veers off into tragicomedy. For him, neither art nor human nature can be predictable; his characters have mixed attributes. EMF does not believe in rigid antitheses or simplistic ones; for him human nature is complex, compounded of "good-and-evil." His values are revealed through tone and atmosphere; in his work there is an expert fusion of theme and form. He downplays the story element. There is a colloquial quality in his work, sometimes the result of the presence of the author's own voice. His style reinforces the tone of his work. Most distinctive is a tension in his work between incident and the rendition of it. His handling of incident best reveals his skill; he handles large incidents or catastrophes casually. With EMF, more becomes apparent to us as we expose ourselves repeatedly to his work. In his novels there is an outer kernel of realistic art that encloses a segment of central or symbolic meaning; there is a still deeper locus of more general significance. Absurdity is stressed in his universe, as in the circumstances of Leonard Bast's death in *Howards End*. In this novel, as elsewhere, EMF is interested in defining moral abstractions, but he also realizes the difficulty of doing so. In method he is an ironic realist. He stresses the element of good will, the importance of the eternal moment, and the value of the spontaneous. The heart's imagination represents his most cherished value. In his work there is a blend of realism and mysticism; he is a worldly mystic. [Sound but not inspired commentary.] [In German.]

534 Heilman, Robert B. (ed). "Fantasy: E. M. Forster," MODERN SHORT STORIES: A CRITICAL ANTHOLOGY (NY: Harcourt, Brace, 1950), pp. 306–11.
[Rpt and brief analysis of "Mr. Andrews," stressing EMF's use of irony, his constant reversal of our expectations, the difficulties involved in the attempts of men to define for themselves a permanent state of happiness, and EMF's accomplished use of a casual, understated style.]

535 H[obson], H[arold]. "E. M. Forster Dramatized," CHRISTIAN SCIENCE MONITOR, "Magazine," 4 March 1950, p. 4.
EMF's novels have not been previously dramatized because of the rarefied, diaphanous quality of his mind and because of the muting of the story element. Stephen Tait and Kenneth Allott fail in their adaptation of *A Room with a View*, since they are unable to invest the scene when George Emerson kisses Lucy Honeychurch with the sense of crisis that it possesses in the novel.

536 de Mendelssohn, Peter. "Wie man Romane Schreibt" (How to Write Novels), DIE WELT (Hamburg), 11 Feb 1950.
Aspects of the Novel is a series of chats from EMF's workshop. Although chaotic and formless, it is stimulating if only because of EMF's own informality. [Review of German translation of *Aspects*. Comments on EMF's reputation as the most important living English novelist.] [In German.]

537 *"A Room with a View,"* TIMES (Lond), 8 Feb 1950, p. 9.
The dramatization by Stephen Tait and Kenneth Allott fails because the events in the play lack the intensity of those in the novel and because the characters verbalize their half-formed thoughts instead of maintaining their reticences as in the novel.

538 Warner, Rex. E. M. FORSTER (Lond: Longmans, Green, Writers and Their Work, No. 7, 1950); rptd with additions to bibliography, 1954; rvd completely by John Morris, 1960; 1960 ed rptd in BRITISH WRITERS AND THEIR WORK, No. 3, ed by J. W. Robinson (Lincoln: University of Nebraska P, 1964); see entry for John Morris (1960).

EMF is part of the liberal tradition but is capable of standing outside it; he is creative beyond its usual bounds. His work is prophetic and intense; he writes of the middle class, but opposes to it something radically different (Italy, illegitimacy, poverty, India). In his novels the middle class is seen from within and without. He is a philosophical novelist; the comic manner veils but does not conceal his purpose. The judgments passed on Agnes Pembroke (*The Longest Journey*) and Charles Wilcox (*Howards End*) are pitiless. In *Where Angels Fear to Tread* EMF insists on the truth and stresses the difficulties in discovering it. He is not successful in rendering sexual love. His method is symbolical and allegorical; his writing is poetic, not realistic. Mrs. Herriton trades on her respectability; Philip, her son, develops beyond Sawston though he never overcomes his passivity. Lilia Herriton is the slave of a different set of conventions in Italy, made for men and not for women, just as binding as those of Sawston. The novel has "neat and dexterous construction"; melodrama is of great importance so that the explosive depths below a delicate surface can materialize. The melodramatic death of Gino's baby is appropriate, but the cruelty of Gino and the transfiguration of Caroline Abbott into a goddess are not. EMF needs violence and sex for his art but distrusts them. Rickie Elliot in *Journey* is conscientious, but a failed intellectual. He is not attractive though EMF presents him with great sympathy; his conscientious quest for the light gives him dignity. Stephen Wonham lacks the stature for his role in the novel and is seen from the outside. *Journey* is "strangely moving and revealing," though not a full success. *A Room with a View* is less serious and passionate and dramatizes the dichotomies existing between truth and falsehood, art and life, the misunderstanding of life and the misunderstanding of art. Mr. Beebe's change to an ascetic in the novel reveals EMF's dislike of committing himself even to Truth or Life; EMF can be blamed for irresolution or esteemed for skepticism. In *Howards End* the melodrama is more firmly related to the symbolism than in the earlier novels. Two great symbols from this novel reappear in modified form in *A Passage to India:* the wise, elderly woman as Mrs. Wilcox becomes Mrs. Moore; the "panic and emptiness" suggested by the Scherzo of the Beethoven Fifth Symphony becomes the echo in the Marabar Caves. In *Passage* the contrast between hope and "panic and emptiness" becomes more stark since the latter attains an almost physical reality in India. After her experience in the Caves, Mrs. Moore deteriorates, becoming "a wise woman without any evident wisdom, a Christian lapsed into emptiness," a kind of Magna Mater who elicits "a willing or reluctant emasculation" from her admirers. In EMF's fiction the worlds of nightmare and vision are conjoined. His standards are good sense and good will, but they are undermined by the world as it is. [Many insights and interesting judgments in a short pamphlet, still of much value.]

539 Westland, Peter. CONTEMPORARY LITERATURE 1880–1950 (Lond: English Universities P, The Teach Yourself History of English Literature, Vol. VI, 1950), pp. 58–59, 102.
EMF ranks high because he embodied and solved the greater part of his problem in his fiction [debatable]. His novels are well-constructed; they have little in the way of plot but work through "suspense." He writes "a rhythmical prose of great unevenness." His characters are not vital but are all puppets speaking for the author [an obtuse judgment]. Their meaning and EMF's own view is that "individual life is of supreme value."

540 W[hite], E[ric] W[alter]. "Edward Morgan Forster," CHAMBER'S ENCYCLOPAEDIA (Lond: George Newnes, 1950), V, 804; 1961 and 1964 eds, V, 804, discussion unchanged; updated in 1967 ed (Oxford, Lond, & NY: Pergamon P), V, 774.
Where Angels Fear to Tread and *A Room with a View* develop "the tragicomedy of the 'undeveloped heart' "; *The Longest Journey* is a "passionate parable" of the inner life and its destruction. [Comment on *Howards End* and *A Passage to India* is more standard. Brief sketch of career with some incidental insights.]

1951

541 Aldridge, John W. AFTER THE LOST GENERATION: A CRITICAL STUDY OF THE WRITERS OF TWO WARS (NY, Lond, Toronto: McGraw-Hill, 1951), pp. 216–17.
A contemporary writer like Truman Capote is no longer sure that an audience will share his view of life or understand it. Though they contended with the same problem, Conrad in VICTORY, Joyce in ULYSSES, and EMF in *A Passage to India* could invest their novels with a significance that transcends the characters and situations in them. In *Passage* EMF writes a tragedy based on the evil in all men, and yet a story about Aziz. These writers treated their materials symbolically. They were nearer to life than Capote is and so could invest their private experience with greater meaning. They communicated an insight into life that became mythical in significance. Such a range of creation is beyond Capote.

542 Ames, Alfred C. "New Forster Essays Are Unhurried," CHI-
CAGO SUNDAY TRIBUNE, "Magazine of Books," 4 Nov 1951, p. 12.
In *Two Cheers for Democracy* the political essays date and the aesthetic
theorizing does not stay in the mind; the best essays are on individual
writers, books, and places and are notable for their "spare, polished, unhurried, terse" style.

543 Annan, Noel Gilroy. LESLIE STEPHEN: HIS THOUGHT AND
CHARACTER IN RELATION TO HIS TIME (Lond: MacGibbon & Kee,
1951; Cambridge, Mass: Harvard UP, 1952), pp. 2, 117, 123, 241,
246, 251, 259, 276.
Sir Leslie Stephen exemplifies in his life the same concern with class values
that English novelists from Fielding to Forster were concerned with. The
idealism and seriousness of evangelical Clapham were formative for Stephen and thus formative for Bloomsbury through his children, Virginia
Woolf, Vanessa Bell, Adrian Stephen, and Thoby Stephen. The same influence came into Bloomsbury from another direction in the Thornton ancestry of EMF, the Thorntons also being identified with Clapham. [Traces
connections between the Clapham evangelical tradition and Bloomsbury.]
Stephen had reacted against Christian orthodoxy with an evangelical seriousness. His children and Bloomsbury as a whole were to react with that
same determination against constricting Victorian moral standards. EMF,
along with Yeats and D. H. Lawrence, reacted against the atrophied liberal
imagination that Stephen in part protested against and that he in part
exemplified. Stephen tried to place the individual's behavior in a wider
context of principles: Beatrice Webb, on the contrary, saw the individual in
light of group behavior or of service to the community, and Virginia Woolf
and EMF saw it in terms of personal relations. The Bloomsbury critics,
including EMF, tended to reject principles and to focus on the work of art
as an entity in itself. Stephen exemplified in his criticism those strong
principles that Trilling finds absent in EMF's criticism. The element of
personal involvement, present in the sensibility of Virginia Woolf and EMF
as it reacts to the work of art, is lacking in Stephen's criticism (to its
detriment). [Many references to EMF, his Clapham ancestry, his Bloomsbury affiliations, and his practice as novelist and critic.]

544 Barzun, Jacques. "Why Not the Third Cheer?" GRIFFIN. I
(1951), 1–3, 7.
Two Cheers for Democracy reveals that, in essence, EMF is a novelist: "The
strongest impression left by the book is of dialogue, dramatis personae, and
settings, and that confident hand of the master showman to which the
novels have accustomed us." In politics, EMF stresses individuality, which
for him means participation; but for him, being a democrat also means
making no direct effort in this direction. Democracy permits, within reason,

variety and self-fulfillment. EMF hates barriers and categories, whether of rank, color, wealth, or power. Democracy, however, tends to create categories that an industrial system has the means to enforce; it can raise up a dictator for roundabout self-worship; it can also destroy true culture by appeals to numbers and vulgarity. EMF finds an internal and not an imposed kind of order in art works. The chief dilemma he faces is seen in this book: "The incompatibility of human talents and human loves with social existence." Thus freedom for self development is also freedom for rivalry and the competition that can snuff out talents; but he deplores as well the existence of a protected elite. EMF would try to reach a compromise between self-expansion and self-restraint, which he calls good taste. He defends the freedom of the artist but perhaps does not see that the artist is at war with all who would harness him. But EMF's intimacy through concreteness outweighs his arch humor and his diffidence. His style is the perfect medium for his thought. [Interesting commentary.]

545 Beaumont, Ernest. "Mr. E. M. Forster's Strange Mystics," DUBLIN REVIEW, CCXXV (Third Quarter, 1951), 41–51.

There are transcendental implications in EMF's *Howards End* and *A Passage to India* embodied in women (Mrs. Wilcox and Mrs. Moore) who have strong intuitive wisdom and understanding but who have rejected a doctrinal Christianity. People matter greatly to Mrs. Wilcox and to the earlier Mrs. Moore; to the later Mrs. Moore the people matter but their relationships do not. Mrs. Moore is a Mrs. Wilcox who experiences India and the Marabar Caves. EMF leaves us in doubt as to whether he is portraying a spiritual progression or a spiritual eclipse in Mrs. Moore's experiences at the Caves. Mrs. Wilcox in the company of Margaret's friends seems to be out of focus with daily life; similarly, Mrs. Moore is out of focus with the Anglo-Indians because of her democratic and humane views and with the universe after her experience in the Marabar Caves. Mrs. Wilcox is intimately related to a place, while Mrs. Moore has kinship with the universe as a whole, although this kinship is severely strained after her shattering experience at the Caves. In India the God she had once known serves her less fully; she seems to become aware of something beyond God, whether "an ultimate nothingness" or "an infinity" that she cannot comprehend. In "the twilight of the double vision" that now descends on her, this life and the after-life are both dimmed. She undergoes a period of spiritual darkness that is not resolved in light, although her darkness may be fading as she leaves India. Yet the novel implies that Mrs. Moore had an understanding of ultimates. Since Mrs. Wilcox and Mrs. Moore "know," they are mystics, having knowledge about the relationship of the human to the divine and of a transcendent realm. Both women have a posthumous influence, giving rise to a kind of communion of saints, or caricature thereof, in both books. The intercessory role attributed to the women is not altogether convincing; it is not quite prepared for and is too marvelous to be acceptable. They are not convincing as mystics because they do not embody unambiguously the force of love. Their influence is asserted rather than fully incorporated into the books. Both have a pantheistic sensitivity to nature, something also present in Hinduism, whose all-embracing quality EMF celebrates in the concluding pages of *Passage*. The festival balances the sequences in the Caves: There is equality, and all things have value. In the festival Mrs. Moore's vision is righted, and she is rightly at its heart, in the mind of Godbole and in Ralph, her son. As to the success of the characterizations of Mrs. Wilcox and Mrs. Moore, it is difficult to draw the line between the complex and the confused, the genuine and the spurious. But their fascination for us lies in their elusiveness. [Some insights of value.]

546 Brome, Vincent. H. G. WELLS: A BIOGRAPHY (Lond & Toronto: Longmans, Green, 1951; Westport, Conn: Greenwood P, 1970), pp. 77, 101, 108 (1970 rpt).

Jane Wells belonged to the world of EMF, Proust, and Virginia Woolf, and she was temperamentally different from her husband, H. G. Wells. In KIPPS and some of his other fiction, Wells lacked the capacity to get inside his characters as EMF was able to do. TONO-BUNGAY might have been better if Wells's vitality and creativity had been allied to the artistry of EMF, whereby ordinary experience might have gained an added dimension.

547 Brooke, Jocelyn. "Four Cheers for Mr. Forster," SPECTATOR (Lond), CLXXXVII (9 Nov 1951), 609.

Rather than being great or important, EMF is compelling by being a free mind. He is a liberator, especially in the moral sphere; but his influence represents also a triumph of art. A possible weakness in EMF's humanism is his failure to commit himself. *Two Cheers for Democracy* is greater than the sum of its parts; the essays, though often occasional in origin, entertaining, and readable, are also serious. Some of EMF's qualities: casualness, wit, occasional malice, oblique and sinuous manner, wisdom, and subtlety. The tone is firmer than in his earlier essays.

548 Brower, Reuben A. "The Twilight of the Double Vision: Symbol and Irony in *A Passage to India*," THE FIELDS OF LIGHT: AN EXPERIMENT IN CRITICAL READING (NY: Oxford UP, 1951), pp. 182–98; rptd in MODERN BRITISH FICTION: ESSAYS IN CRITICISM, ed by Mark Schorer (NY: Oxford UP, Galaxy Books, 1961), pp. 210–24; and in E.M. FORSTER: "A PASSAGE TO INDIA": A CASEBOOK, ed by Malcolm Bradbury (Lond: Macmillan, Casebook Series, 1970), pp. 114–31.

In *A Passage to India* there are scenes of social comedy recalling Jane Austen. EMF's habitual irony in the novel is expressed through metaphors that are symbolic. The predominating ones are Mosque (with its associated arch), Caves (with its associated echo), and Temple (with its associated sky). These contribute to the symbolic, ironic, dramatic design peculiar to *Passage*. "Mosque" is a symbol of friendship (see the encounter in the Mosque between Mrs. Moore and Aziz) and a symbol of possibilities of communication between racial groups and between individuals. The symbols are multiple in significance and often suggest their opposites: the black and white aspect of the mosque, the stillness of the mosque ranged against the "complex appeal" of the night. The Mosque also expresses Fielding's friendship with Aziz and Fielding's liberal hope that the races can get together. Adela's strident attempts to know Indians and her shifting relationships to Ronny Heaslop provide negative meanings for the Mosque symbol. In the Caves Mrs. Moore is shaken; no frame for human life now seems possible. The Caves suggest two things: on the one hand, mystery and order, on the other hand, disillusionment and muddle. The Cave symbol is not antithetic to Mosque but repeats it; there are the same oppositions (especially, the possibility of communication and the failure to attain it). The contrast is sinister between the cordial tea party outside the Caves and the collapse of human relationships after the Caves have been entered. Mrs. Moore loves mystery; she had found it in her first mystical vision of the sky in the Mosque, but that vision there is undercut by her disillusioning experience with the echo at the Cave. Sky and arch are also symbols of infinity, and connect with the echo. Mrs. Moore's vision of infinity at the Caves is less and more than she had hoped for. The Caves stand for a religion accessible only to a particular kind of Oriental intelligence, the Hindu mind (Godbole as "Ancient Night" has intuitive knowledge of them, and their ambiguity is suggested by the song he sings at Fielding's tea party, with its indiscriminate noises). Mrs. Moore's indifference and moral confusion are focused in her loss of faith in Christian marriage. The echo in the Caves, linked with sky and arches, promises a revelation, but Mrs. Moore's vision turns out to be a nightmare. It is a vision characteristic of the twentieth century: Chaos prevails instead of unity, and the older religions no longer seem tenable. "Temple" is a symbol of Hinduism, also a symbol implying both reconciliation and division. This part of the novel is inferior to the other two. Mau cannot be a symbol for unity and peace because it is itself so disorganized [misses the creative aspect of the muddle]. [Feels the preparation for the influence exerted by Mrs. Moore as a spirit-force after her death in "Temple" is lacking or unconvincing. The negative comments are asserted, not proved. An essay with some good insights but unappreciative of EMF's achievements in *Passage*.]

549 Canfield, Dorothy. "Other New Books to Know About," BOOK-OF-THE- MONTH CLUB NEWS, Nov 1951, p. 10.
The essays collected in *Two Cheers for Democracy* have helped "to shape our collective human intelligence." There is little unity but much richness

in the volume; all of the essays are "civilized, intelligent, discriminating, stimulating."

550 Chapin, Ruth. "Variety and Criticism," CHRISTIAN SCIENCE MONITOR, 21 Nov 1951, p. 11.

The heart and intellect combine in *Two Cheers for Democracy* to give it a unique quality. The study of history for EMF was the discovery of those "who carried whimsicality into action." He has an overriding concern with humanity. His politics are inseparable from the man, a politics characterized by tolerance, fair play, and individualism. A deep sense of love is his strength; his failure to apply this emotion widely is his weakness. The book is "a distinguished testament to the finest sort of individualism."

551 Church, Richard. THE GROWTH OF THE ENGLISH NOVEL (Lond: Methuen, Home Study Books, 1951), pp. 78, 208.

Novelists of sensibility such as EMF and Elizabeth Bowen keep alive a concern with moral values and keep fresh the tired minds of readers overcome with the confusions of modern life. EMF, "a gentle liberal platonist," and the dignified Elizabeth Bowen reveal a confidence and quiet irony that allows them to be proponents of admirable standards for civil behavior and thought. Those motivated by cynical despair and by barbarous zeal attack these standards. EMF and Miss Bowen have resisted these attacks, not so much by "superior aloofness" as by a "noble stoicism."

552 Collins, A. S. "E. M. Forster and D. H. Lawrence," ENGLISH LITERATURE OF THE TWENTIETH CENTURY (Lond: University Tutorial P, 1951), pp. 193–203, and passim; 4th rvd ed, 1960, with discussion of EMF's nonfiction added.

Superficially disparate, EMF and D. H. Lawrence have much in common. They were precursors, and creators and symbols of the moral disintegration that has transformed English life and literature since 1920. They are moderns because their "discomfort of soul" made them critics of contemporary civilization. Both emphasize the need for "right" personal relationships: EMF relied on intelligence, culture, and an awakening of the heart; Lawrence, on passions of the blood and sexuality. Both felt the need for the individual to be free in his inner life: see in his early novels EMF's admiration of vitality in his male figures, who embody a semi-mystical paganism akin to Lawrence's. EMF's first four novels were youthful in inception and impression conveyed; they criticized convention as an inhibiting force. The contrasts between characters are too stark in *Where Angels Fear to Tread.* The characters in *The Longest Journey* are not vitally created but are embodied aspects of good and evil in the struggle between convention and spontaneity. Total effect of *A Room with a View* is "one of stimulating pleasure." In *Howards End* EMF no longer tilts one-sidedly at convention.

The business mind has strong qualities, which need, however, to be mellowed by the Schlegels's "sensitive understanding of moral and aesthetic values." The book is a trenchant exposé of the pre-1914 era. In *A Passage to India* personal relationships are more difficult than EMF had thought earlier. Intelligence, good will, and culture are insufficient to solve problems of empire, or of human beings themselves. On the surface *Passage* gives us "the magnitude, mystery and complexity of India." Symbolically, it underscores "the complex mystery of all life" and the problem of evil in the universe. At the end there is a hint of "ultimate goodness behind the mystery of the universe." The West might be helped by learning "the uninhibited naturalness" of the East, its capacity to be happy, its blending of the serious and humorous. Aziz is the one character with full life in the novel. [Discussion of EMF's influence on the modern novel.] EMF gave intellect a greater share in the creation and direction of the genre. Theme becomes more important than plot and persons; idea reigns supreme in EMF's novels. [Cites and quotes from EMF's *Virginia Woolf* (1942).] [Much incisive comment.]

553 Crozier, Eric. "How 'Billy Budd' Became an Opera," LONDON CALLING, No. 639 (20 Dec 1951), 14–15.
[Describes notes and manuscripts for the opera BILLY BUDD upon which he and EMF collaborated, the process of bringing the libretto together, and the modifications made in it by Benjamin Britten.]

554 Davis, Robert Gorham. "E. M. Forster: An Indifferent Liberal," NEW LEADER, XXXIV (10 Dec 1951), 21–22.
The essays composing *Two Cheers for Democracy* are full of "wit, luminosity of image and devotion to beauty." The political essays are less good than the literary ones, though the whole book is a protest against totalitarian culture. EMF is susceptible to ideas but only when they approach him obliquely; he is not interested in ideas as such. His analyses of Nazism are convincing because they can be couched in personal terms, but he is not a rigorous enough thinker to deal with the complexities of Marxism. His attitude toward politics, reflected in his mild endorsement of democracy, is essentially negative. He distrusts all order except that found in art and most motivations except love. But he feels that the artist can only thrive in a society based economically on capitalism, politically on liberalism, and philosophically on individualism. EMF feels that it is difficult to do as he would prefer, to combine the old morality and art with the new economy. In his emphasis on anarchistic individualism, he tends too readily to equate Russian and American politics as equally repressive. In the uneasy world of today, EMF can only recommend, for the preservation of liberty, our thinking clearly, our writing good prose, and our asserting individuality and tolerance against all odds. His prose and perceptions are better than his

thinking. He has little sense of the social nature of the individual and of the role of ideas, traditions, customs, institutions, and symbols in the individual's mediating with the group or their role in forming his mind. But EMF's sensibility and perceptions are excellent. His perceptiveness and detachment allow him to see our present situation with "disturbing clarity and honesty." We must not forget the overwhelming importance of creativity and individualism, as EMF sees them, in our international struggle. [Extremely perceptive article.]

555 Fremantle, Anne. "Books," COMMONWEAL, LV (9 Nov 1951), 126.

EMF is perhaps a bit remote, but his essays in *Two Cheers for Democracy* show us what it is to be civilized in the twentieth century. He is at his best when he is most personal. He exemplifies "the slow accretion, in one lifetime, ... of wisdom in one man."

556 Gill, Brendan. "Two Self-Portraits," NEW YORKER, XXVII (17 Nov 1951), 179–80.

In *Two Cheers for Democracy* EMF regards the past as something to be both cherished and spoofed. The contents of *Two Cheers* are more varied and more vivid than those of *Abinger Harvest*. World War II was as crucial to him in his later life as "the blunt fact of India" was in his earlier phase. It caused him to appraise and defend the value of his own double existence: the detached life of the artist conjoined to the committed life of the citizen. He will live because of his novels, but the essays help us to define the person whose struggle against conventions was real, though it was sometimes carried on remote from the market place. [Perceptive commentary.]

557 Greene, Graham. "François Mauriac," THE LOST CHILDHOOD AND OTHER ESSAYS (Lond: Eyre & Spottiswoode, 1951; NY: Viking P, 1952), pp. 69–73 (NY ed); rptd in COLLECTED ESSAYS (NY: Viking P; Lond: Bodley Head, 1969), pp. 115–21.

With the death of Henry James, the religious sense was lost to the British novel and with its loss went the importance of the human act. The world of fiction lost a dimension, with the result that characters in the novels of Virginia Woolf and EMF are like "cardboard symbols" in a "paper-thin" world.

558 Harrod, R. F. "Undergraduate at Cambridge," "Bloomsbury," THE LIFE OF JOHN MAYNARD KEYNES (NY: Harcourt, Brace; Lond: Macmillan, 1951), pp. 55–104, espec 63, 75n, 84, 94, 172–94, espec 186; also 109.

EMF and Desmond MacCarthy, Keynes's seniors at Cambridge, were much impressed with his fine intellect. H. O. Meredith, Cambridge fellow, was an early admirer of EMF's works. EMF is regarded as part of Bloomsbury. [Chapters, cited above, are invaluable for information about EMF's Cambridge and Bloomsbury milieu.]

559 Howe, Irving. "The Pleasures of Cultivation," NEW REPUBLIC, CXXV (10 Dec 1951), 16–17.
EMF does not share the distrust of American writers for the cultivated mind; his virtues are "an utter freedom from stuffiness, an enviable assurance in dealing with the English literary tradition, a readiness to converse with the reader on terms of intellectual equality, and a shy humility. . . ." His political essays in *Two Cheers for Democracy* are too relaxed and do not confront the issues squarely. His literary essays get at the heart of his subjects. Here EMF is similar to Virginia Woolf in his personal, imaginative method and in his distrust of abstractions: his essays presuppose a cultivated audience. He is entertaining, urbane, at home with the past, charming, creative, and impressionistic in the best sense. [Penetrating commentary.]

560 Krutch, Joseph Wood. "In Defense of Values," SATURDAY REVIEW OF LITERATURE (NY), XXXIV (1 Dec 1951), 25–26.
EMF's *Two Cheers for Democracy* is noteworthy for its revelation of a unified personality. The temperament and opinions may be old-fashioned, but EMF upholds them with conviction. He has no faith in any system as such, including democracy. EMF is concerned with the arts wherein human achievement has been possible; these are now threatened, since democracy, like all other forms of power, discounts, discourages, and destroys them. As a lover of the arts, EMF can neither give up his society nor give in to it. He has detachment enough to see clearly and involvement enough to understand what the issue is. [Stimulating remarks.]

561 Moore, Harry T. THE LIFE AND WORKS OF D. H. LAWRENCE (NY: Twayne Publishers; Lond: Allen & Unwin, 1951), pp. 132, 249.
In Lawrence's "The Last Laugh," the three central characters have been brushed by supernatural experience in the same way that Eustace becomes possessed of the Pan spirit in EMF's "The Story of a Panic." [EMF's visit to the Lawrences at Greatham is mentioned.]

562 Neill, S. Diana. "Satire and Experiment between Two Wars," A SHORT HISTORY OF THE ENGLISH NOVEL (Lond: Jarrolds, 1951; NY: Macmillan, 1952), pp. 294–324, espec 294, 298–302 (NY ed); rvd ed (NY & Lond: Collier-Macmillan, 1964), pp. 339–375, espec 340, 343–49, also 376 (EMF materials unchanged).
EMF as a liberal based his philosophy on reason; it was not enough, but the alternatives were alarming and uncontrollable. EMF's problem became the

reconciliation of "civilized order with imaginative awareness and the world of feeling." Order, culture, and toleration were often accompanied by hardness, complacency, insensitivity, the absence of vitality. The Englishman too often evinced these latter traits because of his "undeveloped heart." EMF's chief theme becomes "the confused complexity of human characters and relationships." He contrasts two opposing modes of existence in his novels: the official way and the way of the heart, the way of the "crustaceans" and the way of the "vitalists" (Ronny Heaslop, Charlotte Bartlett, Major Callendar, and the Turtons versus Fielding, Mrs. Moore, and George Emerson). The characters, however, are not all black and white; e.g., Gino Carella's capacity for parental love in *Where Angels Fear to Tread* is balanced by his cunning, cruelty, and indifference in other relationships. *The Longest Journey* is an "intellectual" novel, a criticism of life rather than a presentation of it. In *A Room with a View*, the room with a view becomes the symbol of those who love life and want to share this emotion with others. In *Howards End* (as in *A Passage to India*) "the skeins of life are tangled." *Passage* is distinctive by its presentation of racial conflict, its evocation of Indian atmosphere, its economy of incident, and its revelation of character through dialogue. The events surrounding the trial reveal prejudice in both camps; sympathy and intelligence are the first victims on either side. EMF's presentation of Aziz is marked by both sympathy and realism: he is slightly ridiculous in addition to being appealing. EMF believes in the good life but also feels that the confusion and mystery of life extend beyond our capacities to comprehend it. He is an advocate of "intellectual *laissez faire*," placing his trust in reasonableness and tolerance. Violence and melodrama in his work have the inevitability that they often possess in real life. [Suggestive insights.]

563 Paulding, Gouverneur. "An E. M. Forster Miscellany, Generous and Civilized," NEW YORK HERALD TRIBUNE BOOK REVIEW, 4 Nov 1951, p. 12.

Two Cheers for Democracy demonstrates how EMF has held to civilized values in a time of crisis and disturbance. He is sympathetic to the detachment of Montaigne and Gibbon but knows how difficult it is to achieve in this age. He therefore writes the obligatory essays defining democracy, though his best work is on purely literary subjects. He reveals in *Two Cheers* a modesty yet also a persistence and a belief in the relevance and strength of his values, despite the fact that they can only prevail for brief moments in a time of violence.

564 Porter, Katherine Anne. "E. M. Forster Speaks Out for the Things He Holds Dear," NEW YORK TIMES BOOK REVIEW, 4 Nov 1951, p. 3; rptd as "E. M. Forster," in THE DAYS BEFORE (NY: Harcourt, Brace; Lond: Secker & Warburg, 1952), pp. 116–19; and

in THE COLLECTED ESSAYS AND OCCASIONAL WRITINGS OF KATHER-
INE ANNE PORTER (NY: Delacorte P, 1970), pp. 72–74.
In EMF's work a "beautiful, purely secular common sense" can hardly be
distinguished from "a saintly idealism." He lives in a "constant state of
grace," deriving from his complete self-knowledge; and he pokes fun at all
sorts of pretentiousness and oppressiveness. *Two Cheers for Democracy* is
an extension and enlargement of his thought; and in it he defends, by means
of personal commitment and example, the arts, civilization, and personal
relationships. [It is as champion of liberty that Katherine Anne Porter best
remembers EMF.]

565 Praz, Mario. "Panorama Letterario Inglese 1949" (Panorama
of English Literature 1949), CRONACHE LETTERARIE ANGLO-SASSONI,
II [Cronache Inglesi e Americano] (Anglo-Saxon Literary Chronicle: English and American) (Roma: Edizione di Storia e Letterature, 1951), pp. 104–19, espec 112–13.
British novels and short stories during the period between the two wars can
only be arbitrarily analyzed for trends and movements. Of the pre-World
War I writers who were in vogue around 1940, Henry James remains the
dominant figure. It is not easy to evaluate the influence of the late Joyce
(the verbal disintegrator of FINNEGAN'S WAKE) or the influence of his technique of "the continuous flux of conscience" as practiced by Virginia Woolf.
During the period EMF was achieving new recognition. His novels belong
to a climate that is not modern, "the Bloomsbury climate." They contain
a realistic and well-defined system of ethics, supplemented by certain values
from romanticism (the cult of the Noble Savage and the cult of Life and
Passion). [In Italian.]

566 Pritchett, V. S. "A Private Voice," NEW STATESMAN AND NA-
TION, nsXLII (3 Nov 1951), 496, 498.
EMF is "extreme" like other writers of the age, but in the cause of tolerance
rather than of faith. His extremism is revealed in his dislike of the will and
the intellect as such. EMF speaks with the private voice in public. He is
capable always of objectivity. In "Mrs. Miniver," he deflates one of his own
characters as it were, a Schlegel or a Miss Abbott or possibly even himself.
EMF has a decisive manner also with ideas and theorizing about the arts;
in general, his critiques reveal the wisdom of the contemplative man and
of the nonparticipant. The critiques on individual writers are below his best
standard. One form of his extremism is similar to that of H. G. Wells; he
abandoned art in order to teach, to propagandize for the good life. Although
the word "Will" is symptomatic of all that EMF loathes, still the artist needs
to exercise his will if he is to achieve the internal order in his work that EMF
prizes. EMF is skeptical of the Will and Greatness simply because these
counters had too often been brought to bear upon men in the immediate past

and had diminished thereby "the returns for the individual and for the value of living." [Review of *Two Cheers for Democracy*. A dense and elliptically written, but thoughtful, critique].

567 [Putt, Samuel Gorley]. "Considering Mr. Forster," TIMES LITERARY SUPPLEMENT (Lond), 27 July 1951, pp. 461–62; ptd under Putt's name as "The Strength of Timid Hearts: E. M. Forster," SCHOLARS OF THE HEART (Lond: Faber, 1962), pp. 35–42.

Neither Rose Macaulay in THE WRITINGS OF E. M. FORSTER (1938) nor Lionel Trilling in E. M. FORSTER (1943) supplies us with a firm basis for our admiration of EMF. Maturity, subtlety, intelligence, discrimination are present in EMF; but what wins us is "the beautiful simplicity of heart." EMF is concerned with the eternal moral possibilities of human nature. He is "a dictatorial Liberal" who insists on seeing both sides of every question. Herein may lie a weakness: when he finds so much to be said for matters that are questionable, the good is often overshadowed. Certain unrealities in the books are the result of a lack of creative vitality; otherwise his characters in action would act more truly and decisively. His characters have discrimination but are sometimes untouched by their experiences (as EMF has presented Mrs. Miniver in his *Two Cheers for Democracy* essay). His great strength is in dialogue. His characters are immensely alive in their immediate dimension; consequently, we forget that their external lives are incompletely presented. EMF is not a spectator of life; rather, his characters do not participate actively enough in life. The attitude toward a feeling rather than the feeling itself too often matters with them. His heroes in the novels are often those of the stories: pagan boys become liberal men who are nostalgic for a mode of existence different from that possible in the modern world. In the Italian stories (and elsewhere) the effect of the foreign place or person on the British visitors is all-important (Gino Carella in *Where Angels Fear to Tread*, for example, is only alive as he impinges on the British). EMF teaches us that passion is best but does not show us inevitably in his works that it is so. He is neither the romanticist nor the disillusioned cynic but the philosopher and novelist who "can show us in the lives of decent baffled cultured folk as imperfect as ourselves, the residual possibilities of courage and of love." [Review-essay on 3rd English ed of Lionel Trilling's E. M. FORSTER (1943). A perceptive, thoughtful, and knowledgeable essay.]

568 "A Qualified Tribute," TIMES LITERARY SUPPLEMENT (Lond), 16 Nov 1951, p. 724.

EMF's miscellaneous works, collected in *Two Cheers for Democracy*, do add up to a book with intellectual, emotional, and moral substance, and a creative impact. There is less whimsy and more tartness, impatience, and defiance in them than in the essays collected in *Abinger Harvest*. The political and aesthetic writings are closely related. His essays on literature are "recommendations" rather than critical discussions and are perceptive and persuasive. The emphasis of *Two Cheers* is both political and ethical. In the short term EMF stresses tolerance, in the long term, love. In his work there is always a rich complexity. [Perceptive review.]

569 Rantavaara, Irma. "E. M. Forster ja Bloomsbury" (E. M. Forster and Bloomsbury), VALVOJA (Helsinki), LXXI (Aug 1951), 257–61.

In WORLD WITHIN WORLD Stephen Spender casts new light on the Bloomsbury group. He feels that while EMF was a close friend of the Woolfs, he was too individualistic to be fenced in by a group. Nevertheless, some affinities between the Bloomsbury people justify the term "circle," and Virginia Woolf and EMF share these affinities. Both seek the way to mature life, the balanced relationship between one's self and the outer world, through aesthetic and ethical experience. Clive Bell's programmatic CIVILIZATION (1928) was spectacular, but it contained little that EMF had not earlier proposed. Bloomsbury had as its sworn enemy the bourgeoisie; whereas Bell attacks the middle class directly, EMF and Woolf are less obvious in their hostility. In spite of similarities in content, EMF and Woolf differ as to the form of their novels. Woolf appeals to the intellect; EMF writes a good story for the public. The general reader is apt to be passive; in order to awaken him, EMF will use sudden deaths and melodramatic incidents. The differences between EMF and Woolf are surface ones: he uses the old-fashioned story; she utilizes visual and rhythmic elements. For EMF there can be no novel without story, and he criticizes writers such as Woolf and Gertrude Stein for trying to eliminate this "atavistic" element. Although both writers have reservations about each other, they share a common philosophy: Man must be freed from limitations imposed upon his self-knowledge and vision. Both stress change and the unconscious aspects of the psyche; they foreshadow psychoanalytical ideas or incorporate them in their novels. Both writers, however, suffered from restrictions imposed by their personalities. EMF's self-criticism created inhibitions; he refused to be great. When he escapes such self-consciousness, he creates a small masterpiece, i.e., *A Passage to India*. Then he shows his ability to see into the human heart and creates an almost prophetic synthesis by using small gestures and few words. During the twenty-seven years since *Passage*, EMF's popularity has increased "with every book that he has not published." EMF feels that this type of liberal thought will disappear now that mass thinking is gaining ground. EMF's cardinal values are the stress on individuality and the importance of mental maturity. Although he does not seem to appreciate fully enough man's relation to religion, he emphasizes certain basic truths: Life does not last forever, the struggle for money and power is not the most important activity, and the need exists for everyone to contribute to social progress. [In Finnish.]

570 Scott-James, R. A. "Above the Battle," FIFTY YEARS OF ENGLISH LITERATURE 1900–1950 (Lond & NY: Longmans, Green, 1951), pp. 66–71; also 34, 54, 163; 2nd ed, FIFTY YEARS OF ENGLISH LITERATURE 1900–1950: WITH A POSTSCRIPT—1951–1955 (1956), pp. 240–63, espec 251; rpts, slightly rvd, "Re-Assessments—II: E. M. Forster," ADELPHI, XXVII (First Quarter 1951), 137–41.

EMF draws upon Jane Austen and Samuel Butler rather than Shaw or Wells. He is aware of the social incongruities of the time, but relates them to the inner lives of his characters. "Other Kingdom" is a small masterpiece. EMF found in Greek culture an inspiriting union "of physical beauty and immortal strangeness." *Where Angels Fear to Tread* reveals youth but not immaturity. The power derives from the ebullient Gino Carella. The novel reveals a youthful perspective but a mature understanding of the clash of cultures involved. Many people and places in *The Longest Journey* evoke "the Spirit, and its magic." Stephen Wonham represents the Spirit of Life. In *A Room with a View* the little god Pan ostensibly rules over the picnic in the hills, but the great god returns to life when George Emerson kisses Lucy Honeychurch among the violets. The theme of the novel is the sacredness of passion, especially as it opposes the conventions. In *Howards End* the individual tries to hold on to the best of tradition under "the assaults of soulless undirected change." In *A Passage to India* EMF values characters insofar as they have the courage to be individuals and confront the restrictions imposed upon them by the tribe. EMF's later miscellaneous writings exemplify the same preciseness, strength, and stylistic power. [Other incidental references.]

571 Shrapnel, Norman. "Mr. E. M. Forster," MANCHESTER GUARDIAN, 6 Nov 1951, p. 4; rptd in abrgd form in E. M. FORSTER: THE CRITICAL HERITAGE, ed by Philip Gardner (Lond & Boston: Routledge & Kegan Paul, 1973), pp. 411–12.

EMF's ideas in *Two Cheers for Democracy*, especially his valuation of tolerance, are heartening, but the diversity of these essays is a liability as much as an asset. He pursues nothing. The diversity in style does not always tell to their advantage. The longer essays are the best, especially "George Crabbe and Peter Grimes" and "John Skelton."

572 Spender, Stephen. WORLD WITHIN WORLD: THE AUTOBIOGRAPHY OF STEPHEN SPENDER (NY: Harcourt, Brace; Lond: Hamish Hamilton, 1951), pp. 127–28, 152, 219; rptd (Berkeley & Los Angeles, University of California P, 1966), pp. 140–42, 167, 241.

Bloomsbury substituted for the university, and it transplanted the influence of turn-of-the-century Cambridge into Edwardian and post-World War I London. EMF is "the best English novelist of this century, and one of the most acute of its moralists." EMF reveals a strange mixture of qualities and "is one of the most comforting of modern writers, and at the same time one of the most uncomfortable." [Mainly on Spender's connections with Bloomsbury.]

573 S[teinhoff], W[illiam] R. "E. M. Forster: 'The Machine Stops,'" STUDY AIDS FOR TEACHERS FOR "MODERN SHORT STORIES," ed by Marvin Felheim, Franklin Newman, and William Steinhoff (NY: Oxford UP, 1951), pp. 11–12.

In order to escape the danger of making his characters mere abstractions in a prophetic, ideologically oriented work, EMF in "The Machine Stops" limits them so that their identity will not be lost. The machine derives its power from promising to fulfill certain social needs. In the process, people are persuaded to concede their individual freedom (also their sense of integrity and their vitality) for the sake of other apparent values. But the natural impulses and the human will survive even in a regimented regime: Kuno refuses to be wholly conquered by the machine.

574 Tait, Stephen, and Kenneth Allott. "A ROOM WITH A VIEW": A PLAY (Lond: Edward Arnold, 1951).

[Play adapted from EMF's *A Room with a View*. It reveals EMF's mastery of characterization through dialogue and of the comedy-of-manners mode. The Misses Alan become more formidable figures than in the novel and Charlotte Bartlett's subtle hypocrisies register quite clearly. Some interpretative dialogue is excellent, e.g., George Emerson's comment to Lucy Honeychurch about the stabbing in the Piazza Signoria in Florence: "Nobody is likely to be stabbed in Summer Street or Tunbridge Wells ... to convince you that blood's thicker than afternoon tea." Not enough is done with sequences involving music, including Freddy Honeychurch's delightful debunking of the song that Cecil Vyse has given Lucy, "Look not thou on beauty's charming"; and the out-of-doors aspect of the novel is scarcely conveyed. An interesting moderately successful adaptation.]

575 Tillotson, Geoffrey. "Henry James and His Limitations," CRITICISM AND THE NINETEENTH CENTURY (Lond: Athlone P, University of London, 1951; NY: Barnes and Noble, 1952), pp. 244–49.

[Point of departure for this essay is the somewhat negative account by EMF of Henry James in *Aspects of the Novel*. EMF's judgment that the characters lack "fun," carnality, and heroism and that they are too removed from social fact is challenged.]

576 "Untidy Old Bird," TIME, LVIII (19 Nov 1951), 118–19.

In *Two Cheers for Democracy* EMF has written skeptical, urbane, relativistic essays: they are the work of "a man who prefers to stand in the cool draft of a perpetually open mind." He is opposed to absolutist values, but has one absolute of his own: moral courage. EMF is an exponent of excellence and quality with respect to culture, but he would not want any kind of conformity to be imposed.

577 Zabel, Morton Dauwen. "Trophies of the Mind," NATION (NY), CLXXIII (Dec 1951), 480–81.

The title of EMF's *Two Cheers for Democracy* well suggests its prevailing content and its angle of vision and of justice. His praise of democracy is tentative and qualified; it is worth two cheers, not three. EMF's temperament is much like Gide's, whom he praises for his sophistication, flexibility of mind, and relativity of vision. EMF continues to show the traits evident in his work from the beginning: "sympathy in justice, reason in conviction, moderation in loyalty, vivacity in passion." He believes in Freedom, Democracy, Humanity, and culture, but he is wary lest these entities become abstractions and thereby become brutalized or impotent. EMF believes still more in "lower-case realities," "in tolerance, in harmony, in personal relations, and in art." EMF's voice is unmistakable as he speaks in these essays; it reveals a man stubbornly honest and at the same time various and catholic in his interests and tastes. EMF speaks authoritatively in a time of world crisis because he has always been aware of evils and dislocations in the universe at large and in human nature itself. His intelligence is uncomforming, but it is also unyielding when its values are threatened. EMF is seen in a public and social role in this book to a greater extent than before. The book also reveals EMF in his life-long aspect as "the kind of artist who conceives of his art as a mediator between art's rightful superiority to use and the humanity that does not care about art at all." He adopts a reconciling function and knows that the opposite of a desired value may have its provisional truth or applicability. He has always acted in accordance with the principle of "art in action" and reveals that he continues to do so in *Two Cheers.* [Zabel's third essay on EMF, like all his others, is illuminating; it is largely incorporated into "E. M. Forster: The Trophies of the Mind," in CRAFT AND CHARACTER: TEXTS, METHOD, AND VOCATION IN MODERN FICTION (1957), to which this essay gave its title.]

1952

578 C., E. "Brief Mention," FREEMAN (NY), II (11 Aug 1952), 780.

In *Two Cheers for Democracy* EMF questions rather than affirms. He gives new life to an old form by using the techniques of the novelist.

579 Cazes, René. "Comptes Rendus" (Reviews), ÉTUDES ANGLAISES (Paris), V (Aug 1952), 266–67.

In *Two Cheers for Democracy* EMF struggles to make human values prevail, to reject overprecise formulations of them, to choose the least of evils, and to further freedom and liberty. EMF has never surrendered to his inherent pessimism; rather the nihilist has chosen combat. [In French.]

580 Cook, Thomas I. "Two Cheers," HOPKINS REVIEW, VI (Fall 1952), 129–31.

EMF is not politically minded. He tends to regard means as corrupt. Democracy deserves the third cheer withheld from it by EMF, because democracy does encourage all varieties of seeker and creator. [Review of *Two Cheers for Democracy*, negative in tone.]

581 Ferry, David. "The Miracles of E. M. Forster," HARVARD ADVOCATE, CXXXVI (Dec 1952), 8–10, 34–35.

EMF's novels represent "the victory of miracles over experience, the wonderful over the probable, the innocent over the worldly." [This antithesis is somewhat arbitrary and absolute, as is the whole essay.] The way of rationalism and probability is the way of experience, worldliness, and knowledge; the way of irrationalism and improbability, championed by EMF, is the way of inexperience, innocence, and wisdom. When his characters remain innocent they cannot fail; when they lose their innocence they are defeated. Innocence and wisdom are victorious in his novels. [Why innocence and wisdom are to be equated is not demostrated, only asserted.] EMF does not trace the passage from innocence to experience (except in *A Passage to India*). In *A Room with a View* the characters do not have the fullness of lifelike people. We are conscious that they illustrate a truth and that the narrator is manipulating them out of interested ends. Action is denigrated because EMF champions innocence and wisdom; the novel becomes a morality play. Lucy Honeychurch is passive, scarcely human, and acted upon. Charlotte Bartlett, in essence, is the champion bad angel and is a pure abstraction. (Cecil Vyse and Mr. Beebe are also in this camp.) They challenge the good angels, the Emersons (who are as "descended gods or messenger spirits"), and are finally defeated by them. Mr. Emerson saves Lucy by heavenly intervention and by miracle. EMF's novels show us the nature of mystery but do not define it satisfactorily. EMF convincingly analyzes failure, but his successes are not always convincing because they are symbolic and therefore inexplicable, miracles being necessary for them. In *Passage* muddle is confronted, and not evaded, by miracle. The miracle convinces because it brings knowledge and this time dispels innocence.

582 Fuller, John. "E. M. Forster at Seventy," ADELPHI, XXVIII (May 1952), 592–93.

EMF's is "the strangest, the most persistent, the most dominant reputation in contemporary literature." There is a fuller coming to terms with the world in *Two Cheers for Democracy* than in his other books. In earlier books EMF did understand passion and cruelty, but he had been diffident and reserved. EMF is not able to stay pertinaciously with the newer attitudes and values he propounds; perhaps he has not had enough average worldy experience to have full knowledge of modern problems. Perhaps the retirement to Cambridge has isolated him too greatly from his contemporaries. [In part, review of *Two Cheers.*]

583 Hart-Davis, Rupert. HUGH WALPOLE: A BIOGRAPHY (NY & Lond: Macmillan, 1952), pp. 49, 59, 113, 255, 313.

Walpole enjoyed *The Longest Journey* when he read it at Nassenheide [the German home of Elizabeth, Countess von Arnim, where EMF had been Walpole's predecessor as her children's tutor; see Leslie de Charms (1958).] EMF praised THE WOODEN HORSE when Walpole sent him the manuscript. Walpole wrote to Pinker (1914) to complain that Henry James in "The Future of the Novel" slighted Conrad's CHANCE, Lawrence's SONS AND LOVERS, and EMF: "he can put the rest of us in his pocket." In 1924, EMF praised THE OLD LADIES.

584 Hewitt, Douglas. CONRAD: A REASSESSMENT (Lond: Bowes, 1952; 2nd ed, 1968), pp. 132–33.

The classic nineteenth-century novelists were concerned with temporality, especially as it determined and ordered the psychological development of characters responding to the laws of cause and effect. In the work of Joyce, Woolf, EMF (*A Passage to India,*) and Conrad, the processes of fiction are less orderly. The works of these writers proceed more by shifts in time and viewpoint and by recurrent images and verbal patterns; thus, they approximate the richness of lyrical poetry. The echo and wasp images in *Passage* are not concerned with emotional cause and effect, and they often cut across such concern.

585 Johnson, Edgar. CHARLES DICKENS: HIS TRAGEDY AND TRIUMPH (Boston: Little Brown, 1952; Lond: Gollancz, 1953), p. 1148.
In *Aspects of the Novel* EMF criticizes the characters of Dickens for being flat but is forced to admit their depth and Dickens's greatness. Actually, all literary portraits are selections and to a degree "flat"; their reality is a result of the art by which they are conceived. There need not be, for the illusion of reality, any great number of accumulated details, such as EMF posits for "round" characters, whom he tends to regard as aesthetically superior to flat characters.

586 Keir, W. A. S. "*A Passage to India* Reconsidered," CAMBRIDGE JOURNAL, V (April 1952), 426–35; rptd in TWENTIETH CENTURY INTERPRETATIONS OF "A PASSAGE TO INDIA," ed by Andrew Rutherford (Englewood Cliffs, NJ: Prentice-Hall, Spectrum Books, 1970), pp. 33–44.
In India will be found "the strangest experience of all"; it is the essence of this that EMF tries to convey, "the mystery of India, its complexity, its lack of form, its lack of meaning." EMF often does so impressionistically, by suggestion. At Turton's "bridge party" the gap between the races is suggested by the image of the receding arches. The action of the novel forms a complex pattern with clear-cut cause and effect in abeyance. Through Mrs. Moore's experience, EMF shows the inadequacy of the British drawing-room Christianity confronted by India. To Mrs. Moore, good and evil do become the same. She rejects all things, whereas Godbole accepts all things. Neither mode is necessarily EMF's. EMF would say that we can neither include everything as Godbole does nor exclude everything as Mrs. Moore does. There is only irony for the futile halfway house of the Christian missionaries, old Mr. Graysford and young Mr. Sorley, who include some things and would exclude others, such as the wasp. EMF is tender to religion because it expresses, though it does not solve, the complexities of life and suggests connections impossible to attain through other means. Even God seems strange, unexpected, and absurd in India. [Approaches *A Passage to India* first as work of art or as an impression, and then as an argument or political tract or social document. A good though not profound essay; the contrast developed between Mrs. Moore and Godbole is discerning.]

587 Levin, Harry. "Essays on Several Occasions," YALE REVIEW, nsXLI (June 1952), 615–18.
EMF's pejoratives are "childish" and "silly"; his terms of praise are "adult" and "grown-up." EMF admits a descent from, and liking for, such "liberals"

as Butler, the Webbs, Gibbon, Voltaire, and the Milton of the AREOPAGITICA; he also celebrates his own Clapham ancestors. Along with Bertrand Russell's, his is the voice of the "authentic and impenitent British liberal," although he is aware that liberalism is on the defensive. His own qualities are highly civilized as he reveals them in "What I Believe." In his criticism he goes beyond his "self-imposed limitations," proceeding readily from the aesthetic to the ethical. EMF may well be remembered as a moralist from "a bright epoch" before "The Second Darkness." [Review-essay on *Two Cheers for Democracy* and other books of essays.]

588 Louis-Chevrillon, Hedwige. "Revue des Livres" (Book Reviews), ÉTUDES (Paris), CCLXXIII (June 1952), 427–28.
The Longest Journey is dense and complex, with Rickie Elliot getting free ultimately of the chains of convention in his marriage to appreciate again the forces of poetry and humanity. [Review of *Le plus long des Voyages* (*The Longest Journey*), trans by Charles Mauron.] [In French.]

589 Lynskey, Winifred. "Comment and Question," READING MODERN FICTION: THIRTY STORIES WITH STUDY AIDS (NY: Scribner's, 1952), p. 208; also 2nd ed (1957), READING MODERN FICTION: TWENTY-NINE STORIES WITH STUDY AIDS; not included in 4th ed (1968).
[Comments on "The Other Side of the Hedge," stressing EMF's opposition to science and to the mechanistic, materialistic civilization that has followed in the wake of science; stresses also pedometer symbol and EMF's use of the two gates (ivory and horn) motif. Story rptd, pp. 203–8.]

590 Oakeshott, Michael. "Book Reviews," CAMBRIDGE JOURNAL, V (April 1952), 436–38.
The essays in *Two Cheers for Democracy*, if not greatly important in themselves, do reinforce one another in a way that might not have seemed possible if they had not been collected. They reinforce each other as manifestations of a temperament or disposition: "civilized without being overcivilized, detached without being olympian, flexible but not flabby, sympathetic but not sentimental." EMF is suspicious of extremes of any kind, especially that of greatness. The organization of the world for the enjoyment of personal relations is never complete, but these relations are always possible. So EMF is optimistic without being progressive, a rebel without being a reformer. The arguments advanced in favor of this point of view are not arresting, but the point of view is consistently reflected in the style whereby everything is presented as a "personal relationship"; his suspicion of greatness appears in his use of understatement, his distrust of power as a lack of force. But EMF is less large in his sympathies and less serene in manner than his master Montaigne. There is something ultimately

too tentative and incomplete in EMF's work. His skepticism is genuine but not profound enough to be convincing at the level of argument. [Densely written, closely argued, but extremely perceptive discussion.]

591 Riggs, Thomas, Jr. "English Literature Since 1910," THE VOICE OF ENGLAND: A HISTORY OF ENGLISH LITERATURE, by Charles Grosvenor Osgood (NY, Evanston & Lond: Harper & Row, 2nd ed, 1952), pp. 591–630, espec 592, 602, 607–8, 620, 621; 1st ed, 1935, has no references to EMF.

EMF is in the comedy of manners tradition of the novel; he is more conservative in idea and form than D. H. Lawrence. EMF's attack on gentility in the cause of Nature and Eros is more oblique than Lawrence's. The confrontations between convention and vitality take many forms in EMF. His English people are caught off guard in a foreign milieu as they confront atavistic forces. An air of fantasy obtrudes in EMF's work, even in *A Passage to India*, which embodies (or disembodies) undefined and primitive forces that menace the individual but with which he must come to terms.

592 Rolo, Charles J. "A Civilized Man," ATLANTIC MONTHLY, CLXXXIX (Jan 1952), 90.

Two Cheers for Democracy is more impressive as a whole than in its component essays. The book expresses a civilized credo: "a liberalism quietly aglow with moral courage." The essays reveal EMF's distrust of absolutes, his belief in the individual, his passion for art, and his qualified faith in democracy (which is consonant, he feels, with the existence of a spiritual aristocracy).

593 Sandwell, B. K. "E. M. Forster on Society: Cost of State Interference," SATURDAY NIGHT (Toronto), LXVII, No. 23 (15 March 1952), 4–5.

EMF is an interesting thinker in *Two Cheers for Democracy*, "the typical civilized, free, educated man of the age before the cataclysm." The EMF age is already behind us; we are in the post-Forsterian age wherein society and state are the same. The more that society interferes (and it is certain to do so) by virtue of its improved modes of communication, the less will there be Forsters to protest. The penalty of state interference is the extinguishing of the artist.

594 Sisson, C. H. "New Books," WORLD REVIEW (Lond), ns, No. 36 (Feb 1952), 68.

Although some of the essays in *Two Cheers for Democracy* deal with politics, EMF is not really concerned with the world of political action but rather with outer events as they impinge on a narrow circle of people. He is concerned with the great community but barely believes in a world outside his own. He is "exquisite" so long as he stays within this world of his own.

595 Spencer, Hazelton, Walter E. Houghton, and Herbert Barrows (eds). "Edward Morgan Forster," BRITISH LITERATURE, II, FROM BLAKE TO THE PRESENT DAY (Boston: D. C. Heath, 1952), p. 1027; 2nd ed., 1963.

EMF is not to be considered as either Edwardian or Georgian. Rather, he is contemporary in his significance. His works are marked by "a clear intelligence," a desire to expose cant and hypocrisy, by "a warmth of heart," and by an appreciation of "the difficulties inherent in the human situation." He demands courage of his characters as they confront the crises in their lives. ["The Road from Colonus," rptd pp. 1027–32.]

1953

---

596 Adams, J. Donald. "Speaking of Books," NEW YORK TIMES BOOK REVIEW, 27 Sept 1953, p. 2.

The people novelists like are present in sympathetic characters who are often transformations of people actually known in real life. EMF is right in thinking that Tolstoy attains a state of detachment concerning his characters that lesser novelists like Thomas Wolfe fail to reach. A second kind of person, "the person whom I think I am," is the author's voice unmistakably present in a major portion of all fiction. A third sort, the people who irritate the novelist, are well-captured by Sinclair Lewis in his satiric portraits. Despite Tolstoy's attaining it, dispassion is likely to remain an impossible ideal for the novelist. [The three categories of characters discussed are those that EMF said he placed in his fiction. See PARIS REVIEW interview (with P. N. Furbank and F. J. H. Haskell 1953).]

597 Arvin, Newton. "A Private Secretary for the Maharajah," NEW YORK TIMES BOOK REVIEW, 25 Oct 1953, pp. 3, 49.

The Hill of Devi is not a major work but has much of "the novelistic liveliness and intellectual acuteness" that one expects in an EMF work. The book centers on the tragic character of the Maharajah of Dewas State Senior, whose virtues outweighed his limitations.

598 Berland, Alwyn. "James and Forster: The Morality of Class," CAMBRIDGE JOURNAL, VI (Feb 1953), 259–80.

Both Henry James in THE PRINCESS CASAMASSIMA and EMF in *Howards End* deal with class and class conflict: in James the dichotomy is that of revolution versus civilization, in EMF that of commercial civilization versus culture. CASAMASSIMA is a fuller and richer novel than *Howards End*, with its willed symbolism. *Howards End* is not one of the best modern novels; its encapsulated life and its art are of a lower sort than James's. *Howards End* represents England, the Earth as a way of life, and the vital past of England. The great house, Medley, in CASAMASSIMA, is a better realized symbol of place than Howards End house. Henry Wilcox's unfaithfulness to Ruth is too contrived for Margaret's grand denunciation of him to be effective. James is the advocate of civilization in CASAMASSIMA, whereas EMF rejects civilization in *Howards End* for primitive, pastoral values. James feels that culture can be inherited; EMF feels that high intelligence and fine sensibility are determined by the conditions of life, as in Leonard Bast. Bast is killed by a bookcase toppling over him; Hyacinth Robinson (CASAMASSIMA) dies that the bookcase may stand. In *Howards End* each character represents some unique sort of action or thought in the social scene, whereas in CASAMASSIMA the characters are symbols of forces which clash within Hyacinth. The question posed by both men is whether history can compensate for the impaired potentialities of each man. Bast is real in his own terms but not in terms of the action of the novel as a whole or in his relationships to others. *Howards End* wavers between realism and symbolism; the two modes of writing are never fully reconciled. Although the scenes of Leonard with Jacky are well-done, his relationship to the Schlegels is never exactly defined. How England will devolve to Helen Schlegel's son or at what cost to the other characters we are never told. As a novel of the class war it says nothing of the lower class, except that it will triumph. The son is not really classless. He does not bridge the classes since his mother (Helen) does not symbolize the middle class so much as the world of culture. Margaret symbolizes the spiritual aspects of culture, Helen the emotional, Libby the intellectual. The return to the earth is as prominent a theme in *Howards End* as in the earlier books. At the end Margaret's happiness is based more on love than money; connection depends on love, though love may not be enough to bring about connection if other attributes are lacking as they are in Henry Wilcox. In effect, Margaret recruits another to her way of life rather than connecting with him.

Leonard's death makes use of every symbolic strand and thematic concern in the novel. The symbol of honor, the sword, becomes an instrument of dishonor in Charles Wilcox's hands, and the bookcase is the symbol of an irrelevant culture that stifles Leonard's spontaneity. His death is seen on a number of levels that fail to merge. Margaret, at the end, recreates a new life for all at *Howards End*, which she acquires and wills to her nephew. The outer world in other Wilcoxes goes off grudgingly at the end. The inner life is sanctified in the land; Leonard has returned to the land in the form of his child. Love and Death—EMF's transcendent values—thus ultimately triumph, as do the inner world and the earth. Henry James regards civilization as "purifier and censor." It can also be regarded as a mask behind which lurks a sinister reality: this is the demonic vision. Or one can adopt the beatific view which bypasses civilization and disregards the terrifying vision; under such aegis the pastoral vision stresses that man is good and that civilization is unnecessary. EMF advocates the pastoral vision, though occasional instances of the demonic obtrude. EMF's characters are victorious over civilization but do not represent triumphs of civilization; his evil characters are dupes of civilization. D. H. Lawrence [letter to EMF (20 Sept 1922)] was right in regarding Henry Wilcox as essentially an innocent, a man corrupted from the outside only, by civilization. [Extended analysis of CASAMASSIMA. A subtle, interesting, provocative article, and essential to any consideration of EMF's relationship to James, much superior, for example, to V. A. Shahane's "Formative Influences on E. M. Forster: Henry James— A Study in Ambivalence" (1961).]

599 Blythe, Ronald. "Shelley Plain," NEW STATESMAN AND NATION, nsL (15 Oct 1953), p. 466.
[Recounts a meeting with EMF, who was kind to the tongue-tied Blythe.]

600 Bowen, Robert O. "Kipling's India Revisited," ACCENT, XIII (Autumn 1953), 268–69.
The value of *The Hill of Devi* is its revelation of the mind and heart of an English public school man active in Indian affairs. The tone of the book is one of propriety and restraint; it shies away from the discovery of the meaningful. EMF and the Maharajah of Dewas State Senior are vastly different people, yet similar in standing aside from life. [Criticism interesting in view of EMF's well-known hostility to the English public school.]

601 Bridge, Ursula (ed.). W. B. YEATS AND T. STURGE MOORE: THEIR CORRESPONDENCE 1901–1937 (Lond: Routledge & Kegan Paul; NY: Oxford UP, 1953), pp. 20–21.
T. Sturge Moore to W. B. Yeats (26 April 1911), EMF ought to be nominated (along with Shaw) to the Royal Society of Literature. EMF has always been seriously interested in literature and has a following of the right sort.

602 Burlingham, Russell. FORREST REID: A PORTRAIT AND A STUDY (Lond: Faber 1953), pp. 19, 20, 37, 78, 158, 165, 166, 167, 170, 172, 208, 219, 229, 237, 249.
In Forrest Reid's novels morality is less explicit than in EMF's novels. In EMF's novels morals are less integrated into his art than inculcated by it. In EMF's novels plot and moral are identical and cannot exist without each other. EMF lacks Reid's sensuous delight in beauty [this is debatable] and his mystical immersion in nature [again too absolute a statement]. Both

novelists have common ground in their affinity for youth, naturalness, and innocence as opposed to intolerance, narrowness, and unimaginativeness. Both novelists protest against the pretentious. There are parallels between the persecutions of Denis in THE BRACKNELS and of Gennaro in "The Story of a Panic." Both novelists believe in EMF's aristocracy of "the sensitive, the considerate and the plucky" ["What I Believe," *Two Cheers for Democracy.*] EMF's novels are about ideas and also are a criticism of life; the result is that EMF eventually stepped out of fiction into public life, for which Reid cared little, and stopped writing novels. EMF also lacked Reid's interest in the metaphysical [this again is too categorical a statement]. [Numerous other references, especially to EMF's essays on Reid in *Abinger Harvest* and *Two Cheers.*]

603 Fraser, G. S. "The Novel: Indian Summer," "The Trends of Criticism: The Bloomsbury Tradition," THE MODERN WRITER AND HIS WORLD (Lond: Derek Verschoyle, 1953; NY: Criterion Books, 1955), pp. 58–70, espec 66–70; 313–18; 2nd ed (Harmondsworth, Middlesex & Baltimore: Penguin Books, 1964) revises and expands basic discussion.

In EMF we have the best revelation in literature of the Edwardian Age. He is interested in the rational solution to moral problems rather than in philosophical problems. He is interested in the perverse element in human psychology that causes "nice" people to behave detestably. His correct people are not just afraid of passion but of mental disloyalty to their inherited code. His chief theme, emphatic in *A Room with a View,* is the individual's need to respond positively to a stranger, at the cost even of sacrificing tradition to do so. The inability of his characters to respond creatively to others is comic in *Room,* tragic in *A Passage to India.* In *Passage* EMF emphasizes the difficulties in the way of achieving individual sincerity and loyalty. A note of sadness intrudes; even the most enlightened individual is unfairly weighed down by conventions. EMF is the best English novelist of the liberal tradition, and he stresses the difficulties involved in determining one's own conduct and in living up to his responsibilities. In the upper middle classes, in administrators, professional men, and scholars, this liberal tradition is seen at its best. EMF notes the barriers to communication and the fairness in the English professional and administrative classes that enables them to break down these barriers. EMF is the novelist not only of "isolated individualism" but of a tradition of moral independence which has helped the cause of social justice.

"The Trends of Criticism: The Bloomsbury Tradition": The two chief criticisms frequently made of Bloomsbury are that it is highbrow and that it is sterile and aggressively clever. The criticisms are not greatly relevant. The members of Bloomsbury were belated upper-middle-class Victorian agnostics, emancipating themselves from Victorian Puritanism. Their "religion" was that of the good life, deriving from G. E. Moore and stressing the cult of the personal and the aesthetic. EMF's own criticism is minor; it has charm but intellectual limitations in its acceptances and rejections. Like Virginia Woolf as critic, EMF is best when dealing with moderate-size figures. Perhaps Bloomsbury was most lacking in original and creative thought. [Suggestive brief account.]

604 Fremantle, Anne. "A Civilization," COMMONWEAL, LIX (4 Dec 1953), 232–34.

In *The Hill of Devi* EMF sees nonpolitical men neither as gods nor as beasts but perhaps as both. The depth and the dimensions established in the book are remarkable. EMF truly understands India in a way not possible today; her captivity, even if it was vile, was a form of communication. EMF has "absolute pitch," a quality of mind that enables him to convey the complexity of his Indian characters.

605 Furbank, P. N., and F. J. H. Haskell. "E. M. Forster: The Art of Fiction I," PARIS REVIEW, No. 1 (Spring 1953), 27–41; rptd as "E. M. Forster," in WRITERS AT WORK: THE PARIS REVIEW INTERVIEWS, ed by Malcolm Cowley (NY: Viking P, 1958), pp. 23–35; in part in A LIBRARY OF LITERARY CRITICISM: MODERN BRITISH LITERATURE, ed by Ruth Z. Temple and Martin Tucker (NY: Frederick Ungar, 1966), I, 312–14; and in part in E. M. FORSTER: "A PASSAGE TO INDIA": A CASEBOOK, ed by Malcolm Bradbury (Lond: Macmillan, Casebook Series, 1970), pp. 27–31.

EMF did not finish *Arctic Summer* because he could not settle upon his major event. Such an event is necessary for organizing a novel, to provide an area in which concentration can take place. Such an event, the incidents in the Marabar Caves, did organize *A Passage to India:* "They were something to focus everything up: they were to engender an event like an egg." His antithesis for writing fiction is this: to be "true" and "lovable" in analyzing a dilemma. EMF has had characters run away with him. Some of his technical problems: how to make Rickie Elliot and Stephen Wonham intimate in *The Longest Journey,* how to get Helen Schlegel back to Howards End house. The Hindu festival in *Passage* was architecturally necessary; a "lump" was needed, but there ought to have been more of it. He had no personal knowledge of the home life of Leonard and Jacky Bast, but he believes that he brought it off. He had to be removed from India in space in order to complete *Passage.* EMF feels that he handled violence acceptably in *Where Angels Fear to Tread* and that the Marabar Caves scene provided an acceptable substitute for violence in *Passage.* Gerald's death in *Journey* had to be passed by; perhaps the sudden death was not the right way of doing it. The seduction of Helen Schlegel in *Howards End* was the result of a need to surprise Margaret and the reader, but he may have sacrificed too much to secure this effect. He has not been consciously symbolical as some of his critics have implied; he did not think of Mrs. Moore having further echoes in her children. He does not keep a notebook but does refer to diaries and letters. He never says of an experience that it might be useful in a novel. He has, however, been inspired on the spot, as in the writing of "The Story of a Panic," "The Road from Colonus," and "The Rock." He is too unvisual to imagine clear-cut patterns for his novels. In his use of repeated motifs, he has been influenced by music and musical methods. He writes only when inspired. *A Room with a View* came first to him, but only half of it. He usually finds names for his characters at the start, though sometimes he will run through several names before the final one is determined. Characters quite often begin as real people but then trail off into book characters. [Originals of some EMF characters are given.] He has gotten three types of characters in his fiction: the people he likes, the person he thinks that he is, and the people who irritate him [see also K. W. Gransden, "E. M. Forster at Eighty" (1959).] Those who describe the variety of life inclusively and dispassionately, like Tolstoy, are the real novelists. Rickie Elliot, Philip Herriton (*Angels*), and Cecil Vyse (*Room*) have elements of EMF in them. He likes thinking about the further fates of some characters, such as Rickie, Stephen, and Margaret Schlegel. A novelist is not really conscious of his own technical expertise. From Jane Austen EMF learned the possibilities of domestic humor, from Proust the modern subconscious way of looking at character. He did not read Freud or Jung. EMF admires the way in which one thing opens into another in Meredith's novels. He is more interested in a writer's achievement than in his development; he is interested in himself only as producer of books. He regrets that the corpus of his work is not larger, but he has enjoyed writing. [Description of EMF's quarters at King's College Cambridge. This is the most comprehensive of the EMF interviews and is indispensable for understanding him and his work.]

606 Fussell, Paul, Jr. "E. M. Forster's Mrs. Moore: Some Suggestions," PHILOLOGICAL QUARTERLY, XXXII (Oct 1953), 388–95.

Mrs. Moore in *A Passage to India* can be identified with the theosophist Helena Petrovna Blavatsky (1831–1891). To Mrs. Wilcox (*Howards End*) EMF added elements from Mme. Blavatsky in forming Mrs. Moore. Among the parallels are these: both women were fond of playing patience but did so irritably; both visited India, had extraordinary experiences in caves, and had telephathic perceptions there; both had similar critical views of the British in India; both left India when ill; both wished for a union of East and West to solve the problem of British India; and both came to be regarded as demigoddesses because of their wishing to bridge, intuitively, the gap between East and West. [Evidence is interesting but hardly conclusive.]

607 Garnett, David. THE GOLDEN ECHO (Lond: Chatto & Windus, 1953; NY: Harcourt, Brace, 1954), pp. 225–26 (NY ed).
In the excitement of proposing marriage a Cambridge don ran naked about the woods before declaring himself later that day. EMF's novels are thus true to life, and so [Garnett wonders,] "Did Pan visit the dons before they read Forster, or only after they had read him?" [Book is valuable for its recounting of Garnett's associations with those in the Bloomsbury circle in its early days until about 1915. See also the two succeeding installments of the autobiography, THE FLOWERS OF THE FOREST (1955) and THE FAMILIAR FACES (1962).]

608 Godden, Rumer, "The Eternal Charm of a Gilbert-and-Sullivan Kingdom in India," NEW YORK HERALD TRIBUNE BOOK REVIEW, 1 Nov 1953, p. 5.
The Hill of Devi is absorbing as EMF is drawn into the tawdry but fascinating Indian scene: the birth of the heir, the festival, the official insult, and the intrigues and evil which sapped the idealism of the Maharajah of Dewas State Senior. The offhand manner and the attention to details of the moment interfere with the dramatic rendering of EMF's subject and with making his people live. The book has little life but great depth and dignity and an "afterglow" that remains in the mind and heart.

609 Hartley, L. P. "Life with the Maharajah," TIME AND TIDE, XXXIV (24 Oct 1953), 1392; rptd in E. M. FORSTER: THE CRITICAL HERITAGE, ed by Philip Gardner (Lond & Boston: Routledge & Kegan Paul, 1973), pp. 416–18.
Whether EMF is great or not, he is one of the most "enchanting" writers of our age. His refusal to be great may arise from his disinclination to reconcile "a serious intention and an 'amusing surface.' " EMF refuses to be great if he must sacrifice his desire to be amusing. In *The Hill of Devi* we get not only "melody, or perception of the truth," but we get a story as well. His two main subjects are friendship and religion, and he has caught "the waywardness, playfulness and inconclusiveness of the Indian mind, and its awareness of mystery." [Perceptive review.]

610 Hughes, Richard. "Mr. Forster's Quandary," SPECTATOR (Lond), CXCI (16 Oct 1953), 432–33; rptd in abrgd form in E. M. FORSTER: THE CRITICAL HERITAGE, ed by Philip Gardner (Lond & Boston: Routledge & Kegan Paul, 1973), pp. 413–16.
Is *The Hill of Devi* the masterpiece we expect from EMF, or is it a casual and slight work? EMF's 1921 visit to India is reconstructed with insight and intensity. The character of Bapu Sahib (the Maharajah of Dewas State Senior) is more real than any of the people in *A Passage to India*, who were,

perhaps designedly, types. The justification of *Devi* is that it opens up "a way of living and feeling and thinking and worshipping that were not there already." The artistic method is subtle; it is almost impossible to define how EMF produces his effects. Whether *Devi* is a minor or major work no reviewer can determine.

611 Jungel, Renate. "Die Zeitstruktur in den Romanen E. M. Forsters" (Time Structure in E. M. Forster's Novels). Unpublished dissertation, Graz University, 1953.
By means of clearly demarcated chronology, from chapter to chapter and episode to episode, EMF creates a time-world of his own for his analysis of human problems; he does not rely on an historical time order. [In German.]

612 Kapur, R. K. "The Other India," NEW REPUBLIC, CXXIX (2 Nov 1953), 28–29.
In *The Hill of Devi* we have an act of historical recreation; the editing of letters gives the book movement. EMF's enthusiasm for India yields to despair at the dying culture of the princely state and the insults heaped upon it by an unimaginative and insensitive imperialism. There is a close relationship between the contents of *Devi* and the characters and incidents in *A Passage to India*, especially the depiction in both of the monsoon season and the Gokul Ashtami ceremonies. The tone of the letters in *Devi* is more flippant, irreligious, and mocking than the tone in *Passage*. In both books the Indians have charm but little dignity, and the English delight in being ignorant, insensitive, and rude.

613 Kettle, Arnold. "E. M. Forster: *A Passage to India*," AN INTRODUCTION TO THE ENGLISH NOVEL, Vol. II: HENRY JAMES TO THE PRESENT (Lond: Hutchinson, Hutchinson University Library; NY: Longmans, Green, 1953; 2nd ed, 1967 with rvd bibliography; NY: Harper, Harper Torchbook, 1960), pp. 152–63; rptd in part in TWENTIETH CENTURY INTERPRETATIONS OF "A PASSAGE TO INDIA": A COLLECTION OF CRITICAL ESSAYS, ed by Andrew Rutherford (Englewood Cliffs, NJ: Prentice-Hall, Spectrum Books, 1970), pp. 45–49.
A Passage to India is EMF's best book; *Where Angels Fear to Tread* is also a success; *Howards End* is his least good book. Is it possible for an Indian to be friends with an Englishman? This is the theme of *Passage*. EMF's characters fail to master life, perhaps more than necessary; the result is that life is made to seem more casual are more arbitrary than it really is. To a certain point the arbitrariness is a virtue: the violence, horror, deaths, and indifference of the cosmos reinforce the unexpected quality of experience and counteract the urbane comedy of EMF's narrative manner. The rela-

tionship between Aziz and Fielding does not survive when the arbitrariness in the way of understanding is removed; imperialism corrupts all that it touches. Yet the construction of *Passage* is not arbitrary. The themes and symbols are skillfully used in the novel; EMF is particularly good in imagining the highly significant incident (e.g., Fielding's tea party). The atmosphere is one of "profound skepticism"; the negative side comes through superbly, the positive does not do so; worldliness and a "tough delicacy of feeling" predominate. EMF is honest, sophisticated, and realistic in depicting personal relationships. His characters are sometimes too relaxed, wistful, and anti-heroic; he tones down or evades significant issues because at times they may give rise to humbug. The Mrs. Moore–Hindu theme represents an attempt by a liberal agnostic to get beyond his own skepticism. The vagueness in the Mrs. Moore–Godbole material is a defect [questionable; the tentativeness and humility here, which Kettle mentions, may be more of a value for other readers.] [Some insights, but does not achieve the depth of the best accounts of *Passage*.]

614 "Letters from India," TIMES LITERARY SUPPLEMENT (Lond), 16 Oct 1953, p. 654.

The achievements of the Maratha Princes are being forgotten now that they have lost power, but *The Hill of Devi* preserves something of their character and culture. The book also answers the question as to where EMF acquired his understanding of India expressed in *A Passage to India;* it was his experiences in Dewas State Senior that gave him this knowledge. His letters and diary "serve to immortalize a fantastic, fairy-tale-like, but now vanished chapter in the evolution of modern India." The abuses of personal power frustrated EMF, while he felt admiration for the person and suffered as he saw tragedy overtake the Maharajah. EMF was powerless to help a friend whose virtues caused a disaster that a lesser man might have escaped.

615 Liddell, Robert. SOME PRINCIPLES OF FICTION (Lond: Jonathan-Cape, 1953), pp. 37, 75, 97–98, 115–16, 139–47; rptd in ROBERT LIDDELL ON THE NOVEL WITH AN INTRODUCTION BY WAYNE C. BOOTH (Chicago: University of Chicago P, 1969).

The artist, as he is depicted in literature, is not always a person of the highest intelligence; his mind, like Rickie Elliot's in *The Longest Journey*, is imaginative rather than philosophical. There is more carnality in Jane Austen than in EMF. This element is lacking in EMF where it is necessary, in depicting Helen Schlegel's relationship with Leonard Bast and in presenting Margaret Schlegel's momentary attraction to a waiter. [EMF's essay on Forrest Reid is quoted appreciatively.]

616 "The Listener's Book Chronicle," LISTENER, L (22 Oct 1953), 695.

Few Englishmen would have come to accept so easily as EMF did the muddle and the chaos that is India; but if he found muddle and chaos, he also found warmth and affection. Richness and variety are part of *The Hill of Devi*, though sometimes the approach is too allusive and casual for maximum effectiveness.

617 Longaker, Mark, and Edwin C. Bolles. "Fiction 1918–1950: Edward Morgan Forster," CONTEMPORARY ENGLISH LITERATURE (NY: Appleton-Century-Crofts, Handbooks of Literature, 1953), pp. 323–27; also 303, 346, 424.

EMF's work is Edwardian in time yet contemporary in temper and feeling, especially in his protest against authority. He writes novels of ideas, relying on character and discussion rather than plot. In this respect EMF is similar to Meredith. *Howards End* is his best novel, which analyzes the failure of relations between two British families and, by analogy, of all human relations. *A Passage to India* dramatizes the power of conventions to keep the races apart; the inconclusiveness of the novel is striking. His essays reveal "a generous culture" and wide range; he is best when dealing with character, at his worst as a critic [most critics on EMF would disagree]. He establishes ease and intimacy with the reader. [Conventional biographical summary. Bland account.]

618 Maclean, Hugh. "The Structure of *A Passage to India*," UNIVERSITY OF TORONTO QUARTERLY XXII (Jan 1953), 157–71; rptd in PERSPECTIVES ON E. M. FORSTER'S "A PASSAGE TO INDIA," ed by V. A. Shahane (NY: Barnes & Noble, 1968), pp. 19–33.

Whitman's "Passage to India" describes the movement of EMF's *A Passage to India* to some kind of transcendence. Its tendency, like EMF's book, is optimistic. Part I, "Mosque," in *Passage* is dominated by Aziz, who is emotional; even his thought has an emotional cast, as he conceives everything in black and white. The spirit of this part is negative; separation is emphasized; harmony is absent. Fielding is the spokesman for Part II, "Caves," representing the force of logic and intellect. At the Caves Adela Quested is overwhelmed by the forces on her mind—love, marriage, sensuality—when she enters; as a result she thinks that a rape has taken place there. Mrs. Moore's experiences in the Cave result in radical disillusionment, withdrawal from life, and a yearning for death. Only after death can she become a reconciling influence and free good influences to act in a positive way. In Part III, "Temple," intuition, represented by Godbole, replaces the emotion and logic of the first two sections. Aziz and Fielding are now drawn into the complex of infinite love. The drift of the novel is to stress the need for men to relax their efforts to impose form on life and to allow life to take on its own form. [Maclean's method is descriptive; it is difficult to separate out from his discourse the points that he wishes to make. His method, associating each book with one specific force, and followed by Glen O. Allen, "Structure, Symbol, and Theme in E. M. Forster's *A Passage to India*" (1955) and by Keith Hollingsworth "*A Passage to India:* The Echoes in the Marabar Caves" (1962), seems to me to be reductive and false to the spirit of the novel.]

619 McConkey, James R. "The Novels of E. M. Forster," DISSERTATION ABSTRACTS, XIII (1953), 811–12. Unpublished dissertation, University of Iowa, 1953; see McConkey, THE NOVELS OF E. M. FORSTER (1957).

620 "Mr. Forster in India," TIMES (Lond), 17 Oct 1953, p. 9.
The Hill of Devi can be read as a vivid recreation of a bygone age or as a personal tragedy. The Maharajah of Dewas State Senior was likable and impulsive, but inefficient as ruler. EMF was on his side, but there were grounds for official impatience and irritation. EMF is a vivid letter writer and open to every impression.

621 Muehl, John Frederick. "Old Tyrannies Dies," SATURDAY REVIEW (NY), XXXVI (12 Dec 1953), 12.
In *The Hill of Devi* EMF traces the decline and fall of the Maharajah of Dewas State Senior from "quaint inefficiency to the inevitable extremes of capricious despotism." The collapse of this feudal regime also anticipated that of the British Raj. EMF also makes us feel that he was indeed betrayed by fate when the facts of life at the court caused him to pass from enthusiasm about his Indian experience to cynicism. Inevitably this was EMF's progress as it was any other Englishman's in India; he was no more fortunate in the consequences to his humanism than was Fielding in *A Passage to India*. [Perceptive discussion.]

622 Plomer, William. "Books in General," NEW STATESMAN AND NATION, nsXLVI (17 Oct 1953), 457–58.
The Hill of Devi is important because it sheds light on EMF's most significant and influential book, *A Passage to India*. The Maharajah of Dewas State Senior and EMF are the two most important figures in *Devi*. EMF reveals himself in all his work as a man "with a forceful, complex, and altogether fresh comment to make about human beings." He knows how they behave and has also an idea of how they ought to behave. He is more important as critical commentator, philosopher, and moralist than as yarn-spinner. Submitting as he does to the dictates of the heart, he endows his work, without our quite realizing it perhaps, with a revolutionary dimension. In the letters in the book there is playfulness and gaiety. Confidence, affection, and intimacy are the most prized qualities developed between Bapu Sahib (the Maharajah) and EMF. The flowers die in the court grounds

because of Indian (and British) inefficiency; their fate is emblematic of the dying of the local civilization as a result of inefficiency, incompetence, and extravagance. The showpiece of the book is the description of the Gokul Ashtami festival. In this sequence EMF tries to understand religious emotion and to make allowances for it. [Excellent article for understanding EMF.]

623 Poore, Charles. "Books of the Times," NEW YORK TIMES, 22 Oct 1953, p. 27.

The Hill of Devi might have been called "The Maharajah and I"; it is "a superb memoir of fantastic experiences in the princely India of far away and long ago." The fantastic quality of EMF's experiences recalls ALICE IN WONDERLAND. He wished to achieve full identification with India; the humor in the letters composing the book is meant for the amusement of others. His work as Secretary to the Maharajah of Dewas State Senior was incongruous with his abilities; he also had little success as sponsor of the arts at Court.

624 "Prince of India," NEWSWEEK, XLII (26 Oct 1953), 119–20.

EMF was wise in *The Hill of Devi* to present not his mellowed second thoughts about the India that he had known as a young man but his first thoughts as he had recorded them in his letters and diaries. These reveal "the simplicity of genius." An element of strain developed on his second visit as a result of the ill-advised "improvements" taken up before EMF's arrival. On the second visit the Maharajah of Dewas State Senior became more boisterous and more mystical, EMF more irritable. The tragic end to the Maharajah's career is presented movingly.

625 Rama Rau, Santha. "A Tribute to Ghosts," NATION (NY), CLXXVII (14 Nov 1953), 403.

The Hill of Devi is a sketch book for *A Passage to India*. In the first part of *Devi*, a callowness and a vexed incomprehension about India obtrude; both are states of mind foreign to the mature EMF. The book with its comic and frustrating occurrences, the account of the destruction of the Maharajah of Dewas State Senior, and the moving portrait of the Maharajah (whom EMF loved and admired, whose jokes puzzled him, whose kindness and manners appealed to him, whose administration he deplored, and whose philosophy and religion he did not understand), takes on stature with EMF's return to India. *Devi* is characterized by the undramatic, the suggested, the never-realized climax. It is about a minor prince in a minor situation whose significance for EMF was great, great also for us in some lights. *Devi* is important as "a tribute to ghosts" and as the raw material of a great novelist. [Excellent discussion.]

626 Rantavaara, Irma. VIRGINIA WOOLF AND BLOOMSBURY (Helsinki: Annales Academiae Fennicae, 1953), pp. 28, 34, 42–48, 51*n*, 55–56, 63, 64–65, 68*n*, 83–84, 89, 92, 97*n*, 114, 126–36, 153.
EMF describes accurately in *Goldsworthy Lowes Dickinson* the Cambridge of J. M. E. McTaggart, Nathaniel Wedd, G. E. Moore, and Goldsworthy Lowes Dickinson. *The Longest Journey* also captures the essence of this era at Cambridge. EMF is centrally part of the Bloomsbury Group, and not just on its outer fringes, by virtue of his temperament and underlying values. EMF is indebted to G. E. Moore [although EMF says he never read Moore] for his moral and aesthetic outlook, and there are close parallels between his views on art and those of Clive Bell. There are close similarities between his novels and the most Jamesean and least experimental of Virginia Woolf's novels, NIGHT AND DAY.

627 "Recent Books: Mr. Forster in India," TIMES (Lond), 17 Oct 1953, p. 9.
The Hill of Devi is both an acute account of a vanished age and a sketch for a personal tragedy, in the career of the Maharajah of Dewas State Senior. EMF displays detachment and much wit. EMF overrates the Maharajah, but his motive for doing so—extreme affection—is understandable.

628 Rolo, Charles J. "A Passage to India," ATLANTIC MONTHLY, CXCII (Nov 1953), 108.
In *The Hill of Devi* EMF has shaped unpromising materials (letters written on his visits to India in 1912 and 1921) into a memorable picture of a vanished civilization. He recreates vividly the personality of the Maharajah of Dewas State Senior, who is interesting, if not the genius and saint that EMF thought him to be. The book is noteworthy for containing source materials for *Passage to India*.

629 Rosselli, John. "Miss Schlegel, Meet Mr. Angus Wilson," NEW STATESMAN AND NATION, nsXLV (14 March 1953), 290–91.
[Hilarious but not altogether fair satire of the Schlegel sisters and *Howards End*. The sisters have survived as maiden lady and widow into the postwar 1950s. Angus Wilson as modern liberal humanist and novelist visits the Schlegel sisters in old age. They have been able to keep one meadow at Howards End; the "new town" houses are only a few hundred yards away; Mr. Wilson must feel that the aspect of the house inside is that of "disorder without heat . . . stagnant"; Margaret still feels, as she might have forty-five years ago, that " 'things have got better in so many ways; we might still muddle through.' "]

630 S[cott]-J[ames], R. A. "Edward Morgan Forster," CASSELL'S ENCYCLOPEDIA OF LITERATURE, ed by S. H. Steinberg (Lond: Cas-

sell, 1953); as CASSELL'S ENCYCLOPEDIA OF WORLD LITERATURE
(NY: Funk & Wagnalls), II, 1784; rvd ed as CASSELL'S ENCY-
CLOPEDIA OF WORLD LITERATURE, ed by J. Buchanan-Brown (Lond:
Cassell; NY: William Morrow, 1973), with rvd bibliography, II,
489.
EMF's chief subject is the conflict between the spontaneous and the inhibit-
ed. In his work gradations occur from light comedy to beautiful descriptions
to terror. He emphasizes the place as well as the persons. In *A Passage to
India* the conflict is not between the British and the Indians, but between
personality and tribalism.

> **631** Spender, Stephen. "Movements and Influences in English Lit-
> erature, 1927–1952," BOOKS ABROAD, (University of Oklahoma),
> XXVII (Winter 1953), 6–32, espec 14–18.

EMF is aware of the evil of power but sees no solution to our political
problems except through the use of power. He believes in personal relations,
but there is a growing pessimism regarding them in *A Passage to India.*
After this novel EMF saw that the problems of living could only be solved
"by power accompanied by impersonal ruthlessness and violence." For him
this realization was an unsatisfactory basis for creativity; he saw no future
in fiction for the personal values that had inspired him. In *Abinger Harvest*
and *Two Cheers for Democracy* he saw the world destroying his values and
was led to support causes that he had regarded as stopgaps, the least of
several evils. His growing political rather than cultural orientation has
forced EMF to support communism against fascism, democracy against
authoritarianism. To give the present world a satisfying projection in art,
EMF would have to write a tragedy; and he does not believe, as writers of
tragedy must, that the spirit can triumph over those physically defeated by
life. Unlike EMF, Yeats took the side of things, and of the tyrants who
would preserve them, rather than of the people. Like Yeats, EMF saw
danger in the challenge to the social order that also threatened the intellectual order which produces art; but he could not agree to preserve art at the
cost of oppression of the many. EMF is on the side of modern victims,
though in being so he must endure a bureaucratic socialism that is often an
enemy to art and distinction. [A shrewd analysis that is part of an extended
survey of English literary history for the period 1927–1952.]

> **632** Spender, Stephen. "Personal Relations and Public Powers,"
> THE CREATIVE ELEMENT: A STUDY OF VISION, DESPAIR, AND OR-
> THODOXY AMONG SOME MODERN WRITERS (Lond: Hamish Hamil-
> ton, 1953), pp. 77–91; rptd in part in A LIBRARY OF LITERARY
> CRITICISM: MODERN BRITISH LITERATURE, ed by Ruth Z. Temple and
> Martin Tucker (NY: Frederick Ungar, 1966), I, 311–12.

EMF's values are provisional. Though he believes in an aristocracy of the mind and heart, he voices his belief only in a whisper. EMF "resists—with a deceptive air of ineffectiveness—the crudely powerful methods of business and politics; he rejects the simplifications of spiritual salvationism, whether in religion or in art; and he reinforces human relations and solitude." He insists also on the double aspect of things; "that Faith with a big F may fail if it deceives the faithful into thinking that they can govern the world by Christian principles; but that with a little f it may enable one to stick to one's friends and to enjoy the better rather than the worse life." He has been criticized by both revolutionaries and conservatives for his mediating position. He is uncompromising about the great importance of personal and aesthetic values. Personal relations produce "the concentric circles of a human comedy including hell, purgatory, and paradise." Hell would be the "panic and emptiness" often mentioned in *Howards End;* Purgatory would be the domain where Henry Wilcox dwells after his exposure and before he wins his way back into Margaret's heart; and Paradise would be the emotional aura and spiritual significance investing Howards End house itself. EMF's comedy is neither Dante's divine comedy nor Balzac's human one, but rather a "Human-and-Divine" sort. His most sublime characters are those who are alone with themselves, who understand others rather than commune with them. Awareness of a mystery that is religious in essence provides the ultimate center of the books and of his commanding characters; but this awareness does not make EMF a mystic, a dogmatist, nor an authoritarian irrationalist (like Kafka). The center of his vision is love, but "love which only attains definition within a relationship." Morality also does not follow fixed rules; his novels emphasize the contradictory elements in experience yet also the need to judge it, in spite of its refractory quality. In EMF's novels the moral situation results in the moment of revelation and does not consist in good people posed against bad people. In EMF's work, for a character to feel or act rightly in a moment of action "means the triumph of values which are realized in the action." Some of EMF's chief values are these: "affection, truth (with a small t); respect for passion (in the physical as well as the spiritual sense); love of aesthetic beauty; reverence for the past; freedom."

In EMF, personal relations "imply affection, loyalty, and sometimes a sharing of values which amounts to shared vision." They imply also a Christian ethic divorced from orthodoxy. Sometimes they act as a mediating force to bridge attitudes and values that seem to be irreconcilable. They can become tragic when social forms and edicts intervene. In *Howards End* and *A Passage to India* the force of power and the forces representing personal values are imaginatively projected into believable characters and are wonderfully balanced. But EMF fails to make the connection firm between the two and to show how the personal values can prevail in a world where all exists in terms of power. The public and private worlds are sometimes too far apart in EMF's novels; he has never created "a character in which his two worlds, the public and private, connect and meet on a high level of explicitness and conscience." This limiting of a wider problem to a purely personal sphere accounts for the unreality of the epilogue in *Howards End.* The impression emerging from EMF's fiction is that personal values cannot solve the problem of society and that society cannot tolerate personal values. Yet he suggests, too, that they can and must prevail. His uncertainty about their power to do so may have inhibited him from writing fiction after 1924. [An important essay, rarely listed in EMF bibliographies.]

> **633** Strong, L. A. G. "E. M. Forster," PERSONAL REMARKS (NY: Liveright; Toronto: Smithers & Bonnellie; Lond: Peter Nevill, 1953), pp. 205–9.

EMF was part of the generation whose "character has been to hate fecundity, deprecate romance, sneer at the grand manner, and stake everything on will and intellect. Lytton Strachey was its historian, THE WASTE LAND its epic, its favoured critics a small group of dons at Cambridge, and, final perversity, it chose E. M. Forster as its novelist." He has not, however, been in sympathy with the attitudes and values of this generation. His own direction has been positive; he has always attacked the fears that lead to conformity, the inability to accept experience, and the cultural inhibition engendered by emotional inhibition. EMF's defense of order and benevolence is "religious"; this order is best expressed for EMF in the work of art. Trilling's view of EMF emphasizes too greatly the intellectual element. [Remarks on EMF occasioned by Lionel Trilling's E. M. FORSTER (1943).]

> **634** Thompson, Ralph. "Other New Books to Know About," BOOK OF THE-MONTH CLUB NEWS, Nov 1953, p. 6.

The Hill of Devi is a remarkable document, casual in approach and seasoned with a dry, "pawky" wit. EMF evokes well the vanished India of "spoiled princelings" and "bumbling, top-lofty, apoplectic British colonials." He appreciated this India but saw its shortcomings. *Devi* is a rare combination of personal history and "the truths of political history."

> **635** Walker, Gordon. "Three Views of India," CHRISTIAN SCIENCE MONITOR, 31 Dec 1953, p. 7.

The Hill of Devi is an absorbing book with its detailed presentation of eroded aristocracy against which modern India still is struggling. The book has brilliant vignettes, though the style is less brilliant than in EMF's other books.

> **636** Wasserman, Earl R. THE FINER TONE: KEATS' MAJOR POEMS (Baltimore: Johns Hopkins UP; Toronto: Burns & MacEachern; Lond: Oxford UP, 1953), p. 228.

The difficulty of understanding works like Emily Bronte's WUTHERING HEIGHTS and *A Passage to India* results from our not yet bringing to these works "the proper controlling cosmos" created by the author of each book.

637 White, Gertrude M. *"A Passage to India:* Analysis and Revaluation," PUBLICATIONS OF THE MODERN LANGUAGE ASSOCIATION, LXVIII (Sept 1953), 641–57; rptd in PERSPECTIVES ON E. M. FORSTER'S "A PASSAGE TO INDIA," ed by V. A. Shahane (NY: Barnes & Noble, 1968), pp. 1–17; rpt in E. M. FORSTER: "A PASSAGE TO INDIA," A CASEBOOK, ed by Malcolm Bradbury (Lond: Macmillan, Casebook Series, 1970), pp. 132–53; and in TWENTIETH CENTURY INTERPRETATIONS OF "A PASSAGE TO INDIA," ed by Andrew Rutherford (Englewood Cliffs, NJ: Prentice-Hall, Spectrum Books, 1970), pp. 50–67.

The dialectical pattern of *A Passage to India* that binds its social, psychological, and philosophical aspects into a harmony has not yet been fully explored. In *Passage* EMF is concerned with a contrast between the world of action and being, or as Rose Macaulay formulates it, the antithesis "between Real and not-Real, being and not-being." As in Whitman's "Passage to India," the theme is that of "fission" and "fusion," "of separateness and desired union." The threefold division of the book suggests a kind of Hegelian Thesis–Antithesis–Synthesis; that is, the statement of the problem and two opposing resolutions. In Part I, EMF points up separations and divisions—between the English and Indians, between the Indians and Indians, between the English and English, between man and the rest of creation. The fact is multiplicity; the desire is for union. This unity may be of two sorts, the one emphasizing exclusions (or negation), wherein differences and separations are stressed, the other emphasizing inclusions, wherein differences are reconciled in a larger synthesis. The first is *against* rather than *with;* it is hostile and evil in essence, breeding more hostility and more evil. The second sort of unity tries to leave behind differences and separations and to reconcile them by good will, sympathy, kindness, and love. Fielding, Mrs. Moore, and (to a degree) Adela Quested try to attain this kind of unity. Part I, wherein the forces of reconciliation often prevail, is the Hegelian Thesis; Part II, wherein the forces of division and evil triumph, is the Hegelian Antithesis. To the problem of oneness, the Caves utter an answer of horror and despair. For the Christian mystic, Mrs. Moore, the communication of a bleak oneness is annihilating; the Marabar Caves tell her that the universe is muddle rather than mystery; the answer to its riddle is Nothingness. For Adela the Marabar bespeaks the horror of a union without love, a sexual oneness that is rape. The keynote to her character is "an honest but arid intellectualism." When Adela thinks of the Caves in relation to sex, some of the same forces of fear and violence prevail that divide the English from the Indians. She also feels herself linked to Ronny Heaslop by these forces since she does not love him; a complete hysterical revulsion against love occurs. The forces of understanding crumble. Adela is upset before the trial because she has attempted union without love. An echo in her mind intuitively suggests that she may have committed a crime, though her intellect rejects such a possibility. Mrs. Moore's spirit arrests ultimate disaster when it leads to Adela's recantation at Aziz's trial, but nothing good is left. Evil, force, fear, and division have indeed triumphed. The answer of the Marabar may not, as Mrs. Moore herself has had intimations, be the final one; she has had glimpses of a more positive view at Asirgarh as she left India, a positive attitude that deepens in "Temple."

"Temple" presents Hinduism as a possible agency for the reconciliation of differences, not in negation but in a larger synthesis (a Hegelian one). "Temple" suggests a universe that is more a mystery than a riddle; and the rains, as a token of renewed life, regeneration, and hope, descend. Godbole is unfitted for the life of action, dwelling only in a world of being; he is diametrically opposite to Ronny Heaslop and most of the Anglo-Indian administrators. He stands for the universality of Hinduism, which makes no distinctions between humanity and the rest of creation as Islam and Christianity do; for if all aspects of creation are linked, "all is one in the Divine." The Hindu god does exist and posits the unity of all men in love; the fact of God's existence is more important than His presence at a given place or time. Hinduism implies that existence is mystery rather than muddle. In "Temple" we have reconciliation rather than real union (the latter is not possible on earth). Through the agency of Mrs. Moore and her children, love and intuitive understanding triumph at last. Mrs. Moore's defeat had been a personal one but not one in understanding or love. *Passage* is not quite a full success in its almost impossible aim, to fuse the world of social comedy and human conflict with a larger world, to impose on experience the pattern of a moral vision. Some difficulty arises in EMF's fusing his double vision of the realistic and the symbolic aspects of his experience. He is, not always successfully, "both poet and satirist, both comedian and moralist, both preacher and artist." Lionel Trilling (E. M. FORSTER, 1943) correctly holds that the characters, especially the redemptive ones, are not large enough for the story. [It is about time, I think, that this judgment be forever abandoned.] Neither beliefs nor action, but only the understanding heart can save us; such is the message of *Passage*. It dramatizes the inadequacy of the liberal–bourgeois–agnostic mind when it confronts ultimate reality; it also reveals the hollowness of Margaret Schlegel's world in *Howards End*. EMF's skill at character portrayal is everywhere apparent in the novel. Aziz is the most fully conceived and realized of all of EMF's characters. [A standard essay, which is at its best when its author analyzes characters in terms of theme and vice versa.]

638 Wood, Percy. "In Era of Princely Pomp," CHICAGO SUNDAY TRIBUNE, "Magazine of Books," 1 Nov 1953, p. 5.

In *The Hill of Devi* EMF records the pomp and extravagance characteristic of the Indian princely states by his presentation of life in Dewas State Senior and of its Maharajah. The book reveals both EMF's knowledge of India and his mastery of the English language.

639 Woolf, Virginia. A WRITER'S DIARY: BEING EXTRACTS FROM THE DIARY OF VIRIGINIA WOOLF, ed by Leonard Woolf (Lond: Hogarth P, 1953; NY: Harcourt, Brace, 1954), pp. 11–12, 76, 99, 171–72, 234–36, 270, 297, 325–26, 328–29.

Entry (12 April 1919), EMF has never read Defoe; as he shakes hands with her, he seems to shrink from her as a clever, up-to-date woman. Entry (6 Nov 1919), EMF likes Woolf's NIGHT AND DAY less than THE VOYAGE OUT. EMF is the best of critics because he has the artist's mind and says the simple things that clever people overlook. Entry (19 May 1925), EMF likes MRS. DALLOWAY better than JACOB'S ROOM. He was pleased about the book; his approval lifts a weight off her mind. Entry (13 Sept 1926), EMF thinks that THE WAVES is a classic. This praise, coming from EMF with his high standards, especially reassures her. [Entry (9 April 1935), Woolf is angry with EMF for quoting remarks made by the London Library Committee disparaging to women and thinks that her name may have been one of the ones discussed (and rejected) for possible membership on the Committee.] [Entry (2 April 1937), Woolf is downcast when EMF judges THE YEARS to be "dead and disappointing," though she herself had judged it to be an "odious rice pudding of a book," and "a dank failure."] [Entry (22 Nov 1938), Woolf is disturbed that her reputation seems lower than EMF's or T. S. Eliot's, but she will continue writing even if she has to go against the current.] [Entry (24 and 25 July 1940), Woolf will be relieved if EMF approves of ROGER FRY.] Entry (10 Aug 1940), EMF does slightly "damp" her.

1954

640 "The Air of Bloomsbury," TIMES LITERARY SUPPLEMENT (Lond), 20 Aug 1954, pp. 521–23.

The man or woman in Bloomsbury was similar to Virginia Woolf's "high-brow," "a man or woman of thorough-bred intelligence who rides his mind at a gallop across country in pursuit of new ideas." The aesthetics of Bloomsbury go back to G. E. Moore. Its members were less grave than J. K. Johnstone presents them as being in THE BLOOMSBURY GROUP; they spent much time laughing at each other. Jacob in Woolf's JACOB'S ROOM is an early Bloomsbury figure resembling her beloved dead brother, Thoby Stephen. "The six young men" in the novel who were to determine the fate of the world and of whom Jacob felt himself one are Bloomsbury in affiliation. G. E. Moore made the Bloomsbury intellectuals feel as though they were forerunners of a new dispensation. Such ardent feeling links them with their serious and altruistic Victorian forbears and reveals how morally preoc-cupied they really were. They rebelled against tradition in morals and religion but not in literature. In Bloomsbury there was a close relationship between the art of painting and the art of writing. Virginia Woolf's pene-tration to what lies behind the semblance of the thing may be the essential aspect of her genius. Strachey and EMF are less commanding figures, though Strachey writes with talent and EMF writes with inspiration in *A Passage to India*, especially in his portrait of Aziz, whom he depicts with devotion and amusement. In EMF's work, even at its weakest, there is "delicate originality." Pan and EMF's boorish young men are his own and signify not only his impatience with the modern mechanized world but with himself. His symbolism is sometimes not clear, and this is a defect. The members of Bloomsbury tended to regard evil as something removed or remote from them. For EMF the personal relationship, or G. E. Moore's "love of love," is all-important; the Christian tradition is concentrated in personal relationships. His characters also have their "moments of timeless or passionate contemplation." EMF, like the other Bloomsbury writers, often fails to define the ineffable, what he means by "moments of vision," "life itself," "spirit," "our spiritual life." Perhaps concealed in these terms are religious or mystical associations that the members of Bloomsbury distrusted with their minds. Mrs. Woolf and EMF tended to discover pat-tern rather than to impose it on external reality (though they imagined they were doing the latter). Perhaps this tendency resulted in EMF's view that life is a mystery, not a muddle. Lytton Strachey knew, however, that life is a muddle, and he imposed form on it. [Review of J. K. Johnstone's THE BLOOMSBURY GROUP (1954). An excellent, perceptive discussion.]

641 Allen, Walter. THE ENGLISH NOVEL: A SHORT CRITICAL HISTORY (Lond: Phoenix House, 1954), pp. 54, 72, 112–13, 188, 225, 236, 312, 319–25; (NY: E. P. Dutton, 1955), pp. 19, 50, 73, 126–27, 227, 276, 291, 390, 400–409.

EMF's novels are technically old-fashioned and are most distinctive for the authorial voice and individual style found in them; these features of his work are closely related to his use of the omniscient point of view. Outside his fiction he is the exponent of the liberal tradition: agnostic, anti-imperialist, anti-authoritarian, concerned with social justice. In EMF's fiction a sharp contrast exists between the surfaces of life and what lies beneath these surfaces; his perceptions of the nature of reality are presented obliquely through symbols. EMF is a tragic humanist for whom man is justified by self-awareness, the products of his imagination, and the arts, especially music. He stresses the need for connection but sees that wholeness is seldom attained. The first four novels exploit this theme and are a mingling of social comedy and poetry. [Extensive analysis of *Where Angels Fear to Tread* and *The Longest Journey*.] The social comedy is the best since Jane Austen's; the poetry doesn't work. The failure of *Howards End* is pronounced; the characters and situations are not ample enough to carry the themes. *A Passage to India* is more successful. The characters fail in their attempts to communicate with each other; yet there is hope that such communication may at some time transpire. *Passage* is superb as a realistic novel and convincing as a symbolic novel because the character of Mrs. Moore is adequate to EMF's purposes. She is a multi-dimensioned figure and acts as a brooding presence in the novel; she embodies some elemental reality. [Other incidental references to EMF throughout. Standard short account.]

642 Bachrach, A. G. H. "Redevoering Van prof. dr. A. G. H. Bachrach" (Citation of A. G. H. Bachrach), RIJKSUNIVERSITEIT TE LEIDEN: EREPROMOTIES VAN JEAN SCHLUMBERGER, EDWARD MORGAN FORSTER, VICTOR EMANUEL VAN VRIESLAND, OP 23 JUNI 1954 (Leiden University: Honorary Degrees of Jean Schlumberger, Edward Morgan Forster, Victor Emmanuel Van Vriesland, 23 June 1954), *A Passage to India* is a modern classic because a political problem of magnitude and delicacy is expressed in the terms of personal relations. EMF has approached his materials through implicit rather than explicit means. He has used the method of antithesis and confrontation which, with him, is not mechanical or contrived. EMF has a "poet's touch" whereby his plots become poetic and symbolic; he has used irony, understatement, and innuendo to voice an honest criticism of his society. His social, ethical, and metaphysical interests have developed in his miscellaneous writing since 1924. [Citation for EMF's honorary degree conferred by the University of Leiden. An excellent summation of EMF's significance, literary and cultural, for the modern age, and superior to many of the critical articles on EMF.]

643 Brewster, Dorothy. EAST-WEST PASSAGE: A STUDY IN LITERARY RELATIONSHIPS (Lond: Allen & Unwin, 1954), pp. 7, 170, 185. EMF protested in a 1915 review of Chekhov and Sologub the tendency to read Russian literature to find out about "soul" instead of literary values. Chekhov's despair is curiously aligned with the despair, devoid of dignity and grandeur, experienced by Mrs. Moore in the Marabar Caves in *A Passage to India*. [Book traces relationships established, primarily after 1800, between Russian literature and English and American authors.]

644 Cazamian, Louis. "Years of Strain 1914–1950: The Novel," A HISTORY OF ENGLISH LITERATURE, with Émile Legouis (Lond: Dent; NY: Macmillan, 1954, rvd ed), pp. 1382–90, espec 1383–84; also 1957, 1960 eds. The intelligence found in *Aspects of the Novel* marks all of EMF's work. His diffidence may affect his popularity but not his reputation with the elite. His work is uneven. In *Where Angels Fear to Tread* the social comedy of Jane Austen is present with its deftness, irony, and humor; but there is also much powerful drama leading to somewhat incongruous mixtures of tones. The elements are better blended in *A Passage to India*, which is remarkable for its symbolic effects. *Howards End* leaves the impression of being EMF's most successful book, though it is not "free from the hesitation of an art at times more thoughtful than perfect." The satire of Victorian smugness and philistinism recalls Meredith; EMF's deepest note, however, is that of "seriously felt moral and social responsibility." His subdued emotion is embodied most notably in the "carefully shaded portraits" of Mrs. Wilcox and Margaret Schlegel.

645 Chaudhuri, Nirad C. "Passage To and From India," ENCOUNTER (Lond), II (June 1954), 19–24; rptd in PERSPECTIVES ON E. M. FORSTER'S "A PASSAGE TO INDIA," ed by V. A. Shahane (NY: Barnes & Noble, 1968), pp. 115–20; and in TWENTIETH CENTURY INTERPRETATIONS OF "A PASSAGE TO INDIA," ed by Andrew Rutherford (Englewood Cliffs, NJ: Spectrum Books, 1970), pp. 68–77. *A Passage to India* became a powerful weapon in the hands of anti-imperialists and contributed to the British departure from India. Also, by painting Anglo-Indians unattractively, it contributed to British indifference and aversion to the Indian empire. *Passage* focuses upon the least significant aspects of the Indian situation; it does not concern itself with the important conflict between Indian nationalists and the British administration. Contrary to Aziz's situation, personal humiliation did not motivate nationalist Indians, nor did the desire to gain the friendship of Englishmen. More typically considered, the political situation in India after World War I would have resulted in "a tragedy of mutual repulsion," not in "a tragi-comedy of mutual attraction." EMF's humanitarian consciousness caused him to simplify certain situations and led him to pure negation in solving a political problem, such as that of Anglo-Indian relations, by eliminating it. It also led him to waste his politico-ethical emotion on characters who do not deserve it. He makes his white officials too absurd; they were never guilty of cowardice with respect to fears from race reprisals. He is too charitable with the Indians; Aziz does not merit the full sympathy that EMF gives him. EMF's Hindus come from the princely states and are too conservative. Godbole is not a serious Hindu but a clown. The Muslims were not at the center of India but were wooed by the English as a counterpoise to Hindu nationalists. The Muslims exploited the British so successfully that they got a separate state in 1947. The Muslims either hated the British or were toadies to them. To present Indio-British relations EMF needed a Hindu for a protagonist rather than a Muslim. EMF shares the liking of the British for the Muslims and their dislike of Hindus. Islamic order was the natural enemy of Christian-European order; the West and Hindus shared the same Indo-European affinities, a fact which was then ignored. *Passage* shows the imperial system at its worst—not as evil but as drab and asinine. The snobbery and pettiness of the Indians is matched by the imbecility and rancor of the British. India's sufferings in EMF's novel are deprived of all dignity; the mental life of India is seen as childish and querulous. The problems could not be solved at the personal level. The Westerners tended to scorn the educated Indians. The contrast between the generosity of Indian leaders, who admitted the advantages of British domination, and British narrowness furnishes the key to the real failure of the British in India. England was at fault for being unwilling to extend its civilization and its spiritual citizenship. [The most searching of the negative critiques on the politics of *Passage*, although the mean-spirited intolerance deplored by EMF is akin to the larger intolerance deplored by Chaudhuri. Jeffrey Meyers in "The Politics of *A Passage to India*" (1971) and M. M. Mahood in "Amritsar to Chandrapore: E. M. Forster and the Massacre" (1943) indicate that EMF was more sensitive to the contemporary political scene in India and to the Nationalist Movement than is sometimes thought.]

646 Cranston, Maurice. "Book Reviews," LONDON MAGAZINE, I (Sept 1954), 77–81.

J. K. Johnstone's purpose in THE BLOOMSBURY GROUP (1954) is confused.

Can we isolate in Strachey, Woolf, and EMF the essence of Bloomsbury, or did Bloomsbury form them? Johnstone tries to answer both questions. Assimilating the earlier G. E. Moore, Bloomsbury felt confidently backed up by philosophy, though Bloomsbury did not really believe in logic. In contrast to the aesthetes of the 1890s, they were not for art against morality but on the side of both art and morality as opposed to false morality. Hence the great self-confidence of the members. The Puritanism of the members became relaxed as they began to publish. Strachey was the natural leader of the group, and Johnstone should have stressed this fact. EMF was only loosely attached to the group: he upheld their standards, but Moore and Fry meant less to him than did Dickinson with his Platonism. EMF is a moralist and something of a mystic; his cardinal principle, "Only connect," has little to do with Moore and Fry and everything to do with Dickinson. [Perceptive review.]

647 Gide, André. JOURNAL 1939–1949; SOUVENIRS (Journal 1939–1949; Memoirs) (Paris: Gallimard, 1954), pp. 272, 290 [original publ of JOURNAL, c. 1950]; as THE JOURNALS OF ANDRÉ GIDE, Vol IV, 1939–1949, trans by Justin O'Brien (NY: Knopf; Lond: Secker & Warburg, 1951), pp. 243, 259 [trans does not include SOUVENIRS].
Entry (12 June 1944), *The Longest Journey* is difficult to get into. Not much remains from a reading of *Howards End* except esteem for EMF. Entry (24 Jan 1946), *A Passage to India* is "a marvel of intelligence, of tact, of irony, of prudence, and of cleverness." Many things escape the reader of EMF's *Passage*, but what EMF suggests and insinuates is often more significant than what he says. EMF's sentences often compel his reader to a kind of complicity with him. [In French.]

648 H., W. "Book Notes," TWENTIETH CENTURY, CLVI (Oct 1954), 381–82.
J. K. Johnstone in THE BLOOMSBURY GROUP (1954) reveals that Bloomsbury was not composed of a group of pretentious Bohemiam poseurs, "highbrow, snobbish, irresponsible and arty." They were single-minded and unworldy but also had a highly organized mode of life that was profoundly moral. Its spirit was gentle, fastidious, fearless, serene.

649 Hafley, James. THE GLASS ROOF: VIRGINIA WOOLF AS NOVELIST (Berkeley & Los Angeles: University of California P, 1954), pp. 4, 8, 9, 34–35, 50, 89, 145–46, 173.
The opening conversation of *The Longest Journey* is typical of the conversations that the Cantabridgian circle (which later formed the Bloomsbury Group) must have had. In NIGHT AND DAY Virginia Woolf reveals the same inability to fuse fact and vision of which she accused EMF in "The Novels of E. M. Forster" (1927). Some such fusion of the two realms she did

achieve in a 1927 novel, TO THE LIGHTHOUSE. EMF judged NIGHT AND DAY to be unsuccessful because Woolf was using uncongenial tools. JACOB'S ROOM is not Woolf's "great departure" as EMF maintained. Striking similarities exist between TO THE LIGHTHOUSE and *Howards End.* Both have a house as a unifying force; a woman who dies part way through the books (Ruth Wilcox and Mrs. Ramsay) dominates them until their final scenes; EMF's dichotomy between love and truth, passion and prose, is similar to Woolf's between matter and memory. EMF's judgment that THE YEARS is a failure is questionable. Woolf does harmonize private and public values in the book, and the style is better controlled than it is in THE WAVES.

650 Hamilton, Mary Agnes. "Books to Read," LONDON CALLING, No. 775 (9 Sept 1954), 12.

The physiognomy and the *feel* of Bloomsbury and, incidentally, its passionate concern with social and political problems do not come through in J. K. Johnstone's THE BLOOMSBURY GROUP (1954).

651 Heiney, Donald W. "E. M. Forster," ESSENTIALS OF CONTEMPORARY LITERATURE (Great Neck, NY: Barron's Educational Series, 1954), pp. 170–73; also 153, 158, 256.

Psychological conflict is paramount in EMF's novels; their social content is latent and secondary. The characters seek understanding, brotherhood, kinship, and broad experience but are frustrated by conventions. EMF is more an individualist than a moralist. His characters are presented from within, though we learn much about them in their interactions with each other. EMF's stress is on relativity, not only of values but in the estimate of human character. His prose is terse and economical without being laconic. He recreates rather than describes events. As artist, he has a feeling for image and metaphor, a flair for dialogue, and a sense of structure. His principal defect is lack of originality and of positive thought for the solution of the dilemmas he presents. [EMF is considered under "The Reaction to Realism." Informed summaries of *The Longest Journey, A Room with a View,* and *A Passage to India.*]

652 Hickley, Dennis. "Ou-boum and Verbum," DOWNSIDE REVIEW (Bath, England), LXXII (Spring 1954), 172–80.

EMF's position in his early novels is that of the agnostic and humanist, into which he penetrates more deeply as he goes along, until in *A Passage to India* he expresses the negation and despair to be found among agnostics and humanists today. EMF is thus a microcosm of the tendencies of a whole age. The goblins of *Howards End* reappear in *Passage.* India appears to have caught EMF unarmed and unprepared. Mrs. Moore regards it as nightmare and succumbs to her anti-vision. When the double vision is in proper focus, a vision results; when it is out of focus, nightmare results. The supernatural haunts the pages of *Passage* just as the echo haunted Mrs. Moore. EMF seems to ignore Christianity, but then becomes aware of it in India because of its absence. He then dismisses it in favor of Eastern religions. A religious type of society exists in the East: people love their religion and are not self-conscious about it. In the East, Christianity seems trivial to EMF. Modern Christianity is too self-conscious, too identified with an external propriety to please EMF, too tied to a sense of behavior that is purely European. EMF responds to religion in India as "an outburst of mystery, joy and love." EMF is probably in Fielding's dilemma, between a Cave that mirrors its own darkness infinitely in every direction and "the spirit in a reasonable form, with flesh and blood subsisting." One must bring into focus the double vision to realize that muddle may be mystery and mystery may exist in muddle. Mrs. Moore is overwhelmed by the transcendence of God without understanding His immanence. There is some religious susceptibility necessary for characters to respond to the echo: Mrs. Moore, Adela Quested, and Fielding have it in some degree; the other officials, as Ronny Heaslop, do not have it. Adela's religion is one of comfort; so is Mrs. Moore's. EMF, the religious humanist, and Mrs. Moore, the religious woman, hear the echo and are distraught; but the echo and its nightmare aspects provide a religious experience, in which "ou-boum" might yet be transposed into "I am." [An interesting discussion, from an unusual angle of approach.]

653 Hughes, Richard. "Bloomsbury," SPECTATOR (Lond), CXCII (11 June 1954), 716, 719.
[Review-essay on J. K. Johnstone, THE BLOOMSBURY GROUP, (1954). Discusses at length the influence of G. E. Moore on Bloomsbury. Stresses the active aspect of Bloomsbury, the fact that it was not an ivory-tower group. The reason for this misapprehension is the fact that Bloomsbury rejected the pursuit of personal power and success in comparison with the propagation of ideas. Roger Fry, for example, wished to convert the public to Postimpressionism. Johnstone's book is better in the first part than in the second; he fails to catch any suggestion of greatness in discussing the work of Virginia Woolf, EMF, and Lytton Strachey.] [Valuable comment.]

654 Johnson, Elaine H. "The Intelligent Mr. E. M. Forster," PERSONALIST (University of Southern California, Los Angeles), XXXV (Jan 1954), 50–58.
Intelligence is EMF's overriding quality, accounting for his characteristic virtues (and some defects). Despite his plea for irrationality, he is a rationalist in emphasis. A novelist of ideas, he is saved from sterility by his concern with people. He understands them and also the fact that good and evil are intermingled in human life. His luminous intelligence is greater than his faults as novelist. [Thin discussion.]

655 Johnstone, J. K. "Bloomsbury Aesthetics," "Values: E. M. Forster, Lytton Strachey, Virginia Woolf," "Composition: E. M. Forster," THE BLOOMSBURY GROUP: A STUDY OF E. M. FORSTER, LYTTON STRACHEY, VIRGINIA WOOLF, AND THEIR CIRCLE (NY: Noonday P; Lond: Secker & Warburg, 1954), pp. 36–95, espec 62–76; 99–156, espec 99–113; 159–266.

Where Angels Fear to Tread derives from the clash of cultures, also from the clash between hypocrisy and sincerity, between a society that represses impulses in people and one that allows people to express themselves naturally. EMF's sympathies are with the Italians, but he can see their flaws; he is also able to appreciate the good qualities in the English. Mrs. Herriton provides the clash at Monteriano and is there as a force. She is an offshoot of her nationality and has no basis in tradition, as does Gino Carella, her Italian antagonist. [Other comment is mostly obvious.] In *The Longest Journey* the three themes of *Angels* are further developed: (1) to lie is to risk spiritual ruin; (2) an act, or a failure to act, may have infinite consequences; (3) a true, sacred racial strain will inevitably survive. [Other comment is again mostly obvious, as is the entire discussion of *A Room with a View.*]

In *Howards End* the Schlegel sisters discover the unseen intellectually, not intuitively like Mrs. Wilcox. Aunt Juley Munt is the only muddled and conventional character who is likable. The Beethoven Fifth Symphony implies a cyclic view of reality; "panic and emptiness" threaten the "splendour" and "heroism" in life and all but overwhelm them, yet life also persists and splendor and heroism may again return. Periods of civilization and freedom alternate, therefore, with those of war and oppression; force is only insecurely shut within its box. The umbrella is a symbol of Leonard Bast's respectability. The graveyard scene (Mrs. Wilcox's burial) assimilates Mrs. Wilcox to the earth. Though he is sometimes petty and sometimes ridiculous, Leonard is never muddled at heart; he has some affinity with the large-minded Mrs. Wilcox, at least in dying at Howards End house. Henry Wilcox is not convincing; he acts merely to illustrate a sociological and theological theorem. The structural rhythm associated with Margaret convinces us that she is heroic, but her heroism does not convince us that her marriage is real.

The style of *Howards End* is distinctive and distinguished. In *A Passage to India* "panic and emptiness" are abstract, not human. The inclusiveness of the novel is great, taking in both infinite time and space. EMF's presentation is without insistence, argument, or didacticism. The relationships in the novel are inexhaustible. Evil is externalized by the echo; only Hinduism makes an adequate provision for it. Through Mrs. Moore's influence, the echo is overcome though it had disabled her earlier. She is central to the

novel [an interpretation with which I agree, in opposition to Edwin Nierenberg's "The Withered Priestess: Mrs. Moore's Incomplete Passage to India"
(1964).] The character drawing is superb; the natural and the supernatural
are fortunately kept separated into different characters. The divisions of the
novel accord with its inner development, as it runs from the peaceful seclusion of theism to the undeniable reality of evil and then to the synthesis
supplied in Hindu pantheism. In *Passage* EMF's style reaches its culmination of strength and brilliance.

[Opening chapters, "Bloomsbury" and "Bloomsbury Philosophy," sketch in
the background for the group, notably in the philosophy of G. E. Moore.
He would isolate the good through the agency of intuition, reason, and
knowledge. For him the greatest goods are the pleasures deriving from
human contact and the enjoyment of beautiful objects (beauty is an essential
component of the good). Human relationships and personal affection are
complex. The "ideal" for Moore is the greatest good that we can perceive;
as such it must be mental, as such it must also be based on the material. In
"Bloomsbury Aesthetics" the aesthetics of the group are established
primarily through a discussion of Clive Bell and Roger Fry. The autonomy
of the work of art is stressed, and the role of mental vision in creating and
apprehending the work of art is paramount. Sensibility or feeling is also
essential for the artist or spectator, but feeling must be subordinated to (or
comprehended in) form. The "visual relations" in a work are all-important
and are to be fastened upon in preference to its dramatic or psychological
aspects. Extended analysis of *Aspects of the Novel* in this chapter, though
EMF's ideas are hardly ever related to Bell's and Fry's; also fails to use
EMF's miscellaneous essays on art in *Abinger Harvest* and *Two Cheers for
Democracy* that are more central to this discussion than *Aspects*. In "Values" some of the principles that organized EMF's life and fiction are mentioned, but little is done to relate them to the ambience of the group. These
values comprise an emphasis on the sensuous and the sensual, an embracing
of nature over convention and industrialism, a respect for tradition, a recognition of an immaterial scale of values that fosters the visionary, a valuing
of personal relations, a belief in an intellectual elite, and a support of
tolerance and the spirit of paradox. These attitudes are deduced from
EMF's separate works, but there is no meaningful synthesis of them. Some
insights in a readable discussion, but there are too few judgments and
profound formulations; the novels are considered *in vacuo* and are not
clearly related to Bloomsbury, as the writer had promised to do.]

656 Leach, Elsie. "Forster's *A Passage to India*, XXXVI," Ex-
PLICATOR, XIII (Nov 1954), Item 13.
In the Mau tank incident in *A Passage to India* in which the main outsiders
are upset and thrown into the water, these outsiders come to share the

Hindu sense of the union of all creation by returning to the watery element. Thus, they become part of the ceremony itself. [Comment is mostly obvious.]

657 "The Listener's Book Chronicle," LISTENER, LI (24 June 1954), 1103–4.
Though the members of the Bloomsbury Group thought that art was autonomous, they realized that it had spiritual dimensions. Beneath Strachey's irony and affected style, there was great devotion to truth and humanity; this devotion became a passion in the work of EMF and Virginia Woolf. J. K. Johnstone's THE BLOOMSBURY GROUP (1954) is a work of literary criticism, not a comprehensive study of this group of intellectuals.

658 Mansfield, Katherine. JOURNAL OF KATHERINE MANSFIELD, ed by J. Middleton Murry (Lond: Constable; Toronto: Longmans, Green, 1954), pp. 120–21; rptd in E. M. FORSTER: THE CRITICAL HERITAGE, ed by Philip Gardner (Lond & Boston: Routledge & Kegan Paul, 1973), p. 162.
Entry (May 1917), *Howards End* is not good enough. EMF only warms the teapot but produces no tea. It is uncertain whether Leonard Bast or his forgotten umbrella got Helen Schlegel with child.

659 Marcus, Steven. "Forster's India," PARTISAN REVIEW, XXI (Jan–Feb 1954), 115–19.
EMF vividly presents in *The Hill of Devi* the farcical aspects, the impersonality, and the stage machinery of colonial government and also the inefficiencies, the intrigue, and the mess of daily life at the Court of the Maharajah of Dewas State Senior. Life there illustrates Hegel's analysis of the spiritual life of India, where the spiritual is trying to get clear of the material. There results an alternating obliviousness to, and worship of, the material. EMF abjured typically English attitudes and roles in India and instead embraced attitudes of disinterested intelligence and enlightened sympathy. The character of the Maharajah does not come through, though the affection leading to the relationship is well conveyed. The description of the State of Dewas Senior is strong, the book being "an excellent account of what it was to be an Englishman and a liberal in a decrepit Anglo-India." [Thoughtful review.]

660 Mayne, Richard. "Mr. Forster," CAMBRIDGE REVIEW, LXXV (16 Jan 1954), 208–10.
EMF's chief note is "a faint but firm critical query," the note of dissent typified in *Two Cheers for Democracy*. EMF's Edwardian novels reveal a depth and a divergence from attitudes and are more nearly Laurentian. Along with Virginia Woolf, EMF did respond to Bloomsbury's chief virtue,

its toleration and encouragement of nonconformity. Critics were puzzled by his books and did not realize that the books were accomplishing "a bloodless revolution." EMF emphasized the unpredictable in psychology and behavior, and he quietly struck at established values and institutions. EMF realized with *A Passage to India* that what he wanted to say did not lend itself to storytelling; and literary history since the 1920s bears out EMF's instinct that "the interesting, the profound, the private, the urgent things in the world were bigger than novels." Reportage, biography, poetry, and criticism are the finest manifestations of the intellectual life today, and *The Hill of Devi* but emphasizes the minor role of fiction in that life. The art of the book conceals its depth and passion. EMF recreates his experiences in a casual, half-comical way. The heart of the book is in the portrait of the Maharajah. EMF's communication with him was often fleeting, but at their meeting was "the moment of truth." [Interesting discussion.]

> **661** Mercier, Vivian. "Finding an Epicurean Basis for a Victorian Culture," COMMONWEAL, LXI (15 Oct 1954), 42–43.

The members of Bloomsbury were Epicureans, not stoics. They did not reject life but wanted to organize its data into illuminating works of art. EMF's novels are unforgettable because so much goes on in them above and below their surfaces; his works are distinctive by their rich texture. [Review of J. K. Johnstone's THE BLOOMSBURY GROUP (1954).]

> **662** Moore, Harry T. THE INTELLIGENT HEART: THE STORY OF D. H. LAWRENCE (NY: Farrar, Straus, & Young, 1954; Lond: Heinemann, 1955), pp. 183, 309, 443; rvd and rptd as THE PRIEST OF LOVE: A LIFE OF D. H. LAWRENCE (NY: Farrar, Straus, & Giroux, 1974), pp. 217, 229, 293, 366, 514, containing some references to EMF and a few other incidental ones.

[Lawrence's letter of 12 Feb 1915 to Bertrand Russell, describing EMF, is cited; see Lawrence. Katherine Mansfield is quoted to the effect that EMF and Lawrence would have understood her life at the Gurdjieff Institute at Fontainbleu where she died. EMF's 1930 estimate of Lawrence as "the greatest imaginative novelist of his generation" is cited.]

> **663** Mortimer, Raymond. *"The Hill of Devi,"* TIMES LITERARY SUPPLEMENT (Lond), 6 Aug 1954, p. iv.

Fineness rather than greatness is the quality that EMF most exemplifies. He is less outspoken and less lyrical and versatile than André Gide whom, among contemporaries, he most resembles. He is demure and oblique; his prose is enlivening, with its unexpected words and turns of phrase. He is idiosyncratic and has his special angle for viewing experience. His novels contrast a delicacy of portraiture and a vigor of situation, in the service of illuminating moral issues. The English professional classes have undergone great changes in their circumstances and beliefs because EMF wrote about these people in his novels, but the moral thrust of the novels, with these characters, remains strong. EMF is always on the side of the individual against the state; he is "a mystic of rationalism," disbelieving in belief yet wanting us to heed our hearts as well as our heads. This ethic is explicit in the essays in *Abinger Harvest* and *Two Cheers for Democracy*, which must not be dismissed as scrappy. *The Hill of Devi* is his most vivid book. [Describes method used in writing and its contents.] It is a portfolio of sketches to the finished painting, *A Passage to India*. *Devi* reveals the reciprocal relationship of his philosophy and heart; it also has great historical value. The flaw of the book is that EMF does not illustrate convincingly the qualities of the Maharajah of Dewas State Senior. EMF does not make quite clear just how the Maharajah was genius and saint. Perhaps the true theme of *Devi* is that a Maratha prince may be a devoted friend yet a detestable ruler, though EMF does not state it so bluntly. The prince also reveals that a man may be religious and not be righteous. EMF forgave the Maharajah everything because he was witty, gay, complicated, affectionate, and "out of step." EMF's ethic is an individual one, demonstrating that he is against all the systems, Christian or rationalist, accepted in Europe. This ethic is difficult to defend in theory, but in practice it often yields advantages and richness. [Mortimer regards EMF with admiration and perplexity. Discerning discussion by a younger associate of Bloomsbury.]

664 Muir, Edwin. "A Study of Bloomsbury," OBSERVER (Lond), 30 May 1954, p. 9.

G. E. Moore's philosophy was germinal among the Bloomsbury Group, though it may have sponsored a world view that was perhaps too narrow for the genius of Virginia Woolf and EMF, in spite of its liberating aspects. In THE BLOOMSBURY GROUP (1954), J. K. Johnstone brings out the element of allegory in EMF's work, an aspect of it that readers too often overlook. The new age that Bloomsbury wished to inaugurate could never have come into being; the twentieth century would have been too much for it. The genius of the Bloomsbury Group still survives along with the limitations of thought and fashion that defined it.

665 Nicolson, Benedict. "Highbrows Unashamed," NEW STATESMAN AND NATION, nsXLVII (19 June 1954), 792, 794.

In THE BLOOMSBURY GROUP (1954), J. K. Johnstone well states the influence of G. E. Moore and has a detached and objective attitude toward his materials, but there is little else to be said for his book. Johnstone regards the group as being more tightly knit than it in fact was, and there is little justification for regarding EMF as part of it. Johnstone disregards certain influences, especially the continental ones, governing its chief figures. It was less political than Johnstone assumes, and it was aloof and did not propagandize. It became influential by example rather than by exhortation. The group was isolated and detached, and for this reason it came to be regarded as snobbish.

666 Paul, David. "Time and the Novelist," PARTISAN REVIEW, XXI (Nov–Dec 1954), 636–49.

The Longest Journey represents the "first complete break with the self-confident smoothness of the Victorian narrative tradition." EMF breaks with the Jamesean concept of ordered plot as the prime necessity in fiction. EMF eschewed the tragic or the comic integration of his characters, and presents them and their environment in unordered, nonconsecutive, chaotic fashion. With *Journey* the nineteenth-century concept of smoothly evolving time in the writing of fiction came to an end. [A somewhat perfunctory discussion of time in the novel. Remarks on *Journey* are interesting.]

667 Pritchett, V. S. "Genius and Saint," NEW YORKER, XXIX (30 Jan 1954), 85–89.

In writing of the Indian state of Dewas Senior and its Maharajah in *The Hill of Devi*, EMF reveals that his "genius has always been for the casual touch, the seemingly amateur and personal view." [Extensive summary of contents of *Devi.*] EMF was evidently puzzled by the conjoining of fatuousness and exaltation in the Maharajah. The vulgar facts are transmuted into symbols in *A Passage to India.* Although the Maharajah lived by the heart, he was also involved in intrigue, "the heart's seamy side." This aspect of the Maharajah EMF does not adequately encompass. Although he was a rare spirit, the Maharajah did some odd things, such as planning carefully for his apparently spontaneous exile from Dewas Senior when the British officials grew insistent about his carrying out reforms. EMF's values are these: the importance of weakness and of the unofficial and the personal as opposed to the official and impersonal. With respect to India, EMF's sympathy and insights are those of the disengaged. He does not understand fully the sensuality of the Indian temperament; he lacks full knowledge of the British in India, who also "had their allegory and symbols" and who were committed whereas he was not. He does not understand action because it is based on passion and will, and they commit. *Devi* does help us understand the making of an original mind. [A speculative, rich review.]

668 Pritchett, V. S. "Some Talkers in the Sunset," NEW YORK TIMES BOOK REVIEW, 26 Sept 1954, 36–37.

The members of Bloomsbury thought that after Victorianism a cultural renaissance would occur. They inaugurated one of sorts, an aspect, in fact, of "that splendid Western European sunset" which was to linger until the 1930s. The Bloomsbury affiliates were the pre-Raphaelites of the twentieth century with their colorful lives, letters, memoirs. D. H. Lawrence and

Wyndham Lewis were excessive in their attacks on the allegedly exclusive, insulated, and rationalistic aspects of the Bloomsbury Group. Though the members of the circle placed emphasis on the private and the personal, they were generous in their wish to have culture prevail at large and in their social conscience. Their emphasis on taste may have been a weakness, but their influence has been great in the diffusion of culture, in the organizing of such institutions as the Arts Council. Though they had little direct influence on the younger generation, they did bequeath something generous and rich to present-day culture. Their valuation of personal freedom still has relevance. Johnstone emphasizes, correctly, the importance of Roger Fry's aesthetics for the Group, especially his conception of the autonomy of the art work and the importance of the visual image. Bloomsbury aesthetics and attitudes were paradoxical. Hedonism consorted with intellectual analysis, mysticism with skepticism, agnosticism with a religion of art. Insularity, detachment, and inherited wealth were not inhibiting factors upon the development of a group of original and gifted minds. [Provocative review of J. K. Johnstone's THE BLOOMSBURY GROUP (1954).]

669 Raymund, Bernard. "Book Reviews," WESTERN HUMANITIES REVIEW, VIII (Summer 1954), 267–69.

In *The Hill of Devi* the mental landscape is all-important, especially the complex personality of the Maharajah of Dewas State Senior and the intricate situation in which EMF found himself. In *Devi* there are no prominent European women who complicate the situations as in *A Passage to India*. This book is obviously based on fact, but might it not also be "the supreme fiction" of all EMF's work?

670 Sigworth, O. F. "Book Reviews," ARIZONA QUARTERLY, X (Spring 1954), 87–88.

EMF's work is a monument to the liberal mind, but it reveals also some of the "destructive difficulties" encountered by a man who is incapable of dogmatic action. In *The Hill of Devi* is presented an India, the truth about which is stranger than fiction. *Devi* is a richly humorous, but tragic, book. The description of the Gokul Ashtami festival is relevant to the ceremony presented in "Temple" in *A Passage to India*, but the themes from EMF's other books are also present in *Devi*, especially these: the undeveloped heart and the difficulty of living with good-and-evil. EMF perfectly comprehends India, but one wonders whether EMF could not have acted decisively to some degree. Does artistic detachment preclude direct action of any sort? The manner of the vision is important in this book, not the facts; but we could wish that EMF saw more, though seeing in his particular way testifies to an unusual integrity of vision. [Excellent review.]

671 Temple, Phillips. "Books," AMERICA (NY), XCII (2 Oct 1954), 20–21.

The Hill of Devi reveals the fascination that India has for the European mind. The "youthful exuberance" of the letters contrasts with the deliberateness of EMF's later commentary upon them.

672 Trevelyan, G. M. "Mr. E. M. Forster on Scott," A LAYMAN'S LOVE OF LETTERS (Lond & NY: Longmans, Green, 1954), pp. 96–105.

In *Aspects of the Novel* EMF fails to recognize the vitality and reality of Sir Walter Scott's Scottish characters and Scott's mastery of dialogue. EMF criticizes Scott for his provinciality, but Scott is only provincial in that he writes of men close to the soil: EMF's suburban characters are actually more provincial than Scott's. EMF is unduly critical of THE HEART OF MIDLOTHI-AN. This book and GUY MANNERING are not "trivial, heavy and ill-constructed." Scott put Scotland on the map, founded the historical novel, and altered man's views of history by filling his canvases with flesh-and-blood human beings, treating history essentially as "social history."

673 Voorhees, Richard J. "The Novels of E. M. Forster," SOUTH ATLANTIC QUARTERLY, LIII (Jan 1954), 89–99.

EMF's subject is in part the failures of human perception; thus in *The Longest Journey*, Rickie Elliot fails to see the real Agnes (whom he marries and by whom he is destroyed). The Agnes he sees does not exist. In all his novels EMF is concerned with the difference between the genuine and the spurious in human personality. In *A Room with a View* Lucy Honeychurch's conflict lies less between duty and love than between the real and the pretended. EMF's clerics differ from Samuel Butler's; they fail to be on the side of the angels because of muddle, not because of malice. But EMF dislikes their "medieval" asceticism. However, by the time of *A Passage to India* he becomes tolerant of clerics, treating Mr. Sorley with a tolerable humor. The witty description of Santa Deodata in *Where Angels Fear to Tread* is out of tone with the rest of the novel. [Fails to see how Deodata reflects on Philip Herriton and the question of his noninvolvement.] EMF recreates well Greek wholeness when he is not solemn about doing so. He presents a successful contrast between muddle and spontaneity in the contrast between Italians and Englishmen in *Angels* and *Room*. The characters he dislikes find the idea of fertility more terrifying than death; those he likes embrace fertility and accept death with equanimity. Mr. Emerson in *Room* presents the two main facets of EMF's moral philosophy: (1) the need to accept life without any trust in personal survival beyond it (rhythms of life and death interweave in the novels; see especially the scene of Mrs. Wilcox's burial in *Howards End* and the murder of one Italian by another in the Florentine piazza in *Room*); and (2) the need to accept the brotherhood of man. The scenes revealing man's capacity for unity have great power and a kind of religious quality, but the difficulties in the way of brotherhood are fairly stressed, with the result that "the good and wise characters unite Christian charity with Lucretian toughness." EMF finds limitations in any moral formulation or any moral system. The novels become protests against the use of black and white distinctions, "against abstractions from human complexity." *Angels*, not without its complexities, has nevertheless the simplicity of a morality play when compared with *Passage*. In the characters of Mrs. Wilcox and Mrs. Moore, EMF would stress "that wisdom cannot be verbal and formal." The Wilcox men are efficient businessmen and manage people as workers, but they fail at human relations. They lack the power to synthesize facts and think of human qualities in empiric terms or assimilate them to abstract precepts, failing to realize that there are no simple answers to complicated questions. Even the overwhelming negations experienced by Mrs. Moore in the Marabar Caves in *Passage* are not final; yet neither are they irrelevant. EMF feels that meaningful brotherhood requires a broad basis in civilization and concedes that in feudalism such a basis existed more perceptibly than in modern society. The English countryside may provide a milieu in which people will be organically related to one another. EMF has no enthusiasm for a cosmopolitan world that might promote a kind of spurious unity among men. [A discussion, regretfully too brief, with much feeling for the novels and many discerning insights].

674 Woodruff, Philip [pseud of Philip Mason]. THE MEN WHO RULED INDIA: II, THE GUARDIANS (NY: St. Martin's P; Lond: Cape, 1954), p. 282.

In the North and South of India the English officials did not live in the state of semihysteria that EMF depicts in *A Passage to India*, nor were they so arrogant as they are in the EMF novel. Perhaps EMF may have reflected the more unsettled situation prevalent in Bengal.

1955

675 Allen, Glen O. "Structure, Symbol, and Theme in E. M. Forster's *A Passage to India*," PUBLICATIONS OF THE MODERN LANGUAGE ASSOCIATION, LXX (Dec 1955), 934–54; rptd in PERSPECTIVES ON E. M. FORSTER'S "A PASSAGE TO INDIA," ed by V. A. Shahane (NY: Barnes & Noble, 1968), pp. 121–41.

The three main divisions of *A Passage to India* are definitely symbolic. "Mosque" is to be associated with man's emotional nature (or Islam), "Caves" with the intellect (or a liberal, idealizing Christianity), and "Temple" with the capacity for love (or Hinduism). The Shri Krishna ceremonies of Hinduism, with their mysticism, deny the intellect and disintegrate the categories that make distinctions (and thought) possible. Hence, Fielding and Aziz cannot understand these ceremonies. The religion associated with "Caves" stresses reason, form, and sense of purpose [questionable; the Caves, I am sure, subvert reason; see Louise Dauner's "What Happened in the Caves? Some Reflections on *A Passage to India*" (1961).] As representatives of futile reason, Fielding and Adela Quested dominate the Caves, just as Aziz dominates "Mosque" and Godbole, "Temple." Mrs. Moore has qualities found in all three parts of the book. She has a strong though subtle resemblance to Fielding and Adela; she is also akin to Aziz's spontaneity and sensitive to Godbole's mysticism. Her strongest moorings are intellectual; she is not intellectually disposed, but intellectually committed, to Christianity. She exerts influence in all three sections of *Passage* but is central to the second, "Caves." Indian religion embraces the three Ways associated with the three books: the Way of Activity ("Mosque"), the Way of Knowledge ("Caves"), and the Way of Devotion ("Temple"). The threefold division of *Passage* dramatizes three attitudes toward life, in their regularized religious aspect and in their aspect as "expressions of varying types of culture and of individual character." A web of fascinating detail is absorbed by this structure: for example, Mrs. Moore's blessing of the wasp (which represents Forsterian good-and-evil); Mr. Sorley's rejection of the wasp (which represents his need to make intellectual distinctions and his repugnance for mysticism); and Godbole's recalling of the wasp (which illustrates his indifference to the intellect and its distinctions).

The structural principle of rhythmically achieved repetition is illustrated in EMF's use of the wasp. Another instance of such structural rhythm concerns Adela's accident in the road caused by an animal, which is ambiguously natural and supernatural, as that accident relates to the "accident" in the Caves (to which can also be assigned tangible and intangible explanations). There is a distinction between rhythms and symbols: symbols (which have a stable meaning) include the Marabar Hills, the Caves, the sun, echoes, serpents, snakes, and worms; rhythms (which vary according to the context) include the wasp, the accident on the road and the affair of the Cave, the speculations of the missionaries, Godbole's song, and the Tank of the Dagger. The Marabar Hills and related symbols derive meaning from sources outside the novel [perhaps questionable]. The attribute of Nothingness assigned to the Caves aligns them with the mysterious aspects of the Hindu deity. In the UPANISHADS, Atman (the self) and Brahman (the Not-Self) are associated with a cave; when Maya or illusion is dissipated, Atman and Brahman become one: "Atman and Brahman, the Self and the Not-Self, which are truly identical, dwell in the cave on the highest summit." The relation between the highest self (Brahman) and the soul (Atman) is analogous to that between the snake and its coils; Brahman and Atman are

279

ultimately one. The "oum" sound in the echo corresponds to the mystic syllable "om" in Indian religion. Meditation on the syllable will lead the Atman to Brahman. Light imagery in the Caves is associated with intelligence, but EMF is also revealing the limits of intelligence, something he does by following the struck match with darkness. This sequence also suggests that time is followed by the irrational idea of eternity, that space yields to an irrational idea of the infinity of space, and that all rational conceptions lead to irrationalities. The striking of the match and the resulting little worms of coiled light imply the existence of the whole serpent.

There are also Schopenhauerean elements in *Passage*. [The monisms of Schopenhauer and Shankara are discussed.] The ultimate monism of Hinduism is one that attributes no qualities to ultimate being. Some Schopenhauerean interpretations [debatable]: The fists and fingers of the Hills denote the intellect under the service of the will (as in the Schopenhauerean description of the body, the hands betoken the will); the sun is seen as a source of light (knowledge) and a source of heat (warmth, or will and power). Like Schopenhauer, EMF stresses the insignificance of human behavior. The Western attitude, in its valuing of the measurable and rational, is opposed to the Oriental; the Orient stresses the inadequacy of the intellect to apprehend deity. Mrs. Moore and Adela in "Caves" reveal these inadequacies of the Christian-ordered mentality in confronting the elemental sides of experience. The indeterminacy of the events in the Caves are an asset to the novel, not a defect; "the double vision" that EMF uses allows us to see the actors in a natural, realistic way and also in a supernatural, mythic way. Neither Fielding nor Aziz as intellectually oriented men can ever understand what happens at the Marabar; it transcends their intellects. Mrs. Moore does capture the final meaning of the Caves, though she is unprepared for it. The costs of being at one with the Universe are ultimately too great for her to bear: the loss of "a transcendent sanction for values," of the distinction between good and evil, of an ultimate reward for good works, and of the sublimity of God or the infinite. She sees eternity as a serpent composed of other wriggling serpents, as a mass of struggling wills, and she is overwhelmed. Her intuition at Asirgarh of another India implies that the anti-vision in the Caves is not final, but it comes too late to restore her.

EMF emphasizes the reconciliation of various antitheses, as in the Shrines of the Mind and Body (which signify that religion all too often includes partial allegiances). The Shrine of Mind equals the Way of Knowledge, which equals the Caves (or the West); the Shrine of the Body equals Aziz's Way of Works (or Islam). The Tank near the Shrines signifies the Way of Love (or Hinduism); the fusion of the three Ways takes place when the boats collide in the tank at Mau. Something is always lacking in any one Way of life and the characters who represent it. The Mediterranean gives us the final norm, the vital kind of proportion and reconciliation of extremes inculcated in *Howards End*. [Most critics do not agree; they regard the muddle at Mau as potentially more creative than the order and seemliness associated with Fielding's view of Mediterranean culture. Attempts to discover EMF's "cosmos" in *Passage* and to relate structure, symbol, and theme to it. An overschematized presentation. It is questionable that the Caves represent rationality; and they also relate, as Wilfred Stone in THE CAVE AND THE MOUNTAIN (1966) and others have indicated, to their obverse, the possibilities to which sublime visionary experience can attain. Despite these reservations, the insights in the critique are abundant and have made it a standard essay. The discussion of the Caves as they relate to Oriental religion and to Schopenhauer provides fertile suggestions for interpretation, though few succeeding critics have agreed all the way with Allen.]

676 Allen, Walter. THE NOVEL TO-DAY (Lond & NY: Longmans, Green, Bibliographical Series of Supplements to "British Book News," 1955), pp. 24, 27.

EMF's *A Passage to India* has metaphysical overtones that are absent from P. H. Newby's THE PICNIC AT SAKKARA. The two novels are concerned with the difficulties of understanding between people from conflicting cultures. Angus Wilson's HEMLOCK AND AFTER fails much in the same way as *Howards End*, in inadequately symbolizing the actual culture that is being criticized.

677 Allen, Walter. "Reassessments—*Howards End,*" NEW STATESMAN AND NATION, nsXLIX (19 March 1955), 407–8.

The influence of EMF and of *Howards End* as his most representative and typical work has been enormous. How relevant and how valuable still are EMF and his novel? EMF claims too much for personal relations that do not go so far as he contends. EMF finds it hard to be fair to the public and civic virtues in the Wilcoxes because he presents them at the rationally explicit level, whereas his emotions find the Wilcoxes repugnant. He does not know the Wilcoxes and Leonard Bast (though he does know the Schlegels, including Tibby, completely). Bast is a literary creation only; he is not sharply in focus. Thus, the Wilcoxes are caricatures of a type, while Bast is "a dummy based on sentimentality." We see all the characters through Margaret Schlegel's or EMF's eyes; this throws too much on the personality of the author, especially if we disagree with him. The epigrams are sometimes untrue, and some of the actions proposed (i.e., Margaret's proposal to give some of her money to people like the Basts) are unfeasible. Margaret is too superior, is "a passionless prig." She accepts the virtues of her own class with complacency, though she is aware of other worlds. Her regard for the Wilcoxes is genuine, though her attitude towards them is once again superior. If one cannot accept Margaret—her characterization and her formulations—he will not be able to accept the novel as authoritative. The comedy and the beauty of the style are outstanding, and one will continually return to *Howards End*, but with diminished enthusiasm. [A stimulating minority report.]

678 Bazalgette, Diana. *"Howards End,"* NEW STATESMAN AND NATION, nsXLIX (26 March 1955), 438.
In view of women's lack of emancipation in the Edwardian age, they would probably not show more than Margaret Schlegel's "academic interest" in the poor. [Letter occasioned by Walter Allen's "Reassessments—*Howards End*" (1955).]

679 Bensen, Alice R. "E. M. Forster's Dialectic: *Howards End*," MODERN FICTION STUDIES, I (Nov 1955), 17–22.
In *Howards End* EMF is much less concerned with the ramifications of his symbols as such than with the coexistence of the Schlegels (with their concern for the inner life and sensitivity) and the Wilcoxes (with their drive toward power and external life). Margaret Schlegel and Henry Wilcox are the principals in their respective camps; they are defined not only in relationship to one another but in relationship to people from their own circles who are in a less tenable position (e.g., Helen Schlegel and Charles Wilcox). The most productive kind of reconciliation would not destroy the identity of opposing forces but preserve them in tension with each other. Howards End house becomes a bulwark and support to the accord achieved by Margaret, Helen, and Henry at the end rather than the reason for the accord. [A sound statement concerning the most apparent way in which EMF's dialectic works in *Howards End.*]

680 Blotner, Joseph L. "E. M. Forster: The Problem of Imperialism," "The Fruits of Imperialism," THE POLITICAL NOVEL (Garden City, NY: Doubleday, Doubleday Short Studies in Political Science, 1955), pp. 22–23, 50.
In *A Passage to India* the two themes are the divisions that split India and the love that alone can make it whole. England has taken India without love in a union, which is rape. This act is paralleled by the projected loveless marriage between Adela Quested and Ronny Heaslop; an ironical parallel also occurs when Adela, the English woman, accuses her Indian host, Aziz, of trying to rape her at the Marabar Caves. Mrs. Moore dispels some of the evil through her spiritual influence. *Passage* is a political force as an appeal either for love or for withdrawal from India. The clannishness, snobbery, and militaristic attitudes of the Anglo-Indians are the prime causes of India's (and Britain's) imperial tragedy.

681 Bowra, C. M. "Beauty in Bloomsbury," YALE REVIEW, nsXLIV (March 1955), 461–64.

In THE BLOOMSBURY GROUP (1954) J. K. Johnstone devotes much of his attention to EMF, Lytton Strachey, and Virginia Woolf and may give the mistaken impression that Bloomsbury was concerned with the arts primarily. The aesthetic emphasis may cause Johnstone to be somewhat narrow in approach: what held the group together was not admiration for the arts but a special approach to life appealing to the postwar generation. Following G. E. Moore, Bloomsbury did believe in aesthetic states and personal relations, and therein lies its strength and weakness. The three writers were careful and conscientious writers, and they are less to be thought of as the heirs of Victorian and Edwardian literature than of the aesthetic cult of the Word deriving from Flaubert and Mallarmé. Bloomsbury's weakness was a narrowness of outlook and a possible inhumanity. The three writers were critics of life but limited in outlook and constricted in sympathy. Strachey's essays are overelaborate, Woolf is interested in objects as much as people, and EMF excludes too many types from his purview. [Intelligent and perceptive discussion of EMF's milieu.]

682 Brooks, Benjamin Gilbert. "Three English Novelists and the Pakistani Scene," CRESCENT AND GREEN: A MISCELLANY OF WRITINGS ON PAKISTAN (Lond: Cassell, 1955; NY: Philosophical Library, 1956), pp. 120–30.

A Passage to India seemed to correct the picturesque, fairy-dress conception of India to be found in Kipling's KIM; *Passage* seemed to be an honest attempt at understanding. EMF does convey some sense of the Muslims as part of a world-wide culture. *Passage* is more adult than Kipling's novels or A. E. Mason's (THE BROKEN ROAD is Mason's best book on India). The subtlety of *Passage* makes it a good example of Anglo-Pakistan fiction. It is more of a tour de force than Kipling's KIM. EMF's experience is transferred to the Muslims who value personal relations as did the Dorset shepherds, the Italians, and the cosmopolitan intelligentsia in his early novels. Noteworthy are his skilled craftsmanship, delicate irony, and poetic feeling merged with his "power of orchestration," at least through to the trial scene. Thereafter, these gifts are dissipated and attenuate into delicate fantasy in the Hindu episodes at the end. But *Passage* does have full power in the presentation of Aziz's and the other Muslims' characters.

683 Cazamian, Madelaine. "Conteurs Irréalistes: Rêves et Enchantments: E. M. Forster" (Anti-Realistic Fiction Writers: Dreams and Miracles: E. M. Forster), LE ROMAN ET LES IDÉES EN ANGLETERRE, 1860–1914, III: LES DOCTRINES D'ACTION ET L'AVENTURE, 1880–1914 (The Novel and Ideas in England, III: The Doctrines of Action and Adventure, 1880–1914) (Paris: Société d'Édition: Les Belles Lettres, Publications de la faculté des Lettres de l'Université de Strasbourg, 1955), pp. 453–57.

In "The Other Side of the Hedge" and "The Celestial Omnibus" a note of serenity and repose contrasts with a wrenching, sinister, and universal fatality. In "The Point of It" death is seen as a prolongation of life: a futile life will result in a futile life after death. In "Mr. Andrews" an abstract, impersonal, inhumane idea of heaven is rejected. EMF's fantasizing is colored with explicit mythologizing in "The Story of a Panic," "The Curate's Friend," and "Other Kingdom." EMF's antirealism contributes these qualities to his literary philosophy and practice: a detachment from the dogmatic, an ongoing sense of the complexity of reality, a preference for the instinctive and spontaneous, a persistent symbolism, and a susceptibility to forces that free and enliven and a rejection of those that confine. [Analysis of some of EMF's short stories as good examples of an antirealistic, supernatural mode of writing.] [In French.]

684 Charrington, Charles. RUDYARD KIPLING: HIS LIFE AND WORK (Lond: Macmillan, 1955), p. 360; as THE LIFE OF RUDYARD KIPLING by C. E. Carrington (Garden City: Doubleday, 1956), pp. 280–81.

Only EMF's *A Passage to India* can compare with KIM as a novel reflecting life in India. KIM withstands the comparison. EMF, not Kipling, is the political writer, and he appraises more sharply and critically than does Kipling the Indian scene and character. Kipling is, however, more sympathetic to the land and its people.

685 Ford, George H. DICKENS AND HIS READERS: ASPECTS OF NOVEL CRITICISM SINCE 1836 (Princeton: Princeton UP; Lond: Oxford UP, 1955; 2nd ed, NY: W. W. Norton, Norton Library, 1965), pp. 68, 191, 196, 211, 225, 226.

In comparison with the sentimental quality of Dickens's death scenes, an implied sentimental streak obtrudes in EMF's deliberate down-playing and casual treatment of death that also makes it unreal. The questions and the dramatization of characters confronted with metaphysical ultimates, characteristic of Dostoevski and of the episode of Mrs. Moore in the Marabar Caves in *A Passage to India*, are lacking in Dickens. [Some interesting EMF references in this standard book of Dickens scholarship. Other references to *Aspects of the Novel* appear.]

686 Garnett, David. THE FLOWERS OF THE FOREST (Lond: Chatto & Windus, 1955; NY: Harcourt, Brace, 1956), pp. 33–35.

[Vol. II of Garnett's autobiography, covering years ca. 1914–ca. 1924 (see also THE GOLDEN ECHO [1953] and THE FAMILIAR FACES [1962]). The books are invaluable for their insider's insights into EMF's Bloomsbury milieu. On Garnett's first visit to Lady Ottoline Morell's Bedford Square house, both

EMF and D. H. Lawrence were present. As a boy of fifteen, Garnett had first met EMF when EMF came to tea at the Garnetts' Hampstead flat. Edward Garnett had written favorably about EMF's work in the NATION and had encouraged him by letters (see "Villadom" [1910]). The Garnetts thought *A Room with a View* was EMF's best novel. EMF was also present when Garnett and the Lawrences visited Duncan Grant's studio. After Lawrence began a tirade of adverse criticism on Grant's paintings, EMF left to catch a train to Weybridge. Following Garnett's and Francis Birrell's visit to the Lawrences in Sussex in 1915, Lawrence wrote famous letters to Lady Ottoline Morell and to Garnett likening the Bloomsbury set to "black beetles."]

687 Gerber, Richard. UTOPIAN FANTASY: A STUDY OF ENGLISH UTOPIAN FICTION SINCE THE END OF THE NINETEENTH CENTURY (Lond: Routledge & Kegan Paul, 1955; reissued, NY: McGraw-Hill, 1973), pp. 56, 85, 115, 121, 138.

In "The Machine Stops" EMF dramatizes a paradox: improved communication leads to renewed isolation among human beings. (Kuno is dissatisfied but his mother is not). Passages from the story support the view that a modern writer often deliberately invents an imaginative construct for his Utopia. [EMF quoted from "Fantasy" (*Aspects of the Novel*) on fantasy requiring something extra from the reader and having an improvised air.]

688 Havighurst, Walter. "E. M. Forster: The Road from Colonus," INSTRUCTOR'S MANUAL FOR "MASTERS OF THE MODERN SHORT STORY" (NY: Harcourt, Brace, 1955), pp. 9–10.

EMF stresses the deficiencies of middle-class life and character by contrasting the English with simpler races and cultures in Greece, Italy, or India. He follows this method in "The Road from Colonus." In this story pastoral existence in Greece is genuine, in contrast to sophisticated existence in London. The irony is effective, when, for example, Mr. Lucas's daughter Ethel congratulates him on his escape from physical death when he has, in fact, lost "strength, wisdom, and love" as a result of her forcing him to leave Greece.

689 Havighurst, Walter. "Symbolism and the Student," COLLEGE ENGLISH, XVI (April 1955), 429–34, 461.

One must take cognizance of the author's whole work and intentions in interpreting a work. "The Road from Colonus" is a symbolic rather than an allegorical tale. The work means what it suggests: the water in the tree is truly that, but it also suggests the "quickness of life" that has now come to Mr. Lucas in Greece.

690 Jones, E. B. C. *"Howards End,"* NEW STATESMAN AND NATION, nsXLIX (26 March 1955), 438.

[Modifies some of Walter Allen's strictures expressed in "Reassessments—*Howards End*" (1955), especially on the attitude of the Schlegel sisters toward Leonard Bast. They have personal feeling for him but not personal regard, since clerks as a class did not associate socially with well-to-do Edwardian Londoners. EMF reveals that he has an exact insight into the "past shades of social outlook."]

691 Jump, J. D. MATTHEW ARNOLD (Lond, NY, & Toronto: Longmans, Green, Men and Books, 1955), pp. 79–80.
"Dover Beach" expresses "a horror of the utterly negative" characteristic of modern literature, especially in *A Passage to India* and "The Waste Land."

692 Karr, Harold Solomon. "Samuel Butler: His Influence on Shaw, Forster and Lawrence," DISSERTATION ABSTRACTS, XV (1955), 587–88. Unpublished dissertation, University of Minnesota, 1953.

693 Kunitz, Stanley J. "E. M. Forster," TWENTIETH CENTURY AUTHORS: A BIOGRAPHICAL DICTIONARY OF MODERN LITERATURE, FIRST SUPPLEMENT (NY: H. W. Wilson Co., 1955), pp. 334–35.
Though EMF has written no novels recently, he has been busy as essayist, lecturer, broadcaster, pageant-writer, film-script writer, and librettist. *The Hill of Devi* is an incisive, dramatically conceived portrait of an Indian prince and his court. [Discusses with relative fullness EMF's career since about 1943, when he achieved his current reputation.]

694 Leavis, F. R. D. H. LAWRENCE: NOVELIST (Lond: Chatto & Windus, 1955; NY: Knopf, 1956), pp. 25, 335, 378 (NY ed).
Lawrence's expertise in rendering the Florentine English-speaking colony in AARON'S ROD contrasts with EMF's callow treatment of such a Florentine colony in *A Room with a View*. Egbert in "England, My England" represents the element of traditional culture, similar to that embodied in the Schlegels in *Howards End*.

695 Lehmann, John. THE WHISPERING GALLERY: AUTOBIOGRAPHY I (Lond: Longmans, Green; NY: Harcourt Brace, 1955), pp. 141, 154, 167, 191, 243, 292; rptd, slightly rvd, in IN MY OWN TIME: MEMOIRS OF A LITERARY LIFE (Boston: Little, Brown, 1969).
[Many incidental references. Most important: (1) a passage from William Plomer's SADO that reveals the influence of EMF's philosophy of mediating extremes and that influenced Lehmann greatly, and (2) a discussion of, and quotations from, EMF's essay on the Soviet Pavilion at the Paris Exhibition,

the essay confirming Lehmann's own frustrating experiences with censorship of the arts in Russia.]

696 Lennartz, Franz. "E[dward] M[organ] Forster," AUSLANDISCHE DICHTER UND SCHRIFTSTELLER UNSERER ZEIT: EINZELDARSTELLUNGEN ZUR SCHÖNEN LITERATUR IN FREMDEN SPRACHEN (Foreign Poets and Novelists of Our Age: Specific Examples of Good Literature in Foreign Languages) (Stuttgart: A Kröner, 1955), pp. 215–16.

EMF is a humanistic individualist without pathos, and he is in the tradition of Erasmus and Montaigne. [Quotes Virginia Woolf to the effect that there is something composed and withdrawn in the nature of EMF's gifts.] In *Where Angels Fear to Tread* EMF humorously and ironically, then tragically, contrasts temperamental and national types. As in *Angels*, *The Longest Journey* contrasts the conventional and the spontaneous ethos. *A Room with a View* is finely modulated. In *Howards End* EMF presents a contrast of idealistic and materialistic types: the conflict ends in manslaughter (of Leonard Bast) and in clearer relations among men. *A Passage to India* reaches its high point in Aziz's trial, wherein nothing is solved or resolved. [Summary of the remainder of EMF's career, briefly mentioning his short stories and his principal books of nonfiction.] [In German.]

697 Maclean, Hugh N. "Forster's India," UNIVERSITY OF TORONTO QUARTERLY, XXIV (Jan 1955), 208–10.

The Hill of Devi belongs to the Maharajah of Dewas State Senior. He rescued EMF in India from his superior air of Cantabridgian amusement. This book is a labor of love in his behalf, as *Goldsworthy Lowes Dickinson* was in Dickinson's. EMF betrays some unease, uncertainty, and unpleasant surprise in India. The effort to grasp the subtleties of the Indian imagination, moreover, blinded him sometimes to its emotional directness. EMF reveals himself as displeased with *A Passage to India*, perhaps because he was unable to create in Godbole a true replica of the Maharajah.

698 Marshall, Kenneth Bland. "Irony in the Novels of E. M. Forster," DISSERTATION ABSTRACTS, XV (1955), 587–88. Unpublished dissertation, University of Michigan, 1955.

699 Moore, Geoffrey. "The Significance of Bloomsbury," KENYON REVIEW, XVII (Winter 1955), 119–29.

In THE BLOOMSBURY GROUP (1954), J. K. Johnstone's view of Bloomsbury is parochial or one-sided; Bloomsbury was a political, social, and general cultural force as well as a literary one. [Corrects Johnstone's view and notes how far-reaching Bloomsbury influence became in the 1920s and the 1930s, to include R. C. Trevelyan, G. W. R. Rylands, T. S. Eliot, and the Pylon

Poets and New Writing groups (William Plomer, Stephen Spender, John Lehmann, and their circles).] G. E. Moore's influence was general and diffused. He synthesized what was already in the atmosphere; his work became an intellectual, Cambridge version of Paterism. His philosophy of good taste became a kind of hedonism. Bloomsbury did not have a program; and Virginia Woolf and EMF, although sharing areas of sensibility and literary talent, were different in aim—EMF was more interested in people and their moral problems, Woolf in impressions. The similarities between them and Strachey are only the most general and intangible. Johnstone oversimplifies in failing to present the controversial aspects of Bloomsbury (and the controversies in which it engaged); the attempts by these university intellects to dominate the cultural scene were not always enthusiastically received. The "Bloomsberries" were criticized by Wyndham Lewis and others for their archness, their high pitch of sensibility and assumption of artistic superiority, and their lack of gusto. They were also theoretical and intellectual by nature and sometimes seemed to lack sympathy for those outside the group. EMF came closest to attaining the wholeness demanded by great art, but even he sometimes seemed more interested in embodying convictions than in presenting "the human comedy for its own sake." Conversation was Bloomsbury's best joy and gift: its members had wit, humor, wide range, assurance, and pettiness. EMF called Virginia Woolf a snob; EMF was too conscious of class perhaps in his patronizing presentation of Leonard Bast. But EMF was also trying to present a social problem that Woolf was not interested in. EMF "stands in fact at a sort of midway point between the socially-conscious and socially-unconscious elements of Bloomsbury." What stays in mind longest about the group is "a sense of style, an unerring ability to use words delightfully and persuasively." Their insights were intuitive, and to these they applied intellectual candor and integrity. Johnstone's book misses much, but it does indicate that the major Bloomsbury figures were artists, each deserving study; it is the first attempt to treat the subject comprehensively. [William Van O'Connor's "Toward a History of Bloomsbury" (1955) and this article are the most authoritative essays on Bloomsbury.]

700 O'Connor, William Van. "Toward a History of Bloomsbury," SOUTHWEST REVIEW, XL (Winter 1955), 36–52; rptd in BACK-GROUNDS TO MODERN LITERATURE, ed by John Oliver Perry (San Francisco: Chandler Publishing Co., 1968), pp. 92–116.

EMF could not have developed from Roger Fry, since Fry joined the Woolf-Bell gatherings after EMF had published four novels. Possibly EMF's essays on art owe something to Fry. EMF says that he does not think he knew Fry when he was writing his fiction and that Fry, to his knowledge, did not have a theory of fiction. EMF has much less of class-consciousness, exclusiveness, and snobbishness than Virginia Woolf. EMF satirizes these as aberrations in his fiction: e.g., his exposé of Lucy Honeychurch in *A Room with a View*. Though they relied on intellect as did the other members of Bloomsbury, Keynes and EMF were also skeptical of the intellect. As a young man EMF was no orthodox liberal; whereas he wished to achieve proportion, he knew that mind was not all-powerful: "His Italian fauns can be natural and also cruel, and not all gentlemen of the cloth are hypocrites or fools. His hopefulness is dark-shadowed. *The Longest Journey* presents an almost Conradian world, though caught more lightly, gently, almost playfully." EMF, like Bloomsbury in general, was interested in politics, but from a liberal and not a revolutionary standpoint. [A most succinct and informative account of Bloomsbury and EMF's background in the group.]

701 O'Connor, William Van. "A Visit with E. M. Forster," WESTERN REVIEW, XIX (Spring 1955), 215–19.
EMF denied that he was indebted to Roger Fry's theory of fiction, as J. K. Johnstone maintained in THE BLOOMSBURY GROUP (1954). David Garnett, EMF observed, has received some attention in England in contrast with the neglect of him in America. EMF says that Bloomsbury, politically, stood for tolerance. EMF is aware, but not overly, of his high position in modern letters. [The visit to EMF took place in the summer of 1954.]

702 Spilka, Mark. THE LOVE ETHIC OF D. H. LAWRENCE (Bloomington & Lond: Indiana UP, 1955), p. 88.
In Lawrence's THE WHITE PEACOCK the close relationship established between the men, Annable and Cyril Beardsall, who suffer from women, is similar to the friendship theme developed in *Where Angels Fear to Tread* and *A Room with a View*.

703 Stone, J. A. A HISTORY OF ENGLISH LITERATURE, by Edward Albert (Lond: George G. Harrap, 3rd ed, rvd by J. A. Stone, 1955), pp. 519–20, 561; materials on EMF not in 1st ed (Lond: Harrap; NY: Crowell, 1923); 2nd rvd ed, STORY OF ENGLISH LITERATURE (Lond: Collins, 1930), unattainable.
Howards End and *A Passage to India* are EMF's masterpieces; they treat misunderstandings between individuals (*Howards End*) and races (*Passage*). *Passage* is unrivalled in depicting the tensions between races and capturing India in its "magic" and "wretchedness." EMF is concerned with the individual personality and the adjustments it must make when confronted with values different from its own. He is an advocate of culture, toleration, and civilization as against barbarity and provincialism. In characterization he has subtlety of insight and appreciation of the unconscious; most of his characters are "round" and vital. He has great storytelling ability, though he is unconventional in devising plot, relying often on startling, unexpected incidents. He has detachment, irony, the ability to

present all aspects of an imagined situation with fairness, and a feeling for place. His true field is comedy, though he touches tragedy. He has an easy style, a gift for dialogue and description, "lightness of touch and precision, and conciseness of presentation."

704 Tindall, William York. "The Stuffed Owl," "Trotting Mouse," "Strange Relations," THE LITERARY SYMBOL (NY: Columbia UP, 1955; Bloomington: Indiana UP, 1965), pp. 102–44, espec 142–44; 145–90, espec 146–49, 189–90; 191–236, espec 217–20; also 86.

A Passage to India begins and ends its first chapter with a reference to the Caves. "Caves" is central among the three principal elements. ("Mosque" and "Temple" are the two others.) Everything subserves the Caves: Adela being bumped in the automobile at night by an unidentified beast, Godbole's song, and the punkah-wallah untouchable at the trial who is "mindless, aloof, eternal, reducing Western machinery to nothing." The Caves are older than time itself or spirit; they seem beyond good and evil, they are meaningless yet full with meaning—"their finiteness, denying while implying infinity, suggests that the abyss itself may be mean and petty though none the less abysmal." Even Temple and Mosque are caves of a sort and related by their shape to the Marabar Caves; the Universe of "Mosque" is formal and limited, that of "Temple" is a divine mess. (God is, however, present in both.) "Temple" comes last in the novel to reconcile the abysmal Caves with the formal Mosque; "God si Love" expresses not only confusion but compromise. Action and character also relate to the Caves. Ronny and Aziz know nothing about them; what Godbole knows he won't tell; Mrs. Moore finds out too much about them; Adela is reborn in them to see herself incapable of sexual love. The Caves include the primitive, the unconscious, and the sexual, and are an image of the multifariousness and confusion of India. In EMF the violence had always been there but in latent form; when the iolent act occurs, it shakes the fable into meaning and releases internal tensions. [Analyzes symbolism connected with Leonard's death at Howards End.] Leonard Bast is killed by the Schlegel sword in the hands of a Wilcox and by the Schlegel books; all classes are present in the house at Leonard's death; it is his posthumous son who will inherit Howards End (emblematic of England). In *Passage* the formlessness of the rich rituals in "Temple" is a form for the ineffable; the shapeless shape of these ceremonies releases tensions generated by the formal Mosque and by the abysmal Caves. [Discusses "rhythm" in the sense that EMF had used it in *Aspects of the Novel*, especially the "internal" rhythm supplied by repeated motif. Remarks on *Passage* are provocative.]

705 Ward, A. C. "The Present Age, 1930–1955," AN OUTLINE HISTORY OF ENGLISH LITERATURE, by William Henry Hudson (Lond: G. Bell, new and rvd ed, 1955), pp. 289–312, espec 301–2.

EMF is an outstanding critic in *Abinger Harvest* and *Two Cheers for Democracy*. He is a liberal but not an optimist; his awareness of the darker side of life is revealed in his spare style and in his emphasis on spiritual and mental isolation in his characters. He is "a novelist's novelist." *A Passage to India* coincided with the mood of the questioning of imperialism. Aziz is a subtly studied character. *Passage* dramatizes the tragic incompatibility between the races. The bulk of EMF's writing is Edwardian in time but contemporary in its influence.

706 Zabel, Morton. "Introducción al Arte de E. M. Forster," (Introduction to the Art of E. M. Forster), SUR: REVISTA BIMESTRAL (Buenos Aires), Numero 236 (Sept–Oct 1955), 35–52.
[Earlier form of "E. M. Forster: The Trophies of the Mind," CRAFT AND CHARACTER: TEXTS, METHOD, AND VOCATION IN MODERN FICTION (1957).] [In Spanish.]

1956

707 Annan, Noel. "Honesty about an Aunt," MANCHESTER GUARDIAN, 25 May 1956, p. 4.
Marianne Thornton reflects the milieu from which sprang the Honeychurch and Schlegel families; Battersea Rise had for the Thorntons the sanctity that Howards End house or Abinger had for EMF. EMF tries to be candid even when aspects of his subject, such as Evangelicism, do not appeal to him. The censoriousness of his ancestors derived from integrity, their distrust of imagination from the fear of the consequences of its use in society. As for Marianne, she was irritating in small matters but measured up in a crisis. EMF implies that the ideals of the Thorntons were perhaps too prescriptive and not often enough set in conflict with each other. The book is important as a link to our personal, cultural, and national past. [Excellent review.]

708 "At Home in Battersea Rise," TIMES (Lond), 10 May 1956, p. 15.
In *Marianne Thornton* EMF writes a biography of his great-aunt to tell us something about himself. The book is also important for its intimate view of the Clapham Sect and for its dramatic portrait of Henry Thornton. EMF makes of Marianne Thornton a fully presented presence, a woman of extraordinary interest. [Excellent review.]

709 Baird, James. ISHMAEL (Baltimore: Johns Hopkins UP; Lond: Oxford UP, 1956), pp. 124–25, 134.

A Passage to India is regarded as a fine example of a traditional novel; as such, it tends to embody "objectivity" and "singularity" rather than "subjectivity" and "multiplicity." If it were to embody subjectivity and multiplicity, its form would be less traditional. [Whether *Passage* so little reflects EMF's own values and emotions and whether it, in fact, fails to be "subjectively symbolic" is questionable. EMF's disparaging judgment of Pierre Loti is quoted.]

710 Bell, Clive. OLD FRIENDS: PERSONAL RECOLLECTIONS (Lond: Chatto & Windus, 1956; NY: Harcourt, Brace, 1957), pp. 28, 131; rptd with Bell's CIVILIZATION (Chicago: University of Chicago P, 1973).
[Describes EMF's visits to Cambridge, origins of the Bloomsbury group, and the values espoused by its members. EMF is described as a close friend, but he was not at the center of the group. Valuable first-hand observations.]

711 Bloomfield, Paul. "The Bloomsbury Tradition in English Literary Criticism," THE CRAFT OF LETTERS IN ENGLAND, ed by John Lehmann (Lond: The Cresset P; Toronto: Ambassador Books, 1956), pp. 160–82.
Cyril Connolly was influenced by, but critical of, Bloomsbury. Its spirit lives on in the works of Lord David Cecil, Sir Harold Nicolson, Raymond Mortimer, L. P. Hartley, and Edwin Muir. George Orwell seceded from Bloomsbury with its university affiliations. In literary criticism, the work of Lytton Strachey and Virginia Woolf owes much to the example and ideas of G. E. Moore, Roger Fry, and Clive Bell. These critics regard intelligence as a primary value but distrust pure rationality. EMF has "continued to speak calmly in the unregenerately civilian, reflective accents of Bloomsbury." [Excellent essay on Bloomsbury and its survival into the present age in the work of David Garnett, V. S. Pritchett, Philip Toynbee, and others.]

712 Blotner, Joseph L. "Mythic Patterns in TO THE LIGHTHOUSE," PUBLICATIONS OF THE MODERN LANGUAGE ASSOCIATION, LXXI (Sept 1956), 547–62, espec 558; rptd in VIRGINIA WOOLF "TO THE LIGHTHOUSE": A CASEBOOK, ed by Morris Beja (Lond: Macmillan, Casebook Series, 1970), pp. 169–88, espec 182.
EMF may have influenced Virginia Woolf in her writing TO THE LIGHTHOUSE. Mrs. Ramsay, the central life-infusing figure whose influence continues or even intensifies after her death, is similar to Mrs. Moore and her reconciling influence after her death in *A Passage to India*.

713 "Briefly Noted," NEW YORKER, XXXII (1 Dec 1956), 238–39.
The Thorntons, like their friends the Darwins, Trevelyans, Macaulays, and

Wedgwoods, represent English greatness more than do the statesmen of the age. EMF is in this book "modest, witty, charming, and honest"; these qualities, in conjunction with an informed scholarship, have contributed to the making of a major work in his canon. [Summary of *Marianne Thornton*.]

714 Brown, Ivor. "Mr. Forster's Great-Aunt," NEW REPUBLIC, CXXXIV (28 May 1956), 17–19.

EMF's *Marianne Thornton* is an act of homage; he gives Marianne Thornton a second, more gracious life. It is also a contribution to the social history of Georgian and Victorian England.

715 Bryden, Ronald. "Books," CAMBRIDGE REVIEW, LXXVII (12 May 1956), 573, 575; rptd in E. M. FORSTER: THE CRITICAL HERITAGE, ed by Philip Gardner (Lond & Boston: Routledge & Kegan Paul, 1973), pp. 420–23.

Marianne Thornton is a memorial to EMF's great-aunt and benefactress, "a work of piety and affection, and also of extraordinary fascination and art." Part of its fascination is historical, part of it is its revelation of EMF's life and personality. The mythology implicit in the book is compelling: Battersea Rise house is the lost Eden of the family, the fall comprises the marriage of Henry Thornton to his deceased wife's sister, and Marianne is the Moses who guides her clan through the wilderness, "the custodian of the family covenant and laws." In this book we see "the tradition from which he [EMF] escaped, by which he is still held." The chief theme of *Marianne* is the insecurity of personal lives in our contingent world and the need for us to establish connections to withstand the chaos of our lives. Marianne Thornton emerges as "a heroine of the war against panic and emptiness" and stands beside Mrs. Wilcox and Mrs. Moore. [Extremely perceptive reivew.]

716 Cecil, Lord David. "A Touch of Jane Austen," SUNDAY TIMES (Lond), 13 May 1956, p. 4.

On the surface, the members of Clapham Sect divided their lives between business, Puritan religion, and philanthropy. In actuality, the contrast between their principles and the warmth of their home lives was odd and charming. In *Marianne Thornton*, Marianne is seen as combining the virtues of her tradition—piety, uprightness, and unselfishness—with humor, shrewdness, sensitivity, and zest for life. "Though pious she was not intolerant; though an idealist, she was no fool." Her letters are striking; the art of EMF as biographer is equally so. But sometimes his liberal agnosticism gets between him and his subject, especially when her religion is in question. [Excellent discussion.]

717 Chase, Mary Ellen. "E. M. Forster Weaves a Delightful Family Biography," NEW YORK HERALD TRIBUNE BOOK REVIEW, 20 May 1956, p. 1.

Howards End, A Passage to India, and *Aspects of the Novel* have continuing freshness and relevance. *Two Cheers for Democracy* reveals EMF's mastery of expression and his wisdom, "a wisdom which only gains in strength and sanity by its qualities of temperance and tentativeness, humor and humility." *Marianne Thornton* has all of EMF's reassuring and delightful qualities but is different in method and subject from his earlier books. He uses personal commentary, reminiscences, and letters to define his subject: the cohesion of a family maintained by the talents and personal qualities of the spinster elder sister.

718 Crompton, L[ouis.] "Thornton's End," CHICAGO REVIEW, X (Autumn–Winter 1956), 83–86.

The Thorntons come out well in EMF's presentation of them in *Marianne Thornton,* despite their kinship to the "Pontifex-Butlers" (see their Evangelicism, their wealth, and their worship of success). There are also differences from the Pontifex world in Samuel Butler's THE WAY OF ALL FLESH: a lack of parental bullying and the presence of a humorous detachment. The Thorntons had a firm sense of their own identity but showed no contempt for outsiders. The cult of family and of houses influenced EMF. EMF is more casual concerning death than the Thorntons were, but the meaning of death is a dominant theme in his work. EMF's biography of Marianne Thornton reveals a hard-won but genuine acceptance of his Victorian ancestors. [Excellent discussion.]

719 Dunlea, William. "E. M. Forster's Homage to Another Time," COMMONWEAL, LXIV (6 July 1956), 352.

Marianne Thornton (*Marianne Thornton*) is more of an Enlightenment figure than a Victorian. She dominated gently because she was never called upon for any great self-affirmation; she adopted, rather, the genteel stoicism of her class. She is beloved though we do not love her. She lived in an age when moral comfort was desired above all else. There is a commendable lightness in the way she developed her religious and moral conclusions. She is well seen as a social individual.

720 Harvey, John. "Imagination and Moral Theme in E. M. Forster's *The Longest Journey,*" ESSAYS IN CRITICISM, VI (Oct 1956), 418–33; rptd in FORSTER: A COLLECTION OF CRITICAL ESSAYS, ed by Malcolm Bradbury (Englewood Cliffs, NJ: Prentice-Hall, Spectrum Books, 1966), pp. 112–27.

In *The Longest Journey* structural flaws are not superficial blemishes but "the inevitable correlatives of a confused or inadequate vision of life." Through analysis of the novel's form, we can best approach and evaluate its substance. Lionel Trilling in E. M. FORSTER (1943) sees in it a shapeliness of form and clarity of outline that it does not possess. The book is richer and untidier than Trilling concedes, but the novel's complexity slides into confusion because of EMF's inadequate control. As Trilling indicates, Rickie Elliot's imagination is "diseased," and he falsely idealizes Mrs. Elliot, Agnes Pembroke, and Stephen Wonham. In the novel a dialectic of sight versus blindness converges on Rickie; the forces of insight are Stewart Ansell and Stephen, whereas the forces of darkness are Herbert Pembroke, Agnes, and Mrs. Failing. Rickie is at the point of balance between them. His imagination is a valid mode of insight, but a vulnerable one; it can be perverted into fashioning false images or it can be stifled by convention. *Journey* proceeds by parallels and contrasts and is clearly directed by EMF's moral intention. His impulse to judge comes into conflict with his sense of life's complexity; his tendency to divide his characters into sheep and goats is mitigated by this sense of what is true. The content of the novel is not amenable to the form imposed on it. We are torn between an impulse to judge and the impulse to withhold and qualify; EMF never resolves the tension between the two impulses. He is successful within the framework of social comedy that he uses to explore two themes: (1) the wrong demands that society makes upon the individual (convention in the lives of the blind chokes up personal feeling and encourages the shadows of unreality); (2) the wrong demands that individuals make on one another. Herbert manipulates others, but Mrs. Failing and Mr. Elliot do so in a more sinister way. They are puppet masters who manipulate people for their own amusement. Rickie tends to impose his own ideal patterns upon human life. The promise exacted from Stephen not to get drunk is "moral blackmail." *Journey* becomes confused when it deals with the positive side of EMF's vision. When he presents the positive through symbol or dramatic contrasts, the book is successful; it fails when he rejects symbol for statement and drama for assertion. In the novel, truth, freedom, and love lack their correlatives, so that the abstractions never come to life. EMF's language betrays him, as in the overwrought passage when Rickie watches Agnes and Gerald Dawes embrace. Nor does Stephen bear his assigned moral values. The moral emphasis and the dramatic power in the book are at odds; EMF's ambition has outrun his technical resources. [This is an incisive and thoughtful, if severe, essay; the alleged defects of *Journey* can be construed more positively if the book is seen as romance or symbolic parable. See George H. Thomson's THE FICTION OF E. M. FORSTER (1967).

721 Hobson, Harold. "Mr. Forster and His Great-Aunt," CHRISTIAN SCIENCE MONITOR, 17 May 1956, p. 7.
Marianne Thornton is important because it bears the impress of EMF's mind throughout, because it is a family biography, because it shows the

religious seriousness of thoughtful people during the regency period, and because it shows that religion is not necessarily allied to solemnity and severity. The Thorntons loved daily life. They were greatly absorbed in national affairs, even if they were also devout.

722 Hoskins, Katherine. "Forster's Act of Gratitude," NATION (NY), CLXXXII (30 June 1956), 554–55.
In *Marianne Thornton* there are too many details and explanations for the reader's imagination to work comfortably. Nor do the characters invite interest: they have too few contacts with people different from themselves. When EMF wrote about the Thorntons, "satire was ruled out and irony dispersed by affection." EMF seems to have admired the moderation that he half-praises and half-deplores in his great-grandfather. As for personality, EMF probably derived more directly from the Forster grandfather (an Irish clergyman), from his father (an architect), and from his mother and her family than from the typical Thorntons. He got material help at least from the Thorntons in becoming a writer, in the form of Marianne's legacy.

723 Hough, Graham. "Bachelor Aunt," SPECTATOR (Lond), CXCVI (11 May 1956), 663; rptd in E. M. FORSTER: THE CRITICAL HERITAGE, ed by Philip Gardner (Lond & Boston: Routledge & Kegan Paul, 1973), pp. 419–20.
In *Marianne Thornton* EMF fails to enlighten his readers appreciably concerning the Thornton Clan. "Good works, money and dense family conceit form their principal preoccupations." There is an officiousness and meddlesomeness in the Thorntons, and EMF reveals a partial reconciliation with the "high-minded communal bullying" that he formerly rejected.

724 Hutchens, John K. "A Note on the Author of *Marianne*," NEW YORK HERALD TRIBUNE BOOKS, 20 May 1956, p. 2.
[Miscellaneous comment on EMF's personality, American trips, influence, and stature.]

725 Geismar, Maxwell. "The Higher and Higher Criticism," NATION (NY), CLXXXIII (10 Nov 1956), 107–10.
EMF is able to "get into the minds and hearts of the writers" whom he criticizes. [Brief notice of Harvest reissue of *Aspects of the Novel* in review of many recent books of criticism.]

726 Lewis, Naomi. "Aunt and Nephew," NEW STATESMAN AND NATION, nsLI (12 May 1956), 534, 536; rptd in abrgd form as "A Cri-de-coeur," in E. M. FORSTER: THE CRITICAL HERITAGE, ed by Philip Gardner (Lond & Boston: Routledge & Kegan Paul, 1973), p. 424.

In *Marianne Thornton* EMF is modest before his ancestors and wishes to explain them; and he captures the drama of their lives, particularly when Henry Thornton married his deceased wife's sister. We share EMF's reserve about his great-aunt. She lacks the quality of fiction; in the end she is "a monument only to the comfort and solidity of the century she spanned."

727 Lindsay, Jack. AFTER THE 'THIRTIES: THE NOVEL IN BRITAIN AND ITS FUTURE (Lond: Lawrence & Wishart, 1956), pp. 28, 204, 218.

EMF was part of a national movement of writers pledged to work against fascism: he was a Liberal, Ralph Fox a Communist, and Herbert Read an Anarchist. EMF praised T. S. Eliot for trying to keep something vital alive in our culture ("T. S. Eliot," *Abinger Harvest*); but Eliot's revolt was minimal. EMF is out of sympathy with both the oppressors and the oppressed in the present epoch. [Some interesting incidental references.]

728 "The Listener's Book Chronicle," LISTENER, LV (10 May 1956), 607, 609.

Through his patience, his curiosity, and his selective and shaping powers, EMF has created in *Marianne Thornton* a book that evokes upper-middle-class life in the early and middle nineteenth century. There are affinities between Clapham (the group to which the Thorntons belonged) and Bloomsbury. Clapham is seen to be high-minded, philanthropic, and intellectually, rather than aesthetically, oriented. EMF is as strongly principled, as generous, and as philanthropic as his ancestors but is individualist and rationalist rather than evangelical in disposition.

729 "Maiden Aunt," TIMES LITERARY SUPPLEMENT (Lond), 11 May 1956, p. 282.

Marianne Thornton is enthralling both as nineteenth-century social history and as a chronicle of a family at whose center stood EMF's maiden aunt, Marianne Thornton, and the house at Battersea Rise. The Thorntons' way of life was perhaps narrow and complacent with respect to social evils, but it had a consistency and an admirable integrity within its own set limits. [Full and discriminating article.]

730 Miller, Betty. "Book Reviews," TWENTIETH CENTURY, CLX (July 1956), 87–88.

In *Marianne Thornton* the change from the certitude present in the first part of the book to the uncertainty of the last part is marked, a change from the world of Jane Austen to that of Ivy Compton-Burnett, a change out of all proportion perhaps to its cause—the challenge to convention posed by the marriage of Henry Thornton to his deceased wife's sister.

731 Nicolson, Harold. "Mr. Forster's Great-Aunt," OBSERVER (Lond), 13 May 1956, p. 13; rptd in large part in A LIBRARY OF LITERARY CRITICISM: MODERN BRITISH LITERATURE, ed by Ruth Z. Temple and Martin Tucker (NY: Frederick Ungar, 1966), I, 312.

In *Marianne Thornton* EMF demonstrates "his dominating powers of selection and statement." EMF's books reveal "an original and combative view on life," "an independent, tolerant, critical, unconventional, observant and very lively mind." His "saints" in this book are seen as "tolerant and gay," not "unctuous and narrow." He conveys in this book a sense of continuity; he establishes the relationship of foreground and background, of major and minor figures; and he reveals insight into the minds of dissimilar people. As stylist, his "sudden comments and turns of phrase" are noteworthy. This book is a model domestic biography. [Perceptive review.]

732 Pendry, E. D. THE NEW FEMINISM OF ENGLISH FICTION: A STUDY IN CONTEMPORARY WOMEN-NOVELISTS (Tokyo: Kenkyusha, 1956), pp 27, 66, 71, 82.

Virginia Woolf was much influenced by EMF, Joyce, and Proust, as were other contemporary women writers. EMF was to Woolf and other women novelists what Richardson was to Jane Austen. Like EMF, both Woolf and Elizabeth Bowen were aware of tensions existing between vulgarity and refinement in society, and their works reflect a fear of the former and a veneration of the latter. In *A Passage to India* EMF presented the elderly matron in Mrs. Moore, revealing the same interest in the middle-aged and elderly women as did modern women writers. Under EMF's influence Woolf came to believe that character and relationship are enough, that the writer can do without plot. [Some scattered insights.]

733 Pickrel, Paul. "The Sense of Identity and the Sense of Society," HARPER'S MAGAZINE, CCXII (June 1956), 80, 82.

In *Marianne Thornton*, the upper middle-class Thorntons are shown as having had a sure sense of self-identity; they were at home in the world, not alienated from it. Marianne's life, for better or worse, was rooted in domesticity. Even the great crisis of her life was domestic: the marriage, regarded in England as illegal, between Henry Thornton (her brother) and his deceased wife's sister. The spinsterish nature of EMF's subject reflects, to some degree, his own spinsterish qualities. He has commemorated a style of life not remarkable for imagination or "intellectual grace," but it was "affectionate, self-assured, and solid."

734 "Portrait of a Family," NEWSWEEK, XLVII (21 May 1956), 120.

Marianne Thornton is chiefly notable in recapturing the enthusiasm for life that the English gentry could still feel before mid-Victorian conventions became too powerful.

735 Pryce-Jones, Alan. "The Personal Story," THE CRAFT OF LETTERS IN ENGLAND, ed by John Lehmann (Lond: The Cresset P; Toronto: Ambassador Books, 1956), pp. 26–43.
The typical 1930s writer was greatly influenced by EMF and his cult of personal relations. [Discusses the writing of autobiography.]

736 Rolo, Charles J. "Period Piece," ATLANTIC MONTHLY, CXCVII (June 1956), 76–77.
Marianne Thornton is a triumph of artistry over subject matter. Marianne Thornton herself is not arresting nor greatly talented, but EMF finds her interesting. In his sketch of her early years, he reveals pre-Victorian family life at its best. In depicting her adult life, he brings us an "intimate and representative" view of British upper-middle-class life in the nineteenth century.

737 Russell, Bertrand. "Adaptation: An Autobiographical Epitome," "Some Cambridge Dons of the Nineties," PORTRAITS FROM MEMORY AND OTHER ESSAYS (NY: Simon & Schuster; Lond: Allen & Unwin, 1956), pp. 1–12, 60–66.
[Mainly gives a view of the Cambridge EMF knew. Mentions EMF as belonging to Russell's circle of immediate friends: Edward Marsh, Desmond MacCarthy, Lytton Strachey, and John Maynard Keynes.]

738 Sen, Ela. "A Room with a View: E. M. Forster Talks to Ela Sen," ENVOY (Lond), (1956), p. 12.
EMF pays homage to his Aunt Marianne Thornton and explains her kindness to him. [The interview took place soon after the publication of *Marianne Thornton*.] He feels he does not know much about contemporary India, and the interviewer agrees. EMF feels that the Indians of the newest generation are competent and confident; they do not have the mannerisms or gaucheries one saw in the older generation. EMF is appreciative of the Indian writers who use English, since he learned much about their country from them; he praises Raja Rao's KANTHATPURA in particular. He deplores the lack of rising young poets in England. He feels, however, that Auden is a poet who has developed; and he reads him, including his later work, with enthusiasm. He is skeptical about literary criticism, feeling it to be "a parasitic trade." He feels that critics too often breathe discouragement into those who write, and he deplores their "unrestrained way as of passing eternal judgment." He plans to allow Santha Rama Rau to dramatize *A Passage to India*. EMF has an active intellect and greatness of vision, and he does not, in old age, live in seclusion.

739 Stewart, J. I. M. "Biography," THE CRAFT OF LETTERS IN ENGLAND, ed by John Lehmann (Lond: The Cresset P; Toronto: Ambassador Books, 1956), pp. 6–25.

Strachey's creations are alive even when they are wrong, EMF affirms. Many distinguished biographies have been written by novelists. This fact emphasizes the legitimacy of the methods drawn from the writing of fiction for the composing of biography. EMF himself has written the admirable *Goldsworthy Lowes Dickinson.*

740 Trilling, Lionel. "Mr. Forster's Aunt Marianne," GRIFFIN, V (Summer 1956), 4–12; rptd as "The Great-Aunt of Mr. Forster," A GATHERING OF FUGITIVES (Boston: Beacon P, 1956; Lond: Secker & Warburg, 1957), pp. 1–11.

The family presented in *Marianne Thornton* stands for a massive cultural tradition. *Marianne*, in addition to being a domestic biography of EMF's aunt, celebrates "the cultural-familial continuity." [Extensive and informed descriptive summary of *Marianne.*]

741 Wagenknecht, Edward. "E. M. Forster Writes Vivid Biography of His Great-Aunt," CHICAGO SUNDAY TRIBUNE, "Magazine of Books," 20 May 1956, p. 2.

EMF in *Marianne Thornton* writes about a person unknown to fame, but he has done so compellingly, giving us characters and a social milieu as vivid as can be found in his novels.

742 Ward, A. C. TWENTIETH-CENTURY LITERATURE 1901–1950 (Lond: Metheun, 1956) [12th rvd ed]), pp. 17–18, 68–69, 77, 79; 14th rvd ed as TWENTIETH-CENTURY ENGLISH LITERATURE (1964), pp. 11, 15, 69–70, 76, 77, with EMF materials unchanged, except for note on his affiliation with Bloomsbury, p. 11; rptd in large part in CONTEMPORARY LITERARY CRITICISM, ed by Carolyn Riley (Detroit: Gale Research Co, 1973), I, 104.

EMF's chief theme is "only connect," as it portends the loneliness of the sensitive individual in the modern age. The theme is commonplace, but EMF treats it with "austere grace and distinction of language." [Repeats materials in first edition and seventh edition; see Ward (1928 and 1940). Adds that *Two Cheers for Democracy* further reveals EMF's art of the essay. Notes his spreading reputation and his popularity with novelists.]

743 Warner, Rex. "Book Reviews," LONDON MAGAZINE, III (Nov 1956), 79–80.

Marianne Thornton not only presents an interesting and significant family relationship but a social history as well. The book shows how we have tended to overemphasize the smugness of the Victorians at the expense of their feelings of insecurity. EMF has presented his materials too meticulously but has yet managed to convey the rhythms, the lifelike aspect, and the lights and shadows of a past society.

744 Webb, Beatrice. BEATRICE WEBB'S DIARIES 1924–1932, ed by Margaret Cole (NY & Lond: Longmans, Green, 1956), pp. 34–36.
Entry (10 July 14), The EMF of *A Passage to India* is a genius: he has admirably expressed a significant experience of old age in portraying Mrs. Moore's overpowering sense of disillusionment after the Marabar Caves. [Mrs. Webb finds herself undergoing Mrs. Moore's "twilight of the double vision" and her "spiritual muddledom," as the subjects about which Webb was once enthusiastic (trade unions, local government, cooperation, political organization) no longer interest her. She is conscious of the past and of the future, but is disenchanted with the present. Like Mrs. Moore, Mrs. Webb has experienced the corroding effects of modern philosophical relativism, and she has no clear standpoint from which to judge past and future.]

745 Welty, Eudora. "The Thorntons Sit for a Family Portrait," NEW YORK TIMES BOOK REVIEW, 27 May 1956, p. 4.
"The perspicacity, the virtue and the persuasion" of *Marianne Thornton* as a domestic biography are unsurpassed. Battersea Rise, the house, is at the center of the book. EMF recreates to the full the personality of Marianne. His powers as a novelist which have enabled him to make imagined people real have helped him to make real the people who were, not too long ago, alive. [Sensitive, imaginative, enthusiastic summation of the book.]

746 Wilcox, Stewart C. "The Allegory of Forster's 'The Celestial Omnibus,'" MODERN FICTION STUDIES, II (Winter 1956–1957), 191–96.
The allegory in "The Celestial Omnibus" centers on the little boy's possession of imagination and Mr. Bons's disastrous lack of it. [The imagery of the story is discussed as it supports the allegory. Commentary is mostly obvious.]

747 William, Sister Mary. "Non-Fiction," BEST SELLERS, XVI (1 Oct 1956), pp. 228–29.
Marianne Thornton not only deals with the life of EMF's great aunt but also provides a record of her contemporaries and their inner and social life. It is truly the domestic biography that EMF says it is. [Summary of contents.]

748 Winterich, John T. "Other New Books to Know About," BOOK-OF-THE-MONTH CLUB NEWS, Aug 1956, p. 7.
Subject and biographer meet in happy conjunction in *Marianne Thornton*,

in that the voluminous Thornton family records fell into a craftsman's hands. EMF's impartiality is notable.

749 Woodcock, George. "Piety and Peacocks," SATURDAY REVIEW (NY), XXXIX (26 May 1956), 19, 31–32.

Marianne Thornton in her long life encompasses an age of social change. In *Marianne Thornton* EMF uses his gifts as novelist to render his characters "with self-effacing competence," and he does not make them unrealistically complex. Marianne Thornton represents the best aspects of her world; she accepted its values but was also capable of satiric detachment and could express herself with literary distinction. EMF is to be commended for letting her speak for herself. His craftsmanship is praiseworthy.

750 Wyndham, Francis. "Twenty-Five Years of the Novel," THE CRAFT OF LETTERS IN ENGLAND, ed by John Lehmann (Lond: The Cresset P, 1956), pp. 44–59.

EMF's silence adds urgency to his humanism and may have led to the great number of post-World War II novels that have asserted that humanism is not enough to resolve contemporary social and metaphysical issues. For a time, EMF's influence, and that of Henry James and Virginia Woolf, may have frustrated the return to realism in novelists such as Patrick Hamilton and Angus Wilson.

1957

751 Brenan, Gerald. SOUTH FROM GRANADA (Lond: Hamish Hamilton; NY: Farrar, Straus & Cudahy, 1957), pp. 36, 142, 143. Virginia Woolf admired EMF's novels because she felt that they had a solid basis in "reality" that her own books lacked. Lytton Strachey could not read EMF's novels, though he and EMF were good friends. Strachey remarked apropos *Pharos and Pharillon* that EMF would have been better at history writing than at novel writing. Desmond MacCarthy and EMF did not think of themselves as belonging to Bloomsbury, but they were accepted on an equal footing by members of the group. [Chapter 13, "Virginia Woolf's Visit" provides excellent commentary on Bloomsbury by one who was himself affiliated with it.]

752 Brocklehurst, A. G. "E. M. Forster Looks Back: *Marianne Thornton*," MANCHESTER LITERARY CLUB PAPERS, LXX (1955–1957), 75–86.
[Extended review-article, mostly description and synopsis, of *Marianne Thornton*.]

753 Enright, D. J. "To the Lighthouse or to India?" THE APOTHECARY'S SHOP: ESSAYS ON LITERATURE (Lond: Secker & Warburg, 1957), pp. 168–86.
Virginia Woolf's approach to personal relationships is excessively direct; EMF's is less so. Woolf strains after significance, and the stream of consciousness method sometimes simplifies her materials. EMF's purposes are less idiosyncratic. *A Passage to India* is a tightly constructed novel and for subject has public as well as personal relationships. *Passage* is symbolic, but less arbitrarily so than are Woolf's novels. EMF's omnipresent sense of moral subtlety is revealed in the caves disaster, which hinges on the length of Godbole's prayer. Adela Quested's curiosity contributes to the disaster, though she is decent and conscientious. If power corrupts the Anglo-Indians, servitude corrupts Dr. Lal, and injustice corrupts Aziz. If Aziz's heart guides him in personal relationships, it also proves in part to be a fallacious guide when he suspects Fielding of having married Adela. Fielding is worthy but not very interesting. The great character is India herself. The result is that the human characters dwindle against India as a "vast amor-

phous Anti-Character—and dwindle in the direction of types or even caricatures." The human situation is made to seem insignificant, but we are more truly aware of it than we are in Woolf's TO THE LIGHTHOUSE. The ending of *Passage* reveals "Forster at his best and firmest—neither cynic nor sentimentalist: one who believes in love, but doubts whether it will ever quite drive out fear and hatred." [Takes issue with Trilling's judgment in E. M. FORSTER (1943) that *Passage* is "comfortable" and "conventional" and is the least "surprising," "capricious," and "personal" of the novels. Excellent critique.]

754 Gerard, Albert, "E. M. Forster, Romancier de la Compréhension" (E. M. Forster, Novelist of Understanding), REVUE GÉNÉRALE BELGE (Brussels), No. 6 (1957), 77–89.

In EMF's life the negative pole is represented by Tonbridge School, the positive by Cambridge University. The cosmopolitan spirit of the Edwardian Age inspired the two Italian novels (*Where Angels Fear to Tread* and *A Room with a View*). [Rather pedestrian analysis of plot and characters of *Angels.*] Gino's baby is a Euphorion figure (the child of parents of different cultures to correspond to the mixed heritage found in Faust's child, Euphorion, by Helen). [Note that Lionel Trilling in E. M. FORSTER (1943) claims that Helen Schlegel's child is a Euphorion analogue.] EMF's chief theme in *Angels* is that heterogeneous cultures cannot be bridged through personal relations. His chief philosophical theme is the need to attain from our imperfect experience a personal understanding based on affection and respect. His early novels have a prophetic aspect: the unity of intelligence and feeling that they recommend is a state that men will try to reach in the future. [Sketches in the Cambridge and Bloomsbury background; notes the skepticism of these men at King's College and their challenging of existing values.] [In French.]

755 Haugh, Robert F. JOSEPH CONRAD: DISCOVERY IN DESIGN (Norman: University of Oklahoma P, 1957), pp. 36–37.

As for EMF's complaint about the fogginess or obscurity of Conrad's work ("Joseph Conrad: A Note," *Abinger Harvest*), perhaps the fault is as much in the viewer (the critic) as in the object.

756 Howe, Irving. "Conrad: Order and Anarchy," POLITICS AND THE NOVEL (NY: Horizon P, 1957; Lond: Mayflower, 1958; Cleveland & NY: World; Lond: Mayflower Meridian Books, 1958), pp. 76–113, espec 110.

Emilia Gould in NOSTROMO lacks the boldness of Mrs. Moore in *A Passage to India* and reveals, in comparison, a life which "narrows into a ritual of controlled deprivation."

757 Isherwood, Christopher. [Headnote, "The Story of the Siren,"] GREAT ENGLISH SHORT STORIES, ed by Christopher Isherwood (NY: Dell, Laurel Edition, 1957), pp. 172–73.

In "The Story of the Siren" the notebook is a symbol of a dry rationalism (which in itself provides no meaningful clue to the mystery of existence). It becomes mysterious and beautiful when it is immersed in the water of the Blue Grotto at Capri and rescued by the boatman, a beautiful child of Nature. The Siren is a vital if unsettling force. The man who sees it, like the boatman's brother Giuseppi, will be unable to resume a conventional life, and he is likely to be destroyed by the guardians of that life. However, the dangerous search for the siren must go on if the world is to be saved. The story is saturated with EMF's own personality, boyish but not näive, emotional but not sentimental, frank but not aggressive, ironical but not spiteful.

758 Jyoti, D. D. "Mystical and Transcendental Elements in Some Modern English and American Writers in Relation to Indian Thought: R. W. Emerson, H. D. Thoreau, E. M. Forster, T. S. Eliot, A. Huxley." Unpublished dissertation, University of London (King's College), 1957.

759 Løgstrup, K. E. DEN ETISKE FORDRING (The Ethical Demand) (Copenhagen: Glydendal, 1957 [Scandinavian University Books, publ in cooperation with publishers in Oslo and Stockholm]), pp. 20–22, 203–4; trans into German by Rosemarie Logstrup as DIE ETHISCHE FORDERUNG (Tübingen: H. Laupp, 1959), pp. 11–12, 200–201.

Disappointed expectations exert powerful influence over an individual's conduct, largely because he will be reluctant to admit such disappointments. Both the Schlegel sisters and Leonard Bast in *Howards End* are reciprocally disappointed but are unable to admit this fact. Both sides are largely blind to what constitutes reality for the other. Neither conscious motives nor ethical standards of right and wrong determine the disastrous conflict between them; it arises from Leonard's balked expectations for a life of culture and intellectual adventure and from the Schlegels' desire to do something material for him and to direct his drive toward the achievement of culture. In the moment of conflict between herself and Henry Wilcox, Margaret judges her husband's behavior and sees that the same traits of narrow-mindedness and hypocrisy that she had previously regarded as harmless and tolerable are moral weaknesses. She passes from a psychological understanding of her husband to an ethical judgment of him. [In Danish.]

760 McConkey, James. THE NOVELS OF E. M. FORSTER (Ithaca: Cornell UP, 1957; Lond: Oxford UP, 1958); rvd from "The Novels of E. M. Forster," Ph.D. dissertation, University of Iowa (1953); "The Prophetic Novel: *A Passage to India*," rptd in PERSPECTIVES ON E. M. FORSTER'S "A PASSAGE TO INDIA," ed by V. A. Shahane (NY: Barnes & Noble, 1968), pp. 77–90; and in E. M. FORSTER: "A PASSAGE TO INDIA," A CASEBOOK, ed by Malcolm Bradbury (Lond: Macmillan, Casebooks Series, 1970), pp. 154–64.

Chap 1, "Introduction": The transcendent and the physical worlds (knowledge of each is achieved by feeling and by reason, respectively) are always present in EMF; his characters generally have incomplete knowledge of the transcendent world. The more such knowledge they achieve (Margaret Schlegel in *Howards End* and Godbole in *A Passage to India*) the more removed they become from the physical world. The Forsterian voice also assumes this mediating stance between extremes from a midpoint position; this voice in its purposeful asceticism is perfectly embodied only in Godbole. [Dubious whether the reconciliation between the seen and unseen involves this degree of asceticism or, if it does, if this position centrally represents EMF.]

Chap 2, "People": EMF's point of view is omniscient; its very omniscience indicates its remoteness. In Philip Herriton of *Where Angels Fear to Tread* and Fielding of *Passage*, self-knowledge brings an increasing sense of remoteness from the human scene. The visionaries and the protagonists in EMF's novels, characterized by their asceticism and detachment, reveal the impress of the feminine spirit, which for EMF implies a heightened sensitivity to the inner life and to the unseen. Opposed to this principle is masculinity, with its extraverted stress on the outer life and with its spiritual (and sexual) imcompleteness. It is best represented by the Wilcoxes in *Howards End*. Fielding (*Passage*) and Rickie Elliot (*The Longest Journey*) have feminine sensitivity but must still assert their masculinity; the conflict results in their failure to achieve a satisfying sexual relationship. Rickie fuses, but not successfully, the intellectuality of Stewart Ansell, the humanitarianism of Tony Failing, and the nature worship of Stephen Wonham. He is weaker than the three people he models himself upon, but he attempts more than they do. [Other characters are discussed.]

Chap 3, "Fantasy and Prophecy": [Discussion based on chapter of this title in *Aspects of the Novel*. McConkey goes on to discuss EMF's endeavors to achieve "a suitable mythological referent" in his fiction.] EMF's fantasy is unalloyed in the short stories. In the first four novels fantasy becomes mixed with prophecy, but only in *Passage* does EMF attain the bardic quality he associates with prophecy. In the first four novels earth provides a source of spiritual integration, a resource that fails in *Passage*. Fantasy predominates in *A Room with a View;* a movement toward prophecy occurs in *Angels* and *Journey*. Philip Herriton of *Angels* is denied fruition and fertility; so are

EMF's other central intellectuals: Rickie, Margaret Schlegel, and Fielding. Rickie is the first character concerned with EMF's overriding problem: the reconciliation of the seen and the unseen. Rickie tries to make permanent the perceived world of flux—a disastrous activity. The Christian myths emphasize the divisions between the physical and the transcendent. *Journey* and the book of Genesis both project the individual's double relationship with man and with divinity. Rickie is an Adam analogue, Agnes an Eve analogue, and Mrs. Failing a Satan analogue, whose mission it is to nullify human attempts to achieve spiritual integration. Such integration will come through pagan rather than Christian means—through Stephen Wonham, through the twin deities of Artemis and Demeter who speak through him, and through the earth, whose child he is. Stephen is not a plausible redemptive agent because *Journey* is less concerned with the acceptance of the physical than with the reconciliation of the physical and the transcendent. EMF approaches, without fully attaining, the prophetic in *Howards End.* Margaret Schlegel combines elements of Stewart Ansell (an awareness of superhuman reality), Tony Failing (a trust in brotherhood), and Stephen Wonham (earth as a satisfying force). She lays greater stress on the imagination than they do and finds through imagination and nature a sense of connection between man and spiritual reality. She gradually verges toward the transcendent world and becomes more separate and alone in the human world. Ruth Wilcox best illustrates the inability of the two positions to merge, and she becomes a statement of transcendent unity rather than a plausible character or the true carrier of EMF's voice. The commitments to the physical and the transcendent have not been bridged in this novel. In *Passage* the two worlds are bridged through Godbole and his all-encompassing Hinduism, and a valid prophetic work is the result. Earth is no longer an assured repository of value; Mrs. Moore possesses Ruth Wilcox's attributes, but her love does not have the reinforcement of earth. In India earth is now alien to man; and the God, the order, and the unity once apprehended through it must be discovered elsewhere. "Temple" stresses rebirth after exhaustion, or an attempt at inclusiveness. Godbole does bridge both worlds, but impersonally; he is the only truly prophetic figure in EMF's fiction. He emphasizes that love for individuals in the physical realm can be valid only when one is removed from that realm. Only through the concrete forms of reality (the triad of Vishnu, Siva, and Brahma) can reality (Brahman) be reached, intermittently and momentarily. Hinduism is the mythological referent, therefore, in *Passage.* In the future some connection between the seen and the unseen may be attained, a connection symbolically suggested in the yet unborn child of Stella and Fielding; it will be through a love divorced from nature and from human relations.

Chap 4, "Rhythm": [McConkey is concerned with EMF's use of easy rhythm (repetition with variation) and "difficult" rhythm (the overall ineffable impression produced by a work of art) in his novels.] In *Angels* and *Room* there is less use made of rhythm than in the later novels. In *Room*, the water is symbolic (unity and creative force); in *Angels*, the towers (a complex symbol of good and evil), Santa Deodata (her irresponsibility relates to Philip's), and the dark wood (a symbol of vitality, also of grim fatality) are analyzed. [Exhaustive discussion of images, symbols, and rhythms in *Journey*.] In *Howards End* hope from the earth remains but has become dimmer than it was in *Journey*. Howards End house, the cherished place, contrasts with the nomadic society of London. At Howards End there is ordered flow; the world outside is full of motion without order. The water images represent both kinds of motion. In *Passage* Godbole's love extends to stones but cannot include them; in love he can abnegate his consciousness only this far. The experience of Mrs. Moore in the Marabar Caves is central: she finds there a disturbing transcendent principle, a negation, that reorients her view of divine reality and that dramatizes the lack of connection between that reality and human traditions. She experiences an empty Absolute, though in Hinduism absolute reality is also without attributes. Her identification with the Absolute is incomplete because she hears an echo, but it is complete enough for her to lose interest in the physical world. In her mystic experience she is to be identified with Siva, the apathetic member of the Hindu Triad. She does not realize that her apathy and disillusionment are the prelude to new growth, which is to be achieved through Godbole and his power of love. Godbole, unlike Mrs. Moore, does not need to believe in the personal presence of God or in the principle of Good. Mrs. Moore requires a divine order amenable to the reason; Godbole is able to renounce more fully the reason than she is. The difficulties of reaching the Absolute are real; Godbole cannot surmount stone; the lit match in the Caves is separated from its reflection (the Brahman) and only is made one with Brahman by the extinction of the flame (or consciousness) and merging in Nirvana, which signifies the extinguishing of life. The Caves signify not only a cosmic negation but an infinitude existing beyond time and space to which man's consciousness cannot reach or to reach which man's consciousness is a barrier. As the cave arch implies a series of arches, so the echo implies further echoes, ultimately all of India and all of the world. The echo is sound reverberating in a world from which God is missing; it implies an order, however, beyond the phenomenal world. At Asirgarh (which appears, vanishes, and reappears when Mrs. Moore leaves India), we have an echo symbol that contrasts with the negations present in the earlier echoes; here the evil forces give ground, and Mrs. Moore begins to be transformed into an Indian deity and a redemptive force. Through the wasp, Mrs. Moore is affiliated with Godbole. The image of Mrs. Moore and the wasp in Godbole's mind suggests that her love has been encompassed by his and that his is the greater. The echo of the Caves is drowned by the noise of the ceremonies at Mau; the thunder clap without lightning suggests a universe from which evil has gone and in which unity has been attained. But the union is momentary, because the sky and rock unite to keep Aziz and Fielding apart. Fielding's qualities are necessary but bring no new integration. The way of Godbole is the only way to salvation: love existing in detachment. [Selected bibliography. A perceptive book and the harbinger of the detailed textual and philosophical criticism that EMF was to receive in the 1960s. This book had great indirect impact, though it was not much noticed on publication. The analysis of images, symbols, rhythms is acute. Excellent on *Passage* and instrumental in the revision upward of that novel. The Hindu interpretation of *Passage* has been challenged but not superseded. For reviews see "The Listener's Book Chronicle," LISTENER, LIX (15 May 1958), 304–5 and George H. Thomson, "The Perils of E. M. Forster's Critics," (1962).]

761 McCormick, John. CATASTROPHE AND IMAGINATION: AN INTERPRETATION OF THE RECENT ENGLISH AND AMERICAN NOVEL (NY & Lond: Longmans, Green, 1957), pp. 65, 73, 75, 80, 82, 155.
EMF's *A Passage to India* is one of the modern works that owes much to tradition and also to the experimentation of the less-than-great innovators. The success of the work of a writer like EMF depends partly on the contrast established between appearance and reality. Anthony Powell and Joyce Cary are similar to EMF in writing superb minor fiction and in their reluctance to risk "the possibly imperfect major performance."

762 Nehls, Edward (ed). D. H. LAWRENCE: A COMPOSITE BIOGRAPHY (Madison: University of Wisconsin P, 1957), I, 265, 266, 269, 272, 273–74, 573,n83.
[Rpts account of EMF's meeting with Lawrence in David Garnett's FLOWERS OF THE FOREST (Garnett, 1955), two EMF obituary letters on Lawrence (23 March and 22 April 1930), and letter from Lawrence to Barbara Low (11 Feb 1915); also in COLLECTED LETTERS, ed by Harry T. Moore (1962), pp. 315–16. Vol. II (1958) and Vol. III (1959) have no significant EMF references.]

763 "Notes on Current Books," VIRGINIA QUARTERLY REVIEW, XXXIII (Winter 1957), p. xiii.
Marianne Thornton is valuable not only as social history and biography but for the insight it gives into EMF's backgrounds and ancestors.

764 Oliver, Harold J. "E. M. Forster: The Early Novels," CRITIQUE, I (Summer 1957), 15–33; rptd, slightly rvd as "The Minor Fiction," THE ART OF E. M. FORSTER (Parkville, Australia: Melbourne UP; Lond & NY: Cambridge UP, 1960), pp. 19–38.
EMF expresses his themes less convincingly in *Where Angels Fear to Tread*,

The Longest Journey, and *A Room with a View* than he does in *Howards End* and *A Passage to India.* The two later novels have the virtues of the earlier ones while they avoid their defects. Two kinds of human beings figure in EMF's novels—those who believe in personal relationships and those who do not. Characters in both groups are associated with places; in *Angels* Gino Carella is associated with Italy, whereas Mrs. Herriton and Harriet Herriton are associated with Sawston. In these three novels, an element of choice is allowed the protagonist as to which side he will join. In *Angels,* Philip Herriton and Caroline Abbott decide to give over the pursuit of the Carella baby; in *Journey,* Rickie Elliot responds to Stephen Wonham and leaves his wife; in *Room,* Lucy Honeychurch finally accepts love, and George Emerson. In these novels EMF uses symbolic scenes and actions to carry his works beyond realism. EMF is more successful with his comic treatment of the false than with his presentation of the true; the Pembrokes in *Journey* are more convincing than Gerald Dawes and Stephen. EMF also takes sides too readily, making assertions about his characters without showing them in action. His treatment of sex is bloodless, yet he writes well about sexless women. EMF has notable skill in conversation and dialogue; his characters are credible when they talk. He is not a great storyteller; realism and symbolism do not always fuse in his work. He is at times overcasual and makes excessive use of surprise. EMF's style is distinctive. He produces the effect of urbane, but never stilted, conversation; he reveals an "elegant colloquialism" when he interrupts dialogue, and he has the perfect ironic manner for his own omniscient method. The generalizations are not obtrusive but rather give the novels their effect of humane, genial wisdom. He combines the conversational charm of Lamb with the ironical, satirical mode of Pope or Byron. The vagueness of some of the "poetical" passages is a blemish.

765 Schorer, Mark. THE NOVELIST IN THE MODERN WORLD (Tucson: University of Arizona P, Riecker Memorial Lecture No. 3, University of Arizona Bulletin Series, XXVIII, No. 2, 1957), p. 17.
EMF is a "beautifully balanced novelist" between the extremes of exploiting personal sensibility and regarding the claims of social organization. Though his novels possess artistic unity, the personal and the social are not integrated in them. He solved his problem by ceasing to write fiction; he was seemingly overpowered by the "Boum" in the Marabar Caves to which he, along with Mrs. Moore, responded.

766 Wagner, Geoffrey. WYNDHAM LEWIS: A PORTRAIT OF THE ARTIST AS THE ENEMY (New Haven: Yale UP; Lond: Routledge & Kegan Paul, 1957), pp. 238, 241, 285.
Lewis's TARR is stripped of the normal aspects of narrative to the greatest extent possible, and what remains is kept by Lewis only as an annoying

necessity. In *Howards End* EMF's attitude toward narrative elements is similar. EMF, like other modern novelists, is ambiguous toward the time element in fiction in *Aspects of the Novel:* he is impatient with the time-sequence as a narrative necessity but feels that it is still important as providing a means for the expression of value.

767 Wilson, Angus. "A Conversation with E. M. Forster," EN-COUNTER (Lond), IX (Nov 1957), 52–57.
[Some of EMF's incidental remarks: a failure to love marks his "goats" in his fiction; he did not demean Leonard Bast in *Howards End* (circumstances were against EMF, perhaps his inadequacy of technique); Mrs. Moore's vision in *A Passage to India* is a negative one, a vision with its back turned; he is indulgent toward those people who possess instinctive moral feeling (his Italians prove that "there is a graciousness that leads into grace"); passivity and gentleness can be destructive, but active cruelty is more reprehensible; his plots and the attributes of his characters are fully formed in his mind before he begins writing; theme for him is antecedent to plot when he writes fiction; he is gratified by Wilson's high opinion of *The Longest Journey.* Wilson states that EMF's ethic has influenced him both directly and in his reactions against it, while EMF thinks highly of Wilson's work, especially his short stories. EMF's best remark, possibly, is on Dickens: Concerning Wilson's contention that we can guess Mr. Micawber's inner being in DAVID COPPERFIELD, though he is drawn in the flat, EMF said, "Yes, but we couldn't guess that he would make good in Australia, could we?"]

768 Zabel, Morton Dauwen. "E. M. Forster: The Trophies of the Mind," CRAFT AND CHARACTER: TEXTS, METHOD, AND VOCATION IN MODERN FICTION (NY: Viking P; Lond: Gollancz, 1957), pp. 228–52; rptd in part in PROSE AND CRITICISM, ed by John Hamilton McCallum (NY: Harcourt, Brace & World, 1966), pp. 725–30.
In *Where Angels Fear to Tread*, Caroline Abbott and Philip Herriton are partially redeemed; they return to Sawston from Italy freed of complacency and fear. *Howards End* depicts a tragic struggle between the forces of intelligence and those of power. In *A Passage to India* Mrs. Moore is a part of the English middle class but also is an alien to it. In *Passage* the divisions between individuals are more fundamental than ever before; but EMF has gone profoundly into the problem and again suggests the need for integration and wholeness, his chief theme from the beginning. EMF has not been false to the Indian "facts" in the book. [Essay gathers the chief points made in Zabel's earlier essays: "E. M. Forster," NATION (NY), CXLVII (22 Oct 1938); "A Forster Revival," ibid, CLVIII (7 Aug 1943); and "Trophies of the Mind," ibid, CLXXIII (1 Dec 1951). In addition, contains running commentary, (pp. 233–44), on the novels, largely plot summary with some thematic analysis. Essay also based on Morton D. Zabel, "Introducción al

Arte de E. M. Forster," SUR: REVISTA BIMESTRAL (Buenos Aires, Argentina), No. 235 (Sept–Oct 1955).]

769 Zwerdling, Alex. "The Novels of E. M. Forster," TWENTIETH CENTURY LITERATURE, II (Jan 1957), 171–81.

EMF's first three novels pull in two ways: subtle and ironic social commentary is opposed to a positive affirmation of personal ideas. These two sides of EMF's novels are bridged by the development of the characters from an almost total absorption in the social community to a concern with a personal ethos. These first books feature the development of personality within an atmosphere stressing the reconciling of opposites. In *Where Angels Fear to Tread* the opposites are communal, not individual. The symbols for England (Sawston and its denizens) emphasize its rejection of the young, the natural, and the passionate in man's nature. For EMF, good is the acknowledgment and acceptance of love, evil its rejection or denial. In his work when nature and passion are suppressed, violence and disaster follow. Love and involvement are EMF's two chief standards. In *The Longest Journey* Stephen Wonham and Rickie Elliot are both incomplete; Stephen comprehends the physical, Rickie, the heart and the head. EMF's compassion for Rickie foreshadows EMF's humanity in *A Passage to India* in which the characters have also little control over their actions and their personalities. In *A Room with a View* Lucy's home life is less repressive than Sawston daily life, but it is shallow. It is a springtime novel in which the main characters blossom and unfold. This expansion is seen in terms of a favorite EMF dichotomy between fertility and barrenness. EMF's "forgiving irony" is emphasized in this novel, EMF being especially charitable to those who reverse their firm stands—Cecil Vyse and Miss Bartlett (though Mr. Beebe becomes more rigid). EMF fails as "a passionate prophet" because of his balanced, sane view of experience. Despite his insistence on the need for participation, he remains a detached spectator of his own creations. Possibly his irony is too benevolent. The forgiving attitude is wise rather than strong; it results in an occasional failure of energy. "The dramatic eye" also fails EMF, when he tends to substitute essay for narrative. Violence and passion are not convincing in EMF, since reflective comment sometimes replaces action. He also tends to overwrite in such scenes, as in the bathing pool sequence in *Room*. He has great success, however, in dealing with "unfelt life," i.e., with the dead. He wishes to manipulate symbols in his fiction rather than narrate; this accounts for his casual attitude toward plot. Thus, the early novels appeal to those who accept EMF's moral position from the start; others are not so readily convinced. His characters and situations do not make his ideas as vital as they deserve to be.

Howards End reveals greater maturity and firmer control. EMF now questions his own values; the issues and characters are not so clear-cut. The need to connect prose and passion is the theme of *Howards End*. EMF reveals sympathy with the Schlegels but is aware of their insufficiency; they belong to the past, whereas the Wilcoxes belong to the present. The novel poses the question: Can the task of connection be accomplished by a human being? The novel's proportions demand a hero, and Margaret Schlegel is all too human. The novel is not always convincing in its spectacle of heroics; the disturbing goblins loom too large. The final note of promise is unjustified in the novel itself. It is more convincing in its private than in its public ranges of meaning. Its true theme is a disenchantment with the power of human relationships. In it EMF urges that compromise is appropriate in a twilight world, wherein the highest virtue is that of simple acceptance. *Passage* is a genuine triumph of the dramatic eye. The cause of good and evil is shown to be communal rather than individual. EMF now questions the efficacy of intimacy and human life. Are they possible in a hostile world? He would seem to say that between people only civility, not intimacy, is possible. A note of weariness and fruitlessness obtrudes; a world of isolation and solitude is portrayed in which people never quite come into each other's focus. Again, the note is acceptance rather than hope and expectation. Through tolerance and acceptance, a compromise position between extremes is reached, a position founded upon an awareness of imperfection. [Essay is at times low pressured, but some interesting formulations and judgments are given.]

1958

770 Arnold, Arnim. D. H. LAWRENCE AND AMERICA (Lond: Linden P; Toronto: Smithers & Bonellie, 1958), pp. 170, 171, 173, 177–80, 183, 185.
[Discusses all of EMF's critiques and defenses of D. H. Lawrence in their contexts.]

771 Austin, Edgar Allen. "Techniques of Detachment in the Novels of E. M. Forster." Unpublished dissertation, University of California, 1958).
[Listed in Lawrence F. McNamee, DISSERTATIONS IN ENGLISH AND AMERICAN LITERATURE (NY & Lond: Bowker, 1968).]

772 Brewer, D. S. "E. M. Forster and Sawston: The Divided Mind," PROTEUS: STUDIES IN ENGLISH LITERATURE (Tokyo: Kenkyusha, 1958), pp. 198–232.
Sawston is important in EMF's fiction though it has now actually ceased

to exist. Sawston revealed a great capacity for management that ran the country; its deficiency was "the undeveloped heart," the failure to love. In the novels through *A Room with a View* Sawston is challenged by foreign cultures, by mind, and by nature. The "mother-figures" (Mrs. Elliot and Tony Failing, Mr. Emerson, Mrs. Wilcox, and Mrs. Moore) oppose Sawston values. Confrontation between the inhabitants of Sawston (the outer world) and the humanistically or intuitively minded (those who dwell in the inner world) is a wide-reaching theme in EMF's early books. In *Howards End* the opposition between the Schlegels and Wilcoxes has an apparent resolution in Margaret's marriage to Henry Wilcox, but in reality the opposition is pushed farther back—the Schlegel qualities are subsumed in a transcendent and beneficent nature mysticism, the Wilcox qualities in the goblins that threaten spiritual serenity by their hints of evil, dislocation, and disharmony (the goblins are in essence the nothingness of the Marabar Caves). Mrs. Wilcox as the Earth Mother represents the positive reality in the book. In *A Passage to India* Mrs. Moore has wider and more radical implications than Mrs. Wilcox because nature ceases to be one source for a positively functioning reality. In *Passage* there is again a conflict between Sawston and a civilization where the heart's affections find their true place. The inner Indian culture, however, lacks the practical virtue of an outer kind of culture as that is represented in Sawston. Fielding and Mrs. Moore attempt in different ways to merge the two cultures, without great success. To Mrs. Moore alone descends the negative vision of the Marabar, offset in part by her enduring influence upon Adela, by her mystical connection with God-bole, and by her more positive vision at Asirgarh on leaving India. The vision in the Caves is, like Sawston, a negation of something positive; and EMF wishes, therefore, to reconcile it with something more positive.

As one aspect of a fundamental unity, Sawston attracts EMF even as it provokes antipathy. EMF is Sawstonian in his high valuation of success, in his desiring tangible benefits from the earth, in his wish for a practicality more far-reaching (because it utilizes love) than the businessman's, in his tacit support of the British Empire, and in his pragmatic view of the worth of culture (as in *Howards End*). EMF reveals an unconscious allegiance at times to what he condemns; he condemns virginity and infertility, but his novels everywhere illustrate his acceptance of them. Even the earth-mother figures have a Sawstonian aspect in their secularized saintliness and in their close connections with Sawstonians (husbands and sons). EMF's veiled hostility to the mother-figure extends to most of the women in his books; the result is a relative failure in the portrayals of the mother image, of marriage, and of parent-child relationships. In the novels, personal relations are less explicit than we expect from EMF's abstract valuation of them (EMF's subject is really the failure of such relations), nor is there much given of the inner lives of his characters. He is divided in his reactions to his experience, and this division extends even to Sawston itself. His divided mind is a source of strength, however, as well as of weakness. [Searching and informed essay, but not fully convincing in tracing EMF's alleged Sawstonian leanings.]

773 Cowley, Malcolm. "Introduction: How Writers Write," WRITERS AT WORK: THE PARIS REVIEW INTERVIEWS, ed by Malcolm Cowley (NY: Viking P; London: Secker & Warburg, 1958), pp. 3–21, espec 5, 18.

EMF gave new direction to the series of interviews for the PARIS REVIEW by placing more focus on the craft of fiction than had been intended. The practice of submitting questions to the authors ahead of time to be pondered was inaugurated with him.

774 Daiches, David. THE PRESENT AGE IN BRITISH LITERATURE (Bloomington: Indiana UP, 1958), pp. 86, 260–61, 265, 281; as THE PRESENT AGE: FROM 1920 (Lond: Cresset P, Introduction to English Literature, Vol. 5, 1958).

EMF illustrates how the theme of modern fiction is not the relationship between gentility and morality but between loneliness and love. "The little society" in EMF's view is opposed always to "the great society" (Stewart Ansell's formulation in *The Longest Journey*), which, as in D. H. Lawrence also, is always the enemy. EMF is a minor classic among British novelists. His theme is the spiritual deficiencies of the English middle class, a theme he treats with irony and a delicate symbolism. *Howards End* is the most mature development of this theme in an English context; when he sets his characters among Indians, the result is a "richer and profounder novel." [Bibliographical listing and brief discussion of EMF's work, pp. 260–61.]

775 Datta, V. N. "Reflections on E. M. Forster," ILLUSTRATED WEEKLY OF INDIA (Bombay), LXXXIX (6 July 1958), 8–9.

EMF combines humanity and lightness of touch. He feels that the English language should be used in India for its vitality and international status. He alleges that Thomas Babington Macaulay was all too typical of the British in India in the past: he had integrity but a complete lack of sympathy. Love, goodwill, and sound reasoning are EMF's primary values, but he distrusts "the preachers of love and the propagandists of morality." EMF feels that Indians have done much with English and recommends Orwell as a stylistic model. EMF's view toward Hinduism changes from indifference in *A Passage to India* and *The Hill of Devi* to a present sympathy for it [the indifference is questionable.] EMF loves solitude, is an apostle of truth, is notable for his integrity, and has intolerance of all that is ambiguous and "makeshift."

776 de Charms, Leslie. ELIZABETH OF THE GERMAN GARDEN (Lond: Heinemann, 1958), pp. 72–73, 101–5, 257.

Reading EMF's essay on "Cardan," Elizabeth said he must go on writing and win; but she was also jealous of EMF's abilities and disliked *Where Angels Fear to Tread* for its vulgarity when she read it in proof. She disliked the first part of *Howards End* when she read it in 1923 and disapproved of the women in the novel, but she also mentioned his "curious effect of sidling up to one with his whimsies—then suddenly real power." [EMF's reminiscences of the German Garden during his stay in 1904 at Nassenheide, his experiences as tutor for three of Elizabeth's children, and his contacts with Elizabeth (Elizabeth Mary, Countess Russell and von Arnim).]

777 Faverty, Frederic E. "Forster under the Spell of India," CHICAGO SUNDAY TRIBUNE, "Magazine of Books," 27 July 1958, p. 2; rvd and rptd as "E. M. Forster's *A Passage to India*," YOUR LITERARY HERITAGE (Philadelphia & NY: Lippincott, 1959), pp. 193–95.

EMF attacks consistently such subjects as nationalism, imperialism, Christianity, racial division, and society's hostility to the artist. In India the English officials are efficient and just, but they withhold sympathy, understanding, and respect. Christianity is too rational in outlook and too restricted in sympathy to cope with the Indian chaos. In Godbole and his Hinduism there is a convincing synthesis of opposites, a recognition of evil as well as good. Characters, settings, and atmosphere all convince. [Brief critique of *A Passage to India*.]

778 Fielding, K. J. CHARLES DICKENS: A CRITICAL INTRODUCTION (Lond, NY, & Toronto: Longmans, Green, 1958), pp. 109, 115–16; 2nd rvd ed (1965), pp. 131, 137–38.

Too much has been made of EMF's distinction, formulated in *Aspects of the Novel*, between round and flat characters, since Dickens was after the creating of live characters rather than the analysis of them. Miss Mowcher and Mr. Micawber in DAVID COPPERFIELD are such intensely conceived characters as to make the distinction between round and flat characters absurd. How Dickens made his flat characters forceful EMF never explains.

779 Fricker, Robert. "E. M. Forster," DER MODERNE ENGLISCHE ROMAN (The Modern English Novel) (Göttingen: Vandenhoeck & Ruprecht, 1958), pp. 77–92.

EMF means more to us than most of his contemporaries. He has affinities with Meredith and with the fantasy writing of Shakespeare, as in THE WINTER'S TALE. EMF is modern chiefly by virtue of his symbolism. He is a Lawrence with the sexuality implicit, a Wells without a belief in the future; and he has affinities with Shelley in his wish to get to the depths of human nature. Mr. Emerson's aphorism in *A Room with a View* underlies EMF's novels and his world view: "Distrust every enterprise that requires new robes." Like Butler, he is temperamentally a modern; like Butler he does not write experimentally. *Where Angels Fear to Tread* is a small masterwork. There are many resemblances to James's THE AMBASSADORS, but *Angels* is less massive. Lilia and Philip Herriton in Monteriano are like Chad and Strether in Paris, and Gino Carella reveals the same natural energies as Mme. de Vionnet. *Room*, like *Angels*, reveals EMF's comic mastery. In both novels people encountered in Italy—Gino Carella and George Emerson—become life-enhancing forces. In *The Longest Journey*, the influences of Shelley and Neoplatonism predominate. It is an education-by-life novel that ends in despair. The theme is the nature of reality; in the terms that Ansell defines, he is right in saying that Agnes Pembroke does not exist. The symbolism in *Journey* is paramount and intricate. Rickie Elliot's death is a comment on his blindness. Stephen Wonham, though illegitimate, is a force for life and reveals EMF's sympathy with the revolt of spontaneous human nature nature against Victorian standards. Stephen is a full man, and he attains mystical proportions by the end of the novel. England rather than Italy is the home of the reality that Rickie would have found had he followed the path of Stewart Ansell, Stephen, and Mrs. Elliot and rejected Sawston, the Pembrokes, and Aunt Emily Failing.

Howards End and *A Passage to India* are more complex and mature novels. *Howards End* stresses the inner life. It is a novel full of tension, surprise, and the unexpected workings of fate. Howards End house is a symbol of the inner life, of the possibilities of communication among men, and of a society characterized by wholeness. At the end, the principle of the inner life triumphs over separation. The novel is carefully constructed, though the incidents often seem casual. They always suggest that in the inner life alone resides the truth for men. The house becomes a standard of truth against which the incidents and symbolic patterns are measured. In *Passage* the symbolic elements are more closely integrated with the realistic. *Passage* is concerned with men attempting to form a world view from the diversities of experience. EMF sees not just the externals of India but India herself. He does not begin the novel with a stress upon racial division; the racial division (at the trial) comes later. The problem is not to be solved by humanistic means but only by a general world view, such as Hinduism, that erases differences among men. The sky is aligned with the Marabar Caves, since both are emblems of infinity. EMF emphasizes that the inner life cannot withstand racial hatred. But the inner life does eventuate in deeper understanding; in the Mau tank the central characters are brought together and reconciled. Aziz forgives Adela Quested, and Fielding draws closer to Ralph and Stella Moore. The festival is a symbolic occurrence in which men achieve union with one another, but only momentarily. *Passage* is a symbolic novel with universal dimensions: the echo and the Caves are powerful symbols. The echo distorts, and it initiates distrust, dividing even those with the best intentions. The Caves indicate that good and evil are not clearly demarcated entities but blend into each other even while they are each other's opposites. *Passage* fuses convincingly the temporal and the divine aspects of experience and is one of the century's great novels. [Competent general survey. Summary of EMF's life and career.] [In German.]

780 Hall, James. "Forster's Family Reunions," ENGLISH LITERARY HISTORY, XXV (March 1958), 60–78; rptd, slightly rvd, as "Family Reunions: E. M. Forster," THE TRAGIC COMEDIANS: SEVEN MODERN BRITISH NOVELISTS (Bloomington: Indiana UP, 1963), pp. 11–30.

In EMF's work a conservatism about the family balances his liberalism about institutions. In *Where Angels Fear to Tread* and *A Room with a View* there is rebellion against passive acceptance of the family; *The Longest Journey* is concerned with restoration of the family. The concern with perpetuating the family provides the "sympathetic" as opposed to the formal structure of *Howards End*. The strongest connection is made not between intellectual (Margaret Schlegel) and businessman (Henry Wilcox) but between intellectual (Margaret) and intellectual (Helen Schlegel). In their separation and reconciliation something from both their values is preserved. The most incisive scenes are the comic and those in which the sense of space predominate; these are invariably the scenes that pit Schlegel against Schlegel. The writing about the Wilcoxes is thinner and more irritable. Another connection is also important, that between Margaret and Ruth Wilcox; when Margaret most fully connects with her, she takes over Ruth's role in the Wilcox clan and also connects most fruitfully with Helen. Helen rebels against the managing, authoritarian spirit represented for her in Henry and to a degree in Margaret. In this revolt she champions Leonard Bast, from personal rather than humane motives, however. Margaret and Henry deserve each other because they are both managers of life and the emotions; from the point of view of the novel, Margaret's commitment to Henry is real but wrong. The main threat of the novel is not the triumph of the Wilcoxes but the possibility that they may "inherit" Margaret.

EMF is also interested in the relationship between the class conflict and the family conflict. Those are rewarded who connect the present with the past, as the sisters do; those who cannot make this connection are routed like the second generation of the Wilcoxes and like the patriarch (Henry) who is deprived of power by defending the Wilcox values. The ending is like that of JANE EYRE: The offenders are punished, the husband is gelded (needing only a nurse), and the feminine principle prevails. Leonard is given an absurd but good death, since he would not have fitted into Howards End house. The family is reconstituted at the end; Henry and Leonard fill emotional needs for each of the sisters at a crucial point but are themselves changed. Henry loses force and Leonard dies, but both have deeply affected the sisters' development. By the end Margaret learns to be impulsive at times in handling Henry; Helen learns to contain her impulsiveness. Margaret loses her sense of uprootedness, Helen her sense of being an outcast. Margaret becomes Mrs. Wilcox but grows beyond her predecessor as well. The novel points up the necessity, and the difficulty, of the inner life, especially for those who do not understand it. It is pessimistic concerning social connection, though the concluding scene symbolizes a stable family life. In part, Leonard exists to illustrate EMF's view of the need to balance the pursuit of the inner life with a recognition of one's limitations. For Leonard, Ruskin is unnatural. The combination of affection and irony with which EMF conceives Leonard is one of his finest achievements. The Wilcoxes of the second generation make Margaret what she is really not, a rebellious rather than a flexible personality; but her rebellion (which is not revolt) allows her to achieve deeper awareness and to establish more fully her understanding with her sister. The rebellion and the sympathy, comprising EMF's liberalism, are enveloped by (and contribute toward) the preservation of family continuity. This conservatism about the family deepens the sense of identity and reality in the Schlegels but also leads to a distrust of experience itself, so marked in *A Passage to India*. The past is sometimes used not so much to bolster the present as to resist it. [Excellent, deep-probing, and wide-ranging essay; one of the best essays on *Howards End*.]

781 Hammelmann, Hans. A. "Der Romancier E. M. Forster" (The Novelist E. M. Forster), Die Neue Rundschau (Frankfurt amMain), LXIX: 3 (1958), 539–48.
EMF is the greatest contemporary living English novelist though he has not published a novel since 1924. He has withstood the test of time better than Edwardian contemporaries such as Bennett, Wells, and Galsworthy. He is not a programmatic realist; he is less heavy and serious than these contemporaries; he has a universal dimension; and he gives a positive view of the world. "The Road from Colonus" dramatizes the theme of all his fiction—the need to exchange the life rooted in custom for a more vital life. *Where Angels Fear to Tread* contrasts true and false attitudes toward life in the Italian and British characters respectively: Harriet Herriton's self-righteousness contrasts with Gino Carella's spontaneous love for his son and his involvement in parenthood. *The Longest Journey* continues the contrast between convention and the necessity to rebel against it. The prescriptive is lacking from EMF's work, except as something to be condemned. The short stories illustrate his ideas and values, in particular, his stress on individualism and the need for communications and reconciliation with one's fellow men. In *Howards End* the house is a reconciling force; the positive role of personal relationships is paramount. *A Passage to India* goes beyond political questions to consider more fundamental relationships. No clear

solution to pressing problems is presented in *Passage;* EMF regretfully emphasizes the separations that must obtain among men. *The Hill of Devi* again stresses men's tragic insufficiency—mankind's failure in general, not just a failure in understanding between races. Only our inner instinct can give us the sense of order and disorder by which we can regulate our lives. As EMF says in *Howards End,* love alone will confer immortality upon men. [In German.]

782 Hennecke, Hans. "Wonnen und Bitternisse der Musse" (Delights and Bitternesses of Leisure), Kritik: Gesammelten Essays zur Modernen Literatur (Criticism: Collected Essays on Modern Literature) (Gutersloh: C. Bertelsmann, 1958), pp. 188–95.

EMF's early novels and stories reflect the slow loss of "sweetness" in the world. EMF in *A Passage to India* is skeptical about interracial understanding. The basic problem of all the novels is establishing and sustaining the true and creative relationships between men. EMF the artist and psychologist is always at the service of EMF the inquiring moralist. The apparent nihilism of *Passage* (EMF is comparable to other pessimists such as Byron, Leopardi, [Christian Dietrich] Grabbe, and Baudelaire) is a sort of zero-point of the soul. "The Eternal Moment," which is akin to *The Longest Journey,* is EMF's best story. EMF has two main themes: the consequences of the undeveloped heart, and the ineffable dimension of mystical experience that reveals a further reality behind the perceived reality. [In German.]

783 Hoggart, Richard. "The Unsuspected Audience," New Statesman and Nation, nsLVI (6 Sept 1958), 308–10.

In British fiction there is a more definite sense of social identity between writer and reader than in America. American writers do not assume a homogeneous audience, and they establish their emotional pitch and their rapport with the reader as they go along. British fiction is socially assured and tends to know how syntax should be employed to express a definite quality and attitude. This assurance, for example, is everywhere present in the opening description of Chandrapore in *A Passage to India.* This ability to communicate to a well-defined and civilized group marks the fiction of Elizabeth Bowen, C. P. Snow, Angus Wilson, and L. P. Hartley, among others. This group is the upper middle class. With the widening of the reading public, readers now come from classes other than the upper middle class. This audience finds itself more at home in the expansive atmosphere and indefiniteness characterizing American novels. EMF represents, typically, this upper-middle-class culture not only in his subject matter but in his art as well.

784 Iyengar, K. R. Srinivasa. "India in Anglo-American Fiction," Tennessee Studies in Literature, III (1958), 107–16.

A Passage to India is "a supreme triumph of modern prose fiction." It stresses the need to overcome categorization and compartmentalization through the intuitions—love and the understanding that results from it. Edward Thompson was the best of EMF's imitators. [Many other English and American writers cited, John Masters possibly being the most important.]

785 Kermode, Frank. "Mr. E. M. Forster as Symbolist," LISTENER, LIX (2 Jan 1958), 17–18; rptd as "The One Orderly Product: E. M. Forster," PUZZLES AND EPIPHANIES: ESSAYS AND REVIEWS, 1958–1961 (Lond: Routledge & Kegan Paul; NY: Chilmark P, 1962), pp. 79–85; as "Mr. E. M. Forster as a Symbolist" FORSTER: A COLLECTION OF CRITICAL ESSAYS, ed by Malcolm Bradbury (Englewood Cliffs, NJ: Prentice-Hall, 1966), pp. 90–95; and as "The One Orderly Product," E. M. FORSTER: "A PASSAGE TO INDIA," A CASEBOOK, ed by Bradbury (Lond: Macmillan, Casebook Series, 1970), pp. 216–23.

A Passage to India tells a story and is a parable in the service of tolerance and liberalism. But EMF also has intuitive, mystical faculties that some of his critics regret and that find expression in his conscious symbolism. However, the story element is strong, and EMF values greatly the "impure" element in art, deriving from life. Only by conscious effort of "faking" can these elements be included in a work of art. Also in EMF's emphasis on organic form there is a tendency for him to "fake" his materials so that he can produce his intended effects. EMF does a brilliant job of "faking" in *Passage*, as in his repeated use of the epithet "extraordinary" to refer to the Caves. Aziz's last mention of the echo (as drowned in the Mau ceremonies) and the thrust-up rocks on the last page (depicted as analogous to the fist and fingers of the Marabar) are other instances of "faking," of making the parts bear an excess weight of meaning. The securing of unity under the aegis of Krishna is also faked; order is achieved in life and in the novel at the expense of some contrivance. EMF's belief in the mystical significance of art as itself "the one orderly product" is a symbolist heritage and an idea that our age has found congenial. As such, art can be made to include, in orderly fashion, the extraordinary. EMF's conception of organic unity as an attribute of the work of art may have derived from G. E. Moore and J. M. E. McTaggart. This conception allowed him to do his consummate faking, to discern that muddle could also be mystery. Story, parable, and image coexist in *Passage;* its harmoniousness makes *Passage* modern (though our conceptions of harmony may differ somewhat from EMF's). His book is exemplary by its very inclusiveness, an inclusiveness that would be impossible, EMF asserts, without "love," which "cheats" and turns muddle into mystery or into art, "our one orderly product." [Quotes John Middleton Murry that a novel should be a story, a parable, and an intuited image of reality. Argument is cryptic, elliptical, and contorted; Kermode's precise valuation of "faking" is difficult to determine.]

786 Klingopulos, G. D. "E. M. Forster's Sense of History and Cavafy," ESSAYS IN CRITICISM, VIII (April 1958), 156–65.

In large part EMF fails in *Howards End* to achieve the integration and connection that was his intent. He achieves much more of this integration in *A Passage to India;* part of the reason for this was the deepening of his sense of history by his contact with Eastern life in Alexandria during World War I and his getting to know the Alexandrian poet C. P. Cavafy, with his sense of vital tradition. *Pharos and Pharillon* is a crucial book in EMF's development. In "The Return from Siva," there is a repudiation of an earlier insular Hellenism; his Hellenism is now broadened and international in scope. Stephen Wonham in *The Longest Journey* does not adequately register Hellenic values. EMF in *Howards End* tries to treat more responsibly the issues of vitality and sterility, England and Empire, but the result is a simplifying and an abstracting of the issues. EMF in *Passage* renounces the pastoral mode and realizes there is no easy good to be set against bad. Its enlarged historical perspective encourages a supple irony and freedom rather than pessimism. A more realistic and comprehensive view of history is the result in *Passage*, though it also reflects the widened views EMF had acquired in World War I, largely as a result of Cavafy's influence (see "The Poetry of C. P. Cavafy," *Pharos*). [Persuasive essay.]

787 Leavis, F. R. "Joseph Conrad," SEWANEE REVIEW, LXI (Spring 1958), 179–200, espec 183–85; rptd as "The Shadow-Line," ANNA KARENINA AND OTHER ESSAYS (Lond: Chatto & Windus, 1967; NY: Pantheon Books, 1968), pp. 92–110, espec 95–97.

Neither Conrad nor Henry James, at the end of their careers, could confidently count on being appreciated for what was central in their work. Virginia Woolf and E. M. Forster did not help Conrad's reputation essentially, guided as they were by irrelevant concern with Bloomsbury decorum. EMF wrongly asserts that Conrad's philosophy cannot be precisely defined; Conrad's ideas must be taken more seriously than EMF seems willing to do.

788 "The Listener's Book Chronicle," LISTENER, LIX (15 May 1958), 823.

In EMF's works the element of rhythm is all-important, an element that manifests itself in his use of image and symbol. American critics have been more interested in the work itself than in the accent in which it is written. By the close reading of EMF's texts, these critics have helped expand their dimensions. For EMF, men's acts and relations still have meaning, even in face of a frightening void, and are seen to be both little and great. [Review of James McConkey's THE NOVELS OF E. M. FORSTER (1957).]

789 McConkey, James. "The Voice of the Writer," University of Kansas City Review, XXV (Dec 1958), 83–90.

"Voice" is a term not often enough considered in discussions of technique. It is more inclusive and more fundmental than "tone"; it represents the author's total personality, his response to the world. Theme and voice become in most cases identical. EMF's work reveals the presence of voice as a controlling force. EMF's "voice" is the midpoint between the unseen and seen worlds, seeking to connect the two yet expressing a sense of its own apartness. In *Howards End* the marriage between Margaret Schlegel and Henry Wilcox is a forced connection at the level of statement; EMF's voice is unconvincing with respect to this incident. One can't believe in the marriage because EMF betrays through his voice the fact that he cannot. In *A Passage to India* his commitment to personal relations is negated by the accents of his voice, and no reconciliation between opposed types is attempted. In *Passage* he has comprehended his own problem, and the accents of his voice ring true in almost every scene. The sadness of Fielding's and Adela Quested's farewell ("dwarfs shaking hands") is validated by EMF's voice, which has always sensed the gap between men rather than the possibilities existing for connection between them.

790 Magill, Frank, and Dayton Kohler. "E. M. Forster," Cyclopedia of World Authors (NY: Salem P, 1958), pp. 374–76.
[Lucid and informed survey of EMF's career and of EMF as writer. Bibliography of secondary materials to date of publication.]

791 Menon, Narayana. "A Tribute to E. M. Forster," Sunday Statesman (Calcutta & Delhi), "Magazine Section," 28 Dec 1958, pp. I, III.

EMF will survive as a man of letters. He is a great man: honest, civilized, generous, witty, humane, mischievous, lovable, aesthetically sensitive, and courageous. He wrote what he felt with simplicity, candor, and grace. "What I Believe" (*Two Cheers for Democracy*) is a central utterance. His writing has to be savored. *Howards End* is his best novel, *A Passage to India* his most famous. He got all of India into *Passage*.

792 Plomer, William. "The Shield of Achilles," "A Broken Chain," At Home: Memoirs (Lond: Cape, 1958), pp. 99–111, espec 107–11; 140–52, espec 144–46; also 114.

EMF has consistently related his ideas "to the phases of the revolution through which he has lived, without deserting what he has believed to be true, and without relaxing that 'moral intelligence,' without lowering that 'shield of Achilles.' " He has avoided an ivory tower existence. Of "all my uncomfortable friends he has had . . . the clearest, subtlest, deepest mind, the most generous understanding, and the most fruitfully revolutionary influence." EMF is no recluse; he belongs to the world of the present and future, and is a harbinger of change. [Stresses EMF's independence rather than his affiliations with Bloomsbury. Stresses the positive aspects of EMF's philosophy of experience and maintains that his works are too truthful to date.]

793 Pompili, Guiliana Aldi. "Nota" (Note), *Camera con Vista* (*A Room with a View*) (Milan: Rizzoli Editore, 1958), pp. 5–7.

EMF's fame is due to the quality, not the quantity, of his writings, which are characterized by a richness of ideas, a psychological and moral investigation of men and their conflicts, and a message of freedom against every type of restriction. These inner aspects of his work are expressed in a brilliant and rapid style and become more incisive and vivid because of his detached but constant humor. *A Room with a View* is perhaps EMF's freshest and most attractive novel: every sentence smells of spring. His characters seem to be ordinary English tourists, but each contributes to the precise and contradictory picture that EMF wished to present of the early twentieth-century middle class. The protagonist, Lucy Honeychurch, stands out because of her intense inner life and individualism. EMF's religious faith in the necessity of reform, proceeding from interior as well as exterior change, charges the work with much nobility and subtlety. [Standard opening biographical summary.] [In Italian.]

794 Pritchett, V. S. "Mr. Forster's New Year," NEW STATESMAN, nsLVI (27 Dec 1958), 912–13; rptd in THE WORKING NOVELIST (Lond: Chatto & Windus, 1964), pp. 49–55; and as "Mr. Forster's Birthday," THE LIVING NOVEL AND LATER APPRECIATIONS (NY: Random House, 1966), pp. 244–50.

EMF has had great influence over people in the cultivated class by teaching them "to disengage themselves from their inherited official, not to say imperial, personality." In writing against imperialism he also wrote against totalitarianism. EMF's chief gift has been "the private voice, carrying without effort, in the public place." Even the utterances that seem to countenance withdrawal do not do so. EMF is a moral realist in his fiction. He has written comedy, and a comedy of ideas. His people are often ordinary, so that they do not show in the novel as extraordinary handlers of ideas in debate. These characters are often jolted alive, and EMF exhibits "no sentimental indulgence for weakness" in presenting them. His people are either disinterested or benighted. "His comedy is positive and spiritual; it has one most alarming trait, assurance. It is lonely. It has courage." In manner he is often casually disrespectful or abrupt. "The intellectual must face causality; but he had better remember casualty and the inexplicable." EMF's contribution to present collective society is to remind us "that it will

be an arid and destroying desert if we remove the oasis of private life."
[Densely written but perceptive account.]

795 Raleigh, John Henry. "Victorian Morals and the Modern Novel," PARTISAN REVIEW, XXV (Spring 1958), 241–64; rptd in TIME, PLACE AND IDEA: ESSAYS ON THE NOVEL (Carbondale & Edwardsville: Southern Illinois UP: Lond & Amsterdam: Feffer & Simons, 1968), pp. 137–63.

EMF is part of a tradition in the novel that includes Samuel Butler and D. H. Lawrence (as opposed to the "Joyce tradition," which includes Henry James, Conrad, and Virginia Woolf). The Butler–Forster–Lawrence line is formally "nonliterary," is kinetic and dynamic, and is anti-bourgeois.

796 Rees, Richard. BRAVE MEN: A STUDY OF D. H. LAWRENCE AND SIMONE WEIL (Lond: Victor Gollancz, 1958; Carbondale; Southern Illinois UP, 1959), pp. 170–71.

[John Middleton Murry's "Lemonade?" (1926) is discussed. Of the writers compared to Lawrence, Rees regards Proust and Joyce as no longer "religiously" relevant for us. EMF's books, on the contrary, are not dead; and Lawrence's work retains its full vitality.]

797 Stebner, Gerhard. "Edward Morgan Forster: Ein Beitrag Zur Einführung in sein Werk" (Edward Morgan Forster: A Contribution to an Introduction to His Work), DIE NEUREN SPRACHEN (Frankfurt amMain), VII (Oct 1958), 449–61.

EMF works in the traditions of the English novel rather than being an innovator. EMF is a realist in the tradition of Fielding, Jane Austen, Meredith, and Henry James. He is also interested in the individual's defining reality for himself (see the opening chapter in *The Longest Journey*). His work is built around the dichotomy of the natural versus the conventional. EMF is a psychologist in his fiction but does not analyze human motives minutely. Despite his disclaimers as to the story element in fiction expressed in *Aspects of the Novel*, the story is essential in his fiction. The plot is sometimes involved but still important. EMF places much emphasis upon the element of mystery in life. He also stresses the moment of crucial choice, "the symbolic moment." His fiction is organized according to a dialectic; the forces that generate life, light, fertility, and intelligence are set against those that generate death, darkness, sterility, and stupidity. He is interested in exploring the complexities of the moral life, in analyzing the mixture of good and evil in human nature. He is a writer of tragicomedy rather than of tragedy. As to his style, elements of pathos and greatness, of poetry and conversation are intermingled; it is complex and subtle. He makes use primarily of the omniscient convention in telling a story. He is also interested in exploring the dichotomy of the seen versus the unseen, the real world versus its symbolic intonations—in exploring the double vision. In the short story genre, he writes parables or fables. He often uses in his narratives an animistic nature and the Greek deities associated with nature. Living close to nature, the individual will be protected from narrow convention, cant, and snobbery; and he will see that salvation is primarily a matter of the physical body. In living the good life, one must envision the relationship of love to death and the importance of each, one must be in contact with nature, and one must appreciate art. EMF places much stress upon the need to connect outer and inner, and puts his final stress upon the inner. He advocates individualism and the value of personal relations. He has a modified faith in democracy, but he also believes in an aristocracy of talent. He places much emphasis on the role of good will and feeling. He is interested in order and sees its most compelling projection not in politics or in science but in the work of art. [Summary of EMF's life and career. Sound but mostly obvious commentary.] [In German.]

> **798** Stebner, Gerhard. "Edward Morgan Forster: Ein Beitrag zur Einführung in sein Werk: 2. Teil und Schluss: Drei Short Stories als Beispiele für seine Thematik" (Edward Morgan Forster: A Contribution to an Introduction to His Work: 2. Part and Whole: Three Short Stories as Examples of His Themes), DIE NEUREN SPRACHEN (Frankfurt amMain), VII (Nov 1958), 507–15.

"The Celestial Omnibus" contrasts the everyday world with fantasy and contrasts the boy's true and spontaneous appreciation of poetry with Mr. Bons's pretentious appreciation of it. For the boy the omnibus is a reality, since he had first apprehended it in dreams. EMF stresses the importance of art in itself; but he does not adopt an art-for art's sake view that stresses form alone, but rather an art-for-art's sake view that stresses the influence which art exerts upon the soul of the one who appreciates it. On their trip to heaven, the boy and Mr. Bons react differently to the Shield of Achilles that they encounter; the boy accepts it, while Mr. Bons recoils from it and wants to go back to earth. In "Other Kingdom," EMF is more concerned with the spiritual influence of nature than that of art. Harcourt Worters represents the conventions and materialism, and a life of artifice; he mistakes luxury for the valid life of the spirit. Evelyn Beaumont represents the worth of the spontaneous; she is the exponent of the inner life and of personal relations, in contrast to Harcourt. Harcourt's materialism alienates him from others, as do his egotism and possessiveness. Evelyn embodies wildness, the desire for freedom, and an impatience with restraints. Her transformation into a Dryad is no ordinary change; rather, it represents her attainment of an "other kingdom" wherein she can know a full life without experiencing irrelevant restrictions. In "The Road from Colonus" the element of fantasy is less insistent; the use of myth is subordinate to an emphasis upon the influence of nature, conceived romantically and pantheistically. The central conflict is between nature and convention (as in "Other Kingdom"); the conflict is internal, rather than among individuals. Greece offers Mr. Lucas redemption from a sterile old age; he experiences a sense of harmony and unity within the plane tree. Subsequently in London his existence is a living death. He loses the possibility of redemption when convention, exemplified in his daughter, triumphs over the free life in nature. [Detailed thematic analysis of "The Celestial Omnibus," "Other Kingdom" and "The Road from Colonus." Commentary is rather obvious.] [In German.]

799 "Televised Version of E. M. Forster's Novel," TIMES (Lond), 3 July 1958, p. 5.
Stephen Tait's and Kenneth Allott's adaptation of EMF's *A Room with a View* (1951) lacks on television the atmosphere of repression and the conflict between the generations that formed the essence of the novel.

800 Toynbee, Phillip. "E. M. Forster at Eighty," OBSERVER (Lond), 20 Dec 1958, pp. 8, 10.
EMF is ironical, skeptical, rational, and humane. He commends the epical quality of Josef Pasternak's DR. ZHIVAGO, the sense of time and space that it conveys, though the characters are inadequate. He likes the fiction of William Golding, largely because Golding seems to enjoy writing. He likes Salinger's CATCHER IN THE RYE and "For Esmé with Love and Squalor." He feels that there is no limitation on the kinds of language a writer may use nor the number of times he may use a special kind, such as demotic argot. He agrees that many novelists lack an individual tone of voice. EMF is now reading Diderot's LE NEVEU DE RAMEAU, which he finds difficult. The social situation at present is not auspicious for the novel; for poetry the future is brighter. The clear class structure that supported fiction in the past is now gone. DR. ZHIVAGO is distinctive by its poetry rather than its traditional fictional properties, though it has enough of them. The nuclear terror is not something with which the novelist can deal adequately; only the poet can do such a cataclysmic subject justice. He is not oppressed by the luxury situation of the English people and will enjoy comforts while he can. His religious position has remained the same since he was twenty-four. He is now more than ever convinced that "reason can't solve everything, but I want it to solve as many things as it can." He is also more aware of his own smallness and the smallness of the planet. He has not read philosophy, though G. E. Moore is reputed to have influenced him. He did not read Moore but knew him a little and liked him a lot. He does not understand the young but is not hostile to them. He prefers grammar schools to the public schools, though public schools may now be different from those he once knew. He is glad that others than public school boys have now begun to come to Cambridge. The widespread contemporary appreciation of music

impresses him, as does the appreciation of painting. Of all the arts literature is now having the worst time. [Important interview.]

801 Werry, Richard R. "Rhythm in Forster's *A Passage to India*," STUDIES IN HONOR OF JOHN WILCOX, ed by A. Dayle Wallace and Woodburn O. Ross (Detroit: Wayne State UP, 1958), pp. 227–37. EMF in "Pattern and Rhythm," *Aspects of the Novel*, distinguishes between an easy rhythm of "discernible notation" and a difficult rhythm integral to the whole work. Some "easy rhythms" in *A Passage to India* are the wasp, the echo, the phrases "Come, come, come, come" and "God is love," the mud-like inhabitants at Chandrapore in Chapter I, and the gods formed of mud in "Temple." There is a parallel between the description of the sunrise and that of the Marabar Caves echo. In both scenes the rhythm mounts to a moment of meaningfulness and then cancels into meaninglessness. The "easy rhythm" is often woven into the action proper and seems to foretell events. Also there is a parallel between the ride of Adela Quested and Ronny Heaslop in the helpful Nawab Bahadur's car and Aziz's offering hospitality by organizing the picnic at the Marabar Hills. The accident to the Nawab's car caused by an animal (in Mrs. Moore's view a ghost) is parallel to the accident at the Caves, with its indeterminate cause and with Miss Derek's rescuing of Adela a second time. The difficult rhythm in *Passage* is a matter, first, of the total effect produced by the book and, second, of its total structure. In *Passage* EMF has shaped his materials centrifugally. Like a symphony, the novel's sections, though created in different keys and tempos, possess at the conclusion "a modal unity" that interlocks the sections, almost superimposing them on one another. A "self-generating synthesis of creation" informs the whole work; it can be felt but scarcely defined; it is to be measured in terms of expansion and opening out.

802 Wilde, Alan. "The World of E. M. Forster." Unpublished dissertation, Harvard University, 1958; rvd as ART AND ORDER: A STUDY OF E. M. FORSTER (NY: New York UP; Lond: Peter Owen, 1964).

1959

803 Allott, Miriam. NOVELISTS ON THE NOVEL (NY: Columbia UP; Lond: Routledge & Kegan Paul, 1959), passim.
[Numerous excerpts from EMF's writings on art and the novel, especially from *Aspects of the Novel*. In discussion of a novelist's use of the marvelous, she uses EMF's concept of the prophetic writer's reaching back to elemental experience. Thus the symbols in novels by Hardy, Emily Bronte, Melville, Conrad, and EMF enlarge the experience presented in them. Makes much use of EMF's views in her discussion of "Structural Problems." The "civilized simplicity" of EMF's style should enable it to wear well.]

804 Anand, Mulk Raj. "E. M. Forster, the Writer," AKASHWANI (New Delhi), XXIV (22 March1959), 41.
EMF's personality and writings reveal a Janus-like subtlety. His canon is slender, but his influence has been enormous. If he is not great, he is the most self-conscious writer of his generation, and he represents the best English traditions. His preoccupation has been the contrast between what the world is and what it might be like. He unites both the empirical and the romantic aspects of the British tradition. He has also been influenced by the expansive Hellenic and Eastern traditions. He rose to the challenge presented by the human situation in India and reached the finality of great art in *A Passage to India*. In *Passage* he accepts life and judges those who do not accept it. He has been the champion of personal relations and of political and intellectual liberty. In *Nordic Twilight*, written during World War II, he revealed the courage and sensitivity of a man profoundly committed to his values.

805 Belvin, Betty June McLain. "Expanding Themes in the Novels of E. M. Forster," DISSERTATION ABSTRACTS, XIX (1959), 2610–11. Unpublished dissertation, University of Washington, 1958.

806 Berry, John. "Notes of a Novelist," NATION (NY), CLXXXIX (14 Nov 1959), 351–54.
In *A Passage to India* Aziz and Fielding are betrayed by the national forces behind them; the mystical Moores provide the only go-betweens for the two sides. The two men may also lack the innate superiority that might have

enabled them to achieve this union of spirit. [Berry was also influenced in his writing by EMF's views on prophecy and pattern in the novel (pattern is not to be achieved at the expense of humanity) expressed in *Aspects of the Novel.*]

807 Crews, Frederick C. "E. M. Forster, An Historical and Critical Study," DISSERTATION ABSTRACTS, XIX (1959), 2951. Unpublished dissertation, Princeton University, 1959; rvd as E. M. FORSTER AND THE PERILS OF HUMANISM (Princeton: Princeton UP; Lond: Oxford UP, 1962).

808 Crews, Frederick C. "*The Longest Journey* and the Perils of Humanism," ENGLISH LITERARY HISTORY, XXVI (Dec 1959), 575–96; rptd, in slightly rvd form, in MODERN BRITISH FICTION, ed by Mark Schorer (NY: Oxford UP, 1961), pp. 176–94; further rvd as "*The Longest Journey*," E. M. FORSTER AND THE PERILS OF HUMANISM (Princeton: Princeton UP; Lond: Oxford UP, 1962), pp. 50–70. EMF is a skeptical humanist by temperament and conviction; the emphasis is upon the preservation of individual values and the disregard for organized systems of belief. This process is accompanied by an atmosphere of "casual disenchantment." In *The Longest Journey* EMF is working with a set of clashing values and philosophies as they affect the characters. The confusion in the novel is more aesthetic than philosophical; EMF tries to embody his philosophical point of view in a too complex narrative. He represents various points of view in the characters as seen through Rickie Elliot's mind, while he simultaneously criticizes Rickie's symbolic approach to life as an error. The short Chapter 28 in *Journey* reveals that EMF's point of view is this-worldly. Rickie is unable to harmonize the extremes of asceticism and commitment to life but vacillates between the two, to a disastrous end. Rickie's problem of "arriving at a moderate and discerning humanism" is explored in the novel. Cambridge represents the life of the mind; Wiltshire, natural piety; Sawston, "a Cave of Error or a House of Pride," which yields for Rickie spurious rewards of sexual love and a position of authority. These rewards lead to "bankruptcy," the discipline of which he does not learn in time to save himself. Yet his efforts make Stephen Wonham richer in the end. Anti-asceticism and the wrongful suppression of human values in the interest of incorruptibility represent the chief thematic lines of the novel. Rickie's enchainment and resurgence are measured in terms of his subservience to his wife Agnes. Shelley decries in "Epipsychidion" a possesiveness similar to Agnes's. Both Stephen and Stewart Ansell distrust "the longest journey" made in the company of one person and condemned by Shelley. Ansell is a prophet of the religion that Stephen illustrates, "the religion of freedom from spiritual constraint." The relationship between Rickie and

Agnes is partly masochistic. Rickie's chief weakness is his tendency to view experience symbolically rather than realistically. When Stephen persuades Rickie to desert Agnes, he is performing the same service for him that Robert did for Mrs. Elliot: enabling an individual to escape from the confines of a deadening marriage to a free life beyond the conventions.

Ansell retains an unclouded view of the good since for him it does not have to be reflected in the world outside him. He finds his good in books. Stephen and Robert find their good in nature, though they recognize that nature is sometimes cruel and destructive. Their virtues of masculinity, practicality, and independence derive from the soil. Rickie either excessively poetizes nature or else becomes too readily disillusioned by it. His disillusionment with nature is rectified when he learns that Stephen is his mother's son and that natural selection may preserve the best as well as the worst hereditary strain. He now learns that the spiritual and the natural need not be exclusive, that love is to be based in the earthly side of our lives, and that one must live in nature rather than erect "a rival world of impossibly sexless ideals." This is the "clear reckoning" that emanates from his "bankruptcy." The humanism in the novel is reinforced by the complex and contradictory symbols in it, the Cadbury Rings and the Cathedral at Salisbury, which imply the coexistence of unity and mutability, the persistence of human love amidst the flux of nature. The weaknesses of Rickie's symbolic mind are reflected in his short stories, in which the symbolism is largely mechanical rather than organic. The same evasiveness and the same divorce from social reality are present in EMF's own short stories, to their detriment. The symbolic moment that EMF stresses in *Journey* must not be mishandled but must be related to the actual facts of nature; meaning must be found in the real world, but meaning must not be attributed to people, objects, or events that will not support it. The search for meaning is difficult and perilous, especially if one loses his critical perspective; to the extent that one cannot find this meaning in the world of actuality, he will be disillusioned. *Journey* therefore is concerned "with the aesthetic consequences of Forster's pessimism." The pessimism is more profound in *A Passage to India*, which reflects the bankruptcy of all attempts to find human meaning in the physical universe. EMF's genial despair gives him his detachment in *Passage*: his best fiction stems from his combining a philosophical pessimism with a recognition of the uniqueness of art. [A searching critique, later incorporated into Crews's first-rate book on EMF.]

809 Engel, Monroe. THE MATURITY OF DICKENS (Cambridge, Mass: Harvard UP; Lond: Oxford UP, 1959), pp. 16–17.
Somewhat perplexed, EMF admits Dickens's success with "flat" characters and their variety. [EMF's opinion, expressed in *Aspects of the Novel*, as to the success of Dickens's "flat" characters is cited.]

810 Gerber, Richard. "The English Island Myth: Remarks on the Englishness of Utopian Fiction," CRITICAL QUARTERLY, I (Spring 1959), 36–43.

The English novel is "insular" and never achieves the greatness and expansiveness of Tolstoy, Dostoevski, or Proust. In some representative instances English fiction is insular in a more literal sense, in its use of the island myth: UTOPIA, GULLIVER'S TRAVELS, and ROBINSON CRUSOE. English fiction, however, has not given us a sea myth, such as that contained in MOBY DICK. In EMF's use of the terms, MOBY DICK would be aligned to "prophecy" and GULLIVER'S TRAVELS to "fantasy." EMF also distinguishes between "flat" and "round" characters; he recognizes, however, in Dostoevski's characters an element surpassing roundness, suggesting some infinite dimension. "Thin" (for flat), "round," and "deep" might be appropriate terms to use to cover the three instances. These terms could also be applied to fictions or myths embodied in them. Fantasy would embody "thin myth" (GULLIVER'S TRAVELS), prophecy would embody "deep myth" (MOBY DICK), and the normal realistic novel would embody "round myth." As in the three English "island fictions" cited, the English novel moves near thin myth; contemporary utopias, such as Orwell's 1984 and Huxley's BRAVE NEW WORLD, provide examples of such thin myths. EMF ostensibly admires deep myth, but in his own work he explores it in "a thin, didactic and programmatic form." [This judgment I do not see as following from Gerber's premises.] EMF is at his best in describing, as in *A Passage to India*, the flight from the deep forces embodied in continental myth. [This essay is elliptically and obscurely reasoned, it does not advance its subject mesurably, and it fails to redefine EMF's terms helpfully.]

811 Gransden, K. W. "E. M. Forster at Eighty," ENCOUNTER (Lond), XII (Jan 1959), 77–81.

The surprises and abruptnesses in EMF's fiction (for which he has been censured) put him on the side of life. There is much tough-minded criticism of life in his essays but also in his novels. He does not agree with Margaret Schlegel as to putting places first; rather his priorities are people, books, places. He thinks that modern writers are too preoocupied with ideas, not people. His current interests: Byzantine art (he had revisited Ravenna), Alban Berg, medieval composers, and W. H. Auden among modern poets. EMF says he gets pleasure from writing. The critical consensus is that EMF communicates this pleasure. This double pleasure keeps his books alive; they have "not only life but a continuous response to life." In *Where Angels Fear to Tread*, the physical and the person are exalted; Philip Herriton, the acute observer, is changed by his visionary experience in Italy. Rickie Elliot in *The Longest Journey* is also an observer rather than a doer; he is the outsider who understands and values the experience of others. When he tries to be a doer, he is false to himself. The book, after Gerald's death, becomes "Agnes' revenge against Rickie for having understood her without being able to satisfy her." For EMF man divides into the rational part and the animal part. For him the Christian concept of Will is not important. *A Room with a View* recalls Jane Austen's comedy and anticipates through George Emerson the vital theories of D. H. Lawrence. *Howards End* is marked by solidity but also lacks some of the hardness and ruthlessness of the early novels. There is an excess of sweetness and light; the sordid bits do not come off. But Leonard Bast is an interesting attempt to portray the submerged and a new slave class, the clerks. The Wilcoxes are hard for the reader to manage, but the victory of the Helen and Margaret relationship is moving and the best thing in the book. Like Butler, EMF places a proper value on money, but only as it is used in and for freedom. The Edwardian age was a heyday of both Wilcoxes and Schlegels who flourished side by side. As a result of economic shrinkage and other factors, we are no longer so free and so individual as we once were. *A Passage to India* brought EMF outside himself and enabled him to transcend his limitations, to work in a truly cosmopolitan scene instead of the insular scene of his earlier books. Aziz and Fielding take their stand on enlightenment; when that fails, they part, defeated. EMF thus reveals the limitations of the rational faculties in human behavior. Hinduism is important in rounding out the perspectives of this book; it comprehends the whole of creation, not just a "civilized minority." [In part an interview, in part a critique. Penetrating discussion.]

812 Green, Martin. "British Decency," KENYON REVIEW, XXI (Autumn 1959), 505–32, espec pp. 526–27; rptd in A MIRROR FOR ANGLO-SAXONS: A DISCOVERY OF AMERICA, A REDISCOVERY OF ENGLAND (NY: Harper, [1960]; Lond: Longmans, [1961]), pp. 95–127, espec 116–17.

EMF is an upper middle-class mind that is "out of touch." *A Passage to India* is impossible to place in time and ignores what has happened in the world. His removed attitude has made his work static. [For a contrary view, see Jeffrey Meyers, "The Politics of *A Passage to India*" (1971).]

813 Grubb, Frederick. "Homage to E. M. Forster," CONTEMPORARY REVIEW, CXCV (Jan 1959), 20–23; rptd in part in A LIBRARY OF LITERARY CRITICISM: MODERN BRITISH LITERATURE, ed by Ruth Z. Temple and Martin Tucker (NY: Frederick Ungar, 1966), I, 314–15.

Three strains predominate in EMF's temper and background: Clapham with its moral seriousness; Cambridge, with its agnosticism, its emphasis on the present moment, its liberal ethics, and its interest in personality; and Hertfordshire, with its implication of rejuvenation through nature. EMF advocates the "yeoman" ideal; in the broadest sense the yeoman would be one who, by being close to nature, apprehends it directly and then tries to embody it in his everyday existence. In short, he is the "aristocrat" in essence. There are no dynamic people in EMF's fiction; rather, he elevates the insignificant or the idiosyncratic. In *A Passage to India* he emphasizes decent social living, especially as this concept is embodied in Fielding. Fielding is "a kind of 'civilised' new picaresque hero, relevant and positive for modern times," a solidly based yet flexible man. The same insight that EMF reveals in analyzing racial differences abroad he reveals in analyzing class differences at home. The Wilcoxes and Schlegels in *Howards End* represent the same social group; both families recognize the importance of the middle class for English civilization. Ernst Schlegel's sword in *Howards End* is at once a lethal weapon (it figures in Leonard Bast's death) and the sword of the spirit. EMF's appreciation of music is all important: Music gives his works symmetry of design. *Abinger Harvest* and *Two Cheers for Democracy* explode the myth that EMF is "the Retiring Don." These books contain a corpus of relevant social criticism, second only to that of Arthur Koestler and George Orwell. In his social criticism EMF is concerned with the adverse effect of bad political situations upon feeling, conduct, and personal relations. He is a "gentleman of letters," one for whom good writing and moral concern are coterminous, a writer who persuades us by his natural authority. [A discerning appreciation but somewhat densely written.]

814 Hassall, Christopher. A BIOGRAPHY OF EDWARD MARSH (NY: Harcourt, Brace; Lond: Longmans, 1959), pp. 148, 168, 169, 184, 187, 227, 509, 522, 611.

EMF reveals enthusiasm for Masefield's NAN, reservations about Frank Harris as critic, and in 1910 a baffled attitude toward Gauguin and Van Gogh. Marsh was greatly impressed by *Howards End* in 1910, but Edmund Gosse refused to share his enthusiasm, feeling EMF's book was "coarse" in its morals and obtrusively brilliant in style. [See Edmund Gosse, letter to Marsh (27 Dec 1910); Charteris (1931).] In 1913, Marsh reports that EMF supposedly has "run completely dry," but has just heard from EMF that he is now writing again. EMF was often a guest at Marsh's house, Gray's Inn, before the war and after it. Marsh praised *A Passage to India* on its appearance as a masterpiece but spoiled for him by a strain of occultism typical of some of EMF's other works as well.

815 Hill, Roland. "Dichter der unentwickelten Herzen" (Poet of the Undeveloped Hearts), FRANKFURTER ALLGEMEINE ZEITUNG, 2 Jan 1959.

EMF is the creator of a literary monument to the bourgeois English middle classes. His novels not only contrast values held by the various characters but analyze differences between appearance and reality. He contrasts sharply with "museum figures" like Wells, Bennett, and Galsworthy; but he evinces a distant relationship to D. H. Lawrence in the emphasis on instinct and feeling. The special quality of *A Passage to India* lies in the tension presented between hope on the one side and panic and emptiness on the other. [In German.]

816 Jones, David. "E. M. Forster on His Life and His Books," LISTENER, LXI (1 Jan 1959), 11–12.

EMF maintains that Cambridge is a place for the very young and the very old. In his middle age a writer ought to go away and find other experiences, to go out into the world and meet more types. In his own case he started writing because of the congenial atmosphere of Cambridge and because Nathaniel Wedd suggested that he do so. He has not written as much as he would have liked and especially regrets his few novels. He dried up after *A Passage to India* because the social aspect of the world had changed so drastically. He can think about the new world but can't embody it in his fiction. His desire to write has been directed into the writing of discursive prose. He is conceited about his novels. He is delighted that *Passage* has been a political success, although it is not chiefly a political book. He likes *The Longest Journey* best because in it he came nearest to putting down what was inside him and what he wanted to say. *Howards End* is all right, but he gets a bit bored with it because of its excessive social preoccupation. He enjoys his Italian novels because he enjoys Italy. He is sure that he is not a great novelist, because he gets only three kinds of people into his work: the person that he thinks he is, the people who irritate him, and the people he would like to be. A really great novelist like Tolstoy gets hold of all types. Jane Austen and Samuel Butler were influential when EMF was young, and Proust was later (EMF admires his depth and delicacy). Music has had an enormous influence over him; the visual arts also mean more and more to him. His musical taste was formed by the nineteenth century (his liking for Beethoven and Verdi). He can get along with new composers but does not understand the new pictorial art. He values most personal relationships, tolerance, and pleasure, and he likes people who are "cheerful, courageous, brave, and tolerant," people who can put themselves in another person's place and do not do harm because they do not wish to hurt. He likes gaiety, also earnestness of purpose, except when it gets out of hand. As to the future, one must be worried and not worried; we will get no further help from science, other than psychological help. A change of heart in some appreciable sense must eventuate. [Important interview.]

817 Karl, Frederick, and Marvin Magalaner. "Introduction," "E. M. Forster: Life," "E. M. Forster: Works," A READER'S GUIDE TO GREAT TWENTIETH CENTURY ENGLISH NOVELS (NY: Noonday P, 1959; Lond: Thames and Hudson, 1960), pp. 2–41, 100–102, 103–

24; also 61, 126, 134, 138, 149, 150, 155; extracts rptd in CONTEM-
PORARY LITERARY CRITICISM, ed by Carolyn Riley (Detroit: Gale
Research Co., 1973), I, 103–4.

["Introduction" defines the essential characteristics of the modern novel in
England, as opposed to the novel of tradition.] The modern novel illustrates
economy in the use of detail and disillusion with Victorian values and
narrative techniques. (EMF's break with them is less total than that of
Conrad, Lawrence, Joyce, or Woolf). The modern novel is psychologically
oriented and deals with an inner reality; EMF, along with Conrad, anticipates this development. Most of the English novelists in the twentieth
century strove for a middle road between the aesthetic anarchy of the 1890s
and the didacticism of the Victorian age. Along with other major twentieth-
century novelists, EMF consciously uses symbols (most obvious are the
Caves in *A Passage to India*, and Beethoven's Fifth Symphony in *Howards
End*). In searching for an internal, often ineffable and elusive reality, these
novelists (EMF included) sought new forms and deliberately experimented.
These writers proceed by indirection and allusiveness when they use symbols, in contrast to the Victorians. Motifs and recurrent themes (as in
Passage) are of extreme importance. Along with the other moderns, EMF
stresses the psychological, the self-analytic (*Howards End* and *Passage*),
and the antiheroic. EMF is modern also in his relativistic point of view and
in his emphasis on "relationships." The new interest in sexuality also figures
in EMF but less explicitly and confidently. With the popularity of Jung,
novelists increasingly used mythical elements in their fiction; EMF emphasizes the mythical elements of vitality and animism in unsophisticated
cultures and persons. The modernist distrusts politics as a subject; even a
politically oriented novel like *Passage* is not only about politics. The modern responsiveness to, and preoccupation with, technique is not an end in
itself; the images and innovations in modern fiction expand its meaning and
human significance.

["E. M. Forster: Life" is a full, informed account of EMF's career. "E. M.
Forster: Works" analyzes *Where Angels Fear to Tread, Howards End* and
Passage.] *Angels* presents the clash of cultures, as in Henry James; EMF
stamps his own liberalism and directness of statement on his book. Among
the antitheses explored are these: true communication versus suburban
small talk, great love versus the convenient alliances of Sawston, reality
versus jealously guarded illusion, the formless currents connecting individuals versus the sterile forms of "civilization" (machinery), ancient myths
versus their modern application. Words lead to communication and are
important, but they are not the highest kind of communication. The marriage of Lilia Herriton and Gino Carella represents a seeking for communication, but this goal is not attained. Material progress in civilization
improves the means for connection, but men ironically drift farther apart.

In primitive Monteriano it is easier to connect than in "civilized" Sawston. The well-organized characters (Mrs. Herriton) are the least sympathetic. As Caroline Abbott looks at Gino's baby, she sees the machinery of Sawston for what it is and rejects it. Love is EMF's most serious thematic concern: maternal affection, spiritual love, sexual love, paternal love, the absence of love, the perversion of love. Italy affects all but the unregenerate (Harriet Herriton). With Lilia's death, attention shifts to an unheroic hero (Philip Herriton) and heroine (Caroline) who both learn the importance of love, but too late. Caroline saves Philip not only from death but from "death-in-life." For EMF illusion is necessary, but a bogus illusion is pernicious. He is honest enough to recognize the ambiguities of experience and the complexities of individuals and cultures; Italy and Sawston alike have virtues and defects. In Saint Deodata are linked the "sweetness and barbarity" characteristic of Italy; like the saint, Philip sacrificed reality to an abstract ideal.

In *Howards End* EMF stresses the health-giving quality implicit in attaining true proportion. In his novels there are guardians or saints who see farther than others and who influence them by the strength of their elemental natures. Mrs. Wilcox is such an instinctively reacting figure whose saintliness, as she approaches death, is evident when the light throws a halo about her. She is, however, more a maternal image than a person. EMF speaks more decisively through Margaret Schlegel who illustrates not only "being" (at the apex of life, as with Mrs. Wilcox) but also the possibility of becoming. Howards End house passes from Ruth Wilcox, the great mother and natural aristocrat, to Margaret, the new aristocrat of "culture, refinement, intelligence, money, and liberal democracy." The Wilcoxes oppose this transfer of the house, but Margaret accedes to power as well as to property by dominating Henry Wilcox. The child of Helen Schlegel and Leonard Bast, the result of union between a depressed civil servant and a woman from the enlightened upper middle class, will replace the money interests. The flux of London life is presented in terms of real estate development. EMF regards machinery, particularly the motorcar, as devitalizing. In *Passage* the English pretend to be gods, but they are only efficient. The tension between the races is felt as a human, not a political problem. The reordering of society implies nothing less than "the re-evaluation of the place of reason, of feeling, and of the super-rational in the individual psyche." EMF's aim is to present "a mystical, highly symbolic view of life, death and human relationship." [Follows Glen O. Allen in "Structure, Symbol, and Theme in E. M. Forster's *A Passage to India*" (1955) by relating "Mosque," "Caves," and "Temple" to the emotions, the mind, and the human capacity for love, respectively; or to the path of activity, the path of knowledge, and the path of devotion.] These three sides to life are fused when the boats collide in the Mau tank: Fielding (mind), Aziz (emotion), the rituals (love). Some characters are stereotypes, but those who are types like Ronny Heaslop and

Adela Quested are also individuals. Aziz is unpredictable but probable. The fate of the characters is a bit arbitrary: Mrs. Moore's end is not determined by her personality conjoined with her fictional milieu. Everywhere in EMF's fiction is the presence of his genial, ironic, humorous personality. [Several other references: Mrs. Gould in Conrad's NOSTROMO is the forerunner of intuitively perceptive women like Mrs. Moore and Mrs. Ramsay (Woolf, TO THE LIGHTHOUSE); Virginia Woolf's Mrs. Dalloway (MRS. DALLOWAY) and Mrs. Ramsay wish, like EMF characters, to connect but find it difficult to do so; EMF anticipates D. H. Lawrence in a deemphasis of mental consciousness. Excellent, perceptive commentary.]

818 "King's Messenger," TIMES (Lond), 1 Jan 1959, p. 9.
EMF's reputation has been growing despite his own aloofness and his lack of effort in its behalf. He has asserted the same values as D. H. Lawrence but brings to them a discipline lacking in Lawrence. EMF both feels and thinks: "his thought, like his prose, is lucid and cool." His precision and delicacy are musical in origin. His failure to write a novel since *A Passage to India* is compensated for in the example he has set. He has backed sensible liberal causes and been critical of excesses in public life. [Editorial.]

819 Lombardo, Agostino. "Prefazione" (Preface), *Casa Howard* (*Howards End*) (Milano: Feltrinelli Editore, 1959), pp. 7–20.
EMF's silence since *A Passage to India* (1924) has made him less known than writers of equal or inferior stature. He is, nevertheless, a great contemporary writer. His major accomplishment has been the creation of an artistic form that reveals the deepest zones of human consciousness. The tradition to which he is anchored is that of Sterne, Jane Austen, George Eliot, Hawthorne, and Henry James. He began to write when James was at the peak and conclusion of his career. In many ways EMF's fiction is a continuation of James's. James's Mrs. Gereth in THE SPOILS OF POYNTON and EMF's Mrs. Wilcox in *Howards End* are similar. Both women are attached to their country houses and to their legacies from the past that comprise for them the meaning of life. As Mrs. Gereth sees in Fleda Vetch the only person able to preserve this legacy, so Mrs. Wilcox sees Margaret Schlegel as the only person worthy of possessing Howards End house. But the relationship between *Howards End* and Henry James's fiction extends further. Leonard Bast, the proletarian, resembles Hyacinth Robinson of THE PRINCESS CASAMASSIMA, who, like Bast, becomes involved with a social class higher than his own. The society in which the Schlegels move is the same as that presented in numerous works by James, especially THE AWKWARD AGE. And the comparison could also include other EMF works that focus, as so many of James's books do, on the "international theme." There are also many differences between EMF and James. EMF has greater interest

in social issues, as evidenced in *Howards End* and *Passage*. In *Aspects of the Novel* EMF takes issue with James's emphasis upon aesthetic perfection and the rigidity that such emphasis implies. As opposed to James's preference for the pure Racine-like beauty of form, EMF tries to capture in the novel the rhythms and the expansiveness of music. The well-known fifth chapter of *Howards End*, which features the reactions of his characters to Beethoven's Fifth Symphony, indicates the importance that the concept of rhythm had for EMF. The goblins that Helen Schlegel hears or sees, evoked by the music, return in the course of the work and assume rhythmic and symbolic significance, as the music of Vinteuil does in Proust. The goblins signify "panic and emptiness," one aspect of reality present in the novel.

EMF weaves a dense, yet extremely subtle, pattern of themes that he repeats with variations. He also tries for the more arduous rhythm of expansiveness and openness that he finds in WAR AND PEACE. In *Howards End* there is nothing rigid or schematic. The narrator, for example, continually intervenes. The absolute objectivity sought by James gives way to an accentuated subjectivity. Convinced of the "impurity" of the novel form, EMF does not hesitate to write an "impure" novel wherein a lyrical passage interweaves with an essay-like meditation, sociological observation with realistic representation, and the comic outburst with the elegaic note. EMF's debt to Henry James concerns not so much technique as the fictional object itself. As with James and the other writers formative upon EMF, EMF responds to their presentation of the complex, mysterious, and ambiguous life of the consciousness. EMF pursues this interest in the inner life in all his narratives. His first novel, *Where Angels Fear to Tread*, while melodramatic, announces his future development. The action is symbolic and concerns an interior struggle between diverse attitudes toward life (the conventional versus the free, the intellect versus the heart). In EMF a clash of the two moral worlds is characteristic. This clash is demonstrated through differences in geography or social class. In *The Longest Journey*, the attempt to reconcile the two worlds ends with Rickie's death. In *A Room with a View* there appears to be a reconciliation between the two worlds, but in reality it is a compromise, for the conflict remains substantially unresolved. In *Howards End* and *Passage* the contrast is dramatized in all its complexity. There is also a romantic aspiration for a total image of life. In these two novels, EMF attempts to go further than the literal. He aspires, like his greatest characters, to connect, to identify with life's contradictions. This identification between author and work tends to remove these two novels to a sphere more moral and metaphysical than aesthetic. Nevertheless, EMF succeeds by the elasticity of his form in maintaining an equilibrium between the different spheres, while his personal presence gives to his fiction a warmth and intensity reminiscent of Melville. [Full, suggestive, interesting account.] [In Italian.]

820 McDowell, Frederick P. W. " 'The Mild, Intellectual Light':
Idea and Theme in *Howards End*," PUBLICATIONS OF THE MODERN
LANGUAGE ASSOCIATION, LXXIV (Sept 1959), 453–63; rptd in part
as " 'Glimpses of the Diviner Wheels': *Howards End*," E. M.
FORSTER (NY: Twayne Publishers, Twayne's English Authors Se-
ries, 1969), pp. 64–80.

The characters in *Howards End* are more human and interesting than those
in *A Passage to India*, though the novel is not so accomplished artistically.
Howards End, despite its weakness, is to be regarded highly for its expert
fusion of character and situation with idea, for its technical skill in bringing
all segments of the middle class together, for its interweaving of the comic
with the serious, and for its style. The subtlety and suggestiveness of the
novel justify an exhaustive thematic analysis with incidental judgments
upon its characters and its aesthetic aspects. The enlightened imagination,
in EMF's view, must modulate the inner and outer lives of the individual,
to enable him not only to see life steadily but to see it whole. The emphasis
is upon the inner life with its sensitivity to the transcendent on the one hand
and to the personal on the other. In establishing the primacy of the inner
life, Ernst Schlegel is important as a liberating influence though he is now
dead. He works better than does Ruth Wilcox, who is too undeveloped to
achieve EMF's intention of making of her a convincing guardian figure. She
may be too real as a crotchety woman to attain easily a serene, mythical
dimension. In EMF's view reason is both important and unimportant, with
the ultimate appeal being made to the intuition, the ineffable, the unseen.
EMF advocates an Arnoldian flexibility of mind that does in fact characterize Ernst Schlegel and his daughter Margaret; this flexibility is lacking in
the extravert Wilcoxes. In relating to both the inner and the outer worlds,
Margaret is more successful than Ruth Wilcox. She is midway between
Ruth Wilcox's detachment and Helen's excessive commitment; she is devoted to the ideal of continually seeking proportion. The Wilcoxes are
suspicious of the inner life or the subjective; they either fail to acknowledge
it or fear it.

Several themes are developed in *Howards End;* the high valuation of personal relationships, of art and intellectual pursuits, and the insight that these
ranges of experience give into the immaterial and the infinite; the need to
apprehend the eternal through the solid impressions of the senses and the
valuing of earth as a primary means to approach the supernatural; the
life-giving aspects of tradition; the primitive as a vital source for spiritual
renewal; the respect for generosity and graciousness as personal attributes;
the recognition of a true cosmopolitanism as a means for achieving the
widest understanding; and the need for an individual to possess an absolute
moral honesty and spiritual self-reliance. The Schlegel sisters are more
impersonal with Leonard Bast than they realize, and Helen's influence on

Leonard is destructive. A major flaw is EMF's failure to illustrate Wilcox virtues in sequences as arresting as those in which he embodies their defects. The marriage between Henry Wilcox and Margaret Schlegel is real, but EMF is confused between his emotional antipathy to Henry and his high valuation of Henry's accomplishments. Wholeness, represented by Margaret's sensitivity to the unseen, is more to be cherished than is steadiness, represented by Henry's appreciation of the seen. Leonard Bast is convincing as an individual precariously existing on the fringe of the middle class, but he is the victim of EMF's undue disparagement. The circumstances of his death are both vivid and heavy-handed; his death after he is struck by Ernst Schlegel's sword in a parody of the knighthood ceremony is compelling, but the bookcase as a symbol of the culture that eludes him except to cause his death by toppling on him is contrived. Margaret is generally convincing in her elaboration of ideas since EMF is emotionally implicated in her humanist values. She and Leonard are to be seen as victims of the Wilcoxes when they cut their fingers on broken glass covering portraits of Jacky and Dolly Wilcox, respectively. Helen and Leonard are linked by the cupids on the mantle shelf in his sitting room that correspond to those on the concert hall ceiling by which Helen is intrigued. [The first of the many extensive essays on *Howards End* to appear in journals in succeeding years.]

821 Markovich, Vida. "Stare Forme i Novi Sadržaji E. M. Fostera" (The Old Forms and New Substance of E. M. Forster), SAV-REMENIK (Belgrade), V (June 1959), 627–33.

EMF's intellectual dilemma is this: he believes in a rational universe but realizes intuitively the impotence of such a universe. This unresolved contradiction detracts from the intellectual stability of his works. EMF is uneasy with the liberal tradition as set forth in the essays in *Two Cheers for Democracy* and embodied in novels like *Howards End* and *A Passage to India*. Certain recurring phrases from *Howards End* ("panic and emptiness," "telegrams and anger," etc.) symbolize EMF's attempts to reconcile the world of rational appearances with an irrationality that may underlie appearances. The contrast of Western rationalism with the traditional, intuitive culture of India presented in *Passage* also embodies the intellectual cleavage in EMF's mind. EMF's own plight is likened to that of his own Mrs. Moore in *Passage* whose certainties are undermined by her experiences with the echoes in the Marabar Caves. EMF's own uncertainties have resulted in his failure to produce a novel since 1924. [In Serbo-Croation.]

822 Meyerstein, E. H. W. SOME LETTERS OF E. H. W. MEYERSTEIN, ed by Rowland Watson (Lond: Neville Spearman, 1959), pp. 154–55, 296–98, 298–99, 326–27; letter to R. M. Dawkins rptd in E. M. FORSTER: THE CRITICAL HERITAGE, ed by Philip Gardner (Lond & Boston: Routledge & Kegan Paul, 1973), pp. 367–68.

Letter to R. M. Dawkins (14 Aug 1933), *Where Angels Fear to Tread* is completely satisfying as art; the courtroom and trial descriptions in *A Passage to India* represent classical prose. EMF has the mind of a poet and a sensitive heart. His issues are not always vital and realized, but his works will be remembered. Letter to Donald Mitchell (1 Nov 1944), EMF lacks the "repetitive boredom" of many modern novelists, as seen in Virginia Woolf's To THE LIGHTHOUSE. Letter to Donal Mitchell (24 Nov 1944), contrary to John Middleton Murry's opinion, Virginia Woolf is not like EMF except, at times, stylistically. Letter to EMF (30 Nov 1944), Beethoven was anticipated by Haydn and Mozart in his preference for the key of C minor [see EMF's "The C Minor of That Life," rptd in *Two Cheers for Democracy*]. [Other remarks on EMF's essay.] Letter to Rowland Watson (18 Dec 1943), [Meyerstein, no enthusiast for contemporary literature, is seen to admire EMF's work and person.] Letter to Walter de la Mare (1 Nov 1946), EMF had his own "program" for Beethoven's "Appassionata" sonata that he would not divulge.

823 Milano, Paolo. "*Casa Howard:* La Prosa e la Passione" (*Howards End:* The Prose and the Passion), ESPRESSO (Rome), 31 May 1959, p. 25; rptd as part of "E. M. Forster in Italia" (E. M. Forster in Italy), IL LETTORE DI PROFESSIONE (The Profession of Letters) (Milano: Feltrinelli, 1960), pp. 99–102.

Fifty years after its publication, *Howards End* is offered in Italian in the new series, "I Classici Moderni." *Howards End* is allusive, resembling a symphonic score. As Lionel Trilling said in E. M. FORSTER (1943), *Howards End* is a vast fictional canvas depicting the destiny of England. This subject is reflected in the tensions governing the segments of the dominating middle class, which alone figure in the novel, especially in the arduous reconciliation of the intellectual Schlegel sisters with the magnate Henry Wilcox and the petty bourgeois Leonard Bast. EMF wished the novel's conclusion to be affirmative. Margaret Schlegel discovers the innate moral value in her role as an enlightened and sensible woman at the side of a powerful man. But because in EMF's view the world is controlled by money, there is throughout an underlying vein of nihilism, conveyed in the constant motif in the novel, "panic and emptiness." Yet the innate irony of EMF's style is often lost in translation, and the Italian version seems opaque, a villa without windows, which this novel is not at all. Yet the English original is also unsatisfactory. The psychology is biting, the structure calibrated, the dialogue exact, the analysis of manners and conventions convincing; but the novel suffers from the British failing, "insularity." Despite EMF's desire to uncover secret zones of consciousness, his horizon remains somewhat narrow and the heart of his work is "exquisitely" bourgeois. [In Italian.]

824 Milano, Paolo. "Incontro a Roma: E. M. Forster in Conversazione" (Encounter in Rome: E. M. Forster in Conversation),

Espresso (Rome), 29 Nov 1959, p. 25; rptd as part of "E. M. Forster in Italia" (E. M. Forster in Italy), Il Lettore di Professione (The Profession of Letters) (Milano: Feltrinelli, 1960), pp. 103–6.

EMF, nearing his eighty-first birthday, resembles Italo Svevo during his last years, not only in appearance but in self-expression, combining good nature and irony. Like Montaigne, the greatest of his personal gods, EMF loves to travel in order to pursue intensely the spectacle of life. In his lecture on the occasion of the Italian translation of *Howards End*, EMF spoke of the three countries that have inspired his work: Italy, England, and India. The exceptional zeal with which he approached the writing of his greatest novel, *A Passage to India*, was due to its origin in two intense personal relationships. Above all, as he wrote in "What I Believe," fanaticism is his enemy, while tolerance is sovereign among virtues. Pleasure, even physical, is an indispensable ingredient of the moral life, he maintains; but he is distrustful of success as such. EMF is a serene man belonging to an age that today seems remote. He is an aristocratic writer who feels neither an obligation nor a compulsion to write. The most profound thought that EMF revealed during his conversations in Rome is this: life's supreme tragedies are those that are imperceptible in our daily lives. EMF spoke of the three countries mentioned above but hardly mentioned a fourth, Greece, for which he has a preference so strong that it must remain silent. [In Italian.]

825 Panter-Downes, Mollie. "Profiles: Kingsman," New Yorker, XXXV (19 Sept 1959), 51–52, 54, 57, 60, 62, 64, 66, 68, 70, 72, 77, 78–80.

EMF was one of the Bloomsbury Group but a bit withdrawn from it. He has led no retired existence but has had a full social life in Cambridge and London. One of his friends characterizes him as "relentlessly in favor of pleasure." He is accessible to the young who appreciate his interest in them and his deference to their opinions, but he does not suffer fools gladly. He is glad that many now come to Cambridge by a route other than that of the public school. He is himself against class distinctions and class consciousness. In his nonconformity he owes much to the traditions (anti-worldly, anti-establishment, anti-clerical) of King's College where he went to the University and has since returned. King's has always encouraged personal relationships and distinction in the arts, particularly music and drama. As to the novel, EMF still reads Jane Austen; he reads much French; he finds the outlook for the modern novel in England not reassuring because family life is disappearing; and he finds Lolita boring in its erotic parts. Nowadays his writing is fragmentary; when cameos from his experience suggest themselves, he begins a new project. As a secularist he is disturbed by the BBC's reluctance to give equal time to churchgoing and agnostic arguments and by the Christian revival at Cambridge. He is therefore much interested in the progress of the Cambridge Humanists, of which he has accepted the presidency. [Description of manuscripts, first editions, and foreign editions of his work for a recent exhibition at King's College Library; description of his gifts of books to King's College, especially Blake's own copy of SONGS OF INNOCENCE AND EXPERIENCE.] His collaboration with Eric Crozier on the libretto for Melville's BILLY BUDD (Benjamin Britten's opera) was a meaningful experience, the theme of the work being congenial to him: the conflict between good and evil forces or the combination of good and evil in each human being. He was pleased with the first version of Santha Rama Rau's adaptation of *A Passage to India*. He was also much affected by a concert given by King's College Musical Society in honor of his eightieth birthday. [Unusually full sketch of EMF as resident fellow at King's College, Cambridge, written shortly after his eightieth birthday (1 Jan 1959). Details of Noel Annan's salutation to EMF given, stressing his Socrates-like influence at Cambridge, and of EMF's reply (he is "a child" in comparison to aged Cambridge).]

826 Pederson, Glenn. "Forster's Symbolic Form," KENYON REVIEW, XXI (Spring 1959), 231–49.

Mrs. Moore in *A Passage to India* achieves form on the symbolic level; her passage contrasts with Adela Quested's mortal, formless one. The characters achieve "form" as they relate to Mrs. Moore. In the novel the characters at the literal level represent separation and diversity, but at the symbolic level they achieve union and unity. Adela is lost in muddle. Aziz is muddled in mystery and vacillates between the physical and the spiritual; his feelings are not reliable, but he does grow. Fielding is involved neither in mystery nor in muddle at the beginning but later becomes involved in mystery—the essence of Mrs. Moore, whose form influences other characters in various degrees. There is an element of supernature to Mrs. Moore's character that accounts for the success of her "passage" (see her instinctive recognition of a "ghost" as cause for the accident to the automobile in which Ronny Heaslop and Adela are riding). Adela is led to the truth through the agency of Mrs. Moore, but she lacks the capacity for vision, and her "passage" to India is not a success. Mrs. Moore is a visionary and often sees the truth that is obscure to others. She truly needs patience when they do not see it. She is concerned with the man, not the institution, as at Aziz's trial. The effect of the Caves on Mrs. Moore is catastrophic, however. They equal "Nothing"; confronted with Nothing, she can only become silent. The echo in the Marabar Cave is frightening because it originates nothing (or from Nothing). Aziz experiences a progress from "Mosque" to "Temple"; the Caves (or Nothing) lie between Islam and Hinduism. The Hindus would complete themselves, not reconstruct others. Godbole transcends differences among Hindus and exact definitions of the Birth of Krishna (or love). When Godbole attempts objects of love beyond Mrs. Moore (and the wasp), he fails. Her completeness is more than his own. [This judgment is not the usual one.] Where Godbole fails, she succeeds by "intuitive logos" rather than by logic.

But Hinduism has its successes. It stresses and includes merriment, for example. "Temple" is not dynamic enough to effect India's salvation; it is too detached to will the salvation by baptism of others. Mrs. Moore, however, is symbolic of the external influences necessary to effect change in lesser natures; through her, the other characters are united in "the eternal, baptismal waters" at Mau. Aziz is happy only in the company of Fielding and Mrs. Moore and learns that it is more blessed to receive than to give. Fielding also experiences regeneration in his increasing hospitality to the supernatural. His faith is in man, not in God; but after his marriage this faith makes him receptive to the supernatural. Stella and Ralph Moore are incarnations of Mrs. Moore's spirit and return to India to complete Aziz's regeneration. The final movement on the water is essentially "a great baptism into rebirth." Water is the indispensable agency for rebirth. Mrs. Moore had in death been committed to the water; her children at Mau also move on the water. Fielding has married one of these children; his union with Stella Moore represents a fusion of earth and sky, field and stars. At the tank Ralph and Stella influence Fielding and Aziz to overcome their antagonism to each other when the two boats collide and throw all four people into the water. The following also figure in the scene: the dead Rajah and the symbolically "quick" Krishna, the Radhakrishna chant, the hand-wrought images of the Indian deities, and Ronny's and Adela's presence through their letters. Only when the integrating unconscious forces are in the ascendancy can Aziz and Fielding be friends. In the final scene between them, the action in the Caves is repeated. Just as the two friends virtually kiss and draw apart, so did the flames touch one another, kiss, and expire on the polished walls of the Cave when a match was lit. The physical union of Fielding and Stella will lead to a spiritual union between the two. The novel illustrates the truth of one of EMF's statements in it: "In space things touch, in time things part." Only outside of time can things unite; so Fielding and Aziz are united during the festival but part when the normal routine begins in time. When in "Temple" the Indian prisoner is released, so is Aziz, who had come from the Mosque through the Caves to the Temple to Mrs. Moore and what she symbolizes. [Essay is diffuse, impressionistic, confused in approach and execution, but is also most suggestive. The conception of Mrs. Moore as the "structural principle" of the novel is illuminating; and the essay corrects the denigration of Mrs. Moore in Edwin Nierenberg's "The Withered Priestess: Mrs. Moore's Incomplete Passage to India" (1964).]

827 Plomer, William. "Foreword," LONDON MAGAZINE, VI (Jan 1959), 7–9.

Those who deplore EMF's not having written more can be answered in two ways: he has written much since 1924, and he has been guided by his sense of what he has to say. EMF has not regarded himself as "the Grand Old Man"; there is an element of playfulness to offset his seriousness; and he has always remained faithful to the ideal of personal pleasure. Part of his influence has been his plain speaking, especially in his critical writings. His angle to the universe is fresh and individual; he has evolved into "a resonant old man." His resonances and illuminations are enclosed in a view of life seen in terms of art and reason. His work gives out warmth as well as illumination.

828 Postel, Elisabeth. "Symbol und Leitmotiv in den Romanen E. M. Forsters" (Symbol and Leitmotif in E. M. Forster's Novels). Unpublished dissertation, Kiel University, 1959. [Listed in Lawrence F. McNamee, DISSERTATIONS IN ENGLISH AND AMERICAN LITERATURE (NY & Lond: Bowker, 1968).]

EMF's symbols provide a timeless reality in conflict with the normal flow of time; his plots revolve about this conflict and other conflicts between differing views of life. [In German.]

829 Randles, W. G. L. "The Symbols of the Sacred in E. M. Forster's *Howards End*," REVISTA DA FACULDADE DE LETRAS (University of Lisbon), Ser. III: 3 (1959), 89–102.

In *Howards End* all the characters seek contact with the permanent and the nontransient. There are three symbols for "the Other World, this home of the soul": (1) Howards End house (the sacred center of existence and also the symbol of the immortality that all men yearn for); (2) the wych-elm (the tree of life, the living cosmos regenerating itself); and (3) the wisp of hay (the spiritual expressed in bucolic terms). Other symbols include Leonard Bast's umbrella (a symbol of respectability) and the vinaigrette sent by the Wilcoxes to Margaret Schlegel (a symbol of the guilty conscience of the Wilcoxes when they fail to give up Howards End house to Margaret, as Ruth Wilcox had requested them to do in a will). The spiritual associated with immortality is found in Mrs. Wilcox; the spiritual associated with regeneration and with this life is found in Henry Wilcox. [This interpretation of Henry is unusual but not implausible.] Mr. Wilcox's regenerative spirituality is associated with the idea of plenitude and is often expressed by acquatic and nautical symbols. London is a sort of sacred center yet is vitiated by flux. Possessions, when they are approached in spiritual terms, are positive forces; when they are worshipped for themselves, they are destructive forces. Possessions as instrumental to something else are to be valued highly. Possessions thus may give rise to the spiritual or serve as obstacles to reaching it. In their quest for the spiritual, the characters search out other people as well as places or possessions. Gestures made toward another can be solicitory or donatory. The Schlegel sisters, for example, fail to respond to Leonard's interest in culture; he fails to solicit their interest. The characters frequently misinterpret the donatory gesture, or the gift-request relationship. It is a failure of insight to refuse a gift spontaneously offered, as when the Wilcoxes refuse from Miss Avery her wedding present for Evie. Margaret fails to respond initially to Mrs. Wilcox's gift of hospitality when the older woman invites her to Howards End house. In *Howards End* there also operates the notion of the "Geis," a modified curse or injunction from one of higher rank to a subordinate. One geis is Mrs. Wilcox's command to leave Howards End to Margaret; another is Helen Schlegel's peremptory, imperious, and disastrous championing of the Basts. Helen's irresponsibility causes Leonard to sink lower, and the gift-requests that he makes to his relatives reveal him as corrupted through Helen's "facile totalism in the application of her beliefs." Tragedies in EMF's work are partly social in origin but more often are the result of the consequences deriving from the chance collisions of human beings. [Some interpretations of the symbols are not found elsewhere.]

830 Robbins, William. THE ETHICAL IDEALISM OF MATTHEW ARNOLD: A STUDY OF THE NATURE AND SOURCES OF HIS MORAL AND RELIGIOUS IDEAS (Toronto: University of Toronto P, University of Toronto Department of English, Studies and Texts No. 7, 1959), pp. 199, 202.
The effect of Arnold's prose writing has been in the direction of EMF's championing of tolerance. Yet tolerance needs to be supplemented by imagination and sympathy, as EMF would be the first to recognize.

831 Shahane, V. A. "A Study of the Works of Edward Morgan Forster with Special Reference to His Place in the Tradition of the English Novel." Unpublished dissertation, Leeds University, 1959; rvd as E. M. FORSTER: A REASSESSMENT (Delhi: Kitab Mahal, 1962; Lond: A Probsthain, 1964).

832 Spence, Jonathan. "E. M. Forster at Eighty," NEW REPUBLIC, CXLI (5 Oct 1959), 17–21; rptd in THE BEST OF GRANTA, 1889–1966, ed by Jim Philip, John Simpson, and Nicholas Snowman (Lond: Secker & Warburg, 1967), pp. 178–84.
EMF's greatness is not alone the result of his published work but is diffused —"a combination of gentleness, toughness, reticence and longevity." He has maintained in a difficult time his confidence in himself and his values. In *Where Angels Fear to Tread, A Room with a View,* and the short stories, the characters are neatly categorized (though some complexities are present), and the issues are simplified. A simple solution is supplied for a

situation in which the forces of light are ranged against those of darkness. In *The Longest Journey* and *Howards End* the same antithesis and the same neatness in solution are retained, but the characters and their situations gain in breadth and complexity. In *Journey* there is a twofold development; EMF goes from a contrast between good and evil to a conception of the moral life as good-and-evil, and he uses repetition with variation to place his characters in a wider context. He achieves his humorous effects from his comments on the characters. The final solution in *Journey* is inadequate to compensate for Rickie Elliot's sufferings and for Herbert Pembroke's stupidity; the solution is too neat in *Howards End*. The Schlegels ought to be presented as still engaged in conflict at the end. EMF is also not equipped to deal with material privation or class suffering. His voice is that of the superior Ruskin when he writes of Leonard Bast. The greatness of *A Passage to India* lies in its comprehensiveness, EMF's sense of the gradations within English and Indian societies, and the complexity of the levels existing between the human and the transcendent in both societies. On the one side is the anti-vision of Mrs. Moore, on the other the mystical, harmonious vision of Godbole; between them stands the decent prosaic world of Adela Quested and Ronny Heaslop, Fielding and Aziz, wherein a degree of stability is sustained despite failures in social communication and certain disastrous events. The direction of *Passage* is positive; existence may remain a mystery but need not be muddle; the horror of the universe can be offset by a sense of its harmony and its transcendent implications. We get a sense of "deities reconciled" in *Passage* though the process is difficult and the gods are formidable. [EMF's daily life at Cambridge described, his universal friendliness, and his idiosyncratic mind. Excellent discussion; especially challenging in its positive view of *Passage*.]

833 Wright, Andrew. JOYCE CARY: A PREFACE TO HIS NOVELS (Lond: Chatto & Windus; NY: Harper, 1959), pp. 57–58.

Cary's African novels are not colonial, as is EMF's *A Passage to India*. Cary lacked EMF's desire to explain a foreign country to England. The interest of Cary's novels is in laying bare human motivation. In AISSA SAVED the opening invites comparison to the opening of *Passage*. Cary writes more from within and is more concerned with the individual's religious experience than is EMF, who writes primarily about the conflict of cultures as symbolizing the isolation of human beings. [EMF is concerned, basically, with religious experiences in *Passage*.]

1960

834 "Albert Camus," TIMES LITERARY SUPPLEMENT (Lond), 8 Jan 1960, pp. 1, 2.

Camus is a liberal existentialist. His humanist cast of mind aligns him not with Jean Paul Sartre, Gabriel Marcel, and Martin Heidegger so much as with the EMF of *Two Cheers for Democracy*. Both men reveal the same deep humanity, the same sanity, the same impatience with mysticism [overstated for EMF], the same optimism concerning men, and the same skepticism toward ideologies.

835 Alvarez, A. "West End Is West End," NEW STATESMAN, nsLIX (30 April 1960), 620, 622.

Santha Rama Rau's adaptation of *A Passage to India* does stand as drama. It has an "intense ominousness"; but it lacks the novel's distinction, possibly because the contemporary theater demands that characters be simplified into "humours."

836 Bachrach, A. G. H. "Reviews," ENGLISH STUDIES (Amsterdam), XLI:5 (1960), 338–40.

EMF was to the novel of his time what Shaw was to the drama, by virtue of his humor, wit, and irony; he teaches us that one need not be solemn to be great. Other distinctive aspects of EMF: his immense culture, his counterpoint of violence, his capacity for the symbolic and for sympathy. [Review of H. J. Oliver's THE ART OF E. M. FORSTER (1960).]

837 Blair, Thomas M. H. "E. M. Forster: 'Mr. and Mrs. Abbey's Difficulties,'" FIFTY MODERN STORIES, ed by Thomas M. H. Blair (Evanston & Elmsford, NY: Row, Peterson, 1960), pp. 543–44.

[Includes "Mr. and Mrs. Abbey's Difficulties" as one of the fifty "stories." This work, while more of a sketch than a story, reveals EMF's tendency to apply the methods of fiction writing to the writing of biography.]

838 Brien, Alan. "Words Made Flesh," SPECTATOR (Lond), CCIV (22 Jan 1960), 109–10.

The power of Santha Rama Rau's adaptation of *A Passage to India* is that of the novel, presenting black and white as shades of gray. The revelation that we all take part in good and evil is true but paralyzing; the conflict between those who want to be loved and those who want to be respected is common to all empires.

839 Crews, Frederick C. "E. M. Forster: The Limitations of Mythology," COMPARATIVE LITERATURE, XII (Spring 1960), 97–112; rptd, slightly rvd, as "The Limitations of Mythology," E. M. FORSTER: THE PERILS OF HUMANISM (Princeton: Princeton UP; Lond: Oxford UP, 1962), pp. 124–41.

Neitzchean (or Dionysian) elements obtrude in some of EMF's short stories, e.g., "The Story of a Panic," "The Other Side of the Hedge," and "The Story of the Siren." The characters in them confront the passionate side of their natures. These individuals work toward an Apollonian ideal of self-knowledge, so that the stories are only incidentally Dionysian. In stories like "Other Kingdom," "The Curate's Friend," and "The Road from Colonus" the Dionysian identification with nature also points toward the Apollonian ideal of self-knowledge. EMF's paganism works in the direction of perfecting the moral nature and is akin to that expressed by most writers in the Victorian age. Under the influence of Lowes Dickinson, EMF appreciated the Greek freedom from asceticism. He accepted passion within the ideal of proportion, as did Meredith, who held that man should steer between the ascetic rocks and the sensual whirlpools. In *Where Angels Fear to Tread* the pagan gods do not appear, though there are some traces of the Dionysian in Gino Carella. It is not passion but repression that produces the central catastrophe in *Angels*. In *A Room with a View* passion predominates: it is valuable for Lucy Honeychurch and George Emerson; it is fatal in the case of the two quarrelers in the Piazza Signoria. Pagan gods, who inculcate experience, preside over the scene of the murder in the piazza. Here the hero might become as a god to the heroine, and vice versa. The gods in the piazza operate also to subdue Lucy's propriety and George's *Weltschmerz*. Phaethon (personified in the carriage driver) advocates impulse and passion when George kisses Lucy for the first time; when George kisses her in Surrey, Phaethon has yielded to Apollo. The deities of Aphrodite and Pallas Athene are reconciled when Lucy accepts George. *The Longest Journey* is the most mythological of the novels. The plot in the novel goes from middle-class prejudice toward a kind of pagan clear-sightedness; and then, in Rickie Elliot's case, toward a reacquisition of pagan enlightenment, after his defection at Sawston. Rickie's mythological way of apprehending the world (in abeyance at Sawston) is contrasted with the literal and arid way of the Pembrokes. The Pembrokes make a gesture toward paganism, with their bust of the Hermes of Praxiteles (but not the nude figure) in their drawing room. Their patronizing attitude toward mythology reveals the flaw in Rickie's own paganism: he is too eager for the great world to validate the truth of the pagan myths in which he believes. Though

Rickie will never be capable of the pagan life, Stephen Wonham and Stewart Ansell rescue him from the conformism of the Pembrokes. Rickie had idolized Gerald Dawes as the Greek athlete, and then idolizes Stephen, who superficially resembles Gerald; but Stephen resists Rickie's efforts at idolization. Stephen's function is to draw Rickie out of his symbolic way of interpreting things, to indicate to him that reality should not be mentalized. Stephen insists on being an actual human being before being seen as a brother. The Demeter image has many complexities of meaning. She embodies the harmony with the earth which Stephen possesses and for which Rickie seeks. She is an embodiment of suffering and hope, of disappointment and salvation, and so is relevant to Rickie's quest for his dead mother and lost brother. Her shattered knees ally her to Rickie, whose knees are broken by the train; she is allied to Mrs. Elliot as a fertility figure. Demeter provides a principle with which Rickie tries to come to terms. He wishes to marry and to make his peace with Demeter, though he is not well-qualified to do so, and Ansell is not qualified to do so at all. Stephen is the one character who can bind himself to future generations of mankind and be Demeter's true representative. Submission to Demeter betokens a state of mind opposite that of the allegorical consciousness that informs Rickie's short stories and EMF's own. EMF's use of Demeter is a concession to the old allegorical spirit that EMF would repudiate in the novel. But he works in a direction of realism, away from an extraneously applied Greek mythology. In *Howards End* the legends are English and local, not Greek and literary. What they signify is similar to what myths signify in *Journey:* "the characters' involvement with the common lot of humanity, living, dead, and unborn." The local myths, which emphasize tradition and continuity, underlie the theme of connection in the novel. In becoming the mistress of the myth-haunted Howards End house, Margaret Schlegel becomes the transmitter of the strength and wisdom accruing from the past. She makes her peace with the prosaic side of the world sooner than Rickie does. For this reason the Wilcoxes emerge as more credible figures than the Pembrokes. In *Passage* the mythology of harmony with the earth is inconspicuous because harmony with the Indian earth would mean madness. The human order and the divine, or natural, order remain irreconcilable. The humanistically envisioned harmony between earth and the works of man disappears in an implacable India. The dominant symbol of Caves, with their nihilistic echo, precludes the possibility of meaning to be found in myths descending from the past. The punkah wallah in the courtroom, however, does function mythologically in exuding vitality and sexuality. *Passage* is Apollonian in its dismissal of romantic illusion; but it is also the most poetic of the novels in that its images project a felt relationship, even if a negative one, between man and the cosmos. The imaginative control evinced in *Passage* indicates that EMF has now produced a novel that has in itself the dimensions of a myth. [The essay explores the possible correlations between EMF's abandonment of specific references to Hellenic mythology in *Howards End* and *A Passage to India* concurrent with the changes in his technique and the broadening of his total outlook. Standard discussion and the most enlightening available on its subject; part of Crews's excellent book on EMF.]

840 Ellmann, Richard. "Two Faces of Edward," EDWARDIANS AND LATE VICTORIANS, ed by Richard Ellmann (NY & Lond: Columbia UP, English Institute Essays, 1959, 1960), pp. 188–210, espec 195, 198, 200, 209.

Though EMF is an agnostic like most of his literary contemporaries, he, like them, uses Christian imagery in his novels and is interested in the "salvation" of his characters. He is ambiguously for both Christ and Pan, for "deities reconciled" to the greatest extent possible. Startling coincidences are used in *A Room with a View* and in James's THE AMBASSADORS to imply that life is much more than it appears to be. To complement the secular miracles prevalent in Edwardian fiction, writers characteristically use for thematic purposes some single unifying event or object, some external symbol used exhaustively, such as the word "view" in *Room*. In *A Passage to India* the secular miracles are not as easily wrought as in EMF's prewar novels. More brutality is present, and the realizations of the characters are less ample and reassuring.

841 Hale, Nancy. "A Passage to Relationship," ANTIOCH REVIEW, XX (Spring 1960), 19–30; rptd, in rvd form, as "The Novel: A Passage to Relationship," THE REALITIES OF FICTION: A BOOK ABOUT WRITING (Boston: Little, Brown, 1962; Lond: Macmillan, 1963), pp. 67–84.

There must be a commanding theme in a novel to support an illusion of life. EMF's theme in *A Passage to India* is separateness and divison, the opposite of relationship, which is the most commanding novelistic theme. *Passage* is not merely concerned with relationships but with the subject of relationship itself and the obstacles that individuals must surmount in order to attain it. EMF makes his novel real by recreating the tempo of life in India, by composing indelible scenes, and by his rendering of character. EMF successfully creates character through comic means and embodies his themes obliquely. What Adela Quested thought happened in the Caves never happened at all; it was a meaningless "boum." EMF used a Moslem to represent India because he wanted the hate and violence of Islam to be a suitable counterpoise to the love and activity emphasized in Fielding's western culture. The echo did not negate Western values any more completely than the British negated Eastern values. Aziz and Fielding in their final conversation negate, between them, the Eastern values of Hinduism [but the Hindu values are not negated for the novel]. In the philosophy found in the BHAGAVAD-GITA and in *Passage*, "relationship is seen to consist in the acceptance of relationship." Godbole alone accepts the fact that everything in the universe has its echo and that an echo also has its echo, "that opposites exist to everything. . . . The fact of the existence of two opposed things *is* the relationship between them." Aziz and Fielding do not accept their relationship. EMF suggests "that behind the Moslem God, and the Christian God, sits enthroned a God of acceptance, who embraces all things, not because they are sensible, or admirable or right, or pitiable, or lovable, or in any way worthy, but simply because he *is*, and they *are*." [Suggestive and appreciative essay.]

842 Hasan, Aley. "The Life and Thought of E. M. Forster," HINDUSTAN TIMES WEEKLY (Delhi), "Sunday Magazine," 11 Dec 1960, p. 4.

[Interview with EMF. EMF thinks that Santha Rama Rau's adaptation of *A Passage to India* is excellent and sensitive. EMF went to India in 1912 as a result of his prior acquaintance with Syed Ross Masood; says his first visit was a Muslim one; his second (in 1921), a Hindu one; his third (1945), a national one. EMF judges that *Passage* has lost its political relevance, some of its social relevance, little of its poetic and personal relevance. EMF is more optimistic about future understanding between races now that the English have left India. EMF regards B. Rajan's THE DARK DANCER as an excellent novel, especially in its Indian sequences; he also admires Raja Rao's KANTHAPURA, and R. K. Narayan's comic mastery. EMF feels that we are in a "global mess," in part due to the population explosion, in part due to the nuclear threat. He is both pessimistic and optimistic (illogically so) about the nuclear threat, favoring an abolition of nationalities as a way to avert catastrophe. A prose writer could deal with this problem but would have to deal imaginatively with it (as would the poet).]

843 Hewett, R. P. "Some Prose Passages Examined: V," READING AND RESPONSE: AN APPROACH TO THE CRITICISM OF LITERATURE (Lond: George G. Harrap, 1960), pp. 155–62.

Adela Quested expresses to Aziz a desire not to become a typical Anglo-Indian after her marriage. There is a similarity of attitudes between the two, but sympathy is dispelled by her doctrinaire way of expounding ideas that Aziz himself believes in. She also displays some lack of imagination in insisting upon incontestable social truths at a time when Aziz is putting forth a great effort to bridge the gap between the races. This excerpt reveals incisive character portrayal, a subtle presentation of the difficulties in the way of understanding, and the complexities in all human relationships. [Analysis of an excerpt from Chap 14, *A Passage to India*, beginning "But wasn't Akbar's new religion very fine?"]

844 Hough, Graham. IMAGE AND EXPERIENCE: STUDIES IN A LITER-ARY REVOLUTION (Lond: Gerald Duckworth, 1960), pp. 7, 69, 212, 213, 217.

The British appreciation of EMF always starts with response to his specific milieu, in contrast to an American critic such as Lionel Trilling, who sees EMF "in a dateless, unlocalised sense" or relates him to currents of ideas. Can the essential obscurity that EMF describes in "Joseph Conrad: A Note" (*Abinger Harvest*) be regarded in CHANCE as a result of Conrad's indirect method of presentation to which he may have been forced by his lack of knowledge about the extended lives of his characters?

845 Hoy, Cyrus. "Forster's Metaphysical Novel," PUBLICATIONS OF THE MODERN LANGUAGE ASSOCIATION, LXXV (March 1960), 126–36.

Howards End is a metaphysical novel because it deals with clashing motives and purposes that are then subsumed by conflicting principles expressed in terms of opposites that must be reconciled in order to determine the nature of reality; such opposites are "the real and the ideal, the tangible and the intangible, the body and the soul, the many and the one." The conflicts are projected through the contrasting values represented by two groups in the novel, the Wilcox family and the Schlegel family. In this conflict the phrase "only connect" represents for Margaret Schlegel the ideal end of life, while the phrase "panic and emptiness" connotes for her sister Helen the doom that threatens us all. Ruth Wilcox represents the unseen, with its uncertain impact upon the seen. As for the outer life, Margaret at first reflects its grosser form in her alliance with the other Wilcoxes; in contrast is its firmer aspect in the life of nature, cherished by Ruth Wilcox. Leonard Bast reveals the same desire to identify himself with nature that motivated Ruth Wilcox. By trying to acquire the culture to which he is not really suited, he is false to his feelings for nature and fails to become the strong, intuitively percep-tive natural man that he might have been. Margaret's inclination to turn to the Wilcoxes is partly the result of her conviction that culture has had its day. Accordingly, she welcomes Henry Wilcox's proposal, though in so doing she partly betrays her values. The extravert Wilcoxes are interested in sex, but pretend not to be. They keep their women in a kind of glass cage, bestowing on them every comfort but becoming overprotective by virtue of possessive, primitive sexual feeling. Images of glass (the glass shade between the married couple and the world; the railway carriage with its glass salon) connect with the idea of sex, as does Leonard's shattering the glass frame on Jacky's photograph and Margaret's shattering the glass on Charles Wil-cox and his bride Dolly's photograph. Both Leonard and Margaret cut their fingers, and both photographs become blood-stained. These two incidents link Leonard and Margaret, both of whom are seeking reality. Leonard truly exemplifies the honor, courage, and strength that Margaret wrongly seeks in the Wilcoxes. Both Leonard and Margaret are seeking a comradeship transcending sex. Near the novel's close, Margaret attains such an apogee of comradeship with Helen, rather than with Henry, in the presence of Howards End house and the wych-elm tree that symbolizes it. Leonard Bast contrasts sharply, in his honesty and sensitivity, with Henry Wilcox, especially in the closing sequences. Leonard is again linked with Margaret when, seeking beauty and adventure, he finds it in the country, as Margaret, in effect, also does. There are also links between Leonard and Ruth Wilcox: they both come from yeoman stock. EMF condemns imperialism through his treatment of the materialistic, exploitative Wilcoxes. The real struggle lies between the yeomanly heritage of Ruth Wilcox and the imperialistic attitudes of the rest of the family. Ruth Wilcox has reconciled the two forces, but Margaret is caught between them. By exposing herself to them, Margaret learns that the Wilcox standards are unworthy ones; and she, in effect, rejects them by turning to the country heritage of Ruth Wilcox and by abandoning the corrupting city that the Wilcoxes dominate. (They are not at home at Howards End and dislike it.) Margaret is more intelligent than Helen by virtue of achieving a truth that reconciles the seen and the unseen; Helen, on the contrary, pursues the unseen so intently that she ends by pursuing an abstraction. Margaret reconciles sameness and difference, the one and the many. She also learns by the end of the book to reconcile the elements in another dichotomy: flesh and spirit, body and soul. This she finds can be done only in nature, not in the city dominated by Wilcoxes. This reconciliation of the human and the divine is the most important task that Margaret undertakes. *Howards End* also anticipates the issues that have been with us since 1910. It portended the World War; it presents urbanization, industrialization, and mechanization; it heralds the victory of the imperialist over the yeoman (though this triumph turned hollow); it chronicled the replacement of agrarianism by cosmopolitanism. The city is seen as satanic and chaotic. EMF's remedy is love; but love with him means companionship, a not altogether satisfactory concept. Though all the themes may not be thoroughly dramatized in the novel, they are symbolically intense and meaningful. The novel works in a transcendent direction: "As love transcends human bestiality, life itself transcends the corruption of mortality." Symbolic of such transcendence is the wych-elm, which becomes an emblem of the unity underlying the diversities of experience. [Stimulating discussion; a standard essay on *Howards End*.]

846 Kain, Richard M. "Vision and Discovery in E. M. Forster's *A Passage to India*," TWELVE ORIGINAL ESSAYS ON GREAT ENGLISH NOVELS, ed by Charles Shapiro (Detroit: Wayne State UP: 1960), pp. 253–75.

Humor, mystic contemplation, and a stress upon the absurdities of reality alternate in *A Passage to India*. Chaucerian whimsicality, the comedy of humors, the comedy of situation with a metaphysical cast, and the more blatant satire on the English are all present. In EMF's fiction there is a mixture of amusement and respect for life, and there is a wisdom in his humor. His dominant theme is the attainment of harmony among individuals, groups, ideas, and attitudes. He also deals with the contrary motifs of the separation between men and the separation between man and nature. The letters from *The Hill of Devi* are instructive as a comparison with the finished novel. India becomes a symbol of human awareness and of the human condition, as well as a social and political entity, in EMF's novel. The standard in the novel for judging character is the degree of tolerance and sympathy possessed by the individual. Aziz, Fielding, and Godbole represent the best in their respective groups; Mrs. Moore transcends and includes all of the characters, who are grouped "radially" around her as she takes her place at the center of a circle, the segments of which include the religious and ethnic groupings presented in the novel. "Mosque," "Caves," and "Temple" represent the Muslim, Brahman, and cosmic aspects of India. *Passage* resists the simplicities of allegory because it is so firmly and fully orchestrated in its development. It does not exemplify any specific thesis because of EMF's traditional irony, the richness and complexity of his outlook, and the indirectness of his approach. Social conflict and cosmic mystery become intertwined in EMF's development of materials. In India all identities are lost, as Mrs. Moore learns. Her initial viewpoint is that of EMF's earlier philosophy of good will and tolerance. In *Passage* this view confronts a stark violence in man and nature to which it is as first unequal. [Her plight is surveyed extensively.] The quiescent tolerance that she finally attains becomes a pervasive influence after her death. Her tolerance is central to the ethos of the novel, as is the expansiveness, the inclusiveness, and the religious fervor present at the Mau festival. The theme of awareness connects the political and social theme in *Passage* with the religious. Aziz is EMF's triumph as a character. EMF also traces the corrupting influence of prejudice and the herd instinct. His liberalism is put to the test in India both by bigotry and by the nihilism suggested in the Caves. [Stresses the comedy of manners aspect of *Passage*. Despite occasional insights, the commentary is too level and derivative to make it an outstanding critique.]

847 Lee, Lawrence Lynn. "The Moral Themes of E. M. Forster," DISSERTATION ABSTRACTS, XX (1960), 1790–1791. Unpublished dissertation, University of Utah, 1959.

848 Lehmann, John. I AM MY BROTHER (NY: Reynal; Lond: Longmans, 1960), pp. 101–2, 179–80, 246, 289; rptd, slightly rvd, in IN MY OWN TIME: MEMOIRS OF A LITERARY LIFE (Boston: Little, Brown, 1969).

[Quotes an important letter from EMF, critical of "proletarian" writing as it was practiced in the 1930s, à propos of Lehmann's NEW WRITING IN EUROPE. EMF feels that doctrinaire political writers often fail to create living characters; he praises W. H. Auden (especially the poems in JOURNEY TO A WAR) and William Plomer as socially oriented poets. Recounts EMF's critical attitude toward the pretentious bureaucrats whom World War I brought into power, although he also recognized that the war had to be fought. Other incidental references.]

849 McDowell, Frederick P. W. "Forster's Many-Faceted Universe: Idea and Paradox in *The Longest Journey*," CRITIQUE, IV (Fall–Winter 1960–1961), 41–63; rptd in part as " 'The Union of Shadow and Adamant': *The Longest Journey*," E. M. FORSTER (NY: Twayne Publishers, Twayne's English Authors Series, 1969), pp. 64–80.

EMF's personal presence in *The Longest Journey* lends force to the novel, as well as contrivance, overemphasis, and distortion in characterization. EMF's identification with Rickie Elliot gives sympathy to his characterization despite his frailties. Rickie organizes the novel and defines (at least initially) most of its values; he also becomes (toward the end) an object lesson in the failure of certain qualities of mind. On balance, Rickie is more admirable and wise than misguided and foolish. The intellectuals in the novel (Rickie Elliot, Stewart Ansell, Jackson, and Tony Failing) all are humanists seeking the truth. Stephen Wonham knows by instinct what these others apprehend intellectually and is also to be counted as a humanist. All believe in the authority of Greek and Roman culture. They emphasize self-fulfillment, they appreciate dynamic personal relationships, and they realize man's potential worth as well as his inherent weakness. In the opening chapter Rickie evinces a poetic version of reality that contrasts with the concrete view of Ansell and the abstract view of Tilliard. Imagination is Rickie's great but fatal gift. For Rickie reality is both concrete and visionary, and inexhaustible as well: such is the significance of the circle within the square diagram in Ansell's exercise, Ansell's matches striking in the opening scene, the flameboats at the end, and the dell at Cambridge. All are microcosmic symbols of a macrocosmic reality that they either represent or contain. Rickie stands on the middle ground between permanence and change. He appreciates the tangle of good and evil in human nature; he gains added insight thereby but is sometimes rendered immobile. Imagination misleads him (even though it allows him posthumously to achieve literary distinction); thus he interprets the embrace of Gerald and Agnes in more extravagant terms than it deserves, and he expects too much from Stephen at the end (though Rickie is partly justified in his disillusionment with Stephen's broken promise). The cracked bell signifies Rickie's aborted career, his truncated development, his deflection from wholeness, and his defeated aspirations, rather than his deficiencies.

Before Sawston enchains him, Rickie reveals Christian and humanist values that are admirable. He dislikes negative emotions. His kindness, generosity, and tact derive from his mother; his father is reprehensible in his lack of feeling and is presented in terms of serpent and whip imagery. Mr. Elliot and Mrs. Failing are characterized in part by diabolical laughter. Rickie also reveals that, for EMF, principles of right and excellence have an absolute existence; one should never think in terms of reward for acting in light of them. In *Journey*, EMF explores the complex relationship existing between beauty and ethics: beauty leads to spiritual enlargement, but a purposive aestheticism can become sterile and inhumane. The humanist ethic that Rickie represents depends on reason but more fundamentally on values transcending intelligence. EMF places high value on the spontaneous as it is revealed in art or as it can be achieved through identification with nature. Country life is superior to urban; the picture of Demeter in Stephen's attic room is associated with agrarian values. This Demeter of Cnidus is not only to be associated with Stephen but also with Rickie; the goddess's shattered knees link with Rickie's mutilation when he saves Stephen's life. Rickie's sensitivity to nature aligns him with Stephen. Rickie and Stephen are connected also by their reverence for Greece and Rome, Stephen's being a physical paganism, Rickie's an intellectual appreciation. The humanist ethic also encompasses a reverence for the past and for tradition. A respect for the personal and for "the holiness of the heart's imagination" links Stephen and Rickie (and both characters with Ansell, as opposed to the Pembrokes). [The essay merits consideration because of its attempt to define EMF's humanism through the characters of *Journey*.]

850 Morris, John. E. M. FORSTER (Lond: Longmans, Green, Writers and Their Work, No. 7, 1960) [complete revision of Rex Warner's E. M. FORSTER (1950)]; rptd in BRITISH WRITERS AND THEIR WORK (No. 3), ed by J. W. Robinson (Lincoln: U of Nebraska P, 1964); see Warner (1950); extracts rptd in CONTEMPORARY LITERARY CRITICISM, ed by Carolyn Riley (Detroit: Gale Research Co., 1973), I, 106.

[Discussion of short stories added, pp. 8–9. Discussion of *Where Angels Fear to Tread*, especially the comparisons with D. H. Lawrence, omitted (1950 ed, pp. 14–15). In discussion of *The Longest Journey* material added (p. 18) on the "shocks" in the novel. Discussion of Agnes Pembroke, Gerald Dawes, and Stephen Wonham dropped (1950 ed, p. 17). Quoted materials from *Howards End* added (pp. 23–24). Material from *The Hill of Devi* added in discussion of *A Passage to India* (p. 25). Material added in discussion of *Passage* on p. 29, citing EMF's exactness of observation, the accuracy with which he records the English speech of the Indians, and the prophetic nature of the closing paragraph. Material on pp. 30–32, concerning EMF's role as broadcaster, *Two Cheers for Democracy*, *Devi*, and *Marianne Thornton* added.]

851 Oliver, H. J. THE ART OF E. M. FORSTER (Parkville, Australia: Melbourne UP; Lond & NY: Cambridge UP, 1960; rpts, slightly rvd, as "The Minor Fiction," "E. M. Forster: The Early Novels," CRITIQUE, I (Summer 1957), 15–33; discussion on *Aspects of the Novel* rptd as "*Aspects of the Novel*" in A GARLAND FOR E. M. FORSTER, ed by H. H. Anniah Gowda (Mysore: The Literary Half-Yearly, 1969), pp. 83–89.

Chap 1, "Introduction": EMF's work is the most interesting product of the cultured mind in modern literature. His subject matter and point of view are modern; he is modern in writing novels with so many levels of significance. Tonbridge School gave him one set of symbols, Cambridge another, in his life and work: the public school attitude and the undeveloped heart versus true culture and spontaneity. Chap 2, "Subject and Method": EMF's humanist credo is to be found in "What I Believe" (*Two Cheers for Democracy*) and his method in *Aspects of the Novel*. [Both works summarized.] Chap 3, "Short Stories and Early Fiction": Goldsworthy Lowes Dickinson complained of the cleft in the short stories between their mythological materials and real life. EMF is concerned in them with the life of the imagination and its practical opposite; his literary skill is often sharpest in drawing people on the opposite side: Harcourt Worters, Tytler, etc. The best story is "The Celestial Omnibus," which represents a more expert blending of the fantastic and the real than does "The Story of a Panic." "The Machine Stops" lacks continuous narrative interest and ingenuity; "The Point of It" is uneven; "Mr. Andrews" is a greater aesthetic success. The second six stories (collected in *The Eternal Moment and Other Stories*) focus upon aspiration versus damnation, and are less good. [Remaining contents of this chapter are summarized in "E. M. Forster: The Early Novels"; see Oliver (1957).] Chap 4, "*Howards End*": Henry Wilcox is clearly seen and "magnificently portrayed." The value of bodily passion is more convincingly defined in the negative through Henry Wilcox's hesitations than in positive characters such as the Emersons and Gino Carella. The Wilcoxes breed continually but are incapable of real sexual love. EMF is not willing to condemn "the wrong side" without saying for it what can be said; but his concessions do not mean complete approval. Helen Schlegel is impetuous rather than idealistic; Margaret Schlegel is steady and aware, but not steady in any pejorative sense. The marriage between Margaret and Henry was not necessary, and Margaret was no better for having become Mrs. Wilcox. The Helen-Leonard Bast affair is not probable. EMF is uneasy with Leonard, who is explained rather than observed and who is more satisfying as a symbol than as a character. The coming together of Basts and Schlegels will be disastrous for the Basts because Helen does not show enough real goodwill toward them. Mrs. Wilcox is gifted with intuitive perception and is not sentimentalized. She does not represent so much England's past as a continuing tradition. Hay is attached to both Mrs. Wilcox and Margaret as an anti-symbol to connote their opposition to nomadic London. Through the various symbols, EMF achieves the effect of expansion, the difficult rhythm that he describes in *Aspects*. Chap 5, "*A Passage to India*": Ronny Heaslop is callow but has some redeeming features. Aziz is far from perfect but is generally an appealing character. Aziz stresses personal affection and becomes a triumph of inconsistency. The impracticality, inconsistency, and flamboyance of the Indians promote a gulf between them and the English. The famous Caves incident is somewhat contrived, but it is an absurd incident like this that drives people apart. What happens in the Caves is inexplicable, as is the accident involving the Nawab's car. Through Mrs. Moore, EMF demonstrates how to come to grips with inexplicable India; she has a kind of mystic sensitivity that takes her straight to the truth. Stella and Ralph Moore in "Temple" replace Mrs. Moore but exert her same reconciling influence. Hinduism, if it does not give the complete answer to human problems provides a better solution to them than Christianity does. Hinduism at least embraces everything, including merriment and wasps. "Mosque," "Caves," and "Temple" can be associated with the cold weather, hot weather, and rains, respectively; with Islam, Christianity, and Hinduism; with personal relationships, the failure of personal relationships, and the resolving of differences. One must stop short of saying that Hinduism represents a solution for India; the idea of India is an oversimplification, and there is no easy solution to India's problems. The fists and fingers of the Marabar Hills, described in the first chapter, establish the fact of evil from the first. It is difficult in India to know what is real and what is illusion. EMF counters the amorphousness of his subject matter with careful attention to structure, including the skilled use of recurrent phrases or incidents. Chap 6, "Retrospect": [Unexciting summary statement.] EMF was to the novel of his time what Shaw was to its drama; both writers revealed that a work could be comic without ceasing to be serious. [Adequate and appreciative survey, but the general observations on EMF's art do not originate from any depths of perception. Reviews: Miriam Allott, "Reviews," MODERN LANGUAGE REVIEW, LVI (July 1961), 420; A. G. H. Bachrach (Entry no. 836); Cyrus Hoy (Entry No. 955); E. Lacotte, "Étude Critique: Études Récentes sur E. M. Forster" (Critical Essay: Recent Studies on E. M. Forster), ÉTUDES ANGLAISES, XX (Oct–Dec 1967), 425–31; Frederick P. W. McDowell, "The Newest Elucidations of Forster," ENGLISH FICTION IN TRANSITION, V:4(1962), 51–58; and Paul West, "Reviews of Books," ENGLISH, XIII (Spring 1961), 154–56.

852 Panter-Downes, Mollie. "Letter from London," NEW YORKER, XXXVI (14 May 1960), 181–84, 187–88, espec 184, 187.
Santha Rama Rau's adaptation of *A Passage to India* has pleased everyone

(including EMF); it conveys a sense of the vastness and the ominousness of India. Zia Mohyeddin epitomizes the mercurial quality of Aziz; Norman Wooland captures in Fielding "the right Airedale qualities of kindness and fidelity," and Enid Lorimer as Mrs. Moore convincingly portrays her abrupt change from serenity to harsh indifference after the visit to the Marabar Caves.

853 "*A Passage to India* by No Means a Novelist's Play," TIMES (Lond), 20 Jan 1960, p. 6.

A Passage to India lends itself better to dramatization than *A Room with a View*, since it provides "a definite picture with a set subject—the incompatibility of East and West," instead of being only a creative imagining. The result is a formally taut play. The third act in the Oxford production is the least successful because the Anglo-Indians in the club scene are caricatures.

854 "Passage to the Stage," TIME, LXXV (1 Feb 1960), 53.

Santha Rama Rau has managed to extract the center of *A Passage to India* in her adaptation of it "without damaging its heart." In a personal appearance at its Oxford premiere, EMF alleged that in his novel he had attempted "to depict the diversity of human types."

855 "People," TIME, LXXVI (4 July 1960), 30.

[Friends of the London Library sell, to help raise money for taxes, the final handwritten draft of *A Passage to India* for $18,200 to a Manhattan rare books dealer. Manuscript is now at the Humanities Research Center, University of Texas.]

856 Priestley, J. B. "Mostly before 1914," LITERATURE AND WESTERN MAN (NY: Harper; Lond: Heinemann, 1960), pp. 336–69, espec 355–56.

Though EMF's novels are Edwardian in date, they belong in spirit to the 1920s and 1930s, for which EMF served as remote advance guard. As with Wells, Bennett, and Galsworthy his work dates. His kind of fiction dates as much as theirs, but it came into fashion later and so is now held in higher esteem. He rejected the idea of an inclusive realism; rather he "works in brilliant flashes, sudden revelations of character, glimpses of heights and depths, action that is not realistic and typical but symbolic." His symbolic method is demanding for the novelist, so that is perhaps why he turned to the essay form. *Aspects of the Novel* produces the impression that EMF has no great regard for the novel as such. EMF reveals himself in his fiction as a poet, a psychologist, and a philosopher of sorts; but he never truly satisfies as a novelist. He wobbles in his narratives; his work is real but not steadily there. There is a kind of willfulness in his writing that is positive as well as negative in its implications, since it is in the service of "all that is life-enhancing, sensuous, personal" as opposed to all that is life-denying, conventional, and impersonal. In *Howards End* and *A Passage to India* this conflict between the life-enhancing and the life-denying forces becomes more complex and complicated.

> **857** Rama Rau, Santha. "*A Passage to India:* A Brilliantly Successful Play Dramatizes the Classic Novel's Conflict between East and West," LIFE INTERNATIONAL (Chicago), XXIX (24 Oct 1960), 76–77.

EMF in *A Passage to India* does get beyond an "atavistic" story to capture a "melody, or perception of the truth," as he would have wished to do. EMF put no difficulties in the way of Santha Rama Rau's dramatizing the novel. After she encountered difficulties in getting the play accepted and produced, it opened in London to critical approval beyond her expectations. EMF cushions his melodramatic plot with "insight, philosophy, mysticism, satire, outright farce and sober comment." He writes about relations between races, ruler and subject, Hindu and Muslim, different individuals; the breadth of his vision prevents his novel from becoming dated. The inner experience that characterizes the last five chapters ("Temple") cannot be satisfactorily projected onto the stage, though they are deeply important to the form and content of the novel.

> **858** Rama Rau, Santha. "A PASSAGE TO INDIA," A PLAY BY SANTHA RAMA RAU FROM THE NOVEL BY E. M. FORSTER (Lond: Edward Arnold, 1960; Samuel French; NY: Harcourt, Brace & World, 1961); rptd in THEATRE ARTS, XLVI (April 1962), 25–26 (abstract based on NY ed).

[A well-known adaptation of *A Passage to India* for the stage, about which critical opinion varies. Act One admirably captures the social tensions and cross-purposes operating among characters from different races, as does Act Two in the events leading up to Mrs. Moore's and Adela Quested's experiences in the Caves. The comedy-of-manners and racial-tension aspects of *Passage* are convincingly dramatized. What comes through less successfully is Mrs. Moore, who is less of a presence than in the novel and who loses credibility to a degree by having to articulate responses that had appeared as her thoughts in the novel. Godbole, whose gospel of Hindu inclusiveness is so central to the novel, fails to register decisively without the concluding "Temple" sequence of the novel. Aziz and Fielding have their famous contretemps (in which they realize that "No, not yet" and "No, not there" can they be intimate friends) after the trial, a too complete *volte-face* for Aziz and Fielding to make after Fielding has just contributed to Aziz's liberation. The inevitable simplification of characters and issues in the play has the effect of making Ronny Heaslop more sympathetic than EMF ever intended. Philosophically, the adaptation is disappointing; a comedy of cross-purposes is inadequate to encompass the radical disparities in Anglo-India between alien cultures.]

859 Rideout, Walter B. "E. M. Forster, 'The Machine Stops,'" INSTRUCTOR'S MANUAL FOR "THE EXPERIENCE OF PROSE" (NY: Crowell, 1960), pp. 40–41.

Though ironic, EMF is serious about the future in "The Machine Stops." EMF shows how technology may imprison man, dry up his emotions, stifle original thought, and cause him to lose "the mythopeic imagination"; man's closed society then becomes a beehive. In EMF's view man must be restored to nature, first-hand experience, and a sense of his own individuality; EMF is sympathetic, therefore, with Kuno in his abortive revolt against the machine.

860 Seward, Barbara. "The Contemporary Symbol," THE SYMBOLIC ROSE (NY: Columbia UP; Lond: Oxford UP, 1960), pp. 118–55, espec 131–32.

EMF is more socially conscious than Virginia Woolf; in EMF the love that the rose signifies implies a fulfillment for the individual that is based in part upon a social reorientation. The rose is for Rickie Elliot symbolic of a reality he had sought in humanity, literature, his wife, and the memory of his mother. His ideal is complex and intangible, but it is attainable. The rose relates also to a humanity pursuing real values of love, integrity, and freedom of the spirit; the pursuit of this rose will stifle class consciousness. The rose will be attained by a fusion of Stephen Wonham's earthiness and Rickie's romantic dreamings. Stephen attains the rose in his rural life and in his child, through Rickie's help.

861 Shahane, V. A. "Beethoven's Fifth Symphony in *Howards End*," INDIAN JOURNAL OF ENGLISH STUDIES (Calcutta), I (Dec 1960), 100–103.

The Fifth Symphony performance in *Howards End* relates closely to Helen Schlegel's problems, values, and personality. EMF uses music "in the manner of an analogy or metaphor, to convey the delicate subtleties of a view of life."

862 Shahane, V. A. "E. M. Forster's *The Longest Journey:* A Moral Fable," LITERARY CRITERION (Mysore), IV (Dec 1960), 1–8.

The Longest Journey expounds EMF's basic values. The conflict between appearance and reality is the chief theme. The conflict often takes the form of a clash between pseudo-culture and instinct, between impersonal organization and personal relations. All the characters have their virtues as well as their defects. [Extended summary of the novel. Superficial essay.]

863 "Smooth Passage to India," TIMES (Lond), 21 April 1960, p. 16.

The London production of Santha Rama Rau's adaptation of *A Passage to India* is "a sensitive and faithful rendering" of EMF's novel. The end of the play is stronger than at its Oxford performance, and the Anglo-Indians at the club no longer evoke derision.

864 Stallybrass, O[liver] G. W. "The Wobblings of E. M. Forster," MANCHESTER GUARDIAN, 20 June 1960, p. 5.

[Earlier, much less developed version of the 1969 essay with the same title, included in ASPECTS OF E. M. FORSTER, ed by Oliver Stallybrass.]

865 Stebner, Gerhard. DAS PHÄNOMEN DES TODES IM WERKE E. M. FORSTERS (The Phenomenon of Death in E. M. Forster's Works). Unpublished dissertation, Marburg University, 1960.

[Listed in Lawrence F. McNamee, DISSERTATIONS IN ENGLISH AND AMERICAN LITERATURE (NY & Lond: Bowker, 1968).] The abrupt presentation of death is not a stylistic weakness in EMF's fiction, but an effective artistic device. [In German.]

866 Stevenson, Lionel. THE ENGLISH NOVEL: A PANORAMA (Boston: Houghton, Mifflin, 1960; Lond: Constable, 1961), pp. 453, 462, 472, 476, 515, 532.

EMF is in the Jamesean tradition, dealing with "the elusive misunderstandings and adjustments experienced by ordinary people." *Where Angels Fear to Tread* and *A Room with a View* deal with the special Jamesean theme of international differences (the English are baffled by the Italians); and *The Longest Journey* and *Howards End* are analyses of the social environment, also then being examined by Galsworthy. EMF is more aloof and his sympathies are more diffused than Galsworthy's. Virginia Woolf's THE VOYAGE OUT has much in common with EMF's work, in its combination of factual narrative with symbolism. EMF is "of the old school of social analysis" [a fallacious judgment] writing his best book, *A Passage to India*, after World War I. EMF gives priority to individual feelings and moral decisions rather than to social pressures, but he is aware of the adjustments that people must make to replace the struggles they once engaged in to minimize the injustices characterizing a self-contained class system.

867 Symons, Julian. THE THIRTIES: A DREAM REVOLVED (Lond: Cresset P; Toronto: Ambassador Books, 1960), pp. 160–61.

In 1938 EMF expressed in "What I Believe" (rptd in *Two Cheers for Democracy*) a disillusionment with political faiths and political causes and emphasized instead personal relationships and virtues such as tolerance, good temper, and sympathy, a "political quietism." [This was only one side of EMF; his "Notes on the Way" and *Nordic Twilight* are explicitly anti-Fascist.]

868 Thespis. "Theatre Notes," ENGLISH, XIII (Summer 1960), 60–63, espec 61.

In Santha Rama Rau's adaptation of *A Passage to India*, the problem of bridging of gaps between races is as compelling as ever. The paradox in *Passage* of the characters' desire to understand leading to yet deeper misunderstanding is powerfully conveyed in the play. Zia Mohyeddin captures the essence of Aziz, especially his contradictions, a man anxious for friendship yet greatly sensitive to slights.

869 Thurston, Jarvis, O. B. Emerson, Carl Hartman, and Elizabeth V. Wright. SHORT FICTION CRITICISM: A CHECKLIST OF INTERPRETATION SINCE 1925 OF STORIES AND NOVELETTES (AMERICAN, BRITISH, CONTINENTAL) 1800–1958 (Denver: Alan Swallow, 1960), pp. 58–60.

870 Trewin, J. C. "A Pair of Old Masters," ILLUSTRATED LONDON NEWS, 7 May 1960, p. 788.

Santha Rama Rau has selected material with so much art that her adaptation of *A Passage to India* seems to be an original play. She has given us "the pith of the book with a quite extraordinary skill."

871 Woolf, Leonard. SOWING: AN AUTOBIOGRAPHY OF THE YEARS 1880–1904 (Lond: Hogarth P; NY: Harcourt, Brace & World, 1960), pp. 171–72, 202; rptd in part in A LIBRARY OF LITERARY CRITICISM: MODERN BRITISH LITERATURE, ed by Ruth Z. Temple and Martin Tucker (NY: Frederick Ungar, 1966), I, 315.

Phase I (c. 1905–1911) of Bloomsbury began after Sir Leslie Stephen's death in 1904, when his children (Adrian, Thoby, Vanessa, and Virginia) moved to Gordon Square and kept alive the intellectual circle formed earlier at Cambridge (consisting of Lytton Strachey, Saxon Sydney-Turner, Thoby Stephen, John Maynard Keynes, G. E. Moore, with EMF and Desmond MacCarthy on its fringes). The Cambridge circle (and Bloomsbury) had its inception in the agnosticism of the late nineteenth century, the spiritual pessimism of the age, and an opposing approbation of the essentially optimistic liberators of this age (Henry James, Meredith, Butler, Hardy, Swinburne, Wells, Ibsen, and Shaw). Also influential was "the clarity, integrity, tenacity, and passion" (and the inspired common sense) of G. E. Moore. [The reverence for Cambridge apparent in SOWING recalls EMF's similar attitude, expressed in *The Longest Journey* and *Goldsworthy Lowes Dickinson*.] By being an Apostle, EMF established contact with those who came after him at King's or at Trinity. EMF's elusiveness, strangeness, and evasiveness fascinated his friends, as did the entire cast of his personality, with its subtlety, sensibility, and odd sense of humor. Strachey's designation of EMF as the "taupe" is exact, in view of his mole-like appearance and his startling observations when, after long periods of quiet and rumination, he would surface in a discussion as if burrowing up from underground. [The first of Woolf's autobiographies, indispensable for understanding Blooms-bury and, by implication, EMF; the series continued with GROWING (1961), BEGINNING AGAIN (1964), DOWNHILL ALL THE WAY (1967), and THE JOUR-NEY NOT THE ARRIVAL MATTERS (1969); see entries for these years. Woolf sketches in his life at Cambridge with his associates in "The Apostles," which also centered about Thoby Stephen (Virginia Woolf's brother, who died in 1906). Letter from EMF (14 Nov 1904) reproduced, regretting Woolf's departure to Ceylon, his not knowing Woolf well, and offering to help him in England in any way possible.]

1961

872 Austin, Don. "The Problem of Continuity in Three Novels of E. M. Forster," MODERN FICTION STUDIES, VII (Autumn 1961), 217–28.

EMF's dominant concern in *The Longest Journey, A Room with a View,* and *Howards End* is continuity, especially as it is expressed in and through the institution of the family. The family reconciles past with present. A member of the older generation in each novel passes on the torch; the individual who receives it must rebel (but not revolt) in order to connect the values of the older generation with his own. He can attain freedom only by assuming responsibility, not only to himself but to the race (or society). In *Journey,* Anthony Failing directs his message to both Rickie Elliot and Stephen Wonham, but fails with Rickie [oversimplification]. In *Room,* Mr. Emerson is a priest to Lucy's initiate. In *Howards End,* Ruth Wilcox exerts power both in life and in death. Margaret Schlegel is the intellectually free woman but lacks, at first, the quality of being the traditional mother of a family. Initially, she does not get Howards End house when it is willed to her; she must learn to recognize its importance. The connection established between Margaret and Ruth Wilcox is all-important; thereafter, connections follow between Margaret and Helen Schlegel, Margaret and Henry Wilcox, prose and poetry, mind and heart, past and present, the "whole" view versus the "steady" view. Cadover, Windy Corner, and Howards End are houses that become symbols of tradition; members of the newer generation must learn to recognize their importance. [Reasonable assumptions, but discussion is a bit thin.]

873 Bantock, G. H. "The Social and Intellectual Background," THE MODERN AGE, ed by Boris Ford (Harmondsworth, Middlesex & Baltimore: Penguin Books, The Pelican Guide to English Literature, Vol. VII, 1961), pp. 13–48, espec 14, 21, 26–27, 29, 46.

EMF's protest in *A Passage to India* is of the heart on behalf of fellow feeling in which social oppression and political subjection are absent. He also protests against the fragmentation resulting from the unchecked will to power and against that "intellectual hatred" which Yeats regarded as the "worst." His assumption that goodwill and culture and intelligence will work betrays "insularity" in the age of Freud and Hitler, yet he does acknowledge the power of the irrational and of the demonic in the echo in the Marabar Caves and in the goblins that Helen Schlegel discovers in the scherzo of Beethoven's Fifth Symphony. [EMF is quoted on the disoriented society after World War I, the solace provided by the hedonistic Huysmans during that war, the failure of the English middle class to be interested in persons, and the nearness of fiction to music.]

874 Bayley, John. CHARACTERS OF LOVE: A STUDY IN THE LITERA-TURE OF PERSONALITY (NY: Basic Books; Lond: Constable, 1961), pp. 6, 34, 66, 84, 185, 215, 258, 267, 289.

In the novel since the mid-nineteenth century, discernment (EMF's "connection") rather than achievement has been paramount, whereas the Elizabethan drama often subordinated discernment to achievement. In the novels of D. H. Lawrence and EMF (e.g., WOMEN IN LOVE, *Howards End*), symbolism is more rigid than in Henry James (THE GOLDEN BOWL). Mrs. Wilcox in *Howards End* and Mrs. Moore in *A Passage to India* reveal a moving outer effect but have no inner depth of individuality, in contrast to a character like Sergeant Troy in Hardy's FAR FROM THE MADDING CROWD. These women are a tribute to EMF's vision, but they are not people such as Charles Wilcox and Aziz, whom we might actually meet. [Numerous incidental references.]

875 Bergonzi, Bernard. THE EARLY H. G. WELLS: A STUDY OF THE SCIENTIFIC ROMANCES (Manchester: Manchester UP, 1961; Toronto: University of Toronto P, 1962), pp. 89, 171.

H. G. Wells's "The Wonderful Visit" is more like an EMF short story in its fantasy than like a work by Jules Verne. The Wellsian Utopia is based on the limitless possibilities of science and large-scale social engineering characterizing A MODERN UTOPIA and THE SHAPE OF THINGS TO COME. EMF satirizes this kind of utopia in "The Machine Stops."

876 "Bloomsbury Group," LISTENER, LXV (4 May 1961), 768.

In the group there was a reaction against the "moral-toned, story-telling aspects" of Victorian literature and art, and against the materialistic world of Wells, Bennett, and Shaw. Bloomsbury wished to produce the novel that was suffused with poetry, the painting featuring color and design, and the history written aesthetically. For them the arts were intertwined. They were not passive or escapist as the politically inclined John Maynard Keynes and Leonard Woolf reveal. Clive Bell and Roger Fry educated public taste and fostered appreciation of modern French and nonacademic British painting. They protested the conventional and the tawdry, and possessed "the integrity of belief and a vision of beauty." [Incidental mention of EMF.]

877 Booth, Wayne C. THE RHETORIC OF FICTION (Chicago: University of Chicago P, 1961), pp. 2, 17, 17*n*, 53*n*, 106–9, 121*n*, 137, 188–89, 213*n*, 286*n*.

Writers usually wish to appeal to the reader and will resort to rhetorical stratagems to do so. Thus the meeting between Aziz and Mrs. Moore in "Mosque" (*A Passage to India*) prepares the reader for what is to come and gives him clues to the meaning of the novel. The rapport established between Mrs. Moore and Aziz makes us unsympathetic with the intolerant Ronny Heaslop, who feels that Aziz is presumptuous in having spoken to his mother at all. For the novel to accomplish its goal we must experience this friendship deeply and truly. The scene is necessary, both dramatically and rhetorically. [On pp. 188–90 comments on the way in which an author can see his characters in a complex light, as EMF does Fielding and Adela Quested when he describes them as "dwarfs shaking hands." Quotes from EMF's *Aspects of the Novel:* his views on limited authorial intrusion, the denigration of story, etc. Principal discussion, pp. 106–9.]

878 Bottrall, Ronald. "L. H. Myers," REVIEW OF ENGLISH LITERATURE, II (April 1961), 47–58, especially 47–48, 51, 53, 58.

EMF, unlike L. H. Myers, was not affluent and reveals "inner uncertainty"; accordingly, EMF sentimentalizes Cambridge. EMF, Myers, Virginia Woolf, and D. H. Lawrence were all concerned with personal relationships; but EMF is too eclectic to attain valid universals, as do Myers and Lawrence. Myers and EMF are linked in the influence on each of G. Lowes Dickinson. THE ORISSERS presents a conflict of forces similar to that presented in *Howards End;* the surviving child is as symbolically unconvincing as Helen Schlegel's child in *Howards End.* In *A Passage to India* EMF fails to concern himself, as did Myers in THE NEAR AND THE FAR, with universal ethical and philosophical issues, with what lies beyond human relationships [an inexplicable judgment]. For EMF and Woolf, personality and communication were the chief problem, whereas Myers ranges beyond these considerations. [Scenes from *The Longest Journey* and Woolf's THE YEARS are compared with Myers's work.]

879 Bowen, Elizabeth. "Where the Pharos Stood," REPORTER (NY), XXIV (27 April 1961), 49–51; rptd as "Alexandria" in SEVEN WINTERS AND AFTERTHOUGHTS (NY: Knopf, 1962), pp. 223–27; and in AFTERTHOUGHTS (Lond: Longmans, 1962), pp. 159–62.

EMF has managed to distill in *Alexandria: A History and a Guide* the evasive personality of Alexandria, which never knew a period of infancy, but sprang into existence "immediate, adult, and dazzling." Dramatic, magical, ancient, and complex, Alexandria met its inevitable chronicler in EMF, who was sent there by chance during World War I. EMF has encompassed his difficult subject by means of art and a touch of sixth sense. His ability to discuss abstract ideas, his dramatic sense, his irony, his passion for exactitude, and his love of color are all revealed in his re-creation of the city. [Review of *Alexandria* (1961 ed).]

880 Bradbook, Frank M. "Virginia Woolf: The Theory and Practice of Fiction," THE MODERN AGE, ed by Boris Ford (Harmondsworth, Middlesex & Baltimore: Penguin Books), pp. 257–69.

Virginia Woolf is not really mystical; the lighthouse in TO THE LIGHTHOUSE is a symbol like the house in *Howards End*, a clear if suggestible one. With EMF music replaces poetry as the source of aesthetic experience. EMF is less successful with his poetic effects than Woolf, though the Fifth Symphony in *Howards End* provides the larger rhythm and theme comparable to Woolf's image of the waves in her various novels. [EMF quoted on Woolf (pp. 260, 268).]

881 Bryden, Ronald. "E. M. Forster," ILLUSTRATED WEEKLY OF INDIA (Bombay), LXXXII (29 Jan 1961), 64.

EMF's statement at the Paris P. E. N. Conference in 1935, "I believe in liberty," may reveal Bloomsbury inadequacy in relating to social issues, but it remains impressive. EMF has written copiously since 1924, and he has served worthy causes. In his novels he is the poet of undermined Victorian confidence, but he also saw that this confidence had shaky foundations and was not all of life. His later work is not nihilistic but demonstrates that, in a vast universe without value or meaning, we must make our own values. In the midst of muddle and anger EMF inspires trust. [Stimulating article.]

882 Churchill, R. C. "The Novel Since Henry James," THE CONCISE CAMBRIDGE HISTORY OF ENGLISH LITERATURE, by George Sampson (Cambridge: Cambridge UP; Toronto: Macmillan, 2nd ed, 1961), pp. 974–1007, espec 981–85, 994, 997; also 916, 962, 1014, 1017.

EMF is the most important contemporary humanist in literature, comparable to Bertrand Russell in philosophy. The fact that EMF's novels are not dated attests to the strength of the humanist tradition (which has been attacked by both Christians and Marxists) and to EMF's concern with universal problems of morality and personal relationships. *The Longest Journey* is his only failure; *Howards End* is as great as any novel in the twentieth century. Its strength lies in the marriage between Margaret Schlegel and Henry Wilcox. EMF does not spare the Schlegels (the impetuosity of Helen, the priggishness of Tibby); the Wilcox virtues are to the fore in Ruth Wilcox. [An untenable assumption since she is only a Wilcox by marriage and had come rather from the yeoman strain antagonistic to the Wilcoxes.] The one weakness of the novel is Leonard Bast. His characterization reveals the chief weakness of Bloomsbury—a social complacency. (The Schlegels apply fashions of taste, not literary standards, to their condemnation of Leonard's reading.) Some of the essays in *Abinger Harvest* are also spoiled by a similar complacency. In *A Passage to India*, EMF's India is transitional between the country described by Kipling and present-day partitioned India. *Passage* is his most important book though *Howards End* is his best. *Passage* is really a tragedy; in it the failure to connect has more disastrous results than in the other novels. His style is his own, owing little to preceding writers, being at once colloquial and reflective. EMF is closer to D. H. Lawrence than to any of his other contemporaries. Margaret Schlegel is much more alive than Wells's heroine in ANN VERONICA; in contrast to Ann, Margaret is much more than the sum of her opinions. [Perceptive insights; other incidental mentions.]

883 Dauner, Louise. "What Happened in the Cave? Reflections on *A Passage to India*," MODERN FICTION STUDIES, VII (Autumn 1961), 258–70; rptd in PERSPECTIVES ON E. M. FORSTER'S "A PASSAGE TO INDIA," ed by V. A. Shahane (NY: Barnes & Noble, 1968), pp. 52–64.

A Passage to India is elusive because the potentialities to be found in an archetypal symbol, the Caves, are not readily exhausted. There is confusion as to what the Caves mean and as to what happens there to Adela Quested. The Caves are, however, the structural core of the novel, and they imply that the greatest insight is to be derived from the collective unconscious, the primordial experience of mankind. The Caves are not oriented toward rationalism but are a setting for the irrational and the archetypal. In primitive cultures caves were places of communal activity and also of burial; this fact implies that the Caves work ambiguously. *Passage* is a novel of barriers (between matter and essence, races, castes, religions, sexes), yet it is paradoxically about connection. The Caves thus represent the opposites of unity and death or separation. A separation of death aspect obtrudes when Mrs. Moore is sucked into the black hole of the Cave. The echo heard within it undermines her life, and she never recovers a sense of the positive. She is lost because she cannot comprehend the existence of good-and-evil as part of the same divinity but must see good and evil as polarities and as absolutes. She is paralyzed because her Oriental intuition is not developed enough to counteract her Western rationality. Her spiritual death precedes her physical, but in her actual death she achieves mystical dimensions and a positive influence. Adela's experience in the Caves elaborates this good-and-evil motif. The difference between what the Cave is and what Adela thinks happens there is great. The strength of her illusion recalls Plato's Cave of Illusion (wherein the object that casts the shadow is also artificial) and the Indian concept of Māyā ("the illusion superimposed upon reality as an effect of ignorance"). Adela's experience in the Cave of Illusion is also an instance of Māyā, including her illusion, her misconception of the truth, and the reality. Adela's flight down the hill is a symbolical rejection of cave values, of union with either the human or the divine. She lacks the intuitive capacity—or love—to harmonize all the paradoxical elements in the Cave. For primitive people the cave was the site of mundane activity and, as the place where religious or ceremonial dances took place, the site, too, of divine power. Mythic ancestors emerge from the caverns or the earth under them; novice magicians experience rebirth in them; churingas that unite the animal and the divine are kept there, as are amulets or blocks bearing female symbols. Primitive peoples regard the cave as the Mother from which they are born, and the rites of passage taking place there unite the human with the divine. The cave is polyvalent. Cumulatively, the cave is "the site of the Divine Mystery, the creative Life-Force." Modern psychology supports some of these interpretations. For psychology the cave is an archetype and a female symbol. A parody of the sex act is involved in Adela's ascent, going into the Cave, and her descent from it. For Jung and Neumann the cave is an archetype for the Great Mother. Neumann sees it as both womb and tomb. Psychologically, the cave is the site of divinity, a symbol of the Good Mother, an aspect, too, of the Terrible Mother (and therefore of the unconscious), and the Way of spiritual rebirth. Beyond Māyā there exists illumination, but Adela is too limited to attain it. Adela is sexually underdeveloped; all the feminine implications of the Cave—union, initiation, potency—are experienced by her as rape, an ironic perversion of them. She is blind to its positive potentialities, and so the Cave for her is evil. Therein she experiences the male principle—the Animus—which she rejects, to her detriment. She fails to achieve significant identity, and she represents the split between the conscious and unconscious natures in modern man. The Cave reveals to Adela knowledge of her own limitations; but the Cave also contrasts "Western rationality against Eastern mysticism; time against eternity; the conscious against the unconscious." For modern man the integration of these polarities is not easy, though the Cave as Mother and Tomb, beginning and end, hints that it may be possible. [A classic article on *Passage* that demonstrates convincingly the ambivalence of the Caves and their symbolic implications. Refutes the more limited conception of the Caves as symbolic of Western rationalism and intelligence; see Glen O. Allen's "Structure, Symbol, and Theme in E. M. Forster's *A Passage to India*" (1955) and Keith Hollingsworth's "*A Passage to India*: The Echoes in the Marabar Caves" (1962). Dauner's interpretation of the Caves to be developed further by Wilfred Stone in his discussion of *Passage* in THE CAVE AND THE MOUNTAIN (1966).]

884 Enright, D. J. "Tales of Alexandria," NEW STATESMAN, nsLXII (26 Aug 1961), 244–45; slightly rvd as "Too Many Caesars: The Poems of C. P. Cavafy" in CONSPIRATORS AND POETS (Lond: Chatto & Windus; Chester Springs, Pa: Dufour, 1966), pp. 160–66; section concerning *Pharos and Pharillon* rptd in its original form as "A Passage to Alexandria" in A GARLAND FOR E. M. FORSTER, ed by

H. H. Anniah Gowda (Mysore, India: The Literary Half-Yearly, 1969), pp. 49–50.
In *Pharos and Pharillon* EMF is "a sort of genteel Cavafy," a less astringent observer of the Alexandrian scene. [Discusses comparative merits of Cavafy translations by John Mavrogordato and Rae Dalven.]

885 Garnett, David. "Some Writers I have Known: Galsworthy, Forster, Moore, and Wells," TEXAS QUARTERLY, IV (Autumn 1961), 190–202, espec 190–95.
[Contains in somewhat altered form the first half of the discussion on EMF (excluding the remarks on *A Passage to India*) to be found in "E. M. Forster and John Galsworthy," REVIEW OF ENGLISH LITERATURE (1964).]

886 Gransden, K. W. "The Listener's Book Chronicle," LISTENER, LXV (30 March 1961), 579.
In *Alexandria: A History and a Guide*, EMF reveals a light touch, and his prose conveys "the accumulated cosmopolitan charm" of Alexandria as the last outpost of Mediterranean civilization. The guide is no longer up-to-date: all things change in Alexandria except its unmatched climate.

887 Haüsermann, H. W. "Begegnung mit E. M. Forster" (Interview with E. M. Forster), NEUE ZÜRCHER ZEITUNG (Zurich), 2 Dec 1961, p. 19.
EMF showed an interest in the extent of Voltaire's land. EMF described his days at the DAILY HERALD, based on his letters to a fellow journalist and a music critic in those days, Walter James Turner. [Extracts from letters are given in English.] He agrees still with his statement to Turner: "So true what you say—that if one begins enquiring into the character of one's associates one might never stop. Yet if one never enquired one might never stop in another direction. My whole life has been an undignified vacillation between non-enquiring and enquiring, and for the moment enquiring has it." He also declared (1961), "My work is finished." [Account of meeting with EMF who was in Geneva as guest of honor at a reception of the Voltaire Research Institute. His physical appearance is described, and his remarks made during a visit to the Voltaire Exhibition are noted.] [In German.]

888 Heilbrun, Carolyn G. THE GARNETT FAMILY (Lond: Allen & Unwin; NY: Macmillan, 1961), pp. 139–40, 186.
Edward Garnett admired EMF's novels more than the short stories, though EMF thought differently as to their relative merits. Garnett, as anonymous reviewer of *Howards End* in the NATION, recognized EMF's importance as a novelist and as a critic of "villadom," but thought that in his social criticism EMF had permitted himself some "clever ingenuity that robs the work of artistic inevitability" (see Edward Garnett, "Villadom," NATION

[Lond: 1910]). In a letter EMF admitted the justness of Garnett's criticism but said, "It is devilish difficult to criticize society and also create human beings. Unless one has a big mind, one aim or the other fails before the book is finished." Another letter from EMF records his failure to recognize at first the merits of Constance Garnett's translations from Turgeniev.

889 Hoffman, Frederick J. "*Howards End* and the Bogey of Progress," MODERN FICTION STUDIES, VII (Autumn 1961), 243–57; rptd in rvd and abrgd form in THE MORTAL NO: DEATH AND THE MODERN IMAGINATION (Princeton; Princeton UP, 1964), pp. 64–87.

H. G. Wells moves away from humanity in his vision of a planned society; EMF's vision is rooted in humanity. Wells's vision is simplistic, deriving from the programmatic rationalism of the eighteenth- and nineteenth-century scientist-philosophers, especially Herbert Spencer; EMF's subtle and complex vision derives from Humean rationalism, which G. E. Moore redefined and which then found expression in the Bloomsbury valuing of personal relationships. (These derive ultimately from Hume's "relations.") Wells sees history as a linear progression, EMF as a slow cyclical figure who acknowledges the fact of death as a limit beyond human ability to control. EMF realized that fear of death becomes a barrier to full commitment to secular affairs, a fact that secular man attempts to evade. Only with the recognition of the limits imposed by death can man survive and progress within them. Against the abstractions formulated by secular man as bulwarks against his fears, EMF recognizes the importance of human and humane values. The influence of such values and an acknowledgment also of man's limitations will result in his potential achievement of wholeness. To their detriment, some of EMF's characters persist in being only partly themselves. "Muddle" results when there is excessive reliance placed upon abstractions and when, as a result, the reality of the tangible thing beneath the word gets lost. EMF has much insight into the fraudulence and fear resulting from the failure to reconcile the polarities of experience. *Howards End* is EMF's most thorough and subtle exploration of human frailty and the failure of human beings to connect. EMF distrusts absolutes because they force a person into violent self-vindication. For EMF the only acceptable absolute is "the center of the human consciousness of self," especially as it relates to other selves and to natural and biological existence. EMF is anti-intellectual in his distrust of absolutes, anti-passional in his distrust of uncritically expressed emotion. In the opening pages of *Howards End* "prose," represented by the Wilcoxes (projected in images of dust and undirected motion), and "passion," represented by the Schlegels (Helen's reversals in the early pages comment upon the Schlegel inadequacy in the practical world), are far apart. Ruth Wilcox connects the two groups: she and Howards End house are centers of balance. As such an agent, her situation is precarious; she has barely enough time before she dies to find her successor in Margaret. To carry on for Ruth Wilcox is easier for Margaret than becoming and remaining the second Mrs. Henry Wilcox. The marriage dramatizes the difficulties of connecting prose and passion; the collision between them leads to violence and death. Leonard Bast is a remarkable mixture of hero and caricature; he illustrates what Wilcox-dominated London has done to Howards End, causing the uprooting of the solid yeoman stock. The Schlegels in their misplaced idealism are as wide of the mark with respect to Leonard as is Henry Wilcox with his dismissal of Leonard as a man who should keep to his station in the class structure. As the problem of Leonard grows, the Schlegels move apart; he becomes what each Schlegel and Wilcox makes of him, but in the process he also becomes "a plausible human being." At the end we see him amid "the calamitous anonymities" into which both people of goodwill and people of determination have forced him. Charles Wilcox fails to connect (to adjust his passionate outrage to prosaic fact) and strikes Leonard "a blow at the heart." Leonard's death shakes the Wilcoxes because they cannot now evade the reality of death, which they fear. They lack subtlety and fail to appreciate Ruth Wilcox's wisdom that in this world there are no plain answers to plain questions. The novel is a critique on the principles and the scene of contemporary "progress," and it dramatizes vividly the gradual mechanizing of society, the pollution caused by industry, and the excessive revering of the abstract and the material. Connection between prose and passion is a necessity in the reconstitution of society, though such connection can only be imperfect in an imperfect world. Thus there is need for Margaret's mediation, unsuccessful as she may sometimes seem to be. [H. G. Wells and EMF are presented as contrasting figures in order to judge the impact of "progress" on mankind in the Edwardian era. A subtle and interesting essay and especially helpful in its analysis of Leonard Bast.]

890 Holloway, John. "The Literary Scene," THE MODERN AGE, ed by Boris Ford (Harmondsworth, Middlesex & Baltimore: Penguin Books, The Pelican Guide to English Literature, Vol. VII, 1961), pp. 51–100, espec 74–75.

Like Virginia Woolf, EMF shows in his fiction a concern with "the immediacy of private living" and a sense of this life being threatened by meaningless violence, the result "of random change or of uncomprehending self-assertiveness." EMF is less exciting but more reassuring than Woolf because he does not obscure his central values with technical viruosity. He ranges farther than she and is more aware of the need to share private experience. *A Passage to India*, by virtue of its humanity and modesty, reveals a plain and strong sense of values and "a half-poetic imaginative-ness" that puts it above EMF's other novels and those of Woolf. The works of Woolf and EMF are a first probing into the inadequacies of polite liberal culture in confronting the twentieth-century world.

891 Hutchens, John K. "*Alexandria,*" NEW YORK HERALD TRIB-
UNE, 8 Feb 1961, p. 21.
The practical usefulness of *Alexandria: A History and a Guide* may now be
in question, but that consideration does not matter. *Alexandria* is clearly
Forsterian: "learned, chatty, original-minded, slyly entertaining, and . . .
fresh in the phrasing. . . ." EMF is a perfect visitor: he lets a place reveal
itself to him and does not impose himself on it.

892 Irwin, W. R. "The Survival of Pan," PUBLICATIONS OF THE
MODERN LANGUAGE ASSOCIATION, LXXVI (June 1961), 159–67.
In modern literature Pan is most often seen as a power figure, malign or
benevolent. As a power figure he can serve as a model for those who would
seek to use best their own energies. He can be a punisher, a destroyer, and
an incarnation of the diabolic; or he can be a benevolent and protective
deity. He is often seen in relation to Christ, who may be regarded as the
fulfillment of Pan, with the elder god supplanted by the younger. Or else
Pan may survive as a pagan exponent of freedom, protesting Christian rigor
before he fades away. [Within this context Irwin discusses the work of
Hawthorne, Lawrence, and EMF.] In "The Story of a Panic," Pan redeems
the boy Eustace. He also liberates the Wiltshire clergyman in "The Curate's
Friend." The spirit of Pan is implicit in "The Celestial Omnibus," "The
Point of It," and "The Road from Colonus." In the novels, Gino Carella,
George Emerson, and Stephen Wonham achieve a Pan-like freedom. Mrs.
Wilcox and Margaret Schlegel respond to his influence in *Howards End*,
and in *A Passage to India* the festival reveals a radical disorder that is
Pan-like. The Pan-genius pervades EMF's fiction, and his characters reach
wholeness to the degree they achieve Pan-like rapport with nature.

893 Isherwood, Christopher. DOWN THERE ON A VISIT (NY: Simon & Schuster, 1961; Lond: Methuen, 1962), pp. 162, 175–76.
[EMF is E. M. in the "Waldemar" section of this novel. Herein Isherwood
figures as the first-person narrator of the frustrated love affair between a
German refugee and an English girl on the eve of Munich. In those trying
days E. M. was a profoundly steadying influence, advising men to live as
if they were immortal rather than as if they were going to die. He represents
the best possible aspect of the British ethos and culture. Pays homage to
EMF's sanity during a period of crisis and to his absolute flexibility. Even
his silliness is constructive because it emanates from his humanity. Substan-
tiates the view that during the late 1930s and World War II EMF was
influential upon intellectuals by virtue of what he was and represented; see
G. D. Klingopulos, "Mr. Forster's Good Influence" (1961).]

894 Klingopulos, G. D. "Mr. Forster's Good Influence," THE
MODERN AGE, ed by Boris Ford (Harmondsworth, Middlesex &

Baltimore: Penguin Books, The Pelican Guide to English Literature, Vol. VII, 1961), pp. 245–56.

EMF's work raises this question: To what extent can one go along with it? He is a consistent moralist and intellectual, and he provided a heartening voice during World War II, because he demanded so little. He represented "an attractive, though not easily imitable, intellectual shrewdness, delicacy, and responsibility." There is danger that EMF's public aspect will influence judgment of his work. He is one of the few modern English writers whose work reveals the process of assimilation and a growth in sensibility. His masters are Jane Austen, Hardy, Meredith, Cavafy, Butler, and Proust. In his work there is "a quality of interest, sympathy, and judgment," independent of the will: a genuine experiencing center. The terms "liberal" and "humanist" are inadequate to encompass his fiction with its profound inwardness. In his early work, especially the tales, he is poised between forms of resistance and escape. The tone and the direction of "The Story of a Panic," and "The Curate's Friend" place the stories near Stevenson's slight fantasies. At their best the stories open vistas for the regimented and evoke for them remote memories of other kinds of existence. *The Longest Journey* has some of the arbitrary fancifulness of *The Celestial Omnibus* stories. It is the weakest of the novels; it has less autobiographical value for the reader than for EMF. The theme: how can the sensitive individual remain loyal to his best impulses in a cold and conventional world, and how can he achieve a good relationship with nature and other men, yet avoid the rigidity and self-sufficiency deriving from pride and the hardness of the will? *Journey*, while it is readable, is mostly a sketch; the marriage deserves more of a chance. The equation between the dead Gerald Dawes and the living Stephen Wonham does not convince; Stephen lacks the symbolic power of Giles Winterborne (Hardy's THE WOODLANDERS). The patterns and rhythms in *Journey* are not organic but appear in set passages. Only in *A Passage to India* are the descriptive passages firmly evocative, yet secure against the incursions of the Comic Spirit or of the little god Pan. Nevertheless, the early novels repay study and reveal affinities with the works of Hardy and Lawrence. The continuity between the short stories and the novels is felt in *Where Angels Fear to Tread* and *A Room with a View*, both successes. In these two novels Italy either liberates the Sawston visitors or confirms their prejudices. The projected rescue of the Carella baby is confused by the living significance of the infant. The violence in these novels signifies EMF's earnestness. His discontent with middle-class manners later becomes more radical, as he recognizes the need of a more substantial basis for relationships. The satire on the Rev. Mr. Beebe and the Rev. Mr. Eager would be better in *Room* if we knew more of their inner selves. Mr. Emerson's inner being is likewise vague. In his retreat to a rectory study he indicates that his own free thinking has limits; his attitudes are sometimes not precise and are sentimental as a result. In *Howards End* the harmonizing, genial, and patriotic sides of EMF are at odds with his radicalism. The writing of *Passage* was an act of courage and an educative work. With it, the influences of Hardy and Meredith are outgrown. In the earlier novels, the correction of one character by another sometimes creates an impression of falsity or sanctimoniousness. In *Passage* EMF does not offer solutions and alternatives. India becomes a solvent not only for the "churchy serenity" of Mrs. Moore but for the rationalism and self-confidence of Fielding. The novel is not pessimistic, because values must be affirmed even when it is difficult to attain them. Mrs. Moore is unable to affirm value; she is punished, in effect, for having said that she likes mysteries but not muddles. The Hindu ceremonies signify that the acceptance of muddle is preferable and nearer truth than "more orderly religious systems and patterns of belief." The greatness of *Passage* is to be measured in terms of its masterly balance of antipathy and sympathy. [An incisive essay, especially valuable for the remarks on EMF as a public presence during World War II.]

895 Lawrence, Frieda. THE MEMOIRS AND CORRESPONDENCE, ed by E. W. Tedlock, Jr. (Lond: Heinemann, 1961; NY: Knopf, 1964), p. 196 (NY ed).
[EMF's complaint in Frieda Lawrence's letter of Feb 1915 to S. S. Koteliansky is cited. Since Frieda added her own views in a letter of D. H. Lawrence's to him, EMF said that he did not wish to deal with a "firm."]

896 Lever, Katherine. THE NOVEL AND THE READER (Lond: Methuen, 1961), pp. 16, 34, 36–37, 41, 56, 66, 67–68, 80, 106, 113, 114, 119; as THE NOVEL AND THE READER: A PRIMER FOR CRITICS (NY: Appleton, Goldentree Books, 1961).
The imagined worlds of fiction are divided by class, wealth, education, and profession and, in *A Passage to India*, by race and religion especially. *Passage* dramatizes the effects of varying spiritual powers: the Anglican God, Mohammed, Shri Krishna, the punkah wallah, and the echo in the Marabar Caves. Addressing the reader directly as EMF does in *Passage* is not a reprehensible technique. The adjudication among conflicting moral perspectives is difficult in reading a novel such as *Passage* wherein people of good intentions rather than of evil impulses precipitate the fiasco of the picnic at the Marabar Caves and of the trial. Yet the finale to *Passage* is not disastrous; the forces making for enlightenment or vision are not defeated in any absolute sense. In *Passage* the intellect cannot bridge Christianity, Hinduism, and Mohammedanism, but Mrs. Moore, Godbole, and Aziz are united by a mystical love that transcends their own understandings. [Many references to *Aspects of the Novel* and to P. N. Furbank and F. J. H. Haskell, "E. M. Forster: The Art of Fiction I" PARIS REVIEW, I (Spring 1953), 28–41 in the definitions presented of novel, novelist, the reader of novels, the critic of novels, and the student of novels.]

897 Macaulay, Rose. LETTERS TO A FRIEND 1950–1952, ed by
Constance Babington-Smith (Lond: Collins, 1961; NY: Atheneum,
1962), pp. 19, 229, 254–55, 264, 266–67, 284, 295, 298, 302, 313.
[Numerous mentions of EMF in letters to the Rev. John Hamilton Cowper
Johnson.] *Howards End* has real characters, excellent style, and a delightful
humor; and it discusses serious problems. EMF is "a person of very strong
and continuing affections" [28 Nov 1951 and 19 Jan 1952]. EMF drives to
Abinger Hammer to visit the grave of his mother and is circumspect in
distributing mimosa sprays on the graves of his other relatives, as if he were
trying to avoid the arousing of jealousies among the dead [1 Feb 1952]. *A
Room with a View* is a very amusing and sometimes moving novel, and the
family life of the Honeychurches is a delight. However, Mr. Beebe is not
adequately explained and Mr. Emerson a bit of a bore. *Room* is good in
detail, conversation, wit, and writing style, but it is not on the scale of
Howards End [2 Feb 1965]. EMF is profoundly a moralist, believing in
personal relationships, affection, and goodness, but not in God [11 Feb
1952]. EMF has an attractive mind [22 March 1952]. EMF's philosophy—
"one of affection in personal relationships and sympathy and comprehension"—is not a bad philosophy; it is not technically Christian, but has many
Christian elements in it. Margaret Schlegel would never have married
Henry Wilcox [though Rose Macaulay isn't surprised at odd marriages];
Helen's affair with Leonard Bast is not believable [Easter Monday, 1952].
Where Angels Fear to Tread is "a queer, *young*, interesting book" [12 May
1952].

898 MacDonald, Alastair A. "Class-Consciousness in E. M.
Forster," UNIVERSITY OF KANSAS CITY REVIEW, XXVII (March
1961), 235–40.
EMF elicits his social values, especially in *Howards End*, from English
upper-middle-class society. At its best (in the Schlegels) its values are
inspiriting and are EMF's own; at its worst (in the Wilcoxes) it is a destructive force. His social criticism is authentic to the extent that it emanates
from well-known materials; it reveals weakness because the attitudes and
milieu thus presented are of doubtful universality. EMF is akin to Meredith,
Butler, and Henry James in tracing "the development of a gentlemanly
status of the spirit." His social values ultimately have a quality of the
indeterminate because he argues on both sides of a question and works from
assumptions, such as the survival of the middle class (which he does not
explicitly state). The victories are those of the individual; he does not posit
a reformed upper middle class. Those who represent positive values (the
Schlegels) are not employed, whereas the Philistines from the upper middle
class are absorbedly employed (there is thus something to be said for them).
The Schlegel sisters enjoy the fruits of Philistine effort and feel compelled
to justify their lives of privilege. They are far removed from simple humani-

ty, which often has a strong lesson to teach them. Simple humanity also has a romantic appeal. Yet if the Schlegel sisters go back to nature, they don't stay there. The Schlegel sisters especially feel the need to justify themselves when victims of Wilcoxism—Ruth Wilcox and Leonard Bast—act upon them. Both, acting through the Schlegels, triumph over Wilcoxism. The sisters are fascinating but a bit unreal, perhaps being too conscious of their superiority. Leonard Bast remains less a person than a problem. Both EMF and the sisters regard Leonard with "patronizing levity"; the result is that EMF's design fails to incorporate "the comically tragic." Too much depends upon the attitudes of the Schlegels in the novel for the social values to have a firm foundation. The Wilcoxes make possible for others leisure, tolerance, and cultivation of the spirit though they do not themselves have recourse to them. EMF views with tolerance both the Schlegels and the Wilcoxes; he sees no final solution, though the enlargement of the individual spirit may contribute to change. The moments of power in EMF's works derive from a world of fundamental realities beyond the limits of class. But he does not remain long in this world. Rather, he soon comes back to his comic manner and to a consideration of the serious through the trivial; his dependence on class considerations constricts him, and his values and emotions are not really representative of mankind and of universal issues. His central values and situations are arbitrary because they are tied to a privileged caste. This fact diminishes the significance of his novels. [A deft discussion of a complex issue in *Howards End.*]

> **899** McDowell, Frederick P. W. "Forster's 'Natural Supernaturalism': The Tales," MODERN FICTION STUDIES, VII (Autumn 1961), 271–83; rptd in part as "The Italian Novels and the Short Stories," in E. M. FORSTER (NY: Twayne Publishers, English Authors Series, 1969), pp. 42–64.

When EMF relies totally on fantasy as in "Mr. Andrews," "Co-ordination," "The Machine Stops," and "The Curate's Friend," he fails to dramatize conclusively his complex and original concepts. [Most critics judge "The Machine Stops" to be a success, e.g., Wilfred Stone in THE CAVE AND THE MOUNTAIN (1966), pp. 152–56 and Irving Howe, CLASSICS OF MODERN FICTION (1972), pp. 233–40; I now agree.] "The Celestial Omnibus" and "The Other Side of the Hedge" also combine too arbitrarily the fantastic and the metaphysical for these stories to become richly textured works. [Judgment is excessive.] "Other Kingdom" and "The Story of a Panic" are more authentic weldings of the realistic and the supernatural. In these stories the use of a naive, ignorant, or complacent narrator involves a contrast between his illusion and the reality that he is unable to recognize or that he fears. In "Other Kingdom" there is an effective contrast between an extravert, unimaginative husband and a wife whose delicacy and sensitivity he is too unimaginative to grasp. "The Story of a Panic" stresses the imperceptiveness of the bourgeoisie (even of the artist Tytler) to a pagan presence, Eustace, in their midst, though theoretically they revere the culture of the ancients. "The Road from Colonus," "The Eternal Moment," "The Story of the Siren," and "The Point of It" most successfully fuse the realistic and the fantastic and thereby achieve an increased degree of credence for the latter. In "The Road from Colonus," myth, ironically and satirically utilized, gives the work amplitude. "The Eternal Moment" stresses the moral power exerted by the "symbolic moment" and the disastrous effects that follow its denial. Miss Raby is interpreted as a sympathetic character. [In contrast, Stone, pp. 137–44, sees her as presumptuous and arrogant; see also John V. Hagopian, "Eternal Moments in the Short Fiction of E. M. Forster" (1965).] In "The Story of the Siren" the siren acts ambiguously as a destructive force to those who cannot understand her but as an inescapable reality to those who do. [I accept James Missey's correction of my interpretation of the siren as an evil influence; see his "Forster's Redemptive Siren" (1964).] The story is effective in its contrast between the academic narrator and the vital Sicilian boy, and in its use of mythology to serve aesthetic ends. "The Point of It" is a complex work to which previous critics have paid little attention. EMF in it effectively uses allegory for the dramatizing of moral concepts. The structure of the story is this: it goes from a death-in-life sequence (with the sudden death of Harold) to a life-in-death sequence (with Micky's prosperous, smug, complacent life as civil servant and comfortable humanist), to a death-in-death sequence (when for years after his death at the hands of two quarreling slum women, Micky resides in a heaven for the "soft" on a plain outside hell, similar to Dante's Dark Plain), to a life-in-death sequence (when, at the urging of a star-like vital spirit, Micky chooses a life-giving existence, affirms love, commits himself, and employs at last "the keen heroic edge" of his sharpened perception to make contact again with the spirit of his truly vital friend, Harold). Micky learns that instinct is superior to the intellect unaided by it, that there are visionary truths which the rational mind cannot encompass, and that the active will alone can allow one's old self to die and one to be born anew. The union achieved in this story of "the critically acute and the imaginatively ingenious" is the hallmark of EMF's best tales. [Not all my judgments have borne up since 1961, but this article was the first attempt to discuss the stories in detail and to recover them as an important part of EMF's *oeuvre*. The lengthy treatment of "The Point of It" is, I think, justified by its excellence.]

900 Manning, Martin. "Real City," SPECTATOR (Lond), CCVII (4 Aug 1961), 179.

Pharos and Pharillon is notable for development of many of the themes present in *Alexandria: A History and a Guide*. The essay on Cavafy is noteworthy as EMF recreates for us the poet. Better still are the essays in which EMF recreates the ancient events and personalities of the city. He deplores the loss of reason and tolerance that resulted from a powerful and dogmatic Christianity under Athanasius. EMF is moved less to evocation (as is Lawrence Durrell) than to observation and elucidation. EMF, unlike Durrell, does not glamorize, but celebrates what is left of modern Alexandria: "a few stones and its noble history."

901 Maxwell, William. "Mr. Forster's Pageant," NEW YORKER, XXXVII (18 Feb 1961), 129–30, 133–36.

[Best appreciative account of *Alexandria* available, but should be read in conjunction with Robert Tracy's "Old Wine in a New Bottle: *Alexandria: A History and a Guide*" (1961). The essay runs to paraphrase and elucidation rather than evaluation, but it is skillfully done. Particularly good at summarizing EMF's accounts of the changing religious and philosophical dynasties in ancient Alexandria. *Alexandria* is not only a guide book; it is literature, its "architecture" being as remarkable as its style and content.]

902 Moseley, Edwin. "A New Correlative for *Howards End:* Demeter and Persephone," LOCK HAVEN BULLETIN, Series I, No. 3 (1961), 1–6.

The narrative line of *Howards End* has its correlative in the Demeter (Ceres) and Persephone story. Mrs. Wilcox is an earth-bound earth mother. Miss Avery is a kind of priestess, a self-appointed guardian of the memory of Mrs. Wilcox. Henry Wilcox does not sense that his wife wastes away in London, shorn of her contact with the earth. She is also an exile, like the Biblical Ruth. Mrs. Wilcox does not resist Henry's values; she puts up with them, as Margaret does later. He is a Pluto figure, with his lower-world values based on wealth and money. Margaret Schlegel represents intellectual beauty and Helen aesthetic beauty to Mr. Wilcox's petty Faust, with his materialistic values. Margaret is a mother figure, not only to her orphan brother and sister but eventually to the Wilcox family. In her greater capacity to cope with everyday life, Margaret is an even more earth-bound goddess than Ruth Wilcox. When Helen absents herself, Margaret is as Demeter to Helen's Persephone. When pregnant, Helen ate of the seed of her lower middle-class seducer; but she is more the seducer than he is. He is no forceful rapist like Pluto; he belongs to the lower world only in the sense of deriving from a lower social class. Leonard is an ironical Paris figure to Helen, Charles Wilcox a caricature of a Greek defending a maiden's honor. Biblical symbology closes the book: the meek do inherit the earth. [Many suggestive parallels, demonstrating that EMF used myth consciously in *Howards End* but less explicitly than in *The Longest Journey*.]

903 O'Faoláin, Seán, [Afterword: "The Story of the Siren"], SHORT STORIES: A STUDY IN PLEASURE, ed by Seán O'Faoláin (Boston & Toronto: Little, Brown, 1961), 643–44.

"The Story of the Siren" is beautiful and real. In it occurs a masterful blending of the fanciful and the fact; this blend means that we tend to believe in the supernatural Siren when it appears and to identify with Giuseppi, who has seen it. We are relaxed from the everyday, the probable, and the rational faculties. Every artist starts with a realistic basis for his work but tries to get beyond in any way that he can. [Searching questions on the story, pp. 443–44; story rptd, pp. 434–41.]

904 ONE HUNDRED ONE GREAT BOOKS OF OUR TIME (Lond: Sunday Times, 1961), pp. 21, 33.

In *Howards End* the connection between Margaret Schlegel and Henry Wilcox, though revealing a generous authorial intention, is improbable; but the social comedy and humanity of the book are remarkable. *A Passage to India* is the humanist complement to Kipling's embodiment of the Raj in KIM. No cheers are given for the British, but no more than two for anything else. Human affections can alone mitigate the chaos resulting from collisions between East and West. [*Howards End* and *Passage* are two of the 101 books.]

905 Parasuram, A. N. MINERVA GUIDE TO E. M. FORSTER'S "A PASSAGE TO INDIA," (Egmore, Madras: The Minerva Publishing House, rvd ed, 1961); 1st ed, 1954, not obtainable.

[Contents comprise "Introduction," "Character Sketches," "Minor Characters," "Character Contrasts," "General Essays," and "Questions and Answers." Book is mostly descriptive rather than critical. "General Essays" is the best section. The essays comprise "The Racial Issue," "India in the Novel," "Religious Symbolism in the Novel," "Forster's Conception of the Ideal Man," and "Forster's Philosophy of Life as Revealed in *A Passage to India.*" They do not have depth.]

906 "People," TIME, LXXVII (19 May 1961), 40.

[EMF, among others, is honored as "Companion of Literature."]

907 Rahman, Kalimur. "Race Relations in *A Passage to India*," VENTURE: A QUARTERLY OF ENGLISH LANGUAGE AND LITERATURE (Karachi), II (March 1961), 56–59.

A Passage to India is about both race relations and personal relations: the two strands come together at Aziz's trial. The ineffectual romance between Adela Quested and Ronny Heaslop points up the poverty of the human spirit. Mrs. Moore's disillusionment in the Cave undermines her faith in human relations. She also speaks for EMF, revealing his apprehension about the value of human relations. He does not give any group an advantage. His Anglo-Indians (especially the women) are smug, narrow, and dependent upon force. Aziz has his limitations: he is uninterested in politics and administrative problems, indifferent or suspicious about Anglo-Indians, and snobbish toward the plain Adela. Aziz lives in pursuit of his dreamlike illusions and is sometimes far removed from the realities that surround him. When the trial interrupts this dream life, he reacts by violently opposing the British presence in India. He is inordinately suspicious and is capable of embarrassing behavior as at Fielding's tea party. EMF does not understand Hindus. [Others do not agree.] Aziz also is ignorant of Hindus and disdains them. Adela, the most British character, shows least understanding in supposing that Aziz represents India. Her fair-mindedness and truthfulness do not appear to advantage in India, since Indians require more than justice or truth; they expect emotional commitment and emotional demonstrations. No novel has better dramatized the "love-hunger" of Indians. Fielding shows the European's fear of loss of dignity in intimacy. Aziz's proposal to Fielding of an eternal friendship after the trial appears "monstrous" because of the degree of commitment to himself that Aziz expects from him. At the end Fielding does not seek intimacy with Aziz. But at least they are then "serene" with each other, since, as Fielding says, they are "not after anything" as Stella, his wife, seems to be. In the light of the partition of India in 1947 and its ensuing violence, EMF reveals in *Passage* a prophetic insight as he describes the fundamental incompatibility of Hindus and Muslims. [Valuable for reflections on the social and political situation presented in the novel.]

908 Ryan, Marjorie. "Forster, James, and Flaubert: A Parallel," NOTES AND QUERIES (Lond), nsVIII (March 1961), 102–3.
In the opera scenes in EMF's *Where Angels Fear to Tread*, Flaubert's MADAME BOVARY, and James's THE AMBASSADORS, the main character (as a result of romantic presuppositions) makes a faulty judgment with momentous consequences. Philip Herriton still misreads Gino Carella and does not yet give up his plans to secure the Carella child for Sawston; Emma Bovary begins the disastrous affair with Leon; and Lambert Strether meets Chad Newsome at the opera after long separation and concludes, falsely, that Paris has improved him in all ways.

909 Schorer, Mark. SINCLAIR LEWIS: AN AMERICAN LIFE (NY, Lond, Toronto: McGraw-Hill, 1961), pp. 274, 311, 516, 545–46.
EMF was one of the two British writers who congratulated Lewis on winning the Nobel Prize (the other was Hugh Walpole). EMF felt that the academy "have done themselves proud" and that many fellow authors are honored through Lewis's being awarded the prize. [EMF's "Sinclair Lewis" (*Abinger Harvest*) is quoted and discussed (p. 516).]

910 Shahane, V. A. "E. M. Forster: A Birthday Tribute," MODERN REVIEW (Calcutta), CIX (March 1961), 236–38.
[Expresses many well-known facts and conventional judgments.]

911 Shahane, V. A. "Formative Influences on E. M. Forster: Henry James—A Study in Ambivalence," OSMANIA JOURNAL OF ENGLISH STUDIES (Osmania University, Hyderabad), No. 1 (1961), 39–58.

Henry James's chief subject is the impact of different cultures on each other; EMF reveals this same interest. James's innovations in technique, especially as they reveal new possibilities in suspense and revelation, have been fruitful for EMF. In THE AMBASSADORS and *Where Angels Fear to Tread*, the male protagonist learns from experience and achieves increased awareness. Both novelists are preoccupied with the dramatization of good and evil. EMF unfairly criticizes James for his lack of carnality: in James's early fiction it is present, whereas EMF's work lacks such carnality. [Article is inadequate for its subject. It is much inferior to Alwyn Berland, "James and Forster: The Morality of Class" (1953) and to Agostino Lombardo, "Prefazione," *Casa Howard* (1959).]

912 Shusterman, David. "The Curious Case of Professor Godbole: *A Passage to India* Re-examined," PUBLICATIONS OF THE MODERN LANGUAGE ASSOCIATION, LXXVI (Sept 1961), 426–35; rptd in PERSPECTIVES ON E. M. FORSTER'S "A PASSAGE TO INDIA," ed by V. A. Shahane (NY: Barnes & Noble, 1968), pp. 91–100; and, in large part, in Shusterman's THE QUEST FOR CERTITUDE IN E. M. FORSTER'S FICTION (Bloomington & Lond: Indiana UP, 1965), pp. 182–202.

Godbole in *A Passage to India* is not a man of goodwill nor is he EMF's spokesman for cosmic and divine truth. [Shusterman challenges interpretations like those of James McConkey (1957) and Hugh Maclean (1953) who put Godbole at the center of the novel. I am of the Godbolean persuasion, as are almost all critics who feel that "Temple" contains the truth of the novel. Shusterman protests attempts to turn EMF into a transplanted Hindu and *Passage* into a tract glorifying Hinduism and Godbole.] In contrast to Hinduistic love EMF's love is not detached from the physical world or from human relationships. The center of *Passage* is the humanist Fielding rather than the Hindu Godbole or the mystically oriented Mrs. Moore. Fielding is one of the aristocracy of the "sensitive, considerate and plucky" (see "What I Believe," *Two Cheers for Democracy*) and represents in his actions the sort of humanly concerned love that EMF champions. For an eclectic like EMF, Hinduism would probably have been only one strand in his philosophical outlook. Godbole does not trust people; he tends to let them down; his influence is nonbeneficial and works in the direction of evil. The whole evil in the novel derives from Godbole's reluctance to say anything about the Caves [but he knows that his audience would not understand his cryptic knowledge of them]. Those critics who contend that he represents India are wrong, since EMF is careful to say that no one character can do so. Godbole does not harmonize the East and the West. He is a calculating individual, purposely miscalculating the length of his prayer so that he and Fielding will miss the train to the Caves. Godbole is treacherous, but he is still baffled and never achieves passage or ultimate knowledge. The carpet in "Temple" separates Godbole from God; they are at its opposite ends. "Temple" does not represent a reconciliation or synthesis; it is only among many possible passages for the soul. EMF is skeptical of the Hindu ceremonies, not enamored of them. Godbole's mystical experiences are only a partial success. Godbole, in concealing crucial information from Aziz, is not ultimately his friend. Godbole is not a positive force so much as a Forsterian mixture of good-and-evil. His very imperfections reveal EMF's skill in creating an individual with all his ambiguities. [This essay attempts, without success, to revise the consensus judgment of Godbole's central importance in *Passage*. Even if he is less important than consensus critics generally regard him, to view him as an Iago-like character represents a misreading of EMF's purposes. Shusterman's interpretation I do not find verified by the context of the novel nor by EMF's experiences and his attitudes expressed elsewhere.]

913 Thomson, George H. "Symbolism in E. M. Forster's Earlier Fiction," CRITICISM, III (Fall 1961), 304–30.
[Early version of some materials in "The Italian Romances" and "*The Longest Journey*," THE FICTION OF E. M. FORSTER (1967).]

914 Thomson, George H. "Thematic Symbol in *A Passage to India*," TWENTIETH CENTURY LITERATURE, VII (July 1961), 51–63; rptd in PERSPECTIVES ON E. M. FORSTER'S "A PASSAGE TO INDIA," ed by V. A. Shahane (NY: Barnes & Noble, 1968), pp. 101–114.
[Much expanded and rvd in THE FICTION OF E. M. FORSTER (1967).]

915 Thomson, George H. "Theme and Symbol in *Howards End*," MODERN FICTION STUDIES, VII (Autumn 1961), 229–42.
[First version of the discussion of *Howards End* in Thomson's THE FICTION OF E. M. FORSTER (1967). The article was completely rewritten for the book, but almost all the points in it are included in the book, except for the remarks on Beethoven as manipulating artist in his Fifth Symphony and the tenuous association of the nine windows of Howards End house with nine different people in nine different rooms. See discussion of Thomson's book (1967).]

916 Tracy, Robert. "Old Wine in a New Bottle: *Alexandria: A History and a Guide*," CARLETON MISCELLANY, II (Summer 1961), 113–17.
The chief merit in the book is the joy of the verbal game well played, the

takeoff on Baedeker or doing him one better. Sometimes in this game EMF oversimplifies because of his inadequate knowledge, especially in his treatments of ancient theological dispuations, of Islam, and of modern Egypt. *Alexandria's* true significance is a heralding of *A Passage to India.* Both books explore the same problem: divinity and man's relation with it, the relationship between men and a God both near to, and far from, human beings. The lesson of this book is what Mrs. Moore learns in *Passage:* "There is no theological way to God." EMF's distrust of intellectual speculation is to the fore in both books. [Important review-essay for understanding *Alexandria.* Lists the surprising number of inaccuracies in the work in both its 1st and 3rd ed; Doubleday has chosen to publish the uncorrected 1st ed. Should be read in conjunction with William Maxwell's "Mr. Forster's Pageant," NEW YORKER (1961).]

> **917** Turnell, Martin. "The Shaping of Contemporary Literature," MODERN LITERATURE AND CHRISTIAN FAITH (Lond: Darton, Longmans & Todd, 1961; Westminster, Md: Newman P, 1961), pp. 24–45, espec 34–39, 43–44.

Since he did not seek a new mode of life as did D. H. Lawrence, EMF was sensitive to what was valuable in the pre-1914 world but was also honest in his realization that its values were inadequate to keep it intact. In *Howards End,* as Mrs. Wilcox lies sick in London, "a strange atmosphere of dissolution" invests her and becomes symbolic of the social and intellectual world of the novel. The primary value of the genteel characters is that of personal relationships, which rests ultimately on the possession of wealth rather than on firm beliefs. *A Passage to India* presents throughout the same disintegration of society; in the first pages the tone is set when the inhabitants are assimilated to the mud of India. This sense of dissolution, which recalls the atmosphere surrounding Mrs. Wilcox's sickbed, attains stark and tragic expression in Mrs. Moore's disabling vision in the Marabar Caves, wherein all exists but "nothing has value." Since EMF's characters lack faith, their world falls apart. Their civility is superficial, as is their philosophy. They are readily replaced by still more negative individuals, the "sub-men" of Hemingway or the "rutting herd" of Henry Miller, whose behavior is dictated alone by physical impulse. [Interesting correlation between *Howards End* and *Passage.*]

> **918** Voorhees, Richard J. THE PARADOX OF GEORGE ORWELL (Lafayette, Indiana: Purdue University Studies, Humanities Series, 1961), pp. 21, 54–55, 77, 104.

Orwell in BURMESE DAYS tried to make an Oriental country intelligible to a Western reader but did nothing with religion; there is not even a remote equivalent of the religious ceremonies dramatized in *A Passage to India.*

[References to EMF in Orwell's "Inside the Whale" (see entry for 1940) are given.] BURMESE DAYS is less aesthetically successful than *Passage*. The style is flat rather than imaginative and resonant like EMF's. Orwell's insights suffer because, if he is just, he lacks charity for both the British and the Burmese. In his essays Orwell celebrates the gentleness of English civilization in passages akin to EMF's lyrical celebrations of England in his novels. EMF praises England's splendor and strength; Orwell, her peacefulness.

919 Wagar, W. Warren. H. G. WELLS AND THE WORLD STATE (New Haven: Yale UP, 1961), pp. 31, 238, 253.

H. G. Wells was shocked by the First World War in the same way that EMF describes Dickinson as being in *Goldsworthy Lowes Dickinson*. The somber, lopsided quality of Wells's Utopian vision in THE SHAPE OF THINGS TO COME was exposed in EMF's "The Machine Stops" and Aldous Huxley's BRAVE NEW WORLD. "The Machine Stops" was one of a number of inverted utopias originating in reaction to Wells's Utopia.

920 Wilde, Alan. "The Aesthetic View of Life: *Where Angels Fear to Tread*," MODERN FICTION STUDIES, VII (Autumn 1961), 207–16; rptd in ART AND ORDER: A STUDY OF E. M. FORSTER (New York: New York UP; 1964; Lond: Peter Owen, 1965), pp. 16–27.

In *Where Angels Fear to Tread* melodrama is a structural counterpart to the great moment, since both emphasize the extraordinary. The melodrama also has links with the fantasy elements of the early stories. Sharp oppositions in values are represented in the characters as they are associated with England or Italy. Caroline Abbott and Phillip Herriton are subtle figures, however, contrasting with the melodrama that dominates the action. Sawston represents the spectator's view of life, a world of convention and appearances; Monteriano represents the ideal of active participation. Mrs. Herriton is the chief representative of Sawston and loves power. Involvement—a meaningful, active life—is epitomized in the opera scene in Chapter 46. Gino Carella in his animal vitality is the chief of the Italian figures. He reveals naturalness when he is behaving spontaneously, vulgarity when he is trying to make an impression. He is elemental in his desire for continuance through his child. In the kidnapping of the baby, convention kills nature; and nothing cancels out the horror of this event. Philip is the spectator to Gino's participant. His Italy is make-believe. On his second trip he is liberated in part from the aesthetic view of life. All the English characters except Harriet discover personal relations in Italy for the first time. Philip's love for Caroline and hers for Gino do not quite ring true. Philip too easily accepts defeat and retreats to his aesthetic view of life. He learns what is real in life but can't connect with it. The book conveys an impression of sadness since wholeness is difficult to achieve in England.

921 Williams, Raymond. "Realism and the Contemporary Novel," THE LONG REVOLUTION (NY: Columbia UP; Lond: Chatto & Windus, 1961), pp. 274–89, espec 282.

A Passage to India is a personal rather than a social novel, because some of the Indians in the novel romanticize their civilization to accord with the needs of certain of the British characters.

922 Woolf, Leonard. GROWING: AN AUTOBIOGRAPHY OF THE YEARS 1904–1911 (Lond: Hogarth P, 1961; NY: Harcourt, Brace & World, 1962), pp. 63–75.

[Woolf helps establish the social and psychological truth of EMF's Leonard Bast in *Howards End*, a character whom EMF's critics have often dismissed as "unreal" (e.g., Frank Swinnerton, THE GEORGIAN SCENE [1934], p. 398). In his mixture of social crudity and cultural aspiration, a civil servant named Dutton was, for Woolf, a flesh and blood Leonard. Dutton's unsympathetic but dominating wife also resembles the fictional Jacky Bast. Woolf reacted to the actualities of empire administration with the same sensitivity and critical sympathy for all the problems involved that EMF did in his writings on India. Woolf also reveals the same eventual distrust of outside rule over an alien people that EMF does in *A Passage to India*. His conclusions were EMF's: no imperial regime can be fair, because it cannot appreciate the total complications of maintaining order in another culture. The similarity of the two writers' views on the imperial question helps account for Woolf's strong counsel to EMF not to give up writing *Passage* (see *The Hill of Devi*, "Note on *A Passage to India*," p. 144, Lond ed). Refutes those who contend that EMF was unfair to the Anglo-Indian officials in *Passage*.]

1962

923 Adams, J. Donald. "Speaking of Books," NEW YORK TIMES BOOK REVIEW, 21 Oct 1962, p. 2.

No one has ever written better about the art of fiction than EMF in *Aspects of the Novel*. He is aware of the infinite possibilities of fiction. One of his assumptions is that the arts depend on one another for definition: hence he uses terms from painting and music (e.g., "Pattern and Rhythm") in writing about the novel. EMF recognized that if the meticulous pattern or structure is extended too far, the vitality of a book may be sapped.

924 Albérès, R. M. [pseud of René Marill]. "Plongées dans les Profondeurs l'Impressionnisme" (Excursions into the Depths of Impressionism), HISTOIRE DU ROMAN MODERNE (History of the Modern Novel) (Paris: Albin Michel, 1962), pp. 181–98, espec 186; also 132, 169, 181.

In the evolution of the British novel toward the total impressionism of Virginia Woolf, there has been a progressive disappearance of dramatic plotting. Henry James's THE AMBASSADORS was concerned with contrasting two cultures and frames of mind, as was EMF in *Where Angels Fear to Tread*. Story as such disappears as a prime element by the time of *A Passage to India*, wherein the essences of two modes of life are evoked, the mystery of customs and sensibilities as well as the mystery of souls. The reality of the novel is no longer on the surface. In France a parallel movement from realism to "irony" corresponds to the movement in England from naturalism to "impressionism." English "impressionistic" fiction has remained more responsive to the impalpable aspects of experience than French "ironic" fiction. EMF is the defender in *Aspects of the Novel* of such an "open" form of the novel. [In French.]

925 Alvarez, A. "Before the Crash," NEW STATESMAN, nsLXIV (6 July 1962), 23.

EMF is a writer of interest more for his re-creation of the Edwardian period than as one who is in all respects our contemporary. "The cool elegance" of his prose signifies that he is of another age. His overpowering desire to understand muddle is admirable but debilitating. Only the overpowering muddle of *A Passage to India* still speaks to later artists (and readers). His rank as a writer who misses greatness is similar to Kafka's. Both are concerned with the interaction of fantasy with social reality, but Kafka's inclusiveness increases as he becomes more fantastic, while EMF's lessens. Kafka is basically the realist, while EMF is the idealist. With the disappearance of his self-possessed world and the predominance of the Marabar echo, EMF rightly judged that others would have to carry on the work of civilization. "He was right, but the loss is ours." [Review-essay on J. B. Beer's THE ACHIEVEMENT OF E. M. FORSTER (1962) and K. W. Gransden's E. M. FORSTER (1962).]

926 Arnold, Bruce. "Book Reviews," DUBLIN MAGAZINE, I (May–June 1962), 54–55.

Since he finished writing fiction, EMF has turned to the exploration of life unhampered by the responsibilities of artistic creation. He is what Rickie Elliot would have been had he survived: "a man deprived of a functional part of himself." *Howards End* is his greatest novel, which "rises brilliantly out of the shadow of Hardy's imagination and Conrad's 'new language.' ''; *The Longest Journey* is his most moving novel; and *A Passage to India* is overrated. [Review of K. W. Gransden's E. M. FORSTER (1962).]

927 Bartlett, Phyllis. "The Novels of George Meredith," REVIEW OF ENGLISH LITERATURE, III (Jan 1962), 31–46.

EMF's negative criticism of Meredith in *Aspects of the Novel* is often adduced by contemporary detractors without recognition of EMF's praise of Meredith for his sense of structure and his ability to order his narratives. EMF also uses in his fiction the personal style of Meredith.

928 Bayley, John. "The Cambridge Humanist," MANCHESTER GUARDIAN WEEKLY, 5 July 1962, p. 11; rptd, in large part, in A LIBRARY OF LITERARY CRITICISM: MODERN BRITISH LITERATURE, ed by Ruth Z. Temple and Martin Tucker (NY: Frederick Ungar, 1966), I, 317–18.

The reading of EMF's novels was a meaningful experience, gratifying and liberating. EMF's message [to Bayley as a youth] was that by feebleness people can be saved and that lack of grit and determination and the desire to be liked and to confide in others are not shameful qualities. In later years, EMF seemed more censorious and evangelistic, more serious in his approach to life though he clothed the seriousness with whimsical humor. EMF has always had to "fake," to render by indirection and obliqueness; he lacks the directness of the prophetical novelist. J. B. Beer's THE ACHIEVEMENT OF E. M. FORSTER errs by the critic's adulation; more astringency is required in the critic of EMF. [Review of J. B. Beer's ACHIEVEMENT.]

929 Beer, J. B. THE ACHIEVEMENT OF E. M. FORSTER (Lond: Chatto & Windus; NY: Barnes & Noble, 1962); Chapter VI, "The Undy-

ing Worm," rptd in E. M. FORSTER: "A PASSAGE TO INDIA," A CASE-
BOOK, ed by Malcolm Bradbury (Lond: Macmillan, Casebook
Series, 1970), pp. 186–215; excerpts rptd in A LIBRARY OF LITER-
ARY CRITICISM: MODERN BRITISH LITERATURE, ed by Ruth Z. Temple
and Martin Tucker (NY: Frederick Ungar, 1966), I, 315–17.

Chap 1, "Aspects of a Novelist": Whether social comedy predominates in
EMF's fiction, as some critics allege, is questionable, as is the validity of an
exclusively moral approach like Trilling's. EMF is a romantic writer, the
heir of Blake, Coleridge, Shelley, Beethoven, and Wagner. He has Jane
Austen's upper-middle-class sense of humor (an anti-romantic trait) but he
is more direct, more aware of violence and death, and more admiring of
spontaneous passion. A conflict emerges between his gift for domestic
comedy and his cherishing of the spontaneous. There are three nexuses in
his work: comedy, moral seriousness, and imaginative passion; they are all
three valid and important, but they sometimes fail to merge. In romantic
art like EMF's, a conflict persists between rational analysis and imaginative
vision, with the latter suggesting an ineffable dimension to life (and to the
literature that reflects it). EMF's most distinctive gift is his power to evoke
states of vision and nightmare, and at moments of heightened imagination
he reveals mystical tendencies. The visionary moment provides the standard by which values are to be judged. Chap 2, "The Earth and the Stars":
EMF's stories reveal a love of the stars, a love of music (especially Wagner
and Beethoven), the influence of Shelley, and a dialectical mode of reasoning as in the German idealists. [Perceptive discussion of stories, contrasting
their visionary moments of truth with lifeless social convention.] Chap 3,
"From a View to a Death": In *A Room with a View* the characters are
abstractions as well as human beings: George Emerson is Life, Cecil Vyse
is Art, and Charlotte Bartlett is Anti-Life. Cecil loves Lucy Honeychurch
as a work of art, not as a person. When EMF's characters fail with their
hearts, they become peevish; when they fail with their heads, they become
muddled. The characters do not divide easily into the good and evil: Cecil
has his complications and goodness, displaying unselfishness and lack of
rancor when Lucy breaks the engagement. Cecil, Mr. Beebe, and Miss
Bartlett all fail to acknowledge passion, yet at times they can pay tribute to
it. The symbolism connected with the music that Lucy plays is intricate;
Schumann corresponds to "the witty weariness" of the Vyses; Gluck's
"Armide" is associated with George's arrival; Lucy refuses to play "Parsifal" music for Cecil; before the final encounter with Mr. Emerson, she plays
the less profound Mozart and Schumann and a song that Cecil gives her,
warning against an assertion of life. These contrasts are also achieved in
terms of painting. The central organizing theme and image group has to do
with views and rooms. Phaethon, the sun-like god of love represented in the
primitive Florentine coachman, encompasses Eros and Pallas Athene, as

Lucy will have to learn to do. The Carella house at Florence, described as
a labyrinth of decay with some life at the heart of it, is a central image for
Where Angels Fear to Tread. Sawston is a society which thinks that people
are to be treated as business items, whereas Italy is a community which
makes mistakes but never this one. The lack of syntactical astringency and
the absence of wit from the humor are planned to show the life-tenacious
(if sometimes decadent) qualities of a society that rejects Sawston's categories. Lilia's vision of Gino Carella is fallacious, unlike Lucy's of George,
because she is conventional at heart. The climax is Caroline Abbott's realization that Gino's son is not a thing or a word but a living being. Caroline
emphasizes that there is in life a moment of crucial choice; Philip Herriton
responds only aesthetically to this pronouncement, though in his conduct
he goes from aesthetic detachment to an involvement with life, when he
confesses to Gino the death of the baby. Philip's final vision of Caroline is
existential as well as aesthetic; he now sees her with glory and passion.
Likewise, Caroline's passion for Gino, which she regards as partly coarse,
is transformed by imagination. A true morality or judgment is thus dependent on vision.

Chap 4, "Flame Boats on a Stream" [All Beer's discussions are excellent,
but this chapter on *The Longest Journey* may be his best.]: The relationship
between the moment of vision and the moment of moral choice is explored
with subtlety in *Journey.* Ansell represents the disinterested pursuit of
truth, a Cambridge virtue. He pursues it vigorously, just as he pursues the
symbolic projection of this quest: the pursuit of the innermost figures as he
places squares within circles. Rickie Elliot has his moment of truth when
he feels that imagination must enter all discussions of reality, but his imagination achieves too powerful a role in his life. He is also too inexperienced
to know how to deal with Mrs. Failing's revelations. Stephen Wonham is
an imaginative construct rather than a living person. As for the piece of
chalk that breaks Mrs. Failing's teacup, the solid earth can be seen as
crushing the finer clay (Rickie's death is prefigured). Unwillingness to accept the symbolic moment is fateful. Psychologically, the rejection of it
results in dulling the inner sense of reality. In the dialectical interplay
established between earth and the imagination, the true sense of reality that
emerges encompasses both. Sawston negates both the imaginative values of
Cambridge and the pagan values of Wiltshire, but Cambridge is more easily
deceived by Sawston than is Wiltshire. At the conclusion Rickie's imagination transfigures the passion of Stephen in a final synthesis of the two. There
are no "sheep" and "goats"; even Herbert and Agnes Pembroke have something to be said in their favor. Rickie is correct in feeling that his visionary
experiences comprise a high form of reality; his mistake lies in identifying
this vision with the suburban girl who called it into being and in thinking
that he can gain permanent access to it by marriage to her. Ansell is the high

priest of Cambridge but has his limitations; his devotion to truth needs to be ballasted by Rickie's imaginative enthusiasm and by the wisdom of true experience. As for Rickie's autobiographical aspect, EMF was imagining what might have happened to a young man (like himself) who followed his (EMF's) enthusiasms to the exclusion of all others: "The result is not autobiography but imaginative self-caricature." The central symbolic episode occurs close to the end: Rickie's and Stephen's sailing of flame boats under a bridge at Cadover. Stephen's lasts longer, and it is his progeny that will inherit the earth. The Demeter symbolism is also important, signifying Stephen's full identification with the earth, Rickie's fear of it, and Ansell's inability to deal with it. The novel calls for the reader's indulgence with Rickie, in view of the latter's Christian virtues of seriousness, kindliness, and truthfulness. Chap 5, "In Country Sleep": The Wilcoxes in *Howards End* are extraverted and muddled. In contrast, Margaret Schlegel's sense of wholeness and her sense of music are great qualities. Henry Wilcox's proposal to Margaret is a fulfillment of Ruth Wilcox's subconscious wish. Margaret wishes for harmony rather than intensity; her sister Helen's reaching out to the absolute reflects intense passion, not self-serving. Margaret's experience of the meaningless sights and sounds in Saint Paul's Cathedral prefigures Mrs. Moore's in *A Passage to India:* Helen is stimulated by this kind of despairing vision to heroic action. The novel misses greatness because there is too great a modal conflict between the domestic comedy of Jane Austen and the exploration of serious moral issues. Leonard Bast is not quite convincing as a clerk and an aspirant to culture; he is a kind of Caliban figure and tonally unsuited to the novel. Margaret becomes a value in herself, since EMF places his emphasis on a visionary person rather than a visionary moment, a person whose discords are transmuted into music. Her vision and her music triumph at Howards End house, despite her failure to get Henry to connect (he provides the realistic grit in the novel). As Margaret becomes more fully identified with Ruth, she also shares her capacity to transcend sex to attain a complete, androgynous vision. In her development she turns from London and the public world to a private one and excludes some ranges of experience. In being impelled to action by her vision, Helen achieves a victory also. She exerts a spiritual influence comparable to that associated with the madonna, with whom she is aligned at Howards End estate. EMF has not completely solved his problem of giving roundness to the novel while still bringing vision and realism into full tension. The identification of the darker side of life with the Wilcoxes and the Basts does violence to them as human beings, with the result that EMF's vision is not completely articulated. But the novel has great richness of conception and detail.

Chap 6, "The Undying Worm": In *A Passage to India* Sawstonians are in a situation where their influence is unchecked and where they complacently assume superiority to a civilization that is more comprehensive than their own and that is potentially as powerful. Since the Indians need the British, the real failure is the one to connect. The British are most to blame because the initiative should have been theirs. The British achievement has been the securing of justice; the British defect, complacency. Fielding's sweet reasonableness is inadequate to solve the problems posed by India. *Passage* explores extremes, not normality; EMF's control keeps his whimsicality in check, and the humor is concentrated. The alleged ghost that bumps the Nawab's automobile at night and the snake on the way to the Caves that turns out to be an illusion establish the aura of uncertainty investing the trial and Adela Quested's part in it. At the beginning the benevolent sky and hostile earth establish the attractiveness and sinister aspect of India; sky and earth are close in the Mau festivities but draw apart again at the end. All elements in the book tend to be similarly ambivalent. The conflict between the British and the Indians broadens to a metaphysical struggle between earth and sky, spirit and matter, love and the intractable. *Passage* is concerned in part with the Forsterian theme of the need to connect head and heart in order to reach reality. In the courtroom the punkah wallah assumes the guise to Adela of an incarnate god, an Indian Apollo, a real but visionary figure reminding her continually of Mrs. Moore. Her sense of reality is restored at the thought of Mrs. Moore, and her testimony marks her recovery from hysteria. The Caves go beyond the time process itself, and they are untouched by any human quality. Mrs. Moore is crucial. The echo undermines her because she is not ready for a radical reorientation of reality. But her spirit is not extinguished; she undergoes a redemptive immortality, as do Rickie in *Journey* and Mrs. Wilcox in *Howards End.* The Caves are not a revelation of reality but a touchstone by which reality is tested. They transform: Adela is made a person; Mrs. Moore is destroyed in body, but her soul lives on. Through her influence Aziz is released from hatred, in the muddle associated with the capsizing boat in the Mau tank. Fielding fails by his disregard of mystery, Mrs. Moore by her dislike of muddles. They are half in touch with Sawston, which tries to evade both muddles and mysteries. The reality of India is casual: this reality is broad and attractive, but it can also become terrifying and incomprehensible in the Cave echoes and reflections. Vision informs the activities of Fielding and Mrs. Moore, but it can also be intensified to ecstatic Hindu love. Vision and reality are not one in India, but in India there is a connection between them. Chap 7, "Serving the World": *Passage* was an advance on EMF's early works in style and subject matter; the language is controlled, there is greater toughness in dialogue, and a cynical realism prevails. Edwardian idealism and sensibility, represented in EMF's early fiction, fought the Germans and were routed by them. The blow to European sensibilities dealt by the war corresponds to the impact of India on EMF's characters. [Recounts EMF's service in World War I in Alexandria, and publication of *Alexandria* and *Pharos and Pharillon.*] EMF became a figure of wide authority during and after World War II. Chap 8, "In and Out of Time": There is charm in EMF's essays, but they lack intellectual astringency. In his novels he displays a mastery in social comedy and dialogue; when he goes toward poetic symbolism, he has often elicited disparaging judgments. Despite his romantic affinities, EMF tends to be an intellectual rather than an intuitive novelist. His greater novels possess visionary experience but are not possessed by it. Vision and realism coexist in EMF's work, the "music" being the ultimate expression of his vision, the detachment being a quality demanded by his realism. His writings stand as important documents by virtue of their social commentary and as works remarkable for their wide, mythologic implications. [One of the standard books on EMF, notable for its sensible and imaginative readings of individual works, for its grasp of EMF's career and canon, and for its persuasive presentation of EMF as romanticist and symbolist. The cogency of the discourse obscures such minor defects as a tendency to use too much plot summary and to quote excessively. Select bibliography. Reviews: A. Alvarez (Entry No. 925); Malcolm Bradbury, "Reviews and Comment," CRITICAL QUARTERLY, V (Spring 1963), 92–94; Ronald Bryden (Entry No. 936); "Comic Moralist," TIMES (Lond), 2 Aug 1962, p. 13; H. H. Anniah Gowda, "Book Reviews," LITERARY HALF-YEAR-LY (Mysore), VI (Jan 1965), 93–94; Barbara Hardy, "E. M. Forster: Interpretation and Judgment," ESSAYS IN CRITICISM, XIII (April 1963), 181–87; W. J. Harvey, "Reviews," REVIEW OF ENGLISH STUDIES, nsXIV (Nov 1963), 426–28; J. K. Johnstone, "The New Books," QUEEN'S QUARTERLY, LXX (Summer 1963), 289–90; E. Lacotte, "Étude Critique: Études Récentes sur E. M. Forster" (Critical Essay: Recent Studies on E. M. Forster), ÉTUDES ANGLAISES, XX (Oct–Dec 1967), 425–31; John Lehmann (Entry No. 967); Frederick P. W. McDowell, "The Newest Elucidations of Forster," ENG-LISH FICTION IN TRANSITION, V: 4 (1962), 51–58; "Only Connect" (Entry No. 973); Piero Mandrillo (Entry No. 1129); Hermann Peschmann, "Reviews of Books," ENGLISH, XIV (Spring 1963), 156–58; "Search for Connexion" (Entry No. 979); William Kean Seymour, "Reputations and Opinions," CONTEMPORARY REVIEW, CCI (Sept 1962), 159–60; George H. Thomson (Entry No. 987); Frank Tuohy (Entry No. 988); Frederick T. Wood, "Current Literature, 1962," ENGLISH STUDIES, XLIV: 5 (1963), 392–93; Andrew Wright, "Reviews," MODERN LANGUAGE REVIEW, LVIII (April 1963), 253–54.]

930 Berthoff, Warner. THE EXAMPLE OF MELVILLE (Princeton: Princeton UP, 1962; Lond: Oxford UP, 1963), pp. 18, 59, 186, 202. [EMF's various pronouncements on MOBY DICK and BILLY BUDD are cited with approbation.]

931 Bradbury, Malcolm. "E. M. Forster's *Howards End,*" CRITI-
CAL QUARTERLY, IV (Autumn 1962), 229–41; rvd and rptd as "*How-
ards End,*" in FORSTER: A COLLECTION OF CRITICAL ESSAYS, ed by
Malcolm Bradbury (Englewood Cliffs, NJ: Prentice-Hall, Spectrum
Books, 1966), pp. 128–43; much rvd and rewritten as part of "E.
M. Forster as Victorian and Modern: *Howards End* and *A Passage
to India,*" POSSIBILITIES: ESSAYS ON THE STATE OF THE NOVEL (Lond,
Oxford, NY: Oxford UP, 1973), pp. 91–120, espec 98–109.

Howards End is written from an enlarged social perspective and has an
enlarged social and moral significance; it is written in the comic mode, and
EMF in it emphasizes the necessity of making compromises in society. As
for EMF's avowed liberalism, he is at once its adherent and its ironic critic.
The affirmations are in another mode of utterance that might be called
"poetic." This mode forms a dynamic antithesis to the social criticism which
is done predominantly in the comic mode. The action of the novel is
essentially moral; it enjoins the need to recognize social and ethical responsibility. The morality implies that inheritance is not a legal or institutional
right but a spiritual right (the worthiest shall inherit England and the earth).
The events in the novel are less important than the apparatus by which they
are to be perceived and interpreted; this apparatus inculcates "sensitivity,
significance, a sense of large and formidable issues often not perceived even
by the characters themselves." The action is incremental, building from
various points of view, and it involves the modulation of the comic with the
poetic modes. These two modes help formulate the dialectic worked out in
the novel between the national and the international, the seen and the
unseen, the practical and the romantic, the prose and the poetry (and
passion). The novelist as essayist (or as omniscient narrator) allows EMF
to solve the technical problem in the novel and to make the needed modulations between the two modes. In his poetic mode, EMF appeals to a largely
vanished feudal order and a threatened agrarian liberalism (of which Howards End house is the symbol, with its evocation of the warrior-yeoman
spirit). The poetic aspect of the book intensifies as it develops; the characters who change do so near the house and its attendant wych-elm. Margaret
Schlegel finally realizes her mistake in thinking of Henry Wilcox as a
potential figure of light; but she also appreciates the fact that it is through
the Wilcoxes that she has gained Howards End and a new stability. [One
of the classic essays on *Howards End;* deeply perceptive and places the
novel in its widest context, for the most part convincingly; works from the
premise that the "poetry" is not adventitious but mostly organic.]

932 Brander, Lawrence. "E. M. Forster and India," REVIEW OF
ENGLISH LITERATURE, II (Oct 1962), 76–84.

In *A Passage to India* EMF gets inside his Muslim characters because they
represent in exaggerated form the best part of the Western psyche; the

Hindus, however, are more inscrutable and are less well portrayed. [Connects, with little sense of EMF's purpose, the muddle of the festival in "Temple" with the negating "boum" heard in the "Caves."] "Caves" presents the sense of unreality that pervades life under the distorting influence of the Indian sun. The disillusionment in the earlier novels is here intensified; violence also obtrudes but is made more probable (see the accident to the Nawab Bahadur's car and the events in the Caves). EMF effectively uses dramatic irony and physical beauty in the novel's plot (as in the courtroom punkah wallah). [Emphasizes the presence of muddle as an evil in the novel, though muddle is also potential order.] For the Hindu all is illusion, and the European humanist and religionist (Fielding and Mrs. Moore) find little comfort in India, which as "ancient night" has little respect for the order and seemliness of Mediterranean civilization. Completeness and fulfillment are momentary in the Gokul Asthami ceremonies; muddle and uncertainty return [but the fact that transfiguration is possible represents, I think, the thrust of *Passage*]. [Essay is inadequate in sum.]

933 "Bridge Party," TIME, LXXIX (9 Feb 1962), 61.
The reduction in scale imposed upon Santha Rama Rau's adaptation of *A Passage to India* makes it true in its shape to the novel, but there is less breadth and depth. It is difficult in the play to prepare the audience for the radical reactions of the women in the Marabar Caves. The play trails off as the novel does not.

934 "Briefly Noted," NEW YORKER, XXXVIII (17 March 1962), 187–88.
Pharos and Pharillon admirably supplements *Alexandria: A History and a Guide*. *Pharos* is more relaxed, includes more details, and is "often wildly funny." [Résumé of contents of *Pharos*.]

935 Brustein, Robert. "Strindberg: The Victor and the Vanquished," NEW REPUBLIC, CXLVI (19 Feb 1962), 20–23.
Santha Rama Rau's adaptation of *A Passage to India* is contrived. The author's narrative, with its "cool, qualifying intelligence" is excised; EMF's subtlety becomes external and melodramatic, and the dialogue of the novel is not good enough to bear the weight of the play. The point of the novel is lost, i.e., that no Westerner can grasp the "otherness" of India. The play becomes a conflict between stupid bureaucrats and innocent Indian victims.

936 Bryden, Ronald. "The Listener's Book Chronicle," LISTENER, LXVIII (2 Aug 1962), 181–82.
Beer is too simplistic in defining EMF's romanticism. EMF's myths represent not so much "some mystic union of man and nature" as man's "perpetual endeavour to come to terms by imagination with his habitat." EMF's

"poetry" has to be read with the rest of his prose, in the context of agnostic twentieth-century humanism. This is what Crews does, and he corrects Beer on EMF's use of myth: EMF uses Dionysian imagery as "a dramatic device, set up to be overthrown by a sadder Apollonianism, the poetry of human individuation." Against his surrounding darkness, EMF can set only "tiny islands of light and order." [Review-article on J. B. Beer's THE ACHIEVEMENT OF E. M. FORSTER (1962) and Frederick C. Crews's E. M. FORSTER: THE PERILS OF HUMANISM (1962). Short but important article.]

937 Churchill, Thomas. "Place and Personality in *Howards End*," CRITIQUE, V (Spring–Summer 1962), 61–73.
The characters in EMF's fiction have difficulty in making connections; the only two who do so are the aristocratic Lucy Honeychurch and the Marxian George Emerson in *A Room with a View*. EMF's dialectical temper wished for connection between people from different ranks, intellects, and sensibilities, but his conscience saw that it could not be. He does find wholeness in some people of yeomen ancestry, personalities like Ruth Wilcox, though her completeness is momentary because of her precarious health. Margaret Schlegel seems the best person to carry on for her after her death, but the tone of the book wavers in the scenes with Leonard Bast and in those describing her courtship and marriage. She seems to have been the result of EMF's conscious ideas, whereas his poetical energy went, after Ruth's death, into depicting Howards End house. The difficulties in tone result from EMF's ambivalence toward Bast and his animosity toward Henry Wilcox. His patronizing of Bast makes him a parody figure; and he is killed too conveniently to get Charles Wilcox into prison or else to keep him from embarrassing the Schlegel sisters. The sisters are culpable in regarding Bast as a subject for discussion, as a non-human object; Ruth would not have so discussed him. Her greatness resides in what she is equated with and in her pervasiveness after death. Howards End house is not England, only a small section thereof, but it is "a center of value and order in a disproportionate country." [But EMF regards it as the best in England and symbolic, therefore, of what she can attain.] Howards End has an almost animistic power; it can banish the unsuitable and wait for its rightful heir. Chapter 25 reveals EMF's power to illuminate place in the description of the Welsh Hills and his relative failure with people. (Most of the chapter is a feminist tract.) Apparently Charles Wilcox and his breed will inherit England. The real problem of the book is finding an heir for the aristocratic values and order embodied in Howards End and its spiritual owner, Ruth Wilcox. Margaret's jumping from the automobile near Oniton is quixotic, her courtship with Henry is sophistical, and her treatment of him at the end is unpitying [Wilfred Stone feels similarly in THE CAVE AND THE MOUNTAIN (1966)]; the question obtrudes, is she really Ruth's spiritual heir? Margaret can never become Ruth, because the soul does not have offspring; Ruth is feminine while Margaret is feminist. Margaret comes off better early in the book

when Ruth's presence supplies an implicit criticism of her, which the novel lacks after Ruth's death. Ruth is more admirable than Margaret because Margaret insists, in these early scenes, on intellectualizing instinct, thereby killing it. But Ruth loves her because she expresses so dramatically her intellect and has a sense of humor, qualities lacking in Ruth's family. The funeral chapter is the finest, "a Winter's Tale in miniature." Proportion is lacking at the conclusion because at Howards End the masculine principle is absent, dead in Leonard, submissive in the tired Henry. The Schlegels, in effect, dream of "a snob's heaven of Transcendent Planes." The child is not the symbol of a classless society but will belong too narrowly to the Schlegel women. [Judgment is begrudging.] But Howards End itself may exert a corrective influence on the child. [An interesting essay with many valid insights, especially for those who dislike Margaret Schlegel.]

938 Clurman, Harold. "Theatre," NATION (NY), CXCIV (17 Feb 1962), 153.
A Passage to India and Santha Rama Rau's stage adaptation of it are incompatible. The virtue of the book does not lie in its plot but in the feeling it gives for India—the atmosphere and life of this country, not its ethnic aspects but its spiritual and philosophical aspects. In short, the book contains an essential poetry that conveys India as an Idea. Put into their speeches, the semi-mystic ideas of the characters seem flat. The play becomes a social drama of a particular time and fails to convey the permanent significance of Indian culture.

939 [Compton-Burnett, Ivy.] "Interview with Miss Compton-Burnett," REVIEW OF ENGLISH LITERATURE, III (Oct 1962), 96–112, esp 103.
EMF is overestimated. He is a man of high talent but not a genius. [But she admires his books, preferring *Howards End* to *A Passage to India* because she is insular.]

940 Crews, Frederick C. E. M. FORSTER: THE PERILS OF HUMANISM (Princeton: Princeton UP; Lond: Oxford UP, 1962); rvd from "E. M. Forster, An Historical and Critical Study," unpublished dissertation, Princeton University (1959); rpts, in rvd form, "*The Longest Journey* and the Perils of Humanism," ENGLISH LITERARY HISTORY, XII (Spring 1960), 575–96 and "E. M. Forster: The Limitations of Mythology," COMPARATIVE LITERATURE, XII (Spring 1960), 97–112; Chap 7, "The Comic Spirit," rptd in FORSTER: A COLLECTION OF CRITICAL ESSAYS, ed by Malcolm Bradbury (Englewood Cliffs, NJ: Prentice-Hall, Spectrum Books, 1966), pp. 96–105; Chap 10, "*A Passage to India*," rptd in E. M. FORSTER: "A PASSAGE TO INDIA," A CASEBOOK, ed by Malcolm Bradbury (Lond: Macmillan, Casebook Series, 1970), pp. 165–85, and in part in TWENTIETH CENTURY INTERPRETATIONS OF "A PASSAGE TO INDIA," ed by Andrew Rutherford (Englewood Cliffs, NJ: Prentice-Hall, Spectrum Books, 1970), pp. 78–89.

Chap 1, "Introductory": EMF is "a lapsed Victorian" of the upper middle class, whose intellectual loyalties continued to be those of 1896 Cambridge. He remained intellectually and spiritually loyal to the tenets of nineteenth-century liberalism and humanism, but as a novelist he found himself questioning these. His artistic growth runs parallel to his disappointments with humanism. Chap 2, "Forster and Religion: From Clapham to Bloomsbury": EMF is an agnostic and anti-Christian, but his books are religious in their concern with the meaning of life. He retains the Clapham Sect moral fervor and interest in ultimate realities, but he rejects the formulas of its Christianity. His agnosticism and moral seriousness are akin to those evinced by Sir Leslie Stephen, the most famous of the Bloomsbury "parents." EMF's sense of the mystery in the universe is accompanied by philosophical despair. [This chapter and the next two are standard for EMF's background.] Chap 3, "The Refuge of Liberalism": EMF remains fundamentally an individualist. His liberalism owes much to John Stuart Mill: both distrusted the power of the state; and both stressed diversity. Both would advocate laissez-faire in the world of the spirit but not in the economic world. Although EMF has not been completely removed from practical affairs, he has embraced the world of order that he finds in art, concomitant with his retirement from "the unmanageable world" of politics. Chap 4, "Cambridge and 'The Good' ": the good comprises, for EMF, sincerity, art, private freedom, diversity, the exercise of personal relationships, and sensitivity to the countryside and its traditions. EMF's attitudes are "toughminded"; he is empiric, pessimistic, apparently irreligious, fatalistic, pluralistic, skeptical, though he is also basically religious. King's College, especially the Apostles Group, fostered his romanticism and humanistic idealism and, at the same time, his skepticism. At Cambridge he came under the influence of Nathaniel Wedd, Goldsworthy Lowes Dickinson, and G. E. Moore (the latter's influence was indirect but crucial). Yet EMF also has ties to the previous generation—his reverence for Shelley, his skepticism of formalism in art, his distrust of aesthetic experimentation, his Platonic and Victorian idealism, and his agnosticism and romanticism in general. He retained to the end the vital contradictions represented in the intellectual "left" of Cambridge, "between idealism and empiricism, collectivism and individualism, religiosity and common sense."

Chap 5, "The Longest Journey": [For contents of this chapter see Crews (1959).] Chap 6, "The Italian Novels": In the Italian novels EMF finds Italy rich in melodramatic moral and emotional extremes. For EMF passion is preferable to respectability, but he is aware of its dangers. He is certain of his ethical philosophy in these books; as a result, they are controlled and formally excellent. The emphasis is social, not metaphysical; and EMF is concerned in them with verbal and dramatic irony rather than with subtlety of meaning. Irony and rhythmic repetition and variation organize the books. The realities are elemental in Monteriano: extravagance, superstition, theatricality, violence, coarse democracy among men, subjugation of women. Harriet Herriton is the villainess because she cannot understand passion. Gino Carella is the decisive influence over the four Sawstonians in Monteriano—Lilia Herriton expected passion and did not find it, since Gino wanted an heir, not a mistress; Caroline Abbott is more intelligent than Lilia and more inhibited, but Gino as a man overcomes the influence of Sawston; Philip Herriton finds his romantic provinciality dispelled with Gino's friendliness at the opera; Harriet Herriton, as an enemy of life, remains impervious to Gino. Rhythms as repeated images and symbols are abundant, e.g., the great tower that becomes emblematic of a complex reality, embracing both heaven and hell. There are also subtle allusions to Dante and similarities to James's THE AMBASSADORS, especially between the characters of Strether and Philip. George Emerson in *A Room with a View* has a view of man's tininess and isolation in the universe; Cecil Vyse has no view at all; Lucy Honeychurch ratifies George's view of love in marrying him instead of Cecil. In most comedies of manners the characters fail to fulfill their social roles, but in *Room* they take these roles *too* seriously. Those who survive are those whose "views" allow them to see through the social code and to recognize enduring relationships with nature and their fellow men. Mr. Emerson, like Tony Failing in *Journey*, prefers the life of instinct to social repressions; his humanism, like EMF's, is sharpened by a romantic sense of doom. George is like Thomas Carlyle in his "Everlasting Nay" phase in SARTOR RESARTUS, while his father is like Carlyle in his "Yea" phase. The Rev. Mr. Eager and the Rev. Mr. Beebe represent Christian repression, and they try to keep the lovers apart. With Charlotte Bartlett and Cecil Vyse, an ingrained asceticism is indistinguishable from an enslavement to social forms. Cecil wishes for women to be dependent, whereas EMF believes in sexual equality within the relationship of passionate love. The complexity of *Room* derives from its comic tangles and the interpenetrations of the rhythms (flowers and violets [symbols of life and passion], passage of the seasons, images of music and water). A climactic episode, like the murder in the Piazza Signoria at Florence, binds up the rhythms.

Chap 7, "The Comic Spirit": EMF is a symbolist wishing to discover a timeless reality in time. In the short stories, an overbalance of meaning prevails at the expense of represented life; the symbolism is unearned. In the novels EMF's sense of comedy prevents them from slipping too far toward allegory. The comedy and the irony present in EMF's vision in the Italian novels restrains too intense a search by his characters for private meaning and restrains EMF himself from imposing too symbolic a significance upon his materials. Fantasy represents the most overt kind of symbolism and is deterministic in essence. EMF used it sparingly, especially in his novels. Generally, he allows the muddle to exist and comments on it through the agency of the comic spirit. Like Butler he uses a comic irony to indicate a discrepancy between fixed values and the complexity of actual experience. The influence of Jane Austen enables EMF to contrast the proper with the reasonable. The standard for judgment is an Augustan love of good sense. Elizabeth Bennett (PRIDE AND PREJUDICE) and Lucy Honeychurch take their places in the world that they criticize, despite their attaining disparaging knowledge of that world. EMF's comedy differs from Jane Austen's in the heightening of witty reversals, the density of the thematic irony, and the tendency to relate his characters to general human nature. EMF is also indebted to Meredith with his theory of a chastening comic spirit. Like Meredith, EMF is concerned in the early novels with the administering of comic justice, especially with the exposure of egoism, which comprises all sorts of pretense and self-deception. In *Journey* the egoists are punished, and though he disapproves of Mrs. Failing, EMF allows her to explode the concept of the romantic hero. Stephen is the ordinary man who escapes from the categories of both hero and mock-hero. The idea of comic justice becomes less relevant in EMF's last two novels, in which he is concerned with the ultimate meaning of existence rather than with the exposure of egoism. The skepticism in these books precludes a belief in a moral order that brings retribution to egoists. Man's isolation from meaning, implicit in these novels, brings to their comedy a sardonic quality. Chap 8, *"Howards End"*: The framework of *Howards End* is a series of antitheses between liberalism and its opposite, a blunt and humorless materialism. Unlike the Italian novels *Howards End* tests liberalism's ability to come to terms with its antagnoist (entrenched convention), and it demonstrates the difficulties involved in preserving ideals in the actual world. EMF has projected the anti-liberal forces in a complex and human character, Henry Wilcox. Liberalism needs Henry's political and economic power, while he needs the civilized force of liberalism. The Wilcoxes distrust the personal element or do not realize its importance. They are a threat to English culture and are antagonistic to the rural, traditionally minded England that EMF loves. EMF asks us to sympathize with the Wilcoxes when it is impossible to do so, though he and Margaret think that a *modus vivendi* with them should be achieved. In working out his scheme, EMF places his sympathies too heavily on the Schlegel side, though it is natural for him to have done so. It is ironical that the rural-minded Schlegels live in the city and that the urban-minded Wilcoxes buy up country estates. London frustrates the life of personal relations; religion cannot flourish there because it is too far from its support in rural nature. The posthumous role of Mrs. Wilcox is important. She and Margaret are sisters in spirit; the denial by

404

Ruth's family of her bequest of Howards End house to Margaret indicates that the latter has not yet earned the right to the house and the traditions for which it stands. The real bequest of Mrs. Wilcox is her superhuman tolerance and self-control. Margaret has these virtues in embryo but must learn to exercise them and to accept those (the other Wilcoxes) who go contrary to her clearest values. By the end she does assume Mrs. Wilcox's civilizing role. Rather than representing England, as Trilling contends, Howards End house represents the integrated family life led there by Ruth and to be continued by Margaret; and it represents an ideal or standard by which each of the characters must be judged. The proper relation between the spiritual and the physical is also inculcated there. In London, Margaret had led the life of an intellectual; at Howards End, she will lead the life of a woman and wife. Howards End reconciles the feminine and masculine natures; there, the Schlegels will avoid being effeminate, the Wilcoxes brutal. Margaret must adjust to the realities of Henry's nature; she learns that physical love can be a binding force when rationality would be insufficient. Helen is too spiritual and too feministic; and her narrow view almost triumphs. Helen and Margaret at Howards End must combine to become an adequate surrogate for Ruth Wilcox, as mother and wife. Helen distrusts sex because it complicates life beyond her power of mastery; Henry distrusts it on religious gounds. The other side of Henry's prurience is a chivalrous protectiveness toward women. But Henry draws Margaret toward sexual tenderness, while Helen draws her toward spirituality. Margaret is saved from Helen by a desire to be truthful to her nature as a woman and a sexual person. EMF regards Margaret's achievement of proportion as all-important. Concerning the theme of social responsibility, Leonard Bast is important. He is a symbol to the Schlegels (and to EMF) of the worst consequences of the capitalism which encourages rootlessness and denies self-fulfillment to the disadvantaged. The Wilcoxes do not see that Leonard is as he is because of their exploitation of his class. Margaret's belief in individual love and tolerance demonstrates a yearning for permanence and a realistic sense of limitation. *Howards End* is not EMF's masterpiece, because the outer world to which he tries to give credit remains alien to him. The novel shows development in that he wishes to admit his prosaic world into his fiction, but he fails to reconcile that world with his own values. Chap 9, "The Limitations of Mythology": [For contents of this chapter see Crews (1960).]

Chap 10, "*A Passage to India*" [Crews believes with Trilling that *Passage* restates our dilemmas without offering us guidance.]: The book is fundamentally concerned with the contrast between aspiration and reality. *Passage* continues the humanistic struggle against meaninglessness but implies that a victory is no longer possible. Adela Quested's hallucination represents a symbolic breakdown of effort directed toward mutual sympathy between two races and countries; human relationships are inadequate to bridge this gap. The discords in the novel proceed from a conflict of civilizations and from defects in human nature itself. The characters, even the most developed, are "flatter" than Rickie Elliot or Margaret Schlegel. EMF utilizes expansive metaphors (receding circles, the theme of invitation) to suggest that humanity is insignificant. The ordering effects of invitations are annulled when cobras, tigers, and wasps may be involved. The rationalistic Westerners and the Moslems find some aspects of creation inimical: flies, bees, wasps. Godbole's Hinduism and Mrs. Moore's mystical propensities allow them, in contrast, to accept all aspects of creation as parts of God's being. *Passage* does not advocate the acceptance of Hinduism. It is one more religion, along with Islam and Christianity, which has its strengths and its limitations. Hindu inclusiveness is not completely satisfactory because it sacrifices the values of Western humanism that EMF cherishes—man and the need for order, selfhood, proportion. EMF likes Islam for its combination of mysticism and selfhood, and Hinduism for its theology but not its rituals. Though Hinduism is treated sympathetically, its chief function is to discredit the Christian and Moslem emphasis on the personal, which is often irrelevant to the welter of India. Hinduism also emphasizes our isolation from meaning and the powerlessness of man before the nihilism of the Marabar Caves. In the Caves, Aziz, Mrs. Moore, and Adela find the formidable, real India that is indifferent to selfhood. Mrs. Moore's experience is a parody of the Hinduistic union with Brahma; instead of an ecstatic experience, it is nihilistic. Adela and Mrs. Moore lose the sense of time; at this point, unconscious feelings rush up from below and overwhelm them. Mrs. Moore perceives nothing positive in the Caves and reduces the world soul to the scale of her own wearied ego; but when she leaves India, she learns at Asirgarh that the Caves were not the whole of India. The Caves echo what is brought into them; in Adela's case their meaning is sexual since she had been preoccupied with sex. Mrs. Moore's indifference to all values makes it appropriate that she be resurrected as a Hindu goddess; for the Hindu, the mortal becomes immortal when the individual becomes indifferent to the ties of the heart. Chap 11, "The Importance of Reason": When the liberal faith is tested in EMF's fiction, it is most often found wanting. Characters emerge with a chastened humanism. The ironies and the sudden deaths, the surprises and the coincidences contribute to an atmosphere of instability and uncertainty. The higher order is not friendly and its attributes are unknowable. If anything, there is an excess of control and lucidity in EMF's fiction. His virtues are honesty, incisiveness, sympathy, irony, rigor, and a classic sense of plot. Yet his novels are deficient in imaginative vigor, and his imagination lacks power. *Passage* escapes the limitations of his other novels because its subject is these limitations. The result is a masterpiece of pessimism. In EMF we have the self-scrutiny of a mind anchored in liberalism yet aware of weaknesses in the liberal tradition. The liberalism in *Passage* veers from the programmatic to a concern with elemental, if disconcerting, realities. [The best book on EMF and the most comprehensive and lucid introduction to his fiction, except for the discussion of *Passage*. Crews discounts too greatly the relevance of Hinduism; *Passage* is also too open-ended to be regarded as solely pessimistic. The discussions of the novels through *Howards End* are superb, despite Crews's view that *Passage* is EMF's only novel of permanent importance. Reviews: Joseph L. Blotner, "Book Reviews," SOUTH ATLANTIC QUARTERLY, LXII (Winter 1963), 122–23; G. Gordon Bolam, "New Books," HIBBERT JOURNAL, LXI (April 1963), 156; Malcolm Bradbury, "Reviews and Comment," CRITICAL QUARTERLY, V (Spring 1963), 92–94; Ronald Bryden (Entry No. 936); "Classified Books," BOOKLIST, LVIII (1 May 1962), 598; "Confused Liberal," TIMES LITERARY SUPPLEMENT (Lond), 17 Aug 1962, p. 626; "Current Books," NINETEENTH CENTURY FICTION, XVII (Sept 1962), 196: Naomi Diamond, "Books in English," BOOKS ABROAD, XXXVII (April 1963), 199–200; David A. Downes, "Book Reviews," THOUGHT, XXXVIII (Spring 1963), 652; Lloyd W. Griffin, "New Books Appraised," LIBRARY JOURNAL, LXXXVII (June 1962), 2380–81; Barbara Hardy, "E. M. Forster: Interpretation and Judgment," ESSAYS IN CRITICISM, XIII (April 1963), 181–87; W. J. Harvey, "Reviews," REVIEW OF ENGLISH STUDIES, nsXIV (Nov 1963), 426–28; H. W. Häusermann, "Besprechungen" (Reviews), ANGLIA, LXXXI: 2(1963), 260–63; Granville Hicks, "Pencraft from Dickens to Durrell," SATURDAY REVIEW (NY), XLV (23 June 1962), 26; E. Lacotte, "Étude Critique: Études Récentes sur E. M. Forster" (Critical Essay: Recent Studies on E. M. Forster), ÉTUDES ANGLAISES, XX (Oct–Dec 1967), 425–31; Perrin Lowrey, "Aspects of a Novelist's Art," MODERN AGE, VI (Summer 1962), 328–29; Alastair MacDonald, "The New Books," QUEEN'S QUARTERLY, LXIX (Winter 1963), 652; Frederick P. W. McDowell, "The Newest Elucidations of Forster," ENGLISH FICTION IN TRANSITION, V: 4 (1962), 51–58; Piero Mandrillo (Entry No. 1129); "Notes on Current Books," VIRGINIA QUARTERLY REVIEW, XXXVIII (Autumn 1962), cxviii; Hermann Peschmann, "Reviews of Books," ENGLISH, XIV (Spring 1963), 156–58; "Reader's Guide,' YALE REVIEW, nsLII (Autumn 1962), x, xiv; David Shusterman, "Book Reviews," CRITICISM, V (Spring 1963), 195–97; George H. Thomson (Entry No. 987); Frederick T. Wood, "Current Literature, 1962," ENGLISH STUDIES, XLIV: 5 (1963), 392–93; and Andrew Wright, "Reviews," MODERN LANGUAGE REVIEW, LVIII (April 1963), 253–54.

941 Driver, Tom. "Two Lines of Vision," CHRISTIAN CENTURY, LXXIX (7 March 1962), 296–97.

Most writers would fail in dramatizing *A Passage to India*, but Santha Rama Rau fails badly in making it an oversimplified drama of race relations. The fears engendered by the Marabar Caves fail to register when they are verbalized. She misses the point that two people of different cultures cannot understand each other and says, rather, that they do not yet understand each other.

942 Echeruo, M. J. C. "E. M. Forster and the 'Undeveloped Heart' " ENGLISH STUDIES IN AFRICA, (University of Witwatersand, Johannesburg), V (Sept 1962), 151–55.
The intellectualism of the Schlegel sisters in *Howards End* and the public school toughness of Fielding in *A Passage to India* are inhibiting influences; these characters lack the fully developed heart to be found in Mr. Emerson (*A Room with a View*), Mrs. Wilcox (*Howards End*), and Mrs. Moore (*Passage*). [Rather obvious interpretation of the novels in terms of the dire consequences of the "undeveloped heart" for the characters.]

943 "Elusive," NEWSWEEK, LIX (12 Feb 1962), 52.
Santha Rama Rau's adaptation of *A Passage to India* is subtle, perceptive, and only occasionally dramatic. She understands the inner quality of her people and the bluff façade of their one-time overlords. The play trails out indecisively.

944 Fadda, Anna Maria. EDWARD MORGAN FORSTER E EL DECADENTISMO (Edward Morgan Forster and Decadence) (Sassari [Universita de Cagliari]: Palumbo, 1962).
Until now a basis for understanding EMF has been lacking. Critics must concentrate upon both the profundity and the stylistic excellence of his work, and they must attempt to place him within his historical milieu. They have too long focused upon his relationship to the society in which he moved, ignoring his psychological and intellectual ties to modern European culture. The influence of Virginia Woolf and Bloomsbury has been overemphasized. EMF's artistic independence is to be measured by the extraordinary coherence of his works and by his fidelity to his individual psychological attitudes and intellectual values. His narrative form does not derive from the Edwardian naturalistic view of reality but from a different tradition, i.e., continental decadent writing and symbolism. Cambridge, with its refined atmosphere and idealistic values, was also allied to this tradition and verified its influence in EMF's work. His manner of interpreting reality and his consciousness of his historical position, even in his later works, reflect spiritually the uncertain and divided Edwardian period. His themes and attitudes express the same spiritual uneasiness and discord to be found in the European decadence, contemporary with him. EMF was, moreover, Victorian in point of view and temper. Like the Victorians, EMF aspired to reach a supreme Order, a supreme Harmony (Reality, Truth), while he saw the impossibility of reconciling the ideal and the real. EMF's narratives describe both an everyday reality and a poetical, mysterious reality that transcends tangible experience. From the examination of EMF's

work emerges this certainty: in confronting the disharmonies of life, he has always maintained an attitude of inner acceptance, being conscious of a world in ruins, which precludes the chance for renewal and progress. In all of his work he reveals the essential solitude of man. In his representation of the world, the tragic is never contained in a single event or in a single character; but it seems, rather, to inhere in the universal human condition. Rather than being a cold and self-controlled writer, as some critics assert him to be, EMF observes the world not with detachment but with keen interest and keen love for England. EMF's compassion for the universal human condition that condemns men to inefficiency and impotency mixes with his criticism for its apathy of bourgeois society. In *Where Angels Fear to Tread*, the chief theme is man's isolation. In *The Longest Journey* (as in *Angels*), there is a contrast between two worlds—Sawston and Cambridge, symbols respectively of conventional and intellectually open worlds. Yet EMF's purpose is not so much to denounce the bourgeoisie as to emphasize the necessity for accepting life, for discovering amid appearances a deeper reality. Sawston and Agnes Pembroke become symbolic of the "unreality" of the material world that EMF opposes to the "reality" that is imagination. But as EMF's world is controlled by fate, the concept of guilt does not and cannot exist. The drama of the novel is not in the events themselves but in man's absurd and total submission to destiny.

EMF's novels reveal opposition between the hypocrisy of the British bourgeoisie and other historical-cultural entities (India, Cambridge, Italy) that encourage a life of immediacy, passion, and instinct. The question then becomes how is EMF's constant use of an unchanging subject to be aesthetically explained and justified? EMF's symbolical conception of art—as knowledge of a reality difficult to know—and his view of the novel as representing the daily, irreconcilable human experiences provide an answer. EMF is interested in the harmonious connection of ideological opposites rather than in the representation of historical truth. Italy or Cambridge or Germany are important then as terms of contrast. In spite of his emphasis on the dichotomies of experience, EMF does not exclude the possibility of one ideology being transformed into its opposite, but such a transformation mainly derives from elements that symbolize "passion" or "truth" rather than from those which connote "prose" or everyday "unreality." The final desired "proportion" is never reached because the fracture caused by such opposition always continues to exist. *A Room with a View* is the only EMF novel that ends "happily," yet the ending is only superficially happy. The symbolism in this first conceived novel is not resonant. The happy ending also is belied by the tragic, desolate conception of life clearly evidenced throughout the novel. The tragedy of EMF's characters lies, then, in their having to live a life governed entirely by Fate, or a destiny over which they can exert no control. In EMF's novels there is a lack of psychological development, an overabundance of tragic elements, and a particular way in which these elements are presented. Rather than representing defects in EMF's artistry, they demonstrate EMF's affinity with other decadent writers. EMF represents not motives but actions, not interior reasons but facts. His narrative manner, perfectly in accord with the sentimental and ideological premises which nurtured him, underlines the presence of tragedy in everyday life. This effect, too, harmonizes with the decadent valuation, according to which a drama does not exist so much for an individual but as a part of humanity. This is why EMF chooses, in order to narrate the human tragedy, a small segment of life as an example and symbol. While he describes all the particulars of social life in a traditional sense (births, marriages, deaths), these events are reduced to normal, even banal proportions while they assume symbolic meanings of great import. Reading *A Passage to India* is like rereading his earlier novels because so little has changed. What little change there has been is in the direction of greater professional knowledge and capacity, a greater control of his own expressive means, an artistic coherence never before reached. But this theme is still the same: a conflict between two worlds, this time, England and India. EMF's search as writer is again the same: for an ideal reality, an harmonic composition of ways of life that seem irreducibly opposed. In spite of its symbolic aspect, there is in *Passage* an unforgettable realistic dimension. EMF is a symbolist who limits the provenance of the external world but does not deny it. India and England are terms in a valid symbolic contrast at the same time that they are terms in a concrete, actual contrast. In this merging of abstraction and reality *Passage* achieves its artistic validity. Not only are EMF's characters symbolic, but so are objects and places (see the tree under which Rickie composes his stories in *Journey*, the "room with a view" in *Room*, the tree and house in *Howards End*, the Marabar Caves in *Passage*). EMF's mystical, even animistic, conception of nature is remarkable, and his symbolism transcends ordinary human experience to aspire toward poetry, mystery, passion, ecstasy, music. Because the symbolism of the Caves is essential for the narrative and because it is fused with the novel's realistic plot, *Passage* is the novel that has the greatest artistic coherence. EMF was silent as a novelist after *Passage* because his interior world was expressed with such clarity and force in *Passage* that had he written other novels, he would only have repeated himself. [Fadda's use of her terms is sometimes not clear, but she writes a sympathetic account. For review, see. H. W. Häuserman, "Besprechungen" (Reviews), ANGLIA, LXXX: 4 (1962), 478–79.] [In Italian.]

945 "First Play by an Indian on Broadway," AMERICAN REPORTER (U. S. Information Service, Delhi), XII (21 Feb 1962), 6.
[Information concerning inception, American production, and reception of Santha Rama Rau's adaptation of *A Passage to India*.]

946 Garnett, David. THE FAMILIAR FACES (Lond: Chatto & Windus, 1962; NY: Harcourt, Brace & World, 1963), pp. 110–12.
EMF had been first commissioned to edit a collection of T. E. Lawrence's letters; Garnett took over the project from EMF [see T. E. Lawrence (1938)]. [Garnett's autobiography from about 1924; see also THE GOLDEN ECHO (1953) and THE FLOWERS OF THE FOREST (1955). The autobiography is a primary document of great value for understanding EMF's Bloomsbury milieu.]

947 Gassner, John. "Broadway in Review," EDUCATIONAL THEATRE JOURNAL, XIV (May 1962), 169–77, espec 174–75.
The characters in Santha Rama Rau's adaptation of *A Passage to India* are in some cases given added dimensions of richness, but the rich novel becomes a thin, unresolved play. The need for dramatizing the subject of colonialism is still imperative.

948 Gilman, Richard. "Sows' Ears Out of Silk Purses," COMMONWEAL, LXXV (2 March 1962), 597–98.
Santha Rama Rau is too faithful to the story in *A Passage to India* to make her play a meaningful adaptation. She fails to integrate the theme of cultural differences with the suspense, violent effects, and the evocation of metaphysical mystery to be found in the novel.

949 Gransden, K. W. E. M. FORSTER (Edinburgh & Lond: Oliver & Boyd, Writers and Critics; NY: Grove P, Evergreen Pilot Books, 1962); rvd ed (Edinburgh & Lond: Oliver & Boyd, 1970); pp. 101–6, Chap 7, "India," rptd in PERSPECTIVES ON E. M. FORSTER'S "A PASSAGE TO INDIA," ed by V. A. Shahane (NY: Barnes & Noble, 1968), pp. 167–72.
Chap 1, "Introduction": [Summary of career; explores briefly the influences of Butler, Meredith, and Jane Austen on EMF.] Chap 2, "Exploration": Fantasy predominates in EMF's short stories and tends to be muted in the novels. EMF urges a dangerous view of reality rather than the conventional. "The Machine Stops" is the most tedious story that inculcates this view; "The Point of It" does not live up to its opening section; "The Road from Colonus" explores the theme at a more aesthetically subtle and satisfying level. "The Celestial Omnibus" is insipid but interesting in its attack on culture as artifice (and by implication, on Bloomsbury). "Other Kingdom" is EMF's best "faun piece"; it is irresistible but overlooks the deeper realities of classical culture. "The Eternal Moment" and *Where Angels Fear to Tread*, the first novel, both go from social comedy to a moment of climactic psychological intensity, and Miss Raby and Caroline Abbott achieve a similar kind of awareness and self-knowledge. In EMF's works passion can be great and sustaining even when it is not consummated or when it has to

be renounced. When the intellectual atones for his physical failures, he achieves his greatest insight into reality. Chap 3, "Italy": The "operatic" quality of the last part of *Angels* is impressive, especially the scene at the opera where heart and head are reconciled. EMF demonstrates in this novel that, when humanist values fail, death is likely to come in. There is a sharp contrast between the quiet ("tea-tabling") manner and the shocking events of the novel. Caroline Abbott is EMF's first "guardian" figure, a person who becomes the medium through which the truth is revealed to others; she is the most touching and surprising of these figures. Neither Philip Herriton nor Caroline will know physical satisfaction in love, but they are transformed by the force of unrequited or renounced love. As in *A Room with a View*, Italy measures the inadequacies of the English middle class. Italy confronts this class with direct experience; Italy counters indifference by insisting on love. In *Room*, Cecil Vyse, though enlightened intellectually, dwells in the dark. An "advanced" person, he belongs to the Middle Ages spiritually. The conventions against which EMF works as a moralist aid him as an artist. The Rev. Mr. Beebe becomes a figure of darkness, whereas Charlotte Bartlett becomes a figure of light. Mr. Emerson is not convincing; George Emerson is a pre-Lawrencian hero but does not come fully to life. Pagan elements are in the ascendancy; the kiss in the violet bank is, for example, a pagan ceremony. Chap 4, "Portrait of the Artist" [Excellent pioneering discussion of *The Longest Journey*.]: *Journey* is a romantic novel, the subject of which EMF sees from the inside; it is "a meditation on the dangers and attractions of romanticism, the more impressive and subtle in that it is itself romantically conceived and presented." *Journey* is epic in structure, symphonic in pattern, tragic in its implications. It is anti-domestic, friendship being valued more than marriage. Friendship results in freedom and the survival of the real self, marriage (especially with an unsuitable mate) results in slavery and the death of the authentic self. *Journey* traces the disintegration of a personality and is profoundly felt. Stewart Ansell (the intellect) and Stephen Wonham (the physical) come together to save Rickie Elliot's soul; in turn, Rickie achieves his posthumous salvation and place through Stephen. The rhetorical outburst when Ansell condemns Rickie at Sawston School for failing to acknowledge Stephen is symbolic and poetic, not realistic. EMF kills off living characters in the novel but brings dead ones to life. His mother's calling to Rickie in dreams is a kind of back-to-the-womb pattern; he expects too much from people, even from his mother who did not shrink from physical contact and passion. He does not grow up or adjust to reality, but the examples found in the grown-up world about him are disastrous. Sawston represents all that is wrong with England: bogus tradition, money-worship, the appeal to the herd instinct, prudishness.

Chap 5, "England" [Brilliant discussion of *Howards End.*]: Margaret Schlegel is EMF's most fully realized character. The novel is international as well as national in scope; the breakdown of liberal values is not only England's fate but Europe's. In the dialectic of the novel, the inner is ultimately more important than the outer, but the outer does matter; in fact, money is sometimes better as an inheritance than ideas (Leonard Bast's ideas would have been better if he had had money). Howards End house is a guardian agency along with Mrs. Wilcox and Miss Avery, who are most closely associated with it. The advancement in EMF's art is in his two central characters, Margaret Schlegel and Henry Wilcox. Howards End is important to Margaret, but she does not get there until late in the book. As for Ruth Wilcox she is shadowy, inarticulate, and self-effacing. Because, or in spite, of these qualities she is central. She identifies with Howards End as a home, in contrast to the nomadic Schlegels and Wilcoxes. In putting her sister before her husband, Margaret shows the primacy of personal relations. Leonard Bast is a good and interesting guess on EMF's part, an attempt at portraying the all-but-submerged. The Basts are the new slave class, without which the commercial technocracy could not flourish. The Wilcoxes represent the "head" in Edwardian society, the Schlegels its "heart," and Bast, in being a victim, its "conscience." Margaret finds Henry to be a manager in a managerial age and loves him for what he is not rather than for what he is. She wants to put down roots but he will not let her; however, he does finally give her some roots, and she gives him some sense of a need for them. The wrong sort of patriotism develops: the Wilcoxes want to exploit England, not love it, and the social results of their activity are undesirable. *Howards End* is a historical novel, since the premises of pre-war liberalism are no longer viable, and a prophetic novel, predicting, as it were, the demise of the society that it presents. Chap 6, "India" [Excellent discussion of *A Passage to India*, beginning with a consideration of the circumstances under which it was written.]: In *Passage*, the visionary element undermines the surface responses of the characters and their rationality. In this novel EMF contrasts a national India, based upon exclusiveness, and an international India, based upon the acceptance, and the power, of Hinduistic love. In the novel all details count, as they do in Hinduism itself. There is little mediation between cause and resultant chaos; Godbole and Mrs. Moore act as influences but not as controlling agents in confining chaos. The arrangement and structure are symphonic and musical; the novel is a series of echoes. Aziz represents India with all her faults and virtues, Godbole her ancient wisdom. Godbole and Mrs. Moore are guardian figures, although they do not communicate lucidly at Fielding's tea-party. India conquers Mrs. Moore by "negation, absence, vagueness." The Caves, in addition to the nothingness attached to them, bring into action the hidden, often unconscious, forces that control an individual and dramatize the effects of such forces upon him. The Caves reflect the unconscious fears and desires of those who enter them, and they hasten whatever is to come: Adela's spinsterhood, Mrs. Moore's death, Aziz's rejection of the British. Mrs. Moore, after the Marabar Caves, is humanity at its extreme moment of "inarticulate insight which immediately precedes death." For Godbole the incident in the Caves is unimportant in his long perspective; he sees beyond the temporal incident and the illusions of men to the Infinite. Despite her indifference, Mrs. Moore remains a force for good. At the trial, under the spell of Mrs. Moore, Adela Quested acts with courage but not with love in withdrawing her accusation against Aziz. Godbole's religion is inclusive, and his humility is in marked contrast with the pride revealed by the other characters. He reveals the dwarfing aspect of Hinduism, its vital truth, and the self-effacing quality in the love that it inculcates. The parting of Fielding and Aziz represents a fragmentation of what Hinduism would have wanted. The novel's pattern signifies the endless process of sundering and reconciliation in human experience; fragmentation may occur but a mystical sort of reunion is also possible. [In a paragraph added to the 1970 ed, Gransden stresses the darkness suffusing the novel, even through to the final pages.] Chap 7, "Afterwards": EMF will be remembered as a novelist rather than as essayist. [Gransden follows Trilling's begrudging estimate of the nonfiction and the criticism. Gransden is right, I think, in judging the introductory essays in *Two Cheers for Democracy* (under the rubric, "The Second Darkness") as EMF's best occasional writings.] EMF has had influence upon the writers of the 1930s (Auden, Spender, Isherwood) and upon some later novelists (Elizabeth Bowen, Angus Wilson, Iris Murdoch). [In "Postscript" to 1970 ed, Gransden celebrates EMF's tenacity, and also the tenacity with which the novels maintain their hold on readers.] [A most informed and enlightened summary of EMF's career, influence, and fiction, compressing much information and many fresh judgments into short compass. Select bibliography. Reviews: A. Alvarez (Entry No. 925); Bruce Arnold (Entry No. 926); Malcolm Bradbury, "Reviews and Comment," CRITICAL QUARTERLY, V (Spring 1963), 92–94; Ronald Bryden (Entry No. 936); H. H. Anniah Gowda, "Book Reviews," LITERARY HALF-YEARLY (Mysore), VI (Jan 1965), 93–94; E. Lacotte, "Étude Critique: Études Récentes sur E. M. Forster" (Critical Essay: Recent Studies on E. M. Forster), ÉTUDES ANGLAISES, XX (Oct–Dec 1967), 425–31; John Lehmann (Entry No. 967); "Lives and Works," TIMES (Lond), 12 April 1962, p. 19; Frederick P. W. McDowell, "The Newest Elucidations of Forster," ENGLISH FICTION IN TRANSITION, V: 4 (1962), 51–58; Piero Mandrillo (Entry No. 1129); "Only Connect . . ." (Entry No. 973); William Plomer (Entry No. 975); "Search for Connexion" (Entry No. 979); George H. Thomson (Entry No. 987); and Frederick T. Wood, "Current Literature," ENGLISH STUDIES, XLIV: 5 (1963), 392–93.]

950 Gurko, Leo. JOSEPH CONRAD: GIANT IN EXILE (NY: Macmillan, 1962), pp. 2, 4, 77, 248.

EMF's judgment in "Joseph Conrad: A Note" (*Abinger Harvest*) that a vapor rather than a jewel is in "the secret casket of his genius" is dubious; there is in the casket the jewel of a created universe. Joseph Conrad's inscrutability has been mistaken by critics, including EMF, for obscurity. The tentative nature of Conrad's values was easily misunderstood. EMF, who illustrates the predominant Western temper of the last century, typically believed in "the objective existence of a moral element in the universe" and so had difficulty understanding Conrad. [The last judgment ascribes too much absolutism to EMF's beliefs.]

> **951** Hale, Nancy. "The Novel and the Short Story: Differences," "The Novel: A Passage to Relationship," "Through the Dark Glass to Reality," THE REALITIES OF FICTION: A BOOK ABOUT WRITING (Boston: Little, Brown, 1962; Lond: Macmillan, 1963), pp. 28–47, espec 42–43; 67–84; 225–47, espec 236–39; also 153; rpts, considerably rvd, "A Passage to Relationship," (1960) as "The Novel: A Passage to Relationship."

EMF is skillful in rendering the transitions in "Mosque" (*A Passage to India*) as Aziz goes from Hamidullah, to Major Callendar's house, to the mosque. The novel progresses as opposed to the short story, and the writer must convey the feeling of life by revealing its various tempos, as EMF has done in *Passage*. A transition must serve many purposes, as EMF's does in "Mosque." EMF shows us how to balance values in fiction as he conjoins tea-table niceties to violent happenings. The machine in the story "The Machine Stops" is the mechanism of the imagination, of wish-fulfillment, and of escape from reality. The denizens within the earth are artists, critics, and others who believe that art is an end in itself for which the real world can be lost. There is no love in this interior civilization. Life and love are of greater worth than thought, in EMF's scale of values. [Interprets (dubiously) the civilization within the earth of "The Machine Stops" as the inner world of imagination.]

> **952** Hannah, Donald. "The Limitations of Liberalism in E. M. Forster's Work," ENGLISH MISCELLANY (Rome), No. 13 (1962), 165–78.

Howards End, in its pretensions and failures, indicates where the achievement of *A Passage to India* resides. The values apparently defined, substantiated, and integrated into *Howards End* are often only asserted. The characters and the plot are contrived, so that they cannot bear the importance attributed to them. EMF asserts that the Wilcoxes are indispensable to a revivified England, but his adverse criticism of them destroys his advocacy; and he praises the Schlegels excessively. The characters refuse to come alive and transcend the formulas they represent. The balancing of forces implies, wrongly, that opposed forces are equal in value. In *Passage* the issue is faced in all its magnitude and complexity. There is no simplification nor easy solution of the problem, nor indeed any solution. Mastery in style, a firm balancing of the comic and the tragic, and sureness of characterization prevail in *Passage*. EMF sees the shortcomings as well as the virtues of the liberal characters Fielding and Adela; and Mrs. Moore is a capricious old woman after the incident in the Caves, as well as a redemptive character. The Wilcoxes of *Howards End* have become the insensitive Anglo-Indians of *Passage*. The commentator is in the background, and contrivance is absent; the characters and events develop naturally and organically. "If the major defects of *Howards End* spring from an insufficient awareness of the limitations of liberalism, the greatness of *A Passage to India* originates from a clear perception of them." *Howards End* is important, however, as an inevitable stage in EMF's progress to the writing of *Passage*. [Exellent essay, although there are other facets to *Howards End* than the political and the social.]

> **953** Hewes, Henry. "Aspic of the Novel," SATURDAY REVIEW (NY), XLV (17 Feb 1962), 48.

The slow movement of *A Passage to India* and its atmosphere are reduced to action in Santha Rama Rau's stage version. The most vivid sections of the play are, however, incidental scenes which do not move it forward. Much more so than the novel, the play features the contrast between "an esthetic but weakened civilization and the practical but inhibited people who govern it."

> **954** Hollingsworth, Keith. "*A Passage to India:* The Echoes in the Marabar Caves," CRITICISM, IV (Summer 1962), 210–24; rptd in PERSPECTIVES ON E. M. FORSTER'S "A PASSAGE TO INDIA," ed by V. A. Shahane (NY: Barnes & Noble, 1968), pp. 36–50.

A Passage to India has for its theme the need for communication. Appropriately, a central symbol is the echo, which is a mockery of communication. The echo image occurs several times before the visit to the Caves: when Adela Quested finds herself trying to surmount "the echoing walls" of the Indians' civility, when Mrs. Moore sees arch beyond arch and is conscious of a silence beyond the remotest echo, when Ronny Heaslop's angry calling of his servant named Krishna creates echoes, when Godbole's invocation to Krishna in his song produces no echo, when Aziz (showing Fielding a picture of his dead wife) removes her from the barrier of purdah and says that she would have found the contemporary world bewildering—or echoing. Mrs. Moore's disillusion is prepared for by her physical fatigue, indifference, and lassitude on the train to the Caves. After the experience in the Caves, human love and divine love both become meaningless for her; she becomes selfish, weary, and cynical. Everything changes for her, except her sibylline aspect and her belief in Aziz's innocence. When "the undying worm" speaks to her, this is presumably "unrelenting death." [Perhaps an oversimplified interpretation because the serpent may be a symbol of both life and death; see George H. Thomson, "A Note on the Snake Imagery of *A Passage to India*" (1966)]. Before she leaves India "the twilight of the double vision" is opposed by the double view which she has of graceful Asirgarh, promising a more positive (or ambiguous) vision of the ultimate. Her original pronouncement that God is love is reasserted in other circumstances at Mau. For Adela also the Caves represent "communication stopped and love denied." Her situation is ironic: the woman who loves the truth makes a false accusation; the person who most wanted to meet and know India causes greater division than any actions of the unsympathetic Turtons and Burtons. The echo is in her case realistic (a part of her neurotic disturbance), as well as symbolic. Mrs. Moore is disillusioned with speech and marriage—two ways of establishing relationships. Adela recovers a temporarily displaced honesty and intelligence; she is through with love but wants others to want it. The Caves are aligned with Western culture and its rationalism; the allegory is concerned with the contrast between Western order and Indian spirit. The West has worshipped science since the Renaissance, and science and technology have given it a peculiar focus. Human curiosity may open up more caves, but such activity does not add to good or evil: the echo is what people find when they look to science for the meaning of life. Mrs. Moore is the Western religious believer who, in the midst of a rationalistic, scientific culture, poses ultimate questions about values; the echo is the empty answer that is returned. With Christian meaning lost as a result of the pretensions of science, the will to live is also lost. Godbole does not mention the echo, for Hindu culture is not faced with the same problem as the Western. Loss of belief, the sinister echo as reality is foreign to the Hindu views of life since Hinduism sees matter not separately as does Western science, but as "part of a single continuum of existence." Adela's English rationalism is also inadequate to the challenge of the echo. She is not religious, however, and is not so fundamentally affected by the Caves as is Mrs. Moore. Adela has been led astray by the new schools of psychology, which stress the divisions in personality and its irrational elements. As a result of going to the Caves she loses faith in the wholeness of personality and in the conscious mind, also in the reality and nobility of love. The self is as much an illusion as Christianity. Her approach to the Caves is marked by "illusion": no one knows what the mounds signify, and the snake is or is not a snake depending on the angle of vision. The snake is also a symbol of her sexual fixation in the Caves, which causes her to believe that she has been assaulted. The binoculars, a symbol of her rational intelligence, are torn from her. Fielding finds that the echo is "evil." The echo is at least modern; there is no stopping it (i.e., the mechanistic forces controlling modern civilization). If the Indians adopt Western modes and values, the disintegration of their society will be accentuated. The women

417

are the ones most drastically affected by the Caves because they have more recently become participants in the intellectual concerns that had formerly been the provenance of men. (They seem more vulnerable to the disillusionment caused by science.) The disquieting reverberations in the "Cave-wombs" accord with a modern disillusion that denies love and with a tendency in our age toward sterility, both spiritual and physical. But a resurgent hope animates "Temple" and the motto "God si love" demonstrates the triumph of the spirit over the letter. [Many insights of value, though I question whether the Caves can be so conclusively identified with rationalism and the spiritually desolating effects of science. Glen O. Allen in "Structure, Symbol, and Theme in E. M. Forster's *A Passage to India*" (1955) interprets them in the same way. The Caves more convincingly embody a terrifying irrationality, I think.]

955 Hoy, Cyrus. "Book Reviews," AUMLA (Australian University Modern Language Association), No. 17 (May 1962), 117–19.

Certain failures in EMF's imagination (his inadequate characterization of the hero in *A Room with a View* and *The Longest Journey;* his lapses into the artificial, when he laments Leonard Bast's loss of his bucolic heritage, for instance; the contrived famous ending of *Howards End;* his failure in depicting love; and his substitution of abstractions, like Margaret Schlegel's ideal of companionship, for a real emotion) are outweighed by his distinctive virtues as an artist (his ability to dramatize man's inability to bridge dichotomies [body and soul, the public and the private] in an age widening the gulf between them; his reinterpretation of romanticist values; his combating inhumanity, especially the "inhumanity of the pernicious kind which man inflicts upon himself by denying a part of his nature"; and the open-endedness of his novels.) [Stimulating remarks in a review of H. J. Oliver's THE ART OF E. M. FORSTER (1960).]

956 Humphreys, A. R. MELVILLE (Edinburgh & Lond: Oliver & Boyd, Writers and Critics; NY: Grove P, Evergreen Pilot Books, 1962), pp. 113–14.

EMF has said the best things yet on BILLY BUDD.

957 Jarvis, William. "Reintroducing *A Passage to India,*" SUNDAY STATESMAN (Calcutta and Delhi), 4 Feb 1962, "Magazine," p. 1.

EMF held that Syed Ross Masood transformed his conception of India; there is something of Masood in Aziz of *A Passage to India.* [Describes EMF's three visits to India. Discusses the essays on India in *Abinger Harvest* and the geographical locations in the novel as EMF gives them in his notes to the Everyman Edition of *Passage* (1942).]

958 Jeffares, A. Norman. "Foreword," E. M. FORSTER: A REAS-
SESSMENT, by V. A. Shahane (Delhi, Kitab Mahal, Masters of English Literature Series, 1962; Lond: A Probsthain, 1964), p. v.
In his work, EMF makes moral and courageous comments on many of the
ethical and aesthetic issues confronting modern man. His art is important
as it asks searching questions about the purposes of life and civilization; in
so doing, EMF often affirms both.

959 Kaiser, Rudolf. "E. M. Forster: Gedankliche Analyze seines
Romanes Howards End im Rahmen des Gesamtwerkes" (E. M.
Forster: Thorough Analysis of His Novel *Howards End* in the
Setting of His Total Work), DIE NEUREN SPRACHEN (Frankfurt am-
Main), XI (Aug 1962), 341–63.
Although little known in Germany, EMF is of interest to Germans for the
parallel natures he assigns to the Germans and the English (especially in
Margaret Schlegel, whose ancestry is part German, and Ruth Wilcox, who
derives from English yeoman stock). Although *A Passage to India* is agreed
to be the high point of EMF's work and is more complex than *Howards
End*, it is not so philosophical as the earlier novel. The problem of *Passage*
is the practicality of close friendship in view of racial differences. The
common problem of EMF's first four novels is resolved in *Howards End*:
the opposition between the "outer" life of appearances and the "inner" life
of spiritual truthfulness. The characters in *Where Angels Fear to Tread* and
A Room with a View illustrate either provincial conventions or spontaneous
feeling. In *The Longest Journey*, EMF expresses for the first time his love
of England. Stephen Wonham, a "natural man," is a spiritual brother of
Gino Carella in *Angels* and a forerunner of Ruth Wilcox in *Howards End*.
It is strange that the intellectual and ironic EMF, who to some readers
seems overly philosophical and not spontaneous enough, should produce
two children of nature like Gino and Stephen. In the first three novels there
is no alternative to the conflict between outer and inner but only the rejection of the former for the latter. In *Howards End*, the active life is not
rejected but grounded on an inner life. Unlike *Angels* and *Room*, *Howards
End* depends upon no narrow relationship, by study and travel, with the
older cultures of Italy and Greece. The Schlegels represent a German type
common about 1860, the type of person imbued with German idealism. It
is on this idealistic basis of much German poetry and thought that the
Schlegels' respect for the inner life is founded. In *Howards End*, the Wilcoxes represent those who have made England powerful, and the Schlegels,
those who can see the whole island of England at once. By observing his
motto, "concentrate" (for five minutes at a time), Henry Wilcox has become
an obtuse burger who sees the world with only a half-open eye; he has no
regard for the inner life or for personal relations. For him love means only

the preparations for a marriage, and death, inheritance. He cannot connect the prose of life with its passion. Helen Schlegel sees things as they ought to be, she disapproves of the Wilcoxes, and she is less stable as a result of her insistent idealism. Margaret sees things as they are, she finds character or "grit" in the Wilcoxes, and she admits that their active life has made possible the contemplative life for others. By the end of the novel Ruth Wilcox's spirit has a pantheistic, universal dimension. Her influence and that of her house and landscape upon Margaret represent mystical powers, a mystical or even mythic reality behind things. Although the foreground of his novels would make EMF an intellectual realist, the deepest aspect of his work lies in its mystical or mythic background or implications and in its romantically envisioned symbols. EMF finds a mythic reality not only at Howards End house, but also in an Italian theater (*Angels*), a male bathing scene (*Room*), a night on the downs (conclusion to *Journey*), in the Marabar Caves (*Passage*), and in the Mau tank boat collision and the immersion of the characters during the Shri Krishna festival (*Passage*). EMF is a Greek, a humanist in the modern age. Reminiscent of the Greek ideal of harmony is his view in *Howards End* that the connection of inner and outer lives can be achieved by "proportion," by a testing of the contrasting sides of life. Howards End is a symbol of peace, concord, understanding, and reconciliation. *Howards End* is more a critical philosophical discussion than a novel and is freighted with ideas. [Sound though not arresting discussion.] [In German.]

960 Karl, Frederick R. A READER'S GUIDE TO THE CONTEMPORARY ENGLISH NOVEL (NY: Noonday P, 1962; Lond: Thames & Hudson, 1963), pp. 6, 11, 18, 86, 109, 111, 195, 272; 2nd ed (NY: Farrar, Straus & Giroux, 1972), additional reference, p. 362.

Not many of EMF's successors were so optimistic as he about survival through "connecting." Along with their predecessors (Thackeray, Meredith, and George Eliot), EMF, Conrad, Joyce, Lawrence, and Virginia Woolf helped bring about the demise of the romantic hero. EMF, with his emphasis on the contradictions and odds and ends of human behavior, played down such a hero. The scientist Rock in Henry Green's CONCLUDING recalls Mr. Emerson of *A Room with a View* by his strong knowledge of what life is. In THE PICNIC AT SAKKARA, P. H. Newby combines the social ideas of EMF and Evelyn Waugh's sense of confusion. In Anthony Burgess's THE LONG DAY WANES, Victor Crabbe is "fumbling and decent," but lacks Fielding's stature in *A Passage to India.*

961 Kerr, Walter. "First Night Report: *A Passage to India*," NEW YORK HERALD TRIBUNE, 1 Feb 1962, p. 10.

Santha Rama Rau in her adaptation of *A Passage to India* has accomplished the difficult feat of talking about the mystery of India and dramatizing the mystery of character. Zia Mohyeddin admirably captures the "perilous balance between pride and open-heartedness" in Aziz's character. The unexpected develops in Aziz's vindictiveness after the trial. Adela Quested and Mrs. Moore reveal similar depths and complexities. Miss Rau has been adept in drawing her characters, yet the experience as theater is not altogether satisfying, since she seems reluctant to move forward in the play. Other characters are thinly drawn, notably the Anglo-Indian officials. The attempt to be complex and oblique detracts from the force and tension of the situation. In the play we pursue "several provocative portraits across attenuated terrain." [Excellent discussion.]

962 Khan, I. Y., and A. Q. Khan. CRITICAL GUIDE TO "A PASSAGE TO INDIA" (E. M. FORSTER) (Malipura, Ujjain: Gupta Prakashan, 1962).
[Extensive summary of *A Passage to India* and leading features of the characters, its background, and its themes. The account is descriptive rather than critical but is of interest as it reflects the Indian attitude toward the novel.]

963 Killham, John. "PICKWICK, Dickens and the Art of Fiction," DICKENS AND THE TWENTIETH CENTURY, ed by John Gross and Gabriel Pearson (Lond: Routledge & Kegan Paul; Toronto: University of Toronto P, 1962), pp. 49–64.
Lady Dedlock in BLEAK HOUSE lacks representative importance, as EMF contends in *Aspects of the Novel.* The story is basic in fiction rather than plot, and Dickens's narrative art is skilled (contrary to EMF's view). Pickwick as a flat character is not necessarily inferior aesthetically to the round characters that EMF prefers. Pickwick is different and functions admirably within the narrative, and he is also distinctive by being an end in himself, embodying qualities that Dickens admires.

964 "A Language in Common—VII: Colour and Local Colour in the English Novel," TIMES LITERARY SUPPLEMENT (Lond), 10 Aug 1962, p. 598.
EMF is superior in his rendition of India to the insular Kipling because of the sharpness of his characterizations and his ability to portray Indians without condemnation or flattery. His sympathy and universality make him as accessible to Indian as to English writers. Joyce Cary and Graham Greene also have his range of insight into their native characters, and they are also non-insular. Nevertheless, there are aspects of milieu that only native writers can fully elucidate.

965 Lawrence, A. W. (ed). LETTERS TO T. E. LAWRENCE (Lond: Jonathan Cape, 1962), p. 140.
Frederic Manning to Lawrence (12 Jan 1931), EMF's praise of SCENES AND

PORTRAITS (by Manning; rvd ed, 1930), is welcome. EMF's work, point of view, and way of writing have always been impressive. He has individuality. [EMF's letters to Lawrence ptd pp. 58–75.]

966 Lawrence, D. H. THE COLLECTED LETTERS OF D. H. LAW-RENCE, ed by Harry T. Moore (NY: Viking P; Lond: Heinemann, 1962), I, 315, 316–19, 323; II, 716, 799, 800, 811, 1024, 1122–24. [Rpts letters from THE LETTERS OF D. H. LAWRENCE, ed by Aldous Huxley (1932) except for postcard to EMF, Summer 1924. Rpts letter to Bertrand Russell (12 Feb 1915) in D. H. LAWRENCE'S LETTERS TO BERTRAND RUSSELL, ed by Harry T. Moore (1948). Letters that follow are new in this collection. Letter to Barbara Low (? 11 Feb 1915), Wonders if "grip" has gone out of EMF and gets a sense of "acute misery" from him, "the acute, exquisite pain of cramp." Lawrence may have been imbued by EMF with this feeling. They talked (apparently to little purpose) about a "revolution." Letter to Mary Cannan (24 Feb 1915) complains that EMF "is dying of inanition." EMF is angry when Lawrence tells him about himself (EMF). Letter to Carlo Linati (8 Aug 1924) calls EMF "about the best of my contemporaries in England." Letter to S. S. Koteliansky (22 Nov 1927) asserts that EMF has become a "piffler" now and that *The Celestial Omnibus* is "rather rubbish." (This letter rptd in THE QUEST FOR RANANIM: D. H. LAWRENCE'S LETTERS TO S. S. KOTELIANSKY 1914 TO 1930, ed by George J. Zytaruk (Montreal & Lond: McGill-Queen's UP, 1970), pp. 330–31.)]

967 Lehmann, John. "E. M. Forster: A Refusal to Be Great?" LONDON MAGAZINE, nsII (Oct 1962), 74–78.
EMF retains hold on our imaginations despite his limited output and the wish in some quarters to bury him. His books reveal the causes for his survival: the subtlety of his craftsmanship and the depth of his convictions as poet-philosopher. His masterpieces are *Howards End* and *A Passage to India* "because they are so full of marvels of organization, character drawing, ironic comedy, philosophic wisdom and poetic vibration"; and they impress us more strongly the oftener we read them. *Howards End* has a universal aspect, as it is concerned with the influence of the traditional pieties and with the need to connect. *Passage* is universal because it drama-tizes a central situation of the modern age: what are we to do when our meaningful activities are brought up against a void? EMF has not fallen silent after *Passage*, but he has continued to show the strength of his moral commitment in *Two Cheers for Democracy*, especially. *Two Cheers* reveals "the quiet voice of the philosopher, gently engaging in tone but penetrating and ruthless in judgement." He has not refused to be great, actually, but "has chosen to be great in the only way that matters." [Review-essay on K. W. Gransden's E. M. FORSTER (1962) and J. B. Beer's THE ACHIEVEMENT OF E. M. FORSTER (1962). A most perceptive critique.]

968 McCarten, John. "India: 1920," NEW YORKER, XXXVII (10 Feb 1962), 94–95.

Santha Rama Rau in her adaptation of *A Passage to India* conveys the tone, style, wit, and wisdom of EMF's novel, but there is lack of decisive action.

969 Macaulay, Rose. LAST LETTERS TO A FRIEND FROM ROSE MACAULAY 1952–1958, ed by Constance Babington-Smith (Lond: Collins, 1962; NY: Athenaeum, 1963), pp. 18, 142–43, 211, 237.

Letter (31 Jan 1954), EMF and Virginia Woolf would never have retained Christianity when they became adult; all of EMF's principles and most of his actions are Christian in a moral sense, but he could never accept Christianity with his intellect. Letter (18 Nov 1955), [EMF's opinions of Billy Graham who recently visited Cambridge.] Current religious revival at Cambridge is little to EMF's liking. EMF thinks that Graham is "a nice, simple, friendly person, not 'civilised,' but 'a good type' " and that he was nicer and more tolerant than the members of the Cambridge Inter-Collegiate Christian Union.

970 Millgate, Michael. "Scott Fitzgerald as Social Novelist: Statement and Technique in THE GREAT GATSBY," MODERN LANGUAGE REVIEW, LVII (July 1962), 335–39.

EMF's description in *Howards End* of the tide in Poole Harbor (end of Chap 19) is comparable to the last four paragraphs of THE GREAT GATSBY in imagery, use of symbols, display of rhetoric, and feeling for one's native land. Each novelist is concerned with the conflict between the outer life and the inner life, between those who feel and those who do not. The resolution and reconciliation in *Howards End* are not completely satisfying; in GATSBY the circular movement of the novel obviates this dissatisfaction, but the expansion of Gatsby's story into a parable of human fate is inadequately prepared for.

971 Moseley, Edwin M. "Christ as One Avatar: Forster's *Passage to India*," PSEUDONYMS OF CHRIST IN THE MODERN NOVEL: MOTIFS AND METHODS (Pittsburgh: University of Pittsburgh P, 1962), pp. 153–63.

Mrs. Moore is a goddess-ideal in each of three sections of *A Passage to India:* in "Mosque" she is the goddess of love found in all religions; in "Caves" she becomes "the voice of the absolute nothingness of creation," and in "Temple" she is resurrected in the rainy season following the heat of "Caves" and enters the consciousness of the Brahman Godbole when he is participating in the Shri Krishna rites (Krishna is the preserver of Indian religion, in contrast to Brahma the Creator and Siva the Destroyer). In that Krishna is correlative to Christ in his life and influence, the identification of Mrs. Moore with Krishna through Godbole suggests that she has undergone resurrection. She is more pointedly Kali, the Mother Goddess of India. Mrs. Moore's death when people most need her is less a comment on her than on the society that has produced people who are unresponsive to what she represents. In *Passage* Mrs. Moore has potentialities for the healing of mankind, but she does not quite fulfill them, though EMF wishes that she had been able to do so (as Margaret Schlegel is able to do in *Howards End*). Though the resurrected god is not completely effective, yet EMF in *Passage* and Faulkner in LIGHT IN AUGUST would agree that Christ-Krishna is a "spring-god," all too often forgotten by Calvinists in their emphasis on abnegation. EMF is more pessimistic than Faulkner in his suspicion not only of "group action for social ends" (e.g., Fielding) but of the individual and the attainment of justice for him.

972 Mukherjee, Sujit. "Forster's Passage to Broadway," SUNDAY STATESMAN (Calcutta and Delhi), "Magazine," 11 March 1962, p. 11.

Santha Rama Rau's adaptation of *A Passage to India* has had much success in the theater. The acting of Zia Mohyeddin (Aziz) and Sayeed Jeffri (Godbole) is perhaps responsible. The adaptation oversimplifies the novel: the first act is the only fully convincing one. The Marabar Caves do not seem formidable, and the characters are so foreshortened as to be distortions of those in the novel.

973 "Only Connect . . ." ECONOMIST (Lond), CCIV (21 July 1962), 226.

EMF is both accessible and relevant to us; his Edwardian subject matter allows us to see him in perspective. Structure in his novels is dense. His "moral lessons" are sustained by a series of interconnections, symbols, and references; and they benefit by critical exegesis. Frederick C. Crews is mistaken to grade the novels by importance of theme and to downgrade *A Room with a View* because it is pure comedy. If EMF is dated, it is because many of his ideas have helped form our minds. [Remarks are part of review of K. W. Gransden's E. M. FORSTER, (1962), J. B. Beer's THE ACHIEVEMENT OF E. M. FORSTER (1962), and Frederick C. Crews's E. M. FORSTER: THE PERILS OF HUMANISM (1962).]

974 Phelps, Gilbert. A SURVEY OF ENGLISH LITERATURE: SOME OF THE MAIN THEMES AND DEVELOPMENTS FROM BEOWULF TO 1939 (Lond: Pan Books, 1962), pp. 341, 343, 344–47, 351, 352.

Martin Decoud's vision of nothingness in the Placid Gulf in Joseph Conrad's NOSTROMO connects with Mrs. Moore's mystical but negative experience in the Marabar Caves in *A Passage to India.* In EMF's books, violence, cruelty, accidents, and hatred are "the expression of despair in the presence of a void that has neither meaning nor hope." In part the despair derives from the realization that man is heading for world war; in part it is a response to the uneasiness experienced by megalopolitan man. Against the forces of external violence, cruelty, internal skepticism, and nihilism, EMF asserts values similar to those of Conrad. Both writers are anxious that man express fidelity to his best impulses in a world that is governed by conventional standards which, under a civilized veneer, are heartless and materialistic. In EMF's work Greece and Italy represent a more spontaneous mode of life than does middle-class England. In *Howards End,* issues are not altogether clear-cut; the Schlegels are guilty of lapses in understanding, and the Wilcoxes claim compassion. The theme of connection is most beautifully represented in *Passage.* EMF's characters do not struggle heroically, but the values that emerge from his novels are tough and uncompromising. He returns to an older tradition in the English novel represented by Jane Austen, despite his modernity in some aspects. He admired Hardy and was influenced by Samuel Butler and George Moore. He is not Jamesean since he does not exclude the omniscient narrator. [Scattered references also to EMF's views on Conrad and Arnold Bennett. Short but fresh account.]

975 Plomer, William. "The Listener's Book Chronicle," LISTENER, LXVII (26 April 1962), 740.
There is something "wizardish" in EMF; he also has had staying power. He is more multifaceted than he is sometimes seen to be. The impact of his books to a generation "half suffocated by the jingoistic smugness of Victorian-Edwardian accepted ideas" was revolutionary. His views were as unacceptable to the die-hards then as they apparently now are to the newest intransigents. [Remarks are part of review of K. W. Gransden's E. M. FORSTER (1962).]

976 Rama Rau, Santha. ["Introduction"], "Indian Entries from a Diary," by E. M. Forster, HARPER'S MAGAZINE, CCXXIV (Feb 1962), 46–47. [British publication of "Indian Entries" (ENCOUNTER, XVIII, [Jan 1962], 20–27) lacks this intro.]
A Passage to India was a shock when it came out to both British and Indians (for the Indians it was a shock to find a writer who understood them so well). The entries from EMF's diary printed herewith formed the raw material for *Passage.* EMF sketches well in the diary the feel of the progress by boat through the Mediterranean toward India and the new-formed impressions he first received of India itself. In these notes figure the people (Syed Ross Masood, the model for Aziz, for instance), the places, and the events that were to be transformed in *Passage.*

977 Rama Rau, Santha. "A Passage to Broadway," THEATRE ARTS, XLVI (Feb 1962), 66–67, 75.
A Passage to India means much because in it EMF for the first time

presented real Indians acting in Indian ways and "thinking as Indians in their own society and philosophy." The novel poses the question: how is it possible to be intimate with a "lesser" race when the real questions about the situation are not understood? [Details given of writing and producing the play in England and New York.] EMF liked the play though it took five years to get produced. [She was glad to refuse movie rights for the novel, to know that EMF was someone who could not be bought.]

978 Rodrigues, E. L. "Towards an Understanding of E. M. Forster," JOURNAL OF THE MAHARAJA SAVAJIRAO (University of Baroda), XI: 1 (1962), 91–105.

One source of EMF's art is revealed in *Goldsworthy Lowes Dickinson.* EMF saw in Dickinson a disillusioned idealist. The other source of EMF's art derives from his interest in personal relations and in the workings of the intelligence as such. *Howards End* is a bit manipulated with respect to theme; in the earlier novels, in which the themes had been simpler, this objection is less pronounced. In *Howards End* the problems set forth, especially in the Wilcoxes with their aggressive materialism and its effects on England, are not solved. Helen Schlegel's belief that Love is superior to Death forms much of the thematic context of *A Passage to India.* EMF is at least intellectually interested in Hinduism. [Rodrigues is dissatisfied with the resolution in *Passage* and is a "Temple" decrier.] "Temple" is not strong enough in its effects to counteract the evil let loose in "Caves." The exorcizing of evil is not embodied in the plot: Mrs. Moore is too shadowy and insignificant, the festival too far from the story to be effective. [The essay is pedestrian and over-relaxed.]

979 "Search for Connexion," TIMES LITERARY SUPPLEMENT (Lond), 22 June 1962, p. 460.

EMF is empiric and eclectic in outlook, but he also desires essence. He is aware, moreover, of the greatness and incompleteness of life. As a result he desires connection, though he knows the achievement of it is improbable; the result is that his novels, except *A Room with a View*, do not end happily. This cast of mind explains the alternation of lyricism and comedy, mysticism and irony, vision and realism, grandeur and deflation in his work. His lack of intellectual robustness may be due to his being brought up in a household of women and being given a legacy by Marianne Thornton. In considering his work, the critic ought to acknowledge the limitations of Cambridge for EMF, as well as its importance. The influence of G. E. Moore upon EMF is also not recognized enough. *A Passage to India* is "an impression and not an argument." There is no solution to the problems it broaches; its tentative solution is aesthetic primarily [questionable]. [This review-essay on J. B. Beer's THE ACHIEVEMENT OF E. M. FORSTER (1962) and K. W. Gransden's E. M. FORSTER (1962) is provocative.]

980 Seymour, William Kean. "Reputations and Opinions," CON-TEMPORARY REVIEW, CCII (Sept 1962), 159–60.

EMF is an unassuming master of the novel, using conversation to achieve a sense of reality and of inner vision. His faintly romantic characters, depicted with humor and ironic compassion, are examples of his "creative certainty." [Remarks are part of review of J. B. Beer's THE ACHIEVEMENT OF E. M. FORSTER (1962) and other books on literature.]

981 Shahane, V. A. E. M. FORSTER: A REASSESSMENT (Delhi: Kitab Mahal, Masters of English Literature Series, 1962; Lond: A Probs-thain, 1964), with "Foreword" by A. Norman Jeffares (Entry No. 958); rvd from "A Study of the Works of Edward Morgan Forster with Special Reference to his Place in the Tradition of the English Novel," unpublished dissertation, Leeds University (1959); Chap 5, "*A Passage to India*," rptd in part as "Symbolism in E. M. Forster's *A Passage to India:* 'Temple,'" ENGLISH STUDIES (Amsterdam), XLIV (Dec 1963), 423–31 and in PERSPECTIVES ON E. M. FORSTER'S "A PASSAGE TO INDIA," ed by V. A. Shahane (NY: Barnes & Noble, 1968), pp. 143–50.

Chap 1, "Introductory": [Fragmented sketch of EMF's career and present reputation.] Chap 2, "Forster's Credo": [Superficial sketch of EMF's mind and attitudes, with attention given to "What I Believe" (*Two Cheers for Democracy*), to EMF's enthusiasms for music and athleticism (the latter emanating from his love of Greece and the Greek classics), and to his preoccupation with death.] Chap 3, "Forster's Short Stories: A Search for Themes": EMF's short stories explore the contrast between "the life of imagination" and "practical hardheadedness." The stories anticipate the themes and situations of the novels. Chap 4: "Forster's Novels: The Pre-War Phase": [Sketchy treatment of *Where Angels Fear to Tread*. Commends the symbolic aptness of the baby-washing scene, stresses the duality in Gino Carella, and is severely critical of Philip Herriton's lack of feeling.] In *The Longest Journey* the narrative does not keep pace with shifts in meaning of the symbols and ideas. *Journey* has intensity of expression and lyrical passion. Rickie Elliot's forgetting to come for the Pembrokes at the Cambridge station reveals how his subconscious mind is more trustworthy than his conscious mind. [Shahane overstresses Rickie's "perverted imagination" and his inheritance of evil qualities from the Elliots.] There is constant use of symbolic imagery having to do with rivers, streams, and chalk. Robert is unduly idealized, while Stephen Wonham lacks the symbolic power of Giles Winterborne in Hardy's THE WOODLANDERS. [Routine discussion of *A Room with a View.*] [Discussion of *Howards End* is more full though still too much tied to opinions of other critics, to summaries of plot and situation, and to character sketches.] The schism between the Schlegel sisters in *Howards End* leads to the dramatic action. Ruth Wilcox epitomizes the intuitive order of the past; Margaret, the realm of intelligence. Margaret is a mediating character, moving from involvement with the incorporeal to an embracing of the corporeal. [James McConkey (1957) more convincingly sees a contrary movement.] Both Schlegels and Wilcoxes suffer from sexual deficiencies. The marriage of Margaret to Henry Wilcox is unbelievable, as is the affair between Helen Schlegel and Leonard Bast (whose death is contrived and whose character is unreal). [Routine discussion of symbols.] Margaret's high valuation of the Wilcoxes is similar to the sensitive Jolyon Forsyte's valuation of the Forsytes in Galsworthy's THE FORSYTE SAGA: Jolyon is appalled by their materialism but recognizes that their wealth is an indispensable substratum for the higher life of culture. Chap 5: "A Passage to India": In Passage the theme of fusion and fission predominates. [Shahane here borrows from Gertrude White (1951).] The Caves represent evil and negativity, nothingness and illusion; their influence and their echoes cannot be contained by Mrs. Moore's poetic intuition and by Adela Quested's arid intellectualism. Three aspects of "Temple" support the view that Passage is symbolic: (1) Godbole's role in the Shri Krishna festival, (2) the meeting of Fielding and Aziz near the Temple of the Shrine, and (3) the boating episode in the Mau tank. EMF in "Temple" stresses harmony and reconciliation, and it is Godbole's role to abet this process. Fielding, and especially Aziz, suffer from false preconceptions (they have paid too much attention to the "head") and are ultimately liberated from them by Godbole and Mrs. Moore—in her spiritual presence and through the influence of her children, Ralph and Stella. Fielding is drawn closer to his wife Stella as a result of their experiences in India. The novel is not defeatist; EMF's symbols reveal his ideas on what life ought to be, whereas his moral realism lets him see that that reconciliation is transient. But possibilities for transcendence do exist. The characters are inadequate. [Follows uncritically Lionel Trilling's questionable premise.] Chap 6, "Forster's Prose: Essays, Biography and Criticism" [Uncritically follows Trilling in denigrating EMF as writer of nonfiction]: In Aspects of the Novel EMF's critical terms lack originality and exactness [a pompous misjudgment in my view]. [The three biographies written by EMF are then summarized: Goldsworthy Lowes Dickinson, The Hill of Devi, and Marianne Thornton.] Chap 7, "Conclusions": EMF is a minor writer. [The bromide that he refuses to be great is cited.] [Bibliography. Discussions tend to be summary and superficial. Shahane quotes ad nauseam from secondary sources. It is not always clear to what extent he agrees with his authorities or to what use he is putting them. His discourse lacks consecutiveness, logic, and clear development. Occasional insights of value come through, especially in the discussions of Howards End and Passage, but there are not enough of them.]

982 Shahane, V. A. "A Note on the Marabar Caves in E. M. Forster's *A Passage to India*," OSMANIA JOURNAL OF ENGLISH STUD-

IES (Osmania University, Hyderabad), No. 2 (1962), 67–75; slightly rvd as "The Marabar Caves: Fact and Fiction," AMERICAN NOTES AND QUERIES, V (Sept, Oct, Nov, Dec, 1966), 3–4, 20–21, 36–37, 54–55.

[Discusses the Marabar Caves in *A Passage to India* in relation to their originals in the Barabar Caves.] EMF dates the Caves further back than do his chief authorities, but he agrees with them as to the heightened internal polish of the cave walls. He denies in *Passage* the associations the Barabar Caves have had in actuality with Buddhism and Hinduism. EMF's description of the Kawadol Cave agrees with that of travelers and archeologists. [Some of this material, from a different point of view, will be found in Sujit Mukherjee's "The Marabar Mystery: An Addition to the Case-Book on the Caves" (1966) and Wilfred Stone's THE CAVE AND THE MOUNTAIN (1966).] The Caves are "the voice of negation and nullity, chaos and primeval darkness." Adela Quested recoils from the thought of a union with Ronny Heaslop, lacking love for him; this idea of a union by force and fear causes her to recoil from the hostile rock out of which the cave is made, and this revulsion impels her to level her charge of rape against Aziz. She is released from muddle when she becomes aware of her irrational revulsion from the hostile rock and when she sees the malicious effect upon her own mind of her charge of attempted rape.

983 Simon, John. "Play Reviews: *A Passage to India*," THEATRE ARTS, XLVI (April 1962), 57–58; rptd as "Novels into Plays: *A Passage to India*, THE ASPERN PAPERS," ACID TEST (NY: Stein & Day, 1963), pp. 89–93.

Santha Rama Rau in her adaptation of *A Passage to India* fails to understand the novel. She is concerned with externals, especially political aspects, whereas *Passage* is primarily about other things: (1) the ambivalence and ambiguity of all human relations, and the misunderstandings which arise with others; (2) the supreme importance of the Marabar Caves; (3) the "helpless" relativity and mutability of the human condition, expressed by EMF in his pervasive irony; (4) the passages of poetry and profound insight in which the author speaks to us directly. The adaptation is literal and slack.

984 Spender, Stephen. "Two Landscapes of the Novel," THE MAKING OF A POEM (NY: Norton, 1962), pp. 73–94.

The two landscapes are the objectively rendered nineteenth century and the subjectively oriented twentieth century. The latter stresses the sensibility of the novelist. The writers to whom we ought to feel most grateful are those like EMF and D. H. Lawrence who connect the outer with the inner, who direct us "out of isolation into personal, or instinctual, relations." [Several mentions of EMF.]

985 Taubman, Howard. "Theatre: Timely Theme," NEW YORK TIMES, 1 Feb 1962, p. 23.

In Santha Rama Rau's adaptation of *A Passage to India* there is immediacy in the collision between the Western colonists and people who wish to rule themselves, and there is timeliness in the conflict that divides men of good will. The run-of-the-mill administrators are perhaps too unrelievedly villains; but Rau, like EMF, conveys in the other characters a complex sense of both their failings and their virtues.

986 Taubman, Howard. "Worth Adapting," NEW YORK TIMES, 11 Feb 1962, II, 1.

Santha Rama Rau's adaptation of *A Passage to India* brings fresh and human characters into the theater and dramatizes ideas that evoke our sympathetic response. She captures much of the novel's atmosphere, emotion, and thought. Rau's play emphasizes "in moving dramatic terms, the great divide of injustice, humiliation and misunderstanding that keeps apart even men of goodwill."

987 Thomson, George H. "The Perils of E. M. Forster's Critics," DALHOUSIE REVIEW, XLII (Winter 1962–1963), 492–98.

Books on EMF all follow the same pattern. Short stories are dismissed; *Where Angels Fear to Tread* and *Room with a View* are lightweight; *The Longest Journey* is treated with respect and caution; *Howards End* is a notable advance; *A Passage to India* is the apotheosis of EMF's art (except for Trilling who awards top place to *Howards End*). The development of EMF's exploration of reality is too grossly equated with his artistic achievement. Some new books on EMF should be written according to different principles from those illustrated in the works under review: (1) one that will take stories seriously [Alan Wilde's ART AND ORDER: A STUDY OF E. M. FORSTER (1964) does this]; (2) one that will analyze carefully EMF's symbols and symbolic approach [Beer's book had already done so, but Wilfred Stone's THE CAVE AND THE MOUNTAIN (1966), George H. Thomson's THE FICTION OF E. M. FORSTER (1967), and many recent articles were to carry this approach further]; (3) one that will analyze his style [this one we are waiting for still]; (4) one that will analyze exhaustively his literary origins in terms of the novelists who influenced him [this one we are also still waiting for]; (5) one that will challenge the canons of realism as providing the exclusive approach to EMF and will recognize the provenance of "romance" in his fiction [Thomson's THE FICTION OF E. M. FORSTER (1967) was to do so superbly]. [Review-essay on K. W. Gransden's E. M. FORSTER (1962), J. B. Beer's THE ACHIEVEMENT OF E. M. FORSTER (1962), Frederick C. Crews's E. M. FORSTER: THE PERILS OF HUMANISM (1962), James McConkey's THE NOVELS OF E. M. FORSTER (1957), and Lionel Trilling's E. M. FORSTER (1943). Perceptive and informed discussion.]

988 Tuohy, Frank. "The English Question," SPECTATOR (Lond), CCIX (6 July 1962), 30–31.

J. B. Beer devotes his attention to the visionary aspect of EMF with which Lionel Trilling had been impatient in E. M. FORSTER (1943). It is the rightness of EMF's moral approach, not the metaphysical element, that keeps his novels alive. The influence of *A Passage to India* has been moral; it is a novel marked by availability, in the sense that people have read it and applied its values to their own lives. This availability has persuaded people going to work or to serve abroad to model themselves on Fielding rather than on Ronny Heaslop. This merit of availability is lacking from *The Longest Journey*, which has other merits but whose "poetry" is sometimes over-emphatic or factitious. Criticism of EMF has gotten too far away from concern with truth to life. Thus there is something unreal about Margaret Schlegel, something voracious about her sitting beside the humiliated Henry Wilcox; and there is something sadistic in Ruth Wilcox exposing the vulnerable members of her family to hay fever, as she walks with sprigs of hay in her hand. EMF's work is not a full criticism of life, but he asks social questions that are not easily answered, questions having to do with social morality and the nature of English experience. The dialogue between the Schlegels and the Wilcoxes goes on and on, though the Wilcoxes seem to have inherited England. [Review-essay on J. B. Beer's THE ACHIEVEMENT OF E. M. FORSTER (1962). A fresh and stimulating essay.]

989 Watts, Stephen. "Forster on 'India'—Author Talks About Novel-into-Play," NEW YORK TIMES, 28 Jan 1962, Section II, pp. 1, 3.

EMF is pleased with the adaptation for the stage by Santha Rama Rau of *A Passage to India* but has resisted all film offers. EMF was surprised at the commercial success of the play but attributes it in part to the racial question that has lately come to the fore, especially in Africa. EMF's main achievement in *Passage* is his capturing in Aziz the essence of Indian character. Part of the success of the London run was due to the Pakistani doctor, Zia Mohyeddin, who will also play Aziz in the New York production. EMF attributes his abstention from novel writing to the disappearance of the stable society he was used to before the first war. EMF agrees with the definition of his work by John Sparrow (1929), that it "deals with the interaction of two types of character, the intersection of two planes of living ... the conflict of those who live by convention and those who live by instinct." This conflict is primarily revealed in *Passage* in the relationship between Aziz and Fielding. EMF says that Fielding is not autobiographical, though some of Fielding's attitudes may be his. Fielding was based on a man in the Indian Education Service "not a bit like me, really." [An interview with EMF at his rooms in King's College. Comments on current theater and the novels he is reading: Iris Murdoch and Hardy's THE WOODLANDERS.]

990 Weimer, Sanford R., and David H. Stewart. "Forster's *A Passage to India*," EXPLICATOR, XX (May 1962), Item 73.
The various means of transportation used by the characters in *A Passage to India* define character and assist the action. Means of transportation reveal, with Western mechanization, each person's new position and aspirations and dramatize "the dynamic flux" now characterizing Indian society.

991 West, Paul. "Turning New Leaves," (1), CANADIAN FORUM (Toronto), XLII (Sept 1962), 132.
EMF is difficult to write about because he either takes us toward allegory or causes us to laugh at his preoccupation with the Absolute. He values the creative effort to understand human beings and their problems; the quality of our responses to them is all-important. The moment of vision may be self-deception, but it is reprehensible to avoid the possibility of illumination for this reason. He is skeptical of the too arduous attempts to project the self into a system and of too intense (or cosmic) a spiritual isolation. [Remarks are part of review of Frederick C. Crews's E. M. FORSTER: THE PERILS OF HUMANISM (1962).]

992 [Williams, William Carlos]. "Four Unpublished Letters by William Carlos Williams," MASSACHUSETTS REVIEW, III (Winter 1962), 292–97.
[Letter to James Laughlin (15 Nov 1943), *The Longest Journey* tore Williams apart. The book builds up a convincing modern hell, "the hell of failure to remember the gods." The journey back to love is brilliantly presented after the depiction of this hell. The authority of EMF's writing is "wonderful."]

1963

993 Allott, Kenneth, and Miriam Farris. THE ART OF GRAHAM GREENE (NY: Russell & Russell, 1963), pp. 13, 86, 108, 175.
Anthony Farrant in ENGLAND MADE ME is an instance in Greene's work of EMF's "undeveloped heart." In THE POWER AND THE GLORY the Mexican setting and the Catholic situation do not alter greatly Greene's view of life, just as India and its religions did not alter EMF's in *A Passage to India.*

994 Antonini, Giacomo. "Singolarita di E. M. Forster" (The Uniqueness of E. M. Forster), OSSERVATORE POLITICO LETTERARIO (Milan), IX:5 (1963), 91–100.
In every way EMF is an extraordinary if hitherto neglected writer. His fame has increased not because of his occasional nonfiction but because of the six works (five novels and a volume of short stories), most of them written fifty years ago. Why he stopped writing fiction after *A Passage to India* is not clear, but it was not the result of being unsuccessful or the incomprehension of his contemporaries. With each book, critical praise increased. *Passage* in 1924 provoked an interest in EMF's work beyond the Bloomsbury group and outside of England. After the war young intellectuals and writers saw in EMF's seriousness and engagement an example to emulate. EMF and his work, in certain aspects, seem anachronistic. In order to appreciate and understand his works, one must consider them in connection with the culture which they reflect. The class differences which EMF observed at Tonbridge School and their pernicious influence were parallel to the racial incomprehension and intolerance that were to engage him later. His years at Cambridge fostered his liberal politics that, too, became almost anachronistic. Fifty years after its conception *Where Angels Fear to Tread* still preserves the grayness and unhappiness created by the narrow-minded, hypocritical, provincial bourgeoisie. The element of color derives from Italy, the Tuscany toward which EMF felt attracted. The influence of Henry James upon the plot is patent: the contrast between the narrow-minded bourgeoisie and the more sanguine, instinctive Tuscans. Italy and Tuscany return in EMF's third novel, *A Room with a View*, his freshest book, a richly suggestive one, and the only one with a happy ending. The Italian moral climate contrasts with that of provincial England and provides for a life of greater sincerity and liberty. As in *The Longest Journey*, EMF attacks the

rigid bourgeois standards prevalent in Edwardian England. He never tried to represent the transformation of Edwardian society into a freer, more chaotic society, following World War I.

Passage concerns British colonial administrators whose mentality and mode of living belong to the first part of the twentieth century. One reason for EMF's premature silence is his inability to adapt spiritually to a transformation of morals and customs. Once the obstacles to such transformation had disappeared, EMF found himself in an artistically embarrassing situation, because the result was different from what he had desired. *Journey* occupies a central position in EMF's work because he elaborated in it for the first and last time his personal life. He has maintained, however, an absolute narrative objectivity, following Flaubert's example in L'EDUCATION SENTIMENTAL. EMF's theme is the vanity of exalted friendship when it alone has to fill man's life. For EMF love in its broadest sense is basic. In *Howards End* through the contrast between the liberal, spiritual Schlegel family and the conservative, materialistic Wilcox family, EMF poses the question of the future destiny of England. The foreboding of a future cataclysm inspired EMF to write *Howards End*, where the world of his adolescence is yet intact with its privileges and prejudices. The novel has immediacy and is not merely an exercise in sentimental nostalgia. The theme of *Passage*—the difficulty of comprehension between people of different races and religions—has become crucial for our age. Yet the interest of the novel is not limited to this aspect of it. EMF, a valiant defender of European civilization and of Western liberalism, becomes aware, in contact with the civilization of India, of the weaknesses of a liberalism incapable of curbing materialistic appetites and of correcting narrow-minded prejudices. Moreover, the novel's irrational, supernatural element should be noted. What has preserved the novel's charm and led to its esteem is the vigor and polish of EMF's narrative. His greatest singularity is, then, to have suddenly stopped writing fiction when he had achieved full artistic maturity. [In Italian.]

995 Bien, Peter. L. P. HARTLEY (Lond: Chatto & Windus; Toronto: Clarke, Irwin; University Park, Pa: Pennsylvania State UP, 1963), pp. 31, 32, 50, 78, 99–100, 102, 103, 159–160, 177, 187, 189, 201, 264, 265.

Man for L. P. Hartley, as for EMF, must succeed in personal relations. Hartley, like James and EMF, makes use of the international novel but does so less consistently than either James or EMF. EMF either sends his bourgeois figures abroad (*Where Angels Fear to Tread*) or imports a foreign or half-foreign element to confront them at home (*Howards End*). Barbara (Eustace's sister) in Hartley's trilogy EUSTACE AND HILDA represents the same kind of intuitive feminine wisdom as do Mrs. Wilcox in *Howards End* and Mrs. Moore in *A Passage to India*. The women in the trilogy serve the same purpose as the great-mother figures in modern novels, among whom are Mrs. Moore and Mrs. Wilcox. The same distending and distortion of the real occurs in Hartley's fantastic fiction as EMF prescribes for fantasy in *Aspects of the Novel*. Hartley, like EMF, did his best work when his characters achieved symbolic and multiple dimensions. Hartley's technique with use of leitmotifs in THE GO-BETWEEN approximates that of Thomas Mann in "Tonio Kröger." Mann uses them more organically than EMF does in *Howards End* but less so than Joyce does in "The Dead." Like EMF, Hartley is irresolute as to whether the world is one of good and evil or one of good-and-evil. In MY FELLOW DEVILS Margaret Pennyfeather remains completely inhibited and is not thrown into the fullness of life by melodramatic incidents as are so many of the prigs in EMF's fiction. A PERFECT WOMAN fails relatively because there is not the congruity between style and characterization which Lionel Trilling finds in *A Room with a View* [E. M. FORSTER (1943)]. In his unpublished lectures on the novel Hartley cites EMF as a novelist who evinces moral responsibility and who favors his good characters over the morally deficient. In order to establish his preferences for his good characters, Hartley relies less on tone and ironic effect than does EMF.

996 Clubb, Roger L. "*A Passage to India:* The Meaning of the Marabar Caves," COLLEGE LANGUAGE ASSOCIATION JOURNAL, VI (March 1963), 184–93.

The Marabar Caves are associated with "the vast, unknowable expanse of geological time." The minds of Mrs. Moore and Adela Quested cannot function at the primitive level required of them in the Caves; the Caves also represent mysteries that human beings cannot understand, the riddle of life itself. In particular, the Caves represent the mystery inherent in the development of life from non-life, the inescapable but still unbridgeable gap between the organic and the nonorganic. The Caves are also symbolic of the womb and connote, accordingly, the mystery of the origins of life, in both a metaphysical and a sexual sense. The experiences of Mrs. Moore are metaphysical. Her sympathies broaden with her continued exposure to India, but her intellect does not keep pace with them. She is disabled by the echo until she sees Asirgarh on her way home and can place the Marabar in perspective. Her journey home is physically one toward death but spiritually one toward life (and a return to the values represented by the Mosque in Part I; see the Mosque at Asirgarh). For Adela the Caves signify the unconscious mind, suggesting the sexual attractiveness of Aziz when she realizes that she is pledged to marry a man she does not love. Thinking of Aziz, she suffers from a delusion that he has attacked her, the Caves symbolizing at this point "the womb or sexual consummation." Adela lacks Mrs. Moore's breadth and sympathy, but even Mrs. Moore does not penetrate fully "the mystery behind the existence of the conscious spirit in the universe." No one can. [A perceptive and illuminating article.]

997 Cooperman, Stanley. "The Imperial Posture and the Shrine of Darkness: Kipling's THE NAULAHKA and E. M. Forster's *A Passage to India*," ENGLISH LITERATURE IN TRANSITION, VI:1 (1963), 9–13. In Kipling's THE NAULAHKA the protagonist Tarvin experiences climactic negation at "The Cow's Mouth" shrine comparable to that experienced by Mrs. Moore in *A Passage to India*. Tarvin defies "complexity, futility, and nothingness," whereas Mrs. Moore gives in to them. EMF develops his theme of negation so that at the end of *Passage* there is simply a recapitulation of the negation and separation introduced in the first chapter. [An oversimplified judgment of EMF's direction in *Passage*.] Tarvin, faced with negation, does not deny his morality and ethic but denies negation itself, and he turns to a life of action. Linear progress in THE NAULAHKA is in contrast with the "cyclic futility" of *Passage*. EMF's introspective relativism has deeper implications than imperialistic action, but affirmations like Tarvin's did build up the Empire and shape the world's civilization.

998 Cox, C. B. "Introduction: The Liberal Dilemma," "Henry James and the Art of Personal Relationships," "E. M. Forster's Island," "Angus Wilson: Studies in Depression," "Conclusion: The Modern Novel," THE FREE SPIRIT: A STUDY OF LIBERAL HUMANISM IN THE NOVELS OF GEORGE ELIOT, HENRY JAMES, E. M. FORSTER, VIRGINIA WOOLF, ANGUS WILSON (Lond & NY: Oxford UP, 1963), pp. 1–12, 38–73, espec 39, 42, 47; 74–102, 117–53, espec 118, 120, 123, 126, 127, 129, 133, 152; 154–84, espec 161, 162, 164, 165, 168, 171; "E. M. Forster's Island" rptd, in part, in TWENTIETH CENTURY INTERPRETATIONS OF "A PASSAGE TO INDIA," ed by Andrew Rutherford (Englewood Cliffs, NJ: Spectrum Books, 1970), pp. 90–93.
The liberal tradition owes much to John Stuart Mill: faith in historical progress, individual freedom, tolerance, and power of reason, and the confidence that evil can be overcome by effort. The greatness of George Eliot, Henry James, EMF, Virginia Woolf, and Angus Wilson lies in their attempts, only partly successful, to relate their liberalism to social realism. They tend to distrust political action and to concentrate on personal relationships. Stephen Wonham in *The Longest Journey* is a sentimentalized character enabling EMF to escape from a hard analysis of moral dilemmas (Stephen is like Will Ladislaw in Eliot's MIDDLEMARCH or James's Princess Casamassima in RODERICK HUDSON and THE PRINCESS CASAMASSIMA). Like EMF, James's urbane manner in THE PORTRAIT OF A LADY does not encompass all the materials of his experience; his later stylistic fastidiousness goes beyond such irony.

"E. M. Forster's Island": EMF presents in his fiction the values of the liberal tradition (freedom, humanitarianism, progress, intelligence), but his comic art emphasizes the flaws in these when they are put into practice. James's moral order seems to EMF an impossible ideal. George Emerson in *A Room with a View*, with his direct affirmation of life, is impatient of subtle moral distinctions like those voiced by the Jamesean free spirit. EMF emphasizes the need to accept the muddle of life; those who use the will to impose an alien order upon the abundance of life distort it. Rickie Elliot in *Journey* is enslaved to his idealistic faith in the goodness of other people. The attempts of the intellect to discover harmony and of the will to impose order on experience result in frustration. Abundance and variety are more important for EMF than order. He advocates tolerance and respect for the individual, but he withdraws from difficult political and social problems; his acceptance ends in exclusion. He is sympathetic toward withdrawal into limited, secure areas of experience. His sympathies are engaged by the Schlegels and Fielding, whose tolerance is sincere but dependent on economic security. These characters are uneasy about their lives of cultured privilege; Margaret extends herself to Henry Wilcox, Helen to Leonard Bast, but both relationships are unconvincing. There is no adequate solution in *Howards End* "to the problem of supplying the commercial world with tolerance, tact, and sensitivity"; the idyllic closing scene is sentimental. EMF realizes that happiness depends not only on financial independence but on personal relationships, "a refinement of consciousness." As a novelist he is more secure in this area; his concern for people and his hatred of those who try to impose their wills on others are well realized. Only a few reach the island of personal relations, however. EMF is not only exclusive, but he fails to engage us in his portraits of Jacky and Leonard Bast. His last standard is provided by the individual self and its need for fulfillment; tolerance and the need for understanding are necessary for the cult of the personal, but they sometimes result in the inability of his central characters to act decisively, a limitation which EMF accepts too readily. He lacks sympathy for the creative impulse as it is directed against low standards of living, or for the energy of the man who works for order and justice in society. His satire and comedy, as a result, lack compassion. His satire of the Wilcoxes and the Anglo-Indians reveals in part his own disgust with will power and energy; his dislike for administrators runs so deep that his picture of the Anglo-Indians in *Passage* is incomplete. His stress on freedom is so great that a man like Fielding steers clear of full commitment and full participation in human relationships. Stephen Wonham's desire in *Journey* to keep his wife "in line" reflects a fear of complete commitment in love; Mrs. Moore's distrust of marriage and Adela Quested's of sex in *Passage* also convey a similar emotional withdrawal. Both the women and Fielding distrust social involvement. When Fielding marries, EMF is less sympathetic with him. EMF usually ascribes the lack of vitality in his free spirits to the repressive effects of an industrial society upon them and advocates renewal through the means of earth and a return to a romanticized feudal England. His pastoral, Wordsworthian view of nature and its renovating effects on the spirit accounts for the fantasizing present in the conclusions to *Journey* and *Howards End;* Stephen bears no relationship to his social environment, the child in the hay likewise. A dreamlike quality invests Howards End house, Ruth Wilcox, and the reunion of the sisters at Howards End. On the one hand, EMF bolsters his humanism by faith in some kind of supernatural force; on the other hand, his ironical mocking of the whole human situation is too radical. His casual treatment of death ends also by devaluing action and life itself. His love for the formless and chaotic is illustrated in his relish of India. With the recognition of evil and complexity, EMF finds it difficult to resolve conflict in his novels; the result is a lack of development in the central characters of *Passage.* His hatred of the will means that he seeks continually for "islands of quiet tolerance"; the impassive punkah wallah in the courtroom in *Passage* seems at times to represent for EMF "the Spirit of Life." He has great comic talents, however, and his portraits of Rickie Elliot, the Schlegels, Fielding, and Aziz are compelling and incisive.

"Angus Wilson: Studies in Depression": Wilson has lost EMF's assurance. Where EMF is evasive, Wilson is savage and uncompromising: he refuses to suffer fools gladly. Unlike EMF, Wilson feels that humanism must take into account the facts of modern life: its suffering, the power of evil, the failure of most human aspirations, the essential loneliness and separateness of all human beings. "Conclusion: The Modern Novel": The liberal hopes for social reform and evolutionary progress were deflected by World War I. In *Room* the plot reveals an evolutionary progress as Lucy Honeychurch travels from blindness to enlightenment; in *Passage* (1924) there is the vision of meaninglessness in the Marabar Caves, and the novel ends with Fielding and Aziz unable to achieve a satisfying relationship. James, EMF, and Woolf do not understand "the rich vitality of the ordinary man"; as a result, their fiction lacks compassion. Since the main characters in Woolf and EMF (unlike those of Eliot and James) lack a sense of duty and responsibility toward others, they are often cut off from each other by insurmountable barriers. EMF's and Wilson's irony would suggest that human life is at times absurd. Security in EMF and Wilson is achieved by withdrawal and non-interference. EMF is therefore attracted to Hindu religion; he also preached "apathy," "uninventiveness," and "inertia" after World War I. These novelists are all valuable because they do stress the ordering element of intelligence. This element is sometimes underestimated by Christianity, which, on the whole, provides a more comprehensive frame for the definition of value (as in the Christian-oriented work of William Golding) than does liberal culture. [A searching, highly critical analysis of

EMF's liberal humanism in conjunction with other humanistic novelists. Excellent for relating EMF to novelists in the English tradition and to an important contemporary, Angus Wilson. In tone and conclusions reached, the book is largely negative; but Cox's integrity and his sensitivity not only to his ideological premises but to the literary values of his authors are impressive.]

999 Delbaere-Garant, Jeanne. "The Call of the South: *Where Angels Fear to Tread* and THE LOST GIRL," REVUE DES LANGUES VIVANTES (Brussels), XXIX:4 (1963), 336–57.

Where Angels Fear to Tread and D. H. Lawrence's THE LOST GIRL are novels that explore the relationship of an English woman (at various times Lilia Herriton and Caroline Abbott in EMF's book, Alvina Houghton in Lawrence's) to a primitive Italian (Gino Carella in EMF's book, Ciccio in Lawrence's). In both novels an English girl escapes the provincialism of her native town, Italy becomes a new way of life, and a confrontation of cultures ensues. The problem varies with the two writers, and their values differ. In EMF's novel neither Sawston nor Monteriano is superior in all respects, though Monteriano has much that Sawston lacks. EMF is more concerned with the differences between the cultures than with ranking them. Neither Gino nor Lilia evolves, whereas Philip Herriton and Caroline do. Philip's enlightenment is the result of several physical blows he receives from Gino (he is toppled onto a bed on his first trip to Monteriano; he is jostled at the opera on his second trip; and he is tortured after the death of Gino's baby). Caroline is the agent for his regeneration, and she links with Mrs. Elliot, Mrs. Wilcox, and Mrs. Moore as an elder sister figure or goddess for the other characters. Her enlightenment is in the direction of learning that human nature is mixed and complex. EMF does not make a god of Gino (as Lawrence does of Ciccio): "What he condemns . . . is not so much Gino's avarice and stupidity or Italy's vulgar side as the false idea with which his English characters approach it." Philip and Caroline understand Italy better but remain alien to its way of life, just as EMF does. The difference between *Angels* and THE LOST GIRL is that EMF wishes to find a mean between the rationalism of the Anglo-Saxon mind and the primitivism of Italy, whereas Lawrence asserts the superiority of the primitive. Lawrence has no patience with the Philip Herriton character and does not wish to save his Albert Witham. Gino's vulgarity is the result of his lack of education, Ciccio's the result of the education he has had. Alvina does not change as a result of her contact with Italy; her qualities are only intensified. In both novels the picture of Italy is not greatly convincing; it is more a country of the mind ("the South") and a symbol of what is lacking in England. EMF's book is theoretical and abstract, and the dialectic in it is obtrusive. Lawrence's book, in contrast, is replete with the luxuriousness of life and is not schematized. EMF is concerned with the life of the mind and is intrigued by the complexity of the situation in which different cultures conflict with each other in *A Passage to India.* Lawrence wants a new culture of his own devising, in the Mexico of THE PLUMED SERPENT, "deeply rooted in the primeval life of the blood." [An intelligent analysis, and almost the only extended treatment of *Angels* in journals. *Angels* is, in my opinion, a better book than THE LOST GIRL.]

1000 Downes, David A. "Book Reviews," THOUGHT (Fordham University), XXXVIII (Spring 1963), 130–31.
EMF's work exemplifies the fact that the humanist's dilemma is insoluble: his need to affirm values that exceed the empirically derived facts basic to his thought and then his reluctance to embrace a "faith" that goes beyond the rational. With the humanist neither reason nor the heart prevails; the real and fictional worlds remain sundered as they do in EMF. [Remarks form part of a review of Frederick C. Crews's E. M. FORSTER: THE PERILS OF HUMANISM (1962).]

1001 Eapen, Karippacheril Chakko. "E. M. Forster and India," DISSERTATION ABSTRACTS, XXIII (1963), 3897. Unpublished dissertation, University of Colorado, 1962.

1002 "Forster Issues Simplified," TIMES (Lond), 7 June 1963, p. 15.
In Elizabeth Hart's adaptation of *Where Angels Fear to Tread,* an old-fashioned play results that conveys little sense of the moral ambiguity and the complexity of the characters to be found in EMF's novel.

1003 Gellert, Roger. "Passage to Italy," NEW STATESMAN, nsLXV (14 June 1963), 913.
In her stage adaptation of *Where Angels Fear to Tread,* Elizabeth Hart has preserved most of the liveliness and much of the irony of EMF's novel. The love-hate relationship between Civilization (Philip Herriton) and Nature (Gino Carella) emerges beautifully. Keith Baxter as Gino has the right mixture "of passion and sloth, puppyish warmth and sly calculation"; and Dulcie Gray as Caroline Abbott reveals "unexpected reserves of feeling" in her confession to Philip at the end.

1004 Gordon, Robert. "Questions for Discussion: 'The Road from Colonus,'" THE EXPANDED MOMENT: A SHORT STORY ANTHOLOGY (Boston: D. C. Heath, 1963), pp. 301–2.
"The Road from Colonus" explores the collision between the repressed British middle class and the spontaneous, instinctive, pagan Greeks. EMF is judicious in appraising such conflicts, but in this story he is decisive in

favoring the Greeks, though they do throw stones. [Also questions for discussion of story.]

1005 Gowda, H. H. Anniah. "E. M. Forster's India," LITERARY HALF-YEARLY (Mysore, India), IV (July 1963), 45–52.
India has inspired a new dimension in EMF as creative artist. He is sensitive to India's spiritual and historical heritage. He utilizes a poetic method in his evocation of India. He has also the gift of assimilating his characters to their surroundings. He has understood both Hinduism and Mohammedanism intellectually and creatively. [Descriptive comment on EMF's evocation of Indian scene.]

1006 "Graceful Play from Novel," TIMES (Lond), 10 July 1963, p. 13.
Elizabeth Hart has skillfully dramatized *Where Angels Fear to Tread* but has not been able to suggest in her characters "the elaboration of motive and the ratiocination of purpose obscurely corrupted by a self-interest fiendishly adept at disguise."

1007 Griffin, Lloyd. "New Books Appraised," LIBRARY JOURNAL, LXXXVIII (15 Dec 1963), 4761–62.
The contributions to E. M. FORSTER: A TRIBUTE, ed by K. Natwar-Singh (1964), reveal a blend in EMF of sensitivity, humility, and overcivilized sophistication, with confidence, belief in principle, courage to stand against conformity, and intuitive understanding of the Indian spirit.

1008 Grigson, Geoffrey (ed). "E[dward] M[organ] Forster," THE CONCISE ENCYCLOPEDIA OF MODERN WORLD LITERATURE (NY: Hawthorn Books; Lond: Heinemann, 1963), pp. 160–63; 2nd ed (Lond: Heinemann, 1970; NY: Hawthorne Books, 1971), pp. 126–30.
EMF's greatness consists in his acute social conscience combined with his depiction of moments of vision. EMF is one of those liberals who take sides "because they feel that everyone should have the right to practise private values." Actually, EMF, for the purposes of his art, supported a regime (notably in *Howards End*) that meant a balancing of opposites "in which material achievement somehow kept going anti-materialist value"; in his theory and in his actions, he supported progressive ideas which upset this balance. In his essays EMF now often deplores a world that he has helped bring about and that he was too honest not to help bring about: "The period he lives in has forced him to abandon his art and tell nothing but social truth." Truth in EMF's fiction consists in the *pursuit* of a vision which can also *be* the vision: "a playfully applied, wholly serious, secular, part-pagan, part-Christian doctrine of salvation is the 'pattern in the carpet' of Forster's work." *The Longest Journey* is perhaps the least satisfactory but the most

revealing of the novels. This novel emphasizes that men should remain loyal to the vision of their youth. Stephen Wonham is not successful because he is presented as a perfect character with superficial blemishes, a conception which is unconvincing. *Journey* reveals "that Forster's morality lies in his art, that it is not the position taken, but the search itself which leads to the moment of revelation." The novels are wonderfully planned and possess "the uninterrupted movement of choreography." They are not moralities but mysteries; EMF himself is concerned with the conflict between the forces of life and those that are against life. [An original and stimulating essay in appreciation.]

1009 Hall, James. "Forster's Family Reunions," ENGLISH LITER-ARY HISTORY, XXV (March 1958), 60–78; rptd, slightly rvd, as "Family Reunions: E. M. Forster," THE TRAGIC COMEDIANS: SEVEN MODERN BRITISH NOVELISTS (Bloomington: Indiana UP, 1963), pp. 11–30.

In EMF's work a conservatism about the family balances his liberalism about institutions. In *Where Angels Fear to Tread* and *A Room with a View* there is rebellion against passive acceptance of the family; *The Longest Journey* is concerned with restoration of the family. The concern with perpetuating the family provides the "sympathetic" as opposed to the formal structure of *Howards End.* The strongest connection is made not between intellectual (Margaret Schlegel) and businessman (Henry Wilcox) but between intellectual (Margaret) and intellectual (Helen Schlegel). In their separation and reconciliation something from both their values is preserved. The most incisive scenes are the comic and those in which the sense of space predominate; these are invariably the scenes that pit Schlegel against Schlegel. The writing about the Wilcoxes is thinner and more irritable. Another connection is also important, that between Margaret and Ruth Wilcox; when Margaret most fully connects with her, she takes over Ruth's role in the Wilcox clan and also connects most fruitfully with Helen. Helen rebels against the managing, authoritarian spirit represented for her in Henry and to a degree in Margaret. In this revolt she champions Leonard Bast, from personal rather than humane motives, however. Margaret and Henry deserve each other because they are both managers of life and the emotions; from the point of view of the novel, Margaret's commitment to Henry is real but wrong. The main threat of the novel is not the triumph of the Wilcoxes but the possibility that they may "inherit" Margaret. EMF is also interested in the relationship between the class conflict and the family conflict. Those are rewarded who connect the present with the past, as the sisters do; those who cannot make this connection are routed like the second generation of the Wilcoxes and like the patriarch (Henry) who is deprived of power by defending the Wilcox values. The ending is like that of JANE EYRE: The offenders are punished, the husband is gelded (needing only a nurse), the feminine principle prevails. Leonard is given an absurd but good death, since he would not have fitted into Howards End house. The family is reconstituted at the end; Henry and Leonard fill emotional needs for each of the sisters at a crucial point but are themselves changed. Henry loses force and Leonard dies, but both have deeply affected the sisters' development. By the end Margaret learns to be impulsive at times in handling Henry; Helen learns to contain her impulsiveness. Margaret loses her sense of uprootedness, Helen her sense of being an outcast. Margaret becomes Mrs. Wilcox but grows beyond her predecessor as well. The novel points up the necessity, and the difficulty, of the inner life, especially for those who do not understand it. It is pessimistic concerning social connection, though the concluding scene symbolizes a stable family life. In part Leonard exists to illustrate EMF's view of the need to balance the pursuit of the inner life with a recognition of one's limitations. For Leonard, Ruskin is unnatural. The combination of affection and irony with which EMF conceives Leonard is one of his finest achievements. The Wilcoxes of the second generation make Margaret what she is really not, a rebellious rather than a flexible personality; but her rebellion (which is not revolt) allows her to achieve deeper awareness and to establish more fully her understanding with her sister. The rebellion and the sympathy, comprising EMF's liberalism, are enveloped by (and contribute toward) the preservation of family continuity. This conservatism about the family deepens the sense of identity and reality in the Schlegels but also leads to a distrust of experience itself, so marked in *A Passage to India.* The past is sometimes used not so much to bolster the present as to resist it. [Excellent, deep-probing, and wide-ranging essay; one of the best essays on *Howards End.* Same as entry 780.]

1010 Hall, James. THE TRAGIC COMEDIANS: SEVEN MODERN BRITISH NOVELISTS (Bloomington: Indiana UP, 1963), pp. 31, 32, 35, 36, 65, 67, 100, 151, 152, 153, 155; rpts "Forster's Family Reunions" (1958) slightly rvd as "Family Reunions: E. M. Forster," pp. 11–30; see Hall (1958).

In EMF there is a domesticated romanticism, in his upholding of natural man (George Emerson, Mr. Emerson, Leonard Bast), his worship of the idyllic and primitive (*The Longest Journey*), and his passion for Greece and Italy. Domesticated romanticism is also Victorianism, the manners of which EMF finds unsatisfactory. He gives his romanticism the authority of tradition in *Howards End* by making the tradition and its chief exponent, Ernst Schlegel, German. Helen Schlegel's reactions to the Beethoven Fifth Symphony are a set piece of such domesticated romanticism; also Leonard Bast's walk at night comments on the role of romantic ideals in the city. Nothing descends from the past in Huxley's work as it does in EMF's; the individual has no help from tradition in making his life and decisions. The avant-garde represented by Huxley went back to attitudes preceding EMF's evolutionary romanticism, much damaged by the war. The intellectual family (*Howards End*) is defeated by society; Huxley uses in his novels groups of people with common views (families of a kind) who have accepted such defeat. Waugh's sympathetic characters are like EMF's in struggling for community of spirit and, for the time, attaining it. With Huxley, Waugh, and Henry Green, the comic novel no longer puts primary emphasis on truth to nature as the comic novel had done from Meredith to EMF. For Henry Green continuing conflict, not struggle-and-resolution, is his concern. The confidence man does not appear in EMF's novels with "their ideal of honest and imaginative self-management." EMF gets rid of the old with ease through the means of satire. The evolutionary aspect of EMF's novels results in an adjudication of past and present; the child at the conclusion of *Howards End* will have some of Margaret Schlegel's control, some of Helen Schlegel's sympathy, and some of Leonard Bast's honesty. The threats to continuity are anger, misunderstanding, and isolation; but EMF is hopeful that those of similar temperaments may attain community through sympathetic intelligence. Such an evolutionary spirit may have died with the war.

1011 Hart, Elizabeth. "WHERE ANGELS FEAR TO TREAD:" A PLAY IN TWO ACTS (Lond: Samuel French, 1963).
[Adaptation of *Where Angels Fear to Tread* for the stage, revealing the intrinsically dramatic qualities in EMF's fiction. Lilia Herriton does not appear, and the Carella baby is smothered instead of being killed in a carriage accident; but the play captures the essence of EMF's novel and some of its complexities.]

1012 Hay, Eloise Knapp. THE POLITICAL NOVELS OF JOSEPH CONRAD (Chicago: University of Chicago P, 1963), pp. 1, 13, 109, 185.
Conrad outdistances novelists like Virginia Woolf, Ford, and EMF by his total commitment. EMF may have been thinking of "Heart of Darkness" when he asserted ("Joseph Conrad: A Note," *Abinger Harvest*) that the "casket" of Conrad's genius held a vapor rather than a jewel. [Hay agrees with Irving Howe (1957) that Emilia Gould in NOSTROMO does not have the boldness of Mrs. Moore in *A Passage to India* and therefore lacks political incisiveness.]

1013 Hepburn, James G. THE ART OF ARNOLD BENNETT (Bloomington: Indiana UP, 1963), pp. 18, 51, 63–64, 95, 143.
EMF in *Aspects of the Novel* maintains that the dog Fosette in THE OLD WIVES TALE is a symbol of age and withering time, but it also suggests renewal at the time of its mistress's death. Hardy, Conrad, Lawrence, EMF, and Joyce are preoccupied with religion and ambiguously so: The phenome-

non is not to be explained exclusively in psychological, aesthetic, or philosophical terms. Bennett shares in part this preoccupation.

1014 Izzo, Carlo. "Il Novecento: Da Joseph Conrad a E. M. Forster" (The Nineteenth Century: From Joseph Conrad to E. M. Forster), STORIA DELLA LETTERATURA INGLESE DALLA RESTAURAZIONE AI NOSTRI GIORNI (The History of English Literature from the Restoration to Our Own Time) (Milano: Nuova Accademia Editrice, 1963), pp. 713–36, espec 734–36.

EMF seems suspended between two worlds: the traditional (for he ignores the innovations of Conrad and Joyce) and the world represented by the Bloomsbury Group, which favored a formalized refinement. Critics agree that *Howards End* and *A Passage to India* are EMF's best novels. Compared with his earlier novels, *Howards End* reveals a more mature treatment of the theme of conflict between the intellectual and spiritual life on the one hand and the practical life on the other, and an increased control over form. Yet EMF's insistence on this earlier theme causes one to suspect a certain narrowness of vision. As in the earlier works there is no true resolution to this conflict; the refined victors seem pallid. The fact that EMF after *Passage* gave up so-called creative writing is not then altogether inexplicable. *Passage* is EMF's most convincing novel. Since it focused on not only the political problems but the human relationships between Indians and British, the timing of its publication no doubt had an historical significance. Although the problem of bridging the fundamental differences between individuals is undeniably monotonous, the novel's solidity cannot be denied. As long as one group continues to be the oppressor and the other the oppressed, a true rapport between the Indians and British can never be established. Yet the possibility of such rapport is not excluded. EMF should be recognized for being more politically far-sighted than his contemporaries. Among his nonfictional works *Aspects of the Novel* is outstanding. [In Italian.]

1015 Lambert, J. W. "Mr. Forster at the Play," SUNDAY TIMES (Lond), 4 Aug 1963, p. 20.

EMF is enthusiastic about Elizabeth Hart's stage adaptation of *Where Angels Fear to Tread* and the quality of the performances. EMF likes a fenced-off art, as in the theater with a proscenium arch. Racine, for EMF, is the ideal or the fixed point in the theater; the barriers he sets up must be broken even while one still respects them. EMF praises the adaptation of Henry James's WASHINGTON SQUARE and asserts that neither James nor he succeeded as a dramatist. Santha Rama Rau's adaptation of *A Passage to India* is excellent. [Mainly reports EMF's opinions on films, music, people's voices, Eliot's readings, Matthew Arnold, verse, his love of Cambridge.]

1016 Liddell, Robert. THE NOVELS OF JANE AUSTEN (Lond: Longmans; Don Mills, Ontario: Collins, 1963), pp. 19–21, 48, 146–49. It was not Jane Austen who refused to face adequately the facts of carnality, but EMF who, in *Howards End*, has Helen Schlegel become pregnant, unconvincingly, with a natural child. [Defends Jane Austen against some other criticisms which EMF, her admirer, makes about her in his essay "Jane Austen" (*Abinger Harvest*).]

1017 Nierenberg, Edwin. "Two Essayists on Man: A Study of Alexander Pope and E. M. Forster," DISSERTATION ABSTRACTS, XXIII (1963), 4678. Unpublished dissertation, University of Pittsburgh, 1962.

1018 Rueckert, William H. KENNETH BURKE AND THE DRAMA OF HUMAN RELATIONS (Minneapolis: University of Minnesota P; London: Oxford UP, 1963), pp. 110–11, 179–90.
A Passage to India, in "The Analysis of Poetry as Symbolic Action," illustrates Burke's view of literature as sometimes representing a dialectic of the Upward or Mystic Way (essentially the kind of structure found in the Platonic dialogue). "In structure, the dialogue is characterized by a movement from error through dialectic to absolute truth, and thence to summary of the particular truth and the translation of the Idea or Ideas into mythic images. . . . In *A Passage to India*, the over-all movement is from mosque to caves to temple, or from widespread ignorance and a glimmering of knowledge (Aziz and Mrs. Moore in the mosque), to abysmal ignorance and near total division (Adela and Mrs. Moore in the caves), to revelation (Adela in court), to the knowledge necessary for unity between the races, to the mythic, visionary representation of a means of unity (the festival in Part III)." The downward movement in "Caves" is countered by an upward movement in "Temple," and the alleged pessimism of the novel's concluding sequence has to be modified by the certain knowledge that some characters (Stella and Ralph Moore, and Godbole) achieve of ultimate truth. [In "The Dramatistic Theory of Literature" an important image in *Howards End*—the wych-elm—is analyzed as in itself a basis for a cluster of images and meanings essential for a full understanding of the novel.] The wych-elm and its associated meanings illustrate Burke's dramatistic view of literature as composed of dynamic images which continually interact in kinetic fashion. The tree is identified with Howards End House, Helen Schlegel, Ruth Wilcox, and Margaret Schlegel; and it opposes the Wilcox values. After Ruth Wilcox's death the tree is increasingly associated with Margaret Schlegel and represents the Schlegel values as they contrast with the Wilcox standards. The tree is also to be seen as a symbol of England, since Ruth Wilcox, Miss Avery, and the Schlegel sisters (to whom the tree means most) represent the best in England. Leonard Bast is excluded from the values

represented by the elm instead of being presented as opposed to them. The tree is a symbol of orderly and affectionate growth, a symbol of both strength and tenderness, and a symbol of spiritual independence. During the night the sisters spend at Howards End, the elm teaches them that continuity and growth are important. When at the end of the novel Margaret maintains that she, Helen, and Henry Wilcox are all fragments of Ruth Wilcox's mind, then the elm, the house, and the principal characters are collapsed into one symbolic complex and made interchangeable with one another, a complex "which embodies and defines the essence of Forster's ideal way of life." [A stimulating and provocative discussion.]

1019 Sorenson, Philip E. "E. M. Forster: A Brief Memoir," CLAREMONT QUARTERLY, XI:1 (1963), 5–9.
[Sorenson came to know EMF in 1961 when he went to King's College for research in economics. Miscellaneous reminiscences of EMF's personality, attitudes toward people and ideas, e.g. "his idealistic concern for mankind is matched by an equal humanity and love for the individuals around him."]

1020 Stewart, J. I. M. EIGHT MODERN WRITERS (Lond & NY: Oxford UP, THE OXFORD HISTORY OF ENGLISH LITERATURE, Vol. XII, 1963), pp. 16, 32, 76, 111, 128, 245, 264, 465.
EMF disliked Joyce's ULYSSES on its publication, but *A Passage to India* would be a different novel without the great works of 1922 in the background: ULYSSES and T. S. Eliot's "The Waste Land." The influence of Hardy (as in the Egdon Heath sequences) may not have worked to greatest advantage for EMF in his descriptions of the Marabar Caves (*Passage*). There are affinities between the Rhineland sequence in Shaw's WIDOWERS' HOUSES and EMF's use of comedy of manners, e.g., in *A Room with a View.* William, in Kipling's "William the Conqueror," is the antitype of the English women (except for Mrs. Moore and Adela Quested) in *Passage.* The idealization of public school life found in Kipling's STALKY AND COMPANY was given its deathblow for the younger generation by *The Longest Journey.* [EMF quoted on James's later fiction and on ULYSSES.]

1021 Swinnerton, Frank. FIGURES IN THE FOREGROUND: LITERARY REMINISCENCES 1917–1940 (Lond: Hutchinson, 1963; Garden City, NY: Doubleday, 1964), pp. 27, 35, 50, 56, 61, 141, 145, 146, 147, 165, 234, 236.
[Cites Hugh Walpole's high praise of EMF, presents EMF's experiences with "Elizabeth" at Nassenheide, substantially as recounted in Leslie de Charms's ELIZABETH OF THE GERMAN GARDEN (1958), praises EMF for relying upon his earlier triumphs and for not writing any more fiction when he had nothing further to say, and discusses his Bloomsbury background. In a discussion of Virginia Woolf, disagrees with EMF's statements that the

story element in fiction should be discounted (though Mrs. Woolf must have found comfort in the statement).]

1022 Trewin, J. C. "From the Novel," ILLUSTRATED LONDON NEWS, 22 June 1963, p. 982.
The opening of Elizabeth Hart's adaptation of *Where Angels Fear to Tread* is clogged and artificial, but the play becomes "forcible, theatrical, and enthralling" once it reaches Italy. The events surrounding the death of the baby and Gino Carella's frenzy on learning about it are "undeniably and painfully dramatic."

1023 Warner, Rex. "A Passage to India and Beyond," NEW YORK TIMES BOOK REVIEW, 29 Dec 1963, pp. 1, 18.
EMF's creed is personal relationships, but he has also expressed national characteristics precisely: English, Greek, Italian, or Indian. The tributes in Natwar-Singh's book are personal and revealing. In EMF's books the situations, though firmly placed in time, are not out of date; he is concerned with perennially pertinent issues such as the difficulties of communication, the conflict of values, the clash of egotisms, the gleams of understanding possible among men. With EMF, truth and beauty are personal and are never to be worshipped as abstractions. A lightness, a playfulness, and a humanity set him apart from "the splendid severity" of Bloomsbury. All the books are admirable, charming, and sometimes prophetic; "The Machine Stops" is especially praiseworthy. The novels are all concerned with moral and political issues, at least in the broad sense. His characters sometimes fail to live up to our expectations; in this they are life-like, though EMF is not primarily a realist. Like Beethoven in *Howards End*, EMF excites the trust of his friends and admirers. [Review-essay on E. M. FORSTER: A TRIBUTE, ed by K. Natwar-Singh (1964). A perceptive and deeply felt essay.]

1024 West, Paul. THE MODERN NOVEL (Lond: Hutchinson University Library, 1963), pp. 7, 22, 36, 60, 61, 64–66, 67, 68, 69, 71, 72, 76, 85, 98, 104, 105, 175, 268, 290, 331, 359, 409, 410.
In his fiction EMF "contrives instances of vitality, cosmic force or sheer charity bursting through the net of cramped *mores.*" His cult of devotion and friendship is atavistic and shows a revulsion from class-consciousness. The deaths in his novels reinforce the theme of loneliness. His irony legitimatizes his self-consciousness. He sometimes resorts to burlesque, as if to indicate that his ideas are more important than the conveying of aesthetic tone; he plays many games with idiom and circumstance. His novels are "contrived demonstrations" with only a few of the characters being alive: "His ideas are fiendishly accurate whilst his portrayal of life is only approximate." His handling of fact fits in with the myth-mindedness of Kafka, D. H. Lawrence, and Hemingway. His quiet voice has few heirs, but his ethic of "charity" is a common modern European tradition.

1025 *"Where Angels Fear* is Staged in London," NEW YORK TIMES, 8 June 1963, p. 4.
Where Angels Fear to Tread is not well-adapted for the stage, but Elizabeth Hart's version is faithful to the original in spirit. Dulcie Gray captures the enlargement of sympathy that occurs in Caroline Abbott.

1026 Wickes, George. "Postwar," "E. M. Forster," MASTERS OF MODERN BRITISH FICTION (NY: Macmillan, 1963), pp. 221–23, 225–26.
EMF probably stopped writing fiction because he found human existence too bleak for a man of his temperament to write about. "Notes on the English Character" (*Abinger Harvest*) provides an explanation for the incompleteness of the typical Englishman and for the failure of many of his characters to "connect." The divisions among his characters into sheep and goats are not sharp; his characters are muddlers rather than heroes or villains. "What I Believe" (*Two Cheers for Democracy*) reveals a skeptic who still believes in humanity. [Rpts "English Prose between 1918 and 1939" and section from *The Hill of Devi*, pp. 227–49. Postwar literary scene and Bloomsbury milieu described (pp. 221–23); discussion of EMF, pp. 225–26.]

1027 Wilson, Angus. "Evil in the English Novel," LISTENER, LXVIII (27 Dec 1962), 1079–80; LXIX (3 Jan 1963), 15–16 [main entry for EMF]; (10 Jan 1963), 63–65; (17 Jan 1963), 115–17; rptd in KENYON REVIEW, XXXIX (March 1967), 168–94, espec 178–179.
EMF's moral distinctions are not clear in *The Longest Journey* and *Howards End;* he tends to equate right and wrong with good and evil, respectively, as did Henry James. Evil becomes cosmic and generalized, however, in the goblins in *Howards End* and the echoes in the Marabar Caves in *A Passage to India.*

1028 Woodward, A. "The Humanism of E. M. Forster," THEORIA (University of Natal), XX (15 June 1963), 17–33.
"Forster holds in solution metaphysical and religious agnosticism, belief in 'personal relationships' . . . and a strong infusion of Pantheist Vitalism in the early books, for which there is substituted in *A Passage to India* a tentative metaphorical use of some aspects of Hindu theology to express a sense of some other world of mystery that lies behind the daylight prose of secular Humanist goodwill." [Outlines the Cambridge background for this humanism in the work of G. E. Moore.] EMF favors an overplus of feeling as opposed to the intellect. In his early books the detailed texture is full of subtlety and nuance, while the overall design is schematic. In *Howards End* there is too much strain after unity. Ruth Wilcox hints at a divineness of mystery behind the empirically apprehended world, as a complement to EMF's agnostic humanism. This is also the purpose of *Passage.* Fielding,

Adela, and Aziz see mystery as muddle; Mrs. Moore encounters it first as a "dark night of the soul." "Professor Godbole is the serio-comic vehicle of an insight which sees what Mrs. Moore sees, but sees it in a wider, serener perspective, though what he sees is disconcerting to Western Humanist (or Christian) eyes—so disconcerting that I think Forster himself suffers some imaginative tension between the featureless depersonalized Hindu Pantheism that Godbole and Mrs. Moore jointly intuit and his feelings as a sensitive Humanist of the West." EMF attempts to create the mystery lying behind personal relations and ordinary action (1) by natural description rendered symbolically, (2) by breaking tone, disconcertingly, of the effects first produced, e.g., reducing Mrs. Moore's mysterious experience to a portentous depression rhetorically conveyed. The first method is more successful than the second. At the bridge party the connections between the races are frustrated by the same "aggressive nullity" which leads to Adela Quested's accusations after the picnic at the Caves. The message of the book is this: Human life is part of a process eluding the either/or of good and evil; but we must struggle after the good. "So Godbole prays to Krishna, though not expecting Krishna ever, effectively, to come, because the Good is only a phenomenal category of a Reality that is beyond good and evil—or rather, that is Good-Evil. To know this (humanly) terrible double vision may destroy one—it almost does Mrs. Moore; but it may also bring its own gift of a totally depersonalized joy of communion with that featureless Reality; and that is what Forster tries to render in the Temple scene." There are some qualifications to EMF's temperamental advocacy of the depersonalized view of Hinduism. It is difficult for him to relate the humanist-realistic and the religious-symbolist levels of the book. The marriage of Stella Moore (a descendant, spiritually, of her mother) to the humanist Fielding allows him to be in contact with an intuitive scale of values that he may not fully apprehend but that gives him also some point of outside reference to which the problems of good and evil can be related; thereby he can avoid disillusionment. In Hinduism one becomes as God, can suspend one's reason, and need not solve the problem of good and evil to one's rational satisfaction; irony holds all in solution; the process of self-deification that Hinduism encourages can also enable one to achieve a transcendent rationale. Yet such deification is achieved only by a personal effacement that bothers EMF. [Analysis of "Mosque" is best detailed analysis of EMF's style, especially as it relates to his philosophical purposes, that we have. A subtle, most interesting article deserving to be more widely known. Compare this article with Michael Spencer, "Hinduism in E. M. Forster's *A Passage to India*," JOURNAL OF ASIAN STUDIES (1968).]

1964

1029 Ali, Ahmed. "Recollections of E. M. Forster, III," E. M.
FORSTER: A TRIBUTE WITH SELECTIONS FROM HIS WRITINGS ON INDIA,
ed by K. Natwar-Singh (NY: Harcourt, Brace & World, 1964), pp.
33–39.
EMF's world is one that mediates between opposites. To achieve self-
fulfilling relationships is difficult, but the attempt has to be made. "Conciliation and reconciliation" are to be striven for "until the vision is blurred in
filth." EMF's way is that of Kung Fu-Tze's chun-tze who continues to seek,
no matter what the outcome; the search becomes the goal, while the seeker
is unmindful of the "goblins" and "nightmares" that may beset him. This
is the humanistic rather than the liberal tradition. EMF is aware of the
goblins but sees other things too. In the end, he would transcend the world
of Maya and achieve the vision of Nirvana. EMF's mother is behind the
supernatural force of the old women in his novels; she has made his women
as they are, foolish and irresolute in youth, ludicrous and improbable in
love, supremely wise and mystical in old age. EMF is instinctive and feminine in his approach to life. [Interesting essay.]

1030 Allen, Walter. THE MODERN NOVEL IN BRITAIN AND THE
UNITED STATES (NY: E. P. Dutton, 1964), pp. 33–39, 110, 185, 237,
247; as TRADITION AND DREAM: THE ENGLISH NOVEL FROM THE
TWENTIES TO OUR TIME (Lond: Phoenix House, 1964), same pagination; extract rptd in CONTEMPORARY LITERARY CRITICISM, ed by
Carolyn Riley (Detroit: Gale Research Co, 1973), I, 104.
[Brief treatment of EMF, somewhat similar to the more extended account
in Allen's THE ENGLISH NOVEL (1954). Other incidental references to EMF
throughout book.]

1031 Amend, Victor E., and Leo T. Hendrick (eds). "E. M.
Forster," TEN CONTEMPORARY THINKERS (NY: Free P of Glencoe
[Macmillan], 1964), pp. 86–121.
[EMF is one of the thinkers, along with R. M. Hutchins, George Orwell,
Joseph Wood Krutch, Archibald MacLeish, Carl L. Becker, Walter Lipp-
mann, C. S. Lewis, Julian Huxley, and E. B. White. Routine sketch of
EMF's career and enumeration of his themes, stressing his emphasis on the

private life and the individual, followed by reprinting of four of EMF's best essays: "Anonymity: An Inquiry" (1925), "What I Believe" (1939), "Does Culture Matter?" (1940), and "Art for Art's Sake" (1949). "Bibliography" includes other essays from *Abinger Harvest* and *Two Cheers for Democracy*, with summaries. Contains "Study Questions" on the individual essays and on general matters suggested by them.]

1032 Anand, Mulk Raj. "Recollections of E. M. Forster, IV," E. M. FORSTER: A TRIBUTE WITH SELECTIONS FROM HIS WRITINGS ON INDIA, ed by K. Natwar-Singh (NY: Harcourt, Brace & World, 1964), pp. 41–49.

EMF is a great Englishman who brought to India the liberal ideals of "generosity, tolerance, and sensitiveness." He has inculcated a philosophy in the novels despite his disclaiming that he has done so. He was also friendly to the Nationalist movement in India in the 1930s. He is a Christian Protestant, always holding to "the primacy of conscience." He is individualistic to the point of contrariness. At the same time he does not always seem sympathetic to the profuseness of Indian culture and its frank sensuality. But he has always looked gift-horses in the mouth and is unafraid of his own convictions. His smile is the symbol of his nature—"disillusioned, urbane, clever, and yet gentle in its tender regard for every human failing."

1033 Austin, Edgar A. "Rites of Passage in *A Passage to India*," ORIENT WEST (Tokyo), IX (May–June 1964), 64–72.

The plot of *A Passage to India* is built around Adela Quested's experience in the cave, but it is Mrs. Moore's experience which arrests the reader and holds the meaning of the book. [Accepts the Hindu interpretation of Mrs. Moore's experience with reservations.] EMF was influenced by the Cambridge anthropologists who were important at the turn of the century when EMF was at Cambridge. "Passage" refers to *rites de passage*, which Jane Harrison, J. G. Frazer, and others argued were essential rituals in primitive civilizations. The events in the Marabar Caves serve "as signs of 'passage,' of initiation, of a ritualistic death and rebirth without which actual death cannot be a spiritual promotion." The echo in the cave parallels the noise of initiation ceremonies, and the cave is like a monster-hut where initiations take place. In the Caves, Mrs. Moore is made ready for the propitiatory act she subsequently performs, that of expiatory death. She dies that Aziz might live; her influence saves him when the crowd invokes her name at the trial. As a result of her preparations for the ritual expiation, she loses her former values and identity; however, as an expiatory influence she has only a limited influence. She is reborn in the consciousness of Aziz and Godbole and is also present in Ralph, her son. For a truly significant passage to have occurred, the steps in Mrs. Moore's are inadequate: "Birth and Death are suffered without love and without volition. Rebirth is aborted. The ways of thought and action that it should have combatted—dissension, the inability to love or to communicate—go on as before." The book does not end in pessimism and disillusionment. The tone of "Temple" is not triumphant, but "Temple" celebrates muddle rather than salvation: "Its affirmation is the acceptance of chaos." By implication EMF rejects the saving aspect of all gods or human beings who become as gods, because as powerful figures they cannot love their inferiors. The cave experience is the death of everything, and the new life that comes from it is "stillborn." But the surge upward from the echo is all important, the release made possible through accepting it. [Interesting and challenging article, although Godbole and his Hinduism are more central and Mrs. Moore is a more dynamic figure than the author allows.]

1034 Bergonzi, Bernard. "Before 1914: Writers and the Threat of War," CRITICAL QUARTERLY, VI (Summer 1964), 126–34; rptd as "Preludes," HEROES' TWILIGHT: A STUDY OF THE LITERATURE OF THE GREAT WAR (Lond: Constable, 1965; NY: Coward-McCann, 1966), pp. 20–31.

EMF's worshipful attitude toward the countryside and the past in *Howards End* heralds that of the Georgian poets. In *Howards End* he foresaw many modern problems: traffic in the London streets, demolition of landmarks and buildings, and the spread of the suburbs into the countryside. The violence in his books is modern. Margaret Schlegel's vision of traditional England, of a countryside that would, if left to itself, vote liberal, was undermined in the years before World War I.

1035 Bess, Donovan. "Forsterism—a Force for Healing," SAN FRANCISCO CHRONICLE, 9 Feb 1964, p. 31.

EMF and conscientious men like him probably helped avert violent conflict between the English and Indians and did act as a counterforce to the arrogant Anglo-Indians presented in *A Passage to India*. His works have been a force for healing, especially in imperial and racial relations. In spite of the inadequacy of his thought to interpret worlds in India beyond his own, his effort to understand gave distinction to his work. [Review of E. M. FORSTER: A TRIBUTE, ed by K. Natwar-Singh (1964).]

1036 Campbell, Sandy. "Mr. Forster of King's," MADEMOISELLE, LIX (June 1964), 80–81, 120–24.

[First met EMF in America in 1947; about 1959 visited him at Cambridge with Donald Windham, the writer. Many details and impressions of visit given, including a London excursion (three weeks later) to Sotheby's where King's College was purchasing Max Beerbohm's caricature of EMF (EMF seen "in the act of withdrawing"). Details of another overnight visit to King's College given.]

1037 Dawson, E. W. "Two 'Flat' Characters in JUDE THE OB-SCURE," LOCK HAVEN REVIEW, 6, Ser. 2, No. 1 (1964), 36–44.
[Uses EMF's distinction between round and flat characters to comment on "Father Time" and the "physician" Vilbert in Hardy's JUDE THE OBSCURE.] Both are flat characters: Father Time is unsuccessful because he "surprises" us as only round characters ought to do (the "surprises" are not convincing), while Vilbert is a believable flat character since his motivation is simple and consistent (an unrelieved selfishness). [Pedestrian.]

1038 Draper, R. P. D. H. LAWRENCE (NY: Twayne Publishers, Twayne's English Authors Series, 1964), pp. 162, 163, 164, 167.
[EMF's crucial estimates of Lawrence before and after his death are cited.]

1039 Enright, D. J. "Who Is India?" ENCOUNTER (Lond), XXIII (Dec 1964), 59–63; rptd as "The Sensibility of V. S. Naipaul: Who Is India?" MAN IS AN ONION: REVIEWS AND ESSAYS (Lond: Chatto & Windus, 1972; LaSalle, Illinois: Open Court, 1973), pp. 204–11.
Although reviled as presenting a distorted picture of India, EMF in *A Passage to India* has gotten nearer the essence of the country than any other writer. [Discussion of V. S. Naipaul's JOURNEY INTO DARKNESS.]

1040 Evans, [B.] Ifor. A SHORT HISTORY OF ENGLISH LITERATURE (Lond: MacGibbon & Kee; Toronto: Ambassador Books, rvd ed, 1964), pp. 169–70; for 1st ed see entry for 1940.
[Consult 1940 entry for commentary on *A Passage to India;* the following discussion added in rvd ed.] In *Where Angels Fear to Tread* and *A Room with a View* EMF finds English life to be emotionally incomplete when it is contrasted with the Italian. *The Longest Journey* is uneven and emphasizes the inner, personal life. *Howards End* develops the themes of the earlier books with greater maturity. *Passage* features the difficulties experienced by the races in understanding each other. EMF has by now achieved great authority in the literary world.

1041 Faverty, Frederic E. "Homage to a Personal and National Friend," CHICAGO TRIBUNE, "Magazine of Books," 23 Feb 1964, p. 2.
EMF is not only a great artist but will be remembered for his lifelong interest in the people and problems of India. [Review of E. M. FORSTER: A TRIBUTE, ed by K. Natwar-Singh (1964).]

1042 Fraser, G. S. "Indian Summer," THE MODERN WRITER AND HIS WORLD (Baltimore & Harmondsworth: Middlesex, Penguin Books, 2nd ed, 1964), pp. 81–95, espec 90–95; also 117, 138, 170, 173, 312; completely rvd and expanded version of 1st ed, 1953.

[For basic line of discussion, see entry for first ed, 1953; commentary below is added in 2nd ed.] In *The Longest Journey* Cambridge stands for the virtues of the intellect; Wiltshire, for nature and spontaneity; and Sawston, for pretense and propriety. EMF's "correct" people are reluctant to face reality. The "code" figures in EMF's novels approach life intuitively. They are either vitalists or saints (Mr. Emerson, Stephen Wonham, Gino Carella, Mrs. Wilcox, Mrs. Moore); they balance vitality and saintliness, and they always reveal simplicity. P. H. Newby's Egyptian books, PICNIC AT SAKKARA and A GUEST AND HIS GOING, are similar to EMF's *A Passage to India*. Perry is like an EMF hero (Fielding), dry but kind, unaware of his own inadequacies. Muawiya is like Gino Carella, an unreliable and dangerous representative of an older civilization, who instructs Perry in the values of spontaneity. [The extended discussion of Bloomsbury in first ed is omitted.]

1043 Friedman, Albert B. "Forster, Dostoevsky, Akutagawa and 'St. Peter and His Mother,'" ENGLISH LANGUAGE NOTES, I (June 1964), 286–91.

EMF found that the Indians in Dewas State Senior liked only one European Story: Dostoevski's "An Onion" (related by Alyosha in Part II, Book VII, Chapter 3 of THE BROTHERS KARAMAZOV). The story is not Russian but a folktale widely diffused in Europe. Akutagawa (author of RASHOMON) gives one version in "Kumo no Ito" ("The Spider's Thread"). There is no extant Buddhist version, to indicate why the court cherished this tale. Akutagawa most likely borrowed from Dostoevski and invented the "spider thread sky-rope" let down from heaven for the sinner, a happier expedient than Dostoevski's onion ladder. Akutagawa may have drawn upon other Oceanic, African, and Asian folktales where such thread ladders figure. His alterations in his Buddhist tale from Dostoevski's Christian one reveal his unconscious absorption of a motif familiar to the Oriental mind and indicated why EMF's audience reacted so appreciatively to the Dostoevski version.

1044 Fuller, Edmund. "A Birthday Tribute," WALL STREET JOURNAL, 7 Jan 1964, p. 18.

Few men of the West (certainly no statesmen) have ever earned such spontaneous praise as that accorded EMF by the Indian contributors to E. M. FORSTER: A TRIBUTE, ed by K. Natwar-Singh (1964). His perception has earned him these tributes, a perception deriving from his artist's and humanist's vision, and from his capacity for intense personal loyalties. *A Passage to India* was prophetic of India's political history after 1945, though the contributors do not mention this aspect of *Passage*. Our literature has been enriched by the quiet integrity of the whole corpus of his work.

1045 Gallagher, Michael P. "Book Reviews," STUDIES: AN IRISH QUARTERLY REVIEW (Dublin), LIII (Summer 1964), 213–16.

Aspects of the Novel provides commentary on EMF's own novels—see EMF's judgment that a writer can confide in the reader concerning the "universe" and his own tendency to do so in his novels; his downgrading of plot and his own weaknesses in plotting; his emphasis upon fantasy and prophecy and his own tendencies to shift from prose to poetry in his books; and his preferring rhythm to strict formal patterns and his own tendency to repeat motifs that attain thereby symbolic purport as they echo through his novels. His humanism is tied too greatly to gentility to be entirely adequate as a philosophy for the modern age. His judgment of Gide's LES FAUX MONNAYEURS can be applied to his works: "among the more interesting of recent works: not among the vital." [Review of Penguin Books ed (1962) of *Aspects* and Frederick C. Crews's E. M. FORSTER: THE PERILS OF HUMANISM (1962).]

> **1046** Garnett, David. "E. M. Forster and John Galsworthy," REVIEW OF ENGLISH LITERATURE, V (Jan 1964), 7–18; considerably expanded version of materials in "Some Writers I Have Known: Galsworthy, Forster, Moore, and Wells," TEXAS QUARTERLY, IV (Autumn 1961), 190–202.

Both EMF and Galsworthy were the writers whom the intelligentsia in England between 1907 and 1914 found most meaningful because these writers attacked from the inside the British upper middle class for its complacency and money values. [Brilliant description of EMF as sly, equivocal, humorous.] In *Where Angels Fear to Tread* as in Galsworthy's THE ISLAND PHARISEES, the inhumanity of the British upper middle class is exposed by a foreigner (Gino Carella). In *The Longest Journey* (the worst of EMF's novels), we learn much about EMF: His experiences at Tonbridge School are transmuted into Sawston School, and he reveals his hatred of the vulgarity and materialism of the middle class, especially as it is revealed in schoolmasters. In EMF's as in Galsworthy's novels, someone from outside the social class exposes it; a foreigner, someone from another social class, an elderly person. Kindness is stressed in *A Passage to India* and in Galsworthy's FRATERNITY. EMF progressed in his art as Galsworthy deteriorated. *Passage* is noteworthy for excellent construction, freshness and fullness of the characters, and piquancy and pungency of the authorial asides. *Passage* may have been the most effective propagandistic novel of this century. [Many stimulating observations from a Bloomsbury insider.]

> **1047** Glenavy, Lady Beatrice. TODAY WE WILL ONLY GOSSIP (Lond: Constable, 1964), p. 98.

[Letter from D. H. Lawrence to Gordon Campbell (1917) is cited, stating that Campbell, John Middleton Murry, himself, and perhaps EMF might be suited for his Rananim scheme.]

1048 Greiff, Louis K. "E. M. Forster—A Bibliography," BULLETIN OF BIBLIOGRAPHY, XXIV (Sept–Dec 1964), 108–12.
[This is purportedly an exhaustive listing, but B. J. Kirkpatrick's A BIBLIOGRAPHY OF E. M. FORSTER (1965) exposes the lack of inclusiveness and the errors in this listing. Only details of interest are those connected with the Canadian publication of EMF's works, material not found elsewhere. This bibliography is careless and inconsistent, and it ought never have been published in its present form.]

1049 Hagopian, John V., and Martin Dolch. "E. M. Forster," INSIGHT II: ANALYSIS OF MODERN BRITISH LITERATURE (Frankfurt amMain: Hirschgraben, 1964), pp. 117–40.
Howards End is pessimistic not comedic; no "connection" is made at the end. The First Movement, "Margaret Was Left Alone," begins with the Schlegels at Queen's Hall listening to the Beethoven Fifth Symphony and ends with Mrs. Wilcox's death and the burning of her will by the members of her family. Margaret's relations with Mrs. Wilcox are analyzed, and her failure to achieve any true connection with Howards End and the Wilcoxes is stressed. The Second Movement, "Her First Real Love Scene," focuses on Margaret's awakening romantic interest in Henry Wilcox and Helen's opposition to Margaret's engagement. Margaret's desire to connect the "prose" and the "passion" of life in her marriage to Henry is the dominant motif. In the Third Movement, "But She Failed," the starting point is Margaret's sermon, with her injunction, "Only connect." The movement demonstrates in detail the defeat of Margaret's aspirations and her inability to realize them in her marriage with Henry Wilcox. Helen and Margaret are complementary: "Helen has her trifling affair with Paul, Margaret marries Mr. Wilcox; Helen becomes pregnant, Margaret becomes a mother to the family." [Account of EMF's career, followed by analyses of "The Road from Colonus" and "The Eternal Moment," by John V. Hagopian, substantially as they appear in "Eternal Moments in the Short Fiction of E. M. Forster" (1965). Some paragraphs of added background material are present in the book version of this article. Stimulating analysis of *Howards End* by Hagopian and Dolch, going counter to the general view of the novel as a comedy (with sinister and tragic overtones) ending in some sort of reconciliation. The ritualistic aspects of the conclusion and the fact that the Schlegel sisters have survived in an alien world temper the alleged pessimism of *Howards End* to a greater extent than the writers allow.]

1050 Hardy, Barbara. "Dogmatic Form: Defoe, Charlotte Brontë, Thomas Hardy and E. M. Forster," THE APPROPRIATE FORM: AN ESSAY ON THE NOVEL (Lond: University of Lond P, 1964; NY: Oxford UP, 1965), pp. 50–82.
Defoe, Charlotte Brontë, Hardy, and EMF suffer because of their use of

"dogmatic form," an oversimplified belief "which excludes much of the varied causality to be found in life, which is metaphysical in character and has precise moral consequences." Some of EMF's conclusions are tentative, but they are still too definite for the freedom that should characterize the writer's vision. In *Where Angels Fear to Tread* the renunciations are symbolic acts rather than human demonstrations. In *The Longest Journey* and *Howards End*, plausible action and psychology are again subordinated to ideological pattern. Ruth Wilcox is an arbitrary figure, dependent too greatly upon symbolism and fantastic machinery to be an effective moral agent. Her unreality is that of Virginia Woolf's Mrs. Ramsay (TO THE LIGHTHOUSE): both Woolf and EMF overvalue the aesthetic qualities of human beings, in contrast to writers like Henry James and James Joyce. With Mrs. Moore in *A Passage to India* EMF "creates a character who ... depends on symbolic stature and fantastic action but whose virtues are properly enacted, so that we respond not to an idea but to an individual portrait." Her respect for other creatures means that she can embody the value of love. The novel is essentially (and programatically) optimistic [contrast Frederick C. Crews (E. M. FORSTER: THE PERILS OF HUMANISM [1962]), and others.] The anti-visions of Mrs. Moore and Adela in the Caves are supplanted by Mrs. Moore's positive views of India when she leaves it and by Adela's recantation. The miracle-working Mrs. Moore is too dependent on EMF's use of fantasy; this aspect of Mrs. Moore is incommensurate with what EMF has to say about "the big gods" in the novel. "The events which are mysterious or ambiguous suggest that love may be powerful, even if we do not go so far as to say that God is love. And the Hindu apotheosis is appropriate rather than ironical, or provides irony to criticize sects, not beliefs and visions." But EMF simplifies India to make it more manageable or to implement his desire to attain unity. The most considerable effects of *Passage* are achieved independently of the fantasy contained in it. [An interesting, well-reasoned, and challenging discussion.]

1051 Hardy, John Edward. "*Howards End:* The Sacred Center," MAN IN THE MODERN NOVEL (Seattle: University of Washington P, 1964), pp. 34–51.

Howards End is a novel with an exceptional interdependence of structure and theme. Its dominant concern is with personal integrity. It has characters rather than personalities; its people are accountable for their actions (or failures to act). Their quest is for self-knowledge and assumption of responsibility. The old-fashioned emphasis on character presupposes another older emphasis on plot. The complex and rich symbology exists to support the action that becomes significant as it embodies human intentions. Coincidence (or lack of foreknowledge) does not excuse the individual from moral responsibility. To define the active principle of the integrity sought is difficult: How, EMF asks, are the rifts between men to be healed? The opening sentence contains the essence of the book: "It's not going to be what we expected." A different connection between the families takes place from the one promised in the first pages. Mrs. Wilcox brings Henry Wilcox and Margaret Schlegel together as she had separated Paul Wilcox and Helen Schlegel, and the final scene refers back to the first. The progress of the novel reveals the healing of division: international conflict, conflict between people and families, and, most centrally, the conflicts within the self. In seeking connection the Schlegels are also seeking self-justification; they can do nothing except seek the life of inner perfection but intermittently have some doubts as to how self-nourishing it can be. They are truly convinced that a person can only know himself in relation to the inner self of another, but they find few relations that are truly personal. Helen applies her formula —the exalting of public relations—without much scrutiny, confusing an abstraction with a person. Her changeability is really insecurity and incipient fanaticism. Her reading of the Beethoven Fifth Symphony, seeing in it heroism and sinister goblins, is personal and idiosyncratic. Margaret tries to see the music as it is and tries to get away from the theory of the interchangeability of the arts. Helen's carelessness about Leonard Bast's umbrella foretells the pattern of her relationship with him. Circumstances defeat him in his quest for identity, but Helen will not recognize his limitations or his lack of appeal to her as a person. He is for her an embodiment of an idea; as such she has sexual relationships with him, and in so doing she violates him and herself both. The doctrine of human relationships stands refuted with Helen, although it is also EMF's. Margaret develops it in truer, less rigorous fashion. By her reluctance to commit herself to the doctrine, she becomes its best champion. She possesses irony and so can see the danger of committing herself to either the world of the Basts or that of the Wilcoxes. Her attitude of indifference does greater justice to Leonard's human dignity than Helen's righteous anger, which makes of him a victim. Margaret knows that human beings can never quite act disinterestedly; she recognizes the value of, even the necessity for, the stereotypes of attitude deriving from class and inheritance. She knows that the Wilcoxes are more her sort than the Basts; but she can also recognize Henry's moral evasiveness. Her knowledge of, and respect for, convention means that she is not deceived by it and can at crucial junctures transcend it, demanding integrity of herself and others.

The house at Howards End is another repository of value; Margaret succeeds to it because she is indifferent to possessing it but is knowledgeable as to what its spirit means. The survival of the house depends upon the personal integrity of its inhabitants. The building metaphor relates to characters and moral values, and it signifies the stability of tradition; the automobile signifies the loss of that stability in modern society. The loss of manners, of humane moral perspective, is associated with the blurring of the aesthetic outlook; men deteriorate when they are so concerned with speed and progress that they forget the forms of their dwelling places. Margaret's leap from the motor car in Shropshire is a defense of Oniton Grange and an attempt to preserve distinctions and proportion. She is right about Henry; he evinces habitual dishonesty but has good stuff in him and fundamental decency, qualities lacking in his son Charles. The hope is to be found more in Howards End house than in the connection between Wilcox and Schlegel. The house stands for extrapersonal values to which we must be faithful, and pursue even in the face of death. The hope symbolized in the house transcends both the Wilcox progressivism and the Schlegel personalism (or any compromise between the two forces); that hope does not inhere in the marriage. The extrapersonal principle to which EMF makes his final appeal in the last chapter is a fertility principle. Ruth Wilcox, in spirit, presides over it, even though she is dead. Helen's fanaticism is mitigated in her child, who will reconcile Schlegels, Wilcoxes, and Basts (and unite their best qualities). Fatherhood redeems Leonard's absurdity. The fertility principle transcends the individual sexual shortcomings of each character. The feminist liberalism of the Schlegels is, for all its insight, sterile. The fields are even more important than the house. The house is to be kept going as long as possible, but the field is eternal. Howards End as wych-elm and meadow will endure longer than Howards End as country house. In the fields at Howards End the drama of human survival finds its most appropriate locale, its "sacred center." [An original, sympathetic, and imaginative reading of *Howards End;* one of the best essays on the novel.]

1052 Harris, Wendell V. "Style and the Twentieth-Century Novel," WESTERN HUMANITIES REVIEW, XVIII (Spring 1964), 127–40; rptd in CRITICAL APPROACHES TO FICTION, ed by Shiv K. Kumar and Keith McKean (NY, Lond: McGraw-Hill, 1968), pp. 131–46.
The style in much contemporary fiction has lost the "assuredness" that nineteenth-century novelists revealed; style is now more personal, idiosyncratic, and imprecise. One undesirable tendency of the nineteenth-century style is the overworking of a facile symbolism, like that of rooms in EMF's *A Room with a View.* [Most critics do not find this symbolism so obtrusive.]

1053 Harrison, Gilbert A. "The Modern Mr. Forster," NEW REPUBLIC, CL (11 Jan 1964), 15–16.
[Recounts EMF's delight at Harrison's not being moved by services in King's Chapel but remembers little of their conversation. Harrison stresses unity of EMF's literary works: "Every line speaks for the individual, for the possibilities of the spirit against brutality or indifference or coercive pride."] For EMF tolerance is a major value, and fanaticism repugnant. Against suspicion and indifference, EMF asserts trust and concern. He offers hope without hallucinations and is optimistic in a fitful and tentative way. EMF

is "the moralist without Belief; the reformer without program, the prophet of personal relations who knows how often they fail." What EMF found in Forrest Reid's work, Harrison finds in EMF's—"not moral precepts, but moral fragrance." The imagination may go far to redeeming the individual, EMF thinks, and great literature will also help illuminate his life. [Interview with EMF and a general critique of EMF's achievement.]

1054 Hoffman, Charles G. Joyce Cary: The Comedy of Freedom (Pittsburgh: University of Pittsburgh P, Critical Essays in Modern Literature, 1964), pp. 27, 29, 81, 83.

Louis Aladai in The African Witch is like Aziz in *A Passage to India*, a victim of his own emancipation. As in *Passage* the racial intolerance is more vehement in the officials' wives than in the officials themselves. Dryas Honeywood is like Adela Quested in precipitating the interracial violence; Judy Coote is like Adela in seeking out Aladai and offering friendship. Captain Rackham and Honeywood are complementary aspects of the conscientious but intolerant Ronny Heaslop. Tolbrook Farm in To Be a Pilgrim is, like the house in *Howards End*, a symbol of England. Who inherits England is, in both books, the principal question. In its complexity Tolbrook Farm is closer as symbol to the lighthouse in Virginia Woolf's To The Lighthouse than to Howards End house.

1055 Hoffman, Frederick J. "Violence and Decorum," The Mortal No: Death and the Modern Imagination (Princeton: Princeton UP, 1964; Lond: Oxford UP, 1964), pp. 23–93, espec 64–87; also 9–10, 289.

G. E. Moore's final influence was to encourage a rationalism based on "a limited analysis of forms and values inhering in objects and states of consciousness" for "futuristic extensions and utopian anticipations." Henry James rather than EMF becomes Wells's polar opposite. [Discussion of *Howards End* is less full than in the first version.] The house at Howards End gives firm insight into death and the possibilities of immortality, at least intimations of the possible salvation to be achieved in death. [Pp. 64–87 rpts in rvd and abrgd form "*Howards End* and the Bogey of Progress," Modern Fiction Studies, VII (Autumn 1961), 243–57. Some new commentary added, especially discussion of the relationships of G. E. Moore to Bloomsbury and EMF.]

1056 Horowitz, Ellin. "The Communal Ritual and the Dying God in E. M. Forster's *A Passage to India*," Criticism, VI (Winter 1964), 70–88.

The dominant Hinduism of Part III of *A Passage to India* cannot be ignored as Lionel Trilling in E. M. Forster (1943) tends to do. The orientation of *Passage* is neither sociological nor mystical but "socio-anagogical," a framework that includes and dissolves opposites. EMF utilizes the cyclic pattern of fertility rituals to organize his novel and to embody its life-giving impulses; the novel moves freely between social conflict and religious ritual and allows an ordinary English woman to become a Hindu deity. The characters' rite of passage in the novel involves, as for the poet in Whitman's "Passage to India," a passage to mystery and to more than India. This movement implies separation but also a dissolution of such separateness. In this passage to mystery, Mrs. Moore becomes a grail-quester, who through her sacrifice of life will redeem the land; she is a kind of Earth Mother, a husbandless Mary who gives birth to a new god. As a twice-born figure she represents duality and continuity; and she can embrace the opposites of action and being, intellect and love, the Christian way and the Hindu way, England and India. The process of Indianization begins with her contact with Aziz in the mosque and her sympathetic thoughts about the wasp. Even before her horrible experience in the Caves, Christianity had seemed wanting. The Caves are a testing place for Mrs. Moore as a grail knight; here she must undergo trials before she can bring fertility to the land. The reality in the Caves is incomprehensible to rational man; the loss of the distinction between good and evil and the loss of form and meaning in the cosmos disable Mrs. Moore, rather than the loss of a transcendent sanction of values or the loss of ultimate reward. In the events involving Mrs. Moore there is the death-renewal archetype. Her sacrifice of self brings life to others (the experience in the Caves is preparation and purification for her sacrifice, as in vegetation rituals). Her leavening influence upon the groups that surround her is great in terms of the union between group members, fertility, and new life. Aziz has a sacrificial-god aspect and becomes the scapegoat for racial hostility. Mythically, he becomes to the English the dark rapist, with Adela as the violated virgin. For England's rape of India, Mrs. Moore atones by her death, and thereby saves an Indian accused of raping an English woman. In her death she is, as a vegetation god, thrown into the water. In the court scene, the peripeteia of ritual occurs, with the intervention of the reborn Mrs. Moore, who is now a goddess. The action proceeds thence from sorrow for the old to joy for the new. After the trial there is the ritualistic victory procession, a symbolic marriage as Fielding and Adela are garlanded, and an actual marriage in "Temple" which Adela, as Mrs. Moore's representative, brings about between Fielding and Stella Moore. "Temple" features union, fertility, and the god's reappearance following struggle and sacrifice. The unborn child of Stella and Fielding symbolizes a union of intellect and mysticism and a parallel to the reborn Krishna. On the water Aziz knows that Ralph is Mrs. Moore's son and that union is now possible; the Mau festival is a moment of triumph and reconciliation when the goblins, or forces of division, are stilled. In the festival, friendship is reaffirmed with the positive aspects of ritual: passage, rain, fertility of the land, the birth of a child. Aziz is parallel to the English mumming-play doctor, symbolically restoring the sacrificial god in order to heal the land. But the reconciliation is only momentary, for division will obtrude after the festival is over. EMF seems to have distrusted the absolute reconciliations found in the Hindu rituals and seems to have preferred that the forces of mystery and middle-class values, of mysticism and pragmatism, be in continued tension with each other. [An astute and subtle interpretation of *Passage;* the exposition is masterly. One of the best essays on *Passage* and deserves to be better known.]

1057 Hudson, Derek. "Reading," EDWARDIAN ENGLAND 1901–1914, ed by Simon Nowell-Smith (Lond & NY: Oxford UP, 1964), pp. 303–26, espec 315.

EMF had no great commercial success with his novels; in the years 1908–1913, *A Room with a View* sold 2,312 copies and *Howards End,* 9,959.

1058 Hynes, Samuel. "The Old Man at King's: Forster at Eighty-Five," COMMONWEAL, LXXIX (21 Feb 1964), 635–38; rptd in EDWARDIAN OCCASIONS: ESSAYS ON ENGLISH WRITING IN THE EARLY TWENTIETH CENTURY (NY: Oxford UP; Lond: Routledge & Kegan Paul, 1972), pp. 104–11.

We approach EMF with a deference that is deserved, though his gracious personality and liberalist views may have disarmed criticism. His short stories are slight but reveal his values: his Hellenism, his visionary romanticism, his opposing of heart to head, his feeling for the *genius loci. Where Angels Fear to Tread* and *A Room with a View* are charming comedies of manners and perfect for their kind. *The Longest Journey* does not succeed. *Howards End* sets head against heart without the help of alien myth or locale (the means used to do so in EMF's other narratives). Why, after *A Passage to India,* did he drift out of novel writing? In one of his reviews he admits that the Edwardian Age was wrong in its confidence that problems could be solved. After the war he found that he could not continue to write Edwardian problem novels because the problems were irresoluble. The novels express a nineteenth-century humanism based on the need to reconcile heart and head, the faith that man can be good and happy if he chooses. The values were too clear and simplistic. But in *Howards End* the dichotomies became more complex, and EMF acknowledged the disagreeable aspects of reality and the divisive elements in life. *Howards End* is about the failure to connect, as is *Passage.* The novels seem to say, "If only we could connect." His honesty in admitting the failure of communication and connection gains for him our approbation and admiration. He was evidently reluctant to write additional fiction to convey this same conclusion. For EMF his personal values remained; they were strong enough to live by but not to create by. The novels with their wit, intelligence, and decency "will survive their failure to be more perfect than life has seemed to the Old Man at King's." [A most perceptive discussion.]

1059 Joseph, David I. THE ART OF REARRANGEMENT: E. M. FORST-ER'S "ABINGER HARVEST," (New Haven & Lond: Yale UP, Yale College Series, 1964).

The Thorntons, described in "Battersea Rise," shared the Wilcox concern in *Howards End* for material well-being, a strong business-sense, energy, lack of interest in literature and the arts, and distrust of a mystical as opposed to a practical religion. But the Wilcoxes also differ from the Thorntons: the latter valued "noble public spirt," "constant self-examination," and the sense of place, qualities in abeyance in the Wilcoxes. Ruth Wilcox never became part of her family's life; she is anti-modern, even reactionary in temper (see her anti-feminism); she is never able to adapt her rural values to new, urban England as Margaret Schlegel is able to do. Margaret preserves Mrs. Wilcox's values and makes her more than a skeleton from the past, though Margaret has to learn the truth of Ruth's ideas, especially the value of a home. Margaret meets a real test at Oniton Grange; if she had not forgiven Henry Wilcox for his sexual trespass against Ruth, she would have indicated her inability to adapt to a new situation. She is also able to deal with the unexpected situation and shows that preparedness is not all-important. It is difficult for her to inculcate, in a culture based on telegrams and anger, the importance of the Greek ideal of proportion. Helen Schlegel gives up the definiteness required for human relationships and for meaning in art. She is so forgetful of demarcations that she is unable to achieve an inner life of true significance. In *Passage* the structure consists of a series of touchings and partings. The ordered values of Western culture and civilization are at odds with the hostility of the Indian soil to them (though the traditions of India respond to hospitality and kindness). A contest results between formless India and the forms that natives and outsiders alike would try to impose upon her. Not much progress toward order and light is possible in a country whose ceremonies partake of "sacred bewilderment," and whose general aspect is that of muddle. [Analysis, seriatim, of essays in *Abinger Harvest*, to determine the principles underlying EMF's rearrangement of the essays under topics and to relate the essays to the novels. The first aim is nowhere accomplished; the second is scarcely accomplished since *Howards End* is analyzed purely on its own terms after Joseph discusses the essays collected under "The Past," and *A Passage to India* is analyzed similarly after he discusses the essays collected under "The East." The essays are minutely analyzed, but the analysis adds nothing to what a careful reader of *Abinger* can gain for himself. The confinement of his discussion to the essays in *Abinger* is artificial, since there are numerous uncollected essays from the same time-span as that covered in *Abinger* and since there are some essays in *Two Cheers for Democracy* that date back to 1935 or before, the cut-off date for *Abinger*. Joseph's assumption that the essays were written simultaneously with the novels is incorrect; only four in *Abinger* predate *Howards End*. The majority were written after *A Passage to India* (1924). No attempt is made to synthesize EMF's philosophy as he expresses it in his nonfiction. The discussions of *Howards End* and *Passage* are the best sections of the book, though the discussions are at best only loosely integrated with the other contents.]

1060 Las Vergnas, Raymond. "The Twentieth Century (1914–1963): The Novel and the Short Story," A HISTORY OF ENGLISH LITERATURE, by Louis Cazamian and Émile Legouis (Lond: Dent; NY: Macmillan, 1964, rvd ed), pp. 1366–1416, espec 1370–72.

Marianne Thornton is crucial to an understanding of EMF's early life and his later values. He rejected the public school ordeal and accepted Cambridge as all that a true education should be, a fusion of anti-snobbery, tolerance, and "a synthesis of intellectual magnanimity and emotional impulse." Breadth of mind and rejection of racial superiority are among his characteristic traits, also his "refusal to exploit the serious in a tragic sense." Art for him is "a planned birth," but an open process: "No hard patterns then, no absolute principles; only wide windows on the universe in order to be able to construct a fictional world true to reality." This open quality, revealed as suppleness in the fiction, assures him immortality; elasticity is characteristic of a fiction that is sometimes rigidly modeled from the dramatic point of view. He is on a level with his characters who exist independently of the motives assigned to them. The plots are not artificial; the victories are not won in advance nor are they decisive. Yet he is not entirely free and easy; he is serious as an artist, adept at suggesting the half-tones implicit in his people and situations. His works suggest "a sort of negative urbanity" or "gentlemanly anguish." Such reserve at times leads to an excessive detachment, especially in the rendition of passion; sexuality is deemphasized in his fiction. He is an artist of extraordinary talent whose books have vitality though they may lack full intensity.

1061 Lombardo, Agostino. "L'Elegia di Forster" (Forster's Elegaic Note), IL MONDO (Milan), 14 Jan 1964, pp. 15–16.

EMF is now receiving the attention due a great twentieth-century writer who has contributed, despite his traditional technique, to the renewal of the novel. Even his first novel, *Where Angels Fear to Tread*, aided in this renewal by its insight into interior experience and by its formal qualities that so convincingly express a conflict between two worlds and attitudes toward life. All of EMF's novels reflect his attempts to transform such conflicts into a harmony, but the resolution of such conflicts is not fully possible. Only in *A Room with a View* is there an impression conveyed of resolution. Like Joyce and Virginia Woolf EMF is animated by a strong sense of life and by the faith, perhaps absurd and contradictory, that art can arrest life through images and thereby reveal its mysteries. In *Howards End* EMF leads us beyond a representation of contrasts to an investigation of the total nature of life. Such an aspiration to know life (found also in *A Passage to India*) accounts for EMF's greatness. Symbols provide a chief means of investigating life's mysteries and the symphonic "rhythms" of experience. In addition to the symbolic method to be found in all his novels, *Howards End* and *Passage* reveal a more complex symbolism that invests objects with multiple significances—the house in *Howards End* and India itself in *Passage.* India, in particular, embodies a perfect equilibrium between observed reality and symbolic meaning. Every aspect of India that the characters and author succeed in capturing becomes a spiritual conquest. Nevertheless, *Passage* testifies to the impossibility of "connecting" different worlds, as does *Howards End.* Only Mrs. Moore has known the "mystery" of India and ultimately (but not immediately) has found some harmony. Like Mrs. Wilcox in *Howards End,* she dies with her secret. Only silence thereafter was appropriate to this failure to reconcile opposing worlds, a silence that had as harbinger EMF's sad, elegaic music of defeat. [Suggestive essay.] [In Italian.]

1062 Loofbourow, John. THACKERAY AND THE FORM OF FICTION (Princeton: Princeton UP; Lond: Oxford UP, 1964), pp. 3, 4, 9, 161, 165, 172, 180–83, 211.

EMF, Virginia Woolf, and Henry James write in a different artistic world than do the eighteenth-century novelists. They are conscious of the expressive medium itself, the use of metaphor and image for striking aesthetic effect. Thackeray is transitional in the evolution of the novel from Fielding to EMF. Thackeray reconceived the process of writing fiction and anticipated Meredith, James, and EMF. In *Howards End* the images are symbolically allusive and organic to the novel's inner consistency. Lord Castlewood as a Grand Lama or Marlborough as a triumphant god in HENRY ESMOND are similar in the effect they produce to the Collector as an Olympian presence in *A Passage to India* at the time of Aziz's arrest. [EMF is quoted on the organic quality of rhythm in excellent fiction.] The dissociation of texture and content does not occur in *Passage,* or it is a problem solved in the novel. EMF saw two commanding figures when he surveyed English fiction, Emma and Esmond. In EMMA and ESMOND the novelists explore the relationship of fact and fantasy. In EMMA the fantasy is always implicit in the dramatized fact; in ESMOND it is revealed in the narrative texture, creating its own expressive forms. The literal events in *Passage* become reference points for the major symbolisms of Mosque, Caves, and Temple to devolve and develop around. Recurrent musical motifs provide the means for developing this symbolism, but the symbols always eventuate from definite objects. The thematic continuities in *Passage* are expressed in the novel's elaborate structure; in ESMOND, in the narrator's consciousness.

1063 Macauley, Robie, and George Lanning. TECHNIQUE IN FICTION (NY, Evanston & Lond: Harper & Row, 1964), pp. x, 28, 31, 49, 68, 127–28, 153, 156, 158–60, 161.

Percy Lubbock's THE CRAFT OF FICTION and EMF's *Aspects of the Novel* remain unrivaled as discussions of fiction because they are by writers who are also novelists. EMF also illustrates in *A Passage to India* the importance of actualizing place in his opening chapter. The opening chapter of *A Room with a View* illustrates a "low" rather than a "high" tone: casual, quiet, somewhat discursive, and humorous. EMF reveals the use of the informal style at its best in his description of the characters in *Passage*. He reveals much skill in conveying information about India; it is always made part of the lives of the characters and is never superimposed on them or irrelevant to them. [Incidental discussions of EMF's critical terms in *Aspects* and of his remarks therein on Proust.]

1064 Macaulay, Rose. LETTERS TO A SISTER, ed by Constance Babington-Smith (Lond: Collins; NY: Atheneum, 1964), pp. 154, 195, 251, 252.

[Brief references to EMF's broadcast on Indian art, journey to Portugal (6 Sept 1935), and EMF on desiring foreign visitors (15 July 1956).]

1065 McConkey, James. "The Exemplar at Eighty-Five," SHENANDOAH, XV (Spring 1964), 68–70.

E. M. FORSTER: A TRIBUTE (1964) demonstrates that in EMF's own life personal relationships are important, since the six Indian contributors attest to EMF's warmth in friendship. EMF's concern with his own values and his knowledge of their limitations give his fiction integrity even when his plots are contrived. Some of the writers feel that the modern world does not favor a man of EMF's temper; but we are forced to return to his personal apprehension of experience by the blackness of our present situation. As he was shaped by the Victorian Age he may be the vanishing man; but he also represents what will not vanish in human experience. [Review-essay on E. M. FORSTER: A TRIBUTE. A meaningful appreciation of EMF and his influence.]

1066 McLuhan, Marshall. "The Medium Is the Message," UNDERSTANDING MEDIA: THE EXTENSIONS OF MAN (NY, Toronto & Lond: McGraw-Hill, 1964), pp. 7–21, espec 15–16.

A Passage to India dramatizes the inability of opposed cultures to meet, the "oral and intuitive oriental culture" and the "rational, visual European." "The moment of truth and dislocation from the typographic trance of the West" occurs in the Marabar Caves. Adela Quested's limited rationality cannot cope with "the total inclusive field of resonance that is India." The novel becomes "a parable of Western man in the electric age," and is only incidentally political.

> **1067** Marcus, Steven. "The Art of Fiction XXXII: Norman Mailer, an Interview," PARIS REVIEW, No. 31 (1964), 29–58, espec 41–42; rptd as "Norman Mailer," WRITERS AT WORK: THE PARIS REVIEW INTERVIEWS, THIRD SERIES, Intro by Alfred Kazin (NY: Viking P, 1967), pp. 253–78, espec 264–65.

Norman Mailer has learned much from EMF. Gerald Dawes's sudden death in *The Longest Journey* taught Mailer that character is more fluid, shifting, inexact, and unpredictable than he had thought. After reading EMF, Mailer felt a novel written in the third person would be impossible for him for many years (despite the fact that EMF never wrote a first-person novel and wrote in third person), since EMF so radically revised Mailer's "notion of personality."

> **1068** Menon, Narayana Menon. "Recollections of E. M. Forster, I," E. M. FORSTER: A TRIBUTE WITH SELECTIONS FROM HIS WRITINGS ON INDIA, ed by K. Natwar-Singh (NY: Harcourt, Brace & World, 1964), pp. 3–14.

EMF is almost overcivilized, generous, witty, humane, mischievous, lovable, sensitive to music and art, and courageous. His mind is independent. EMF's work is not shy, unworldly, and diffident as some critics assert [see George Sampson, THE CONCISE CAMBRIDGE HISTORY OF ENGLISH LITERATURE (1941).] The sheer quality of his writing has secured for him his reputation. His style is relaxed, colloquial, eloquent, resembling good conversation. His novels give us perceptions of truth. *Howards End* is his greatest work. In this novel the rapprochement between Wilcoxes and Schlegels is not always convincing; but the novel finally persuades through its shrewd analysis of minor details, motives, and actions. *A Passage to India* reveals EMF's supreme interest in India.

> **1069** Meyet, Marc. "*A Passage to India:* Notes on Forster's Scepticism," ÉTUDES ANGLAISES ET AMÉRICAINES (Aix-en-Provence), II (1964), 149–56.

EMF's skepticism is not the expression of an uncertain mind or of a doubt-ridden soul but of a philosophical viewpoint. *A Passage to India* goes further and arraigns the Western faith in the powers of the mind to make meaningful discriminations and so undermines the criteria upon which Western skepticism is based. EMF identifies in part with the inertia and spiritual quietism represented in Godbole's view of the interchangeability of good and evil and in his inability to act. EMF goes beyond this quietism to a "self-imposed voluntarism which transcends disbelief." The "ulterior" humanism that emerges as EMF chooses the forms and order of Mediterranean and British civilization over the muddle and quietism of India is far less confident (but firmer) than the "anterior" humanism represented early in the novel by Mrs. Moore and Fielding before they were confronted with the challenge of India. [Misses the thrust of *Passage:* the reconciliation and harmony achieved in "Temple" and the implied superior richness of Indian muddle over the ordered forms of Western civilization.]

1070 Miller, James E., Jr., and Bernice Slote (eds). NOTES FOR TEACHING "THE DIMENSIONS OF THE SHORT STORY: A CRITICAL ANTHOLOGY," (NY: Dodd, Mead, 1964), pp. 20–21.
"The Story of a Panic" develops a basic paradox: an unsympathetic narrator obtrudes but sympathy is nevertheless generated for the protagonist.

1071 Missey, James. "Appearance and Reality in the Fiction of E. M. Forster," DISSERTATION ABSTRACTS, XXIV (1964), 2037–38. Unpublished dissertation, University of Pennsylvania, 1963.

1072 Missey, James. "Forster's Redemptive Siren," MODERN FICTION STUDIES, X (Winter 1964–1965), 383–85.
The siren is a redemptive presence. Giuseppi and Maria (who have both seen the siren) are analogues of Joseph and Mary; their unborn child (who is killed with Maria when a priest pushes her over a cliff) may be the redeemer who might have done much to save the world had he been allowed to live. The siren is undoubtedly God, the spiritual progenitor of the unborn Christ. [Corrects (justifiably) Lionel Trilling's interpretation of the siren (E. M. FORSTER, 1943) as death in "The Story of the Siren" and Frederick P. W. McDowell's view of the siren as an evil force ("Forster's 'Natural Supernaturalism': The Tales," 1961).]

1073 Nakano, Yukito. "Art in E. M. Forster," EIGO EIBUNGAKU RONSO (Fukvoka, Japan), No. 14 (Jan 1964), 23–32.
EMF's skepticism and anti-systematism result in an impressionistic method of criticism; he combines effectively humanism with his skepticism. [Demonstrates by discussion of several of EMF's essays that his overriding concept in aesthetics is the autonomy and importance of the individual work of art. Statement is much less clear and comprehensive than in Mark Goldman's "Virginia Woolf and E. M. Forster: A Critical Dialogue" (1966), Frederick P. W. McDowell's "E. M. Forster's Conception of the Critic" (1965) and "E. M. Forster's Theory of Literature" (1966).]

1074 Natwar-Singh, K. (ed). E. M. FORSTER: A TRIBUTE WITH SELECTIONS FROM HIS WRITINGS ON INDIA (NY: Harcourt, Brace & World, 1964).
[Contents, abstracted separately: K. Natwar-Singh, "Introduction"; Narayana Menon, "Recollections of E. M. Forster, I"; Raja Rao, "Recollec-

tions of E. M. Forster, II"; Ahmed Ali, "Recollections of E. M. Forster, III"; Mulk Raj Anand, "Recollections of E. M. Forster, IV"; Santha Rama Rau, "Recollections of E. M. Forster, V"; K. Natwar-Singh, "Recollections of E. M. Forster, VI." By EMF, not abstracted: "Mahatma Gandhi" (1949, uncollected); "The Nine Gems of Ujain" (1914, *Abinger Harvest*); "Syed Ross Masood," (1937, *Two Cheers for Democracy*); ["On the Death of Bapu Sahib"], (1953, *The Hill of Devi*); "Two Books by Tagore" (1914, 1919, *Abinger*); "The Emperor Babur" (1921, *Abinger*); "Note on *A Passage to India*," (1953, *The Hill of Devi*); "Caves" (1924, Chapter XII, *A Passage to India*); "India Again" (1946, *Two Cheers*); "The Mind of the Indian Native State" (1922, *Abinger*); "Gokul Ashtami" [in part], (1953, *The Hill of Devi*); "Hymn before Action" (1912, *Abinger*). Reviews: Donovan Bess (Entry No. 1035); L. D. Clark, "Book Reviews," ARIZONA QUARTERLY, XX (Spring 1964), 275–76; Frederic E. Faverty (Entry No. 1041); Edmund Fuller (Entry No. 1044); Lloyd Griffin (Entry No. 1007), James McConkey (Entry No. 1065); Frederick P. W. McDowell, "E. M. Forster's Most Recent Critics," ENGLISH LITERATURE IN TRANSITION, VIII:1 (1965), 49–60; "Notes on Current Books" (Entry No. 1079); Orville Prescott, "Mr. Forster and His Indian Friends," NEW YORK TIMES, 1 Jan 1964, p. 23; Alan Pryce-Jones (Entry No. 1083); Bradford Smith, "Six Who Came to Praise," SATURDAY REVIEW (NY), XLVII (4 Jan 1964), 83–84; and Rex Warner (Entry No. 1023).

1075 Natwar-Singh, K. "Introduction," E. M. FORSTER: A TRIBUTE WITH SELECTIONS FROM HIS WRITINGS ON INDIA, ed by K. Natwar-Singh (NY: Harcourt, Brace & World, 1964), pp. ix–xiv.
[This is a volume written by Indians whom EMF had affected, whose lives he had "uplifted and enlarged." Sketch of his career. His life is characterized by "love of truth, love of friends, love of beauty, love of music, understanding, sympathy, courage, kindness, generosity, tolerance, wit and wisdom." Records conversations with EMF. EMF does not like the orderliness of Islam; the political influence of *A Passage to India* was incidental since he was interested in the story and characters primarily. William Golding is trying to do his sort of thing in the novel but in a different way.]

1076 Natwar-Singh, K. "Recollections of E. M. Forster, VI," E. M. FORSTER: A TRIBUTE WITH SELECTIONS FROM HIS WRITINGS ON INDIA, ed by Natwar-Singh (NY: Harcourt, Brace & World, 1964), pp. 65–75.
[EMF taught the English to disengage from imperialism. Account of his associations with EMF at Cambridge. EMF appreciates Natwar-Singh's praise of *The Hill of Devi*: its outlook, said EMF, is like that in *A Passage to India*, only the political situation has changed, so that *Devi* will be no more acceptable to present-day India than *Passage* was to the India of forty

years ago. Cites EMF's praise of Nehru. EMF's correspondence reveals his current pessimistic view of the world; when EMF reflects on what human beings might feel and do and don't do and feel, he inevitably gets "depressed." Essay striking by its personal quality.]

1077 Nierenberg, Edwin. "The Prophecy of E. M. Forster," QUEEN'S QUARTERLY, LXXI (Summer 1964), 189–202.

As a prophet EMF would contend that some spiritually basic meaning to life must be searched out and the spiritually desiccated orthodoxy exposed for its weaknesses. The spiritual life is necessary, mysterious, real. EMF utilizes this principle to criticize traditional Christian concepts, his spiritual philosophy being an amalgam of classical and romantic, Christian and non-Christian attitudes. He believes in the self and personal relations, despite evidence that they may be only partly effective. At the peak of the struggle for meaning, the depths of non-meaning must be recognized, confronted if not fully resolved. He advocates no either/or position but asserts a yes-and-no complexity, seeing life not in terms of good and evil but in terms of good-and-evil. The ultimate is not to be conceived as a static force or frozen power, denying the possibility of the freedom of the will and promising us a maximum security. Absolute despair also is too simplistic an interpretation of life. Institutional Christianity has failed both as a local and as a universal religion. For EMF the answer may lie in a synthesis of religions, any one religion often becoming intolerant, tyrannical, and exclusive, as Christianity did, for example, in ancient Alexandria. He is opposed to asceticism, and while he does not deny the need for a conscience, he deplores its abuse by religion itself (see his attacks on Cecil Vyse's "medievalism" in *A Room with a View* and his deploring the death of Mrs. Emerson as due to an hysterical religiosity). He does not deny man's badness but starts with the idea of his goodness and a realization of his need for happiness and fulfillment in this world. What EMF finds of value in Christianity is its contributions to a tradition of individuality, of conscience that urges personal integrity against the tyranny of the state, of scholarship and tolerance in such men as Clement and Origen. Santa Deodata in *Where Angels Fear to Tread* becomes a living force to the Italians because of her powerful indwelling spirit which unites the extremes of "love and cruelty, sacrifice and barbarism, patriotism and ignorance, the nobility of the spirit and the poverty of the flesh." EMF is not Christian but religious, sympathetic to the open and tolerant religion of Voltaire, Erasmus, Montaigne, and above all, the Greeks. In *A Passage to India* EMF's prophetic aim is to bridge a gap "between East and West, laughter and conscience, man and god." Its structure may provide a kind of passage for twentieth-century man from optimism to disillusion to a qualified hope for spiritual integration. EMF would support any religion that allows men to connect. In "Mr. Andrews" EMF celebrates a vital religion allowing for the element of choice. In "The Story of the Siren" EMF analyzes the need for a change in our current religious institutions if the spirit of religion is to be saved. Giuseppi, Maria, and their unborn child are Holy Family figures destroyed by an institutional church; it has destroyed the possibility of redemption through love and the universal brotherhood that it enjoins. EMF believes in something over and beyond life but does not raise death to a fearful domination over life. Death, in fact, makes life more precious. Virtue is its own reward and not to be rewarded after death. In an age of alienation EMF's prophecy urges a passage to a more "plentudinous" world where choice and the creation of value are realities. By recognizing the complexity of life, he would hope to restore "the concept of synthesis" to human life. [Extensive analysis of "The Story of the Siren." A substantial essay, of value in fixing the contours of EMF's "religion" and especially his complex relations to Christianity.]

1078 Nierenberg, Edwin. "The Withered Priestess: Mrs. Moore's Incomplete Passage to India," MODERN LANGUAGE QUARTERLY, XXV (June 1964), 198–204; rptd in PERSPECTIVES ON E. M. FORSTER'S "A PASSAGE TO INDIA," ed by V. A. Shahane (NY: Barnes & Noble, 1968), pp. 66–72.

Mrs. Moore in *A Passage to India* is not a heroine. The existing criticism stresses her benevolent and superhuman qualities. She is neither a saint nor a devil, neither redemptive nor fallen, but a figure with concurrent attitudes of sincerity and self-deception. She sometimes displays tolerance and wisdom, and the desire to act well, to create goodwill, and to establish communication between the races. But she fails in an understanding love and reveals, in her ignorance, an uninformed heart. She is not wise enough to accept muddle and mystery in a friend, in God, or in India. She does not have the capacity, in a world that is complex, to love when the issues are not clear, to envision a God who comes and doesn't come, a God of mystery who is also a muddle. Her religion is incomplete; she has no true notion of evil, and she has no acts of love to her credit. She does not ever show love in action. Instead of love she obeys a sense of duty, "in a universe of obligation and due reward." She has a naïve faith in progress, until it is undermined by her experience in the Caves. She does not spontaneously give of her self; she has few insights into her own nature upon which valid personal relationships might be established. She is concerned with the letter rather than the spirit of her Bible. As a result of her visit to the Caves, she abjures action because she has lost belief, not in love but in rewards. Her disillusion after the Caves over "God's never-coming and never-rewarding reality" is overwhelming. She is pitiable but not heroic or great. Her being remembered after death by Godbole, Aziz, and Fielding is an unexpected reward but not a heroine's reward for inspirational greatness. Her incomplete, deficient nature is also to be measured by her lack of response to the waters of India. The image of the Ganges (with dead bodies and crocodiles in it) provides a contradictory view of reality to which she cannot accommodate. At the Marabar, the experience with the ablution tank signifies Mrs. Moore's incompleteness, her inability to immerse herself in the waters of life. Wishing a reward for having never faced up to her truth-thwarting reason, Adela Quested wants a reasonable marriage; Mrs. Moore wants proof of a just God without facing up to her reliance upon a promise of reward for actions that ought to be disinterested. They are blind to the elusiveness and the mystery of human experience, a beauty and elusiveness symbolized by India. After the visit to the Caves, they are left defenseless before the disorder of an unreasonable universe. Mrs. Moore overcomes despair to a degree when she leaves India. She has failed to achieve a passage for and by herself, but she gives hope to others. [This article is blind to the *magna mater* aspect of Mrs. Moore, who after radical disillusion achieves transcendental sanctions for what she is and does. The article fails to upset the consensus view of Mrs. Moore as a redemptive figure (see Glenn Pederson, "Forster's Symbolic Form," KENYON REVIEW [1959]) and fails even as a cogent minority report.]

1079 "Notes on Current Books," VIRGINIA QUARTERLY REVIEW, XL (Spring 1964), p. lxxii.

All the contributions in E. M. FORSTER: A TRIBUTE (ed by K. Natwar-Singh) reveal EMF's understanding of India and Indians ("so remarkable, so intuitive and free"), and a conception of him as a saintly presence: "Not a saint of God, certainly, but an anthropocentric apostle—to whom the intellectual appetites of men, the obese vocabulary of boys, the indiscrete discretions of Indians, the violence of Italians, the passions of a Maharaja, the awkward straightness of an Englishman, so many faces and despairs, are signs of an internal music, of a pure human truth, aspects of an earthly logos."

1080 Panichas, George A. ADVENTURE IN CONCIOUSNESS: THE MEANING OF D. H. LAWRENCE'S RELIGIOUS QUEST (The Hague, Lond, & Paris: Mouton, 1964), pp. 42, 66, 92, 170, 178.

Angus Guest and Francis Dekker in Lawrence's AARON'S ROD bring to mind EMF's indictment of public-school men in "Notes on the English Character," *Abinger Harvest*. [Lawrence's mild dislike for EMF during World War I is cited.] Like Dostoevski and Blake, Lawrence reacted to horror in life by escaping through it to a further vision. This is one of three kinds of persons described by EMF in "T. S. Eliot" (*Abinger Harvest*); the other two kinds comprise those people who do not react or those who suffer continually. The vision of felicity in the Epilogue to Dostoevski's CRIME AND PUNISHMENT is not incongruous with the tensions and strife previously present; and its note of hope is an indispensable part of Dostoevski's prophetic art. The endings of Lawrence's THE RAINBOW, Hardy's THE DYNASTS, and EMF's *Howards End* are similar in scope and intent. Svidrigailov in CRIME AND

PUNISHMENT and Loerke in WOMEN IN LOVE represent an unmitigable evil, a *meta*-evil which is overwhelming, similar to the all-pervasive evil cited by EMF as characteristic of Claggart in Melville's BILLY BUDD. [Materials in preceeding two sentences are part of chapter, "F. M. Dostoevsky and D. H. Lawrence: Their Visions of Evil," rptd in THE REVERENT DISCIPLINE: ESSAYS IN LITERARY CRITICISM AND CULTURE (Knoxville: University of Tennessee P, 1974), pp. 205–28.]

1081 "People," TIME, LXXXIII (10 Jan 1964), p. 37.
[Description of EMF's spending his eighty-fifth birthday with his friend Robert Buckingham.]

1082 Pl[omer], W[illiam]. "Edward Morgan Forster," ENCY-CLOPAEDIA BRITANNICA (Chicago & Lond: Encyclopaedia Britannica, 1964), IX, 631–32; and in succeeding eds, updated in 1973 ed. In his rejection of the received values of his society, EMF reveals a revolutionary temper. His view of human nature is consistent: religiously he is agnostic and anti-clerical; as to politically, he is liberal and democratic, but individualistic. For him, personal emotion and impulse are more important than social convention, which tends toward narrowness, shallowness, rigidity, and lack of generosity and imaginative sympathy. *Aspects of the Novel* is written in a resilient, unpompous style and has had a lasting influence, though some of the judgments are faulty. "What I Believe" (*Two Cheers for Democracy*) is central to the understanding of EMF. In *Marianne Thornton*, we get a glimpse of the piety, philanthropy, and cultivation characterizing one group of his ancestors, the Clapham Sect. [Summary of life and career.]

1083 Pryce-Jones, Alan. "Forster at 85: The Endurance of a Case Well Stated," NEW YORK HERALD TRIBUNE BOOK WEEK, 5 Jan 1964, p. 3.
[Tries to account for the reason people now regard EMF as a great writer, considering the slenderness of the canon and his failure to handle great themes and personalities. The answer is that "in a machine-made age he has constantly asserted the value of the human heart and mind. He has always sought to enrich the private life wherever public events might lead." Like others in the Bloomsbury Group, he has tried to define the "something essential" in the civilization he writes about. He writes a fiction of emancipation; he stresses sensuous responsiveness, the importance of human relationships, and the necessity of connecting and making the pattern of life comprehensible. He presented the dilemma in *Howards End* of the human values of liberalism being dependent upon the obtuse efficiency of the rest of the world. In his last years at Cambridge he has become the guardian spirit of liberal civilization, without losing touch with ordinary people.

Intelligent remarks; in part of review of E. M. FORSTER: A TRIBUTE, ed by
K. Natwar-Singh (1964).]

1084 Rama Rau, Santha. "Recollections of E. M. Forster, V," E.
M. FORSTER: A TRIBUTE WITH SELECTIONS FROM HIS WRITINGS ON
INDIA, ed by K. Natwar-Singh (NY: Harcourt, Brace & World,
1964), pp. 50–64; rptd as "*A Passage to India* as a Play," PROSE
AND CRITICISM, ed by John Hamilton McCallum (NY: Harcourt,
Brace & World, 1966), pp. 745–52.

[In a program note to Santha Rama Rau's adaptation of *A Passage to India*
EMF said that he had described political and social conditions which date
and human beings who do not date so much. He wanted to dramatize "the
human predicament in a universe which is not, so far, comprehensible to our
minds."] EMF admitted that Mrs. Moore in *Passage* is a "tiresome"
woman; what he meant was that she lived in the novel and outside the novel
on her own terms. In *Passage* EMF has three roles: the sharp-eyed critic,
the creative artist, and the subtle social philosopher. The novel was written
from inside the Indian mind yet convinced Indians that it was telling the
truth. One of its remarkable qualities is that the Indians speak differently
when talking among themselves and when talking to the British. [Back-
ground information given about her adaptation.] The English finally accepted it, realizing that EMF had caught "a moment of history" and that
such moments are being continually experienced by human beings throughout the world. EMF posed many questions for India that have not yet been
answered, now that India is free from Great Britain. [Excellent, authoritative essay.]

1085 Rao, Raja. "Recollections of E. M. Forster, II," E. M. FORST-
ER: A TRIBUTE WITH SELECTIONS FROM HIS WRITINGS ON INDIA, ed by
K. Natwar-Singh (NY: Harcourt, Brace & World, 1964), pp. 15–32.
EMF strikes one as being a saint but an "anthropocentric" one for whom
the experiences of this world are parts of a complex reality. He is also
something of "an unfrocked priest" who would confess for others; he is also
something of a Hamlet. EMF once proclaimed, "I believe in man"; EMF
finds in every man "the rational saint." EMF reiterated his view that the
Maharajah of Dewas State Senior in *The Hill of Devi* was a "saint."

1086 Reed, John R. "Made in England: The Gentleman Abroad,"
OLD SCHOOL TIES: THE PUBLIC SCHOOL IN BRITISH LITERATURE (Syracuse: Syracuse UP, 1964), pp. 124–56, 259.
The public school promotes the qualities of enterprise, practicality, materialistic concern, anti-intellectualism, anti-aestheticism, and deficiency in
feeling characteristic of the middle-class inhabitants of Sawston (the Herritons in *Where Angels Fear to Tread* and the Pembrokes in *The Longest*

Journey), the Wilcoxes (*Howards End*), and the Anglo-Indian bureaucrats (*A Passage to India*). EMF criticizes the deficiencies of the middle class in these figures, although the Wilcoxes have developed the wealth and political power that have made England and her empire great. The qualities of enterprise and practical initiative in this class (and in the British public schools) must be supplemented by the Schlegel respect for culture, humanitarian feeling, and personal relations. In this way the inhumanity, complacency, and occluded vision too often characteristic of this class will be eliminated. In *Journey* occurs the first extended analysis of the public school by a major English novelist. [An interesting but superficial discussion of the role of the public school in EMF's novels.]

1087 Saunders, J. W. "The Mass Market," THE PROFESSION OF ENGLISH LETTERS (Lond: Routledge & Kegan Paul; Toronto: University of Toronto P, 1964), pp. 199–224, espec 223–24; also 243.
EMF's career was less full of distress than that of a writer like Hardy, Joyce, or Lawrence. These writers contended more directly than did EMF with the mass market. EMF, by his valuing of the story element and his love of suspense and surprise, of melodrama, made his work appeal to the mass market of the Penguins. EMF's view of life was original, with its emphasis on the chance collisions of human beings, the tenderness possible in the sexual relationship, and the inconstancy and instability of all relationships. EMF offered no easy comfort but wrote so that the reader might understand those matters which might perplex him in real life.

1088 Stead, C. K. THE NEW POETIC (Lond: Hutchinson; NY: Hillary House, 1964), pp. 85–87.
The Georgian Poets belong to the new liberal intellectual group (1900–1910), and the Schlegel sisters of *Howards End* best illustrate this type. The Schlegels were interested in social problems; they championed the claims of the individual; and they rejected cant. EMF's lyrical passages reveal softness as well as honesty, qualities characterizing the Georgian poets as well as the Schlegels. [Provocative discussion.]

1089 Trilling, Lionel. "Preface to the Second Edition," E. M. FORSTER (NY: New Directions, New Directions Paperbacks, 1964), pp. 1–4.
The books which EMF wrote since 1943 [date of first ed of Trilling's book] add to his stature as a writer but do not fundamentally change our conception of him. The large bulk of criticism written since that date also attests to his stature as a writer. [Trilling's polemical purpose, he says, his quarrel with the socially oriented literature of the 1930s and 1940s, would now prevent him from revising his critique convincingly. Also his friendship with

EMF, which developed since 1943, inhibits him from revising his book. These arguments are not altogether cogent.]

1090 Wagner, Geoffrey. "John Bull's Other Empire," MODERN AGE (Chicago), VIII (Summer 1964), 284–90.
[Several mentions of EMF's *A Passage to India* in this general discussion of novels of empire.] The Army racist is too familiar a type in this fiction, in contrast with the hardworking servant of empire; the natives were not unfavorable toward strong control by the ruling powers (Aziz says "we need a king"). Race is an inevitable factor in the colonial scene, but it was no more important than that to the average colonial administrator. Many characters in colonial literature are sympathetic to the native populations; Mrs. Moore is described by Aziz as "an Oriental." The chasm would often be greater between Hindus and Moslems than between Indians and British. The cultivated Indians tend to think mainly that England has assumed excessive importance. However, the native populations, as Aziz says, need more than justice. There are three classes of people in the empire: (1) the good "white" man (of whatever color), (2) the rest of the majority population, (3) the bad "white" man. The vulgarization of class structure in American segregationist literature cannot be attributed to British colonial writers or the scenes they write about. (There are only two characters in *Passage* who use the derogatory term "nigger.") The job sense sustained the civil servant even under physical discomfort. (McBryde is not defeated by the heat which, he maintains, unmans the natives.) The creation of character by hardships was something which the colonial administrator knew and which Whitehall and even the general public at home did not know. (EMF's Collector is furious with a bumbling Parliament but prevents the looting of an accused India's belongings when he is beside himself with rage at the Indians.) The English to Indians in *Passage* are all alike—for better or for worse.

1091 Waugh, Evelyn. A LITTLE LEARNING: AN AUTOBIOGRAPHY, THE EARLY YEARS (Boston: Little, Brown; Lond: Chapman & Hall, 1964), pp. 37, 198–99.
[EMF's *Pharos and Pharillon* was one of Waugh's favorite books.]

1092 Westburg, Barry R. "Forster's Fifth Symphony: Another Aspect of *Howards End*," MODERN FICTION STUDIES, X (Winter 1964–1965), 359–65.
Helen Schlegel's reactions in *Howards End* to the Beethoven Fifth Symphony reveal her creative cast of mind, though she mixes genres in doing so (a tendency of which both Gotthold Lessing and Margaret Schlegel would disapprove.) Though Margaret is the main character, Helen is a catalyst, responsible for whatever action takes place. She is on the side of reflectiveness, passion, and the inner life. But she is also active and eventually gains

enough worldly knowledge to make her a bridge to the outside world—the world of the Wilcoxes. Her creative aspect is seen in her imposing her own fantasies on Beethoven's symphony, in her role in the plot, and in her being the mother of a child. In her reaction to music, she implies that a work of art is less valuable for its own sake than for its moral or social meaning to the individual who exposes himself to it. Those for whom the symphony is an enclosed entity (the pure aesthete like Tibby or the Philistines like the absent Wilcoxes) are deficient in one way or another. Helen sees a vision involving social commentary, even prophecy (an adumbration of Leonard Bast's death occurs in her vision of gods and demi-gods contending with swords), while the aesthete and the Philistine see nothing. The Schlegels, especially Helen, want to get the Wilcoxes to look beyond themselves, "to see their fundamental weaknesses and responsibilities to the rest of mankind." Eventually, aided by love, they may be able to connect spirituality with their materialism. Helen's synaesthesia (interpreting one art in terms of another) in the concert hall embodies also EMF's desired synthesis "of unity of being won through encompassing all of life—even life beyond the concert hall." [An excellent essay, mostly justified by the novel's context, concerning Helen's positive role in the novel despite her deficiencies (the aspects of Helen usually emphasized by critics).]

1093 Wheeler, Robert Harvey. "Poetry, Comedy, and Vitalism in the Novels of E. M. Forster," DISSERTATION ABSTRACTS, XXIV (1964), 2045. Unpublished dissertation, University of Rochester, 1963.

1094 Wilde, Alan. ART AND ORDER: A STUDY OF E. M. FORSTER (NY: New York UP, 1964; Lond: Peter Owen, 1965); rvd from "The World of E. M. Forster," unpublished dissertation, Harvard University (1958); rpts "The Aesthetic View of Life: *Where Angels Fear to Tread*," MODERN FICTION STUDIES, VII (Autumn 1961), 207–17; discussion of "Temple," *A Passage to India* from Chapter Four, "The Search for Order," rptd in PROSE AND CRITICISM, ed by John McCallum (NY: Harcourt, Brace & World, 1966), pp. 740–45.

Chap 1, "Art and Life: Biographical and Introductory" [Informed summary of life and career]: The dominant theme in EMF's work (especially the early writings) is the conflict between an aesthetic view of life (that ideally life ought to have the coherence of a work of art) and the need to react spontaneously to the challenges of life. Characters like Gino Carella, Stephen Wonham, and the Emersons have EMF's approbation, but they are fantasy figures and inadequately realized. His deeper sympathies are with his failures and problem children, although he sometimes treats them cruelly. The early books stress the need for the removal of obstacles to self-realization; the later ones, the fact that order is not easily attained in a chaotic universe. In *A Passage to India* the search for order resulted in despair and moral paralysis. Thereafter EMF turned to the essay, away from concern with the horror of existence, although death, chance, and separation inform the background of the essays. In his late years EMF found a positive order and vitality in art; in his early fiction, he had been concerned with the limitations of the aesthetic view of life. He reaches his highest achievement as artist in *Passage;* but in the essays which followed, the dialectic of his thought reached its equilibrium.

Chap 2, "The Aesthetic View of Life" [For discussion of *Where Angels Fear to Tread*, see Wilde (1961)]: In *The Longest Journey* Rickie Elliot, like Philip Herriton in *Angels*, adopts an aesthetic view of life, transforming his experience into artistic configurations that lack fullness and flexibility. Stewart Ansell is interested in finding an ultimate meaning to experience, as his exercise with squares and circles indicates; one can discover meaning in the universe but one cannot fathom its ultimate meaning. The opening discussion about the reality of the cow indicates that *Journey* is concerned with what is "real." For EMF, through Ansell, reality is seen to consist of (1) the indisputable existence of the phenomenal world (a psychological matter); (2) a perception of what is valuable in the world (an ethical matter); and (3) an awareness that behind the valuable is some unattainable final meaning (a metaphysical matter). When Rickie sees Agnes Pembroke and Gerald Dawes embracing, he makes of her a goddess, as does Philip of Caroline Abbott in *Angels*. This passage is not purple prose but a depiction of Rickie's false perceptions. After his marriage to Agnes and his symbolic rejection of Stephen Wonham, Rickie falsely judges on the basis of the outer man rather than the inner. Later, sympathy for Rickie is maintained by our remembrance of his better self and by his glimmerings of what is happening to him. In responding finally to Stephen's voice, Rickie hears his mother's voice, about which he dreams. At the end, his perceptions are disordered because he allows Stephen's momentary behavior to take precedence over what the man really is. In Rickie's case the search for order leads to ultimate disorder, chaos, and death. Stephen's final triumph does not fully balance Rickie's defeat. The realistically presented ploughboy does not comport with the symbolic values that EMF attributes to him. The other characters try to achieve an aesthetic harmony (Mr. Elliot, Mrs. Failing, Rickie) or an intellectual one (Ansell); only Stephen's harmony with nature is a fulfill-ment. In elevating Stephen and devaluating Rickie, EMF loses too many desirable values: the intellect, books, poetry, Cambridge. *A Room with a View* is the best controlled and most perfectly realized of the novels. [In-formed discussion of characters and conflicts follows.] Mr. Emerson refuses to view life aesthetically and provides the touchstone of reality. At the end, good is triumphant but evil is not worsted: see the wish of Mr. Beebe to separate the lovers.

Chap 3, "Two Worlds and Their Ways: The Short Stories" [The first full and excellent discussion of the stories to appear in book form]: In the stories there is a disjunction between the realm of the real and that of the ideal. The satire and destructive aspects of the stories are convincing, but their fantastic, positive, and poetic aspects are not. [Perceptive analysis of many of the stories.]

Chap 4, "The Search for Order": In *Howards End* EMF reveals his passion to achieve order: the plot, symbolism, and motifs work in the direction of this ordered view of life as it should be; the psychological dramatization works in the direction of what life is, in all its variety, disappointments, and failures. Mrs. Wilcox represents the desired unity of forces, but she is more symbol than human being; her complexity is static. She is EMF's symbol of salvation against the flux, the motion, and the machinery of modern life, and the mediocrity and the instability characterizing London. In the dialectic of the novel, the new and better product will have in it more of Schlegel than of Wilcox. Henry Wilcox tends to treat people as representatives of abstract categories; the Schlegel sisters deal with people individually. They are confident of their standards, but they recognize the need to reexamine them. The Wilcoxes, however, do not see the need to revise theirs. Margaret Schlegel is the active agent in connecting the antitheses in the novel, and she realizes that life itself is meaningless unless an individual tries to invest it with meaning. She tries to find proportion though she knows that life and twentieth-century society are chaotic. She is admirable despite her faults; she does what is correct even when it is not congenial to do so. Henry Wilcox is ascetic and afraid of the emotional life; his mind works in stereotypes and clichés. Why does Margaret marry him? She perhaps does not fully know him; she feels the intellectual desire and the emotional need to connect; she hopes that he will change; she thinks that order can only be achieved by doing violence to her own wishes and impulses. EMF's development of her is firm, and she does achieve new depths as a result of her experiences; but she is disappointed in her hopes for the outer life and for connection with Henry. In the conclusion, a symbolic reconciliation is effected, with some violence done to realism; one does not believe in Margaret's return to Henry, nor is Henry worthy of her. A forfeit of principle or else the impossible connection is involved. In becoming an anti-intellectual person like Ruth Wilcox, she loses her most attractive qualities—her intelligence, her awareness, and her conscious approach to life. She becomes a figure no longer searching for harmony, but one who patches worn and wasted lives. Helen is more vacuous than she was before; Leonard Bast at the end is a better but smaller character. The Wilcoxes undergo severe misfortunes without becoming better people. Henry makes his connection by submission rather than by the active will. The only satisfactory relationship at the end is that between Margaret and Helen. If the sisters break up lives, it is not their fault, considering that life and society are as they are; but their destructiveness would be more clearly justified if they were bigger people. In the conclusion the search for meaning becomes EMF's, not Margaret's, with the result that more is imputed to the characters and events than they can support. Helen's baby is an inadequate symbol for the continuance of life and the inheritance theme. EMF through this and other symbolic means expresses hope, but the undertone is sadness. In effect, EMF does not achieve proportion, but the half-way meeting of opposites that Margaret (and EMF through her) deplores.

In *Passage* the straight roads at right angles to each other in Chandrapore comment on the opposition of ordered British rule to the untidiness of India. In India the strength of the non-human world is overwhelming. The British do not understand the true nature of India so that their rule is unsuccessful. The atmosphere of discord and misunderstanding is present from the beginning, but in "Mosque" the major characters try to establish confidence and friendship with each other. Fielding is more rational and self-conscious than Aziz or Mrs. Moore; his rationality leads to clarity but is a limitation in personal relationships, as in his relationship with Aziz. Communication fails to emerge at Fielding's tea party. The muddle that Mrs. Moore says, at this point, she dislikes, changes in the course of *Passage* to its cosmic counterpart, chaos; and the lives of all the characters are then undermined. Godbole's appearance, song, and silences are unnerving to the Westerners, especially to Adela Quested and Mrs. Moore: his affinities are with eternity, not time; with the one, not the many. The two women assume an order in the universe that does not exist, and they fail to realize the power of the forces making for disruption. The difficulty of communicating is in bridging the gap between Anglo-Indian rigidity and the utter shapelessness of India. In India people are caught between an infinity that is immeasurably small and an infinity that is immeasurably large; as a result, they can communicate only with difficulty. Isolation yields to unwonted indistinction in a hostile universe; but this indistinction or unity also means loss of communication. Primal India, the world before civilization or even life developed, broods over the "Caves" section. EMF concenters primal India in the Marabar Caves symbol so that men can grasp its presence and purport. The Caves are impressive because they are inexpressive yet suggest meanings that they do not yield. In fact, they suggest nothing, yet nothing so definite as evil. Mrs. Moore is brought to the abyss in her vision of chaos in the Caves. Her disquietude has universal implications, and her echo spreads disastrous effects to those around her. Adela's reactions to the Caves are psychological

481

and physiological, also more general, resulting in her inability to cope with the strangeness about her. Alone, Godbole perceives the connection between evil and the ultimate nothingness of the Caves in which good and evil are the same. One must acknowledge the reality of chaos before he can explain or build on it. Godbole is alone able to accept a pessimistic view of the universe and to continue to live in a purposeful way. The caves imply to Fielding his own incompletness. Adela's statement is true that in space things touch (for a moment men may communicate) but in time things part (men are separated after their moments of understanding). On her return home, Mrs. Moore realizes that the nihilistic views emanating from the Caves do not comprise all of India or all of reality. Her new knowledge helps push evil in India back into its confines after her death. The punkah wallah in the courtroom as a reality symbol has a great effect on Adela and prepares her to receive the influence of Mrs. Moore and to withdraw her charge against Aziz. At this point the values that meant so much before the trip to the Caves—love, friendship, and intuitive understanding—are reasserted, but the values of reason or the possibility of verbal communication are not. Things are not quite as they were before the Marabar. The echo is never completely extinguished; affirmation is not strong enough to overcome negation in *Passage;* the abyss still continues to exert power. After the trial, the celebration is less able to bind Aziz and Fielding together than the crisis had been. In "Temple," the way of Hinduism, expressed through Mrs. Moore and Godbole, is that of love and instinctive understanding, the way of inclusion, and it contrasts with the form and order that Fielding finds in Venice. His ideal seems to be EMF's; and at this point, form, harmony, and reason receive their due, as in Part III sub-rational communication does. EMF cannot accept completely Fielding's view, because EMF is also aware of the welter of the world's cultures and beliefs. EMF's sympathies with Hinduism have limits, however. He admires the inclusiveness of Hinduism and the fact that under its aegis men can love each other and the universe. Godbole has from the beginning the knowledge that Mrs. Moore gains by painful experience—inadequacy and incompleteness are indelible features of the universe, but one must still go on. "Temple" balances hope and despair. After the festivities are over, discords obtrude; Fielding and Aziz no longer communicate. During the festival an adjustment seemed possible between man's recognition of chaos and his ideals. With the collision of the boats, the discords between people are eased. The new personal understandings are not easy to effect, and they do not last; but they are never quite erased (this is the meaning of Aziz's last ride with Fielding). The vision of the Caves is compelling but not overriding, as Reuben Brower suggests (1951). One can either deny the vision or give in to it as Mrs. Moore did at first. The whole question of order is never explicitly resolved, and EMF stops short of a final synthesis in *Passage.* Chap 5, "Art and Order": In his essays EMF finds in art the order, permanence, and unity he has tried to find in life but has failed to find. [An excellent, standard book on EMF, remarkable for the depth and subtlety of its insights and judgments. Select Bibliography. Reviews: Ben W. Fuson, "New Books Appraised," LIBRARY JOURNAL, LXXXIX (1 May 1964), 1967; Barbara Hardy, "The Personality of Criticism," SOUTHERN REVIEW, nsIII (Autumn 1967), 1001–9; E. Lacotte, "Étude Critique: Études Récentes sur E. M. Forster" (Critical Essay: Recent Studies on E. M. Forster), ÉTUDES ANGLAISES, XX (Oct–Dec 1967), 425–31; Frederick P. W. McDowell, "E. M. Forster's Most Recent Critics," ENGLISH LITERATURE IN TRANSITION, VIII: 1 (1965), 49–60; George A. Panichas (Entry No. 1135); and Richard Whittington-Egan, "Literature," BOOKS AND BOOKMEN, X (May 1965), 28.]

1095 Woolf, Leonard. BEGINNING AGAIN: AN AUTOBIOGRAPHY OF THE YEARS 1911–1918 (Lond: Hogarth P; NY: Harcourt, Brace & World, 1964), pp. 22–25.

[Woolf discusses Bloomsbury and his understanding of its origins. For him Old Bloomsbury got under way between 1911–1914, when his Cambridge associates (see SOWING, 1960) began to meet regularly at the Woolfs' and the Bells'. These were years of emerging fame for the members of Old Bloomsbury, after Woolf's return from Ceylon and his marriage to Virginia Stephen. He stresses, like Quentin Bell in BLOOMSBURY (1968), the nondoctrinaire quality of Bloomsbury: It was a group of people with similar tastes who enjoyed each other's company. The chief figures were Vanessa Stephen Bell, Virginia Stephen Woolf, Adrian Stephen and wife Karin Costello, Lytton Strachey, Clive Bell, Woolf himself, John Maynard Keynes, Duncan Grant, EMF, Saxon Sydney-Turner, Roger Fry, Desmond MacCarthy, and his wife Molly. Any cohesion the group possessed went back to Cambridge and G. E. Moore's astringent influence: a radical clarity verging on iconoclasm. This part of Woolf's autobiography is also absorbing in its accounts of Virginia Woolf and her bouts with insanity.]

1965

1096 Bateson, F. W. A GUIDE TO ENGLISH LITERATURE (Garden City, NY: Doubleday, Anchor; Chicago: Aldine Publishing, 1965; rvd ed, Aldine, 1968), pp. 191–92 (rvd ed).
[Sound survey of recent critical and scholarly work on EMF.]

1097 Bedient, Calvin Bernard. "The Fate of the Self: Self and Society in the Novels of George Eliot, D. H. Lawrence, and E. M. Forster," DISSERTATION ABSTRACTS, XXV (1965), 1187. Unpublished dissertation, University of Washington, 1964; rvd as ARCHITECTS OF THE SELF: GEORGE ELIOT, D. H. LAWRENCE AND E. M. FORSTER (Berkeley & Los Angeles: University of California P, 1972).

1098 Bergonzi, Bernard. "Georgians in Peace and War," NEW YORK REVIEW OF BOOKS, 30 Sept 1965, pp. 22–24; rptd in THE TURN OF A CENTURY: ESSAYS ON VICTORIAN AND MODERN LITERATURE (NY: Barnes & Noble; Lond: Macmillan, 1973), pp. 146–52.
The tendency of the Georgian poets to stress England both as a poetic subject and as a state of mind was paralleled in EMF's *Howards End*, with its stress upon house and wych-elm tree as symbols of English tradition. EMF's liberalism approximates also the political views of these poets. [See also Bergonzi (1964).]

1099 Bergonzi, Bernard. "Preludes," HEROES' TWILIGHT: A STUDY OF THE LITERATURE OF THE GREAT WAR (Lond: Constable, 1965; NY: Coward-McCann, 1966), pp. 20–31, espec 21–22, 30; also 35, 37, 177; ["Preludes" appeared as "Before 1914: Writers and the Threat of War," CRITICAL QUARTERLY, III (Summer 1964), 126–34 (see entry for 1964).]
Rupert Brooke's life is that of a figure from an unwritten or suppressed novel by EMF. Brooke's celebration of the English landscape in "An Unusual Young Man" (NEW STATESMAN, III [29 Aug 1914], 638) is similar to EMF's in *Howards End*. The Georgian poets at the time of World War I were in the melting pot described by EMF in the concluding pages to *Howards End*.

In Ford Madox Ford's PARADE'S END, Tietjens' England reaches further back than the liberal England of EMF and the Georgian poets.

1100 Boyle, Ted E. "Adela Quested's Delusion: The Failure of Rationalism in *A Passage to India,*" COLLEGE ENGLISH, XXVI (March 1965), 478–80; rptd in PERSPECTIVES ON E. M. FORSTER'S "A PASSAGE TO INDIA," ed by V. A. Shahane (NY: Barnes & Noble, 1968), pp. 73–75.

The Marabar Caves challenge the conscious, rational, and intellectual values on which Adela Quested has been reared; the subconscious, the irrational, and the emotional overwhelm her in the Caves. She suffers also from repressed sexuality. The field glasses are a symbol of her shallow rationalism; the phallic-like snake, emblematic of her repressed sexual longings which she observes enroute to the Caves, turns out to be a lifeless palm stump when it is viewed through the glasses. Adela is a better person after she can learn to accommodate the irrational. Adela's initial untempered rationalism also comments on the failure of rationalism to destroy the barriers that exist between men.

1101 Bradbury, Malcolm. "A Short Guide to Forster Studies," CRITICAL SURVEY, II (Summer 1965), 113–16; rptd, rvd, and enlgd, as "Introduction," FORSTER: A COLLECTION OF CRITICAL ESSAYS, ed by Malcolm Bradbury (Englewood Cliffs, NJ: Prentice-Hall, Spectrum Books, 1966), pp. 1–14; abstracted under this date.

1102 Brien, Alan. "Living Legends: E. M. Forster," VOGUE, CXLV (1 Jan 1965), 124, 125, 168.

EMF's personality and writings appeal to all ages, classes, and nationalities. He is a romantic optimist by virtue of his distrust of science. In his five novels he reveals his flawed heart, his faith in the civilized virtues of "humanity, decency, sensitivity, generosity, tolerance," and his perception that they must be complemented by "energy, vulgarity, sensuality, disorder, masculinity." The intentions—the mediations suggested in *Howards End* between opposed social types—are admirable, yet EMF may also be guilty of betraying his cause "by secret negotiations with the enemy." Two streams meet in EMF's work: "muddy melodrama and crystal-clear comedy, irrelevant violence and muted sexuality, sharp-eyed naturalistic observation with sociological and psychological improbabilities, limpid flowing prose with vague viscid poeticisms, simple explicit dialogue with muddled obscure monologues." One is uncomfortable with EMF's belittling references to sexual pleasure. What sort of man will replace the beast and the monk (see *Howards End*)? The books can be reread with pleasure through a lifetime. [Short, but vigorous and fresh article.]

1103 Campos, Christopher. "The Salon: Bloomsbury," THE VOICE OF FRANCE FROM ARNOLD TO BLOOMSBURY (Lond & NY: Oxford UP, 1965), pp. 208–37, espec 211, 230.
[Traces French sympathies and affiliations of the Bloomsbury Group in which EMF figured peripherally.]

1104 Chattopadhyay, Sisir. THE NOVEL AS THE MODERN EPIC (Calcutta: K. L. Mukhopadhyay, 1965; 2nd rvd ed), pp. 14, 28–30.
The novel is "the epic of the era of human liberation." The future of the novel is auspicious because, as EMF maintains in *Aspects of the Novel*, it makes man's secret life visible. In the modern novel heroes and villains are less important than the social factors determining human beings. The emphasis in the modern novel, beginning with Dorothy Richardson, has tended to be on the inner consciousness of the individual. [The disappearance of the "story" as primary and crucial is noted. (EMF quoted from *Aspects.*)]

1105 Connolly, Cyril. THE MODERN MOVEMENT: ONE HUNDRED KEY BOOKS FROM ENGLAND, FRANCE, AND AMERICA 1880–1950 (Lond: Deutsch, 1965; NY: Atheneum, 1966), pp. 28, 50–51 (NY ed).
The Longest Journey is more a key book than *Howards End*, because of its personal and passionate quality. EMF "angrily" contrasts free friendship among undergraduate men to the possessiveness of marriage. *A Passage to India* is the other key book. In it EMF explores the limitations of humanism and finds in religion and philosophy some solution to his problems. His visual sense is given over to delight instead of to nausea.

1106 Ethridge, James M., and Barbara Kopala (eds). "E[dward] M[organ] Forster," CONTEMPORARY AUTHORS: A BIO-BIBLIOGRAPH-ICAL GUIDE TO CURRENT AUTHORS AND THEIR WORKS (Detroit: Gale Research Co., 1965), Vols. 13–14, pp. 156–58; rptd in 200 CONTEM-PORARY AUTHORS: BIO-BIBLIOGRAPHIES OF SELECTED LEADING WRIT-ERS OF TODAY WITH CRITICAL AND PERSONAL SIDELIGHTS, ed by Barbara Harte and Carolyn Riley (Detroit: Gale Research Co., 1969), pp. 116–17.
[Summary of career; exhaustive listing of posts, memberships, and honors; full bibliography. Interesting collection of comment by EMF and by others about him.]

1107 Ford, George H. DOUBLE MEASURE: A STUDY OF THE NOVELS AND STORIES OF D. H. LAWRENCE (NY: Holt, Rinehart & Winston, 1965; Norton, 1969), pp. 23, 72, 78, 94n, 95–96, 127–28 (1969 ed).
D. H. Lawrence is a master of the device of "rhythm" as EMF defines it in *Aspects of the Novel:* the use of recurring allusions and motifs and variations upon them—e.g., the echoing caves in *A Passage to India.* In "The

Prussian Officer," characters reverse roles as they do in EMF's analysis of Anatole France's THAIS in *Aspects*. "The Last Laugh," with the god Pan showing himself to several characters, is reminiscent of EMF's short fiction. In fiction, trivial and unpromising objects and incidents inaugurate "epiphanies," e.g., Mrs. Moore's hearing the echo in the Caves in *Passage*. The parallel imagery used to describe the bedroom in Will and Anna Brangwen's cottage and the cathedral at Lincoln is an instance of musical technique as EMF uses the term. The gargoyles in the cathedral, which Anna calls to Will's attention to dispel his ecstasy, are disturbing presences like the goblins in *Howards End*, in intimating that the beautiful, confined world of marriage bed and cathedral is incomplete.

1108 Freund, Philip. THE ART OF READING THE NOVEL (NY: Collier Books, 1965), pp. 101, 110, 152, 166–68, 171, 202–4, 278, 335, 345; 1st ed, HOW TO BECOME A LITERARY CRITIC (NY: Beechhurst P, 1947) has no significant references to EMF.

In *Aspects of the Novel*, EMF appreciates the bardic aspect of D. H. Lawrence. [Other cited opinions of EMF are also from *Aspects*.] Contrary to EMF's assertion, author intrusion (even concerning his characters) is not necessarily heinous. [EMF is quoted on the tenuousness of Henry James's universe, the lack of robustness in his characters, and his overconcern with form and pattern.] EMF overstates the case against James. EMF's distinction between flat and round characters is valid, but Edwin Muir's insistence, in THE STRUCTURE OF THE NOVEL (1928), that flat characters are not less important than the round ones is preferable. EMF rightly held that André Gide was over-concerned with method. In his own fiction EMF is to be aligned with modern pessimists like Nietzsche, Tolstoy, Conrad, Lawrence, Twain, Galsworthy, Kafka, and Maugham.

1109 Friedman, Alan. "The Turn of the Novel: Changes in the Pattern of English Fiction since 1890 in Hardy, Conrad, Forster, and Lawrence," DISSERTATION ABSTRACTS, XXV (1965), 6622. Unpublished dissertation, University of California, 1964; rvd as THE TURN OF THE NOVEL: THE TRANSITION TO MODERN FICTION (NY & Lond: Oxford UP, 1966).

1110 Gilbert, S. M. E. M. FORSTER'S "A PASSAGE TO INDIA" AND "HOWARDS END" (NY: Monarch P, Monarch Notes and Study Guides, 1965).

[Summary of life and career; summary of each chapter of *Howards End* and *A Passage to India*, followed by competent but not profound interpretive comment for each chapter; character analyses provided following the summaries of each novel. Summary of *Passage* is skillfully managed, with the main lines of the novel kept clear. Under "Critical Commentary" presents the opposed views of F. R. Leavis and Lionel Trilling on relative importance of *Howards End* and *Passage;* among recent critics the views of K. W. Gransden and Frederick C. Crews are summarized. For what they are worth, there are eight pages of "Sample Questions and Answers." An annotated bibliography of general accounts, accounts of the two novels, and accounts of EMF and Bloomsbury may be useful to the beginning student. On the whole this pamphlet shows little insight into EMF's work.]

1111 Grubb, Frederick. "In but not of: E. M. Forster, Julian Bell, and the Liberal Critique," A VISION OF REALITY: A STUDY OF LIBERALISM IN TWENTIETH-CENTURY VERSE (NY: Barnes & Noble; Lond: Chatto & Windus, 1965), pp. 164–78; also 14, 56, 67, 74, 82, 83, 128, 147, 151, 217n, 222, 228, 241.

[The section "In but not of: E. M. Forster, Julian Bell, and the Liberal Critique" contains extended discussion of EMF, regarded as the moral center of this book on poetry, since his thought touches poetry and since the inner lives of his characters have their poetic aspects.] EMF is closely allied to Bloomsbury by his intellectual interests but is considerably apart from it in his emotional and instinctual emphases. Julian Bell felt that his predecessors in Bloomsbury altered conventions rather than challenged them. Bell appeals to EMF when he [Bell] rejects the pacifistic and permissive aspects of Bloomsbury since EMF was more activist than Bloomsbury in general. Bell's values, moreover, were EMF's, especially the need to connect the prose and the passion of life. EMF's own heroes are reluctant rather than dynamic, and Fielding in *A Passage to India* is their type—"a picaresque hero positive for our time" who possesses both detachment and sympathetic concern. EMF judges his characters by his own ideas of what civilization should be, and his judgments are pertinent since our difficulties have much in common with those experienced by his Edwardian characters. As artist EMF has recourse to music to give his work symmetry of design, and one measure of his strength is that he does not dissolve the informative into the sensational modes. Bell rejects the dogma of the 1930 Leftist but feels that the cultivated middle class—Bloomsbury—is too removed from action and social interest. He recognizes that the *literati* must define standards of taste and right values. This is not a democratic procedure, but it must be connected with efforts to persuade the masses to practice "rational behavior." In his letter to EMF (rptd in JULIAN BELL: ESSAYS, POEMS, AND LETTERS, ed by Quentin Bell, 1938), Bell defines his activist views and feels that EMF himself may be too passive. [See also Peter Stansky and William Abrahams, JOURNEY TO THE FRONTIER (1966). An excessively abstract and difficult essay.]

1112 Hagopian, John V. "Eternal Moments in the Short Fiction of E. M. Forster," COLLEGE ENGLISH, XXVII (Dec 1965), 209–15.

E. M. Forster

[Confines his discussion to "the realistic psycho-moral narratives," "The Road from Colonus," and "The Eternal Moment."] "The Road from Colonus" is related to Sophocles's Oedipus at Colonus, but EMF's use of *from* in the title is significant, since the story "leads away from the willing submission to death that transfigured the aged and deposed king of Thebes into the *genius loci* of a foreign place. Mr. Lucas at Plataniste, far from his native England, also feels that he may have found his apotheosis, but he is robbed of his transfiguration by the stout common sense of his mock-Antigone of a daughter and her crass friend Arthur Graham." In the two stories EMF shows the contrast between English and Mediterranean cultures. The conflict is embodied with greater authority in "The Eternal Moment" than in "The Road from Colonus." Both stories also embody a subjective philosophy of time. "The Eternal Moment" raises ambiguous questions: (1) Are Miss Raby's guilt and gestures of atonement noble? (2) Is Colonel Leyland correct in thinking Miss Raby's conduct unbecoming, highhanded, and silly? [Hagopian answers "No" to the first question and "Yes" to the second. His discussion is fruitful in defining the complexities of the tale, but he reaches his conclusions by treating Miss Raby ironically and satirically. That EMF intended her to be unsympathetic and Colonel Leyland moderately sympathetic is dubious, though Wilfred Stone in The Cave and the Mountain (1966) would support Hagopian. Concludes with an illuminating discussion of the scenic symbolism of the tale; especially revealing is Miss Raby's identification with the Cumaean Sibyl in the fresco at the Hotel Biscione.] The central characters in the stories "present not the permanent victory of the race over cruelty and chaos, but rather—as in his great novels—the pathetic defeat of characters who aspire to his notion of saintliness."

1113 Hamill, Peter. "Totem Is Taboo," Washington Post Book Week, 27 June 1965, p. 2; rptd as "The Totemization of E. M. Forster," in E. M. Forster: The Critical Heritage, ed by Philip Gardner (Lond & Boston: Routledge & Kegan Paul, 1973), pp. 425–27.
[Protests the recent uncritical adulation (the "totemization") of the EMF novels, but praises the shrewdness and wisdom present in the EMF essays.]

1114 Harrison, Robert Ligon. "The Manuscripts of *A Passage to India*," Dissertation Abstracts, XXV (1965), 474. Unpublished dissertation, University of Texas, 1964.
[Collation of the variant manuscripts with the published text of *A Passage to India* (first English printing, 1924). Introduction points up the most significant variations, additions, and deletions to the published novel. An indispensable study for the textual criticism of *Passage* and for insight into EMF's creative processes. George H. Thomson's "Appendix" to The Fic-

TION OF E. M. FORSTER (1967), June Perry Levine's CREATION AND CRITICISM:"A PASSAGE TO INDIA" (1971; also her 1967 thesis and her PMLA article, 1970), and Oliver Stallybrass's "Forster's Wobblings: The Manuscripts of *A Passage to India*" (1969) draw upon Harrison's thesis.]

1115 Harvey, W. J. "The Human Context," "Conclusion: An End to Theory," CHARACTER AND THE NOVEL (Ithaca: Cornell UP; Lond: Chatto & Windus, 1965), pp. 52–73, espec 64–67; 83–90; also 12, 192, 195.

In the novel the modulation from the intense to the relaxed, the exceptional to the mundane, is achieved in terms of structure and the relationships of the characters rather than in terms of a heightened style (resort to the "poetic" style may result in the detachable purple passage; in *A Passage to India*, however, the Caves embody such modulations structurally). The significance of Mrs. Moore's negative vision in the Marabar Caves must be diffused through many characters and many relationships to become as effective as EMF makes it. Structurally, there is reason for her death so that she does not have to work out the significance of her vision for herself. Adela Quested helps enlarge Mrs. Moore's vision and its consequences, because she shares Mrs. Moore's vision of the inhuman and the absolute. [Other incidental references to EMF as novelist and critic.]

1116 Heilbrun, Carolyn. "The Woman as Hero," TEXAS QUARTERLY, VIII (Winter 1965), 132–41; rptd with additions in TOWARD A RECOGNITION OF ANDROGYNY (NY: Knopf, 1973), pp. 44–112, espec 93, 97–101.

From 1900 to 1940 women could more readily strike out for a new vision since they had less at stake in the old order than men did. After World War II women in fiction have again lost their heroic potential, being important mostly as parts of the life of men. In *Howards End* EMF made Margaret Schlegel a "hero." The Schlegel sisters seek a reality not sanctioned by their society. The marriage with Henry is improbable. The sisters avoid approved feminine attitudes, and they search for a new identity; in so doing they still shock us. In Adela Quested (*Passage*) we have the limited heroine who is not sexually attractive but who performs the difficult feat of making a fool of herself for justice. She is a heroine in the sense of affecting external events rather than being content to be wife, mother, or mistress. [Considers women protagonists in novels written by men: Henry James's THE PORTRAIT OF A LADY, EMF's *Howards End* and *A Passage to India*, and D. H. Lawrence's THE RAINBOW and WOMEN IN LOVE. Informed discussion.]

1117 Heine, Elizabeth. "Thought and Form in the Novels of E. M. Forster." Unpublished dissertation, Harvard University, 1965. [Listed in Lawrence F. McNamee, DISSERTATIONS IN ENGLISH AND AMERICAN LITERATURE, SUPP 1 (NY & Lond: Bowker, 1969).]

1118 Howarth, Herbert. "E. M. Forster and the Contrite Establishment," JOURNAL OF GENERAL EDUCATION, XVII (Oct 1965), 196–206.

[Traces some of EMF's liberal and humanistic attitudes to his friends on the editorial staff of the INDEPENDENT REVIEW and to their contributions and those of others to the periodical.] The editors were "young humanitarians who belonged to, and felt the onus of belonging to, the Establishment of 1900." They were men of good families who nevertheless felt guilt at the fact of there being "two nations" in England. EMF's novels are pervaded by the ethos of the INDEPENDENT group. In *Howards End* EMF says that landlords and capitalists must give to the poor; Margaret gives away her money, Helen her body. EMF nevertheless values money and property perhaps more than did his friends, and he was less confident about the effects of education. Fielding in *A Passage to India* is a figure of contrition; he has the humanitarian ideals of the contrite group and perhaps their deficiencies in feeling. EMF's sympathy with Helen and Fielding against the official and conventional point of view was his "innovatory force" as a writer in his own time, while his poetry (in the style of his books) is his enduring distinction. The INDEPENDENT group also opposed the imperialism of Joseph Chamberlain. EMF questions the imperial theme in *The Longest Journey* and *Howards End*, but such questioning reaches its fulfillment in *Passage*. EMF's INDEPENDENT friends helped him become socially responsible rather than a dilettante; they helped enlarge his sympathies and made him aware of social issues. They influenced him to adopt a terse and direct style in order to express himself honestly and forcefully. [Interesting and illuminating article.]

1119 Husaid, Syed Hamid. "A Study of the Novels of E. M. Forster." Unpublished dissertation, Agra University, India, 1965.

1120 Ingli, James G. "The New Criticism and the New Morality," CHRISTIAN SCHOLAR, XLVIII (Winter 1965), 279–97.

The sequence wherein Caroline Abbott discovers Gino's baby to be a real human being rather than an abstract entity over whose possession and training the people in *Where Angels Fear to Tread* struggle supports the contention that the "newest" criticism will be imbued with the "new morality" which rejects impersonal, abstract, absolutist principles. [Discussion of *Angels* on pp. 283–84.]

1121 "Intelligent Adaption [*sic*] of a Novel," TIMES (Lond), 21 July 1965, p. 15.

Adaptation of *Howards End* by Lance Sieveking and Richard Cottrell reduces the novel "to a dated problem play on the theme of Edwardian social hypocrisy." The adaptation is faithful and intelligent but lacks the nuances and rich texture of the original.

1122 Kilner, G. "Some Questions of Interpretation in *A Passage to India*," USE OF ENGLISH (Lond), XVI (Summer 1965), 302–7. In *A Passage to India*, Fielding fails in moral and spiritual terms because the pressures on him are too great. His shortcomings are emphasized; Aziz's are admitted but created more sympathetically. The Caves signify an ambiguous ultimate reality, as Wilfred Stone also maintains (THE CAVE AND THE MOUNTAIN [1966]). EMF's symbolism is successful because it is organic to the novel. [Analysis of the characters and symbols in *Passage* that says little that was not said before its publication.]

1123 Kirkpatrick, B. J. A BIBLIOGRAPHY OF E. M. FORSTER (Lond: Rupert Hart-Davis, 1965; 2nd rvd ed, 1968, incorporating John Shipley's "Additions to the E. M. Forster Bibliography" (1966). [Standard and indispensable bibliography of primary writings, correcting the impression that EMF ceased, in large part, to write after publication of *A Passage to India* (1924). Bibliography is subdivided into Section A, "Books and Pamphlets"; Section B, "Contributions to Books"; Section C, "Contributions to Periodicals" (over 500 entries); Section D, "Translations"; and Section E, "Syllabuses." Reviews: Wilford E. Fridy, "E. M. Forster Bibliography," AMERICAN BOOK COLLECTOR, XVI (March 1966), p. 3; "Language and Literature," CHOICE, (Feb 1966), p. 850; Frederick P. W. McDowell, "E. M. Forster: Recent Extended Studies," ENGLISH LITERATURE IN TRANSITION, IX:3 (1966), pp. 156–68; R. J. Roberts, "Book Reviews," BOOK COLLECTOR, XV (Spring 1966), 75–76, 79; "Works of E. M. Forster," TIMES LITERARY SUPPLEMENT (Lond), 1 July 1965, p. 568; and Stephen Wall, "The Qualities of Forster," NEW STATESMAN, nsLXXVI (19 July 1968), 87.]

1124 Knoepflmacher, U. C. RELIGIOUS HUMANISM AND THE VICTORIAN NOVEL: GEORGE ELIOT, WALTER PATER, AND SAMUEL BUTLER (Princeton: Princeton UP; London: Oxford UP, 1965), pp. 22, 131. Dorothea Brooke's disillusionment with Christianity and her passage from faith to stoicism in George Eliot's MIDDLEMARCH prefigures the conversion of Mrs. Moore in *A Passage to India*. Christianity becomes "poor" and "talkative" when placed against the alien order of the natural universe. Catherine Arrowpoint in George Eliot's DANIEL DERONDA anticipates EMF's Schlegel sisters and the heroines of D. H. Lawrence in her defiance of provincialism and indentification with continental culture.

1125 Koljević, Svetozar. "E. M. Forster: Sceptic as Novelist," MAD RIVER REVIEW (Dayton, Ohio), I (Fall–Winter 1965), 3–15. *Where Angels Fear to Tread, The Longest Journey,* and *A Room with a View* are interesting by what they are skeptical about; *A Passage to India* achieves its significance by the skeptic's realization of what his skepticism is about. The opposing force to skepticism is not, as in *Howards End*, so much an attitude as it is the radicalism of vision that is fully prepared to test itself, "to explore the ultimate areas of human significance, of doubt, delusion, and uncertainty." In *Angels* the contrasts are too stark for skepticism to be transcended; in *Journey* interpretation, statement, and comment do not belong organically to the novel as a literary form. EMF's statements in *Howards End* are projected organically into story and character, although the exploration of the issues is not so firm as in *Passage*. In *Howards End*, the poignancy derives from Margaret's naïveté, which encourages her to assume "an integral order in nature, society and man." But this is an illusion insofar as she depends on the Wilcoxes to help her to realize this order. Uncertainties result from Margaret's association with the Wilcoxes; her connection with them goes counter to EMF's exposure of them. In *Passage* the skeptical vision is more thoroughgoing: "The novel embodies the tragic urge to establish correspondences between what has to be separate for the simple reason that separation is the form of its identity." The English and the Indians both suffer from misunderstandings: "The ways in which people resist the ironies of their relationships are explored within a general framework of radically agnostic futility." The Caves sequence derives its power and significance not only by virtue of what is being expressed but by the resistance—by the characters and by EMF—to what is being said. The light and warmth of the flames reflected in the cave surfaces symbolize EMF's own creative qualities, which he opposes to his skeptical vision; but the divisions and misunderstandings are universal in their implications. "So this vision of an imaginative passage to India grows into a complex allegory of a modern pilgrimage in which the pilgrims are left with few illusions and no beliefs except, perhaps, in the moral dignity of their journey." The last ride of Fielding and Aziz expresses both a separation and an implicit protest against it. The novel reveals EMF's skepticism, but writing the novel represents EMF's attempt to counteract that skepticism. [Stimulating, but somewhat obscurely reasoned and written.]

1126 Lemon, Lee T. THE PARTIAL CRITICS (NY: Oxford UP, 1965), p. 73.

Howards End is merely a good novel while Tolstoy's WAR AND PEACE is a great one, because it is a work of greater complexity. The characters in *Howards End* are adequate to the function they serve in the novel, and the novel is large enough to contain them; the facets of reality assimilated in WAR AND PEACE are more numerous and extensive.

1127 McDowell, Frederick P. W. "E. M. Forster's Conception of the Critic," TENNESSEE STUDIES IN LITERATURE, IX (1965), 93–100.

EMF is skeptical about the validity of general principles in literary criticism and about their usefulness for the critic. Still, some tentative principles determine EMF's view of the critic and his function, despite his own impressionistic bias. EMF faces two ways: He distrusts analytic criticism because it interposes itself between the work of art and the individual reacting to it; but he values the critical intelligence as it clarifies the work of art and makes it more available to the public. The critic's function is to apply "logic to the illogical"—an endless task. Sometimes, the lack of a critical instinct in the artist himself is harmful to his work. Legitimate tasks for the critic are the correction of untutored appreciation by "education through precision" and the awakening of interest in a writer. Criticism can also help "civilize the community," by encouraging the individual to appreciate the world of the senses and by exposing the fraudulent and the pretentious. It helps the artist only minimally. Criticism is twofold in practice: It can be concerned with (1) the general bearings of the artist and his works, or (2) the elucidation of specific texts. The successful critic needs a ranging imagination and a wide perspective. Sympathy and detachment are his two chief qualities.

1128 Mander, Gertrud. "Suche nach Indien: Ein Plädoyer für E. M. Forster" (The Search for India: A Plea for E. M. Forster), FRANKFURTER ALLGEMEINE ZEITUNG, 21 Dec 1965.
The main qualities of *A Passage to India* are the humane sensibility of the author, the analysis of both specific and general psychological problems, and the author's talent for presenting a complete world in miniature. For EMF India is formless and opaque, it suggests many meanings, and it becomes a mystical nothing that confounds definition. Mutual understanding between the races is not possible, since both sides start from the wrong premise—enthusiasm and optimism—instead of from sensitivity and tolerance. *Passage* is a parable about the problem of human relations in general; the search for India is mankind's search for its true self. [Review of German translation of *Passage*, rpt of 1960 ed.] [In German.]

1129 Mandrillo, Piero. "E. M. Forster e la Critica" (E. M. Forster and Criticism), RIVISTA DI LETTERATURE MODERNE E COMPARATE (Florence), XVIII (1965), 211–27.
EMF's novels were discovered in Italy after World War II as a result of EMF's admiration for Italy, his interest in Italian humanism, his wide reading in Italian writers, and above all, his poetic quality and his beautiful prose. Principal Italian critics of EMF are Linati, Guidi, Rebora, Praz, Baldini, and Lombardo. Lombardo has written one of the most penetrating aesthetic and thematic discussions of EMF's world and art ("Prefazione," *Casa Howard*, 1959). Anna Maria Fadda in EDWARD MORGAN FORSTER E EL DECADENTISMO (1962) is perhaps too reductive, but her book demonstrates

how EMF illustrates in a later age the characteristics of the continental symbolist and decadent movements prevalent in the late nineteenth century. [Survey of recent EMF criticism, including Lionel Trilling's E. M. FORSTER (1943), K. W. Gransden's E. M. FORSTER (1962), J. B. Beer's THE ACHIEVEMENT OF E. M. FORSTER (1962), and Frederick C. Crews's E. M. FORSTER: THE PERILS OF HUMANISM (1962).] [In Italian.]

1130 Martin, John S. "Mrs. Moore and the Marabar Caves: A Mythological Reading," MODERN FICTION STUDIES, XI (Winter 1965–1966), 429–33.

Frederick C. Crews (E. M. FORSTER AND THE PERILS OF HUMANISM [1962]) is correct in seeing EMF's *A Passage to India* as less oriented toward Greek mythology than is his earlier work. Nevertheless, two of the chief elements in *Passage*, Mrs. Moore and the Marabar Caves, can be seen "as re-enactments of Greek mythological archetypes." The Marabar Caves have many similarities with the caves of the Cumaean Sibyl (both have a hundred mouths, and in both an echo externalizes the visitor's own mental state). Mrs. Moore resembles the Sibyl herself (both are elderly and possess insight into the unknown; both are votaries of a god; both are, or become, priestesses and oracles; both wrap their truths in darkness; both inhabit caves [Mrs. Moore's is mental]; and both experience a vision of reality which makes them long for extinction). By relating the caves and Mrs. Moore to these aspects of myth, EMF makes these elements in his novel far more convincing than they could be if he were only to view them realistically. [Interesting and perceptive.]

1131 Mason, W. H. A PASSAGE TO INDIA (E. M. FORSTER) (NY: Barnes & Noble; Oxford: Blackwell Notes on English Literature, 1965).

"Significance": The reader's surprise or discomfort at the presence of "Temple" section is due to EMF's need to secure a wide perspective (by which to see the characters and events in the first two sections) and his poetic intentions. The characters serve EMF's purposes; those who achieve a significance beyond the plot (Professor Godbole and Mrs. Moore) are less interesting in themselves than in the quality of their vision. EMF's art is notable for integrating the action with the situation and scene. Thus the life of the Anglo-Indians at Chandrapore, with its racial arrogance and cruelty, intensifies the treatment of the central incident, the trial of Aziz. The incident at the Marabar Caves also integrates action, sense, and metaphysical significance. As for his Anglo-Indians, EMF has not given us a complete picture of British activity in India. Rather, he has shown some representative officials and the effects of their attitudes upon problems of race and empire. Nor does he sentimentalize the Indians. His purpose is not only realistic and political but ethical and philosophical; he wishes to show the supreme value of human relationships attained through love. The balancing of contrasting experiences, particularly the Krishna celebration against the sinister echo of the Marabar Caves, expresses the profundity of his vision; love contends with nihilism and is in a measure victorious. The Caves symbolize all forces hostile to belief in the meaningfulness of the universe. To offset such negation we have the tentative but genuine affirmation of "Temple" with its message of "God si love."

"Structure and Style": In "Caves," a narrowing and a concentration takes place. In "Temple," the novel opens out and achieves transcendental significance. Noteworthy is the skill with which EMF throughout switches point of view and makes use of repetition or echo. The style is characterized by idiomatic naturalness, simplicity, and supple rhythms.

"Characters": The characters are not larger than life, and EMF views them from a distance, thereby decreasing their charm and immediate appeal. They do not have a markedly individual idiom, and they often are presented from a shifting viewpoint. Aziz impresses by his vitality; his human weaknesses make him convincing. Adela is a well-developed but not an appealing character. Fielding is partly Forster, but not completely so. EMF is more sensitive to the intuitive and the mystical than Fielding, but Fielding's kindness, courage, sympathy, and intellectual honesty are humanistic attributes which EMF values. The characterization of Mrs. Moore is marked by realism and by her transcendental sensitivity; she impresses more as a presence than as an individual. The same can be said of Godbole. He is animated by a spirit of prophecy; his detachment from the physical world is a measure of his love of all who are within it. [A lucid, comprehensive account with many valid insights and interpretations.]

1132 Moore, Harry T. E. M. FORSTER (NY & Lond: Columbia UP, Columbia Essays on Modern Writers, No. 10, 1965); extracts rptd in CONTEMPORARY LITERARY CRITICISM, ed by Carolyn Riley (Detroit: Gale Research Co., 1973), I, 106–7; rptd, with additions, in SIX MODERN BRITISH NOVELISTS, ed by George Stade (NY & Lond: Columbia UP, 1974), pp. 220–69, 283–86, with updated bibliography; see entry for 1974.

From the first, EMF has written of the schisms between people and between the worlds in which they live. The stories illustrate his interest in fantasy, mythology, magic, and the supernatural, whereas the novels are in "the vein of everyday realism." [This judgment is debatable.] "The Story of the Siren" sums up all themes explored in EMF's short stories, especially the contrast between the natural-supernatural and the conventional-social. "The Eternal Moment" is EMF's best story. In *Where Angels Fear to Tread* accident and coincidence take the place of fantasy. Many scenes reveal EMF's finesse, especially the LUCIA DI LAMMERMOOR sequence. EMF sees the admirable and questionable aspects of the contrasting cultures. Gino Carella is a convincing natural man; Philip Herriton not only is passive but has the ability to change. In *The Longest Journey* the characters convince except for Stephen Wonham (as child of nature he is not so authentic as Gino Carella). The comic, sardonic mode derives from Jane Austen and Samuel Butler. EMF had already begun to use the repeated motif (the "easy rhythm" described in *Aspects of the Novel*). The paintings in Rickie Elliot's room are symbolic; Watts's "Sir Percival" comments on Rickie's failure to "recapture the Holy Grail," the cheap brown madonna contrasts with the madonnas of merit owned by the Pembrokes, and the picture of Stockholm refers to the Swedish idyll in which Stephen was conceived. *A Room with a View* is thin; no "atmospheres" clash with each other; and the characters lack energy and force. [Overlooks the book's freshness.] George Emerson has some of the vitality of the Renaissance, in contrast to Cecil Vyse with his "medievalism." In *Howards End* Leonard Bast becomes increasingly unreal. [Mentions but does not analyze some of the repeated images: hay, the wych-elm, the motor car.] The connections between the Schlegels and the Wilcoxes do not take place despite Margaret's eagerness that they should; she triumphs because of circumstances. The novel reveals EMF's gifts of comedy and irony, the strength of his style, the suggestiveness of his symbols, and the "romantic" aspect of his temper. In *A Passage to India* there is more dramatization and less adventitious description. Its characters are convincing; it again exhibits EMF's skepticism concerning the ability of human beings to connect. His interest in sustained connection or continuity again appears. Ruth Wilcox becomes the Mrs. Moore of *Passage;* both women are *magna mater* figures. *Passage* also manifests the influence of Proust, in EMF's preoccupation with the unconscious depths of behavior and his use of repeated images. The novel expresses EMF's deepest conviction: the causes of separation among men run deep. "Blindness of heart" prevents conciliation and reconciliation among men as it has among larger groups in the history of the modern age. [Extended summary of the nonfiction (pp. 12–17). A readable survey of EMF's life and work; it runs to description and summary, and few judgments of importance are made. Selected bibliography.]

1133 Mukherjee, Sujit. "India's Entry into English Fiction," QUEST (Bombay), No. 47 (Autumn 1965), 51–55.

KIM and *A Passage to India* reveal Kipling's and EMF's attitudes toward India. Kim and Fielding, respectively, are Kipling's and EMF's central intelligences. The mystery surrounding the Lama is paralleled by the mystery surrounding Mrs. Moore. She and the Lama are more real in their effects on others than as individuals. In the two works there are similarities in structure but divergences in manner, treatment, and achievement. EMF is more tentative and cautious. He is less confident of understanding India than is Kipling, and he emphasizes various levels of understanding the country, its people, and its culture. EMF is more symbolic in his method, and his characters are more various and real. Kipling's view is retrospective; EMF's interest is in the present and the present as harbinger of the future. The quest theme predominates in both novels. It is simplified in KIM, the Lama's and Kim's searches being those of individuals; in *Passage* a character's search is an individual one, but transcends the human. Symbolism in *Passage* gives it a dimension lacking in Kipling's more straightforward romance. Kipling's somewhat simplified art found a more satisfying projection in the short story than in the novel. [Competent but not arresting discussion.]

1134 O'Grady, Walter. "On Plot in Modern Fiction: Hardy, James and Conrad," MODERN FICTION STUDIES, XI (Summer 1965), 107–15; rptd in CRITICAL APPROACHES TO FICTION, ed by Shiv E. Kumar and Keith McKean (NY, Lond: McGraw-Hill, 1968), pp. 57–65.

[Uses EMF's distinction in *Aspects of the Novel* between story and plot for a discussion of plot in fiction.] There are more qualitative distinctions between characters and situations than EMF allows for, and situations differ as they are interior or exterior. [O'Grady's chief concept resides in plot as an interacting flow between situations and events, a flow which may be forward and inward (THE AMBASSADORS) or backward and outward (TESS OF THE D'URBERVILLES).]

1135 Panichas, George A. "Book Reviews," MODERN LANGUAGE JOURNAL, XLIX (Nov 1965), 456–57.

Critics fail to appreciate the vitality and positive quality in EMF's art and thought, largely because of D. H. Lawrence's charges of inanition and F. R. Leavis's adverse comments upon the Bloomsbury influence. [Review of Alan Wilde's ART AND ODER: A STUDY OF E. M. FORSTER (1964).]

1136 Raina, M. L. "The Use of the Symbol by English Novelists 1900–1930, with Particular Reference to E. M. Forster, D. H. Lawrence and Virginia Woolf." Unpublished dissertation, Manchester University, 1965.

[Listed in Lawrence F. McNamee, DISSERTATIONS IN ENGLISH AND AMERICAN LITERATURE, SUPP I (NY & Lond: Bowker, 1969).]

1137 Rao, G. Nageswara. "Gokulāstami: The Resolution of the Antithesis in Forster's Art," VISVABHARATI QUARTERLY (Sankiniketan, West Bengal), XXXI: 3 (1965–1966), 273–300.

EMF's purpose in writing *A Passage to India* is metaphysical rather than political. EMF presents the clash of opposites in his fiction and their ensuing reconciliation into some kind of harmony or unity. The process of social dissociation becomes acute and explicit in *Howards End*, whereas *Passage* is the most complete rendition in EMF's fiction of this alienation. Nevertheless, *Passage* makes a positive statement about the human condition: Unity is possible and can be achieved through human and cosmic love (the leading principle of Hinduism). Although some aspect of James McConkey's (1957) and Glen O. Allen's (1955) Hindu interpretations of *Passage* are questionable, they point the way to fuller understanding. The experiences in the Caves are religious in the sense that each character is brought to experience the ultimate reality for him and to recognize the meaninglessness of life in its isolation (the nullity of the isolated life is epitomized in the identification of the echo sound with the Brahman "aum"). Through his characters' experience of negation EMF is preparing for a rejuvenation of faith and is driving at something positive, "the root-concept that is the basis for the Brahman of Hinduism, the total renunciation of jainism [*sic*], the *nirvana* (suggested in the merge and extinction of flame in the cave) of Buddhism, the revelation of christianity [*sic*], the puzzle of the agnostic." At the Gokulāstami ceremony "there is the birth of a hope which will bring the chaos of life under the order of Infinite love." In *Passage* the universal disillusionment and exhaustion are more fully present than in the other novels, but there is also a compensatory sense of positive direction in it: a "completeness" not just a "reconstruction." [Article is well-considered, if too long, and refutes pessimistic interpretations of *Passage*, e.g., Brower (1951) or Crews (1962).]

1138 Shusterman, David. THE QUEST FOR CERTITUDE IN E. M. FORSTER'S FICTION (Bloomington & Lond: Indiana UP, Indiana University Humanities Series, 1965); includes, pp. 182–202, most of "The Curious Case of Professor Godbole: *A Passage to India* Reexamined," PUBLICATIONS OF THE MODERN LANGUAGE ASSOCIATION, LXXXVI (Sept 1961), 426–35.

Chap 1, "Motivations of Life and Art": EMF's creative writing (until 1924) was a forerunner to the reflective writing of an older man. His fiction resulted from his discoveries about self and life. He is a skeptical humanist who finds little certainty in experience. His attitudes fluctuate between pessimism and optimism. He can give credence only to the organic order to be found in a work of art, not to the divine order posited by religion. He tries to find still another kind of order within the limits set by life and society, a vision which would reconcile outer and inner. He works toward such a unity and such a certitude in *Howards End*. The reconciliation is only transient, and disllusionment with the possibility of this synthesis sets in after World War I and forms the undertone of *A Passage to India*. He wished to see life steadily and to see it whole, but he never attained this state firmly. Chap 2, "The Quest": EMF experienced a unification of his powers at Cambridge. To restore such unity to modern man and to find it himself again became EMF's purpose as writer. But he was not able to achieve it in any full and lasting sense. Chap 3, "The Short Stories: The Uneasy Truant": In his stories EMF made his first attempt to reconcile art (with its implicit sense of order) with all other aspects of man's life. The fuzziness revealed in the stories reflects his own uncertainty at the time. "The Story of a Panic" reveals the divisive aspects of human nature; "The Other Side of the Hedge" contrasts the aesthetic view of life favorably with the materialistic; "The Celestial Omnibus" reveals the need to worship wholeheartedly the things of the spirit; "The Road from Colonus" (containing EMF's finest merging of theme and symbol) dramatizes the life-giving impulses deadened by the social conventions; "The Machine Stops" protests the forces making for division; "The Point of It" dramatizes EMF's conviction that Love and Truth are both necessary in order to see life steadily and to see it whole (and the difficulty of so seeing it); "The Story of the Siren" reveals how the dogmatic priest can extinguish the life-giving impulses; and "The Eternal Moment" reveals EMF's use of fiction to indicate the arduous nature of the quest to reach understanding and peace. Chap 4, "*Where Angels Fear to Tread:* The Fair Myth of Endymion": In *Aspects of the Novel* EMF maintained that the writer of fiction must try both to create a work of art and to catch life itself (only once, in *Passage,* was EMF completely successful in doing so). In the dialectic of the Italian ethos in opposition to the Sawston ethos, EMF is aware of complexities; Italy, for example, has sinister as well as life-enhancing qualities. Philip Herriton represents the best in England and humanity; Gino Carella, though he represents the truth inhering in the primitive, does not fundamentally engage EMF. Caroline Abbott gives to Philip a vision of aesthetic harmony; it will regenerate him, but whether the aesthetic vision alone is sufficient is questionable.

Chap 5, "*The Longest Journey:* Endymion Again, or the Cup and the Chalk": In *Journey* EMF is more concerned than he was previously with the nature of reality and with the conflict between art and convention (and materialism). The confused vision of life presented in *Journey* may be the only one possible in modern life. Rickie Elliot is misguided by his intense idealism and does not interpret reality aright. He wishes to achieve more than aesthetic order; the union of opposed qualities at Cambridge represents for him an ideal mode of existence. But such unity is difficult to maintain in the actual world; Sawston exists to undermine it. The book poses the problem of how the ordinary individual can fight free of the claims of the Philistine world to attain a sense of integration. *Journey* is a tragedy concerned with man's fate rather than a comedy concerned with man's shortcomings in society. At the end there is not the fusion of the ideal and the actual, as some critics maintain, but Rickie as artist is vindicated in the life he makes possible for Stephen Wonham, his half-brother. Stephen is too centrally dominated by the body; and his character in the epilogue lacks dignity and wholeness, though the ritualistic sequences when he recalls Rickie and realizes that Rickie has sanctified his life for him are moving. After he associates freely with Stephen, Rickie accepts the earth too uncritically in revulsion from the life of art: the result is that something precious, Mrs. Failing's teacup, is broken when the piece of chalk falls on it. For the intellectual like Rickie, the realm of art is not to be deserted for the earth, which can be destructive of the higher faculties as well as a source of renewal. Mrs. Failing is right in seeing that Rickie's domain is the world of culture, humanism, the intellect, and art, and not the natural world. He is the modern man assailed by various winds of doctrine. In the understanding which the brothers reach in the flameboat episode, a reconciliation occurs between chalk and teacup, nature and art. [Discussion of *Journey* is most perceptive.] Chap 6, "*A Room with a View:* The Seizure of the Moment": The tonal difference between the two parts of *Room* is a defect in so far as unity may be violated; but the presence of evil, tragic undercurrents, and complexity at the end denote EMF's maturing over the five years since he began the novel. The Emersons carry things along too easily, and there is more to be said for Cecil Vyse, who in some respects is a sacrifice to the plot. *Room* lacks the wit and penetration of *Angels*, though the concluding chapters are noteworthy for their large utterance and great expanse. Alone in EMF's fiction, *Room* celebrates the unifying power of love between human beings and the glory of the moment in sexual fulfillment.

Chap 7, "*Howards End:* Synthesis Achieved": In *Howards End* EMF does not dismiss the materialisitic as an illusion, as he had done earlier, but he sees it now as a reality to be grappled with. EMF prefers to see life "whole" (as Margaret Schlegel tries to do) in preference to seeing it "steadily" (as the Wilcoxes tend to do). Ruth Wilcox is a force making for "connection"; she stands for tradition, opposed to the flux of the modern age. Margaret's marriage to Henry Wilcox is possible and not a violation of probability or of Margaret's integrity. The ending, though contrived, does project EMF's wish for unity. In the novel he reaches a synthesis between the opposed forces in modern life, but it is an uneasy one. Chap 8: "*A Passage to India:* Synthesis Broken, or No One is India": From 1910 to 1914 EMF's optimism slackened and his mind deepened into pessimism. *Passage* is harsher in tone, more subjective, and more organic in its symbolism than the prewar novels. The personal connections stressed in *Howards End* are inapplicable in *Passage*. The theme of division predominates. Fielding, if anyone, is the protagonist and EMF's spokesman. The novel is about two Indias, the literal and the figurative (a cosmic entity relevant to all humanity). The Marabar Caves symbolize the unfriendly universe in microcosm, and Mrs. Moore is humanity trapped in its flux and unfathomable mystery. She experiences an extreme nihilism, characteristic of the twentieth century after the War had undercut the synthesis propounded in *Howards End.* All the characters seek for a certainty that they do not find. Fielding, for example, is frustrated in his search for a meaning beyond his humanism, but he is reaching toward a deeper wisdom at the end. Even Godbole is not India; no one character is; and far from being a character for good, he exerts evil influence. [Most of Shusterman's 1961 discussion of Godbole as a malign character is rptd; see entry for 1961.] *Passage* is EMF's masterpiece with its scope and grandeur. Chap 9: "The End of a Quest": EMF's writings show increasing awareness of the complexities involved in attaining the unity of man's faculties which he had elaborated in *Howards End.* The optimism of that book yields to the negations expressed in *Passage.* Irrespective of the failure of his quest for unity, EMF is one of the dozen most important twentieth-century writers because he affirmed "the importance of art, of love, of friendship, of justice." [This book presents an overview of EMF that has many valuable insights. However, Shusterman stresses unduly the worth of the unitary vision and EMF's alleged compulsion to attain it. EMF is, I think, tentative and flexible in temper, conceives that truth may lie in the continued opposition obtaining among dichotomies, and is mostly happy that we should be thus suspended. The upward revision of characters like Herbert Pembroke and Cecil Vyse is excessive. More convincing are the arguments advanced against regarding Gino Carella and Stephen Wonham as ideal figures. Discussion of *Journey* is excellent. For my comments on Shusterman's treatment of *Passage,* see Shusterman (1961). Despite the pertinence of some of the discussion and the ease of the writing, this book is too idiosyncratic to serve as a reliable introduction to EMF. Reviews: Barbara Hardy, "The Personality of Criticism," SOUTHERN REVIEW, nsIII (Autumn 1967), 1001–9; "Language and Literature," CHOICE, V (Oct 1966), 651; Frederick P. W. McDowell, "E. M. Forster: Recent Extended Studies," ENGLISH LITERATURE IN TRANSITION, IX: 3 (1966), 156–58; Richard Wasson, "Book Reviews," JOURNAL OF ENGLISH AND GERMANIC PHILOLOGY, LXV (Oct 1966), 745–48;. Alan Wilde, "Book Reviews," MODERN PHILOLOGY, LXV (Nov 1967), 183–85; Paul L. Wiley, "E. M. Forster," CONTEMPORARY LITERATURE, VIII (Summer 1967), 459–62; and Andrew Wright, "Where Critics Adore to Dabble," KENYON REVIEW, XXVIII (June 1966), 405–15 (see also Shusterman's rejoinder, "Comment," KENYON REVIEW, XXVIII [Nov 1966], 711–15).]

1139 Smart, William, (ed). EIGHT MODERN ESSAYISTS (NY: Saint Martin's P, 1965), pp. 38–40; 2nd ed, 1973, pp. 2–4.

There are two main themes in EMF's work: (1) "poetry, mystery, passion, ecstasy, music" are what count, and (2) personal relationships are more important than public duty. EMF is a true humanist, and his hopes for mankind are moderate. This attitude is reflected in the casual, offhand quality of the style that alienates some readers. They think him excessively urbane, whereas he is perhaps too "civilized" for them. [Full and informed summary of EMF's life and career, updated in 2nd ed. Rpts "Notes on the English Character," "My Wood," "Not Listening to Music," "What I Believe," and "Art for Art's Sake," pp. 41–75. Second ed, pp. 5–45, omits "Art for Art's Sake" and includes "Voltaire's Laboratory."]

1140 Spender, Stephen "Introduction," THE STRUGGLE OF THE MODERN (Berkeley & Los Angeles: University of California P; Lond: Methuen, 1965), pp. xi–xiii.

EMF thinks that human nature remains the same in the present as it had been in the past; Virginia Woolf feels that the nature of modern man changed about 1910. As a "contemporary" instead of a "modern," EMF was content to write a traditional kind of novel, even though he uses modern subjects; Woolf and the self-conscious moderns tried to define man's changed nature by evolving new forms. [Contrasts EMF's novels and his critical utterances on the novel with those of Woolf.]

1141 Stebner, Gerhard. "E. M. Forster: *A Passage to India,*" DER MODERNE ENGLISCHE ROMAN, INTERPRETATIONEN (The Modern English Novel, Interpretations), ed by Horst Oppel (Berlin: Eric Schmidt, 1965), pp. 135–59.

A Passage to India is less a political work than a reflection on EMF's view of the undeveloped heart. He places his emphasis upon intuition rather than rules, and he reveals how the practical man becomes unpractical because such a man darkens the truth. Though love disintegrates with time, still the importance of deep feeling cannot be overestimated. [In discussing the Caves, Stebner reviews existing interpretations.] The Caves emphasize ulti-· mately the gap existing between individuals: The flame in the Caves strives to achieve, unsuccessfully, union with its reflection in the Caves' walls. The Caves are not a symbol of reality but a means by which reality is to be measured. [Stebner agrees with J. B. Beer, 1962.] They are also a symbol of the incommensurability of India with the rational faculties of Western man, a symbol therefore of the absurdity of existence. The echo undermines Mrs. Moore's hold on life because her mental equipment is inadequate to allow her, soon enough, to discern the full complexities of reality. She does not see that the answer to her own desolating vision is to be found in Godbole's unquestioning, yet somewhat tentative beliefs. Adela Quested's thoughts had been running on the subject of love and sex before she entered the Caves, so that she is easy prey to the sensation that she has been attacked there. The punkah wallah in the courtroom is a reality symbol that begins to dispel her illusion, a process that is completed by the crowd's invocation of Mrs. Moore and Adela's recollection of her. The result is Adela's recantation. Both Adela and Fielding, as a result of the Marabar experience, become conscious of some ineffable dimension to existence, which they find difficult to define. The casual nature of Mrs. Moore's death aligns her more with Indian culture than with Western. She remains central in the novel: Ronny is still unregenerate in his hostility to her after her death, Adela and Fielding change because of it, and Aziz feels it sharply, achieving through her surviving influence some sense of reconciliation. In her personality there is a collocation of opposites: love versus loss of personal feeling, hope versus despair, harmony versus the absurd. In Part III, men come together after their radical separations in Part II. Mrs. Moore and her blessing of the wasp are set against Godbole's remembering her and a wasp. Her belief that "God is love" achieves a tougher, more universal formulation in the Hindu transliteration, "God si love." The death and resurrection symbolism in the Gokul Ashtami ceremonies sums up the meaning of the novel: rebirth through death, achieving harmony from chaos and disunity. The direction of the novel is not pessimistic: if infinite love descends only momentarily to men, there is always the promise of its return. EMF derives not only from the humorous-ironic tradition of Fielding, Jane Austen, Meredith, and Henry James, but also from the philosophical and didactic tradition of Defoe, George Eliot, and Hardy. An element of fantasy also obtrudes, but it is fantasy with a basis in EMF's firm, realistic perceptions. In *Passage* absurdity and hope, muddle and mystery, coalesce into a cosmic unity; the result is a novel with a poetic structure. [Extended descriptive summary of the contents and ideas expressed in *Passage* with some original insights.] [In German.]

1142 Thomas, Edward M. ORWELL (Edinburgh & Lond: Oliver & Boyd, Writers and Critics, 1965; NY: Barnes & Noble, 1968), p. 28. In BURMESE DAYS Orwell lacks "that delicate arrangement of coincidence and circumstantial irony" through which EMF, in *A Passage to India*, suggests order and meaning in the events of his novel. Orwell's outlook may not have been clear enough for a novelist; he could not distinguish very well "poetic truth" from everyday fact.

1143 Thomas, Roy, and Howard Erskine-Hill. "*A Passage to India:* Two Points of View," ANGLO-WELSH REVIEW, XV (Summer 1965), 44–50.
Thomas: EMF gives a convincing picture of India in *A Passage to India*, although it is not inclusive. EMF has a strong social sense and a sense of his own limitations. In *Passage* a restricted scene and group of characters contain larger meanings and suggest the difficulties involved wherever minority groups exist—difficulties that are complicated by the presence of fallible but well-intentioned individuals on either side. EMF's approach is intelligence supported by sensitivity; irony and detachment characterize it. The detachment extends from the Indians to the English and thence to all mankind. The last section of the book is wry in tone; there is no evidence

to show that EMF is a religionist. A possible limitation is EMF's inadequate comprehension of social and metaphysical evil. Erskine-Hill: The novel emphasizes the barriers between one individual and another. EMF stresses the need for open-mindedness as opposed to closed-mindedness. The symbolism of *Howards End* is inadequate and even "phoney"; the characters are unable to encompass EMF's subject. EMF in *Passage* concentrates his efforts upon overcoming the second of two deficiencies in *Howards End:* lack of substance and range in the characters, lack of authority in the symbolism. In *Passage* symbolism is more ambitious and convincing, while the characters bear much less responsibility for the success of the novel than in *Howards End.* The characters are far less complicated. At the liberal humanistic level, the significance of *Passage* is clear; EMF's method is to use trivial social details to indicate a deep moral and human significance. "Mosque," "Caves," and "Temple" arch over and extend the meaning of the novel. The Mosque suggests man's aspirations toward human unity; the Caves suggest nullity and human insignificance ("the novel is not only about racial or social prejudice; it is also about that unacknowledged terror at the insignificance of our lives which, Forster seems to suggest, prompts men to resort to it"); and the Temple expresses the multiplicity of our experience. There are no solutions to the problems presented in the book, but EMF "is providing us with an image of life and the acceptance of its diversity, an image which startlingly balances and contrasts the dominant symbols and concerns of the two earlier sections of the novel, and which carries with it, at least, obscure implications of hope." [Some valuable perceptions.]

1144 Vidal, Gore. "Afterword," THE CITY AND THE PILLAR REVISED (NY: E. P. Dutton; Lond: Heinemann, 1965), pp. 245–49; rptd as *"The City and the Pillar* after Twenty Years," in REFLECTIONS UPON A SINKING SHIP (Boston: Little, Brown; Lond: Heinemann [1969]), pp. 118–22.
On visit to EMF at Cambridge, after publication of THE CITY AND THE PILLAR (1948), EMF confessed to having written a homosexual novel also, in which the characters "talked" when in bed together. [This novel, *Maurice,* was published in 1971.]

1145 Wickes, George. "An Interview with Christopher Isherwood," SHENANDOAH, XVI (Spring 1965), 23–52, espec pp. 31–34. Concerning presence of "E. M." in the "Waldemar" section of Isherwood's DOWN THERE ON A VISIT (1961), Isherwood admits that E. M. is EMF. He meant more to Isherwood than any other writer. Isherwood singles out EMF's approach, its lightness and seriousness, and his ability to handle all kinds of material. Isherwood stresses EMF's involvement with contemporary issues and controversial questions. Isherwood cherishes EMF's range of subject and his ability to reach a kind of comedy beyond both comedy and tragedy. Isherwood feels EMF has not dried up as writer since 1924, as he has written copiously in forms other than the novel.

1146 Yoneda, Kazuhiko. "E. M. Forster no Tachiba" (E. M. Forster's Attitudes), EIGO SEINEN (Tokyo), CXI (1 Sept 1965), 698–99.

EMF's attitudes toward Christianity, people, and culture as revealed in *Abinger Harvest* and *Two Cheers for Democracy* are agnostic, humanistic, and democratic. They remained unchanged throughout his life. EMF values the individual. He believes that individuals should enjoy freedom, though he is pessimistic on the future of the race. He himself is aware of his limitations: he is as race-bound and class-bound as any Victorian liberal. [In Japanese.]

1966

1147 Adams, Robert M. JAMES JOYCE: COMMON SENSE AND BEYOND (NY: Random House, Studies in Language and Literature, 1966), pp. 88, 215.

The term "epiphany" is not particularly useful in understanding the short stories in DUBLINERS if it does not refer to a transcendent reality. If it is merely a moment of evocation, other writers such as Stendhal, Meredith, and EMF have been adept at revealing a character in a phrase or a trivial action. Thus EMF in *A Room with a View* exposes Cecil Vyse's entire personality by the way in which he refuses to play tennis with Freddy Honeychurch. FINNEGANS WAKE is closer to embodying the full world in which people live in 1966 than the novels of EMF or John P. Marquand.

1148 Anderson, George K., and William E. Buckler (eds). "The Modern Period: Disillusioned Truth Seekers" and "Edward Morgan Forster," THE LITERATURE OF ENGLAND: AN ANTHOLOGY AND A HISTORY, Vol. II: FROM THE DAWN OF THE ROMANTIC MOVEMENT TO THE PRESENT DAY (Glenview, Ill; Scott, Foresman, 5th ed, 1966), pp. 1620–28, espec 1625; 1646–47; earlier eds by George B. Woods, Homer A. Watt, Karl J. Holzknecht, and George K. Anderson do not contain EMF materials, or mention EMF only incidentally.

"The Modern Period": *A Passage to India* is an ironic protest against material realism; the irony is even more incisive in EMF's realistic portrayals in *Howards End* and *A Room with a View*. He wishes to expose the insularity of liberal middle-class English society. His results are ambivalent because he finds it difficult to reach a general view of his subject. His style is low-pitched and understated; he is pessimistic, though his humor and irony mitigate the pessimism. "Edward Morgan Forster" [Summary of his career]: Quietness and unobtrusiveness mark both EMF's life and his work. In his work he is inclined toward fantasy and the romantic, although he is capable of powerful effects by utilizing his ironic potentialities. His chief theme is the tension of the collison between the idealistic and the aesthetic on the one hand and the conditional and the pragmatic on the other. In "The Road from Colonus" the preposition "from" is important: Mr. Lucas is led away from a willing submission to a possibly transfiguring death, like that of Oedipus, and his daughter, a mock-Antigone, prevents him from following his instincts and thereby attaining self-fulfillment. ["The Road from Colonus" rptd pp. 1647–54.]

1149 Bayley, John. "The Quest for E. M. Forster," MANCHESTER GUARDIAN, 22 July 1966, p. 9.
Stone's quest in THE CAVE AND THE MOUNTAIN (1966) finds EMF in the temple, cave, and mountain symbolism of *A Passage to India;* but this approach is misguided since EMF, like Jane Austen, has created in his fiction a composite self greatly at variance with his actual one. Like Jane Austen EMF has to be approached through his art and not through his imputed personality. [Challenges the validity of Stone's assumption that everything about a novelist is in itself illuminating.]

1150 Bergonzi, Bernard. "Introduction," TONO-BUNGAY, by H. G. Wells (Boston: Houghton Mifflin, Riverside Edition, 1966), pp. v–xxvii, espec xv–xvi, xxii–xxiii; rptd as "H. G. Wells," THE TURN OF A CENTURY: ESSAYS ON VICTORIAN AND MODERN ENGLISH LITERATURE (NY: Barnes & Noble; Lond: Macmillan, 1973), pp. 72–98, espec 84–85, 93–94.
Both TONO-BUNGAY and *Howards End* are intensively sociological novels, concerned with the condition of England. Howards End house and Bladesover House (TONO-BUNGAY) are both symbols of a vanishing feudal mode of life. *Howards End* lacks the panoramic sweep of Wells's novel; it is concerned with large social issues only by implication. The focus of EMF's novel is more with characters as personalities and with the reconciliation of the sensitive Liberal, the activist Tory, and the emergent lower-class elements in the British middle class. In presenting the newly arrived lower middle class, EMF was less adept than Wells: Leonard Bast is not so sure a characterization as Kipps or Mr. Polly. Both books convey a sense of foreboding that the Edwardian certainties cannot last much longer. In discussing the characterizations of Dickens and Wells in *Aspects of the Novel,* EMF uses "round" and "flat" as evaluative terms (round characters showing more creative force than flat); the terms are useful as applied to the two writers if they are restricted to a descriptive function (Aunt Susan in Wells's novel is more a round character than Uncle Teddy).

1151 Boulton, J. A. NOTES ON E. M. FORSTER "A PASSAGE TO INDIA" (Bath [England]: James Brodie, Notes on Chosen English Texts, [1966]).
A Passage to India is more than a political novel: "Alien rule imposes not simply political subjection but a distortion of natural normal ways of social intercourse. . . ." As for satire, EMF is gentler with the Indians than with the English. Place in the novel is used to underline thematic content and

to establish the emotional register of the novel. [Competent but obvious commentary as Boulton discusses "Muddle," "The Echo and Evil" (this equation is too simplistic), "Hallucination," "Symbols," "Personal Relationships," and "Style." The analysis of characters is better.] Fielding's moderate liberalism is tested, explored, and deepened by his Indian experiences; Mrs. Moore's instinctive wisdom is overcome by apathy and spiritual despair, but she is positive in effect as she lives on in the minds of others and influences them; Godbole's aloofness is the result of spiritual serenity, and EMF draws his character with "humorous love." [A helpful map gives the most probable location of the principal places in *Passage*. An excellent and complete biographical account to 1924 cites recent primary sources. A chapter by chapter synopsis of *Passage* is given, to which is appended for each chapter unexciting commentary. Relationships between *Passage* and *The Hill of Devi* are also indicated. Except for the geographical information and biographical summary, this study is pedestrian and not as good as similar studies by W. H. Mason ("A PASSAGE TO INDIA": E. M. FORSTER [1965]) and by John Colmer (E. M. FORSTER: "A PASSAGE TO INDIA," [1967]).]

1152 Bradbury, Malcolm (ed). FORSTER: A COLLECTION OF CRITICAL ESSAYS (Englewood Cliffs, NJ: Prentice-Hall, Spectrum Books, 1966).

Contents, abstracted under date of first publication: Malcolm Bradbury, "Introduction" (1966); I. A. Richards, "A Passage to Forster: Reflections on a Novelist," FORUM (1927); Peter Burra, "The Novels of E. M. Forster," NINETEENTH CENTURY AND AFTER (1934); F. R. Leavis, "E. M. Forster," SCRUTINY (1938), as rptd in modified form in THE COMMON PURSUIT (1952); Austin Warren, "E. M. Forster" [in part], A RAGE FOR ORDER (1948), first ptd in AMERICAN REVIEW (1937); D. S. Savage, "E. M. Forster" [in part], THE WITHERED BRANCH (1950), first ptd in Now, III (c. 1944); Lionel Trilling, "Forster and the Liberal Imagination," E. M. FORSTER (1943); Hyatt Howe Waggoner, "Notes on the Uses of Coincidence in the Novels of E. M. Forster," CHIMERA (1945); Frank Kermode, "Mr. E. M. Forster as a Symbolist," LISTENER (1958); Frederick C. Crews, "E. M. Forster's Comic Spirit," E. M. FORSTER: THE PERILS OF HUMANISM (1962); H. A. Smith, "Forster's Humanism and the Nineteenth Century" (1966), first ptd in this vol; John Harvey, "Imagination and Moral Theme in E. M. Forster's *The Longest Journey*," ESSAYS IN CRITICISM, (1956); Malcolm Bradbury, "E. M. Forster's *Howards End*," CRITICAL QUARTERLY (1962), rvd for this vol; E. K. Brown, "Rhythm in E. M. Forster's *A Passage to India*," RHYTHM IN THE NOVEL (1950); and Benita Parry, "Passage to More than India," (1966), first ptd in this vol. Also contains "Chronology of Important Dates," "Notes on the Editor and Authors," and "Selected Bibliography" (of secondary sources).

1153 Bradbury, Malcolm. *"Howards End,"* FORSTER: A COLLEC-
TION OF CRITICAL ESSAYS, ed by Malcolm Bradbury (Englewood
Cliffs, NJ: Prentice-Hall, Spectrum Books, 1966), pp. 128–43.
[Rvd version of "E. M. Forster's *Howards End,*" CRITICAL QUARTERLY
(1962); see 1962 entry for essential line of argument in the essay. Pp.
128–29 on the existing criticism of the novel is added; conclusion is modified (pp. 142–43) to suggest that the irony and comedy partly signify an
anarchic force, never far removed from the instances of alleged connection
in EMF's fiction. At best the optimism in *Howards End* is muted.]

1154 Bradbury, Malcolm. "Introduction," FORSTER: A COLLEC-
TION OF CRITICAL ESSAYS, ed by Malcolm Bradbury (Englewood
Cliffs, NJ: Prentice-Hall, Spectrum Books, 1966), pp. 1–14; rptd,
rvd, and enld, from "A Short Guide to Forster Studies," CRITICAL
SURVEY, II (Summer 1965), 113–16.
EMF's work has recently seemed more complex and modern than previously; recent critics have now seen the complexity and resource of his fictional
method. Most critics now have focused on EMF's rhythms and symbols; the
danger is that we may forget the comic social novelist. Too often EMF has
been regarded as a scion of Victorian liberalism; but his traditional romantic
and political liberalism recognizes and confronts a modern disquietude. In
Howards End, EMF records this disquietude in his intellectuals. He is only
partly the Edwardian liberal humanist, since he is also "criticising Benthamite organization from the point of view of the need for diverse individualism, and criticising the indulgences of individualism with a deep commitment to the demands of the 'unseen.' " He is a mystic as well as a rationalist.
His visions, if they imply unity, also embrace anarchy and imply an incomplete redemption. He has affiliations with the Bloomsbury philosophy of
personal relationships and aesthetics based on a personal vision, but his
attachment to Bloomsbury is also critical. His complexity and ambiguity
lead him into uncertainties of tone, archness, and a damaging variety of
intentions, qualities difficult for critics to assimilate and assess. To the
extent that a modern chaos permits, his visionary qualities enable him to
achieve harmony and a full sense of life in *Howards End* and *A Passage to
India*. EMF combines experimentalism and symbolism with an enlargement of the social-moral novel. Early critics of EMF, such as F. R. Leavis
and Virginia Woolf, noted the split between a poetic mysticism and a social
realism. American critics have been largely concerned with the "poetic" or
symbolic aspect of EMF, and English critics with the social and realistic.
[An illuminating general survey of EMF's literary reputation and of tendencies in recent EMF criticism. Surveys EMF's principal critics since I. A.
Richards's "A Passage to Forster" (1927).]

1155 Burke, Kenneth. "Social and Cosmic Mystery: *A Passage to
India*," LUGANO REVIEW, I (Summer 1966), 140–55; rptd in LAN-

GUAGE AS SYMBOLIC ACTION: ESSAYS ON LIFE, LITERATURE, AND METHOD (Berkeley & Los Angeles: University of California P, 1966; Cambridge: Cambridge UP, 1967), pp. 223–39.

A Passage to India may be seen in terms of a four-part definition: (1) "A long realistic prose narrative, tinged with mystery, and employing dialogue and description" (2) "The descriptions treat of the overall situation, of the particular scenes in which the many episodes take place, of the mental attitudes involved in the agents' acts and relationships, and of the crises wherein private relations merge into the behavior of groups." (3) "Though the descriptions contribute functionally to the total context, at times they have a design that sets them off like arias in music." [Analyzes the description of the interior of the Marabar Caves in Chap XII as such an "aria."] (4) "The story is told from a novelistic point of view that transcends the perspective of any one character, and that is designed to evoke in the reader a mood of ironically sympathetic contemplation." [Considers the fourth part of the definition and shows how the plot and the situation provide the materials for "a comedy of ironically sympathetic contemplation."] The muddle of castes and classes in India is the situation that provides much subtle comedy. Not only do the traditional formalities operate in this situation, but with India in transition the formalities have to be adjusted and made flexible, often under comic strains and stresses. Such a situation leads to embarrassed "improvisings" by all castes and classes, "the improvising of protocol." Adela's retraction of her accusation against Aziz is the most extreme example of these embarrassed improvisings; but the relations between Aziz and Mrs. Moore illustrate more consistently this kind of tentative, exploratory behavior [also one would judge that the uneasy relationships between Aziz and Fielding would be applicable here.] The plot can be viewed from two vantage points. The first strand features Adela Quested and leads finally to the ironic relationships between the classes and castes. Attitudes of "gallantry" can mitigate social tensions. The second strand features Mrs. Moore and her surviving influence after her death (elements both of mystery and of mysticism are present here).

The characters tend to reflect the element of divisiveness in human relationships. There is no villain in the book but "only a comic scale of errors," and the characters are seen as, in various ways, contributing to the main mystery-muddle dichotomy. Godbole is the comic representation of the book's serious message. Also, in the courtroom punkah wallah the "mystery and muddle meet. Here, tentatively, is a silently drastic step beyond Fielding's rationalism. Here one of the most supernumerary characters in the book is enigmatically invested with an unresolved tangle of motives such as one experiences at bewildering moments when 'values' are not so much 'transvalued' as thrown into a state of total suspension. The entire logic of both empire and resistance to empire becomes mute, merging into a realm of untouchability that is both vexing and enticing to a mind burdened with the norms of progress, tradition, and order." [Traces the significance of recurring words and phrases as they provide an internal consistency for the novel: "attendant terms" such as "extraordinary," "star," "half-way," "bump" versus the "pomper" of the train wheels, "echo."] Finally, *Passage* alleges that distinctions are to be transcended, but a doubt lingers that, in our imperfect world, they can be. [A closely reasoned, involuted essay, with some sharp insights, but difficult at times for even an informed reader to gain clear impressions from.]

1156 Carens, James F. THE SATIRIC ART OF EVELYN WAUGH (Seattle & Lond: University of Washington P, 1966), p. 138.

Waugh's BLACK MISCHIEF and SCOOP are satires of empire, but Waugh in them is not hostile to imperialism as such and to the injustice of its assumptions as a liberal might be. He does, however, ridicule its practices. The two novels do not reveal the qualified humanism to be found in *A Passage to India* or in Orwell's BURMESE DAYS.

1157 Chaudhuri, Nirad C. THE CONTINENT OF CIRCE: BEING AN ESSAY ON THE PEOPLES OF INDIA (Lond & NY: Oxford UP, 1966), pp. 68, 93, 128.

The influence of *A Passage to India* with its emphasis on putting Anglo-Indian relationships on a "human" footing may have led to a sentimentalizing of the Indian aborigines that paved the way for their disintegration as a part of India. In *Passage* EMF is ostensibly pro-Indian, but really treats his Indians as perverted, clownish, or quixotic. EMF is satirical and uncomplimentary, especially to the Hindus. The English were victims of life in the tropics, for which they were not suited. Many were arrogant and self-centered and disinclined to share English culture with Indians; but many showed intense compassion, as EMF reveals in *Passage*. The book's message might be phrased thus: "However impossible and even provoking an Indian might be, an Englishman has no right to forget that he is a Christian gentleman." [Most of discussion appeared as "On Understanding the Hindus," ENCOUNTER (Lond), XXIV (June 1965), 20–33.]

1158 Daleski, H. M. "Rhythmic and Symbolic Patterns in *A Passage to India*," STUDIES IN ENGLISH LANGUAGE AND LITERATURE, ed by Alice Shalvi and A. A. Mendilow (Jerusalem: The Hebrew University, 1966), XVII, 259–79.

The meeting of Mrs. Moore and Aziz contrasts with the bridge party, presenting a true as opposed to a false unity between the races. Aziz's relationship with Mrs. Moore depends on the heart, that with Fielding on the mind. Neither relationship has been tested at the end of "Mosque." The

Caves are non-human, divisive, represent negation, and deny and defy connection (e.g., the effect of the Caves on Adela Quested, Mrs. Moore, Aziz, Fielding and their various relationships). The Temple, like the Mosque, is a symbol of unity, but a unity attained through the submerging of individual differences rather than through a reconciliation of opposites. Mrs. Moore (through her children Ralph and Stella) and Godbole are the presiding spirits at the reconciling rituals in "Temple." Mrs. Moore's presence merges with the rumors of salvation, associated with the Temple ceremonies, to save Aziz from the spirit of division, associated with the Caves. The reconciliation of Aziz and Fielding depends on the religious ceremonies at Mau. Stella Moore brings the men into physical contact by causing the wreck of the boats in the tank, when the tray bearing the Hindu effigies reaches her and causes her to capsize her boat. Some aesthetic confusion occurs at the end when EMF presents the primordial differences between Fielding and Aziz in terms of political differences. [Stresses, as in Wilfred Stone's THE CAVE AND THE MOUNTAIN (1966), the cyclic aspects of *A Passage to India.* Persuasive and original discussion, although there is too much quotation from EMF and too little consideration of other accounts of the novel. Skillfully contrasts the various scenes and characters and makes many striking observations. The account of Mrs. Moore, her function and her influence, is especially perceptive.]

1159 Davis, Robert Gorham (ed). "Introduction," "E. M. Forster," TEN MASTERS OF THE MODERN ESSAY (NY: Harcourt, Brace & World, 1966), pp. 1–15, 17–37.

"What I Believe" (*Two Cheers for Democracy*) is a model essay, EMF subjecting idea and intuition to the test of his own experience, values, likes, and dislikes. In "What I Believe" EMF modulates between an unrestrained colloquialism and more formal eloquence. *A Passage to India* is concerned with issues deeper than merely political ones. In his early novels EMF had treated both national and class differences. By virtue of his wit, modesty, and love of style he is an ideal familiar essayist. [Praises conversational quality of many of EMF's essays: "Trooper Silas Tomkyn Comberbacke" (*Abinger Harvest*) and "The United States" (*Two Cheers*). Three cited essays ptd, pp. 19–37.]

1160 Friedman, Alan. "E. M. Forster: 'Expansion not Completion,'" THE TURN OF THE NOVEL: THE TRANSITION TO MODERN FICTION (NY & Lond: Oxford UP, 1966), pp. 28, 29, 106–29; rvd from "The Turn of the Novel: Changes in the Pattern of English Fiction since 1890 in Hardy, Conrad, Forster, and Lawrence," unpublished dissertation, University of California (1964).

The formal element in fiction is the "stream of conscience," the self confronting the world outside it. In the nineteenth- and twentieth-century novel there has been a movement away from the closed form to the open form. In the closed form, the stream of conscience is contained; in the open, it is not so contained. EMF's novels exemplify the open form, wherein "expansion, not completion" is the rule. In an EMF novel we have an expansion of experience, followed by a tapering; from that point, an expansion and an opening out again develops. In *A Room with a View* the characters are pushed "expansively" from rooms to views, from the life led according to conventions to the expression of desire, from English viewpoints to Italian vistas. In *Where Angels Fear to Tread* a marriage with Gino Carella would have been as constricting for Caroline Abbott as it was for Lilia Herriton. Both Caroline and Philip Herriton undergo an expansion of conscience, of moral apprehension and emotional grasp. The sense of life ahead, made more difficult by expanded awareness, is greater here than in *Room*. In *A Passage to India* EMF's insistence on an open flow of conscience also organizes his material. Mrs. Moore's experience is expansive, as is Adela Quested's at the trial and after. The movement is from separation to mutual friendship, which reaches its consummation under the stars on the roof of Aziz's house that night after the trial. Countercurrents of suspicion undermine the relationship and contract it. In "Temple" the relationship again opens out, with Mrs. Moore acting as a hidden catalyst. [A stimulating if somewhat simplified interpretation.]

1161 Friend, Robert. "The Theme of Salvation in 'The Point of It,' " Studies in English Language and Literature, ed by Alice Shalvi and A. A. Mendilow (Jerusalem: The Hebrew University, 1966), XVII, 243–57.

In "The Point of It," the protagonist Micky achieves salvation by re-embracing the spirit of youth and by eschewing his own apathetic senility. Youth's desire for strength and beauty represents the desire for unity of being. Harold embodies the spirit of youth and Micky that of corroding senility. Harold is uneducated, innocent, and inartistic compared to Micky, but these are qualities that bring Harold closer to reality. He is also to be associated with Christ and with Pollux, and is thus an allegorical representation of truth. Micky is the flawed and imperfect man who must learn from experience; as such, he is more suitable to be the protagonist than is Harold. The "plain in Hell sequence" is unsuccessful as a mixture of allegory and symbolic realism. [There are a few new observations in this article, but it largely repeats Frederick P. W. McDowell in "Forster's 'Natural Supernaturalism': The Tales" (1960) and Alan Wilde in Art and Order: A Study of E. M. Forster (1964).]

1162 Goldman, Mark. "Virginia Woolf and E. M. Forster: A Critical Dialogue," Texas Studies in Literature and Language, VII (Winter 1966), 387–400.

Virginia Woolf and EMF represent opposing views on the nature of the novel. Woolf felt the need to break with the Edwardian past in order to capture the Georgian sensibility and reality; she criticized EMF for trying to capture the Georgian sensibility without abandoning the Edwardian form. In "The Novels of E. M. Forster" (1927) she finds EMF torn between Edwardian fact and Georgian vision. As a novelist of complex ideas his balancing of attitudes is crucial; but he works from the outside in. Mrs. Woolf's balancing is formal or aesthetic; her points of view are discovered from the inside, and they irradiate from a subjective center. EMF is too conscious of human comedy, too much the novelist of ideas, too involved in the liberal tradition to commit himself to the novel of sensibility. EMF, in his essays on Virginia Woolf, celebrates the beauty of her poetry but feels that life sometimes eludes her. EMF feels that the poetic method may fail to achieve for the novel its characteristic, traditional reality. In *Aspects of the Novel* he illustrates the modern preoccupation with psychology and inner experience but resists assaults upon form. In "The Art of Fiction" (1927) Mrs. Woolf asserts that EMF judges narrative art from the humane rather than the aesthetic point of view, and she feels EMF is thereby disloyal to the art of fiction. In EMF's later essays, such as "Anonymity" and "Art for Art's Sake," he approaches more closely the aesthetic view of art. EMF also has more reservations about the value of criticism as a discipline and as a help to the artist than do Clive Bell, Roger Fry, or Virginia Woolf (see EMF's "Raison d'Etre of Criticism in the Arts" in *Two Cheers for Democracy*). Perhaps his impatience with the critical faculty, especially as it bears upon the writing of fiction, accounts for his failure to write more novels after *A Passage to India*. [A carefully thought-out essay, though EMF had, possibly, a higher view of the critic than Goldman admits; see Frederick P. W. McDowell, "E. M. Forster's Conception of the Critic" (1965).]

1163 Hampshire, Stuart. "Two Cheers for Mr. Forster," NEW YORK REVIEW OF BOOKS, 12 May 1966, pp. 14–16; rptd as "E. M. Forster," MODERN WRITERS AND OTHER ESSAYS (Lond: Chatto & Windus, 1969; NY: Knopf, 1970), pp. 47–55 (NY ed), all references to Stone's book are deleted.

EMF is divided between two attitudes: an inherited liberalism (which stresses the authority of individual conscience and sensitivity and lucidity in personal relations within the setting of a civilized private life) and the natural order (which is sublime, unknown, unlimited, and not well-adapted to our powers of understanding). Art is the means of bridging the "upper" and "lower" consciousness. In his earlier work EMF had stressed values of inner truthfulness and lucidity of feeling and had implied that self-knowledge was possible. By the time of *The Longest Journey* and *Howards End*, he suggests, by the texture of his prose, the incompleteness of these values.

The presence of such doubt in EMF's work places him in the modern movement; he is the link between the nineteenth-century novel, which focuses upon the individual and his moral responsibility (as in Henry James and George Eliot), and the modern novel, which is generally broader in its implications and less given to rational analysis. In *A Passage to India* EMF's vision is perfectly realized, and Indian art and thought vindicate his distrust of liberal humanism. The characters in the novel, British and Indian, achieve identity as they are seen against the backgrounds of India and its monuments, wherein reside intimations of a reality that eludes the intellect. [Ostensibly a review of Wilfred Stone's THE CAVE AND THE MOUNTAIN (1966). Lucid, important, wide-ranging discussion.]

1164 Heilbrun, Carolyn. "Speaking of Books: A Modern Among Contemporaries," NEW YORK TIMES REVIEW, 30 Jan 1966, p. 2.

Only James, Conrad, and EMF possessed the "imagination of disaster" in their work as a countercurrent to the confidence of the Edwardian age. *Where Angels Fear to Tread* traces the inner development of two inhibited Sawstonians, Philip Herriton and Caroline Abbott; it embodies "sexuality, moral impulses, the tragic vision—the whole world of modern fiction." The "moderns" of the Edwardian age wrote a literature of "encounters," "encounters which did not receive the sacraments, but which were sacramental for all that." Writers such as EMF, James, Conrad, Joyce, Woolf, and Lawrence all realized "that there was no certainty but the truth of the imagination, that, if old claims were no longer sacred, the heart's affections now were holy." The "moderns" also possessed a metaphoric imagination and a sharp insight into the tragic dimensions of existence. EMF attained the modern vision earlier than most, and kept it. [Authoritatively relates EMF to his contemporaries.]

1165 Hunt, John Dixon. "Muddle and Mystery in *A Passage to India,*" ENGLISH LITERARY HISTORY, XXXIII (Dec 1966), 497–517.

The disorder of Indian life and the mystery of the Hindu religion are intimately related in *A Passage to India.* British order is at best superficial; it is, in actuality, a form of disorder because it gives rise to chaos and ill-feeling. The novel's essential theme "suggests that formlessness, disorder and inappropriateness are holier than British precision." Fielding, Mrs. Moore, and Godbole (in that ascending order of insight) take their visions beyond strict categories and divisions, and they perceive that truth lies elsewhere. Godbole alone survives physically and spiritually. Fielding does not survive as a spiritual force because he disregards mystery; Mrs. Moore does not survive as a person because she dislikes muddle. [A sprawling essay that could have condensed its insights into a few pages. The thesis is valid and valuable but inadequate for such an extended essay.]

1166 Lehmann, John. THE AMPLE PROPOSITION: AUTOBIOGRAPHY III (Lond: Eyre & Spottiswoode, 1966), pp. 74, 102–3, 152, 187; rptd, slightly rvd, in IN MY OWN TIME: MEMOIRS OF A LITERARY LIFE (Boston: Little, Brown, 1969).

[EMF assisted Lehmann with NEW WRITING. Lehmann describes his friendship and admiration for EMF, EMF's painstaking reading of manuscripts for his friends, and his continued help to Lehmann in matters literary. Quotes letters from EMF describing his busy activity with manuscripts in 1952 and his valuing Lehmann as friend, editor, and writer.]

1167 Lekachman, Robert. "Education and Early Career," THE AGE OF KEYNES (NY: Random House, 1966; Lond: A. Lane, 1967), pp. 6, 11–27, espec 14–15, 21, 24n.

EMF's *Marianne Thornton* shows the prosperity of the nineteenth-century upper middle class into which Keynes was born. Through Marianne's legacy to EMF, Henry Thornton (the banker-founder of the family who died in 1815) has to his credit *Howards End* and *A Passage to India.* The members of Keynes's circle needed Marianne Thornton legacies to realize their full potential. Keynes's absolute loyalty to a friend in August 1914 helped him get back to Austria. This gesture reveals a motivation similar to that behind EMF's pronouncement in "What I Believe" (1939; also in *Two Cheers for Democracy*) that if he had to choose between betraying friend or country, he would hope to have the "guts" to betray his country. [Cited chap valuable for knowledge of EMF's Cambridge and Bloomsbury ambience.]

1168 Lodge, David. LANGUAGE OF FICTION: ESSAYS IN CRITICISM AND VERBAL ANALYSIS OF THE ENGLISH NOVEL (NY: Columbia UP; Lond: Routledge & Kegan Paul, 1966), pp. 154, 201, 243.

EMF is a master of implied derogatory repetition (*A Room with a View*). EMF is a major novelist though Spender regards him mostly as "contemporary." [Quotes EMF concerning the insubstantial nature of James's characters. Adopts Stephen Spender's view in THE STRUGGLE OF THE MODERN (1965) that James, Conrad, Joyce, Lawrence, and Woolf are "modern" rather than "contemporary."]

1169 Lucas, John. "Wagner and Forster: PARSIFAL and *A Room with a View,*" ENGLISH LITERARY HISTORY, XXXIII (March 1966), 92–117; rptd in ROMANTIC MYTHOLOGIES, ed by Ian Fletcher (Lond: Routledge & Kegan Paul; NY: Barnes & Noble, 1967), pp. 271–97.

EMF's great passion for music suffuses his novels: the Beethoven references in *Howards End* and the use of music in *A Room with a View* to modulate mood and to cause Lucy to admit unwelcome truths about herself. PARSIFAL was the most cherished of the Wagner operas in Edwardian times because it revealed how an artist could be simultaneously secular and religious.

PARSIFAL was the source of myths that EMF put to productive use in *Room*. In this novel EMF's emphasis on "Love" and "Truth" becomes religious in implication because of the metaphors which surround these terms. The radical theme of the novel relates to PARSIFAL: the paradox that the guardians of society can be killers (Klingsor, Charlotte Bartlett, Cecil Vyse, the Reverend Beebe) and the outcasts who threaten it have "the vitality which is life itself" (Parsifal, Amfortas, Titurel, the Emersons). In EMF vital political and social attitudes are raised to the level of moral perceptions: the contrast between the Emersons' easy but sincere democracy and Cecil's empty exclusiveness, snobbishness, and complacency. But like the other main characters, Cecil is deficient in a typical sense and in an absolute or mythic sense; he is "medieval" as well as insufferable. George Emerson, Lucy, Miss Bartlett, and Reverend Beebe also attain mythic stature in part.

Both PARSIFAL and *Room* are on the side of life or of "religion," although the pagan is exalted in *Room* and the Christian in PARSIFAL. Mr. Emerson and George Emerson are similar to Titurel and Amfortas. The Emersons, like their analogues, cherish values that are sustaining and quickening. George's wound is that caused by love in a magic garden on a hillside. Lucy is a kind of Kundry figure, love for whom brings disaster to the hero. Like Kundry, she is indecisive and vacillating. George suffers from a death-in-life melancholia similar to Amfortas's sufferings and inability to die. Miss Bartlett and the Reverend Beebe are Klingsor analogues; she employs Lucy to hurt the enemy (the hero), and he is sexless and repressive. Lucy is saved by the Holy Fool, Mr. Emerson. Mr. Emerson is the Parsifal as well as the Titurel analogue. As Parsifal, Mr. Emerson saves his son by curing his wound, and he converts Lucy by his wisdom and example (in the opera, Parsifal is responsible for Kundry's baptism). Mr. Emerson has perhaps too many functions in the novel and is too exclusively mythic to be altogether convincing. [The analogues suggested are stimulating, although I find it difficult to envision the valetudinarian Mr. Emerson as a holy fool. Article is too diffuse and relaxed in method, but excellent for articulating the background of EMF's Edwardian novels. Article convincingly traces the great popularity of Wagner in Edwardian times.]

1170 McDowell, Frederick P. W. "E. M. Forster's Theory of Literature," CRITICISM, VIII (Winter 1966), 19–43.

EMF is no systematic critic; but if rigid principles are lacking, a point of view is present. For EMF the artist is a god-like creator whose works exist with individual authority as "heterocosms." EMF regards each work as self-contained, in which part and whole are mutually dependent. He also stresses internal order and coherence, which result from the shaping mind of the artist. EMF stresses the need for both formal tautness and the relevant, aesthetically impressive detail. The writer must be attentive not only to form but to style. He will be guided mainly by his need to secure a single, sustained effect. The artist must combine, therefore, critical acuteness and an active sensibility. Great art is self-contained, but its influence, paradoxically, radiates far beyond its self-contained universe. It is at once aesthetic and ethical in nature and influence; individual and social in its orientation. The artist is awake, therefore, to the complexities of life and is inclusive in his vision. He is a realist in that the external world influences his vision and forms part of his finished work, but he must also be aware of the underlying symbolic and general implications of his materials. Craft and the need to attain beauty are important, but the importance of theme and psychology cannot be underestimated. Art matters greatly, but it is not all that matters.

1171 Mackenzie, Compton. MY LIFE AND TIMES: OCTAVE 5, 1915–1923 (Lond: Chatto & Windus, 1966), pp. 144, 246.
Disillusionment resulted from rereading *Where Angels Fear to Tread*, which had been impressive ten years earlier. Now it seems "a completely artificial drama of Italian life imagined by a cloistered introspective temperament." EMF's Italians are academic caricatures. Letter from John Hope-Johnstone (1922) is skeptical of the refined, high-toned aspects of EMF's work; his writing is "automatic" in the sense that we can predict what he will say.

1172 "Major or Minor," TIMES LITERARY SUPPLEMENT (Lond), 13 Oct 1966, p. 936.
EMF is not best served by his academic admirers, like Wilfred Stone in THE CAVE AND THE MOUNTAIN, who discuss him as a major author rather than as a delightful minor one. Stone does not find, or fails to convey, EMF's "distinction, toughness, and warmth." "Moral certainty and final shapeliness" are less EMF qualities than his ironic and nostalgic tone; "the compromises and sad timidities" with which the novels end measure the way that things are (in EMF's view) rather than EMF's indecisiveness.

1173 Marshall, Rachelle. "On E. M. Forster," PROGRESSIVE (Madison), XXX (6 Dec 1966), 46–48.
For EMF sanity is essential; a choice between extremes is not necessary, and "simple decency" is the only value that will work in the long run. In THE CAVE AND THE MOUNTAIN (1966), Wilfred Stone is best on *A Passage to India*, which is one of the great books of social protest. It explores "the psychological and social ravages of imperialism," showing that the domination of one group by another damages the oppressor more than the oppressed. *Passage* is much more than a sociological novel.

1174 Martin, Kingsley. FATHER FIGURES: A FIRST VOLUME OF AUTOBIOGRAPHY 1897–1931 (Lond: Hutchinson; Toronto: Nelson, Foster & Scott, 1966), pp. 98, 102, 123, 126.

[EMF was a member of Cambridge Apostles at turn of the century. Though Martin did not come to Cambridge until after World War I, he got to know most of the members of this group. He was profoundly influenced in his undergraduate thinking by EMF's first four novels. In his chapter on Goldsworthy Lowes Dickinson, quotes EMF on magical quality of prewar Cambridge and regrets that EMF was unable to be frank in his biography about Dickinson's homosexuality.]

1175 Mendilow, A. A. "The Triadic World of E. M. Forster," STUDIES IN ENGLISH LANGUAGE AND LITERATURE, ed by Alice Shalvi and A. A. Mendilow (Jerusalem: The Hebrew University, 1966), XVII, 280–91.

The protagonists in *A Passage to India* are trapped in a cyclic pattern. Unity and divisions are continually present; the conflicts are often expressed in a triadic rather than a dualistic pattern. The Mosque represents the social or civilized aspects of man's life, suggests the human and the rational, and is associated with the cool season and with activity in society. Characters associated with Mosque are Aziz, Mrs. Moore, Fielding, and Adela Quested. The Caves represent the biological aspects of man's life, suggest the instinctual and subhuman, and are associated with the hot season and with sex. The anonymous guide who may (or may not) have tried to rape Adela is the chief embodiment of these aspects of the Caves. The Temple represents the spiritual aspect of man's life, suggests the superhuman and the mystical, and is associated with the rainy season and religion. Characters associated with the Temple are Godbole, Stella, Mrs. Moore, and Ralph Moore. The Mosque projects the historical past, the Caves project the geological past, and the Temple projects the legendary past. The movement of the novel is in a pessimistic direction. Aspiration to love and unity, dramatized in "Temple," is defeated by the facts of human life. No satisfying communication with man, god, or nature is possible; "one cannot blend or become one for there is no unity." [This essay suggests more than it develops; too much commentary consists in character sketches and a retelling of the plot. A far more sophisticated discussion of the "triads" in the novel is in Wilfred Stone's THE CAVE AND THE MOUNTAIN (1966). The alleged pessimism of the novel is also questionable.]

1176 Moore, Katherine. CORDIAL RELATIONS: THE MAIDEN AUNT IN FACT AND FICTION (Lond: Heinemann, 1966, Don Mills, Ontario: Collins, 1967), pp. 4–5.

The maiden aunt has been something of an archteypal presence in British social life and fiction. EMF is one genius who has devoted a whole book to such an aunt, *Marianne Thornton*. Marianne Thornton is typical of this type, a devoted woman yet a strong personality.

1177 Morton, A. L. "An Englishman Discovers India," THE MAT-TER OF BRITAIN: ESSAYS ON A LIVING CULTURE (Lond: Laurence & Wishart, 1966), pp. 150–54.

There is an average quality to the Chandrapore setting and the characters in *A Passage to India*. Still, the characters come to experience profound human emotions: "pity, terror, love, hate, fear and exaltation, friendship and the final loneliness of the soul in the waste places." EMF is great by virtue of his attitude toward life; life does not teach us, it changes us. His fundamental problem: How are men to establish contact with one another and yet preserve their individuality? EMF believes not so much in formal democracy as in true democracy—in "Love the Beloved Republic." He believes that other people are as real as oneself. He condemns the Anglo-Indians for not realizing the importance of this precept. The sun, a character in the novel and a symbol of power without beauty and of intellect without love, operates in *Passage* to prevent true understanding between English-man and Englishman and between Englishman and Indian. EMF presents the waste, frustration, and bitterness that inequality produces on both sides. Powerlessness corrupts the Indians just as power corrupts the English. The political situation must become a function of the personal. [Some valuable insights.]

1178 Mukherjee, Sujit. "The Marabar Mystery: An Addition to the Case-Book on the Caves," COLLEGE ENGLISH, XXVII (March 1966), 501–3.

Most of the interpretations of the Marabar Caves in *A Passage to India* are unreliable. Firmer interpretations would follow if critics recognized the actual prototypes of the Caves, their attributes, and the sects associated with them. The Caves in the Marabar Hills are based on those in the Barabar Hills south of modern Patna (Chandrapore). The Barabar Caves are as-sociated not with the Hindu religion but with the atheistic Ajivika sect, sponsored by the Emperor Asoika in the third century B. C. but now defunct. Its philosophy was marked by "quietism and determinism, inaction and denial, asceticism and negation," attributes that EMF associates with his characters' reactions in the Marabar Caves. "Thus whatever may be the symbolic doctrine of the caves in the novel, in actuality they have had no association with the theory and practice of Hinduism." [Mukherjee disre-gards too greatly the associations, made by EMF, of the Caves with the Hindu Professor Godbole; he has intuitive knowledge of them which the other characters lack.]

1179 Nicolson, Harold. DIARIES AND LETTERS 1930–39, ed by Ni-gel Nicolson (NY: Atheneum; Lond: Collins, 1966), pp. 87, 148. [Incidental references: EMF's enthusiasm for Gerald Heard (14 Aug 1931), and EMF's being elected to the London Library Committee (8 May 1933).]

1180 Panichas, George A. "E. M. Forster and D. H. Lawrence: Their Views on Education," RENAISSANCE AND MODERN ESSAYS PRESENTED TO VIVIAN DE SOLA PINTO IN CELEBRATION OF HIS SEVENTIETH BIRTHDAY, ed by G. R. Hibbard (Lond: Routledge & Kegan Paul, 1966), pp. 199–214; rptd in THE REVERENT DISCIPLINE: ESSAYS IN LITERARY CRITICISM AND CULTURE (Knoxville: University of Tennessee P, 1974), pp. 157–69.

Both EMF and D. H. Lawrence were concerned with the meaning, needs, and trends of education in the twentieth century. EMF, with his liberal humanism, saw education as a corrective process, working to remold civilization; Lawrence was more individualistic and apocalyptic, stressing a need to redefine concepts in order to promote the individual's development. EMF's vision is "mediate," "the result of delicate interweavings of and tensions between 'actions and meditations.' " In education, as in his art, EMF reveals "the habit of intellect and a predisposition towards introspection." Lawrence's vision is "immediate" and iconoclastic. Lawrence has some use for the mind, but his view is not primarily rational. Too often education imposes a pattern, Lawrence says, and forgets the need to restore a "non-ideal, passional" element to human relations. Both EMF and Lawrence recognize "mystery" in human life, and they fear that education may extinguish it. [Does not get below the surfaces of the subject.]

1181 Parry, Benita. "Passage to More than India," FORSTER: A COLLECTION OF CRITICAL ESSAYS, ed by Malcolm Bradbury (Englewood Cliffs, NJ: Prentice-Hall, Spectrum Books, 1966), pp. 106–16; rptd in PERSPECTIVES ON E. M. FORSTER'S "A PASSAGE TO INDIA," ed by V. A. Shahane (NY: Barnes & Noble, 1968), pp. 151–65.

EMF's characters in *A Passage to India* work in two directions—they aspire to understand themselves and the universe, but they are also alienated from their fellow men, especially when differing cultures are involved. Despite the muddle of India and the implacable and malignant quality of nature in India, the various Indias may encourage modes of growth and harmony hitherto unknown to us. The Indian mind and the Indian landscape are linked to values that the Moslem and British invaders do not understand. The Hindu flabbiness is really passive resistance and stoic endurance; man's inherent activity and creativeness are signs of his humanity and counterbalance the negations of "Caves." Godbole reveals the mystery and many-textured quality of Hinduism; he harmonizes, as a "wise fool," its contradictions. Hinduism balances the impulse toward division and the impulse toward inclusion. The message of the book is not proportion, in view of the divisive tendencies present throughout. Fielding too readily compromises as a representative of normality and proportion. Incompleteness is present not only in the characters but in developing the spiritual theme. The reconciliations suggested in the novel are only tentative; and the transcendental allusions move between uncertainty and whimsicality. The tendency of the book is toward a muted hope, however. EMF would suggest that the "not yet" of the concluding paragraph will at some time be transcended. [Essay reveals knowledge and insight but lacks clear development.]

1182 Penman, E. M. "Moments of Apperception in the English Novel: A Study of Henry James, Virginia Woolf, E. M. Forster and James Joyce Related to Psychiatric and Philosophic Developments in the Late Nineteenth and Early Twentieth Centuries." Unpublished dissertation, University of London (University College), 1966. [Listed in G. M. Paterson, INDEX TO THESES ACCEPTED FOR HIGHER DEGREES IN THE UNIVERSITIES OF GREAT BRITAIN AND IRELAND, XVI (1965–1966).]

1183 Price, Martin. "E. M. F. and D. H. L.," YALE REVIEW, nsLV (Summer 1966), 597–601.
EMF's remarks, defending D. H. Lawrence from T. S. Eliot's attack, reveal EMF's eloquence and "ironic outrage" and impart his own affinities with Lawrence. Both writers are interested in the struggle of the individual to attain reality; both are impatient with a society that obstructs this struggle; both show us an image of full descent into being, which either regenerates (in EMF's and Lawrence's work in general) or overpowers [see EMF in "Caves," *A Passage to India*]; both search for an ultimate reality. For EMF this search does not preclude a skeptical irony, but Lawrence loathes such irony. EMF is a more courageously detached thinker. His skepticism is a serenity that is not passive but "warm-blooded, unstable, and profoundly curious." In his treatment of *Howards End*, Wilfred Stone reveals an insensitivity to EMF's irony and self-criticism. [Review-essay on Stone's THE CAVE AND THE MOUNTAIN (1966) and H. M. Daleski's THE FORKED FLAME: A STUDY OF D. H. LAWRENCE (Evanston: Northwestern UP, 1966). Daleski has written an informed, penetrating book in which EMF is only tangentially mentioned. Price's essay-review is illuminating on the relationships between the two writers.]

1184 Putt, S. Gorley. HENRY JAMES: A READER'S GUIDE (Lond: Thames & Hudson, Reader's Guide Series; Ithaca: Cornell UP, 1966), pp. 79, 337.
In "Adena," a young Italian avenges himself on a theft of a topaz by luring away the thief's wife, just as one of EMF's Italians might have wreaked havoc on the hearts of English ladies. Lambert Strether in THE AMBASSADORS is a figure resembling EMF.

1185 Raina, M. L. "A Forster Parallel in Lawrence's ST. MAWR," NOTES AND QUERIES (Lond), nsXIII (March 1966), 96–97.

Monroe Engel, in "The Continuity of Lawrence's Short Novels," HUDSON REVIEW, XI (Summer 1958), 207, remarks on the similarity of Mrs. Moore's anti-vision in the Marabar Caves in *A Passage to India* to the experience of Lou Witt in D. H. Lawrence's ST. MAWR during her ride to the Devil's Chair Rock. There are verbal parallels between Adela Quested's disillusioning experiences at the Marabar and Lou Witt's succumbing to apathy on her ride. [The parallels are interesting but scarcely so conclusive as the author would maintain.]

1186 Raina, M. L. "Traditional Symbolism and Forster's *Passage to India*," NOTES AND QUERIES (Lond), nsXIII (Nov 1966), 416–17.

The divisions of *A Passage to India* into three sections conforming to the three seasons (cold weather, hot weather, and rain) of the Indian year (often seen by critics to symbolize "on the plane of human relationships the disruption and re-creation of cosmic order") has firm basis in Indian mythological literature. The ravages of Vishnu as the Sun in the hot weather are neutralized by the torrential rain he thereafter sheds. The earth comes to know at last its final relief—extinction or Nirvana. [Wilfred Stone in THE CAVE AND THE MOUNTAIN (1966) makes the same points.]

1187 Rama Rau, Santha. "Oranges, Birds and Crystals," REPORTER (NY), XXXIV (March 1966), 54, 56.

Wilfred Stone in THE CAVE AND THE MOUNTAIN (1966) has explored convincingly a "developing myth," i. e., EMF's complex view of the human situation in the context of a philosophic and social "symbology." In India EMF's work reached fruition as he analyzed incisively the need for understanding among individuals and the social, political, and religious forces that prevent it. [Fresh, personal approach.]

1188 Rao, K. Bhaskara. RUDYARD KIPLING'S INDIA (Norman: University of Oklahoma P, 1966; Folkstone, Kent: Baily Bros. & Swinfen, 1967), pp. 4, 10, 48, 51, 52, 82, 108–9, 112, 115, 155–57, 159.

EMF represents the liberal, more tolerant and understanding approach to India. Unlike EMF, Kipling could not see that India is a spirit as well as a physical country. According to Kipling, Ronny Heaslop in *A Passage to India* would be the ideal British administrator. Mrs. Moore and Fielding are more sympathetic than the other Anglo-Indians; they participate in Indian life without losing their individuality. The closing chapter of *Passage* indicates that EMF was aware of the development and influence of the Indian National Congress when he has Aziz reject friendship, for the moment, with Fielding and the British. Kipling's LETTERS OF MARQUE is superficial compared with EMF's *The Hill of Devi*. In Kipling's NAULAHKA, Rhatore is shown in a more realistic light than are the princely states in LETTERS OF

Marque, and Rhatore has similarities to the intrigue-ridden court at Dewas State Senior in EMF's *Devi*. Kim "achieves much more in effective interpretation of India in terms of permanence and universality than *A Passage to India.*" [For contrary view, see Sujit Muhkerjee, "India's Entry into English Fiction," Quest (1965).] The purpose of *Passage* is too specific to show India effectively. The central character is Aziz, who is a Moslem. The picture of India cannot therefore be a true one, since Mohammedans were, like the English, conquerors of India rather than its original inhabitants. [Overlooks the view of EMF and many of his critics that this novel is not primarily political but metaphysical. Also seems not to have considered carefully the role of Godbole and of the "Temple" section.] EMF does not mention enough the Indian National movement. [K. Natwar-Singh in "Only Connect . . . : Forster and India," Aspects of E. M. Forster, ed by Oliver Stallybrass (1969), points out that the novel comes from an India earlier than that of the 1920s, when the Indian Nationalist movement got underway; Jeffrey Meyers, "The Politics of *A Passage to India*" (1971) establishes that *Passage* reflects, often by implication, the political India of the early 1920s; and M. M. Mahood, "Amristrar to Chandrapore: E. M. Forster and the Massacre" (1973) indicates how central the Amritsar massacre was to EMF and his projection of a state of psychic disillusionment in "Caves" section of *Passage.*]

1189 Rola, Dionsia. "On E. M. Forster's *Howards End:* Some Generalizations," Diliman Review (University of the Philippines), XIV (July 1966), 285–86.
[Pedestrian discussion of *Howards End* as it reflects a conflict between the two different worlds of value represented by the Wilcoxes and the Schlegels.]

1190 Rosenthal, M. L. "Only Connect," Spectator (Lond), CCXVII (23 Sept 1966), 383–84.
Wilfred Stone's efforts in The Cave and the Mountain are commendable, but EMF also speaks well for himself and may not need all this apparatus. Stone's book is at once superb, over-elaborate, and competitive with EMF. EMF is in the aesthetic tradition but cannot escape the tragic implications of experience when he examines it. EMF writes of certain modern preoccupations: the confrontation of classes and a mystique of liberating sexuality. EMF has not been so tough-minded as Yeats or Joyce in accepting the tragic condition of man and the impersonality of the sexual principle; but "a mystique of a dynamic, liberating sexuality" informs all his work. This aspect of EMF Stone does not deal with adequately (perhaps he is too occupied with the homosexual aspects of Cambridge and Bloomsbury to seize upon this mystique as central). [Review-essay on Stone's The Cave and the Mountain (1966). A most provocative essay.]

1191 Scott, Paul. "How Well Have They Worn?—1: *A Passage to India*," TIMES (Lond), 6 Jan 1966, p. 15.

A Passage to India was the right book at the right time to influence opinion. After 1947 it no longer exerted a political influence. By 1947 the Fieldings in Parliament were powerful enough to remove the Turtons from power in India. A more important subject is the failure of Fieldingism or liberal humanism: "It is this self-awareness of failure as inevitable but darkly mysterious that makes *A Passage to India* not only one of the great tragic works of twentieth-century fiction but one that we have still not wholly grown into, let alone grown out of." Mrs. Moore declares that human beings are important but that human relationships are not. She means that people do not know accurately what a human being is; a new definition of a human being is essential. To such a definition we are painfully progressing. EMF stands astride the whole period between the old Middle Ages and the new. "One might think of him . . . as one of the first of the considerable artists of the Post-Renaissance." [Stimulating article; unusual angle of approach.]

1192 Shipley, John B. "Additions to the E. M. Forster Bibliography," PAPERS OF THE BIBLIOGRAPHICAL SOCIETY OF AMERICA, LX (Second Quarter 1966), 224–25.

[Lists several additions to B. J. Kirkpatrick's A BIBLIOGRAPHY OF E. M. FORSTER (1965) that have been incorporated into 2nd ed (1968).]

1193 Smith, H. A. "Forster's Humanism and the Nineteenth Century," FORSTER: A COLLECTION OF CRITICAL ESSAYS, ed by Malcolm Bradbury (Englewood Cliffs, NJ: Prentice-Hall, Spectrum Books, 1966), pp. 106–16.

In the novels Sawston (illiberal England and the insensitive Philistine middle class) is opposed by two forces, the instinctive wisdom of Ruth Wilcox and Stephen Wonham, and the good will plus culture plus intelligence of Fielding and Stewart Ansell. These are differing humanisms, the one Dionysian or romantic, the other Apollonian and rationalistic. The adherents of either philosophy are generally flawed characters, however. Instinct and intelligence, culture and nature, reason and religious insight can sometimes be combined in one person (e.g., Rickie Elliot, Helen Schlegel, or—preeminently—Margaret Schlegel) who represents imaginative reason. EMF is at the end of a long succession of social critics (Carlyle, Ruskin, Morris, Arnold, and Dickens) who attack "the inner darkness in high places which comes with a commercial age." The principal method of confronting this darkness, established long before EMF began to write, is a confrontation of different points of view with one another, of past with present, a method of juxtaposition and apposition that approaches but does not become allegory. The positive alternative to an alien civilization often takes the form of a humanism like EMF's. In some writers, as in EMF, this humanism has an equivocal quality; it expresses a double vision, or a double vision gives rise to it. The imaginative or religious humanism stemming from the romantic movement is ultimately more important to EMF than the rational, skeptical humanism stemming from the Enlightenment. EMF measures his characters not against a commonly accepted social norm but against ideal standards; this lends a prophetic or apocalyptic note to his fiction. The worst failure people can reveal is a failure in imagination and in the affections. But EMF is less sure of the power of love and passionate understanding than were his romantic predecessors; the natural order and the human, social order no longer appear so benevolent as they did to the romantics. [An original, perceptive, illuminating essay.]

1194 Stansky, Peter, and William Abrahams. JOURNEY TO THE FRONTIER: TWO ROADS TO THE SPANISH CIVIL WAR (Boston: Little, Brown; Lond: Constable, 1966), pp. 5, 7, 9, 10, 12, 71, 261, 277, 279, 281, 299, 303–4, 394, 397, 409–10.

Bloomsbury was in essence the upper middle class of culture whose wealth and talents were inherited. EMF celebrates the life of this class in the Schlegels of *Howards End;* foreign to Bloomsbury was the deprivation of Leonard Bast depicted in the same novel. Julian Bell's reactions to life in China, as they were colored by his reactions to the outbreak of the Spanish War, are given in a 1937 essay; "War and Peace: A Letter to E. M. Forster" [see JULIAN BELL, ed by Quentin Bell (1938)]. The detached aestheticism of Roger Fry is more consistent than the humanitarian liberalism of Leonard Woolf and EMF; it is preferable to approach social matters with Fry's detachment, when an external menace such as fascism is not too imminent. [A dual biography of Julian Bell and John Cornford, prominent younger poets of the 1930s who were killed in the Spanish Civil War. See also Frederick Grubb, A VISION OF REALITY (1965).]

1195 Stewart, J. I. M. RUDYARD KIPLING (NY: Dodd, Mead; Lond: Gollancz, 1966), pp. 123, 140, 157.

"The Bridge-Builders" gathers a resonance from EMF's *A Passage to India* wherein bridge parties are an unsuccessful means of bringing the races together. "In the Rukh" contains a Mowgli who is a combination of the noble savage, the subservient Indian native, and a Greek god. The latter aspect recalls the figures in EMF's short stories. The blood on the books and papers in "Slaves and the Lamp" (from STALKEY & CO.) recalls EMF's use of blood on Lucy Honeychurch's pictures in *A Room with a View.* In both narratives the blood symbolizes a need to confront the powerful if violent truth.

1196 Stone, Wilfred. THE CAVE AND THE MOUNTAIN: A STUDY OF E. M. FORSTER (Stanford: Stanford UP; Lond: Oxford UP, 1966).

Chap 1, "Introduction: Poetry and Prose": EMF is a Colderidgean rather than a Benthamite, a romanticist rather than a rationalist, an anti-Utilitarian rather than a Utilitarian. He exemplifies the Coleridgean reconciliation of opposite and discordant entities. Like Coleridge and Arnold, EMF experienced at an early age a withering of his creative powers. He is conscious of fragmentation, though he wishes for an integration of man's powers. The novels are "dramatic installments in the story of his own struggle for selfhood—and for a myth to support it." [This is Stone's chief premise, which he overuses in his discussions of individual works.] Chap 2, "Clapham: The Father's House": His father's people, Henry and Marianne Thornton and their relatives, EMF respected; but he felt more affection for the impulsive, less pragmatic Whichelos on his mother's side. The conflict between the two groups of anscestors provided a constant tension in EMF's life that was at times also reflected in his art. The distance he develops from Clapham is a measure of his development as artist and individual. Chap 3, "The Apostolic Ring": EMF joined the Cambridge Apostles in 1897; this was a crucial experience for him. Rickie Elliot's problem in *The Longest Journey* was also EMF's: how to enter the great world without being contaminated by it. The Apostles were religious without being dogmatic and were anti-Utilitarian. They emphasized the dictates of conscience and right reason over convention or law. They stressed the need to be good rather than the doing of good. As did the Bloomsbury liberals, they resorted to "apolitical politics." They distrusted action; they were radical in their individualism yet conservative in preferring the individual over the state. J. M. E. McTaggart's philosophical idealism influenced EMF, and both men were "extravagant" individualists. From G. E. Moore EMF derived his faith in personal relations and aesthetic states, also the elevation of fact over judgment and the tendency to conceive of love as a timeless ecstasy, to emphasize "the love of love." Roger Fry emphasized intrinsic qualities in a work of art, as EMF at times also did. Nathaniel Wedd inspired in EMF a love of the classic and a witty irreverence; he encouraged him to write and was the closest of his Cambridge friends. Chap 4, "Goldsworthy Lowes Dickinson": Dickinson's ideas on Greece influenced EMF. For EMF and his compeers, to embrace Greek culture was to be at once unorthodox and moral, individualistic and traditional. Dickinson's formulation of a personal myth in his literary work was less successful than EMF's. EMF's mind was tougher, and he was able to utilize the distancing resource of humor. EMF ended by outgrowing Dickinson.

Chap 5, "From Words to Music" [Routine analysis, by way of synopsis, of *Aspects of the Novel*]: EMF was interested in the novel as art but not in technique as such. He stressed vision rather than method—the importance of the novel as an end in itself and as a source of spiritual revelation. Chap 6, "The Stories: Fantasy": With EMF, fantasy, which finds its purest ex-

pression in the stories, is a substitute for action, a way of facing imaginatively what cannot be faced in reality. In "The Story of a Panic" Pan represents
a liberation from convention and prudery toward a freedom allowing one
to move to a boundless, ineffable ideal. In "The Eternal Moment" Miss
Raby is presumptuous; she plays the goddess and makes absolute moral
judgments. She is unscrupulous, and in trying to revive Feo's love for her,
she is guilty of self-deception or sadism or both. She achieves love without
men and in defiance of sex. [She is, I think conscientious, responsible, and
honorable.] In "The Road from Colonus" the ineffectual Mr. Lucas returns
to the womb when he goes inside the plane tree and withdraws from reality.
[Mr. Lucas is unduly downgraded.] In "The Other Side of the Hedge" there
is a geographical representation of an eternal moment; behind the hedge,
those without will power achieve beatitude. "The Celestial Omnibus" is one
of EMF's better stories and presents a total separation between society and
art. When the boy's problems get too insistent he returns to the heaven of
art. "The Machine Stops" again depicts the psychic escape of a boy hero;
he wills his escape and suffers for so doing. He is heroic by virtue of having
the right attitudes, rather than by his actions. "Other Kingdom" is self-
conscious and academic. [Severe judgment.] "The Point of It" demonstrates
the essayist moving in on the story writer. EMF is drawn toward both
Harold's heroism and Micky's civilization. The narrator of "The Story of
the Siren" is a Prufrock with heroic impulses but unheroic capacities. [The
focus of the story is less on the narrator than on the Sicilian's encounter with
the siren and his brother's and sister-in-law's violent deaths, by the forces
of the church and conventional society.]

Chap 7, "*Where Angels Fear to Tread*: The Fool as Prophet": *Angels* is a
book notable for its gaiety; social and political issues enter only by implication. Vulgarity, not right or wrong, becomes the standard for the judgment
of people and their acts. [This view of *Angels* is misleading.] The book is
a comedy insofar as it satirizes the usages of society, a romance insofar as
it is concerned with the inner development of individuals. Caroline Abbott
and Philip Herriton are rebels who do not rebel. They are not partial people
in a healthy society but the remnants of life in a dead society. Caroline must
turn life into art to be moved by it; so must Philip. They are fools [extreme
judgment] to Harriet's and Mrs. Herriton's knaves. The book is uncertain
in effect because it hovers between comedy and prophecy. [Abstract ideas
about genre interfere with Stone's interpretation of the book.] *Angels* is
autobiographical in that Philip is the artist as young man exploring his
possibilities for experience. At the end both Philip and Caroline find that
love of love is sufficient for them. The novel "screams" the panic and
emptiness of the main characters. [Extreme judgement; they are conscientious and sympathetic though not heroic.]

Chap 8, "*The Longest Journey:* The Slaughter of the Innocent": The presentation of the protagonist, Rickie Elliot, is ambiguous—both ironical and sympathetic. The book is divided between confession (as it presents Rickie's alienation), romance (as Rickie—and later, Stephen Wonham—illustrate the hero tested by various crises), and novel (as it presents Rickie's adjustments to contemporary social life, especially in Sawston). In Sawston, Rickie chooses to endure convention rather than to break with it. [Stone prefers to read *Journey* as romance and will study Rickie's tests or ordeals.] Though Rickie is Prufrockean, he reaches tragic dimensions in that he is no puppet or victim; he also gives his life freely for another by an exercise of the will. He lives for the future rather than for the present, and he is a prophetic hero rather than a tragic one. In marrying Agnes he challenges all the Cambridge values, which he also embraces with a part of his nature. [Extensive, but not fully convincing, analysis in Jungean terms of Rickie's character follows.] In Sawston he tries to do good instead of seeking the good in itself; this urgency toward moral action comes between him and art, with the result that he is fatefully self-divided. At Cambridge, Rickie escaped from the curse lying on his father's house; but when Agnes allies herself with his aunt, Mrs. Failing, he is brought back under its influence. The Cadbury Rings (where Mrs. Failing tells Rickie about his half-brother, Stephen) are mounds, a Madingley dell (Rickie's retreat at Cambridge) with wider vistas. The Rings signify his marital imprisonment; they are also a womb symbol to which Rickie, the unheroic hero, wishes to retreat. He shrinks from reality, never facing Stephen or himself adequately. In his weakness Rickie needs Stephen for a hero, as an instrument of sexual deliverance and as an agent to assure continuance of his mother's line. Rickie illustrates Jung's infantile hero with an obsessive desire to return to the mother. EMF sacrifices him so that his libido may be released for an active life through transference of this force to Stephen. Rickie is a totem for all the childish disabilities that EMF finds in himself, and he must therefore be sacrificed. He is EMF's ego character and his anti-ego character; the healthy emerging ego is Stephen. *Journey* is apocalyptic rather than tragic, a book of revelation. A new hero is adumbrated, combining Stephen's body, Ansell's mind, and Rickie's soul. *Journey* is in essence a coming-of-age ceremony for EMF, who reveals in it that he is both man and artist.

Chap 9, "*A Room with a View:* Sex and Sensibility": *Room* is EMF's "nicest" book because its experiment in self-discovery takes place in the open. The plot concerns Lucy Honeychurch's "gradual escape from her Sawstonian confinement (the lie) into Emersonian freedom (the truth)." The Emersons are not successful characters (Mr. Emerson is too rigid; George is too "incredible" as romantic lead), but they do provide standards of value whereby the reader can judge the conformists, Cecil Vyse and Charlotte Bartlett, for the conventional people they are.

Chap 10, "*Howards End:* Red-bloods and Mollycoddles": *Howards End* broadens EMF's concerns from the private to the public, and the book is "a test of the ability of Bloomsbury liberalism to survive a marriage with the great world." EMF stresses the need for connection rather than for salvation and escape, as in the earlier works. He would test the possibility of achieving a middle path between decadence and brutality. EMF no longer attempts to compete as a man or to project characters who do so; he scorns that masculine part of his identity, lets it live briefly in Henry Wilcox, and turns to the Schlegel sisters as identity figures for himself—with their feminine values, methods, and attitudes toward life. EMF wishes to conjoin power and sensibility, the heroic and the civilized, the male and the female; and he attempts, in the process, to elicit universality from his personal experience. But he seems to face the world out of duty rather than inclination. Houses are crucial in this novel; the men do not have the credentials— the sensitivity and the imagination—for inhabiting them. The Schlegels are Bloomsbury; they test the provenance of the Arnoldean ideas of culture. Ernst Schlegel is formative upon his daughters; he belongs to the tradition of German and Coleridgean idealism with its separation of utilitarian and aesthetic functions. He champions the Arnoldean light within, rather than Pan-Germanism and materialistic values. His daughter Margaret connects an idealistic spaciousness with the idea of present-day England rather than with the concrete (and disturbing) realities to be found in England. Too many of the connections are thus made within the mind and so evade the dramatic problem of the novel, which requires a firm connection between outer and inner. The Schlegels at least realize that their liberalism, untested, is more aesthetic than political. One of the book's chief narrative rhythms is the sisters' drifting apart and coming together again. Helen Schlegel finds the world empty because she does not know how to direct the libido toward objects. She lacks internal poise; she is frigid; she is ultimately a force making for death in her relationships with Leonard Bast. [Extreme, perhaps fallacious, judgments about Helen.] The Schlegel sisters are representatives of EMF's ego in the novel: Helen represents a continuation of Rickie Elliot (they both withdraw into absolutes with disastrous consequences to their personal lives), and Margaret continues Stephen (Helen's withdrawal gives Margaret the chance to connect, as Rickie's death gives such a chance to Stephen). [In many respects Margaret as humanist is closer to Rickie than is Helen, and Helen, in her instinctual disposition, is closer to the anti-intellectual Stephen than to Rickie.] Leonard Bast is one of EMF's most interesting and least convincing characters. In his connections with the Schlegels EMF expresses his social conscience. The Schlegels play god with him without realizing that they are so doing. He becomes the victim of Helen's idealism and her absolutist zeal. Her view that the idea of death saves a man is an expression of a death wish. [Extreme judgment, though through her, EMF rejects the soft kind of liberalism or Philistinism that evades or sentimentalizes death.] Helen's ideas are right, but her actions are intolerable. In Margaret's connection with Henry Wilcox, she is honest about him but less than honest about her own motives. She seems ultimately less interested in a relationship with a man than in attaining a relationship in marriage that transcends sex. She is much influenced by Ruth Wilcox, whose spiritual authority in the novel is unquestioned. Ruth was not successful in changing the Wilcoxes, so how can Margaret be? The problems involved in the rapprochement of the Wilcoxes and Schlegels indicate the difficulty for EMF of combining myth and realism in a book that is flawed by an ethical evasiveness. In marrying Henry, Margaret also marries Ruth, the one (Henry) in the flesh, the other (Ruth) in the spirit. She grows more like Ruth away from the city and the active concerns of life to an attainment of a "proportion" that becomes disinterestedness and finally a withdrawal from life. Her marriage to Henry has some of the sentimentality which accrues when an actual person is seen also as an abstraction; Henry is not only a man to her but "men" as well, about whom she generalizes. She is virginal from the beginning. [Questionable.] Her desire is to save Henry, not to marry him; the result is that their relationship becomes a power struggle. At the end women are in control of Howards End house, and the people with whom the Schlegels have connected are maimed, imprisoned, or dead. [But is the Wilcox influence really dead, and is the reduced existence of the Schlegels totally of their own choosing?] Under Schlegel influence Howards End becomes a place of "sterile quarantine against the enemy." [Overstated; the situation is not so closed as Stone sees it.] The symbolic heir, Helen and Leonard's child, will come under the malign Schlegel influence. EMF seems to want not connection but the rewards of connection, not sex but an heir. It is the love of love (G. E. Moore's ideal) that is attained, not a connection with people. EMF has presented a moral failure as a triumph. [Not fully demonstrated.] Technically, the book is possibly a masterpiece. Its texture, even-voiced and urbane, is distinctive, as is EMF's use of rhythm. The book has humor but is mainly prophetic; the mixture is not always successful and accounts for the book's thematic failures. It does, however, convincingly flow from lightness to seriousness. The leitmotifs are dense and complex. [The question obtrudes: Is the artistry of *Howards End* as separable from content as Stone implies? Could the book be so distinctive aesthetically and such a failure ideologically?]

Chap 11, "A Passage to Alexandria": The years 1910–1924 closed the gap for EMF between memory and experience, and the writing of *Alexandria* and *Pharos and Pharillon* helped prepare him for his great work, *A Passage to India.* Chap 12, "*A Passage to India:* The Great Round" [This discussion is, possibly, the most searching and provocative yet written on *Passage*]: EMF in his art has always made use of circular images that suggest motions of expansion and contraction. They are feminine images and function ambiguously as prisons and paradises, dread coils and "cradles of an ideal, harmonious peace." These motions suggest that the tumescence of creation has an underside of nothingness, that life lives on death. The circle represents also the cyclic unity of life, of God himself. In *Passage* EMF tried to put together the pieces of a broken circle, "to relate the broken arcs of his own experience to some final scheme of ultimate value," to formulate aesthetic representations of "the Great Round." The nucleus of the Round is formed by the Marabar Caves, which are at the center of the novel. The Marabar Hills and the Caves that they contain are "archetypal picturings of life's origin, of the primal inside and outside from which creation springs." The Hindu Godbole understands the Caves, but they terrify, puzzle, or bore the others. The Hindus in *Passage* are the group closest to elemental knowledge of the meaning of ancient myth. The Hindu view of life gives the book its final thematic and aesthetic focus. Fundamental to its structure is the temple as World Mountain, whose exterior reveals life in all its forms, and an ur-temple (small, secret, and dark), similar to a cave, at its center. Inside lies the realm of the unconscious, the source of "prophecy." On the outside is the realm of the ego, consciousness, and history; a corridor connects the two, suggesting the inevitable link among opposites. The Caves represent a reality far more antecedent than that represented by the inner cell of the World Mountain. The nothingness in the Caves is not an emptiness; they are primal womb and tomb, the darkness before existence itself, which some can contemplate, others cannot. EMF uses symbols from Indian religion and art: the egg, the tree, the cave, stones, the serpent, the Indian Gods (especially Kali [the Earth Mother] and Vishnu [the destroyer]). Like the serpent, all these other symbols are both life-inducing and death-bringing forces. EMF is sensitive to the duality of consciousness and unconsciousness (most vividly projected in the action in the Caves). Consciousness and unconsciousness pursue each other in the novel; they do not meet, and therein lies world tragedy. In visiting the Caves the characters return from consciousness to unconsciousness, to a prehistoric and subrational reality that is still present though it may have been long suppressed. The Caves are at the center of *Passage,* and "the vaulting arms of the macrocosmos" circumscribe them; their circles are intersected and triangulated by the multitudinousness of created life, the forms on the World Mountain. God's symbol is the circle, man's the straight line, especially in the triad or trinity form. Much of the organization of the book is tripartite— it is composed of three parts, "Mosque," "Caves," and "Temple"; and three races dominate it, the Moslem, suggesting the emotions, the Anglo-Indian, the intellect, and the Hindu, the capacity for love; also sky, water, and earth govern the book. From one point of view *Passage* is a political novel; from another, human politics seem insignificant measured against historic and geologic time. The figure presented in *Passage* is that of a mandala, or encircled squares; that of a unity around a disordered multiplicity. Estrangement or division is one principal theme; there is not only division among the three chief groups but divisions within the groups themselves (even Godbole, the Brahman, is separated from his god for most of the time). Aziz is a bridge between East and West; but he lacks the ability to adjust his mind to Western categories, and British insensitivity defeats him. The question of personal relations and friendship subsumes politics, but impediments to friendship (and to politics) are subtle and insidious. EMF does not feel that personal relations can take the place of government, but for him the personal is primary and cannot be disregarded. Fielding is a Bloomsbury intellectual—liberal, decent, sensitive, reflecting EMF himself, in the descent of Cecil Vyse and Rickie Elliot. The failure of Aziz and Fielding to come together at the end represents a postponement rather than an abandonment of hope. They cannot come together because in them consciousness and unconsciousness are separated. Mrs. Moore experiences the dark mysteries that are closed to Fielding, and they overwhelm her. She discovers a reality (the echo as an emanation from the unconscious) that destroys her but which might also have been a redeeming force. "Temple" is integral to the novel, not only architecturally but thematically. Adela Quested in the Caves sees what Mrs. Moore and Godbole find there, a glimpse into the ultimate negation at the bottom of consciousness, "the archetypal emptiness preceding existence itself." Mrs. Moore is sensitive to this force of the unconscious, though it overpowers her. For this reason the Indians are sympathetic to her, and for them she ultimately becomes a goddess without fixed attributes or character. Proportion is still EMF's recommendation for the meaningful life, but his perspective on it has greatly widened. He honors the Hindu religion above the Christian and the Moslem because it is the most inclusive, "the least resistant to the unconscious and the instinctual, the least dogmatic and theological, the least appalled by the vision of the shadow." Hinduism, in fact, restores a sense of the Shadow and its echoes; they are not good, but the reality which they encompass cannot be disregarded. Hinduism also brings the conscious and the unconscious together into a fruitful harmony. The novel's message is the need for unity rather than division; it is prophetic in essence, revealing the dangers inherent in man's separation from his instinctual nature. Technically, the book is masterful, especially in its exploitations of rhythms.

Chap 13, "Criticism: The Near and the Far": After 1924 EMF's main preoccupation was sensitivity to what was going on. His humanistic vision persisted despite his clear sense of negation. He has not been a man fundamentally engaged by politics; but in those places where politics touch personal relations, violate individual freedom, or repress civil liberties, he has been a strong partisan. In his literary criticism, when heart combines with intelligence, his work is first-rate. [Discusses with discernment the writers who influenced EMF and about whom he wrote as critic: Proust, Tolstoy, Virginia Woolf, Henry James, Meredith, Gide, T. S. Eliot, and D. H. Lawrence. Thorough and standard discussion of similarities and differences between EMF and D. H. Lawrence.] The measure of EMF's success as a writer is in his fusion of the tangible with vision. [This is a monumental book and a controversial one. The consensus view follows. The treatment of EMF as person and writer is sometimes ungenerous or mistaken; the reliance upon Jung in the analysis of the man and his fiction is excessive; the analyses of the first four novels, though often brilliant, are sometimes idiosyncratic and insensitive to EMF's own views, implied or expressed in his fiction and nonfiction. But the critique of *Passage* is superb. The book contains much information; it is a challenging rather a definitive book. Reviews: Dudley Barker, "Contrast," ECONOMIST, CCXX (6 Aug 1966), 566; John Bayley (Entry No. 1149); Gion Bionco (Entry No. 1209); Merlin Bowen, "Forster's Progress," CHICAGO REVIEW, XVIII (Autumn–Winter 1966), 181–87; Alfred A. Carey, "Reviews," CITHARA (St. Bonaventure University), V (May 1966), 66–67; C. B. Cox, "Reviews," REVIEW OF ENGLISH STUDIES, XVIII (Nov 1967), 497–98; Stuart Hampshire (Entry No. 1163); Elaine Hedges, "Criticism, 1965," CONTEMPORARY LITERATURE, VII (Summer 1966), 227–28; Herbert Howarth, "Book Reviews," SOUTH ATLANTIC QUARTERLY, LXV (Autumn 1966), 548–49; "In Brief," NEW YORK TIMES BOOK REVIEW, 13 Feb 1966, p. 32; Dan Jacobson, "Forster's Cave," p. 560; Gene Koppel, "Book Reviews," ARIZONA QUARTERLY, XXII (Autumn 1966), 284–85; Marion Labistour (Entry No. 1230); E. Lacotte, "Étude Critique; Études Recentes sur E. M. Forster" (Critical Essay: Recent Studies on E. M. Forster), ÉTUDES ANGLAISES, XX (Oct–Dec 1967), 425–31; Robert Langbaum (Entry No. 1277); "Language and Literature," CHOICE (Chicago), III (Dec 1966), 902; Daniel Leary, "New Books," CATHOLIC WORLD, CCIII (Sept 1966), 373–74; "Liberal Prophet," TIMES (Lond), 30 June 1966, p. 16; James McConkey, "Reviews," MODERN LANGUAGE QUARTERLY, XXVII (Dec 1966), 485–88; Frederick P. W. McDowell, "E. M. Forster: Recent Extended Studies," ENGLISH LITERATURE IN TRANSITION, IX: 3 (1966), 156–68; Frank MacShane, "Book Reviews," DALHOUSIE REVIEW, XLVI (Summer 1966), 254–55; "Major or Minor," (Entry No. 1172); Rachelle Marshall (Entry No. 1173); Keith Mitchell, "Morgan," TABLET, 2 July 1966, p. 754; K. Natwar-Singh, "Return Passage to India," SATURDAY REVIEW (NY), XLIX (5 March 1966), 43; "Notes on Current Books," VIRGINIA QUARTERLY REVIEW, XLII (Summer 1966), xcix; Martin Price (Entry No. 1183); Santha Rama Rau (Entry No. 1187); Irma Rantavaara, "Besprechungen" (Reviews), NEUPHILOGISCHE MITTEILUNGEN (Helsingfors), LXX: 2 (1969), 353–57; John Raymond, "Morgan's Way," PUNCH, CCLI (17 Aug 1966), 271; S. P. Rosenbaum (Entry No. 1242); M. L. Rosenthal (Entry No. 1190); Lawrence A. Ruff, "Book Reviews," THOUGHT (Fordham), XLII (Spring

1967), 132–34; Theodore F. Simms, "New Books Appraised," Library Journal, XCI (1 Jan 1966), 112; Tony Tanner (Entry No. 1197); Gilbert Thomas, "Reviews of Books," English, XVI (Spring 1967), 151–52; Richard Wasson, "Book Reviews," Journal of English and Germanic Philology, LXV (Oct 1966), 745–48; Stanley Weintraub, "Books in English," Books Abroad, XLI (Autumn 1967), 466–67; Alan Wilde, "Book Reviews," Modern Philology, LXV (Nov 1967), 183–85; and Andrew Wright, "Where Critics Adore to Dabble," Kenyon Review, XXVIII (June 1966), 405–15.]

1197 Tanner, Tony. "Selected Books," London Magazine, nsVI (Aug 1966), 102–9.

EMF's qualities are those of liberal humanism: "The gentleness, the tolerance, the sensitivity, the quiet perspicacity, the unfailing humour, the respect for the private life, the hatred of brutality and a distaste for politics coupled with an unassertive faith in the high value of art and personal relationships—these are the qualities manifested in the man as well as the virtues extolled in his writing." Wilfred Stone in The Cave and the Mountain (1966) attempts to determine the origins of these qualities in EMF, in the Thornton family and the Clapham sect, and in his mother's contrasting values. EMF found a rationale at Cambridge that fostered the inner as opposed to the outer life. He accepted this ethos of Cambridge (and later of Bloomsbury) with reservations; he wanted to relate to other human beings and to the unknowable. He espoused, but was critical of, liberal humanist values. In EMF's work and temperament there is the conflict between the satirist and the mystic, the humanist and the poet, the moralist and the prophet. Stone's view that *Howards End* reveals a failure to connect is correct. The resolution in this novel is not a marriage between spirit and action but a "vengeful victory of sensibility over power." Stone's is an excellent analysis of *A Passage to India*. There is some failure of power in EMF; the "restless energy of perception" that makes a great writer is often in abeyance. The music of EMF's art diminishes while it orders "the rich confusions of actual life." [Discriminating review-essay on Stone's book.]

1198 Temple, Ruth Z., and Martin Tucker (eds). A Library of Literary Criticism: Modern British Literature (NY: Frederick Ungar, 1966), I, 306–18.

[Rpts extracts from Bonamy Dobrée, The Lamp and the Lute (1929); Cyril Connolly, Enemies of Promise (1938); Rose Macaulay, The Writings of E. M. Forster (1938); Virginia Woolf, "The Novels of E. M. Forster," Atlantic Monthly (1927; rpt date, 1942); F. R. Leavis, "E. M. Forster," Scrutiny (1938; rpt date, 1965); Stephen Spender, The Creative Element (1953; ptd under 1952); Harold Nicolson, "Mr. Forster's Great-Aunt," Observer (1956); P. N. Furbank and F. J. Haskell, "E. M. Forster," Paris

REVIEW (1953; rpt date, 1958); Frederick Grubb, "Homage to E. M. Forster," CONTEMPORARY REVIEW (1959); Leonard Woolf, SOWING (1960); J. B. Beer, THE ACHIEVEMENT OF E. M. FORSTER (1962); and John Bayley, "The Quest for E. M. Forster," MANCHESTER GUARDIAN WEEKLY (1962).]

1199 Thomson, George H. "A Note on the Snake Imagery of *A Passage to India*," ENGLISH LITERATURE IN TRANSITION, IX: 2 (1966), 108–10.

In *A Passage to India* the Caves signify the absence of God; Temple (and jungle) His presence—a theme present in both the major and minor symbols. Among the notable symbols are snakes and images of snakes. The only important actual snake is the cobra seen by Aziz and Fielding on their last ride. Snake images (snakes, serpents, scorpions, dragons) are abundant earlier, especially in the events and descriptions connected with the Marabar Caves. Sometimes the snake suggests the instinctive, the unconscious, the primordial and the transcendent, but mostly EMF uses the image "to reinforce the absence that prevails in the wasteland and the negation that prevails in the Marabar." The real cobra at the end stresses once again the difference between presence and absence. In "Temple" the "monster" image, with its positive implications, contrasts with the snakes of illusion and "nightmare vision" in the earlier part of the novel. [Illuminating note.]

1200 Watson, Ian. "E. M. Forster: Whimsy and Beyond," EIGO SEINEN (Tokyo), CXV (1 May 1969), 282–85.

EMF's work goes from whimsy (or fantasy) to prophecy, only attaining authentic prophecy in *A Passage to India*. The short stories are self-contained and enclose their mystery without undue strain; the strain becomes pronounced in the realistic novels of social observation wherein fantasy or mystery is an alien element. The phrase "only connect" is characteristic of all his work, "a quiet cry from the heart of the romantic sceptic." In *Howards End* the regenerative aspects of nature are emphasized, but its world is less defined by place than by time and is static and withdrawn. It is a period piece. The sense of "otherness" in this novel is conveyed by the joyous life of the spirit and the demonic "goblin footfall" associated with those who betray this life. The sanctified pastoral life celebrated in *The Longest Journey* and *Howards End* does not yet attain to prophecy. EMF's imagination goes beyond pastoralism and whimsy, Pan and Wagner, in *Passage*. Hinduism is a religion not only of contradictions but of synthesis; it accepts absurdities through love. The festival acts as a counterpart to the demonic absurdity of the Marabar Caves, balancing them structurally and spiritually. The Caves (stressing "devastating absurdity") are balanced by the Hindu temple (stressing "an equivocal synthesis through love"). Neither a pert, meager Pan nor a whimsical Krishna are present. [A good article with some challenging insights. Same as entry 1383.]

1967

1201 Abe, Yoshio. "Works: *The Longest Journey*," E. M. FORST-
ER, ed by Ineko Kondo (Tokyo: Kenkyusha, 1967), pp. 69–82.
The Longest Journey is a novel of manners, based on the idea that truth
reveals itself in momentary revelations. *Journey* gives much insight into
EMF's views of women and love. [Extended plot summary.] [In Japanese.]

1202 Abe, Yoshio. "Works: *A Room with a View*," E. M. FORSTER,
ed by Ineko Kondo (Tokyo: Kenkyusha, 1967), pp. 83–92.
A Room with a View is comic and melodramatic like *Where Angels Fear to
Tread*. It differs from *Angels* in that (1) the focus is on the development of
the protagonist (Lucy Honeychurch), (2) the ending is happy, and (3)
nature is used organically throughout, not merely as contrast to an effete
civilization. *Room* is also concerned with the damaging effects of misunderstanding between social classes. [Extended plot summary.] [In Japanese.]

1203 Abe, Yoshio. "Works: Short Stories," E. M. FORSTER, ed by
Ineko Kondo (Tokyo: Kenkyusha, 1967), pp. 146–50.
The essence of "The Celestial Omnibus" as a fantasy might be lost by
regarding it critically. In "The Road from Colonus" and "The Eternal
Moment," EMF is concerned with the contrast between corrupt civilization
and an uncorrupted life in nature. EMF relates man's life to the change of
the seasons and proposes that a return to nature may bring maturity and
spiritual fruition. [In Japanese.]

1204 Abe, Yoshio. "Works: *Where Angels Fear to Tread*," E. M.
FORSTER, ed by Ineko Kondo (Tokyo: Kenkyusha, 1967), pp. 58–68.
Where Angels Fear to Tread is comical and melodramatic in comparison
with EMF's later works. [Extensive plot summary. Discusses the central
theme of personal relationships and questions EMF's attitude toward natural, instinctive men. Are they used too simply as the means for dramatizing
moral issues and contrasts?] [In Japanese.]

1205 Ando, Toshio. "Biographies," E. M. FORSTER, ed by Ineko
Kondo (Tokyo: Kenkyusha, 1967), pp. 188–202.
In *Goldsworthy Lowes Dickinson* and *Marianne Thornton* EMF makes
compelling books from uneventful lives. [In Japanese.]

1206 Ara, Masahito. "Works: *A Passage to India*," E. M. FORST-ER, ed by Ineko Kondo (Tokyo: Kenkyusha, 1967), pp. 113–45.

EMF is pessimistic regarding the force of personal relationships in *A Passage to India*, but he does not give up his view that ideal personal relationships or harmony are possible. EMF's India is only the India of the Hindus and the Moslems, not the complete India. [Extended plot summary.] [In Japanese.]

1207 Araujo, Victor de. "The Short Story of Fantasy: Henry James, H. G. Wells and E. M. Forster," DISSERTATION ABSTRACTS, XXVII (1967), 200A. Unpublished dissertation, University of Washington, 1965.

1208 Bell, Vereen M. "Comic Seriousness in *A Passage to India*," SOUTH ATLANTIC QUARTERLY, LXVI (Winter 1967), 606–17; extract rptd in CONTEMPORARY LITERARY CRITICISM, ed by Carolyn Riley (Detroit: Gale Research Co., 1973), I, 107.

The symbolic and mythic interpretations of *A Passage to India* do not go far enough. *Passage* is also comic, and it moves fluently "back and forth from shrewd social comedy to the most exacting kind of metaphysical speculation." The comedy in the novel is both social and psychological. [The discussion is perfunctory, dealing *in extenso* with plot; it contributes little to our understanding of *Passage*.]

1209 Bianco, Gino. "Il Grand Vegliardo Forster" (Forster, the Venerable Old Gentleman), LA FIERA LETTERARIA (Rome), 26 Jan 1967, p. 15.

EMF's fame is still increasing in spite of the silences between *Howards End* (1910) and *A Passage to India* (1924) and between 1924 and today. Wilfred Stone's THE CAVE AND THE MOUNTAIN gains importance because it is the first book written on EMF with his cooperation. The title of Stone's book symbolizes EMF's belief that reality is hidden in the secret and shadowy places of man's consciousness. Although EMF is sympathetic toward various members of the Bloomsbury circle, he is opposed to their spirit because of his desire for a world of instincts. In spite of the strengths of EMF's fiction his work suffers from "insularity." For his characters a world different from their British bourgeois world would be inconceivable. While presenting EMF as a moralist Stone realizes his elusive nature, together with the influence that Cambridge had upon him. Stone concludes by demonstrating that EMF's influence has been more philosophical than literary. [In part a review-essay on Wilfred Stone's THE CAVE AND THE MOUNTAIN (1966).] [In Italian.]

1210 Bredsdorff, Thomas. "E. M. Forster," Fremmede Digtere i
Det 20. Arhundrede (Foreign Writers in the Twentieth Century),
ed by Sven Kristensen (Copenhagen: G. E. C. Ged, 1967), I, 533–
44.

The experiences that went into shaping EMF's works derive from the four
stages of his life: home, school, university, and travel. His middle-class
background, dominated by female relatives, made him aware of social values. Public school showed him the results of the perversion of these values.
At Cambridge he realized that unity and order were possible, and this
conviction became essential. He was keenly aware of the society from which
he came, and he foresaw the tragic aspects of modern industrialism. He
revealed this orientation in his novels—or his "novel," for in a sense he
wrote only one. His first three novels prepared the way for his greatest work,
Howards End, which together with his greatest success, *A Passage to India*,
belong to the world rather than to English letters alone. Aside from his five
novels—and a few short stories—the rest of his work is made up of clever,
witty, good, but also wordy and weak essays and critical studies. [This is not
the usual judgment of his nonfiction.] EMF's style—a blend of dialogue,
description, allusion, and authorial comment—and his realization of the
conflict between a humanistic past and an inhuman industrialized present
were fully matured when he wrote *Howards End*, which is in many ways
reminiscent of Dickens. Unlike Dickens, who could incorporate the demonic, EMF conceived of characters who are guided by reason. [Overstated.]
He knows that the demonic is to be found in man, but his logical, objective
prose is inadequate to encompass it. To express the demonic he resorts to
other arts or to violent, melodramatic situations. This incompleteness in
presenting human nature prevents EMF from ranking with the greatest
writers, although *Howards End* approaches greatness. Only once, fourteen
years later, in *A Passage to India* did a work of his approach the stature of
Howards End. *Passage* suffers from the author's moralizing voice; its
boundless tolerance is in danger of becoming an undiscriminating relativism. *Passage* led to a new era in England's relationship to colonials but not
in English literature. EMF's traditional form reveals its limitations in *Passage;* its contradictory and irrational situations are resolved in a too contrived manner by an all-knowing author. EMF's love of the past and his
hatred of modern society were not unqualified. He found good in twentieth-
century developments, and he did not glorify the past without reservation.
He maintained that order is possible in chaos, and he cherished the conviction that the best of the past, the relationship of man to man, can be carried
on into a new era. EMF's ideal—his humanistic inheritance—and the means
for implementing it—tolerance, integrity, and unprejudiced thought—inheres in the academic traditions of Cambridge that continually influenced
him. In these traditions his limitations also inhere, for beyond the bounds

of the intellect lurks the irrational. [EMF's romanticism is downplayed.] [In Danish.]

1211 Burgess, Anthony [pseud of John Anthony Burgess Wilson]. THE NOVEL NOW: A STUDENT'S GUIDE TO CONTEMPORARY FICTION (Lond: Faber, 1967), pp. 15, 23, 32–33, 36, 113, 154, 162, 212; rvd ed (Faber, 1971); material on EMF is unchanged but pagination differs slightly; as THE NOVEL NOW: A GUIDE TO CONTEMPORARY FICTION (NY: Norton, 1967); rptd in part in CONTEMPORARY LITERARY CRITICISM, ed by Carolyn Riley (Detroit: Gale Research Co., 1973), I, 107.

EMF's technique is traditional. The plot elements stem from melodrama rather than from the sophisticated modern novel, "but his originality and subtlety lie in the dry, often sceptical, frequently witty, always civilized commentary." In the novels two worlds persistently try to connect but fail to do so: that of society with formal conventions and that of the sensitive individuals who are outside it. These individuals are often failures in direct action; but they are aware of their limitations, and at moments of crisis they are better able to act with insight than their more extravert counterparts. The epigraph to *Howards End*, "Only connect," is ironically reflected in the "No, not yet" and the "No, not there" of *A Passage to India*. [Numerous incidental mentions of EMF.]

1212 Colmer, John. E. M. FORSTER: "A PASSAGE TO INDIA" (Lond: Edward Arnold, Studies in English Literature No. 30, 1967).

EMF's emphasis is always on the individual rather than on society. EMF uses contrasts and abrupt juxtapositions as symbolic indices to the mystery or muddle that underlies reality as human beings experience it. The novel is relativistic in implication, so that the promise of infinity is not truly satisfying, and varying perspectives become all-important. *A Passage to India* is, in essence, optimistic, since a new situation may always evolve in which discordant forces can be more thoroughly reconciled. In a relativistic novel, the author's superior, ironic, and compassionate vision becomes important; in *Passage* such vision is established from the beginning.

At the beginning the moment of contact and revelation between Mrs. Moore and Aziz in the Mosque contrasts with the disunity engendered at the "bridge party." The Indians show greater delicacy and tact than do the brusque and perfunctory English. Turton's complex motives for staging the party compensate for EMF's tendency to make caricatures of the Anglo-Indians. Fielding, a Ulysses figure, is host thereafter at a tea party that successfully bridges the gap between the nationalities. In Aziz's company Adela implies that she will reject Ronny, and she is more truthful and direct about herself than she generally is. Attempts by human beings to identify with the divine usually fail, but the two worlds do interpenetrate; likewise, identification with other people is a positive impulse that is often frustrated. EMF balances the romantic ideal that the imagination can penetrate ultimate reality with the sceptical humanistic view that the natural world is alien to man. Adela Quested's bloodlessness is not a weakness, as EMF depicts her. Unacknowledged sexual jealousy is one factor leading to the breakup of the affair between her and Ronny. In Fielding, a fine characterization, EMF recognizes his own humanistic creed but steps outside him and views him and his humanism critically. Aziz's abundant imagination (in contrast with Fielding's overdeveloped intellect) is his potential strength and besetting weakness. Comedy and compassion are expertly fused in the sequence in which Aziz shams sickness, and his friends, including Fielding, visit him.

In the Marabar Caves the characters are shown a differing order of experience than their religions or philosophies can account for. The imagined assault in the Caves reflects Adela's divided being and also her lack of self-knowledge. The comedy surrounding Godbole indicates that EMF only partially subscribes to his views while still regarding him as a touchstone of reality. Before the trial and after, Fielding is in the difficult position of being accused of perfidy by both Aziz and the British. Fielding is unresponsive both to visions of beauty and heroism and to unknown spiritual forces; he is essentially unaffected by his experience at the Caves. Mrs. Moore realizes that she has become a worse rather than a better woman as a result of the visit to the Marabar. Despite her present disillusionment, her initial desire for the happiness of others is a great value. The modification of her pessimism as she leaves India, or the sense that she ought to modify it, prepares us to see her as a life-giving force at the trial and in "Temple." Indian irrelevance at the trial—the dispute over Mrs. Moore's being sent away— saves the situation; the invocation of her name causes Adela to see the truth about her situation. She has renounced her people but is also disowned by the Indians. Both Adela and Fielding attain a degree of self-knowledge and thus reveal their integrity. In his one-sidedness Fielding reveals the inadequacies of Western civilization in India: a conscientious humanist who lacks abundant intuitive wisdom is unable to recognize the complexities of an alien and ancient culture. EMF's irony when Adela returns to Christianity indicates her incomplete acceptance of it.

The ceremonies at Mau reveal "the imperfect attempts of all too fallible human beings to give objective form to an ideal vision of harmony." Godbole's own humanism is universalized and generalized, and it is offered as one positive spiritual vision. Both Aziz's suspicions of Fielding and Fielding's own rationalism are absurd when compared with the glimpses of the Eternal seen intermittently at the Mau ceremonies. The forces making for good are dispersed among several characters: Mrs. Moore, Fielding, and

Aziz. The celebrated last paragraph "epitomises the oscillations between affirmation and retraction, vision and anti-vision, that have characterised the novel," and is neither pessimistic nor optimistic. The final effect is one of qualified optimism. The novel works "to make us more sensitive to the importance of love and imagination in human affairs, to make us sceptical of putting our trust in any one religion or creed, and to believe in the unique power of beauty and personal relations." [A linear and chronological analysis of *Passage;* stresses parallel scenes, events, and characters, and indicates EMF's extensive foreshadowing of major incidents. Many valuable comments, unexciting method.]

1213 Colmer, John. "Form and Design in the Novel," AP-PROACHES TO THE NOVEL, ed by John Colmer (Edinburgh & Lond: Oliver & Boyd; Adelaide: Rigby, 1967), pp. 1–16.
No comprehensive aesthetic exists for the novel. [Follows Lord David Cecil in thinking that a novel must reconcile two claims, those of life and art.] Patterns in *A Passage to India*, for example, are both ethical and aesthetic: "Forster's great triumph in that novel is his discovery of an appropriate form to express his unique vision of man's limitations and the fascination of the infinite." Readers must cooperate with an author to discover his form and pattern (the Jamesean "figure in the carpet"). The author rather than the critic gives us the best guide for reading. It is valuable to know the germ of a work or the actual life from which it grew. For *Passage* there are three such sources: (1) the letters in *The Hill of Devi*, (2) EMF's remarks on the difficulty of turning this experience into fiction, (3) Whitman's poem "Passage to India." Internally, the form and design of *Passage* result from its three-part division. "Mosque" chronicles meetings and separations; "Caves" reveals the limits of Western rationalism and of human endeavor. In "Caves" suspicion and hatred triumph, but Mrs. Moore acts as a healing influence. "Temple" is a "vision of faith," with Hinduism seen as transcending the duality of animate and inanimate life. The book ends with a qualified optimism, and in a very minor key. The "minor key" gives us a clue to EMF's conception of form and design. Recurrent images act like musical phrases; *Passage* is in essence a symphony. [Some valuable insights.]

1214 Confalonieri, Mariachiara Beneduce. "I Racconti di E. M. Forster" (The Short Stories of E. M. Forster), ENGLISH MISCELLANY (Rome), XVIII (1967), 163–205.
As Virginia Woolf observed, EMF gives the impression of building "cages" (mistaken education, misunderstood religion, frustrated artistic effort, and inhibited psychology) in his works which he later criticizes and/or demolishes and which his characters must elude. His stories present tentatively the problems that he wishes to define and his solutions to them. Only in the novels will problem and solution be appropriately merged. The theme of

"The Story of a Panic"—an escape from suffocating society into nature—is elaborated in "The Other Side of the Hedge," "The Celestial Omnibus," "Other Kingdom," and "The Curate's Friend." In "The Road from Colonus" this theme merges with another that reappears in EMF's second volume of stories and in the tensions present in the *The Longest Journey* and *A Passage to India:* the aspiration to harmonize the life of man with that of the universe. In "Panic" Eustace's discontent and apathy reappear in George Emerson of *A Room with a View.* The story's motif, "to get in touch with nature," is found in the stories written by Rickie Elliot in *Journey* and in the desire that drives Leonard Bast in *Howards End* to wander about the outskirts of London at dawn. In "Panic" British middle-class conformity is offset by the Italian Gennaro. In "Other Kindom," because of her attachment to nature, Evelyn Beaumont is the younger sister of Mrs. Wilcox in *Howards End,* but is incapable of sacrificing herself by marrying her Worters-Wilcox. Instead of the need for solidarity expressed in *Howards End,* here the theme is self-realization. In the sensible, intellectual Ford, EMF attempts to harmonize idealism and practicality, the spirit of classical culture with modern life. In "The Celestial Omnibus" the "other spiritual kingdom" of man is a literary Olympus to which one is led by writers whose works serve as allegorical omnibuses between this world and the world of art and poetry (Sir Thomas Browne, Dante, Shelley). Reverend Bons, like Herbert Pembroke in *Journey,* is a cultural "snob" who is unable to participate in the boy's trip to the world of poetry and art. In "The Road from Colonus" Mr. Lucas, like the boy in "Omnibus," searches for the universal but this time in everyday reality. Ethel Lucas is a mixture of Harriet Herriton in *Angels* and Agnes Pembroke in *Journey,* with her false Sawstonian values. "The Curate's Friend" dramatizes a rejection of society that is more psychological than romantic or mythic.

In "The Other Side of the Hedge" EMF expresses the same satirical view of social "progress" that reappears in "The Machine Stops" and in *Howards End.* The "other" world, opposed to that of modern industrialism, presupposes a harmony of life and thought. Within the science fiction atmosphere of "The Machine Stops" EMF also satirizes a deadening industrialism. The faith of the protagonist Kuno in individuality and in a connection between the past and the future is also Margaret Schlegel's in *Howards End.* In "The Eternal Moment" Miss Raby's failure to preserve a great spiritual moment dramatizes EMF's view that it is difficult to achieve form and vital influence for our ideals and to attain release from the cages that contain us. The two protagonists of "The Point of It" anticipate most markedly the preoccupations of EMF's novels. Although Micky is similar to Rickie Elliot, he passes through all the stages that his own nature requires, from love to sympathy, to tolerence, and thence to apathy. Janet, Micky's wife, resembles Agnes in *Journey* because of her rigidity and egoism. Between these extremes of idealistic emotion and egotism the heroes of EMF's fiction fluctuate: Philip Herriton, Rickie, Fielding. The final story, "The Story of the Siren" is EMF's most allegorical. The young boy who "will fetch up the Siren from the sea, and destroy silence, and save the world" parallels EMF's personal mythic quest and the conclusion of *Howards End*. EMF's need for social and creative purpose corresponds to the need which he felt to counter his own skepticism. [Inclusive account.] [In Italian.]

1215 Craig, David. "Fiction and the Rising Industrial Classes," ESSAYS IN CRITICISM, XVII (Jan 1967), 64–74; rptd in rvd form as "Fiction and the 'Rising Industrial Classes,'" THE REAL FOUNDA- TIONS: LITERATURE AND SOCIAL CHANGE (Lond: Chatto & Windus, 1973), pp. 132–42.

Dickens in BLEAK HOUSE and George Eliot in FELIX HOLT are too impatient with the hard-won reforms achieved by the workman agitators or by social leaders who try to work with the actualities of social dislocation and ine- quality to improve conditions. They both ascend too easily to the moral plane and suggest that reform is meaningful only if it is moral and apocalyp- tic as well as social and political. So George Eliot sentimentalizes the humanism of Felix Holt; so D. H. Lawrence finds in WOMEN IN LOVE no promise or hope in the activities of the tycoon Gerald Crich; so EMF proposes in *Howards End* an unreal rapprochement between intelligentsia and business man upon the questionable basis of personal values which turn out to be inadequate to make the desired connection. In *A Passage to India* he came to see that "the facts of inequality and exploitation were so clamant that wishful idealisms could hardly survive." [Suggestive account.]

1216 Dooley, D. J. THE ART OF SINCLAIR LEWIS (Lincoln: Univer- sity of Nebraska P, 1967), pp. ix, 261, 264.

Sinclair Lewis did what EMF said that Lewis did in "Sinclair Lewis" (*Abin- ger Harvest*): lodge a piece of continent in our imagination. EMF praises Lewis for his skill at photography in the novel but implies that such skill is a youthful attribute and a dead end for a developing artist.

1217 Eagle, Dorothy. "Edward Morgan Forster," THE OXFORD COMPANION TO ENGLISH LITERATURE, by Sir Paul Harvey (Oxford: Clarendon P, 4th ed, 1967), pp 308, 401, 621.

[Short sketch of life and career. Summary of *Howards End*, stressing the thematic complications developing between Wilcoxes and Schlegels. Sum- mary of *A Passage to India*, stressing Aziz's importance and his passing from British influence to a Hindu-Moslem *entente*.]

1218 Edwardes, Michael. BRITISH INDIA 1772–1947: A SURVEY OF THE NATURE AND EFFECTS OF ALIEN RULE (Lond: Sidgwick & Jack- son, 1967; NY: Taplinger, 1968), pp. 172, 317.

A Passage to India is just as offensive in describing Indian characters as were the novels written by previous Anglo-Indian writers. EMF's novel reflects less knowledge of India than do the novels of Edward J. Thompson. EMF uses few Indian words in *Passage* because of his inability to understand India or the world of the British in India. [This is the minority view of *Passage*. The opposing view is best presented in E. M. FORSTER: A TRIBUTE, ed by K. Natwar-Singh (1964) and in Benita Parry's DELUSIONS AND DISCOVERIES (1972).]

1219 Fleishman, Avrom. A READING OF MANSFIELD PARK: AN ESSAY IN CRITICAL SYNTHESIS (Minneapolis: University of Minnesota P, Minnesota Monographs in the Humanities, Vol. 2, 1967), pp. 74–75, 95n.

Jane Austen's MANSFIELD PARK affirms the abiding reality of society and resembles *Howards End*, which may be the last novel to make this affirmation. Both books take titles from country houses; both are ambivalent in their treatment of the gentry; both explore the theme "Only connect"; both emphasize the class divisions in the way of effective personal relations; and both envision an ideal of human connection in symbolic terms.

1220 Godshalk, William Leigh. "Some Sources of Durrell's ALEXANDRIA QUARTET," MODERN FICTION STUDIES, XIII (Autumn 1967), 361–74.

EMF's *Alexandria* provided Lawrence Durrell with historical and religious motifs for his ALEXANDRIA QUARTET. [The indebtedness is fully documented and convincing.]

1221 Green, Martin. YEATS'S BLESSINGS ON VON HÜGEL: ESSAYS ON LITERATURE AND RELIGION (NY: Norton; Lond: Longmans, Green, 1967), pp. 25, 93–94, 225.

T. S. Eliot was able to reject the impulse to synthesize everything good, and EMF was able to reject the rational and the polite both without exclusively committing themselves to the poetic as did Yeats when he rejected the values of contemporary life. Brian Wicker in FIRST THE POLITICAL KINGDOM (Lond & Melbourne: Sheed & Ward, 1967) and elsewhere maintains that liberalism as a political philosophy is much weaker than socialism. Wicker defines liberalism much as EMF did in "What I Believe" and "The Challenge of Our Time" (*Two Cheers for Democracy*). Along with Lionel Trilling, Wicker agrees that EMF's politics are commendably not "eschatological"; rather they focus on humanity in the here and now. Wicker's criticism of liberalism is incisive, but socialism as he envisions it needs a liberal component. As a symbolical novel dealing with politics, Pasternak's DOCTOR ZHIVAGO lacks the integration of EMF's *A Passage to India*.

1222 Hillegas, Mark E. THE FUTURE AS NIGHTMARE: H. G. WELLS AND THE ANTI-UTOPIANS (NY & Lond: Oxford UP, 1967), pp. 85–95, and passim.

"The Machine Stops" is the first important anti-utopian work in the twentieth century, appearing five years after H. G. Wells's A MODERN UTOPIA. EMF's tale was influenced by Wells's book and his preceding science romances, at the same time that it was a reaction against Wells's views on utopia. EMF helped define the line which the anti-utopians were to take: in spirit and detail his story is an inversion of the glorious future prophesied by Wells in A MODERN UTOPIA. EMF thought that his own values (personal relationships, freedom of the individual) were threatened by the Wellsian world-state; and he also attacked the machine as subversive of humanist values in general, to contrast with Wells's optimistic view of its role in human progress. In spite of his satire upon Wellsian views, EMF adopts many of Wells's ideas and images (though EMF usually inverts them), and he borrows many elements from the scientific romances of Wells's early career. Ideologically, EMF is closer to the Wells of THE TIME MACHINE; "The Machine Stops" is an imitation of this Wellsian book rather than an attack on it as Wilfred Stone asserts in THE CAVE AND THE MOUNTAIN (1966). In turn, EMF anticipates many of the later inventions exploited in the anti-utopian novels written by Yevgeni Zamyatin, Aldous Huxley, George Orwell, and C. S. Lewis. [Valuable for placing EMF's short story in its tradition.]

1223 Holroyd, Michael. "Bloomsbury: The Legend and the Myth," LYTTON STRACHEY: A CRITICAL BIOGRAPHY, Vol I: THE UNKNOWN YEARS 1880–1910 (Lond: Heinemann, 1967; NY: Holt, Rinehart & Winston, 1968), pp. 395–424; also 123, 129–30, 168n,, 173, 205, 238, 316, 353, 375; most of these materials on EMF rptd in Michael Holroyd, LYTTON STRACHEY AND THE BLOOMSBURY GROUP: HIS WORK, THEIR INFLUENCE (Harmondsworth, Baltimore: Penguin Books, 1971).

The role of sympathetic friendship and a paradoxical frame of mind were paramount in the Bloomsbury Group: "a superfine mixture of arrogance and diffidence, of ambitious talent and crippling shyness." [EMF is quoted to emphasize the aristocratic reserve of the members, how they "would have shrunk from the empirical freedom which results from a little beer."] In Bloomsbury there was an absence of clearly defined trends; rather, Bloomsbury represented "a mood, an atmosphere, a culture." [Holroyd disagrees with J. K. Johnstone (THE BLOOMSBURY GROUP [1954]) and others who assimilate all the Bloomsbury figures to one or more generalizations. Johnstone in Holroyd's view overstresses the influence of G. E. Moore.] The members of the Group were neither so irresponsible as they have sometimes been viewed, nor so courageous as some of their partisans have seen them.

They placed greatest value upon independence after the Hellenic model and were individualists, if anything. They were detached, remote, and overcultivated; they were also hopeful and interested in vague social reform, in accordance with the spirit of a "neo-Platonism" which motivated them. If they were reformers, they were not revolutionaries. Though they rejected much of the Victorian social and sexual heritage, they were essentially the last of the Victorians.

As for EMF, he was ill at ease with Strachey. Both men had natures too esoteric to allow for ease of communication, at least initially. EMF was withdrawn and reflected, perhaps uncomfortably for him, a mirror image of Strachey. EMF was dubbed the "taupe" by Strachey, because of his resemblance to a mole in appearance and habits. [EMF's *The Longest Journey* is quoted to recapture the exciting atmosphere at Cambridge at the beginning of the century.] Strachey found *Journey* to be "a dreary fandango," although he was sensitive to its evocation of Cambridge. Rickie Elliot is EMF himself, Strachey thinks; the other principal figure is Hom [H. O. Meredith; is Stewart Ansell referred to here? (letter to Duncan Grant, 30 April 1907.) EMF is quoted on the founding of the INDEPENDENT REVIEW: "a new age had begun."] EMF, unlike Strachey, is not the thorough atheist or agnostic; Strachey found EMF's novels unreadable.

1224 Howe, Irving. THOMAS HARDY (NY: Macmillan; Lond: Macmillan-Collier, Masters of World Literature, 1967), pp. 73, 191.
In TWO ON A TOWER Hardy dramatizes the incongruities of human experience with something of EMF's hard, comic tone. EMF was one of Hardy's admirers in a younger generation, along with Siegfried Sassoon, John Masefield, and others.

1225 Hutchins, Francis G. THE ILLUSION OF PERMANENCE: BRITISH IMPERIALISM IN INDIA (Princeton: Princeton UP; Lond: Oxford UP, 1967), pp. 27, 28, 36, 44, 70, 153.
EMF's *A Passage to India* reveals that the Anglo-Indians retained their sense of superiority to the Indians as had their Victorian forebears but without their concern to provide inspiriting exemplars to the Indians. [EMF cited on dislike of India by British administrators, their public-school values, their Olympian attitudes toward India, and the alleged sexual antipathy of the fairer races to the darker.]

1226 Kelvin, Norman. E. M. FORSTER (Carbondale & Edwardsville: Southern Illinois UP; Lond & Amsterdam: Feffer & Simons, Crosscurrents Modern Critiques, 1967).
Chap 1, "Introduction": The tone of EMF's prose work reveals detached self-appraisal combined with a frank attachment to values. [Discusses EMF

as continuer of romantic tradition and then considers his intellectual biography.] Chap 2, "Short Stories and *Arctic Summer*": Realism—reflecting class distinctions—and fantasy are the polar opposites in EMF's stories. The Greek myths substitute a "moral-poetic statement" for action in the characters' struggles to escape the constraints of middle-class life. In "The Story of a Panic" EMF reveals that the middle class, though it may lack sensitivity, is the most likely to undergo transformation. In "The Eternal Moment" EMF implies that a superior, educated class needs to assume responsibility and to develop sensitivity. In "Other Kingdom" Evelyn Beaumont finds that she is unable to live in her husband's fantasy world of money and power and so escapes into her own fantasy kingdom. Mr. Lucas in "The Road from Colonus" may be a Moses figure; the spring gushes for him inside the tree as it did for Moses; and like Moses, Mr. Lucas never sees the promised land. "The Story of the Siren" is unsatisfying because the precarious existence of love is too large a theme. Chap 3, *"Where Angels Fear to Tread"*: Two main themes are developed: The characters become engaged with culture and history, and romance is necessary for all human beings. Many important scenes are presented as tableaux. EMF distills true perceptions from apparently worn-out ideas; his aphorisms are both pointed and dynamic. Philip Herriton becomes the spokesman for romance and the cause for Caroline Abbott's awakening although she is not engaged sexually by him. EMF is on Philip's side as a champion of romance rather than Caroline's. [Demonstration not conclusive, since Kelvin does not define "romance" exactly.] EMF removes Caroline from the confines of history by exposing her to romance. He then reintroduces history (or social fact) to negate in part her newly acquired moral vision. Romance—the enlargement of vision—is divorced from sexuality in *Angels;* hence the influence of Caroline and the rebirth of Philip are incomplete. He is saved by a woman who cannot save herself. Chap 4, *"The Longest Journey"*: Some themes relate to Rickie Elliot's poetic imagination. These are Stewart Ansell's intellectual search for truth and his moral action, and Stephen Wonham's relation to earth, the past, and living people. Other themes arise out of the negation and denial of truth by the Pembrokes and Mrs. Failing. Broader themes relate to conventional society in the early twentieth century, the meaning of England's history and tradition, and the philosophical quest to find what reality is. Agnes Pembroke is to be associated with a predatory social Darwinism. Robert is a kind of Holy Ghost who saves Mrs. Elliot from a loveless life and who fathers Stephen. The symbolic moment is essential to the continuance of life, but it is fatal to turn people into symbols as Rickie does. The persisting image of his dead mother prevents him from getting into a right relationship with the earth. The gods Dionysus and Demeter are associated with Stephen as a vital force; and Rickie, as the dying god analogue, has also a moment of association with Dionysus.

Chap 5, *"A Room with a View"*: Sexual love in *Room* becomes an extension of EMF's humanism; his increasing pessimism puts him on the defensive in developing this subject. Character, as in Mr. Emerson, controls and generates plot and gives to the events moral meaning. Mr. Emerson's aphorisms are structurally necessary. His faith in physical reality is one determinant of the plot. He is prophetic but not mythic, and he is anti-Platonic in urging the importance of a concrete reality. He provides a more effective secularization of Hellenism than did Goldsworthy Lowes Dickinson, EMF's Cambridge friend and mentor. George Emerson's individualism is as much his strength as a source of alienation. In Mr. Emerson's view the conventions and the fears that create obstacles for George and Lucy Honeychurch also inhibit the social and political life of mankind. The Surrey landscape performs a life-infusing function as does the view at Florence. Yet Surrey's middle-class society is also conventional, with Mr. Beebe representing its denial of the heart. Surrey society is not only defeated but attains increased stature by the strong heroism required for its defeat. After her interview with Mr. Emerson, Lucy seems like a squire about to do battle for religious truth. By her decisive actions she strikes a real blow at Surrey, although Surrey will not acknowledge it. Surrey's philosophical ignorance lies in the fact that life being perilous, love ought to be cherished. Surrey is mistaken in feeling that life is solid; it is, rather, fragile and vulnerable, marked by peril and by death. [Kelvin's best discussion.] Chap 6, *"Howards End"*: *Howards End* is filled with insoluble dilemmas, antitheses that provide a framework for the plot but which lead to no synthesis. Margaret Schlegel tries to connect the outer and the inner, but fails. Margaret's aphorisms are a structural device, working on the level of social and economic realism and then on the level of their being negated. [Defines the numerous antitheses.] Margaret marries Henry Wilcox but does not love him. [Questionable.] Connections occur only infrequently, and when they do, they are mostly envisaged ironically (see the opening connection—or collison—between Mrs. Munt and Charles Wilcox). [Expounds the glass symbolism in the novel, also noted by McDowell (1959) and Cyrus Hoy (1960).] The connection between Helen Schlegel and Leonard Bast proves disastrous to him. Helen points out that love and justice are often antithetical, since love involves exclusions. As a result of Margaret's connection with Henry, the Wilcox children are excluded from his. As realism, the final scene is not convincing; rather, EMF was positing certain images and values for the cure of middle-class deficiencies. He develops the concept of an elitist aristocracy, which can, through the imagination, merge the real and the ideal. Ernst Schlegel and Ruth Wilcox are such figures, as are the Schlegel sisters and Miss Avery. The affair with Helen permits Bast to rise to a heroic and tragic level. The child of Helen and Leonard is also mythical, the forerunner of a new elite, classless in origin and imbued with rural values.

Chap 7, *"A Passage to India"*: [The discussion is thematic; and for a novel so dependent on its multi-faceted images and symbols for its meaning, the method is limited. Kelvin argues that EMF comes down on the side of concretions, but the novel is more intrinsically metaphysical than Kelvin grants.] Reality is expanded in *Passage* and is best served when it is not devoured by the illusions which challenge it but lives side by side with them. A "post-metaphysical empiricism" is necessary in order for the reality of persons and objects to be reasserted. The compartmentalization, so common in India and elsewhere, helps in the assertion of this empiric reality. Illusion is a threat to empiric reality in the forms of misunderstanding and metaphysical seduction. Adela Quested at the Marabar Caves experiences both forms of illusion. Personality and self become the basic realities in India, not the personal relationship; compartmentalization, also (and primarily) a Western concept, again helps to assert this sort of reality. Thus Aziz's identity and selfhood survive the trial and the breakup of his friendship with Fielding. Fielding's identity is so firm as to be emblematic; and he exemplifies two of EMF's coordinates for personality: rationalism and honesty. His appreciation of the concrete realities of Italy on his voyage home is essential to EMF's meaning in *Passage.* [Most critics do not agree.] Compartmentalization is a good-and-evil which tries always to get rid of evil. Evil is thus mitigated in "Temple," wherein compartmentalization is in abeyance. Mrs. Moore loses hold of reality and is overcome by an evil vision of transcendent unity. Godbole aspires to an all-inclusive love and fails to attain it. [Most critics do not agree.] He knows that the effort to transcend the self, however abortive, guarantees the existence of the self; the failure to recognize this truth defeats Mrs. Moore. [The downgrading of the symbolical, the philosophical, and the ineffable results in an inadequate reading of an intricate work of art.] Chap 8, "Literature, the Past, and the Present": [Summary of *Aspects of the Novel* and individual essays from *Abinger Harvest* and *Two Cheers for Democracy*, with commentary on some essays but little attempt made to reach a synthesis or to discuss them philosophically.] [Kelvin's book is uneven; his method and approach are idiosyncratic, and his abstract terms are not precisely defined. There are insights of value to the EMF tyro, especially on *Room* and *Howards End.* Kelvin is best when he uses his sensibility and focuses upon actual characters and situations. The haphazard framework provided for his insights lessens their value. Bibliography. Reviews: "Language and Literature," CHOICE, V (April 1968), 721; Frederick P. W. McDowell (Entry No. 1281); and Stephen Wall (Entry No. 1312).]

1227 Kettle, Arnold. "E[dward] M[organ] Forster," ENCYCLOPEDIA OF WORLD LITERATURE IN THE TWENTIETH CENTURY, ed by Wolfgang Bernard Fleischmann (NY: Frederick Ungar, 1967), I, 395–96.

[Competent but routine review of EMF's career, ideas, and work.]

1228 Kondo, Ineko (ed). E. M. FORSTER (Tokyo: Kenkyusha, Introductions to Twentieth Century and American Literature, 1967). Contents, abstracted separately: Ineko Kondo, "The Man and His Life"; Yoshio Abe, "Works: *Where Angels Fear to Tread*," "Works: *The Longest Journey*," "Works: *A Room with a View*"; Takeshi Onodera, "Works: *Howards End*"; Masahito Ara, "Essays"; Yoshio Abe, "Works: Short Stories"; Kazuhiko Ara, "Essays"; Toshio Ando, "Biographies"; and Tatsuo Matsumura, "Appraisal of E. M. Forster," Chronology and Bibliography. [In Japanese.]

1229 Kondo, Ineko. "The Man and His Life," E. M. FORSTER, ed by Ineko Kondo (Tokyo: Kenkyusha, 1967), pp. 1–56.
EMF stopped writing novels after *A Passage to India* because of the decline in the prestige and wealth of the upper middle class after World War I. After the war EMF became involved in the campaign for the writer's freedom. [Leonard Woolf informed a friend of Mrs. Kondo that EMF was homosexual; this fact may help clarify EMF's personality and works. Account of EMF's life, treating successively EMF's family background, his childhood, school life, the influence of Greece, Italy, and Germany, and his trips to India.] [In Japanese.]

1230 Labistour, Marion. "Reviews and Comment," CRITICAL QUARTERLY, IX (Summer 1967), 191–92.
EMF's norm is that of the absurdity of existence; his vision is one of resignation in the face of human confusion, misunderstanding, and absurdity. Speaking of human absurdity, delight, and inclusiveness, EMF in his novels forms a mock-epic commentary on Wilfred Stone's ambitious critical apparatus in THE CAVE AND THE MOUNTAIN (1966).

1231 Larrett, William. "E. M. Forster," THE ENGLISH NOVEL FROM THOMAS HARDY TO GRAHAM GREENE (Frankfurt amMain: Moritz Diesterweg, 1967), pp. 70–92; also 9, 14, 17, 23, 95, 111.
The tone and handling of his chief theme sets EMF apart from other writers: the need for understanding and toleration and the desire to set human values in their right perspective in a materialistic world. His themes succeed on a linguistic plane by his use of motifs and images, in the larger view by his sense of structure. *Howards End* is his best novel because of its perfect fusion of content and form. [Larrett applies EMF's concepts of "pattern" and "rhythm" formulated in *Aspects of the Novel*.] Pattern is a static, spatial element; rhythm is a dynamic, temporal element. These elements are juxtaposed in *Howards End* through the human relationships charted among the three groups of characters. A circular framework prevails; this novel begins and ends at Howards End house. Leonard Bast and Charles Wilcox

are the polar characters; they are too far apart ever to come together amicably. The hopes for a better future are embodied in Howards End itself and Helen Schlegel's and Bast's child. The rural setting represents a fusion of the worlds of Howards End and London. The house is alive and a dynamic force; the Schlegel furniture fortuitously appearing in this house, owned by the Wilcoxes, represents a fusion of the two families. The novel is stitched internally through recurring phrases or motifs like "telegrams and anger," "hands on the ropes," books and umbrellas, "abyss," "see steadily," "see whole," flux (and related words), motor car. In *A Passage to India* the Caves are an emblem of a mystery and an evil that cannot be explained. The echo springs from the evil of confusion and nullity, and engenders this confusion and nullity. The symbols and motifs in *Passage* comprise chiefly caves and noises [including the echo, chants, and repeated sounds (train wheels, songs at the Hindu festival, and others).] *Passage* does not have the same closely woven texture of *Howards End*, nor "the same clearly intentioned manipulation of language." In *Where Angels Fear to Tread* EMF uses as motif the Baedeker guide; in *A Room with a View*, he uses rooms and views; in *The Longest Journey*, he uses trains, streams, Orion. His style is sometimes inadequate to his intended effects of surprise and horror (the last scene of *Angels*). He uses surprise well. The chapter titles for *Room* indicate the action in each case except for the two crucial ones (Chapter 4 and Chapter 12, containing respectively the stabbing in the Piazza and the nude bathing scene, the most dramatic and surprising occurrences in the novel). [Numerous other references. Pleasant and informed though not profound discussion.]

1232 McDonald, Walter R. "Forster's *A Passage to India*," Ex-PLICATOR, XXV (March 1967), Item 54.
EMF withholds comment in *A Passage to India* concerning what happened to Adela Quested in the Marabar Caves. This strategy tells us more than if EMF had been explicit: the "withheld knowledge enforces the theme of unresolved tension, ambivalence, and suspicion." [Short and rather obvious note.]

1233 Martin, John H. "Theme and Structure in the Novels of E. M. Forster," DISSERTATION ABSTRACTS, XXVVII (1967), p. 4258A. Unpublished dissertation, University of Connecticut, 1966.

1234 Matsumura, Tatsuo. "Appraisal of E. M. Forster," E. M. FORSTER, ed by Ineko Kondo (Tokyo: Kenkyusha, 1967), pp. 203–32.
Critics have often addressed themselves to two issues: to what degree is EMF a traditional "liberal," and to what degree is his juxtaposition of

realism and symbolism aesthetically viable? [Survey of EMF criticism in English and in Japanese.] [In Japanese.]

1235 Mitchell, Nancy H. "Metaphysical Relativism in the Works of E. M. Forster," DISSERTATION ABSTRACTS, XXVII (1967), 4260A. Unpublished dissertation, Catholic University, 1965.

1236 Müllenbrock, Heinz-Joachim. "Presse und Literatur in den Jahren vor Ausbruch des ersten Weltkrieges: Anzeichen für ein positiveres Deutschlandbild bei Forster und Wells" (The Press and Literature in the Years before the Outbreak of the First World War: Signs of a More Positive View of Germany in Forster and Wells), LITERATUR UND ZEITGESCHICHTE IN ENGLAND ZWISCHEN DEM ENDE DES 19. JAHRHUNDERTS UND DEM AUSBRUCH DES ERSTEN WELT-KRIEGES (Literature and History of the Age in England between the End of the 19th Century and the Outbreak of the First World War) (Hamburg: Cram, de Gruyter, 1967), pp. 137–52.

In *Howards End* EMF reveals an ambiguous view toward Germany as he describes Ernst Schlegel and the Germanic influence on his daughters. Ernst is presented as deeply appreciative of the idealistic aspects of the German temperament that had become widespread about 1860; he disapproves the pan-Germanism and the imperial pretensions that followed, though EMF is also critical in the novel of English imperial pretensions. EMF still regards contemporary Germany as more favorable to the life of the mind than England, although there is more liberty of action in England. Margaret Schlegel regards England and Germany as the two greatest nations and as complementary to one another. EMF is highly critical in *Howards End* of the chauvinists in both England and Germany: Aunt Juley Munt and Fräulein Mosebach. The Philistine business man (Charles Wilcox) who hates cosmopolitanism, and German cosmopolitanism in particular, is also a force making for international misunderstanding. In *Howards End* EMF reveals a sincere British patriotism, but also a tolerant and informed view of Germany. [In German.]

1237 Nicolson, Harold. THE WAR YEARS 1939–45: VOLUME II OF DIARIES AND LETTERS, ed by Nigel Nicolson (NY: Atheneum; Lond: Collins, 1967), p. 434.

EMF was upset by excesses of communist leaders in Greece, especially since his own political views had been consistently leftist. "In Spain there was no doubt at all which side was in the right and which was in the wrong. But this Greek thing disturbs me. I hate tyranny as much as I hate anarchy." [This under 12 Feb 1945.]

1238 Onodera, Takeshi. "Works: *Howards End*," E. M. FORSTER, ed by Ineko Kondo (Tokyo: Kenkyusha, 1967), pp. 93–112.

EMF places the spiritual above the materialistic, since Henry Wilcox is ultimately dependent on Margaret Schlegel, the embodiment of the spiritual. [Extended plot summary. The contrast between the spiritual and the materialistic is stressed.] [In Japanese.]

1239 Peskin, S. G. "An Examination of Some Themes in the Novels of E. M. Forster," UNISA ENGLISH STUDIES (University of South Africa), I (1967), 1–22; II (1967), 1–14.

In *Where Angels Fear to Tread* passion and hope are alien to Mrs. Herriton and Harriet Herriton. In *The Longest Journey* Stephen Wonham is no more successful in connecting with others than are Rickie, Agnes, or Ansell. In *A Room with a View* Lucy is less hampered by sham and convention than by English Puritanism. In *Howards End* Margaret Schlegel's ability to connect makes possible the survival of her nephew, who is Margaret's and Ruth Wilcox's child as well as Helen's. Leonard Bast is vividly realized as a character; we are drawn to him too powerfully as a person for EMF's adverse reaction to him to be convincing. EMF wants him to be seen as a symbol; as it is, he generates sufficient sympathy so that sympathy for Helen and Margaret is deflected. [Little that is new in this extended commentary on all five novels. First four novels treated in first article; *A Passage to India* in second. Extensive paraphrase, obvious comment, repetition of ideas made by other critics with no acknowledgment that others have written on EMF. Abstract gives only the comments that seem not to have been made before. Nothing of note in second article on *Passage.*]

1240 Raina, M. L. "Imagery of *A Passage to India:* A Further Note," ENGLISH LITERATURE IN TRANSITION, X:1 (1967), 8–9.

The snake image in *A Passage to India* can be more closely related to cave-temple, arch-echo symbolic pivots in the novel if it is juxtaposed to imagery (connoting forboding and doom) of birds, insects, and animals. Bird images are to be associated with the hostile sun energy; they are negative symbols connoting man's frustrated attempts to achieve order and regeneration; and they are seen to be in tension with snake images which are associated with the fertilizing power of earth. [A follow-up to George H. Thomson's "A Note on the Snake Imagery of *A Passage to India*" (1966).]

1241 Rawlings, Donn. "E. M. Forster, 'Prophecy,' and the Subversion of Myth," PAUNCH (Buffalo, NY), No. 30 (Dec 1967), 17–36.

According to *Aspects of the Novel,* prophecy in fiction suspends humility and the sense of humor, it reaches back to something elemental, it gives us sensation or sound, and it looks toward unity; realism is only intermittent. EMF is apprehensive about the loss of individual freedom involved in any kind of program of externalization that results in the formulations of myth, but does recognize that myth enables us to discern "lost portions of man and his world which need winning back." The present is disruptive; we need to recover a sense of harmony and wholeness through the means of myth. Prophecy in fiction will appear to affirm the establishment while presenting "a series of signals pointed to the subversion of it"; it works through parodying recognized institutions and rituals and through implication. In EMF's fiction the elemental or myth figures (Stephen Wonham, Gino Carella) are less interesting and convincing, however, than the aesthetic spectators of life (Philip Herriton, Rickie Elliot, the Schlegel sisters). The latter figures, especially the Schlegels, are caught between the worn-out conventions of society and a vitality that would subvert these conventions, and they have glimpses of the prophetic (though they are not "mythic" in their own right like Gino or Stephen). The conflict arises when valued personal realities are opposed to "the claims of an attractive but potentially destructive transcendental myth." Such a myth works on the Schlegels (to subvert their personal standards), rather than on the Wilcoxes or Leonard Bast (through the Schlegels). The conflict is intense in Margaret; and as she embraces some mythic elements, she loses some ground in her personal life. Her connections with Howards End house are a kind of death. In this kind of novel the myth also loses ground and is punctured at various points, but total human awareness is increased. This interpenetration of myth (especially as it presents the extraordinary or Faustian man) with everyday circumstances and the modifications of each force by the other is also illustrated in Dostoevski's CRIME AND PUNISHMENT. [A densely written and conceived article, not altogether clear in its logic and development; a first try at a subject that needs more precise definition.]

1242 Rosenbaum, S. P. "Virginia Woolf and E. M. Forster," UNIVERSITY OF TORONTO QUARTERLY, XXXVII (Oct 1967), 109–12.
[Review of Wilfred Stone's THE CAVE AND THE MOUNTAIN and Jean Guignet's VIRGINIA WOOLF AND HER WORKS. Questions the applicability of cave and mountain and their being united in the temple (which fuses the conscious and the unconscious) as a central symbol for the earlier fiction.] Stone misunderstands G. E. Moore. Moore was only incidentally an idealist and, in fact, ended the split in English moral thought between Bentham's Utilitarianism and Coleridge's Kantianism. Moore ended influence of idealism among the Apostles. Stone's book is useful because of its inclusiveness.

1243 Roy, Chitra. "D. H. Lawrence and E. M. Forster: A Study in Values," INDIAN JOURNAL OF ENGLISH STUDIES (Bombay), No. 8 (March 1967), 46–58.
[Descriptive comparison, only incidentally analytic, of EMF and D. H. Lawrence, inferior to Martin Price's "E. M. F. and D. H. L." (1966) and

Wilfred Stone's discussion of the two writers in the last chapter of THE CAVE AND THE MOUNTAIN (1966).]

1244 Sandison, Alan. "Rudyard Kipling: The Imperial Simulacrum," THE WHEEL OF EMPIRE: A STUDY OF THE IMPERIAL IDEA IN SOME LATE NINETEENTH AND EARLY TWENTIETH-CENTURY FICTION (Lond: Macmillan; NY: St. Martin's P, 1967), pp. 64–113, espec 79, 84, 97.

In Kipling's "The Education of Otis Yeere" Mrs. Mallowe has some of Mrs. Moore's insight into the potential destructiveness of India. The Club members in Kipling's "The Mark of the Beast" are racially exclusive, like the Anglo-Indians in *A Passage to India*. "On the City Wall" by Kipling reveals the gap between the Anglo-Indians and the native Indians in a scene similar to EMF's "bridge party." By its formlessness and omnipresent diversity, India sends Kim (KIM) back to the forces making for law, order, and control —to the British Civil Service—just as it sends Fielding in *Passage* back to the world of clear definitions and distinctions embodied in Italian and British culture.

1245 Schmerl, Rudolph B. "Fantasy as Technique," VIRGINIA QUARTERLY REVIEW, XLIII (Autumn 1967), 644–55.
[Starts from EMF's discussion of fantasy in *Aspects of the Novel*. Disagrees with EMF that we must suspend our disbelief when we read fantasy (that is, "pay something extra") but agrees there can be objectively described characteristics of fantasy that can help us define it as a genre.] The fantasist can dispense with "pretenses of actuality"; but he must be "responsible" in relating his work to external reality, and he should have a purpose in writing. [Inconclusive essay on the characteristics of literary fantasy.]

1246 Shahane, V. A. "Forster's *A Passage to India*, Chapter VII," EXPLICATOR, XXVI (Dec 1967), Item 36.
Godbole's song at the conclusion of Fielding's tea party in *A Passage to India* has thematic significance and is not presented for ironic and humorous effect alone. It is a poetical expression of the Hindu view of God (of the need for complete surrender to Him), a mystical assertion of the Immanence of the Divine (a pantheistic view; God is already within the milkmaidens; they forget this fact when they pray to Him to "Come").

1247 Shahane, V. A. "A Visit to Mr. E. M. Forster," QUEST (Bombay), No. 53 (Spring 1967), 42–46.
EMF does not regard the sudden deaths in his novels as evidences of a definite philosophical predisposition, but he realizes more than he used to do that death takes place frequently. EMF says that Meredith no longer means much to him. EMF emphasizes the important influence of Proust upon him after 1920, in "the way I look at my characters, I suppose, and

also the manner in which I try to fathom the depth of their beings." EMF maintains that in writing *A Passage to India* he had no particular person in mind for Godbole or Aziz [see Wilfred Stone, THE CAVE AND THE MOUNTAIN (1966), p. 319*n*, for persuasive evidence, including EMF's own statements, that Aziz was modelled on Syed Ross Masood and Godbole on another friend (possibly the Maharajah of Chhatarpur)]. Chandrapore is Bankipore, a cantonment town near Patna. Godbole's song about Tukaram was given EMF by a friend, but the first song about gopis was pure invention. The title of *Passage* derives from Walt Whitman's poem, but EMF looks at matters differently from Whitman. The novel, like the poem, has a deep religious meaning according to EMF. Again EMF says that *The Longest Journey* is the novel he likes the best though the critics do not think highly of it: "Yet I like it most because it is so close to me . . . to what I am." [Interview.]

1248 Stevenson, Lionel. "The Earnest Realists," THE HISTORY OF THE ENGLISH NOVEL, Vol XI: YESTERDAY AND AFTER (NY: Barnes & Noble, 1967), pp. 60–110, espec 87–102; passim.

[Gives extended review of EMF's career.] EMF has four nineteenth-century antecedents: Jane Austen and Henry James, the first of whom influenced him through style, the second through his moral preoccupation; Meredith, who influenced him on plot and form; and Butler, who influenced him to hate the latent cruelty of family life. In *Where Angels Fear to Tread* EMF is uncomfortable in dealing with sex and violence. EMF was "captive of the very tyranny of good taste and decency that he was striving to discredit." [Extreme judgment.] Gino Carella is judged to be a "dull materialist" and incapable of genuine love. *The Longest Journey* reveals EMF's portrayal of himself in Rickie Elliot. Butler's THE WAY OF ALL FLESH was a considerable influence upon the satire associated with Sawston school in *Journey*. EMF in *Journey* stresses that primitive violence underlies civilization and that modern complacency makes men and women incapable of handling such violence. In *A Room with a View* the influence of Meredith is paramount. The chief theme, as in *Angels*, is the contrast between English stolidity and continental sensitiveness. In *Howards End* EMF views established English society as approaching cataclysm. The essential emphasis is in the idyllic last chapter: the individual seems to matter little, and the incidental damage to the Wilcoxes is unimportant in view of Margaret's muted triumph. [Interprets a number of the elements in *A Passage to India* incorrectly: that Fielding takes over Mrs. Moore's role of guardian after her death (whereas his rationalism cuts him off from her insight into the verities; her role is taken over, rather by Godbole and by her son and daughter, Ralph and Stella); that there is a guidebook quality about the descriptions (in contrast to almost all recent critics, he does not regard the descriptions of the Caves and the Mau festivities as organic); that Chap 32, with its description of Egypt and Italy, is irrelevant (it is central, as it contrasts Western order and form with life-enhancing Eastern muddle and chaos).] The novel lacks full dramatic force to bring the two cultures of East and West together. EMF does not "play fair," because he fails to tell us what happened in the Caves. The trial scene, as good as it is, comes too early in the book and so vitiates suspense. The Mau festivities violate the unities, especially when Godbole takes over as central character. [But it is EMF's purpose to reconcile as many polarities and antagonisms as possible through a man (Godbole) who at once is of this world and has glimpses of Eternity.] Fielding's marriage to Stella Moore is extraneous and implausible; the marriage indicates Fielding's severance of his Indian affiliations and a reversion to his natural English background. [Oversimplified; Fielding gains some insight as result of his wife's influence and her affinity with Hinduism.] Godbole's Hinduism is "a passive but compassionate admission of our human futility." [Makes too much of one polarity, the pessimistic, in the book and in human experience.] The thematic pattern is not fully related to "the normal elements of action and character," and the book has inequalities in style. The novel "lapses into buffoonery" in these sequences: when Aziz's friends visit him as he lies sick and when the boats collide in the tank at Mau. These sequences rupture the consistency of tone. [They offer needed variety, and the boat collision is symbolically organic to the novel.] "The author does not seem to be a skillful craftsman constructing a trim artifact, but a considerate amateur, impelled to grapple with the onerous task of communicating his impressions and his anxieties." [This is an inexplicable summation for a 1967 criticism.] [Like C. B. Cox in "E. M. Forster's Island," THE FREE SPIRIT (1963) and other social critics, Stevenson views EMF as a liberal humanitarian, realist, and moralist in the succession of George Eliot; he underplays the Jane Austen and Meredith lines of descent, overlooks the influence of romanticism, and seems unaware that James McConkey, J. B. Beer, George H. Thomson, and others have written of EMF's symbolism, and his mystical and transcendental qualities. The judgment that EMF is essentially a realist (in company with Hugh Walpole, W. Somerset Maugham, Compton Mackenzie, and others) is surprising and misleading. Interpretations sometimes perceptive, more often inept; excessive plot summary. Old-fashioned in method and point of view. Numerous incidental references to EMF throughout.]

1249 Thomson, George H. THE FICTION OF E. M. FORSTER (Detroit: Wayne State UP, 1967); includes, in much rvd form, "Symbolism in E. M. Forster's Earlier Fiction," CRITICISM, III (Fall 1961), 304–20; "Thematic Symbol in *A Passage to India*," TWENTIETH CENTURY LITERATURE, VII (July 1961), 51–63; and "Theme and Symbol in *Howards End*," MODERN FICTION STUDIES, VII (Autumn 1961), 229–42.

"Introduction": (1) EMF's works of fiction are romances rather than novels, (2) symbolism is central to his works considered as romances, (3) the main source of his symbols is ecstatic experience, (4) through his ecstatic perceptions his symbols attain archetypal and mythic significance. EMF for the most part presents myth as experienced personally rather than myth as known abstractly. EMF's works do not belong to the tradition of realism, though most critics have focused upon his alleged physical realism, social realism, psychological realism, or moral realism. The critics then find shortcomings which they cannot explain. EMF's liberal humanism (to the fore in discussions since Lionel Trilling's E. M. FORSTER [1943]) and the discovery that such humanism is inadequate for interpreting the works of fiction are irrelevant considerations when the works are regarded as the embodiment of myth. What matters is EMF's ability to express, through the means of myth, the polarities of man's experience from an absolute negation to an ultimate affirmation.

Chap 1, "E. M. Forster" [EMF's affiliations with Cambridge and Bloomsbury are described]: The great problem for EMF was the survival and development of the individual personality in an urbanized, industrialized, and routinized culture. Though EMF had no direct contact with his contemporary Jung, they both agree that modern man should search for his soul, that he should search for it by developing his personality to the full, and that he should reach beyond his individuality to a more impersonal and universal entity, the spirit. Myth and symbol would be the most effective means for achieving these goals. EMF was in advance of his time in this search for soul and universality and in his bold use of myth and symbol to fulfill the psychological needs of the modern age. The myth theorists (Andrew Lang, Frederick W. H. Myers, Jane Harrison, J. A. Stewart, B. F. Westcott, all contemporary or antecendent to EMF) are proto-Jungean and provide the Gestalt out of which EMF developed his interest in symbol, myth, and romance. He agrees with these theorists as to the oneness of man and universal nature, the importance of a deeper self and its relationships to a higher self, the use of myth to express the paradox of man's unchanging yet evolving nature, and the value of a life-oriented art to provide new insights and new myths. He differs from them in his greater emphasis on individuality and self-development. His approach to symbol is inseparable from his approach to nature. The romantics had self-consciously achieved an identification with nature, whereas EMF and the myth theorists wished to achieve identity with nature. The unconscious helps man to achieve a bond with nature that is not possible through means of the self-conscious intellect. In EMF the moment of identity with nature is an impersonal, visionary experience, and is central to his art.

Chap 2, "Romance Moralities": The fiction of EMF is primarily romance, with some elements of the novel in it. In romance there is projected an unfallen world with characters who exist in a strange and beautiful setting. The world of romance is one of innocence and energy into which forces of evil intrude, such as the wasteland, monsters, ogres, and demonic villains. In EMF's work the romance vision of innocence is conveyed intensely, but the vision of evil is mostly social, a vision taken over from the Fielding-Austen tradition of the novel. Transcendent evil also exists in his fiction, with the presence of evil characters who are, as in romance, perverted innocents rather than morally responsible individuals. As in romance, in EMF's typical short stories experience-and-evil is contrasted with innocence-and-goodness. His ultimate moral vision, because it is based on a sense of transcendent good and evil, is decisive and prophetic, emphasizing a wholeness not found in the separate components of his art. The "eternal moment" intensifies all his work but is presented in its purest form in the short stories (the novels tend to be more diffident, tentative, and modest in actualizing such moments). [Full discussion of short stories.] "The Eternal Moment" is a relative failure because it does not embody romance criteria. The best stories are "The Point of It," "The Celestial Omnibus," "The Story of a Panic," "The Road from Colonus," "Other Kingdom," and "The Story of the Siren" because, in one way or another, they do illustrate such criteria.

Chap 3, "Narrator as Archetype": The instrumental cause of mythic order is the ecstatic experience of the character; the final cause is the ecstatic experience of the creator, the author-narrator, who assumes archetypal dimensions in EMF's Italian romances. The narrator objectifies the inner life by giving it an outward representation (such is the method of romance). The forces which contend for man's soul (life and death, good and evil) are each dramatized and contend openly for the souls of the characters. In *A Room with a View* there is the romance division of characters into positive and negative kinds. Lucy Honeychurch is a romance heroine; her character is fixed; the question is not whether she will change but whether her nature will triumph or fall. George Emerson is primarily the romance hero. It is not the psychology of the lovers but their fate that matters, the great forces that make or break an individual. The characters in *Where Angels Fear to Tread* are more purely romance characters than those in *Room*. EMF uses melodrama and tightly structured plot in order to dramatize the moral confrontations that are the staple of romance.

Chap 4, "Hero as Archetype": The hero is a uniting symbol, transformed by ecstatic apprehension into a mythic presence. He is fixed in his attributes, representing being rather than becoming; he is godlike in epitomizing man's nature and destiny. The problem in presenting him: How is his individual aspect to be prevented from obscuring his universal aspects? EMF limits our view of the hero and endeavors to debar him from situations that reveal his individual nature. In the short stories he limits the appearances of the hero; in the novels (except for Stephen Wonham of *The Longest Journey*), he confines himself to archetypal characters who represent only certain aspects of the hero's total nature or destiny. They have a limited significance, but within their limits they are typical and universal. Thus Gino Carella of *Angels* is unmistakably archetypal in his role as father. As natural man he is too involved in social circumstance for his heroic dimension always to register decisively. The same hazard of overexposure endangers the effectiveness of the archetypal characters from *Journey:* Stewart Ansell, Mrs. Elliot, and Stephen Wonham. Stephen's presence in the novel in ordinary situations sometimes obscures the mythic power of his role as hero. The hero's ambiguous aspect interferes with the novelist's presentation of him—seen mythically he is "the bringer of civilization, order, and spiritual advance;" seen pragmatically, he is "the bringer of mob rule and tyrannical authority." In order to circumvent the distasteful second aspect, EMF uses boys or children for his heroes, and later the Great-Mother archetype. Stephen is unique in not being either one. In Stephen, EMF faces the full range of difficulties in presenting the hero archetype, and is moderately successful in so doing. Rickie Elliot begins as hero and is then supplanted by Stephen. Rickie's foundling background is similar to a typical hero's. Cambridge and Madingley Dell allow Rickie to succeed in the first of the hero's quests, the attainment of his own identity. He is, thereafter, less successful in mastering the world. Agnes is the shadowy figure he ought to have fought against but whom he embraces. Ansell is the spiritual guide to whom he ought to hearken; Stephen is a Pan-like figure who betokens Nature's reality. Mrs. Failing is the dragon who must be slain by the hero. His test is contained in Mrs. Failing's disclosure of his relationship to Stephen. Rickie is unable to meet the test implicit in this knowledge of his past and is unable to proceed to rebirth or renewal. Mrs. Elliot is the Great-Mother in her benign aspect; Mrs. Failing, in her terrible aspect. Agnes prevents Rickie from accepting Stephen, the son of the benign Earth Mother. Rickie's marriage to Agnes is not a holy one; through its agency, he undergoes a journey to the underworld of Sawston. Dunwood House is the heart of this low-grade hell, symbolized in its proprieties; a certificate praising the drains, the bust of the Hermes of Praxitiles (but not the complete nude figure), and a teakwood monkey. Herbert is his false guide. No purification for Rickie results from this dark journey; he emerges bankrupt. The railroad is symbolically allied to the Elliots; in this novel it brings death. It symbolizes arbitrary and meaningless death; when it is bridged, it is brought into harmony with the world of comedy in which death is a meaningful event in the life of each generation. In Part III Stephen emerges as hero, but Rickie remains the central character. Ansell (associated with trying to find the true reality at the innermost figure in his drawing of circles within squares), Mrs. Elliot (associated with Demeter), and Stephen (associated with Orion) are subordinate characters existing to guide the hero. [Extensive discussion of circle images and of circles within squares figure.] In Wiltshire it is Stephen, the hero or divine man, who stands at the central tree in the Cadbury Rings where Rickie first hears the truth about his relationship to him. His being at the inmost circle connects him with Ansell, the drawer of squares within circles. Stephen is thus the reality that is at the center of the circle and square diagram. This central point at the heart of both past and present (in the Cadbury Rings) is a symbol of rebirth (as it was thought to be the center of creation in primitive myths). Rickie cannot achieve such rebirth. The Cadbury Rings are also a symbol of the past, and the circles are associated with the most potent figure for Rickie from that past, his mother. Mrs. Elliot, as Demeter, is represented by the tree at the center of the Rings; she is also related to the stars, associated with Stephen. Demeter appears in a supporting, not a subsuming, role in relation to the hero. The Demeter of Cnidus with its shattered knees is associated with Rickie and the other Elliots rather than with Mrs. Elliot and Stephen. Mrs. Elliot (Earth) is the mother of Stephen (as Earth was the mother of Orion, with whom Stephen is continually associated). Stephen as hero is a kind of foundling. His parents are heroic and divine, the Earth-Mother and the heroic, impregnating, disappearing god (the farmer Robert). Mrs. Failing is his foster parent and is androgynous in nature, reminiscent of the sardonic Mr. Elliot, her brother. Through Mrs. Failing, Stephen shares the same carnal father with Rickie; in Mrs. Elliot they share the same divine mother. As a boy Stephen appears as the child-hero on the roof, betokening his future role as mediator, bringer of wholeness, and reconciler of opposites. Like the hero he has to labor in youth at the command of another. Stephen is heroic by virtue of "his primordial humanity, his animal simplicity, and his resemblance to the elements." His adventures in Sawston, London, and Wiltshire have a heroic cast. His bathing at the ford is a ritual of purification and rebirth. The rose (of the flame boat) signifies the unfolding of a higher self, the transfiguration of the body united with Earth and aligned with the circle (in the form of a rose) of Ansell. Stephen is ready for the supreme event and comes to represent all reality, whether it is found in books, earth, or man. The stream is a river of life, and Stephen is a bridge between the dead and those yet to be born. The theme of the death wish and the loss of reality in Rickie is balanced by that of the spirit of life, which is to be found in the symbols of *Journey* and in Stephen as hero. The mythology of the twins is represented in the brothers: one of the two must die that the other have life and immortality. Though Rickie is sacrificed as a person, what he stands for—individuality—is included in, and reconciled with, Stephen's impersonality. In another (and perhaps more profound sense) Rickie's individuality is sacrificed to the universality and impersonality of the hero. [This is a classic discussion of *Journey*.]

Chap 5, "Object as Archetype": In *Howards End* there is only one archetypal character, Mrs. Wilcox. Helen and Margaret Schlegel are not archetypal but support Mrs. Wilcox by, in effect, becoming like her. Having only one such character, EMF can confer much greater authority on objects. These all support and find their focus in Mrs. Wilcox. [Among symbols (objects) discussed intelligently and exhaustively are the Beethoven Fifth Symphony, Howards End house, hay and grass, the wych-elm, the Danish tumuli, Ruth Wilcox as Demeter and Sophia, Wickham Place (the Schlegel's London home), London (and its links with the Wilcoxes).] The symbols often dramatize the collocation of opposites: beast-monk versus love, life versus death, the seen versus the unseen, the past versus the present. The happy ending is not faked, because the monster, London, is not destroyed. *Howards End* is a comedy also in which light triumphs over darkness, though the triumph is an uneasy one. In describing Beethoven, EMF sees him achieving effects that unite the sinister and the triumphant. This he does himself in *Howards End.*

Chap 6, "Novel as Archetype": *A Passage to India* presents three stages in the spiritual history of mankind and the individual, which correspond to the three parts of the novel—"Mosque," "Caves," and "Temple." The first stage is that of superficial optimism; the second, of disillusionment; the third, of qualified spiritual achievement. Mrs. Moore goes through all three stages, though she has to be transfigured by death, in the third stage, to achieve oneness. As in romance fiction, the characters divide into good and bad, with the individual not incurring moral responsibility. The Anglo-Indian officials are evil, Mrs. Moore and Godbole are good, and the other chief characters, Aziz, Fielding, and Adela Quested are somewhere in between. The truth emerges as revelation, as visual images and symbolic moments of good and evil. Evil is not transcendent, in that its source lies beyond man; it is universal and transcends the individual because all contribute to it—the responsibility is universal rather than individual. As narrator EMF is responsible not to his characters but to the total order of experience in which they participate. He judges Aziz, Fielding, and Adela and finds them wanting. Mrs. Moore is not the all-pervasive character, as is Mrs. Wilcox in whom all the symbols meet and fuse. Rather, she acts as an influence but does not encompass or contain the novel (or the trial scene). The Marabar Caves and Hills form the most important symbol in the novel but are balanced by the Indian Temple. Mrs. Moore's moment of anti-vision and Godbole's impelling her to completeness balance one another, but neither the moment of desolation nor the moment of vision controls the novel. The narrator seems swallowed by the novel. Frequently no character dominates. When one character does so, intimacy is absent. The perspective of the narrator comes through in the description of India or Indians, but he cannot reduce his materials readily to the requirements of form. The truth resides in India, which if it is contained at all is contained only within the confines of the whole novel. Hence the novel is archetypal; the total order of *Passage* is itself visionary. In *Passage* the approach to the Marabar Hills is as through a dream or nightmare, but the Chapel Perilous is an empty cave. The Hills epitomize the universe of matter; the Caves are as bubbles within the matter, which have been frozen into stillness. The Caves "epitomize the universe of man, isolated, turned in upon itself, spiritually dead." They are best viewed through the echo, which expresses the absence of the original sound yet implies its existence. The echo implies the existence of God while expressing His absence; and therefore it is to be conceived as always evil. [Reasoning here is somewhat obscure.] The call of "Come," echoing through India, signifies the absence of God in the natural universe, while in Godbole's song the call signifies His absence in the world of man. The echoes in India imply the existence (though remote) of God; the echoes in the Caves are absolute negation. [A commonly held view; I think, rather, that the negation also implies the existence of its opposite.] Fielding, Adela, and Aziz are all deficient in ranges of intuitive and mystical insight and do not fully appreciate the mystery of the Marabar Hills and Caves. However, the limited achievement of the Western rationalists is more important than their failure. Fielding, Adela, and Aziz feel that they exist in themselves; this is pride to the Christian (or Moslem); in any case a form of egotistic isolation which is also signified by the Caves. This narcissistic isolation is not restricted to individuals only but is present in every human organization or activity—personal relations, formal religion, government, and race are a series of vast caves, hovering over the spirit of man. Every organization is based on exclusiveness and tends toward spiritual emptiness. The silence beyond the remotest echo is a sign of a godless universe; the failure of the Marabar Hills to echo implies the nonexistence of God. The Cave is not the unconscious or the womb, but the negation of these and other realities. The light in the Caves when the match is struck connotes "supreme isolation in all its insidious charm and deathlike beauty"; it glimmers a while and then reflects its own darkness. Mrs. Moore, alone of the English, has the spiritual capacity to comprehend the echo; her vision, full of self-perpetuating snakes and echoes, is one of insanity and nightmare. It represents a negation of distinctions and of the spirit's life. Central to *Passage* is the proposition that Mrs. Moore has an overwhelming awareness of the absence of God and an awareness of evil, while Godbole has a corresponding awareness of the presence of God and an awareness of good. The existence of God is, therefore, asserted as much by one as by the other. The themes of death and the absence of God are intertwined; Mrs. Moore's initiation into death began in India with her reactions to Godbole's song. Her vision is a twilight one, and so her darkness is not complete; hope is always implicit in her despair. On leaving India she goes from her state of withdrawal to a state of possible rebirth; she becomes, in effect, one of the echoes of India and an influence thereby. In "Temple" Mrs. Moore becomes one with the universe through Godbole and his love. The reconciliation between Aziz and Fielding is partial: "But at least there is *some* light and song and there *is* a struggle." The festival cancels the Marabar in the episode of the flooded Mau tank, wherein momentarily Fielding and Aziz are in harmony. This flooded tank contrasts with the Tank of the Dagger at the Marabar, where evil, under Aziz's escort, was let loose and an accident caused evil to spread out to and beyond Adela. At the Mau tank an accident, under Ralph Moore's aegis, brings harmony and union from muddle and confusion. Water, hills, and sky become friendly in "Temple," where they had been inimical in "Caves." Sound in "Temple" also becomes pleasurable and meaningful. The thunderstorm symbolizes the marriage of heaven and earth; it nullifies the last silence, the invisible arch beyond all arches, and the Marabar Caves with their snakes of light and echoes of sound. The Mau festival is not necessarily a force making order; it ends as a muddle with only some hints of order being asserted. The universe is not really comprehensible or susceptible to order, EMF implies; and the desire for precise order or comprehensibility is, in fact, suspect. *Passage* captures at the same time the multiplicity and the oneness of India. The muddle of the hundred Indias signifies the absence of order, whereas the mystery of the one India signifies "a supreme order" unlike the one which Fielding and Adela understand. The Indian Temple and the Marabar Hills are antithetical, symbolizing the presence and the nonexistence of God, respectively. The narrative interdependence of good and evil, of being and not being, of Temple and the Marabar, is essential to EMF's success in rendering his complete novel archetypal. The key to *Passage* is Mrs. Moore and her vision of desolation following upon her ecstatic vision in "Mosque." Good and evil lodge side by side in her, whereas in the earlier fiction they were separated into different characters. Mrs. Moore thereby provides the human center for that narrative interdependence of opposites, just described. Her conflict, in short, helps establish the novel as archetypal.

Appendix A, "Forster and the Nineteenth-Century View of Nature and Symbol": In his identity with nature EMF breaks with the self-consciousness dominating nineteenth-century literature, which culminated in aestheticism and symbolism. The mythic writer regards myth and symbol as life-enhancing; the self-conscious symbolist regards them as art-enhancing. Appendix B, "The Manuscripts of *A Passage to India*": [Discussion of the manuscripts of *Passage* and the rejected readings found therein, making use of Robert L. Harrison's thesis (1965) and anticipating the more complete discussions by June Perry Levine (1967, 1970, and 1971) and Oliver Stallybrass (1960 and "Forster's Wobblings," 1969)]. [A path-breaking book. It will be difficult ever again to disregard the symbolical and mythical elements in EMF's fiction and its romance aspects. Although EMF is ultimately the poet and romancer, Thomson overstates his case to the point of implying that EMF is almost entirely a romancer instead of a novelist with an acute critical, comic, realistic sense of character and the social scene— his Jane Austen rather than his Hardy or D. H. Lawrence aspect. EMF also has a George Eliot or Henry James side, with an intense interest in his characters, in their psychic experiences, and in the analysis of moral values. But he is more than a realistic and comic novelist, and in that lies the difference between him and the majority of his contemporaries in fiction. It is this difference which Thomson explains fully. For more on this subject, see my review-article "E. M. Forster: Romancer or Realist?" (1968). For other reviews see: Philip Armato, "Reviews," STUDIES IN SHORT FICTION, VI (Spring 1969), 344–45; Annabel M. Endicott, "The New Books," QUEEN'S QUARTERLY, LXXV (Winter 1968), 762–63; "Language and Literature," CHOICE (Chicago), V (Oct 1968), 962; Karen McLeod, "Reviews," REVIEW OF ENGLISH STUDIES, nsXX (Feb 1969), 111–12; Elgin W. Mellown, "Book Reviews," SOUTH ATLANTIC QUARTERLY, LXVII (Autumn 1968), 712–13; "Passage to the Universe," TIMES LITERARY SUPPLEMENT (Lond), 4 April 1968, p. 335; Wilfred Stone, "Reviews," MODERN LANGUAGE QUARTERLY, XXIX (Dec 1968), 504–8; Richard Wasson, "Book Reviews," JOURNAL OF ENGLISH AND GERMANIC PHILOLOGY, LXVIII (April 1968), 312–15; and "Writer of Romances," ECONOMIST, CCXXVII, Supp (17 April 1968), xviii.]

1250 Trelford, Donald. "From Gladstone Onward, Russell Told Them All," OBSERVER (Lond), 19 Feb. 1967, p. 13.
EMF could not accept Bertrand Russell's credo that men must be made decent now to insure a decent society in the future. EMF sympathized with Russell when the latter was imprisoned for his pacifism in 1918. [Russell's correspondence was prolific and many-sided.]

1251 Trilling, Lionel. "Commentary," THE EXPERIENCE OF LITERATURE: A READER WITH COMMENTARIES (NY: Holt, Rinehart & Winston, 1967), pp. 683–84.
In "The Road from Colonus," Mr. Lucas had an intuitive experience of another mode of reality from his customary one. He understands it, though he is unable to formulate it definitely. He experiences peace and an acceptance of death. Oedipus in OEDIPUS AT COLONUS transcends his pride, anger, and bitterness by his acceptance of death; Mr. Lucas is raised by a like acceptance to something of Oedipus' dignity. Mr. Lucas demonstrates the truth of Helen Schlegel's dictum in *Howards End:* "Death destroys a man, but the idea of death saves him." [Accepts the partial identification of Mr. Lucas with Sophocles' hero rejected by Wilfred Stone, THE CAVE AND THE MOUNTAIN (1966), p. 146.]

1252 Walker, Warren S. TWENTIETH-CENTURY SHORT STORY EX-PLICATION: INTERPRETATIONS, 1900–1966, OF SHORT FICTION SINCE 1800 (Hamden, Conn: Shoe String P, 1967, 2nd ed), pp. 188–93. [Lists criticism of EMF's short stories in books and periodicals. Incorporates 1st ed, 1961; SUPPLEMENT I TO FIRST EDITION, 1963; and SUPPLEMENT TO FIRST EDITION, 1965.]

1253 Woolf, Leonard. DOWNHILL ALL THE WAY: AN AUTOBIOGRA-PHY OF THE YEARS 1919–1939 (Lond: Hogarth P; NY: Harcourt, Brace & World, 1967), pp. 107, 114, 129, 130, 163. [Mostly an account of Woolf's political activities in the years after World War I and his publishing activities as founder and manager of the Hogarth Press (EMF was one of the authors published). In his distress with Fascism as a political evil, Woolf illuminates EMF's similar reactions to the threat posed by Nazism to Western Civilization (see the mostly uncollected "Notes on the Way" from TIME AND TIDE, *Nordic Twilight*, and the first section of *Two Cheers for Democracy*). For Woolf the last phase of Bloomsbury began in 1920 with the founding of the Memoir Club. At each meeting one or more members would read a "memoir" or reminiscence; reader and audience strove to achieve absolute candor in the writing and the discussion following. Through these meetings continuity in the Bloomsbury Circle was assured, although intellectually it still remained fluid and divergent. EMF was a member of the Memoir Club; Quentin, Julian, and Angelica Bell of the next generation; and David Garnett, among others, came into the Group as some of its original members died. Its last meeting was in 1956. Woolf ascribes the death of Bloomsbury to the death of Lytton Strachey in 1932. An indispensable first-hand account of Bloomsbury during the 1920s.]

1254 Yoneda, Kazuhiko. "Essays," E. M. FORSTER, ed by Ineko Kondo (Tokyo: Kenkyusha, 1967), pp. 151–87. The ideas expressed in EMF's essays over forty years remain consistent. His essays reveal an aversion to Christianity, but EMF has a personal religion; he accepts the universe in a mode somewhat similar to the Hindus. He places much faith in the order-producing aspect of personal relationships in our modern chaos. He accepts democracy as preferable to a society emphasizing class distinctions. He is an apostle of culture, he stresses the need for personal and intellectual freedom, and he regards art as another means of ordering chaotic reality. In the essays EMF is a "liberal individualistic humanist." [The essays are discussed in terms of EMF's life, and how his essays grew out of his experiences.] [In Japanese.]

1968

1255 Ackerley, J. R. MY FATHER AND MYSELF (Lond, Sydney, Toronto: The Bodley Head, 1968; NY: Coward, McCann, 1969), p. 132.

[EMF is the friend who counsels Ackerley not to give up the possibility of love in his homosexual encounters, or of response in the individual with whom he may be having a relationship. Ackerley did not need the response and did not necessarily relish it when he aroused it.]

1256 Armytage, W. H. G. "The Disenchanted Mechanophobes in Twentieth Century England," EXTRAPOLATION (College of Wooster), IX (May 1968), 53–59, espec 29–41, 44, 46.

[Descriptive summary of plot and action of "The Machine Stops," in the context of other modern utopian and dystopian works.]

1257 Ashley, Leonard R. N., and Stuart L. Astor. "E. M. Forster," BRITISH SHORT STORIES: CLASSICS AND CRITICISM, ed by Leonard Ashley and Stuart Astor (Englewood Cliffs, NJ: Prentice-Hall, 1968), p. 174.

"The Celestial Omnibus" illustrates EMF's characterization of the INDEPENDENT REVIEW as "decency touched with poetry." The welding of the fantastic to the ideal reveals an ingenuousness more disturbing to critics than to readers. [Story rptd, pp. 175–89; "Reviews and Criticism," with helpful excerpts from EMF's critics, pp. 189–90; and informed biographical sketch, pp. 390–91.]

1258 Barrière, Françoise. "Forster et Ses Morts" (Forster and His Dead), LES LANGUES MODERNES (Paris), LXII (Jan–Feb 1968), 79–86.

The dead in EMF's books are of two kinds: those who die in the course of the novel and those who have posthumous life. EMF prefers violent deaths to natural. Characters often die at a moment when they have become precisely defined in the eyes of one or more individuals; the image of the character as he was when he died is eternally fixed. So in *Howards End* Leonard Bast for the Wilcoxes dies as Scandalous Lover; in *The Longest Journey* Gerald dies as Triumphant Athlete, Mr. Failing as Scorned

Philosopher. The laconic style describing the death is often in contrast to the sharp effects produced by the event. In EMF the dead rebound into life; they guide the living and become reference-points for them; they represent a stable world in contrast to the chaos of life. Death also provides a passage, which we can all learn something of, between the visible and the invisible worlds. As to EMF's images, death is allied to the earth, life to water. The concept of race continuity becomes a victory of sorts over death. Sometimes a character (Rickie in *Journey*) dies that another might live (Stephen) or live in a different way (Mrs. Wilcox, dying in *Howards End*, makes way for Margaret's marriage to Henry Wilcox). Death destroys the body but not that universal element in the spirit of man which returns to the earth and nourishes it. Death takes away personality but liberates the deepest elements in personality. Those who have no profound fibers in their personalities (Mrs. Failing and Mr. Elliot in *Journey*) go into nothingness at death. Fascination with death is not allegorical with EMF. Rather, it expresses his incertitude before the infinite, now that Christian certitude has yielded to modern humanistic existential anxiety. [Interesting though not profound treatment.] [In French.]

1259 Batchelor, J. B. "Feminism in Virginia Woolf," ENGLISH, XVII (Spring 1968), 1–7; rptd in VIRGINIA WOOLF: A COLLECTION OF CRITICAL ESSAYS, ed by Claire Sprague (Englewood Cliffs, NJ: Prentice-Hall, Spectrum Books, 1971), pp. 169–79.

Mrs. Woolf rejects a programmatic feminism as aesthetically unappealing but is feminist in her passionate concern with the nature of women. [Refutes EMF's contention in *Virginia Woolf* that Mrs. Woolf's feminism impaired her writing and that her concern with the status of women was anachronistic.]

1260 Bayley, John. "The 'Irresponsibility' of Jane Austen," CRITICAL ESSAYS ON JANE AUSTEN, ed by B. C. Southam (Lond: Routledge & Kegan Paul, 1968; NY: Barnes & Noble, 1969), pp. 1–20.

In *Aspects of the Novel* EMF contends that George Eliot in MIDDLEMARCH is to be linked with the Tolstoy of WAR AND PEACE. [Bayley challenges this judgment, asserting that Jane Austen is more akin still to Tolstoy by virtue of the complete authority in her novels.]

1261 Beachcroft, T[homas] O. "Edwardian Developments: Who is the Narrator?" THE MODEST ART: A SURVEY OF THE SHORT STORY IN ENGLISH (Lond & NY: Oxford UP, 1968), pp. 149–61, espec 157–58.

EMF's stories anticipate the intense stories of Katherine Mansfield. In "Other Kingdom" EMF changes a persecuted girl into a dryad; Katherine Mansfield would have shown her only as longing to be thus transformed.

EMF's worlds of fantasy are more allegorical than those of Beerbohm or Saki. "The Celestial Omnibus" is characteristic of EMF in this genre, with its contrast between the boy's imaginative encounters with literature and the stodginess of the adults who surround him. [Useful for placing EMF's stories in context of the English short story as a whole.]

1262 Bell, Quentin. "Introductory," "Bloomsbury before 1914," "The War," "The Character of Bloomsbury," BLOOMSBURY (Lond: Weidenfeld & Nicolson, Pageant of History, 1968; NY: Basic Books, 1969), pp. 9–22, espec 14–16; 23–65, espec 50; 66–82, espec 70–71; 103–18, espec 106.

EMF is on the fringes of Bloomsbury, though he was a member of the postwar "Memoir Club." Prior to 1910 the members of the Bloomsbury circle had not produced much, except for EMF and Roger Fry. [The uneasy relationship of EMF with D. H. Lawrence is described, one that did not last long and was the result of "mutual admiration and mutual exasperation."] EMF recognized the menace of irrational forces and the violence underlying the forms of civilization more than did most of his Bloomsbury friends. He is also more reverent and optimistic than they, despite his recognition of these darker forces. EMF and his friends would agree, however, that the rational faculties can order and contain these forces. [Bell's book is an important analysis of the Bloomsbury temper and traits by one who knew it from the inside (Bell is Virginia Woolf's nephew and was to write her biography, VIRGINIA WOOLF: A BIOGRAPHY, 1972).] The common attitude towards life held by Bloomsbury members was complex; it involved an irreverence toward the Victorian past, a moral seriousness deriving from the past, a questioning approach to all absolute systems of value, a cherishing of friendship and personal relations, and a skepticism originating in large part from G. E. Moore. Its radical skepticism and its criticism of tradition are Bloomsbury's most positive contributions; its tendency to dwell on the formalities of life rather than its essential issues is its greatest weakness. The rationalistic humanism of Bloomsbury ceased to be influential (and Bloomsbury came to an end) with the death of Lytton Strachey (1932), the Spanish Civil War (1936–1938), and the rise to power of the Nazis. [Many indispensable pictures, prints, and photographs; this small book does more to capture the essence of Bloomsbury than J. K. Johnstone's more ambitious but pedestrian THE BLOOMSBURY GROUP (1954).]

1263 Brander, Laurence. E. M. FORSTER: A CRITICAL STUDY (Lond: Rupert Hart-Davis, 1968; Lewisburg, Pa: Bucknell UP, 1970).

Where Angels Fear to Tread is "gay fun," and Philip Herriton therein is inhibited from making love to Caroline Abbott at the end because she has just shown herself sexually drawn to an Italian peasant. [*Angels* is a serious book, and Philip is not this priggish.] *A Room with a View* would have been a slight performance without Mr. Emerson. [He registers far less decisively than the great comic creations, Cecil Vyse and Charlotte Bartlett.] Mrs. Elliot in *The Longest Journey* is "colourless and lacks taste." Agnes Pembroke reaches "tragic proportions" late in the novel, and Rickie Elliot is "the average untruthful man." [These observations on *Journey* are, at best, inexact.] Friendship and love are the themes of *A Passage to India*, and Adela Quested is to be equated with the Schlegel sisters in *Howards End*. All the characters in *Passage*, except Mrs. Moore and Fielding, are "paper" people; the events of the arrest and trial are improbable and devoid of reality; the falseness in the English characters contributes to the convincing nature of EMF's abstract and symbolic ideas by way of contrast; and Fielding, married, loses EMF's approval. [None of these judgments on *Passage* is capable of being fully substantiated if one considers the book as a total configuration.] [Only a sampling of the contents of this book is possible because it adds so little to our understanding of EMF. The book is mostly descriptive; the method is primarily that of paraphrase and plot summary. Speculative comment about the novels, the man, and his ideas is mostly absent. There is little intellectual analysis, and the discourse seldom rises to an abstract level of discussion. At best, the book reveals an impressionistically sensitive mind; at worst, a disorderly one. The book provides a rudimentary, but scarcely reliable, introduction to EMF. Select bibliography. Reviews: "Aspects of E. M. Forster," TIMES LITERARY SUPPLEMENT (Lond), 18 July 1968, p. 754; Lewis Bates, "Eminent Edwardian," PUNCH, CCLIV (12 June 1968), 863; Frederick P. W. McDowell, "Recent Books on Forster and on Bloomsbury," ENGLISH LITERATURE IN TRANSITION, XII: 3 (1969), 135–50; Edward Thomas (Entry No. 1308); and Stephen Wall (Entry No. 1312).]

1264 Brooke, Rupert. THE LETTERS OF RUPERT BROOKE, ed by Geoffrey Keynes (Lond: Faber; NY: Harcourt, Brace & World, 1968), pp. 172, 173, 190, 198, 229*n*, 261, 385, 404, 674.

[Numerous references to EMF.] Letter to Erica Cotterill (July 1909), She must read G. E. Moore's PRINCIPIA ETHICA very slowly and carefully; "the best story ever written is in the July ENGLISH REVIEW, called *Other Kingdom*, by E. M. Forster"; *A Room with a View* is very good but lighter than the other books recommended to read. Letter to Mrs. Brooke (27 Nov 1909), [He is tired and bad-tempered because of the number of people with whom he has been dining lately—Jacques Raverat, Justin, H. F. Garrett, Bob Trevelyan, Eddie Marsh, EMF, Margery and Bryn Olivier, A. Y. Campbell.] Letter to Katherine Cox (18 March 1910), Give "love to the spot by the *Loggia dei Lanzi* where one Italian stabbed another, and Miss Somebody fainted into George's (was it George's?) arms" [reference to *Room*]. Letter to Mrs. Brooke (3 Nov 1910), EMF has been staying two nights; a charming person, "an old King's man of 27 or 28"; *Howards End* is commendable. Letter to A. F. Scholfield (30 Sept 1912), The craze now going among intellectuals for the East—Goldsworthy Lowes Dickinson, EMF, and now Scholfield himself is deplorable; "Why should King's be stripped in this way?" Letter to Katherine Cox (19–24 March [Postmark: 6 April 1915]): Mentions WORKING MEN'S COLLEGE JOURNAL, with lecture by EMF in it ["The Function of Literature in War-Time"]; EMF is typical of the liberal who is aloof from, or critical of, the war; EMF is on the outside of things, and war brings out such "exteriority" in well-meaning non-combatants; EMF does not realize that the nobilities he wishes for are more readily attained in war than in peace.

1265 Daiches, David. "The Twentieth-Century Novel," A CRITICAL HISTORY OF ENGLISH LITERATURE (Lond: Secker & Warburg, 2nd ed, 1968; NY: Ronald P, 1970), pp. 1152–78, espec 1155, 1158–60; also 1013 (pagination is NY ed); lst ed, 1960, has no significant references to EMF.
EMF's chief theme is human relationships (after he exhausted it, he wrote no more fiction). EMF is the exponent of the liberal imagination (as it was at a historic moment and as it contains something permanent). He inherits a nineteenth-century religious benevolence, and he is a literary artist with a strong sense of aesthetic form. *The Longest Journey* dramatizes life and death in human relationships and satirizes conformity and respectability, *A Room with a View* contrasts conformist England with passionate Italy, and *Howards End* explores inward feeling versus outward behavior. The complexities in *Howards End* are resolved too easily and too aesthetically; an impression of evasiveness results. In *A Passage to India*, EMF as the English liberal humanist on the side of Indian independence is also the "connoisseur of human littleness and absurdity." His comic mysticism undercuts the tragic aspects of the book. He does not push his insights far enough, even in *Passage*, his masterpiece. His novels are unsatisfactory but also substantial in revealing the English liberal imagination at its best. The conflict between humanity and honesty is interesting in his books: the valuation of cultivation versus the realization of its cost.

1266 Das, Gaur Kishore. "Call Me An Unbeliever: Interview with E. M. Forster," STATESMAN (Delhi), 23 Sept 1968, p. 6
EMF denied he was interested in India politically before he had contact about 1907 with Syed Ross Masood; he did not meet Gokhale, or Edwin Montagu (spokesmen for India before World War I). EMF remarked that *A Passage to India* attracted little attention when it was published. His own trend, he says, has been toward matters other than political. EMF agreed that Godbole has the shrewdness and power of a "Chitpavan Brahmin" but maintained that Godbole had no original. [For evidence to the contrary, see Wilfred Stone, THE CAVE AND THE MOUNTAIN (1966), p. 319n.] EMF never

met anyone like him, and he was an entirely created character. Though Sir Malcolm Darling's Indian social sympathies were similar to Fielding's, EMF did not have Darling in mind when he conceived Fielding. EMF was influenced in his non-belief by Hugh Meredith. He would regard himself as a non-believer rather than an unbeliever. He does not believe in Krishna any more than in anyone else but likes things about Krishna worship.

1267 Das, G. K. "Shonfield and Forster's India: A Controversial Exchange," ENCOUNTER (Lond), XXX (June 1968), 95.

The politics presented in *A Passage to India* are not distortions of the facts for the novel's period of time, and the spirit of understanding between the races was lacking in the way that EMF sees it. The reforms made in the Indianization of the Civil Service and other administrative improvements came too late to undo the damage done by the unimaginative rule of the British Raj in the earlier twentieth century. [Challenges the assumptions made by Andrew Shonfield in "The Politics of Forster's India," ENCOUNTER (Jan 1968), 62–69.]

1268 Decap, Roger. "Un Roman Pascalien: *A Passage to India* de E. M. Forster" (A Pascal-like novel: E. M. Forster's *A Passage to India*), CALIBAN (Toulouse), V (Jan 1968), 103–28.

The direction of *A Passage to India* is metaphysical, and the book demonstrates that the mystery of the universe is best related to, or subsumed by, mystical experience. The theme of separation and disunity and the theme of the transcendence of separateness in mystical experience are central to the book. *Passage* shows the falseness of a God based upon human hopes and aspirations; the prideful individual can obtain no notion of religious truth or understanding (a Pascalian concept). *Passage* also shows the fallacy of trying to replace God or religious experience with intellectual formulations such as humanism (see Fielding's ideas). They are inadequate or irrelevant. The novel accomplishes the humiliation of the self-centered individual and of the anthropomorphic god. The individual as such is not important nor can nature be fully known. The absence of God in this world presupposes his presence in another; this is the gist of Godbole's views. Achieving a religion not susceptible to logical formulation or amenable to human wish-fulfillment—implied in the Hindu distortion of the phrase "God si love"—is the final thrust of *Passage* and of EMF's own point of view. Those who laugh at Godbole as representative of mystical truth reveal their own limitations and enslavement to decorum. Godbolean mysticism is the only possible solution to the problems explored in the novel, which stresses the falsity of hope but the need for hopefulness. [Important in emphasizing the significance of "Temple."] [In French.]

1269 Fagan, B. W. "Forster and His Publishers," BOOKSELLER, no. 3288 (28 Dec 1968), 2070–72; rptd in ASPECTS OF E. M. FORSTER, ed by Oliver Stallybrass (NY: Harcourt, Brace & World; Lond: Edward Arnold, 1969), pp. 93–98.

[Informative article, coming out of thirty years association (from 1930 to 1960) as EMF's publisher. Fagan's conclusion: "Never was a mind more acute allied with a spirit more modest, more natural, more unassuming, more unpompous." EMF was always informal and considerate in his visits and arrangements. Recounts the libel action involving the first ed of *Abinger Harvest.* "A Flood in the Office" was reprinted at Fagan's suggestion, without his or EMF's knowledge that the book under review, THE NILE PROJECTS by Sir William Willcocks, had been successfully prosecuted for libel by Sir Murdoch MacDonald. The first ed of *Abinger* had to be withdrawn, and later eds have appeared without the offending essay.]

1270 Fasanelli, James A. "Berenson without Baedeker: Some Notes on His American Sources," HARVARD LIBRARY BULLETIN, XVI (April 1968), 156–66.

Lucy Honeychurch (*A Room with a View*) has been influenced by Bernhard Berenson's FLORENTINE PAINTERS (either directly or indirectly; she appreciates paintings without the help of a Baedeker). She has appropriated Berenson's term "tactile values"; she has become aware of their significance in the appreciation of painting in terms of touch. EMF's use of Berenson's term indicates how pervasive his influence had become in the Edwardian era.

1271 Fleishman, Avrom. CONRAD'S POLITICS: COMMUNITY AND ANARCHY IN THE FICTION OF JOSEPH CONRAD (Baltimore: Johns Hopkins P, 1967; Lond: Oxford UP, 1968), p. 62.

From Coleridge largely descends the "organicist social criticism" that was to inform the work of modern writers like Conrad, Lawrence, and EMF.

1272 Furbank, P. N. "Tribute to Forster," TIMES (Lond), 28 Dec 1968, p. 15.

The prevailing note in the contributions to the volume is gratitude rather than awe. Possibly EMF could have demonstrated his real powers if he had been engaged in more significant debates than his life afforded him. He had an expertise in controversy that he never fully realized. World War I was an oppressive influence and drove him back to privacy. EMF was fitted by temperament to be a political teacher, but he lacked a philosophy of the state. He did the next best—and an excellent—thing; he addressed himself to defining his private situation *vis-à-vis* the state's pretensions. If this is a limitation it defines his range. He is uncomfortable with his political position, but has had, ironically, a tremendous indirect political influence. Another aspect of his genius is his compulsion to project himself into another person when writing an essay or review (this is not the main duty of the educated man, but it is his first). EMF may have had only one thing to say, but he has dedicated himself to saying it, even at the risk of manipulating his materials. Such manipulation is "the calculation of a talent knowing its limitations, in the service of a genius which made no compromises at all." The talent is great, as in his modulation of style; it enables him to adjust delicately large masses of material "so that consonances and cross-perspectives breed." His intrusions as narrator—his apparent compromises with technique—signalize his artistic integrity. He does not want his characters to have too much independence; he wants, instead, to indicate clearly their strangeness. In *A Passage to India* people are mysterious in the sense that their feelings are more concrete than their physical identities and have a destiny and posterity of their own (see Ralph Moore's magical appearance at the end of *Passage* in the succession of his mother, an appearance that continues the notion that feeling is paramount and permanent). The young EMF's truest likeness is in Ralph Moore, not in Rickie Elliot. [Review-essay on ASPECTS OF E. M. FORSTER, ed by Oliver Stallybrass (1969). A profound and provocative article.]

1273 Godfrey, Denis. E. M. FORSTER'S OTHER KINGDOM (Edinburgh & Lond: Oliver & Boyd; NY: Barnes & Noble, 1968).
In EMF the visionary impulse is primary: the influence of the "unseen" world, the intuitive, the spiritual, the intangible upon his characters from within and without. [The point is an obvious one. Godfrey, moreover, overlooks the paradoxical basis of EMF's art. For EMF the unseen is valued only so long as it is made firm by the seen. Godfrey operates at the level of statement and simplified idea, with the result that he fails to consider the other components of EMF's fiction, such as symbolism, myth, pattern, structure, irony, and style. His method relies almost exclusively upon synopsis and paraphrase. Some of his interpretations are questionable: the assertion that Mrs. Moore is less endowed spiritually than Mrs. Wilcox, and Aziz's alleged sensitivity to the unseen. To date, the poorest book on EMF. Select bibliography. Reviews: "Aspects of E. M. Forster," TIMES LITERARY SUPPLEMENT (Lond), 18 July 1968, p. 754; James Ginden, "Recent Books on Modern Fiction: British," MODERN FICTION STUDIES, XV (Summer 1969), 316; John Gray, "Author as Mystic," BOOKS AND BOOKMEN, XIII (Aug 1968), 17; Daniel J. Leary, "A Nonagenarian's Threefold Philosophy," SATURDAY REVIEW (NY), LII (15 Feb 1969), 49, 106; James McConkey, "Reviews," MODERN LANGUAGE QUARTERLY, XXX (June 1969), 305–7; Frederick P. W. McDowell, "Recent Books on Forster and on Bloomsbury," ENGLISH LITERATURE IN TRANSITION, XII: 3 (1969), 135–50; Karen McLeod, "Reviews," REVIEW OF ENGLISH STUDIES, nsXX (Feb 1969), 111–12; Devendra P. Varma, "Book Reviews," DALHOUSIE REVIEW, XLIX (Spring 1969), 123–25; and Stephen Wall (Entry No. 1312).]

1274 Heilbrun, Carolyn G. "The Bloomsbury Group," MIDWAY (Chicago), IX:ii (1968), 71–85; rptd, much rvd and enlg, in TOWARD A RECOGNITION OF ANDROGYNY (NY: Knopf, 1973), pp. 116–67, espec 134–36; as TOWARDS ANDROGYNY: ASPECTS OF MALE AND FEMALE IN LITERATURE (Lond: Gollancz, 1973).

Reason which excludes violence but not passion was possible in the Bloomsbury Group because masculinity was infused, or actually merged, with femininity. The ideal sought was androgynous; it scorned the assertive masculinity of the Victorian Age, and it revered love of any kind (heterosexual, homosexual, or whatever) wherever it was found, or as EMF expresses it in the concluding chapter to *Howards End*, "eternal differences." The excellence of Bloomsbury lay partly in the art of conversation, but mostly in what it accomplished in various fields. [Excellent article.]

1275 Holroyd, Michael. LYTTON STRACHEY: A CRITICAL BIOGRAPHY, Vol II: THE YEARS OF ACHIEVEMENT 1910–1932 (Lond: Heinemann; NY: Holt, Rinehart & Winston, 1968), pp. 80, 86, 106, 141*n*, 145, 149, 370, 457, 486, 515, 517, 520, 531–32, 570, 575, 614, 645–46, 655, 656; most of these materials on EMF are in Michael Holroyd, LYTTON STRACHEY: A BIOGRAPHY (Harmondsworth, Middlesex & Baltimore: Penguin Books, 1971; Lond: Heinemann 1973).

[Bloomsbury expands to include the younger generation; a division takes place between those who frequented Angelica Bell's at No. 8, Fitzroy Street and those who frequented the Woolfs' at Tavistock Square after their return to London from Richmond in 1924. The events and personalities in this volume provide the ambience of EMF after 1910. He is a background presence in Strachey's life, not unlike the "guardian" figures of his own novels. He was a frequent visitor at Ham Spray house as Strachey's guest (see also CARRINGTON: LETTERS AND EXTRACTS FROM HER DIARIES, 1970).] Strachey is disillusioned with EMF's high estimate of pension life in Italy. At the Savile Club in 1914 Strachey described EMF as "a mediocre man" but as one who knows it or suspects it (he is treated rudely by the waiters and is not really admired by middle-class dowagers). EMF wants to read Strachey's "Manning" (EMINENT VICTORIANS) so that he won't go mad (letter, 17 May 1915). Strachey's sketch of EMF at Tidmarsh in 1919 streses "his 'curious triangular face, and a mind, somehow, exactly fitting.'" EMF has his differences with the brusque younger generation, represented by Carrington's admirer, Ralph Partridge, who regards EMF as unduly involved with his mother and aunts and wanting friendship without intimacy. Strachey likes *Aspects of the Novel* less well than Edwin Muir's THE STRUCTURE OF THE NOVEL. EMF reads two "improper" stories to Strachey and Carrington. [Stories probably similar to those in *The Life to Come*.] EMF has a favorable opinion of Strachey's ELIZABETH AND ESSEX. EMF introduced Strachey to "a human weasel" (Strachey's words), the Italian novelist, Alberto Moravia, who writes novels too shocking to translate.

1276 Hynes, Samuel. THE EDWARDIAN TURN OF MIND (Princeton: Princeton UP, 1968), pp. 62, 146–47, 153, 328; passim.
EMF is indicative of the decline of realism in art and literature in the Edwardian age; he turned to the intelligentsia away from concern with the masses. Fantasy and mythic stories were common literary modes; scientific romances were really anti-scientific and exercises in fantasy, as in "The Machine Stops." Both H. G. Wells and EMF were anti-scientific in two ways: they liberated the imagination by repealing scientific laws, and they demonstrated the inadequacy of science to accomplish human happiness. EMF's judgment of Edward Carpenter is definitive; he will not have much immortality, but he will be remembered by students of the age as a pioneer. In fact, Carpenter was probably formative upon EMF, with his emphasis on tolerance and personal relations; also Carpenter in his INTERMEDIATE SEX anticipated EMF's Englishman of the undeveloped heart. Carpenter is among the ancestors of Bloomsbury with his "religion of art, intelligence, and human relationships that was born in Edwardian London and died in the Second World War." [Interesting incidental commentary and valuable for defining EMF's Edwardian background. Carpenter must also have encouraged EMF to confront his own homosexuality; see "Terminal Note," *Maurice* (1971).]

1277 Langbaum, Robert. "A New Look at E. M. Forster," SOUTHERN REVIEW, nsIV (Winter 1968), 33–49; rptd, in rvd form, in THE MODERN SPIRIT: ESSAYS ON THE CONTINUITY OF NINETEENTH AND TWENTIETH CENTURY LITERATURE (NY: Oxford UP; Lond: Chatto & Windus, 1970), pp. 127–46; extract rptd in CONTEMPORARY LITERARY CRITICISM, ed by Carolyn Riley (Detroit: Gale Research Co., 1973), I, 107.
EMF wrote two masterpieces, *Where Angels Fear to Tread* and *A Passage to India*. *Angels* is "a perfect little comedy of manners," and critics too often overlook its comic aspects. EMF lacks the same clear standards that Jane Austen had, and his irony plays over all the characters and all the alternatives proposed to middle-class standards. Because he lacks precise standards, he becomes unduly concerned with a mystical "reality" lying behind the shifting surfaces of experience. In *Passage* there is a concern with three different cultures, in this ascending order of significance: European Christianity, emphasizing will and order; the Moslem, emphasizing emotion and erotic love; and the Hindu, emphasizing disorder and impassivity. The last has "a comprehensiveness that dissolves distinctions and manifests itself as nothingness." As for Hinduism, neither EMF nor his chief character Fielding can accept it completely, although EMF appreci-

ates its inclusiveness. In *Angels* (as in the other novels) there are three grades of Englishmen: Philistines, who never see beyond middle-class values; the tourists or sensitives, who try to break away from these values but cannot quite do so; and the authentic people, who are, or become, what they ought to be. In *Angels* Gino Carella is authentic because of his mixed qualities and because he successfully evokes erotic force (only in *Passage* is this force ever again successfully evoked). The sensitives (Philip Herriton and Caroline Abbott) are as potentially destructive in their transcendentalizing tendencies as Harriet Herriton is in her blindness. [Questionable.] Wilfred Stone in THE CAVE AND THE MOUNTAIN (1966) incorrectly asserts that EMF reaches the prophetic in this book but correctly says that the next three novels are experiments in self-confidence [to me a doubtful judgment], as EMF peers out at the world from his ivory tower of pure speculation and sensibility. In *The Longest Journey*, despite the tone of ironic realism, Rickie Elliot's antagonists are unconvincing because they are melodramatic in essence; and Stephen Wonham is a failure because only his brutality registers, not his erotic force. *Journey* is successful in its *Bildungsroman* aspect as it records Rickie's adjustments, and failures to adjust, to his circumstances. The Schlegels in *Howards End* are classless representatives of the tourist mentality. The novel fails because eroticism is not successfully evoked. [A frequently made, but not entirely valid judgment.] Personal connections in this novel can only be interpreted allegorically and cannot be seen as actual relationships between people. Ruth Wilcox is a successfully envisaged character since she carries her own atmosphere with her and suggests an order of existence completely different from any other found in the novel. The Schlegel culture is feminine and feminized, and as Stone says, Helen's child (the heir of England) will turn out only to be another Tibby Schlegel. [Such judgment overlooks Margaret's highly critical view of Tibby, and her desire to achieve a culture devoid both of brutality and effeteness.]

Passage is the most successful novel because it is set in a larger universe. Here EMF's former themes are played out to their conclusion: the comedy of manners (it now becomes sinister and sardonic), the romantic belief in experience and personal relations (these now take us only so far), the liberal search for a just political order (reality and justice can be no further fused than they are in Hinduism, wherein all their external characteristics are softened). "Temple" is integral to the novel and the consummation of its dramatic and thematic lines. Hindu myth gives the best explanation, in its blurring of distinctions, of the formlessness of reality and becomes the human equivalent of the experience in the Caves. The mythic aspect of the book and the "Temple" sequence are efficacious, especially as they record the transformation of Mrs. Moore into a reconciling agent. Frederick C. Crews (E. M. FORSTER: THE PERILS OF HUMANISM [1962]) wrongly main-

tains that the ending is pessimistic. We gather from it "the fortifying pleasure of seeing all things in their due place, of understanding the validity of
things because we understand the limits of their validity." EMF's vision of
reality is not completely nihilistic; rather, "the very void projected by the
echo is a spiritual presence." [A review-essay of Stone's THE CAVE AND THE
MOUNTAIN (1966), but in reality an independent essay full of useful and
challenging insights.]

1278 Lehmann, John. A NEST OF TIGERS: EDITH, OSBERT AND SA-
CHEVERELL SITWELL IN THEIR TIMES (Lond: Macmillan; Boston: Little, Brown, 1968), pp. 62, 199.
[EMF was part of Bloomsbury background of the Sitwells' London in the
1920s. EMF is appreciative of Lehmann's "account of that immortal evening at the Churchill Club" when, in the autumn of 1944, Edith Sitwell read
"Still Falls the Rain" during a doodle-bug raid.]

1279 Lester, John A. JOURNEY THROUGH DESPAIR 1880–1914:
TRANSFORMATIONS IN BRITISH LITERARY CULTURE (Princeton:
Princeton UP, 1968; Oxford: Oxford UP, 1969), pp. 11, 21, 107,
168, 186, 187.
As a transitional figure between the Victorian and the modern age, EMF
throws light on the intellectual climate of Edwardian England. *The Longest
Journey* expresses in part the need for women's freedom. "What I Believe"
(*Two Cheers for Democracy*) shows the difficulty involved in, and the necessity for, believing in some eternality of truth. "Art for Art's Sake" (*Two
Cheers*) shows art to be an "orderly product." *Aspects of the Novel* shows
the coexistence in our lives of a "life in time" and a "life by values"; the
latter argues the influence of an unseen world beyond the seen. *Journey*
asserts the importance of "the symbolic moment" and its ecstatic character
(it is one way of escaping the flux of existence). Joseph Conrad would also
"impose firm subjective order on life." "Joseph Conrad: A Note" (*Abinger
Harvest*) asserts lack of creed in Conrad [refuted].

1280 Levine, June Perry. "E. M. Forster's *A Passage to India:*
Creation and Criticism," DISSERTATION ABSTRACTS, XXVIII (1968),
3189A–3190A. Unpublished dissertation, University of Nebraska,
1967; rvd as CREATION AND CRITICISM: "A PASSAGE TO INDIA" (Lincoln: University of Nebraska P, 1971; Lond: Chatto & Windus,
1972).

1281 McDowell, Frederick P. W. "E. M. Forster: Romancer or
Realist?" ENGLISH LITERATURE IN TRANSITION, XI:2 (1968), 103–22.
[Review-essay on Norman Kelvin's E. M. FORSTER (1967) and George H.
Thomson's THE FICTION OF E. M. FORSTER (1967). Explores question raised

by Thomson as to whether EMF is romancer or realist. Despite excellence of his critique, Thomson goes too far in claiming that EMF is a romancer; however, he does give convincing data for rejecting the exclusively realistic appraisal of the fiction. (see F. R. Leavis, "E. M. Forster" [1938] or John Harvey, "Imagination and Moral Theme in *The Longest Journey*" [1956]).]

1282 Moody, Phillipa. A CRITICAL COMMENTARY ON E. M. FORSTER'S "A PASSAGE TO INDIA" (Lond: Macmillan; NY: St. Martin's P, Macmillan Critical Commentaries, 1968).

EMF celebrates in *A Passage to India* the dull average aspects of life that are in reality anything but dull, as his characters are goaded into awareness. In Indians contrasted with Englishmen, EMF demonstrates the over-developed heart and the undeveloped, respectively. The Indians are too demonstrative and offer no full release for the inhibitions of the English. The Indians, as EMF see them, are more complicated than the English. Divisions between Indians and English and between Muslim and Hindu are cultural; between the Hindus they are social and religious (Brahman and non-Brahman). In *Passage*, Islam is a personal religion, precisely because its God is less personal than the God of Christianity; and the Mosque stands for the developed heart. EMF is drawn to Hinduism despite its untidiness; for the novel, Hinduism is less a complex religion than "a social expression of the true India." [A questionable judgment.] In *Passage* there are two conflicting voices: one finds life endlessly significant; one finds nothing that is significant. EMF is conscious of a reverence for life in India, though this life is not only human. The conditions surrounding life there make it precarious (the forces making for life and anti-life, vision and anti-vision are closely intertwined).

In "Mosque" a threefold point of view is developed characterizing *Passage* as a whole: the view from outside (the realistic, concentrating on Indian muddle), the view from the inside (the romantic, sensitive to Indian mystery), and the view from "the overarching sky" (which combines the two viewpoints at a distance). Though muddle vitiates personal and social relationships and is common in India, Indian muddle—because it is spontaneous—is preferable to British order, which is bureaucratic. The differences between the best representatives of the two races are temperamental. Thus Aziz has impulsiveness without patience, and Fielding has patience without impulsiveness. Moments of vision in the novel are validated or invalidated by the overarching sky. India both promotes aspiration toward God and thwarts it. In "Caves" the line between everything and nothing is thin. Adela Quested's experience in the Caves is less extreme than Mrs. Moore's because it is still personal. Mrs. Moore's vision is neither to be considered as final nor to be dismissed. Aziz is blind to Adela's sacrifice in her recantation and to Fielding's in his taking up Aziz's cause. In *Passage* characters who are lovable (Aziz) oppose those who are true (Adela, Fielding); both sorts have their virtues and their limitations.

"Temple" is inadequate as a close to *Passage*. It is descriptive rather than dramatic; and the meetings between Aziz and Fielding to which it leads are too brief. EMF does not fully achieve his intention of attaining an expanding perspective, transcending the nihilism of the Cave's echo. Hinduism and India preserve a precarious balance between everything and nothing (this the Europeans and Aziz fail to achieve). In "Temple" the vision is communal and positive (at the end the lovable and the true are nearer than before), but this vision is not so convincing as the negative vision that is less extrinsic and more fully part of us. EMF is not fully able to express the inexpressible; he vacillates between rhetoric and flippancy, and an uncertainty of tone results. EMF is not qualified by temperament to capture a religious experience, and he does better when he tries to express the ineffable through the aesthetic vision. [These criticisms reveal an incomprehension of EMF's aims and achievements in "Temple" and a patronizing tone; Moody follows critics like Reuben Brower, Frederick C. Crews, and David Shusterman who downgrade this part of the novel.] Characters are not big enough for their functions; Mrs. Moore and Godbole, for instance, are seen from the outside only. [A fallacious judgment, following Lionel Trilling in E. M. FORSTER (1943).] As a "liberal novelist," EMF expands our awareness of life's complexities to the extent that all solutions seem inadequate. [Bibliography. Some perceptive commentary, but the book as a whole fails to reach the standard of the best essay and book treatments of *Passage*.]

1283 Moraes, Dom. MY SON'S FATHER: A POET'S AUTOBIOGRAPHY, (Lond: Secker & Warburg, 1968; NY: Macmillan, 1969), pp. 126–27 (NY ed).
[Moraes met EMF through Stephen Spender, and found him to be "a small, comfortably plump man, with a grey moustache in a face which, like that of some intelligent hare, was both inquisitive and withdrawn." In conversation he advanced and withdrew recurrently. Notes his gentleness, tact, and consideration. EMF was diffident about poetry in general and Moraes's in particular.]

1284 Moran, Ronald. " 'Come, Come,' 'Boum, Boum,' 'Easy' Rhythm in E. M. Forster's *A Passage to India*," BALL STATE UNIVERSITY FORUM, IX (Spring 1968), 3–9.
[Traces the appearance of the phrases "Come, Come" and "Boum, Boum," at various points in the novel and rather too easily equates them in significance. An elementary and unoriginal essay.]

1285 Mortimer, Raymond. "E. M. Forster: The Art of Being Individual," SUNDAY TIMES (Lond), 29 Dec 1968, p. 51.

At ninety EMF is still in fine fettle; recently he spent a whole night, with equanimity, locked in Cambridge Guildhall after a concert, and he also took his first flight in a glider. He is elusive and peers at life from an unusual angle. EMF enjoyed Marx Brothers films, though he had not thought he would; earlier EMF had said as only he could say, "I don't care for the Marx brothers: one wouldn't like to meet them, if one were mad." [Many other EMF sayings quoted.] EMF is unpredictable in temper, inconspicuous in appearance. He is really unworldly; he does not despise comfort but does not seek luxury. He is munificent to his friends, King's College, and the London library; he loves Cambridge, not only for its high thinking and beauty but also for its plain living. EMF is reserved rather than shy; he is diffident, considerate, assuming good manners from others, but he is not humble. Humor is constant in his speech. He reveals himself most fully in *The Hill of Devi.* As for ASPECTS OF E. M. FORSTER (ed by Oliver Stallybrass), the essays are illuminating, but unfortunately the book lacks contributions by Leonard Woolf, John Morris, W. H. Auden, Christopher Isherwood, and Glenway Wescott. EMF's writings on moral and political issues have spread his influence. Works of biography and criticism, when truly memorable, like EMF's, spring from the subconscious, as do other forms such as the novel and poem. In connection with Stallybrass's "Forster's Wobblings: The Manuscripts of *A Passage to India*" (1969), EMF's revisions are important to an understanding of *A Passage to India.* [In part a review-essay of ASPECTS OF E. M. FORSTER, ed by Oliver Stallybrass (1969). Affectionate and illuminating reminiscences and character analysis by a Bloomsbury associate.]

1286 Mukherjee, Asim Kumar. "The Split Personality of E. M. Forster," QUEST (Bombay), No. 56 (Winter 1968), 49–55.
The essential EMF is "classical," interested in style, and revealing a remarkable emotional poise and ironic stance. Romantic emotionalism, utopian and Platonic idealism, and visionary experience are foreign to his genius. EMF expresses himself more memorably as a satirist of the middle class than as a romantic sensibility. The shallow Hellenism derived from King's College, Cambridge, "debauched" his sensibility. As realist, he was a formidable critic of the English middle class and imperialism; as an idealist, he subverted the structure and the values present in his novels. In *A Passage to India* Mrs. Moore's transcendent influence is only vaguely realized and is philosophically suspect. Fielding, who represents an enlightened rationalism, is undercut by his affection for the "impulsive, headstrong, mendacious and vulgar" Aziz. [Discusses the "split" in EMF observed by F. R. Leavis, Virginia Woolf, Walter Allen, and others, with the implied judgment that the poetry does not "work" in EMF's novels; but unlike these critics, finds *Passage* vitiated by the same "split." This article is overstated and asserts

its contentions without proving them. Interpretation of *Passage* is idiosyncratic and unjustified by novel's context and the general consensus of critics.]

1287 Nelson, Harland. "Shonfield and Forster's India: A Controversial Exchange," ENCOUNTER (Lond), XXX (June 1968), 95.
A Passage to India is more than a political novel, or it is only incidentally political. The English and Indian characters are not distortions; EMF was within his rights as artist to place a Moslem at the center of the novel, and "Temple" restores the balance and gives Hinduism its preeminent position in the novel. [Argues against the explicit political criticism of *Passage* presented by Andrew Shonfield in "The Politics of Forster's India."]

1288 Orwell, George [pseud of Eric Blair]. THE COLLECTED ESSAYS, JOURNALISM AND LETTERS OF GEORGE ORWELL, 4 vols, ed by Sonia Orwell and Ian Angus (NY: Harcourt, Brace & World; Lond: Secker & Warburg, 1968).
[Rpts "Some Recent Novels" (1936) and "Inside the Whale" (1940), Vol I; "Rudyard Kipling" (1942), Vol II; "As I Please" (1944), Vol III; and "Through a Glass, Rosily" (1945) Vol IV; see entries for these years. Many other scattered references to EMF.]

1289 Panichas, George A. "Introduction," PROMISE OF GREATNESS: THE WAR OF 1914–1918 (NY: John Day, 1968), pp. v–xxxvi, espec xxvii; rptd as "Promise of Greatness: The War of 1914–1918," THE REVERENT DISCIPLINE: ESSAYS IN LITERARY CRITICISM AND CULTURE (Knoxville: University of Tennessee P, 1974), pp. 34–53, espec 45.
Mrs. Moore's intuitions in the Marabar Caves (*A Passage to India*) that pathos, piety, courage, and filth are identical and that everything exists but that nothing has value reflect, unforgettably, the collapse of the discriminating, civilizing faculty during the 1914–1918 war, the recrudescence of barbarism as a continually threatening influence, and the tenuous and possible worthlessness of civilization in a world of force.

1290 Parker, G. B. "Introduction," E. M. FORSTER SELECTED WRITINGS, ed by G. B. Parker (Lond: Heinemann Education Books, The Twentieth Century Series, 1968), pp. ix–xv.
EMF voiced his fears for the individual's possible loss of liberty before Lawrence or Orwell did. EMF's fears derive from the omnipresent influence of the public school ethos upon the character of the middle- and upper-class Englishman. In the personal and social spheres, the influence of the matriarchy was also oppressive. EMF's constant subject is the exposure of pretense and hollowness and the championing of spontaneous emo-

tion. EMF conceives of the individual in "What I Believe" (*Two Cheers for Democracy*) as a creative being rather than as a passive entity. The conscientious attempt to live creatively is all-important; the failure to achieve such an ambition is irrelevant. [Biographical Note. Rpts the following—from *Abinger Harvest*, "Notes on the English Character," "Me, Them and You," "My Wood," "Liberty in England," "Malcolnia Shops," "The Mosque," and "The Suppliant"; from *Two Cheers for Democracy*, "Our Deputation," "What I Believe," "The Duty of Society to the Artist," and "Jew-Consciousness"; from *The Hill of Devi*, "Gokul Ashtami"; "The Celestial Omnibus" and "The Road from Colonus"; and excerpts from *Where Angels Fear to Tread*, *A Room with a View*, and *A Passage to India*.]

1291 Phelps, Robert, and Peter Deane. THE LITERARY LIFE: A SCRAPBOOK ALMANAC OF THE ANGLO-AMERICAN LITERARY SCENE FROM 1900 to 1950 (NY: Farrar, Straus & Giroux, 1968).
[Several references to EMF and interesting portraits and pictures.]

1292 Pritchett, V. S. "E. M. Forster at Ninety," NEW YORK TIMES BOOK REVIEW, 29 Dec 1968, pp. 1, 2, 18, 19.
EMF's private voice has been more powerful in converting the educated man about the evils in imperialism than have any of its formal political opponents. EMF is against the Victorian obsession with great men. The offhand manner in his prose, so much a part of our own sensibilities, was once shocking. In the years 1900–1930 his liberal humanism was an effective weapon against British complacency. The bankruptcy of the middle class (his chief characters) was complete by 1918. The novels may now seem archaic despite their literary distinction. Not only did the class he wrote about disappear, but he lost his fictional subject. EMF's characters are less apprehensible than Trollope's or Austen's because these novelists never asked intellectual questions that their characters could not answer. In EMF's books people from the dull middle class are put out of their moral and intellectual depth and are compelled to face issues that would normally never occur to them. His good characters are disinterested; his bad, benighted. In EMF's own case he was subject to attack from the right and the left, when he kept to his ideal of detachment; however, the 1939 war was fought to preserve some of the liberal principles he stood for. EMF is a skeptic and an inquirer. He had enormous influence on the educated and the educable, but the influence redresses a balance instead of being formative. He is not whimsical in his cult of privacy and personal relationships because he has some Victorian or puritan sternness. As for the fiction, EMF's use of melodrama is purposive. The moral life is etched in with clarity, and in his comedy, people are exposed to moral danger. Before *A Passage to India* EMF lacked a powerful scene and an antagonist removed from all-too-familiar Cambridge. The stories, except for "The Machine Stops," are fail-

ures because the Mediterranean scene is still too near to EMF for him to use it effectively. The serious intention behind his comedy and melodrama is to illuminate nature or things as they are. [A fresh and wide-ranging essay.]

1293 Raban, Jonathan. "Narrative: Point of View," THE TECHNIQUES OF MODERN FICTION: ESSAYS IN PRACTICAL CRITICISM (Lond: Edward Arnold, 1968; South Bend: University of Notre Dame P, 1969), pp. 35–44, espec 35–36, 41; also 56 (American ed).
EMF rightly asserts, in *Aspects of the Novel*, that the shifting of viewpoint to omniscience is justified when it "bounces" the reader into acquiescence. In *Howards End* EMF blends most skillfully the possibilities of omniscience and limited point of view. EMF is sympathetic with many characters, and it is difficult to know his full valuation of them. The "bounced" (quasi-omniscient) narrative is a natural mode for the ironist. Angus Wilson in ANGLO-SAXON ATTITUDES follows EMF by playing "fast and loose" with his characters.

1294 Richler, Mordecai. "A Sense of the Ridiculous: Paris, 1951 and After," NEW AMERICAN REVIEW (NY & Toronto: New American Library, 1968), pp. 114–34, espec 128–29; rptd in SHOVELLING TROUBLE (Toronto: McClelland & Stewart, 1972), pp. 23–46.
[Mostly an account of Richler's 1951–1953 stay in Paris as an apprentice writer. Recounts a brief visit to Cambridge, where Richler did not "connect" with EMF. EMF seemed, along with the Cambridge he symbolized, irrelevant to Richler's chief concerns. EMF could not understand F. Scott Fitzgerald's high reputation, apparently admired Angus Wilson's HEMLOCK AND AFTER, and did not like Nelson Algren's THE MAN WITH THE GOLDEN ARM, which Richler had left with EMF.]

1295 Riley, Madeleine. BROUGHT TO BED (Lond: J. M. Dent, 1968), pp. 11, 43–45, 124.
[Book explores attitudes expressed in the English novel toward pregnancy and childbirth, the circumstances of childbirth, and the effects of childbirth upon fathers and the immediate family. In this context *Howards End* is cited to demonstrate that Helen Schlegel is vulnerable as an unwed mother, although her adversary, Henry Wilcox, has not suffered at all for a sexual transgression in the past. In *Where Angels Fear to Tread* Gino Carella's desire to have a son outweighs solicitude for his wife, Lilia, who dies in childbirth. Gino wants a son to assure him of his own immortality and does not even think of the possibility that he could have a daughter.]

1296 Scott, Virgil, and Adrian H. Jaffe (eds). STUDIES IN THE SHORT STORY (NY: Holt, Rinehart & Winston, 1968; 3rd ed), p. 271.

["Questions for Discussion" for "The Other Side of the Hedge"; rpts this story, pp. 267–71. EMF not included in 1st ed (1949) and 2nd ed (1960).]

1297 Shah, Syed. "The Empire in the Writings of Kipling, Forster and Orwell." Unpublished dissertation, University of Exeter, 1968. [Listed in G. M. Paterson, INDEX TO THESES ACCEPTED FOR HIGHER DEGREES IN THE UNIVERSITIES OF GREAT BRITAIN AND IRELAND AND THE COUNCIL FOR NATIONAL ACADEMIC AWARDS, XVIII (1967–1968).]

1298 Shahane, V. A. (ed). PERSPECTIVES ON E. M. FORSTER'S "A PASSAGE TO INDIA": A COLLECTION OF CRITICAL ESSAYS (NY: Barnes & Noble, 1968).
Contents, abstracted or noted under date of first publication: V. A. Shahane, "Introduction" (1968); Gertrude M. White: "*A Passage to India:* Analysis and Revaluation," PUBLICATIONS OF THE MODERN LANGUAGE ASSOCIATION (1953); Hugh Maclean, "The Structure of *A Passage to to India,*" UNIVERSITY OF TORONTO QUARTERLY (1953); Keith Hollingsworth, "*A Passage to India:* The Echoes in the Marabar Caves," CRITICISM (1962); Louise Dauner, "What Happened in the Cave? Reflections on *A Passage to India,*" MODERN FICTION STUDIES (1961); Edwin Nierenberg, "The Withered Priestess: Mrs. Moore's Incomplete Passage to India," MODERN LANGUAGE QUARTERLY (1953); Ted E. Boyle, "Adela Quested's Delusion: The Failure of Rationalism in *A Passage to India,*" COLLEGE ENGLISH (1965); James McConkey, "The Prophetic Novel: *A Passage to India,*" THE NOVELS OF E. M. FORSTER (1957); David Shusterman, "The Curious Case of Professor Godbole: *A Passage to India* Re-examined," PUBLICATIONS OF THE MODERN LANGUAGE ASSOCIATION (1961); George H. Thomson, "Thematic Symbol in *A Passage to India,*" TWENTIETH CENTURY LITERATURE (1961); Nirad C. Chaudhuri, "Passage To and From India," ENCOUNTER (1954); Glen O. Allen, "Structure, Symbol, and Theme in E. M. Forster's *A Passage to India,*" PUBLICATIONS OF THE MODERN LANGUAGE ASSOCIATION (1955); V. A. Shahane, "Symbolism in *A Passage to India:* 'Temple,' " E. M. FORSTER: A REASSESSMENT (1962); Benita Parry, "Passage to More Than India," FORSTER: A COLLECTION OF CRITICAL ESSAYS, ed by Malcolm Bradbury (1966); K. W. Gransden, "The Last Movement of the Symphony," E. M. FORSTER (1962).

1299 Shahane, V. A. "Introduction," PERSPECTIVES ON E. M. FORSTER'S "A PASSAGE TO INDIA": A COLLECTION OF CRITICAL ESSAYS (NY: Barnes & Noble, 1968), pp. xi–xxii.
[Traces the criticism of *A Passage to India.*] Critics at its publication were mostly interested in its political implications, then shifted to a wider perspective following publication of Lionel Trilling's E. M. FORSTER (1943). The most recent criticism of *Passage* tends to be philosophical or psycho-

logical rather than social or political, with considerable emphasis on its structural and symbolical properties. Critics have also tended to shift their focus from "Caves" to "Temple." The inconclusiveness of *Passage* is part of the reason for its greatness and the reason for the varied interpretations accorded it. [Pedestrian account, discussing essays seriatim with little concentration on the issues being debated by critics of this novel.]

1300 Shonfield, Andrew. "The Politics of Forster's India," EN-COUNTER, XXX (Jan 1968), 62–69.

No Hindu is given a central part in *A Passage to India*. [The best critics of the novel (Glen O. Allen, James McConkey, Wilfred Stone, and George H. Thomson) have all seen the centrality of Godbole and the Mau festivities ("Temple").] "Temple" is "rather insubstantial and in places positively banal." [Condescending judgment.] It is unfortunate that Aziz, a Moslem, is ostensibly the protagonist [Aziz is no more central than Mrs. Moore, Fielding, Adela Quested, and Godbole; for refutation of Shonfield's view, see K. Natwar-Singh, "Only connect . . . : Forster and India," ASPECTS OF E. M. FORSTER, ed by Oliver Stallybrass (1969)]. Regrettably, Godbole is disreputable and makes Hinduism seem foolish. [EMF was showing that in him—and in his Hinduism—all extremes meet and are reconciled; see John Colmer, E. M. FORSTER: "A PASSAGE TO INDIA" (1967).] The Anglo-Indian officials (Turton, Callendar, Ronny Heaslop, McBryde) are caricatures and unsympathetic, inhumane, and self-centered. [For essential truth of EMF's depiction of these Anglo-Indians, see Henry W. Nevinson, " 'India's Coral Strand,' " SATURDAY REVIEW OF LITERATURE (1924) and K. Natwar-Singh (1969); also George Orwell's BURMESE DAYS and Joyce Cary's THE AFRICAN WITCH; also Benita Parry's DELUSIONS AND DISCOVERIES (1972)]. EMF does not show sympathy to the National Congress Movement, which got under way in India in the early 1920s. [*Passage* shows India at an earlier moment of time and presents the conditions that helped lead to the Indian agitation for independence, as Natwar-Singh demonstrates; see also Jeffrey Meyers, "The Politics of A Passage to India," (1971) wherein EMF is seen to have been sympathetic to Indian nationalist aspirations.] That *Passage* says something true about India, EMF's Hindu friends and disciples attest. [See E. M. FORSTER: A TRIBUTE, ed by K. Natwar-Singh (1964)]. [Critical, like Nirad C. Chaudhuri in "Passage to and from India," ENCOUNTER (1954) of EMF's treatment of the political scene in India in *Passage*, but makes a poorer case. This article proceeds, I think, from mistaken assumptions and complete misreading of EMF's intentions and achievements.]

1301 Shonfield, Andrew. "Shonfield and Forster's India: A Controversial Exchange," ENCOUNTER (Lond), XXX (June 1968), 95.
[In answer to Harland Nelson, "The Politics of Forster's India," (1968), Shonfield holds that his own explicitly political interpretation of *A Passage*

to India is more tenable than the now current "metaphysical" interpretations. In answer to G. K. Das, "Shonfield and Forster's India: A Controversial Exchange" (1968), Shonfield holds that Anglo-Indian administrators were more conscientious than EMF presents them.]

1302 Spencer, Michael. "Hinduism in E. M. Forster's *A Passage to India*," JOURNAL OF ASIAN STUDIES (Ann Arbor), XXVII (Feb 1968), 281–95.

Three problems are posed when we think of EMF's relationship to Hinduism in *A Passage to India:* (1) Was EMF knowledgeable about it? He was. (2) Is religion important in the design of the novel? Is Hinduism more than "cultural background"? Yes. (3) Is Mohammedanism more important than Hinduism in viewing the novel as a whole? No, though Aziz is more lovable than the characters associated with Hinduism, Godbole and Mrs. Moore. The Marabar Caves are a source of evil, of negation; they express a monistic reality that figures in more positive terms in "Temple," the antithesis of the Caves. The vision in the Caves stresses renunciation and the fact that the world is illusion. In Bkahti Hinduism the world is not Maya or illusion; it blends flesh and spirit. The Caves lead to rejection of human action; the festival gives it purpose. The Caves call for renunciation, not for incorporation, as the festival does. Bkhati devotion also erases caste and all other distinctions; the festival reflects the confusion and muddle at the heart of India and the positive synthesis of Bkahti Hinduism. The myth is attractive by its inclusiveness; it helps sustain the values of living men, but it is in its turn prescriptive. Evil to the Hindu can be overcome but not transformed into good. The struggle against evil is eternal; and man has to be reincarnated constantly to engage in this struggle (also Shri Krishna is perpetually reincarnated in the fight against evil). This cycle from good to evil to good is repeated in the three sections of the novel, although there are contrasting and complicating elements in each section. Without religious sensibility, the characters only understand half of the double vision, their physical environment; and this is true even of the best of the English, Fielding. Godbole represents well the force of Hinduism in the novel. His goal is inclusiveness and unity; but EMF implies that his disinterestedness toward people may be extreme. EMF cannot incorporate personality into Hindu characters to the degree that he might wish, though he is committed to Hinduism, and Godbole is admirable. He is not lovable, and EMF reserves personality for Aziz. Likewise, Mrs. Moore, who is finally an exponent of Hindu values, is more a character than a personality. [Interesting essay. Answers critics like Reuben Brower, David Shusterman, and Frederick C. Crews who discount the Hindu influence. Covers some of the same ground as Wilfred Stone in THE CAVE AND THE MOUNTAIN (1966), which Spencer seems not to have consulted. Spencer's view that Hinduism appealed to EMF's imagination but that he has some reservations about it is sound. Should be read in

conjunction with A. Woodward's "The Humanism of E. M. Forster," THE-
ORIA (1963).]

1303 Stewart, J. I. M. JOSEPH CONRAD (NY: Dodd, Mead; Lond:
Longmans, 1968), p. 218.
The comic element in CHANCE, especially that connected with the Fynes,
is excellent. It defines the limitations of the convention-bound English
upper middle class, a rendition similar to that found in EMF's novels.

1304 Stewart, J. I. M. "Tradition and Miss Austen," CRITICAL
ESSAYS ON JANE AUSTEN, ed by B. C. Southam (Lond: Routledge &
Kegan Paul, 1968; NY: Barnes & Noble, 1969), pp. 123–35.
The novelists at a round table, described in the first pages of EMF's *Aspects
of the Novel* as a symbol of a common aesthetic tradition, would not really
understand each other; and a synoptic view of the novel is much more
difficult to attain than EMF imagined. Jane Austen was central to the
concerns of the later novel, in placing the personality at the center of the
moral life.

1305 Stone, Wilfred. "E. M. Forster et Matthew Arnold" (E. M.
Forster and Matthew Arnold), LES LANGUES MODERNES (Paris),
LXII (Jan–Feb 1968), 65–77.
EMF reveals manifold influence of Matthew Arnold, especially in *Howards
End*. According to John Stuart Mill's distinction between the Benthamite
and the Coleridgean positions, Arnold and EMF are Coleridgeans, opposing
an organic vision of life to a mechanical one, creative synthesis to analysis,
imagination to logic. For EMF, the absolute entity is art; for Arnold, culture. But EMF like Arnold is also concerned with the role of culture in
society. *Howards End* is a living dialogue based upon Arnold's idea of
culture, which EMF discusses in terms of the need to avoid the extremes
of decadence and brutality. The Schlegels, exemplifying Arnold's moral via
media, would be part of his "saving remnant." [Proceeds to an analysis of
Howards End, following some lines of discussion found in THE CAVE AND
THE MOUNTAIN (1966).] The mediation between the two poles, Schlegel
culture and Wilcox worldly action, is not achieved. We cannot, therefore,
truly support Margaret's "triumph" in the novel; her victory in the larger
view is a defeat. Technically the novel is a great achievement. [An attempt,
with partial success, to discuss a relationship between two important writers. Discussion is too centered on *Howards End* to be definitive. Arnold's
ideas, as they apply to EMF, are not exhaustively analyzed, e. g., Hebraism
versus Hellenism, the English reliance on machinery, the scientific passion
for knowledge versus the social passion for doing good, the varying views
of the middle class. Arnold's literary criticism as it influenced EMF is not

discussed; the ideas contained in Arnold's religious writings are not mentioned. Arnold as a liberal, a humanist, and an agnostic is not fully presented, as EMF represents these same tendencies. No mention is made of Arnold's poetry.] [In French.]

1306 Talon, Henri A. "E. M. Forster: Récit et Mythe personnel dans les premiers Romans (1905–1910)" (E. M. Forster: Story and Personal Myth in the Early Novels [1905–1910]), ARCHIVES DES LETTRES MODERNES (Paris), No. 88 (1968).

In *Where Angels Fear to Tread, A Room with a View,* and *The Longest Journey,* a contrast exists between those who have a full interior life and those who do not. Those with the full interior life experience the call of the unknown and are vital and mythic figures. Gino Carella (*Angels*) and Stephen Wonham (*Journey*) are the best examples of this type of individual. Figures of this sort, in harmony with a primitive nature and representing a primitive human nature, disappear after *Journey,* although the aspiration in EMF that led to their creation survives in the creation of some of his characters in *Howards End.* In embodying such aspiration "the story" is a more important element in the novel than EMF realizes (in *Aspects of the Novel* EMF regards pattern and rhythm as more important than story). In the first three novels, as in *Howards End,* the inability of the characters to realize fully their aspirations results in a pervasive sadness. In *Howards End,* the polarity is not between the conventional individual and the primitive individual but between the intellectual and the man of affairs. As intellectuals, the Schlegel sisters are much less on the sidelines than are Philip Herriton in *Angels* and Cecil Vyse in *Room.* EMF's "personal myth" is more securely based in *Howards End;* primitive and sexual feelings are only incidentally present, as in the rustic in the cemetery who plucks a flower for the girl he loves. In *Howards End,* the masculine and the feminine worlds are both incomplete because authentic sexual feeling is so largely absent from them. A conscious effort to "connect" is substituted for a vital primitivism. The marriage between Henry Wilcox and Margaret Schlegel is inadequate to the aspiration that led to the creation of the book. As if in tacit recognition of this inadequacy, a note of renunciation, defeat, and cultural failure is implicit or explicit in this marriage. Margaret becomes too passive and so reveals the failure of the metropolitan culture that she had so enthusiastically espoused. Her drift now toward repose negates her previous preoccupation with culture and her belief in its spiritual power. She gives up the culture of the city too readily as she turns to a pastoral existence. Her culture is narrow as it excludes those who are less privileged. It is also too greatly dependent on money. Howards End house is an inadequate symbol, because it is less commanding at the close (when it becomes a feminine refuge from the shocks of active life) than it was in the beginning (when it seemed to convey a sense of expanding horizons). The Beethoven

Fifth Symphony is a far more expansive, vital, and positive symbol than Howards End house. [In French].

1307 Taraporewala, M. P. *"A Passage to India:* Symphonic Symmetry," SIDDHA III, ed by Frank D'Souza and Jagdish Shivpuri (Bombay: Siddarth College of Arts and Sciences, 1968), pp. 58–86. Music relates to the problems of structure in *A Passage to India.* The following leitmotifs, present in "Mosque," recur with variations in "Caves" and "Temple": (1) Sky and earth; (2) India as muddle; (3) the wasp; (4) God is Love and He is everywhere; (5) the phrase, "Come, Come." [Discusses these leitmotifs and the principal characters as they relate to the two principal subjects of EMF's extended "symphony": the racial question and the need for an understanding heart that will permit Love to exist. Interestingly traces the persistence of those motifs throughout the novel but arbitrarily implies that these are *the* motifs. Another reader could come up with five different, but equally plausible, "motifs." Subdivisions of these motifs are not clearly defined. Resorts to synopsis in the place of hard analysis. The article says little that other critics have not said before.]

1308 Thomas, Edward. "Selected Books," LONDON MAGAZINE, nsVIII (July 1968), 84–87.
"Forster and Orwell, seemingly such poles apart, are with Chesterton the only writers . . . in this century who have written memorably about England and the English character, seeing the country as an entire organism with its characteristic and interwoven strengths and weaknesses." Orwell notes that the Bloomsbury and socialist intellectuals came from the same families; EMF says that they marry each other: "Either way the cohesiveness of English society is maintained." The case for EMF is the case for the England of the liberal intellectuals, for the inner life, the bridging of the gaps between classes and races, the view that imagination is life and Philistinism is death. There is also a case against EMF and the middle-class liberal intellectuals. He would try to justify his private income by an excessive desire to sympathize with the underprivileged. A private sympathy and a generous stoicism are not enough to effect improvement. The release at the end of *Howards End* and *A Passage to India* is on the level of beauty, and EMF's epigrams reveal the supremacy of style over rigor of content. There seems to be a vicarious enjoyment of the violence and sudden deaths in the novels, at least a zest in recounting them. "The stoicism, the style, and the frivolity all show forth an unwillingness to immerse in the destructive element of life." In EMF's novels marriage and work are seen as threats to the spirit. But EMF did overcome, to considerable degree, the limitations of his class, and his books are modern, not Edwardian, in temper. Laurence Brander's book (E. M. FORSTER: A CRITICAL STUDY) is sympathetic to EMF's work, though his own predilections obtrude a bit too greatly in his "thorough, fair, evocative book." EMF may have less influence in the future

over our lives because his is a voice from the sidelines, advocating art, leisure, and personal relations in a time when one leads a refractory, multi-dimensioned, and interrelated life. [Review of Laurence Brander's E. M. FORSTER: A CRITICAL STUDY (1967). A fresh and stimulating essay.]

1309 Thomson, George H. "E. M. Forster and Howard Sturgis," TEXAS STUDIES IN LITERATURE AND LANGUAGE, X (Fall 1968), 423–33.

EMF was influenced by his friend Howard Overing Sturgis. Sturgis treated sexual ambivalence in ALL THAT WAS POSSIBLE (1895) playfully, to contrast with EMF's serious presentation of it in *The Longest Journey* and else-where. EMF avoids Sturgis's "crude instruments of emotional pitch and narrative attention" in *Journey*, and thus escapes self-revelation. In TIM (1891) a sensitive boy, tormented by public school life and emotionally attached to a hero, may have been formative upon EMF in writing *Journey*. EMF was much impressed by BELCHAMBER (1904), and it also may have affected him in writing *Journey*. An affinity exists between Sturgis and EMF, the writer of short stories and two Italian novels. In BELCHAMBER Santy is similar in his experiences and attributes to Rickie Elliot of *Journey*. Sturgis was more direct in presenting the horrors of the public school, but he still managed to combine intimacy with irony. EMF eschews intimacy, partly by presenting his characters as undergoing visionary or mystical experiences that are individual rather than communal in nature. "The Story of a Panic" and "The Road from Colonus" illustrate not only EMF's desire for detachment but also his willingness to become engaged with his charac-ters in those moments of visionary experience that by their nature prevent undue intimacy. EMF is able to extend this visionary element and the resulting aesthetic control of his characters over increasing lengths of narra-tive in the novels that succeeded the short stories. [An interesting relation-ship convincingly explored.]

1310 V., S. V. "Interview: Concern for the Individual, Santha Rama Rau: *A Passage to India*," TIMES OF INDIA (New Delhi), 25 Feb 1968, p. 12

[Circumstances given of Santha Rama Rau's adapting *A Passage to India* for the stage.]

1311 Wakefield, G. P. "HOWARDS END" (E. M. FORSTER) (Oxford: Basil Blackwell, 1968).

The "only connect" concept is important in EMF's fiction, especially in *Howards End;* in Margaret Schlegel EMF has created "the articulate apolo-gist of his own philosophy." In EMF's work the idealist is always conduct-ing a dialogue with the realist. In *Howards End* EMF is more concerned with class struggle than he is elsewhere; nevertheless, this aspect of the novel is secondary to his presentation of the intellectual, emotional, and spiritual contrasts among his characters. Throughout, the inner Schlegel world of culture and personal relations is in equipoise with the outer Wilcox world of materialism and mobility. EMF shows us, however, the weaknesses in the Schlegel values and the strengths in the Wilcoxes. The Schlegels do make inward connections, and all the failures of the Wilcoxes can be ascribed to their failure to do so. In applying to *Howards End* EMF's own terms (story and plot), plot is more important and depends on the Schlegel sisters; as for story EMF is not averse to rousing interest by the use of surprise, coincidence, and the dubiously probable. The structure of *Howards End* shows seven main climactic incidents: (1) The affair of Helen and Paul Wilcox (Chap 1–4); (2) The unbrella episode (Chap 5 & 6); (3) The death of Ruth Wilcox (Chap 7–12); (4) Henry's proposal of marriage to Margaret (Chap 13–24); (5) The arrival of the Basts at Oniton (Chap 25–29); (6) Helen's return (Chap 30–38); (7) Leonard's death (Chap 39–43). EMF's style is a true familiar style. He reveals a skilled use of imagery and has the ability to suggest life in inanimate things: the countryside, trees, houses. He is skilled in his dialogue and is able to adapt his style to the character portrayed. He makes sophisticated use of repeated words and phrases. His style is fused with the novel's structure in his dramatic scenes; in them the dialogue is flexible and functional. EMF reveals a fondness for long descriptive passages and for didactic comment, effective techniques as EMF uses them, though they are now out of fashion. EMF's humor is distinctive. It is present in his descriptive characterizations and revealed, too, in the actions and speech of his characters. The comic scenes are relevant to his main theme, and his writing is marked by understatement, innuendo, or the directly humorous effect. The characters are incrementally revealed instead of being presented descriptively at the onset. Margaret Schlegel is subtly portrayed, although she represents EMF's own values. The realism of her marriage is not really in question; EMF prepares us for it and the occurrence can remain a mystery. Helen Schlegel might have given herself to Leonard Bast, but we need more motivation for this act than we get. Leonard is relatively successful as a character and is not flat. Henry is a round character but has little mystery about him; his common sense and good nature are less strong than his shortcomings. Ruth Wilcox is an earth spirit more than a woman; in general, however, she is convincing. The novel requires a multiple and complex response from its readers. Though EMF may not be a great novelist, the truth of *Howards End* as a whole transcends all partial criticisms of it. [Sound but hardly profound analysis. The section on style is the best in the book.]

1312 Wall, Stephen. "The Qualities of Forster," NEW STATESMAN, nsLXXVI (19 July 1968), 87.
One of EMF's qualities of appeal is his personal conduct and supervision

of his stories. He can get away with this technique by virtue of the quality of his personality. Also the modernity of his mediating tone prevents the early books from dating. His wisdom, far-sightedness, and truth attract us. His kind of mind allows for moral seriousness without undue earnestness. "His view of man as both a creature of sex and possessed of reason shows a rare and sane balance." His work has a counterbalancing, refreshing element of play and irresponsibility. The fact that we trust EMF (and the personality he reveals in his books) allows us to assimilate without great distraction the implausibities in situation and character. His characters do not always achieve solidity of line; we would rather meet him than his characters. The reader's relationship to EMF has been too little discussed. [Review-essay on B. J. Kirkpatrick's A BIBLIOGRAPHY OF E. M. FORSTER (2nd 1968); Laurence Brander's E. M. FORSTER: A CRITICAL STUDY (1968); Norman Kelvin's E. M. FORSTER (1967); and Denis Godfrey's E. M. FORSTER'S OTHER KINGDOM (1968). Excellent essay, rightfully avoiding the discussion of inferior studies to concentrate on the man and his work.]

1313 Webb, R. K. MODERN ENGLAND FROM THE EIGHTEENTH CENTURY TO THE PRESENT (NY & Toronto: Dodd, Mead, 1968), pp. 464–65, 556.
EMF was gentler than Shaw but as corrosive, turning from conventions and proprieties to naturalness. In *Howards End* he predicted the inheritance of England 'by the unclassed, the alien, and the intellectuals.'

1314 Wood, Russell. "The Masque of E.M.Forster." Unpublished dissertation, Occidental University, 1968. [Listed in Laurence F. McNamee, DISSERTATIONS IN ENGLISH AND AMERICAN LITERATURE, SUPP I (NY & Lond: Bowker, 1969).]

1969

1315 Anand, Mulk Raj. "Profile of E. M. Forster," A GARLAND FOR E. M. FORSTER, ed by H. H. Anniah Gowda (Mysore, India: The Literary Half-Yearly, 1969), pp. 3–7.

The subtlety and elusiveness of EMF's mind and art mean that they escape clear definition. EMF's canon is slight, but his influence is enormous. He continually contrasts what is with what might be. He reveals an empirical sense of fact and a common sense realism juxtaposed with a romanticism in the succession of Wordsworth and Meredith. He is not academic in any narrow sense, because he desires pleasure as well as knowledge. He appreciates Oriental as well as Hellenic wisdom; India brought his creativeness to full growth and helped him to fuse into a harmony the polarities of his experience. But EMF does not stress harmony at the expense of actual life; he has strong regard for the individual and his rights, for personal relationships, and for communication between human beings. [An admirable tribute by a man who knew EMF for forty years, more remarkable for its consistently respectful tone than for the novelty of its ideas.]

1316 Appaswamy, J. B. *"The Hill of Devi,"* A GARLAND FOR E. M. FORSTER, ed by H. H. Anniah Gowda (Mysore, India: The Literary Half-Yearly, 1969), pp. 51–53.

The Princes in India were supplanted politically by the British Raj, but the British also upheld them in the forms of their power as a counterweight to the Indian middle class. The Princes, in effect, have reappeared as an English educated elite in the government and the professions. Under later British rule the courts of the Princes revealed frustration and meaninglessness because they had no positive function in diplomacy or war. Present-day Indians regard their former princely rulers with nostalgia, which EMF evokes in *The Hill of Devi*. EMF is noteworthy for having tried to participate in the life of Indians.

1317 Arlott, John. "Forster and Broadcasting," ASPECTS OF E. M. FORSTER, ed by Oliver Stallybrass (NY: Harcourt, Brace & World; Lond: Edward Arnold, 1969), pp. 87–92; printed in slightly variant form as "E. M. Forster at the Microphone," LISTENER, LXXXI (2 Jan 1969), 8–9.

EMF gave valuable service during World War II to the BBC in its program-grouping called "English to India." After the war he contributed a monthly book review to the BBC's Eastern Service. He contributed these talks because of his love of India. These broadcasts ranged "from the coolly objective to the completely unguarded subjective." His talks were composed of "complete, terse thoughts producing a cumulative effect." He was always open to suggestions and was appreciative of stylistic nuances appropriate to the wireless medium. He concentrated on clarity, but he also expected efforts to be made by his audience as they listened to him. [Illuminates a little-known side of EMF.]

1318 Barnes, Clive. "On the Scene," HOLIDAY, XLV (March 1969), 12, 17–18, espec 18.

EMF outlived his time; he said what he had to say and then as a novelist preferred silence. History trampled over his genius, but his reputation survives.

1319 Beer, J. B. "Forster's Ninetieth," CAMBRIDGE REVIEW, XC (17 Jan 1969), 199–201.

EMF's liberalism is strenuous enough to face the persistent challenge to it. As in *Howards End* (in the scene wherein the Wilcoxes discuss and then destroy Ruth Wilcox's bequest), EMF can condemn the liberal tendency to muddle the past and ignore the central issue. His literary stature is a matter for debate. Some have challenged *A Passage to India* on the grounds that it is not a realistic rendering of India (it was not meant to be). Others say he is spinsterish (but so was Jane Austen); others condemn his authorial intrusions (though these establish the flavor of the books and enrich them). ASPECTS OF E. M. FORSTER (ed by Oliver Stallybrass) has little adverse criticsm but is free of uncritical adulation. [Reviews contents of volume, citing Malcolm Bradbury's "Two Passage to India" (1969) for special praise.] Elizabeth Bowen's "A Passage to E. M. Forster" (1969) is the biography of an EMF reader. [As an undergraduate, he was attracted to *Passage* for its social implications and for its complexities, especially in Fielding's problems. (This is Trilling's approach.)] Another reading finds *Passage* a great novel of the human heart with Mrs. Moore at its center. (Angus Wilson's view.) *Passage* is, finally, a novel like *The Longest Journey*, concerned with the nature of reality and how reality depends on one's own sense of the external world (Adela Quested is central here). This interpretation gives the novel a passionate core and suggests hope for renewal in spite of the disruption of friendship between Aziz and Fielding; it satisfies curiosity about what happened in the Cave and establishes a connection with EMF's earlier work. Earlier, EMF had argued that the deepest failure in man is his failure to fulfill his own body and its potentialities. That failure is translated into the "panic and emptiness" of *Howards End* and the nullity of the Marabar

Caves in *Passage*. EMF's positive values are the importance of the unmuddled head and the development of the heart's affections. Behind these values lies a conviction that man's psychic health depends on maintaining a link between earth and his imagination, a link that is much challenged at present. But man's native resources may see him through. EMF's very presence in Cambridge is reassuring as a reminder of the resources that humanity can muster against its own nightmares. [Review-essay of ASPECTS OF E. M. FORSTER ed by Oliver Stallybrass (1969). A challenging and deep thrusting, if somewhat refractory, essay.]

1320 Bey, Hamdi. "The Novels of a Ruling Caste—II," THOUGHT (Delhi), XXI (10 Sept 1969), 15–16.

EMF is the least unpleasant reminder of the two hundred years struggle between Britain and India, the British prizing action and the Indians gesture. [Reviews EMF's connection with India and his evaluation of, and assistance to, many Indian writers. Describes EMF's relations with Iqbal, Tagore, and Ross Masood.]

1321 Booth, Wayne C. "Introduction," ROBERT LIDDELL ON THE NOVEL (Chicago: University of Chicago P, 1969), pp. xiii–xx.

Liddell's work ranks with EMF's *Aspects of the Novel* and Percy Lubbock's THE CRAFT OF FICTION (1921). His mind, like EMF's, is "richer than its overt categories." We can learn more about story as such from Liddell's work than from EMF's *Aspects*. Liddell is concerned with the values and truths to be found in fiction and demonstrates conclusively how incorrect values as in *The Longest Journey* and *A Room with a View* (where all depends on one "great refusal" to value properly a "noble savage" character) can vitiate a work of fiction. [Rpts A TREATISE ON THE NOVEL (1947) and SOME PRINCIPLES OF FICTION (1953); for Liddell's discussions of EMF, see Liddell 1947 and 1953.]

1322 Bowen, Elizabeth. "A Passage to E. M. Forster," ASPECTS OF E. M. FORSTER, ed by Oliver Stallybrass (NY: Harcourt, Brace & World; Lond: Edward Arnold, 1969), pp. 1–12.

[EMF is the writer who more than any other has influenced her view of life and the way she writes. His books did not seem like the work of any other writer when she read them, though they were "professionally" written, as Edwardian novels tended to be. Her first contact with EMF was *The Celestial Omnibus and Other Stories*, a landmark experience for her.] The subject matter of the short stories was not impressive, but their manner was. Their electric climate, in which anything could happen, produced an aesthetic shock. Impressive were the fusing of the banal and inexplicable, the way in which irony held mockery in curb and made it superfluous, the satirizing of complacent and pretentious people rather than the woolly-minded, the feeling for place revealed in them, and the conversations in which the talkers precipitated action and illustrated the "striking-power of the thing said." EMF enlarged rather than developed so that his earliest works are closely connected with his latest. The novels sometimes reveal an unjust and intemperate attitude, but they are deeper and more comprehensive than youthful novels generally are. In fact, they seem to prophesy later fiction, since they belong as much to our time as to the age in which they were written. From the first, EMF presented a world of conflict (but not *in* conflict); as a result, the schisms and the oppositions between its people stand out clearly, as does the exterior gentleness contained in them. The conflicts are inherent and inevitable, "part of the continuous struggle for integrity" and the desire to achieve understanding. In particular, EMF comes out against falsification between the sexes. [Bowen celebrates the passion contained in the works, especially in *Howards End*, which seethes with it. An impressionistic yet discriminative account of EMF's work, and a companion piece to her essays in Collected Impressions (1950) and Seven Winters and Afterthoughts (1962; see Bowen, 1961).]

1323 Bradbury, Malcolm, "The Fictiveness of Fiction," What Is a Novel? (Lond: Edward Arnold, Arnold's General Studies, 1969), pp. 31–38, espec 34–35; also 19, 42.
EMF defines the novel (*Aspects of the Novel*) as "a fiction in prose of a certain extent" (not less than 50,000 words). [Agrees with EMF that point of view should not be rigidly observed in fiction. Discusses EMF's intrusions into *Howards End* (especially the one about King's Cross station suggesting infinity to Margaret Schlegel). Defends this intrusion because it helps set tone and gives distance to presentation of Margaret so that she does not reflect EMF's values too directly.] EMF also achieves by his intrusions a comic command over the "telling," the comic mode mediating between the ordinary prose life in time and the poetic life by values (another discrimination deriving from *Aspects*).

1324 Bradbury, Malcolm. "Two Passages to India: Forster as Victorian and Modern," Aspects of E. M. Forster, ed by Oliver Stallybrass (NY: Harcourt, Brace & World; Lond: Edward Arnold, 1969), pp. 123–42; rptd in E. M. Forster: "A Passage to India," ed by Malcolm Bradbury (Lond: Macmillan, Casebook Series, 1970), pp. 224–43; much rvd and rewritten as part of "E. M. Forster as Victorian and Modern: *Howards End* and *A Passage to India*," Possibilities: Essays on the State of the Novel (Lond, Oxford & NY: Oxford UP, 1973), pp. 91–120, espec 110–20.
The division in EMF's mind and sensibility results in contrasting, often contradictory, elements in his fiction. EMF regards art as a repository, first, of intelligence and honesty and, second, of passion and imagination. The

first comprises a heritage from eighteenth- and nineteenth-century human-ism and rationalism and from certain aspects of romanticism; the second comprises a heritage from nineteenth-century romanticism as that has been modified by a modern sense of the contingent, of the complex, and of the apocalyptic. EMF is Victorian in believing that art is a responsible power, and modern in viewing it as a transcendent entity. He is a transitional figure, then, between the nineteenth and twentieth centuries; and he has tried, sometimes unsuccessfully, often with power and insight, to bring together the contingent world of history and the transcendent realm of the spirit as that realm may be embodied in mystical intuitions, in nature, or in the work of art. Throughout his career he wished for the real, the contingent, the historical to be modified through the effects of the infinite. He has, however, become aware of the difficulties involved in bringing the two realms to-gether and has often had to substitute, especially in *A Passage to India*, a vision of anarchy, with its disabling influence, for a vision of wholeness. The disturbing possibility exists that multiplicity may absorb or supplant the unitary vision. In *Passage* EMF has extended his sensibility to include a recognition of the difficulty of achieving wholeness and attaining—and making effective in the world of history and time—the unitary vision. In this book he has emphasized the desolating effects of the vision of anarchy. India is a metaphor of multivalence, of the contingent (as London is in *Howards End*); and only at moments (as in the prophetic vision of Godbole and Mrs. Moore at the festival) can the anarchic and the historically contin-gent be assimilated to a spiritual view of the universal. In *Passage* EMF is even more aware than he customarily is of the complications present in the social and the contingent realm; he exhibits no preference for the values of any group (India's resistance to English rationalism and civilization is salu-tary, but the passive comprehensiveness in India and Indians is a kind of social decay). In fact, the efforts of any individual or group are of miniscule importance in the cosmic scheme and are those that would only benefit intellectual dwarfs. "Human relationships are dwarfed not only by the scale of the historical and social world, which is potentially redeemable, but by the natural world, which is not." The transcendence expressed in the novel is less the inclusive and confident synthesis of a Whitman than the uncertain and ambiguous transcendence of a Melville, "where the universe is a diabolical cipher, where the desire to penetrate meaning ends only in our being swallowed up in the meaning we have conferred." Technically, the mode of symbolism and postimpressionism in the novel, conveying a mod-ernist sense of historical apocalypse and spiritual abyss, is juxtaposed with the mode of traditional story, conveying by implication the presence of meaningful social and spiritual values as they derive from the humanist tradition. The tone induced by EMF's poetic sensibility suggests the possi-bility of a timeless symbolic (and symbolist) unity, while the tone induced by his irony and a sense of the comic suggests the refractory and contingent nature of the social world in time. [As in his 1962 essay on *Howards End*, Bradbury uses positively the existence of a "double vision" in EMF. Critics such as F. R. Leavis, Walter Allen, and Virginia Woolf have found the operations of the double vision aesthetically confusing or debilitating and have condemned EMF for this. Like H. A. Smith in "Forster and the Nineteenth Century" (1966), Bradbury tries to account for the presence of this double vision in EMF's sensibility and his strategic use of it in art. For Bradbury, EMF's poetic stance is not simply a survival of some aspects of romanticism, as it is for Smith. It is for Bradbury the result also of the modern sensibility operating upon certain elements of that romantic heritage and redefining them. An intelligent essay and invaluable for the subtle interpretation of EMF's mind and art.]

1325 Brander, Laurence. "Aspects of E. M. Forster," A GARLAND FOR E. M. FORSTER, ed by H. H. Anniah Gowda (Mysore, India: The Literary Half-Yearly, 1969), pp. 95–104.

The rank of *A Passage to India* is assured and the other novels are also potential classics because they have fullness of life and because they yield increasing significance. EMF had more somber views than did most Edwardian writers; he knew our troubles in advance and suggested how they could be met. EMF is Edwardian to the extent that he did not comprehend fully the problems of Mass Man. The Victorian middle class, from which EMF came, was supplanted by one segment of it, the industrial entrepreneurs. Mass Man was degraded in the process, or he himself degraded his society. EMF preferred a feudal regime (an organic community based on the land) to a society based on bureaucrats and technicians. EMF is bothered by the muddle in which modern man finds himself. His novels survive because stylistically they are alive and full of magic. The magical quality gives his novels their prophetic overtones. His prose was influenced also by the King James Bible, as in the opening chapter of *Passage*. In general, EMF has been content with his humanism and has not pursued mystical experience. [Review comment on ASPECTS OF E. M. FORSTER, ed by Oliver Stallybrass (1969). Appreciative and interesting essay, though not profound.]

1326 Britten, Benjamin. "Some Notes on Forster and Music," ASPECTS OF E. M. FORSTER, ed by Oliver Stallybrass (NY: Harcourt, Brace & World; Lond: Edward Arnold, 1969), pp. 81–86.

EMF is "our most musical novelist." [Noted are the well-known passages in *Where Angels Fear to Tread*, *A Room with a View*, and *Howards End;* "The C Minor of That Life," *Two Cheers for Democracy* (EMF feels that specific keys suggest music of a specific kind); the uncollected "Revolution at Bayreuth" (LISTENER, LII, 4 Nov 1954, 755–57; EMF at his musical best); and "Not Listening to Music," *Two Cheers* (EMF reveals a romantic tendency to let music suggest emotional states and suspects an analytic approach to art.). Britten writes appreciatively of his collaboration with Eric Crozier and EMF on the opera BILLY BUDD.] EMF is perceptive, witty, energetic, and constantly inspired. [Goes somewhat less deeply into its subject than one could have wished, but presents us with a modicum of valid fact and sharp insight.]

1327 Burkom, Selma. " 'Only Connect': Form and Content in the Works of Doris Lessing," CRITIQUE, XI: 1 (1969), 51–68.
Doris Lessing's humanism is similar to EMF's: the reconciling of dichotomies is central to both novelists as is the repudiation of modern fragmentation. Both writers attempt to reconcile the public and the private spheres, and the inner and outer realms (they both stress the interfusion of spirit and matter). For both writers connection is the right key to personal relationships; failure to connect results, ultimately, in disaster.

1328 Chanda, A. K. "The Failure of Humanism—A Study of the Structure of E. M. Forster's *A Passage to India*," BULLETIN (Calcutta University, Department of English), V: 2 (1969–1970), 2–19.
In *A Passage to India* the indifference of the cosmos to man is stressed less than the death and despair that result when human solidarity is undermined. In *Passage* a dynamic relationship exists between social comedy (the horizontal line) and the poetry (reflecting elemental qualities—the vertical line). The horizontal line culminates in the disruption of personal relationships, largely through muddle, after the Marabar Caves; the vertical line culminates in the Caves and their echo enclosing Western Humanism, Christianity, and Islam, and is further extended in "Temple." In "Temple" the horizontal structure consists of the healing, at least partly, of broken relationships; the vertical structure extends over "Caves" and dissipates the despair engendered in the Caves by including it. [Good analysis of subject of personal relations.] Fielding has something of an undeveloped heart in comparison to the Indians. Both the Englishman's rationalism and the Indian's emotionalism have positive aspects. The Englishman's capacity for generalization indicates a lack of spirituality but a firm grasp of reality. The Englishman believes that the complexities of life can be analyzed by rationalist means; the result is that all the English characters, except Mrs. Moore and her children, are emotionally stunted. EMF condemns the extremes of both British rationalism and Oriental emotionalism in the novel. In the vertical line of "Mosque" and "Caves," the Indian landscape (especially the Caves) and climate provide an image of formlessness, chaos, and dreariness. The horizontal structure connects with the vertical in four major episodes in "Mosque" and "Caves": the bridge Party, Fielding's tea party, the ride in the Nawab's car, and the picnic at the Caves. Because they suffer Mrs. Moore and Adela Quested establish the connection between the two lines

in the first two parts of *Passage*. EMF does not deny the importance of personal relationships in *Passage* but exposes their insignificance and powerlessness when faced with the chaos of the Caves. "Caves" exposes the impotence of humanism and Christianity, but "Temple" presents a superior way of life (Hinduism) because it can neutralize the echo of the Caves and makes of it a mystery rather than a sinister force. The harmony and completeness of Hinduism are all-inclusive; it engenders a collective and impersonal love that is more powerful than the personal relations of humanism or the personal god of Christianity. Disorder at Mau is creative in contrast to that at the Marabar Caves and includes all racial and national divisions and death itself. The Mau section gives the negatives of the Caves a positive value by merging them "in a higher order of absolute values." The novel's two structures meet in "Temple" in the relationships developed between Aziz and Fielding, more importantly in Godbole, especially in his connections with Mrs. Moore (who is assimilated to Hinduism—a process requiring the disintegration of her western values). [Some valuable insights, and contributes to our knowledge of the relationships between the Marabar Caves and Mau festival. However, Chanda's concept of structure is not completely clear and his discussion is not placed clearly in the context of existing criticism on *Passage*.]

1329 Choudhury, A. F. S. I. "The Enemy Territory: A Study of Joseph Conrad, E. M. Forster and D. H. Lawrence in Relation to Their Portrayal of Evil." Unpublished dissertation, University of Leicester, 1969.

[Listed in Geoffrey M. Paterson and Joan E. Hardy, INDEX TO THESES ACCEPTED FOR HIGHER DEGREES BY THE UNIVERSITIES OF GREAT BRITAIN AND IRELAND AND THE COUNCIL FOR NATIONAL ACADEMIC AWARDS, XIX (1968–1969).]

1330 Collins, J. A. "Novels into Plays; Where Angels Fear to Tread: A Criticism of Santha Rama Rau's *A Passage to India*," A GARLAND FOR E. M. FORSTER, ed by H. H. Anniah Gowda (Mysore, India: The Literary Half-Yearly, 1969), pp. 77–81.

Rau's adaptation has dramatized only the bare incidents in the novel, and her work lacks the poetry and the psychological subtlety of the original. EMF's art is one of shadows; this aspect of his work Rau's play does not convey.

1331 Colmer, John. "*Howards End* Revisited," A GARLAND FOR E. M. FORSTER, ed by H. H. Anniah Gowda (Mysore, India: The Literary Half-Yearly, 1969), pp. 9–22.

In *Howards End*, EMF dramatizes three kinds of harmony: that to be found in personal relationships, that to be found in connecting the private and the public spheres, and that to be found in communion between man and the earth (two other forms of harmony are also possible: that to be found in religion and that to be found in art). The presentation of these dichotomies is convincing, although EMF sometimes makes an unwarranted appeal to aesthetic values to secure a solution to pressing problems of individual and social morality. The characters in his best novels seem to expand. In *Howards End* and *A Passage to India*, he combines comedy and prophecy, prophetic vision and ironic commentary. In *Howards End* he uses the "easy" kind of rhythm represented by internal "stitching." This stitching is of three sorts: recurrent images, recurrent antitheses, and recurrent words and phrases. To a degree he attains the more integral, expanding, and difficult kind of rhythm; he does reach back to elemental realities and outward again to society as a whole. EMF achieves this dimension by purposeful withholding of information and then suddenly releasing it; by adoption of the Gothic mode of aesthetic concentration and contraction (the meaning of England is contracted into that of a single house); by a supernatural vision being achieved through physical shock, "the Gothic *frisson*"; and by intensive descriptions of houses and landscapes. Characters, houses, landscapes all have symbolic value, and EMF stresses a realizable harmony whereby the horrors of industrialization can be transmuted into "a plausible atavistic pastoral dream." The horror of city life and its sterility, presented so vividly in *Howards End*, herald T. S. Eliot's "The Waste Land." Strain develops in *Howards End*, in EMF's passing from a critique of industrialism and the commercial ethic to an idyllic pastoralism; a gap results between desired wholeness in life and EMF's artistic design, which is inadequate to his ambitious purpose. In spite of such reservations, EMF has been more successful in *Howards End* than D. H. Lawrence was in LADY CHATTERLEY'S LOVER in dramatizing the dislocations in human beings attributable to a spoliated environment. EMF's prophetic passages stand up to ironic scrutiny better than do Lawrence's, and they show EMF's firm control of his materials. [Perceptive article, especially in its discussion of the rhythms to be found in *Howards End*.]

1332 Delavenay, Émile. D. H. LAWRENCE: L'HOMME ET LA GENÈSE DE SON OEUVRE, LES ANNÉES DE FORMATION: 1885–1919, 2 Vols (Paris: Librairie C. Klincksieck, 1969), pp. 283, 291, 295, 319, 330, 337, 338, 349, 350, 376, 544, 687, 697; trans as D. H. LAWRENCE: THE MAN AND HIS WORK, THE FORMATIVE YEARS: 1885–1919, trans by Katharine M. Delavenay (Lond: Heinemann; Carbondale & Edwardsville: Southern Illinois UP, 1972), pp. 225, 232, 235, 251, 259, 260, 261, 276, 277, 436 (Vol. II, DOCUMENTS, not trans, contains references to EMF).
[English trans used in citing references to EMF in Vol. I. EMF's objection to Frieda's domination of Lawrence is cited (see Frieda Lawrence [1961]).]

EMF brings to Greatham in 1915 a rumor that police might intervene to stop the sale of THE PRUSSIAN OFFICER because of the homosexuality present in the title story. EMF was one who felt the charm of Lawrence (along with John Middleton Murry, Richard Aldington, Bertrand Russell, and John Maynard Keynes). EMF was thought of as a possibility for participation in Lawrence's Utopian experiment, "Rananim." [Letter of 12 Feb 1915 to Bertrand Russell is cited, giving Lawrence's opinions on sex, resulting from his reactions of EMF's visit (see Lawrence, 1948); EMF's short-lived relationship with Lawrence is described.] EMF disliked the tensions in the Greatham circle and was suspicious, like Bertrand Russell, of Lawrence's authoritarian tendencies and his egotism. Lawrence's censorious attitude to the frigid, isolated Bertie in "The Blind Man" reflects possibly his opinions about Bertrand Russell and about EMF's lack of passion. [Vol. II, DOCU-MENTS, in the French ed contains letters from Jessie Chambers to Delavanay with references to EMF. Letter (25 Jan 1935), she does not know if EMF or Aldous Huxley or either will write the preface to her book, D. H. LAW-RENCE: A PERSONAL RECORD (Lond: Cape, 1935). Letter (30 Oct 1935), she cites a student writing on Lawrence who is using a difficult approach, that of Lawrence as prophet, suggested by EMF in his *Aspects of the Novel*.]

1333 Delbaere-Garant, J[eanne]. "Who Shall Inherit England? A Comparison between *Howards End*, PARADE'S END and UNCONDITIONAL SURRENDER," ENGLISH STUDIES (Amsterdam), L (Feb 1969), 101–5.

Howards End, PARADE'S END and UNCONDITIONAL SURRENDER all end with an illegitimate child's inheriting a family property that symbolizes England. Like Matthew Arnold, EMF believes that the future of England depends on a revitalized middle class. The worlds of intellect and money are painfully reconciled in Margaret Schlegel's marriage, but this delicate equilibrium is seriously upset by the intrusion of Leonard Bast, who is not yet prosperous enough to find his rightful place in the framework of the social classes. Bast's child owes his existence to conflict between two antagonistic views of the lower classes: Helen's committed altruism and Henry Wilcox's complacent indifference. Margaret at the end is keeping a precarious balance among conflicting forces in a refractory present. In Ford Madox Ford's PARADE'S END the conflict is between the rising middle class and the aristocracy. There is no "connecting," since Christopher Tietjens breaks with his past by leaving his wife Sylvia and by turning over Groby House in Yorkshire to his child by Sylvia. He enters on a new life with the middle-class girl, Valentine Wannop, and their unborn child; the break is painful but necessary. In Evelyn Waugh's UNCONDITIONAL SURRENDER, the illegitimate child of Guy Crouchback's wife inherits the ancestral manor at Broome in Somerset to the exclusion of Crouchback's own children. Waugh has a contempt for the proletarian hero Trimmer that EMF never shows for Bast. [Traces some interesting literary relationships.]

1334 Dobrée, Bonamy. " 'Kindness and More Kindness,' " A GARLAND FOR E. M. FORSTER, ed by H. H. Anniah Gowda (Mysore, India: The Literary Half-Yearly, 1969), p. 1.
[Letter from Dobreé to Gowda asserts that EMF's two chief questions are: "What is 'the personality?' " and "What is reality?"] EMF holds that connection is only possible through intuition. He is a brilliant, convincing delineator of character, though he says you can never really "know" anyone. EMF "seeks and produces beauty in people, places and things"; and he is always eminently readable.

1335 Emerson, Gloria. "E. M. Forster, 90, Named by Queen to Order of Merit," NEW YORK TIMES, 1 Jan 1969, pp. 1, 2.
[Gives circumstances surrounding EMF's being named to Order of Merit on his ninetieth birthday.]

1336 "E. M. Forster at Ninety," TIMES LITERARY SUPPLEMENT (Lond), 2 Jan 1969, p. 12.
EMF has stood for the unheroic virtues and emotions: tolerance, good temper, sympathy, personal relationships, pleasure, and love. The quality of his personality is everywhere in EMF's work; he does not believe in the impersonality of art. *A Passage to India* is a first-class book despite EMF's denigration of his achievement. EMF celebrates the life of courage and integrity; and his realism, revealed in his dignified acceptance of the undesired situation, is heartening. [Same as entry 1351.]

1337 Garnett, David. "Forster and Bloomsbury," ASPECTS OF E. M. FORSTER, ed by Oliver Stallybrass (NY: Harcourt, Brace & World; Lond: Edward Arnold, 1969), pp. 37–50.
EMF was elusive at Cambridge and elusive later with respect to his Bloomsbury affiliations. Although EMF did not know G. E. Moore too well, he was his disciple insofar as EMF believed that states of mind are important and that one must take into account the immediate results of an action (since final effects are not possible to calculate). Bloomsbury grew out of Cambridge but also revealed the strong catalytic effect exerted by London and the influence there of Virginia and Vanessa Stephen. The Bloomsbury group had strong intellectual substance and great originality. EMF was more like a Cheshire cat than a comet in his relationships with the group. He was introduced there by Leonard Woolf, whose advice he always sought and who encouraged him to go with the writing of *A Passage to India*. Virginia Woolf came to respect and depend on his opinion and judgment. He was possibly influenced by the rationalistic ambience of Bloomsbury to restrain his vein of fantasy, as he did in *Passage*. The friendship between Lytton Strachey and EMF grew out of shared jokes and a common attitude toward

life rather than an admiration for each other's work. EMF was also a friend of Roger Fry and of Charles Mauron (EMF's French translator). EMF was greatly sensitive, capable of expressing a "wince of pain" when something displeased him and a genial humor at other times. One remembers best EMF's laughter, "appreciative, anguished, but always critical." [Valuable for firsthand commentary on Bloomsbury by a younger member.]

1338 Gordon, Robert C. UNDER WHICH KING: A STUDY OF THE SCOTTISH WAVERLEY NOVELS (NY: Barnes & Noble: Edinburgh & Lond: Oliver & Boyd, 1969), pp. 8, 9, 19, 64, 170–71.

EMF admired Sir Walter Scott's ability to introduce new characters. The opera sequence in *Where Angels Fear to Tread* depends for its comic effect upon the contrast between English reverence for a classical novel by Scott and the wayward performance of LUCIA DI LAMMERMOOR (based on THE BRIDE OF LAMMERMOOR) by a provincial opera company. EMF's novel reveals that Donizetti captures in his sextet Scott's scenic power and invention, qualities especially prominent in Chap 33 of Scott's narrative. EMF perhaps demands too much aesthetic purity when he berates Scott for talking about the early Christians, in THE ANTIQUARY, at a time when some of the characters are in danger of drowning. In THE TWO DROVERS Edward Lowland's difficulties among the Highland Scots anticipate EMF's conclusion in *A Passage to India* that human divisions are not easily overcome. [The directness of Scott's narrative technique in OLD MORTALITY is defended against EMF's strictures expressed in *Aspects of the Novel.*] Scott had more passion, especially in the novel, than EMF credits him with.

1339 Gowda, H. H. Anniah (ed). A GARLAND FOR E. M. FORSTER (Mysore, India: The Literary Half-Yearly, 1969); rptd from LITERARY HALF-YEARLY, X (July 1969), E. M. Forster Special Number, except the "Foreword" and five EMF letters to R. C. Trevelyan.

Contents, most abstracted for 1969: Mulk Raj Anand, "Profile of E. M. Forster"; J. B. Appaswamy, *"The Hill of Devi";* Laurence Brander, "Aspects of E. M. Forster"; J. A. Collins, "Novels into Plays"; John Colmer, *"Howards End* Revisited"; Bonamy Dobrée, " 'Kindness and More Kindness' "; D. J. Enright, "A Passage to Alexandria" (see Enright, 1961); H. H. Anniah Gowda, "Foreword," "A Case Book: Perspectives on E. M. Forster," and " 'To the Caves' "; Wilson Harris, "A Comment on *A Passage to India";* E. F. C. Ludowyk, "Return to *A Passage to India";* Darshan Singh Maini, "John Colmer on *A Passage to India";* Sudhakar S. Marathe and Sujit Mukherjee, *"A Passage to India:* A Check-List"; K. Natwar-Singh, "Only Connect . . . E. M. Forster and India" [same essay as in ASPECTS OF E. M. FORSTER, ed by Oliver Stallybrass (1969)]; Stanley F. Rajiva, "E. M. Forster and Music"; P. Spratt, "The World Citizen"; and Michael Thorpe,

"E. M. Forster's Short Stories"; passage on *Aspects of the Novel* rptd from H. J. Oliver's THE ART OF E. M. FORSTER (1960). Letter (29 Oct 1905) is important for interpretation of *Where Angels Fear to Tread* (EMF intended for Philip Herriton to improve until he appreciates and finally exceeds Caroline Abbott), and letter (6 Aug 1917) gives details of EMF's acquaintance with C.P. Cavafy.

1340 Gowda, H. H. Anniah. "Foreword," A GARLAND FOR E. M. FORSTER, ed by H. H. Anniah Gowda (Mysore, India: The Literary Half-Yearly, 1969), pp. i–ii.

[Gowda emphasizes India's debt to EMF which derived from the pervasive influence of *A Passage to India* and the increased understanding of India resulting from the book, EMF's advocacy of her cause at the time of Chinese attack in 1962, and his help to her writers.] EMF is Edwardian in time but contemporary in his spirit.

1341 Gowda, H. H. Anniah. " 'To the Caves,' " A GARLAND FOR E. M. FORSTER, ed by H. H. Anniah Gowda (Mysore, India: The Literary Half-Yearly, 1969), pp. 23–34.

A Passage to India is inexhaustible; authorial comment in this novel helps EMF project his views of life. *Passage* is only incidentally a political novel; EMF's genius is comic and ironic, also lyrical. *Passage* presents a passage, symbolical and literal, to EMF's mind. Nature and human nature coalesce in the book, and there is a close relationship between the Caves and Indian heroes and demons. In her conscience Adela Quested detests her contemplated marriage to Ronny Heaslop but cannot go deep enough to understand India and, by extension, the irrational aspects of human nature. [Appreciative essay, though excessive plot summary interferes with its occasional striking insights.]

1342 Green, Robert. "Messrs. Wilcox and Kurtz, Hollow Men," TWENTIETH CENTURY LITERATURE, XIV (Jan 1969), 251–59.

The Wilcoxes in *Howards End* are as truly caught up in colonial exploitation as Kurtz is in Conrad's "Heart of Darkness." *Howards End* is not only concerned with the domestic situation of England but with the situation in the Empire. The Schlegel sisters detest nationalism, materialism (beyond a certain point), and imperialism, as their father Ernst had before them; they express anti-imperialistic views throughout the novel, to contrast with the imperialistic views of the Wilcoxes. The attitudes associated with imperialism stain the private lives of the Wilcoxes and account for their emotional and personal inadequacies. Margaret is EMF's Marlow; Henry Wilcox, his Kurtz. Margaret attains enlightenment on British imperialism and reflects EMF's own views. In the end Henry is a shattered man like Kurtz. "All the characteristics of England that Forster detested—obtuseness in personal relationships; chauvinism; opposition to female emancipation and socialism —converge in the Wilcox family, those bastions of Imperialism." In this novel, EMF explores the effects of imperialism at home; in *A Passage to India* he will study its effects abroad. [Sound and perceptive essay.]

1343 Greenberger, Allen J. THE BRITISH IMAGE OF INDIA: A STUDY IN THE LITERATURE OF IMPERIALISM 1880–1960 (Lond & NY: Oxford UP, 1969), passim.

EMF is in a tradition of novelists not widely known who tried to portray objectively the facts about British rule in India. George Orwell and EMF attacked the British Raj because British rule was actually destroying the British in India. Britain was judged a failure by Orwell, EMF, and others, not because she failed to bring law, order, or education but because she did it superficially and condescendingly. Only the non-official British are represented favorably in Orwell, EMF, and Edmund Candler. Like other anti-Raj writers (Edward Thompson, Dennis Kincaid, Candler), EMF blames British women for erecting social barriers between the British and the Indians. In *The Hill of Devi*, EMF expresses the muddle that defeats many Englishmen in India. In *A Passage to India*, radical reorientation occurs in the Caves for all characters except Fielding, who doesn't visit them (in contrast with Kipling's THE NAULAHKA in which positive action is stressed as the answer to an unsettling experience in a cave.) The Indians are naïve, undependable or child-like as they are pictured by British writers; the Indians are sensitive and quick to take offense (see Aziz, who is hardly idealized). Contrary to Nirad Chaudhuri's opinion expressed in "Passage to and from India" (1954), EMF does not distort seriously the Indians he presents in *Passage*. For Anglo-Indian writers, including EMF, personal relations were so important that they saw little need for public reform as such. As Virginia Woolf suggests, the Caves represent the soul of India; the inability of Adela Quested to understand them or of Fielding to go into them indicates that Europeans do not understand the soul of India. For EMF it is difficult for men to achieve intimacy in any place; but is is even more difficult in India where racial, imperial, and communal divisions prevail so strongly. Most Anglo-Indian writers following EMF agreed that it was impossible under colonial rule for an Englishman and an Indian to be close friends. [Perceptive remarks, which agree, in the main, with those expressed in Benita Parry's DELUSIONS AND DISCOVERIES (1972) and Jeffrey Meyers's FICTION AND THE COLONIAL EXPERIENCE (1973).]

1344 Harea, V. "Două concepţie asupra romanuli" (Two Concepts of the Novel), IASUAL LITERAR (Writers' Union of the Romanian Republic, Bucharest), XX: 9 (1969), 81–82.

In EMF's lectures (*Aspects of the Novel*) there is informality and lack of ceremony. The novel, according to EMF, is not a specifically modern creation, and the idea of its evolving is fallacious since human nature, its province, does not change. EMF's seating all his authors at a round table stresses the similarities between novelists. EMF has written a readable book, not on systematic premises but following a logic of ideas that seem to be more random than they really are. A novelist himself, EMF should be read for what he says about the novel by anyone writing at present. [Review of two books recently translated into Romanian, R. M. Albérès's Histoire du Roman Moderne (1962) and EMF's *Aspects*.] [In Romanian.]

1345 Harris, Wilson. "A Comment on *A Passage to India*," A Garland for E. M. Forster, ed by H. H. Anniah Gowda (Mysore, India: The Literary Half-Yearly, 1969), pp. 35–39.

In EMF there is "a curious lack of grasp," "a certain self-deception which passes for order in his predilection for limited human beings such as Aziz and Fielding." EMF, in *A Passage to India*, is deeply conscious, however, of the spiritual void in the lives of his characters and is sympathetic with their spontaneous and irrational behavior as they face the inscrutable. EMF achieves an art that depicts complicated psychic states, and he exploits "unconformable legacies of psyche" rather than the facts and pressures which surround his characters. It is at such a level of psychic incompatibility that the affair between Adela Quested and Ronny Heaslop breaks up.

1346 Hewitt, John. "An Hour with E. M. F.," Listener, LXXXI (13 March 1969), 353.

[Short poem, commemorating the survival in EMF of "an edge of sharpness in that gentle mind."]

1347 Hill, Roland. "Ein grosser Liberaler: E. M. Forster 90 Jahre" (A Great Liberal: E. M. Forster at Ninety), Frankfurter Allgemeine Zeitung, 31 Dec 1969.

EMF has been the teacher of an entire English generation. If he has not had as decisive an influence as Bertrand Russell, he has yet exerted influence as a convinced liberal and as one who has actively contributed to the diminishing of the British imperialistic syndrome. World War I was a watershed for EMF. Human hope had previously been possible; afterwards, human helplessness predominated. EMF no longer accepts the liberal "laissez-faire" view in the sphere of economics and politics but regards it as still valid in the world of the spirit. [In German.]

1348 Hoskins, Katherine Bail. Today the Struggle: Literature and Politics in England during the Spanish Civil War (Austin & Lond: University of Texas P, 1969), pp. xiv, 83, 87, 110, 111, 142, 181, 218, 233–34.

EMF's opinion of Christopher Caudwell's ILLUSION AND REALITY, that it is propaganda, reveals that EMF fails to see how Caudwell raises fundamental questions about human liberty. EMF in 1935 had supported the communist cause but had by 1938 become skeptical of its alleged long-term benefits. EMF he is skeptical of causes in his "Credo" of 1938 ("What I Believe," *Two Cheers for Democracy*). After Christopher Isherwood's Chinese experience, pacifism seemed the only answer to him, but a pacifism recognizing the individualistic skepticism of EMF, with its emphasis on personal integrity and distrust of ideology. Toward the end of the 1930s, Auden and Isherwood embraced the political quietism of EMF, while Louis MacNeice became more militant against fascism. [Scattered references.]

> **1349** Houk, Annelle S., and Carlotta L. Bogart (eds). UNDERSTANDING THE SHORT STORY (NY: Odyssey P, 1969), pp. 272–76; also pp. 253, 255, 262.

[Rpts "The Other Side of the Hedge," followed by commentary.] This story is allegorical rather than symbolical, because the details can be precisely equated to abstractions (the details are "metaphorical") and are not in themselves indefinitely suggestive. [A possible overstatement since the garden and some other details do have a symbolical aura.] The gate of ivory is the one through which come empty dreams, and it is the starting place for the active, spiritually empty life on the road. The gate of horn is the one through which come dreams that really happen and is the one through which man will reenter the paradise of the park. The pedometer is misused to register life and time, not distance. EMF thus implies the enslavement of man to things rather than to truth, the irresponsible use of the instrumentalities of science, the anti-human aspect of a scientific society, and the tyranny of materialism over man. [Rather tenuous association of the number 25 on the pedometer with the twenty-five centuries that have elapsed since Greek culture flourished and modern science had its origins. Fresh, if somewhat rigid, discussion.]

> **1350** Huxley, Aldous. LETTERS OF ALDOUS HUXLEY, ed by Grover Smith (Lond: Chatto & Windus; NY & Evanston: Harper & Row, 1969), pp. 345, 391, 855.

[Letter to Matthew and Ellen Huxley (20 Oct 1955) mentions seeing EMF in the London social whirl. Letter to EMF (17 Feb 1935) declines post of committeeman for London Library, if expert in Italian literature is needed. Shares EMF's gloom about the period and cannot agree with Bertrand Russell that the really important things are those "conditioned by scientific techniques." Invites EMF to visit him.]

> **1351** [Hynes, Samuel.] "E. M. Forster at Ninety," TIMES LITERARY SUPPLEMENT (Lond), 2 Jan 1969, p. 12; rptd, with additions and

revisions, as "E. M. Forster: An Obituary," EWARDIAN OCCASIONS: ESSAYS ON ENGLISH WRITING IN THE EARLY TWENTIETH CENTURY (NY: Oxford UP; Lond: Routledge & Kegan Paul, 1972), pp. 111–14.

EMF has rejected the superhuman as tending to be inhuman; he has rejected the heroic virtues for the non-heroic: "tolerance, good temper, sympathy, personal relationships, pleasure, love." He exists more surely in his books than do his characters. The morality and technique of the books is old-fashioned but reassuring; he commits himself to the moral issues of his invention and so inspires trust. He rightly judges his novels to be less than first-class, but this judgment is not true of *A Passage to India.* His books do not contain him; beyond them stretches a life inspiriting by its courage and integrity. He has been aware of much in his time that is distressing, but he has been "a realist" in his approach, accepting what cannot be altered, with regret but also with dignity. [In rvd form as obituary, essay is cast in past tense and material is added concerning EMF's honesty, his honest treatment of death, his survival in the history of the English novel, and his humanist's faith, which stresses "the supremely valuable individual, the sense of duty, the sense of delight." Stimulating critique.]

1352 Knies, Earl A. THE ART OF CHARLOTTE BRONTË (Athens, Ohio: Ohio UP, 1969), pp. 175–76.

Lucy Snowe in VILLETTE is not so dependable a narrator as Jane Eyre. Her lack of consistency reflects back, adversely, upon her integrity, as EMF contends in *Aspects of the Novel.*

1353 Lee, Robert A. ORWELL'S FICTION (Notre Dame & Lond: University of Notre Dame P, 1969), pp. 21, 156.

BURMESE DAYS does not possess the philosophical complexity of *A Passage to India.* Orwell seems not to have shared EMF's sense of despair over man's isolation. Orwell's ultimate reputation should be comparable to EMF's. EMF and Orwell share a common theme in fiction—"the tenuousness of human community."

1354 Lewis, Anthony. "Humanist and Sage: Edward Morgan Forster," NEW YORK TIMES, 1 Jan 1969, p. 2.

Concerning a glider ride at age 89, EMF has said, "There is absolutely nothing in it. You go up, and you come down." This remark typifies the EMF matter-of-factness, also the fact that he is "a master of understatement, the enemy of hyperbole." *A Passage to India* dramatizes the unbridgeable differences between the races, with an air of mystery and an attitude of kindness to both sides. *Passage* had a real influence in changing Britain's colonial policy. [Résumé of life and career.]

1355 Ludowyck, E. F. C. "A Return to *A Passage to India*," A GARLAND FOR E. M. FORSTER, ed by H. H. Anniah Gowda (Mysore, India: The Literary Half-Yearly, 1969), pp. 41–47.

Excitement and discomfort follow a reading of *A Passage to India*. Excitement depends on appreciating the social comedy, the range of tone in the irony and satire. *Passage* reveals "the confrontation of a highly cultivated artistic sensibility with a reality outside the normal round of its experience." The ideas need clearer articulation than their musical rendering provides for them, but through musical means EMF does render their uncertain aspect forcibly. The themes are the need for human beings to communicate and their failure to do so; and the quest for vision, and disillusion at its rapid passing. [Too relaxed, derivative, and general to be an effective essay.]

1356 McDowell, Frederick P. W. E. M. FORSTER (NY: Twayne Publishers, Twayne's English Authors Series, 1969); rpts in part " 'The Mild Intellectual Light': Idea and Theme in *Howards End*," PUBLICATIONS OF THE MODERN LANGUAGE ASSOCIATION, LXXIV (Sept 1959), 453–63; "Forster's Many-Faceted Universe: Idea and Paradox in *The Longest Journey*," CRITIQUE, IV (Fall–Winter 1960–1961), 41–63; and "Forster's 'Natural Supernaturalism': The Tales," MODERN FICTION STUDIES, VII (Autumn 1961), 271–83; extracts rptd in CONTEMPORARY LITERARY CRITICISM, ed by Carolyn Riley (Detroit: Gale Research Co, 1973), I, 107–8.

[Extensive chronology.] Chap 1, "E. M. Forster: Writer, Moralist, and Thinker": EMF's humanism embraces such attributes as intelligence, emotional sensitivity, and humanitarian sympathy. His humanism derives somewhat from eighteenth-century rationalism, but more directly from nineteenth-century sources: romantic writers, the social critics of the Victorian age, the agnostics of the time, and the renewed enthusiasm for the classics of Greece and Rome. EMF found in Matthew Arnold and in Greek culture an emphasis on bringing man's powers into harmony, of achieving a middle way between extremes. Like Arnold, he celebrates the "junction of mind with heart," a balancing of the forces of intuition and reason; neither force is more to be valued than the other, though intuition may be regarded as more basic. The need to achieve proportion is all-important. A belief in the fecundity of earth and its regenerative powers provides one link between EMF and the romantic writers; his reverence for the past and racial tradition is another such link. Ultimate reality for EMF is psychological as well as mystical, e.g., his high valuation of personal relationships. He protests all pressures which add to the failure of communication among men and promote their alienation, especially the adverse influence upon them of repressive social conventions and "the undeveloped heart." He celebrates love as the force that welds men together but also feels that love should be in the service of the intelligence. Tolerance is in some respects a greater, if less exciting, virtue than love. His liberal and humanistic values are revealed in his cherishing of the individual, and they explain his impatience with the official attitude in politics. Both the individual and the community are important; however, neither one should be served at the expense of the other. Socially, he is both committed and uncommitted. He prizes the liberty possible under democracy but is elitist in stressing the development of the individual and an aristocracy composed of sensitive and imaginative individuals. Underlying his world view is a sense of the contradictory and ambiguous aspects of experience. Problems tend to be more complicated than they first appear; the unpredictable aspects of life run counter to our expectations. Such a realization qualifies the optimism of EMF's humanism, as does his increasing realization of man's inherent potentialities for evil. [This analysis of EMF's mind is wide-ranging and considers uncollected works as well as the collected.]

Chap 2: "The Italian Novels and the Short Stories": The structure of *Where Angels Fear to Tread* consists of two journeys undertaken by Philip Herriton. The first is aesthetically rather than morally motivated, i.e. when he tries to prevent Lilia Herriton's marriage to Gino Carella; the second results in Philip's spiritual regeneration. Fundamental to the novel is the Dantean concept of the "life-pilgrimage" and the need for the characters, especially Philip and Caroline Abbott, to find "the true way." Italy provides both a structural and a moral principle in the novel. Monteriano, signifying a unity of intellect, soul, and body, symbolizes the truth concerning Italy as a force that helps create a vital harmonizing of man's powers. In *A Room with a View* nature is a redemptive influence, as is the life of instinct and passion. The Pension Bertolini in Florence and Windy Corner in rural England provide focuses for the two parts of the novel. Structure depends on Lucy's several encounters with George, which result in her liberation from convention and his liberation from *Weltschmerz*. EMF's art triumphs in the rendition of the pillars of convention, Cecil Vyse and Charlotte Bartlett. [Comments on stories follow in abrgd form, the discussion in "Forster's 'Natural Supernaturalism': The Tales" (1961).]

Chap 3, " 'The Union of Shadow and Adamant': *The Longest Journey*": [Discussion follows that in "Forster's Many-Faceted Universe: Idea and Paradox in *The Longest Journey*" (1960). Some comments on the novel's three-part structure are added; also the inadequacy in EMF's portrayal of Stephen Wonham as an inclusively archetypal character is discussed.] Chap 4, " 'Glimpses of the Diviner Wheels': *Howards End*": *Howards End* lacks the full maturity of *A Passage to India* but is a more engaging and zestful work. Its structure depends on bringing two segments of the middle class into conflict: the materialistic Wilcoxes and the spiritually oriented Schlegels. The concluding sequence, regarded as improbable by many critics, is a fertility ritual presided over by the spirit of Ruth Wilcox [indebted here to John Edward Hardy's "*Howards End:* The Sacred Center" (1964)]. The Schlegel values are only triumphant within limits; London and the Wilcox values are still encroaching on Howards End house at the close. Mrs. Wilcox is an archetypal character, representing transcendent values with which all the other characters must come to terms. There are three well-defined movements: the first, presenting the relationships of the Schlegels with the Wilcoxes, until the death of Ruth Wilcox when they are separated; the second, chronicling Margaret's engagement to Henry Wilcox, which leads to the climactic confrontation of all the characters at Evie Wilcox's wedding at Oniton Grange; the third, tracing the separation between Margaret and her sister Helen and their reunion at Howards End, which leads to Margaret's attack upon Henry for his failure to connect his sexual lapses in the past with Helen's present lapse. The novel is partly organized through evocative symbols: Howards End house, the wych-elm, the Wilcox motor car, the Wilcox life of "telegrams and anger," Helen's obsession with the "goblin footfall" in the Beethoven Fifth Symphony, the abyss associated with the Basts, the grayness of London, hay and grass, the Schlegel bookcase, the Schlegel sword. The dialectical motion is complex; Margaret not only brings outer and inner together in her connection with Henry but attains more durable and spiritually significant connections with Ruth Wilcox and with Helen. As a result of her trials, her fuller understanding of Ruth Wilcox, her critical insight, and her own continued growth, Margaret achieves a more dynamic reconcilation between the earthly and the transcendent than Ruth Wilcox had. She attains true proportion by rejecting the extremes represented by Helen, the Wilcoxes, and even by Ruth Wilcox. The novel is distinctive by its fusion of social realism and poetic symbolism. EMF's mastery of social comedy is indisputable; his attempts at a poetic symbolism have led to controversy. Actually, the comedy and the poetry give distance and perspective to each other. Margaret embodies convincingly EMF's values. Ruth Wilcox does not quite achieve the greatness which EMF imputes to her; too great a disparity remains between what she symbolizes and the kind of woman she really is. Helen Schlegel is real as a passionate woman; and her affair with Leonard Bast, given her impulsiveness and imperiousness, is not so "unreal" as most critics have alleged. EMF, contrary to the opinion of some critics, does well with the Basts, projecting into his picture of them the elements of "tenderness, squalor, humor, and vulgarity." Leonard's characterization is successful when he is presented in action and is unsuccessful when EMF comments disparagingly upon Bast's aspirations. Henry Wilcox is a convincing portrait, though EMF's disparagment of the man negates his abstract valuation of Henry's accomplishments. The marriage between Margaret and Henry is plausible as an alliance between opposites, though EMF's unconcealed dislike of Henry undercuts its effectiveness. The intense and evocative style in certain arresting scenes results in the most memorable effects produced by *Howards End.*

Chap 5, " 'A Universe . . . not . . . Comprehensible to Our Minds': *A Passage to India*": *Passage* is linked to the earlier books in being a masterful ironical comedy, though the novel is much more than that. In it EMF best expresses his double vision and so achieves metaphysical dimensions unique in his work. His view of life is paradoxical and is supported by the inclusiveness of Hinduism. (EMF intellectually agrees with much of Hindu thought, though he has some reservations about Hindu forms and ceremonies.) The absence of God implies His presence and vice versa; evil is not to be desired but endured as only one polarity. So the nihilism that Mrs. Moore finds expressed in the echoes of the Marabar Caves implies its opposite—the beatific, transcendent reality symbolized in the Temple ceremonies at Mau. Mrs. Moore's philosophical ideas, the result largely of a sentimentalized Christianity, are inadequate for the experience she has had in the Caves; but she is capable of vision. As a result she achieves regeneration in death, and afterwards she becomes a Hindu goddess and a pervasive spiritual influence. Hinduism means more to EMF than Islam and Christianity because in its scope it can account for the muddle of India as well as man's dream of order ("the Mediterranean norm" as experienced by Fielding on his way home from India). The Marabar Caves and Hills represent a primordial reality that is extraordinary and elusive, sinister but capable of effects of beauty when the Hills are seen at a distance or when a match is struck within the Caves. Mrs. Moore and Adela Quested at the Marabar Caves experience only the negative aspect of this primordial reality and do not then have the power to envision its opposite. Eternity may be more ominous than reassuring, yet it exists and lends stability and meaning to a chaotic universe. The Caves comprise the sum total of experience, death and life, the womb and tomb of existence, the unconscious and the conscious. [Discussion is here indebted to Louise Dauner's "What Happened in the Cave?" (1961) and to Wilfred Stone's THE CAVE AND THE MOUNTAIN (1966)]. The imagery, in large part associated with the four elements (air, earth, fire, and water), irradiates the novel from within, illustrates the polarities of negation and affirmation, and results in the novel's ineffable quality. The characters are defined through their reaction to, or connections with, the Marabar Caves and the Temple ceremonies. EMF's people are complex and fully developed, especially Aziz.

Chap 6, " 'Unexplored Riches and Unused Methods of Release': Nonfictional Prose and General Estimate": The nonfiction, coming mostly after 1924, is important and adds to EMF's stature. The books after *Passage* are important for what they reveal about EMF's mind, art, and personality. *Alexandria* and *Pharos and Pharillon*, written from EMF's unusual angle of combining fact and personal vision, are memorable evocations of the past. So also are many of the biographical studies collected in *Abinger Harvest* and *Two Cheers for Democracy*. EMF has a flair for writing biography, capturing both the essence of the person he writes about and his milieu. He also does so in two full-length biographies, *Goldsworthy Lowes Dickinson* and *Marianne Thornton*. In *The Hill of Devi* he reveals the savor and complexity of a whole civilization. In his personal, political, and social commentary, to be found especially in *Abinger* and *Two Cheers*, he is subtle, shrewd, and wise. His literary criticism is distinctive for its impressionistic insight and stylistic felicity. In writing his own novels EMF was concerned not only with reflecting the society he knew but with communicating his personal vision as a writer of fable and romance and as prophet. His highly individual style gives his work "its freshness, individuality, and resonance." His creative imagination gives his work, despite its flaws, its incandescence. The recent interest in EMF attests to the widespread recognition of his worth as a critical intelligence and as novelist. [Annotated bibliography. For reviews see George H. Thomson, "E. M. Forster: Realist and Romancer," ENGLISH LITERATURE IN TRANSITION, XIII: 1 (1970), 81–84; Norman Kelvin, "Annual Review Number: Individual Writers, E. M. Forster," JOURNAL OF MODERN LITERATURE, I (1971 Supplement), 97–99; and Mark Goldman, "Recent Books on Modern Fiction: British," MODERN FICTION STUDIES, XVII (Winter 1971–1972), 581–83.]

1357 Marathe, Sudhakar S., and Sujit Mukherjee. "*A Passage to India*: A Check-List," A GARLAND FOR E. M. FORSTER, ed by H. H. Anniah Gowda (Mysore, India: The Literary Half-Yearly, 1969). [A reasonably complete checklist of secondary criticisms on *A Passage to India*.]

1358 Maskell, Duke. "Style and Symbolism in *Howards End*," ESSAYS IN CRITICISM, XIX (July 1969), 292–307; extracts rptd in CONTEMPORARY LITERARY CRITICISM, ed by Carolyn Riley (Detroit: Gale Research Co., 1973), I, 108.
Too much elucidation of the symbolic aspects of *Howards End* has obscured its deficiencies in style and the inorganic nature of its symbols. As to the style, the "poetic passages" are marked by clichés and stock associations; they exemplify, too neatly, ready-made emotions. EMF's second style, the "ironic," is too chatty, and the ironic self-doubts are not rigorous or scrupulous enough. A novel that does not work at the level of language cannot work at all. *Howards End* is "dead to the living surfaces of things." Nor does the symbolism really work; the symbols are too self-conscious in EMF's formulation and development of them. Mrs. Wilcox fails as a symbolic character who is also engaged in actions or with objects that are perpetually symbolic. Some of the trouble is that the rural metaphors and symbols have

no basis in EMF's experience. The symbols are often not fully enough incorporated into a dramatic context. [Some of the strictures are justified, but EMF's language is fresher and more integral to his creative intentions, I feel, than this critic believes.]

1359 Merivale, Patricia. "The Sinister Pan in Prose Fiction," PAN THE GOAT-GOD: HIS MYTH IN MODERN TIMES (Cambridge: Harvard UP, Harvard Studies in Comparative Literature, No. 30, 1969) pp. 154–93, espec 158–59, 175–76, 180–91, 193; also 123, 138, 140, 194, 199–200, 204, 226.

EMF and D. H. Lawrence are the two major modern writers who have made use of the Pan myth. The legend in some form runs throughout all of EMF's fiction written before 1914. [Confines attention to "The Story of a Panic" and *The Longest Journey.*] In "Panic," EMF sees Pan as ambivalent, in any case as "the representative of the ineffable 'beyond the veil,' "; to encounter him is death and/or fulfillment. The conventional English people dread such encounters even when they appreciate Pan as a literary convention (the artist Leyland), mourn him as a lost Arcadian presence (Sandbach), or become bewildered by his ambiguity (the narrator Tytler). Eustace has a true apprehension of Pan but cannot articulate it; he is a "wraith," whereas it is the cerebral, fearful, conventional narrator who comes to life. *Journey* contains most references to Pan: EMF uses the legend to emphasize the artificial and literary quality of much modern nature appreciation, as opposed to the vital reality Pan originally signified and ought still to signify. The phrase "Pan ovium custos" (Pan the herder of sheep) links Stephen Wonham as schoolboy with Rickie Elliot as schoolmaster. [Discusses exhaustively and intelligently the presence and artistic use made of the Pan legend in modern literature. Emphasis on overt use of the legend confines the subject and limits effectiveness.]

1360 Missey, James. "The Connected and the Unconnected in *Howards End,*" WISCONSIN STUDIES IN LITERATURE (Oshkosh), No.6 (1969), 72–89.

Howards End is to be understood in terms of the polarity existing between "the connected and the unconnected." This polarity assumes two guises in the novel. It forms the structure of the novel, as opposites clash in the Schlegel-Wilcox confrontations, the country-city dichotomy, the Wilcox-Ruth Wilcox relationship, and the Margaret-Helen misunderstanding and reconciliation. The strain between connection and its lack also refers to the life of the individual; lack of connection results in a chaotic, fragmented life for him, especially if he prefers the one-sided "steady" view to seeing life "whole." [The country-city opposition is developed at great length in this article.] In the course of the novel the Schlegels become increasingly identified with the country, while Leonard Bast is undermined by the city as

Henry Wilcox represents its values; the forces of culture in the city also ruin Leonard, as does its communal life. It is difficult for Leonard to reach the country from the city; his second foray into the country results in his death. The reconciliation between city and country is only partly achieved; cf. the inconclusive nature of the last chapter. The Wilcoxes (even Henry) are not changed, and London may one day engulf Howards End. If the country triumphs momentarily, the city threatens ultimately to conquer. The breach between Ruth Wilcox and the rest of her family is never closed in realistic terms, though it is symbolically closed in the final reconciliation of Margaret and Helen. Individual personalities are often incomplete or fragmented in the novel. Henry is thus unconnected, and Margaret wants to get him "connected." Ruth Wilcox and her successor, Margaret, alone integrate the whole view and the steady view. [A thorough and sympathetic article, although there is little in it that earlier critics have not noted.]

> **1361** Muecke, D. C. THE COMPASS OF IRONY (Lond: Methuen, 1969), pp. 154, 230, 239.

The echo of the Marabar Caves in *A Passage to India* becomes a perfect image for the potential nihilism characteristic of irony. An example of "protective" irony occurs when, to placate his angry superiors, Dr. Panna Lal behaves like a buffoon before them.

> **1362** Müllenbrock, Heinz-Joachim. "Gesellschaftliche Thematik in E. M. Forster's *Howards End*" (Social Themes in E. M. Forster's *Howards End*), ANGLIA (Tübingen), LXXXVII: 3/4 (1969), 367–91.

Howards End is the deepest of EMF's four early novels. The social preoccupation of the first three novels (*Where Angels Fear to Tread, The Longest Journey, A Room with a View*) lies in the contrast presented between the conventional and the natural, the outer life versus the inner life. In these books EMF analyzes a social problem but is not primarily interested in reform. *The Longest Journey* is the most philosophical, metaphysical, and complex of these three novels. In *Howards End*, Leonard Bast represents an individual from a lower segment in society than any present in the earlier novels. Class feeling on the part of others is fatal to Leonard, but class feeling also results in untoward consequences to the Wilcoxes (Charles's imprisonment and Henry's loss of power at the novel's close). In *Howards End*, EMF's interest in social problems is more direct and explicit than it was in the earlier novels; it ignores for the moment his high valuation of the inner life as contrasted to the outer. Perhaps here he comes to feel that the outer and inner must be reconciled, and he has a higher valuation on the outer than he had ever revealed previously. In the epilogue he puts into the future the risks and the difficulties involved in instituting radical change in society. He is more interested in the present than in the future; he is interested in attaining a social unity, which he feels may in part be attained by resorting to patriotic feeling. He emphasizes the importance of a sense of responsibility. *Howards End* is not a symbol of England nor a symbol of reality, but a symbol by which reality is to be measured. EMF is conscious of the debt of England to its enterprising middle class and so is led to become more of an apologist for this class than he had been earlier. In his fiction there is a movement from a protest against a society inhibiting to the individual to a concern with the formulation of viable social order. In considering the social order as a whole EMF did not feel that he could ignore the Wilcoxes and their significance. Edwardian England was in a period of drastic change. Intellectuals such as Wells, Galsworthy, and EMF came to think that, for the dangerous times lying ahead, the help and guidance of the classes responsible for England's material and political greatness would be necessary. In their works Galsworthy and Wells are advocates of an aristocracy of the elite. In EMF as in Galsworthy there is the same lack of a radical criticism of the upper middle class. The time-spirit encouraged a reliance upon the ruling classes that EMF then reflects in *Howards End.* He makes no such apology for them in *A Passage to India* or his other postwar works. [An interesting and challenging article expounding EMF's social concern in his novels. For a further development of this neglected aspect of EMF, see Willis H. Truitt, "Thematic and Symbolic Ideology in the Works of E. M. Forster: In Memoriam" (1971).] [In German.]

1363 Natwar-Singh, K. "Only Connect . . . : Forster and India," ASPECTS OF E. M. FORSTER, ed by Oliver Stallybrass (NY: Harcourt, Brace & World; Lond: Edward Arnold, 1969), pp. 37–50; rptd, without the notes, in A GARLAND FOR E. M. FORSTER, ed by H. H. Anniah Gowda (Mysore, India: The Literary Half-Yearly, 1969), pp. 105–14; rptd abrgd, as "The Face of a Friend," THE TIMES OF INDIA, "Magazine," (New Delhi), 19 April 1969, p. 1.

EMF has connected with Indians through affection, loyalty, a warm heart, and a sensitive understanding. Despite his being relatively unknown in India, he has been influential with the Indian intelligentsia as friend, critic, and creative artist. The kind of energy represented by Kipling and his imperialism was alien to EMF. He realized that the British Raj had to go before cordial relations could exist between England and India. He was the first writer to portray Indians as human beings and not as caricatures or shifty natives. But he has not been uncritical of India. The criticism has been easy to take, however, because he wished to learn from India, and he was harder on his own people than on the Indians. His view of Anglo-Indians has been challenged (cf. Andrew Shonfield, "The Politics of Forster's India," ECOUNTER [1968]); but the conditions in India were generally as EMF had presented them. *A Passage to India* has been criticized because it makes no mention of the postwar nationalist movement. In reality, the book is largely drawn from India before World War I, though it also presents in part the India of the 1920s. The book's political influence has been ambivalent; it annoyed the British without satisfying Indian political aspirations. EMF's choice of a Moslem for his main character has not bothered his Hindu readers unduly. Godbole, the Hindu, is also an important character and the last scene of the book is the Hindu festival at Mau. EMF was interested in highlighting the human predicament. So any reasonable choice for the protagonist which would allow EMF's creative faculties to expand was justified. EMF understands Hindu philosophy and thought or he could not have written *The Hill of Devi.* His continued interest in, and support of, India has been heartening. [Valuable essay, correcting interpretations that EMF was not interested in, or knowledgeable about, India and Hinduism.]

1364 Park, Clara Claiborne. "Civility in an Age of Muddle," CHICAGO TRIBUNE BOOK WORLD, 2 Feb 1969, p. 4.
EMF's gift is to draw his reader into intimacy. EMF is naturally reticent and distrusts brilliance. In spite of his gentleness and moderation, his work is dynamic in impact: he is "an enemy of accepted ideas, of uptight moralism and outworn convention," a proponent of "openness, truth-telling, love." He forwards these positive qualities by manners and civility. For him, "proportion, precision, self-deprecation, humor, control" have moral as well as aesthetic implications. He would not have people fear to be irrational and passionate, but he would have them recognize the limits within which freedom can be secure. [Review of ASPECTS OF E. M. FORSTER, ed by Oliver Stallybrass.]

1365 "People," TIME, XCIII (10 Jan 1969), 37.
[Account of awarding Order of Merit to EMF on eve of his ninetieth birthday. EMF would not wish to have his death commemorated in King's Chapel: "It would be letting the humanists down."]

1366 Perrott, Roy. "The Quiet Revolutionary," OBSERVER (Lond), 5 Jan 1969, p. 21.
From Edwardian days "Forster has acted as a renegade corpuscle in the English bloodstream, doggedly moving against the accepted direction of flow in order to demonstrate what was deeply amiss with English life and attitudes." EMF is characterized by self-deflation, has carried "deeply held values with an easy-going, ironic flexibility," and has been distrustful always of the abstract morality of the West. EMF is an agnostic, skeptical of authority, a moralist not believing in moral systems. EMF was helped by G. E. Moore to dissect the conventions of the morality surrounding him. In *A Passage to India* he expressed the untenable basis of British imperialism without any moralizing. His wide influence was helped by the accessi-

bility of his writing. EMF was aware of the defeat of liberalism in the twentieth century without lapsing into authoritarianism. [Excellent brief account of EMF's life and career.]

1367 Plomer, William. "Forster as a Friend," ASPECTS OF E. M. FORSTER, ed by Oliver Stallybrass (NY: Harcourt, Brace & World; Lond: Edward Arnold, 1969), pp. 99–105.

Visits to Abinger Hammer were reminiscent of the Edwardian social life presented in the early EMF novels. Friends mean much to EMF; he cherishes them personally and also objectively, as a novelist might. As a friend, EMF brings out the unusual qualities of "ordinary" persons. EMF discovered Cavafy in Egypt and encouraged J. R. Ackerley (HINDOO HOLIDAY) to write. The individual quality of EMF's letters is admirable. The range and variety of EMF's friends is remarkable; and he has also been able to avoid muddle in these relationships. [A pleasant, informative, but not profound essay.]

1368 Rajiva, Stanley F. "E. M. Forster and Music," A GARLAND FOR E. M. FORSTER, ed by H. H. Anniah Gowda (Mysore, India: The Literary Half-Yearly, 1969), pp. 55–68.

EMF prefers an absolute, nonprogrammatic music and regards form, though not the first consideration, as important because it implies an artist's sensitiveness to the demands of his experience and of his craft. EMF distrusts criticism of the arts although he recognizes its importance in causing us to become "infected" with the artist's work. A spontaneous response of "love" is necessary in comprehending the fine arts; and music is an equivalent for love in EMF's purview. Music is a totality fusing the extremes of innocence and experience and other polarities; it fosters spiritual expansiveness and moments of vision. *A Passage to India* combines pattern and rhythm as EMF defines them in *Aspects of the Novel;* and it also achieves the difficult rhythm of "expansion" defined therein. [Commentary mostly obvious; inferior to Benjamin Britten's "Some Notes on Forster and Music" (1969).]

1369 Ramsaran, J. A. "An Indian Reading of E. M. Forster's Classic," IBADAN STUDIES IN ENGLISH (University of Ibadan), I (1969), 48–55.

Hindu religion seems more congenial to EMF's humanistic bent than the pantheism of *A Room with a View* or the naturalistic symbolism of *The Longest Journey. A Passage to India* represents the human yearning for self-realization as a result of one's finding the meaning of earthly existence. India connects many disparities and becomes a microcosm of history. Godbole represents the supreme bliss and unity of being when the human and divine mingle; Mrs. Moore pursues the same experience but inadequately;

Fielding is satisfied with the Mediterranean harmony between the works of man and the prospects of nature and only reluctantly goes further; Aziz wishes for an integration of reason and emotion; Adela Quested reveals how a vague romanticism yields to a wise disillusionment (she never subscribes to the Burton-Turton ethic, no matter how limited she may seem to be). Three men are united by a love of poetry: Fielding, Aziz, and Godbole. All three desire to grasp a reality, beyond the intellect, of which they all have some intimation: Aziz follows Sufi friendship, Godbole follows religious emotionalism of the Vaishnava, and Fielding follows art and human relationships. By force of the Temple ceremonies and the Gokul Ashtami celebrations, Fielding achieves greater integration in his relationship with Stella (daughter to Mrs. Moore); and Aziz and Ralph Moore come together. Godbole has greater faith in the infinite and achieves greater unity in his religious ecstasy than do the other characters (see his reaching out to Mrs. Moore and the wasp); Adela and Ronny Heaslop fail in their relationship because they do not respond to India. Fielding comes to realize the need for "the link outside the human participants" and that good will, culture, and intelligence are not enough to explain life. [A refreshing article, seeing *Passage* from a new angle, in particular the character of Fielding.]

> **1370** Randall, Alec. "Forster in Romania," ASPECTS OF E. M. FORSTER, ed by Oliver Stallybrass (NY: Harcourt, Brace & World; Lond: Edward Arnold, 1969), pp. 51–60.

EMF delighted in his Romanian travels. He refused to visit Randall in fascist Italy and was shocked by aggressive Hungarian displays of nationalism, on the way to Romania. [Some informed insights into EMF's life and personality.]

> **1371** Rising, Clara Lucille Coates. "From Hegel to Hinduism: The Dialectic of E. M. Forster." Unpublished dissertation, University of Florida, 1969.

[Listed in Lawrence F. McNamee, DISSERTATIONS IN ENGLISH AND AMERICAN LITERATURE, SUPP II (NY & Lond: Bowker, 1974).]

> **1372** Roerick, William. "Forster and America," ASPECTS OF E. M. FORSTER, ed by Oliver Stallybrass (NY: Harcourt, Brace & World; Lond: Edward Arnold, 1969), pp. 61–72.

[Roerick persuaded EMF to come to America, knowing that the kindness of Americans and surviving places of interest in America would please EMF; persuaded him to come to Music Symposium at Harvard in 1947; helped him revise his talk later printed as "The Raison d'Etre of Criticism in the Arts" (*Two Cheers for Democracy*); gives details of EMF's travels and of a trip in 1949 when EMF stayed in New York with the painter Jared French.] EMF has had only one thing to say in his own work, "love"; he was much impressed by the abrupt good manners of Americans. [Quoted letters are interesting, especially EMF's expression of loss at President Kennedy's death.]

1373 Spratt, P. "The World Citizen," A GARLAND FOR E. M. FORSTER, ed by H. H. Anniah Gowda (Mysore, India: The Literary Half-Yearly, 1969), pp. 91–94.
EMF's pieces on art in *Two Cheers for Democracy* can make an ordinary reader despair even as he learns something of the quality of the artist's vision. EMF would have preferred to ignore political and social problems, but he could not do so in the 1930s and 1940s. [This observation ignores EMF's protests made in the 1920s against World War I to be found in *Abinger Harvest*.] EMF fails to mention Gandhi. [Seems ignorant of EMF's tribute to Gandhi in 1948, rptd in E. M. FORSTER: A TRIBUTE ed by K. Natwar-Singh (1964).] EMF gives us some notion of the informed liberalism to be realized in the future. [Shallow, uninformed essay.]

1374 Sprott, W. J. H. "Forster as a Humanist," ASPECTS OF E. M. FORSTER, ed by Oliver Stallybrass (NY: Harcourt, Brace & World; Lond: Edward Arnold, 1969), pp. 73–80; rptd in part in MANCHESTER GUARDIAN, 1 Jan 1969, p. 6.
As sage and humanist, EMF has illustrated the facets of the humanistic temper he mentions in "Gide and George" (*Two Cheers for Democracy*): "curiosity, a free mind, belief in good taste, and belief in the human race." [Perfunctory essay by a long-time friend of EMF.]

1375 Stallybrass, Oliver (ed). ASPECTS OF E. M. FORSTER: ESSAYS AND RECOLLECTIONS WRITTEN FOR HIS NINETIETH BIRTHDAY JANUARY 1, 1969. (NY: Harcourt, Brace & World; Lond: Edward Arnold, 1969).
Contents, abstracted: John Arlott, "Forster and Broadcasting"; Elizabeth Bowen, "A Passage to E. M. Forster"; Malcolm Bradbury, "Two Passages to India: Forster as Victorian and Modern"; Benjamin Britten, "Some Notes on Forster and Music"; B. W. Fagan, "Forster and His Publishers" (see 1968); David Garnett, "Forster and Bloomsbury"; K. Natwar-Singh, "Only Connect . . . : Forster and India"; William Plomer, "Forster as a Friend"; Alec Randall, "Forster in Romania"; William Roerick, "Forster and America"; W. J. H. Sprott, "Forster as a Humanist"; and Oliver Stallybrass, "Forster's 'Wobblings': The Manuscripts of *A Passage to India*"; Wilfred Stone, "Forster on Love and Money"; George H. Thomson, "A Forster Miscellany: Thoughts on the Uncollected Writings"; and Patrick Wilkinson, "Forster and King's." [Reviews: Clive Barnes, "End Paper," NEW YORK TIMES, 27 Feb 1969, p. 39; J. B. Beer (Entry No. 1319); "Briefly Noted," NEW YORKER, XLIV (15 Feb 1969), 123–24; Laurence Brander (Entry No.

1325); Keith Cushman, "The Book Review," LIBRARY JOURNAL, XCIV (1 March 1969), 998; P. N. Furbank (Entry No. 1272); Julian Jebb, "The Inner Man," NEW STATESMAN, nsLXXVII (17 Jan 1969), 86–87; Daniel Leary, "A Nonagenarian's Threefold Philosophy," SATURDAY REVIEW (NY), LII (15 Feb 1969), 19, 106; Frederick P. W. McDowell, "Recent Books on Forster and Bloomsbury," ENGLISH LITERATURE IN TRANSITION, XII: 3 (1969), 135–50; Raymond Mortimer (Entry No. 1285); Clara Claiborne Park (Entry No. 1364); "Passage into the Nineties," ECONOMIST, CCXX (4 Jan 1969), 36; Joel Porte, " 'Only Connect . . .': He Did What He Said," CHRISTIAN SCIENCE MONITOR, 10 April 1969, p. 11; and Barrie Ryan, "Book Reviews," ARIZONA QUARTERLY, XXVI (Spring 1970), 89–90.]

1376 Stallybrass, Oliver. "Forster's 'Wobblings': The Manuscripts of *A Passage to India*," ASPECTS OF E. M. FORSTER, ed by Oliver Stallybrass (NY: Harcourt, Brace & World; Lond: Edward Arnold, 1969), pp. 143–154.

[Expands and enlarges an earlier article on the same subject in MANCHESTER GUARDIAN, 20 June 1960, and makes extensive use of Robert L. Harrison's dissertation, "The Manuscripts of *A Passage to India*," (University of Texas, 1964). As curator of the London Library, Stallybrass arranged manuscript of *A Passage to India* for sale, and it was bought by the University of Texas. Harrison follows Stallybrass's earlier division of the manuscript into Manuscript A (main MS, with the greatest number of leaves—399 in all—in their completest and latest forms), Manuscript B (101 miscellaneous leaves, mostly corrected versions of leaves in MS A), and Manuscript C (a typescript carbon of various passages in intermediate stage between MS A and published book).] EMF seems to have written fast and to have used the act of writing as part of the creative process. Published book shows much improvement over the existing manuscript variants. Narrative is converted into dialogue, and explanatory comment is omitted. Some interesting passages are omitted that occur in the MS (those concerning Fielding's past, the chauffeur's origins, and the rumors of Adela's death). Changes in characterization have resulted between the MS and the published book. In the manuscript version Fielding has lost his motor bicycle, smokes cigarettes instead of a pipe, and practices the Wilcox ritual of looking at his watch. Adela is more aggressive in the early versions, and her name had been Violet, Janet, and Edith. Variant versions of many incidents occur. Of Chap 14–16 (the Marabar Caves sequence)fifty-five earlier drafts exist. The MS indicates that it was EMF's original intent to have had Adela assaulted at the Caves. The manuscripts confirm doubtful readings in the published text or can be used to correct misprints. [An interesting and careful article. See also June Perry Levine, "The Manuscript of *A Passage to India*," CREATION AND CRITICISM: "A PASSAGE TO INDIA" (1971) and George H. Thomson,

"The Manuscripts of *A Passage to India,*" Appendix, THE FICTION OF E. M. FORSTER (1967).]

1377 Stone, Wilfred. "Forster on Love and Money," ASPECTS OF E. M. FORSTER, ed by Oliver Stallybrass (NY: Harcourt, Brace & World; Lond: Edward Arnold, 1969), pp. 107–22.

EMF in his work, particularly in *Howards End,* overcame the Victorian reticence about money, illustrated in his fiction by the inhabitants of Sawston (*Where Angels Fear to Tread, The Longest Journey*) and by the Wilcoxes (*Howards End*). In realizing the cultural and spiritual implications of the possession of money, Margaret Schlegel is EMF's spokesman; and Helen Schlegel realizes the power of money to raise the economic and spiritual standards of the submerged classes. Her role in regard to Leonard Bast is akin to that of Overton with respect to Ernest Pontifex in Butler's THE WAY OF ALL FLESH. Helen tries to help Bast, but she also tempts him to renounce his class (he resists the temptation), and she would like to salve her conscience at his expense. EMF (and the Schlegel sisters) illustrates the same pragmatic attitude toward money that Butler does. EMF would agree with John Maynard Keynes in accepting the difference between love of money as a possession and love of money "as a means to the enjoyments and realities of life." Money can be either sacred or profane; it can lead to connection or severance among human beings. The intelligentsia in EMF's fiction are uneasy about the wealth they have done nothing to earn; unearned money implies disregard of merit and the work ethic so prominent in the Victorian ethos. EMF feels guilt about his inheritance from his Aunt Marianne Thornton [questionable]. EMF felt the need to harmonize the Thornton wealth, power, and sobriety (as represented in his father's family) with Whichelo poverty, inefficiency, and love (as represented in his mother's family). Escape from the world of money is possible in the worlds of nature and space, perhaps also in works of art. In EMF's work, money or its lack is less important than "certain psychological and moral attitudes that money can evoke or demonstrate." With money one can purchase God's things as well as Caesar's. EMF has not fused convincingly the realistic dimensions of his tale in *Howards End* with its romance or allegorical aspects. [Comments on the inadequacies of *Howards End* follow the line Stone established in THE CAVE AND THE MOUNTAIN (1966). Interesting and provocative article. Stone attains extraordinary insights into EMF's mind and work, in view of the commonplace premises from which he starts.]

1378 Szladits, Lola L. "New in the Berg Collection: (1962–1964)," BULLETIN OF THE NEW YORK PUBLIC LIBRARY, LXXIII (April 1969), 227–52, espec 237.

[Describes new accessions to the Berg Collection, especially the MS of "The Early Novels of Virginia Woolf" (*Abinger Harvest*) and two EMF letters praising Woolf's JACOB'S ROOM and TO THE LIGHTHOUSE.]

1379 Thomson, George H. "E. M. Forster, Gerald Heard, and Bloomsbury," ENGLISH LITERATURE IN TRANSITION, XII: 2 (1969), 87–91.

EMF in "Bloomsbury, an Early Note: February, 1929" denies implicitly Michael Holroyd's judgment ["Bloomsbury: The Legend and the Myth," LYTTON STRACHEY, I, 395–24 (1967)] that Bloomsbury was a "largely fictitious coterie." EMF acknowledges its tangible existence by saying that it can be understood in light of Gerald Heard's analysis of intellectualism. For EMF, Bloomsbury is the only genuine movement in modern civilization; its members are "gentlefolks," eschewing in their culture "gamindon" and the aristocracy alike. They are possibly too detached. EMF explains Bloomsbury by quoting from Heard's THE ASCENT OF HUMANITY to the effect that intellectuals (like Bloomsbury members) are irritated by emotionalism because such intellectuals are not wholly intellectual. In admitting the claims of emotion, the intellectuals fear their individuality will be destroyed, says Heard; they thus resist emotion in favor of the intellect. EMF no doubt thought this intellectualism constricting if we can judge by the intuitions whose resulting illumination he celebrates in his fiction and elsewhere. [An interesting though overconcentrated note.]

1380 Thomson, George H. "A Forster Miscellany: Thoughts on the Uncollected Writings," ASPECTS OF E. M. FORSTER, ed by Oliver Stallybrass (NY: Harcourt, Brace & World; Lond: Edward Arnold, 1969), pp. 155–76.

There are 210 contributions by EMF to periodicals uncollected, about one third of which deserve to be collected. [Discusses (1) Fiction, (2) Early Writings, (3) India and Egypt, (4) History, Society, and the Arts; (5) Literature; (6) Autobiography. Thomson does not discuss EMF's contributions to books, some of which are significant. He demonstrates that the uncollected writings are important; and he has collected the fugitive pieces until 1915 in *Albergo Empedocle and Other Writings* (1971). Perceptive comments.]

1381 Thorpe, Michael. "E. M. Forster's Short Stories," A GARLAND FOR E. M. FORSTER, ed by H. H. Anniah Gowda (Mysore, India: The Literary Half-Yearly, 1969), pp. 69–75.

EMF's short stories have an aura of the Edwardian period about them. In their classical references they presuppose a culture available to all cultivated people in the age. They also include satirical comments on contemporary middle-class manners or probings of certain stock ideas. EMF exposes a "humanity" that lacks heart and conventions that no longer have life. In his attacks on fixed ideas, he reveals an Arnoldian realism and a conviction that individuals are more important than progressive notions. In "The Point of It," there is a testing of liberal humanistic values under the pressures of experience. EMF is a humanist with vision; and he regards a true Hellenism as stressing the command, "Know thyself." In "The Machine Stops," the side of the story that stresses man as a measure of all things is superior to the "Anglo-animist" or mystical side, revealed in Kuno's nature-worship at the end. "The Story of the Siren" is hardly worth second reading. [Most other critics regard it as one of EMF's best.] The summits of EMF's art in the short story are "The Road from Colonus" and "The Eternal Moment." In these tales the chief theme is the difficulty of reconciling one's relationships with others to the need of being at peace with one's self. "The Eternal Moment" possesses the greater weight and suggestiveness. Except for these last two stories, the stories are dated by the fantasy in them. [A sound and provocative essay.]

1382 Thorpe, Michael. Matthew Arnold (Lond: Evans Brothers, Literature in Perspective, 1969), p. 87.
William Arnold, Matthew Arnold's brother on whom Arnold wrote two elegies ("Stanzas from Carnac" and "A Summer Night"), was an early exponent of the humane treatment of Indians and a caustic critic of imperialistic complacency in the vein that receives its finest literary expression in *A Passage to India.* [See EMF's "William Arnold" in *Two Cheers for Democracy* and Irene A. Gilbert, "Public and Private Virtue in British India" (1974).]

1383 Watson, Ian. "E. M. Forster: Whimsy and Beyond," Eigo Seinen (Tokyo), CXV (1 May 1969), 282–85.
EMF's work goes from whimsy (or fantasy) to prophecy, only attaining authentic prophecy in *A Passage to India.* The short stories are self-contained and enclose their mystery without undue strain; the strain becomes pronounced in the realistic novels of social observation wherein fantasy or mystery is an alien element. The phrase "only connect" is characteristic of all EMF's work, "a quiet cry from the heart of the romantic sceptic." In *Howards End,* the regenerative aspects of nature are emphasized; but its world is less defined by place than by time and is static and withdrawn. It is a period piece. The sense of "otherness" in this novel is conveyed by the joyous life of the spirit and the demonic "goblin footfall" associated with those who betray this life. The sanctified pastoral life celebrated in *The Longest Journey* and *Howards End* does not yet attain to prophecy. EMF's imagination goes beyond pastoralism and whimsy, Pan and Wagner, in *Passage.* Hinduism is a religion not only of contradictions but of synthesis; it accepts absurdities through love. The festival acts as a counterpart to the demonic absurdity of the Marabar Caves, balancing them structurally and spiritually. The Caves (stressing "devastating absurdity") are balanced by the Hindu temple (stressing "an equivocal synthesis through love"). Neither a pert meager Pan nor a whimsical Krishna are present. [A good article with some challenging insights.]

1384 Watt, Donald J. "G. E. Moore and the Bloomsbury Group," ENGLISH LITERATURE IN TRANSITION, XII: 3 (1969), 119–34.

G. E. Moore's influence on members of the Bloomsbury group was both personal and intellectual. The lucidity of his language and his precision, when he tried to present a reality beyond the perceiver but apprehended by him, is a possible influence upon the stylistic experiments by Virginia Woolf and EMF. His emphasis on the importance of aesthetic enjoyment led to a view among his followers that art was autonomous, to the promulgation of the concept of "significant form" in Clive Bell and Roger Fry, to a view that the novelist presents a reality divorced from all programmatic considerations (Virginia Woolf), and to an emphasis upon the importance of art expounded by EMF, notably in "Art for Art's Sake" (*Two Cheers for Democracy*). Moore's view of ethics, as determined by the search for what is good in itself, led to a rejection of conventional standards and to a relativistic view of morality and conduct. The emphasis is upon the individual conscience: Keynes emphasizes the resulting freedom; Leonard Woolf, a sense of his increased responsibility, starting from Moore's "liberating" influence. In Moore is implicit the Bloomsbury emphasis on friendship and personal values. [Extends J. K. Johnstone's view expressed in THE BLOOMSBURY GROUP (1954) that G. E. Moore's influence on Bloomsbury was strong. Watt utilizes materials provided by Leonard Woolf's autobiographies and Michael Holroyd's LYTTON STRACHEY (1967 and 1968). Interesting and perceptive article; consolidates available information and views rather than being strikingly original.]

1385 White, Margaret B. "An Experiment in Criticism," DISSERTATION ABSTRACTS, XXIX(1969), 1521A. Unpublished dissertation, University of Rochester, 1968.

[Applies the critical theories of EMF, Kenneth Burke, Gaston Bachelard, and Northrop Frye to a reading of *A Passage to India*.]

1386 Wilkinson, Patrick. "Forster and King's," ASPECTS OF E. M. FORSTER, ed by Oliver Stallybrass (NY: Harcourt, Brace & World; Lond: Edward Arnold, 1969), pp. 13–28.

Nathaniel Wedd was for EMF the supreme influence. He not only encouraged EMF's literary, classical, and cultural development, but encouraged him to write. EMF was sponsored for the Apostles by H. O. Meredith, later Professor of Economics at Belfast, an intellectual with a lasting passion for the Greek drama and a lifelong friend. Alfred Ainsworth, a brilliant scholar and devotee of G. E. Moore, was the model for Stewart Ansell, just as Rickie Elliot is in part drawn from EMF and his first experiences at Cambridge. Goldsworthy Lowes Dickinson was a great influence upon EMF as a Socratic thinker and as a presiding genius of the discussion societies. Other friends at Cambridge included J. E. Dent (musicologist and model for Philip Herriton in *Where Angels Fear to Tread*), H. O. Meredith, and George Barger (later Professor of Chemistry at Edinburgh). Others connected with Cambridge whom EMF came to know were Roger Fry (an older, nonresident Kingsman, but later Honorary Fellow of King's and Slade Professor for three years), John Maynard Keynes (a younger Apostle), and W. J. H. Sprott (eighteen years EMF's junior and later Professor of Philosophy, then of Psychology, at Nottingham). EMF became resident fellow at King's after 1945, cultivated undergraduates, and became greatly popular with them. He has also been credited with many "clandestine generosities," and he has been kind to all on the college staff. In his view, the third-year man "owns" the college of which he is a part. EMF has been much interested in attending concerts and has been president for some years of the Cambridge Humanists. [The article closes with an account of EMF's eightieth birthday celebration, which was attended by most of his surviving friends. A valuable article, especially for EMF's biography.]

1387 Woolf, Leonard. THE JOURNEY NOT THE ARRIVAL MATTERS: AN AUTOBIOGRAPHY OF THE YEARS 1939–1969 (Lond: Hogarth P, 1969; NY: Harcourt, Brace & World, 1970), pp. 53, 75–77, 125. [EMF was one of the friends the Woolfs saw often on their intermittent trips to London in 1940; he was one of the important writers published by the Hogarth Press; and he asked Virginia Woolf in 1940 to become a member of the London Library Committee, forgetting that in 1937 he had scoffed at the idea of a woman being on the committee (see Virginia Woolf, A WRITER'S DIARY, 1953). This book concludes Woolf's five-volume autobiography and is a kind of epilogue to his life in the Bloomsbury Group. Like EMF, Woolf respected the values of liberalism in the intellectual and personal spheres; both men came to see that liberal ideals must be related, in some viable manner, to the facts of political power.]

1388 Yoneda, Kazuhiko. "E. M. Forster to Orwell" (E. M. Forster and Orwell), EIGO SEINEN (Tokyo), CXV (1 June 1969), 348–50. Ineko Kondo should include the following in her "Forster and His Life," in E. M. FORSTER, ed by Ineko Kondo (1967) concerning the relationship of EMF and George Orwell: EMF was in charge of the British Broadcasting Corporation's fifteen-minute bookshelf program for the broadcasts to India. Orwell was at first Talks Assistant and later became Talks Producer. EMF contributed "Edward Carpenter" (rptd in *Two Cheers for Democracy*) to the TRIBUNE at the request of Orwell, its literary editor. EMF was active also in defending freedom of speech and the press in the 1940s. In 1944, he protested censorship in a letter of protest against the suppression of the anarchistic WAR CORRESPONDENT because of its alleged antiwar propaganda; Orwell signed a separate letter of protest. EMF, with Orwell, was reputedly active on the Freedom Defence Committee, headed by Herbert Read; Orwell became its vice chairman three months after its founding. Orwell was shocked when EMF left the National Council for Civil Liberties in March 1948. Certain characteristics of EMF and Orwell are clarified through "George Orwell," a review written by EMF of SHOOTING AN ELEPHANT AND OTHER ESSAYS (rptd in *Two Cheers*). EMF maintains that 1984 presents a frightening picture of a possible totalitarianism. There are similarities between the anti-Wells, anti-utopian 1984 and EMF's "The Machine Stops." EMF and Orwell are both humanists and agnostics; but Orwell felt that the true problem of the modern age lies in its recovering a truly religious attitude, impossible to effect until the problems of poverty and economic slavery are solved. EMF agrees with Orwell on nature (they have nostalgia for the England of tradition and the countryside), the undesirable aspects of nationalism, and concern for the purity of language. One chief difference is Orwell's belief in "the people"; EMF places his reliance on the individual. EMF was less an activist than Orwell, putting his faith in the individual and in tolerance. Hence EMF regarded Orwell as a "bit of a nagger." Orwell felt that EMF's "tradition" could only be preserved by active efforts to change the status quo. But he would surely have approved of EMF's courage and integrity, although Orwell's COLLECTED ESSAYS does not have an essay on EMF. [In Japanese.]

1970

1389 Akbar, Syed Ali. "E. M. Forster in India," ILLUSTRATED WEEKLY OF INDIA (Bombay), XCI (18 Oct 1970), 25, 27.
EMF was interested in India because of his friendship with Syed Ross Masood, which began in 1907 and lasted until Masood's death in 1937. [Documents EMF's travels and friendships in India and includes some of Akbar's own reminiscences of EMF's visits. Mentions EMF's love for birds, his being covered with cactus thorns when visiting a deserted fort, and his relish of ruins, forts, temples, and Indian architecture in general. Asserts that *A Passage to India* was disliked both by the Anglo-Indians and the Indians because of EMF's candor. Important for biographical fact.]

1390 Anderson, Patrick. "E. M. Forster," SPECTATOR (Lond), CCXXIV (13 June 1970), 793.
EMF is the last of the benign voices expressing a love affair between Cambridge and ancient Greece. EMF was an individualist and a liberal expressing sympathy based upon reason and tolerance. His tone, charm, grasp of subject, and healthiness of vision rescue his work when melodrama ensues or symbolism is too obtrusive. Individual scenes of his novels lodge in the imagination, as his concepts and phrases embodying them remain in the mind. Honesty and fairness characterize his fiction. [Sympathetic obit comment.]

1391 Annan, Lord [Noel]. "Morgan Forster Remembered," LISTENER, LXXXIII (18 June 1970), 826.
EMF was severe in judgment about people, less so about art. He was offended by insensitivity more than by anything else. He was admired by the young in four generations: Bloomsbury (after 1918), Auden and Isherwood in the 1930s, the 1939–1945 war generation, and the post-World War II generation (as "a grand old man of literature"). He was able to say new things about freedom and tolerance in the 1930s and later. In doing so he never thought of his audience (in the sense of having to write to it), and he never forgot it (addressing each person in a perfectly normal way). [Stresses humor in the novels and the enlivening aspects of EMF's own humor. Judicious and appreciative account.]

E. M. Forster

1392 "Aspects of the Novelist," TIME, XCV (22 June 1970), 82; rptd in part in CONTEMPORARY LITERARY CRITICISM, ed by Carolyn Riley and Barbara Harte (Detroit: Gale Research Co., 1974), II, 134.

[Stresses elusive and complex aspect of EMF's art. Notes his affinities with Henry James, D. H. Lawrence, and Jane Austen and maintains that he had only modest hopes for fiction as a shaper of men and history.]

1393 "Author Forster Is Dead; Literary 'Shy Giant': E. M. Forster is Dead at 91," SAN FRANCISCO CHRONICLE, 8 June 1970, pp. 1, 33.

[Obituary article, containing standard account of EMF's career.]

1394 Babu, M. Sathya. "Godbole in 'The Temple,'" LITERARY CRITERION (University of Mysore), IX (Summer 1970), 70–78.

A considerable distance exists between Forsterian skeptical humanism and the mystical, metaphysical position reached in *A Passage to India.* EMF presents the latter as a possible human experience of considerable value without necessarily embracing it himself. Fielding represents EMF's humanistic values, but they are inadequate to encompass the reality of India; in different ways, Adela Quested and Mrs. Moore fail to bridge the gaps between East and West. For India (but not necessarily for EMF) Godbole's spiritual intuitions represent the only possible way in which the complications of India can be truly apprehended. Godbole represents the path of devotion: "to believe in God, to love Him, to be devoted to Him and to enter into Him." Adela's method is based on observation, Fielding's on understanding, Mrs. Moore's on intuition, Aziz's on activity. Godbole's devotional approach, which often precludes direct action, exposes the fallacy of David Shusterman's interpretation in THE QUEST FOR CERTITUDE IN E. M. FORSTER'S FICTION (1965) that Godbole is negative and demonic by his neglect of social responsibility. EMF finds the rituals of Hinduism absurd but its theology attractive. Fielding, who respects the individual man, is a true Westerner; Godbole, who blesses the wasp, is a Hindu. In Godbole there is the reconciliation of the sacred and the mundane, of godhead and the comic, of egoism and selfishness, of the community and the individual; his "devotion" comprehends more than do the ways of activity and knowledge. [Reveals feeling for the novel and some fresh insights; but EMF's rational humanism does not exclude for him the mystical side of experience, i.e., Hinduism can be more in *Passage* than an objectively viewed construct.]

1395 Bajpai, Mani Kant. "Kipling and Forster: A Study in Contrast," THOUGHT (Delhi), XXII (10 Jan 1970), 13–14.

Kipling is not a better writer than EMF because Kipling's characters are stronger. Rather, EMF understands India's complexities and is a reconciling force. [Superficial.]

1396 Barger, Evert. "Memories of Morgan," NEW YORK TIMES BOOK REVIEW, 16 Aug 1970, pp. 2, 32.
[EMF was a life friend of the author's father, a science professor at Edinburgh. The friendship began in the Apostles group at Cambridge. EMF and Barger were also friendly with Sydney Waterlow and H. O. Meredith. Recounts Mrs. Forster's great, indirect influence on her son and the warm relationship existing between Barger's mother and the Forsters. Gives details of EMF's strained visit to Barger at Oxford and describes trip with his mother, EMF, and a mutual friend (Mary Grierson) to Bayreuth in 1954. EMF was a devotee of Wagner but did not like the dark, symbolic settings of the Wagner brothers. EMF was diffident about his own achievements; and he never consented to filming of *A Passage to India* because he would have lost control over the production. Informative reminiscences, with many EMF comments.]

1397 Barnes, Clive. "Theatre: 'A Passage to E. M. Forster,'" NEW YORK TIMES, 28 Oct 1970, p. 62.
A Passage to E. M. Forster, is a remarkable dramatic miscellany from the works of EMF, arranged by William Roerick and Thomas Coley. There is something essentially dramatic in EMF's prose which makes an adaptation such as this a success; his writing has about it "the naturalness of human conversation."

1398 Beer, Gillian. MEREDITH: A CHANGE OF MASKS (Lond: University of London, Athlone P, 1970), pp. 127, 187, 193.
EMF is ambiguous toward Meredith in *A Room with a View*: Cecil Vyse is damagingly made an admirer of Meredith, but EMF's poetic rendition of Lucy Honeychurch in the bed of Florentine violets recalls the courtship scenes at the weir in THE ORDEAL OF RICHARD FEVEREL. [Cites EMF's recognition of Meredith's structural *tour-de-force* in THE EGOIST (*Aspects of the Novel*). EMF's comparison of the plot units in Meredith's novels to kiosks, from which the characters emerge changed, hints at Meredith's secrecy.]

1399 Beeton, D. R. "The Message beyond the Marabar: Some Aspects of E. M. Forster's *A Passage to India*," UNISA ENGLISH STUDIES (University of South Africa), VII (Nov 1970), 20–26.
The objects in *A Passage to India* are, to begin with, real and concrete; but they also have secondary meanings. Thus the fists of the Marabar Hills stand for the anger that will transpire after Adela Quested's accusation of Aziz, the fingers for the various accusations that will be made. The novel's greatness largely lies in such expanding perspectives. The landscape at the end first unites Fielding and Aziz, and then the rocks cause division be-

tween them, the rocks signifying the whole of India that comes between them. Pessimism suffuses not only the Caves scene but also aspects like the punkah wallah in the court room, who presides like a mindless god over the proceedings. The punkah is as terrifying as the Marabar Caves; ostensible harmony covers emptiness. But the punkah is also a reality principle despite this mindlessness and is influential upon Adela (along with the memory of Mrs. Moore) in her candid confrontation of her own situation. The punkah's mindlessness and the ou-boum of the Caves are offset by the fumbling efforts of human beings to secure grace and transcendence; Adela's honesty, Aziz's generosity (when he decides not to press for compensation), and Mrs. Moore's vital influence are all positive forces. The novel dramatizes the need for the connection and the difficulties of attaining connection through forces that divide. Humor is an element that makes for connection; so is EMF's affection for his characters despite their weaknesses. Indians secure connection more easily than do the English because they are more fully identified with Mosque or Temple, places of worship that heighten emotion. The English find it difficult to connect conduct with their lofty sentiments. Ultimately, the separations are bridged, and man's higher ideals and love prevail: Mosque and Temple overcome misunderstandings and undergird the sanctity of personal relationships. EMF is more critical of the Anglo-Indians, who as Christians might learn much from Temple and Mosque, than he is of the Indians. The Indians sometimes act in accordance with the herd instinct, as do the British after Adela accuses Aziz of rape. But the British as Sahibs and administrators ought to be more in control of their behavior. Godbole's religion is genuine but somewhat chilling in its impersonality. Yet he is not cold-blooded in spite of his abstract way of regarding good and evil. In the festival scenes there are distancing elements of let-down and humor, but there is also compassion for humanity that must endure through obscurity and muddle. Mankind can control and defeat muddle through sincerity. *Passage*, in short, stresses mankind's muddle and mankind's value: "Man, in sustaining his faith in life, discovers renewal and God may indeed be born." [Contains a number of challenging insights.]

1400 B[eeton], D. R. "Obituary: E. M. Forster," UNISA ENGLISH STUDIES (University of South Africa), VIII (Nov 1970), 17–18.
EMF's career is most distinctive for the "contribution of his undogmatic concern." For him "the individuality of the person was more important than his protest"; the Aziz who in *A Passage to India* rises superior to his vindictiveness is more significant than "the Moslem triumphant." EMF always championed the individual against the establishment. The influences of Cambridge and of India were profound. Charm dominates *Where Angels Fear to Tread* and *A Room with a View*. The vitality and untidiness of Indians are dramatized in *Passage;* the untidiness of the German-English world of the Schlegels predominates in *Howards End*. [Concludes with a

short notice of ASPECTS OF E. M. FORSTER, ed by Oliver Stallybrass (1969).]

1401 Bennett, Arnold. LETTERS OF ARNOLD BENNETT, ed by James Hepburn, III (1916–1931) (NY & Lond: Oxford UP, 1970), p. 188, 208–9.
[Letter to John Middleton Murry (1 May 1923) advises him to secure services of Robert Lynd, EMF, Desmond MacCarthy, and H. M. Tomlinson for Murry's new journal, the ADELPHI. Letter to Radclyffe Hall (28 Aug 1928) fears that EMF's advocacy of Hall's THE WELL OF LONELINESS may be too late to have tangible results. Letter to EMF (1 Sept 1928) advises him to drop his advocacy of Hall's book, since her demands upon him have apparently become drastic.]

1402 Bergonzi, Bernard (ed). THE TWENTIETH CENTURY (HISTORY OF LITERATURE IN THE ENGLISH LANGUAGE, Vol. 7) (London: Barrie & Jenkins, 1970).
[Contents, abstracted (1970), "The Advent of Modernism 1900–1920," Malcolm Bradbury, "The Novel in the 1920s," and David Lodge, "Literary Criticism in England in the Twentieth Century." Other scattered references.]

1403 Bergonzi, Bernard. "The Advent of Modernism 1900–1920," THE TWENTIETH CENTURY (HISTORY OF LITERATURE IN THE ENGLISH LANGUAGE, Vol. 7), ed by Bernard Bergonzi (Lond: Barrie & Jenkins, 1970), pp. 17–48, espec pp. 34–35.
Howards End is better than the early books, but its cultural significance is greater than its literary merit. EMF is conscious of the need to connect the inner and outer realms in the Schlegels and the Wilcoxes and the need for both to connect with the lower middle class in Leonard Bast, who embodies the democratic future. He reveals with insight the divisions between these groups, but the connections he discovers or imposes are melodramatic and strain credulity. Yet the novel is impressive as an attempt to discover England's destiny. His work is traditional until *A Passage to India;* then new forms in the novel allowed him to achieve greater aesthetic intensity and tragic understanding.

1404 Blaise, Bharati Mukherjee. "The Use of Mythology in E. M. Forster's *A Passage to India* and Herman Hesse's SIDDHARTHA," DISSERTATION ABSTRACTS INTERNATIONAL, XXX (1970), 3901A. Unpublished dissertation, University of Iowa, 1969.

1405 Bradbury, Malcolm (ed). E. M. FORSTER: "A PASSAGE TO INDIA": A CASEBOOK (Lond: Macmillan, Casebook Series, 1970).
Contents, abstracted under date of first publication: Malcolm Bradbury,

"Introduction" (1970); P. N. Furbank and F. J. H. Haskell, "An Interview with E. M. Forster," from "E. M. Forster: The Art of Fiction I," PARIS REVIEW (1953); Oliver Stallybrass, "Forster's 'Wobblings': The Manuscripts of *A Passage to India*," ASPECTS OF E. M. FORSTER (1969), ed by Oliver Stallybrass; Virginia Woolf, ["A Failure?"], from A WRITER'S DIARY, ed by Leonard Woolf (1953); D. H. Lawrence, ["Two Letters"], from THE LETTERS OF D. H. LAWRENCE, ed by Aldous Huxley (1932); L. P. Hartley, "Mr. E. M. Forster's New Novel," SPECTATOR (Lond; 1924); Ralph Wright, ["A Review"], "New Novels," NEW STATESMAN (1924); J. B. Priestley, ["A Review"], "Fiction," LONDON MERCURY (1924); Virginia Woolf, "The Novels of E. M. Forster" [ptd in part], ATLANTIC MONTHLY (1927); Lionel Trilling, "*A Passage to India*," E. M. FORSTER (1943); E. K. Brown, "Rhythm in E. M. Forster's *A Passage to India*," RHYTHM IN THE NOVEL (1950); Reuben Brower, "The Twilight of the Double Vision: Symbol and Irony in *A Passage to India*," THE FIELDS OF LIGHT (1951); Gertrude M. White, "*A Passage to India*: Analysis and Revaluation," PUBLICATIONS OF THE MODERN LANGUAGE ASSOCIATION (1953); James McConkey, "The Prophetic Novel: *A Passage to India*," THE NOVELS OF E. M. FORSTER (1957); Frederick C. Crews, "*A Passage to India*," E. M. FORSTER: THE PERILS OF HUMANISM (1962); John Beer, "The Undying Worm," THE ACHIEVEMENT OF E. M. FORSTER (1962); Frank Kermode, "The One Orderly Product" [originally "Mr. E. M. Forster as a Symbolist"], LISTENER (1958); and Malcolm Bradbury, "Two Passages to India: Forster as Victorian and Modern," ASPECTS OF E. M. FORSTER, ed by Oliver Stallybrass (1969). By E. M. Forster and not abstracted: ["Note on *A Passage to India*"], from *The Hill of Devi*. Selected Bibliography.

1406 Bradbury, Malcolm. "Introduction," E. M. FORSTER: "A PASSAGE TO INDIA": A CASEBOOK, ed by Malcolm Bradbury (Lond: Macmillan, Casebook Series 1970), pp. 11–23.

Aspects of the Novel represents EMF's attempt to reconcile the traditional novel with modernism, formalism, and experimentalism. *A Passage to India* is more a novel of the 1920s than of the prewar period. EMF's first three novels were distinctive by (1) the complexity of his moral and social critique (EMF questioned in them liberal, humanist, reformist, romantic attitudes) and (2) the presence of spiritual and moral control, a kind of good sense interested in truth as such. Art can illuminate our lives by fantasy, by the making of formal orders, and by asserting standards of wisdom and truth (the humanist category in which EMF's works are prominent). The early novels revealed a humanistic basis and a moral scepticism; *Howards End* stressed the need for organic wholeness in the community (the need to connect) as opposed to accelerated flux. EMF's unease is still greater in *Passage*. His "moral realism" in it goes deeper "to the most profound questioning of hope, meaning and connection that he ever produced." *Pas-*

sage is full, genial, and bleak; it is characterized by sharp social observation and by an evocation of anarchy and historical disorder; its pessimism is more than an easy assertion. The book's inclusiveness gives even the vision in the Caves a meaning. The world of *Passage* includes the worlds of religion, nature, race, and politics and puts them in relation to each other. "Only connect" is still a necessary imperative in "this unconnected and contingent world," but connection is more a possibility than a probability. Two visions contrast with each other: Mrs. Moore's (nothingness) and Godbole's (completeness). There are also two tones—the poetic, which sees "muddle as mystery" and the comic, which sees "mystery as muddle." The problem in interpretation of *Passage* is one of emphasis: which mode is it written in? In interpretation we must put the human and verbal planes into their right relationship. Earlier interpretations stressed the social and political (or comic) aspects, as in Lionel Trilling's E. M. FORSTER (1943). More recently the poetic (and formal) emphasis has been in the ascendant. Wilfred Stone in THE CAVE AND THE MOUNTAIN (1966) and others maintain that *Passage* articulates a vision of universal oneness; James McConkey in THE NOVELS OF E. M. FORSTER (1957) and E. K. Brown in "Rhythm in E. M. Forster's *A Passage to India*" (1950) discern a fragmented vision but stress the intertwined themes, images, and motifs that give *Passage* formal unity. Frank Kermode in "Mr. E. M. Forster as a Symbolist" (1958) goes further and sees the novel as an artistic construct, where attention to form may even mean the presence of "faking" in subject matter. One can profit from the insights of these formalist critics without losing sight of the novel's social and political dimensions. Its comic aspects are complex and have not been fully explored. [Perceptive commentary.]

1407 Bradbury, Malcolm. "The Novel in the 1920's," THE TWENTIETH CENTURY (HISTORY OF LITERATURE IN THE ENGLISH LANGUAGE, Vol. 7), ed by Bernard Bergonzi. (Lond: Barrie & Jenkins, 1970), pp. 180–221, espec 192–96.
Virginia Woolf is more modernist than EMF, yet her fragile sensibility makes her best novels less significant than *A Passage to India*. In contrast to EMF's other books, *Passage* has neo-symbolistic cohesiveness and rhythmic construction; herein lies the debt, acknowledged by EMF, to Proust. In *Howards End* there is not only the fusion of comedy and the visionary but a sense of historical acceleration. In *Howards End*, EMF works toward a visionary sense of space as against a sense of flux in time. Since the urban state of flux can be contained only by an ideal that may be realized in the future, the thrust of the book is partly ironic. Its centers are given spiritual and moral validity but not historical justification; the unity proposed is symbolical. In *Passage*, EMF's social, political, and historical observation is fuller, and his response to people is deeper. He is less concerned with the challenges within western culture than with the challenges made to that

culture by alien forces. The fullness of his eclecticism results partly in an implied nihilism. The book speaks for human reconcilement and for personal values, but it does so in a world whose edges shade off into a primitive universe that goes beyond time and history and manifests meaninglessness, indifference, and evil. The unity proposed is difficult to envision or to contain within the pages of the book, but the book presses toward fullness with great moral power. On the one side EMF presents the multiplicity of India, the comic mode expressing its muddle; on the other side, he suggests a total unity, the poetic mode suggesting mystery. The interplay between the two conceptions and the two modes suggests the need for both flux and formal order. EMF is both a social novelist and a symbolist. His vision is partly that of the artist who can create in his work "a sense of wholeness, order and completeness." [Challenging discussion.]

1408 Brierre, Annie. "Hommage à Edward Morgan Forster" (Homage to Edward Morgan Forster), REVUE DES DEUX MONDES (Paris), ns8 F (August 1970), 414–18.
[Competent summary of EMF's career, his novels, and his miscellaneous works.] [In French.]

1409 Brogan, Denis. "A First—Without a Star," SPECTATOR (Lond), CCXXIV (20 June 1970), 818.
EMF was put off by Indian culture, though he had superior insight into it; he had closer affinity with the culture of Italy or that of Alexandria. EMF's India is as genuine as Ackerley's, Kipling's, or Nirad Chaudhuri's (1954). At the conclusion of *A Passage to India*, with Fielding's increasing conservatism and Aziz's going "native," "passage" is reversed; connection is unachieved. In *Howards End* EMF apprehends both sides of the Schlegels (their British and German sides) and the deficiencies of the Wilcoxes, and he depicts Margaret's adjustment to the Wilcox world with insight and sympathy. EMF was too despairing about Leonard Bast's possibilities. EMF was a great figure in the enlightenment which ended in 1914, and he helped restore faith in the life of reason. [Excellent obit notice.]

1410 Cahill, Daniel J. "E. M. Forster's *The Longest Journey* and Its Critics," IOWA ENGLISH YEARBOOK, XV (Fall 1970), 39–49.
In the increasing bulk of EMF criticism, *The Longest Journey* has aroused the most controversy. Sympathetic critics see *Journey* as EMF's endeavor to dramatize in Rickie Elliot a failure to mediate between the "real" and the "ideal." Negative critics like John Harvey in "Imagination and Moral Theme in E. M. Forster's *The Longest Journey*" (1956) see *Journey* as a failure in terms of both substance and technique. Rose Macaulay in THE WRITINGS OF E. M. FORSTER (1938) and James McConkey in THE NOVELS OF E. M. FORSTER (1957) have offered suggestive Christian readings, and

Frederick C. Crews in E. M. FORSTER: THE PERILS OF HUMANISM (1962) interprets the novel authoritatively in terms of EMF's values and ideas. [Charts some complexities of its subject, but article is inadequate because analyses by J. B. Beer, Wilfred Stone, John Magnus, and George H. Thomson are not cited.]

1411 Carrington, [Dora de Houghton]. CARRINGTON: LETTERS AND EXTRACTS FROM HER DIARIES, ed by David Garnett (Lond: Jonathan Cape, 1970; NY: Holt, Rinehart & Winston, 1971), pp. 141, 143, 237, 250, 297, 389, 395, 405, 430, 431.

EMF's charm, self-sufficiency, and moodiness (he seems to try to hide his true feelings by his surface gaiety) are emphasized. [Letter to Sebastian Sprott (March 1929) would indicate that Carrington knew EMF well.] [Numerous incidental references to EMF by Lytton Strachey's friend and housekeeper. Excellent portrait of EMF by Carrington. The book is important for enlarging our knowledge of the Bloomsbury Group.]

1412 Carstairs, G. M. "Foreword," A DYING COLONIALISM, by Frantz Fanon, trans from French by Haakon Chevalier (Harmondsworth Middlesex: Penguin Books, 1970), p. 8.

[Fanon's works are concerned with the acute social dichotomy which imperialism brings with it and which vitiates all relationships between the governing and the governed races. This same dichotomy had been explored memorably in EMF's *A Passage to India*. EMF's sympathies were with the governed population, although he was not actively political.]

1413 Casey, Phil. "E. M. Forster, Famed British Writer, Intellectual, Dies in Coventry at 91," WASHINGTON POST, 8 June 1970, pp. 1, 9; in some eds essay is also titled, "E. M. Forster Dies at 91; British Novelist, Critic."

[EMF never had a bad press. Critics, scholars, and fellow writers all regarded him with admiration and affection. EMF had capacity for enjoyment and was always congenial. General account of his work and career, recapitulating facts and judgments already familiar. EMF told Santha Rama Rau that we place our magical island in the past (memory) or in the future (vision), but we cannot locate it in the present: "We call it memory or a vision to lend it solidity, but is is neither, really: it is the outcome of our sadness, and of our disgust with the world that we have made."]

1414 Chapple, J. A. V. DOCUMENTARY AND IMAGINATIVE LITERATURE 1880–1920 (NY: Barnes & Noble; Lond: Blandford P, 1970), pp. 74, 172, 212–19, 265, 332–38.

Some of EMF's short stories are escapist, but "The Machine Stops" reveals some of his basic values. *A Passage to India* reveals the lack of humanity in the English because of their imperialist position; the administrators of empire lack a developed heart. Yet EMF believed in social order and sensed the divisions present in the Indians (religion, race, caste) who are united only against the English. EMF stresses the need to connect across such barriers. At the trial the motive for Adela Quested's withdrawal of her charge and the events in the Marabar Caves are not entirely clear, but they register symbolic intonations. The symbolic pattern is all important, as is the whole Caves sequence. The description of the Caves' interior is masterly. In the Caves the efforts of the flames to reach their reflection comment symbolically on the unity prevented by "ineluctable circumstance." The Caves provide an experience of horror and negation for Mrs. Moore but a positive influence for Adela when she remembers them at the trial. The positive influence of "Temple" and the negating influence of "Caves" are both Indian. The moment of vision is momentary, and personal relationships are difficult; but "not yet" and "not there" imply that somewhere and at some time they will flourish. [Discussion notes the conflict of values in EMF's novels, especially in *Howards End* between the Schlegels and Wilcoxes.] EMF follows Matthew Arnold in emphasizing the need for harmony. *A Room with a View* emphasizes the difficulties in the way of being honest.

1415 Churchill, R. C. "Forster the Novelist: A Passage to Greatness," HUMANIST (Cambridge), LXXXV (Aug 1970), 230.

EMF is a great novelist, and he persuades us that he is so by his modesty about his achievement. He is a master at telling a story, e.g., the first two chapters of *Howards End*. In this book we have EMF's self-criticism at its most relentless; the Schlegel sisters (and EMF and Bloomsbury itself), as well as the Wilcoxes, fail at times to connect. In *A Passage to India*, Aziz is a fascinating character and is a victim of the British failure to connect. *Passage* is *Howards End* on a larger scale; EMF observes the Indian scene with lack of bias and with witty penetration. Aziz and Fielding could connect at the end if the wisdom of East and West could be brought together. In EMF's fiction no character ever gives in, because EMF himself did not; they are as tough as he was. EMF was the backbone of Bloomsbury more so than Virginia Woolf. [An interesting judgment.] In old age he became "the revered heart of English humanism" as Bertrand Russell became its head. In EMF's fiction the characters grow increasingly strong and have greater trials from book to book. EMF will be a surviving presence in literature just as Mrs. Moore becomes such in *Passage*. [Excellent insights.]

1416 "Commentary," TIMES LITERARY SUPPLEMENT (Lond), 13 Nov 1970, p. 1326.

King's College, Cambridge, will become repository for EMF's papers and center for EMF studies.

1417 Das, Gour K. "E. M. Forster as Interpreter of India." Unpublished dissertation, Cambridge University, 1970.
[Listed in Lawrence F. McNamee, DISSERTATIONS IN ENGLISH AND AMERICAN LITERATURE, SUPP II (NY & Lond: Bowker, 1974).]

1418 Das, Manoj. "E. M. Forster: The Strong Rationality," THOUGHT (Delhi), XXI (20 June 1970), 18.
[Brief article stressing EMF's intellectual grasp of his subjects.]

1419 Davis, Edward. "E. M. Forster (Died July 1970)," STANDPUNTE, XCLI (1970), 24–25.
EMF's "major" theme: "the innocence, trustworthiness and depth of man's instinctive self contrasted with deviousness, insincerity and shallowness of the self which submits to the conventions of the social environment." Some of his works are secure by their sense of justice, some by their faith in nature. His work, despite his criticism of the public school, also comprises the finest existing tribute to its ideals. His works decry the abuses of power and are imbued with the principle of *noblesse oblige.* The EMF in every Englishman caused England to relinquish her final hold on India.

1420 Draper, R. P. (ed). D. H. LAWRENCE: THE CRITICAL HERITAGE (Lond: Routledge & Kegan Paul; NY: Barnes & Noble, The Critical Heritage Series, 1970), pp. 19, 23, 244, 287, 318–21, 341, 343–47.
[Details are given of EMF's defense of Lawrence in the 1920s, of J. Middleton Murry's comparison of Lawrence with EMF and others (see "Lemonade?" [1926]), and of EMF's obit notice of Lawrence. Other incidental references to EMF in articles by Edwin Muir, V. S. Pritchett, and Arnold Bennett. Rpts "Mr. D. H. Lawrence and Lord Brentford" (NATION AND ATHENAEUM, 11 Jan 1930) and "D. H. Lawrence" (LISTENER, 30 April 1930), both by EMF.]

1421 Drews, Jörg. "Humaner Skeptiker: zum Tode des englischen Romanciers E. M. Forster" (Humane Skeptic: On the Death of English Novelist E. M. Forster), SÜDDEUTSCHE ZEITUNG (Munich), 9 June 1970.
EMF's inability to write novels after 1924 is the result of the change after World War I in the society that he had known. Although *A Passage to India* marked a departure from his subtle moral comedies, it begins with the same initial groupings of characters found in *Where Angels Fear to Tread.* EMF is a master of the subtle nuance that hints at reality; only the "developed heart" can understand such indirections. [In German.]

1422 Dyson, A. E. THE INIMITABLE DICKENS: A READING OF THE NOVELS (Lond: Macmillan; NY: St. Martin's P, 1970), p. 130.

EMF was wrong in his criticism of Dickens in *Aspects of the Novel* when he called the characters in DAVID COPPERFIELD "flat." They have the inexhaustible life that EMF reserves for "round" characters.

1423 Eagleton, Terry. EXILES AND ÉMIGRÉS: STUDIES IN MODERN LITERATURE (NY: Schocken; Lond: Chatto & Windus, 1970), pp. 12, 38–40, 68, 219–20.

The central contradiction dramatized in *Howards End* is one within the upper middle class—the conflict between its deviant humanists and its Philistine economic architects. EMF is more honest than Virginia Woolf in seeing the parasitism of the upper middle class as resting on the social structure that it criticizes. He perceives the problem but is unable to solve it. His reconciliations are at a formal level and do not concern themselves with "an open conflict of values in the real world." We are asked to admire Wilcox qualities and overlook Wilcox activities and to believe that Leonard Bast is real. What is questionable is the implied equivalence between Bast and the Wilcoxes from the Schlegel point of view, as representing a real world in contrast to their own contemplative one. The true antinomies in the novel are the upper-middle-class world of the Schlegels and the Wilcoxes versus the exploited, patronized existence of Bast. This division is finally recognized in the marriage of Henry Wilcox and Margaret Schlegel and in the death of Bast, with his survival in Helen Schlegel's child. In *A Passage to India* Mrs. Moore's liberal humanism allows her to reject the formal upper-class ideology of her son. But to the extent that she identifies with the "amorphous, alien and opaque reality" which is India, she finds her traditional Western values weakening. Her futility is structurally related to the satirized orthodoxies as their only viable alternative. There is a similarity between *Howards End* and Evelyn Waugh's BRIDESHEAD REVISITED: traditional values (liberal or conservative) "cannot be foregone" but neither can they be "advanced or defended without a destructively opportunistic alliance with their enemies." [Incidental but pointed commentary.]

1424 "E. M. Forster," THE INDIAN P. E. N., XXXVI (July 1970), 191–93.

[Account of life and career based on standard facts.]

1425 "E. M. Forster: India Inspired His Greatest Novel," THIS IS BRITAIN (New Delhi), II (June–July 1970), 5–6.

[Summary of EMF's life, career, achievement, and sojourns in India; also the honors awarded him.]

1426 "E. M. Forster: Legacy of the Dominating Females," MANCHESTER GUARDIAN, 13 July 1970, p. 8; similar to "Forster's Earlier Life—Extracts from a Radio 3 Discussion," LISTENER, LXXXIV (16 July 1970).

[Section covering EMF's reactions to the Wolfenden Report is omitted, but discussion concerning EMF's women characters has been added. Andrew Shonfield asserts that EMF's women, apart from the Schlegel sisters, tend to be dominating rather than sexually magnetic. W. J. H. Sprott mentions EMF's mastery with the mature, elderly woman (Ruth Wilcox and Mrs. Moore), and K. W. Gransden stresses EMF's vivid portraits of ruthless, manipulating upper-middle-class women (Mrs. Herriton and Mrs. Failing). Interesting discussion.]

1427 "E. M. Forster," NEW YORK TIMES, 10 June 1970, p. 46.
EMF's books identify and "impale" racial and social predjudice, "the human flaws of hypocrisy and repression." He and others in the Bloomsbury circle were, if insular in some ways, "creative visionaries," dedicated to the cause of personal and scholarly freedom.

1428 "Forster's Earlier Life—Extracts from a Radio 3 Discussion," LISTENER, LXXXIV (16 July 1970), 82 [radio discussion, 12 July, Andrew Shonfield, Chairman, with Lord Noel Annan, K. W. Gransden, and W. J. H. Sprott (EMF's literary executor)]; differs in detail from "E. M. Forster: Legacy of the Dominating Females," MANCHESTER GUARDIAN, 13 July 1970.
[Annan asserts that EMF stopped writing novels because the morality he had known before World War I did not correspond to that he found in India. Also EMF knew more personal happiness in the 1920s than before; and writers, Annan feels, often work best out of unhappiness. Gransden mentions the negative influence on EMF of World War I. Annan adheres to a more personal explanation for EMF's cessation of novel writing: the widening of his circle of friends to include some that were homosexually oriented and the diminution of his mother's influence (and that of other women relatives). Annan discusses EMF's homosexuality and EMF's own disingeniousness and lack of candor in writing in behalf of the Wolfenden Report, legalizing adult homosexuality. Gransden cites EMF's "homosexual" influence in the early novels of Angus Wilson. Feels that Lucy Honeychurch in *A Room with a View* is a boy *en travesti* and that EMF's homosexuality gave him a detached insight into the inner lives of women. Notes that D. H. Lawrence may have been latently homosexual and that the Brangwen sisters in WOMEN IN LOVE reveal the same depth of authorial insight as do the Schlegel sisters in *Howards End.* Sprott describes *Maurice* and EMF's intent to bring this homosexual novel to a happy ending, disregarding the then current assumption that such novels should end tragically. Informative discussion.]

1429 Freedman, Richard. "A Brief Triumph over Panic and Emptiness," CHICAGO TRIBUNE BOOK WORLD, 12 July 1970, pp. 1, 3.

EMF has a secure if narrow position in the great traditions of English ficiton and English liberalism. From the ancestral Thorntons came the high Victorian moral tone that EMF mocked and yet felt nostalgic toward. He was an individualist and was aloof, even from Bloomsbury. *A Passage to India* is the classic novel about India but also a novel about all barriers to human communication, not only between races but between the sensitive and the boorish, the young and the old, and the different sects of a country. The problems of misunderstanding go too deep to be solved by politics or goodwill, yet they must be solved. At Cambridge after 1945 he was sympathetic with the aspirations of the young and was a benign presence there. His overwhelming concern was with continuity—moral, spiritual, personal—as an offset to "panic and emptiness."

1430 Furbank, P. N. "The Personality of E. M. Forster," ENCOUNTER (Lond), XXXV (Nov 1970), 61–68.

It is too early to pronounce definitively on EMF. But he is a man who did know how to live in daily touch with his own depths. A biographer of EMF faces difficulties: his life stood still, and there are no accounts of EMF and his conversation before he became famous. But his contemporaries assure us that he was the same at twenty as at ninety. EMF had a passion for friendship but never gave himself fully to his friends. He did not like being laughed at or teased; he was not good at quarrels, which always loomed too large and to which his reactions were always personal. There was something self-pleasing in his approaches to others, especially when sex was involved. Gratitude marked his sexual experiences, but he did not want to establish a permanent relationship with anyone. He fretted at having to write marriage fiction when he believed that there were finer possibilities than those offered by marriage. EMF did have vanity; he felt a strong respect for his own work and his position and was not really humble. EMF's "dowdiness" was a deliberate choice. An element of self-punishment obtrudes; he would like to have displayed himself, but his Puritan background would not allow him to do so. EMF was also capable of jealousy. But Ackerley is right in saying that EMF was without envy; he was worried about his reputation and sterility after *Howards End*, but he did not let envy creep in. Ackerley was right also about EMF's great generosity. The most important characteristic in his life and writing was his moral passion. His technical originality consisted in his being more Victorian than George Eliot or Thackeray. He is more godlike even than they in manipulation of characters and in commenting on them, and he worked "his godlike intrusions" more closely into his fictional fabric. The moralizing increases with time, so that *A Passage to India* reveals his presence more than ever: "He found moralizing a device of endless potentiality; there was room for his genius in it." This bent he inherited in part from his mother; but he makes of his moralizing something elusive, flexible, and complicated. EMF's moralizing also made him formidable. As a literary critic he looked at a work as if it had never existed before. He then expressed his empirically derived impressions and "emerged with a brand new, freshly-minted formula" for the work. For better or worse, his approach made him distrustful of intellectual systems. The virtue of his criticism was that it expressed his mind, which was "a vast breeding-ground for discriminations." In his fictions as in his essays EMF was "a master of angle," but his angles were not the product of whimsicality. His deepest originality lies in his feeling for life and its possibilities. For him all of life's potentialities might be contained in any one moment of it. [Praises J. R. Ackerley's account of EMF (OBSERVER, 14 June 1970), but does not agree with all aspects of it. Extremely perceptive and fascinating account by EMF's official biographer.]

1431 Gilbert, Elliot L. THE GOOD KIPLING: STUDIES IN THE SHORT STORY (Athens: Ohio UP, 1970), pp. 11, 120–21.
Kipling in "The Ballad of East and West" is less absolute in positing a gulf between the English and the Indians than is EMF in the conclusion of *A Passage to India.* [EMF is quoted from *Howards End,* along with Ruskin, Tennyson, Carlyle, Conrad, Housman, D. H. Lawrence, and T. S. Eliot, to indicate that Kipling was not the only writer in recent literature to celebrate the British empire.]

1432 Gillen, Francis. "*Howards End* and the Neglected Narrator," NOVEL, III (Winter 1970), 139–52.
Recent criticism of the novel has failed to attend to the narrator's function and has asserted that EMF has failed to "connect" values. The study of EMF's use of the narrator reveals that connection is made and provides us with a "running *exemplum*" of how it is made. EMF's comments make it clear that *Howards End* is not primarily a realistic novel. The narrator modulates between idealistic and realistic visions in the novel. Margaret Schlegel is the character best exemplifying such a modulation, both in her actions (as EMF sometimes directly comments on them) and in her character itself (as she comments on others and the action in general). The closing scene is to be placed in the context of Margaret's modulations between these two visions. At the end her realism and idealism are both operative: one clears the rubble from the past, the other looks to the future. In the Schlegel family Tibby is too cynical, Helen too idealistic; each represents one-sided and extreme views. EMF implies in the novel that the ideal is latent in the real and that the two can be accommodated: a reconciliation between the two occurs in the narrator's voice and in the whole conspectus of the novel itself. The particular and the universal are held in tandem. Melodrama also takes the reader from the realistic level to the abstract. The narrator, moreover, involves the reader directly in some of his comments.

The visionary and the idealistic formulations are sometimes undercut by EMF's "ironic realism." The narrator will often correct himself and thereby involve the reader in his own search for realism or truth. "The current critical prejudice against the 'intruding narrator' has caused us not only to neglect the subtlety and delight of his comments but to miss that very aspect which conveys the major vision of his novel." [Provocative and illuminating article, noting the same contrasting worlds in *Howards End* as Malcolm Bradbury does in "E. M. Forster's *Howards End*" (1962).]

1433 Gillen, Francis Xavier. "The Relationship of Rhetorical Control to Meaning in the Novels of Henry James, Virginia Woolf, and E. M. Forster," DISSERTATION ABSTRACTS INTERNATIONAL, XXX (1970), 1525A. Unpublished dissertation, Fordham University, 1969.

1434 Haas, Willy. "Ein Unsterblicher stirbt: E. M. Forster oder der letzte Viktorianer" (An Immortal Dies: E. M. Forster or the Last Victorian), DIE WELT (Hamburg), 9 June 1970, p. 23.
E. M. Forster will prove immortal. He has celebrated freedom in his novels. We know more about his characters than we do about real people because of his genius in character portrayal. He had the unadorned speech of the born novelist and should not be criticized (as Virginia Woolf criticized him) for his lack of self-conscious artistry. [In German.]

1435 Heilbrun, Carolyn. CHRISTOPHER ISHERWOOD (NY & Lond: Columbia UP, 1970, Columbia Essays on Modern Writers, No. 53), pp. 9–11, 33–34.
The personal goodness or gentleness present in Isherwood's work was characteristic of only one other English writer of his age, EMF, whose influence on Isherwood has been strong. Isherwood was more socially conscious in the 1930s than was EMF, but EMF's pacifism and lack of hysteria at the outbreak of World War II impressed Isherwood, who pays homage to him in DOWN THERE ON A VISIT (1962). He derived from EMF the "tea-table" manner of understatement [Isherwood, LIONS AND SHADOWS (1938)] and his determination also not to be great. Isherwood was earthier than EMF and would have found love for humanity impossible without some kind of religious basis.

1436 Hennecke, Hans. "Der unbeirrbare Romancier: zum Tode des englischen Schriftstellers Edward M. Forster" (The Imperturbable Novelist: On the Death of the English Storyteller Edward M. Forster), FRANKFURTER ALLGEMEINE ZEITUNG, 9 June 1970.
The EMF legend applies not so much to the writer and his work as to his radiating humanity and his mode of thought. He seems to be a messenger

from more auspicious times. His tragic humanism keeps him from an unconditional nihilism. He is the toughest individualist of our age. His lack of convinced ideology never led him to an arid, devitalizing pragmatism. [In German.]

1437 Hoggart, Richard. SPEAKING TO EACH OTHER: ESSAYS BY RICHARD HOGGART: Vol. II, ABOUT LITERATURE (NY: Oxford UP; Lond: Chatto & Windus, 1970), pp. 34, 97, 165, 194–99, 248.

"Literature and Society": The opening paragraph from *A Passage to India* and from D. H. Lawrence's SONS AND LOVERS illustrate different "rhetorics," deriving from each author's tone and manner and from his assumptions about his society, about his prospective readers, and about literature in relation to social class. [In Section "A Question of Tone" these paragraphs are analyzed at length.] There is a difficulty in controlling "tone" in autobiographical writing and of finding a style for discussing social questions. The first paragraph from *Passage* reflects "the voice of a civilized, literate, English middle-class observer of the early twentieth century" which is assured of its own relationships to its material and the response of its audience. There are traditions in style available for EMF as a middle-class rentier that are not available for the working-class writer. Lawrence in SONS AND LOVERS did manage to capture through tone and style the essence of working-class life, and he reveals such mastery even in his first paragraph. The paragraph has a directness and colloquial quality absent from the first paragraph of *Passage.* "A Matter of Rhetoric: American: American Writers and British Readers": The British novel is the voice of the English middle class. EMF would ask the middle class to be more demonstrative, to respond to the call of the heart (in *The Longest Journey* Rickie's advice to Agnes is to "mind" Gerald's death with her whole being). Yet EMF senses in British fiction this lack of the character's emotional involvement by indicating in *Aspects of the Novel* that such involvement is typical of the prophetic novel, which is not typically British. "Samuel Butler and THE WAY OF ALL FLESH": EMF's views on money, expressed in *Howards End*, are similar to Butler's (in THE WAY OF ALL FLESH). [Essays much rvd for book publication: "Literature and Society" first appeared in LITERATURE AND SOCIETY: A GUIDE TO THE SOCIAL SCIENCES, ed by Norman Mackenzie (Lond: Weidenfeld & Nicolson; NY: New American Library, 1966), pp. 225–48; "A Question of Tone" (The Tredegar Memorial Lecture of the Royal Society of Literature) first appeared in ESSAYS BY DIVERS HANDS, XXXIII (Lond and NY: Oxford UP, 1965), pp. 18–38; "A Matter of Rhetoric" first appeared in NATION, CLXXXIV (17 April 1957), 361–63; "Samuel Butler and THE WAY OF ALL FLESH" first appeared as "Introduction," THE WAY OF ALL FLESH (Lond: Penguin, 1966).]

1438 Holloway, David. "Unique Place: Founded No School," DAILY TELEGRAPH (Lond), 8 June 1970, p. 10.

EMF's influence on literature was great but indirect. No one has ever written of human relationships in the way he did. He has only two unquestioned masterpieces, *Howards End* and *A Passage to India*, but the Marabar Caves section of the latter stands near the top of twentieth-century fiction. EMF has one chief defect: an inability to deal with sexual passion. He tended to run away from it and "took refuge in implications of sadism and impotence or simply condemned his characters to death." For him, Cambridge, with its slightly hothouse atmosphere, was paradise. His political thought was weak: "a wishy-washy Leftish liberalism that allowed token protests on many causes—but rarely full commitment." [Extreme statement; ignores his passionate hatred of Nazism. Summary of career and personality, stressing his modesty, whether it brought him into public or kept him in private. Excellent discussion.]

1439 Howarth, Herbert. "Whitman and the English Writers," PA-PERS ON WALT WHITMAN, ed by Lester F. Zimmerman and Winston Weathers (Tulsa: University of Tulsa, The University of Tulsa Monograph Series, No. 11, 1970), pp. 6–25, espec 7–14.

Vaughan Williams, Goldsworthy Lowes Dickinson, Edward Carpenter, Roger Fry, Bertrand Russell, and R. C. Trevelyan all reveal in their letters, work, or actions the influence of Whitman, who had therefore become popular at Cambridge by the time EMF was there. Whitman's humanitarianism was especially an influence. EMF refers directly to "Song of Myself" in *The Longest Journey* and lets it establish the mood for the Swedish idyll between Mrs. Elliot and Robert (the parents of Stephen Wonham). In *Where Angels Fear to Tread*, Mr. Emerson (appropriately named in recognition of Whitman's chief forbear) is Whitmanic in his idealism and romantic championing of instinct. Whitman also influenced EMF to an appreciation of the tangible and visible world (e.g., "the existence of the cow" motif in *Journey*). Whitman influenced the writing of *A Passage to India* (the Whitman poem, "Passage to India," has the same theme, the voyage to transcendence, best represented in the novel by Godbole, a perfect "Whitmanite pantheist.") Whitman optimistically assumes that men cannot help but become brothers and spiritually unified, but EMF is aware of the difficulties on the way. [Excellent critique. Goes on to discuss D. H. Lawrence as an even more ardent English disciple of Whitman.]

1440 Johnson, Edgar. SIR WALTER SCOTT: THE GREAT UNKNOWN (NY: Macmillan; Toronto, Collier-Macmillan; Lond: Hamish Hamilton, 1970), p. 538.

In *Aspects of the Novel* EMF is wrong in asserting that the action of THE ANTIQUARY is a series of melodramatic episodes. The so-called melodramatic episodes are organic to the themes and action of the novels.

1441 Kermode, Frank. "Forster," LISTENER, LXXXIII (18 June 1970), 833.

EMF's moderns were Wagner, Ibsen, and Butler, not Gertrude Stein; G. Lowes Dickinson, Nathaniel Wedd, and J. M. E. McTaggart, not G. E. Moore and Bertrand Russell. He was not much interested in the experiments of James, Conrad, or Ford; for him the great contriver was Meredith. Like the great Edwardian novelists, EMF saw his task as registering the crisis or decline of a culture, but he did not see this duty in terms of making radical formal innovations. His great subject is the British bourgeoisie—the complications, evasions, hypocrisies, and restrictions of their lives, and how these lives end by the stifling of creativity. His earlier books were restricted by the society they represented; hence, passion in them is not convincing. For EMF love binds together the elite. Translated into works of art, love enables him to attain a completeness there that is lacking in life. In *A Passage to India*, the wholeness of the novel includes the incompleteness that he earlier wrote about so extensively. His range widened in *Passage* to focus on "the possibilities and limits of love in a whole world" rather than on "tribal quirks." *Passage* is a complicated, passionate, wide-ranging novel; it will live because of "its complicated passion." [Stimulating obit appreciation.]

1442 Kéry, László. "Edward Morgan Forster," AZ ANGOL IRODALOM A HUSZADIK SZÁZADBAN (English Literature in the Twentieth Century), ed by László Báti and Kristó-Nagy Istaván (Budapest: Gondolat, 1970), I, 181–206.

EMF criticizes the capitalist world and its bourgeois value system but does not realize the full significance of socialism. He sees how far capitalist reality departs from bourgeois humanist ideals and is conscious of its interference with the free exercise of man's full capabilities. EMF's skepticism exceeds that of the Renaissance humanists because he rejects Christian belief. He idealizes late feudal civilization as it is passing into modern capitalism and rejects a technological civilization. He is aware of his intellectual contradictions; in 1935 he admitted that he might be a Communist if he were younger ["Liberty in England," *Abinger Harvest*], while he remains a middle-class Englishman. His ideal society is not the product of revolution but a republic of love brought about by contacts among individuals. Since he rejects orthodox religion, he feels that this chaotic and muddled world can only be ordered through aesthetic means. He is too aware of contemporary social problems to be satisfied with the ivory tower attitude encouraged by Bloomsbury, but he is not brave enough to seek human fulfillment actively through revolution. His social insights are valid but do not go far enough. His public school years and his Cambridge days gave him his basic experiences: the opposition between the man of "vestigial" heart, who has been despoiled by contemporary social chaos, and the man of developed heart, who is fulfilled in spirit. This dichotomy informs the fantasy present in his early stories: Pan, a god of the fulfilled Greeks is not dead for the sensitive individual in "The Story of a Panic," although he is out of sight for the Philistines in it. "The Road from Colonus" and "The Eternal Moment" present this opposition without using the means of fantasy. "The Eternal Moment" goes beyond the opposition of the effete, "civilized" Englishman to the poor, foreign "natural" man. EMF sees class conflict and prejudices as hindering human connections. *Where Angels Fear to Tread* is pessimistic concerning the ideal of wholeness; Philip Herriton's desire for completeness can only be realized by combining his aesthetic perceptiveness with Gino's sense of the actual. *The Longest Journey* works at three levels in three places: Cambridge signifies humanist completeness, Sawston signifies Philistinism, and Wiltshire signifies natural vitality. Rickie Elliot, who seeks vital reality, finds it finally in his instinctual half-brother, Stephen Wonham, but does not connect with him successfully. EMF succeeds in *Journey* in his ironic satire of Sawston but does not elicit adequately the tragic pathos and the mystical symbolism inherent in the situation. *A Room with a View* is a love comedy threatened by tragic forces. Lucy Honeychurch almost chooses wrongly between staid, middle-class Cecil Vyse and the vital George Emerson, from the working class, whose nature is complete.

EMF first successfully combines realism and symbolism in *Howards End*. The house and its owner, Mrs. Ruth Wilcox, are actualities while they are also symbols of traditional, natural vitality. Mrs. Wilcox bequeaths the house, not to her practical middle-class sons, but to the cultured, "progressive" Margaret Schlegel. Margaret realizes that culture depends on middle-class money, and her marriage to Henry Wilcox represents—unconvincingly—the harmonizing of opposing value systems. Similarly, the house will pass to the child of Helen Schlegel and Leonard Bast (from the lower middle class). In Bast and his child EMF again reveals the triumph of his hopes for reason, humanity, and vitality as forces to counterbalance their opposites in the real world (incarnate in a Henry Wilcox who does not change fundamentally). In *A Passage to India*, a postwar EMF loses his illusions. He shows how circumstances prevent vital human relationships: the bourgeois English colonial administrators and the Indian intellectuals misunderstand each other because of their mutual suspicion. The experiences of the humane Fielding and the instinctively wise Mrs. Moore (EMF's finest figure of this type) make this clear. Aziz's final words to Fielding indicate that significant human contact depends on social equality and political freedom, possible only after colonialism is overthrown. (This prophecy was accurate.) The novel's central symbol, the Marabar Caves, is masterfully evocative and significant; in them Mrs. Moore glimpses creations's final indifference to all values. Here EMF also places Adela Quested's "incident," which, a disaster at first, leads ultimately to values still worth affirming. EMF insists, finally, that revolution must precede the possibility of firm affectionate relationships in India. EMF is modern in this radical social and political perceptiveness rather than in his technical innovating; he is a master of the traditional realistic novel. [In Hungarian.]

1443 Kim, Yong-Chul. "E. M. Forster and the Humanist Theory of Art," ENGLISH LANGUAGE AND LITERATURE (Seoul, The English Literary Society of Korea), No. 34 (Summer 1970), 51–78; rptd in SEOUL UNIVERSITY FACULTY PAPERS, I (15 Oct 1970), 66–81.

EMF contends that escapism can be valid when it allows the individual to escape the bondage of communal life. He emphasizes the ordered world presented to us by the work of art. The artist's true nature is his lower, unconscious one. The great work of art exerts a transforming quality and thereby is able to exert a renovating effect on civilization (notes kinship here with both Shelley and Arnold). EMF stresses three terms in his aesthetics: permanence, disinterestedness, and apathy. EMF emphasizes both the intrinsic value of the work of art and its relationships to other aspects of experience. [Analysis of EMF's aesthetic theories, citing principally "The Ivory Tower" (ATLANTIC MONTHLY, CLXIII, Jan 1939, 5–58), "Anonymity" (*Abinger Harvest*), *Aspects of the Novel*, and the following from *Two Cheers for Democracy:* "The Challenge of Our Time," "Art for Art's Sake," and "The Raison d'Etre of Criticism in the Arts." Intelligent discussion that, however, discusses essays *seriatim* and does not build to a compelling synthesis.]

1444 Kirkup, James. "In Memoriam E. M. Forster: Love, the Beloved Republic—a Memoir of Morgan Forster," EIGO SEINEN (Tokyo), CXVI (1 Sept 1970), 510–15.

EMF expressed a truth about the English in a foreign country in *A Passage to India;* they are uninterested in the natives who bore them. EMF impressively conveys the sense in *Passage* of unexplained mysteries in human relationships. EMF embodied the sense of deep happiness and inexhaustible patience and sympathy. He revealed a lack of class-consciousness and conceit. Friendship and love between human beings became for EMF an end in itself. He regarded the East as a source of cultural renewal for the West in the future, as Italy and Greece had been in his generation. EMF was in old age much interested in the subject of sex (he had become one of Kinsey's interviewees in America in 1947). EMF admired pornographic writing in which he himself engaged during his last years; but he felt that this kind of writing ought to have style and be aesthetically satisfying. EMF felt that such writing should excite the reader sexually. Unfortunately the repressed and puritanical British will not allow the publication of these works. [These stories were published as *The Life to Come and Other Stories*, Vol 8 in *The*

Abinger Edition of E. M. Forster, ed by Oliver Stallybrass (1972). Kirkup and EMF corresponded during World War II and met afterwards through J. R. Ackerley; see also THE LETTERS OF J. R. ACKERLEY, ed by Neville Braybrooke (1975).]

1445 Kondo, Ineko. "Forster no Koto" (Forster), EIGO SEINEN (Tokyo), CXVI (1 Sept 1970), 516–17.
EMF was a kindly, gentle, human, humane, sensitive man with a sharp and quiet sense of humor. [Kondo's impressions derive from a meeting with him, from letters that he wrote her, and from comments by others. Enthusiastic eulogy for EMF.] [In Japanese.]

1446 Kondo, Ineko. "Virginia Woolf to E. M. Forster" (Virginia Woolf and E. M. Forster), EIGO SEINEN (Tokyo), CXVI (1 Feb 1970), 64–66.
In spite of their contemporaneity, similar social and intellectual milieu, and friendship, Virginia Woolf and EMF are divergent as writers. She trusted his criticism of her work and other subjects, but as a critic she analyzed sharply his problems as writer. He appreciated her talent, calling her a poet while he defined her problems as novelist. EMF and Woolf influenced each other's work. According to A WRITER'S DIARY, she recommended MOLL FLANDERS to EMF, who wrote about it in *Aspects of the Novel*. A WRITER'S DIARY indicates EMF's influence. Only five days before she completed the first draft of TO THE LIGHTHOUSE (13 Sept 1926), she had not decided whether to make Mr. Ramsay or Mrs. Ramsay the protagonist. In December 1925 she read *A Passage to India;* and it is possible that the dominance of Mrs. Ramsay was inspired by EMF's Mrs. Moore, whom Mrs. Ramsay resembles. [In Japanese.]

1447 Langbaum, Robert. "A New Look at E. M. Forster," THE MODERN SPIRIT: ESSAYS ON THE CONTINUITY OF NINETEENTH- AND TWENTIETH-CENTURY LITERATURE (NY & Lond: Oxford UP, 1970), pp. 127–46; rvd version of essay published in 1968 (qv).
The combination of idealism and pessimism (the stress on individualism by Bloomsbury and the writers for the INDEPENDENT REVIEW, and their misgivings about it) is the infusing spirit of *A Passage to India*. [First three paragraphs of essay are revised, and materials on EMF's intellectual milieu (on Clapham, the Cambridge Apostles, and influence of Arnold and Mill have been added).]

1448 Lask, Thomas. "An Eye for Individuals: The Young Found Forster Relevant Because He Challenged Conventions," NEW YORK TIMES, 8 June 1970, p. 37.
Closeness, sympathy, and understanding prevailed between EMF and Cam-

bridge undergraduates. He also evinced tolerance; he defended individual traits in men; and he revealed "confidence in the human impulse as against ordered conformity." He distrusted intellect as such. EMF was a moralist but no preacher; he made use of an adequate symbolism to convey his ideas, instead of a discursive prose. His characters are more memorable than his scenes. His style is a bit "bloodless," yet it is "full of ironic glints and lights." Style in EMF's books is as much a part of substance as the matter. EMF is good at capturing the mysterious and the unknown; he rejected "literary fashions or innovations in technique" as such, and he expressed his humanism in his own way. [Perceptive obit article.]

1449 Laurent, C. "E. M. Forster et D. H. Lawrence" (E. M. Forster and D. H. Lawrence), LES LANGUES MODERNES (Paris), LXIV (July–Aug 1970), 65–72.

EMF called Lawrence a prophet, but we hardly think of EMF as such. However EMF and Lawrence have much in common: an emphasis on sexuality as life-enhancing, a deploring of the psychic mutilation of individuals through bourgeois conventions, a need for union with nature as source of inner renewal, and the use of symbols organic to the individual novels. [Superficial discussion in contrast to Martin Price's "E. M. F. and D. H. L." (1966).] [In French.]

1450 Levine, June Perry. "An Analysis of the Manuscripts of *A Passage to India*," PUBLICATIONS OF THE MODERN LANGUAGE ASSOCIATION, LXXXV (March 1970), 284–94; rptd, slightly rvd, as "The Manuscript of *A Passage to India*," CREATION AND CRITICISM: "A PASSAGE TO INDIA," (Lincoln: University of Nebraska P, 1971; Lond: Chatto & Windus, 1972), pp. 75–107.

The different versions of the plot in the MS variants of *A Passage to India* reinforce the movement of the completed novel: attraction, rupture, reunion. EMF universalizes his characters in *Passage* and omits many details of their backgrounds and former lives, details which help, however, in understanding the novel. Mrs. Moore's reactions to the echo in the Marabar Caves were earlier given to Fielding, and she is made into a more complex and interesting figure in *Passage*. She becomes impressive from having been a commonplace, orthodox old lady; her blandness becomes vulnerability, her Christianity widens into mysticism, and her idealism turns into radical disillusionment. In the manuscripts Adela Quested is uninterested sexually in Aziz, and this fact should qualify extreme Freudian interpretations of her character (her alleged repressions before she enters the Caves). Aziz becomes more rebellious, volatile, and Moslem in the novel. Fielding's history is more extensive in the manuscript, and he is seen to be a harsher figure. The Anglo-Indian civil servants are more unsympathetic in the novel than in earlier versions. [Examines the MS of *Passage* in relation to plot, themes, creative methodology, and characters. An informed essay to supplement Oliver Stallybrass's "The Wobblings of E. M. Forster" (1969) and George H. Thomson's "The Manuscripts of *A Passage to India*" (Appendix to THE FICTION OF E. M. FORSTER, 1967). See also Levine (1971).]

1451 Levin, Harry. "Reappraisals: Charles Dickens 1812–1870," AMERICAN SCHOLAR, XXXIX (Autumn 1970), 670–76, espec 675; rptd as "Dickens After a Century," GROUNDS FOR COMPARISON (Cambridge, Mass: Harvard UP, Harvard Studies in Comparative Literature, 1972), pp. 339–50, espec 347.

EMF's discussion of "round" and "flat" characters in *Aspects of the Novel* detracted from Dickens's reputation, with EMF's implied derogation of flat characters, found so abundantly in Dickens. In reality, Tolstoy's and Proust's four-dimensional fiction is closer to that of Dickens than to that of Virginia Woolf or EMF.

1452 Lewis, Anthony. "E. M. Forster Homosexual Novel Due," NEW YORK TIMES, 11 Nov 1970, pp. 1, 42.

Publication of *Maurice*, written between 1913 and 1915, is projected. The novel will throw light on EMF's homosexuality and the changing British attitudes toward homosexuality in the twentieth century. EMF left estate of $151,000 in trust to his literary executor, Professor W. J. H. Sprott of Nottingham University, with King's College, Cambridge, as final legatee. EMF suppressed *Maurice* because he wished to avoid "intrusive controversy" during his life. [P. N. Furbank's "The Personality of E. M. Forster," ENCOUNTER (1970) is quoted at length.]

1453 Lodge, David. "Literary Criticism in England in the Twentieth Century," THE TWENTIETH CENTURY (HISTORY OF LITERATURE IN THE ENGLISH LANGUAGE, Vol. 7), ed by Bernard Bergonzi (Lond: Barrie & Jenkins, 1970), pp. 362–403, espec 391; rptd as "Crosscurrents in Modern English Criticism," THE NOVELIST AT THE CROSSROADS AND OTHER ESSAYS ON FICTION AND CRITICISM (Ithaca: Cornell UP; Lond: Routledge & Kegan Paul, 1971), pp. 247–86.

EMF is ambivalent in *Aspects of the Novel* toward modernism; his rejection of story-line as such and his concept of rhythm (reiterated motifs) are modern, but his impatience with formalism as opposed to vitality is antimodern in tone and tendency.

1454 Lucas, John. THE MELANCHOLY MAN: A STUDY OF DICKENS'S NOVELS (Lond: Methuen; NY: Barnes & Noble, 1970), pp. 154, 197–98, 280, 305.

The conventionally respectable Dombey of DOMBEY AND SON has affinities with the Henry Thornton presented in *Marianne Thornton*. Despite the element of artifice in the prose, the deaths of Steerforth and Dora in DAVID COPPERFIELD are described in terms that recall "the sadness of the incomplete," associated with Lucy Honeychurch's playing of Schumann in *A Room with a View*. Doyce in LITTLE DORRIT reveals some of the same self-satisfaction that EMF ascribed to the process of artistic creation. Pip in GREAT EXPECTATIONS undergoes much suffering for his advocacy of Magwitch including physical torture by Orlick which recalls Gino Carella's torturing of Philip Herriton in *Where Angels Fear to Tread*, though Orlick is more brutal.

1455 Maes-Jelinek, Hena. CRITICISM OF SOCIETY IN THE ENGLISH NOVEL BETWEEN THE WARS (Paris: Société d'Editions, "Les Belles Lettres," Bibliothèque de la Faculté de Philosophie et Lettres de l'Université de Liège, Fascicule CXC, 1970), pp. 231, 340, 343, 519.

The Burmese in Orwell's BURMESE DAYS lack the integrity and pride that EMF's Indians possess in *A Passage to India*. In EMF both the Indians and the English are fully wrought human beings. In contrast to Orwell, EMF appreciates from the inside the natives and their civilization. EMF is more optimistic than Orwell in feeling that the Indians as a subject people can one day be self-sufficient politically.

1456 "The Man of the Week," SHENKAR'S WEEKLY (New Delhi), 14 June 1970, p. 4.

EMF exposed English snobbishness and the failure to understand Indian ways and culture as a disaster in *A Passage to India*. The novel revealed that an Englishman could understand India and that "Kipling was hopelessly wrong." [Obit notice.]

1457 Mathur, S. S. "India in Forster's Works," MODERN REVIEW (Calcutta), CXXVII (Aug 1970), 100–103.

[Mostly a perfunctory descriptive account of *A Passage to India*.]

1458 Matsumura, Tatsuo. "Forster no Bungakukan" (Forster's View of Literature), EIGO SEINEN (Tokyo), CXVI (1 Sept 1970), 506–7.

While Percy Lubbock's THE CRAFT OF FICTION and Edwin Muir's THE STRUCTURE OF THE NOVEL (1928) focus on the technique of the novel, EMF's *Aspects of the Novel* emphasizes the value of the novel and is, therefore, a more impressive critique. For example, EMF's terms, "prophecy" and "rhythm" can be regarded respectively as revelation and resonance, if one thinks in terms of how a book affects the reader. But EMF is not merely an impressionistic critic, for he discusses the "story" as basic to the novel. His theory is radical and positive in his insistence that "story" is inevitable in the novel. By contrast, Lubbock's well-constructed theory may lead to the impoverishment of the novel as a record of human experience. In "Anonymity" (1925) and elsewhere, EMF regards art as absolute and self-contained. The Japanese novelist Naoya Shiga expresses a similar concept when he writes that Buddha's image, in any statue of him, emerges as independent of its creator. In *Aspects* EMF emphasizes his idea of anonymity when he envisions novelists from all literary periods working at one round table, freed from the restrictions imposed by chronology and milieu. EMF's elevation of art into an absolute dignifies it but tends to separate life from art, or man from art. [In Japanese.]

1459 Maxwell, J. C. "The Text of *Where Angels Fear to Tread*," NOTES AND QUERIES (Lond), nsXVIII (Dec 1970), 456.
[One slight textual error and one major one are cited for *Where Angels Fear to Tread*. The major error: Caroline Abbott tells Philip Herriton in Chapter 8 to "Fight as if you think us wrong"; the passage should read, "Fight us if . . ."]

1460 Mehta, Ved. PORTRAIT OF INDIA (NY: Farrar, Straus & Giroux; Lond: Weidenfeld & Nicolson, 1970), pp. 142, 440–41.
Film director Satyajit Ray said he would like to film *A Passage to India*. Ray disapproved of the stage adaptation by Santha Rama Rau in which he felt the Indians emerged as caricatures. Ray would have two languages used, to avoid unintentional comedy, the Indians speaking their own language, not English. Calcutta is a city of the dying, and the fable of Lazarus and his extraordinary knowledge (that of the dead) is a symbol of what Calcutta knows. The power that the knowledge of death has over the living is also the central theme of *Passage*. As a result of her shattering experience in the Marabar Caves, Mrs. Moore's hold on life is undermined. Thereafter for her, all human accomplishment exists but has no value. The abyss is not final, as she discovers at Asirgarh, when she leaves India. The abyss in Calcutta is not final. The leper there is one of a hundred Indias, not the final one. Still the image of Calcutta as a city too knowledgeable of death persists. [Interesting in demonstrating that the Indian intellectual often refers to EMF's novel for points of departure in his thinking.]

1461 Meyers, Jeffrey. "E. M. Forster and T. E. Lawrence: A Friendship," SOUTH ATLANTIC QUARTERLY, LXIX (Spring 1970), 205–16.
EMF first met T. E. Lawrence in 1921, but the relationship did not become close until after 1924 with EMF's extended letter to T. E. Lawrence about SEVEN PILLARS OF WISDOM, which T. E. Lawrence had asked EMF to read. In the letter EMF viewed T. E. Lawrence's work as "granular" rather than "fluid" and felt that the "reflective" style was present at the expense of T.

E. Lawrence's other stylistic modes: technical, narrative, emotive. Reading SEVEN PILLARS may have helped inspire EMF to finish *A Passage to India*. EMF's letter helped T. E. Lawrence carry on with the writing of SEVEN PILLARS; Lawrence, in turn reassured EMF that *Passage* could well represent him, as EMF was having difficulties writing further fiction. T. E. Lawrence praised *Passage* in one of his letters, especially the scene at the club after Adela's accusation, the roof-top scene with Aziz and Fielding after the trial, and the orgiastic temple scene [see THE LETTERS OF T. E. LAWRENCE, ed by David Garnett (1938)]. EMF helped T. E. Lawrence organize THE MINT and reviewed it on its posthumous publication. T. E. Lawrence felt that he could be frank with EMF in analyzing his reasons for entering the enlisted ranks. EMF was, in general, more frank with T. E. Lawrence than T. E. Lawrence was with him, though in the letters T. E. Lawrence is more honest, in particular about EMF's unpublished works [*Maurice* and "Dr. Woolacott," *The Life to Come and Other Short Stories*] and homosexuality. The letters to T. E. Lawrence reveal EMF in a different light from his other writings, as a tougher and more practical man, a sharper critic, and an intenser moralist. T. E. Lawrence's letters throw light on his own literary work and his methods, his character, and his estimation of EMF's books. [An important and considered article.]

1462 Meyers, Jeffrey. " 'Vacant Heart and Hand and Eye': The Homosexual Theme in *A Room with a View*," ENGLISH LITERATURE IN TRANSITION, XIII: 3 (1970), 181–92.

The same polarity between life and anti-life forces in *A Room with a View* is explored in *Howards End*. Only Mr. Beebe does not fit the pattern; he begins in the vital group and ends in the morbid one. The Bathing Scene (Chap 12) is crucial to an explanation of this shift. In it Beebe discovers his love for George Emerson, which explains his negative reaction to Lucy as a sexual being and to the prospect of George's marrying her. His asceticism is really a mask for his homosexuality, and his earlier lack of enthusiasm for women as fully vital beings also supports this view. Bathing scenes in EMF's fiction either provide symbolic release from sex inhibitions (as with Mr. Beebe) or become a manifestation of sexual repression. Mr. Beebe's views are symptomatic of EMF's general distrust of heterosexual love. There are numerous instances of this distrust in EMF's books. This negative strain undermines EMF's power and effectiveness and renders his novels spinsterish in tone. Beebe approves of Lucy's song, which counsels a renunciation of the senses; it had been Lucy Ashton's song in Sir Walter Scott's THE BRIDE OF LAMMERMOOR. The song is not suited either to Lucy Ashton's character or to Lucy Honeychurch's and is, therefore, ironically used by both Scott and EMF. Beebe's negative role is also suggested by the imagery in the novel (Virgil's bees, the ascetic church). Though Beebe is negatively presented, he expresses EMF's views on homosexuality, revealed in EMF's total canon. [A convincing exposition.]

1463 Morley, Patricia A. "E. M. Forster's 'Temple': Eclectic or Visionary?" UNIVERSITY OF TORONTO QUARTERLY, XXXIX (April 1970), 229–41.

The "Temple" section of *A Passage to India* is not concerned solely with the Hindu festival. Rather, "Temple" alternates tableau descriptions and scenes featuring personal relationships. The structure indicates EMF's eclecticism and his desire to synthesize the values of East and West. EMF expresses an ambivalent attitude toward Hinduism in *The Hill of Devi*. Godbole's name could be interpreted (from Greek) as "clod of earth" or (from Scottish-Irish) as an aperture. He seems, therefore, related to the individual's aspiration after unity and the force (Caves) which obstructs that aspiration. In Chap 35, in the incident of the freed prisoners, Islam, Hinduism, and Christianity come together. [Reasoning here seems tenuous.] In Chap 36 the muddle contributes to reconciliation. In Chap 37 EMF is concerned primarily with personal relationships. *Passage* is not really prophetic: the ironic tone in "Temple" interferes with expression of the conviction that the whole world needs pity and love. EMF's view is eclectic, not visionary or prophetic. This interpretation is verified by the greater importance of Aziz than of Godbole in the novel. [EMF's ambivalence toward Hinduism is, I think, less great than this critic assumes. Also, tone of "Temple" is not so "dispassionate" as this critic feels. I regard the total impact of "Temple" as more intense and prophetic than she does. The inadequacies of Christianity and Islam in encompassing both ultimate value and India's muddle—in contrast to Hinduism—are insufficiently recognized.]

1464 "Mr. E. M. Forster, O. M.: One of the Most Esteemed English Novelists of His Time," TIMES (Lond), 8 June 1970, p. 10.

EMF's silence after 1924 was the result of his alienation from the age following World War I, wherein his civilized temperament, cultivated sensibility, and liberal moralism could have little scope. EMF lacked the spur of commonplace passion. His scenes of sexual passion are not convincing, and this fact accounts for a melodramatic note in his tragic scenes, despite the "luminous humanity" in his novels. [An informed summary of his career follows. Obit article, penetrating in its formulations and judgments.]

1465 Nagel, James. SUGGESTIONS FOR TEACHING "VISION AND VALUE: A THEMATIC INTRODUCTION TO THE SHORT STORY" (Belmont, Calif: Dickenson, 1970), pp. 2–3.

In "The Celestial Omnibus" the narrator's consciousness is innocent and restricted; his horizon is similar to the boy's. The theme of developing maturity in the boy is measured in terms of his growing sensitivity to art. Bons, in contrast, is insensitive to the deeper meaning of art.

1466 Natwar-Singh, K. "E. M. Forster and India," Illustrated Weekly of India (Bombay), XCI (21 June 1970), 45.
EMF's achievement has been both a private one and one that is wide and universal. In *A Passage to India*, the emphasis is not so much on political issues as on the human predicament. EMF has influenced three generations of Indians; he has achieved this influence "through affection, loyalty and sensitive understanding." EMF has had a great personal influence over Indians. A part of EMF lived spiritually in India. In an interview comment, EMF maintains that he has been attracted by Islamic culture but does not like its orderliness. Aziz was modeled on Masood, EMF's greatest Indian friend, Godbole on another friend; but EMF regards these characters as people, not religious types. EMF feels that William Golding is trying to carry on his tradition in a different way. EMF feels that marriage is many times an admirable institution and regards the "Golden Wedding Anniversary" as a high point of civilization.

1467 Natwar-Singh, K. "Remembering Forster," Hindustan Times Weekly (New Delhi), 14 June 1970, p. 7.
"His reputation and fame grew with each book he did not write." EMF helped the Indian writers Mulk Raj Anand, Raja Rao, and Ahmed Ali.

1468 Onodera, Ken. "E. M. Forster no Shiso: Shinpisei to Kojin-shugi" (E. M. Forster's Thought: The Inexplicable and Humanism), Eigo Seinen (Tokyo), CXVI (1 Sept 1970), 4–5.
EMF's interest in the "inexplicable," which can be comprehended only by man's imagination, grows out of his humanism and his individualism. In EMF's thought a basic duality is characteristic. He recognizes the importance of the "mean," but for him the mean also presupposes the existence of the "radical," the violent, and the irrational. In this sense EMF resembles D. H. Lawrence. EMF places the highest value on the unseen or inexplicable element in man's experience. As a critic of materialistic culture, he is in the tradition of Carlyle, Ruskin, Morris, Dickens, and Arnold. He was a romantic because he valued imagination, but he oscillated between a nineteenth-century love of nature and a Cambridge intellectuality. EMF is modern in his belief that imagination allows one to understand "the inexplicable." An individual must appreciate the inexplicable if he is to break through the corrupt surfaces of present-day civilization. [In Japanese.]

1469 Priestley, J. B. The Edwardians (NY & Evanston: Harper & Row; Lond: Heinemann, 1970), pp. 81, 129.
The widespread influence of G. E. Moore on Bloomsbury (including EMF) and the British cultivated public made intellectual life in the period between the two wars different from what it would otherwise have been. In his first four novels EMF is anti-Edwardian while remaining Edwardian. He is the

reverse of the typically Edwardian sociological novelist; he is poetic and symbolic, achieving his effects by sudden flashes of insight. Nevertheless, he is interested (in *Howards End*) in the conflicts between the two opposing segments of the upper middle class. His fiction is also very personal.

1470 Pritchett, V. S. "E. M. Forster," NEW STATESMAN, nsLXXIX (12 June 1970), 846.

As for EMF's silence since 1924, EMF in writing *A Passage to India* exhausted in advance what he would have said in narrative about totalitarianism. This novel prolongs its significance in Africa and the American Deep South. EMF's power "lay in his startling power of speaking in a natural private voice in public places." But this liberal agnosticism did not mean weakness and passivity. Though an apologist of the heart, he was intellectually hard; his phrases came from "a gentle yet stern and sceptical intelligence and also from a continuous sense of curiosity as moral duty." In his fiction no one is let off, and he is also ruthless in seeing life as a "rotten business." His humanism was conscious of the peril surrounding it. His skepticism and detachment were balanced by a sense that one should continue to seek answers even if one does not find them. His is an austere kind of comedy in which characters are in offhand manner brought to judgment. He viewed our dislocations and perplexities as being more than social; they are ethical and philosophical. His self-possession and self-understanding are qualities to be envied, as was his lack of affectation. [Informed and perceptive obit account.]

1471 Pritchett, V. S. GEORGE MEREDITH AND ENGLISH COMEDY: THE CLARK LECTURES FOR 1969 (Lond: Chatto & Windus; NY: Random House, 1970), pp. 9, 10, 12, 39–40, 55, 108.

Those who attack Meredith using EMF's strictures in *Aspects of the Novel* overlook his positive assertion that Meredith is a great contriver in plotting his novels. EMF's description of Meredith's plotting expresses also the literary ideas of EMF's own generation: plot in Meredith's hands is a series of kiosks, passage through which changes the characters. Meredith is to be linked with contemporary novelists like Virginia Woolf and EMF, despite the fact that he is out of critical favor: the link is provided by Meredith's personal element in his fiction, his psychological approach, his feeling for image, and his rejection of realism. The use of the personal, conversational voice is also present in EMF's *The Longest Journey* and Woolf's THE WAVES. EMF's complaints that the tangible things are not real in Meredith's fiction is irrelevant, since Meredith was writing romance. In BEAUCHAMP'S CAREER, Rosamund Culling's appeal to Romfrey for spiritual honesty in apologizing to Dr. Shrapnel has a Forsterian quality such as might be found in *Howards End:* Romfrey must "connect" or disaster will ensue.

1472 Rao, B. Syamala. "E. M. Forster—*A Passage to India*," CEN-TURY (New Delhi), 4 July 1970, pp. 9, 12.

Mrs. Moore is a link between Christianity and Hinduism (also Islam), since Aziz and Godbole remember her. Nothing is really blessed in a book in which vision and nightmare are so closely conjoined (also the pervasive irony undercuts the positive). Because of their polished manner, EMF's works appeal to other writers before they appeal to ordinary readers. [Routine summary of *A Passage to India* and a few interesting interpretations.]

1473 Raven, Simon. "The Strangeness of E. M. Forster," SPECTA-TOR (Lond), CCXXV (5 Sept 1970), 237.

EMF gave the impression of idleness, although he had a perceptive and curious mind. He was diffident and inconclusive in his personal relationships and would support the underdog as an ethical principle over and against his personal and aesthetic preferences. His own behavior in other instances would go contrary to his expressed principles. He inconsistently condemned Ackerley for not coming to Cambridge, although Ackerley was helping his dog through heat and was illustrating thereby the two chief Forsterian virtues: sensitivity and loyalty. [As an undergraduate, Raven knew EMF but was not intimate; therefore, he could see EMF's day-to-day behavior from the outside.]

1474 Robson, W. W. "The Liberal Humanists: The Bloomsbury Group," MODERN ENGLISH LITERATURE (NY & Lond: Oxford UP, 1970), pp. 93–108, espec pp. 94–97, *passim.*

The world of EMF's Edwardian novels seems more remote than Jane Austen's; in EMF's the conflict between individuality and convention is dated. Yet his light touch and the coolness with which he handles violence attract many modern readers. His chief theme is the relationship between nature and culture. Nature is a primary value and a source of value; in this respect, EMF is a D. H. Lawrence, with less force and more tentativeness. Like Matthew Arnold EMF also respects a genuine culture and is a liberal humanist. So are many of EMF's protagonists, who are often chastened by confrontation with a deadened society and with their irrational selves. There is a didacticism and a melodramatic quality in EMF. EMF has little sense of the unpredictable in human nature [questionable]; his characters are prejudged. Personal relationships are all important for EMF, especially the relationships between man and man (rather than those between man and woman). There are similarities between EMF and Edward Carpenter; both are individualists and democrats. *A Passage to India* is EMF's one great novel. It is little concerned with the topical. It has a somber quality and a religious orientation. None of the three religions presented is satisfactory:

Christianity is parochial, Islam is ethnocentric, and Hinduism is incomprehensible (though it is the most profound). The exact nature of the happening in the Cave does not matter in a symbolical and metaphysical novel. The Great War reverberates in echo, despite the fact that the setting is pre-war. EMF is here noting the inadequacy of his liberal humanism. EMF's half-heartedness may be his virtue, because he can remind us thereby of a world outside politics and of the ends that politics ought to serve. [Excellent discussion in a book the quality of which is not uniform.]

1475 Rose, Martial. E. M. FORSTER (Lond: Evans, 1970; Literature in Perspective Series).
[Chapter I, "Forster's Life and Work," rehearses the known facts. Chapter II, "Literary Background," stresses influence of Shelley on the Cambridge group (of which EMF was part) at turn of the century.] Hardy influenced him with his anti-hero in JUDE THE OBSCURE. Blake, Morris, and T. S. Eliot are in EMF's background, and he respected the achievement of his great contemporaries, Conrad, Joyce, and Lawrence. EMF was fascinated with the new psychology and with the concept of the unconscious. [Succeeding chapters discuss EMF's book-length works, roughly in chronological order.] In his short stories the villains are the "dream-breakers," men who themselves lack insight and imagination. EMF champions the visionary against the realist in his stories. [Also in his novels.] In the short stories, nature is seen as uncontrollable (the Pan influence); places are important, and first-hand experience is always superior to secondhand. In *Where Angels Fear to Tread* there is structural imbalance; the themes of pain and death intrude too suddenly at the end and are not developed. Phillip is not changed with the death of the child. [Actually, his awakening occurs at the opera and just before.] In *The Longest Journey* there is an Oedipus analogue in Rickie Elliot. EMF celebrates carnal love in the novel, with Stephen the devotee of Aphrodite (or of Demeter as fertility goddess). *Journey* will retain its power, as it reveals poetically the artist who goes "from fantasy to reality, from ignorance to self-knowledge." [Little that is fresh in discussion of *A Room With a View* and *Howards End*.] The attempt in *Howards End* to link two ideologies ends in disaster. In *A Passage to India* the friendships between Aziz and Fielding and between Aziz and Mrs. Moore are moderately successful "passages." Mrs. Moore and Adela Quested communicate "telephatically" after the debacle in the Cave. Godbole's harmony includes "love of all men, the whole universe, and 'the tiny splinters of detail.' " A strained relationship exists between Aziz and Godbole, and their songs contrast with each other. The collision of the boats in the Mau tank in "Temple" is a symbol of a fracture rather than a reconciliation. Chap 8, "Achievement": [Stresses EMF's creative use of music, his mystical inclinations, his presentation of a "caged society" at odds with man's impulse for freedom, and the tragicomic nature of his vision wherein separation rather than

connection occurs.] "High seriousness is there, but it is to stress the coexistence of prose and passion, rather than the transmutation of prose into passion." The plots are tight, and EMF is successful as a storyteller; he also uses seasons expertly. Leonard Bast is a successful character, especially in the dialogue sequences, which show EMF's interest in other social classes. In the dialogue of *Angels* and *Passage*, he captures "the gestures and intonations of foreigners." His detachment tends to give his characters objective life. He is great because of "the complexity of his work, the depth of his insight into the human condition and his consummate artistry." [Pleasant and relaxed summary but contains little that is new or challenging. The discussions run to plot summaries and descriptions rather than to analysis and criticism.]

1476 Rosselli, John. "Moralist and Musician," MANCHESTER GUARDIAN WEEKLY, 20 June 1970, p. 16.
The suspicion may obtrude that EMF knew too little of the world and its ways. He is at once moralist and musician, and his novelist's voice drowns out all such suspicions and reservations. In *Howards End*, allegory and story come together in a fugal composition, and the novel stands as one of the last statements about Europe as a complete civilization. *A Passage to India* is also a rich composition. There is a minor quality in all his utterances and in his life, except in the monument of his five novels. [Perceptive obit.]

1477 Rutherford, Andrew (ed). TWENTIETH CENTURY INTERPRETATIONS OF "A PASSAGE TO INDIA": A COLLECTION OF CRITICAL ESSAYS (Englewood Cliffs, NJ: Prentice-Hall, Spectrum Books, 1970).
Contents, abstracted under date of first publication: Andrew Rutherford, "Introduction" (1970); Lionel Trilling, "*A Passage to India*" [in part], E. M. FORSTER (1943); W. A. S. Keir, "*A Passage to India* Reconsidered," CAMBRIDGE JOURNAL (1952); Arnold Kettle, "E. M. Forster: *A Passage to India*" [in part], AN INTRODUCTION TO THE ENGLISH NOVEL (1953); Gertrude White, "*A Passage to India*: Analysis and Revaluation," PUBLICATIONS OF THE MODERN LANGUAGE ASSOCIATION (1953); Nirad C. Chaudhuri, "Passage To and From India," ENCOUNTER (1954); Frederick C. Crews, "*A Passage to India*" [in part], E. M. FORSTER: THE PERILS OF HUMANISM (1962); C. B. Cox, "Mr. Forster's Island" [in part], THE FREE SPIRIT (1963); Barbara Hardy, "Dogmatic Form" [in part], THE APPROPRIATE FORM: AN ESSAY ON THE NOVEL (1964); Oliver Stallybrass, "Forster's 'Wobblings': The Manuscripts of *A Passage to India*," ASPECTS OF E. M. FORSTER (1969). Chronology of Important Dates; Selected Bibliography.

1478 Rutherford, Andrew. "Introduction," TWENTIETH CENTURY INTERPRETATIONS OF "A PASSAGE TO INDIA": A COLLECTION OF CRITICAL ESSAYS, ed by Andrew Rutherford (Englewood Cliffs, NJ: Prentice-Hall, Spectrum Books, 1970), pp. 1–16.

A Passage to India claims attention as a historical document, a philosophical statement, and a work of art. The novel customarily is rooted in social actuality; the accuracy of its representation of that actuality becomes one factor in interpretation, particularly when the reality is in itself controversial and when the book has had political impact (as *Passage* has had). EMF has been praised and condemned for his depiction of the Indian and Anglo-Indian scene. From some points of view he may distort the social reality; but the fact that there was any racial or class discrimination at all in India impelled him to write *Passage*. (British rule in India relied on force, and the Anglo-Indians too often displayed an arrogance and an insensitivity which he found distasteful). *Passage* is about divisions in mankind, the racial being only one; other divisions are those of wealth, class, religion, and caste. To mitigate these forces of division becomes the task, in EMF's view, of the liberal Englishman in India, represented in the novel by Fielding. Fielding is a creditable man whose accomplishments are creditable; yet he lacks certain dimensions of imagination and sensibility, and is inadequate, therefore, to a full understanding of India. A religious as well as a moral vision operates in the novel and cannot be disregarded. EMF rejects the Christianity of the missionaries, Mr. Graysford and Mr. Sorley, which depends on exclusion; he also demonstrates that Mrs. Moore's Christian love is partly irrelevant in India. He implies, especially in "Temple," that Godbole's inclusive and ambiguous Hinduism more nearly comprehends the facts of India. But the Gokul Ashtami ceremonies have a tentative aspect; they are soon over, and Hinduistic love and inclusiveness yield once again to division and separation. EMF's symbolism and the degree of his commitment to Hinduism are not therefore entirely clear. In any case, the novel represents EMF's maturest artistry; and it is a sophisticated and carefully wrought work, despite his reservations expressed about form as such in *Aspects of the Novel*. *Passage* exemplifies a triumphant fusion of form and reality, of pattern and life. It is also a fusion of realism and symbolism, the full success of which in this novel (as in his other novels) has been a matter of continuing debate. EMF is himself both craftsman and creator. [Sensible but hardly inspired remarks.]

1479 Sanders, Charles, Robin R. Rice, and Watt J. Cantillon. "E. M. Forster," WRITER AND PERSONA: CHARACTER INTO PROSE, ed by C. Sanders, R. R. Rice, and W. J. Cantillon (NY: McGraw-Hill, 1970), pp. 221–59, espec 219–21; also vii–x.

In his essays, EMF likes arresting opening sentences, and these have a belligerent aspect. Combat remains central in his prose, and this combativeness compensates for his disdain of conventional middle-class virtues and his leaning to middle-class "vices" (contemplation, personal relationships). In his novels his delicate psychological analysis is interrupted by melodramatic violence; in his essays the pattern is reversed: brusque (and sometimes brash) pronouncements are to the fore and conceal the precision of his thought. His emphatic, assertive, and paradoxical views are in the service of the problems of the age and of an active social consciousness. He chides society for repressing the artist but also chastises the idiosyncratic artist. He vigorously counsels the individual to achieve a mean position between opposing forces. [Rpts "The Menace to Freedom," "Anonymity: An Enquiry," "The Duty of Society to the Artist," and "The Raison d'Être of Criticism in the Arts," from *Two Cheers for Democracy.*]

1480 Schürenberg, Walter. "Graue Eminenz des Romans: zum Tode E. M. Forster" (Gray Eminence of the Novel: On E. M. Forster's Death), Tagesspiegel (Berlin), 9 June 1970.

EMF's trick of casually mentioning birth, love, and death is one of his chief qualities and a quality that has excited admiration in younger writers. EMF's heroines are characteristically well brought-up spinsters, who after crisis or violence become fascinated by foreigners and thereby experience the painful process leading to increased awareness and understanding. In his London club EMF was difficult to converse with; and his use of an ear-trumpet did not help. [In German.]

1481 Scott, Paul. "India: A Post-Forsterian View," Essays by Divers Hands, nsXXXVI (Lond: Oxford UP, 1970), pp. 113–32.

The Turtons and the Burtons, as they are presented in *A Passage to India*, are aesthetically right for the novel but sociologically partly wrong. EMF is not much concerned in *Passage* with the work done by the Anglo-Indians but with the dramatizing of a confrontation between two groups of these Anglo-Indians—the Turtons and the Burtons with their aristocratic paternalism versus Fielding, Mrs. Moore, and Adela Quested with their liberal humanism. The lines between reactionary and liberal thought have since narrowed. In *Passage*, liberalism fails in India; in India itself it has succeeded to a point. In Mrs. Moore, EMF was prophetic because in her anti-vision the liberal premises are challenged and seem not to matter unduly or to be at all clear in their significance. EMF also diagnoses well, in his picture of the alienation of the Anglo-Indians, the alienation now felt by the typical technicians who come out to India and feel lost there. They lack the sense of underlying purpose that had at least steadied the Turtons and the Burtons; they are insular, while the Indians have lost the moral fervor that nationalist agitation provided them with. If anything, Turtonism is even more pronounced now than it was then, as there is no English community to which to retire; alienation leads to an assertion of superiority or Turtonism. The Marabar echo still strikes for those in India: "One may come after Forster, but not, I think, after Marabar. So the final image is of the cave and the echo, and Mrs. Moore motionless with horror, while poor silly Adela

Quested rushes back into the protective arms of defensive prejudice. Mrs. Moore was before her time, and sits motionless to draw attention to our own." [Unusual angle of approach; ideas are stimulating though diffusely developed.]

1482 Seltzer, Leon F. THE VISION OF MELVILLE AND CONRAD: A COMPARATIVE STUDY (Athens: Ohio UP, 1970), p. 49.

The complexity of Conrad's subject matter resists a clear, unambiguous presentation of it. [EMF's charge ("Joseph Conrad: A Note," *Abinger Harvest*) that there is something obscure at the center of Conrad's genius is refuted.]

1483 Seymour, William Kean. "E. M. Forster: Some Observations and a Memory," CONTEMPORARY REVIEW, CCXVII (Aug 1970), 84–86.

[Stresses EMF's modesty and air of "watchful benignity," and doubts if he fully appreciated D. H. Lawrence, appreciative as he was of Lawrence's genius. Pleasant but superficial obit account.]

1484 Shahane, Vasant A. "Theme, Title and Structure in Khushwant Singh's TRAIN TO PAKISTAN," LITERARY CRITERION (Mysore), IX (Winter 1970), 68–76.

Singh's TRAIN TO PAKISTAN owes much to EMF. Singh is indebted to EMF's establishment of a troubled, sinister atmosphere on the train going out to the Marabar Caves and at the Caves themselves. The ambiguous, darkened atmosphere investing the train from Pakistan, which once was a symbol of life, is now a symbol of death (it now carries the bodies of those who perished in the partition war).

1485 Shepard, Richard F. "Forster Dies, Wrote *A Passage to India;* Fame Was Long-Lasting," NEW YORK TIMES, June 1970, pp. 1, 37.

According to his publisher William Jovanovich (president of Harcourt, Brace and World), EMF was a great conversationalist because he listened: "He didn't, in later years, seem to be as acute an observer as it turned out he was." [Obit article, consisting mostly of well-known facts and judgments.]

1486 Spender, Stephen. "E. M. Forster (1879–1970)," NEW YORK REVIEW OF BOOKS, 23 July 1970, pp. 3–4.

Talking of his experiences in Greece to a young writer visiting him in 1968, EMF recalled how his moments of vision often came in the midst of "muck," if they were placed in a wider context (the young writer had just explained to EMF that the Greek Colonels prevented him from visiting

Greece). The vision and the surrounding muddle, this is characteristic of EMF's attitude and work. He spoke at the end of his life with the under-graduate's voice of 1900; he spoke from out of his whole life. He was retiring and unobtrusive, yet he noticed everything; he was affectionate but critical of his friends. As for his ceasing to write novels, the essays often seem like autobiographic fiction wherein EMF finds himself at the center of the contemporary world "like Prufrock in the drawing room." In them he seems not defeatist but like one who has already wryly accepted his defeat—while waiting a chance, too, for a comeback. A complex note of helplessness and defiance prevails in his writings about the contemporary world. He felt that civilized values in the 1930s must be proclaimed, not with defiant rhetoric but with an emphasis upon one's own weaknesses. He abandoned fiction because he could not imagine a world in art in which his values would only appear as entities that had been defeated by the pressures of the age after World War I. *A Passage to India* is about politics only as they contain and condition human nature. Aziz's and Fielding's last ride proclaims political division but also the fact that affection subsists between the friends. Through Mrs. Moore we become aware of the terror as well as the beauty of life. Her mind becomes terrible like Yeats's in his last poetry. The novels show how redeemed characters are in touch with an ineffable reality. Mrs. Wilcox and Mrs. Moore are priestesses "in touch with divine mysteries, hearing terrible secrets." For EMF, art becomes a means of communicating through an infinite series of intercalated images, leading into the unknown (see Ansell's preoccupation in *The Longest Journey* with the series of squares and circles inside each other, with the final reality being in the inmost one). EMF's novels bore inward to the central reality; in his later writing he addressed himself to conditions in the outer sphere because he saw that a wholesome situation there was basic to all other activity. Like Matthew Arnold he turned from creation to criticism, to improve the qual-ity of society as a whole in which art would be written. EMF is a defeated liberal who yet remained articulate and protesting to the end. [Luminous, suggestive obit essay.]

1487 Spender, Stephen. "The Perfectly Candid Man," NEW YORK REVIEW OF BOOKS, 23 April 1970, pp. 24–30.
The Cambridge undergraduates at the turn of the century, who were later to form "Bloomsbury," were fortunate in being able to live their values. EMF (*The Longest Journey*) and Virginia Woolf (THE WAVES) created in fiction pictures of a shared vision among a Bloomsbury-like group of friends over a period of time. The Cambridge group then and later subscribed to the formulation of a nineteenth-century Cambridge Apostle, Henry Sedg-wick: "The pursuit of truth with absolute devotion." Virginia Woolf's efforts to maintain this vision resulted in despair alternating with hope and faith in life. The meeting of Leonard Woolf with the Stephen sisters, who were

visiting their brother Thoby at Cambridge, was like an occurrence in an EMF novel. In GROWING, Woolf reveals forces allowing him to sustain the strain of Virginia's mental breakdown and suicide: his absorption in his work, his ability to love people across a gulf of incommunicability, and his love of solitude. His Ceylon is closer to Conrad's Africa in "Heart of Darkness" than to EMF's India. On his return to England, Woolf recovered to a degree his first vision of idealism mixed with pleasure. We think of EMF, Virginia Woolf, and Roger Fry as being at the center of Bloomsbury because they reveal in their writing this vision in its purest form. The virtue of Bloomsbury lay in a group of friends keeping alive "values of intellect, art, friendship, and social justice" and judging their behavior in terms of these values. They observed proportion (EMF's *Howards End*) and lived their lives according to "invisible values," to use an EMF phrase. The defect of Bloomsbury was its snobbishness, its exclusion of too much: Wyndham Lewis, F. R. Leavis, Eliot's Anglican God, the dark gods of Lawrence. For them religious intensity offended good taste. They were both Apollonians and Dionysians; they combined "temperance with cultivated moments of intemperance" (and for those not initiated it was debilitating). Leonard and Virginia Woolf were exceptional people who flourished in this soil but were individuals as well as members of a group. Candor is above all else the mark of Leonard Woolf as he reveals himself in his autobiographical books and reflects Bloomsbury values. [Review article on Leonard Woolf's SOWING (1960), GROWING (1961), BEGINNING AGAIN (1964), DOWNHILL ALL THE WAY (1967), and THE JOURNEY NOT THE ARRIVAL MATTERS (1969). Important article for understanding EMF and his Bloomsbury milieu by one who knew most of its members; numerous mentions of EMF.]

1488 Stern, Richard. "A Memory of Forster," NATION (NY), CCX (29 June 1970), 795–96.

Perhaps EMF surrendered too early to self-criticism, but he may have been surprised by the survival of his books. He had persistent curiosity. He was "the Man of Sympathy who had invented unsentimental ways of conveying it." His talk had the warmth of the great English books, now a quality almost lost. He was prepared for death and had a young friend read for him in 1964 Tolstoy's "The Death of Ivan Ilyitch" as a kind of preparatory rite.

1489 Stone, Michael. "Operation am unterentwickelten Herzen. Zum Tode des englischen Romanciers E. M. Forster; sein Werk ist für uns noch zu entdecken" (Operation on the Undeveloped Heart. On the Death of the English Novelist, E. M. Forster: We Must Still Discover His Work), CHRIST UND WELT (Stuttgart), 26 June 1970.

EMF and Jane Austen both wrote at the end of an age, both belonged to a middle-class society, both have a universal aspect in the truth of their moral perspective, and both reveal English humor in its furthest development. Jane Austen's ethic is implicit; EMF's is a muted didacticism at the heart of his work. Both embody the best qualities of their class. [In German.]

1490 Thatcher, David S. NIETZSCHE IN ENGLAND, 1890–1914: THE GROWTH OF A REPUTATION (Toronto: University of Toronto P, 1970), pp. 266–67, 268.

In "T. S. Eliot" (*Abinger Harvest*) EMF was typical of the Bloomsbury attitudes and values which Nietzsche would have decried. Huysmans's A REBOURS, EMF maintained, went counter to the moral imperatives of war present in 1917 and stressed the sanctity of sensation rather than of Nietzschean will. Bloomsbury derived philosophically from G. E. Moore with "his Pateresque philosophy of the exquisite sensation" rather than from Nietzsche. In *Howards End* EMF disparaged the superman, through Helen Schlegel, for lacking a personal identity.

1491 Trainor, Edward Alphonsus. "The Role of Setting in the Novels of E. M. Forster," DISSERTATION ABSTRACTS INTERNATIONAL, XXXI (1970), 736A. Unpublished dissertation, University of Michigan, 1969.

1492 Vidan, Ivo. "E. M. Forster's 'Heart of Bosnia,'" STUDIA ROMANICA ET ANGLICA ZAGRABIENSIA (Zagreb University), No. 29/ 30, 31/32 (1970–1971), 623–24.

EMF said the play "The Heart of Bosnia" was never planned for production; it had a romantic, "Ruritarian," violent plot that made it an unlikely stage success.

1493 Vidler, Alec R. "Remembering E. M. Forster," CHRISTIAN CENTURY, LXXXVII (22 July 1970), 894.

EMF was little affected by his public reputation. He valued private life and personal relations; he had a wisdom and a sensibility seasoned with salt, a genuine tolerance and openness combined with "great assurance of conviction." He was "otherworldly without believing in the other world . . . a saint of humanism." He was a non-Christian or an ex-Christian who embodied many of the Christian virtues, "a gracious and graceful doubter" and a salutary influence as a result. In the best sense he revealed "a cloistered virtue." [Revealing discussion and obit by the once Dean of King's College.]

1494 Vogel, Jane Austen. "The Theme of the Journey in the Works of E. M. Forster," DISSERTATION ABSTRACTS INTERNATIONAL, XXXI (1970), 406A. Unpublished dissertation, Cornell University, 1969.

1495 Wagner, C. Roland. "The Excremental and the Spiritual in *A Passage to India*," MODERN LANGUAGE QUARTERLY, XXI (Sept 1970), 359–71.

Mystical yearning does more than qualify the mature, naturalistic, liberal vision which Trilling celebrated in *A Passage to India* (in E. M. FORSTER, 1943); it enters into the very substance of his worldliness. EMF goes beyond the naturalistic; the nothingness that he thinks he may find there becomes a goal in itself, a form of pure being, of infinite essence: "Both the philosophical power and the final fuzziness of the novel suggest Forster's great sense of the complexity of existence and his inability to commit himself to a stable point of view." *Passage* suggests that he is in touch with the nakedly irrational but not in secure imaginative control of it. Godbole is unconcerned about the echo and the "excremental reality" it includes or emphasizes (the comic treatment of Godbole undercuts EMF's full acceptance of his vision); Mrs. Moore is overwhelmed by the echo (and the filth associated with it). The novel itself overcomes Mrs. Moore's (and EMF's) horror of filth. Godbole handles filth without guilt; for EMF Hinduism is attractive because it is free from guilt and accepts filth. Yet Hinduism is marked by moral evasiveness as well as spiritual insight, and EMF's agnosticism prevents him from accepting Godbole's vision completely. Godbole is for EMF a false mystic, as well as a true one. EMF is sympathetic to the inclusiveness of Godbole's vision but personally prefers a version of the infinite free of the excremental, as that is approximated through personal relations, art, and culture. These entities are present in *Passage*, but they are dwarfed therein. The moments of illumination for Mrs. Moore and Adela are earned but are minor ones in the whole conspectus of the novel, "peripheral experiences surrounding a central mystery, not central experiences around which the artist builds his mysterious world." [Illuminating article and persuasive, although EMF is more positive concerning Godbole than Wagner allows.]

1496 Wagner, Geoffrey. "The Novel of Empire," ESSAYS IN CRITICISM, XX (April 1970), 229–42.

English fiction of empire is, in part, an expression of England's commercial prosperity in the nineteenth century. The fiction of Kipling, Conrad, and EMF can yield information as to British colonial conditions, if elements of fantasy, native to fiction, are discounted. Fiction enables us to see that the word "white" did not carry with it associations of racial domination; race did not ordinarily enter into the Englishman's conception of moral value and his judgments of others. Rose Macaulay correctly maintains that *A Passage to India* is not about dissolution of empire but about ill-breeding. England intruded where she was not wanted. Even with the Anglo-Indians in *Passage* only a few use the term "negro" as a hate-absolute. McBryde with his theories of the impossibility of combating climatic factors was himself defeated by them. In the typical novel of empire, not only is character created by colonial hardships, but those back home in England may be regenerated by those who live elswhere. Those in the club at Chandrapore in *Passage* have suspicion of those who have an easier life at home, just as do the club members in Kipling's tales about India. Even EMF's collector has a residual sense of responsibility in preventing the looting of Aziz's belongings prior to the trial. There are moral differences among imperialists; and the nineteenth-century imperialist outlook is not the same as that of the modern gangster. [Argument tends to the tenuous and finespun, and the evidence assembled by Benita Parry in DELUSIONS AND DISCOVERIES (1972) refutes the view expressed here of the alleged tolerance of other races revealed by the administrators of empire.]

1497 Walker, Warren S. TWENTIETH-CENTURY SHORT STORY EXPLICATION: SUPPLEMENT I TO SECOND EDITION, 1967–1969 (Hamden, Conn: Shoe String P, 1970), pp. 73–76.
[Continues Walker's listing of criticism on EMF's short stories; see Walker 1967.]

1498 Ward, A. C. "E. M. Forster," LONGMAN COMPANION TO TWENTIETH-CENTURY LITERATURE (Lond: Longman, 1970), pp. 208–9.
[Good short account, stressing EMF's influence on Virginia Woolf and his role as "a novelist's novelist." Also contains summaries of EMF's novels, *The Celestial Omnibus, Abinger Harvest*, and *Two Cheers for Democracy.*]

1499 Whittemore, Reed. "E. M. Forster—1879–1970," NEW REPUBLIC, CLXII (20 June 1970), 28.
EMF was a "triple-threat" man: a great literary craftsman, a profound observer of the social condition, and a great moralist. EMF was a secular being like his Mr. Emerson, but like him EMF was continually seeking for "the true heartland of relevance." Present-day youth might even understand EMF's statement that he could betray his country before his friend. [Whittemore first connected with EMF in World War II in Italy by reading *A Room with a View*, which a Stalinist friend also liked. The two were connected with EMF by the admiration that all felt for Jane Austen, who did not, in fact, seem irrelevant in wartime; the connecting link between Austen and the men was EMF's high regard for genuine and spontaneous affection. Brief but incisive obit account.]

1500 Zeh, Dieter. "Studien zur Erzählkunst in den Romanen E. M. Forsters," (Studies of Narrative Methods in E. M. Forster's Novels). Upublished dissertation, FrankfurtMain, 1970.
[Listed in Lawrence F. McNamee, DISSERTATIONS IN ENGLISH AND AMERICAN LITERATURE, SUPP II (NY & Lond: Bowker, 1974). Analyzes EMF's

novels in relation to the concept of "significant form," developed by A. C. Bradley, Clive Bell, and Roger Fry.] [In German.]

1501 Zimmerman, Paul D. "E. M. Forster (1879–1970)," NEWS-WEEK, LXXV (22 June 1970), 84–5; rptd in part in CONTEMPORARY LITERARY CRITICISM, ed by Carolyn Riley and Barbara Harte (Detroit: Gale Research Co., 1974), II, 135.

EMF was our last great link with Edwardian England. He was a custodian of civilization especially in *Abinger Harvest* and *Two Cheers for Democracy*, which reveal "a cultivated and wide-ranging intelligence—independent, tough-minded and non-partisan," a humanism that valued the private virtues over the public ones. Like Dickens, EMF was concerned with the heart, as a means not to social reform (with Dickens) but to private salvation, as "an antidote to social injustice but not a cure." EMF was Victorian in his preference for melodrama and struggle, as in his predilection for firm plot and story. He was modern in his projection of moral ambiguities into his melodrama, in his detached tone, his skepticism, and his fine irony. He turned to the essay when the society he knew passed away, and advanced thereby the tradition of the English familiar essay. With his death "the last of a civilized breed" has gone. [Obit article with some good insights.]

1971

1502 Ackerley, J. R. E. M. FORSTER: A PORTRAIT (Lond: Ian McKelvie, 1971); ptd in abbreviated form as "E. M. Forster: A Personal Memoir," OBSERVER, 14 June 1970, p. 7.

EMF adapted to each of his friends, had phenomenal power of judging people, and listened intently. He was entirely lacking in self-consciousness. He retained his faith in human values and human relationships; but his honesty led him always to reject the spurious and to expect much from his friends. He had also the formidable quality and toughness of the saint. He was close to the questioning temper and love of truth embodied in Stewart Ansell in *The Longest Journey*. He was, moreover, our greatest literary critic. [Friendship with EMF was the longest, closest, and most influential in Ackerley's life. Affectionate and revealing reminiscences and character analysis.]

1503 Alldritt, Keith. THE VISUAL IMAGINATION OF D. H. LAWRENCE (Lond: Edward Arnold; Evanston: Northwestern UP, 1971), pp. 149–61.

[D. H. Lawrence's relationships to Bloomsbury are given in detail. Lawrence's uneasy relationship with EMF is discussed as it is reflected in the letter to Bertrand Russell, 12 Feb 1915 (see Lawrence [1948]). Lawrence's blunt criticism of Duncan Grant's paintings in EMF's and David Garnett's presence is given (see Garnett's THE FLOWERS OF THE FOREST [1955]).] Lawrence was more sympathetic to another Bloomsbury painter, Mark Gertler. Gertler's intense, naked, "corrupt" sensibility is akin to Loerke's in WOMEN IN LOVE. In Loerke is satirized Clive Bell's and Roger Fry's doctrine of "significant form." Bloomsbury's interest in primitive art is revealed in the important place in the book given to the sensual African statuary, which Birkin alone among the characters experiences genuinely.

1504 Allen, Walter. "The Least of Forster," DAILY TELEGRAPH (Lond), 7 Oct 1971, p. 10; rptd in E. M. FORSTER: THE CRITICAL HERITAGE, ed by Philip Gardner (Lond & Boston: Routledge & Kegan Paul, 1973), pp. 437–38.

Maurice is dated, as *The Longest Journey* is not, because in *Journey* there is more of EMF. *Maurice* has the least in literary value of any of his novels because it overconcentrates, as a thesis novel tends to do, on a single issue. There is an affinity between Maurice and the Wilcoxes, which makes of him a "bore," something that Rickie Elliot is not. EMF should have written more autobiographically, in fiction or in nonfiction, on homosexuality.

1505 Alvarez, A. "From Snobbery to Love," SATURDAY REVIEW (NY), LIV (16 Oct 1971), 39–40, 42–43; rptd in part in CONTEMPORARY LITERARY CRITICISM, ed by Carolyn Riley (Detroit: Gale Research Co., 1973), I, 109.

EMF's career reveals a common crisis when in early middle age the fact of death is recognized. *A Passage to India* reflects the ten years of public upheaval that transpired in its writing; it also reflects the mid-life crisis. In India EMF felt less alien than in England; India's appeal was strong because of its difference from all that he had previously known. In *Albergo Empedocle and Other Writings* (ed by George H. Thomson) the pieces on India are more detailed and subtle than the other uncollected writings. In England the contrast between the established and the true was less obvious than in India; and only his minority convictions supported him in his alienation: his belief in culture, the truth of the emotions, and his homosexuality. He prepared himself for writing *Passage* by writing *Maurice*, a story about a man in the minority, as Fielding, Adela Quested, and Mrs. Moore are in India. Since he was at his creative zenith, the book is disappointing, despite "its own brand of self-effacing courage and originality." Its reticence is not necessarily a blemish, but EMF failed to maintain the appropriate artistic balance and to order his priorities. The Cambridge section is the weakest; the book improves after its half-way point when EMF has done with Clive Durham and his idealization of homosexual love and turns to the subject he knows—loneliness and snobbery. Maurice's loneliness leads to illumination, though his homosexuality forces him into incomprehensible isolation. In *Passage*, EMF was to move out against not only class prejudice but colonialism and racial prejudice. Though it would have been brave to publish *Maurice* after it was written, EMF's life would have been made impossible. It now seems too much a period piece. In the uncollected essays edited by Thomson, EMF reveals "his decency and tolerance, his subtle but unshowy intelligence." He had none of the self-congratulation of his Bloomsbury associates. Also at the core of his talent is his reticence, which made the writing of a great novel about sexuality impossible for him. [Stimulating, perceptive discussion.]

1506 Annan, Noel. "Love Story," NEW YORK REVIEW OF BOOKS, 21 Oct 1971, pp. 12–19.

In a comparison of *Maurice* with Lawrence's LADY CHATTERLEY'S LOVER, Lawrence's book is better, and he imagines the lower class better than EMF. Lawrence's ambition, range, and achievement are greater, but so is his failure. In *Maurice* the humor and the "fierce contoured" plot of his other novels are absent. The book is thin but not negligible. EMF believed in human beings, the reality of their actions, the possible moral meaning of action, in emotional restraint and emotional expression. He liked the comedy of sex but not sexual boasting, and he expected more from homosexual love than his heterosexual friends did from marriage. The Platonic relationship at Cambridge between Maurice and Clive Durham is credible and historically possible. In so far as the novel expresses the doubts, dilemmas, and fears of the young, it is not dated. The chief theme that EMF explores is the difficulty that someone like Maurice has in learning to trust his heart. The descriptions of Clive's and Maurice's behavior and their conversations are unsatisfactory. Clive finally adopts the values of "the great world" and breaks with Maurice. EMF himself had a working-class friend and knew Alec Scudder's class. He felt that Maurice and Alec had the simplicity that would be needed for a lasting relationship, but he does not prepare us enough for us to believe in their idyllic future life. Both Lawrence and EMF try to portray tenderness as the supreme achievement in love-making, and neither one succeeds. For Lawrence the gamekeeper is a symbol of sex and ruthless vitality, for EMF of coziness. Maurice and Alec have too little in common to live together, nor does EMF convey by inference what the quality of their life together might be. The Georgian reticence he deplores in the marriage of Clive and Anne envelops the affair between Maurice and Alec also. The omission of the details of physical intimacy are here disastrous, as they are not in the Helen-Leonard Bast episode in *Howards End.* His social observations show the moralist at work, and he does well with social comedy, as in the case of Mr. Borenius, the Durhams' vicar. A great homosexual novel is impossible, since the whole subject gets between author and reader. The uncollected essays *Albergo Empedocle and Other Writings* (ed by George H. Thomson) are not of great significance, but Thomson does his job as editor with tact and good taste. The fact that EMF is a great moralist with one great novel assures his continuing reputation. [A wide-ranging, interesting, and perceptive article.]

1507 Appasamy, S. P. "Forster's Attempt to Connect Britain and India," INDO-BRITISH REVIEW (Madras), III (Jan–March 1971), 19–24.

Indians and English did meet under the Raj, but they also failed to connect, largely because the British military and civil servants had been brought up on the external, activist values of the public school (leadership, bravery, initiative, energy, and honesty), which dulled the social imagination and personal sympathies. These men also assumed that they had a mission to educate and improve the civilization of the native races. The glorification of these activist values made Kipling's view of India insupportable to the Indians. Orwell and especially EMF reacted in their personal lives against the public-school ethos and were able as a result to scrutinize critically the English civil and military servants and to view with sympathy the native races who had been encouraged to assume a slave mentality. In *A Passage to India*, EMF analyzes the failure of the civilizing mission of the British; it failed because of the insensitivity of most British officials and the hypersensitivity of most cultured Indians. The novel broadens to a conflict between love and the intractible; this conflict sums up the novel. Those who are sensitive to this conflict have connected with India; the dramatization of this truth represents EMF's attempt in *Passage* to connect Britain with India. [Perceptive article.]

1508 Barber, Dulan. "Disarming not Definitive," TRIBUNE (Lond), XXXV (15 Oct 1971), 10.

Maurice is disarming; it is not a masterpiece nor was EMF "a secret pornographer." It is not a definitive homosexual novel but deserves a minor place in the EMF canon. Its schematic quality is right for revealing the long process involved in Maurice's accepting his nature, for presenting the duel between his carefully nurtured persona and his soul (or his homosexuality). Maurice's sensitivity leads to his regeneration. EMF's homosexual romanticism is at odds with his acerbity and his moral honesty, qualities to the fore in most of his other work. Does the book reveal EMF's inability to get to terms with what is closest to him, or is his homosexuality less important than one had supposed?

1509 Beer, Gillian. "ONE OF OUR CONQUERORS: Language and Music," MEREDITH NOW: SOME CRITICAL ESSAYS, ed by Ian Fletcher (Lond: Routledge & Kegan Paul; NY: Barnes & Noble, 1971), pp. 265–80.

Joyce, Lawrence, T. S. Eliot, and EMF all derived something, at least indirectly, from Meredith's freedom from constraint in ONE OF OUR CONQUERORS and from his experiments in it with language. Wagner dominates the mood of the novel. Meredith's celebration of music in it recalls the exalted description of Beethoven in SANDRA BELLONI: this description anticipates EMF's celebration of Beethoven's Fifth Symphony in *Howards End*.

1510 Beer, John [B.] *"A Room with a View,"* TIMES LITERARY SUPPLEMENT (Lond), 11 June 1971, p. 677.

Edward J. Dent is to be identified with EMF's Philip Herriton in *Where Angels Fear to Tread* (as EMF stated in Angus Wilson's "A Conversation with E. M. Forster" [1957]). In Elizabeth Ellem's "E. M. Forster: The Lucy and New Lucy Novels" (1971), a manuscript fragment identifies Philip very closely with EMF and indicates the depth of EMF's relationship with Dent. Miss Lavish is to be identified with Emily Spender, a popular novelist. Her books A SOLDIER FOR A DAY (1901) and THE LAW BREAKERS (1903) have many resemblances to *A Room with a View*, especially the Italian setting and the repression of the heroine's sex instincts by an elderly relative. Miss Lavish's conventional unconventionality is similar to Emily Spender's.

1511 Birnbaum, Milton. ALDOUS HUXLEY'S QUEST FOR VALUES (Knoxville: University of Tennessee P, 1971), pp. 4, 8, 10, 11, 23, 24, 61, 103, 133, 176, 177, 182, 199*n*.

Contrary to Huxley, EMF thought of art as self-sufficient, not as catalytic, and reflecting, therefore, the spiritual problems of his age. Huxley tried to erode the traditional sources of value in his fiction. Among these were education (the efficacy of the public school was denied also by EMF and Samuel Butler), nature (EMF reveals in the twentieth century the sustaining value of nature when in *The Longest Journey*, Stephen Wonham takes his little girl to sleep with him in the fields at night), and religion (even EMF's denial of belief held men's attention). The effects of the drying up of traditional sources of value are evident not only in Huxley but in the works of Joyce, Lawrence, Woolf, and EMF. To illustrate this tendency, EMF attacks traditional education and champions a life of instinct. *A Passage to India* reflects EMF's pessimism about traditional human relationships. Aziz voices EMF's solution to problems created by British upper-class snobbery in an advocacy of kindness, but EMF's hope for the developed heart was minimal. *Passage* ends pessimistically, and this pessimism was never alleviated in his subsequent writings. [Overstated.] Huxley's characters are representative of his age and throw light on the satirically or ironically envisioned characters of Joyce, Lawrence, Woolf, and EMF (e.g. Herbert Pembroke in *Journey*). Nature is mostly absent from Huxley's work (see the contrast between city life and rural life present in so many novels by Lawrence and EMF). Huxley's view of marital love as unsatisfying is echoed in many twentieth-century novels (see the disastrous marriage between Rickie Elliot and Agnes Pembroke in *Journey*).

1512 "A Bit Behindhand," ECONOMIST (Lond), CCXLI (6 Nov 1971), p. iv.

In *Maurice* there is no new illumination of homosexuality but a conception of it as "an outlaw queerness, a perversion separating its practitioners forever from the 'normal' society of their fellows." The superiority of the Alec Scudder episode to the Clive Durham episode results from the fact that the first is the result of craft rather than of experience. The book as a whole is a failure.

1513 Blakeston, Oswell. "Forster's Stuffed Owl," BOOKS AND BOOKMEN, XVII (Oct 1971), 35.

The subject of *Maurice* is dull. EMF wrote it probably as therapy; his repressions were apparently blocking his creative impulse. EMF regrettably makes a mediocrity of Maurice; EMF makes Maurice boring to punish him for EMF's own daydreams. The real dreams in the novel are dull. EMF was obsessed with his subject to the point of neglecting his art as a writer. Maurice did not have "the intelligence or the sensibility to break down his generation's class barriers." *Maurice* was not worth publishing.

1514 B[lythe], R[onald]. "Bloomsbury Group," PENGUIN COMPAN-ION TO ENGLISH LITERATURE, ed by David Daiches (NY: McGraw-Hill; Harmondsworth, Middlesex: Penguin, 1971), p. 54.
[Informed short account, stressing influences of G. E. Moore, the remote influence of Clapham Sect, and the prime influence of Cambridge upon this small, informal group of twentieth-century intellectuals.]

1515 Borrello, Alfred. AN E. M. FORSTER DICTIONARY (Metuchen, NJ; Scarecrow P, 1971).
[Book has residual usefulness as a reference tool, with respect to the characters and principal places mentioned in EMF's work. Uncollected works are not included; this decision is unfortunate because the best and most seminal of them are indispensable for the interpretation and appraisal of EMF's other works. The well-known facts about places in *A Passage to India* are omitted. Insensitivity to the literary dimensions and significance of EMF's characters is marked: Helen Schlegel in *Howards End* is described as having an affair with Leonard Bast, whereas it is really a one-night onslaught by Helen upon Leonard; Margaret Schlegel becomes "a good wife" to Henry Wilcox (their relationship is not that tranquil); Rickie Elliot and Gerald Dawes in *The Longest Journey* are incorrectly described as "friends" at school; Mrs. Moore is simplified (no mention is given of the evocation of her name at Aziz's trial, of her being remembered by Godbole at the Mau festivities after her death, or of her continuing life as a minor Indian deity). Inaccuracies abound: Cyril Fielding throughout is called Cecil, Ernst Schlegel is Ernest, Lilia Herriton is Lila; names of places, proper names, and literary works, are incorrectly and inconsistently given. Such inaccuracies are deplorable in a reference work.]

1516 Brace, Keith. "Forster's Will and Testament," BIRMINGHAM POST, 9 Oct 1971, "Saturday Magazine," p. II.
The influence of Bloomsbury artists and the intellectuals has gone into our current attitudes of moral tolerance, political and social idealism, and do-goodism. Bloomsbury values of individuality and revolt are in *Maurice*, but it rises above its context by the personal pressure behind it. The shocking nature of the suggestion that a lasting homosexual marriage might be possible was the reason for EMF's delaying publication of his book. It reveals young men in passionate friendship in the pre-1914 era who do not realize what it is about. The tone perhaps too faithfully reflects bourgeois society

of its day, and an act of historical imagination is needed to recreate Maurice's situation. But when EMF's deepest feelings are involved, he wrote in parts of *Maurice* with a dateless eloquence. He does not proselytize and does not maintain that homosexuality is necessarily better than heterosexuality. *Maurice* is an important addition to the Bloomsbury canon, although Bloomsbury might have condemned it for "giving the game away." [An illuminating review.]

1517 Bradbury, Malcolm. THE SOCIAL CONTEXT OF MODERN ENGLISH LITERATURE (Oxford: Basil Blackwell; NY: Schocken Books, 1971), pp. xxiii, xxxiv, 27, 33, 34n, 46, 51, 52, 54, 57, 80n, 93, 115, 254, 255.

A sense of tradition balances a compulsion to experiment in many typical modern writers, as in EMF. The fact that Edwardian society was a half-controlled growth rather than a culture or a community explains the vein of rural nostalgia in EMF, given in *Howards End*. The city in EMF (as in D. H. Lawrence) is a force of cultural disintegration and discontinuity. To compensate for such effects of the city, some writers envision a "new pastoral" in which the country embodies a generally lost organic society (*Howards End*, Lawrence's THE RAINBOW), and the city stands for a "new exposure" to disintegrating forces. In *Howards End* the city is an ambiguous entity; it is a center of culture for the Schlegels and "a creeping red rust" into the countryside. [Other incidental references.]

1518 Brooks, Jean R. THOMAS HARDY: THE POETIC STRUCTURE (Ithaca: Cornell UP, 1971), pp. 90, 91, 257, 307.

Hardy in his poetry often attains the "notable pinnacles" of experience mentioned by EMF. In JUDE THE OBSCURE Father Time as "an enslaved and dwarfed Divinity" recalls EMF's conception in *A Passage to India* of infinity as something ignoble and small. The modern novel has moved closer to poetry in its recognition of unexplained experiences; also the relativity of truth and the haphazard chronology implicit in Hardy's "moments of vision" help determine the themes and forms of experimental novels written after Hardy by Joyce, Woolf, and EMF. [EMF is quoted on the contrast between "the life in time and the life by values," set forth in *Aspects of the Novel.*]

1519 Brophy, Brigid. "The Saving of Maurice," LISTENER, LXXXVI (7 Oct 1971), 481.

The style of *Maurice* is comparable to that of the undistinguished, immensely popular Edwardian novelist Marie Corelli, and it has little distinction. *Maurice* was unpublishable in 1914, but without EMF's name as author, it would still be unpublishable. It is interesting only as an EMF document, although is is not as bad as the worst EMF. *Maurice* is essentially unrealized. The sexual symbolism of windows is overexploited.

1520 Churchill, Allen. THE LITERARY DECADE (Englewood Cliffs, NJ: Prentice-Hall, 1971), pp. 152, 176, 278.

EMF's *A Passage to India*, a British import, was an outstanding novel for the American 1920s. Thornton Wilder achieved critical success with THE BRIDGE OF SAN LUIS REY (1927) by deliberately restricting his canvas, as EMF had done just previously in *Passage.*

1521 Clemons, Walter. "The Love of Comrades," NEWSWEEK, LXXVIII (Oct 1971), 95–96.

Maurice is worth publishing, but it is EMF's "palest" novel. The other novels should not be reinterpreted as homosexual in tendency; if anything, EMF may have exaggerated the influence of women and the themes of fertility and continuity in the early fiction. *Maurice* may, however, give a key to EMF's silence after 1924 as a writer of fiction. [A likely inference; see Oliver Stallybrass's "Introduction," *The Life to Come and Other Stories* (1972).]

1522 Colmer, John. "Comradeship and Ecstasy," AUSTRALIAN (Sydney), 16 Oct 1971, p. 18.

Maurice is both publishable and worth publishing. It is a sketch rather than a masterpiece, although it reveals EMF's subtle characterization, complex vision, and ironic detachment. The homosexual theme distorted EMF's sympathies and forced him into private therapeutic writing rather than allowing him to remain a social conscience. His achievement is placing homosexual relations within a conflict between conventional values and personal integrity. True brotherhood can occur only when people touch the earth and are unashamed of their physical natures. Only such people should inherit England. EMF was able even in private writing to charge details with symbolic power. Alec Scudder is partly wish-fulfillment, though the fear he inspires in Maurice and his attempts at blackmail ring true. EMF was forced by a conservative society to be unduly harsh with the sexual turncoat, Clive Durham. The book is beautiful and poignant, "a charming pastoral eclogue in Edwardian fancy dress." [Incisive comment.]

1523 "Commentary," TIMES LITERARY SUPPLEMENT (Lond), 3 Dec 1971, p. 1506.

[Discussion of E. M. FORSTER, 1879–1970: HEFFER CATALOGUE SEVEN (1971) and A. N. L. Munby's "Introduction" thereto (1971). Notes the absence of contemporary fiction in EMF's library and a preponderance of poetry, criticism, belles lettres, history, biography, and the arts. Introduction and pamphlet are valuable for information on EMF's reading.]

1524 Connolly, Cyril. "Corydon in Croydon," SUNDAY TIMES (Lond), 10 Oct 1971, p. 39; rptd in E. M. FORSTER: THE CRITICAL HERITAGE, ed by Philip Gardner (Lond & Boston: Routledge & Kegan Paul, 1973), pp. 458–61.

EMF's failure to publish *Maurice* when it was written may have been a failure of nerve; in his reticence he is more similar to Gide than to any other contemporary. *Maurice* reveals a "sustained lyricism" and shows the novelist "at the height of his powers"; but the book is unfortunately dated, in its language and in the playful behavior of Maurice and Clive Durham. Platonic love between men was once the backbone of empire and was bred along with responsibility, honesty, and leadership in the public schools. Freud has since taken the experience out of latency, where it tended to remain in Edwardian England.

1525 Craig, David. "Supple Freedom of Forster's Prose," TIMES HIGHER EDUCATION SUPPLEMENT (Lond), 15 Oct 1971, p. 21; rptd as "A Faulty but Brave Attempt at Candour," in E. M. FORSTER: THE CRITICAL HERITAGE, ed by Philip Gardner (Lond & Boston: Routledge & Kegan Paul, 1973), pp. 469–72.

The prose in *Maurice* is supple with a point to point movement of life, yet psychologically the early sections are scanted. The sequences at Cambridge are thin, but the London ones reveal EMF's customary mastery of the dramatic. Maurice is presented with insight in his young manhood; Clive Durham's conversion, however, is stated, not dramatized. The scenes with Alec Scudder are done with great finesse. The end is neither a living happily ever after nor a defeat but a modern kind of opening out of character and situation, as one phase of life yields to the next. *Maurice* lacks "heaviness, a consistent density of evoked life"; it is an attempt, not totally successful, to achieve total candor in the novel in the early twentieth century.

1526 Cronin, John. " 'Publishable—but Worth It?' " IRISH PRESS (Dublin), 9 Oct 1971, p. 12; rptd in E. M. FORSTER: THE CRITICAL HERITAGE, ed by Philip Gardner (Lond & Boston: Routledge & Kegan Paul, 1973), pp. 456–58.

EMF has been a moralist of the possible, warning us against the despair that is likely if we try to reach the unattainable. His intrusions are sometimes obtrusive, but at his best his novels open out into humorous scenes, notable for their accuracy of observation and irony. In his other novels irony and humor obscure the ever-present pain and terror. In *Maurice* a great amount of pain is present, and no humor. The "painful morbidity" of *The Longest Journey* is reflected in *Maurice*. There is less art in *Maurice* than in the other novels; the narrative method is thin, the style fragile. There is a great gulf between the tenuousness of this book and "the expansive wisdom" of *A Passage to India*. EMF was too close to Maurice; he never attains fictional distance from him. The novel, moreover, never really symbolically supports its theme. It will not diminish EMF's reputation though it will not add much to it. [Original remarks.]

1527 Daleski, H. M. DICKENS AND THE ART OF ANALOGY (NY: Schocken Books; Lond: Faber, 1970), p. 85.

The outer life of business and the inner life of personal relations, opposed to each other in *Howards End*, are fused with each other in MARTIN CHUZ-ZLEWIT through Dickens's recurring metaphors of money and business.

1528 Das, Bikram K. "A Stylistic Analysis of the Speech of the Indian Characters in Forster's *A Passage to India*," INDIAN JOURNAL OF ENGLISH STUDIES (Bombay: Orient Longmans), No. 12 (Dec 1971), 42–54.

The breakdown of communication—the central theme of *A Passage to India*—is symbolized by the failures of the Indians and the English to understand each other when the English language is used. When the Indians speak English among themselves, EMF gains credulity for them by the use of a formalized style. When Indians speak in English to English people, misunderstandings occur, not as the result of the use of faulty grammar by the Indians but as a result of their imperfect apprehension of an alien culture and of the total context within which they must speak and act.

1529 Deacon, Andrew. "*A Passage to India*: Forster's Confidence," CRITICAL REVIEW (Melbourne), XIV (1971), 125–36.

A tiredness and emotional flatness in EMF's prose suggests that his vision of human limitation and muddle comes from a lack of vitality and lacks therefore the universal validity that he claims for it in *A Passage to India*. His formulations strive for an urgency that they do not in fact possess, and they reveal an element of softness, or sentimentality, in his humanism. He also overvalues passive states of affection, emotion, and morality and undervalues the active and purposive; as an example of this tendency, the Indians emerge as somewhat smaller than life. He is superb at rendering individuals as part of their groups, less successful in presenting them as individuals. Mrs. Moore is not big enough for her role in the book; her experiences are stated rather than rendered. There are instances of uncertainty in tone and in manipulation of incident in "Temple," but his comic zest shows "a trust in life's variety, energy, and self-sufficiency." With Aziz, EMF is expert in showing that his lack of comprehension of the Caves matters little because of his deep, primal commitment to life. EMF shows perceptiveness in sensing that Godbole's and Aziz's instinct to leave Chandrapore after the trial is the only possible course for them; he also perceptively reveals their lack of self-consciousness and their rejection of "instrumental" living. "Temple" is most affirmative when EMF reveals the creative aspect of

Aziz's new life at Mau. [Interesting, if at times dogmatic in tone; more perceptive when it defines the virtues of EMF's work rather than its limitations.]

1530 Delavenay, Émile. D. H. LAWRENCE AND EDWARD CARPENTER: A STUDY IN EDWARDIAN TRANSITION (NY: Taplinger; Lond: Heinemann, 1971), pp. 8, 160, 231, 233, 248, 273.

The work of Virginia Woolf and EMF owes much to Carpenter's notion of a fluid rather than a fixed personality. [EMF is quoted on Carpenter as a forgotten writer whose work has, nevertheless, passed into our heritage. Also on the mystical aspects of Carpenter, which ally him to Lawrence.]

1531 Dennis, Nigel. "The Love that Levels," SUNDAY TELEGRAPH (Lond), 10 Oct 1971, p. 16; rptd in E. M. FORSTER: THE CRITICAL HERITAGE, ed by Philip Gardner (Lond & Boston: Routledge & Kegan Paul, 1973), pp. 465–68.

In *Maurice* is presented a history of homosexuality as it goes from a Platonic sort (the pre-1914 kind) to the overtly physical (the kind we know today). EMF is angry at class restrictions, possibly because homosexuality levels class barriers. As an angry book, it is sharper, bolder, more belligerent, more indignant than his others. EMF rejects his upper-class characters in favor of those from the middle class, the "commuters," who were so dead, however, that only a "resurrection" could bring them to life (as EMF does with Maurice). EMF in this otherwise excellent book fails to explain homosexuality as a condition. [Provocative review.]

1532 Dick, Margaret. "A Declaration of Love," SYDNEY MORNING HERALD, "Weekend Magazine," 20 Nov 1971, p. 22.

Despite the fact that *A Passage to India* (1924) was his last novel, EMF has remained in the years since "the enduring spokesman for humane and civilized values, the defender and subtle expositor of the inner life, the wise and witty observer of the human scene." EMF's isolation as a result of his homosexuality may have given him the insight that a happier man may lack. *Maurice* lacks the density and cohesiveness of EMF's other fiction, but it has distinction. Maurice Hall suffers because he is normal in all respects except his sexuality and would rather not choose to be at odds with his class. The sequences between Maurice and Clive Durham ring true; those between Maurice and Alec Scudder do not and suggest "that only in fantasy can personal relations triumph over prejudice, convention, and the barriers of class." The fact that the novel had to be concealed for sixty years and the fact that the love in the book should be regarded as criminal are inexplicable.

1533 Doyle, Paul A. "Fiction," BEST SELLERS, XXXI (15 Oct 1971), 310–11.

Maurice does not deserve the prominence it has been accorded because it is "tepid, flat, remote, and lifeless." EMF fails to explain his characters (especially the homosexual ones) and their motivations. Two sections stand out: Maurice's futile interview with Dr. Barry about his homosexuality and the ending.

1534 Duckworth, Alistair. THE IMPROVEMENT OF THE ESTATE: A STUDY OF JANE AUSTEN'S NOVELS (Baltimore & Lond: Johns Hopkins P, 1971), pp. 53, 91, 208, 210.

In MANSFIELD PARK the cutting down of an avenue of trees at Sotherton connects with the idea of the wych-elm tree in *Howards End* as a symbol of social continuity, and with the cutting down of trees as a radical break with the past (Donne's "Satire II" and the giant tree at Groby in Ford's PARADE'S END). In PERSUASION Anne Elliot's constant love for Wentworth is parallel to her care for the estate that she has inherited. Some hint obtrudes that such secular values, inherent in a landed estate, may be inadequate to embody durable moral truths. PERSUASION is thus in the same pessimistic group of novels as PARADE'S END, *Howards End*, and Waugh's UNCONDITIONAL SURRENDER.

1535 Ellem, Elizabeth. "E. M. Forster: The Lucy and New Lucy Novels: Fragments of Early Versions of *A Room with a View*, TIMES LITERARY SUPPLEMENT (Lond), 28 May 1971, pp. 623–26.

[Examines the MS fragments of "Lucy Novel" (written before Dec 1903) and "New Lucy Novel" (written 1904 and after, to mid-1907), and attempts to establish their relationship to *A Room with a View.*] The "Lucy" fragments, set completely in Italy, have as protagonist Arthur/Tancred, a painter, who decides out of idealistic and humanitarian motives to renounce his painting and turn to politics. He also challenges Lucy's adherence to unselfishness. In "Lucy," she undergoes a profound crisis whose exact nature is not clear, but its effects upon her are emphasized. The names of characters vary considerably from those in *Room*. The "New Lucy" fragments dramatize a lighter kind of mood. In "Lucy," geniality is lacking: Lucy is not accomplished, and Miss Bartlett is venemous, malicious, and hypocritical. Part I of "New Lucy" follows the plot line of *Room* closely. Lucy now witnesses the stabbing in the Piazza, the kiss among the violets had occurred, etc. "New Lucy" is more fragmentary than "Lucy"; many internal contradictions among the various drafts exist. In "New Lucy" the character of Arthur/Tancred/George changes most. Arthur/Tancred is priggish and culture-conscious; these aspects in *Room* are transferred to Cecil Vyse. The George Emerson of "New Lucy" is an ideal figure, independent, close to nature, "a cultured rough diamond," though socially inferior to the other characters; he is more colorful and brutal than Arthur/Tancred or the

George of *Room*. The Cecil of "New Lucy" is totally disagreeable. In "Lucy" the influence of Arthur/Tancred and Lucy on each other seemed trivial and anti-climactic. EMF did not exploit his later theme: "The quickening of the conventional by contact with the natural and uncivilized." In "Lucy" the relationship between Lucy and Arthur/Tancred is Platonic; in "New Lucy" it has become full of romance and passion. Florence in "Lucy" is a disagreeable city in November; in "New Lucy" the countryside in spring is featured. In "New Lucy" the overt moralizing and the improving lectures on art are absent; types have also become individuals. After *The Longest Journey* was published EMF turned to a rewriting of "New Lucy," to the composition, that is, of *Room*. [Most informative article analyzing the creative process in EMF; quotes from many unpublished MSS and letters.]

1536 E. M. FORSTER, 1879–1950: HEFFER CATALOGUE SEVEN (Cambridge: W. Heffer & Sons, 1971).
[Contains "Introduction" by A. N. L. Munby (1971) and listing of E. M. Forster books for sale—Part One: Family and Association Items and Books Signed or Annotated by E. M. Forster; Part Two: Copies Presented to E. M. Forster Signed by Authors and Friends; Part Three: Music; and Part Four: Other Books from His Library.]

1537 E. M. Forster. "Terminal Note," *Maurice* (Lond: Edward Arnold, 1971), pp. 235–41; (NY: Norton, 1971), pp. 248–55.
[*Maurice* dates from 1913, the result of a visit to Edward Carpenter at Milthorpe, an advocate of "Uranian" love. George Merrill, Carpenter's associate, touched EMF's backside, and EMF's reaction was intense. The result was the writing of *Maurice* at Harrogate. The three characters came about spontaneously, and the writing was carried through without hitch. A happy ending was necessary, with attendant exile. Maurice was as unlike EMF as possible and is the essence of suburbia, normal in every respect, except for his homosexuality. Clive Durham is Cambridge, and EMF feels that Clive's kind of Platonic homosexuality is not at all unusual for the England of the time. When Clive turns to women, he deteriorates (and so, says EMF, does his treatment of him). Alec Scudder began as "the touch on the backside" at Milthorpe, and he developed constantly over the years. EMF feels that Clive and Alec are capable of loyalty, though Strachey was skeptical of the success of their relationship. Alec had to be led up to and to be led down from. In order to suggest that their love might last, the tests through which each must pass had to be elaborated. The book dates because of its anachronisms but, more importantly, because it belongs to an England, now gone, where one could get lost. As to the homosexuality and

English life, ignorance and terror have yielded now to familiarity and contempt. Indispensable information to understand *Maurice.*]

1538 Epstein, Joseph. "E. M. Forster's Posthumous Novel— More Important to the Man than to Literature," NEW YORK TIMES BOOK REVIEW, 10 Oct 1971, pp. 1, 2, 24, 26, 28, 29.

The sense of loss at EMF's death is widespread. He had stressed the personal in his novels and had indicated what we were to think of his characters; the result was that reading him became a personal relationship. He saw things "with lucidity, sympathy, and absolutely in the round." His wisdom is apparent, but his place in literature is uncertain. He exerts the same kind of appeal as does Chekhov; the two writers were alike "in possessing temperaments of exquisite balance, in being firmly anchored in their respective national cultures, in holding at all times to an essential decency." In a sense EMF died twice, as novelist at forty-five, as man at ninety-one. The first half of his life was devoted to perfection of the work, the second to the perfection of the life. EMF never aged; he only deteriorated physically. He combined a capacity for moralizing with the knack of "impeccable judgment." *Howards End* is his masterpiece; it combines knowledge of life and human nature, fine workmanship, and "a tone of offhand elegance." As for EMF's homosexuality, it must be dealt with because the public life can only be understood in terms of the private. The fact that a great novelist of middle-class marriage and heterosexual love could not partake of it is ironical; yet the homosexual influence in the other novels is negligible. *Maurice* is disappointing. It demonstrates that the passions are more difficult to write about than the affections. The love between Maurice and Clive Durham is heightened by an element of impossibility in it—that two men could come together homosexually in the society in which they lived. EMF's element of surprise is the conversion of Clive to heterosexual love. In EMF's revulsion from Clive there is a loss of distance, a loss of the "magnificent clarity and majestic disinterest" present elsewhere in his fiction. The novel to its detriment becomes a one-character novel, and we are more sympathetic with Maurice's situation than with his character. The novel ends as "an idyll, a homosexual fantasy." EMF's writing of *Maurice* was apparently an act of personal liberation; his writing a flawed book, moreover, makes him seem more human than before. *Maurice* illustrates the aesthetic anomaly that "psyche's gain is often art's loss." [A perceptive review of *Maurice* and thoughtful discussion of EMF as a man and writer. Also brief review comment on *Albergo Empedocle and Other Writings by E. M. Forster,* ed by George H. Thomson.]

1539 Fleissner, Robert F. "Passage from 'Kubla Khan' in Forster's *India*," INDIAN LITERATURE (Sahitya Akademi, Calcutta), XIV (Sept 1971), 79–84.

The influence of Coleridge's "Kubla Khan" was considerable upon EMF's style and thought in *A Passage to India*. [Some influence undoubtedly existed, but some of the alleged parallels are strained or fortuitious.]

1540 Furbank, P. N. "Introduction," *Maurice* (Lond: Edward Arnold, 1971), pp. v–ix ("Introduction" lacking in NY Norton Ed, 1971): ptd in part as "A Period Piece in 'Perversion,'" SUNDAY TIMES (Lond), 6 June 1971, p. 12.

EMF did not publish *Maurice* in the 1960s because he had come to feel that people do not decisively save one another as they do in this book and because some of his friends thought that the book is dated. EMF wrote on the 1960 typescript, "Publishable—but worth it?" [Recounts the circumstances concerning EMF's writing of *Maurice*. Letter to Forrest Reid quoted in which EMF condemns Maurice's society for preventing his free development; EMF suggests also that Maurice is trying to "connect" the "fragments" of his nature, as did Margaret Schlegel in *Howards End*. EMF notes the difficulty of rendering the physical part of love. See also letter from Furbank (SUNDAY TIMES, 13 June, p. 15) protesting title of extract from introduction as "quite gratuitously belittling to the novel."]

1541 Fyfe, Kenneth. "Teddy Bears' Picnic," VARSITY (Cambridge), LXXIV (16 Oct 1971), 15.

Maurice is not a book that adds to EMF's reputation, but it is of interest in adding to a homosexual tradition and for the light it throws on EMF's preoccupations in his other works. It gives proof of EMF's resiliency and of his ability to be "dry" about the morbid Hellenism featured in some of his other works. It also provides insight into the "diffused impotence" of *A Passage to India*. Are Maurice and Alec "sylvan guerrillas" or teddy-bears? The Platonic affair between Maurice and Clive Durham is given in the spirit of a code that is now barely recognizable; there is much shifting and evasiveness about the essential sexual experience. The second part is much more direct and much more readable. The book is fantasy, though EMF does not denominate it as such. His failure to do so is evidence of his confusion in the book; he does not know in which direction to turn his creative energy. EMF is no Genet, but in *Maurice* he is a minor participant in the same tradition.

1542 Gill, Stephen M. "Forster's Message in *A Passage to India*," CALCUTTA REVIEW, nsII (Jan–March 1971), 321–23.

The question of love and unity underlies EMF's *A Passage to India*, as it does Whitman's "Passage to India." EMF likes neither Indians or Anglo-Indians; they are alike fallible. He focuses on the separations and discords between the races. Mrs. Moore acts as an agent of love and divinity. This emphasis upon personal connection aligns together *Passage* and *Howards End*. [Routine discussion; most original observation is on Adela Quested: her contemplated "loveless marriage was not less than a rape."]

1543 Gindin, James, "E. M. Forster," HARVEST OF A QUIET EYE: THE NOVEL OF COMPASSION (Bloomington & Lond: Indiana UP, 1971), pp. 156–78; also pp. 3–4, 6, 10–11, 21–22.

[Attempts to define a form and tradition, "the novel of compassion," that began about 1875. Novelists illustrating this tradition are Trollope, Meredith, Hardy, Lawrence, Bennett, Howells, James, Fitzgerald, EMF, Woolf, James Joyce, Joyce Cary, and Angus Wilson.] "The novel of compassion" is open in form and relativist in philosophy, descriptive rather than prescriptive, realistic rather than allegorical, interested in character and psychology, verisimilar rather than fantastic. EMF exemplifies these criteria. [This assumption is dubious.] EMF's texture is highly controlled and patterned, and his themes are carefully expanded. As in *Howards End*, EMF utilizes contrasting scenes to make his point (both Leonard Bast and Margaret Schlegel break picture frames that contain portraits, respectively, of Jackie Bast and Evie Wilcox and thereby reveal their uneasiness about encounters that will lead them into worlds that they have not known before). At two points of emotional crisis, Helen Schlegel uses the nearest man, with dubious results. In such patterns EMF demonstrates "the repetitious predictability" of human experience and his own control over his subject. EMF often resorts to contrivance in order to serve thematic purposes (arbitrary deaths, coincidences, etc). His initial scenes often adumbrate the principal themes and action. In *A Room With a View*, for example, Lucy regards herself as a medieval lady; the action of the novel consists in rescuing her from the medieval Cecil Vyse. The initial scenes are satiric; the satire then modulates into a statement of theme, and then theme expands into generalizations that express EMF's major conclusions about experience. *Howards End* is his least convincing novel, containing a number of irrelevant essays. [Some incidental insights]: In *Where Angels Fear to Tread* Charlotte Bartlett and Philip Herriton achieve a sensitivity they can nowhere use; in *Howards End* EMF celebrates not only the importance of place but the need to overcome its strong pull toward inaction by conscious effort; in *A Passage to India* the private and public realms are seen to connect but are not congruent and analogous as they were for Margaret Schlegel in *Howards End;* in most of his fiction EMF respects the weak man because of his vulnerability and receptivity toward experience. EMF qualifies his content by his style and comic manner. [Malcolm Bradbury more persuasively set forth this view in "Two Passages of India: Forster as Victorian and Modern" (1969). Account is pleasant to read but, aside from a few scattered insights, is little more than an introductory survey of EMF's novels.]

1544 Gordon, Jan B. "DIANA OF THE CROSSWAYS: Internal History and the Brainstuff of Fiction," MEREDITH NOW: SOME CRITICAL ESSAYS, ed by Ian Fletcher (Lond: Routledge & Kegan Paul; NY: Barnes & Noble, 1971), pp. 246–64.

The Crossways in DIANA OF THE CROSSWAYS is one of the great houses in

English fiction, along with Mansfield Park, Waverly, Bleak House, and Howards End. In her evolution Diana Warwick is an example of the new women to be found in Shaw's plays and EMF's novels.

1545 Gradsden, K. W. "E. M. Forster and 'Morgan': Notes and Memories," ECOUNTER (Lond), XXXVI (May 1971), 59–62.
The relaxed "Morgan," who charmed a generation of intellectuals and Cambridge undergraduates, was not the rigorous "E. M. Forster" who wrote the novels before 1924. The friendly essays composing *Abinger Harvest* and *Two Cheers for Democracy* were written by "Morgan" and are lesser achievements than the novels written by "E. M. Forster." [Interesting reminiscences.]

1546 Hair, P. E. H. "Marianne Thornton, 1886," NOTES AND QUERIES (Lond), nsXVIII (Nov 1971), 419–20.
A letter from Marianne Thornton to Parthenope, Lady Verney [ptd] was not used by EMF in *Marianne Thornton*, but it would have been had he seen it in time. She refers to her evangelical childhood, the abolitionists, and the mob hostility to Robert Inglis (her childhood guardian), who had voted against the popular Queen Caroline.

1547 Hall, M. A. "The Impact of Exotic Culture on D. H. Lawrence and E. M. Forster," DOSHISHA JOSHI DAIGAKU GAKUTSU KENJU NEMPO (Doshisha Women's College of Liberal Arts [Kyoto], Annual Report of Studies), XXII (1971), 246–61.
D.H. Lawrence and EMF register in their work an adverse reaction to the industrial/commercial civilization in the first thirty years of the century. The elements of the spontaneous and the natural are lacking in modern culture, the result of its overemphasis on "the rational, conscious, calculating activity in man" and its severance of man from nature. Both writers used alien and foreign cultures to embody their positive ideas. Both found a source of renewal in Italy (or Greece) before they found it in India or Mexico. EMF reveres Italy and Greece as the homes of Reason and Humanism and as lands characterized by beauty, freedom, and spontaneity, where it is possible to harmonize the inner and the outer. Fielding in *A Passage to India* is the best individual that the middle class and Western humanism can offer, but he lacks the capacity to cultivate the Unseen. Hinduism, on the contrary, insists that the commonplace and the incongruous reveal "an infinite significance." In Hinduism, therefore, EMF finds the fulfillment of his idea of tolerance and reconciliation, wherein dualities can coalesce, and nothing is excluded. In Hinduism everything has transcendent value, or else nothing has value (this latter negative aspect is revealed in Mrs. Moore's anti-vision in the Marabar Caves). After her traumatic experience in the Caves, she rejects verbalization, with its limited, logical thought

modes (she refuses to talk to Adela Quested), but her power for nonverbal communication persists (she finally does communicate, after her death, with Adela in the courtroom). Adela's deficiency lies in her being "theoretical"; she is also a prey to sex-fears. Western Christianity in Mrs. Moore and Adela and Western humanism in Fielding are ultimately inadequate to meet the challenge of India. Lawrence goes back to a pre-Christian past and finds renewal in the rituals and civilization of the North American Indians. Their religion (as does Hinduism) recognizes the divinity in all creation. EMF is more convincing in his rendition of mystical experience as a detached outsider who feels its fascination than is Lawrence, who is too directly a participant in primitive rituals to depict them lucidly. [Traverses well-known material; a few insights of value.]

1548 Harvey, C. J. D. "*Maurice:* E. M. Forster's 'Homosexual' Novel," STANDPUNTE (Cape Town), XCVII (1971), 29–33.
Maurice is not a masterpiece to put beside EMF's other novels, especially *Howards End* and *A Passage to India*, although its composition comes between them. The book has honesty, sympathy, and clarity and precision of style; but it fails to reach the highest distinction because the element of humor is lacking. The nature of his subject, homosexuality, defeated EMF; humorous treatment of it would be liable to misinterpretation.

1549 Hays, Peter L. THE LIMPING HERO: GROTESQUES IN LITERATURE (NY: New York UP, 1971), pp. 141–42, 144.
Rickie Elliot, the crippled protagonist of *The Longest Journey*, has difficulty in finding his proper role and function in life. He is a romantic given to false idealizations. He idealizes people and misinterprets them; he idealizes nature but does not understand it. He is crippled less by his deformed foot than by his distorted view of reality. His life, in spite of his delusions, was not in vain.

1550 Hedberg, Johannes. PILOT BOOK TO E. M. FORSTER "A PASSAGE TO INDIA" (Stockholm: Almqvist & Wiksell, 1971).
"*A Passage to India*—A Forsterean Symphony": [EMF's travels to India and the circumstances concerning the writing of *Passage* are described.] EMF welds story, plot, melody, and perception of truth into a fascinating and disquieting work of art. *Passage* is the only English novel about Indians that has gotten their almost unmixed approval. His picture of the Anglo-Indian officials reveals an eye "trained by Dostoevski." The best representatives (Aziz and Fielding) of the contrasting races attempt to come together but too much divides them. Godbole describes Aziz's poem, his sole one with an international ethos, as *bhakti;* the enlightenment that this word signifies may well be India's message to the world, EMF implies. [The tripartite structure of *Passage* is described, as well as the presence in the

novel of "easy" and "difficult" rhythms; see "Pattern and Rhythm," *Aspects of the Novel*.] EMF's dramatic irony is incisive. Mrs. Moore's nihilism, experienced in the Marabar Caves, is set against Professor Godbole's view that man as part of nature is "invincible, indestructible, and divine." EMF's dramatic irony is revealed in his making Mrs. Moore into a god, as she has so late in life lost her faith in God. He is also expert in utilizing symbols, for aesthetic effect, of varying degrees of complexity. [Other contents: "Notes and Explanations/Glossary," "Indian Words in *A Passage to India*," "Subjects for Discussion and Essays," "Notes" (to "*A Passage to India*—A Forsterean Symphony"), "A Select Bibliography," "Dictionaries and Other Reference Material Used."]

1551 Helfand, Michael Steven. "Liberalism and the Form of the Novel," DISSERTATION ABSTRACTS INTERNATIONAL, XXXI (1971). Unpublished dissertation, University of Iowa, 1970. [On Dickens, Meredith, EMF.]

1552 Hern, Anthony. "Maurice as Hero: the Odd Man Out," EVENING STANDARD (Lond), 12 Oct 1971, p. 20.

Maurice shares the faults of homosexual and romantic novels—a hero with a "fancy" name and a sentimental, soft center to the book. It is a propaganda novel in the sense that EMF must prove that homosexual love is ennobling. About such a novel it is difficult to be objective. There are fine passages of observation and feeling but typical defects: "a mawkishness of phrases, a simpering of style." It will not rank high in the EMF canon.

1553 Hope, Francis. "Resigning from the Club," NEW STATESMAN, nsLXXII (9 July 1971), 56–57.

Viewed in retrospect EMF, in *A Passage to India*, too readily decreed upon Indian virtues and shortcomings. His discussion of the shortcomings betrays certain inflexibilities of his own, especially the view that the English are good at governing and the Indians are not. The English may not be as efficient as EMF depicts them. If present-day Indians are the last Englishmen, present-day Englishmen have become the last of EMF's Indians. A touch of regret with them has become a torrent, as a result of their appropriation of Fielding's defiance of official attitudes at the time of Aziz's trial.

1554 Humphries, Lynda. "Forster behind Times," CAMBRIDGE EVENING NEWS, 23 Oct 1971, p. 5.

Maurice is one of EMF's successes but is not to be regarded as a great work. At the end, when Maurice disappears from view with Alec Scudder, his problems are as unsolved then as they would be now. [Summary of the novel.]

1555 Hunter, Alan. "Novel that Haunted Forster," EASTERN DAILY PRESS (Norwich), 8 Oct 1971, p. 18; rptd in E. M. FORSTER: THE CRITICAL HERITAGE, ed by Philip Gardner (Lond & Boston: Routledge & Kegan Paul, 1973), pp. 451–52.

Maurice haunted EMF and may have been the basis for his "creative eclipse" as a writer of fiction. He was not assured of publication and reception, as was Proust. The novel suffers from the conception of its protagonist and his inconsistency, "a hybrid of an uncultivated athlete and a man of intense sensibility." The dichotomy is worrying, as is the vexed happy ending; Maurice's euphoria is no solution to his problems. *Maurice* reveals EMF's powers of observation and precise expression; it is not his best book but perhaps his most interesting.

1556 [Hynes, Samuel.] "A Chalice for Youth," TIMES LITERARY SUPPLEMENT (Lond), 8 Oct 1971, pp. 1215–16; rptd in T. L. S.: ESSAYS AND REVIEWS FROM THE TIMES LITERARY SUPPLEMENT, 1971 (10), (Lond: Oxford UP, 1972), pp. 15–23; and in E. M. FORSTER: THE CRITICAL HERITAGE, ed by Philip Gardner (Lond & Boston: Routledge & Kegan Paul, 1973), pp. 482–90; rptd, slightly rvd, as "Forster's Cramp," in EDWARDIAN OCCASIONS: ESSAYS ON ENGLISH WRITING IN THE EARLY TWENTIETH CENTURY (NY: Oxford UP; Lond: Routledge & Kegan Paul, 1972), pp. 114–22.

EMF's sexual condition was as central to his art as it was to his personal life. His homosexuality informs his fiction: "the voyeuristic distancing of the narration, the ironic tone, the self-deprecating humour," and it accounts for his unsatisfactory treatment of heterosexual attraction, heterosexual relationships, and marriage. In his fiction, marriage is beyond his range. *The Longest Journey* is "a kind of homosexual nightmare, in which the condition of marriage is imagined—cold, loveless, and degrading." The central relationship is between Rickie Elliot and Stephen Wonham, not between Rickie and Agnes. In *A Room With a View* the male bathing scene is more real than the heterosexual passion. Pan is the presiding deity of EMF's fiction, Pan being not nature so much as natural human behavior. Pan is the supernatural deity who would make homosexual love possible for those imprisoned in the bourgeois Sawston-Cambridge world. EMF is incapable of recording deep feeling; love, birth, and death are treated casually. Since ordinary emotional relationships were beyond him, he had to resort to melodrama to indicate strong feeling. When emotion is explicitly sexual, the failure is complete, as in *Howards End*. *Where Angels Fear to Tread* is a better novel than *Howards End* because it does not attempt sexuality: "What it is really about is the difficulties a homosexual has in understanding the behavior of heterosexuals, and Forster knew a good deal about that." [This judgment is not entirely clear]. *A Passage to India* is the exception;

the relationship between Fielding and Aziz is more moving than any marriage or love affair in his fiction. EMF did have a developed heart in spite of his "donnish reticence." In his work the family tribe makes sexual love unnecessary or impossible. It consists of a fatherless family, a possessive widow and mother, some other feminine hangers-on, and one inadequate son. The tribe represents the forces of convention and repression; to reject the tribe is to be free of convention, to live in the imagination, and to escape to the world of men. The son (Philip Herriton, Freddy Honeychurch, Rickie Elliot, Tibby Schlegel) is ascetic and detached, imperfectly involved in life, slightly ridiculous. He provides a self who can comment on the other characters in the novel but a self that can also be treated satirically. "These are Forster's selves, but seen through the world's eyes, and denied and disinherited by their creator." EMF lived in a world that believed in marriage and marriage novels; his desire to stay in it was stronger than the desire to tell the truth about himself. Homosexuality did not extinguish his gifts; rather a "*creative* tension existed between the impulse and the work, and . . . the effort to transform homosexuality into socially acceptable forms was an ordering force" and provided his characteristic vision and tone. His vision is that of a world devoid of absolutes, lonely and threatening, full of "panic and emptiness." This bleak vision was balanced with a self-deprecating irony that was comic rather than completely serious. With EMF irony and homosexuality consort well together, not tragedy and homosexuality: "He wrote . . . defensively, to preserve his place in the society which would ostracize him if it knew. But cunning defensiveness suited his talent, and he made out of self-deprecation, transference, and evasion a personal and functioning style." *Maurice* is a novel of self-discovery. Maurice is also the young man in the inhibiting female tribe. The happy ending places a human principle above an aesthetic one. The novel fails because here the homosexual imagination and society's restraints are not in tension. EMF sacrifices his excellent qualities, "the ironic tone, the distance, the humour, the touches of shrewd wisdom, the style," and gains no commensurate value. Sentimentality is everywhere; the prose style is inept. The episodes are not fully realized; his imagination is imperfectly made verbal. EMF's attitude about sex is not liberal; the language is that of society, with his acceptance of such terms as "morbidity," "perversity," "abnormality." Maurice accepts (as does EMF) his condition but disapproves of it. He chooses sentimental ostracism from society rather than confrontation with it. EMF's direct treatment of homosexual love is no more successful than his treatment of heterosexual love. Sex continues to be sordid, furtive, repulsive, not innocent or joyous. The novel does not transcend being an Edwardian treatment of homosexuality. It adds nothing to EMF's achievement as novelist nor to his stature as a man. In J. R. Ackerley's E. M. FORSTER(1971), EMF emerges as a man more interested in the immortality deriving from the affections rather than from words and deeds. [This notice of Ackerley not in rptd version. A discriminating and stimulating essay, if harsh in some judgments.]

1557 Jeffares, A. Norman. "The Making of *Maurice*," YORKSHIRE POST (Leeds), 7 Oct 1971, p. 6.

In *Maurice* EMF committed himself to the belief that homosexual love was a good. The notions of class, middle-class conventionality, and medical knowledge have a period flavor; modern youth is less innocent. Maurice is a symbol of suburbia, Clive Durham of Cambridge's Hellenism, Alec Scudder of primitive nature. *Maurice* is well-written in its first and middle parts, less so in the last; it is "sensitive; self-indulgent; the expression of a romantic dream; and certainly dated."

1558 Johnson, Bruce. CONRAD'S MODELS OF MIND (Minneapolis: University of Minnesota P, 1971), pp. 139, 140.

The radical challenges to received values revealed in Conrad's NOSTROMO, THE SECRET AGENT, and UNDER WESTERN EYES might have acted as the Marabar Caves do in *A Passage to India* to spur the positive workings of the "Godbolean spirit." VICTORY is not quite a full resolution to the problem of individualist values versus communal. The Russia of UNDER WESTERN EYES is like the India of *A Passage to India* in being most significantly a country with symbolic dimensions, though the political actuality of each country is not in question.

1559 Johnstone, J. K. "E. M. Forster," THE POLITICS OF TWEN-TIETH-CENTURY NOVELISTS, ed by George A. Panichas (NY: Hawthorn Books, 1971), pp. 15–29.

Intellectually, EMF is a liberal; emotionally, in his ties to rural tradition, he is a conservative. *Howards End* is about the middle class. He approves the part of it represented by the Schlegels, but he distrusts the city and commercialism, middle-class convention, and middle-class insensitivity (its "undeveloped heart"). His belief in human nature is modified by his pessimism. In its structure, *Howards End* forecasts danger (panic is opposed to heroism, gray London to Howards End), though the solution of merging the Schlegels with the Wilcoxes is not convincing. [Essay is superficial and inadequate to its subject.]

1560 Kermode, Frank. "A Queer Business," ATLANTIC MONTHLY, CCXXVII (Nov 1971), 140–42, 144.

Maurice produces a strange impression, perhaps as a result of EMF's own imaginative needs or social limitations. It is a wish-fulfilling fantasy, whose symbolic patterns are inert in comparison with those present in *A Passage to India*. EMF did not know the lower class as did the D. H. Lawrence of

SONS AND LOVERS. What EMF did know best was the way in which the upper classes sin against passion and truth. The poor are spared such crises, apparently because they are poor. In EMF's upper classes, we mostly find Wilcoxes and Pembrokes, but there are also a few elite people who have been nurtured and enlightened by Cambridge. They are frank but like Stewart Ansell in *The Longest Journey* are inclined to believe in the nonexistence of the people who do not resemble them. In the prewar novels, the lovers are scarce and ungentlemanly. In *Maurice*, however, we are dealing with sexual actuality, with sexual good and evil; and the book helped EMF to handle sex in *Passage*. *Maurice* is concerned "with the relation between homosexual freedom and the breaking down of the class barriers." In *Maurice*, the dreams concerning the coming of a friend are important; in *Passage* the coming of a "friend" is elaborated outward into the Krishna who finally does come. EMF in *Maurice* strives for a verisimilitude that will lend actuality to Alec Scudder and a symbolism that will convince us of the truth of the relationship between Maurice and Alec by transcending it. Maurice is "saved" from the perfunctory sexual love that surrounds him, from the conventionality of Clive Durham, and from a rotting society. Women in this society are "bores, nuisances, substitutes, interrupters, and powerful rivals." There is a powerful irony in *Maurice;* upper-class English society created the conditions under which Uranian love flourished and yet was savage in condemnation of it. The result of this social irony was a secret society in England that romanticized homosexuality and gave it a cultural frame of reference. This society then regarded heterosexual love "as *déclassé*, base, and finally unintelligible." To this "queer business," *Maurice* is a monument. [Stimulating article.]

1561 Kettle, Arnold. "All for Love," NEW REPUBLIC, CLXV (9 Oct 1971), 25–26.

The dominant characteristic of an EMF novel is a combination of the realistic and symbolic, of the particular and the general, in the mode of Meredith. *Maurice*, in scale, belongs to the earlier rather than the later EMF. The act of falling in love is a breakthrough for Maurice though not for Clive Durham. Maurice progresses toward life so that with Alec Scudder he feels that the world is well lost for love. EMF invites us to make a comparison with D. H. Lawrence's LADY CHATTERLEY'S LOVER. Both writers stress the value of a relationship which practical considerations make difficult; both regard a personal and sexual relationship as part of a social milieu but also as something that transcends it. In both novels the liberating character is from a lower class. Clive Durham and Clifford Chatterley represent a barren intellectuality as a rationalizing of economic self-interest. *Maurice* is propagandist, or committed, or perhaps a bit abstract. EMF's insistence on the value of love may be vulnerable, but it is not sentimental because he is concerned with society as much as with two people in love.

EMF lacks Lawrence's impact and scale but has a truer sense of actual social life. *Maurice* reveals a wonderful concreteness; EMF's vein is "a modest ironical realism" that lacks pretense. [Excellent review; incidental comment on *Albergo Empedocle and Other Writings by E. M. Forster*, ed by George H. Thomson.]

1562 Kettle, Arnold. "BEAUCHAMP'S CAREER," MEREDITH NOW: SOME CRITICAL ESSAYS, ed by Ian Fletcher (Lond: Routledge & Kegan Paul; NY: Barnes & Noble, 1971), pp. 188–204.

The plot of BEAUCHAMP'S CAREER is something more than contrivance, even in the positive sense of the term as EMF utilized it in *Aspects of the Novel*. Rosamund Culling's realization of her contribution to the horse-whipping of Dr. Shrapnel in the novel is similar to the self-deception-awareness pattern illustrated by Adela Quested in *A Passage to India*, though Meredith is the more skillful novelist. Despite its excellences BEAUCHAMP'S CAREER is less impressive than it ought to be, a matter of style and presentation of character rather than of the falsity of the values presented (EMF's criticism of Meredith's content in *Aspects*).

1563 Kim, Yong-chol. "E. M. Forster and the Heritage of English Humanism: A Study of Forster's Essays on Civilization, Literature and Society," DISSERTATION ABSTRACTS INTERNATIONAL, XXXI (1971), 4168A. Unpublished dissertation, University of California at San Diego, 1970.

1564 Kitchen, Paddy. "E. M. Forster," TIMES EDUCATION SUPPLEMENT (Lond), 8 Oct 1971, p. 23; rptd in E. M. FORSTER: THE CRITICAL HERITAGE, ed by Philip Gardner (Lond & Boston: Routledge & Kegan Paul, 1973), pp. 444–47.

EMF is a noteworthy moral tutor. The young should read EMF and be attracted by his anti-authoritarian temper. *Maurice* is schematic, compared to EMF's other novels. Because he is writing in part a thesis novel, he makes no attempt to flesh out the minor characters. *Maurice* is still relevant; we have changed our laws about homosexuality but not our opinions. EMF's voice in the novel sets up tensions between thought and feeling, with attendant vibrations. EMF contrasts the romantic side of homosexuality (the life of Maurice and Clive Durham at Cambridge) with the drabness, the betrayals, the loneliness that becomes part of that life elsewhere (Maurice's life in the suburbs). EMF made homosexuality romantic in this novel in order to present it in the best possible light. [Excellent critique.]

1565 Kitchen, Paddy. "Gay Edwardians," SCOTSMAN (Edinburgh), "Weekend Scotsman," 9 Oct 1971, p. 3.

The individual chapters in *Maurice* burst and fade as do the symbolic evening primroses therein; but EMF also has a tough central moral purpose

—to show that homosexuality can be a force for good. *Maurice* lacks the subtleties in form and characterization as well as the stature of EMF's other novels; but it reveals him again as a moralist. [Novels by Paul Scott, Peter Forster, and John Hawkes are also noted.]

1566 Kondo, Ineko. "Forster Zakki" (Forster Miscellany), EIGO SEINEN (Tokyo), CXVI (1 Jan 1971), 771–72.

[Details of a visit to Cambridge where, at King's College Library, Mrs. Kondo studied the pencil-written draft of *Where Angels Fear to Tread.*] As Oliver Stallybrass has noted for the manuscripts of *A Passage to India* ("Forster's Wobblings," 1969), EMF's processes of creation are also clearly visible in this draft. Good miscellaneous pieces remain to be collected, such as his BBC talk on D. H. Lawrence and a review entitled "Coleridge in His Letters." EMF's ashes were scattered over the garden at the crematory, and a commemoration concert, instead of a service, was given for him. [In Japanese.]

1567 Lakshmi, Vijay. "Virginia Woolf and E. M. Forster: A Study in Inner Criticism," BANASTHALI PATRIKA (Banasthali Vidyapith P. O., Rajasthan), XVI (1971), 8–18; rptd as "Virginia Woolf and E. M. Forster: A Study of Their Critical Relations," LITERARY HALF-YEARLY (Mysore), XII (July 1971), 39–49.

[Perfunctory analysis of EMF's "The Early Novels of Virginia Woolf" (*Abinger Harvest*) and "Virginia Woolf" (*Two Cheers for Democracy*), and of Virginia Woolf's "The Novels of E. M. Forster" (1927) and "The Art of Fiction" (her review of *Aspects of the Novel* [1927]). Little attempt is made to generalize in any significant way; much inferior to Mark Goldman's "Virginia Woolf and E. M. Forster: A Dialogue" (1966).]

1568 Lebowitz, Naomi. "*A Passage to India:* History as Humanist Humor," HUMANISM AND THE ABSURD IN THE MODERN NOVEL (Evanston: Northwestern UP, 1971), pp. 67–83; also pp. 6, 17–18, 23, 85, 104.

Contrary to Frederick C. Crews's view in E. M. FORSTER: THE PERILS OF HUMANISM (1962), *A Passage to India* is the strongest expression of EMF's humanism, by virtue of the challenges this humanism faces and weathers. The humanist like EMF resists the tendency to make an absolute from an abstract vision, a fixed point of view, or an intellectual stance, in contrast with the absurdist who elevates an extremist view of man's fate to a position of universal validity. EMF also resists the tendency to make an absolute of the past or of a fixed political position. He lives in the present and makes use of his supple irony, his critical cast of mind, and his tolerance to adjudge the contradictions in life and to see in perspective its polar or eccentric aspects. For the humanist "art supports life" instead of "seeking to conquer it." EMF reveals this humanist temper as does his intellectual ancestor,

Montaigne. In *Passage*, EMF's sense of the dullness of ordinary life balances its apocalyptic moments. As humanist he accepts the present and is
not tempted to escape into history or to opt for "aesthetic martyrdom."
Visionary experience, to which EMF is sensitive, does not annihilate for
him the social fact. He is suspicious of the abstract as such and resists all
tendencies to allegorize culture and nature; the movement in *Passage* is
"from overly moral and structured worlds to indifferent, amoral, and
amused ones." *Passage* unites nature's indifference and man's compulsion
to attain order, and its tone goes from compassion to derision [see a similar
view expressed in Malcolm Bradbury's "Two Passages to India: Forster as
Victorian and Modern" (1969)]. A "comic tolerance" alone provides salvation in a difficult world. The mystical intuitions of Godbole and Mrs. Moore
provide a vantage point for criticism rather than for affirmations in themselves. EMF rejects in his novel the rigidly willed ideologies of the West for
the more open, flexible attitudes and mind of the East. As Western humanists, Adela Quested and Fielding are in part overborne by their Indian
experience, but "a tiny charity" helps them keep their humanist perspective.
In Aziz the emphasis is on feeling, which is in part a corrective to rigid
views, provided feeling itself is not historicized and raised to an absolute.
Poetry or religion give us no panacea; at best, they give momentary intuitions into an anti-rational order of truth. Western ideologies are mostly too
rigid for an amorphous culture like India's; but at times Western poetry,
religion, and myth help order the universe and relieve us from absurdity by
stressing the human and the personal. Neither Western values nor Eastern
mysticism contains the entire truth. At the end Aziz makes of Fielding a
public and political abstraction and is false to a humanist imperative. The
personal, the spontaneous, the contingent is always opposed to—and more
valuable than—the institutional or the abstract; the humanist recognizes
this opposition and its frequent absurdity, and he knows that neither love
nor art can mold history, order society, or complete our human relationships. Yet the humanist will not embrace Mrs. Moore's retreat from life. He
cannot grant us easy assurance but does remind us that to be human we must
refuse both glory and despair. [Stimulating, original, at times profound
discussion; but excessively abstract and opaque style impairs its persuasiveness.]

1569 Lee, L. L. " 'Oedipus at Colonus': The Modern 'Vulgariza-
tions' of Forster and Cicellis," STUDIES IN SHORT FICTION, VIII (Fall
1971), 561–67.

The Oedipus myth in literature operates so that the individual discovers the
self (especially in the experience of love) and also his home (the locale and
human society where he can most readily find himself and *be*). EMF's "The
Road from Colonus" vulgarizes the myth, in that its characters are bourgeois rather than heroic, and its protagonist reverses the process of the myth

by losing his identity (instead of finding it) when he fails to take advantage of his chance to live more fully. The English reject earth and love and prevent Mr. Lucas from experiencing them to the full in Greece. Kay Cicellis's "The Way to Colonus" vulgarizes the myth even more. Her characters are in more sordid circumstances than EMF's but, like Mr. Lucas, they still search for meaning that eludes them.

1570 Lehmann-Haupt, Christopher. "A Major 'New' Forster Novel," NEW YORK TIMES, 1 Oct 1971, p. 39.
Maurice is a major novel, "rich in its subtle intelligence, beautifully controlled in its development, deeply moving." We share Maurice's agony because of society's injustice to him. His homosexuality "is not a condition to be explained and defended, but a symbol of human feelings." The obstacles that thwart him are "superbly realized images of British society before World War I." EMF stresses feeling, its repression, and individualism. *Maurice* is a complex work of art and can be related to *Howards End* and *A Passage to India.* It is preferable to *Howards End.* The Forsterian preoccupations with class distinctions and with the need for connection run through it. The central image, the leaking roof in the Durham living room, is a trivial symbol compared to the echo in *Passage.* The happy ending is also difficult to credit. [Highly positive view.]

1571 Levin, Bernard. "The Shield of Achilles," TIMES (Lond), 23 Oct 1971, p. 5.
[Levin was glad that there was a sixth EMF novel, even though he had to wait many years for it to appear, a novel worthy "in its power, its passion and its wisdom" to complete EMF's canon. He has been an admirer of EMF for over thirty years. His introduction to EMF by way of the Fifth Symphony passage in *Howards End* was shattering. He found that EMF's attitudes were intelligible and desirable; he was able to identify with the characters; he responded to EMF's open enthusiasm.] EMF espouses both eighteenth-century rationalism and nineteenth-century romanticism; his incomplete characters raise up reason at the expense of emotion or vice versa. Stewart Ansell in *The Longest Journey* and Fielding in *A Passage to India* approach a balance most closely. [EMF also instructed him that moral absolutes were possible for an individual who lacked a non-radical faith to support them; at the same time, there were no easy solutions to moral dilemmas.] *Maurice* is Forsterian because, among other things, the doctor speaks with an "undeveloped heart." Lucy Honeychurch in *A Room with a View* is one of EMF's great characters because it is not certain that she will be saved until the end. EMF taught above all "that certainty is possible in principle even while it is impossible in practice."

1572 Levine, June Perry. CREATION AND CRITICISM: "A PASSAGE TO INDIA," (Lincoln: University of Nebraska P, 1971; Lond: Chatto &

Windus, 1972); rvd from "E. M. Forster's *A Passage to India:* Creation and Criticism," unpublished dissertation, University of Nebraska, 1967; rpts, with few changes, "An Analysis of the Manuscripts of *A Passage to India,*" PUBLICATIONS OF THE MODERN LANGUAGE ASSOCIATION, LXXXV (March 1970), 284–94.

["Introduction" (Chap 1) covers well-known facts about EMF's life and stresses the dualities that determined his mind. Chap 2, "The Raw Material of *A Passage to India,*" discusses *The Hill of Devi* and some of EMF's essays on India, collected and uncollected, as they bear on *A Passage to India.* Levine also draws upon books by others that have not yet been used in interpreting the novel (she does little speculating, however, on the relationships between these writers and EMF in *Passage*). Demonstrates centrality of Valentine Chirol's INDIAN UNREST (1910), which EMF himself read, for understanding *Passage.* Chirol's attitude is more conservative than Fielding's in *Passage* but more sympathetic than that of the typical Anglo-Indian civil servant. Notes interesting parallels between "Temple" (third section of *Passage*) and the descriptions of the Gokul Ashtami ceremonies in J. R. Ackerley's HINDOO HOLIDAY (1952, rvd ed) and in Goldsworthy Lowes Dickinson's APPEARANCES (1914). Chap 3, "The Manuscript of *A Passage to India*" (the best in the book), rpts with few changes "An Analysis of the Manuscript of *A Passage to India*" (1970). Chap 4, "*A Passage to India* and the Critics," is superficial. Levine fails to define the crucial issues as they have been debated by other critics and merely summarizes seriatim the works of those critics whom she chooses. Her work is incomplete; she stops discussion in 1965 and 1966, though the book was published in 1971. In Chap 5 "*A Passage to India:* An Interpretation," which contributes little that is new, her main principles are that all the characters aspire towards union, and *Passage* revolves around such dualities as transciency and permanency. This discussion is less perceptive than similar treatments by Wilfred Stone (THE CAVE AND THE MOUNTAIN, 1966) and Malcolm Bradbury ("Two Passages to India: Forster as Victorian and Modern," 1969). Stone and H. M. Daleski ("Rhythm and Symbolic Patterns in *A Passage to India,*" 1966) have been before her in discussing the circular images in the novel. Some passing insights of value. Notes that the Marabar Hills are an ultimate reality (along with the religious ceremonies at Mau), which the echo erodes, and views the English and Indian relationships between the central characters as positive. (Mrs. Moore cancels the division between Fielding and Aziz at the end, and they remain friends because of her direct and indirect influence. Author's own critical discourse is more descriptive than analytic, and she considers few other critics. Helpful and informative book at points, but it falls below the highest standards of excellence. Reviews: "Abroad in India," TIMES LITERARY SUPPLEMENT (Lond), 31 March 1972, 354; Oswell Blakeston, "Literary Criticism," BOOKS AND BOOKMEN, XVII (March 1972),

80–81; Frederick P. W. McDowell, "By and about Forster," ENGLISH LITER-ATURE IN TRANSITION, XV: 4 (1972), 332–24; M. L. Raina, "Forster," QUEST (Bombay), LXXXIX (Nov–Dec 1972), 97–99; Harvey Curtis Webster, "Recent Books on Modern Fiction: British," MODERN FICTION STUDIES, XVIII (Summer 1972), 244–46; and Alan Wilde, "Individual Writers; E. M. Forster," JOURNAL OF MODERN LITERATURE, III (Feb 1974), 608–10.]

1573 Lodge, David. "Before the Deluge," TABLET (Lond), 23 Oct 1971, p. 1024; rptd in E. M. FORSTER: THE CRITICAL HERITAGE, ed by Philip Gardner (Lond & Boston: Routledge & Keagan Paul, 1973), pp. 473–74.

Maurice will not enhance EMF's reputation but will not damage it. It is less complex than his other novels, a *bildungsroman* recounted in a straightfor-ward, often summary fashion. An element of wish-fulfillment weakens it as a work of art. It is not without good scenes, penetration, ironical touches, and skilled use of leitmotifs; but written between *Howards End* and *A Passage to India*, it falls far short of them "in complexity, interest, humour and rhetorical skill." His subject may have interfered with EMF's complete effectiveness in *Maurice*. He does best when he expresses his personal concerns deviously and indirectly in heterosexual themes or situations. Writing for himself and his coterie, he no longer had to appeal to an "ideal audience—austere, discriminating, yet catholic—for whom, like all good writers, he wrote his other books." *Maurice* proves that in literary matters artistry is more important than sincerity. [Interesting review.]

1574 Lucas, John. "Meredith as Poet," MEREDITH NOW: SOME CRITICAL ESSAYS, ed by Ian Fletcher (Lond: Routledge & Kegan Paul; NY: Barnes & Noble, 1971), pp. 14–33.

Despite the modern tendency to denigrate the attitudes presented by Mere-dith in his love poetry, they did become ethical norms for some twentieth-century works such as EMF's *Where Angels Fear to Tread*, *A Room with a View*, and *The Longest Journey*. Also EMF follows Meredith in utilizing figures from Greek mythology in an English setting.

1575 Lucas, John. "Meredith's Reputation," MEREDITH NOW: SOME CRITICAL ESSAYS, ed by Ian Fletcher (Lond: Routledge & Kegan Paul; NY: Barnes & Noble, 1971), pp. 1–13.

EMF was used by F. R. Leavis in THE GREAT TRADITION to demolish Meredith without his realizing, as did EMF, Henry James, and Virginia Woolf (all hostile at points to Meredith), that there was something solid in Meredith that his inflated reputation tended to obscure.

1576 Mano, D. Keith. "A Balanced Ticket," NATIONAL REVIEW, XXIII (3 Dec 1971), 1358–59.

The fairy-tale conclusion of *Maurice* is not convincing, but the rest of the novel is. There is the charm in it of a love story from another era. The affair with Clive Durham reveals on EMF's part restraint, dignity, and insight. Homosexuality is not to be regarded as a crime; rather, it elevates and sensitizes Maurice and makes him painfully alive.

1577 Marsh, Pamela. " 'Publishable—but Worth It?' " CHRISTIAN SCIENCE MONITOR, 21 Oct 1971, p. 7.

Affection rather than passion is the keynote of *Maurice*. There are some excellent moments in it. But EMF has not played fair with his characters or with his readers. As for Maurice, we pity him but do not like him. EMF is unfair to Clive Durham after he turns to women. The happy ending is propaganda overriding literature. In "Pessimism in Literature" (1907) EMF had argued, rather, that separation, not easy completion, is the dominating note in modern literature. [Brief notice of *Albergo Empedocle and Other Writings by E. M. Forster*, ed by George H. Thomson (1971).]

1578 Martin, Richard. "Ideal and Reality in the Writings of E. M. Forster." Unpublished dissertation, Ruhr-Universität Bochum, 1971; rvd as THE LOVE THAT FAILED: IDEAL AND REALITY IN THE WRITINGS OF E. M. FORSTER (The Hague & Paris: Mouton, Studies in English Literature, LXXXIV, 1974).

1579 Martin, Richard. "Modern Writers—E. M. Forster," PRAXIS DES NEUSPRACHLICHEN UNTERRICHTS, Heft 3 (Dortmund: Lambert Lensing, 1971), 293–97.

[Overview of EMF's career and achievement, stressing the potentialities of love as an ideal (often in conflict with refractory realities), and discussion of each novel in light of this principle.]

1580 Maskell, Duke. "Mr. Forster's Fine Feelings," CAMBRIDGE QUARTERLY, V (Spring 1971), 222–35.

EMF has received unmerited praise for what he is taken to represent. He has generated in himself and others only an enthusiasm for platitudes, as can be seen if "What I Believe" (*Two Cheers for Democracy*) and *Howards End* are regarded critically. In *Howards End* he professes love and sympathy and reveals the casual snobbishness of an upper-class Cambridge don at the turn of the century (e.g., his treatment of the Basts). The Basts also reveal EMF's lack of social knowledge. *Howards End* never addresses itself to the dependence of bourgeois culture on an exploited proletariat. In this treatment of social issues EMF reveals a failure of intelligence and imagination. He does not deal fairly or imaginatively with the businessman, as does Lawrence with Gerald Crich in WOMEN IN LOVE, although Lawrence comes out finally against him. EMF is unable, moreover, to give reality to upper-class decency and cultivation in the Schlegels. *A Passage to India* is equally unreal and unnecessary as a novel. [The case against EMF is overstated; see also Maskell's "Style and Symbolism in *Howards End*" (1969).]

1581 Masters, Tony. "Books," FREETHINKER (Lond), 9 Oct 1971, p. 326.

Maurice is a major novel; it could have been sentimentalized, but it is not. EMF presents his milieu with accuracy and with "delicate, deadly wit." The novel would have been effective in increasing the awareness of the public if it had been published five or ten years ago. EMF handles his subject with tact and charm; his book has passion. The novel, moreover, has relevance in that the kind of dilemma and suffering presented in it still exists.

1582 Mercier, Vivian. "A Means of Grace," NATION (NY), CCXIII (29 Nov 1971), 565–67; rptd in part in CONTEMPORARY LITERARY CRITICISM, ed by Carolyn Riley and Barbara Harte (Detroit: Gale Research Co., 1974), II, 135.

What has changed since the time when EMF wrote *Maurice* is not so much the heterosexual's attitude toward the homosexual as the homosexual's attitude toward himself. Maurice feels aversion as well as attraction toward Alec Scudder, an aversion deriving more from class distinctions than from sexual disgust. EMF seems to feel that some people can be saved, others not. For Maurice, homosexuality becomes a mode of salvation. Maurice was made suburban and ordinary for the propaganda value involved in such a man being homosexual. The unity and strength of the book derive from this choice of hero as do its weaknesses. EMF knows little of Maurice's outer or inner life. *Maurice* is thin, lacking the irony, symbolism, the sharply differentiated characters of *A Passage to India*. Writing *Maurice* allowed EMF to purge himself of the homosexual obsession, also of snobbery, including the inverted snobbery of liberalism. EMF does give us some of the scope and variety of homosexual love in *Maurice*. EMF demonstrates that a man's acceptance of his homosexuality may be a metaphor for liberation—from the Christian sexual ethic, from the matriarchal family, and from suburbia and bourgeois society. *Maurice* is a smaller book than *Passage* but does not disgrace EMF as man or artist. [Thoughtful discussion.]

1583 Meyers, Jeffrey. "The Politics of *A Passage to India*," JOURNAL OF MODERN LITERATURE, I (March 1971), 329–38; rptd as part of "E. M. Forster: *A Passage to India*," FICTION AND THE COLONIAL EXPERIENCE (Totawa, NJ: Rowman & Littlefield; Ipswich: Boydell P, 1973), pp. 29–54.

A Passage to India is not about India in 1912 but reflects India as it was in 1921–1922 and depicts the inadequacies in a changed political climate of the surviving reactionary pre-war colonial ideas and attitudes. Contrary to charges of critics like Martin Green, Andrew Shonfield, and K. Natwar-Singh, EMF understood and made use of events that occurred in India and the entire world prior to publication of *Passage*. *Passage* thus reflects "the political implications of race relations, fear of riots, English justice and government, Hindu-Moslem unity, Indian Native States, nationalism and the independence movement." The racial intolerance in *Passage* reflects the notorious violence of General Dyer at the 1919 Amritsar Massacre (Mrs. Turton declares the insolent Indians ought to "crawl" before the English as they were made to do by Dyer in 1919). Other violent incidents are reflected obliquely: the Moplah Rebellion on the Malabar Coast (1921) and the Khalifat Movement (1921–1922), which enlisted Hindu-Moslem cooperation. *Passage* dramatizes, in fact, EMF's views that colonial, racial, and political problems result primarily from personal misunderstandings and a lack of imagination. Mrs. Moore, Fielding, and Aziz express the need for charity, kindness, and goodwill in solving imperial issues; the typical Anglo-Indians fail to see that India's problems are not administrative but social and religious. [Gandhi and his son are quoted to this effect.] EMF's belief (voiced by Aziz and and sympathized with by Fielding) that Indians should determine their own destiny is at the heart of the Indian national movement in the 1920s. Aziz's trial is a political allegory on the theme: Adela Quested's accusation and retraction indicate the course of British imperial policy; Aziz's change from subservience to independence dramatizes its effects. Adela's echo is a symbol of British guilt, which disappears when she withdraws her charge. Aziz predicts Moslem-Hindu unity and India's attaining of independence in the next war; EMF was thus a political prophet. [Informative, illuminating article, correcting the views of those who believe that EMF's novel is nonpolitical or noncontemporary in its ambience.]

1584 Miller, Merle. "What It Means to Be a Homosexual," NEW YORK TIMES MAGAZINE, 17 Jan 1971, pp. 9, 10, 48, 49, 57, 60; rptd, with additions, in ON BEING DIFFERENT: WHAT IT MEANS TO BE A HOMOSEXUAL (NY: Random House, 1971), espec pp. 3–5, 54.
["What I Believe" (*Two Cheers for Democracy*), with EMF's declaration that he would betray his country rather than his friend, caused so much discomfort in the McCarthy era that the essay was withdrawn from secondary school textbooks. But EMF did not roll with the tide and wrote, in *Maurice*, of his homosexual inclinations as he knew them. The publication of the story about EMF and his posthumous homosexual novel in the NEW YORK TIMES [Anthony Lewis, "E. M. Forster Homosexual Novel Due" (11 Nov 1970)] inspired Miller to write his essay. Miller has great admiration for EMF as writer and man since his first reading of *Howards End.*]

1585 Mitchell, Julian. "Fairy Tale," MANCHESTER GUARDIAN, 7 Oct 1971, p. 15; rptd in E. M. FORSTER: THE CRITICAL HERITAGE, ed by Philip Gardner (Lond & Boston: Routledge & Kegan Paul, 1973), pp. 439–40.

EMF should have published *Maurice,* if only in a foreign edition. It now seems tame rather than shocking and reveals his limitations. EMF's account of undergraduate romance rings true; the romantic defiance of society does not. EMF seems to have not wished to face the possibility of social acceptance for the homosexual. He does not take his characters into adulthood nor deal with homosexuals in society.

1586 Moore, Harry T. "Age of the Modern," AGE OF THE MODERN AND OTHER LITERARY ESSAYS (Carbondale & Edwardsville: Southern Illinois UP, Lond & Amsterdam: Feffer & Simons, Crosscurrents/Modern Critiques, 1971), pp. 94–118, espec 113–18.

EMF notably describes in *Aspects of the Novel* the affinities of modern fiction with music. The resemblances to music in fiction may be to form as well as to sound. EMF admits this possibility, though he can find in fiction no parallel to Beethoven's Fifth Symphony. If no such parallel can be found in the novel, T. S. Eliot followed such a complex musical pattern in FOUR QUARTETS.

1587 Müllenbrock, Heinz-Joachim. "Die Kunst der Eröffnung im Werk E. M. Forsters: Ein Beitrag zur Poetik Seiner Romane" (The Art of Disclosure in E. M. Forster's Work: An Article on the Poetry of His Novels), GERMANISCH-ROMANISCHE MONATSSCHRIFT (Heidelberg), LII: 2 (1971), 185–203.

The first chapter in a novel by EMF provides the key to, and contains in embryo, all the thematic material developed later in the novel. [Examines in detail the opening chapters of *Where Angels Fear to Tread, A Room with a View,* and *A Passage to India.*] In *Angels,* the formidable characters of Mrs. Herriton and Harriet Herriton and Phillip Herriton's ineffectual nature are foreshadowed. Chance and determinism are emphasized as factors in experience. The later melodrama in the novel is adumbrated in the violence and the purposeful incoherence in style, present in the first chapter, when Mrs. Herriton learns of Lilia's "engagement" to Gino Carella. In *Room,* the major characters are all introduced in the first chapter, which also establishes the atmosphere of English respectability, transplanted to Italy, through which Lucy Honeychurch must eventually break. In the first chapter the characters and action are reflected from Lucy's perspective. She is the protagonist and is seen at a midpoint between the naturalness of the Emersons and the conventionality of Charlotte Bartlett. Through comic means EMF embodies in this chapter the main theme of his novel: Lucy's movement toward the light. In *A Passage to India* the opening chapter is more general in its implications than the opening chapters of the English novels. The drabness of life at Chandrapore is the dominant impression established. An atmosphere of strangeness is generated, and the alienation of the English in India is hinted at: English culture is irrevelant in the vastness of India. In India nature dwarfs man but also allows him to see himself in true perspective. The description of the limitless sky at the end of the first chapter creates much intensity, and nature is seen as protagonist in this novel. The theme of separation is reinforced by the impersonal heavens. The later disastrous occurrences in the Marabar Caves are fore-shadowed in EMF's description of the Marabar Hills as fists and fingers. [In German.]

1588 Munby, A. N. L. "Introduction," E. M. FORSTER, 1879–1970: HEFFER CATALOGUE SEVEN (Cambridge: W. Heffer & Sons, 1971), 1–4 (see E. M. FORSTER, 1879–1970: HEFFER CATALOGUE SEVEN, 1971).

[Describes EMF's haphazard collecting, storing, and giving away of his books; the principal sources of his library; and the acquiring of the most important of his books by King's College Library, the main repository of EMF's MSS and papers. The MS of *A Passage to India* is at the Humanities Research Center, The University of Texas, and the Thornton family papers are at the Cambridge University Library.]

1589 Natwar-Singh, K. "Forster and His *Maurice,*" ILLUSTRATED WEEKLY OF INDIA (Bombay), XCII (12 Dec 1971), p. 57.

The publication of *Maurice* will not damage EMF's reputation in the long run but will affect it adversely in the short run. The parts of the book are better than the whole. The prose is superb, but EMF has not been able to handle his tricky subject with his customary adroitness.

1590 O'Brien, M. D., S. J. "E. M. Forster's Intellectual Heritage," ENGLISH LITERATURE AND LANGUAGE (Tokyo), No. 8 (1971), 27–36.

[EMF's career and Bloomsbury connections are described.] EMF avoided the worst excesses of Bloomsbury (exhibitionism, cliquishness, cultural snobbery, and irresponsible sexual relations) and shared with Bloomsbury its view that the intelligentsia should leaven society. This conviction accounts for EMF's emphasis on value in fiction rather than upon event or plot. Samuel Butler was a chief influence. His mocking, ironic, and skeptical tone, and his emphasis on the importance of money were formative on EMF. In *Howards End* EMF contrasted the ineffectual quality of the Schlegels as intelligentsia with the insensitivity of the Wilcoxes as practical individuals. The Schlegel values are important but so is the Wilcox money. Helen Schlegel's obsession with abstract justice for the Basts is of lesser value, in EMF's view, than Margaret's loyalty to Henry Wilcox as the man she loves. EMF's tentativeness in this novel derives from Butler. EMF also emphasizes the importance of visionary emotion, an emphasis that he combines with the writing of social comedy, designed to expose the shortcomings of modern society. EMF encounters difficulties in *A Passage to India*. The possibilities of friendship are not realized, and an imperfect sympathy with the Indians obtrudes, despite EMF's attempts to be fair to them. He also undercuts in the novel all meaningful values [the fact that strong affirmation of positive values was no longer possible in the postwar era is too greatly discounted]. EMF's range is narrow, but he is an accomplished artist within it.

1591 "Old Sage and Young Turk," HUMANIST (Cambridge), LXXXXVI (Dec 1971), 356.
It is difficult to believe that Bernard Levin ["The Shield of Achilles," TIMES (Lond), 23 Oct 1971, p. 6] could have been so deeply influenced by EMF. EMF's style in the novels made no difference in Levin's own, though the style in the historical sketches (like "Macolnia Shops," *Abinger Harvest*) may have helped Levin draw together the threads of his own historical reconstructions. Levin's fervor sets him apart from EMF's detachment. EMF is, however, more committed in *Maurice* than elsewhere. Levin correctly holds that *Maurice* is not dated; EMF throws light on the homosexual's problems. EMF is a great novelist, though critics are reluctant to use that word for a writer whose canon is small.

1592 Ozick, Cynthia. "Forster as Homosexual," COMMENTARY, LII (Dec 1971), 81–85.
There is an element of shock in EMF's fiction, whereas his life was equable, except for the shock produced by the posthumous publication of *Maurice*. In this book he tries to indict society, but the accusation fails to achieve complexity and authority as it did in *Howards End* (which, with George Eliot's MIDDLEMARCH, is a prototypical wisdom novel). The element of wish-fulfillment in *Maurice* makes of it a fairy tale. Maurice is himself conceived impurely and insincerely, as a kind of Wilcox who is also a homosexual. The efforts to coarsen Maurice, in order for him to be divorced from EMF himself, are unconvincing and embarrassing. *Maurice* suffers because the sex scenes are not really there. EMF seems actually to think that homosexuality is wrong, although he writes about it and was himself implicated in it. He is disturbed by the sterility implicit in it; he reveals a Christian moral bent by subscribing with his sympathies to the Biblical injunction, "Be fruitful and multiply." EMF did not accept the homosexual manners of a Lytton Strachey, his elitism, and his recoil from Christianity. EMF was more mystical than the Cambridge Apostles or Bloomsbury and less skeptical. The revelations about his homosexuality tend to devalue his humanism, to make of it an interested and personal rather than a general

program for tolerance, love, humanity, sensitivity, and courage. [Stimulating discussion.]

1593 Peel, Marie. "Biography," BOOKS AND BOOKMEN, XVI (Feb 1971), 49–50.

J. R. Ackerley's E. M. FORSTER: A PORTRAIT (1971) reinforces the impression of EMF as not being "a seeing, suffering kind of artist" but "a listening one" of great sensitivity.

1594 Peel, Marie. "Women's Lib in Lit," BOOKS AND BOOKMEN, XVII (Nov 1971), 14–17.

[Mostly about other writers, but links Henry James and EMF in their recognition of woman's need for independent significance as a person.] EMF's women may not be attractive, but they are spiritually dedicated. Adela Quested is a forerunner of Doris Lessing's Martha Quest (CHILDREN OF VOLENCE).

1595 Pittenger, Norman. "E. M. Forster, Homosexuality and Christian Morality," CHRISTIAN CENTURY, LXXXVIII (15 Dec 1971), 1468–71.

EMF had all the Christian virtues except faith; his novels reveal that love, understanding, connection, and courage were primary virtues for him. Had he met with tolerance and acceptance of homosexuality by Christianity, his attitude toward it and its faith would probably have been different. *Maurice* may promote a tolerance in society for all forms of love.

1596 "Playboy after Hours: Books," PLAYBOY, XVIII (Nov 1971), 36.

Maurice is dated, but the heterodox opinions that EMF expresses in it will revise academic estimates of him. The purported Hellenic sexual freedom breeds fake emotion, which destroys the relationship between Maurice and Clive Durham. *Maurice* is a story of the achievement of happiness, but the novel only comes alive when things go wrong, when "tempers are flashing," and when EMF can use for satire his celebrated wit.

1597 Porterfield, Christopher. "Boy Meets Boy," TIME, XCVIII (18 Oct 1871), 90, 92.

Maurice is a willed performance. There is less in this novel of surprise and ambiguity than in EMF's other work; he reveals "a one-track mind." A note of prim authorial constraint hangs over the book. EMF did better, as in *The Longest Journey*, when he wrote obliquely of homosexual relationships. As for *Albergo Empedocle and Other Writings by E. M. Forster* (ed by George H. Thomson), it will be useful to specialists, interesting to EMF enthusiasts, but otherwise dispensable.

1598 Pritchard, R. E. D. H. LAWRENCE: BODY OF DARKNESS (Pittsburgh: University of Pittsburgh P, 1971), pp 157, 159, 177.

"St. Mawr" is partly a reply to EMF's *A Passage to India*, Lawrence's empty desert at the end of his tale corresponding to, and answering, EMF's Temple as a vision of what underlies experience. The Shropshire Hills in the early section of the tale are "great shut fingers," reminiscent of the Marabar Hills in *Passage.*

1599 Pritchett, V. S. "The Upholstered Prison," NEW STATESMAN, nsLXXII (8 Oct 1971), 479–80; rptd in E. M. FORSTER: THE CRITICAL HERITAGE, ed by Philip Gardner (Lond & Boston: Routledge & Kegan Paul, 1973), pp. 447–50.

Maurice comes to life when EMF centers on his hero's sexual problems, after the first hundred pages. The novel reveals his "tart gift for moral puncture, all his talent for not forgiving and for not shedding tears." The book invites comparison with D. H. Lawrence's LADY CHATTERLEY'S LOVER. The two books are similar in their preoccupation with snobbery and class-consciousness and with the stagnant quality of English life. Maurice was not a suitable protagonist, being too conventional to be endowed with EMF's own intelligence and sensibility. But he becomes vital when he recognizes his sexual anomaly. *Maurice* reveals expert craftsmanship throughout. EMF recreates the triviality of Maurice's Edwardian society. It is "an upholstered prison . . . in which people settle for continuous irritability and nerves as the most convenient way of not knowing the volcano they are living on socially." [Excellent discussion.]

1600 Raina, M. L. "The Symbol and the Story—The Case of *Howards End,*" PUNJAB UNIVERSITY RESEARCH BULLETIN, II (Aug 1971), 11–26.

The use of symbols in literature is related to the whole problem of a writer's communicating his vision. D. H. Lawrence, Virginia Woolf, and EMF try to fashion a symbolic mode of writing without losing touch with the mimetic aspect of their materials. EMF's skepticism, as in the bathing sequence in *A Room with a View*, renders suspect its imputed symbolic value. EMF not only has difficulty in conferring symbolic value on the factual; he is also unsuccessful in establishing realistic dimensions for certain ritualistic sequences in his fiction as in the flame-boat episode in *The Longest Journey*. [Most critics do not agree concerning this episode.] In the earlier novels, the symbolism is too direct and contrived; in *A Passage to India* EMF goes beyond a symbolism rooted in the actual; in *Howards End* alone does he try to solve the technical problem of rooting symbolism in the actual. EMF is not successful in uniting the conscious direction of his plot with his unconscious valuations. The negative description of London and the positive descriptions of the countryside coincide with EMF's unconscious values, but the plot goes counter to them. Subjectively EMF dislikes the Wilcox hurry, and he values the leisurely dignity of those associated with Howards End (Ruth Wilcox, Margaret Schlegel) as seen in his use of an imagery of "flow" or "floating" in connection with them. Here again, his unconscious valuations go counter to the plot. In the last scene the gulf is again too great between symbolism and plot. There is similar ambiguity and insufficiency in the house symbolism. Howards End does not serve convincingly as a connecting symbol because only the Schlegels see it as such. At best the house is an emblem of hope but never actualizes its potentialities in terms of the dramatic conflict in the novel. EMF is also unsuccessful in conveying a symbolic meaning through Ruth Wilcox while retaining her human dimension as a character. Her realistic dimension is not supported by any sense of established relationships with other people; as symbol, she apprehends harmony but does not communicate it. EMF lacks the "magisterial subjectivity" of a D. H. Lawrence, which would have permitted him to make characters like Mrs. Wilcox and Mrs. Moore more credible. In *Howards End* EMF tries to overcome the limitations of realistic fiction, but he never achieves a harmony of opposing modes. [Most critics of the novel would admit the pertinence of these observations but find that EMF has greater success in combining realism and symbolism than this critic allows. I agree with her analysis of Mrs. Wilcox, which is the best part of the article.]

1601 Raskin, Jonah. "Introduction: Bombard the Critics," "Forster and Cary: Old and New," "Disconnections," "Trips East," "School Lessons: History and Geometry," THE MYTHOLOGY OF IMPERIALISM: RUDYARD KIPLING, JOSEPH CONRAD, E. M. FORSTER, D. H. LAWRENCE, AND JOYCE CARY (NY: Random House, 1971), pp. 3–14, 222–41, 242–56, 257–85, 286–93.

[Critique of the novelists in title, written by a critic from the present-day Left.] "Introduction: Bombard the Critics": EMF divorces art from life. His concept of a writer is that of an individual immune in his ivory tower to all social change. [An oversimplification; in fact, the same protest that EMF makes about Henry James in *Aspects of the Novel.* EMF would balance the claims of the individual and of society (see "The Ivory Tower," ATLANTIC MONTHLY, CLXIII [Jan 1939], 119–30.] "Forster and Cary: Old and New": EMF was finished off by World War I [but he hated the war; see "Me, Them and You" and "Our Graves at Gallipoli," *Abinger Harvest*]; he is fearful of revolution and reverts to Victorianism in his thinking. EMF and Goldsworthy Lowes Dickinson (and others in their circle) failed to take into account the deprivations undergone in the 1920s and 1930s by the majority of the world's population. EMF's turning to the myth of the past represents a denial of the social conflicts taking place in the present; the myth of the invincible British middle class in most forcefully expressed in "Notes on the

English Character" (*Abinger*). [The line of EMF's essay is more disparaging than laudatory.] EMF would tolerate the enemy rather than jail or execute him. In fighting the fascist enemies of Europe, EMF was overwhelmed to inaction by the lack of fixity or stability in modern life [an overstatement]; in India the landscape expresses the discord, confusion, and chaos that disabled him. EMF's colonial world in *A Passage to India* is, moreover, a nineteenth-century one—"Jane Austen shipped to the East." [Other critics attest to the reality of the world pictured by EMF; EMF's point is that its negative character resulted partly from the fact that it was anachronistic.] EMF's fear of the modern world is conveyed by his distrust of modern mass media, the radio, cinema, etc. The apocalyptic note in EMF results from his lack of convictions to oppose to the modern chaos. He refutes Kipling in *Passage* but excuses his politics instead of condemning them. On such matters EMF lacks Joyce Cary's clarity. "Disconnections": *Howards End* is "a sappy, sentimental book." The Schlegel sisters are ineffective politically because of their limited, parochial outlook. EMF patronizes Leonard Bast and shuns the poor. He opts for a static feudal regime, there is no class struggle apparent in *Howards End*, and no communal society is brought into existence at the end. [For the more convincing, opposite, Marxist interpretation of EMF's early novels that finds them, in fact, revolutionary, see Willis H. Truitt, "Thematic and Symbolic Ideology in the Works of E. M. Forster. In Memoriam" (1971)]. EMF cannot imagine revolutionary alternatives. The yeoman is not a fit antagonist to the imperialist; the imperial type needs to be opposed by an international type, which EMF cannot envision. He does not see the Wilcoxes as malignant materialists who were responsible for World War I. *Howards End* is reactionary and counterrevolutionary in content and form, in comparison with a truly revolutionary book like D. H. Lawrence's WOMEN IN LOVE. "Trips East": There is no glamor in EMF's India, nor is there much about Indian politics in *Passage*. He does not write about colonial liberation struggles in the East and sees few possibilities to depict the Gandhi resistance movement in his art. [That EMF is aware of nationalistic ferment in twentieth-century India, Jeffrey Meyers's "The Politics of *A Passage to India*" (1971) proves.] EMF's India is one of diversity. The Caves and echo are overpowering. EMF sports his pessimism unduly; but he fails to be precise about it because we never do learn what happened in the Cave. *Passage* is "a death elegy to nineteenth-century romanticism." EMF is hospitable to Hinduism as a religion for alienated man; it is a religion in which the individual in a chaos can confront personally his own God and find unity. EMF's belief in personal relations and private conversation is broken by India because nothing is private there. The weight of colonialism oppresses him because men are powerless to make friends with people from different races. Fielding is willing to befriend Aziz in his crisis but is not willing to join with him as a nationalist agitator. The Caves, not the courts (or the amelioration of social conditions), hold

EMF's imagination in India; he believes that man's efforts are futile in the infinite Indian universe. It is a social system that prevents communication between men of different races, but EMF is finally not interested in doing away with it, i.e. with British imperialism. The efforts of individual men in their private realms are the important thing for EMF. He does have the human intelligence, however, to see that under imperialism friendship between rulers and ruled cannot be a relationship between equals. He sees the inadequacies of his own liberalism but cannot espouse revolution or communism. *Passage* is, all told, a sad work, holding little promise for the future. "School Lessons: History and Geometry": There are close similarities in underlying philosophy between *Passage* and *Aspects of the Novel*. *Aspects* provides therapy for the EMF of *Passage* by its abrogation of history. He espouses a philosophy of art-for-art's sake to escape the vexing problems of his society [overstated]. His discussions of novels suggest that his own affinities were with architecture, not with music. [Critic assumes that detached intelligence is in itself reactionary and unimportant in a social context.]

> **1602** Ratcliffe, Michael. "The Undeveloped Heart," TIMES (Lond), 7 Oct 1971, p. 10; rptd in E. M. FORSTER: THE CRITICAL HERITAGE, ed by Philip Gardner (Lond & Boston: Routledge & Kegan Paul, 1973), pp. 441–44.

Like EMF's other novels, *Maurice* is concerned with "the profound pathology" (Trilling's phrase) of the undeveloped heart. Alec Scudder is a fantasy of fulfillment; Maurice is too literally the Edwardian stockbroker. He has an undeveloped heart, but not a cold one, illustrating EMF's characterization of the English in "Notes on the English Character" (*Abinger Harvest*). Maurice and Clive Durham are quite typical of Edwardian young men, in that love takes the place of religion; the search for "the one true friend" takes the place of the search for God. EMF had himself already found both God *and* friend in India. Alec as the friend who might be God does not convince. The contrivances in *Maurice* are too bald; lacking are "a transcending command of melodrama" and "a comic genius of Austenite magnitude." It is the least poetic, the least witty, the least dense, and the most immediately realistic of the six novels. The spirit of place and "the fringe of emasculating women" are scarcely utilized. EMF is less successful with a direct presentation of homosexuality than with a more indirect presentation of it in Rickie Elliot and Stewart Ansell of *The Longest Journey*. Possibly EMF wrote this novel too soon, before he had had experience with physical love. [An enlightening and perceptive review.]

> **1603** "Reservations," ANTIOCH REVIEW, XXXI (Fall 1971), 439.

The controlling image in *Maurice* is the Sherwood Forest Woodland, symbolizing a refuge for primitive sexuality as opposed to a deadening society.

EMF reveals that he knew the reality of lust and of spirit hidden behind social conventions. He also realized the difficulty of achieving awareness in modern society.

1604 Rosenbaum, S. P. "E. M. Forster and George Meredith," PUBLICATIONS OF THE MODERN LANGUAGE ASSOCIATION, LXXXVI (Oct 1971), 1037–38.

[Note on June Perry Levine's "An Analysis of the Manuscripts of *A Passage to India*," PUBLICATIONS OF THE MODERN LANGUAGE ASSOCIATION (1970).] Levine wrongly ascribes to Dante the lines from Meredith's "The Woods of Westermain," used by EMF in a cancelled passage of the manuscript in which Fielding (rather than Mrs. Moore) enters the Marabar Caves and experiences the radical disillusionment undergone by Mrs. Moore in the finished novel. The union of faculties—blood, brain, and spirit—celebrated in the poem under the aegis of earth is not possible in the Indian earth (or Caves). The allusion to Meredith is replaced in the novel by a quotation from the King James Bible. The use of Meredith by Fielding reveals a distance between EMF and Fielding, in view of EMF's later denigration of Meredith.

1605 Rosenbaum, S. P. "Himself, His Love and the Greenwood," TORONTO GLOBE AND MAIL, "Globe Magazine: Books," 23 Oct 1971, p. 17.

Maurice was worth publishing despite EMF's own uncertainty about it. It is about class more than it is about sex, and it is frequently a brilliant comedy of manners. The treatment of homosexuality is not melodramatic or clinical. The book fails to achieve absolute distinction because the connections that Maurice makes are few: "Nothing beyond himself, his love, and the greenwood." The struggles between the claims of the private life and the public are not fully enough rendered. The book throws light on why EMF may have stopped writing fiction and on *A Passage to India*. The book is important in itself, in its combining the serious and the comic, and in its stress upon love to overcome "the undeveloped heart" of the middle-class Englishman.

1606 Rosenbaum, S. P. "The Philosophical Realism of Virginia Woolf," ENGLISH LITERATURE AND BRITISH PHILOSOPHY: A COLLECTION OF ESSAYS, ed by S. P. Rosenbaum (Chicago & Lond: University of Chicago P, 1971), pp. 316–56, espec 331–32, 339–40.

As EMF indicates in "The Early Novels of Virginia Woolf" (*Abinger Harvest*), Virginia Woolf's work shows its orientation toward "philosophical realism" in the famous description in MRS. DALLOWAY: "Here is one room; there another" (although there is another dimension in her work that reaches toward mysticism). EMF's fiction reveals the same primacy of the realist impulse, although he too reaches out for mystical experience. Both novelists are basically concerned with "the marvellous, irreducible otherness of people, the plurality of souls, the obduracy of matter." Both are essentially philosophical realists. [EMF quoted as to Woolf's rendering the process of thought itself in her fiction.]

1607 Rosenthal, Michael. "Lytton Strachey's Mistress/Mother/Child/Student/Domestic/Friend," NEW YORK TIMES BOOK REVIEW, 25 April 1971, pp. 2, 16, 18, 20, 22.
[Review-essay of CARRINGTON: LETTERS AND EXTRACTS FROM HER DIARIES, chosen by David Garnett. Excellent discussion of Bloomsbury. Stresses influence, on those in the circle, of G. E. Moore, their rationality, their rejection of conventional pieties, their passionate skepticism, and their essential decency and sanity. The death of Julian Bell in the Spanish Civil War in 1937 marks the end of Bloomsbury. Several mentions of EMF.]

1608 R[oss], A[ngus]. "E[dward] M[organ] Forster (1879–1970)," PENGUIN COMPANION TO ENGLISH LITERATURE, ed by David Daiches (NY: McGraw-Hill; Harmondsworth, Middlesex: Penguin, 1971), pp. 191–92.
EMF was affiliated with Bloomsbury, which continued an inherited evangelical moral concern with a detachment provided by inherited wealth and secularized beliefs. The classics contributed EMF's feeling for the power of myth; he also had sharp observation of life, wit, irony, and a poet's perception. His fiction contrasts pagan vitality with "civilized" convention. His Indian experiences broadened his outlook and allowed him to probe into the weaknesses of European culture. "The Hindu 'openness' to feeling, to experience, to religious awe (with its dangerous concomitant of indecision) is contrasted with the 'practical' English inflexibility, which is necessary to maintain and exercise power." His great gift was to organize his vision into comedy. [Perceptive biographical summary and literary criticism.]

1609 Runyan, Elizabeth. "Escape from the Self: An Interpretation of E. M. Forster, D. H. Lawrence, Virginia Woolf," DISSERTATION ABSTRACTS INTERNATIONAL, XXXI (1971), 5423A. Unpublished dissertation, Kent State University, 1970.

1610 S., C. "Posthumous Postscript," GLASGOW HERALD, "Saturday Extra," 9 Oct 1971, p. 2.
Maurice is not a novel in the sense that EMF's other full length works are, i.e., "complex and subtle accounts of many different people and many different emotions in interaction." Here we have one person, a homosexual, statically presented, who exemplifies only a way of life. Insisting upon a happy ending for his fantasy, EMF was false to social and psychological

reality. His worst vices are present: an archness now becomes coyness; mawkishness takes over in emotional scenes; and brutality is projected towards objects of distaste (especially women). EMF lacks the irony and clear-sightedness of Proust. The concluding sequences represent an attempt to get at reality, but only an attempt. The novel generates a feeling of falseness, of the conventionality resulting when a convention is turned upside down. In contrast to the Caves section of *A Passage to India*, we have a "fantasy of wish-fulfilment" instead of an "imaginative exploration of the truth."

1611 Sainsbury, Ian. "Forster at His Best," MORNING TELEGRAPH (Sheffield), 9 Oct 1971, p. 12.
"The death of England" (at which time EMF thought that *Maurice* might be published, and referred to in his "Terminal Note") may mean the death of restrictive sexual conventions, the death of the class system, or (regrettably) the death of the English countryside. These are also the themes of *Howards End* to which *Maurice* seems to be "a coda." It is worthy to stand with the rest—or best—of EMF's fiction.

1612 Simmons, James C. "Philip Meadows Taylor and the Anglo-Indian Novel with a Check List of His Writings," BULLETIN OF THE NEW YORK PUBLIC LIBRARY, LXXV (March 1971), 154–62.
In his fiction, Philip Meadows Taylor (1808–1876) anticipates the EMF of *A Passage to India* by his sympathy with Indian society and its culture, by his condemnation of the arrogance and cant of many Anglo-Indians, and by his presentation of the schism between Moslem and Hindu civilizations.

1613 Smith, D. J. "The Mem-Sahib in Her Books," LITERARY CRITERION (Mysore), IX (Summer 1971), 42–50.
The mem-sahib in Kipling's work was either an irresponsible flirt, an idealistic woman devoted to altruistic endeavor, or a domestically inclined woman. The first and third types could, on occasion, be intolerant of the natives, as are the officials' wives in EMF's *A Passage to India*. Another, later type of the mem-sahib is the ardent, unconventional, egalitarian, skeptical, somewhat unimaginative woman, Adela Quested in *Passage*. She reflects how the misunderstandings between the races were often the result of differing attitudes toward sex. Anglo-Indian writers, beginning with Kipling, have understood the problems of English women in India better than did their predecessors.

1614 Smith, Robert Francis. "E. M. Forster Transfigured: A Study in Prose Stylistics," DISSERTATION ABSTRACTS INTERNATIONAL, XXXI (1971), 1295A. Unpublished dissertation, University of Pennsylvania, 1969.

1615 Snow, C. P. "Open Windows," FINANCIAL TIMES (Lond), 7 Oct 1971, p. 28; rptd in E. M. FORSTER: THE CRITICAL HERITAGE, ed by Philip Gardner (Lond & Boston: Routledge & Kegan Paul, 1973), pp. 433–36.

Maurice exhibits some of EMF's good qualities but also some of his questionable ones. The novel is sincere, first as an expression of sexual guilt, then as an expression of the belief that homosexual love can be happy and enduring. The ecstatic ending does not ring true; the novel is crippled by being a novel of purpose. The novel accentuates EMF's lack of feeling for those he does not know well from experience, e.g., the business mentality. His characters do not always exist freely. Maurice is well-done, but the rest of his life, apart from the sexual, is shadowy. EMF has little real grip on the physical world. The novel will make little difference in his reputation. For those uncommitted to EMF, *Maurice* but emphasizes "that there is a weakening ambiguity in his novels which is not the result of art but a kind of equivocation." [Excellent discussion.]

1616 Southerington, F. R. HARDY'S VISION OF MAN (NY: Barnes & Noble: Lond: Chatto & Windus, 1971), pp. 34, 35, 107.

[EMF's judgment of Hardy set forth in *Aspects of the Novel* is challenged.] EMF asserts that Hardy's characters are overschematized to fit the demands of a total determinism and that his determinism does not comport suitably with the medium of the novel. Rather, Hardy's characters have some degree of freedom and responsibility and so may fuse ideology with personality more skillfully than EMF admits. A LAODICEAN, though a failure, prefigures EMF's preoccupations in *Howards End*, in the contrast made between the decaying aristocracy and the progressive industrial powers and in the concern expressed with the question of who shall inherit the earth.

1617 Speirs, John. POETRY TOWARDS NOVEL (NY: New York UP; Lond: Faber, 1971), pp. 207, 319*n*.

The contrast between England and Italy in Byron's "Beppo" is similar to that in EMF's *Where Angels Fear to Tread*. In both works two different styles of life are compared, and we have "a comedy of contrasts of peoples and places." Like Conrad, EMF universalizes his setting, characters, and actions. *A Passage to India* is not only an ironic comedy based on the failures of human beings to understand each other, but it deals finally with the insuperable difficulties in the way of such understanding. *Passage* is the equivalent in the English liberal tradition of such works as T. S. Eliot's "The Waste Land" or D. H. Lawrence's ST. MAWR, although there are great differences in the visions of the three authors.

1618 Steiner, George. "Under the Greenwood Tree," NEW YORK- ER, XLVII (9 Oct 1971), pp. 158, 160, 163–66, 169; rptd in E. M.

FORSTER: THE CRITICAL HERITAGE, ed by Philip Gardner (Lond & Boston: Routledge & Kegan Paul, 1973), pp. 475–82.

The conception of *Maurice* and EMF's handling of its theme are "almost risibly hedged and dated." Its happy outcome is forced. While its defects are obvious, *Maurice* has its strengths and its interest in EMF's career. In it he says things that meant much to him and had to be excised from his public (and therefore less honest) writings. The Cambridge chapters are the best in the book. EMF may also be the victim of reticence, with the result that his abstractions are at once strained and hollow, and his style is lush in compensation. Chap 18 [it describes the two-year idyll between Maurice and Clive Durham] is the structural center of the novel and is stylistically a "disaster." The consultation scene with Dr. Barry is excellent, and the scene at the British Museum has an "incisive delicacy" that leads into *A Passage to India*. EMF's ambivalence remains puzzling and damaging. In his presentation of the central theme, there is duplicity, as he does not seem capable of rejecting the guilt that his society has instilled in him: "When he speaks of Clive Durham's 'cure,' of his 'normality,' he does it without irony and in pained defeat." This "defensive pathos" damages the book. Thematically the novel points to *Passage*. In *Passage* EMF expresses with authority his loathing of the class that had destroyed Clive's love for Maurice, its smugness, cruelty, unimaginativeness, and lack of feeling: "The encounters between white and native, between emancipated rulers and 'advanced' Indians, in *A Passage to India* are a brilliant projection of confrontations between society and the homosexual in *Maurice*." In *Passage* he also solved the problem of "physical realization." In *Maurice* there was no sensuous equivalent available to EMF adequate to his vision of sex, but the mysterious outrage in the Marabar Caves is a perfect projection of his vision. The "non-event" in the Hills includes "values that we can now confidently recognize as being both heterosexual and homosexual." Both are aspects of "the unbounded unity of love." *Maurice* may make EMF's achievement seem more narrow than it did formerly. In its light some of his moral dicta also will take on new or added meaning. We now see the personal hurt from which his liberal and individualistic values derived, "an intensely spiritualized yet nervous and partly embittered homosexuality." EMF lacked the force, vigor, and honesty in handling normal and abnormal passion found, for example, in the work of John Cowper Powys. [Profound discussion.]

1619 Stern, Frederick C. "Never Resemble M. de Lesseps: A Note on *A Passage to India*," ENGLISH LITERATURE IN TRANSITION, XIV: 2 (1971), 119–21.

De Lesseps stands for all the worst in Western rationalism, all that interferes with Adela Quested's ambition to encompass India and with her ability to cope with sexual love. In returning to Western society, she will seek out the most Eastern elements in it—Mrs. Moore's children—out of deference to the East. The Eastern experience has taught her something: to abjure, to the degree possible, de Lesseps's pragmatic and soulless activity. For Mrs. Moore the Asirgarh fortress is a symbol of her failure to encompass India, of her mistake in regarding the echo as the ultimate in a vertical arrangement of realities rather than as one element in a hierachy of realities horizontally arranged as in a continuum.

1620 Stewart, J. I. M. THOMAS HARDY (Lond: Longman; NY: Dodd, Mead, 1971), pp. 140, 153.

Grace Melbury in THE WOODLANDERS associates Giles Winterborne with the gods just as Lucy Honeychurch in *A Room with a View* associates George Emerson with the figures of Michelangelo after she has, like Grace, initially contemned her lover. In "The Fiddler of the Reels" Hardy achieves a finer blending of the mundane and the preternatural than did EMF in some of his short stories.

1621 Theroux, Paul. "Forster's Fantasy of Liberation," WASHINGTON POST BOOK WORLD, 3 Oct 1971, pp. 1, 3.

Maurice lacks the moments of poetry to be found in the earlier novels and the dense and thoughtful complexity of *Howards End* and *A Passage to India.* In 1914 the book would have shocked the public because of its views on homosexuality and class, but not now. It is, in actuality, a conventional love story, except for the gender of the lovers. The movement of the novel traces Maurice's development from a man with definite ideas on class and uncertain ones on sex to a man who is classless and passionate (the passion makes him classless). Male friendship is central in EMF's work (here his mentors were Edward Carpenter and Goldsworthy Lowes Dickinson), in "Albergo Empedocle" and *The Longest Journey*, in particular. EMF subscribed to the view of his mentors that the Uranian would be a liberating force and a man of the future. The novel itself is "an Edwardian fantasy of liberation," and dated in consequence. Its slang, its archness, and its proto-apocalyptic aspect also date it. In comparison with Lawrence's LADY CHATTERLEY'S LOVER, "it is less graphic . . . , but as pagan in its determination." It is occasionally satirical, but the satire modulates into mild social comedy. "*Maurice* is not distinguished art, but is is a fine artefact." [In passing, notes that the pieces republished in *Albergo Empedocle and Other Writings by E. M. Forster* (ed by George H. Thomson) are inconsequential except for "Albergo" and "Pessimism in Literature." Stimulating discussion.]

1622 Thomson, George H. (ed). "Introduction," '*Albergo Empedocle*' *and Other Writings By E. M. Forster* (NY: Liveright, 1971), pp. ix–xi; and Headpieces for sections of book as follows: "An Early Short Story" (p. 3), "Cambridge Humor" (pp. 39–43),

"Bourgeois Values versus Inspiration" (pp. 93–95), "For the Workingmen's College" (pp. 125–127), "India" (pp. 187–91), and "The
Arts and War" (pp. 231–34).
[In "Introduction" EMF's uncollected writings are related to his life, career,
and writings collected in books. Headpieces are valuable commentary on
these writings, their relationships to EMF's published books, and EMF's
work as whole. In Headpiece to "An Early Short Story," early composition
of "Albergo Empedocle" is stressed. In Headpiece to "Cambridge Humor,"
EMF's earliest nonfictional writings are perceptively analyzed.] The paro-
dies on Aeschylus are the most suggestive for EMF's later work, revealing
his interest in the dominant woman and his conviction that extreme notions
of fate are untenable. EMF "refused to see life as either dull routine or
grandiose fate." In his third parody of Aeschylus, he rejects the entire
concept of remorse, as he also does in *Howards End*. He values spontaneity
rather than fatality. [In Headpiece to "Bourgeois Values versus Inspiration"
the ambiguity expressed in the uncollected essays from the INDEPENDENT
REVIEW and some other sources is noted.] EMF reveals some attraction
toward bourgeois values but in the main a hostility to them (these were the
values satirized in his fiction and analyzed in "Notes on the English Character" [*Abinger Harvest*]). EMF champions the eccentrics who exposed
these negative values, which the artist must also confront and transcend. [In
Headpiece to "For the Workingmen's College" the significance of the papers delivered to the College is noted.] In "Pessimism in Literature" EMF
is poised between the pessimistic tendencies of the age revealed in its
literature and the optimistic tendencies of his own humanistic, romantic
temperament, which favors comedy and the possibilities of spiritual salvation. "Dante" reveals importance for EMF's mind and art of Dante, with
his valuing of harmony and use of star symbolism (as in EMF's own writings) to convey it. "The Functions of Literature in Wartime" reveals the
Platonic cast of EMF's mind; he sees the writer as a spokesman for the good,
the beautiful, and the true. But EMF is also humanistic in relating these
values to the individual. [The Headpiece to "India" stresses importance of
the uncollected works on India in defining EMF's own views on India and
its culture; and he notes the bearing of these works upon *A Passage to
India*.] These essays, like the novel, convey EMF's sense of the multiplicity
of Indian culture and the irrelevance to it of Western norms, his dislike of
Western arrogance, and his ultimate identification with the the anti-ration-
alistic aspects of Indian religion as they provide a comprehensive view of
ultimate reality. "Hinduism on the one side and the vast confusion of India
on the other made it possible for Forster to express, with clarity of insight
and richness of detail, the supreme paradox of the One and the Many." [The
Headpiece to "The Arts and War" discusses some miscellaneous works, the
most important of which stress the originality and insubstantiality of Virginia Woolf's THE VOYAGE OUT ("A New Novelist") and the necessary

organic fusion of fact and idea in any viable kind of literary symbolism ("Short Stories from Russia").]

By EMF and not abstracted: "On Grinds" (1 Feb 1900) and "On Bicycling" (10 May 1900), CAMBRIDGE REVIEW, XXI, pp. 185, 301–2; "The Cambridge Theophrastus: The Stall-Holder" and "A Long Day," BASILEONA, No. 1 (1 June 1900), 5–6, 13; "A Tragic Interior," "The Pack of Anchises," and "The Cambridge Theophrastus: The Early Father," BASILEONA, No. 2, (21 Nov 1900), 19–21, 21–22, 23–24; "A Brisk Walk" and "A Tragic Interior," BASILEONA, No. 3 (21 Feb 1901), 30–31, 32–34; "Strivings after Historical Style" BASILEONA, No. 4, (June 1901), 43; "Albergo Empedocle," TEMPLE BAR, CXXVIII (Dec 1903), 663–84; "A Day Off," PILOT, IX (14 May 1904), 445–46; "Rostock and Wismar," INDEPENDENT REVIEW, IX (June 1906), 332–35; "Literary Eccentrics: A Review," ibid, XI (Oct 1906), 105–10; "Pessimism in Literature," WORKING MEN'S COLLEGE JOURNAL, X (Jan–Feb 1907), 6–10, 26–30; "Dante," ibid, X (Feb–April 1908), 261–64, 281–86, 301–6; "The Beauty of Life," ibid, XII (Oct 1911) 154–57; "The Functions of Literature in War-Time," ibid, XIV (March 1915), 57–61; "Mr. Walsh's Secret History of the Victorian Movement," BASILEON Z, XIII (June 1911), 4–7; "An Allegory (?)," BASILEON H, XIV (June 1912), 4–7; "Inspiration," AUTHOR, XXII (July 1912), 281–82; "Iron Horses in India," GOLDEN HYNDE, I (Dec 1913), 35–39; "The Indian Mind," NEW WEEKLY, I (28 March 1914), 55; "The Wedding," ibid, I (2 May 1914), 216; "The Gods of India," ibid, I (30 May 1914), 338; "The Age of Misery," ibid, II (27 June 1914), 52; "The Rose Show," ibid, II (11 July 1914), 119; "To Simply Feel," ibid, II (8 Aug 1914), 245–46; "The Elder Tagore," DAILY NEWS AND LEADER, 11 Nov 1914, p. 7; "The Indian Boom," ibid, 2 Feb 1915, p. 7; "A Great Anglo-Indian," ibid, 29 March 1915, p. 7; "A New Novelist," ibid, 8 April 1915, p. 7; "The Mission of Hinduism," ibid, 30 April 1915, p. 7; "Tate versus Chantrey," ibid, 26 May 1915, p. 8; "Short Stories from Russia," NEW STATESMAN, IV (24 July 1915), 373–74; and "Reconstruction in the Marne and the Meuse," WESTMINISTER GAZETTE, 30 Aug 1915, pp. 1–2. Reviews: A. Alvarez (Entry No. 1505); Noel Annan (Entry No. 1506); "Briefly Noted," NEW YORKER, XLVII (18 Dec 1971), 136; Joseph Epstein (Entry No. 1538); Arnold Kettle (Entry No. 1561); Frederick P. W. McDowell, "By and about Forster," ENGLISH LITERATURE IN TRANSITION, XV: 4 (1972), 319–31; Christopher Porterfield (Entry No. 1597); M. L. Raina, "Forster," QUEST (Bombay), LXXIX (Nov–Dec 1971), 97–99; Frank Reynolds (Entry No. 1697); Paul Theroux (Entry No. 1621); and Richard Wasson (Entry No. 1709).

1623 Thompson, M. B. "Forster's Belated Novel: Theme not Taboo Now, but Writing is Opaque," OTTAWA CITIZEN, 20 Nov 1971, p. 37.

In EMF's day homosexual love was impossible; society forced the man to think his proclivity something it was not or to deflect his urges into normal channels. *Maurice* is not a good novel, with its mixture of melodrama, wish-fulfillment, opaque and studied writing, offhand symbolism, and narrow vision. EMF's treatment of class is more subtle than his treatment of sex. *Maurice* is a flawed book but does EMF no disgrace.

1624 Toynbee, Philip. "Forster's Love Story," OBSERVER (Lond), 10 Oct 1971, p. 32; rptd in "Books," CRITIC (Chicago), XXX (Jan–Feb 1972), 71–72, and in E. M. FORSTER: THE CRITICAL HERITAGE, ed by Philip Gardner (Lond & Boston: Routledge & Kegan Paul, 1973), pp. 462–65.

EMF came from a middle-class background which proscribed homosexuality. His experiences at Cambridge then came as a liberation and a revelation. *Maurice* is a *"roman à thèse* with a vegeance." It reveals EMF's chief deficiency as a novelist, except in *A Passage to India:* "a disturbing element of Victorian fine writing, whimsicality and high-minded gush." But in his other novels this tendency was controlled by litheness and toughness of mind, by a pervasive and not always good-humored humor. *Maurice* isolates EMF's faults and is devoid of his great virtues. As in his other novels the protagonist is put to the test, and this time is not found wanting. *Maurice* is "novellettish, ill-written, humorless and deeply embarrassing." EMF misunderstood his talent; he wrote as a moralist to prove his point about the middle class and its "undeveloped heart," but his real ability lay in seeing, understanding, and describing social behavior. *Maurice* shows the undersirable effects of the lack of prohibition and restraint in its direct treatment of its subject. EMF did much better when he did not express his homosexual feelings directly. There is nothing homosexual about the novel except that it is about homosexuals.

1625 Truitt, Willis H. "Thematic and Symbolic Ideology in the Works of E. M. Forster: In Memoriam," JOURNAL OF AESTHETICS AND ART CRITICISM, XXX (Fall 1971), 101–9.

EMF goes far beyond the "liberal" political ideology generally imputed to him and is, in fact, a revolutionary writer. Only a Marxist review of the work can save him from politically "respectable" interpretations. Though he was not Marxist in his conscious convictions, historical materialism can provide a useful means of interpreting his work. In late nineteenth-century and Edwardian times, naturalistic or subjectivistic conventions predominated; both were hostile to theoretical presuppositions. The dominant temper of the age comprised "skepticism, agnosticism, and antihistoricism." EMF protested such "social skepticism and denial of reason," beginning with *The Longest Journey.* In the opening pages he ridicules subjectivistic epistemology; in *Howards End* he reacted to the fragmentation of modern life by formulating the admonition "only connect." In his desire to write a social novel with a progressive ideology, he rejected the nonprogrammatic realism of George Eliot and Dickens and the purely aesthetic criteria of G. E. Moore and EMF's own Bloomsbury colleagues. In EMF's radical fiction the English public school and the Anglican Church become detested symbols of the Establishment. The real subject of *Journey* and *Howards End* is class antagonism and the class struggle. EMF hopes for reconciliation of the class struggle with the merger of the intelligentsia and the working class. In *Journey* the philosophical question is posed in Part I, "Cambridge." EMF not only attacks subjectivism but also "the nominalistic bias of empiricism," which would deny social classes, class-consciousness, and social action as opposed to individual liberty. EMF discards the isolated, self-seeking ego in favor of a reality that is social as well as individual. EMF then turns to the question of who shall inherit society. He emphasizes that Stephen Wonham must do so, since he is the product of a marriage uniting the working man and the bourgeois intellectual. In Part II of *Journey*, "Sawston," the question of action is explored. The failure of Utopian socialism is demonstrated in the career of Anthony Failing. Stephen's link to Failing connects the old socialism with the socialism yet to be, which stresses action and social change. Action is preferable to speculation and theory; thus the academic Hegelianism of Stewart Ansell is seen as ineffective in modern society. In Part III, "Wiltshire," the final struggle and the death of bourgeois society occur. Stephen triumphs; the death of Rickie Elliot leaves unresolved the fate of the intelligentsia. In *Howards End* the child of Leonard Bast and Helen Schlegel is a more decisive symbol of England's inheritor. Leonard's death signifies the need, and the historical inevitability, of the revolutionary struggle; he dies that his son may inherit England, a son of an intellectual mother and of a more politicized member of the proletariat than was Stephen Wonham. The bourgeois-aristocratic attempts to forestall the collapse of capitalism and revolution fail, in the marriage of the merchant (Henry Wilcox) and the sophisticate (Margaret Schlegel).

In *A Passage to India* EMF's revolutionary premises are less sure, or even more insistent, with the implication that the final struggle of capitalism for survival will take place in foreign lands, in its imperial guise. Analysis of the later nonfiction reveals a revolutionary writer. EMF is Marxist in his conception of history, antagonistic to imperialism ("Our Graves in Gallipoli," *Abinger Harvest*), sympathetic to the working class and its potential amelioration in Eastern Europe ("Me, Them and You" *Abinger*), hostile to the assumed right to possess private property ("My Wood," *Abinger*), confident that communism alone holds hope for humanity ("Liberty in England," "A Note on the Way," *Abinger*), and enthusiastic about a socially oriented aesthetic culture ("The Last Parade," *Two Cheers for Democracy*). [A fresh, provocative essay with an original interpretive line. Conclusively proves that the context of EMF's work is more explicitly political and social than commonly considered and that EMF was in certain moods more than a detached liberal. Overstates his leanings toward socialism and communism, but is generally persuasive. Also proves, like Wilfred Stone in his Jungean interpretation of *A Passage to India* in THE CAVE AND THE MOUNTAIN (1966), that major works of art are susceptible to multiple methods of interpretation, all of which add incrementally to our knowledge of them.]

1626 Viswanatham, K. "Forster: *A Passage to India* (The Desperate View)," INDIA IN ENGLISH FICTION (Waltair, India: Andhra UP, Andhra University Series No. 100, 1971), pp. 90–120.

EMF's portrayal of India in *A Passage to India* reveals a limited and unsympathetic mind. Godbole is not EMF's voice, and the views dramatized in "Temple" are not the culmination of EMF's metaphysics. Godbole is a caricature—unreal and silly. The descriptions of Godbole and of the Gokul Ashtami festival reveal EMF's antipathy toward them. [Overlooks evidence to the contrary that reveals EMF's sympathy with India and with Hinduism, e.g., the uncollected writings on India gathered in *Albergo Empedocle and Other Writings by E. M. Forster*, ed by George H. Thomson (1971).] The impression produced by the novel is uncertain because of EMF's ambiguity toward his materials. *Passage* is a *cul-de-sac*, and EMF's comment in it on the human situation is depressing and irrelevant. [Detailed descriptive summary of *Passage* that seldom rises to the level of cogent critical comment. Downgrades *Passage* and then inconsistently terms it a "great" novel. The presentation is muddled and confused.]

1627 Walker, Keith. "Body Depth," NEW SOCIETY (Lond), No. 471 (7 Oct 1971), 80.

Theme molds *Maurice* and distorts the characters. At Cambridge Clive Durham represents Greek thought, mental superiority, and moral excellence; but in reality, Maurice is more admirable than Clive. EMF lacks generosity in depicting Maurice. The book fails because of EMF's "disabling involvement" with the affair between Maurice and Clive. As for the happy ending, we are victims of EMF's design.

1628 Watt, Ian. "Realism and the Novel," ENGLISH LITERATURE AND BRITISH PHILOSOPHY: A COLLECTION OF ESSAYS, ed by S. P. Rosenbaum (Chicago & Lond: University of Chicago P, 1971), pp. 65–85, espec 75–76.

The importance of time in the recent novel is a parallel development to that of realism in philosophy. The "life by time," mentioned by EMF in *Aspects of the Novel*, becomes as important as his "life by values" [though EMF would not agree].

1629 Webner, Hélène L. "E. M. Forster's Divine Comedy," RENASCENCE, XXIII (Winter 1971), 98–110.

The rites of passage in *A Passage to India* represent a passage to the Divine, the Caves represent the absence of God rather than his nonexistence, and the ceremonies in "Temple" are a beatific experience uniting Christian and Hindu elements in a redemptive and unifying experience. Mrs. Moore is most likely based on EMF's mother and his Aunt, Mrs. Aylward, who was profoundly Christian. EMF himself was not opposed to a mystic mythology or religion that would not threaten other values. [Webner agrees with Wilfred Stone (THE CAVE AND THE MOUNTAIN [1966]) that the triadic structure of *Passage* invites a speculative and philosophical interpretation; she agrees with George H. Thomson (THE FICTION OF E. M. FORSTER [1967]) that the novel's parts comprise a prelude, a wasteland, and an escape from the wasteland.] "Mosque" represents this world with its temptations and trials, its rationalism and materialism, and its imperfect intuitions of the divine; "Caves" is a Hell wherein separation occurs and wherein God is absent; "Temple" is a transcendent vision of God with Godbole and Mrs. Moore as mediators of His grace. [Extensive analysis of religious elements in *Passage*, which are more often Christian than is generally supposed.] The novel is not so much an attack upon Christianity as an illustration of some of its aspects. Thus Mrs. Moore's disillusionment in "Caves" is, in effect, "a Dark Night of the soul," which is part of "the Unitive Way." "It is because Mrs. Moore is a devout Christian contemplative that the poisoned atmosphere of Anglo-India and equally of the Marabar Caves affect her so severely." "The ghost" that is imputed to have caused the accident to the car in which Adela Quested and Ronny Heaslop are riding foreshadows Mrs. Moore's own strong influence after her death. The punkah wallah at the trial is associated with Godbole, as a reality principle; the naked man appears also when Godbole sings at Fielding's tea party and again as the servitor in the last scene on the lake. In the Caves, Mrs. Moore incurs disillusionment, but her Christianity is not obliterated; rather, it ultimately saves her and allows her to be a redemptive figure in "Temple." Mrs. Moore causes Adela to atone for her sin against Aziz through the Christian rite of confession, which leads to her conversion. In "Temple" Mrs. Moore figures as a redemptive agent through Godbole's memory of her and through the active presence of her son and daughter, Ralph and Stella. The principals incur a baptism when their boats collide in the tank. Fielding is seen as curious about religion and finally as mellowed by it through Mrs. Moore's agent, Stella, her daughter and his wife. [Interesting for its isolation of Christian elements in *Passage* and convincing discussion of them.]

1630 Wescott, Glenway. "A Dinner, a Talk, a Walk with Forster," NEW YORK TIMES BOOK REVIEW, 10 Oct 1971, pp. 2, 18, 20, 22.

EMF was a man not altogether happy but obliged to seem so, in fairness to others and in love for them. In short, EMF was a kind of saint. [Details given about his plans to publish *Maurice* in America if it could not be published in England (reveals that he was not indifferent about the novel being published). The American publication was to be entrusted to Christopher Isherwood. With the passage of the Sexual Practices Act in England in the wake of the Wolfenden Report, it could be published in England. Isherwood assigned his royalties to the National Institute of Arts and Letters for establishing an E. M. Forster Award to be given from time to time to a British writer residing in America.] EMF was "indomitable and instinctive and abiding"; his literary imperfections, such as the arbitrary deaths of his characters, became "a form of originality, altogether intentional and adamant." [A most revealing account.]

1631 Wilde, Alan. Christopher Isherwood (NY: Twayne, English Author Series, 1971), pp. 18, 20, 30, 32, 33, 34, 39, 40, 42, 55, 58, 84, 92, 127, 150, 153, 154.

[The number of references to EMF demonstrates how central his humanism and art were to the group of writers in the 1930s associated with Isherwood and W. H. Auden and how similar in theme, situation, and ironic method Isherwood's fiction is to EMF's.]

1632 Wilson, Colin. "A Man's Man," Spectator (Lond), CCXXVII (9 Oct 1971), 512–13; rptd in E. M. Forster: The Critical Heritage, ed by Philip Gardner (Lond & Boston: Routledge & Kegan Paul, 1973), pp. 453–56.

Maurice, unexpectedly, supplies the key to EMF's work and to his artistic tragedy. In his early novels he is convincingly an English Ibsen who wishes to shatter middle-class prejudices. But he has no standard of happiness and vitality to serve in these novels as a counterpoise. The violence and sensuality of *Where Angels Fear to Tread* are not much superior to the values that he detests. Honesty and decency also are unexciting. *Howards End* is quite ambiguous; EMF's early approbation of the Schlegels is greatly qualified by the end of the novel. With the publication of *Maurice*, EMF is seen to be a Platonic homosexual, elevating friendship above marriage. *Maurice* is a fine novel though simpler in structure than *Howards End* or *A Passage to India*. The ending of *Maurice* is unsatisfactory. EMF found that he could not express his homosexual predilections in *Passage*, so he stopped writing. He was thus abruptly halted in his progress toward becoming a great writer. [Thoughtful discussion.]

1972

1633 Amsel, Anja. "New Light on the Work of E. M. Forster," SOUTH LONDON ADVERTISER, 6 Oct 1972.
The stories in *The Life to Come and Other Stories* are masterly and add to our knowledge of EMF. "The Life to Come" explores hypocrisy sensitively.

1634 Anderson, Patrick. "Forster's Other Side," SUNDAY TELEGRAPH (Lond), 1 Oct 1972, p. 14.
The stories in *The Life to Come and Other Stories* represent EMF's retreat from the heterosexual novel, and they reveal more fantasy and Voltairean fun than *Maurice* allowed. EMF also wanted to prove that he could still write creatively. The result is as though Jane Austen was discovered to have indulged herself in writing licentious stories. "The Obelisk" is a "subversive romp"; the rest are somber or tragic. Violence is strong. The book has freshness and is beautifully written; it is less didactic and tougher than *Collected Short Stories*. "The Other Boat" has "sustained magic and strangeness" and is the last and best of the stories.

1635 Babington Smith, Constance. ROSE MACAULAY (Lond: Collins, 1972), pp. 103, 142, 200, 213.
Rose Macaulay first met EMF while he was working on *Aspects of the Novel*. She then became his devoted disciple. EMF became increasingly attached to Rose Macaulay toward the end of her life, while she regretted his anti-Christian stance. She agreed with EMF that "Dame" is a silly title, after she was made a Dame Commander of the British Empire in 1958.

1636 Barrett, William. "Ou-Boum or Bou-oum," TIME OF NEED: FORMS OF IMAGINATION IN THE TWENTIETH CENTURY (NY, Evanston, San Francisco, & Lond: Harper & Row 1972), pp. 283–311; also 312, 325–26, 339.
EMF's novels are conventional in form; they are marked by the presence of the novelist as commentator. EMF is the moralist who insists that good and evil are intermixed. His values in the abstract are unambiguous (individuality, decency, tolerance, and reasonableness) but are also capable of being parodied and are sometimes too general for the specific circumstances of life. He is, however, conscious of the abyss beneath "civilization." The

Englishman is particularly muddled in his emotions; it is more important, EMF feels, to educate the emotions than the intellect. In *The Longest Journey* Rickie Elliot's great tragedy is to die accepting his aunt's conventions. In this novel, Salisbury Cathedral and Stonehenge represent twin poles, civilization and the primitive. (The latter EMF accepts with reservations but realizes its importance.) EMF experienced in the Edwardian Age "the forward wave of frantic industrialization," but industrialism and housing developments that helped destroy the old were also a necessity. Like D. H. Lawrence, EMF is a romantic, stressing the need for man's kinship to nature as opposed to the dehumanizing aspects of industrialism and applied science. EMF, like Beethoven in the Fifth Symphony (*Howards End*), knows that the goblins of evil are there. They are present when Margaret Schlegel shivers at discovering the full extent of Henry's duplicity in the closing scene of the novel. In *A Passage to India*, EMF's curiosity ends by making him more sympathetic toward Hinduism than he was initially. He is partly revealed in Fielding but more so in Mrs. Moore. In the Marabar Caves she has a vision of nihilism against which the courage that might have eliminated the goblins in *Howards End* is of no avail. The nihilism induced by the echoes in the Caves is a fact that cannot be explained away, yet it is not the only fact. Another range of value organic to life is dramatized in "Temple." Salvation as it is depicted there will be universal and democratic, all matter and all spirit participating in it. The festival emphasizes that everything exists and that everything has value, in contrast to the Marabar Caves which in their echoes say that everything exists and that nothing has value. Both "Caves" and "Temple" represent indispensable poles in a religious vision; neither can be eliminated. After *Passage* the whisper of the Marabar prevented EMF from indulging in the illusions of fiction. He could not domesticate the Marabar in fiction because he could not bring himself to a state of spiritual excess, the physical violence of a Faulkner or the spiritual violence of a Proust. EMF knows that terror is present in life but keeps it at a distance, as Frost does in his poetry. EMF performs a service, however, in not letting us forget that darkness exists at the heart of being. [Interesting, though not profound observations, more pertinent in view of the book's thesis—that modern life is in a state of metaphysical crisis and ought not break its ties with primitive being—than as independent judgments.]

1637 Bedient, Calvin. "Lawrence and Forster in Italy," "E. M. Forster," ARCHITECTS OF THE SELF: GEORGE ELIOT, D. H. LAWRENCE, AND E. M. FORSTER (Berkeley & Los Angeles: University of California P, 1972), pp. 183–5, 199–65; also pp. 1–2, 21–30, 266–69; rvd from "The Fate of the Self: Self and Society in the Novels of George Eliot, D. H. Lawrence, and E. M. Forster," unpublished dissertation, University of Washington (1964).

"Lawrence and Forster in Italy": Lawrence and EMF sought to "restore . . . a sense of wonder to the body of the world," to reconcile once again "ideation and impulse." Both sought to restore the primacy of the unconscious self, and in so doing they embraced the subjectivity of the romantic writers, with its implied transcendence of the world of objects. They both sought renewal in Italy, not, like George Eliot, the renunciation of the self. She was a novelist of "self-extrusion"; Lawrence and EMF were novelists of "self-occupancy." [This is one of Bedient's typically opaque statements.] The self in Lawrence is to be fulfilled by instantaneous consummations; the self in EMF is to be fulfilled more incrementally by the process of observing proportion. For Lawrence, Italy is an either/or alternative (embrace sensuality or be damned); for EMF it is an opportunity to attain full humanity. In seeking such fullness EMF gives heed to intelligence; Lawrence doubts that it is necessary. In THE LOST GIRL Lawrence reveals his preference for an unalloyed sensuality. A fuller humanity is achieved in EMF's Italian novels; nature in them is positive, wholesome, and life-expansive. Mr. Emerson, however, in *A Room with a View* feels compelled to give intellectual form to what Italy offers. In Italy nature and truth are in perfect accord. In *Where Angels Fear to Tread* this accord is upset by caprice and by the presence of an alien element, "character." The gloriousness of life, as seen in this novel, is less significant than its difficulty. Gino Carella is strong in nature but weak in character and muddled in mind; Philip Herriton is clear-sighted but weak in character and in nature; Caroline Abbott approaches human completeness but lacks a mentor to teach her the holiness of direct desire. At the end the difficulty of being complete proves insurmountable to the characters. The English arrive in Italy too late: "character" has worked on them too early and now inhibits them; they are too cultured for their own good.

"E. M. Forster": EMF is seen as the individualist in an age that crushes the individual; but his is a stubborn, not a deep, faith. His two highest values are the Person and Romance. For EMF the individual and the cosmos both become a manifestation of the sacred. EMF maintains contact between the "I" and the infinite. Truth and seriousness are the final attributes of the Forsterian person. Romance is regarded as "Time's love for Eternity." [This fanciful kind of formulation is characteristic of Bedient's discourse.] Its chief forms and objects are "truth, love, friendship, procreation, art, the earth and its views." In *Howards End* Romance is on the defensive before the modern world; it may inhere in a place if that place suggests the eternal or the infinite. Rural life as the essence of Romance and the Person as an object are both in danger of disappearing. The Romantic person can become heroic when he tries to get the objective man to achieve his soul (see Margaret Schlegel's efforts in behalf of Henry Wilcox in *Howards End*). Margaret is, in short, a heroine of proportion and tries to "make the world safe for Romance." She fails, but EMF does not acknowledge her failure. The novel, as a result, is false and confused at the end, in chronicling a contrived triumph of Romance over Imperialism. The logic of the book requires a defeat by the proponents of Romance. At the end Margaret becomes too identified with the "unseen," as Helen had been previously. EMF's philosophy is more inclusive than either Lawrence's or George Eliot's, but he does not adhere to it steadily; he is not their superior, therefore, in characterization. His characters, objects, and places lack weight and association; a thinness of specification results.

In *A Passage to India* this thinness does not matter; it is redeemed there by an insistent, groping note. EMF's politics have a personal basis. Because of his social conservatism, he does not want class structure to change; his individualism, however, detests social organization. These traits, conservative and liberal alike, indicate his Romanticism. He stared the conservative out of countenance; Individualism and Romanticism remained. He would balance the claims of the community with those of private life, but in the end he comes down on the side of private life. The romantic socialism embraced by Mr. Emerson in *Room* develops into the mystic internationalism of *Passage*. His political realism does not allow him much hope, since he knows the limitations of his politics. In *Passage* the cherished EMF values—romance, individuality, personal relations—are threatened by a hostile macrocosm. India confronts and dwarfs his values: India is (1) the evil and confusion of Imperialism (administration without love, racism with sordid rationalizations); (2) the contemporary condition of man, a world without connection, peace, organic sanctity, romance; and (3) an emblem of the macrocosm—an inclusive, unsorted universe, "a nihilistic cosmos of insidious matter, of blind and ungenerous instinct." In India, Romance fails; beauty of place is lacking. Individuality fares no better; the Person dwindles to a mere individual. Fielding and Adela Quested are too rational to expand into Romantic selves. Plot exists in *Passage* to discover self-limitation rather than to lead to self-development. EMF in this novel is uncertain; his mind is "on the rack between a horrified skepticism as to whether spirit exists at all and a piqued interest in an Absolute Spirit" that is appalling because it is incomprehensible and vast. The Marabar Caves assert that the individual does not exist; they are a denial of spirit. Yet insofar as they assert the absence of God, they also imply His presence, elsewhere if not here. Even stone is not an obstacle to union; the stone hills, for example, are symbols of God. Balked in his quest for the personal, EMF reaches out to the universal and embraces a cosmic mysticism. The assurances of God's existence and influence are not decisive, so that the individual moves baffled between "a doubtful cosmos and a doubtful subterranean psyche." *Passage* is EMF's greatest novel because he was drawn out of himself to confront his basic certitudes; he did so honestly and directly. His own

"Brahma-like inclusiveness" in the novel is truly remarkable. [Bedient's underlying premises are debatable and represent a simplistic view of Victorian literature. The book is schematic and marred by an impressionistic formulation of intellectual constructs, by the elaboration of idiosyncratic or obvious ideas, and by an obtrusive high-flown style. There are many insights of value, however, in this overextended treatment.]

1638 Bell, Quentin. VIRGINIA WOOLF: A BIOGRAPHY (Lond: Hogarth P, 1972), Vol. I: VIRGINIA STEPHEN 1882–1912, pp. 171, 177, 214; Vol. II: MRS. WOOLF 1912–1941, pp. 12, 28, 29, 68, 74, 83, 86, 105, 111, 113, 129, 132–35, 138, 140, 155, 162, 163, 185, 188, 191, 204, 213, 224; publ as VIRGINIA WOOLF: A BIOGRAPHY (NY: Harcourt Brace Jovanovich, 1972), 2 vols in one, same format and pagination.

Virginia Woolf was delighted by EMF's praise of THE VOYAGE OUT. She commented on his timidity and charm. His adverse opinion of NIGHT AND DAY discouraged her, but it was delivered with typical discernment and kindness. Woolf and EMF loved and detested many of the same things, but there were also barriers between them. EMF was an established writer before Woolf published her first novel; his career as novelist was ending as hers began. He was not deeply interested in her experiments with time and psychology. He respected her achievement with her new methods in JACOB'S ROOM, MRS. DALLOWAY, and TO THE LIGHTHOUSE; but he felt that she had departed too far from actual life in her experimentalism. He found her feminism disturbing and felt that she was too sharply critical. He felt more affection for Leonard Woolf than for Virginia, yet he had a genuine affection for her and she respected his writings. In "Mrs. Bennett and Mr. Brown" (1924), she regarded EMF as a Georgian rather than an Edwardian novelist; but he had compromised to an extent with the older traditions of Bennett and Galsworthy. EMF reacted sharply to her critique of *Aspects of the Novel* ("Is Fiction an Art?"; 1927), with her championing of art as opposed to life; he judged her to be wrong rather than annoying in her judgments [correspondence of both quoted]. In his Rede lecture (1941; also in *Two Cheers for Democracy*) he maintained that she just escaped the dullness that her aestheticism threatened to bring with it. Woolf thought that EMF just escaped the dullness inherent in overt moralizing and overt use of classical mythology for symbolic purposes. In her Journal for May 1928, apropos of the suppression of Radclyffe Hall's THE WELL OF LONELINESS, she quoted EMF: he did not wish to be converted from sodomy, but he disliked Sapphism. EMF regarded THE WAVES as a classic and so reassured Woolf. In vain he urged her and Leonard to participate in a 1935 Congress of anti-fascist intellectuals in Paris; but sometimes, against her inclinations, EMF persuaded her in the 1930s to participate in political activity. In 1935 she was angry at him for his failure to support the appointment of a woman to the London

Library Committee; she remembered her interchange with him and refused to become a member of this committee when EMF asked her to do so in 1940, declining thereby to be a "sop" to public opinion. [Numerous incidental references preponderate in Vol. II, suggesting that it was then that EMF's relationship with Woolf became close; the book is valuable for contributing to an understanding of EMF's Bloomsbury milieu; the comments above all derive from Vol. II.]

1639 Birje-Patil, J. "The Way of All Sterility," QUEST (Bombay), LXXVII (July–Aug 1972), 77–80.

Maurice is an odd book to judge. Although its homosexual theme has contemporary interest, the book lacks the "perplexing discontinuities" that one associates with modernism. The grace and elegance of *Maurice* dispel any dated quality. EMF handles Maurice's homosexual awakening and the course of his emotional life with finesse, although EMF tends to obtrude editorially. Both society and nature are against Maurice; the result is EMF's despair concerning the homosexual cause. The defoliation of the greenwood in World War I caused EMF to seek emotional satisfaction in Indian rather than Greek culture. Lacking flamboyance and violence, EMF's book causes us to face the issues we might tend to disregard. Yet disappointment with *Maurice* continues. EMF's stance on heterosexual love is difficult to reconcile with his proclaimed liberal values. He implies that heterosexual love is a tribute paid to convention by the less imaginative and courageous. Perhaps the final rupture between Fielding and Aziz in *A Passage to India* is due more to their "uncompromising heterosexuality" than to the iniquities of the Raj. [An original observation.] [Excellent discussion.]

1640 Borrello, Alfred. AN E. M. FORSTER GLOSSARY (Metuchen, NJ: Scarecrow P, 1972).

[Explanation of allusions (cultural, historical, literary, etc.) in EMF's collected works. The biographical sketches and the summaries of novels are often perfunctory and reveal little sense of the use to which EMF put his materials in his works. The assumptions in the preface are questionable: that EMF's writing suffers from "opacity" as it recedes in time, and that the scholar, student, and interested reader who would wish to know EMF as he really is need only consult this volume rather than "the bewildering commentary" that has been written on his work. At the least, such a statement denigrates the great amount of excellent criticism on EMF. Furthermore, does even the ordinary reader have to have explained to him Falstaff, Faust, Richard Feveral (*sic*), Henry Fielding, Edward FitzGerald, Moll Flanders, Henry Ford, Saint Francis, Freud, The French Revolution (confining myself to entries under F)? There are many spelling and proofing errors. The book has residual usefulness in explaining the obscurer allusions in EMF's works, but it lacks a sure rationale for its existence.]

1641 Brace, Keith. "The Simple Truth behind the Ambiguities of E. M. Forster," BIRMINGHAM POST, 30 Sept 1972, "Saturday Magazine," p. 11.

Maurice showed the tragedy of EMF's life; not that he was homosexual but that he could not write about it openly. The stories in *The Life to Come and Other Stories* pose this question: Can literature be made from sexual situations that still may shock? Yes, when as in "The Life to Come," "The Other Boat," and "Dr. Woolacott," the homosexuality is used as a point of departure for studying human relations; No, in "The Obelisk," "What Does It Matter? A Morality" and "The Torque," when the homosexual situation is used as a basis for propaganda. "The Other Boat" and "The Life to Come" are powerful works.

1642 Bragg, Melvyn. "An 'Indecent' Art," WORLD (NY), I (5 Dec 1972), 58–59; rptd in part in CONTEMPORARY LITERARY CRITICISM, ed by Carolyn Riley and Barbara Harte (Detroit: Gale Research Co., 1974), II, 136.

One regrets EMF's lack of boldness, after perusing *The Life to Come and Other Stories*. If he had published his homosexual tales when they were written, he might have changed the course of literature and culture. "Ansell" contains all of EMF. Because he had to write despite his homosexuality, he sought outlets other than fiction, except for his unpublished stories. The stories are indications "of a possible and glorious future" but are also "a number of sad backward glances." They are often brilliant. They reveal EMF's addiction to melodrama, to which his homosexuality apparently gave new force. There is much to admire in these tales and much to regret in that they were not published when they were written and in that EMF was not then encouraged to write substantial fiction. [Stimulating account.]

1643 Capitanchik, Maurice. "The Novels of E. M. Forster," BOOKS AND BOOKMEN, XVII (May 1972), 14–16, 18; rptd in part in CONTEMPORARY LITERARY CRITICISM, ed by Carolyn Riley and Barbara Harte (Detroit: Gale Research Co., 1974), II, 135–36.

In *Howards End* EMF reveals his valuation of three facets of human life: self- knowledge, imaginative insight, and personal relationships. This novel is a major achievement because of the elegance of its style, the pertinence of the character drawing, and the relevance of its social insight. In *A Passage to India*, India figures as "an archaic, formless continuance of the earth" and as the home of several great civilizations in decay. EMF presents a conflict between religious, primitive, and instinctive life as opposed to the imposed order and "justice" of the British, which is all too often a denial of "the true civilisation of the heart" but which, at its best, defends heroically friendship and truth. Mrs. Moore realizes that the primitive impulse of sex is real power and that civilization is "an impudence." Adela Quested realizes this truth also in the presence of the courtroom punkah wallah. Although EMF values this highly primitive instinct, as an artist he also realizes that intelligence is the only weapon we have against fear and prejudice; it is her intelligence that allows Adela to retract her charge against Aziz. The characters all lack integration, as do the various societies presented in the novel. *Passage* represents a great stylistic achievement; its defect is an "ennuie." [Judgment is hardly substantiated.] In *Maurice* EMF demonstrates that a homosexual relationship can lead to self-fulfillment. EMF's contribution is this: to suggest in the realistic domestic novel the issues that underlie our civilization as a whole and the moral choices that we all have to make. He also poses the question as to whether our institutions and civilization are worth our giving up the sources of primitive renewal in ourselves and in nature. [Intelligent but unarresting summary of plots and themes in *The Longest Journey, A Room with a View*, and *Where Angels Fear to Tread*. Some new and interesting observations.]

1644 Craig, David. "The Clash between Sex and Culture," TIMES HIGHER EDUCATION SUPPLEMENT (Lond), 20 Dec 1972, p. 15.

For sixty years the subject that most concerned EMF, passion between men, was the one subject that as artist he could not treat. His homosexual fiction is not as good as his other writing, which portrays the clash between the genteel and uninhibited (*A Room with a View*), the managerial and the intellectual (*Howards End*), and the colonizers and the colonized (*A Passage to India*). The language was also not suitable for rendering homosexual experience. Also, the class differences made it difficult to enter into feelings of both parties when one of them was drawn from a lower class or an alien culture. In *The Life to Come and Other Stories* "Authur Snatchfold" says as much, or more, about the thoughts of businessman and milkman as it does about their sensuality. "The Life to Come" is more about the effects of "development" on backward nations than about homosexuality. The old English ruling class is etched memorably in "The Other Boat." The evasive language used in the sexual encounters interferes with their effectiveness. In this story Lionel's assault and murder of Cocoanut and his own subsequent suicide were triggered by his remembering his fight with "savages" in a desert war and by his horror at being trapped at his Indian destination by the colonized. In *Passage* there was greater harmony between EMF's material and what he made of it. [Excellent discussion.]

1645 Dick, Aliki Lafkidou. A STUDENT'S GUIDE TO BRITISH LITERATURE (Littleton, Colo: Libraries Unlimited, 1972), pp. 210–41.

[Lists principal books by EMF and on EMF.]

1646 Edel, Leon. "The Younger Generation," HENRY JAMES: THE MASTER, 1901–1916 (Philadelphia & NY: Lippincott; Lond: Hart-Davis, 1972), pp. 388–97, espec 389–90.

[Describes James's relations with the nascent Bloomsbury Group. James came in contact with all the members of old Bloomsbury when they were young. Details presented of EMF's visit to Henry James at Lamb House, Rye, in 1908. The visit to James was EMF's first encounter with a great man, but he claimed "that isn't my road." EMF was to remain "affectionately critical" of James.]

1647 "E. M. Forster," GLASGOW HERALD, 7 Oct 1972, "Saturday Extra," II.

The short stories in *The Life to Come and Other Stories* have a melancholy biographical interest. The death-wish appears frequently in the stories. Their intrinsic literary merit is not high, but the volume has value as psychological evidence.

1648 Emmett, Jr., V. J. "Verbal Truth and Truth of Mood in E. M. Forster's *A Passage to India*," ENGLISH LITERATURE IN TRANSITION, XV: 3 (1972), 199–212.

EMF's concern with language is evident in his consistent use of a distinction, propounded by Fielding in *A Passage to India*, between "verbal truth" and "truth to mood." Carelessness with the first in favor of the second, when factual accuracy is needed, can be disastrous (a failure of the critical faculty), just as the inability to make use of—or to understand—truth to mood can also be disastrous (a failure in imagination). [Excellent discussion follows, conclusively showing how the misunderstandings presented in the novel result from the faulty use of (or the failure to use) language appropriate to the given situation, as verbal truth or truth to mood may be the kind of truth needed at the moment.] In the early scenes Adela Quested is lacking in truth to mood and Aziz in verbal truth; only Fielding appreciates the role of each sort. Truth to mood can also be sinister when the Anglo-Indians allow themselves to become hysterical before the trial. Adela's rationalism is defective; her hysteria represents a truth of mood to her, based largely on her unconscious fears of sex. Mrs. Moore's nihilism, experienced in the Marabar Caves, is also expressed in terms of a disillusion with language as an expressive medium or mode of communication. The trial is the great moral test in the novel, which Mrs. Moore and Godbole fail to meet [though the crowd outside chanting Mrs. Moore's name causes Adela to retract her charge]. "Temple" emphasizes division rather than unity, the promise of which is undercut by disorder, the waywardness of the characters, and their moral decline. The novel is thus pessimistic and provides a negative and ironic gloss upon Whitman's "Passage to India." [Relates EMF to the analytical philosophers G. E. Moore, Bertrand Russell, and Ludwig Wittgenstein, the first two of whom were part of EMF's Cambridge; closer demonstration of his link to them would have been helpful.

Essay is provocative and there are many unusual insights, especially concerning the centrality of Fielding and the kinds of language used by EMF throughout. Other judgments are less persuasive: the alleged decline of Fielding and Aziz (overstated); the negative interpretation of the Mau ceremonies and the alleged identification of Hinduism with Christianity as both untenable religions; the interpretation of comedy (surrounding Godbole and the festival) as a pejorative rather than a distancing element; the failure to see Mrs. Moore as a transfigured individual in death who acts as a reconciling agent at Mau directly or through her children; the symbolic interpretation of rain as a hostile instead of a fructifying agent; and the overlooking of essays on India written from 1913 to 1915 that are friendly to Hinduism (collected in *"Albergo Empedocle" and Other Writings by E. M. Forster*, ed by George H. Thomson, 1971). The consistency of this essay is admirable.]

1649 Espey, David. B. "The Imperial Protagonist: Hero and Anti-Hero in Fiction of the Late British Empire," DISSERTATION ABSTRACTS INTERNATIONAL, XXXIII (1972), 6423A. Unpublished dissertation, University of Michigan, 1971.
[On Kipling, Conrad, Orwell, and EMF.]

1650 Farber, Anne. "Forster's Stature," COMMENTARY, LIII (May 1972), 32, 34, 36.
EMF's references to "friend" in "What I Believe" (*Two Cheers for Democracy*) are not necessarily homosexual in implication, as they are in *Maurice*. But doubts as to EMF's knowledge of the actual relationships of men and women are dispelled when we read his works. The sociological achievement in *Howards End* and MIDDLEMARCH were inseparable from (not prior to) the novelistic visions of EMF and George Eliot. But the novels tell us more than the sociological; they have psychological and moral insight as well. Writers can analyze with authority matters that they might not have known about from their personal experience. Thus it is possible for a homosexual author to write with authority about heterosexual relationships. [Discussion of Cynthia Ozick's "Forster as Homosexual" (1971).]

1651 Faulkner, Peter. "Rabelaisian Humor," NEW HUMANIST (Lond), LXXXVIII (Dec 1972), pp. 341–42.
The stories in *The Life to Come and Other Stories* reveal a Rabelaisian sense of humor, especially in "What Does It Matter? A Morality," in which sexual behavior is deemed a private matter. (As a result, the country of Pottibakia is adjudged subversive.) "The Life to Come" begins well, but the idea of a native's mistaking homosexual for Christian love cannot sustain the story; "The Other Boat," a powerful story, has a romantic ending in which a greater complexity is necessary. "Arthur Snatchfold," a more casual story,

succeeds better, especially in its evocation of static middle-class society and in its protest concerning rigid laws against homosexuality. One regrets the loss to literature caused by EMF's homosexuality and by the repressive attitudes of his society toward homosexuals. EMF's forte was the exploring of human relationships. When he turned to writing of love in terms of casual sexual encounters, he limited his creativity.

1652 Feinstein, Elaine. "Loving," London Magazine, nsXI (Jan 1972), 154–57.

Maurice presents two strong passions: the need for love and the will to maintain dignity in face of its loss. It is not the perhaps arbitrary conclusion that convinces in the book; it is the torment that precedes it. A sharp, simple style befits the subject. The female characters in this novel are petty and contrast with the greatness of soul revealed in EMF's women in other novels. For EMF, Maurice's earlier, cerebral approach to love under Clive Durham's tutelage is less valid than his later spontaneous recognition of his nature and his acting in accord with it in the relationship with Alec Scudder. EMF also leaves us with the sense that Maurice will not escape further loss and pain.

1653 Finkelstein, Bonnie Blumenthal. "The Role of Women in the Novels of E. M. Forster with Parallels to the Role of Homosexuals in *Maurice*," Dissertation Abstracts International, XXXIII (1972), p. 2931A. Unpublished dissertation, Columbia University, 1972; rvd as Forster's Women: Eternal Differences (NY & Lond: Columbia UP, 1975).

1654 Fraser, G. S. "The English Novel," The Twentieth Century Mind: History, Ideas, and Literature in Britain, Vol II, 1918–1945, ed by C. B. Cox and A. E. Dyson (Lond & NY: Oxford UP, 1972), pp. 373–416, espec 373, 377, 394–99; also ix, 7.

EMF is supreme as a novelist, not as a nonfiction writer. *A Passage to India* is a great book. It is the last great English traditional novel and is a book embodying at its best the middle-class ethos. EMF is a novelist of the middle-class mind at its most confident and self-critical. *Passage* is also the last great novel "of unquestionable authorial authority." The moral stance is strong because it is not assertive. The boom in the Marabar Caves is ambiguously a symbol of acceptance and rejection, and Mrs. Moore ambiguously reveals "mystical despair and hopeless sanctity." Civilization ambiguously rests on fine discriminations and a rigid order. In Chandrapore there is contrasted the sterile order of the Anglo-Indians and the vital chaos of Indian culture and religion. Despite their effort involved to supplant sterile institutions, EMF's admirable characters achieve their identity and importance in social circumstances, not by turning from them like D. H.

Lawrence's characters. The effort, even if arduous or futile, is what ultimately matters. (Aziz, Fielding, and Adela Quested make such an effort.) EMF contrasts the rancor of the English community before the trial with the hysterical exultation of the Indians after it; both reactions are signs of weakness. EMF contrasts Mrs. Moore's negative mysticism in the Marabar Caves and later with the positive mysticism, "the creative muddle" of the Hindu festival. Aziz and Fielding may feel attraction because they are both members of races that have conquered the Hindus. EMF places a high value on love that involves conscience, intelligence, and will; but such love is all too often absent. This great stress on brotherly love appealed to such writers in the 1930s as Auden and Isherwood. EMF's central moral quality embodied in his art is "an intelligent patience." There is a rigorous separation in his characters between those who are damned and those who are saved; EMF reveals thereby "a neo-Calvinistic" judgment. In the need of his characters to stand alone, as in the lack of passion in his novels, EMF reveals his own Puritan temperament. [Discerning remarks.]

1655 Friedman, Alan. "The Novel," THE TWENTIETH CENTURY MIND: HISTORY, IDEALS, AND LITERATURE IN BRITAIN, Vol I, 1900–1918, ed by C. B. Cox and A. E. Dyson, (Lond & NY: Oxford UP, 1972), pp. 431–36, espec 430–34; also 221, 407.

Along with Henry James and Joseph Conrad, EMF is modern by virtue of his openendedness, as opposed to the tautness of realists such as Arnold Bennett. EMF emphasizes the self in contrast to the forms of society; he is devoted to symbolism and to "symbolic geography." Like other moderns EMF suggests through place the unconscious levels of experience. EMF's emphasis on growth in the self enables him to open out in his novels, when Lucy Honeychurch in *A Room with a View*, for example, learns the value of human feeling and bodily love. EMF in *Howards End* succeeds in documenting the social world in the Edwardian age. This novel is superior in its comedy, its prophetic tone, its suggestion that Howards End house is "a microcosm of the new century's inescapable fate." At Howards End the main segments of the middle class connect. Howards End is also emblematic of the older, pre-modern England, while Ruth Wilcox represents the natural world, rural tradition, and primitive England. The incidents are often more symbolically arresting than convincing as realistic renditions of experience. Margaret's marriage and Jacky as Henry Wilcox's former mistress strain credibility, but Helen as mother of a child by Leonard Bast is one of EMF's best touches. Despite its flaws *Howards End* achieves the expansion that EMF in *Aspects of the Novel* posits for memorable fiction. [Excellent short account. David Bell in "Philosophy" traces the influence of G. E. Moore upon EMF and Virginia Woolf. John Wain in "Poetry" challenges EMF's views of the early T. S. Eliot: his poetry was not escapist, as EMF maintains.]

1656 Fry, Roger. LETTERS OF ROGER FRY, ed by Denys Sutton, Vol I, 1878–1913, Vol II, 1913–34 [the two vols paginated as one] (Lond: Chatto & Windus, 1972; NY: Random House, 1973), pp. 6n, 92, 94, 95, 284, 285, 485, 486, 540n, 544, 555, 573, 575, 594, 621, 632, 691, 716.

[Many incidental references. "Introduction" establishes the close friendship between Fry and EMF (cf., EMF's "Roger Fry: An Obituary Notice," *Abinger Harvest*)]. Letter to R. C. Trevelyan (May 1907), *The Longest Journey* is fascinating. EMF says some things wonderfully. The book has an atmosphere all its own. EMF has genius of a kind, this book being reminiscent of Gorki. Letter to Virginia Woolf (20 July 1920), "The Story of the Siren" is memorable except as it is repetitive of earlier stories by EMF. Letter to Virginia Woolf (26 Oct 1922), [Fry likes "Our Graves in Gallipoli: A Dialogue," NEW LEADER, 20 Oct 1922; also in *Abinger Harvest.*] This essay is the best thing EMF has done on a small scale. Letter to Virginia Woolf (2 July 1924), Charles Mauron has started translating *A Passage to India*, which has marvelous texture and beautiful writing, though in the late parts of the book there is too much mysticism. Until Aziz's acquittal, the book goes perfectly; after that the design gets "wobbly" and indistinct because EMF then has too many themes to develop. EMF is an artist, but he despises his art and thinks he ought to be more than an artist. Maybe he goes at his art too directly and self-consciously. [See Virginia Woolf, ROGER FRY: A BIOGRAPHY (1940), p. 240; letter in fuller form here.] Letter to Helen Anrep (c. 1928), reports from Virginia Woolf that EMF seems to be unhappy and lacking in confidence. [See a similar report in 1929, CARRINGTON: LETTERS AND EXTRACTS FROM HER DIARIES, ed by David Garnett (Lond: Jonathan Cape; NY: Holt, Rinehart & Winston, 1970), pp. 404–5.] Letter to Gerald Brenan (19 April 1934), EMF's *Goldsworthy Lowes Dickinson* is "beautifully done," and it was a difficult thing to do. Hopefully EMF can get some new subject and construct his narratives more solidly. He exploits too much his own fancy.

1657 Gillie, Christopher. "Novelists of Human Culture: E. M. Forster, D. H. Lawrence," "E. M. Forster (1879–1970)," LONGMAN COMPANION TO ENGLISH LITERATURE (Lond: Longman, 1972), pp. 216–17, 523–24; also 213, 218, 220, 569, 696–97.

"Novelists of Human Culture": EMF lies between the social "materialism" of Wells, Bennett, and Galsworthy and the intellectuality of James and Conrad. EMF's first four novels insist on the material basis of British civilization but satirize the obtuseness that allows people to accept it uncritically. In these books EMF also discriminates the qualities of intellect that allow the individual to escape from this materialism. EMF's enlightenment makes him a central novelist; his keen and subtle comedy gives his work freshness. Except for *A Passage to India* he is not a first-rank novelist because he lacks poetic power, the power to create a substantial image of what it is like to be human. "E. M. Forster": [Review of career.] EMF's books illustrate how blind conformity to social conventions leads to an inability to see the truth in the unexpected, to use the intelligence critically, and to value spontaneous life. His pervasive symbolism is his most signal contribution to the art of fiction. [Informed summaries of *Howards End* and *Passage.*]

> **1658** Gill, Richard. "Disputed Heritage: The Edwardians and the Country House: Wells, Forster, Galsworthy, Ford," HAPPY RURAL SEAT: THE ENGLISH COUNTRY HOUSE AND THE LITERARY IMAGINA-TION (New Haven & Lond: Yale UP, 1972), pp. 95–132, espec 108–15; also 6, 13, 14, 144, 157, 191, 194, 196, 206, 208, 213, 222, 246, 272–73.

Parallels exist between *Howards End* and James's THE SPOILS OF POYNTON, especially in the situation of an elderly woman searching for a spiritual heir for a cherished house. Parallels exist also with H. G. Wells's TONO-BUNGAY: Bladesover house and Howards End are seen in relation to a changing England, and Edward Pondevero and the Wilcoxes come from the same rootless, materialistic milieu. In *Marianne Thornton* EMF shows what Battersea Rise and a rural Hertfordshire house [Rooksnest] (the prototype for Howards End house) meant to him. Howards End is only the most outstanding of the houses that signify much for EMF: Windy Corner in *A Room with a View*, Cadover in *The Longest Journey*, the manor house in *England's Pleasant Land*. The many meanings assigned to Howards End by critics indicate its richness as a symbol: England, nature, the past, the reconciliation of the masculine and feminine natures. It is an integrative symbol and a criterion for assessing characters in the novel: those are most admirable (e.g., Ruth Wilcox and Margaret Schlegel) who are the most closely assimilated to it. It is also a stage for the final reconciliation among the characters. The houses in Virginia Woolf's BETWEEN THE ACTS, Joyce Cary's TO BE A PILGRIM, and Evelyn Waugh's BRIDESHEAD REVISITED are also evocative symbols of England in the succession of Howards End.

> **1659** Gish, Robert. "Forster as Fabulist: Proverbs and Parables in *A Passage to India*," ENGLISH LITERATURE IN TRANSITION, XV: 4 (1972), 245–56.

There is purpose and design in EMF's use of proverbs and parables in *A Passage to India;* they are organically part of the construction and meaning of the book; and they are basic to an understanding of EMF as a fabulist. The proverbs and parables are sometimes used straightforwardly, sometimes ironically.

> **1660** Godfrey, Denis, "Book Reviews," DALHOUSIE REVIEW, LII (Spring 1972), 136–38.

Maurice presents a young man's discovery of his abnormality through the means of tragedy and nightmare. It does not date because the homosexual individual is still anxious about his status and his identity and still feels the need to achieve self-justification. EMF creates sympathy for his protagonist's plight by viewing him with objectivity. This objectivity and the reader's credulity characterize *Maurice*'s love affair with Clive Durham, but disappear when EMF writes about the affair between Maurice and Alec Scudder. In literature, as in life, the permanent homosexual relationship is impossible to achieve. Homosexuality figures overtly only in *The Longest Journey* among the prewar novels, but it may account for EMF's extraordinary insight into the feminine mind. His homosexuality may also have introduced into *Howards End* and *A Passage to India* a note of spiritual reserve that qualifies the optimism expressed in them, a note also characteristic of *Maurice*.

1661 Goldknopf, David. THE LIFE OF THE NOVEL (Chicago & Lond: University of Chicago P, 1972), pp. 136, 178.

EMF in *Aspects of the Novel* somewhat hesitantly defines one truth about the modern novel: it resists the tyranny of plot.

1662 Grierson, Edward. THE DEATH OF THE IMPERIAL DREAM: THE BRITISH COMMONWEALTH AND EMPIRE 1775–1969 (Garden City, NY: Doubleday; Lond: Collins, 1972), pp. 85, 86, 91, 279, 321.

Even sympathetic Englishmen in India such as G. O. Trevelyan found the amalgamation of conqueror and conquered to be "impracticable," the implication also of the closing sequence in *A Passage to India*. Englishmen drifted too easily, in the early nineteenth century, into the idea of being superior to the Indians; the English women did likewise, as EMF shows in *Passage*. After the 1857 Mutiny the world of companionship celebrated in G. O. Trevelyan's THE COMPETITION WALLAH declined into the chilling relationships between the races depicted in EMF's Chandrapore. The Club, as presented in Maugham's work and EMF's *Passage*, was a necessary adjunct to the British rule in colonial dependencies. Despite all defects, the English were incorruptible in the administering of justice: see the EMF character who complains that even if an English official could be bribed, he would find for the other side anyway. [Scattered but interesting references to *A Passage to India*.]

1663 Haskell, Molly. "A Refuge among Contemporary Novels," VILLAGE VOICE (NY), 8 June 1972, pp. 25–26.

EMF's homosexuality in *Maurice* seems more natural than D. H. Lawrence's strident heterosexuality. The character of Maurice is a theoretical construct, but the novel has its successes: the character of Clive Durham, the rendering of two families, and "the delicacy, the humor, the particularity, the feeling, the insights" that make the book "a refuge among contemporary novels." But *Maurice* does seem to be propaganda fiction. The happy ending in *Howards End* has a more provisional quality than it does in *Maurice*, in which it seems to have preceded the characters and determined their relationships. The ending is false because EMF does not feel it viscerally. EMF in *Maurice* tries to embrace the Dionysian spirit as a sexual force rather than as a cosmic force. The element of compromise (underlying the ethos of "connection") is lacking in this novel; in this respect and in its embracing of natural forces, *Maurice* is the most Lawrentian of the novels. Alec Scudder is a fantasy, a literary symbol of total physicality. If EMF satirizes the values and the undeveloped qualities of middle classes he never cuts himself off from them as the classes that he hopes to reach and influence. For EMF, passion is not so much sex as it is a passion for life ranged against the forces of convention; as represented in Margaret Schlegel, passion becomes affection. EMF's portraits of women are remarkable, and he sympathizes with their aspirations for more complete existences. He is also committed to marriage and the family because he values human relationships and civilization so highly; but he also has doubts about them. The other side to this pessimism is the forced optimism of *Maurice*, which celebrates a relationship that can avoid the pitfalls of heterosexuality and marriage. EMF loves his characters, even for their flaws, as he loves the limited Maurice. Maurice has small insight and a limited capacity for love but a great capacity for suffering; and EMF has a great capacity for understanding him. EMF is unfair to Clive Durham, and insofar as Clive represents EMF, to himself. We find it harder to be sympathetic with Maurice when Clive is so slighted. A quality of innocence obtrudes, too, in Maurice; his flight with Alec Scudder "is the triumph of life lived rather than understood, and love enjoyed in the flesh rather than in the imagination." The message of the book may be that possibility for such fulfillment does exist. [Consistently interesting critique.]

1664 Heine, Elizabeth. "Rickie Elliot and the Cow: The Cambridge Apostles and *The Longest Journey*," ENGLISH LITERATURE IN TRANSITION, XV: 2 (1972), 116–34.

The symbols in *The Longest Journey* convey EMF's philosophy; the symbols give immediacy to the ideas but at times make the novel too overtly allegorical. In Stephen Wonham there is projected the reality that must be faced, in Agnes Pembroke the unreality that must be shunned. Mrs. Failing represents embittered experience. In Rickie Elliot and Stewart Ansell EMF presents opposing views of reality to be found in Cambridge: the poetic versus the rational. In the Apostles Group there is discernible over a fifteen-year period a shift from J. M. E. McTaggart's Hegelian idealism to G. E. Moore's rationalism (PRINCIPIA ETHICA, 1903) to Lytton Strachey's psychological probing and John Maynard Keynes's analytic economics. Ansell represents attitudes of both Moore and Strachey, "a symbolic compendium of the friendship, honesty, and rational investigation of reality" that forms one aspect of the philosophies dominant among the Apostles in the early 1900s. Rickie represents the other aspect: the poetic mysticism of Dickinson and McTaggart. Rickie's mysticism is related not only to McTaggart's but also to Bertrand Russell's; both men stressed the unity that is apprehended and the visionary apprehension of it. In MYSTICISM AND LOGIC Russell expresses a concept crucial to *Journey*, that mysticism is valuable as a mode of feeling but erroneous as a way of thinking. G. E. Moore adopted a mean position between McTaggart's and Dickinson's tendency to regard the apprehending of the beautiful as a mystic experience and Russell's stress upon a psychic apprehension of an objective reality. Moore emphasizes the reality of "the Good" rather than the psychological validation of it; Strachey extends the psychical apprehension of reality beyond Russell's position. Ansell's position in *Journey* is similar to the mean position of G. E. Moore. In the development of the novel EMF wishes to synthesize the earthy reality of Stephen Wonham with the contrasting ideals of Rickie and Ansell, to reconcile the spirit of earth in Stephen with the religious "soul" in Rickie and the humanistic "spirit" in Ansell.

The question concerning the reality of the cow is basic to the complex symbolism in the novel. EMF demonstrates how mystical and rational views of reality intertwine and reinforce each other in the eternal cosmic forces of night-and-day and sun-and-moon-and-stars, and in the circles-within-squares image. (At the center of the Cadbury Rings brotherhood and love are implied as the prime reality.) To the extent that Agnes represents the "sun" for Rickie, he is mistaken; to the extent that he divines her unreality, he judges her rightly. After his marriage to her, the cow "disappears," and Agnes's light is insufficient to prevent his world from darkening. The fireboat and Orion images betoken Stephen's and Mrs. Elliot's goodness and immortality. All the symbols of the novel converge at the end to establish its final meaning. Rickie loses faith in what the meaningful symbols signify, and he deserves to die. He is punished for his weakness, but the best part of him, in his stories and novel, survives as an influence on Stephen. *Journey* ends with the affirmation of brotherhood when Stephen salutes his child. He and EMF take the rational view of mysticism: immortality is beyond our grasp, but a possibility thereof exists through memory and progeny; there may be even an immortality of the soul since men persist in thinking about it. Rickie dies because he is powerless to defend the poetry that he and EMF believe in against the pressures of Victorian convention; but EMF implies his essential worth and the worth of his imagination through the symbols used to depict him. The poetry in Rickie will be preserved at the end of the novel through Stephen and Ansell who will control, if not contain, the Sawstonian Pembrokes. EMF wishes to preserve the mysticism of McTaggart and Dickinson; but like Russell he values rational thought, particularly as it may be applied to mystic emotions. EMF's "compromise is also in some ways similar to the move from Cambridge philosophizing to the rational aestheticism of Bloomsbury." [Interesting, well-informed, original, well-developed article.]

> **1665** Hewitt, Douglas. THE APPROACH TO FICTION: GOOD AND BAD READINGS OF NOVELS (Lond: Longman, 1972), pp. 56, 77, 117, 178–79, 188.

The feeling of EMF and Virginia Woolf that the dominance of plot in fiction is deplorable is perhaps exaggerated, since life itself is made up of sequential activity. The tone of *A Passage to India* ("irony confronting muddle") absorbs potentially controversial material so that we yield it provisional assent. The opening chapter conjoins the grotesque, the beautiful, and the muddled, within a consistently ironic vision. EMF therefore can generalize and comment on the action and characters without causing us as readers to reject his world. He only fails when this characteristic tone is in abeyance. [Discussion primarily of Trollope's THE WAY WE LIVE NOW as a realistic novel, Dickens's LITTLE DORRIT as a symbolical novel, and Peacock's CROTCHET CASTLE as a novel of ideas.]

> **1666** Hillman, Martin. "Storytelling Wealth," TRIBUNE (Lond), 1 Dec 1972, p. 9.

EMF's disciplined genius is well-suited for the short story. In *The Life to Come and Other Stories* EMF reveals his notable ability to penetrate the masks of people to reach "the sad-silly, tragi-comic interior realities."

> **1667** Holroyd, Michael. "William Gerhardie," ENCOUNTER (Lond), XXXVIII (March 1972), 83–88; rptd in UNRECEIVED OPINIONS (Lond: Heinemann, 1973; NY: Holt, 1974), pp. 119–48.

William Gerhardie's career is like EMF's: a prolific outpouring of novels and then silence. EMF wrote six novels over nineteen years; Gerhardie, seven over sixteen. EMF wrote no novels after 1924 and lived until 1970; Gerhardie wrote none after 1938 and is still alive. EMF's reputation swelled every year that he failed to write a novel, but Gerhardie vanished from the literary scene altogether. EMF's survival in the public consciousness has largely been due to zealous disciples who have been vociferous and who are agreed on the greatness of *A Passage to India* and *Howards End*. Gerhardie has lacked such disciples, and among his readers there is no such agreement as to his best work. Gerhardie has been long at work on a tetralogy in one volume.

> **1668** Howe, Irving. "Introduction" ["The Machine Stops"], CLASSICS OF MODERN FICTION, 2nd ed, ed by Irving Howe (NY: Har-

court Brace Jovanovich, 1972), pp. 233–40; EMF is not included in 1st ed, 1968.

In "The Machine Stops," people are now content to stay in their own rooms, and that is the source for their social and moral degeneration in a world gone insane through an excess of rationalism. The people have lost their humanity; the line of the story consists in Kuno's realization of this truth, his gradual attempt to recover his humanity, and his inability, therefore, to remain any longer in his own room. The compression of the story, its cleverness of detail, and its unobtrusive style account for its impact. In the opening conversation between Kuno and Vashti (his mother), EMF depicts a horror of direct experience and a desire to pursue ideas only as long as they remain demarcated from actual people and experience. This story embodies the chief characteristic of anti-utopian fiction: it does not deny progress but projects the nightmare reality when progress is realized. At such a time technique outruns a concern with values. The question posed by anti-utopian work is, "Can human nature be manufactured, or completely conditioned?" There are strivings and aspirations in human nature that cannot be suppressed indefinitely, but that can be suppressed at any given moment. In this genre the contrast is present between the misery of the independent individual and the placidity of the obedient. In anti-utopian fiction, characters are not well developed since in such a society they are by nature dehumanized; they can only aspire wistfully to the human relationships that form the preserve of ordinary fiction. The difficulties for a writer in this genre are great since the ordinary emotions that he might wish to utilize are conspicuous by their absence, and characters are simple rather than complex since they predominantly illustrate mental attitudes. Anti-utopian fiction derives its impact in a number of ways: (1) it posits a flaw in the perfect society (Kuno's rebelliousness); (2) it illustrates a passionately projected idea that is dramatically simple but historically complex (a dire transmutation of values has occurred); (3) it makes clever use of substantiating detail (see Kuno's revelling in the fresh air and his rediscovery of human emotions at the end); (4) it strains our sense of the probable but does not violate our sense of the possible (in EMF's story a society similar to our own has gone one step beyond ours to display a humanity devoid of human traits and aspirations); (5) it depends on the reader's ability to recollect historically (especially the power that the idea of a Golden Age has exerted over the European imagination). ["The Machines Stops" rptd, "Notes on the Authors" (Biographical Sketch). An important and germinal discussion, relating "The Machine Stops" to the central features of anti-utopian fiction.]

1669 Hunter, Alan. "E. M. Forster's Remains," EASTERN DAILY PRESS (Norwich), 27 Oct 1972, p. 25.
The stories in *The Life to Come and Other Stories* are not of the first rank.

Their structure is often faulty, the characters lack depth, the narratives are hazy.

1670 Hynes, Samuel. "Introduction: A Note on 'Edwardian,'" EWARDIAN OCCASIONS: ESSAYS ON ENGLISH WRITING IN THE EARLY TWENTIETH CENTURY (NY: Oxford UP; Lond: Routledge & Kegan Paul, 1972), pp. 1–12.

Men were rightly aware that a change in man's consciousness was taking place during the years 1900–1914, but the change was concerned with social rather than aesthetic matters. The notion of literature as being necessarily related to the social thought of the age was Edwardian. The Edwardians were also preoccupied with history, and realistic novelists of the age tried to recreate the age in their works, EMF, for example, recording in his fiction "the historical fact of suburbanism." Also, EMF reveals the pessimism that was perhaps the strongest note, aesthetically and philosophically, in Edwardian literature. Modernism was given a new start by the World War I; the Edwardian concern with society and value was lost, perhaps regrettably, in a self-consciously aesthetic age.

1671 Jennings, Elizabeth. "Aware and Unaware," ENCOUNTER (Lond), XXXVIII (April 1972), 83.

EMF's *Maurice* has considerable value; it is beautifully written and shaped; its artifice does not obtrude. EMF treats his subject with great delicacy and compassion. This subject is that of the other novels: the contrast between "the aware and the unaware mind and heart." This theme is best realized in Maurice Hall and Clive Durham. *Maurice* has subtlety and clarity, the characters are projected in the round, and the incidents and emotions are depicted with great skill.

1672 Kitchen, Paddy. "Different Loves," SCOTSMAN (Edinburgh), 7 Oct 1972, p. 3.

The stories in *The Life to Come and Other Stories* are not satisfying, although "The Other Boat" and "Arthur Snatchfold" are brilliant as narratives with a twist at the end. But the Forsterian "patches" are admirable, as in the description of social life in "Arthur Snatchfold." EMF's darker and "sexier" side is more apparent here than in *Maurice.*

1673 Kondo, Ineko. "Denki to Sakuhin: E. M. Forster to *Maurice*" (Biography and the Work: E. M. Forster and *Maurice*), EIGO SEINEN (Tokyo), CXVIII (1 April 1972), 14–16.

Maurice is important not only in itself but for the insight it gives into EMF's other work. It is a work of art, not a tract or comedy of manners, because of EMF's persistent concern with Maurice's personal awareness of homosexuality and with his relationships to others. Several factors account for the unconvincing happy ending: EMF always kept his intense love for people once he committed himself to them, and it was natural for him to have affairs with those from the working class. *Maurice* is a novel of wish fulfillment. It was written in 1913–1914 before EMF had had satisfying sexual relationships. Though EMF tries to give distance to Maurice, his hero is still closely identified with EMF. If EMF had achieved the imaginative reality of A PORTRAIT OF THE ARTIST AS A YOUNG MAN or of SONS AND LOVERS, the happy ending of *Maurice* would have been more convincing. The biographical approach to *Maurice* is inevitable despite the danger of confusing the work and its author. *Maurice*, as it reflects EMF's own homosexuality, helps us understand his protest (along with Virginia Woolf's) of the banning of Radclyffe Hall's THE WELL OF LONELINESS (1928), a novel that expressed the author's desire for freedom to express homosexual emotion. In *Maurice*, EMF, like D. H. Lawrence, criticized the life style of the English middle and upper classes and affirmed his own fundamental humanity in his appreciation of the working class. *Maurice* reveals some of the same violence underlying EMF's other books, such as *Howards End*. [In Japanese.]

1674 Kubal, David L. OUTSIDE THE WHALE: GEORGE ORWELL'S ART AND POLITICS (Notre Dame & Lond: University of Notre Dame P, 1972), pp. 33, 78, 127, 142, 143, 153*n*.
Orwell's liberal faith is similar to that expressed by EMF in "What I Believe" (*Two Cheers for Democracy*). BURMESE DAYS is not as profound as Conrad's "Heart of Darkness" or as accomplished as *A Passage to India*. Like EMF Orwell deals with imperialism not in the abstract but as it determines human relationships. Like EMF, Orwell in ANIMAL FARM stresses the need for the nonrational as well as the rational. Orwell is to be related to the enlightened liberal thought of Matthew Arnold and EMF.

1675 Lafourçade, Françoise. "Symbole, Symbolisme et Prophétie dans *A Passage to India*" (Symbol, Symbolism and Prophecy in *A Passage to India*), CALIBAN (Toulouse), IX (1972), 122–34.
A Passage to India is a prophetic novel in EMF's sense of "prophecy" as he defines it in *Aspects of the Novel*. The prophet not only predicts the future but is an intermediary between the visible and invisible worlds, the natural and the supernatural. EMF did predict the civil war that occurred when partition took place in India after World War II. But EMF means by "prophecy" something more radical and fundamental than predicting the future. Prophecy is the revelation rather than the prediction of reality. For EMF the personal relationship acquires the sanction of the supernatural, characters become mythical, and symbols evoke an ineffable reality. (The repeated symbol achieves a musical effect.) Repeated symbols expand in *Passage*, achieve a prophetic dimension, and perform a prophetic function. [Article is pedestrian and obvious.] [In French.]

1676 Laws, Frederick. "Forster Miscellanies," DAILY TELEGRAPH (Lond), 14 Dec 1972, p. 7.

[Descriptive review account of *The Life to Come and Other Stories* and *Two Cheers for Democracy* in the Abinger Edition.]

1677 Leavis, F. R. "Élites, Oligarchies and an Educated Public," NOR SHALL MY SWORD: DISCOURSES ON PLURALISM, COMPASSION AND SOCIAL HOPE (Lond: Chatto & Windus; NY: Barnes & Noble, 1972), pp. 201–28, espec. 223–27.

EMF's *A Passage to India* must be seen in its widest possible aspect; and when one considers it in this way, he is disappointed. EMF is unfair to the English in the novel, in that he undervalues the vast creative work done by the English in India. EMF in *Passage* is still too self-enclosed, too much the product, and the object of veneration, of a coterie. On the basis of D. H. Lawrence's criticisms of EMF, EMF misses "the full and profound creativity that draws from sources closed to the selfhood." EMF's ironic poise is equivocal; he has not earned his enlightenment and wisdom. Mrs. Moore's crisis is not genuine; she does not exist, or she only exists for EMF to make a statement impressive to his Bloomsbury peers. What EMF did was to give the Bloomsbury ethos respectability and prestige, and so obscure its essential vulgarity. [Main argument of essay: elites and oligarchies are necessary, but so is an enlightened public to check, control, and use them; this public may be fostered by a concerned, deep-thrusting literary criticism, which will place literary values in their broadest context. That EMF did dramatize an essential facet of British rule in India—its arrogance, insularity, and racial antipathy—is proved by Benita Parry's DELUSIONS AND DISCOVERIES (1972). EMF shows some awareness of the British contribution in the administration of justice and in education; Fielding, Mrs. Moore, and Adela Quested are English but different in temper and ethos from the typical Anglo-Indian officials. The truth about *Passage* is more nearly approximated in Leavis's "E. M. Forster" (1938).]

1678 Lewis, Peter. "Maugham's Mistake," DAILY MAIL (Lond), 28 Sept 1972, p. 7.

"The Life to Come" and "The Other Boat" in *The Life to Come and Other Stories* are first class. EMF had the tact to present sex indirectly in these stories and so heightened his effects. The sex is implicit and presented with commendable detachment. [Also brief review of Robin Maugham's ESCAPE FROM THE SHADOWS.]

1679 McDowell, Frederick P. W. "Second Thoughts on E. M. Forster's *Maurice*," VIRGINIA WOOLF QUARTERLY, I (Fall 1972), 46–59.

EMF's chief failure in *Maurice* lies in the character of the protagonist;

EMF's control of him means that he is not free to develop nor is much sympathy generated for him. He fails to support EMF's projected values because EMF undercuts him too greatly. He is presented as too average a person to be capable of some of his later sexual intensities and social perceptions. The strength of the novel lies in EMF's conception of the Clive Durham-Maurice relationship and, to a lesser degree, of the Alec Scudder-Maurice relationship. The affair with Clive is more convincing in its early stages than in Clive's turning from homosexuality (or bisexuality) to heterosexuality. The conflict in Maurice between desire and the consciousness of his class superiority in his affair with Alex are well realized. What is false in their relationship is the stated happy outcome and the direct rendition of passion, not the encounter itself and its equivocal aspects. There are many truly Forsterian scenes in the novel; and it is excellent for its satirizing of both middle-class and aristocratic values.

1680 McGuinness, Richard. "*Maurice* Is a De-Mailerized Zone," VILLAGE VOICE (NY), 13 July 1972, pp. 21, 22, 24, 26, 28, 29.
Molly Haskell does not understand the problems of the homosexual in society and so unfairly denigrates EMF's *Maurice* as propaganda for homosexuality when EMF is essentially presenting the truth about this subject. *Maurice* is not "a forced fantasy" but "bitter, low-key realism," especially in the Maurice-Alec Scudder relationship. The novel represents not an achievement of innocence but the bitter realization of EMF of the cruel forces aligned against homosexuals in the social world as it actually exists. [Article critical of Haskell's "A Refuge among Contemporary Novels" (1972).]

1681 McGurk, E. Barry. "Gentlefolk in Philistia: The Influence of Matthew Arnold on E. M. Forster's *Howards End*," ENGLISH LITERATURE IN TRANSITION, XV: 3 (1972), 213–19.
The stress in *Howards End* upon the need to achieve proportion, to reconcile the inner life and the outer life, derives from Matthew Arnold's concept of "Harmonious expansion." The Wilcoxes, the exponents of the outer life, exemplify "Hebraic" values in Arnold's sense; the Schlegels, the exponents of the inner life, exemplify "Hellenic" values. Leonard Bast projects an Arnoldian view of the deprived populace, unable to achieve culture through its unaided efforts. In their interest in furthering a life-enhancing culture, the Schlegel sisters are Arnoldian. Margaret, in particular, is Arnoldian in her ability "to see life steadily and to see it whole." The Wilcoxes, in contrast, reveal the deficiencies of both the Philistines and the Populace. The Schlegels are part of the "saving remnant" and are thereby the Arnoldian "children of light"; the Wilcoxes are the Arnoldian "enemies of the children of light." The Schlegels, in their devotion to the inner life, exempli-

fy also Arnold's "imaginative reason." [Contributes to our understanding of Arnold's influence on EMF, but is not exhaustive.]

1682 Mellown, Elgin W. A DESCRIPTIVE CATALOGUE OF THE BIBLI-OGRAPHIES OF TWENTIETH CENTURY BRITISH WRITERS (Troy, NY: Whitston Publishing Co, 1972), pp. 118–20.
[Bibliography of primary works by EMF and annotated notices of secondary writings on him. The listed items are also noticed or abstracted in McDowell's book.]

1683 Meyers, Jeffrey. "Forster's Secret Sharer," SOUTHERN REVIEW (Adelaide), V (March 1972), 58–62.
Maurice is tame and dated, it lacks interesting characters, and EMF fails to analyze them conclusively. Neither the arguments for homosexuality nor the emotions are rendered convincingly. The ironic and balanced structure of *Maurice* gives it some merit. The novel's themes are Forsterian: "how to live frankly," "the connection between love and lust," and the role of "the exposed heart" and the "deepened vision" in sponsoring life. In plot, characters, and theme *Maurice* is closest to *The Longest Journey*. The similarities between the two novels emphasize the imaginative limitations of *Maurice*. The homosexual theme that is "oblique, ambiguous and interesting" in *Journey* becomes in *Maurice* "flat, banal and dull." *Maurice* is a study in repression and guilt. *Maurice* was, however, a therapeutic success: EMF had to exorcise the homosexual themes before he could write *A Passage to India*. EMF was not able to actualize homosexuality as both a nourishing and a destructive force, as Thomas Mann was able to do in DEATH IN VENICE (1913). For EMF homosexuality was mostly destructive. He seems to have been incapacitated by love (or lust) for working-class youths. *Maurice* clarifies our understanding of the homosexual themes in the early novels. In its "gentle satire, elegant style and certain thinness of substance" *Maurice* suggests the work of later English writers (Angus Wilson, Christopher Isherwood, and William Plomer) on homosexual themes. [Informative discussion.]

1684 Morgan, Edwin. "Forster's Other Face," SUNDAY TIMES (Lond), 1 Oct 1972, p. 39.
EMF is interested in presenting homosexual behavior as only one element in the social pattern. This placing of homosexuality in the larger world is useful to EMF as a writer, creating for him in his work many sorts of polarities. EMF was creating for aesthetic and humanitarian purposes "endless metamorphoses of the male-female opposition and attraction." The East-West polarity figures as the strongest polarity in "The Life to Come" and "The Other Boat," two of his best works in the *The Life to Come and Other Stories*.

1685 Mount, Ferdinand. "Awkward Pieces," FINANCIAL TIMES (Lond), 28 Sept 1972, p. 14.

The stories in *The Life to Come and Other Stories* are overwhelmed by the homosexual feeling in them and by the insistent theme of the Puritan prig seduced by the child of nature. The stories give us only the sensually fleeting or the ridiculously conventional.

1686 Mudrick, Marvin. "Fiction and Truth," HUDSON REVIEW, XXV (Spring 1972), 1142–58, espec 1142–44; rptd in part in CONTEMPORARY LITERARY CRITICISM, ed by Carolyn Riley and Barbara Harte (Detroit: Gale Research Co., 1974), II, 135.

Maurice is a bad novel but EMF's only truthful one. *A Passage to India* reveals the crudeness of EMF's sensibility. *Howards End* is mostly false uplift. *Albergo Empedocle and Other Writings* (ed by George H. Thomson [1971]) contains work that is mostly trivial. [Review of *Maurice* and *Albergo*.]

1687 Mulvey, Thomas. "A Paraphrase of Nietzsche in Forster's *Howards End,*" NOTES AND QUERIES (Lond), nsXIX (Feb 1972), 52.

Nietzsche was formative upon EMF in *Howards End.* Nietzsche propounded the "nightmare theory" of the world being dominated by men (like the Wilcoxes) who cannot say "I," and his ideas on women and marriage are voiced by the Wilcoxes, man existing for war and woman for the recreation of the warrior.

1688 "Now They Can be Told," TIMES LITERARY SUPPLEMENT (Lond), 13 Oct 1972, p. 1215; rptd as "E. M. Forster: *The Life to Come,*" T. L. S. ESSAYS AND REVIEWS FROM "THE TIMES LITERARY SUPPLEMENT, 1972" (No. 11), (Lond & NY: Oxford UP, 1973), pp. 68–72.

None of the stories in *The Life to Come and Other Stories* is as good as the best to be found in *Collected Short Stories,* and the worst are not good. They do not detract from EMF's reputation but do not add to it. To write in order to excite oneself, as EMF asserts that he did, is to write pornography. Like pornography, the stories substitute sexuality for character, and they isolate sexual experience that becomes either "sodomic rape" or madness. There is little love, affection, connection. The undeveloped heart was EMF's subject; in its extreme form writing on this subject becomes part of the literature of pornography. He ceased writing because he wanted to write (or felt he was only able to write) about homosexual love. But EMF could not write well on this theme, though he wanted to. "Doctor Woolacott" is the only story that approaches in quality his best short fiction. In it, health is the enemy of love, and homosexuality is a disease ending in death. (The intruding young man is death.) All EMF's fiction has a homosexual aura because all of it concerns constraint and freedom. (The constraint can be equated with society's disapproval of homosexuality.) "Dr. Woolacott" expresses only more explicitly the chief theme of EMF's fiction: "the yearning for free expression through male love, and the repressive power of society." As literature, these stories or sexual fantasies in *The Life to Come* are not sustaining.

1689 Ozick, Cynthia. "Forster's Stature," COMMENTARY, LIII (May 1972), 36, 40, 42.

One feels more affinity with the EMF of the novels than with the EMF of the moralistic essays. With the revelations of his homosexuality, the liberalism professed in the essays becomes the voice of an oppressed minority and is devalued by the presence of a vested interest. His commitment is less to a philosophy of liberation than to one of self-preservation. The personal basis of his morality (in essence, his relativism is a situation ethics) fails to provide the principles necessary to underlie a universal ethics, nor can these relationships stand up well to cosmic disillusion without the notion of law or contract (cf. Mrs. Moore's disillusion in *A Passage to India*, which prevents her doing something positive for her friend Aziz). There is lack of rigor in EMF's morality; it depends too much upon initial hurt or a martyr complex in its manifestations. EMF is not limited to homosexual orientation in writing about human relationships, but some of those he describes are homosexual. [Does not deny the wisdom that Farber imputes to EMF in the novels. With respect to Skir, fertility for Ozick means actual offspring, and EMF celebrates them in many novels despite his own homosexuality.] EMF was also skeptical of causes and may therefore have been skeptical of the Gay Liberation movement. This movement has made politics out of love, sex, and friendship, and EMF would have been opposed to so doing. [Reply to Anne Farber and Leo Skir (both 1972).]

1690 Ozick, Cynthia. "Loneliness," COMMENTARY, LIII (March 1972), 30–32.

In interpreting a literary work, one must always begin with the most basic concretions before he extracts an abstract meaning from the work, and this procedure is especially necessary in discussing a book the subject of which is controversial, as *Maurice* is. [Takes issue with Alfred Sherrard (1972) when he insists that *Maurice* is about loneliness and despair and not about homosexuality.]

1691 Page, Norman. THE LANGUAGE OF JANE AUSTEN (Oxford: Basil Blackwell; NY: Barnes & Noble, 1972), pp. 191, 193.

Jane Austen initiated the trend of witty and ironic dialogue that characterizes the novels of Mrs. Gaskell, George Eliot, Ivy Compton-Burnett, and

EMF. EMF continues the tradition of realistic and self-revealing dialogue and ironic commentary begun in Jane Austen, as does Angus Wilson.

> **1692** Parry, Benita. "Introduction," "The British-Indian Encounter," "Flora Annie Steel, 1847–1929," "Edward J. Thompson, 1886–1946," Rudyard Kipling, 1865–1936," "E. M. Forster: *A Passage to India*," DELUSIONS AND DISCOVERIES: STUDIES ON INDIA IN THE BRITISH IMAGINATION 1880–1930 (Berkeley & Los Angeles: University of California P; Lond: A. Lane, 1972), pp. 1–8, espec 5–7; 9–70, espec 52, 58; 100–130, espec 130; 164–202, espec 181, 187, 188, 194; 203–59, espec 215, 227, 231, 255, 257; 260–320.

"Introduction": The typical Englishman in the nineteenth and early twentieth centuries was alienated from Indian society and culture. Anglo-Indian writers reflected this alienation and their inability to see India truthfully in their fiction. Only Kipling and EMF knew India as a spirit and incorporated their vision of it in literary art. EMF was particularly receptive to the influence of India and penetrated to the truth of it. In *A Passage to India* he reveals how India opened out his "vision of man's experiential range." India for him became "a symbol of man's spiritual history and his experiments in self-understanding." EMF saw in India the possibilities for sensuous and transcendent ranges of experience not to be found in the culture of the West.

Chap 1, "The British-Indian Encounter": [Convincingly describes the prevailing attitudes of the official Anglo-Indians.] EMF and J. R. Ackerley were more human, supple, curious, and openminded than most of the British in India, and were diffident toward, rather than censorious of, those aspects of Indian civilization that may have disturbed them. The lack of logic and rationality in the Hindu synthesis, the vision of cosmic cycles and the blending of opposites in Hinduism, its ultimate emphasis upon the life out of time rather than the life in time, and its fusion of the sensual with the mystical alienated the West. Hysteria characterized British reactions to the life and art of India in which eroticism (sometimes manifested in unusual or "perverted" sexual practices) was often the chief motif or subject. [Invaluable documentation for many of the ideas and attitudes dramatized or satirized in *Passage* or asserted in EMF's occasional writings on India.] Chap 2, "The Romancers: Five Lady Novelists": [The five ladies are Mrs. F. E. F. Penny, Mrs. Alice Perrin, Mrs. B. M. Croker, Mrs. Maud Diver, and Mrs. I. A. R. Wylie.] They reveal in their fiction about India, consciously or unconsciously, the attitudes, prejudices, and values of the Anglo-Indian ruling caste. [These are the ideas that EMF satirized in *Passage;* and he advocates many of the attitudes and values of the Moslem and Hindu cultures in India that the ladies condemn implicitly, self-righteously, or hysterically.] Chap 3, "Flora Annie Steel, 1847–1929": Mrs. Steel reveals the same attitudes and values as the lady romancers above, but her work had wider currency. [Her ability to communicate "the antipathy and fear possessing the British and their consciousness of an abyss separating them from their human environment" (she sympathized with these attitudes) resembles EMF's presentation of the Anglo-Indians and their fears after Adela Quested in *Passage* charges Aziz with rape.] Chap 4, "Edmund Candler, 1874–1926" and Chap 5, "Edward J. Thompson, 1886–1946": [EMF's ability to see India sympathetically and objectively contrasts with the sympathetic but insular and not fully liberated visions of Candler and Thompson.] In AN INDIAN DAY Thompson draws on EMF's *Passage* in his description of Indian hills. In Thompson they express an ancient India alien to British sensibilities and lack the multisymbolic dimensions—metaphysical, atavistic, mythical, unconscious—that they possess in *Passage*. Thompson again echoes EMF when he describes the disquieting effects of these hills upon the Western beholder. Alden's consciousness of an ancient and elemental India rising in rebellion against the British is expressed in a language that echoes Mrs. Moore's sensations of the Caves. [For Thompson's view of *Passage* see 1930.] Chap 6, "Rudyard Kipling, 1865–1936": [Informed and persuasive account of Kipling as the self-righteous voice of Anglo-Indian values and as an artist who evokes multifarious India through the senses.] Kipling's art is greatest when he gets furthest from the imperialist ideology, as in "The Bridge Builders"; fine achievements such as "The Man Who Would be King" and KIM are flawed by his consciously and unconsciously expressing the values of empire. [EMF rejected these values. The conflict between the artist and the ethnocentric Englishman is largely absent in EMF. Refutes Stanley Cooperman's contention in " 'The Imperial Posture and the Shrine of Darkness': Kipling's THE NAULAHKA and E. M. Forster's *A Passage to India*" (1963) that Tarvin in Kipling's novel undergoes any kind of spiritual crisis comparable to Mrs. Moore's in *Passage*. Notes distrust of EMF and J. R. Ackerley by Kipling's avid advocates, as revealed in the KIPLING JOURNAL.]

Chap 7, "E. M. Forster: *A Passage to India*": [Sensitive reading of *Passage* in light of the social and political values expressed in it and the ethical, philosophical, aesthetic, and religious values dramatized in it. Parry does not refer often enough to the minor writers discussed in her earlier chapters and concentrates, perhaps excessively for a book of her sort, upon the intrinsic aspects of this novel. Excellent account, and particularly perceptive as it relates *Passage* to the corpus of Indian literature and religious thought.] *Passage* is not only a socially oriented work but a metaphysical one as well. Both the physical environment and metaphysical states of extraordinary intensity figure in it. EMF is thus concerned with the distance between what men are and their existential capacities, with both the near and the far. Man's social destiny is challenged by his unconscious mind; the human spirit in *Passage* awakens to mystical illuminations or states of pathological fear as a result of the promptings of the unconscious. EMF feels that modern civilization is sick because it tends to repress the instincts and to place taboos on experiences that transcend the norms. EMF is predisposed to be sympathetic toward India because these ordinarily repressed instincts can there attain expression. Both Hindu and Moslem life connect the liberated passions with the intellect, the secular with the sacred. The Hindu yoga rituals connect the conscious and the unconscious and allow escape from the ego into a cosmic awareness. EMF does not accept in all respects the Indian modes of perception but does feel that other modes are inadequate. Illusions and realities are difficult to dissociate in India. There are divisions in India (e.g., the various Hindu sects and the antipathies between Hindu and Moslem), but there the opportunity also exists for wholeness. India is a concrete civilization with glorious manifestations as well as a culture sensitive to the unconscious. India is both the educated magistrate Das and the handsome, instinctive punkah wallah in the courtroom. The "Mosque" accommodates both the material world and spiritual fulfillment, and represents a compromise between these realities. The "Caves" represent the forgotten life of the race in man's unconscious and the ancient ascetic traditions that embody this life and that reject, pessimistically, the world of men and matter. The "Temple" posits the possibilities of superconsciousness and an affirmation of the total universe as a fusion in the One of spirit and matter. The three parts of the novel represent a kind of human passage. EMF is appreciative of the values in both Hinduism and Islam but is critical of both cultures. He brought to India an understanding of the paradoxes in man's situation, matured through his contemplation of other societies. He learned that aspects of man's existential situation are atrophied in other cultures, while they achieve at least tentative expression in India. On one side EMF is a liberal humanist and reverent agnostic; on the other, he has mystic inclinations, feeling a strong need for wholeness and the integration of man's faculties. He supports the liberal ethos that results in free intellectual inquiry and civilized personal relations; these values are rejected by the Anglo-Indian bureaucrats. EMF values Fielding's skeptical humanism but also acknowledges its limitations. In India EMF subordinates his rationalism and contemplates the sublime for the illumination that it may bring.

EMF's *Passage* is a triumphant expression of the British mind exploring India. EMF sees both the unique qualities of India and her more extensive meanings. Adela Quested and Mrs. Moore do not have EMF's inner poise but experience in India a disconcerting reality that goes far beyond what they have previously encountered. They do not realize that visions in India can bring diabolic terror or else the peace that passeth understanding. Islam, a monotheistic religion hospitable to a temperate mysticism, is, from one point of view, a meeting point between East and West; from another, it is intensely Indian. Aziz wishes to identify with India, though, paradoxically, he does not love it as a motherland. He is more aware of the unity of India in Mau, where the British are absent, than he had been in Chandrapore. At Mau, Islam is absorbed into India, though Islam seeks not so much for unity with God as it yearns for His presence. Anglo-Indians resist participation in any of the three aspects of India, symbolized in Mosque, Caves, or Temple; they understand none of them and resent them all. As for the Marabar Caves, they are not oriented toward Hinduism but are aboriginal in essence and are to be associated with the Jain religion that is pessimistic, ascetic, and based on an ancient cosmology. [This discussion is unusually enlightening.] Mrs. Moore's total despair, after she hears the echo in the Caves, is Jain in purport. After Mrs. Moore and Adela visit the Caves, India acts upon them like a hallucinogenic drug, "rearranging their senses, extending the limits of their perceptions and depriving them of the power of choice." There is something fatalistic in the journey to the Caves, even from its inception. As a result of their exposure to the Caves, both women are turned back to a past condition of mankind and are unprepared to cope with such a radical challenge to their accustomed values. The Caves cause Adela to acknowledge her sexuality, which, for a repressed woman like her, is in itself an assault. Her journey is away from easy certainties, such as the sanctity of personal relationships, toward a confrontation with a reality below the surfaces of social life. Mrs. Moore's vision is alien to the culture that has bred her; and she becomes like the ascetic Jains, yearning to escape the body. In Jainism the attaining of such freedom from the phenomenal world is not a mystical identification with the Absolute so much as a stage of complete isolation beyond man or matter. Mrs. Moore's passing to become a Jain savior ends with the Caves episode; thereafter, she is reunited with India as a whole and becomes a redeemer as a Hindu saint. The Caves act obliquely upon the rationalistic Fielding and make him aware of a reality previously unknown to him. As for Aziz, he returns to the glorious Muslim past; the Caves strike at him but bring no psychic dislocation since he is not an alien. For Godbole the "ancient night," with which he associates the Caves, represents the Veda tradition of his Aryan ancestors who invaded Dravidian India and triumphed over the aboriginal religion while absorbing parts of it into their own developing philosophy. As a practitioner of Bhakti yoga he wishes to unite the Self to the Absolute through the agency of Krishna, the Brahmanical tradition familiar to EMF from his residence in Dewas Senior [recounted in *The Hill of Devi*]. Such an affirmation, dramatized in "Temple," is antithetical to the nihilism voiced through the Cave's echo. Hinduism in "Temple" becomes "a mirror-image of India, blending diversity, containing opposites and spanning a continuum from mud to mystery." According to Hinduism, all matter and all spirit participate in the Divine; but man alone, through discipline and effort, can attain "the identity of the Atman-Brahman" and so become one with the Absolute. The paradox of India's being is exemplified in Godbole: the India that comprises a static social order and a dynamic spiritual life. Hinduism embraces all the attributes and enigmas of India; it reconciles Caves and Temple as part of the One. Yet it represents finally an aspiration toward unity rather than an attainment of it (except momentarily). [Bibliography. A milestone book for understanding *Passage.*]

1693 Portnoy, Howard. "The Imperialist vs. the Yeoman: Forster's *Howards End,*" JUNCTION 1972 (Brooklyn College), pp. 73–76.

A contrast is developed in *Howards End* between the materialistic, urban imperialist and the rural, classless, emotional, and spiritually sensitive yeoman, particularly as this dichotomy impinges on the question of the ownership of Howards End house. The Schlegels, though cosmopolitan, are yeoman in their values, and these values triumph when Margaret Schlegel finally comes to own Howards End. [Little that is new; the dichotomy discussed in this article had been developed by Cyrus Hoy in "Forster's Metaphysical Novel" (1960).]

1694 Puri, Meenakshi. "Private Activity," THOUGHT (New Delhi), XXIV (12 Feb 1972), 17–18.

Maurice reveals that the British require uniformity in sexual expression, heterosexual rather than homosexual in kind. *Maurice* fails because Maurice is dull, Clive Durham is dull and respectable, and Alec Scudder is not convincing in his role as lower-class lover.

1695 Reade, Brian. "Books," PSYCHOLOGY TODAY (Del Mar, Calif.), V (April 1972), 20, 22, 110.

Maurice is "unpublishable" but "worth it" because EMF wrote it and because it is one of the few pre-1950 novels with homosexuality as its subject. Its publication in the 1930s would have damaged EMF's image. He is a homosexual author in that men are more important, though not more prominent, than women in his novels. In the novels the sexual potential of women is hardly accounted for. But for EMF's sexual repressions as a young man, we might never have had the novels: they can be classified as "the side effects of youthful anxiety." *Maurice* is in large part a tract. Some of the things that happen can be best explained in terms of post-Wildean hostility to homosexuality. EMF's preoccupation was with how a man of feeling would face, without muddle, the problems posed by sex and friendship. The mechanics of his liberalism should in part be referred to his sexual orientation.

1696 Rees, Goronwy. A CHAPTER OF ACCIDENTS (NY: The Library P; Lond: Chatto & Windus, 1972), pp. 95, 208, 229.

At Oxford during the period between world wars as at Cambridge, the masculine principle prevailed over the female principle. Often the masculine principle resulted in overt homosexuality, but not always. EMF's epigraph to *Howards End* ("Only connect") supplied the rationale for this masculine principle in its more general as well as in its more extreme and overt manifestations. This phrase was extremely influential in shaping the emotional attitudes of the English governing class between the world wars. In light of Rees's relationship with the communist spy Guy Burgess (Rees's close friend) and Rees's decision to inform the government finally of his suspicions of Burgess's activity as a spy, Rees regards as false EMF's statement that if one had to choose between betraying his country or betraying his friend, one ought to choose to betray his country. EMF's antithesis is false, and the betrayal of one's country might mean the betrayal of other friends, wife, and family.

1697 Reynolds, Frank. "Early Forster Writings Reveal Seeds of Genius," ROCKY MOUNTAIN NEWS (Denver), "Startime," 2 Jan 1972, p. 15.

"Albergo Empedocle" is a failure: the theme of the transmigration of souls is hackneyed, and the theme of conflict between glibness and sensitivity is too stark. In the early essays collected in *Albergo Empedocle and Other Writings by E. M. Forster* (ed by George H. Thomson [1971]) EMF reveals how he elicits joy, beauty, and meaning from unlikely materials. The previously uncollected essays on India are interesting and revealing. EMF's reaching toward India as goal is a continuing process, and he appreciated a culture that stressed "ambivalence and paradox as routes to the 'Unknowable.' " EMF's final view was this: the Occident cannot and need not define India but must try to connect with some of its aspects. In the essays in this book he writes with his characteristic "justice, grace, and kindness."

1698 Roby, Kinley E. "Irony and the Narrative Voice in *Howards End*," JOURNAL OF NARRATIVE TECHNIQUE, II (May 1972), 116–24.

The narrative voice does not speak for EMF, and the woman narrator does not reveal a predominantly Fosterian sensibility. Rather, EMF often uses the narrator, presumably a woman, for ironic effects. [An interesting and conscientious presentation, but must we assume that EMF is not speaking in the novel?]

1699 Sherrard, Alfred. "Loneliness," COMMENTARY, LIII (March 1972), p. 30.

In *Maurice*, Maurice Hall finds love and loses it; the affair with Alec Scudder is a fantasy of revenge against Clive Durham for ceasing to love him. The affair with Alec is therefore unreal. The novel is about loneliness and despair, and only incidentally about homosexuality.

1700 Shrapnel, Norman. "Abinger's Harbinger," Manchester Guardian, 28 Sept 1972, p. 16; Manchester Guardian Weekly, 7 Oct 1972, p. 30.

The contents of *The Life to Come and Other Stories* vary in quality but are of great interest. EMF's early stories are revealing with respect to his later mastery. EMF did not use the twist ending; his shocks and surprises are organic. Sometimes, however, the story is unresolved; in "The Rock" the resolution is given but the story left out. Structural slackness but stylistic grace are apparent. Death, homosexuality, and the occult are his themes; books and weapons are favorite symbols. Two stories are outstanding: "The Life to Come" and "The Other Boat." (The latter analyzes sexual and racial taboos.)

1701 Skir, Leo. "Forster's Stature," Commentary, LIII (May 1972), 36.

EMF did not think of homosexuals as sterile, and he would have been in sympathy with the aims and activities of the Gay Liberation Movement. [Discusses some points raised by Cynthia Ozick's "E. M. Forster as a Homosexual" (1971).]

1702 Spender, Stephen. "Forster's Queer Novel," Partisan Review, XXXIX: 1 (1972), 113–17.

Despite EMF's revisions, a certain thinness remains in *Maurice*, since the homosexual theme throws other elements into the background. Maurice comes to know himself but does not, as a result, get to know the world better. (If this aspect of *Maurice* had been developed, the novel would have been more complex.) The relationship between Maurice and Clive Durham is a "pure" homosexuality, more of the spirit than of the body; such an innocent relationship proves unsatisfying to Maurice. EMF too easily identified Clive's reversion to normality and his deterioration thereafter with the decadence of the aristocratic class, so that EMF cannot present persuasively the difference between two kinds of love, homosexual and heterosexual, each acceptable within its own context. (Clive's wife is too undeveloped for EMF to present a convincing heterosexual relationship, something he apparently did not wish to do.) Maurice passes from a relationship based on identity (with Clive) to one based on otherness (with Alec). Maurice rejects the world of normality but does not recognize a homosexual world in which others besides himself and Alec figure. [A most perceptive article.]

1703 Stallybrass, Oliver. "Editor's Introduction," *Two Cheers for Democracy*, ed by Oliver Stallybrass (Lond: Edward Arnold, *The Abinger Edition of E. M. Forster*, Vol. 11, 1972), pp. vii–xii.

Two Cheers for Democracy uses about one-half of EMF's uncollected nonfiction between 1935 and 1951. About one-half of these pieces were done for either the LISTENER or the NEW STATESMAN, largely because J. R. Ackerley and Raymond Mortimer were their respective literary editors [friends of EMF]. There are seven pieces originally given as lectures, and there are a number of broadcast talks revised for the printed page. Occasionally these revisions reflect a change in opinion. EMF was wise to reject a chronological arrangement of the essays in order to secure a more organic unity to this miscellany. *Two Cheers* is a tougher and more serious book than *Abinger Harvest.* [The circumstances of EMF's preparing *Two Cheers* for the press in 1951 are given. "Source and Textual Notes" are invaluable for the scholar and indicate the basis, almost invariably sound, for the adoption of emended readings. The "Annotated Index" is helpful and fascinating (a kind of intellectual concordance and glossary to the contents of *Two Cheers*).]

1704 Stallybrass, Oliver. "Introduction," *The Life to Come and Other Stories*, ed by Oliver Stallybrass (Lond: Edward Arnold, *The Abinger Edition of E. M. Forster*, Vol. 8, 1972), pp. vii–xxi; as "Introduction," *The Life to Come and Other Short Stories* (NY: Norton, 1972), pp. vii–xxi.

The Life to Come contains all the extant complete stories not included in previous collections. The earlier stories, "Ansell," "The Purple Envelope," "The Helping Hand," "The Rock," and "Albergo Empedocle" differ from the later stories in subject matter. "Albergo Empedocle" is superior to some of the stories that appeared in volume form. "Ansell" is the best of these early efforts and superior in many ways to "The Story of the Siren." [These judgments are perhaps excessive.] "The Purple Envelope" may have irritated editors because of its satire on "respectability," its teasing with the supernatural, or its moral ambivalence. "The Helping Hand" is slight and scarcely appeals to any universal values. In "The Rock" the idea is a good one, but the realization of it is faulty. Seven of the eight remaining later stories were written after *A Passage to India.* ("The Life to Come" dates from 1922.) Their homosexual content prevented their publication. These stories, as EMF indicates in his diary (8 April 1922), were written to excite himself rather than to express himself. The few friends who read these stories had varying reactions. So apparently did EMF; he destroyed some that he thought less good than others out of "a craftsman's dissatisfaction," some because he thought them too indecent. After 1922 EMF could write only unpublishable "sexy stories." [This delimitation by EMF provides the most convincing explanation for his ceasing to write novels after 1924.] In his diary (10 June 1911) he had become weary of the subject of the love of men for women and vice versa; in a letter to Siegfried Sassoon (1 Aug 1923) he asserts that his patience with ordinary people had given out; in his diary (31 Dec 1964) he says that his sexual proclivities have prevented him from being a more famous writer. EMF's inner honesty and artistic integrity made the writing of fiction for publication impossible after he accepted himself as homosexual. *A Passage to India* may be a "magnificent rearguard action" in which sex has a minor role. The stories are franker and more robust than *Maurice*, free from the novel's didacticism and sentimentality. There are two sorts of stories: (1) those in which EMF attacked the heterosexual world and some "civilized" institutions (woman, the Church, schoolmasters, town councillors) and which may be regarded as his "facetious" tales: "The Obelisk" (1939), "What Does It Matter?" (c. the 1930s), "The Classical Annex" (1930–1931); and (2) those in which he treats profoundly and powerfully some of his central concerns (love, death, truth, social and racial differences) and which may be regarded as his "serious" tales: "The Life to Come" (1922), "Dr. Woolacott" (1927), "Arthur Snatchfold" (1928), and "The Other Boat" (1957–1958). "The Torque" (c. 1958), an uneven story, falls somewhere between the two groups. "Dr. Woolacott" is reminiscent of "The Point of It" in its "evocation of the twilight boundary between life and death" and in demonstrating the superiority of ecstasy in death to a colorless life. "Arthur Snatchfold" evokes well the social pretenses of an empty society, a Wilcox-like businessman, and a clubroom scene when Conway learns with futile remorse of Snatchfold's sentence to jail. "The Life to Come" and "The Other Boat" show EMF at the height of his powers. These stories reveal "tragic grandeur, unsurpassed even in *A Passage to India.*" [The stories are excellent, but this judgment is excessive.] Both stories involve an East-West encounter. "The Life to Come" develops the theme of passion contrasted with hypocrisy. This story came from deep within him, EMF said. "The Other Boat" reveals unity of scene. The sexual experience is well-realized and not fantasized; the shifting moods and emotions in the post-coital conversation are also convincing. [Describes the writing of EMF's contribution to "Three Courses and a Dessert" (EMF wrote the second part); describes the establishment of a text for this volume (difficult to do because many versions existed of some stories) according to EMF's latest intentions, to the extent that they could be discovered. Indispensable account.]

1705 Stansky, Peter, and William Abrahams. THE UNKNOWN ORWELL (NY: Knopf; Lond: Constable, 1972), pp. 14, 29, 120, 136, 279.
In *Howards End*, the Schlegel sisters' idea of connecting with other social classes is an ideal that would have been difficult to achieve in stratified Edwardian society, an age of privilege that came to an end in 1914. The sisters were also sensitive to the inequalities in the distribution of wealth and to their own favored position.

1706 Stewart, J. I. M. "Old and Gay," SPECTATOR (Lond), CCXXIX (21 Oct 1972), 629–30.
The early stories in *The Life to Come and Other Stories* are of but minor

interest; the admittedly homosexual ones are by a mature writer. The four serious homosexual stories are not unqualified successes but are "moving and impressive attempts at an enlarged artistic integrity." "Arthur Snatchfold" ends with the young man's protecting his elder seducer. "The Life to Come" and "The Other Boat" end in murder and suicide. "Dr. Wollacott" is strange, "confused, incoherent, uncertainly dream-like" and quite powerful. EMF has difficulty in realizing his young lover from out of the greenwood.

1707 Stone, Donald David. NOVELISTS IN A CHANGING WORLD: MEREDITH, JAMES, AND THE TRANSFORMATION OF ENGLISH FICTION IN THE 1880's (Cambridge, Mass: Harvard UP, 1972), pp. 67, 93, 128, 156, 335–36.

Affinities exist between Henry James's Hyacinth Robinson in THE PRINCESS CASAMASSIMA, Leonard Bast in *Howards End*, and Gilbert Grail in George Gissing's THYRZA: the only solution for each one's difficulties is the acceptance of suffering as a value in itself. Clara Middleton (THE EGOIST) is Meredith's greatest human figure. Rickie Elliot uses her in *The Longest Journey* as a touchstone of value along with Beatrice and Brunnhilde and Shelley's view of women. Clara's progress is like that of Lucy Honeychurch in *A Room with a View:* both women develop in heart and mind; personal development goes along with social progress, both women reaching in their inner lives "The End of the Middle Ages" (final title in *Room*). John Crowe Ransom accurately presents Meredith's influence upon English fiction and upon younger writers in "E. M. Forster" (1943).

1708 Thomson, George H. "Forster's *Howards End*, Chapter 43," EXPLICATOR, XXX: 8 (April 1972), Item 64.

[Notes the orderly collocation, in the passage in *Howards End* beginning "Here Leonard lay dead in the garden," of symbols of life and death, though why death is "a blue sky" is not easily resolved.]

1709 Wasson, Richard. "Books," WORLDVIEW (Council on Religion and International Affairs, NY), XV (June 1972), 52–53.

EMF did provide a steadying influence for twentieth-century intellectuals by the fact of his being alive; his moral imagination deserves praise, as do his honesty, his cultural intelligence, his sanity, and his tact in ceasing to write when he had exhausted his vein. Yet we can give only two cheers for EMF's self and his moral values. His imagination failed him at the same point that that of others fails, where the individual is oppressed by social, political, and economic forces. His recognition in *Maurice* of a conflict between class and eros, between middle-class values and joy, remains an intellectual construct. He has sympathy with those from the liberating lower class but lacks full knowledge of them, something revealed in the imprecision of the language used in *Maurice*. He remains in the end committed to class values rather than humanist ones. His delay in publishing *Maurice* and his failure to write other homosexual works indicate that prudence governed his imagination and that the class values he decried overwhelmed him. In the speeches to the Workingmen's College (especially "The Greatness of Literature," *Albergo Empedocle and Other Writings By E. M. Forster*, ed by George H. Thomson), he urges working men to embrace values irrelevant for them: nobleness and gentility. His humanism becomes a bourgeois humanism in which transcendent values rather than possible ones obtain. Because EMF recognized his own limits, we can appreciate him; but those limits of his imagination and value system did circumscribe him. We must recognize his insight into the relationship between love and class but try ourselves to overleap the bounds of class. [Stimulating discussion.]

1710 Watson, Sara Ruth. V. SACKVILLE-WEST (NY: Twayne Publishers, Twayne English Authors Series, 1972), pp. 33–35, 74, 75, 118, 119, 120, 125, 127, 135, 143.

The high valuation placed on personal relationships and mystic contemplation, revealed in *A Passage to India*, is characteristic of Bloomsbury, with which V. Sackville-West was affiliated. Like EMF, V. Sackville-West in her short stories expects reader participation. Like EMF, she loved the countryside but she localized it more. Like EMF, she contrasts the material world and the inner world. Along with Henry Fielding and EMF, V. Sackville-West belongs in the tradition of the satirical novel of manners. The search of the characters in GRAND CANYON (1942) is for honesty, personal fulfillment, and reality, as in EMF. In this novel her attraction for mystical experience recalls the EMF of *Passage*.

1711 Waugh, Alec. "E. M. Forster's World," NATIONAL REVIEW, XXIV (31 March 1972), 335–56.

In A NOVELIST ON NOVELS (1918), W. L. George named EMF as one of seven contenders for first place in the new generation of novelists. (Others were J. D. Beresford, Gilbert Cannan, D. H. Lawrence, Compton Mackenzie, Oliver Onions, and Frank Swinnerton.) Only Lawrence and EMF became great; only Mackenzie and Swinnerton are still alive and still writing. EMF was definitely "the man" George was looking for, as implied in the chapter heading "Who Is the Man?" EMF became a public figure in the way that D. H. Lawrence did not.

1712 Wyatt-Brown, Anne Marbury. "E. M. Forster and the Transformation of Comedy," DISSERTATION ABSTRACTS INTERNATIONAL, XXXIII (1972), 1751A–1752A. Unpublished dissertation, Case Western Reserve University, 1972.

1713 Wilson, Angus. "Books versus Biceps," OBSERVER (Lond), 8 Oct 1972, p. 39.

The publication of EMF's unpublished works, as in the short stories of *The Life to Come and Other Stories*, may not be in his best interests. There is no evidence that he valued any of them. The dichotomies and contrasts are sometimes too simply envisioned and lack subtlety. Sometimes sex does not matter (the gist of "What Does It Matter? A Morality"), for example, but sometimes it does. The more farcical stories are sometimes the most serious ultimately; some of the intended serious ones are closest to farce. Only "Ansell" poses with wit, skill, and ambiguity the problem of brawn versus brains.

1973

1714 Aldiss, Brian W. Billion Year Spree: The True History of Science Fiction (Garden City, NY: Doubleday, 1973), pp. 78, 190–91, 201.

Writers with a feminine sensibility in fiction—Jane Austen, Henry James, EMF, and Ivy Compton-Burnett—have concentrated on personal relations, whereas writers of science fiction have turned to the external. Aldous Huxley's Brave New World superseded EMF's "The Machine Stops" as the reply to Wells's utopian ideas. Huxley's world is more believable than EMF's. C. S. Lewis and EMF, in arguing against Wells, concentrated only on the eternal human condition. Huxley, EMF, and C. S. Lewis, in answering Wells, have accepted his fears and rejected, or challenged, his hopes.

1715 Altman, Peter. "Forster's Short Stories Lack Strength of Novels," Minneapolis Star, 22 May 1973, p. 10-B.

EMF's genius worked best in the enlarged, expansive form of the novel. The stories in *The Life to Come and Other Short Stories* are, however, more substantial than those previously published. The three best are "The Life to Come" (an effective parable of colonialism and personal betrayal), "Arthur Snatchfold" (a poignant, resonant tale of homosexual love that crosses class lines), and "The Other Boat" (a skillfully controlled work, full of sensitivity and shrewd social observation). The other stories are slighter.

1716 Arkin, Stephen E. "Reluctant Moderns: A Study of E. M. Forster and Virginia Woolf," Dissertation Abstracts International, XXXIV (1973), 2603–4A. Unpublished dissertation, Yale University, 1973.

1717 Auden, W. H. "Foreword," *Goldsworthy Lowes Dickinson and Related Writings*, ed by Oliver Stallybrass (Lond: Edward Arnold, *The Abinger Edition of E. M. Forster*, Vol. 13, 1973). pp. vii–ix.

Goldsworthy Lowes Dickinson is EMF's best book. EMF has overcome a great obstacle: writing about a personal friend and a good man, an individual whose life revealed little external action, and a man whose letters were much less arresting than his conversation. [See Auden's review of *Dickinson* (1934).]

1718 B[eer], J. B. "E. M. Forster," WEBSTER'S NEW WORLD COMPANION TO ENGLISH AND AMERICAN LITERATURE, ed by Arthur Pollard (NY: World Publishing; Salisbury: Compton-Russell, 1973), pp. 259–61.

EMF's theme is often the dislocation experienced by the middle-class English person set against a Mediterranean culture that he does not comprehend (e.g., some of his short stories, *Where Angels Fear to Tread, A Room with a View*). *The Longest Journey* juxtaposes three kinds of reality, apprehended through reason, imagination, and passion. In *Howards End*, EMF shows more tolerance toward the British middle class and its commercial values. In *A Passage to India*, EMF stresses mostly separation, not unity. *Passage* is only incidentally political and is primarily concerned with the relationship developing between India and each of three characters: Fielding, who is the fair-minded administrator; Mrs. Moore, who lives by intuition; and Adela Quested, whose "bodily psyche" is undereducated. Modern criticism of EMF is too attentive to his surfaces rather than to his symbolic depths. At his best he depicts perceptively his own middle-class world and suggests the existence of other worlds beyond it that must not be neglected. His understated style when he comments on society in his nonfiction is one of his characteristic qualities. [Sketch of career.]

1719 Bell, Quentin. "Higher Love and High Ideals," TIMES HIGHER EDUCATION SUPPLEMENT (Lond), 14 Sept 1973, p. 15.

Goldsworthy Lowes Dickinson, while not so great an achievement as the novels, is a feat of letters, since circumstances helped EMF so little in writing it. Dickinson's achievements were minimal, his projects often unsuccessful, his life undramatic, and his teaching casual. But EMF reveals Dickinson as an exemplar of "the quiet, gentle and sceptical way of life" in which EMF believed. EMF exerts greater powers in his book than did Dickinson in his AUTOBIOGRAPHY (1973), because EMF wished to convert people, reluctant to believe in it, to a sense of Dickinson's worth. As for his younger friends in Bloomsbury, Dickinson commanded their affection rather than their respect. There was a gap between Dickinson's generation and the ribald, irreverent men of the next generation at Cambridge who were to be the founders of Bloomsbury. Dickinson was too abstract and idealistic to be entirely effective as a person and as a lasting influence. [Review of *Goldsworthy Lowes Dickinson and Related Writings, Abinger Edition*.]

1720 Bolsterli, Margaret. "Studies in Context: The Homosexual Ambience of Twentieth Century Literary Culture," D. H. LAWRENCE REVIEW, VI (Spring 1973), 71–85.

Émile Delavenay's D. H. LAWRENCE AND EDWARD CARPENTER: A STUDY IN EDWARDIAN TRANSITION (1971), CARRINGTON: LETTERS AND EXTRACTS FROM HER DIARIES, ed by David Garnett, Quentin Bell's VIRGINIA WOOLF: A BIOGRAPHY, and EMF's *Maurice* all illuminate the homosexual aspects of the milieu in which D. H. Lawrence wrote. EMF's acknowledgment in his "Terminal Note" of Carpenter's influence legitimizes Delavenay's study of Lawrence. *Maurice* adds to the context of Lawrence's novels by providing details of the period and by describing the place of the homosexual in that society. Edward Carpenter and George Merrill did live in "the greenwood," as EMF wished Maurice Hall and Alec Scudder to do in *Maurice.* The imputed happy ending to *Maurice* is hardly convincing. Possibly the gamekeeper figure (Annable in THE WHITE PEACOCK, Alec in *Maurice*) might have had his origins in Edward Carpenter. One aspect of *Maurice* that is not dated is Maurice's difficulty in accepting his sexual nature and the lack of help offered him by the society of which he is a part. Carpenter's LOVE'S COMING OF AGE, Lawrence's WOMEN IN LOVE, and *Maurice* derive from the same intellectual climate. Rupert Birkin in WOMEN IN LOVE could have functioned more easily without Hermione and Ursula Brangwen than without Gerald Crich.

1721 Borrello, Alfred. E. M. FORSTER: AN ANNOTATED BIBLIOGRAPHY OF SECONDARY MATERIALS (Metuchen, NJ: Scarecrow P, 1973).
[There are about 711 entry numbers, 23 insertions, and some 9 numbers designated as "No entries," for a total of about 725 actual items. An additional 400 items published in various issues of ENGLISH LITERATURE IN TRANSITION are *not* included, and 365 items in Borrello's book had previously appeared in *ELT* (formerly *EFT*). Besides omission of *all* publications appearing between 1911 and 1920, there are other omissions of absolutely essential items, such as George Thomson's THE FICTION OF E. M. FORSTER (1967) and H. H. Anniah Gowda's A GARLAND FOR E. M. FORSTER (1969). Borrello's book is further weakened by the exclusion of all foreign language criticism. Some 56 entries are not annotated, although 30 of these were abstracted in *ELT.* Borrello's book is regrettably marred by an astonishing number of errors, omissions, and inconsistencies, enough to comprise a closely typed list of some six pages. Since a total of more than 765 items on EMF were listed in *ELT* by June 1970, Borrello is less than accurate when he claims that neither the *ELT* nor the listing by MODERN FICTION STUDIES "equals the comprehensiveness of this volume." It should be noted that despite similarities in titles and in format, Borrello's volume is in no way associated with the ASB Series, nor with *ELT.* The ASB Series volume on EMF, further, was announced publicly in June 1969, and frequently thereafter.—H. E. G.]

E. M. FORSTER

1722 Bradbury, Malcolm. "E. M. Forster as Victorian and Modern: *Howards End* and *A Passage to India*," "The Modern Comic Novel in the 1920s: Lewis, Huxley, and Waugh," POSSIBILITIES: ESSAYS ON THE STATE OF THE NOVEL (Lond, Oxford, NY: Oxford UP, 1973), pp. 91–120, 140–63, espec 140–42; also pp. 5–6, 8, 33, 74, 84–86, 89, 90, 122, 130, 134, 215–16, 239; rpts, in rvd form, "E. M. Forster's *Howards End*," CRITICAL QUARTERLY, IV (Autumn 1962), 229–41, and "Two Passages to India; Forster as Victorian and Modern," ASPECTS OF E. M. FORSTER, ed by Oliver Stallybrass (NY: Harcourt, Brace & World; Lond: Edward Arnold, 1969), pp. 123–42.

"E. M. Forster as Victorian and Modern" [Bradbury's earlier essays are completely rvd.]: EMF compels not as the modern, withdrawn, masked, and impersonal artist, nor as a prophet of stress and extremity, but as a rare kind of modern writer who compels because of his centrality, decency, humanity, and respect for culture. In *Howards End*, EMF is often much criticized for the rigidity of his patterns and the schematic quality of his fiction, without the realization that his irony modulates his vision. In *Passage* his irony is equivocal to the end. He embraces transcendence, while his irony undercuts it; he modulates the permanency of art by an insistence on contingency. "The Modern Comic Novel in the 1920s": Even EMF partakes to some degree in the dehumanization of the characters in modern fiction, moving away from his professed humanism and emphasis on personal relationships and sensitivities. Unlike many other modern comic writers, such as Wyndham Lewis, Aldous Huxley, and Evelyn Waugh, he gives the center of human experience its due; these other writers stress the arbitrary far more than do Jane Austen and EMF. [Many scattered references throughout book.]

1723 Brée, Germaine. "Two Vintage Years: France, 1913; England, 1922," VIRGINIA WOOLF QUARTERLY, I (Summer 1973), 19–30. Strong parallels exist between the French literary movement (of the pre-World War I years), *Vaneau*, with André Gide at its center, and Bloomsbury, with Virginia Woolf at its center. Both movements stressed personal relationships. Lytton Strachey and his sister, Dorothy Bussy, were links between the two movements in their personal contacts with Gide. In 1943, Gide read Virginia Woolf; in 1944, EMF's *The Longest Journey* and *Howards End*. Both groups expressed a middle-class ethos and rebelled against it. Sexuality was discussed openly but treated obliquely in the work of both groups; EMF's *Maurice*, an exception, remained unpublished. People in both circles were highly civilized and possessed a devoted sense of aesthetic purpose. Virginia Woolf in the 1920s revealed a "tragic sense of life" that separates later Bloomsbury from earlier Bloomsbury and from *Vaneau*.

1724 Brophy, Brigid. PRANCING NOVELIST: A DEFENCE OF FICTION IN THE FORM OF A CRITICAL BIOGRAPHY IN PRAISE OF RONALD FIRBANK (NY: Barnes & Noble; Lond: Macmillan, 1973), pp. 73, 86, 101, 118, 425.

Firbank, like EMF and some other important writers, enjoyed a private income that enabled him to write fiction. (This is one form of social subsidy of a writer.) EMF wrote an appreciation of Firbank in 1929 that was imperceptive in maintaining that there is nothing "up to date" in him. In Firbank's THE ARTIFICIAL PRINCESS the Baroness alleges that she sees Pan on viewing a goat. (This remark may be a satirical thrust at EMF's early tales.)

1725 Broyard, Anatole. "Raiding the Rag and Bone Shop," NEW YORK TIMES, 4 June 1973, p. 33.

The stories in *The Life to Come and Other Short Stories* seem like a desecration of EMF's grave. Too much contrivance and too much of the gratuitous shock pervade them; the fantasy is clumsy. "Ansell" is the least unsuccessful. Some good moments are present in "The Other Boat," but its ending is bathetic.

1726 Cavaliero, Glen. JOHN COWPER POWYS: NOVELIST (Oxford: Clarendon P, 1973), pp. 178–79, 183.

Powys is a great romantic novelist by virtue of his treatment of nature. He laments, as do Lawrence and EMF, the ravages of the machine age on the English landscape. Powys resorts less to the unseen world and to fantasy than does EMF and finds in the very structure of nature a guarantee against the obliteration of identity. In Powys's novels, unlike EMF's, there are fewer passages that can be regarded in isolation as typical of his work.

1727 Crompton, Louis. "Literature and Our Gay Minority," IOWA ENGLISH BULLETIN YEARBOOK, XXIII (Nov 1973), 3–21.

EMF's *Maurice* is the best novel of stature in existence on the subject of homosexuality and can be taught in any literature course. [Survey of Western literature on homosexual themes.]

1728 Cushman, Keith. "The Book Review: Fiction," LIBRARY JOURNAL, XCVIII (15 June 1973), 1934.

The homosexual stories in *The Life to Come and Other Short Stories* are the most interesting and are definitely to be reckoned with. EMF's non-homosexual fiction is now seen in new perspective, as is his pagan-Christian dialectic, since the paganism now includes homosexuality. EMF has become a more interesting and complex writer.

1729 Deemer, Charles. "Old Master's New Stories," NEW LEADER (NY), LVI (17 Sept 1973), 19–20.
In *The Life to Come and Other Short Stories* the homosexual relationships are depicted with gentleness but resolved in violence. In "The Life to Come" and "The Other Boat" EMF reveals the probable spiritual and psychological consequences of homosexuality: guilt leads to violence and death.

1730 Dick, Kay. "Unfolding of Forster," SCOTSMAN (Edinburgh), "Weekend Scotsman," 22 Dec 1973, p. 3.
The Manuscripts of Howards End (*Abinger Edition*) reveals how a major novel was written. The new *Howards End* (*Abinger Edition*) is also welcome because it reveals how relevant the novel still is as an "ironic drama of personal relationships in a fast-changing world."

1731 Dickinson, G[oldsworthy] Lowes. THE AUTOBIOGRAPHY OF G. LOWES DICKINSON AND OTHER UNPUBLISHED WRITINGS, ed by Dennis Proctor (Lond: Duckworth, 1973), pp. 170, 178–80.
[Principal mentions of EMF concern his travels with Dickinson, R. C. Trevelyan, and G. Luce to India in 1912–1913. Dickinson notes that EMF got closer to Indian realities than he or Trevelyan did. Dickinson notes, in the Forsterian terms of *A Passage to India*, the incomprehensibility of India to the English (a lack of understanding that Dickinson himself experienced) and the great gulf in Calcutta between the educated Indians and the Anglo-Indian bureaucrats. Surprisingly few mentions of EMF considering that EMF was a life-long friend and disciple (later literary executor); he apparently was never a subject of Dickinson's love. Invaluable for its re-creation of the Cambridge milieu (in which homosexuality figured actively) immediately before, during, and after EMF's sojourn at Cambridge, the milieu that formed Bloomsbury in the early century. Supplements indispensably EMF's *Goldsworthy Lowes Dickinson* and Wilfred Stone's useful account of Dickinson's influence on EMF in THE CAVE AND THE MOUNTAIN (1966).]

1732 Donoghue, Denis. " 'Till the Fight Is Finished': D. H. Lawrence in His Letters," D. H. LAWRENCE: NOVELIST, POET, PROPHET, ed by Stephen Spender (NY: Harper & Row; Lond: Weidenfeld & Nicolson, 1973), pp. 197–209, espec 207.
D. H. Lawrence's sense of the decay of old England is like EMF's in *Howards End*.

1733 Edmiston, Susan. "Bloomsbury: A Good Address in the Geography of the Mind," NEW YORK TIMES, X (18 March 1973), pp. 1, 18.
[Most of the standard facts on Bloomsbury are given, including EMF's

tangential relationship to it. Valuable for maps of Bloomsbury and for illustrations of Bloomsbury associates and habitats.]

1734 "Edwardian Taboos," TIMES LITERARY SUPPLEMENT (Lond), 21 Sept 1973, p. 1085.

Goldsworthy Lowes Dickinson is likely to be remembered only as the subject of another man's writing. EMF's biography, *Goldsworthy Lowes Dickinson*, reveals EMF's decency, generosity, intelligence, and reticence, but it lacks his most distinctive literary gift, irony. EMF's *Dickinson* is so bland and inoffensive, because EMF was unable to deal honestly with Dickinson's preferences as homosexual and boot-fetishist. *Dickinson* is incomplete, therefore, as a human document and becomes, instead, "a chapter in the History of Donnishness." In THE AUTOBIOGRAPHY OF G. LOWES DICKINSON, Dickinson did recount truthfully his love relationships and the childhood and adolescence that formed his sexual nature. EMF had access to this autobiography and drew upon it for his *Dickinson*, often echoing Dickinson directly, especially for the early years. This fact reveals the close affinity existing between the two men: EMF was drawn by Dickinson's Platonism, his liberal humanism, and his philosophical earnestness. Above all, both men were homosexuals, realizing that homosexuality in Edwardian England was a burden to be borne but not a fact to be denied. (Both men thus reveal a private honesty.) EMF in *Dickinson* memorializes the public man and writer; in his AUTOBIOGRAPHY Dickinson focuses upon his inner life. He emerges as a more attractive figure there than in EMF's book. Dickinson judged himself with "a blunt severity," knowing that he was a born writer but not a great one and nothing of a poet. He realized that the life of the world went on in circles that were alien to him; he was at ease only in Cambridge. He scarcely mentions his career as a teacher, except in terms of the young men toward whom he was attracted. He does not view them as men to be trained intellectually. His failure to do so reveals how adolescent he remained in his emotional life. Dickinson's books are too abstract, too vaguely idealistic, and often overwritten. These qualities are in abeyance in the AUTOBIOGRAPHY, which is his best book. The personal charm that EMF celebrated in his friend and mentor comes through more persuasively in the AUTOBIOGRAPHY than in EMF's biography of the man. [Review of EMF's *Goldsworthy Lowes Dickinson and Related Writings*, ed by Oliver Stallybrass (Lond: Edward Arnold, The Abinger Edition of E. M. Forster, 1973) and THE AUTOBIOGRAPHY OF G. LOWES DICKINSON, ed by Dennis Proctor (Lond: Duckworth, 1973). Most perceptive account.]

1735 Ellem, Elizabeth. "E. M. Forster's *Arctic Summer*," TIMES LITERARY SUPPLEMENT (Lond), 21 Sept 1973, pp. 1087–89.

Four manuscript versions of the unfinished *Arctic Summer* exist, totaling about 50,000 words and mostly dating from 1911–1912. The manuscripts are concerned with the relationship (or the attempt to establish a relationship) between a professional and intellectual man of about 30, Martin Whitby, and a "youth" named Clesant—or Cyril—March. In the Tramonta version, Martin is an intellectual married to a spiritually aggressive blue-stocking, Venetia Borlase. He regards the bourgeois civilization of his era as a necessary phase in the progress of the race. He has never known passion and is rationalistic, forward-looking, and abstract in disposition. His temperament is challenged when he meets Lieutenant Clesant March, whose ideas are chivalric: "purity, automatic courage, blind devotion to a chosen cause, and that women should be treated with exaggerated courtesy." Clesant dislikes Martin and the help that Martin extends, so that Clesant can visit Tramonta Castle to see there the frescoes depicting the Battle of Lepanto. Martin visits the Castle alone and sees a soldier in a painting who is the image of Clesant. The result is a revelation to Martin about the barrenness of his life, and the fact that he has missed totally the element of romance. He is unsettled as a result of this experience, and further unsettled somewhat later when he leaves a motion picture auditorium after a fire breaks out and before he ascertains that his companion is safe. In desperation Martin applies to Clesant for is friendship. Clesant and his brother Lance, whom he idolizes, have been trained by their uncle to attack self-proclaimed, nonconformist intellectuals such as Martin. Lance is sent down from Cambridge for consorting with women, and, when Clesant turns against him, Lance shoots himself. In the Cyril version, Martin is less a progressive and more an exponent of chivalric ideals who tries to help Cyril overcome his remorse for his brother's disaster, for which he blames himself. In the Radipole Version, the two men meet not on a train platform at Basle but in a public school at Radipole. Martin is a civil servant who makes an unpopular speech at Radipole, inculcating values at odds with the public school ethos. Clesant is the only boy who listens to Martin but undiplomatically proclaims his dislike of the speech. Martin is attracted toward Clesant's affable brother, Lance. In this version Mrs. March is a controlling figure. Captain March, the father, feels disgrace because he did not come to the rescue of a royal princess. The Aldeburgh Version parallels the Tramonta down to the betrayal of Lance by Clesant. In 1951 this alternative was not satisfactory for EMF. In a note EMF describes how Martin and the Borlase women will combine to rescue Lance (though change in characterization would have been necessary for Venetia and for Lady Borlase to do so).

The manuscripts reveal how EMF was searching for a new form in which to express his theme of the meeting of the civilized man and the man of instinct. EMF is trying to escape suburbia, but his choice of romantic medievalism as a source for positive value was not a happy one. EMF was at his best in describing Cambridge or the suburbia that he was trying to escape. The writing, done in 1911–1912, reveals the same ironic and stylistic mastery that EMF had displayed in *Howards End*. In the early chapters the theme is like that in *Howards End*, the need to reconcile oppositions; in the later chapters EMF is preoccupied with the need to bring two men together. His chief problem was to cause the unwilling Clesant to accept Martin and to find an acceptable permanent relationship for the men. The chief difficulty is that Clesant's character is inflexible, undeveloped, and uncritical. The two men were too similar in class origin for them to retire from society altogether as do Maurice and Alec in *Maurice*. EMF was still trying "to reconcile the genteel, womanish world of respectability and the secret world of men: to find a satisfactory relationship for his heroes *within* society." *Arctic Summer* is not a homosexual novel, though with the years EMF became more interested in bringing the two heroes together than in reconciling ideologies. The minor characters are conceived with EMF's customary vigor and incisiveness. The novel was not completed because World War I intervened, to reveal the hollowness of Clesant's values of chivalry and romance and to supplant the Victorian-Edwardian world of the earlier novels, including *Arctic Summer*. "There was no place for Martin and Clesant in this new world, and no likelihood of a happy-ever-after ending for his fairytale." [A most interesting and perceptive article; the quotations reveal the literary excellence of the completed segments of *Arctic Summer*.]

1736 Evett, Robert. "Forster's Homosexual Tales," EVENING STAR AND WASHINGTON DAILY NEWS, Section F, 24 June 1973, p. 2.
The homosexuality of John Maynard Keynes, Lytton Strachey, and EMF has been a significant recent revelation. EMF wished to have his homosexual writings published, but only after his death. Among the earlier works "The Rock" is excellent. In his homosexual tales his characters are promiscuous; the sordid, insignificant encounters described in them could hardly engender "high tragedy and ennobling love." The stories, however, reveal finished craftsmanship.

1737 Finkelstein, Bonnie Blumenthal. "Forster's Women: *A Room with a View*," ENGLISH LITERATURE IN TRANSITION, XVI: 4 (1973), 275–87; rptd in rvd form in FORSTER'S WOMEN: ETERNAL DIFFERENCES (NY & Lond: Columbia UP, 1975), pp. 65–88.
EMF is concerned in *A Room with a View* with the acceptance of sexuality and the life of the body and with sexual equality and the role of women in society. As for sexuality, Lucy Honeychurch must learn to accept George's passion for the positive force that it is, thus overcoming the constraining influences of Cecil Vyse, Charlotte Bartlett, the Misses Alan, and Mrs. Honeychurch. She must also learn to be an emancipated woman (rather than a "medieval" one), capable of expressing her own individuality, because only as man's equal can a woman enter the Garden of Eden with him.

Mr. Emerson is the voice of liberty and freedom on these matters. Italy, George, and music combine to emancipate Lucy. She finds that liberty and emancipation are not easy to accept, but she comes to realize that it is more of an insult to be protected by Cecil than to be kissed by George. Miss Lavish is Mr. Emerson's obverse: his genuine unconventionality is false originality in her. [EMF's fiction is capable of feminist interpretation, despite current emphasis on his homosexuality and evidence of misogyny in the homosexually oriented fiction.]

1738 Fleishman, Avrom. "Being and Nothing in *A Passage to India*," CRITICISM, XV (Spring 1973), 109–25.

In *A Passage to India* EMF is concerned with the movement of the individual between the poles of being and nothing, of negation and affirmation, of birth and death, of the ordinary and the extraordinary, of downward movement and upward aspiration, of mystery and muddle. [The article is sound and occasionally perceptive, but densely written. Other critics who had previously covered much the same subject are dismissed. EMF's paradoxical view of reality is discussed at length in Louise Dauner's "What Happened in the Cave?" (1961), Frederick C. Crews's E. M. FORSTER: THE PERILS OF HUMANISM (1972), H. M. Daleski's "Rhythm and Symbolic Patterns in *A Passage to India*" (1966), and Wilfred Stone's THE CAVE AND THE MOUNTAIN (1966).]

1739 Friend, Robert. "The Quest for Rondure: A Comparison of Two Passages to India," HEBREW UNIVERSITY STUDIES IN LITERATURE (The Hebrew University of Jerusalem), I (Spring 1973), 77–85.

Both EMF's *A Passage to India* and Whitman's "Passage to India" stress spiritual exploration. EMF's purpose is metaphysical or religious, as is Whitman's. Both writers stress the need for "rondure" (connection, completion, unity), though EMF is less sanguine than Whitman that it can be attained in an India where so many gaps, depravations, and confusions occur. [Comparison between *Passage* and Whitman's poem is not always clearly or pointedly developed. Repeats many points made in Hugh Maclean's "The Structure of *A Passage to India*" (1953) and in Wilfred Stone's THE CAVE AND THE MOUNTAIN, Chap 12: "*A Passage to India*: The Great Round" (1966). Account is inferior to Herbert Howarth's "Whitman and the English Writers," PAPERS ON WALT WHITMAN (1970).]

1740 Friend, Robert. "The Rainbow Bridge: Forster's Failure in *Howards End*," FURTHER STUDIES IN ENGLISH LANGUAGE AND LITERATURE, ed by A. A. Mendilow (Jerusalem: The Hebrew University, 1973), XXV, 227–39.

EMF in *Howards End* fails to make credible the marriage between Margaret Schlegel and Henry Wilcox. Margaret is unable to build "the rainbow bridge" between the values she represents and those embodied in her husband. Marriage at any price is not worthy of her. At the end of the novel "connection" between the Schlegels and the Wilcoxes is not made. It is not even necessary, as the Schlegel valuation of the inner life emerges as all-important. [A long article to prove a proposition that other critics, e.g., Wilfred Stone in THE CAVE AND THE MOUNTAIN (1966), had already fully demonstrated. It is not so much the marriage that is unconvincing, I think, as the contradiction between what EMF means Henry Wilcox to represent and what in fact EMF judges him to be.]

1741 Gardner, Philip (ed). E. M. FORSTER: THE CRITICAL HERITAGE (Lond & Boston: Routledge & Kegan Paul, The Critical Heritage Series, 1973).

[Contains "Preface" and "Introduction" and 184 items (reviews, journal entries, published and unpublished letters, and articles), printed in whole or in part, which focus on the reception of EMF's works. The 184 items appear roughly in the chronological order of their publication. Most of the items are abstracted here. In this bibliography, the title line for an item reprinted in Gardner's book will contain this information. Such a notation regarding reprinting is not made for the published letters of D. H. Lawrence and others, reproduced in Gardner's book. Many of the materials reprinted here are difficult to obtain in most libraries. The book also contains unpublished letters not available elsewhere, and these are abstracted. The book is indispensable for EMF scholars. Letters: Frieda Lawrence to EMF (c. 1915), She loves *The Longest Journey*. Rickie is not at all dead; he is appealing. EMF does well with the man-to-man relationship, but he does not understand women. A. C. Bensen to EMF (9 Dec 1910), Bensen's mother finds a kind of conscientious pragmatism in *Howards End* with respect to ethics. Bensen's own view is more determinist. For him the book emphasizes the strength of sturdy, ordinary humanity. In Margaret and Helen Schlegel there is the contrast between the emotional and the intellectual nature, "with and without moral force." Marmaduke Pickthall to EMF (18 July 1924), EMF in *A Passage to India* gives him insight as to what has happened to his fellow countrymen in India. Edward Carpenter to EMF (14 Aug [1924]), congratulates EMF for conveying so well in *Passage* the Anglo-Indian life and portraying the lives of his characters. Robert Bridges to EMF (11 Nov [1924]), congratulates EMF on writing a masterpiece in *Passage* and for his insight into Indian psychology. Edith Sitwell to EMF (30 March 1928), *The Eternal Moment and Other Stories* has beauty, truth, and illumination. "The Machine Stops" is "the most tremendous" short story of our time, "The Point of It" is excellent, and "The Eternal Moment" is "the most terrifying ghost story" she has ever encountered. Edward Carpenter to EMF (23 Aug [1914]), Carpenter has reservations about EMF's impressionist style in *Maurice*, but the atmosphere and Maurice's love affairs are well-realized. He is glad that Scudder was not let go; the end, though improbable, is not impossible. Lytton Strachey to EMF (12 March 1915), Strachey rather questions the end of *Maurice*. The Clive affair is better realized than the Alec one. The ending is mythical because class differences would mean that the two would have no common interests and would part in six weeks. The lack of a physical relationship with Clive is improbable. The upper-class life is presented well. EMF is too uneasy and self-conscious about physical sex, as in the Dicky and the railway carriage episodes. For reviews, see "Patriarch of the Liberal Imagination," TIMES LITERARY SUPPLEMENT (Lond), 26 Oct 1973, p. 1316, and Frederick P. W. McDowell, "The Critical Heritage Series and E. M. Forster," ENGLISH LITERATURE IN TRANSITION, XVII: 2 (1974), 137–39.]

1742 Gardner, Philip. "Preface," "Introduction," E. M. FORSTER: THE CRITICAL HERITAGE, ed by Philip Gardner (Lond & Boston: Routledge & Kegan Paul, The Critical Heritage Series, 1973), pp. xvii–xviii, 1–39.

["Preface": Critical opinion recorded in this book consists of reviews, letters, comments, and articles, primarily from 1905–1928, covering EMF as fiction writer. The cut-off point is 1943, the date of Lionel Trilling's E. M. FORSTER, when the "revival" of recent interest in EMF got under way. A few reviews of EMF's other works after 1943 are included, and a number of reviews for *Maurice* (1971). "Introduction": Informed summary of critical reception of EMF, based on discussion of the reprinted reviews and other commentary in this book. Section IV carries the survey beyond 1943 to 1973. Gardner concludes that at least one more critical study will be necessary on EMF, in view of the recently printed homosexually oriented fiction, but such a study might be premature before P. N. Furbank's authorized life appears.]

1743 Gish, Robert Franklin. "Literary Allusion and the Homiletic Style of E. M. Forster: A Study in the Relationship between the Tales and the Novels," DISSERTATION ABSTRACTS INTERNATIONAL, XXXIII (1973), p. 5678A. Unpublished thesis, University of New Mexico, 1972.

1744 Hanquart, E. "Comptes Rendus" (Reviews), ÉTUDES ANGLAISES (Paris), XXVII: 2 (1973), 236–37.

Maurice is less a work of force than of faith, less a work of illumination than of warmth. EMF is concerned with the realization of the self through love, homosexual love in this case. In the long view the individual is more important than society. The characters in *Maurice* form a romantic triangle; the psychological treatment tends to be unreal and summary, and the characters tend to be disembodied. EMF is also concerned with the malevolent effects of class; its narrowing effects are especially embodied in the women of the novel. *Maurice* is not a masterpiece, but it is of value in understanding more fully the mind of the author of *Howards End* and *A Passage to India*. [In French.]

1745 Hanquart, E. "Comptes Rendus" (Reviews), ÉTUDES ANGLAISES (Paris), XXVII: 2 (1973), pp. 237–38.

The early stories in *The Life to Come and Other Stories* offer little that is new. The homosexual stories are presented with more violence than is present in *Maurice*. Some of them present an extravagant kind of humor ("The Obelisk," "What Does It Matter? A Morality," "The Classical Annex"), a more measured humor ("The Torque"), and a bitter seriousness ("Dr. Woolacott," "Arthur Snatchfold"). The social satire is often bitter, while homosexual love is seen as natural. "The Life to Come" presents Christianity ambiguously and is satiric about colonization. "The Other Boat" presents the milieu of *A Passage to India*, racial snobbery in particular. This snobbery is contrasted with the tenderness of the homosexual passion in the story. The last two stories have creative power superior to that found in *Maurice* and EMF's other novels. [Contains short descriptive review of *Two Cheers for Democracy*, Abinger Edition.]

1746 Hanquart, Evelyne. "E. M. Forster's Manuscript of *Marianne Thornton*," NOTES AND QUERIES (Lond), XX (Sept 1973), 336–40.

The corrections and amendments to the manuscript of *Marianne Thornton* in most cases result in stronger, more precise, more colorful, or more straightforward prose. The major additions to the manuscript, as well as the deletions, serve the same purpose. Some significant deletions occur in the autobiographical "Great Aunt" section. EMF also corrected his personal copy of the book at two different times. [Discussion of the manuscript of *Marianne* as compared to the printed book. Judicious and informative article.]

1747 Hanquart, Evelyne. "Humanisme Féministe ou Humanisme au Féminin? Une Lecture de l'Oeuvre Romanesque de Virginia Woolf et E. M. Forster" (Feminist Humanism or Humanism Based on the Feminine? A Reading of the Novelistic Canon of Virginia Woolf and E. M. Forster), ÉTUDES ANGLAISES (Paris), XXVI: 3 (1973), 278–89.

The advocates of humanism stress the powers of the human being and his or her potentialities. The feminist movement, beginning at the end of the nineteenth century, was humanistic in emphasis, and Virginia Woolf well represented its tenets. The masculine world is one based on intellectualism rather than, like the feminine, on a living intelligence, acknowledging the importance of sensation and intuition. EMF was even more centrally a humanist than Woolf. EMF recognized the importance of the feminine attributes of sensitivity, intuition, and imagination in the formulation of his humanism. His humanism saved him even from the misogyny present by implication in his creation of the feminine characters in *The Longest Journey* and *Maurice*. Although some of his most vividly drawn women are Philistine and Sawstonian, nevertheless his enlightened feminine characters are the most enlightened of all his characters. In the typical EMF novel, it is the humanistically oriented woman who brings salvation to men—Caroline Abbott in *Where Angels Fear to Tread* and the Schlegel sisters in *Howards End*. The Schlegel sisters oppose their humanist values to the materialistic values of the Wilcoxes; and Howards End house, the touchstone of reality, is identified with Margaret Schlegel and her attributes as opposed to the Wilcox attributes. Margaret becomes an apostle of humanism and is analogous, in her dynamic spiritual influence, to Mrs. Ramsay in Woolf's To the Lighthouse. In *Howards End*, the positive values are feminine in purport. EMF emphasized therein the aptitude of women for the interior life as opposed to men of affairs or dilettante men of culture like Tibby Schlegel. Margaret's humanism is the humanism based on the feminine that is so integral a part of the work of both Woolf and EMF. The importance of this feminism cannot be underestimated, though it was weakened by the failure of Woolf and EMF to adopt a sufficiently realist attitude toward the situation of women in their day. [In French.]

1748 Hardwick, Elizabeth. "Bloomsbury and Virginia Woolf," New York Review of Books, 8 Feb 1973, pp. 15–18; rptd, slightly rvd, in Seduction and Betrayal: Women and Literature (NY: Random House, 1974), pp. 125–39.

The style and the sexual freedom of Bloomsbury are the most arresting things about it. Bloomsbury did lack the sense of the demonic; EMF's *Maurice* is really tame and not demonic. The suspense concerning *Maurice* derived from the widespread speculation about it, as it was withheld from publication until after EMF's death. Jealousy and possessiveness were lacking in Bloomsbury. The two transcendent personal loyalties in the circle were Carrington's for Lytton Strachey and Leonard Woolf's for Virginia. Bloomsbury was insular, though the need for excitement, experience, and sex sometimes breaks through; this aspect is to the fore in the homosexuals (Alec Scudder in *Maurice* writes the blackmailing letter that the Bloomsbury members or their partners might have written but did not). Style and the rendering of life from the inside matter. Miss Kilman in Mrs. Dalloway reveals the same lack of the graces and elicits the same feeling of repulsion from the author as does Leonard Bast in *Howards End*. (The girl in Henry James's "In the Cage" is similar.) All these characters earn their creators' excessive dislike, which we as readers need not necessarily share. Virginia

Woolf in her life reveals that the time of Bloomsbury was a larger, more courteous and loyal time than ours. It is all contemporary, yet historical. The aestheticism, the "androgyny," of Mrs. Woolf limits her work and significance, as it limits Bloomsbury as a whole. [Review of Quentin Bell's VIRGINIA WOOLF: A BIOGRAPHY (1972) and LYTTON STRACHEY: THE REALLY INTERESTING QUESTION AND OTHER PAPERS, ed by Paul Levy (Lond: Weidenfred & Nicolson, 1972).]

1749 Heilbrun, Carolyn G. "The Woman as Hero," and "The Bloomsbury Group," TOWARD A RECOGNITION OF ANDROGYNY (NY: Knopf, 1973), pp. 47–112, espec 93, 97–101 and 116–67, espec 134–36; as TOWARDS ANDROGYNY: ASPECTS OF MALE AND FEMALE IN LITERATURE (Lond: Gollancz, 1973).

In his first three novels EMF's central characters seek for a new sexual awareness, though his prophetic vision is more often voiced by the men (e.g., Mr. Emerson's view in *A Room with a View* that men and women must attain deep understanding before they can enter "the garden"). EMF's homosexuality, evident since the publication of *Maurice*, made the creation of women heroes easier for him; they took the place of the homosexual heroes that public opinion did not let him create. More important is EMF's realization that the feminine principle can be best valued in a society that does not limit the woman's role to that of loving wife and mother. Women must also live in a world of far-ranging choices. For EMF the "heart's affections" are basic to spiritual growth and renewal. Hence, he emphasizes friendship even when the friends are, on the surface, unlikely (Aziz and Mrs. Moore in *A Passage to India;* Caroline Abbott and Philip Herriton in *Where Angels Fear to Tread*). [Heilbrun objects (justifiably, I think) to the Freudian interpretation of the relationship between Margaret Schlegel and Henry Wilcox.] In Margaret's relationship with Henry, EMF is not presenting the "gelding" of the male but is dramatizing a conviction that the intelligentsia and businessmen need to discover and support each other. In such encounters the businessman will not survive unchanged. The rapport among Margaret Schlegel, Ruth Wilcox, and Miss Avery emphasizes the importance of feminine values, which are played down in the Wilcox world, though the Wilcoxes provide the material resources that allow these values to flourish. Henry at the end learns something of the feminine spirit and realizes that the masculine and feminine spirits cannot survive isolated from each other, as Charles Wilcox and Helen Schlegel might seem to think. Margaret and Ruth are in touch with the feminizing earth, which has been preserved for them by the masculine virtues. [Rpts "The Woman as Hero," TEXAS QUARTERLY, VIII (Winter 1965), 132–41 with the above additions. Provocative discussion. Also rpts, much rvd in light of the author's increased emphasis on the relevance of the androgynous ideal, "The Bloomsbury Group," MIDWAY, IX (Autumn 1968), 71–85 (1968), with additional sections discussing the androgynous elements in Lytton Strachey (EMF cited in defense of Strachey's temper and art) and in the fiction of Virginia Woolf.]

1750 Heine, Elizabeth. "The Significance of Structure in the Novels of E. M. Forster and Virginia Woolf," ENGLISH LITERATURE IN TRANSITION, XVI: 4 (1973), 289–306.

In achieving "significant form" EMF reveals Clive Bell's idealist view, which presupposes some transcendent reality; in achieving such form, Virginia Woolf reveals Rogers Fry's human-centered view. In Claude Lévi-Strauss's sense EMF reveals "savage" thought in his work; it is "mythic" thought, going from structure to event and is "synchronic" in its repetitions of pattern and motifs. Woolf's thought is "scientific"; it goes from events to structure and is "diachronic" in its concern with historical development and change. In EMF's work abstract pattern and "rhythm" govern; the organization is dialectical. Relatively rigid pattern and easy "rhythms" (repetition and variation as in the leitmotif) prevail in each novel. A belief in aesthetic wholeness and an exposure of unconscious psychological processes result from this combination of rigidity and flexibility. The emphasis is on the difficulties human beings encounter in trying to discover a correct understanding external to them. In Woolf's fiction the thoughts of the characters lead to the form. The pattern is that of life itself (not an imposed dialectic), enriched by love and ending in death. The emphasis is on an internal personal perception of reality. In EMF's fiction the omniscient author is alone aware of the full complexities of the situation. In *A Passage to India* EMF creates a nonhuman absolute to which the characters and their problems are referred. In Woolf's fiction the characters are free to grow and develop in accordance with the inner laws of their own nature; they do not conform to a superposed problem or form. Human beings attempt to shape their own reality. In EMF's fiction an eternity of infinite order is present that only the mystically inclined figures perceive; in Woolf's fiction an eternity of life and death is present in which the uniting force is a human mind, often that of an artist inside the novel rather than the artist outside the novel. In EMF's fiction man is governed by forces beyond his control; Woolf presents individuals as fully developing entities in time. EMF's concern with dialectic that reaches toward a transcendent reality or myth and his antithetical and allegorical bent of mind mean that his fiction is more explicable than Woolf's in terms of the formulas that Lévi-Strauss has worked out in "The Structural Study of Myth." [Perceptive, stimulating, and possibly path-breaking article.]

1751 Hemenway, Stephen Ignatius. "E. M. Forster's *A Passage to India* as a Touchstone for Two Traditions: Anglo-Indian and Indo-Anglian Novels," DISSERTATION ABSTRACTS INTERNATIONAL,

XXXIV (1973), 773A. Unpublished dissertation, University of Illinois, 1972.

1752 Henig, Suzanne. "Interview with John Lehmann," JOURNAL OF MODERN LITERATURE, III (Feb 1973), 91–99.
Lehmann asserts that in recent fiction the greatest richness in imaginative power is to be found in the works of Lawrence, Virginia Woolf, and EMF. EMF did not publish *Maurice* in the 1920s because he was diffident about its worth and its modernity. Most discerning critics have focused on its literary aspects—the adequacy of the writing and the awareness of social differences—not on its sexual side. *Maurice,* at least in its central character, is not autobiographical. EMF was not serious and solemn in his personal relationships; gaiety and humor were always present.

1753 Hynes, Samuel. "Hazards of an Honest Life," WASHINGTON POST BOOK WORLD, 3 June 1973, p. 3.
EMF knew that he was not a great novelist because he was so locked in himself. After 1913 EMF cared to write fiction only with homosexual themes. EMF would have been heroic to have published the contents of *The Life to Come and Other Short Stories* during his lifetime, but he was not heroic. Judged by modern standards, his reticence is extreme; but he was Edwardian. The stories emphasize the major theme in all his fiction: the conflict between repressive society and the individual who desires freedom. The stories are not first rate, though they are of interest. He was honest rather than saintly in his character and attitudes. [Provocative discussion.]

1754 Italia, Paul G. "On Miss Quested's Given Name, in E. M. Forster's *A Passage to India,*" ENGLISH LANGUAGE NOTES, XI (Dec 1973), 118–20.
The name "Adela" suggests "addled," which derives from Anglo-Saxon "adela" (mud). The name "Adela" itself derives from Old High German "adal," meaning "noble." Adela's name is thus emblematic not only of her mixed attributes and actions but of those of all the major characters, who are "rooted in the mud and mire" yet "reach toward something noble." [A somewhat strained interpretation.]

1755 Kennard, Jean E. "*A Passage to India* and Dickinson's Saint at Benares," STUDIES IN THE NOVEL, V (Winter 1973), 441–56.
Wilfred Stone's view of the structure of *A Passage to India* (THE CAVE AND THE MOUNTAIN, 1966) in terms of the Hindu temple as World Mountain with its cave at the center and circular lines on its exterior is reinforced by the Hindu symbol of the tree, described in Goldsworthy Lowes Dickinson's APPEARANCES (1914), and used by EMF as symbolic of the cyclic journey of the soul. EMF makes structural use of this symbol in *Passage.* EMF's use

of this symbol indicates his Hindu sympathies. Hinduism explains much about ultimate realities without being a completely satisfying philosophy. Hinduism allows us to live with political and social problems even if it does not solve them. [A persuasive essay, if at times overly ingenious in its elaborations.]

1756 Kermode, Frank. D. H. LAWRENCE (NY: Viking P, Modern Masters, 1973), pp. 5, 25, 60–61, 137.

Wagner meant almost as much to Lawrence as to EMF, with whom Lawrence has much in common. [EMF is quoted as to the power of Lawrence's "message."] Lawrence probably knew Edward Carpenter, a visit to whom inspired the writing of EMF's *Maurice.* Mellors in LADY CHATTERLEY'S LOVER looks back to the educated gamekeeper in THE WHITE PEACOCK who had dropped out into the greenwood, also a place of retreat for Maurice in EMF's novel.

1757 Kermode, Frank. "The Novels of D. H. Lawrence," D. H. LAWRENCE: NOVELIST, POET, PROPHET, ed by Stephen Spender (NY: Harper & Row; Lond: Weidenfeld & Nicolson, 1973), pp. 77–89, espec 85.

Form in D. H. Lawrence's fiction tends to become a succession of vividly realized sequences or images, "unlike the interactions of social notation, narrative and symbol" in EMF's *A Passage to India* or the surfaces being held in place by underlying myths in Joyce's ULYSSES.

1758 Kermode, Frank, and John Hollander. "E. M. Forster" [Modern British Literature], THE OXFORD ANTHOLOGY OF ENGLISH LITERATURE, Vol. II, 1800 TO THE PRESENT, ed by Frank Kermode and John Hollander (NY & Lond: Oxford UP, 1973), pp. 2128–31 ["What I Believe," *Two Cheers for Democracy*, rptd, pp. 2131–38]; as MODERN BRITISH LITERATURE (The Oxford Anthology of English Literature), pp. 620–23; "What I Believe," rptd pp. 623–30.

EMF had reverence for his Clapham ancestors but criticized them for their indifference to social concerns and their deficient aesthetic and mystical sensibilities. The Cambridge "Apostles" stressed "candor, gaiety, and self-effacing honesty" as indispensable elements in friendship. This group also assimilated the influence of G. E. Moore, with his stress upon the mentalizing of reality and his concept of "complex wholes" in which beautiful objects and personal relations are primary elements. From J. M. E. McTaggart EMF derived his sense of the mystical virtues of friendship; from Goldsworthy Lowes Dickinson he absorbed a similar view and the idea of the supremacy of Greek culture. EMF was a part of the nonconformist Bloomsbury Group, who saw themselves, in Clapham-sect fashion, as a sort of elect. But EMF was apart from this group even as part of it. He was modern but not experimental, his masters being Wagner, Samuel Butler, Meredith, and Hardy, not the late James, Conrad, and Joyce. His first four novels are concerned with the claims of individuality as opposed to those of social class; the individual's primary responsibility is to himself. Structurally the books are complex, though the problems explored are now of less relevance than they once were. *Maurice*, posthumously published, allows us to see that EMF's sinning heroes and heroines are substitutes for the proscribed homosexual hero and enables us to define the exact nature of his Hellenism. *A Passage to India* is an enormous advance on his earlier novels. In it EMF uses a limited world to comment on "the tragedies and mitigations of the larger one." [Cites his subsequent volumes of nonfiction.] He has written one great book, *A Passage to India*, which assures him a permanent reputation. His general influence is more difficult to define since his liberalism is at once pertinent and outmoded. He was "an Edwardian version of a Victorian sage," with a different and individual view of morality, and an artist of strenth and delicacy. "What I Believe" is a classic expression of the Bloomsbury ethos: "intelligent skepticism, the supremacy of personal relations over such external loyalties as may be demanded of one." Auden borrowed in "September 1, 1939" the image of the elect flashing their signal lights to each other through the darkness. [A more independently wrought and significant account than one generally finds in anthology headpieces.]

1759 Lauterbach, Edward S., and W. Eugene Davis. THE TRANSITIONAL AGE: BRITISH LITERATURE 1880–1920 (Troy, NY: Whitston Publishing Co., 1973), pp. ii, 15–16, 23, 148–50, 205.
EMF has been an innovator in his use of imagery and symbolism, but, nevertheless, his debt to earlier fiction is great. Instead of new forms in his earlier work he preferred to use the traditional forms supplied by social comedy (*Where Angels Fear to Tread*), and he made extensive use of author intrusion (*A Room with a View*). He outgrew these propensities in *Howards End* and *A Passage to India*. His striking quality as a writer is his invention of effective symbolic detail. Both *Howards End* and *Passage* achieve resonance by EMF's "harmonizing details of imagery into chords of significance." EMF is a master of the symbolic interaction of scene, character, and incident. The circumstances of Leonard Bast's death in *Howards End* and of Adela Quested's experiences in the Marabar Caves in *Passage* are such symbolically full episodes. EMF's stress is upon the need for people to connect at the same time that he dramatizes the barriers in the way of making meaningful connections. The inability to connect or to communicate is a constant theme in modern literature. Fantasy, magic, and the supernatural are central to EMF's short fiction, in contrast to his novels. "The Celestial Omnibus," "The Story of a Panic," and "The Road from

Colonus" are all concerned with transcendental experiences that cannot be shared and with the alienation felt by the central characters in their resulting isolation. [Selected bibliography.]

1760 McDonald, Walter R. "The Unity of *A Passage to India*," CEA CRITIC, XXXVI (Nov 1973), 38–42.

The meeting of Aziz and Mrs. Moore in "Mosque" (*A Passage to India*) contains in embryo the entire novel. Fielding is the real protagonist of *Passage;* Aziz is increasingly an "antagonist" who resists understanding and union. Fielding is close to the omniscient author in values and attitudes. India is a land of opposites. The Moslems confront the infidel; the Hindus absorb him. The conceptual pattern of the book is this: attempted friendship, confusion and humiliation, and withdrawal. Coincidence is not really present in *Passage;* rather, reality has an absurd and refractory aspect. EMF is good at rendering the passage of time and at handling authoritatively the omniscient author's viewpoint. EMF's symbolism is functional, not esoteric. His artistry is especially prominent in the novel's rich texture. Reality is ultimately baffling and ambiguous in *Passage.* It is difficult to know which came first, Indian suspicion or British hypocrisy; perhaps they both originated simultaneously. [A few new insights, but the ground is well-trodden by now.]

1761 McDowell, Frederick P. W. "E. M. Forster and Goldsworthy Lowes Dickinson," STUDIES IN THE NOVEL, V (Winter 1973), 441–56.

Goldsworthy Lowes Dickinson in the Abinger Edition reveals the same expertise as earlier volumes in the edition. The relationship between Dickinson and Dickinson's "Recollections" (on which EMF based the early sections of his book and which are printed with additional materials as THE AUTOBIOGRAPHY OF GOLDSWORTHY LOWES DICKINSON, 1973) is now apparent. EMF's book continues the record beyond the "recollections" and supplies details of Dickinson's public life, though EMF declined to discuss Dickinson's homosexuality in any explicit way. *Dickinson* reveals that EMF identified himself with Dickinson the classical scholar, the philosophical idealist, the humane rationalist, and the romantic enthusiast. However, EMF revealed an intermittent pessimism, a preoccupation with the irrational and the violent, an appreciation of the unpredictable involutions of the human psyche, an ironic scrutiny of the Meredithean and Arnoldean values that he espoused, and an instinctive realization of the indissolubility of the empirically observed and the visionary—all elements lacking in Dickinson's mind. The Forsterian touches in point of view, characterization, and style give *Dickinson* its literary distinction. In the AUTOBIOGRAPHY the portrayal of the secular saint shown in EMF's biography is supplemented by a view of the frustrated, sexually obsessed man. Both books are necessary for a portrait of Dickinson. It is as patron of Bloomsbury, influential don, and man of singular integrity that Dickinson will be remembered. [Contains full analysis of AUTOBIOGRAPHY and discussion of Dickinson's works.]

1762 McLaurin, Allen. VIRGINIA WOOLF: THE ECHOES ENSLAVED (Cambridge: Cambridge UP, 1973), pp. 3, 5, 27, 39, 98–99, 103, 119–20, 160.

EMF, along with Shaw, Wells, and (less directly) Virginia Woolf, are part of a turn-of-the-century Samuel Butler "school." EMF and Woolf both derive from Butler a view of the world that conjoins contraries; EMF presents them directly, whereas Woolf uses the *images* of such antitheses. Woolf and EMF ("Me, Them and You," *Abinger Harvest*) both disliked the literary and anecdotal character of Sargent's painting, "Gassed." E. K. Brown in RHYTHM IN THE NOVEL (1950) explores fruitfully the element of repetition in EMF's work but does not go far enough in allying this technique with EMF's embracing of Butlerian paradox and antithesis. In Roger Fry's opinion repetition in art should be neither mechanical nor formless and uncontrolled. Indian art for him tended to represent the extreme of formlessness, an aspect of Indian culture that EMF has projected in *A Passage to India*, in which the West represents the extreme of excessive mechanistic order and the East the extreme of formlessness, with its concomitant lack of connection between human beings and an ultimate emptiness at the heart of existence.

1763 Mahood, M. M. "Amritsar to Chandrapore: E. M. Forster and the Massacre," ENCOUNTER (Lond), XLI (Sept 1973), 26–29.

The Amritsar Massacre was in EMF's mind in writing *A Passage to India*, especially in the events centering about the Marabar Caves and Aziz's trial. "Mosque" depicts India in 1912, "Caves" reflects the Amritsar Massacre and its aftermath in 1919, and "Temple" mirrors Dewas State Senior in 1921 and EMF's exposure there to Hinduism. [Supports conclusively Jeffrey Meyers's contention in "The Politics of *A Passage to India*" (1971) that EMF makes numerous references to postwar Indian history and politics in *Passage*.]

1764 Masters, Anthony. "Two Cheers," TIMES EDUCATIONAL SUPPLEMENT (Lond), 12 Jan 1973, p. 22.

The essays on international politics of the late 1930s and on World War II are the most interesting. There is less of the gentleman amateur in them, though even in the political essays EMF needs more power and energy to deal most effectively with his adversaries. He still deserves to be defended. [Review of Abinger Edition, *Two Cheers for Democracy*, ed by Oliver Stallybrass (1972).]

1765 Meyers, Jeffrey. FICTION AND THE COLONIAL EXPERIENCE (Totowa, NJ: Rowman & Littlefield; Ipswich: Boydell P, 1973), passim; rpts, slightly rvd, "The Politics of *A Passage to India,*" JOURNAL OF MODERN LITERATURE, I (March 1971), 329–38.

"Introduction": Kipling invented colonial fiction. It comprises two sorts of works: those in the tradition of Kipling's early stories (romantic-adventure fiction, revealing little involvement with natives, who are stereotyped, or with native culture; the white ethos dominates) and those in the tradition of Kipling's KIM and of works of Conrad and EMF (fiction that regards seriously and humanistically cultural conflicts, race relations, and the problems of empire). This latter kind of fiction focuses, in part, on atavistic survivals in modern man and the influence of the primeval and the primordial upon him. (The visit to the ancient Caves in *A Passage to India* is a return to the depths of an unconscious racial past.) In the tropics an ordered world is often absent: chaos prevails and a frightening reality obtrudes from under the chaotic surfaces of social life. The writers are concerned with men caught between two civilizations. They explore the questions of what happens to the "civilized" white man in an alien tropical culture and the effects of alien rule upon the natives and their culture.

Chap 1, "Rudyard Kipling: Codes of Heroism": The Lama in KIM is superficial compared with Professor Godbole in *Passage;* Kipling did not have EMF's understanding of Hinduism. Chap 2, "E. M. Forster: *A Passage to India*" [Comparison of EMF and Kipling is best available discussion of this subject, superior to that by a Kipling sympathizer such as K. Bhaskara Rao in RUDYARD KIPLING'S INDIA (1966)]: Kipling's view of colonialism prevailed until 1924. One aspect of *Passage*, its realistic depiction of social life in India and of the racial conflict between the British and Indians, dispelled the view, fostered by Kipling, of India as the romantic land of warfare and imperial conquest; but the power and threat of India, dramatized in many of Kipling's stories, remain in EMF's *Passage*. EMF satirized Kipling's imperial values. EMF and his spokesman, Fielding, derive from Bloomsbury, and they value individualism, personal relations, tolerance, and understanding. EMF emphasizes the moral and intellectual aspects of the colonial experience, Kipling the physical. Kipling's heroes—the conscientious Anglo-Indian administrators who lack imagination, sympathy with others, and penetration into the native culture—become EMF's villains. EMF's mind is open and flexible; he appreciates the relativity of cultural and ethical values, and he reveals sympathy and respect for other nationalities and civilizations. Kipling, on the contrary, reveals a "rigid ethnocentric nationalism." He emphasizes the gulf between the races; EMF tries to bridge it in his most sympathetic characters and rejects the tradition of mistrust (and the extravert values) engendered by the British public school. He does not feel that white rule in the empire is necessarily an indication of progress. EMF is antiauthoritarian and opposes the militaristic attitude toward dependent peoples. EMF's values are those of Fielding; Kipling's values survive in Ronny Heaslop. EMF attacks Kipling's racial and political ideas. He rejects Kipling's exaggerated respect for the martial Indian tribes and his disrespect toward the Western-educated Indian. Kipling felt that the English were never sexually attracted by the Indians; but Adela Quested's unconscious sexual gravitation toward Aziz disputes this notion. Kipling regarded Indians as an undifferentiated mass, as character types, or in a negative light; EMF respects the individual Indian. Kipling was antidemocratic and distrusted parliamentary government. EMF is not sympathetic with the Anglo-Indian view of alleged Indian brutality after the Mutiny of 1857; the Anglo-Indians forget the comparable brutality of the British. The Anglo-Indians are opposed in *Passage* to the Ilbert Bill, which allowed Indian magistrates to try the British.

[Rpts "The Politics of *A Passage to India*" (1971).] The role of setting in the novel is crucial and formative upon the characters; they have a metaphysical as well as a physical relation to it. It continually confuses the characters; it is anthropomorphic, reflecting the values and the attitudes of the men who inhabit it. The Marabar Caves exemplify the negative aspects of the characters and of the relations between the races. The English feel threatened by India and try to impose, unsuccessfully, a rational, logical order upon it. Adela Quested, in particular, is too dependent on logic. She does not realize that the Marabar Caves defy and deny reason and that clarity can prevent spiritual intuition. (Fielding has more intuitive insight and a keener sensibility than Adela.) Her field glasses are a symbol of the futility of applying reason to the reality represented by the Caves. The "anti-rational and elusive multifariousness of India" is expressed in EMF's dualistic view of all experience. He advocates a relative rather than an absolute judgment of human and nonhuman behavior. Social misconceptions take on ontological reality once the nature of the reality is questioned. Confusion in *Passage* between illusion and reality is rampant; the English are most often the slaves of illusion. The antiquity of the Caves is their paramount aspect. The flames struggling to unite with each other symbolize the gestures toward friendship made by the sympathetic English and the Indians; the friendship kindles and then is extinguished. The Caves themselves project nothing: both no thing and nothingness. They are an active force that reshapes and redefines the characters who come into contact with them. They deny Western values. They are not entirely evil but represent a fusion of good and evil and exemplify the view that from evil good may spring. The Cave episode thus "prevents the loveless marriage between Ronny and Adela, unifies Hindus and Moslems in a common cause, provides a victory of the Indians over the English, vindicates the Indian character, demonstrates Indian integrity and ability in Judge Das, allows Aziz to regain his personal dignity and self-respect by escaping from British to Indian territory and rejoining his children, and deepens his friendship with

Fielding and Godbole." [This insight is original.] Both Kipling and EMF prefer Moslem clarity to Hindu confusion. EMF's rational, ironic, skeptical cast of mind and the comic tone of "Temple" invalidate the interpretation of it as a positive expression of Hindu mystical union [extreme judgment; EMF is partly sympathetic with the Hinduism that he projects in "Temple"]. The terrifying destructiveness of the echo in the Caves cannot be forgotten, and the climax of "Temple" is really an "anticlimax of a dull ordinary reality." Godbole does symbolize unity. At the conclusion politics preclude friendship, but a passage is made by Fielding: he sounds positive hopes for future friendship between the races.

Chap 3, "Joseph Conrad: The Meaning of Civilization": Conrad, like EMF, was irritated by Kipling's imperialistic values. The Marabar Caves and the heart of darkness, as well as Fielding and Marlow, have many similarities; but in Conrad's Africa and South America the ancient religions and the sophisticated civilizations to be found in India are lacking. EMF's *Passage* is far more philosophical and speculative than are Conrad's books. Marlow is a bluff man of action, whereas Fielding is the highly educated intellectual and teacher, the denizen of Cambridge and Bloomsbury. Chap 4, "Joyce Cary: Authority and Freedom": Cary's THE AFRICAN WITCH and *Passage* have similar plots. Adela Quested and Judy Coote both go to the colonies to learn more about their fiancés before they break their engagements; both EMF and Cary use club scenes to reveal colonial society; and both authors use race relations to test and define their characters. Dryas Honeywood and Adela Quested are similar as imperceptive young women, Jerry Rackham and Ronny Heaslop as extraverted administrators, and Aladai and Aziz as cultured natives who initially desire British approbation. THE AFRICAN WITCH is more pessimistic than *Passage*, since successful personal relationships do not neutralize official failure, and redemptive characters such as Fielding and Mrs. Moore, who represent truly civilized values, are absent. Cary, like EMF, is suspicious of public school attitudes in his colonial administrators (see Burwash in THE AFRICAN WITCH). Both Cary and EMF were prophetic in their distrust of indirect rule, whereby the British helped native potentates to maintain the status quo: only after World War II were they both seen to be correct in their disapproval of this policy. Chap 5, "Graham Greene: The Decline of the Colonial Novel": In Greene's African novels there is no discernible attempt to create political ideas and attitudes about subject peoples. There are no fully developed characters involved in political questions; the political references are imposed from without. Greene's African novels reveal the influence of T. S. Eliot and Baudelaire rather than of EMF. Greene is different from the other four novelists in that he never lived abroad; he also wrote after World War II when the empire was dissolving, and he generalizes his settings to accord with the moods of his characters. "Conclusion": These novelists are noteworthy for the contribution that they made to the native traditions of the people about whom they wrote, supplying them with forms to enable them to express their own visions of social reality. The novelists all interpret the colonial experience in a negative light. The protagonists are both witnesses and critical judges of colonialism, not its advocates. [Important book, though sketchy in the treatment of writers such as Kipling and Conrad, whose canon is considerable. The treatment of Greene is restricted, but the discussion of Cary is excellent. The best critique is that on EMF, which is especially valuable for indicating the relationship of *Passage* to actual events.]

1766 Meyers, Jeffrey. "Fizzling Sexual Time Bombs," COMMONWEAL, XCVIII (21 Sept 1973), 506–8.

In general, EMF left a sexual time bomb that failed to explode. He was inhibited from writing fiction after 1924 because he could not write, as could Proust, of homosexual love in heterosexual guise. The theme of the stories in *The Life to Come and Other Short Stories* is the "call to life," the triumph of the instinctive and the impulsive over the rational and the repressive. EMF's repressed heroes are condescending and patronizing, and any affair never has a future. In his stories, to punish his own guilt, he illustrates the need of his protagonists to be hurt by their lovers. "Dr. Woolacott" is reminiscent of LADY CHATTERLEY'S LOVER with Connie omitted; the ministering gamekeeper is T. E. Lawrence. The stories were better as therapy for EMF than they are as art. [Interesting and perceptive review, supplying some of the homosexual Bloomsbury context for *The Life to Come.*]

1767 Meyers, Jeffrey. THE WOUNDED SPIRIT: A STUDY OF "SEVEN PILLARS OF WISDOM" (Lond: Martin Brian & O'Keefe, 1973), pp. 11, 12, 17, 83, 123, 128.

T. E. Lawrence was attracted to the primitive as EMF and other modern writers were. Lawrence figures in EMF's "Dr. Woolacott." [EMF is quoted on Lawrence's work and style.] EMF is one of a number of homosexual authors who were Lawrence's friends.

1768 Miller, Karl. "Forster and His Merry Men," NEW YORK REVIEW OF BOOKS, 28 June 1973, pp. 9–11.

In *The Life to Come and Other Short Stories*, EMF's fantasy works in the service of homosexuality, as do the tricks resorted to in the stories. Now that the laws against homosexuality have been eased in England, it is an awkward time to publish the stories. Their flaws are accentuated, now that the stories no longer pertain to a cause needing some courage to espouse. Some of them reveal EMF's inexperience with the subject: solitude, dreams, idyllic relationships often characterize them. They reveal how closely tied the expression of homosexuality was to a class system. Exploitation of lower-class men is implicit in them; in their sado-masochistic element EMF reveals some submission to the class system he hated. EMF's misgivings about the stories were justified; they did interfere with the exercise of his abilities as writer of fiction. His daydreams are reflected in them; these dreams were the result of a constricting society imposing celibacy upon him, a society that, in other respects as well, was static and sterile. These works are less impressive than those in which he knows his subject rather than dreams of it. The women in the "indecent writings" lack the stature of those in his other fiction, and they are seen as oppressive and narrow individuals, the product of EMF's misogyny. Hilda in "The Obelisk" is subject to such belittling. "Arthur Snatchfold" is a better, more developed tale of illicit love. "The Other Boat" is the best story: the love-making between the British captain and his Eurasian lover on board ship is both realistic and passionate. The melodramatic end is convincing, as is also the hovering presence of the Captain's mother. It was best to publish these tales, even if they inject doubts as to EMF's stature. To have withheld them would have been cowardly and untruthful, and they are interesting and explanatory about EMF. They are also evidence as to how widespread homosexuality was in the British schools and universities, a form of behavior that both subverted and served the class system. [Provocative discussion.]

1769 Müllenbrock, Heinz-Joachim. "Modes of Opening in the Work of E. M. Forster: A Contribution to the Poetics of His Novels," MODERN PHILOLOGY, LXX (Feb 1973), 216–29.
[Ample discussion of the opening chapters of *The Longest Journey, Howards End*, and *A Passage to India*, as they adumbrate the development of the characters and the later action. The analysis is sometimes illuminating, though the essay develops conclusions that are more often obvious than profound.]

1770 Naremore, James. THE WORLD WITHOUT A SELF: VIRGINIA WOOLF AND THE NOVEL (New Haven & Lond: Yale UP, 1973), p. 8.
The allegorical approach in Woolf's THE VOYAGE OUT links that novel to Howards End.

1771 "Notables," TIME, CII (2 July 1973), 65–67.
EMF reveals in *The Life to Come and Other Short Stories* that, during his silence after 1924, homosexuality was the only theme to fire his imagination. In these stories EMF presents the struggle between civilization and true civility.

1772 Nye, Robert. "Collected Forster," BOOKS AND BOOKMEN, XIX (Oct 1973), 88–89.
EMF's appeal is to the man apart—the critic, perhaps, rather than the novelist. *Goldsworthy Lowes Dickinson* is a sensitive and affectionate biog-

raphy, criticized by some for not mentioning Dickinson's homosexuality. The restraints in force when EMF wrote the biography were perhaps more helpful to EMF than obstructive. EMF's work has had a powerful influence on his followers, because his vision in it goes beyond concepts of right and wrong. In his work there is the confronting by EMF's own moral intelligence of "an experience of life not absolutely explainable in moral terms." EMF suggests Charles Williams in their common search for an order through the means of "patient concentration." EMF is closer to the visionary than to the rationalist in his conviction that "the play of life is more Mystery than Morality." [Christopher Isherwood is quoted from DOWN THERE ON A VISIT (1961) as to the central nature of EMF's reputation but its elusive, obscure character. Review of *Goldsworthy Lowes Dickinson and Related Writings*, Abinger Edition.]

1773 O'Rourke, Matthew R. "Fiction," BEST SELLERS, XXXIII (1 June 1973), 103.

The stories in *The Life to Come and Other Short Stories* are underwritten and sensitive. "Arthur Snatchfold" is among the best. "The Other Boat" has a "grimly ironical and pathetically tragic" concluding scene. This book and *Maurice* fill in our knowledge of Bloomsbury.

1774 Ostermann, Robert. "*The Life to Come:* The Stronger Passions Turn into Art in Mr. Forster's Disinterred Stories," NATIONAL OBSERVER (Silver Springs, Md), XII (9 June 1973), 23.

Despite EMF's remoteness from the 1970s in theme and stance, his unpublished writings are worth disinterring because of his superlative mind and manner. The first five stories in *The Life to Come and Other Short Stories* are trifling, but the nine homosexual ones are fired by EMF's preoccupation or obsession with homosexuality. "The Life to Come" celebrates impulse and condemns a repressive Christianity. "The Other Boat" handles sex explicitly and violence with ease. The interior quality of EMF's vision animates his work, including these stories. They suggest what EMF might have done had he been free to express fully the deepest side of his nature.

1775 "Overdone," ECONOMIST, CCXLIX (22 Dec 1973), 99.

The care with which EMF is being edited would argue that in the Abinger Edition of *Howards End* we have a classical text and in EMF a major novelist. EMF, who is no technical innovator, may not demand the attention he receives in the Abinger Edition volume, *The Manuscripts of Howards End;* but the volume does reveal that EMF's powers of self-criticism were acute. *Howards End* may assert itself as a masterpiece in future generations, but the cult of EMF may decline with the man himself no longer present to disarm criticism. [Review of Abinger Edition, *Howards End* and

The Manuscripts of Howards End (1973), ed by Oliver Stallybrass.]

1776 Page, Norman. SPEECH IN THE ENGLISH NOVEL (Lond: Longman, English Language Series, No. 8, 1973), p. 98.

In Dickens's novels the speech of admirable characters in low surroundings tends to be genteel, as in Oliver's utterances in OLIVER TWIST. Leonard Bast in EMF's *Howards End*, on the contrary, speaks differently from the Schlegels and the Wilcoxes, reflecting his different social origins and his lack of educational opportunities.

1777 Parker, Derek. "On the Way to *Howards End*," TIMES (Lond), 24 Dec 1973, p. 18.

The Manuscripts of Howards End proves to be the best example yet of a work that enables us to follow the activities of a creative mind as it forms a substantial novel. The changes made for the better from manuscript to published novel are staggering. [Review of Abinger Edition, *Howards End* and *The Manuscripts of Howards End*, ed by Oliver Stallybrass. Perceptive discussion.]

1778 Paterson, John. THE NOVEL AS FAITH: THE GOSPEL ACCORDING TO JAMES, HARDY, CONRAD, JOYCE, LAWRENCE AND VIRGINIA WOOLF (Boston: Gambit, 1973), pp. 149, 155, 166, 188, 194, 202, 212, 216.

[References are to D. H. Lawrence's and Virginia Woolf's views on EMF.]

1779 Peel, Marie. "Plot: Pattern or Power?" BOOKS AND BOOKMEN, XVIII (Jan 1973), 34–37.

EMF's conception of plot as pattern is too narrow; it is more "an instrumental power that can change existing patterns and create new ones." There are several kinds of plot: plot as imposed external pattern, with all power left inside the book as in many melodramatic Victorian novels; plot as a recognition that all operative power lies outside the book (in God or Morality or the State or sanctified social creed), wherein symbol and allegory are extremely important; and plot that is to be seen as the artist's own instrument. EMF's plots have a distinctive instrumental quality despite his own downgrading of plot. His plots effect real changes in the lives of his characters (though the awareness of these people is conveyed in terms of their inner lives rather than in terms of their considering action as instrumental). *A Passage to India* is an exception, revealing a close link between plot and EMF's philosophical schema. [Discussion of these three types of plot in the work of many other writers. Uses EMF's remarks in *Aspects of the Novel* as basis, especially EMF's impatience with story, with plot considered as action, and even with plot conceived as pattern. EMF is interested, rather, in the secret personal lives of his characters.]

1780 Pinion, F. B. A JANE AUSTEN COMPANION (Lond: Macmillan; NY: St. Martin's P, 1973), pp. 144, 147, 151.

In "Jane Austen" (*Abinger Harvest*) EMF implies that Jane Austen's people could lead fuller lives than they do in the novels, but their lives are full since she works through impressions rather than by the conveying of knowledge and fact. EMF resembles Jane Austen in the presence of the "coadunating power" in his fiction, the organic fusion of several dimensions of experience. In Jane Austen's letters there is more of the common experience of Mrs. Allen and Miss Bates and less of the triviality, ill breeding, and sententiousness associated with Lydia Bennett, Mrs. Jennings, and Sir Thomas Bertram than EMF admits.

1781 Pochoda, Elizabeth. "Stories E. M. Forster Wrote Only for Friends," GLAMOUR (NY), LXIX (July 1973), 104.

The stories that EMF did not publish during his life and that form the matrix of *The Life to Come and Other Short Stories* provided him relief not only from portraying heterosexual relationships but from the seriousness of his art. The lack of seriousness in the present short stories impairs their worth as art, and the homosexual relationships depicted lack the subtlety with which EMF presented heterosexual relationships in his novels. Some of the authentic EMF is present in the conflict presented between passion and civilized life.

1782 Pownall, David E. ARTICLES ON TWENTIETH CENTURY LITERATURE: AN ANNOTATED BIBLIOGRAPHY 1954 TO 1970 (NY: Kraus-Thomson, 1973), II, 1092–1113.

["An expanded cumulation of 'Current Bibliography' in the journal TWENTIETH CENTURY LITERATURE, volume one to volume sixteen, 1955 to 1970." Entries F1064 to F1167, Vol. II, contain brief annotations of the most important critical articles on EMF in journals for the period 1954–1970.]

1783 Pradhan, S. V. "A 'Song' of Love: Forster's *A Passage to India*," CENTENNIAL REVIEW, XVII (Summer 1973), 297–320.

A Passage to India is a novel with not only social and political implications but metaphysical ones as well. EMF distances his presentation of such metaphysical issues by making his narrator assume, for the most part, Fielding's rationalistic, skeptical, and humanistic stance. [Though EMF is close to him, Fielding can hardly be regarded as narrator because there emerges from the novel a sympathy with Hinduistic mysticism, with Godbole, and with Mrs. Moore in excess of what the rationalistic Fielding could feel. The omniscient comments that judge Fielding to be deficient in sensitivity to mystical experience can scarcely be Fielding's own. The case for Fielding as narrative voice as against EMF is not convincingly made.] Some earlier critics are incorrect in their interpretations of *Passage:* Glen O. Allen ("Structure, Symbol, and Theme in E. M. Forster's *A Passage to India*,"

1955), with his view that the Cave represents the fusion of Atman and Braham; James McConkey (THE NOVELS OF E. M. FORSTER, 1957), with his view that the Cave represents the nothingness of the metaphysical absolute itself; and Ellin Horowitz ("The Communal Ritual and the Dying God in E. M. Forster's *A Passage to India,*" 1964), with her view that Mrs. Moore attains Nirvana and also becomes a force making for salvation. Mrs. Moore's vision in the Caves is to be regarded as exemplifying the asceticism, renunciation, and life-denying properties implicit in Jain religion, with which the Marabar Caves are to be associated. [Earlier critics had erred, possibly, in regarding Mrs. Moore's "anti-vision" as Hinduistic. It can be considered Jain in its negative thrust, as it also is by Benita Parry in DELUSIONS AND DISCOVERIES (1972). Parry correctly assumes that Mrs. Moore emerges from her Jain phase to achieve modified salvation through Hinduism and posthumously to act as a redemptive force, aspects of Mrs. Moore denied in this article.] To contrast with Mrs. Moore's "contempt for the world and her withdrawal from life" after the anti-vision in the Caves, Professor Godbole represents the force of Bhakti Hinduism, with its emphasis on universal love and devotion. Bahkti Hinduism recommends disinterested action, not aversion from the world, and is a theistic rather than an atheistic mysticism. The palm trees at the Mosque and at Asirgarh are symbols of the Bhakti spirit, as is the festival in "Temple." Bhakti Hinduism is in opposition not only to Mrs. Moore's Jainist renunciation but to the Mohammedanism of Aziz, to the doctrinal Christianity of the missionaries, Mr. Sorley and Mr. Gray, and to the "official" Christianity of the English club members at Chandrapore. Mohammedanism and Christianity both fail, as does Jainism, to reach the inclusiveness and the universal love present in Hinduism. Fielding and Aziz achieve a social and political vision through the means of the echo image to correspond to the mystical visions of Mrs. Moore and Godbole. [Whether a "vision" can occur to such mystically insensitive characters as Fielding and Aziz is questionable.] Fielding in deeming that "the original sound may be harmless, but the echo is always evil" is commenting upon the contrast between the worth of an original impulse and the often disastrous consequences of it when actualized in action. [This is a challenging insight.] Fielding has also a social and political vision of India, united through the means of "goodwill plus culture and intelligence." Fielding's vision is, however, inadequate to present political realities. Aziz's more forthright vision of Indian rejection of Empire neutralizes Fielding's retrograde and paternalistic vision. In the spiritual realm, Mrs. Moore's vision is juxtaposed with Godbole's; in the social and political realm, Fielding's is juxtaposed with Aziz's. Both the Indian and British visions are partial. Positive as they are, Godbole's vision is apolitical and Aziz's vision is aspiritual. If Godbole's gospel of universal love and salvation is a valid aim, India must complete an ideal "passage" by uniting Godbole's spiritual wisdom with the political maturity of Aziz's. This vision of an ideal "passage" underlies the novel and composes its "song" (a characteristic feature of prophetic fiction according to EMF in *Aspects of the Novel*). As such, it "flows athwart the action and manifests meaning like an undercurrent." [Article is stimulating and challenging, although the writer takes into consideration too little the work of critics such as E. K. Brown, Louise Dauner, Glen Pederson, A. Woodward, George H. Thomson, and Wilfred Stone. Article is valuable for emphasizing the non-Hindu quality of Mrs. Moore's vision, for elucidating the Bhakti aspect of Godbole's Hinduism, and for underlining the inadequacies of Mohammedanism and Christianity in interpreting Indian culture. The Bhakti aspect of Godbole's Hinduism had previously been analyzed by Michael Spencer in "Hinduism in E. M. Forster's *A Passage to India*" (1968) and by Benita Parry in DELUSIONS AND DISCOVERIES (1972), although she correctly finds more affinities between Godbole and Mrs. Moore than does the writer of this article.]

1784 Price, Reynolds. "What Did Emma Bovary Do in Bed?" ESQUIRE, LXXX (Aug 1973), 80, 144, 146.
Some contemporary writers have abused their freedom to represent sex explicitly, and the line between art and pornography in some instances is not clear. Some other notable books might have gained aesthetically from a more explicit rendition of sexual experience: Flaubert's MADAME BOVARY, Hardy's TESS OF THE D'URBERVILLES, and EMF's *Maurice*. In *Maurice*, explicit eroticism is absent. This absence weakens the book's substance and impact. *Maurice* is "a story of sexual discovery and response; of self-confrontation, self-understanding and finally communication *through* sexual relation." Since the novel is about sex, the veiling of the subject obscures the final meaning. Certain other novelists were not thus crippled by the restraints placed on the expression of sexual experience: Tolstoy in ANNA KARENINA and Emily Brontë in WUTHERING HEIGHTS. But Emily Brontë and Henry James (in THE GOLDEN BOWL) might have been silenced if more freedom to describe sex had been allowed.

1785 Proctor, Dennis. "Introduction," THE AUTOBIOGRAPHY OF G. LOWES DICKINSON AND OTHER UNPUBLISHED WRITINGS (Lond: Duckworth, 1973), pp. 1–32.
EMF took part in an unsuccessful commemoration program for Dickinson at King's College about 25 years after his death. The AUTOBIOGRAPHY acts as a supplement and a corrective to EMF's *Goldsworthy Lowes Dickinson;* Dickinson was not so melancholy as EMF drew him, and he was a far more passionate individual and far more sexually involved than EMF presented him (or felt that he would have been able to present him). Dickinson emerges in the AUTOBIOGRAPHY as a stronger, more positive person than in EMF's portrait. [Recounts circumstances leading to publication of the AUTOBIOGRAPHY, evaluates it as a human document, and supplies materials

additional to those found in the "Recollections" (Dickinson's title for his autobiography). Proctor has decided to publish Dickinson's THE WANDER- ING JEW, an unpublished work of excellence on the blindness of postwar leaders, which neither Dickinson nor EMF mentioned.]

1786 Purkis, John. "WHERE ANGELS FEAR TO TREAD" (Milton Keynes: The Open University Press, The Nineteenth-Century Novel and Its Legacy, Unit 28, 1973).

EMF, in *Where Angels Fear to Tread*, reveals one of the main features of poetry: compression. This compression is compatible with allusiveness, also a poetic quality. The social organization in *Angels* is a matriarchy with Mrs. Herriton as its powerful head. All the details tend to be symbolic: in the first scene, Mr. Kingcroft's footwarmer (a present for the departing Lilia) is associated with his rather doggy love for her, which might still have saved her; Harriet's present (also for Lilia) of an inlaid box with its retinue of handkerchiefs and collars suggests her own and Sawston's respectability. The new life that Philip Herriton prophesies for Lilia glances at Dante's LA VITA NUOVA. A "new life" begins for Philip when he is able to recognize his Beatrice in Caroline Abbott and is in part transfigured by this experience. The novel is notable for its verbal and dramatic irony. Mrs. Herriton's disaster with her garden when the sparrows eat the pea seed implies that she cannot control nature, powerful as she is. [England and Italy are dis- cussed as focal contrasts in the novel.] The real antagonists are Mrs. Herri- ton, who heads the forces of convention at Sawston, and Gino Carella, who heads the life-infusing forces at Monteriano in Italy. Mrs. Herriton has as her opposite also Santa Deodata, for whom willed activity such as Mrs. Herriton's meant nothing. Lilia Herriton has feeling, but the heart needs to be supplemented with intellect, taste, and willpower. Harriet is insensitive but has strength of conviction. EMF seems to have gone beyond the Victori- an novelist, parcularly in his use of violent scenes and inexplicable deaths; the fight between Philip and Gino, the death of Gino's baby, and the offhand death of Lilia are instances. There are both traditional and modern elements in this novel. [Appendix A: quotations from Lionel Trilling, F. R. Leavis, Frederick C. Crews, P. N. Furbank (*Paris Review* interview with EMF), and Virginia Woolf. Appendix B: selected bibliography.]

1787 Quennell, Peter, and Hamish Johnson. A HISTORY OF ENG- LISH LITERATURE (Lond: Weidenfield & Nicolson; Springfield, Mass: Merriam, 1973), pp. 295, 456.

In *Where Angels Fear to Tread* the themes and manner of the later fiction are present: unfulfilled characters are brought into contact with a richer, more primitive civilization. The problem of communication between races and individuals preoccupied EMF. In *Howards End* he is concerned with communication between the conformist Wilcoxes and the intellectual

Schlegels. *A Passage to India* is his only major achievement. Again the problem of communication between contrasting cultures is emphasized. The echo suggests an alien world beyond that of the human reason. His novels are tentative, and this quality deprives them of vital strength.

1788 Rawlings, Carl Donn. "Prophecy in the Novel," DISSERTATION ABSTRACTS INTERNATIONAL, XXXIV (1973), 2575A–76A. Unpublished dissertation, University of Washington, 1973.
[On EMF, D. H. Lawrence, Emily Brontë, Melville, and Dostoevski, based in large part on ideas expressed in EMF's *Aspects of the Novel*, Chap 6, "Fantasy" and Chap 7, "Prophecy."]

1789 Rice, Allen. "Short Stories Span Fifty Years: E. M. Forster and the Wisdom of Self-Restraint," ROCKY MOUNTAIN NEWS (Denver), "Startime," 26 Aug 1973, p. 18.
EMF throughout his career satirized the upper class in England. The homosexual stories in *The Life to Come and Other Short Stories* emphasize the social as well as the psychological aspects of homosexuality. In "The Other Boat" and "The Life to Come" EMF analyzes also the effects of contrasting races and cultures upon homosexual love. "The Life to Come" terminates unconvincingly in EMF's resort to the supernatural. The dreamlike aspect of "Dr. Woolacott" is far more convincing, and the sense of doom it conveys is compelling. The lighter stories such as "The Obelisk" and "What Does It Matter? A Morality" are excellent. "The Classical Annex" and "Three Courses and a Dessert" are thin, whereas the combination of ribaldry and history in "The Torque" is effective. The first five stories, in which homosexual content does not predominate, are the freshest and most appealing to the modern reader. "The Helping Hand" points up the wisdom of self-restraint; "The Rock" illustrates the need in human beings for grossness as well as insight. [Excellent account.]

1790 Riley, Carolyn (ed). CONTEMPORARY LITERARY CRITICISM: EXCERPTS FROM CRITICISM OF THE WORKS OF TODAY'S NOVELISTS, POETS, PLAYWRIGHTS AND OTHER CREATIVE WRITERS (Detroit: Gale Research Co, 1973), I, 103–9.
[Rpts extracts from Frederick R. Karl and Marvin Magalaner, A READER'S GUIDE TO GREAT TWENTIETH CENTURY ENGLISH NOVELS (1959); Walter Allen, THE MODERN NOVEL IN BRITAIN AND THE UNITED STATES (1964); A. C. Ward, TWENTIETH CENTURY ENGLISH LITERATURE 1901–1950 (1956; ptd under date, 1964); Lionel Trilling, E. M. FORSTER (1943; ptd under rpt date, 1964); Rex Warner, E. M. FORSTER (1960; ptd under rpt date, 1964); Harry T. Moore, E. M. FORSTER (1965); Vereen M. Bell, "Comic Seriousness in *A Passage to India*," SOUTH ATLANTIC QUARTERLY (1967); Anthony Burgess, THE NOVEL NOW: A GUIDE TO CONTEMPORARY FICTION (1967); Robert

Langbaum, "A New Look at E. M. Forster," SOUTHERN REVIEW (1968); Frederick P. W. McDowell, E. M. FORSTER (1969); Duke Maskell, "Style and Symbolism in Howards End," ESSAYS IN CRITICISM (1969); and A. Alvarez, "E. M. Forster: From Snobbery to Love," SATURDAY REVIEW (1971).]

1791 Sanders, Scott. D. H. LAWRENCE: THE WORLD OF THE FIVE MAJOR NOVELS (Lond: Vision P, 1973); as D. H. LAWRENCE: THE WORLD OF THE FIVE MAJOR NOVELS (NY: Viking P, 1974), pp. 73, 115, 130, 165.

The violence and intensity of the unconscious world present in D. H. Lawrence's characters illustrate EMF's contention that modern psychology "has split and shattered the idea of a 'Person'" ("What I Believe," *Two Cheers for Democracy*). EMF had recognized such depths in depicting the reactions of his characters to the sinister Marabar Caves in *A Passage to India*. EMF and Lawrence thus discredited the rationalistic analysis of motives that had guided the English novelists from the beginning. During World War I Lawrence had friends among the London intelligentsia, especially in Bloomsbury, in which EMF figured. Lawrence satirized this aspect of his experience in his rendition of London bohemia in WOMEN IN LOVE. Lawrence could not treat homosexual love directly in WOMEN IN LOVE, considering the state then of public opinion. Homosexuality flourished in Bloomsbury but underground, as in Lytton Strachey's life and work and in *Maurice*, which EMF could not publish in his lifetime. Even in 1926 Gide's frank acknowledgment of his homosexuality caused a scandal. *Passage* influenced Lawrence in writing THE PLUMED SERPENT. Kate Leslie is an outsider in an alien landscape and culture which affect her intensely but which she never fully comprehends. Her situation is therefore analogous to that of Adela Quested and Mrs. Moore in *Passage*.

1792 Scruton, Roger. "Love, Madness, and Other Anxieties," ENCOUNTER (Lond), XL (Jan 1973), 81–85.

EMF judged the stories in *The Life to Come and Other Stories* to be too weak or indecent to publish: his feelings ought to have been respected. The main fault is a callow vision of human relationships, existing apart from strong delineation of character or brilliant description. These stories are unpleasant, not harmless like EMF's others. In "Arthur Snatchfold" a tension exists between the unreality of motive and the realism of description to give the story a note of wish-fulfillment. With EMF, in contrast with Jean Genêt, the homosexual encounter is the end rather than the beginning of psychological exploration. EMF sentimentalizes physical passion.

1793 Seymour-Smith, Martin. "British Literature," FUNK AND WAGNALLS GUIDE TO MODERN WORLD LITERATURE (NY: Funk & Wagnalls, 1973), pp. 191–323, espec 202, 208–9, 254; as GUIDE TO MODERN WORLD LITERATURE (Lond: Wolfe Publishers, 1973).

EMF is Great Britain's chief representative of humanism; *A Passage to India* is his finest achievement. The earlier books are flawed and over-contrived, and the old-fashioned technique is a hindrance. In *Passage* ambiguity and symbolism enhance the realistic and psychological aspects of the book. The wisdom of Mrs. Moore, essentially human good will, is as valid now as in 1924. EMF rejects in *Aspects of the Novel* the impersonal and author-effacing aesthetic of Henry James. EMF might have achieved more had he been able to come to terms publicly as a novelist with his homosexuality.

1794 Shaheen, M. Y. "Forster on Meredith," REVIEW OF ENGLISH STUDIES, nsXXIV (May 1973), 185–91.

EMF's denigration of Meredith in *Aspects of the Novel* is qualified by an account of Meredith in an unpublished lecture from the 1930s that focuses on him both as a Victorian liberal and as a full chronicler of his age. EMF appreciated Meredith as a comic writer (perhaps unduly), but he felt that Meredith slighted science in his view of culture. In conversation EMF remained noncommital on Meredith, though he felt that Meredith was in advance of his age. EMF tended to remain undecided on Meredith and his significance, but was less negative than he appeared to be in *Aspects*.

1795 Sharma, D. R. "MR. SAMMLER'S PLANET: Another 'Passage' to India," PUNJAB UNIVERSITY RESEARCH BULLETIN (ARTS) (Hoshiarpur), IV (April 1973), 97–104.

Saul Bellow in MR. SAMMLER'S PLANET, through his Dr. Lal, gets further into Indian life and civilization, "her spiritual identity and her moral tradition," than does EMF in *A Passage to India*. EMF's treatment of India is "horizontal," Bellow's is "vertical." Dr. Lal is far less insular than Godbole. A more reliable "passage" to India occurs in Bellow than in EMF because two citizens from democracies (Sammler and Dr. Lal) in Bellow's book provide a more sustained communication than do representatives from the ruler and the ruled (Mrs. Moore and Aziz) in EMF's book.

1796 Sheed, Wilfred. "The Good Word: On Keeping Closets Closed," NEW YORK TIMES BOOK REVIEW, 2 Sept 1973, p. 2.

The private life of the writer sometimes distorts interpretation. EMF's homosexuality has been proclaimed too loudly, with the result that hasty and improbable critical revisions of his work are taking place. *Howards End* remains an authentic woman's book, for example, and reveals that EMF did (however improbably) know women.

1797 Sherry, Norman. "Towards *Howards End*," DAILY TELEGRAPH (Lond), 27 Dec 1973.

In *The Manuscripts of Howards End* a novelist is discerned at work "seeking greater verbal economy and suggestiveness; modifying his plot; heightening his symbolism." [Review of Abinger Edition, *Howards End* and *The Manuscripts of Howards End*, ed by Oliver Stallybrass, and of E. M. FORSTER: THE CRITICAL HERITAGE, ed by Philip Gardner (1973). Perceptive discussion.]

1798 Shone, Richard. "A Quiet Life," SPECTATOR (Lond), CCXXXI (18 Aug 1973), 219–20.

Goldsworthy Lowes Dickinson is a book revealing EMF's piety touched with humor, his eagerness to praise, and his charity of outlook. EMF's scholarly and imaginative treatment of his material is noteworthy. He manipulates time, for example, to achieve the most subtle effects possible. He reveals his presence in the tone and approach of the book. *Dickinson* reveals Dickinson's distinguished and distinctive qualities as a man, even though he is not impressive as thinker. [Review of *Goldsworthy Lowes Dickinson and Related Writings*, Abinger Edition.]

1799 Spender, Stephen. "D. H. Lawrence, England and the War," D. H. LAWRENCE: NOVELIST, POET, PROPHET, ed by Stephen Spender (NY: Harper & Row; Lond: Weidenfeld & Nicolson, 1973), pp. 71–76.

D. H. Lawrence's criticism of EMF for glorifying business people in *Howards End* is a willful misreading but indicates Lawrence's alienation from England by 1922. He could not tolerate the Wilcoxes in *Howards End* nor even the Schlegels: his England was the prewar countryside near Nottingham. Despite his despair, he had more faith in the resurgence of England than had EMF. The reason for his ultimate despair of England's resurgence is the same as EMF's: the impossibility of "planning" without ruining England. In the 1922 story, "England, My England," Egbert is an instinctual Englishman like Stephen Wonham in *The Longest Journey*. He represents the real England, and is symbolically killed in the war. Lawrence, like EMF and Kipling, identified the essential spirit of England with its primeval people. Egbert is nobler than the other characters because, like Mrs. Wilcox in *Howards End*, he dies for a past that he symbolizes. Like her, he does not resist death, because he realizes that it is the fate of the English consciousness that he embodies.

1800 Stallybrass, Oliver. "The Abinger Edition of E. M. Forster," ENGLISH LITERATURE IN TRANSITION, XVI: 4 (1973), 245–56.

[The circumstances concerning the origin of The Abinger Edition and the principles governing it are given.] The Edition will come down on the side of completeness; it will not be chronologically arranged, so as to keep intact the identity of well-known books like *Pharos and Pharillon*, *Abinger Harvest*, and *Two Cheers for Democracy*. The Edition will gather most of the uncollected writings and the most pertinent works existing in manuscript.

(Most of the contents of the first volume that has been published, *The Life to Come and Other Stories*, existed only in manuscript.) Diaries, journals, etc., will wait until P. N. Furbank's authorized life of EMF appears. The text of EMF's printed works will be scrutinized carefully. The editor will collate the most significant editions and the manuscript versions of these when they exist. To the extent possible, misreadings will be corrected. The new readings thereby established for *Howards End* have been so extensive as to justify a supplementary volume to contain them. [Editorial matter will consist of an introduction to each volume, textual notes, explanatory notes, and an annotated index. Indispensable article for EMF scholars.]

1801 Stallybrass, Oliver. "Editor's Introduction," *Goldsworthy Lowes Dickinson and Related Writings*, ed by Oliver Stallybrass (Lond: Edward Arnold, The Abinger Edition of E. M. Forster, Vol. 13, 1973), pp. xi–xix.

[Recounts circumstances of EMF's writing *Dickinson*. EMF used as basis the "Recollections" of Dickinson, now published as his AUTOBIOGRAPHY (see Dickinson [1973] and Proctor [1973]). EMF left out the sexual element in these "Recollections" in writing *Dickinson*, at Dickinson's own behest. EMF enjoyed writing the book, which has elicited general admiration among readers. The work was motivated by EMF's gratitude and affection for his friend and one-time mentor.]

1802 Stallybrass, Oliver. "Editor's Introduction," *Howards End*, by E. M. Forster (Lond: Edward Arnold, The Abinger Edition of E. M. Forster, ed by Oliver Stallybrass, Vol. 4, 1973), pp. vii–xix.

Diary notice, 26 June 1908, describes the novel that EMF is contemplating: two Schlegel sisters are pitted against the materialistic Wilcoxes. The novel also had its inception before 1908, in EMF's memories of Rooksnest, his Hertfordshire home from his fifth to fifteenth year. [In Appendix, EMF's earliest known composition, dating from 1894 and entitled "Rooksnest," is rptd.] *Howards End* also reflects details from EMF's experiences in Shropshire, London, Manchester, and Germany. [Letters, diaries, and other sources for these aspects of EMF's life are quoted.] The Schlegel sisters were based in part on Goldsworthy Lowes Dickinson's three sisters, possibly also on the two Stephen sisters [later Virginia Woolf and Vanessa Bell]. Diary entries reveal EMF's thematic concerns in *Howards End:* his fascination with opposites, his disgust with the machine, and his preoccupation with money. The Helen Schlegel-Leonard Bast affair aroused reservations from the beginning. As for the novel as a whole, the reception was favorable. EMF had fluctuating opinions about it, as his diaries reveal. In a Commonplace Book of 1958, he is proud of it but does not love any of its characters; yet he singles out many of its true excellences: "all pervading plot that is seldom tiresome or forced, range of characters, social sense, wit, wisdom, colour." In his diary for 6 June 1965, he acknowledges, disarmingly, the merit of both *Howards End* and *A Passage to India*. ["Notes" are excellent as they define and discuss the allusions made in the novel and are indispensable for the general reader and scholar. The rptd text is the result of careful collation of Arnold 1969 rpt of Pocket Edition of *Howards End* with significant earlier eds and the manuscripts. The result is an authentic, authoritative text. See *The Manuscripts of Howards End*, ed by Oliver Stallybrass (1973).]

1803 Stallybrass, Oliver. "Editor's Introduction," *The Manuscripts of Howards End*, by E. M. Forster (Lond: Edward Arnold, The Abinger Edition of E. M. Forster, ed by Oliver Stallybrass, Vol. 4A, 1973), pp. vii–xxii.

First, the manuscripts of *Howards End* provide insight as to the genesis of this major novel, since in many places the final text is different from what was originally written. Second, the discarded material sometimes illuminates EMF's intentions. Third, the differences between the manuscripts and the published version reveal that the text as hitherto published is incorrect (in some editions or in all of them). The majority of the changes from the manuscript to the authentic text are stylistic, aiming at "greater elegance, precision, economy, vividness, vitality." Others affect the novel more radically, "the characterization, the plot, the symbolism, the very tone of the author's voice." [Description of almost complete manuscript of *Howards End* at King's College Library, Cambridge; some superseded or rejected fragments as well as working notes also exist. In this book the manuscripts are compared closely with a copy text, the Arnold 1969 rpt of the Pocket Edition of *Howards End*. Some of the more interesting differences between the manuscripts and the printed versions of *Howards End* are discussed. Appendix A, "Working Notes," rpts notes that EMF did not always follow in his final version. Appendix B, "Variants in Editions," lists (and sometimes discusses) the chief differences between the copy text and other texts or between these texts and the manuscripts. The manuscript variants and rejected or superseded passages are printed meticulously in full detail. The newly established authentic text is printed in Vol. 4 of The Abinger Edition, *Howards End* (1973).]

1804 Stallybrass, Oliver. "Forster's Reputation," LISTENER, LXXXIX (5 April 1973), 449.

Even if EMF's early stories in *The Life to Come and Other Short Stories* are lightweight, they are not negligible. Although he did not publish the later homosexually oriented ones, he did not destroy them. The implication is, then, that he would ultimately have wished them to be published. EMF's reputation will be best served by posterity's access to all his writings, including his less than best. [Objects to Francis Wyndham's review (1973) of *The Life to Come.*]

1805 Stewart, J. I. M. "J. I. M. Stewart on the Slow Growth of a Country House," SPECTATOR (Lond), CCXXXI (8 Dec 1973), 774–75.

The Manuscripts of Howards End is a major bibliographical monument. EMF's corrections almost always improve the lucidity and style of the writing. *Manuscripts* confirms the facts that EMF was an old-fashioned novelist with his intrusions and reflective passages, that the whimsical and fantastic came easily to him, that the characters and what happened to them came less easily, and that he was sensitive to the symbolic implications of his materials. *Manuscripts* also demonstrates that he was not comfortable with the erotic. The "Rooksnest" sketch, used as an appendix in *Howards End*, reveals EMF's great love of the house that was to be featured in the novel. [Review of Abinger Edition, *Howards End* and *The Manuscripts of Howards End*, ed by Oliver Stallybrass. Excellent discussion.]

1806 Swinden, Patrick. UNOFFICIAL SELVES: CHARACTER IN THE NOVEL FROM DICKENS TO THE PRESENT DAY (Lond: Macmillan; NY: Harper & Row [Barnes & Noble], 1973), pp. 196, 225–26, 255.

Richard Hughes's technique in THE FOX IN THE ATTIC proceeds by abrupt movements so that in his novel surprising events do not catch us off guard as did Gerald Dawes's sudden death in the football match in EMF's *The Longest Journey*. Muriel Spark's THE MANDELBAUM GATE has similarities to *A Passage to India*, though it is oriented toward belief rather than unbelief. Freddy Hamilton is parallel to Fielding, Barbara Vaughan to Adela Quested, and Abdul and Suzi Ramdez, collectively, to Aziz. The understanding and misunderstanding, as between Fielding and Aziz, is projected in the relationship between Freddy and Alexandros, the antique dealer. In both novels there is an expedition to a strange place and a strained relationship between two members of the English community which has a disruptive effect on the various social groups present. In *Passage* the events in "Temple" reflect on earlier confusions; in THE MANDELBAUM GATE similar instances of knowing and not knowing produce ambiguous effects. Both novels concern muddles from which the authors extract significant truth. In Iris Murdoch's A FAIRLY HONOURABLE DEFEAT two homosexuals are attracted to each other by a Greek god. To interfere with the god's influence on either individual would be a disaster: see Ethel Lucas's disastrous interference with the influence of local deities upon her father in EMF's "The Road from Colonus."

1807 Thornton, Eugenia. "Forster, Early and Late," CLEVELAND PLAIN DEALER, Section H, 20 May 1973, p. 7.

"Only connect" is the theme of the short stories in *The Life to Come and*

Other Short Stories. Many of these tales contain in embryo the themes and preoccupations of EMF's genius. Even the earliest reveal a manifest modernity. "Albergo Empedocle," "Arthur Snatchfold," and "The Obelisk" are excellent stories. "The Life to Come" and "The Other Boat" are of overpowering distinction. In "The Other Boat" EMF handles perfectly all the taboos of the time: racial, social, and sexual.

1808 Toth, Susan Allen. "Forster's 'Homosexual Stories' Reveal a Passionate Writer," MINNEAPOLIS TRIBUNE, Section D, 24 June 1973, p. 10.

Readers may find it difficult to reconcile EMF's frank celebration of homosexual passion in *The Life to Come and Other Short Stories* with their image of a man "revered for his wisdom, wit and irony." But the stories reveal other qualities that can allay such misgivings: a convincing portrayal of the supernatural, compassion, playfulness, and the absolute importance of personal relationships. The central relationship in "The Other Boat" illuminates the ambiguous relationship between Fielding and Aziz in *A Passage to India.* The collection enlarges our view of EMF.

1809 Turk, Jo M. "The Evolution of E. M. Forster's Narrator," STUDIES IN THE NOVEL, V (Winter 1973), 441–56.

In *A Room with a View*, the narrator is a stage manager, not much implicated in the action of the novel. In *Howards End* the omniscient narrator works through the consciousness of a central character, Margaret Schlegel, though he also maintains his distance from her. In *A Passage to India* the narrator is an observer speaking with much sympathy, understanding, and insight about the social, metaphysical, and moral problems confronting his characters and the human race in general. Fielding and Mrs. Moore gain increased stature through the mediation of the tolerant, perspicuous narrator, and the Gokul Ashtami ceremonies gain authority from the narrator's positive views concerning them. The progress of the narrator is linked to the spiritual history of the twentieth century: he progresses from static adherence to categorical absolutes (even when they are on the side of rebellion) to a flexible embracing of the relative point of view. In his evolved form especially, the narrator is sensitive to both the intellectual and the transcendent, the physical world and the intuitive spirit, the ironic and the poetic aspects of experience. The narrator recognizes the ambiguities of experience and attempts to relate them with tact to each other. [A sound and reasonably illuminating discussion. Malcolm Bradbury's "E. M. Forster's *Howards End,*" (1962) and "Two Passages to India: Forster as Victorian and Modern" (1969) and H. A. Smith's "Forster's Humanism and the Nineteenth Century" (1966) anticipate this discussion of EMF's divided sensibility.]

1810 Wade, Rosalind. "Quarterly Fiction Review," CONTEMPORARY REVIEW, CCXXII (Jan 1973), 47–50.

In the stories in *The Life to Come and Other Stories* there is an absence of explicit physical detail, with respect to the sexual encounters. The denouement to "Arthur Snatchfold" is impressive in its timing and compression, as Conway learns of the arrest of his lover and of his loyalty, over a club lunch. Most of the stories are brief and fragmentary and unlikely to be judged among EMF's best work.

1811 Wagman, Jules L. "Some Passages from Forster," CLEVELAND PRESS, "Showtime," 1 June 1973, p. 18.
The Life to Come and Other Short Stories will add to EMF's reputation. "The Life to Come" is a "savagely brilliant and funny" story, and compassionate as well; its satire on doctrinal Christianity and Western industrialism is acute.

1812 Watt, Ian. "Foreword," SENSUOUS PESSIMISM: ITALY IN THE WORK OF HENRY JAMES, by Carl Maves (Bloomington & Lond: Indiana UP, 1973), pp. x–xi.
EMF and James knew France better than they knew Italy, but both chose Italy to represent a life that was opposite to their own native cultures— Sawston or New England. James found it harder to accept the emotional openness of Italy than EMF did; but James gave greater prominence to the Italian past, both for its imaginative appeal and for its symbolic suggestion of intractable realities with which sensitive foreigners must come to terms.

1813 Webb, Beatrice. "Appendix G, Beatrice Webb on Goldsworthy Lowes Dickinson," *Goldsworthy Lowes Dickinson and Related Writings*, ed by Oliver Stallybrass (Lond: Edward Arnold, The Abinger Edition of E. M. Forster, Vol. 13, 1973), pp. 223–24.
[Letter to EMF, 24 April 1934, in which Mrs. Webb states that EMF's *Goldsworthy Lowes Dickinson* has enabled her to see why she and Dickinson are antithetical; her view of the good is much more pragmatic than Dickinson's. She wants EMF to write another great novel in succession to *A Passage to India*, in which he will pursue the antithesis between those who are motivated to cultivate exquisite relationships within the circle of the "elect" and those who wish for the "hygienic and scientific improvement" of mankind as a whole.]

1814 Welty, Eudora. "A Collection of Old New Stories by E. M. Forster," NEW YORK TIMES BOOK REVIEW, 12 May 1972, pp. 17–28, 30.
Some of the stories in *The Life to Come and Other Short Stories* reveal evidence of cramp and strain because they could not see the light of acceptance. "The Other Boat" carries a freight of emotion with nowhere to go. Regrettably, when the women left EMF's fiction, so did the comedy. There are flaws in the stories but never flaws of feeling. They lack the broader

proportions of "The Road from Colonus," nor do they have that story's nobility of feeling. But Mr. Lucas's desire in "Colonus" to cling to life at its most meaningful point is true of the admirable figures in all of EMF's works. What engaged EMF was not the issue of respectability versus homosexuality but spiritual life versus spiritual death. This volume gives us knowledge of a writing life of fidelity that was both difficult and sad, though with some glints of the comic in it. EMF often appealed to "Eternity" in his work, and it is by eternity that he will be judged. [Appreciative and perceptive discussion.]

1815 Wilde, Alan. "Depths and Surfaces: Dimensions of Forsterian Irony," ENGLISH LITERATURE IN TRANSITION, XVI: 4 (1973), 257–74.

Where Angels Fear to Tread is an exercise in coherent satire, with verbal irony as the chief weapon; but another irony, exposing (and reacting to) the disparities and incongruities of existence, points to EMF's later novels. Love and truth are seen as not quite compatible in *Angels;* nor are sex and love. In *A Passage to India* satire yields to irony, and the confident standards expressed or implied in *Angels* yield to the tentative and relative point of view; the personal yields also to the impersonal. In *Passage* EMF demonstrates the impossibility of all attempts to impose order, yet he also recognizes that the unbounded is chaotic. There is disjunction between existence and value; all is reduced, finally, to Mrs. Moore's cynicism and Fielding's solipsism. Life as mere surface heralds *The Life to Come and Other Stories*, in which tension between surface and deeper meaning disappears in the celebration of surface. The monotony of normal life in *Life to Come* intensifies the moments of pleasure in sex when they materialize. In "The Life to Come," "Dr. Woolacott," and "The Other Boat," sexual fulfillment does not presuppose love but is more likely to lead toward death. An ethic of acceptance characterizes these stories; in seeking the pleasures of the moment, EMF no longer tries to achieve the connections dramatized in *Howards End*. This ethic of acceptance implies an irony, even while EMF rejects the ironic vision of *Passage*. Irony now resides in the reader's awareness of a disagreement with EMF and his reduced values. EMF now accepts a part in place of the whole. A connection is achieved, but a connection by reduction. Self is now joined to the world at the expense of an expanded consciousness. [Tightly reasoned, but original and stimulating essay.]

1816 Williamson, Jack. H. G. WELLS: CRITIC OF PROGRESS (Baltimore: Mirage P, Voyager Series, 1973), p. 131.

As so many of Wells's followers tended to be, EMF is both his imitator and attacker in "The Machine Stops." EMF hates the machines in which Wells places his trust, though he draws many details from Wells's work. EMF's attacks on modern society approximate the pessimistic views of Wells himself in his early THE TIME MACHINE.

1817 Wyndham, Francis. "The Masochist's Success," LISTENER, LXXXIX (22 March 1973), 378–79.

EMF's reputation has not been well served by the posthumous collection of his unpublished and uncollected stories in *The Life to Come and Other Stories*. The early stories are thin; the later, which are homosexual in content, are embarrassing rather than aesthetic successes. EMF's instinct to suppress them while he was alive was correct. The comic ones are dated; the serious ones are either sentimental or reveal "a crazily apocalyptic note." The lesson we learn from them: EMF's novels gained from the fact that his homosexuality had to remain implicit.

1974

1818 "All That the Scholar Could Want," TIMES LITERARY SUPPLE-MENT (Lond), 18 Jan 1974, p. 43.

Howards End is a good novel but full of "the liberal sentimentality" that sometimes substituted for thought with EMF and flawed by his inability to deal incisively with the relationships between men, women, and sex. Stallybrass offers a new and standard text. *Howards End* is primarily the revelation of the author's soul, "gentle, timorous, loving the Greeks for their right feeling, and fearing and distrusting the modern, mechanical, commercial world." *Howards End* demonstrates not connection made between the worlds of commerce and culture but the unbridgeable gap between them. The notes are informative. *The Manuscripts of Howards End* records meticulously the shaping of *Howards End* and the great number of changes made between manuscript and printed novel. [Review of Abinger Edition, *Howards End* and *The Manuscripts of Howards End* (1973), ed by Oliver Stallybrass. Excellent critique.]

1819 Armstrong, Paul B. "E. M. Forster's *Howards End:* The Existential Crisis of the Liberal Imagination," MOSAIC (University of Manitoba P), VIII (Fall 1974), 183-99.

Existential psychology represented in the work of the Swiss Ludwig Binswanger, because of his concern with language, is appropriate for examining the preoccupations of the liberal imagination in EMF's *Howards End:* the problems of "connection" among opposites, the merging of subject and object, and the reconciliation of idealism with materialism. Like Binswanger, EMF raises philosophical questions through the medium of language. EMF seems to acknowledge rather than "reconcile the contradiction dividing subjects and objects, idealism and materialism, spirituality and efficient practicality." Though EMF does not solve his problems in the novel, he and Binswanger both raise profound questions. Both thinkers make similar pleas for openness and authenticity, qualities which both of them feel must be developed in relation to other people, especially through the medium of love, which for Binswanger leads to a state of transcendence and which for EMF leads to a sensitivity toward "the unseen." Both EMF and Binswanger work toward a state that emphasizes the unity of the subjective and the objective. The two men derive from differing traditions, but the troubles of

Leonard Bast with openness and authenticity and those of Margaret Schlegel with love indicate EMF's affinity with Binswanger and his existential premises. The problems are those raised by the liberal imagination, although only "the existential imagination" can answer them. Leonard Bast's problems are those that derive from the conflict between the subjective world of his dreams and the grey objective world of his everyday existence. His conflict is the disastrous one defined by Binswanger as that between an "ethereal world," deriving from his aspirations, and a "tomb world," deriving from his normal activities that circumscribe him. His death does not resolve the contradictions posed by the conflict between prose and passion. The "ground" on which he stands is, throughout the novel, too insecure to support his attempts at greater freedom, and the result is tragedy for him. Margaret Schlegel reveals the same failure of sympathetic imagination that Forster does, the failure to integrate the various polarities of experience. In her views of Leonard, Margaret alleges that he could not have changed "the self-destructive design of his divided world." As a human being, Leonard could do so, in Binswanger's view, if the ground that he stood on were firm enough. Margaret denies to Leonard the capacity for change that she arrogates for herself. Yet she shares some of Leonard's extravagance and lack of critical realism in her attempts to achieve integration with and through her unimaginative husband. Her confidence in the power of love is not securely grounded and reveals some of Leonard's mental extravagance; for this reason, as well as Henry Wilcox's obtuseness, she fails to establish a firm relationship with him. The retreat to Howards End house is not real peace positively attained for Margaret, but a retreat by her to a mere sanctuary. She fails to reach a vantage point from which to judge her experiences disinterestedly; she is too immersed, therefore, in the flux of her ordinary experience to connect the conflicting realms of subject and object. [A stimulating and searching article, proving that *Howards End*, despite its flaws, is substantial enough as a work of art to support readings from many vantage points. Margaret's failures at the end of the novel may be too strongly emphasized in view of her determination to live as fully as she can in her reduced circumstance.]

1820 Arnold, Joseph Henry. "Narrative Structure in *The Collected Tales of E. M. Forster,*" DISSERTATION ABSTRACTS INTERNATIONAL, XXXIV (1974), 7908A. Unpublished dissertation, University of Illinois, 1973.

1821 Baroody, W. G. "E. M. Forster's 'The Celestial Omnibus': All the Way for Boy and Teacher," ARIZONA ENGLISH BULLETIN (Tucson), XVI (April 1974), 129–31.
In "The Celestial Omnibus" the boy's sensitivity to literature as a transcendent experience (in contrast to the smug insensitivity of Mr. Bons)

supports the view that literature is the most dynamic source of spiritual knowledge and power. The story should confirm the teacher of literature in the importance of one principle, e.g., the student should be exposed continually to works of the human imagination.

1822 B[eer], J[ohn] B[ernard]. "E. M. Forster," THE NEW ENCY-CLOPAEDIA BRITTANICA: MACROPAEDIA, (Chicago: Encyclopaedia Brittanica, 1974), VII, 548–49.

EMF's lack of systematic philosophy was deliberate. He adopted many traditional themes in the novel but broke with the intricacies of plotting and the literary style characteristic of nineteenth-century fiction. EMF stressed concerns basic to romanticism: reliance on the earth, the power of the imagination, and cultivation of "the heart's affections." The absorption either in the earth or in the imagination is not enough: earth and imagination must both be present, in harmony or in tension with each other. Such is EMF's drift in *The Longest Journey*. The conclusion of *Howards End* is similar in emphasis; at Howards End house there occurs a reconciliation (though tenuous) between the imagination and the earth. In *A Passage to India* the merging of the earth with the imagination seemed to be impossible, although Adela Quested glimpses their possible concord, momentarily, in the trial scene. [It is rather Mrs. Moore and Professor Godbole who have moments of ineffable insight.] Seriousness and truthfulness are represented in Fielding, an outgoing and benevolent sensibility in Mrs. Moore. Neither character is totally successful nor fails totally. The novel ends not in certainty but in an uneasy equilibrium of forces, dramatized in the Hindu religious ceremonies. The humane and humanistic values of truthfulness and kindness dominate EMF's later thinking. During World War II he became a symbolic figure, standing for the personal and the cultural values challenged by Fascism. [Brief descriptive bibliography. Stimulating short account.]

1823 Bennett, Arnold. ARNOLD BENNETT: "THE EVENING STAN-DARD" YEARS, "BOOKS AND PERSONS" 1926–1931, ed by Andrew Mylett (Lond: Chatto & Windus; Hamden, Conn; Shoe String P, 1974), pp. xxv, 4, 25, 100–102, 122, 145, 162, 207, 212, 257, 276, 364, 416.

"Life and the Novel: Witty Author Laughs at the 'Big Guns' and the Public" (17 Nov 1927): In *Aspects of the Novel*, EMF is not a typical lecturer; he is colloquial and "larkish, witty, humorous, epigrammatic, full of sly fun." EMF is happy to be "pseudo-scholar"; he speaks with the authority, however, of the creative artist. For anyone interested in fiction as an art, EMF's *Aspects* can be read with pleasure and profit because of his perspicacity and the book's order and comprehensiveness. The only element lacking in this treatise is a discussion of "creative power," especially its origins. "A Critic

Can Be a Novelist: E. M. Forster's Startling Ghost Story in the Wells Manner" (12 April 1928): It is possible for a critic to be a creative writer, as EMF proves; he is the outstanding example of this combination of talents in the twentieth century, as Matthew Arnold was in the nineteenth. In 1927 EMF revealed his critical abilities in *Aspects;* now in 1928 he reveals his imaginative creativity in *The Eternal Moment and Other Stories.* "The Machine Stops" is the outstanding story from this collection and is his best work in the mode of fantasy. "It is original; it is full of imaginative invention; it hangs together; it is terrible (but with a hopeful close); it is really impressive in a very high degree." [Other mentions]: Dostoevski, rather than Tolstoy, is probably the greatest Russian novelist, in contrast to EMF's judgment. EMF, among his other excellent qualities as critic, has that of "impishness."

> **1824** Blamires, Harry. "The Twentieth-Century Novel," A SHORT HISTORY OF ENGLISH LITERATURE (Lond: Methuen; NY: Barnes & Noble, 1974), pp. 436–73, espec 445–47, 449.

Basic to EMF's books is his eye for idiosyncrasies of personality and his exposing of self-deception. He writes of the misunderstandings between various cultural and social groups, in an understated rather than a flamboyant manner. In his fiction, people with opposed attitudes fail to bridge the gap between them even when they are motivated by goodwill to do so. In *Where Angels Fear to Tread* the conflict is between English middle-class respectability and Italian "frankness and impetuousity." Gino Carella's baby is a "symbol of the linking of incompatibles" and dies as result of the struggle of opposing characters to possess it. In *Howards End* the conflict is between the subjectively motivated Schlegels, interested in culture and human needs, and the Wilcoxes, interested in commerce and imperialism and Philistine in their attitudes. EMF's artistry makes the alleged improbabilities in the novel acceptable. In *A Passage to India* EMF explores the difficulties of communication between the races. He stresses the need for "passion and truth," "personal relations," and "integrity," as opposed to conventionalism and the rule by formula. EMF's positive values may have become liberal clichés, due in their turn perhaps for "demolition."

> **1825** Bolling, Douglass. "The Distanced Heart: Artistry in E. M. Forster's *Maurice,*" MODERN FICTION STUDIES, XX (Summer 1974), 157–68.

The revelations provided by *Maurice* will aid in reinterpreting EMF's other fiction. The novel is more about the obstacles to love present in a sterile, class-ridden society than it is "a description of achieved communion and consummation." Society must be changed if love of any sort is to flourish. The greenwood is a symbol of renewal through nature and the impossibility of achieving it in modern society. The chief deficiency of *Maurice* is the lack of dialectical tension among the characters: the use of enriching episodes and complicating action is at a minimum. However, *Maurice* is possibly superior as a work of art to *Where Angels Fear to Tread* and *A Room with a View,* but it is inferior to *The Longest Journey.* [This is not the consensus opinion.] Distance is successfully maintained between EMF and the protagonist; Maurice is made to be different from EMF. EMF also secures distance between the reader and Maurice by blunting the reader's ready sympathy for him. As distancing techniques EMF uses a low-keyed rhetoric to describe Maurice, irony and comedy to depict him, and much tonal variety. Maurice is in large part defined through images of heart, darkness, and sleep. [A thorough discussion.]

1826 Booth, Wayne C. "The Ironist's Voice: E. M. Forster as Essayist," A RHETORIC OF IRONY (Chicago & Lond: University of Chicago P, 1974), pp. 185–90; also pp. 176, 193.

EMF has developed in his essays a tone distinctly his own; it is ironic, but the ironies are subtle and various. In "Me, Them and You" (*Abinger Harvest*), the satire, with Forsterian irony as its instrument, is directed against the ruling classes until the final paragraph, when EMF ceases to be ironic as he expresses hope for "the new dawn" in which the suffering of the working class will be lessened. In works by such ironists as Henry Fielding and EMF, the reader must know where to stop in his search for "ironic pleasures," so that other more significant meanings are not lost. [Essay rptd, pp. 186–88.]

1827 Boulton, James T. "E. M. Forster: 'Three Generations,'" NOTES AND QUERIES (Lond), nsXXI (Oct 1974), 376–77.

[Summary by Vivian de Sola Pinto of a talk "Three Generations" given by EMF on 14 Jan 1939 at University College, Nottingham. For discussion of this talk, see M. Y. Shaheen, "Forster and Proust," (1975).]

1828 Bradbury, Malcolm. "Forster," THE ENGLISH NOVEL: SELECT BIBLIOGRAPHICAL GUIDES, ed by A. E. Dyson (Lond: Oxford UP; Pennsauken, NJ: Lehigh P, 1974), pp. 314–33.

An element of ambiguity and uncertainty prevails in many judgments of EMF. [EMF's general reputation and significance, EMF's texts, and the critical studies and commentary on him are discussed. The discussion of the critical studies and commentary on EMF follows the lines established in Bradbury's "A Short Guide to Forster Studies," CRITICAL SURVEY (1965) and "Introduction," FORSTER: A COLLECTION OF CRITICAL ESSAYS, ed by Bradbury (1966), and represents a revision and updating of these accounts. Fairly inclusive bibliography of secondary writings.]

1829 Brenan, Gerald. PERSONAL RECORD 1920–1972 (Lond: Jonathan Cape, 1974; NY: Knopf, 1975), pp. 47, 57, 156–57.

EMF's novels at one time seemed to be woolly and sentimental, with occasional sharp passages in them. As a person EMF seemed to be without distinction because he was more interested in listening to other people than in expressing his own views. *A Passage to India* is a masterpiece. [Brenan did not think so at the outset.] This novel encompasses the ambiguities of the Indian mind and its "clash with English moral positivism" and EMF's own tentative and enigmatic views about the universe. EMF's letters bring out the elusive and elfish side of his nature. Like his conversation they are dry but at times pointed. His impersonality toward people was to change when he faced up to his homosexuality. The astringency and toughness of *Passage* were the result, according to Lytton Strachey, of EMF's having had a love affair with an Indian.

1830 Carnie, Daniel. "The Modern Middle Class: In Premchand and In Forster," INDIAN LITERATURE (Sahitya Akademi, Calcutta), XVII (Jan–June 1974), 25–33.

EMF in *A Passage to India* and Premchand in GODANN are both concerned with well-to-do Indians of the professional classes. In GODAAN, these people are seen in relation to the peasants; in *Passage*, to the Anglo-Indians. EMF judges these people by aesthetic standards; Premchand, by standards of social justice. Premchand regards his Indian professionals as irresponsible but finds in their knowledge and liberalism the answer to India's problems, especially if these people will assimilate some of the peasants' wisdom. EMF sees Indians as strange, difficult, and offensive at times, but underneath he recognizes a sensitivity and a spirituality in them that is aesthetic and admirable.

1831 Cox, C. B. JOSEPH CONRAD: THE MODERN IMAGINATION (Lond: J. M. Dent; Totowa, NJ: Rowman & Littlefield, 1974), pp. 31, 46, 79, 138, 171–73.

Physical disability in Ralph Touchett (James's THE PORTRAIT OF A LADY), Rickie Elliot's club foot (*The Longest Journey*), and Jim's lameness (Conrad's LORD JIM) symbolize the sensitivity of these characters to the realities of a post-Darwin world that incapacitates them for action. EMF and F. R. Leavis are wrong in regarding Conrad's treatment of the wilderness in "Heart of Darkness" as imprecise. Conrad's dark Golfo Placido in NOSTROMO is a more compelling symbol of the chaos and meaninglessness of twentieth-century experience than the echo in the Marabar Caves in *A Passage to India.* Henry James, Joyce, D. H. Lawrence, Virginia Woolf, Conrad, and EMF all use fiction "to explore their own mirror-images." (EMF does this especially in *Journey.*) EMF describes with accuracy Conrad's "double vision" but is incorrect in alleging that such double vision is harmful in fiction ("Joseph Conrad: A Note," *Abinger Harvest*). Such double vision can only be suggested, not defined with precision. EMF's failure to reconcile the nihilism symbolized by the echo in the Marabar Caves with the Hindu mysticism of Godbole inhibited his own creative vitality after *Passage* (1924). He was frustrated in trying to convey his own double vision with more definiteness than the experience would allow.

1832 Curtis, Anthony. THE PATTERN OF MAUGHAM: A CRITICAL PORTRAIT (Lond: Hamish Hamilton, 1974), pp. 77, 108, 136, 158, 161, 198.

Like EMF, Maugham was not prepared in OF HUMAN BONDAGE to reflect his sexual ambivalence in Philip Carey, though in other respects he was fully honest. Others, including EMF in his indictment of Agnes Pembroke in *The Longest Journey*, shared Maugham's view of woman as the enemy of the creative life. In Maugham's late plays there are beneficent, transcendently wise elderly women corresponding to Mrs. Wilcox in *Howards End* and Mrs. Moore in *A Passage to India*. In Maugham's stories of the East he passes over the social snobbishness that EMF emphasized in his writings on the East in favor of an obsession with the effects, mostly debilitating, of interracial sex. In the character of D. O. Alban in "The Door of Opportunity," Maugham was unable to depict imaginatively how a crippled literary intellectual might show more moral courage than an extravert games-playing man, as EMF tried to do, with some success, in Rickie Elliot in *Journey*. Just as the cosmopolitan EMF wrote best about one foreign country, India, so did Maugham. (Spain was his preferred country.)

1833 de Margerie, Diane. "Forster Posthume" (Posthumous Forster), LE MONDE, 15 Feb 1974, p. 18.

Maurice has many affinities with *The Longest Journey*. Rickie Elliot could have been saved by a spontaneous relationship with his primitive and genuine half-brother, as Maurice is to be by his relationship with Alec Scudder. In *Maurice* EMF avoids sudden death so that the characters must confront their situation fully. It is difficult to understand EMF's hesitation in publishing the book or his reticences in depicting sex. [Review of French trans of *Maurice* by Nelly Shklar.] [In French.]

1834 Drabble, Margaret. ARNOLD BENNETT: A BIOGRAPHY (NY: Knopf; Lond: Weidenfeld & Nicolson, 1974), pp. 177, 287, 317, 328, 341–42.

Among modern authors Bennett admired Joyce, Proust, Lawrence, Huxley, the Sitwells, and EMF. Bennett, like EMF, could not in his writing go against the sexual ethos of his times and be convincing when he did so. In *Maurice* the gap between the self and the written word was too great to allow EMF to overcome self-consciousness. Bennett suffered from similar disability in writing about contemporary sexual mores. EMF could not create a credible social future for Maurice and his lover because there was none he could devise; he also could not admit all aspects of sexual reality because of his genteel upbringing. Both EMF and Bennett were men who wanted to live in society and work through it rather than rebel against it.

1835 Fry, Phillip Lee. "An Annotated Calendar of the Letters from E. M. Forster to Joe R. Ackerley in the Humanities Research Center, The University of Texas at Austin," DISSERTATION ABSTRACTS INTERNATIONAL, XXXV (1974), 449A. Unpublished dissertation, The University of Texas, 1974.

1836 Furbank, P. N. "Ger . . ." LISTENER, XCI (31 Jan 1974), 153. EMF is both a current and an Edwardian writer. He achieved his artist's vision early, with the result that he wrote most prolifically when he was in his twenties. The result is that his people are Edwardian, including the Anglo-Indians in *A Passage to India. Howards End* is the Edwardian novel par excellence, interpreting with originality the preoccupations of the Edwardian era. As for the concern with physical degeneracy, EMF advocated athleticism, but an athleticism having its basis in love. As for the obsession with Germany, voiced notably by Henry Wilcox, EMF let the notion of Prussian strength discredit itself, though he went along, to some extent, with the idea of war as purifier. *Howards End* is too often judged unfavorably. It does have one chief flaw, EMF's inability to imagine anyone like Jacky Bast. Both *Howards End* and *The Manuscripts of Howards End* are models of careful editing. [Review of Abinger Edition, *Howards End* and *The Manuscripts of Howards End* (1973), ed by Oliver Stallybrass.]

1837 Gadd, David. THE LOVING FRIENDS: A PORTRAIT OF BLOOMSBURY (Lond: Hogarth P, 1974; NY: Harcourt, Brace, Jovanovich, 1975), pp. 20, 45, 62, 174.
EMF often visited the Cambridge of a later generation when Strachey was an undergraduate. EMF was self-effacing and courteous, an observer rather than a participant. He slips in and out of later Bloomsbury, "recognised, and perhaps then dismissed, as a man of sensitivity and gifts." [EMF seems to have been more central to Bloomsbury or to our later views of it than he is presented as being in this book.]

1838 Gilbert, Irene A. "Public and Private Virtue in British India," SOUTH ASIAN REVIEW (Lond), VIII (April 1974), 209–22.
William D. Arnold's OAKFIELD depicts a hero driven by a social passion for improving the welfare of the Indians. [William D. Arnold (1828–1859) is Matthew Arnold's brother.] This altruistic purpose organized the life of British civil servants in India. EMF denigrates this purpose in *A Passage to India* and portrays the Anglo-Indians as being irresponsibles like Fielding

because they place their emphasis upon personal values rather than upon more objective, social ones. [This article presents a gross misunderstanding of *Passage*. The writer assumes that the British did not abuse their power in India, understood Indian civilization, and were sympathetic to an alien people. How far the British were from full comprehension of the people and the culture that they controlled is conclusively demonstrated in Benita Parry's DELUSIONS AND DISCOVERIES (1972). Parry reveals how Anglo-Indians take their governmental tasks seriously but without the saving grace of imagination. Fielding is sincerely interested in the Indians and is no dilettante; he merely emphasizes that understanding of India and its culture must precede meaningful administration. Leonard Woolf, a devoted servant of empire, came to feel, after ten years of service in Ceylon, that imperialism was morally indefensible in spite of some benefits that it provided. Woolf reaches in GROWING (1961, but covering the period 1904–1911) EMF's conclusions in *Passage*. George Orwell's and Joyce Cary's novels of empire emphasize the same limited vision in the typical British civil servant as EMF did in *Passage*. See also EMF's "William Arnold" (*Two Cheers for Democracy*), wherein EMF views Oakfield as a sensitive man who does not understand the Indians but who is in revolt against the unimaginative attitudes of his contemporaries in India, especially the military. In this revolt he would be akin to Fielding rather than his opposite.]

1839 Goonetilleke, D. C. R. A. "Colonial Neuroses: Kipling and Forster," ARIEL (University of Calgary), V (Oct 1974), 56–67.

The racial fear of the European encountering an alien civilization is one element common to the nightmarish early stories of Kipling and EMF's *A Passage to India*. The nightmarish experiences of Mrs. Moore and Adela Quested in the Marabar Caves parallel the experience of Morrowbie Jukes in the crater in Kipling's "The Strange Ride of Morrowbie Jukes." Yet EMF finds a philosophical dimension in this experience which Kipling does not, and he suggests that in Mrs. Moore's experiences in the Caves there is "the depressed sense of an absence of solidly accepted or acceptable system of values which haunts the modern European mind."

1840 Gregor, Ian. THE GREAT WEB: THE FORM OF HARDY'S MAJOR FICTION (Lond: Faber; Totowa, NJ: Rowman & Littlefield, 1974), p. 24.

EMF in *Aspects of the Novel* reveals a Jamesean progression in his discussion. In an endeavor to reinforce the idea of fiction as an organic whole, EMF denigrates story (which he discusses first) and assumes pattern and rhythm (which he discusses last) to be the most valuable of the novel's "aspects." Hardy's novels do not seem to possess in full degree the unity and coherence emphasized by James and EMF, but do have their own kind of unity and coherence.

1841 Hanquart, Evelyne. "The Manuscripts of Forster's *The Longest Journey,*" REVIEW OF ENGLISH STUDIES, XXV (May 1974), 152–62.

[Describes the MSS of *The Longest Journey* in detail. Notable are the variants for the published version of Chap 31 (when Stephen Wonham comes back to Dunwood House to see Rickie Elliot once again, after Stephen has been dismissed by the Pembrokes) and of Chap 33 (the flameboat episode). Interesting details are given concerning a rejected "fantasy" chapter involving Stephen—his wild ride on a railroad engine, his being ejected therefrom without his clothes, and his wandering naked thereafter in a Lawrentian rapport with nature. Article fails to be definitive in relating closely the characters and incidents in the finished book to their earlier versions in the MS.]

1842 Hersey, John (ed). [Headnote], THE WRITER'S CRAFT (NY: Knopf, 1974), p. 64.

A Passage to India in its own way followed the looser mode of writing fiction illustrated by Joyce in ULYSSES, in opposition to a tightly conceived form for the novel elaborated by Percy Lubbock in THE CRAFT OF FICTION. EMF's *Aspects of the Novel* is a more informal kind of treatise on the novel than Lubbock's, though EMF acknowledges that those who followed Lubbock would be laying "a sure foundation for the aesthetics of fiction." [Excerpts from *Aspects*, "The Story," "People," "The Plot," "Fantasy," "Prophecy," "Pattern and Rhythm," and "Conclusion," rptd pp. 64–80.]

1843 Hotchkiss, Joyce. "Romance and Reality: The Dualistic Style of E. M. Forster's *Maurice,*" JOURNAL OF NARRATIVE TECHNIQUE, IV (Sept 1974), 163–75.

EMF's style is not so relaxed and comfortable as critics tend to think; it is, in reality, tension-creating and dissonant. This aspect of EMF's art can be seen by an examination of *Maurice.* There are two main thematic concerns in *Maurice* or two main modes of coping with life, and there is a style to accord with each of these thematic concerns or treatments of life. One mode is imaginative, poetic, and romantic; the other is prosaic, realistic, and practical. Thematic dissonance is recorded and dramatized through the tension resulting between two kinds of style in *Maurice:* a plain style and an elevated style. The plain style is used to depict the social aspect of the novel and the poetic is used to depict the non-realistic, the mythic, the fantasizing aspect.

1844 Hynes, Joseph. "After Marabar: Reading Forster, Robbe-Grillet, Spark," IOWA REVIEW, V (Winter 1974), pp. 120–26.

In *A Passage to India* there is present only a glimmer of hope for fusing the rational and the intuitive, for achieving a Godbolean synthesis, and for accentuating a sense of life as "mystery" rather than as "muddle." Robbe-Grillet abandons all hope for attaining such a synthesis. Life for him does not yield meaning, and there is no realm beyond the individual's sensibility. For Muriel Spark muddle is what the mind may understand if it does not yet do so; mystery is what we may have intuitive awareness of but what is not fathomable by the mind. She would try to make "illusorily real the double vision of Adela Quested and the potentiality of simultaneous vision as embodied in the attitude of Professor Godbole." The three writers illustrate three kinds of novel, rather than three separate genres of fiction. [The reasoning is elliptical and contorted; the result is an opaque statement excessively difficult to apprehend.]

1845 Jago, David. "School and Theater: Polarities of Homosexual Writing in England," COLLEGE ENGLISH, XXXVI (Nov 1974), 360–68.

The present political activities of homosexuals can be defined in terms of the polarities present in homosexual writing in England in the twentieth century. "Confrontation" has been expressed in literature through the image of the theater, as in the work of Oscar Wilde; "integration" has been expressed through the image of the school, as in the work of EMF. With respect to the tradition embodied in EMF, adolescence is seen as an imperfect stage of life through which one passes. Emotions are then at their purest; they are strong and yet are threatened by an outer world eager to destroy them. The tradition is idealistic; it presents a sheltered and narrow view of life; it embodies a strong sense of moral duty. The literary tradition of realism, dominant in the twentieth century, was a hindrance to the homosexual writer such as EMF who is interested, by the very nature of his imagination, in creating a utopian fiction beyond the bounds of realism. To express his homosexuality EMF had to resort to strategems of flight: "into dreams, the past, the visions of literature, or some kind of divine possession, often by Pan and the rural gods of paganism." To have written realistically upon homosexuality, EMF would have had to deny the possibility of fulfillment for homosexuals; to have written without any basis in realism at all, he would probably have produced pornography. The isolation of the invalid hero in "Dr. Woolacott" is typical of EMF's homosexually oriented stories. The protagonist's problem is solved by a deus ex machina figure, a healthy intellectual laborer who is further to be identified with death and an erotic fulfillment therein. The laboring class, in its primitive vitality, fascinated EMF as it did other Edwardian writers. Another mode of escape from an intolerable present is into the past ("Albergo Empedocle," "The Torque," "The Classical Annex"). Still another kind of escape is provided by a culture that is contemporary but distant in space, such as the Indian culture represented in "The Other Boat," which contends with Victorian, imperialistic British culture. In *Maurice* EMF followed a similar strategy in order to make the happiness of his lovers possible: he removed them from an uncongenial society. Such is the significance of the greenwood, also of the Cambridge milieu, removed as it was from the world. In homosexual activity and in homosexual literature today, the current poles are still revolution and the hope of integration, of promiscuity and idealization. [Interesting and stimulating account.]

1846 Liddell, Robert. CAVAFY: A CRITICAL BIOGRAPHY (Lond: Duckworth, 1974), pp. 10, 29–31, 33, 65, 78, 80, 156–57, 166, 179, 184, 196, 209–10.

Cavafy's homosexuality accounts for "the slight angle" (EMF's phrase in "The Poetry of C. P. Cavafy," *Pharos and Pharillon*) at which he stood to the universe. As EMF maintained, Cavafy was a Greek spiritually but not in any narrow political sense. EMF would have been tolerant, in his Alexandrian stay (1915–1919), of Cavafy's homosexuality. EMF was anxious about Cavafy's literary reputation abroad, but Cavafy himself did little to further it. [Many references to EMF's *Alexandria* and *Pharos and Pharillon*.]

1847 McDowell, Frederick P. W. "A Standard Edition of E. M. Forster's Works and of a Major Forster Novel," ENGLISH LITERATURE IN TRANSITION, XVII: 2 (1974), 134–37.

[Review of volumes to date in Abinger Edition of E. M. Forster, ed by Oliver Stallybrass, especially *Howards End* (Vol. 4) and *The Manuscripts of Howards End* (Vol. 4A). Many of the rejected or variant readings for *Howards End* are described, both those analyzed in "Editor's Introduction" (1973) to *Manuscripts* and those not discussed there.]

1848 Malek, James S. "Forster's 'Albergo Empedocle': A Precursor of *Maurice*," STUDIES IN SHORT FICTION, XI (Fall 1974), 427–30.

The homosexuality implicit in "Albergo Empedocle" prevented EMF from including it among the short stories he collected during his lifetime, despite its superiority to some of the other collected stories. Some of the themes, characters, and situations in *Maurice* are present in embryonic form in "Albergo." As an ordinary but homosexual Englishman, Harold is similar to Maurice; as an impediment to Harold's full development, Mildred Teaslake is similar to the Clive Durham of *Maurice*. Homosexuality in both works enables the chief characters to achieve salvation. In "Albergo" Tommy, the narrator, fails Harold, who achieves homosexual identity and salvation by a retreat to the past and to "Madness." Maurice achieves overt satisfaction in the present with a lover, Alec Scudder, who does not fail him as Tommy fails Harold. The lovers' escape in *Maurice* to the greenwood is analogous to Harold's escape into the past.

1849 Martin, Richard. THE LOVE THAT FAILED: IDEAL AND REALITY IN THE WRITINGS OF E. M. FORSTER (The Hague & Paris: Mouton, Studies in English Literature, LXXXIV, 1974).

Foreword: [The thesis of the book is indicated.] EMF's "ideal" is humanistic, deriving from Mill's rationalistic liberalism, from Matthew Arnold's desire for a human perfection to be attained through culture, and from G. E. Moore's (and his Cambridge associates' and Bloomsbury disciples') emphasis upon personal relations and aesthetic satisfactions. This "ideal" EMF then tested in his fiction by opposing it to "reality," which is either the truth inherent in everyday experience or an ultimate value to which all other experience aspires. [This formulation is rather obvious and the elaboration of it sometimes interferes with Martin's formulation of more important insights.] Chap 1, "Mill, Arnold, and the Liberal Tradition": Both distrust the state, as such. EMF places more emphasis on art and less on culture than does Arnold; both stress reason, aesthetic sensitivity, and a democracy devoid of class principles. Both appreciate the middle class but seek to reform it. Arnold stresses the role of the state more than does EMF. Chap 2, "Moore, Bloomsbury, and Personal Relations": [Sound, but not arresting discussion.] Chap 3, "God or Man: Religion and Humanism": EMF rejects formal Christianity and embraces a humanism that champions reason (but not to the exclusion of emotion), faith in humanity, and the importance of the individual. Chap 4, "The Search for Reality": [Discussion elaborates the terms defined in the "Foreword."] Chap 5, "England and Italy": [Analysis of *Where Angels Fear to Tread* and *A Room with A View* as they illustrate the conflict between the humanistic ideal and the two kinds of reality posited above. Discussion is full and sound but does not break new ground. Martin's method, of commenting on a plot paraphrase, limits his effectiveness as interpreter and critic.] Chap 6, "A Contact with Reality: *The Longest Journey*": [Chapter reveals the same limitations as the preceding one.]

Chap 7, "Love and Money: *Howards End*": [Discussions of *Howards End* and *A Passage to India* transcend at many points the limitations of Martin's method, and he formulates many insights of value.] There is nothing "heroic" about Margaret Schlegel, but she is distinctive and not ordinary. In the connections that she makes EMF illustrates the role of compromise in implementing the ideal. She also reveals the resoluteness of purpose and the strength of will necessary for such activity. Money and its implications connect the Schlegels and the Wilcoxes and determine their relationships to Leonard Bast. The Schlegels fail with Leonard by making him a symbol. For Henry Wilcox love is measured in terms of possessiveness, property instinct, and sex. Margaret's means for reconciling experience with the ideal is her recognition of diversity in human beings. Chap 8, "The Years Between: 1910–1924": [EMF's writings in these years on the East and World War I are discussed perceptively.] Intellectually and aesthetically, EMF prefers Hinduism; humanely and emotionally, he was drawn to Islam. Chap 9, "The Love That Failed: *A Passage to India*": The English, on the heights at Chandrapore, cannot perceive much of the truth about India. In the relationship between Aziz and Mrs. Moore a tone of optimism prevails. More strain is involved in the relationship between Fielding and Aziz. Fielding finds it difficult to keep his humanistic idealism intact in India and is sometimes escapist in his sympathies and actions. In the relationship between Ronny Heaslop and Adela Quested, the two drift apart because of the hostility of the natural environment toward human beings. In Mrs. Moore's reactions at the Caves EMF shows the weakness of conventional middle-class values in confronting a frightening reality; Mrs. Moore is great by virtue of her acceptance of the consequences of her vision. In the Caves Adela's experiences signify the protest of the Indian earth against a union in which love is absent. Fielding, with his rational powers, stands firm against the irrationalism let loose in the Caves and its social and legal consequences at Chandrapore before and after Aziz's trial. Fielding's rational faculties are strong in a social sense but are metaphysically incomplete. "Temple" is necessary to counteract the skepticism of Fielding and Adela in "Caves." [Others see it as balancing the nihilism inherent in the Caves and their "message."] *Passage* is pessimistic, though there are some glimmers of hope. [The downgrading of Mrs. Moore as a spiritual touchstone and woman of prophetic insight, the view that Adela's recantation at the trial is a triumph of reason on her part rather than an illumination caused by the crowd's chanting of Mrs. Moore's name, and the interpretation of Godbole's Hinduism as unimportant for the novel's final meaning are debatable.]

Chap 10, "Grief Generating Action: Miscellaneous Prose": [Informative discussion and summary of much of the uncollected nonfiction.] In the 1920s and early 1930s EMF stressed reason as a bulwark against the fluctuation of values; he prized highly the notion of freedom for artist, intellectual, and citizen; he emphasized the importance of Western civilization and culture, in contrast with his disillusion concerning it in the novels; he valued art as a means for making civilization more flexible and supple; and he saw in tolerance the most favorable climate for the advancement of liberal culture. A faith in mankind's spiritual possibilities rather than an organized religion is basic to his humanism. [This book reveals an enviable command of EMF's novels, a thorough assimilation of the criticism on them, an intelligent use of EMF's uncollected work, a real sympathy for EMF, and a pleasing style. It is sound rather than exciting or originative. It is a useful introduction to EMF's work, though most of the remarks on the novels have already been made by others. Even though the book was written before the extent of EMF's homosexual disposition was known, it is unfortunate that it could not have been revised, with some reference made to EMF's sexual proclivities. The reader has to make his own corrections when Martin discusses "friendship," "the belief in love," "personal relations," "the undeveloped heart," and some of the dilemmas of the key characters. The speculations about EMF's failure to write fiction after *A Passage to India* are also outdated: he did not cease to write it but merely to publish it because of its homosexual content.]

1850 Martin, Robert Bernard. "Notes toward a Comic Fiction," THE THEORY OF THE NOVEL: NEW ESSAYS, ed by John Halperin (NY, Lond & Toronto: Oxford UP, 1974), pp. 71–90, espec 75.
The concert scene in *Howards End* reveals the fallacy of judging a work of art by one's own responses to it. Margaret Schlegel is the only person who encounters the music as it really is.

1851 Meyers, Jeffrey. "The Paintings in Forster's Italian Novels," LONDON MAGAZINE, XIII (Feb–March 1974), 46–62; rptd as "Ghirlandaio and *Where Angels Fear to Tread;* Giotto and *A Room with a View*," PAINTING AND THE NOVEL (Manchester: Manchester UP; NY: Barnes & Noble, 1975) pp. 3–45.
In *Where Angels Fear to Tread* Ghirlandaio's frescoes, "St. Gregory Announces the Death of Santa Fina" and "The Funeral of Santa Fina," and in *A Room with a View* Giotto's "The Ascension of St. John" do much to "suggest the symbols, reveal the characters and emphasize the themes" of the books. The scene in *Angels* in which Caroline Abbott bathes the baby and Gino Carella watches over them both (in a virgin-and-child-with-donor tableau) is central in expressing one chief theme: unfulfilled maternity, a theme that unites Caroline, Lilia Herriton, and Harriet Herriton. The sweetness and the barbarity of Santa Fina's life are reflected in Gino's complex personality. As Santa Fina struggled with the devil, so do Lilia, Caroline, and Philip Herriton struggle with the demonic Gino to achieve self-definition. The violets that spring from Santa Fina's deathbed supply another motive for the two novels. Caroline at the end achieves Santa Fina's resignation. In *Room* George Emerson corresponds to Gino, Cecil Vyse to Philip, Lucy Honeychurch to Caroline, and Charlotte Bartlett to Harriet. In *Room* there is fulfillment in love (in contrast to *Angels*) to correspond to the divine love depicted in Giotto's painting. There are two groups of characters: those who represent instinct, passion, the classical, the truth, and sunlight and who are symbolized through views, violets, music, and water; and those who represent convention, intellect, the medieval, lies, and shadow and who are defined in terms of snobbery, hypocrisy, repression, and sterility. Giotto's painting establishes the differing values of the central characters; it teaches Lucy how life can be enhanced by art; it instructs her how to react directly; and it impels her (through Mr. Emerson's aegis) to move from darkness to light. Lucy changes from an aesthetic or Leonardesque object to a living

woman of Michelangelesque vitality. Italy and its art awaken her passion and assure her development. [Interesting and searching article.]

1852 Moore, Harry T. "E. M. Forster," SIX MODERN BRITISH NOVELISTS, ed by George Stade (NY & Lond: Columbia UP, 1974), pp. 220–69, 283–86; rpts, with additions, E. M. FORSTER (NY: Columbia UP, Columbia Essays on Modern Writers, No. 10, 1965). "Albergo Empedocle" is one of EMF's better symbolic short stories. The best of the group of early stories in *The Life to Come and Other Short Stories* is "Ansell," which anticipates much of the later EMF with its subject of male friendship. As for the homosexual stories, they do not represent EMF at his best because the same self-consciousness that prevented him from publishing them also impeded him in writing them. "The Other Boat," even though melodramatic, is vital. "Dr. Woolacott" is more allegorical, with the forces of love and death being symbolized in an attractive lower-class youth. This figure reappears in "Arthur Snatchfold." "The Obelisk" is a neat sexual comedy in which a man and his wife undergo unexpected sexual initiations. "The Torque" suggests that EMF could have done well in writing historical fiction. "The Life to Come" balances satisfactorily the claims of theme, action, and character: the violent ending is organic to the ironically conceived situation, the misunderstanding by a native chieftain of a male missionary's use of the word *love. Maurice* contains many striking scenes but seems flaccid when compared to EMF at his best. The earlier part reveals deficiency of tension; the novel becomes more vital and poignant in the fourth and last part. [Additions (pp. 228–31, 253–60) to Moore's 1965 study concern the posthumously published works; updated bibliography, pp. 283–86. See Moore (1965) for other commentary.]

1853 Mulkeen, Anne. WILD THYME, WINTER LIGHTNING: THE SYMBOLIC NOVELS OF L. P. HARTLEY (Detroit: Wayne State UP; Lond: Hamish Hamilton, 1974), pp. xiii, 12, 47, 115.
Hartley's use in EUSTACE AND HILDA (the third novel in the EUSTACE AND HILDA trilogy) of the festival of the Ridentore in Venice is reminiscent of the Indian festival scenes in *A Passage to India.* In Hartley's later books symbols approach the status of precise signs, or what EMF in *Aspects of the Novel* called "banner" symbols.

1854 Munby, A. N. L. "Viewpoint," TIMES LITERARY SUPPLEMENT (Lond), 15 Feb 1974, p. 156.
[Remarks on King's College Library as repository of MSS for figures associated with Bloomsbury, including those for EMF.]

1855 Norton, Rictor. "An Interview with Eric Bentley," COLLEGE ENGLISH, XXXVI (Nov 1974), 291–302.

EMF may not have been hindered as an artist by the taboo against homosexuality, despite the consequences to his personal life. As if to bear out this judgment, *Maurice* is not as good as EMF's less overtly homosexual novels. The discomfort of his personal situation may have provided the artistic discipline that he needed. He may have done his best work when he was thrown out of himself and thus forced to be creative in a more objective sense. The women in his early books are convincing, because he did not regard women as essentially passive as did the conventionally thinking heterosexual writers of his time. His homosexual feeling enabled him to imagine women who were not "womanly" in the Victorian sense. He saw women as persons. In *Maurice* EMF wrote "gay propaganda." It is a good novel though not a great one.

1856 Panichas, George A. "The End of the Lamplight," THE REVERENT DISIPLINE: ESSAYS IN LITERARY CRITICISM AND CULTURE (Knoxville: University of Tennessee P, 1974), pp. 54–79, espec 54. The Edwardian Age enjoyed great material prosperity but was insensitive to the welfare of the less privileged classes. The cultured, prosperous Edwardian would have agreed with EMF in *Howards End* that "the very poor . . . are unthinkable." Even an enlightened "liberal humanist" such as EMF could not face squarely the changes wrought by an urban, industrialized England.

1857 Panichas, George A. "Three English Lives: Arnold Toynbee, Vivian de Sola Pinto, Leonard Woolf," THE REVERENT DISCIPLINE: ESSAYS IN LITERARY CRITICISM AND CULTURE (Knoxville: University of Tennessee P, 1974), pp. 89–134. The pessimism that John H. Lester, Jr., in JOURNEY THROUGH DESPAIR, 1880–1914 (1968) attributes to that period is more central to the postwar years. In *The Longest Journey* EMF, contrary to Lester, reveals that *Angst* is a positive psychological and spiritual influence. EMF also celebrates the ordered nature of Edwardian civilization; he felt that the 1914–1918 war undermined this civilization irretrievably. In his "Terminal Note" to *Maurice* EMF reveals that two world wars destroyed forever the pastoral wildness still characteristic of England in the Edwardian Age. In Toynbee, Pinto, and Woolf, the humanism implicit in the Judaeo-Christian and Graeco-Roman cultures managed to survive in some part. In "Arnold Toynbee" the qualities that EMF attributed to the humanist (curiosity, a free mind, belief in good taste, and belief in the human race) are Toynbee's own. He reflects the essence of the liberal and humanist faith that was so strong before 1914, which EMF defines so felicitously in "The Challenge of Our Time" (*Two Cheers for Democracy*). In "Vivian de Sola Pinto" Pinto reveals in his autobiography, THE CITY THAT SHONE (Lond: Hutchinson; NY: John Day [1969]), despite his criticism of the Edwardian Age, an appreciation of its civilization in somewhat the same terms as EMF's. In his reaction to World War I Pinto evinces an initial idealism that evolved into a disillusionment, similar to that expressed by EMF in "T. S. Eliot" (*Abinger Harvest*). [In "Leonard Woolf" (pp. 129–34) Bloomsbury is discussed and said to be notable for its advocacy of Forsterian humanistic values and of a stable culture. The section on Woolf first appeared as "The Bloomsbury Cult," MODERN AGE, XII (Spring 1968), pp. 210–16, as a review of Woolf's DOWNHILL ALL THE WAY (1967).]

1858 Paris, Bernard J. A PSYCHOLOGICAL APPROACH TO FICTION: STUDIES IN THACKERAY, STENDHAL, GEORGE ELIOT, DOSTOEVSKY, AND CONRAD (Bloomington & Lond: Indiana UP, 1974), pp. 5, 10–11, 276, 281.

[EMF's distinction between "life by time" and "life by values" and his belief that fully realized characters in fiction tend to run away with a writer (ideas expressed in *Aspects of the Novel*) partly support the theoretical presuppositions of this book.]

1859 "Passages to India," NEW STATESMAN, nsLXXXVII (14 June 1974), 841–42.

[Rpts, with explanatory comment, some of EMF's letters to K. Natwar-Singh.]

1860 Proctor, Margaret Ruth. "E. M. Forster and D. H. Lawrence as Novelists of Ideas," DISSERTATION ABSTRACTS INTERNATIONAL, XXXV (1974), 1119A. Unpublished dissertation, University of Toronto, 1973.

1861 Richardson, Betty. "Beleagured Bloomsbury: Virginia Woolf, Her Friends, and Their Critics," PAPERS ON LANGUAGE AND LITERATURE, X (Spring 1974), 207–21.

The homosexual works of EMF, recently published (*Maurice* and *The Life to Come and Other Short Stories*), revise our view of Bloomsbury. "The Life to Come," "Arthur Snatchfold," and "Dr. Woolacott" are accomplished stories. "The Obelisk" is far franker than EMF was in the nude bathing scene in *A Room with a View;* a Lawrentian blood lust pervades "The Purple Envelope"; "The Life to Come" and "What Does It Matter? A Morality" present the relationships between sex laws and police states. The affinities of Bertrand Russell's protagonist in his short story, "The Perplexities of John Forsterice," with the liberal, humanistic, mystical EMF of "What I Believe" (*Two Cheers for Democracy*) are noted: the name of his hero suggests these affinities. EMF remains a neglected figure in Bloomsbury. EMF's critical works must be collected. The reticence of Bloomsbury with respect to sex, a reticence shared by EMF, has been misunderstood. Much yet remains to be done on Bloomsbury figures, particularly on their relevance to their age and their contemporaries. [Useful survey of the recent voluminous publications on Bloomsbury and Bloomsbury figures.]

1862 Riley, Carolyn, and Barbara Harte (eds). CONTEMPORARY LITERARY CRITICISM: EXCERPTS FROM CRITICISM OF THE WORKS OF TODAY'S NOVELISTS, POETS, PLAYWRIGHTS, AND OTHER CREATIVE WRITERS (Detroit: Gale Research Co., 1974), II, 134–36.
[Rpts extracts from "Aspects of the Novelist," TIME (1970); Paul D. Zimmerman, "E. M. Forster (1879–1970)," NEWSWEEK (1970); Vivian Mercier, "A Means of Grace," NATION (1971); Marvin Mudrick, "Fiction and Truth," HUDSON REVIEW (1972); Maurice Capitanchik, "The Novels of E. M. Forster," BOOKS AND BOOKMEN (1972); and Melvyn Bragg, "An 'Indecent' Art," WORLD (1972).]

1863 Rising, C. "E. M. Forster's *Maurice:* A Summing Up," TEXAS QUARTERLY, XVII (Spring 1974), 84–96.
Maurice is more than a novel (written in an inept style) that focuses tiresomely on one character; it concentrates on man's need to belong to the earth, to be accepted by his fellows, and to find some central reality at the core of his being. Maurice is a new character in EMF's fiction, one who learns through suffering, and survives. [Other characters do this also: Philip Herriton in *Where Angels Fear to Tread*, the Schlegel sisters in *Howards End*, and Aziz in *A Passage to India*.] EMF "attempts in the here and now what Mrs. Moore attains only in the hereafter: a connection with spirit through love." *Maurice* gives insight into two chief EMF themes: homosexuality as a refuge (sometimes doubtful in its effects) for society's victims, and nature as a sponsor of the passion that enables the elite to attain fullness. Despite his disclaimer that Maurice was unlike him, EMF is closer to Maurice than to the admittedly autobiographical Rickie Elliot of *The Longest Journey*. Elements of EMF's close Indian friend Syed Ross Masood are also to be found in Maurice. *Maurice* may have served as a passage that EMF made through his experience to the more objective and artistically viable rendition of it in *Passage*. *Maurice* makes use of wornout symbols and loses effectiveness thereby [debatable]; these materials required a more straightforward autobiographical approach [also debatable]. *Maurice* is important in dramatizing the main value expressed in EMF's fiction: the need to connect. [This critic assimilates too many of the characters, human relationships, and ideas found in EMF's other fiction to homosexuality.]

1864 Rockwell, Joan. FACT IN FICTION: THE USE OF LITERATURE IN THE SYSTEMATIC STUDY OF SOCIETY (Lond: Routledge & Kegan Paul, 1974), pp. 84, 103–4.
Bourgeois norms tend to reduce personal relationships in literature to an

exchange value, as happens in Galsworthy's THE MAN OF PROPERTY and in *Howards End*. (In recent fiction love tends to rise above such valuation, however.) EMF is conscious of the importance of money. Even the Schlegels, who are interested in sensibility, art, culture, and personal relationships are bourgeois in their recognition of the importance of money in their lives. Idealistic Helen tries to make reparation to Leonard Bast by using money as the "medium" to do so; he refuses it and so survives the "test" that it provides. The house at Howards End represents a prebourgeois England, but it is also taken over and preserved by the Wilcox principles and resources. The bourgeois point of view presupposes a division of function between the sexes: the women are implicated in culture, the men in economic activity. Margaret is finally rewarded in material terms for her virtues when she acquires Howards End. This notion of financial reward for exemplary behavior has become part of the bourgeois novel.

1865 Salter, D. P. M. "Reviews and Comment," CRITICAL QUARTERLY, XVI (Spring 1974), 87–91.

Some of EMF's stories in *The Life to Come and Other Stories* are not coarse, but vulgar. "The Life to Come" is improbable in depicting the young chief as being so sexually patient and long suffering. "The Other Boat" is a compelling study, but it says little that is penetrating about racial conflict, and its melodramatic ending is false. "Dr. Woolacott" is somewhat strained. "Arthur Snatchfold" is the most accomplished and moving later story. In it EMF is concerned less with sex than with the social consequences of sex, and he exposes society's punitive attitudes towards it. The stories are more pornography than literature: the emphasis is on the suggestive image rather than language, and a sense of guilt pervades them. In *Maurice* EMF failed when he tried to make his central character unlike himself. The happy ending seems an impossibility. EMF suffered a sense of guilt at the thought of his own and of his hero's lack of fertility, and EMF's preoccupation with racial continuity emphasizes such guilt. If EMF had come to terms with his own sexual nature, *Maurice* would have been a different novel, erotic or tragic, and a better one. The notes and assembled source materials provide the strength of the Abinger Edition *Two Cheers for Democracy*. In *Albergo Empedocle and Other Writings*, ed by George H. Thomson (1971), the Indian pieces are essential for our understanding of EMF. In "Albergo Empedocle" EMF's dislike of pretended unconventionality is the most stimulating theme. [Review also of E. M. FORSTER: THE CRITICAL HERITAGE, ed by Philip Gardner (1973).]

1866 Schneiderman, Beth Kline. "From Fantasy to Prophecy: A Study of the Fiction of E. M. Forster," DISSERTATION ABSTRACTS INTERNATIONAL, XXXV (1974), 475A. Unpublished dissertation, Purdue University, 1973.

1867 Stade, George. "Introduction," Six Modern British Novelists (NY & Lond: Columbia UP, 1974), pp. vii–xv.

Modernist British writers of stature were not at once English, Protestant, male, middle-class, and heterosexual, whereas writers of the prevailing type (Bennett or Galsworthy) tended to illustrate all those characteristics. Modernists tended to be in an adversary relationship with their cultures, as EMF was with his homosexuality. These writers also tended to see national character not only as a problem but as problematic; it was to be seen ambiguously, as in Conrad's Jim, Gould, and Lingard and in EMF's Wilcoxes and Anglo-Indians.

1868 Spender, Stephen. "Elegies for England: E. M. Forster," Love-Hate Relations: English and American Sensibilities (NY: Random House; Lond: Hamish Hamilton, 1974), pp. 222–33; also xxvi, 207, 211, 217, 220, 234, 243, 251, 259, 279.

Like Henry James, D. H. Lawrence, Joyce, and Woolf, EMF was a poet-novelist. The principal characters in their works often have the sensibilities of poets (see Mrs. Wilcox in *Howards End*). The poet-novelists are subjectively imaginative, contrasted with novelists such as Bennett, Wells, and Galsworthy, who are objectively societal. The novels of EMF, Lawrence, and Woolf are about the English soul at a moment in history. D. H. Lawrence's comments on *Howards End* in 1922, though inaccurate, betray his hatred of contemporary England. In the work of poet-novelists there is usually a character who is alienated from his society and who becomes a critical observer of it. EMF's characters are not divided into sheep and goats; rather, EMF's hatred of the "goats," i.e., imperialists and businessmen, divides society into goats and the rest of us. After World War I the England of Stephen Wonham (*The Longest Journey*) and Mrs. Wilcox died; the aware individual was replaced by the dying civilization of T. S. Eliot's "The Waste Land," and the Wilcoxes were in fact triumphant. Auden from the first in "The Orators" had no faith in the past England celebrated by the early Lawrence, EMF, and Virginia Woolf. [Main discussion, "Elegies for England: E. M. Forster," pp. 222–33, follows.] The poet-novelists wrote elegies of England, and they also projected characters in whom the nature of England could survive. (Nature meant the actual countryside and human nature itself.) In so conceiving characters an ambiguity obtrudes, as in the Stephen Wonham of *Journey* who is more a symbol of moral truth than a successful character. The ambiguity resides in the contrast between EMF's conscious and unconscious portrayal of Stephen. On the conscious level, EMF thinks of him as representing England's past and future. On the unconscious level, Stephen is a symbol of an England dying but one that is also outside time and eternal. He represents English qualities that ended with World War I, as does the hero in Lawrence's "England, My England." Like Mrs. Wilcox in *Howards End*, Stephen haunts the other characters.

Characters like Mrs. Wilcox and Stephen are ghosts. Stephen belongs to a mythical past. Like him, Mrs. Wilcox is also part symbol and part character, and is a touchstone of genuineness in other people's lives. Both characters are rooted in place. Mrs. Wilcox represents values more deeply rooted than the Fabian socialism of Margaret Schlegel and the insensibility of the Wilcoxes. In *Howards End* the idea is to connect; but in actuality EMF's novels record the ritualistic murdering of a vital, unspoiled England. However, EMF is not apocalyptic: England may die but not everyone there will. In EMF's view England is a waste land, dying because the English cannot "connect." He is, however, a patriot of the true England against the false. T. S. Eliot is an expatriate exile who sees in the collapse of Europe a collapse of civilization. EMF's characters live on a reduced scale, measured against the general horror of modern life. EMF regarded Eliot's position in "The Waste Land" as extreme. EMF felt that people can create small societies of much value apart from modern civilization as a whole. The constituted small society provides the EMF "idyll." The idyll is precarious and the larger world may wreck it: thus London encroaches on Howards End and the world intrudes to spoil the relationship between Aziz and Fielding in *A Passage to India*. An idyll between men of different classes occurs in *Maurice*. EMF came to see that the world he cared for was irredeemable: the result was that he wrote essays, not novels, after World War I. Those characters in the novels (Stewart Ansell, Margaret Schlegel) who recognize the natural geniuses (Stephen, Mrs. Wilcox) are important in keeping civilization from decaying. In his work as a whole EMF was concerned with slighter protests against the impersonal and insensitive forces governing modern life, especially in its official and public aspects. [Interesting and important discussion.]

1869 Stallybrass, Oliver. "Editor's Introduction," *Aspects of the Novel and Related Writings*, ed by Oliver Stallybrass (Lond: Edward Arnold, The Abinger Edition of E. M. Forster, Vol. 12, 1974), pp. vii–xvi.

EMF was distrustful of criticism, and his own critical work is "wayward," marked by occasional incisive insights rather than by detailed analysis or by extensive development of a topic. His own distrust of criticism did not prevent him from accepting the invitation to deliver the Clark Lectures for the year 1926–1927, which were to become his *Aspects of the Novel*. *Aspects* has been criticized for being intellectually thin, anarchical, and contemptuous of the artist's craft. Actually, it is "a set of observations somewhat arbitrarily arranged . . . of a man who is a novelist first, a slightly uncommon reader second, a friend third, and an analytical or theorizing critic fourth." In *Aspects*, EMF is sometimes more of a friend than a rigorous critic. James and Scott are slighted, and George Eliot, Conrad, and Mrs. Gaskell are inadequately represented. On the credit side, some of EMF's judgments are astute, his juxtaposing of writers and books such as Sterne and Virginia Woolf, ADAM BEDE and THE BROTHERS KARAMAZOV are striking, his ideas are stimulating even when they are not fully developed, and his own aims and achievements in fiction are illuminated. Thus *Aspects* is an excellent introduction to the novel and a useful adjunct to other more sustained and consistent critical works. [The "related writings" consist of Appendix A, "Extracts from Forster's Commonplace Book"; Appendix B, "The Fiction Factory" (review of Clayton Hamilton's MATERIALS AND METHODS OF FICTION [Lond: Allen & Unwin; Garden City, NY: Doubleday, Page, rvd ed, 1918]); Appendix C, "Materials and Methods of Fiction" (EMF's extracts from Clayton Hamilton's book); and Appendix D, "The Art of Fiction" (broadcast talk, B. B. C. Eastern Service, 24 Nov 1944). Textual Notes. Annotated Index.]

1870 Stallybrass, Oliver. *"Howards End,"* TIMES LITERARY SUPPLEMENT (Lond), 8 Feb 1974, p. 135.

[Letter referring to review of *Howards End* and *The Manuscripts of Howards End*, "All That the Scholar Could Want" (1974). Stallybrass regrets that he left an impression of "ill temper" and defends the inclusiveness of his annotations.]

1871 Tennyson, Sir Charles. "Introduction," BASILEON: A MAGAZINE OF KING'S COLLEGE, CAMBRIDGE 1900–1914 (Lond: Scolar P, 1974), pp. vii–ix.

EMF was one of the chief contributors to BASILEONA. [The first 16 numbers, 1900–1914 are rptd.] EMF was shy and unobtrusive. His early work, first published in BASILEONA, was practice work, lacking his later power and penetration. His contributions of 1911 and 1912 ["Mr. Walsh's Secret History of the Victorian Movement" and "An Allegory"] hint at these qualities.

1872 Wisenthal, J. L. THE MARRIAGE OF CONTRARIES: BERNARD SHAW'S MIDDLE PLAYS (Cambridge: Harvard UP, 1974), pp. 12, 242–43.

Margaret Schlegel's conscientious but unprescriptive mode of reaching proportion in *Howards End*, of finding a middle way between opposed entities, is central to the vision and dramaturgy of Bernard Shaw. There are parallels existing between *Howards End* and MISALLIANCE. Johnny Tarleton parallels Charles Wilcox; the Schlegels, in opposing Charles Wilcox's values, correspond to Bentley Summerhays, who opposes the extravert Johnny and his views. Like Leonard Bast, Gunner is a disaffected clerk from the lower middle class. *Howards End*, in its recognition of the importance of money and of practical affairs, also has similarities to MAJOR BARBARA.

1975

1873 Ackerley, J. R. THE LETTERS OF J. R. ACKERLEY (Lond: Duckworth, 1975), ed by Neville Braybrooke, passim; as THE ACKERLEY LETTERS (NY: Harcourt Brace Jovanovich, 1975).

Letter to Stephen Spender (26 Nov 1958), EMF is large-minded and bears no rancor, though he often takes his friends to task. Letter to James H. Lawrie (13 July 1966) [Details given concerning the shortcomings of the dramatization of *Howards End*, by Richard Cottrell and Lance Sieveking, in performance]. Letter to James Kirkup (16 Feb 1967), In the portrait of EMF that Ackerley has just been writing (E. M. FORSTER: A PORTRAIT, 1971), EMF emerges with many resemblances to Stewart Ansell, the philosopher of *The Longest Journey*. [Many details in many other letters throughout, concerning the particulars of EMF's life, ideas, personality, sexual views, and career.]

1874 Bell, Vanessa. "Notes on Bloomsbury," THE BLOOMSBURY GROUP: A COLLECTION OF MEMOIRS, COMMENTARY AND CRITICISM, ed by S. P. Rosenbaum (Toronto & Buffalo: University of Toronto P; Lond: Croom Helm, 1975), pp. 73–84.

EMF was at home with the Bloomsbury circle, "but vanishing as completely to a world of his own." [Original publication of this important essay on Bloomsbury occurs in this volume.]

1875 Bernstein, Burton. THURBER: A BIOGRAPHY (NY: Dodd, Mead, 1975), pp. 273–74.

Letter to E. B. White (ca. 1936), Thurber praises the individual and unexpected insights from the essays in *Abinger Harvest*. The essay on Sinclair Lewis is the best that Thurber has read; the characterization of Howard Overing Sturgis is vivid; and the remarks on Mickey Mouse are amusing. "The guy is full of swell lines."

1876 Birje-Patil, J. "Ducklings in Glass Troughs," FOCUS ON FORSTER'S "A PASSAGE TO INDIA," ed by V. A. Shahane (Madras & New Delhi: Orient Longman, 1975), pp. 89–97.

EMF's attitude toward the State of Dewas Senior, expressed in *The Hill of Devi*, is ambiguous. In his experiences there, the formlessness of India both

impressed him and inhibited him when he was writing *A Passage to India.*
EMF's own growth in awareness is to be seen in part by his growing
appreciation of the Saturnalian aspects of Indian religious ceremonies. Between EMF's first visit and his second, he composed *Maurice.* Whereas the
Krishna cult is not hospitable to deviant love, it does not necessarily dis-
courage it. The worshippers place themselves, like the milkmaids in Indian
myth, in a position of subservience, in order to seek the favor of Krishna
and to implore the God to "come" to them. The Maharajah adopted the
prostrate position of the milkmaids with respect to Krishna, and in his turn
implored his God to "come" to him. EMF may have had Maurice adopt
a similar stance when he shouts "Come," waking out of a dream, as if
imploring the presence of one who will save him. Alec Scudder answers this
call. Thus Maurice, in calling out to Alec, is analogous to the Krishna
worshipper calling out to his Lord. Dewas state may have been "the greenwood" longed for in the Terminal Note to *Maurice.* The greenwood passed
away in England as a result of the twentieth-century wars and modern
science; and the greenwood of Dewas state was destroyed by the force of
"Western righteousness" in India. Greenwoods belong perpetually to history; or if they are to be found in the actual present, they are worlds much
imbued with fantasy. Even EMF's Dewas "must remain a sort of Dionysian
nightmare where human beings splash about like ducklings in glass
troughs." [A suggestive and informative, if somewhat relaxed, essay.]

1877 Braybrooke, Neville. "Introduction," THE LETTERS OF J. R.
ACKERLEY, ed by Neville Braybrooke (Lond: Duckworth, 1975), pp.
xv–xxxi.
[The friendship with EMF, which began in 1922, was the most momentous
in Ackerley's life. On EMF's suggestion, Ackerley went out to India in
1923–1924, and as a result of his experience there he wrote his widely
acclaimed HINDOO HOLIDAY. EMF did not review this book, probably because he was taken aback by its sexual candor. Details given of Ackerley's
sale of EMF letters to him to the University of Texas.]

1878 Bridge, George Richmond, Jr. "The Belief of an Unbeliever:
The Theological Implications in Edward Morgan Forster's *A Passage to India,*" DISSERTATION ABSTRACTS INTERNATIONAL, XXXVI
(1975), 301A. Unpublished dissertation, University of Pennsylvania, 1974.

1879 Cammarota, Richard S. "Musical Analogy and Internal Design in *A Passage to India,*" ENGLISH LITERATURE IN TRANSITION,
XVIII: 1 (1975), 38–46.
Among major twentieth-century novelists in England, EMF was one whose
connections with, and affection for, music and musical form were perhaps

the most significant. In his novels, EMF makes use not only of musical motifs and references but of musical forms like the sonata. Each section of *A Passage to India* reveals a form analogous to that of the sonata, following an exposition-development-recapitulation pattern. In *Aspects of the Novel*, EMF maintained that pattern must be flexible, supple, and organic. He was still more fascinated by "rhythm," the musical term to which he most often refers. He differentiated between "the easy rhythm" of repeated motifs and variations and "the difficult rhythm" which the sonata or symphony, as an entity, exemplifies. (The novel as a whole can be regarded as such an entity and capable of embodying such difficult rhythm.) In *Passage*, divisiveness and exclusiveness are the thematic motif that is "musically" developed in "Mosque." In "Caves," the triumph of hostility, evil, and negation is developed, and the secret powers of the heart are ineffectual against these forces. In "Temple," inclusiveness and union are stressed, to contrast with the other two sections of *Passage*. The three movements in *Passage*, rhythmically conceived and developed, illustrate "the symmetrical compactness of the sonata or 'ternary' pattern of presentation." "The rhetorically applied sonata form combines with the larger musically centered dialectic to produce a kind of musical-literary symbiosis of aesthetic union." [A suggestive and interesting essay, although the argument at times tends to be a bit nebulous.]

1880 Colmer, John. E. M. FORSTER: THE PERSONAL VOICE (Lond & Boston: Routledge & Kegan Paul, 1975).
Chap 1, "Life and Times": [Review of EMF's life and career in light of known facts and some unpublished materials from the EMF archive at King's College, Cambridge.] Chap 2, "Short Stories": The short stories pose the central critical question about EMF's work: How effectively does he combine poetry and realism? Many of the stories have for subject the cult of Pan and the related cult of the supernatural. "The Story of a Panic" is a representative story because of "the use of an obtuse narrator, the sudden irruption of the supernatural, the contrast between the instinctive and the conventional life, the related themes of salvation and brotherhood." "The Road from Colonus" successfully embodies its themes in the story itself. In "The Story of the Siren" the evocative quality of the prose raises a story of violence and superstition to the level of myth. Most of the stories are concerned with the historical past or with the personal past of the characters; a remarkable story, "The Machine Stops" is compellingly concerned with the the future. Chap 3, "Italian Novels": The great theme of *A Room with a View* is honesty. The symbolical ramifications of certain scenes are powerful: the scene of the murder of the Italian in Florence, George Emerson's kissing of Lucy Honeychurch at Fiesole, and the male-bathing scene in England. The weakness of the novel is that Lucy's emancipation from muddle comes through old Mr. Emerson rather than through his son. The

lovers' happiness is precarious at the end because it is visionary in essence and because its survival into modern industrial society is problematical. In *Where Angels Fear to Tread* EMF plays off spiritual salvation against a mere saving of face. Even with emancipated characters such as Caroline Abbott, prudential values ultimately triumph over more genuine ones. At the end, her experiencing an eternal moment prevents her from achieving a more direct commitment to life. Salvation is the thematic center of *Angels*, and transfiguration is the means used to achieve such salvation. Several scenes involving transfiguration begin with the sequence at the opera house. Philip Herriton is educated by life, but he cannot escape completely the "inveterate custom of translating unmanageable life into manageable art." Philip is similar to EMF, but his irony is cynical rather than genial like EMF's.

Chap 4, *"The Longest Journey"*: In *The Longest Journey* and *Howards End* EMF is preoccupied with the relationship between the individual and the spirit of England, with the supremacy of the imaginative vision, with the need for contact between the individual and the earth, with personal relations (and the necessity "to connect"), and with the superiority of the inner life to the outer life of commerce and worldly pursuits. *Journey* reveals how difficult it is for any individual to be both natural and cultured. There is the inevitability of Greek tragedy and of Ibsen's GHOSTS about this work. Also important are the themes of salvation and illusion versus reality. Rickie Elliot represents the way of imagination; Stewart Ansell, that of intellect; and Stephen Wonham, that of instinct. No one of these modes of apprehending reality can in itself suffice. The completely realized backgrounds against which the characters develop prevent them from becoming thin or allegorical. The conflict between Ansell and Agnes Pembroke is as much sexual as philosophical. She invades (and degrades) both of Rickie's sanctuaries: his Cambridge rooms and the dell at Madingley. The Wessex scenes bring in the themes of brotherhood and of the continuity of England and the challenges to Rickie in the persons of his aunt (Mrs. Failing) and his half-brother (Stephen). In the Sawston scenes EMF demonstrates how the public individual is formed at the expense of the private one. The last section of the novel reveals some confusion between the spiritual view of reality and the ethical. The spiritual view demands that Rickie see Stephen as transfigured by the presence of their mother in him (to enforce the theme of continuity), and the ethical view demands that Rickie see Stephen as a man and as nothing else. The famous flameboat episode supports the symbolic identification of Stephen with the dead mother (the spiritual view) rather than his existence as an individual (the ethical view). In Stephen there is too much "beast" for him to fuse adequately "the monk" and "the beast" in man. Cancelled portions of the manuscript suggest that Rickie's reason for saving Stephen at the end is the result of Rickie's recognition of the dead mother's surviving through Stephen. Rickie's death reveals that

EMF could find no place in Edwardian society for a liberated Rickie, i.e., a Rickie who would have been able to express openly and without guilt the homosexual bent in his nature. In *Journey* the great imaginative scenes result in an impressive work, and it rises superior to its confused vision and technique. Chap 5, *"Howards End"*: The rescue motif has many manifestations in *Howards End:* the attempt to save Helen Schlegel from a misguided marriage, the attempt to rescue a house from ownership by a stranger (and the later rescue of this house by Margaret Schlegel from the unappreciative Wilcoxes), the rescue of a clerk from descent into the economic abyss, the attempt by Margaret to rescue Helen at Howards End house after she has acted mysteriously, and the rescue of Henry Wilcox from collapse and prostration at the end of the novel. EMF is concerned with the condition of England, especially in the episodes connecting the Schlegels and the Wilcoxes with the Basts. EMF's principal theme is the need to attain harmony both in private life and in public life. Diversity is cherished as much as harmony. Houses signify permanence; the London flats, change. The Basts anticipate in their sterile love the characters in T. S. Eliot's "The Waste Land." Leonard Bast's ruin through both the Wilcoxes and the Schlegels suggests that both the capitalist and the liberal idealist are responsible for the state of society. Henry Wilcox is credible as a representative social figure but not as a sexually compelling man. The Basts are presented with compassion and insight as people dwelling on the fringes of the Edwardian middle class and likely to fall into the economic abyss. EMF accommodates the Infinite and the Unseen in *Howards End* by making use of rhythm (particularly internal stitching), which helps communicate a sense of the impalpable and the numinous, by making use of prophecy (through exploiting the sudden illumination into reality), by adaptation of the Gothic mode (inducing of the supernatural vision through psychic shock), and by EMF's own tone of voice. *Howards End* is a representative novel which misses greatness because of a sense of strain and a lack of human warmth.

Chap 6, "Posthumous Fiction": [Discussion of *Arctic Summer.*] *Maurice* seems to be a sketch for a novel rather than a fully articulated work. The lack of tension between author and audience accounts for a thinness in the narrative, a self-indulgent tone, and a lack of ironic perspective. The conclusion makes clear that a classless society in England is to be regarded partly in terms of freedom for the homosexual to communicate across the barriers of class. Maurice Hall has a fineness of perception that is often at odds with the stated nature of his character. Homosexual and social themes reinforce one another toward the end of the novel, where EMF is as much concerned with class as with sex. For example, the partnership of Maurice and Alec Scudder in the cricket match suggests the strength of their love and the promise of a redeemed and classless England. In the British Museum sequence and later scenes, the surface antagonisms are at variance with a deep inner harmony uniting Maurice and Alec. The personal and social triumph at the end is unsure, but the novel is poignant in its presentation of the individual alienated from his society. As for *The Life to Come and Other Stories*, the two best works are "Arthur Snatchfold" and "The Other Boat." In both, powerful sexual instincts lead to retribution, through the agency of an unemancipated and unsympathetic social order. Chap 7, "India, Alexandria, and India Again": [Discussion of "Indian Entries," *Alexandria: A History and a Guide, The Government of Egypt, Pharos and Pharillon*, and *The Hill of Devi.*] Chap 8, "*A Passage to India*": A statement from "Three Countries" (a King's College manuscript) indicates EMF's purpose in writing *A Passage to India:* "It's about something wider than politics, about the search of the human race for a more lasting home, about the universe as embodied in the Indian earth and the horror lurking in the Marabar Caves and the release symbolized by the birth of Krishna." In *Howards End* the principle of diversity validates human relations; in *Passage* they are imperiled by this diversity. The first chapter of "Mosque" sets the tone and suggests the themes for the entire novel: the contrast between native and official Chandrapore, the contrasting entities of earth and sky, and the looming presence of the "extraordinary" Caves in the distance. In "Mosque" kindness and spontaneous affection overcome many barriers. In "Caves" absence and presence are seen as necessary aspects of the divine. The opening chapter stresses the infinity of geological time, the impersonality and the negative aspects of the Caves, and the ambiguity of human experience through the image of the match flame reflected in the cave wall, an image which can be an emblem either of an intense reality or of a passing illusion. The first chapter of "Temple" strikes an apocalyptic note and combines religious mysticism and the comic spirit. The relationship between Ronny Heaslop and Adela Quested cannot accommodate the irrational; that between Aziz and Fielding is more successful in so doing. EMF values the attempts to achieve harmony through "completeness" as preferable to the attempts made to achieve it through "reconstruction." Completeness derives from the influence of love, affection, and imagination; reconstruction, from the intellect. Mrs. Moore, Professor Godbole, and Aziz achieve most in the way of completeness; Fielding and Adela, except in rare moments of visionary insight, follow the path of reconstruction. In *Passage* good actions are preceded by good states of mind—when Professor Godbole recalls Mrs. Moore and the wasp, when Adela retracts her charge against Aziz, and when Aziz at the end writes to Adela. As a result of this close association in his characters of a good state of mind with positive action, EMF escapes the emphasis in the early fiction on internal grace and privileged aestheticism as the means for attaining salvation, and he also avoids the tendency in *Howards End* to formulate the solution to social problems solely in terms of states of mind and aesthetic patterns. The characterizations in *Passage* are convincing because of EMF's deep understanding of human nature, his wit, his humor, and his mastery of dialogue. Life is conveyed through speech and the speech patterns developed in the novel; most of the misunderstandings between Aziz and Fielding are also the result of linguistic difficulties. The superiority of *Passage* is as much the result of EMF's tempered voice as of his vision.

Chap 9, "Criticism and Biography": [Discussion of *Aspects of the Novel*, *Goldsworthy Lowes Dickinson*, and *Marianne Thornton.*] Chap 10, "Essays, Lectures, and Broadcasts": EMF's essays reveal the qualities that give his fiction distinction: imaginative insight and ironic detachment, an appreciation of the complexity of humanism: "the importance of individualism, tolerance, sensitiveness, the capacity to enjoy and endure, personal relations, resistance to authority, and scepticism towards political panaceas." The essays on the arts reveal a skepticism toward criticism and an espousing of the aesthetic tenets of romanticism. His broadcast talks convey his engaging personal qualities and his breadth of view, his wide interests, and his imaginative and critical insight. His essays and talks on political subjects demonstrate his refusal to regard political issues solely in external and institutional terms; he sees that problems of freedom and order have an interior dimension in the struggles that the individual makes in his spirit between the forces of light and darkness. In his essays EMF regards force as an enemy of civilization, though in his fiction violence often has salutary effects in helping individuals break through the conventions. "What I Believe" attains authority more through the voice present in the essay than through its arguments. This essay, while proposing a spiritual elite, is really individualistic in its premises and speaks to the individualist in all of EMF's readers. The source of EMF's strength as novelist and as publicist is the same: "it lies in his capacity to create rhythms of thought and emotion that go on sounding and expanding in our minds long after we have ceased to read the actual words." Chap 11, "Conclusion." [Bibliography. A sound and sometimes exciting introduction to EMF's work, but not a brilliant or a profound critique. The judgments are sensitive and sensible, however, and the quotations from unpublished materials are illuminating.]

1881 Cunningham, Valentine. "Morgan le Fay," NEW STATESMAN, nsLXXXIX (21 March 1975), 288–89.
EMF had little to offer in 1927 when he discussed serious fiction in *Aspects of the Novel*. The fact that he did not is now more apparent with the publication of *Aspects* in *The Abinger Edition* (1974, ed by Oliver Stallybrass). The notebooks from which EMF drew his lectures are more honest about the writers that he discusses than are the published lectures. *Aspects* is marked by "insincere mediocrity."

1882 Delany, Paul. "Lawrence and E. M. Forster: Two Rainbows," D. H. LAWRENCE REVIEW, VIII (Spring 1975), 54–62.

Lawrence's sketch illustrating the final scene of THE RAINBOW, sent to Viola Meynell, 2 March 1915, had its origins in paintings by Fra Angelico, Hans Memling, and Raphael, but it also owed something to a design by Roger Fry from the endpapers of E. M. Forster's *The Celestial Omnibus and Other Stories* (1911), a book that EMF had sent to Lawrence in early 1915, along with *Howards End*. Lawrence did not conceive of the rainbow as a link between divergent realms, such as EMF's earthly and spiritual worlds, prose and passion; with Lawrence, the end of the rainbow rests on objects from this world, the colliery and "the brittle, hard edged new houses," both being symbolic of a moribund social order that must be destroyed before renewal can take place.

1883 Donoghue, Denis. "An Ear for Fiction," TIMES LITERARY SUPPLEMENT (Lond), 31 Jan 1975, p. 103.

In *Aspects of the Novel* EMF's guiding principle is that "in music fiction is likely to find its nearest parallel." The art of fiction "consists of its continuity with the art of music, and . . . the best readers have a practised ear for both." Music represented for EMF the greatest possibility for, and attainment of, order. Accordingly, he appropriated the principles of music for considering critically the art of fiction. The chief defect of *Aspects* is EMF's failure to discuss those aspects of fiction "for which music cannot provide a valid analogy"—social change, political forces, the circumstances determining authorship and readership, conventions of style and communication, and the linguistic ramifications of literature. EMF in his best criticism is sensitive to the rhythmic aspects of a work and the way they determine its form. [Stimulating comments. Review of EMF's *Aspects of the Novel and Related Writings*, ed by Oliver Stallybrass (Lond: Edward Arnold, The Abinger Edition of E. M. Forster, 1974).]

1884 Ebbatson, J. R. "The Schlegels' Family Tree," ENGLISH LITERATURE IN TRANSITION, XVIII: 3 (1975), 195–201.

The Schlegel sisters reveal affinities with the Dashwood sisters in Austen's SENSE AND SENSIBILITY, Elinor Dashwood being similar to Margaret Schlegel and Marianne being similar to Helen. The Schlegels also reveal some similarities to the Pole sisters in Meredith's SANDRA BELLONI. Both sets of sisters reveal much sensitivity and sensibility; both authors give a qualified approval to the sister group in their novels. Like the Schlegels, the Poles have a weak-willed brother, and they adopt an outcast, Sandra Belloni, into their circle (the Schlegels look after Leonard Bast). *Howards End* has affinities also with Meredith's RHODA FLEMING. The seduced girl, Dahlia Fleming, is Helen's counterpart; and a more controlled sister, Rhoda, is Margaret's. A still more convincing case of literary ancestry is demonstrated in the relationship between William Hale White's CLARA HOPGOOD and *Howards End.* Clara is similar to Margaret in her steady good sense, while Madge Hopgood is similar to Helen in her impulsiveness. Frank Palmer is similar to Leonard Bast, and he has a brief love affair with Madge which makes her pregnant, a circumstance similar to Helen's pregnancy as a result of her casual relationship with Leonard. As a repository of instinctive wisdom, Baruch Cohen is not unlike the intuitively penetrating Mrs. Wilcox. Clara's casual death in fighting for the *risorgimento* in Italy is parallel to Leonard's; and Clara's daughter, like Helen's son, carries the promise for the future. [A suggestive article.]

> **1885** Eldridge, Shaila VanSickle. " 'The Life by Value' in the Novels of E. M. Forster," DISSERTATION ABSTRACTS INTERNATIONAL, XXXVI (1975), 2842A. Unpublished dissertation, University of Denver, 1975.

> **1886** Feldmann, Hans Eugene. "The Function of Heresy in Modern Literature: Studies in the Major Fiction of Thomas Hardy, E. M. Forster, and D. H. Lawrence," DISSERTATION ABSTRACTS INTERNATIONAL, XXXVI (1975), 1524–25A. Unpublished dissertation, University of Maryland, 1974.

> **1887** Finkelstein, Bonnie Blumenthal. FORSTER'S WOMEN: ETERNAL DIFFERENCES (NY & Lond: Columbia UP, 1975); rvd from "The Role of Women in the Novels of E. M. Forster with Parallels to the Role of Homosexuals in *Maurice.*" Unpublished dissertation, Columbia University, 1972; rpts, in expanded form, "Forster's Women: *A Room with a View*," ENGLISH LITERATURE IN TRANSITION, XVI: 4 (1973), 275–87.

Chap 1, *"Where Angels Fear to Tread":* In *Angels,* EMF analyzes four main female types: Mrs. Herriton is the woman as manipulator and is the conventional mother figure; Lilia Theobald Herriton Carella is the woman imprisoned by marriage and is an Eve figure; Harriet Herriton is the conventional spinster seeking salvation in religious fanaticism; and Caroline Abbott is the sensitive, intellectual woman who attempts to avoid the fate of the stereotyped women in her society. Caroline Abbott accepts her sexuality, but the brotherhood of man exists at the expense of sisterhood and the freedom of women, so that she is not able to achieve sexual fulfillment. She resists Gino Carella because life in Italy is intolerable for a woman in a society that stresses woman's submission and man's unfettered personal freedom. Chap 2, *"The Longest Journey":* Rickie Elliot must learn to accept individual differences, EMF's great principle. In *Journey,* marriage is destructive not only of fraternity but of one's ability to accept the significance of symbolic moments. Rickie is a figure symbolic of modern alienated man. Women are involved in the opening discussion on the nature of reality; in the male

Cambridge society, they seem hardly real. Women do not come off well in *Journey;* Agnes Pembroke and the elderly Mrs. Failing are variously unreal, and Mrs. Elliot surrendered to convention after breaking from it in her affair with Robert. Stewart Ansell is a voice of reality and wisdom, but he lacks the insight not to be misogynous. Rickie's marriage is a disaster because he identifies with the brutal, negative aspects of both sexes, in his attraction to both Gerald Dawes and Agnes. Agnes's influence is disastrous for Rickie, and she causes him especially to deny the element of brotherhood. As a woman, however, she merits our sympathies, because society provides her with no outlet for her strong energies. She is opportunistic and exemplifies (like Mrs. Failing) an anticonventional conventionality. She has a real feeling for Gerald and thus demands our pity when he dies, but she demands also to be judged by Gerald's brutality. Mrs. Elliot is a woman entrapped by an unhappy marriage. She illustrates the roles of wife and mother; she is repressed and lives only as people react to her. She is the suffering outsider whose sympathies are androgynous. In her lifetime, Mrs. Failing changes from a life-serving, truly anticonventional woman, to a life-denying one who honors the conventions. She is close to Agnes in being a manipulator and in being conventionally unconventional. Rickie is somewhere between the homosexual Ansell and the heterosexual Stephen. Chap 3, "*A Room with a View*": [For contents of this chapter, see Finkelstein, "Forster's Women: *A Room with a View*" (1973).] Chap 4, "*Howards End*": EMF's stress in this novel is on connection: internally, the individual must achieve sexual knowledge, uniting the beast and the monk; externally, he must achieve satisfying personal relationships. In the Schlegel sisters, the "heroes" of this novel, the emphasis is on the personal. Margaret also voices EMF's stress on individuality with her observation that among people there are "eternal differences" that must be respected. Margaret accepts her sexuality and also transcends these eternal differences to exalt the companionship that lies beyond sex. She is the quintessential androgynous hero in EMF's work who accepts his (or her) sexuality, the importance of women in society (and by extension, of other repressed elements such as homosexuals), and the principle of fraternity. As for the end of the novel, the typical critical reaction is negative and antifeminist. Henry Wilcox is not "gelded"; he is simply more human than he was before. As for Margaret, she is able now to connect the prose of life (Henry) and its poetry (Helen). The final vision in *Howards End* is androgynous; no one, and no one sex, controls everything. Equality between classes is stressed as a corollary to the equality of the sexes. Leonard Bast is not antifeminist but is a victim of the male dominance that is concomitant with chivalry. Jacky is the price that society pays for a double standard of sexual morality; and EMF would agree with Helen Schlegel that men are responsible for making Jacky what she is. Helen is active in sex, to the dismay of many critics. Ruth Wilcox is not a feminist, but she is an enlarging spiritual force. Margaret's London life is inadequate when measured against the example of Ruth Wilcox; but Margaret is not personally inadequate. Ruth's chief gift to Margaret is to teach her to have affection for a place. Henry Wilcox is antifeminist in subscribing to a double standard (in particular, he will not connect his own sexual irregularities with Helen's unconventionality), in emphasizing a "chivalric" protectiveness toward woman, and in stressing woman's passivity and delicacy. He ignores the personal aspect of relationships. After her confrontation with him over Helen, Margaret insists on equality between the sexes, on a valid comradeship or nothing. At the end, Henry is more humanized than feminized. Spiritual heredity is more important for EMF than physical (Margaret will not have children, but her influence will be much greater than the physically fertile Dolly Wilcox's). Howards End house is androgynous and connects the two sexes, all the social classes, and all the characters. Men are too closely associated with laws concerning physical heredity, and women are passed over as unimportant in Edwardian society. Howards End house is at the heart of England, but the alterations to the house have somewhat deformed it; so England's body is disfigured because of a false idea of femininity. The house embodies the idea of the companionship that transcends sex rather than sex itself. Chap 5, "*A Passage to India*": To correspond to political imperialism with its repressions and opportunism, Indian men oppress their women, while British women manipulate their men. At the time of Adela Quested's being the victim of rape, the English are motivated by a misguided chivalry but fail to treat Adela as a person. Indian women are entirely passive. The nonexistence of the Indian women behind purdah corresponds to the invisibility of Western women behind their veils of "ladylikeness." Aziz is aware of the political oppression of Indians by other political powers but is never aware of Indian repression of women. Mrs. Moore establishes connections, and her point of view is inclusive, as is that of her son Ralph. Ronny Heaslop is antifeminist in his lack of sympathy for Mrs. Moore. Her experience in the Caves reveals that she cannot incorporate Hinduism into her innermost being by her own will, but Hinduism finally incorporates her. Adela comes to India to find the real India and marriage but instead finds real India, sexuality, and self-knowledge. Adela is prosaic and cannot therefore connect the "passion" with the "prose." In India, however, she can acknowledge her own sexuality; she achieves self-knowledge even if she is not able to gratify her sexuality. Fielding, like Margaret Schlegel, is aware of the eternal differences among people and stresses, like her, the importance of an enlightened individualism. His marriage is a positive act, connecting him more closely with Mrs. Moore than he had been before. He is able to embrace both Stella and Aziz, and he goes further, therefore, than Philip Herriton could in *Angels*, who was unable to embrace Caroline sexually and Gino fraternally. The final effects of Fielding's marriage remain unclear, and there is much that is tentative about it. Chap 6, "*Maurice*": Maurice must be rescued from conventionality by Alec Scudder, as in *Room* Lucy Honeychurch must be rescued by George Emerson. Maurice must learn the lesson that individuals are different. *Maurice* presents three kinds of sexual man: Maurice Hall is both Platonic and physical in orientation and is homosexual; Clive Durham is idealistically homosexual and then becomes ideologically and physically heterosexual; and Alec Scudder is bisexual at the physical level. Homosexuality is often connected with an imagery of darkness, though light is associated with the acknowledgment of homosexuality and a resulting self-awareness. Maurice's salvation occurs in two stages: Clive teaches him to accept homosexuality, and Alec teaches him to accept sex. Agnosticism and homosexuality are linked, while Christianity is linked with the ascetic repression of homosexuality. Clive replaces Christianity with a philosophical Hellenism, whereas Maurice retains his agnosticism to the end and in place of the lost Christianity elevates the personal, sexual relationship. The women in *Maurice* are oppressed by society and by the oppressed men in that society. Clive relies on intellect rather than emotion in his relationships with others. Clive's antisexuality is to be associated also with his class snobbery. [Selected bibliography. This book analyzes EMF's feminism competently and often cogently, EMF being drawn to the cause of women, whom he saw as comprising an oppressed segment in society. The analysis of *Howards End* is especially good. There is perhaps too little acknowledgment of EMF's misogyny as such, of his conviction expressed in *Journey* and *Maurice* and in the posthumous tales of woman herself as sometimes the oppressor, particularly as she becomes an obstacle to sexual fulfillment.]

1888 Fussell, Paul. THE GREAT WAR AND MODERN MEMORY (NY & Lond: Oxford UP, 1975), pp. 106, 272, 285, 306.
The popularity in the postwar era of the epigraph to *Howards End*, "Only connect," implies that things were disjointed or polarized if there was need to connect them, and the epigraph thus reflected upon the fragmentation present in postwar life. EMF expressed in his novels from 1905 to 1910 [and in the short stories] the "period" motif of the sudden death of boys as the most moving image possible for the literary mind to project. The "boys-bathing" sequence in *A Room with a View* contributed to the Great-War writers' use of soldiers-bathing scenes. This sequence in *Room* is more vivid than any heterosexual scene in the novel.

1889 Gillie, Christopher. "Diversification of the Modern Novel: E. M. Forster (1879–1970)," MOVEMENTS IN ENGLISH LITERATURE 1900–1940 (NY & Lond: Cambridge UP, 1975), pp. 112–20; also pp. 92, 111, 133, 134.
Despite his criticism of the British middle class, EMF is himself of this class. Like the middle class he describes, he is sometimes afraid of feeling. Thus when he surrenders to strong emotion, he becomes "sentimentally rhetori-

cal"; when he expresses sexual passion, he becomes commonplace; and when he surrenders to strong emotion, he becomes "sentimentally rhetorical"; when he expresses sexual passion, he becomes commonplace; and when he presents a working-class character, he reveals his social inhibitions. Though EMF is more intelligent and discriminating than Kipling, Kipling often succeeds in ranges of fiction wherein EMF is unsuccessful. Like Matthew Arnold EMF became self-critical in order to criticize the system. Arnold went back to ancient Greece or outward to France for a standard; EMF went to Greek mythology and to other countries (except in *The Longest Journey*). EMF developed a symbolism more organic than Virginia Woolf's, and he combined art-for art's sake with a communicative relationship with the reader. The problems presented in the prewar novels, however, lack depth and persuasiveness. In *A Passage to India* he found a theme of outstanding grandeur which he treated with great depth. *Passage* presents a critique of Anglo-Indian postures before and after the 1914–1918 war; it developed contrasts among cultures (British, Moslem, Hindu), and it explored the subject of religion (the British) by showing a culture that has made religion as inherent in every aspect of life (Hindu). Fielding has genuine virtues but suffers himself from an undeveloped heart (with respect to Aziz). Only Godbole is religious in the full sense of the word. The visit to the Marabar Caves is decisive in many lives. All the characters are responsible for what happens in them. Godbole alone sees the human situation whole, but he is incapable of practical action. In Mrs. Moore there is the disparity between her will for good action and the weakness of her spiritual grasp. Subsequent to her experience in the Caves, she collapses into a total egoism, but paradoxically its intensity is more effective than her good intentions and shakes Adela Quested into a realization of the truth that Aziz did not attack her in the Caves. At the trial the British are defeated and the Indians are triumphant; but the real victory goes to the British intellectuals, Fielding and Adela, who are consistently honest. The distinction of *Passage* lies in the articulated and reiterated symbolism, used to emphasize a double contrast: the confusion of Indian social life in which the British mind imposes order, and the unfathomable aspect of the India that perceives an infinite order which the Western mind is partly unable to grasp. EMF in *Passage* is not guilty of the wishful imposing of values. George Orwell's Burmese Days and *Passage* have similar characters and situations. In Orwell the characters are stereotypes, as are the racial and religious phenomena presented in the novel. The conflicts are more bitterly presented in Orwell but more thinly. In Orwell's characters, unlike EMF's, the dimension of generosity is lacking. [Some perceptive remarks on *Passage*.]

1890 Hanquart, Evelyne. "Notes on 'Monteriano,'" NOTES AND QUERIES (Lond), nsXXII (May 1975), 198–201.
The manuscript of *Where Angels Fear to Tread* was with the Nathaniel

Wedd papers at King's College, Cambridge, and the galley proofs were in EMF's papers at King's College. The College then presented the manuscript to the British Museum. Both documents are labelled "Monteriano." A passage in the manuscript that was later deleted expresses EMF's direct interest in, and involvement with, Italian things and people. In the manuscript Philip Herriton's motivation in confessing to Gino Carella the death of the latter's child is more elaborately analyzed, and Caroline Abbott's confession of love for Gino is more explicit. In the manuscript EMF is more confidential and more romantic in the expression of his deep feelings toward life and human beings. In the published version of *Angels*, the writing gains both in directness and suggestiveness.

> **1891** Harm, Roger Lee. "The Literature of Imperialism: Kipling, Conrad, and Forster," DISSERTATION ABSTRACTS INTERNATIONAL, XXXVI (1975), 2845–46A. Unpublished dissertation, Stanford University, 1975.

> **1892** Kermode, Frank. "Aspects and Points of View," MANCHESTER GUARDIAN WEEKLY, 15 Feb 1975, p. 21.

Aspects of the Novel is often dated and silly, but it has not "wilted." The "shy insights" and the "tentative propositions" advanced in the book still make it challenging. [Review of Abinger Edition, *Aspects of the Novel* (1974), ed by Oliver Stallybrass.]

> **1893** McDowell, Frederick P. W. "A New Edition of E. M. Forster's *Aspects of the Novel*," ENGLISH LITERATURE IN TRANSITION, XVIII: 4 (1975), 257–59.

The most noteworthy aspect of *The Abinger Edition* of *Aspects of the Novel* (1974, ed by Oliver Stallybrass) is the printing of "Extracts from Forster's Commonplace Book," which allow one to compare at several points in *Aspects* EMF's original thoughts with those that he presented in his completed book.

> **1894** Meyers, Jeffrey. A READER'S GUIDE TO GEORGE ORWELL (Lond: Thames & Hudson, 1975), pp. 11, 40, 68–69, 75, 84, 98, 105, 158.

Kipling's image of India inspired other writers to be critical of his views on empire: EMF in *A Passage to India*, Orwell in BURMESE DAYS, Cary in MR. JOHNSON, and Greene in THE HEART OF THE MATTER. Many similarities exist between BURMESE DAYS and *Passage*. BURMESE DAYS is more pessimistic than *Passage* since official failure is not redeemed by personal relations. There are no characters in Orwell's book such as Mrs. Moore and Fielding who maintain civilized values. *Howards End* is a work like Gissing's NEW GRUB STREET, James's THE SPOILS OF POYNTON, Conrad's NOSTROMO, Shaw's MAJOR BARBARA, and Orwell's COMING UP FOR AIR in protesting the mechanization of modern life.

1895 Mukherjee, Meenakshi. "On Teaching *A Passage to India,*" Focus on Forster's "A Passage to India," ed by V. A. Shahane (Madras & New Delhi: Orient Longman, 1975), pp. 98–104.

A Passage to India is a difficult yet rewarding text for Indian students of English literature to study, since it offers many aesthetic and intellectual problems for ready discussion. It is one of the few books of English literature that immediately involves the Indian student and that his own experience may help him to interpret.

1896 Naik, M. K. "Passage to Less Than India," Focus on Forster's "A Passage to India," ed by V. A. Shahane (Madras & New Delhi: Orient Longman, 1975), pp. 63–72.

[This essay presents a generally unconvincing negative view of the novel that does not go conspicuously beyond the similar ideas advanced by Nirad C. Chaudhuri in "Passage to and from India," Encounter (1954) and by Andrew Shonfield in "The Politics of Forster's India," Encounter (1968). (Naik does not refer to this last essay). Many other writers on EMF have implicitly or explicitly refuted the premises developed in Naik's essay. Among them are Michael Spencer in "Hinduism in E. M. Forster's *A Passage To India,*" Journal of Asian Studies (1968) and Jeffrey Meyers in "The Politics of *A Passage to India,*" Journal of Modern Literature (1971).]

1897 Naslund, Sena Jeter. "Fantasy, Prophecy, and Point of View in *A Passage to India,*" Studies in the Novel, VII (Summer 1975), 258–76.

In EMF's fiction fantasy is concerned with the supernatural, prophecy with the universe and the universal. In *A Passage to India* fantasy is all pervasive. Ghosts are a reality, for example: Mrs. Moore's spirit is real when she causes Adela to retract her charge at Aziz's trial and when Godbole recalls her in "Temple." The "ghost" that bumps into the Nawab Bahadur's car in which Adela Quested and Ronny Heaslop are riding is real to Mrs. Moore. The supernatural (or the fantastic) is connected with flexibility of temper and the ability to reverse one's attitudes or to realize that spiritual reality is contingent, unpredictable, and ambiguous. The reader's angle of vision is also to be modulated, and this EMF achieves by enlarging "the reader's spirit in mental overturns through fanciful tonal modulations." In "Caves" and "Temple" EMF thus manipulates the reader. Dual perspectives occur throughout the book, and fantasy is omnipresent and leads toward prophetic vision. Fielding's view that "we exist not in ourselves, but in terms of each other's minds" is to be interpreted in light of J. E. McTaggart's idealism rather than in terms of Hinduism. EMF wishes the reader to visit various angles of vision rather than to observe the universe merely from the vantage point of any one of them. Prophecy is contained within fantasy and exfoliates therefrom. "The voice of the prophet is one of involvement with realistic characters at one of their moments of intensity, narrated with a tinge of fantasy." Mobility of point of view (as in the last scene of *Passage*) combines with fantasy to produce prophecy. [The philosophical premises in this essay are not always clearly formulated, but the demonstration that fantasy is omnipresent in the novel is convincing.]

1898 Novak, Jane. THE RAZOR EDGE OF BALANCE (Coral Gables: University of Miami P, 1975), pp. 11, 13, 17–18, 22–28, 33, 40, 55, 59, 64, 77, 89, 104, 105, 139, 147.

Virginia Woolf was severe with EMF in her two essays on him ("The Art of Fiction," NATION AND ATHENAEUM [1927] and "The Novels of E. M. Forster," ATLANTIC MONTHLY [1927]) for his failure to fuse the world of realism with the world of symbolism. She was severe with him because of her own failure to fuse these worlds, especially in THE VOYAGE OUT and NIGHT AND DAY. She found his novels lacking in conclusiveness since they presented so much of life; he found her novels lacking in the feel of life because of her intense poetic economy.

1899 Price, Martin. "People of the Book: Character in Forster's *A Passage to India*," CRITICAL INQUIRY, I (March 1975), 605–22.

EMF's contrast between the time-bound and social on the one hand and the heroic and impersonal on the other separates the less real from the more real in his portrayal of character. In his characters there are varying levels of consciousness and awareness. In *A Passage to India*, Fielding is close to the omniscient author's mind. We enter frequently into Fielding's mind, less frequently into Mrs. Moore's, and once only into Godbole's. The characters tend to be slight because the design of the novel is so powerful. For them India is not so much a rival force and anti-character as a common predicament. The most troublesome predicament for EMF's characters is that of interpretation; reality is contingent and can only be partially apprehended by any one sensibility. In India, life conveys a sense of power but of uncertain purpose. There is, for example, much sound in India but no abundance of clear meaning. Many aspects of this impassive novel remain uncertain. The problem of incarnation summarizes the tensions explored in the novel: how much spirit is needed to inhabit the flesh, and vice versa. The Caves reveal an extreme instance of matter obstructing and refusing spirit. "Within this common predicament of the need to interpret and of its constant frustration, Forster creates characters who bring different kinds of apparatus for judging." Aziz is the most fully realized character and is in the anomalous situation of being somewhere between the ancient mysteries of Hinduism and the modernity of British administration. He is most marked by anxiety, and sometimes his anxiety makes him unpleasant. He reveals the lack of proportion and of taste characterizing India as a whole. His deepest religious experience is his friendship with Mrs. Moore. Adela Quested and Fielding are trapped within the limits of liberal, rational intelligence as Aziz is not. Adela's crisis is induced by insincerity. Fielding has an excess of detachment and intelligence. Mrs. Moore and Godbole are equivocal characters, lacking "the human centrality that we associate with rational awareness, with moral responsibility, with form on a limited scale." They are less human than the other characters, but are they something more, we ask. Mrs. Moore has, in the early scenes, clairvoyance and insight; in the Caves, she is exposed to the dark side of pantheism. Godbole is the most inscrutable of the characters because his beliefs, unlike Mrs. Moore's, have no history. Godbole, in his Olympian aloofness at the time of Aziz's arrest, seems to be denying the reality of human suffering, or at least reducing responsibility for it. There is an element of fatuity in Godbole's vision of unity. Both he and Mrs. Moore have moved beyond moral involvement. His is an ambiguous presence, suggesting "at once a perfect fool and the nearest approach to the gates of the Divine." "The subtlety of the novel lies in its unrelieved tension of flesh and spirit, exclusion and invitation, the social self and the deeper impersonal self." The characters reveal various aspects of this dichotomy. We can only glimpse the unseen "through paradox, violence, or fear; and each of these contributes something to Forster's conception of character." [Some insights of value, though the characters considered in isolation from the whole organism of this novel is sometimes disturbing, as is the critic's failure to refer to the work of other scholars and critics.]

1900 Rosenbaum, S. P. (ed). THE BLOOMSBURY GROUP: A COLLECTION OF MEMOIRS, COMMENTARY AND CRITICISM (Toronto & Buffalo: University of Toronto P; Lond: Croom Helm, 1975).
[Anthology is divided into four sections, "Bloomsbury on Bloomsbury," "Bloomsberries," "Bloomsbury Observed," and "Bloomsbury Criticisms and Controversies." It contains source materials by members of the Bloomsbury circle and their immediate associates, including Virginia Woolf, EMF, Lytton Strachey, Roger Fry, Clive Bell, Vanessa Bell, John Maynard Keynes, Duncan Grant, Desmond MacCarthy, Adrian Stephen, Saxon Sydney-Turner, Leonard Woolf, Cuentin Bell, David Garnett, Angelica Garnett, Rayriond Mortimer, Lady Ottoline Morrell, and Vita Sackville-West. Anthology contains critical essays by most of the above figures and by Michael Holroyd, Noel Annan, John Russell, T. S. Eliot, R. F. Harrod, Osbert Sitwell, Edith Sitwell, Stephen Spender, John Lehmann, Gerald Brenan, Arthur Waley, William Plomer, Peter Stansky, and William Abrahams. Section, "Bloomsbury Criticism and Controversies" contains selections on or by Wyndham Lewis, D. H. Lawrence, Dmitri Mirsky, Bernard Shaw, F. R. Leavis, and Bertrand Russell. The following items by EMF are rptd: "Bloomsbury, An Early Note (February 1929)," "Desmond Mac-

Carthy," "Virginia Woolf," and Letter (LISTENER, XLVIII [24 July 1952], 142 [Reply to letter by Bertrand Russell, 17 July, 97–98]). Anthology contains relevant Bloomsbury materials from the following items, abstracted in this volume under date of first publication: John Maynard Keynes, TWO MEMOIRS (1949); F. R. Leavis, "Keynes, Lawrence and Cambridge," SCRUTINY (1949); Stephen Spender, WORLD WITHIN WORLD (1951); R. F. Harrod, JOHN MAYNARD KEYNES (1951); David Garnett, THE FLOWERS OF THE FOREST (1955); Clive Bell, OLD FRIENDS (1956); Gerald Brenan, SOUTH FROM GRANADA (1957); William Plomer, AT HOME (1958); John Lehmann, I AM MY BROTHER (1960); Leonard Woolf, SOWING (1960), GROWING (1961), BEGINNING AGAIN (1964), and DOWNHILL ALL THE WAY (1967); David Garnett, THE FAMILIAR FACES (1962); Peter Stansky and William Abrahams, JOURNEY TO THE FRONTIER (1966); Michael Holroyd, LYTTON STRACHEY, I (1967); Quentin Bell, BLOOMSBURY (1968); David Garnett, "Forster and Bloomsbury," ASPECTS OF E. M. FORSTER, ed by Oliver Stallybrass (1969); and Quentin Bell, VIRGINIA WOOLF (1972). Anthology contains "A Bloomsbury Chronology," "Bibliographies," "Identifications" (for important persons and places connected with Bloomsbury), and reproductions of paintings by Bloomsbury artists. The book comprises a compendious anthology of materials essential for the understanding of Bloomsbury and EMF.]

1901 Rosenbaum, S. P. "Foreword," "Introduction" (Bloomsbury Criticisms and Controversies), [Headnotes], THE BLOOMSBURY GROUP: A COLLECTION OF MEMOIRS, COMMENTARY AND CRITICISM, ed by S. P. Rosenbaum (Toronto & Buffalo: University of Toronto P; Lond: Croom Helm, 1975), pp. i–v, 329–31, 24–25, 26–27, 156, 163, 204, 295–96, 331–34, 361–63, 380, 388.

"Foreword": Bloomsbury did exist, and Bloomsbury is worth studying. Bloomsbury, according to EMF, is the only genuine movement in British civilization. Friendship formed the enduring basis of the group. It had no platform or creed nor can its complexities be argued away. EMF was one of the original thirteen people in Bloomsbury. "Introduction" (Bloomsbury Criticisms and Controversies): Various people in the Bloomsbury circle disliked each other's work: Strachey was bored by EMF's novels; Virginia Woolf was critical of Strachey's biographies and EMF's theory of the novel, etc. EMF's *Howards End* and *Maurice* are in part depictions of Bloomsbury milieu and personalities. [Headnote], "E. M. Forster: Bloomsbury, An Early Note (February 1929)": In spite of his detachment expressed in "Bloomsbury, An Early Note" (see George H. Thomson, "E. M. Forster, Gerald Heard, and Bloomsbury," ENGLISH LITERATURE IN TRANSITION [1969]), EMF is still an integral part of Bloomsbury. Though he criticized the members of Bloomsbury in this essay for their excessive intellectuality, he showed strong resemblances to many of them in the convictions expressed in "What I Believe" (*Two Cheers for Democracy*) and elsewhere. A draft for a fragmentary essay in the EMF Archive reveals a more affectionate and involved attitude toward Bloomsbury than he expressed in his 1929 note. The essay concerns his introduction to the group and his early encounters with its members. [Headnote], "Desmond MacCarthy: Bloomsbury, An Unfinished Memoir (1933)": Desmond MacCarthy's conception of Bloomsbury is more limited than EMF's expressed in "Bloomsbury, An Early Note." [Headnote], "Desmond MacCarthy by E. M. Forster": EMF's "tribute" to MacCarthy supports Quentin Bell's estimate of MacCarthy's geniality and tolerance. [Headnote], "E. M. Forster by David Garnett": Garnett's essay conclusively demonstrates that EMF was part of Bloomsbury. [Headnote], "Virginia Woolf by E. M. Forster"; EMF's essay on Woolf is the best available brief introduction to her work and personality. [Headnote], "William Plomer: Evenings in Tavistock Square": Plomer's description of EMF in AT HOME (1958) is vivid and well-known. [Headnote], "Wyndham Lewis": Even the mild EMF did not escape attack in Wyndham Lewis's wars on Bloomsbury. Lewis called EMF the "male opposite number to Virginia Woolfe" [*sic*] in his BLASTING AND BOMBARDIERING (Lond: Eyre & Spottiswoode, 1937). [Headnote], "D. H. Lawrence": Though Bloomsbury may have been hostile to Lawrence's work and though he was critical of Bloomsbury, still Virginia Woolf was favorable to SONS AND LOVERS, Clive Bell and Lytton Strachey opposed the suppression of THE RAINBOW, and EMF called Lawrence "the greatest imaginative novelist of our generation." Lawrence was also enthusiastic about *A Passage to India*. [Headnote], "Dmitri Mirsky": Mirsky criticized EMF as one of the Bloomsbury writers in THE INTELLIGENTSIA OF GREAT BRITAIN (Lond: Gollancz, 1935). [Headnote], "F. R. Leavis": Leavis and his SCRUTINY associates are the most consistent critics of Bloomsbury. Leavis admired EMF's fiction but not his criticism. [Headnote], "Bertrand Russell": Russell's severe criticism of Lytton Strachey in "Portraits from Memory: Keynes and Strachey" (LISTENER, XLVIII [17 July 1952], 97–98) was by one who knew him well. EMF's rejoinder (LISTENER [24 July 1952], 142) was also by one who knew him well. [Perceptive commentary by a scholar whose knowledge of Bloomsbury is impressive and wide-ranging.]

1902 Sahni, Chaman Lall. "E. M. Forster's *A Passage to India* in Relation to Indian Thought," DISSERTATION ABSTRACTS INTERNATIONAL, XXXVI (1975), 1922–23A. Unpublished dissertation, Wayne State University, 1974.

1903 Sahni, Chaman L. "The Marabar Caves in the Light of Indian Thought," FOCUS ON FORSTER'S "A PASSAGE TO INDIA," ed by V. A. Shahane (Madras & New Delhi: Orient Longman, 1975), pp. 105–14.

The Marabar Caves signify a journey taken into a timeless past, and they are connected with infinity, eternity, and vastness in Mrs. Moore's mind. The Infinite in Indian religion and philosophy is seen under the symbol of *Sunya* or the Void, the Absolute which is beyond any human concept of good and evil. The Caves fuse matter and spirit, as does the Indian concept of the Infinite. The novel also illustrates the Jain concept that all unconscious matter is potentially conscious. In a Vedanta interpretation the match flame in the Caves is the symbol of *Atman*, the pure space of the Caves represents Brahman, the walls of granite suggest the phenomenal world, and the flame mirrored in the walls represents the world of appearances created by Maya. The world of appearances must be integrated into the Brahman for the merging of the *Atman* and the Brahman to occur. The Caves are associated with eternity through the recurrent image of the serpent and its coils, with the serpent swallowing its own tail. The Caves suggest the various facets of an all-embracing whole, to be found in the non-Vedic and Vedic schools of Indian thought: "The caves may then simultaneously represent the 'impersonal cosmic principle' of the Ajivika sect, the total renunciation and isolationism of Jainism, the Nirvana or the Void of Buddhism, the irresoluble dichotomy of *purusha* (life-monad, always represented in the Sankhya system as an 'imprisoned spirit') and *prakriti* (matter) represented by Sankhya and Yoga, and the undifferentiated oneness that lies at the root of the concept of Brahman in Advaita-Vedanta." Mrs. Moore's experience in the Cave annihilates her Christian heritage and confronts her with "the Hindu view of the Timeless Absolute," which to her Western point of view seems to be Nothingness. If the echo conveys Nothingness, it is not to be thought of, as some critics contend, as Evil. The echo, rather, goes beyond good and evil. "The undifferentiated oneness suggested by the echo to Mrs. Moore lies at the root of Advaita-Vedanta, and signifies the ultimate perception of the Hindu mystic." For her the echo eliminates all the distinctions she had previously known. Her confrontation "with the Indian view of the Timeless Absolute" immobilizes her, and she hangs suspended between life and infinity, between the phenomenal and noumenal worlds. She yearns for peace and extinction in a state of negative isolation as advocated in Jainism, Sankhya-Yoga, and the Hindu Upanishads. After her physical death she is spiritually reborn in the Krishna festival: her presence in Godbole's mind at that point indicates that she has reached the fulfillment of her destiny by being absorbed in the Absolute. "In the *Bhagavad-Gita* Krishna is represented as the highest Godhead, the physical embodiment of the metaphysical Absolute, and, at the same time, the symbol of Cosmic Love and Unity. The Caves embodied *nirguna* (superpersonal, without attributes) Brahman; the Temple represents *saguna* (personal) Brahmin—both being aspects of the same Lord." [An illuminating and seemingly authoritative discussion.]

1904 Salter, Donald. "That is My Ticket: The Homosexual Writings of E. M. Forster," LONDON MAGAZINE, XIV (Jan–Feb 1975), 5–33.

In *Maurice,* EMF attempts detachment with respect to the experience that he depicted; the detachment is less present in the stories that were unpublished in EMF's lifetime and collected in *The Life to Come and Other Stories* (1972). EMF is correct in alleging that sex prevented him from becoming a voluminous writer in fiction. Nevertheless, in the suppressed homosexual stories he continued to emphasize the need for committed personal relationships. In "The Other Boat" and "Arthur Snatchfold," EMF depicts the tragedy that results when the sensitive individual is confronted with social and moral absolutes that repress his freedom to act as his nature dictates. EMF in "The Life to Come" explores similar issues. He tended to romanticize the man from the working classes not only in his personal life but in stories such as "Ansell," "The Torque," "Dr. Woolacott," and "Arthur Snatchfold." In "Arthur Snatchfold," EMF managed to avoid both romanticism and strident propaganda.

EMF found it difficult to treat the carnal in his fiction; his natural reticence increased the difficulty and the evasiveness. Many of his newly published stories are pornographic; they seek to excite. They tend to regard sexual activity as an end in itself and rely for effect on anatomical details or specific sensations, and sex is seen as more important than the people involved in it, with the result that experience is simplified. Examples of such reductive stories are "The Obelisk" and "The Classical Annex." In pornography an element of guilt obtrudes, which is absent from the openly erotic. The theme of guilt links up with the themes of sterility and continuity developed in *Maurice* and the other novels. EMF's feelings of guilt lead to his uncertainty and the irregularities of tone found in such stories as "What Does It Matter? A Morality" and "The Torque." In these works he is sometimes guilty of vulgarity where coarseness might have led to an artistic success in them. The stories in *The Life to Come* are demeaning to EMF and his reputation, since they are so patently escapist and prurient. Possibly EMF's feelings of guilt with respect to sex caused him to find sexual release only with men from the working class and to romanticize them in his homosexual writings. EMF's friend, J. R. Ackerley, also sought satisfaction with men from the working class. The stories in *The Life to Come* and *Maurice* have as their central sexual agent a vital youth from the lower class. EMF, if somewhat less honest and forthright about homosexuality than Ackerley, did keep his balance and resilence, and he achieved in his journal greater humor and philosophy than did Ackerley in his personal writings. EMF did try to work for the improvement of the position of the homosexual, although he was not optimistic about any radical improvement in this situation. He worked for such a goal without rancor or self-dramatization.

Sensuality plus loyalty were the qualities that enabled EMF to endure the pressures exerted by a conventional society. Still, his views on sex were often inconsistent or dissembling. The tolerance masks the conventional view, and he was especially intolerant of Lesbian love and of women as free agents in society. He reveals that a writer must often express only indirectly his central obsessional interest, if his work is to qualify as art. EMF's homosexual writings are not self-sufficient, as his novels are. Nor do these writings possess the honesty characteristic of Mann's DEATH IN VENICE or of Ackerley's MY FATHER AND MYSELF and the comprehensiveness that such honesty makes possible. Radclyffe Hall's THE WELL OF LONELINESS shares the faults of *Maurice*—overwriting and special pleading for the homosexual. But it is a better book because its range is greater. In *Maurice* something is shirked when EMF fails to deal conclusively with the conflict between the homosexual and a hostile society. EMF disregards this problem too greatly and is overly concerned with the lure of the greenwood for Alec and Maurice. *The Life to Come* and *Maurice* all too seldom draw on the wisdom that informs EMF's major novels. His stories are less "concerned with what it is like to be a homosexual as with creating the minimum background for a sexual exchange." The homosexual writings reveal that it is not necessary for a writer to make public all the different personas that make up his psyche. EMF will be remembered by his best work rather than by his willed or relaxed divagations into homosexually oriented narratives. [An important article, definitive on its subject.]

1905 Savidis, George. "Cavafy and Forster," TIMES LITERARY SUP-PLEMENT (Lond), 14 Nov 1975, p. 1356.
A lasting, far-reaching, and mutually beneficial friendship developed between the Greek poet C. P. Cavafy and EMF when the latter was posted in Alexandria during the period 1955–1919; the two met again in 1922 and 1929. Homosexuality contributed to the relationship, though the two were probably never lovers. EMF, in a letter to Cavafy (1 July 1917), discusses the nature of depravity. Cavafy, in a letter to EMF (15 Oct 1929), expresses satisfaction with EMF's visit and praises *A Passage to India*. The characters and situations in *Passage* have now become Cavafy's "companions." As G. D. Klingopoulos in "E. M. Forster's Sense of History and Cavafy" (ESSAYS IN CRITICISM [1958]) has shown, EMF's view of history became more comprehensive after his acquaintance with Cavafy; and EMF was probably encouraged in the rewriting of *Maurice* and in writing his late short stories by Cavafy's erotic liberation. In turn, EMF's firm view of the imperial question may have helped Cavafy form his view of the Roman Empire.

Letter from EMF to George Savidis (25 Jan 1958) expresses EMF's great satisfaction in having known Cavafy.

1906 Schneider, Daniel S. SYMBOLISM: THE MANICHAEAN VISION, JAMES, CONRAD, WOOLF, AND STEVENS (Lincoln: University of Nebraska P, 1975), pp. 18, 124–27, 130, 146.
A symbolism of North and South occurs in the work of Mann, Stevens, D. H. Lawrence, and EMF wherein spirit, intellect, and will are opposed to animality, instinct, and the unconscious. The developmental pattern of Virginia Woolf's THE YEARS is similar to that in *Howards End* by which she was influenced. In EMF's novel, connections are stressed—between the sexes, between idealism and materialism, spirit and flesh, objectivity and subjectivity—and disconnections are to be overcome to the extent possible. Connection is difficult, since the irrational is always ready to overcome the rational. The Bloomsbury atmosphere in *Howards End* must have appealed to Woolf. The ideal of wholeness, implicit in the novel, was attractive to her, difficult as it was to achieve. Elinor Partiger (THE YEARS) and Ruth Wilcox (*Howards End*) are analogous characters in their search for wholeness in an age of fragmentation. The opposed forces in this struggle to attain wholeness are to be aligned with the Manichean view of Hawthorne, Melville, James, and Conrad. Delia Partiger feels the presence of Rose after her death just as Ruth Wilcox's presence after death is felt by the Schlegel sisters.

1907 Shahane, V. A. (ed). FOCUS ON FORSTER'S "A PASSAGE TO INDIA" (Madras & New Delhi: Orient Longman, 1975).
[Contents, abstracted under date of first publication: V. A. Shahane, "Introduction" (1975); K. Natwar-Singh, "Only Connect . . . : E. M. Forster and India," ASPECTS OF E. M. FORSTER, ed by Oliver Stallybrass (1969); M. Sivaramakrishna, "Marabar Caves Revisited" (1975; first ptd in this volume); H. H. Anniah Gowda, "To the Caves," A GARLAND FOR E. M. FORSTER, ed by H. H. Anniah Gowda (1969); G. Nageswara Rao, "Gokulāstami: The Resolution of the Antithesis in Forster's Art," VISVABHARATI QUARTERLY (1965; rptd in abgd form); Asim Kumar Mukherjee, "The Split Personality of E. M. Forster," QUEST (1968; rptd in abgd form); T. G. Vaidyanathan, "In Defence of Professor Godbole" (1975; first ptd in this volume); M. K. Naik, "Passage to Less Than India" (1975; first ptd in this volume); Sujit Mukherjee, "The Marabar Mystery: An Addition to the Casebook on the Caves," COLLEGE ENGLISH (1966); Bikram K. Das, "A Stylistic Analysis of the Speech of the Indian Characters in Forster's *A Passage to India*," INDIAN JOURNAL OF ENGLISH STUDIES (1971); J. Birje-Patil, "Ducklings in Glass Troughs," (1975; first ptd in this volume); Meenakshi Mukherjee, "On Teaching *A Passage to India*" (1975; first ptd in this volume); Chaman L. Sahni, "The Marabar Caves in the Light of Indian

Thought" (1975; first ptd in this volume); V. A. Shahane, "Search for a Synthesis" (1975; first ptd in this volume). Contains "Itinerary of E. M. Forster's Visits to India."]

1908 Shahane, V. A. "Introduction," Focus on Forster's "A Passage to India," ed by V. A. Shahane (Madras & New Delhi: Orient Longman, 1975), pp. xiii–xix.
This collection of essays is a celebration of the fiftieth anniversary of the publication of *A Passage to India* (1924), and its purpose is to present an image of *Passage* as formed by Indian critics. Few Indian critics have contributed to the great body of criticism on *Passage:* the "Indianness" of the essays in this collection is their important characteristic. All approaches to *Passage* are justified because India developed EMF to his creative limits.

1909 Shahane, V. A. "Search for a Synthesis," Focus on Forster's "A Passage to India," ed by V. A. Shahane (Madras & New Delhi: Orient Longman, 1975), pp. 114–32.
A Passage to India dramatizes the theme of double vision, especially in the contrast provided through the negative implications of "Caves" and the affirmations suggested in "Temple." [A diffuse essay tied too greatly to plot summary of *Passage.*]

1910 Shaheen, M. Y. "Forster and Proust," Times Literary Supplement (Lond), 21 Feb 1975, p. 197.
Denis Donoghue is right ("An Ear for Fiction," 1975) in asserting that EMF pays little attention to Proust in *Aspects of the Novel.* EMF is much concerned with Proust in an unpublished lecture, "Three Generations," delivered at University College, Nottingham, 28 Jan 1939, to a political discussion group. [In the lecture, EMF sees the prewar era as a time of "hope without faith," with Meredith as its representative; the age beginning with 1933 is a time of "faith without hope" and has no completely typical representative; and the time between these two somewhat dogmatic ages, the civilization of the 1920s, is represented by Proust, with his curiosity and tolerance. Some ideas and phrases from the lecture were used in "Our Curiosity and Despair," New York Herald Tribune Books, 21 April 1929, pp. 1, 6, rptd as "Proust," *Abinger Harvest.* EMF has another essay on Proust, not mentioned by the author, "Our Second Greatest Novel," Listener, XXIX (15 April 1943), 454–55, rptd in *Two Cheers for Democracy.*]

1911 Sivaramakrishna, M. "Marabar Caves Revisited," Focus on Forster's "A Passage to India," ed by V. A. Shahane (Madras & New Delhi: Orient Longman, 1975), pp. 5–17.
Like most other works in the novel genre, *A Passage to India* focuses upon the quest for reality, with the social world as basis and with manners as a

index to man's soul. For EMF this reality went beyond the realm of rationality; in *Passage* there is, therefore, a tension between the "realism" of the liberal humanist and the transcendent reality of the symbolist and poet. Indian philosophic thought, by which EMF was attracted, regards rationality "as an indispensable but inadequate criterion." In India the reality is difficult to define, since India obliterates normal distinctions; India serves, consequently, as a testing ground for the characters in their quest for reality. The Caves are at the core of the novel: They suggest a contradictory and dichotomous vision of India and of ultimate reality that is difficult, but necessary, for the liberal humanist to grasp. The Caves do not have, like the Mosque and the Temple, "clearly recognizable semantic, philosophic and religious referents." The Caves, in short, suggest this impasse: "the awareness of the inadequacy of rationality as a norm but an awareness born out of this very rationality." The Caves antedate existence, and they represent nothing (and everything) and so transcend the usual categories of good and evil. [This essay traverses little ground that other commentary has not already traversed.]

1912 Vaidyanathan, T. G. "In Defence of Professor Godbole," Focus on Forster's "A Passage to India," ed by V. A. Shahane (Madras & New Delhi: Orient Longman, 1975), pp. 42–62.

The conception of Godbole as a negative influence and as a clearly evil force, advanced by David Shusterman ("The Curious Case of Professor Godbole: *A Passage to India* Re-examined," Publications of the Modern Language Association [1961]), is not valid. If Godbole had told other people more of what he knew about the Caves, he would not have altered what happened; he is not malevolent or even indifferent. His conception of friendship and love is based on the universality implicit in Hinduism rather than upon the tender regard for the individual implicit in Christianity. Nevertheless, Godbole does show love in sponsoring the rehabilitation of Aziz at Mau, even if he could not act in Aziz's behalf at the time of the trial. In *Passage* it is EMF, not Godbole, who effects reconciliation, seeks a unifying vision, and stresses the provenance of the Absolute. Godbole represents not the Vedantic sort of Hinduism with its stress upon the Absolute but the Vishnu-oriented (or Vaisnavite) Hinduism, with its prophet in Shri Krishna, its emphasis upon a personal God, and its pluralistic (rather than monistic) view of God and the universe. Whatever emphasis is present in *Passage* on the desirability of cosmic unity is advanced by EMF; and such emphasis derives primarily from EMF's aesthetic design rather than from philosophical or religious sources. [The refutation of Shusterman is thorough and convincing. The revisionist view of the Hinduism in *Passage* is suggestive and carefully argued, but the view of the unity advocated in the novel as being primarily based on aesthetic rather than philosophical premises is less convincing.]

1913 Woolf, Virginia. THE FLIGHT OF THE MIND: THE LETTERS OF VIRGINIA WOOLF, Vol I: 1888–1912 (VIRGINIA STEPHEN), ed by Nigel Nicolson and Joanne Trautmann (Lond: Hogarth P, 1975), pp. 372, 499; as THE LETTERS OF VIRGINIA WOOLF, Vol I: 1888–1912 (VIRGINIA STEPHEN) (NY: Harcourt, Brace, Jovanovich, 1975).

Letter to Madge Vaughan (1 Nov [1908]), *A Room with a View* is amusing but repeats what EMF has said already.

Index

AUTHORS

Included here are authors of articles and books on E. M. Forster, editors and compilers of works in which criticism on E. M. Forster appears. Editors and translators are identified parenthetically: (ed), (trans). Numbers after each name refer to the item(s) in the bibliography where the name occurs.

Deutsch, Babette: 197
de Wyzewa, T.: 15
Dick, Aliki Lafkidou: 1645
Dick, Kay: 1730
Dick, Margaret: 1532
Dickinson, G[oldsworthy] Lowes: 118, 281, 1731
Dilly Tante [pseud of Stanley Kunitz]: 262
Dobrée, Bonamy: 255, 279, 280, 351, 1334
Dolch, Martin: 1049
Donoghue, Dennis: 1732, 1883
Dooley, D. J.: 1216
Doughty, Howard M., Jr.: 263
Douglas, A. Donald: 134
Downes, David A.: 1000
Doyle, Paul A.: 1533
Drabble, Margaret: 1834
Draper, R. P.: 1038; (ed): 1420
Drew, Elizabeth: 186
Drews, Jörg: 1421
Driver, Tom F.: 941
D'Souza, Frank (ed): 1307
Duckworth, Alister M.: 1534
Dunbar, Olivia Howard: 396
Dunlea, William: 719
Dutton, George B.: 113
Dyson, A. E.: 1422; (ed): 1654, 1655, 1828

E., E. F.: 80
Eagle, Dorothy: 1217
Eaglestone, Arthur A. [See Dataller, Roger]
Eagleton, Terry: 1423
Eapen, Karippacheril Chakko: 1001
Ebbatson, J. R.: 1884
Echeruo, M. J. C.: 942
Edel, Leon: 1646
Edmiston, Susan: 1733
Edwardes, Michael: 1218
Einsiedel, Wolfgang von: 533
Eldridge, Sheila Van Sickle: 1885
Ellem, Elizabeth: 1535, 1735
Ellis, G. U.: 379
Ellmann, Richard: 840; (ed): 840
Elting, M. L.: 358
Emerson, Gloria: 1335
Emerson, O. B.: 869
Emmett, V. J., Jr.: 1648
Endicott, N. J.: 359, 397
Engel, Monroe: 809
Enright, D. J.: 753, 884, 1039
Entwistle, William J.: 424
Epstein, Joseph: 1538
Erskine-Hill, Howard: 1143
Espey, David B.: 1649
Ethridge, James M. (ed): 1106
Evans, B. Ifor: 384, 510, 1040
Evett, Robert: 1736

F.: 38
Fadda, Anna Maria: 944
Fadiman, Clifton: 421
Fagan, B. W.: 1629
Fanon, Frantz: 1412
Farber, Anne: 1650
Farrelly, John: 486
Fasanelli, James A.: 1270
Fassett, I. P.: 135
Faulkner, Peter: 1651
Faussett, H. I'A.: 360
Faverty, Frederic E.: 777, 1041
Feinstein, Elaine: 1652
Feldman, Hans Eugene: 1886
Felheim, Marvin (ed): 573
Ferry, David: 581
Fielding, K. J.: 778
Finkelstein, Bonnie Blumenthal: 1653, 1737, 1887
Fleishman, Avrom: 1219, 1271, 1738
Fleischmann, Wolfgang Bernard (ed): 1227
Fleissner, Robert F.: 1539
Fletcher, Ian (ed): 1169, 1509, 1544, 1574, 1575
Ford, Boris (ed): 873, 880, 890, 894
Ford, Ford Madox: 200
Ford, George H.: 685, 1107
Forman, Henry James: 119
Forster, E. M.: 281, 1537
Fraser, G. S.: 603, 1042, 1654
Freedman, Richard: 1429
Fremantle, Anne: 361, 555, 604
Freund, Philip: 1108
Fricker, Robert: 779
Friedman, Alan: 1109, 1160, 1655
Friedman, Albert B.: 1043
Friend, Robert: 1161, 1739, 1740
Frierson, William C.: 227, 398
Fry, Philip Lee: 1835
Fry, Roger: 1656
Fuller, Edmund: 1044
Fuller, John: 582
Furbank, P. N.: 605, 1272, 1405, 1430, 1540, 1836
Fussell, Paul, Jr.: 606, 1888
Fyfe, Kenneth: 1541

G., C. W.: 136
Gadd, David: 1837
Gaines, Clarence H.: 137
Galinsky, Hans: 380
Gallagher, Michael P.: 1045
Gardner, Philip: 1742; (ed): 1, 2, 3, 4, 6, 7, 8, 9, 10, 11, 12, 13, 15, 16, 17, 18, 19, 20, 21, 22, 24, 25, 27, 28, 29, 30, 31, 32, 33, 34, 36, 37, 38, 40, 41, 42, 43, 44, 45, 46, 50, 51, 52, 53, 54, 55, 57, 58, 59, 61, 62, 63, 64, 66, 67, 69, 70, 71, 72, 74, 78, 82, 83, 84, 88, 90, 91,

Proctor, Dennis: 1731, 1785; (ed): 1731
Proctor, Margaret Ruth: 1860
Pryce-Jones, Alan: 430, 735, 1083
Pure, Simon [pseud of Frank Swinnerton]: 126, 162, 182
Puri, Meenakshi: 1694
Purkis, John: 1786
Putt, S. Gorley: 567, 1184

Quennell, Peter: 1787

R., G. R. B.: 299
R., J. C. [See Ransom, John Crowe]
R., W. K.: 494
Raban, Jonathan: 1293
Rago, Henry: 495
Rhaman, Kalimur: 907
Rahv, Philip: 431
Raina, M. L.: 1136, 1185, 1186, 1240, 1600
Rajiva, Stanley F.: 1368
Raleigh, John Henry: 795
Rama Rau, Santha: 625, 857, 858, 976, 977, 1084, 1187
Ramsaran, J. A.: 1369
Randall, Alec: 1370
Randles, W. G. L.: 829
Ransom, John Crowe: 338, 432
Rantavaara, Irma: 569, 626
Rao, B. Syamala: 1472
Rao, Guttikonda Nageswara: 1137
Rao, K. Bhaskara: 1188
Rao, Raja: 1085
Raskin, Jonah: 1601
Ratcliffe, Michael: 1602
Ratcliffe, S. K.: 164
Raven, Simon: 1473
Rawlings, [Carl] Donn: 1241, 1788
Raymund, Bernard: 669
Reade, Brian: 1695
Redman, Ben Ray: 166, 496; (trans): 107
Reed, Henry: 476
Reed, John R.: 1086
Rees, Goronwy: 1696
Rees, Richard: 796; (ed): 190
Reid, Forrest: 373, 388
Reilly, Joseph J.: 339
Reynolds, Frank: 1697
Rice, Allen: 1789
Rice, Robin R.: 1479
Richards, I. A.: 209, 1152
Richardson, Betty: 1861
Richler, Mordecai: 1294
Rickert, Edith: 110, 231, 316
Rideout, Walter Bates: 859
Riding, Laura: 241
Riggs, Thomas, Jr.: 591
Riley, Carolyn (ed): 436, 742, 817, 850, 1030, 1106, 1132, 1208, 1211, 1277, 1356, 1358,

1392, 1501, 1505, 1582, 1642, 1643, 1686, 1790, 1862
Rising, C[lara]: 1371, 1863
Riley, Madeleine: 1295
Robbins, William: 830
Roberts, R. Ellis: 167, 406
Robinson, J. W. (ed): 538, 850
Robson, W. W.: 1474
Roby, Kinley E.: 1698
Rockwell, Joan: 1864
Rodrigues, E. L.: 978
Roerick, William: 1372
Rola, Dionisia: 1189
Rolo, Charles J.: 592, 628, 736
Roscoe, Theodora: 407
Rose, Martial: 1475
Rosenbaum, S. P.: 1242, 1604, 1605, 1606, 1901; (ed): 1606, 1628, 1874, 1900, 1901
Rosenthal, M. L.: 1190
Rosenthal, Michael: 1607
R[oss], A[ngus]: 1608
Ross, Mary: 242
Ross, Woodburn O. (ed): 801
Rosselli, John: 629, 1476
Routh, H. V.: 348, 477
Rovere, Richard (ed): 405
Roy, Chitra: 1243
Rueckert, William H.: 1018
Runyan, Elizabeth: 1609
Russell, Bertrand: 737
Rutherford, Andrew: 1478; (ed): 436, 586, 613, 637, 645, 940, 998, 1050, 1376, 1477, 1478
Ryan, Marjorie: 908

S., A.: 300
S., C.: 1610
S., G.: 453
S., J. F.: 243
S.-J., R. A. [See Scott-James, R. A.]
Sahni, Chaman L[all]: 1902, 1903, 1907
Sainsbury, Ian: 1611
Sale, William M.: 529
Salter D[onald] [P. M.]: 1865, 1904
Sampson, George: 392, 882
Sanders, Charles R.: 1479
Sanders, Scott: 1791
Sandison, Alan: 1244
Sandwell, B. K.: 593
Sato, Ineko: 408
Saunders, J. W.: 1087
Savage, D. S.: 454, 1152
Savidis, George: 1905
Schmerl, Rudolf: 1245
Schneider, Daniel S.: 1906
Schneiderman, Beth Kline: 1866
Schnell, Jonathan: 340

Index

TITLES OF SECONDARY WORKS

Titles of articles in periodicals and chapters in books are in quotation marks; book titles are in upper case; translations of article titles originally appearing in a foreign language are in parentheses, without quotation marks, and in lower case; translations of book titles originally appearing in a foreign language are in parentheses and in upper case. Numbers after each title refer to the number(s) of the item(s) in the bibliography where the title appears.

E. M. FORSTER

E. M. FORSTER

E. M. Forster

Index

PERIODICALS AND NEWSPAPERS

Included here are periodicals and newspapers for which entries occur in the bibliography. Numbers after each title refer to the numbers(s) of the item in the bibliography where the title appears.

MINNEAPOLIS STAR: 1715
MINNEAPOLIS TRIBUNE: 1808
MODERN AGE (Chicago): 1090
MODERN FICTION STUDIES: 679, 746, 872, 883, 889, 899, 915, 920, 1055, 1072, 1092, 1094, 1130, 1134, 1220, 1249, 1356, 1825
MODERN LANGUAGE JOURNAL: 1135
MODERN LANGUAGE QUARTERLY: 1078, 1495
MODERN LANGUAGE REVIEW: 970
MODERN PHILOLOGY: 1769
MODERN REVIEW (Calcutta): 168, 910, 1457
IL MONDO (Milan): 1061
MORNING LEADER (Lond): 42, 72
MORNING POST (Lond): 19, 37, 54
MORNING TELEGRAPH (Sheffield): 1611
MOSAIC (University of Manitoba): 1819

NATION (Lond): 27, 43, 59, 93
NATION (NY): 116, 153, 219, 310, 330, 377, 402, 440, 489, 491, 577, 625, 722, 725, 806, 938, 1488, 1582
NATION AND ATHENAEUM (Lond): 118, 175, 212, 216, 233
NATIONAL OBSERVER: 1774
NATIONAL REVIEW (NY): 1576, 1711
DIE NEUE RUNDSCHAU (Frankfurt am-Main): 781
NEUE ZÜRCHER ZEITUNG (Zurich): 887
DIE NEUREN SPRACHEN (Frankfurt am-Main): 797, 798, 959
NEW ADELPHI (Lond): 218
NEW AGE (Lond): 94
NEW ENGLISH WEEKLY (Lond): 335
NEW HUMANIST (Lond): 1651
NEW LEADER (Lond): 149, 554, 1729
NEW REPUBLIC: 108, 125, 144, 204, 251, 252, 268, 290, 332, 375, 396, 419, 427, 486, 501, 559, 612, 714, 832, 935, 1053, 1499, 1561
NEW STATESMAN: 103, 124, 133, 142, 164, 177, 198, 199, 222, 794, 835, 884, 924, 1003, 1312, 1470, 1553, 1599, 1859, 1881
NEW STATESMAN AND NATION: 282, 322, 353, 404, 410, 430, 441, 516, 566, 599, 622, 629, 665, 677, 678, 690, 726, 783
NEW YORK EVENING POST: 197, 217
NEW YORK EVENING POST LITERARY REVIEW: 118, 130, 179
NEW YORK HERALD TRIBUNE: 891, 961
NEW YORK HERALD TRIBUNE BOOK REVIEW: 336, 563, 608
NEW YORK HERALD TRIBUNE BOOK WEEK: 1083
NEW YORK HERALD TRIBUNE BOOKS: 176, 178, 212, 242, 311, 395, 724
NEW YORK HERALD TRIBUNE WEEKLY BOOK REVIEW: 438, 481, 482, 717

NEW YORK REVIEW OF BOOKS: 1098, 1163, 1486, 1487, 1506, 1748, 1768
NEW YORK TIMES: 83, 84, 117, 312, 344, 484, 623, 985, 986, 989, 1025, 1335, 1354, 1397, 1427, 1448, 1452, 1485, 1570, 1725, 1733
NEW YORK TIMES BOOK REVIEW: 102, 119, 120, 138, 203, 229, 288, 326, 374, 391, 400, 414, 415, 418, 458, 480, 483, 484, 497, 519, 564, 596, 597, 668, 745, 923, 1023, 1164, 1292, 1396, 1538, 1607, 1630, 1796, 1814
NEW YORK TIMES MAGAZINE: 1584
NEW YORK WORLD: 128, 170
NEW YORKER: 215, 421, 498, 566, 667, 713, 825, 852, 901, 934, 968, 1618
NEWSWEEK: 624, 734, 943, 1501, 1521
NINETEENTH CENTURY AND AFTER: 277
NORTH AMERICAN REVIEW: 137, 275
NOTES AND QUERIES (Lond): 908, 1185, 1186, 1459, 1546, 1687, 1746, 1827, 1890
NOVEL: 1432
NOW (Lond): 454

OBSERVER (Lond): 14, 52, 66, 151, 292, 664, 731, 800, 1250, 1255, 1366, 1624, 1713
ORIENT-WEST (Tokyo): 1033
OSMANIA JOURNAL OF ENGLISH STUDIES (Hyderabad): 911, 982
OSSERVATORE POLITICO LETTERARIO (Milan): 994
OTTAWA CITIZEN: 1623
OUTLOOK (Lond): 28, 46, 75, 86, 141
OUTLOOK (NY): 193, 211
OXFORD MAGAZINE: 303

PALL MALL GAZETTE: 1, 13, 40
PALL MALL GAZETTE, ILLUSTRATED LITERARY SUPPLEMENT: 77
PAPERS OF THE BIBLIOGRAPHICAL SOCIETY OF AMERICA: 1192
PAPERS ON LANGUAGE AND LITERATURE: 1861
PARIS REVIEW: 605, 1067
PARTISAN REVIEW: 417, 487, 659, 666, 795, 1702
PAUNCH (Buffalo): 1241
PERSONALIST (University of Southern California): 654
PHILOLOGICAL QUARTERLY: 606
PHILOSOPHY: 287
PLAYBOY: 1596
POLITICAL QUARTERLY (Lond): 294
PRAXIS DES NEUSPRACHLICHEN UNTERRICHTS (Dortmund): 1579
PROGRESSIVE (Madison): 1173
PSYCHOLOGY TODAY (Del Mar, California): 1695

Index

FOREIGN LANGUAGES

Included here are the languages in which articles and books listed in the bibliography originally appeared. Numbers under each language refer to items in the bibliography where the foreign-language title is given. English language items are not listed.

Danish: 759, 1210

Finnish: 569
French: 15, 107, 202, 221, 225, 579, 588, 647, 683, 754, 924, 1258, 1268, 1305, 1306, 1332, 1408, 1449, 1675, 1744, 1745, 1747, 1833

German: 254, 380, 523, 530, 533, 536, 611, 696, 779, 781, 782, 797, 798, 815, 828, 865, 887, 959, 1128, 1141, 1236, 1347, 1362, 1421, 1434, 1436, 1480, 1489, 1500, 1587

Hungarian: 1442

Italian: 266, 462, 565, 793, 819, 823, 824, 944, 994, 1014, 1061, 1129, 1209, 1214

Japanese: 317, 1146, 1201, 1202, 1203, 1204, 1205, 1206, 1228, 1229, 1234, 1238, 1254, 1388, 1445, 1446, 1458, 1468, 1566, 1673

Romanian: 1344

Serbo-Croatian: 821
Spanish: 706

Index

PRIMARY TITLES

Included here are all titles by Forster which occur in titles of articles or books or in the abstracts. Numbers after each title refer to the item(s) in the bibliography where the title appears.